HISTORIC SPOTS IN CALIFORNIA

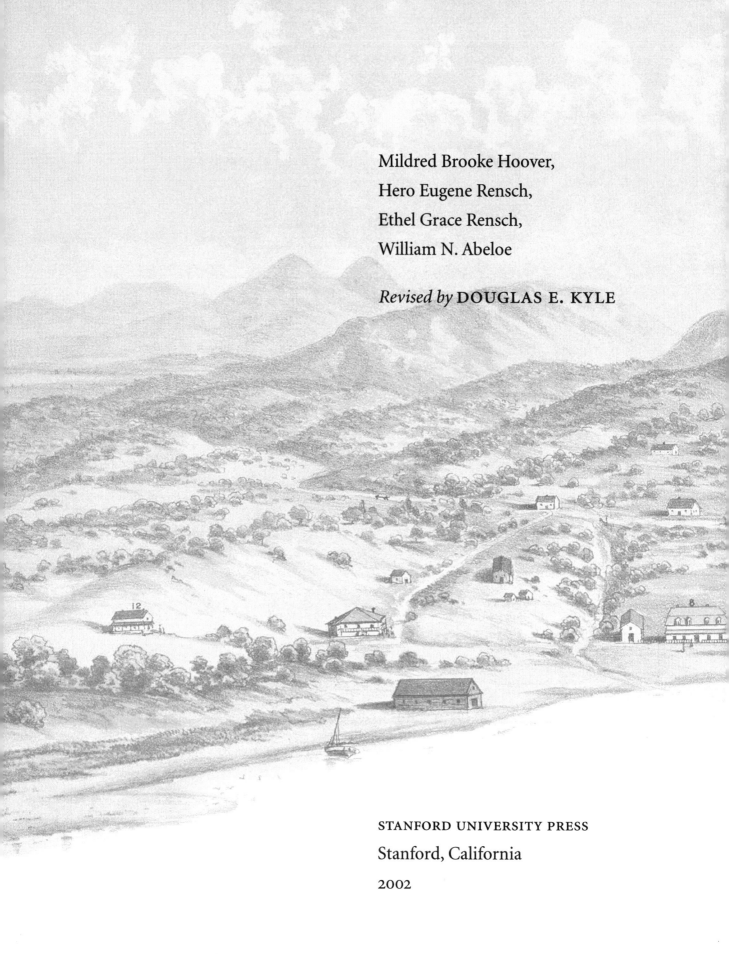

Mildred Brooke Hoover,
Hero Eugene Rensch,
Ethel Grace Rensch,
William N. Abeloe

Revised by DOUGLAS E. KYLE

STANFORD UNIVERSITY PRESS

Stanford, California

2002

FIFTH EDITION

Historic Spots in
California

Historic Spots in California was originally published in
three volumes: *The Southern Counties* (1932), by H. E. and
E. G. Rensch; *Valley and Sierra Counties* (1933), by H. E. and
E. G. Rensch and Mildred Brooke Hoover; and *Counties of the
Coast Range* (1937), by Mildred Brooke Hoover. A revised
edition, in one volume, was published in 1948. A third edition,
revised and expanded by William N. Abeloe, was published in
1966. A fourth edition, extensively revised and updated by
Douglas E. Kyle, was published in 1990.

Stanford University Press, Stanford, California
© 1932, 1933, 1937, 1948, 1966, 1990, 2002 by the Board of
Trustees of the Leland Stanford Junior University

Published with the assistance of the Edgar M. Kahn
Memorial Fund

Printed in the United States of America
on acid-free, archival-quality paper.

Library of Congress Cataloging-in-Publication Data

Historic Spots in California / by Mildred Brooke Hoover ...
   [et al]. — 5th ed. / revised by Douglas E. Kyle.
     p. cm.
   Includes bibliographical references and index.
   ISBN 0-8047-4482-3 (acid-free paper) —
   ISBN 0-8047-4483-1 (pbk. : acid-free paper)
    1. Historic sites—California.   2. California—History, Local.
I. Hoover, Mildred Brooke.   II. Kyle, Douglas E., 1935–
F862 .H57   2002
979.4—dc21   2002001377

Original Printing 2002
Last figure below indicates year of this printing:
11 10 09 08 07 06 05 04 03 02

Designed by Janet Wood
Typeset by James P. Brommer in 10/13 Minion
and Franklin Gothic display

Historic Spots in California is now in its fifth edition and has an interesting history of its own. The work began as a project of the California State Conference of the Daughters of the American Revolution. It was published, then as now, by Stanford University Press. The first edition appeared in three volumes, the first being *The Southern Counties* (1932), written by Hero Eugene Rensch and his wife, Ethel Grace Rensch. In the following year, *Valley and Sierra Counties* appeared, with Mildred Brooke Hoover as coauthor with Mr. and Mrs. Rensch, her brother-in-law and sister. The third volume, *Counties of the Coast Range*, completed the project in 1937 and was entirely the work of Mrs. Hoover.

In the 1930s Californians could see many efforts being made to preserve and to commemorate the history of their state. Anthropologists were publishing extensively on the world of the California Indians. Many crumbling buildings of the missions, perhaps the most famous Spanish enterprise in California, were being restored. In old cities like Los Angeles and Santa Barbara, historic buildings were being identified and refurbished. The Gold Rush period seems to have produced one book or journal article every month in that decade. Historically important State Registered Landmarks were beginning to be identified and labeled. *Historic Spots in California*, therefore, appeared when there was a considerable interest in California's past, and it found a receptive audience.

The second edition of the work was published in 1948. The three original volumes were brought together into a single book, which kept the previous geographic divisions and was updated and revised by Ruth Teiser. This work included the introduction from the first edition by Robert Glass Cleland, an established California historian. A select bibliography followed each county's history in this edition, as it did in the volumes of the first edition.

In 1962, Stanford University Press engaged Reverend William S. Abeloe to make a third edition of *Historic Spots in California*. Father Abeloe was an enthusiastic student of California history and was teaching this, among other subjects, at Bishop O'Dowd High School in Oakland. He quoted with evident approval from the first edition that one of the purposes of this book was "to arouse a state-wide interest in the preservation of those vanishing historic landmarks which still survive." He made some substantial changes to the book, the first of which was to put county chapters in alphabetical order. He added photographs taken on his trips throughout the state and maps for each county. The text was revised to note those buildings or landscapes that no longer existed. This third edition, which was in several places thoroughly rewritten by Father Abeloe, was published in 1966. It became a popular book and went through several printings, and an updated preface was added to the reprinting of 1978.

I am a descendant of Dr. Willard Pratt, mentioned in the Plumas County chapter, who arrived in California in the late 1850s. My late parents Oliver and Helen Kyle (she was his granddaughter) encouraged an interest in California history, and in time I became a teacher of this and other historical subjects at Merritt College in Oakland, where I was on the faculty for nearly forty years, also serving for a long time as chairman of our instructional department. My bachelor's degree in history was taken at Stanford in 1957, and I did further graduate work at San Francisco State (master's degree in international relations, 1959) and at the University of California, Berkeley. In the 1970s, I edited the *Alameda County Historical Society Quarterly*, which brought me in contact with many other historians, and I collaborated on some historical publications. One of these was with Father Abeloe, whom I found to be, as so many others could testify, a friendly comrade and a man who supported fellow historians.

In 1985, a year after Father Abeloe's death, Stanford

v

University Press engaged me to do a fourth edition of the book, which was published in 1990. I decided to eliminate the maps, which were an expensive component of the cost of this large work. Up-to-date maps are available throughout the state, and a book expected to be in print for a couple of decades could no more be current on road conditions than it could on bibliography. The book was extensively rewritten and updated. But, as geologists and historians agree, California is always on the move. As the twenty-first century began, Stanford University Press and I agreed to present a fifth edition of this work. The text has been thoroughly revised and updated to early 2001.

Historic Spots in California has never claimed to be a history of California; rather it is a book about the historical landmarks of the state. To provide historical background, I have written a short introductory essay. The book is divided into chapters based on the current fifty-eight counties of the state, alphabetically listed. Within each chapter is a text that is organized on a mostly chronological basis. The text generally begins with pertinent facts on geography, continuing with Indian life, followed by the coming of the Spaniards and other outsiders, and then the American conquest of the 1840s. Where it had an impact, the Gold Rush following the 1848 discovery is dealt with. The text then continues into the period of statehood in 1850, industrialization, railroads, intensive agricultural development, the growth of cities, and on into more recent times. Since museums are often the best introduction to historical matters, an effort has been made to include the addresses of the museums of the state and their particular subjects. Visitors should make local inquiries as to days and hours when a museum or other historic spot is open.

The reader will find locations of the State Registered Landmarks, and many, but not all, of the list on the National Register of Historic Places. While the latter identify only existing buildings and sites, State Registered Landmarks (SRL followed by a number in the text) include many places that no longer exist and in some cases have not even been marked with a sign or monument. A number of private organizations have also placed markers around the state; among them are the Native Sons of the Golden West, the Native Daughters of the Golden West, the Daughters of the American Revolution, and E Clampus Vitus. The last is a twentieth-century revival of a social group originating in the Mother Lode in the 1850s.

Every photograph used in this edition was taken by the author. The text has been written with the idea that the reader might use the book while traveling around the state, and thus mileage and specific locations have been given where it was thought necessary to do so. Numbered roads are identified as follows: interstates as, for example, I-5, U.S. highways as US 101, and state routes as SR 1.

The bibliography has been updated to the beginning of 2001 and includes some of the established classics in California history as well as more recent material.

When Father Abeloe and I, as members of the board of directors of the Alameda County Historical Society, were among those working with Leonard Verbarg on his book *Celebrities at Your Doorstep*, Verbarg looked around the table after a long session and observed: "It takes teamwork when you deal with history." Certainly this book owes a great deal to the efforts and suggestions of many people, and the following are herewith thanked for their input.

At Stanford University Press, the editorial and design work of Norris Pope, John Raymond, Janet Wood, James Brommer, and Janna Palliser brought readability and order to the manuscript and illustrations. I am much in their debt.

From many counties in the state came information, often from a corresponding secretary of a historical society, and all of this was personally corroborated by the author in a visit at one time or another. Alameda County benefited from the input of Analee Allen, Jim De Mersman, Joy Furth, Philip Holmes, David Nicolai, Sherry Nighswanger, and Carl Wilson. Larry Cenotto gave information on Amador County. Butte County contributors included Marge Holmes, William Kyle, and James Lenhoff. Colusa County has information provided by Billiejean Durst and Kathleen Moran.

Contributors to Contra Costa County included Beth Hansen, Elizabeth Isles, Virgie V. Jones, Betty Maffei, Traci Parent, Robert Ruddick, and Maggie Skinner. Del Norte County received material from Mary Lu Saunier. El Dorado County has information provided by Linda McBeath–Van Gundy and Betty Mitchell. Fresno County had input from Kelly Hobbs, and Gene Russell again helped out on Glenn County material.

Humboldt County has material from Don S. Davis, Raymond W. Hillman, and Ann Roberts. Helpful information on Imperial County came from Eugene Chamberlin, Lynn Housouer, and Phil Porretta. Contributors to Inyo County included Gene Brown, Don Dobmeier, and Beth S. Porter. Kern County information came from Harland W. Boyd, and Tim I. Purdy brought Lassen County information.

Los Angeles County had an impressive list of contributors: Bonnie Beckerson, Casey Berent, Dominique Brummond, Barbara Callarman, Donna Crippen, David D. Earle, Don Esacove, Tim Gregory, Rosemary Hulle, David Johnson, Gloria Ricci Lothrop, Steve Navarro, Ruth Rogers, William Shepherd, and L. R. Utter. Marin County correspondents included Beverly Bastien and Jocelyn A. Moss. Mariposa County had information from Gail H. Tyler; Lila Lee advised on Mendocino County. Merced County had information from Jack Bleiman, Georgia Johnson, and Andrea Morris Metz. Modoc County had information from Dixie M. Server.

Mono County material came from Kent Stoddard. Napa County material came from Dorothy Soderholm. Nevada County was commented on by Lester Simmonds, Edwin L. Tyson, and Patricia van der Pas. Orange County data was provided by Virginia Bannister, Don Dobmeier, Kenneth Leavens, and Stephen H. Smith. Placer County material came from Ralph W. Kummer, George A. Ley, and Dean Moore. Plumas County information was provided by Marge Holmes, Don C. Johns, and Marge Werner. Riverside County information came from Alan Curl and Sally McManus.

From Sacramento County, information was provided by Annie Anderson, Elizabeth Pinkerton, Arleen Towne, and Allen Wilson. San Diego County material was furnished by Eugene Chamberlin, Eldonna Lay, and Olga Puhn. San Francisco benefited from the information given by Robert J. Chandler, Gary Holloway, and Daniel B. Rosen. San Joaquin County had information from Don Walker. San Luis Obispo County material was provided by L. W. Allen. San Mateo County information came from Eleonore M. Fourie, Edna S. Harks, Martha R. May, and Robert Schoeppner. From

Santa Barbara County, information was provided by Jarrell C. Jackman. The Santa Clara County contributors included Martha Bilbrey, Lisa Christiansen, Melissa Heyman, Mary Lou Lyon, Willys I. Peck, Steven Staiger, and Jim Williams.

Shasta County data came from Bert Walsh. Sierra County had advice from Anne Elder. From Siskiyou County came useful information from W. J. McKellar and Richard Silva. Solano County had information from Bertram A. Hughes. Sonoma County's Anne Garrett was a contributor. Sutter County had material supplied by Frances Whyte. Tehama County had material from Eugene Serr and Joan and John Ward. Trinity County once more benefited from the information provided by Alice G. Jones. Tulare County's Terry L. Ommen provided useful data.

Tuolumne County has material provided by Sharon Marovich. The Ventura County chapter benefited from the input of Ynez D. Haase, Patricia Havens, Mary Alice Orcutt Henderson, and Betty McAllister. Helpful material on Yolo County was provided by Shipley Walters and by Allen Wilson, and Yuba County had information from Daniel Barth.

In acknowledging all these contributions from others, I alone remain responsible for the final writing. If there are errors of fact or of interpretation, I would greatly appreciate being notified of corrections, in hopes of incorporating them in future editions.

Judith B. Kyle and I would like to dedicate this edition of *Historic Spots in California* to our children and grandchildren: to Lucile Kyle; to Charles, Erin, Alexander, and Cameron Kyle; and to William, Lynn, and Jennifer Kyle. We are all natives of the Golden State and enjoy living in California.

Douglas E. Kyle

Contents

This overview of California history is intended to provide some background for readers not already acquainted with it and to avoid the need to repeat information throughout the chapters. Readers seeking more detailed information should consult the first section of the bibliography, which lists works on the general history of California.

California's earliest verified historic date is September 28, 1542, when two small ships flying Spanish colors sailed into a harbor on the Pacific Coast of North America. Juan Rodríguez Cabrillo, commander of the expedition, called his anchorage the Bay of San Miguel. Sebastián Vizcaíno, whose expedition entered the port sixty years later, called it the Bay of San Diego, and that name is the one that has survived. Name changes would often happen in the history of California.

Spain, by the middle of the sixteenth century, was the foremost military and naval power of western Europe, with expanding colonies in the Caribbean and on the continents of North and South America, and trade interests that spanned the Pacific to the Philippine Islands and Japan. Voyages by Cabrillo and his contemporary Hernando de Alarcón (who may have been the first European to set foot on California soil, in what is now Imperial County, around 1540) were part of the Spanish program of expansion. This was financed in large part by the incredible wealth that the Spaniards found in Mexico and Peru and was driven both by imperial needs and by dreams of gold and magical lands.

The name California was taken from Garcí Ordoñez de Montalvo's popular romantic narrative published in 1510, *Las Sergas de Esplandían* (*The Exploits of Esplandían*), which referred to a fabulous island ruled by an Amazon, Queen Calafia. The name was later given to the land lying north and west of Mexico, thought at that time to be an island, but actually the peninsula now known as Baja (Lower) California. Also somewhere to the West—which has, in Western civilization, always represented the future, unknown but potentially golden—the land of El Dorado was supposed to lie. The legend of El Dorado told of a kingdom so rich that its ruler was daily anointed with gold dust, thus becoming "El Dorado," the Gilded Man.

Meanwhile, in 1579, Spain's hegemony in the Pacific was briefly challenged by the Englishman Francis Drake. After raiding Spanish ports on the Pacific coast of South and Central America, Drake anchored his ship for three weeks, probably in California's Marin County. On his departure he claimed the land for Queen Elizabeth, a loyal but basically empty gesture. No other English voyager is known to have called on the California coast for more than two centuries.

After Cabrillo's visit, the next official Spanish voyage of discovery was that led by Sebastián Vizcaíno in 1602, in search of a possible anchorage on the North American coast for the great cargo ships that sailed from Manila to Acapulco. Vizcaíno discovered Monterey Bay, which he named for the Conde de Monterey, viceroy in Mexico. However, Vizcaíno's glowing reports of what he saw in traveling perhaps as far north as Cape Mendocino did not stimulate further expeditions. Spain claimed the Pacific Coast of North America as being within her empire, and no other European power challenged that claim. This remained a stable situation until the middle of the eighteenth century.

The area claimed by Spain as Alta (Upper) California was, in fact, already home to some 300,000 indigenous people, whose ancestors had been living there for at least 12,000 years. California's generally mild, dry climate and abundance of plant and animal life made it possible for the native people (usually referred to by outsiders as Indians) to harvest and store a generous supply of food without the need for farming or a nomadic life style. By the time Europeans began to explore the coast of California, the Indians had evolved into a complex of cultures, encompassing 104 language groups and living, usually in permanent settlements

xi

(later called *rancherías* by the Spanish), in every region of the present-day state except the High Sierra. Their life was on the whole peaceable and enriched by cooperative labor and extensive patterns of trade. They were, however, quite unprepared to withstand the Europeans, who showed little understanding or appreciation of the Indian way of life and whose attitude of superiority was to have tragic consequences.

By the 1760s Spain was forced to review her situation in the New World; Britain, France, and Russia were claiming more and more territory in North America. The northwestern frontier of Spain's empire was unfortified and vulnerable to foreign penetration.

The decision was made to colonize Alta California. Spanish subjects would be induced to move into these northern territories, assured of military protection and remission of taxes in the first five years of settlement. The Catholic Church would be provided with a fresh field in which missionary work could be done among the Indians—it was remembered that they were subjects of the king and could be introduced to the benefits of Spanish culture. The military would fortify strategic locations and deal with possible Indian or foreign resistance.

In 1769 a two-part expedition set out for Alta California and arrived at San Diego in the summer of that year. Three ships carried colonists and soldiers from Mexico, and an overland party traveled from Sonora with Gaspar de Portolá, governor of Baja California, as military commander and Father Junipero Serra as spiritual leader. Portolá had been instructed to find the Bay of Monterey of the Vizcaíno reports. Serra was to begin the establishment of the missions to the Indians of Alta California.

After the two groups came together at San Diego, Father Serra and his Franciscan brethren established the first mission. Portolá, after ordering the foundations for a presidio, took a party northward to find Monterey Bay. The settlers took possession of the land. Not unexpectedly, this act was challenged by the local Indians; every activity of the Spanish was protected by a small military force.

Ultimately, four presidios, or fortified places, were established by the Spaniards in Alta California, all before the end of the eighteenth century, at San Diego, Santa Barbara, Monterey, and San Francisco. In addition, twenty-one missions were founded by the Franciscans along the coast, from San Diego de Alcalá in 1769 to San Francisco Solano in Sonoma in 1821. Many became extensive operations, containing churches, a padre's residence, workshops and storehouses, and quarters for both Indian neophytes and soldiers. Using Indian labor, the missions developed gardens, orchards, vineyards, and pastures and began an extensive trade in hides and tallow. Between the missions, usually a day's ride apart, a rough pathway developed—El Camino Real, "The King's Highway." The name has been retained in several communities and is closely followed by today's US Highway 101 between Petaluma and Los Angeles, and Interstate Highway 5 between Los Angeles and San Diego.

A third type of Spanish settlement was also begun in Alta California; this was the pueblo or town, home for Spanish colonists. Many inducements were made to bring settlers into the province. Two pueblos, Los Angeles and San Jose, survived to become major California cities; a third, Branciforte, languished, and its site is now part of the city of Santa Cruz.

Alta California was thought of as a northern extension of New Spain, as Mexico was known in its Spanish days. For a dozen years, overland expeditions brought in settlers, livestock, seeds, and tools, culminating in the founding of the Pueblo of Los Angeles in 1781. In that year, a massacre of Spaniards along the Colorado River by Mojave Indians abruptly brought the overland route to a halt. Henceforth, the connection between inhabitants in Alta California and the governors in Mexico was made by sea, and a separation and sense of distance obtruded between the two areas, which was never overcome, in either the Spanish or the Mexican years.

Spain's rule over Alta California has come under vigorous criticism by many historians in the last hundred years. The attack centers on the impact of Spanish Christian culture and domination upon the native California population. By their words and their actions, Europeans of the eighteenth and early nineteenth centuries believed their ways to be highly superior to the rest of the world, and this was evident in Alta California. Every European who left memoirs of a visit during the Spanish period wrote disparagingly of the Indians, who were described as ugly, naked, lethargic, and behaving much like animals. Rounded up into communities under Spanish rule, the Indians were cut off from their traditional ways; they were also exposed to European diseases, which worked with terrible force. Zealous and devout missionary priests, including the beatified Serra, probably would be horrified to find that a later age would charge them with genocide. One fact can not be denied: the Indian population of California had declined from 300,000 at the time of first

European contact to less than 50,000 by the middle of the nineteenth century. Once in a while rebellion broke out, always to be crushed with military force. It is almost miraculous that Indian culture survived at all.

Several Europeans visited California and left accounts of what they saw. Among them was the Englishman George Vancouver, who twice visited the province in the 1790s and noted the weak defenses of the coast. In 1806 a Russian ship easily entered San Francisco Bay to begin negotiations with the local authorities for supplies to the destitute colony of Sitka in Russian America, now Alaska. Although Spain's mercantile economic policy sought to keep foreigners out of her imperial trade, the officials in remote Alta California agreed to permit a limited amount of commerce between the province and the Russians. When a Russian settlement was established north of San Francisco at Fort Ross (Sonoma County) in 1819 the Spaniards were unable to oust these traders, and indeed were grateful for the services of the colony's artisans.

A new threat to Spain's empire came from the United States of America. An occasional American ship had already been seen along the California coast in the early days of the nineteenth century, as the whaling industry and the China trade began to bring Yankee ships into Pacific waters, which had hitherto been a Spanish monopoly. In 1819, the Adams-Onís Treaty between the United States and Spain drew a boundary line between Spanish and American claims in North America, which followed the 42nd parallel of latitude westward from the Rocky Mountains to the Pacific Ocean, the boundary line between California and Oregon today. The Oregon Country became an American outpost on the Pacific, from which many Americans would emigrate into California in the Gold Rush days.

In 1822 New Spain threw off Spanish rule and became the Republic of Mexico. Alta California had no choice but to accept this political change, although many of her leaders were Spanish by birth or by loyalty, particularly among the padres of the Church. Thus an element of hostility was added to the sense of distance that already existed between Mexico and Alta California. Spain had been an imperial power of global scope; Mexico was an impoverished country with no tradition of political self-government and no system of efficient internal communications.

Mexican rule did bring significant changes from that of Spain. A governor appointed from Mexico was sent to rule the province. The seat of government often moved from one administration to another, usually between Monterey in the north and Los Angeles in the south. (Briefly, in 1832–33, the quarrel between the north and the south resulted in two governors and two capitals. North-south conflict in California is an old story.) A provincial legislature, the *diputación*, was created, but its authority was limited, and its deeds were few. Municipal government appeared, and the *alcalde*, the town's chief official, became the most important person in the region.

By Mexican revolutionary standards, the Church was hopelessly reactionary. As owner of extensive lands, it was also a major economic force in a poor country. Ideology and fiscal needs combined to bring on the secularization of the missions beginning in 1834. The property of the missions was taken over by the state and sold to eager buyers. Those Indians who lived in the vicinity of the missions were supposed to get land of their own in this process, but in fact few did.

Land was the one permanent element in this period of change. In the Spanish days, each of the missions received a grant of land for its sustenance. A few private individuals had also been given the right to occupy specific tracts of land, and most of these two dozen awards were confirmed under Mexican law in the 1820s. Mexico began the policy of making outright grants of land to trustworthy citizens. The land was allocated by leagues; a linear league would be 2.63 miles in today's measurements, and a square league would be about 4,439 acres. These parcels of land were known as *ranchos* and often mark the first attempts made in the history of California to make specific identification of land. Thus many of the historic spots in California have their first mention as ranchos. (The chapters in this book that deal with coastal counties often contain subheadings based on ranchos, followed by the names of the towns that now sit on that land.) About five hundred grants of land were made in the quarter century of Mexican rule.

The economic backwardness of Mexican California invited outsiders. After 1822, more and more of these were young bachelors, American or British, seeking their fortune; many of them married the daughters of established California families after being baptized in the Catholic faith, which accounts for a name such as Juan Bautista Rogers Cooper of Monterey. Jedediah Strong Smith headed the first party of Americans to arrive in Alta California overland from the United States, in 1826; other mountain men and fur traders, some from the Hudson's Bay Company in the Oregon Country, were active in California in the late 1820s and 1830s. Unable to keep them out, Mexico permitted foreigners who were willing to acknowledge Mexican law to become citizens of the republic, and as citizens these newcomers could become landowners. Men such as Robert Livermore and George C. Yount were now peers of established families like the Carrillos, the Lugos, and the Yorbas. These Hispanic grandees were chiefly concerned with cattle raising on their extensive lands. The newcomers tended to dominate the commercial and business life of Alta California.

Overland migration of American settlers into California began in 1841, when the Bidwell-Bartleson party arrived from the Mississippi Valley. The crossing of the West was a formidable undertaking: trails were random and poorly marked, water was scarce, and livestock perished. The people making this crossing endured great hardship in their migration, of which the Donner Party (whose story is told in the Nevada County chapter) was a frightful example. Despite adversities, the newcomers made a considerable addition to the American presence in California by 1846.

Between 1835 and 1846, relations between Mexico and the United States deteriorated. In part, this was the result of Mexican suspicion that the United States was seeking territorial expansion at Mexico's expense. In 1835, Mexico rejected an American offer to purchase San Francisco Bay. In the following year, Americans in Texas staged a successful revolution that drove Mexico out and created the independent Lone Star Republic, officially annexed to the United States in 1845. In 1842, Thomas ap Catesby Jones, commodore of the U.S. Pacific squadron, having heard a rumor that war had broken out, brought his four ships into Monterey Bay and demanded the surrender of the province. In the 1840s, expansion toward the Pacific Coast became the announced goal of the Democratic Party. In the election of 1844 voters chose Democrat James K. Polk as president and put Democrats in control of both houses of Congress. The American annexation of Texas early in 1845 caused Mexico to sever diplomatic relations with the United States, and by May 1846 the two countries were at war. Although the major events of the war took place along the Texas border and on into Mexico, the opportunity to gain control of California was not wasted.

John Charles Frémont, an Army officer and son-in-law of Senator Thomas Hart Benton of Missouri, had begun his career with expeditions exploring passes in the Rocky Mountains. He reached the Oregon Country in 1843 and entered Alta California the following year, where he too noted the weak defenses of the region. His *Report of the Exploring Expedition to Oregon and North California*, written with his wife Jessie in 1845, was very well received and brought California to the attention of American officials. By the end of 1845, Frémont was back in California, where he and his men openly defied the Mexican authorities, going so far as to put up a fortification atop Gabilan Peak in San Benito County, overlooking the Salinas Valley. He abandoned the fort before any formal hostilities ensued. In May 1846, while Congress was receiving President Polk's war message, Frémont returned to California from a short sojourn in Oregon, captured Sutter's Fort at Sacramento, took Captain Sutter as prisoner, and encouraged Americans to rise against Mexican rule.

On June 14, 1846, a party of Americans took possession of the town of Sonoma and raised the Bear Flag of the California Republic over the plaza. Within three weeks, an American naval force appeared on the coast and formally proclaimed American rule over the presidios and coastal towns. Throughout the remainder of 1846, several incidents of Californian resistance to the American conquest took place, the most serious being the Battle of San Pasqual in San Diego County, where twenty-one American soldiers were ambushed and killed in December. On January 13, 1847, Frémont accepted the surrender of Governor Pío Pico and General José María Flores. The captured province was officially annexed to the United States by the Treaty of Guadalupe Hidalgo in 1848, ending the Mexican War.

Just a few days before the treaty was signed, James Marshall, an employee of Captain John Sutter, discovered abundant gold in the bed of the South Fork of the American River, at Coloma in El Dorado County. Nothing could keep this news from spreading, and throughout 1848 there were many other discoveries. President Polk's message to Congress in December acknowledged the bonanza. By 1849 the great gold rush was on. From as far away as Australia, Chile, China, and Europe, gold-seekers came to California by sea. A greater number of Americans ventured overland, on the trails already established by earlier pioneers. The excitement continued even after the easily discovered streambed nuggets were gathered and men realized that they had to mine the foothills of the Sierra in search of more gold.

In this Mother Lode region, new camps and towns set up almost overnight, many lasting no more than a few months. "Dame Shirley," the pen name of one of the few women in a mining camp, left memorable descriptions of Rich Bar, Plumas County, in 1852, which are a classic of reporting. The ruins of these short-lived mining centers are still to be seen throughout the state, from Tumco and Havilah in the south up to Hawkinsville and Timbuctoo in the north. A number of other towns, such as Nevada City and Sonora, have survived and remain important regional centers.

Extensive hydraulic mining was practiced throughout the gold region until halted by a court order in 1884, largely because of environmental damage. Rivers had filled with debris, necessitating levees along the Feather and Sacramento Rivers to hold back the spring floods, an annual problem that persisted into the middle of the twentieth century. Malakoff Diggins State Historic Park in Nevada County and the enormous tailings east of Folsom in Sacramento County were the result of this kind of mining.

California, newcomers realized, presented many other opportunities for wealth beyond the haphazard search for gold. The mild climate and good soil invited the development of agriculture, ultimately the state's most valuable economic activity. The new cities of the Gold Rush—San Francisco, Sacramento, and Stockton in particular—needed skilled workmen and entrepreneurs. California's isolation encouraged the development of domestic industry, which by the federal census of 1860 boasted more than 3,500 manufacturing establishments.

The migration into California was so large that a movement toward statehood was underway even before civil territorial government began. In September 1849 a state constitutional convention met in Monterey. Of the forty-eight delegates, only seven were native Californians. The new state government included a popularly elected governor holding office for two years, a bicameral Legislature, and a hierarchy of courts. A bill of rights contained a ban on slavery. As it happened, fifteen states in 1849 were free soil and fifteen were slave holding, a balance deliberately maintained since the Missouri Compromise in 1820. No slave territory was available to match free-soil California, whose admission to the Union the slave-holding South feared would place that region at a disadvantage when sectional issues were voted on by Congress. Nonetheless, California entered the Union as a free state in the Compromise of 1850, which also included a more stringent fugitive slave law.

When the Civil War broke out, the need to link loyal California to the Union became urgent. As early as 1853, plans for a federally underwritten transcontinental railroad had been discussed, but nothing came of them for nearly a decade. In 1862, Congress enacted the Pacific Railroad Bill, just at the time when the forces of the Union seemed to be losing ground. (Travel by sea from New York to California, even using the shortcut over the Isthmus of Panama, was still a matter of many weeks under the best of conditions.) Before the completion of the railroad in 1869, however, telegraph lines connected California with the Mississippi Valley, and so on to the eastern states. San Franciscans learned of President Lincoln's death the morning after his assassination in April 1865.

Lincoln's Republican Party, which received California's electoral votes both in 1860 and 1864, advocated federal support for internal development; this included extensive land grants to encourage the construction of railroad lines in the West. With Republicans dominating both the federal and the state political scene for many years after the end of the Civil War in 1865, the railroads had friends in high places. The Central Pacific Railroad, the western half of the transcontinental project of 1862–69, became the Southern Pacific Railroad system by the end of the century and exerted a great deal of influence on California politics. Its landholdings created towns such as Barstow, Roseville, and Tulare, and its power brought on such events as the Mussel Slough Tragedy in 1880, a story told in the Kings County chapter.

In these years (1850–80), a major development in California history resulted from policies adopted concerning Mexican land grants. These grants had been made in the days when a registered *diseño* (a sketch map and description of the land) was sufficient evidence of a valid land claim. Virtually none of the ranchos in California had fences or any marked boundaries. Although Article IX of the Treaty of Guadalupe Hidalgo declared that Mexican land titles would be honored under the new American regime, ambitious newcomers into California laid claim to attractive areas of old land grants or simply "squatted" on these lands and defied the owners to drive them out. The early histories of both Oakland and Sacramento give many examples of how effective squatter settlement could be.

A federal statute in 1851 attempted to regularize the process whereby land claims in California could be approved (or "patented") by a commission appointed for that purpose. Holders of Mexican land grants had two years to prove before the courts that theirs was a valid title; the burden of proof was upon the Mexican owners, not the new squatters. The Land Commission met from 1852 to 1856 and, at great length and to the disadvantage of claimants (none of the commissioners knew Spanish, for example), determined the status of each claim. On the average, it took seventeen years for a claim to be patented. Often, the original litigants had died; even more often, the costs of litigation compelled the rancho owners to sell off their land piecemeal. Between 1865 and 1880, to cite one example, the Sepulveda family had to contend with eighty separate lawsuits in their effort to keep Rancho Los Palos Verdes in Los Angeles County. The result of all this litigation was that about three-quarters of the Mexican claims were accepted or patented by federal officials, but in fact most of the litigants had already sold most of their holdings. Albany, Berkeley, Emeryville, and northern Oakland now stand on the lands of José Domingo Peralta, who was so impoverished by legal fees that, at his death in 1865, his family needed financial aid for his burial. Thus the old ranchos became divided into many new holdings.

With railroad transportation into and out of California a reality after 1869, the pace of California life stepped up dramatically. Migration from East to West increased, particularly in the area around Los Angeles. The twenty-seven original counties of California were gradually subdivided and increased to reflect these changes until there were fifty-eight by 1907. Many new towns were incorporated, chiefly in the Los Angeles basin and in the Great Central Valley. A diverse population soon developed, with a significant number from the Far East. Chinese laborers, some who arrived as early gold miners and others brought in to build the railroads, stayed on, and San Francisco's Chinatown had 47,000 inhabitants by an 1875 estimate. Settlers from France, Italy, and the Austro-Hungarian and German empires all established colonies for their countrymen. One could see Chinese joss houses and Jewish synagogues in the towns. The one population group that was declining was the California Indian. A last hard-fought resistance against overwhelming odds, the Modoc War of 1873, ended Native American protests for nearly a hundred years.

In the late nineteenth century California was discovered by artists and writers, attracted to the magnificent landscapes and natural beauty of the state, and to the fascinating spectacle of rapid social and economic change. Some great works of this period, such as the paintings of Albert Bierstadt or the essays of John Muir, were done by men born in Europe but raised in America and who came in their maturity to California. Health seekers flocked to the balmy climate: many tuberculosis sanitariums were established between 1880 and 1920, for example. A new kind of "El Dorado" myth began, comprised of oranges, sunshine, outdoor life, and a wholesomeness that was contrasted with the squalor of Eastern industrial cities.

In these years of great change, some believed that California's past was being obliterated. In 1871 the Cali-

fornia Historical Society was organized at the University of Santa Clara. In 1875 the Native Sons of the Golden West was begun, followed in 1886 by the Native Daughters of the Golden West. These groups were all concerned with the commemoration and recording of California's historic activities and landmarks. Many of these are today State Registered Landmarks (SRL) and are so identified in the text that follows.

California political issues between 1875 and 1924 frequently involved anti-Oriental movements, whose leaders declared that Chinese labor was undercutting white labor and that Japanese entrepreneurs were acquiring excessive amounts of land. Under pressure from the California congressional delegation, the United States in 1882 stopped further immigration from China, the first time that a nationality had been excluded. Japanese immigration was halted by an Executive Agreement in 1908 and banned in 1924. In 1913 California's Webb Act prohibited Japanese not born in the United States from acquiring land in the state. In the years after 1924, official relations between the United States and the Empire of Japan grew more and more estranged: the Pearl Harbor attack on December 7, 1941, brought into the open a long-standing hostility, to which California politics had made some contribution. Although all Japanese on the West Coast were forced into internment camps in the early days of World War II, most Japanese living in the United States were loyal to this country. The Manzanar site in Inyo County remains as a reminder of this period of wartime tension.

Political issues in these years were a chief subject of the press, which was always important as a means of communication in a state as large and diversified as California. Many leading newspapers had joined the concerted effort in the 1910 election to drive the Southern Pacific Railroad from its dominant position in the state; this campaign was successful with the election of Progressive Republican reformer Hiram Johnson as governor and a sympathetic legislature.

The major newspaper publishing names of the twentieth century, among them Chandler, De Young, Knowland, McClatchy, and Storke, were also concerned with historic preservation. William Randolph Hearst, the most influential publisher in California's history, supported several historical restorations. His San Simeon estate, in San Luis Obispo County, is a kind of treasure-house of collections, and is a major tourist attraction today.

Water is an issue that repeatedly makes the headlines, for the simple reason that southern California has the larger population while northern California has 70 percent of the water in the state. Agriculture depends upon irrigation to get through the long, dry summers. Dams and reservoirs, aqueducts, and pumping systems have been installed throughout the state, often after considerable acrimony and debate. The city of Los Angeles acquired water rights in the Owens River valley around 1900, an action that is still hotly debated. Great aqueducts brought the water to Los Angeles, leaving the Owens River basin in a desiccated condition. More aqueducts brought water from the Colorado River; the Salton Sea is the result of an overflow of water from the Colorado in 1905. The federal Central Valley Project, begun in 1935, dammed the Sacramento and San Joaquin Rivers to provide irrigation for the Great Central Valley. The larger State Water Project, begun in the 1960s, involves moving millions of acre-feet of water every year from the northern to the southern part of the state; Butte County's Oroville Dam and Lake Oroville are the biggest elements in this project, without which California might not have grown as it has.

Petroleum became important in California as early as 1880, as numerous oil strikes were made in Kern and Los Angeles counties. By the first years of the twentieth century, the state was the largest oil producer in the nation. Overall, the value of petroleum far exceeds that of gold, although California is still known as the Golden State.

Economic struggles came to the fore in California as the twentieth century began, and workers began to organize, particularly in the industrial city of San Francisco. Often at odds with management, such groups as the International Longshoremen's Association wielded considerable power in the city; in 1934 they led a successful general strike in San Francisco, the only such occurrence in California history. Meanwhile, though the ports continued to be important for the shipment of goods, more and more commerce was being carried by trucks on the expanding highway system. All too often these highways were built through and over old areas of historic interest.

One industry closely connected with California since the early 1900s is motion pictures and, more recently, television, centered around the Hollywood district of Los Angeles. "Hollywood" became synonymous with glamour and opulence, not only on the screen but also in the homes of Bel Air and Beverly Hills. The area has been a tourist attraction for decades. Movies were also shot on location throughout California, creating a new category of historic spots. When the Hooker Oak (SRL 313) in Bidwell Park, Chico, fell in 1977, newspapers identified it chiefly as part of the setting of the 1938 film *Robin Hood*.

World War II brought great changes to California, among them many new or expanded military bases; in the early months of the war there was a Japanese submarine attack on the Santa Barbara County coast. Hundreds of thousands of military personnel were moved through California ports. There had been an influx of migrants from the Dust Bowl states into California in the 1930s, but the new wave was ten times that of the previous decade. The defense industry, which became one of California's most important, sought workers from all over the country. One group that responded in large numbers was black Americans from the South. The 1940 census reported 124,000 blacks in California; by the 1950 census, their numbers had risen to 462,000. Established California cities became larger, and new ones arose seemingly overnight, particularly in the San Francisco Bay Area and in the Los Angeles basin.

In the last decades of the twentieth century, new population movements were occurring, many as a result of war in Southeast Asia. People from Cambodia, Laos, and Vietnam now made their homes in California. Fresno became not only a city of many Armenians; by 1990 it had the world's largest Hmong population. The assimilation that some Californians have feared and others have championed will doubtless continue to add color and new dimensions to the history of California in the future. One encouraging sign is the return of Native Americans. From near-extinction in 1900, the Indian population of California is today more than 200,000, the largest of any state, in part because of migration of Indians into California from other parts of the United States.

From its earliest contacts with the outside world, California has had a strong connection with national policy, international strategy, and military fortifications. A major change in California in the past two decades has been the closure of military bases and the abandonment of lands that have long been off-limits to the public. In the following text, the reader may note that it has not always been possible to say unequivocally just what is happening to land that was formerly an air force base, for example.

Moreover, the account of California's historic spots that follows will inevitably require updating as time, earthquakes, floods, and freeways take their toll. So this must be regarded as a chapter in a history still unfolding, still fascinating, and worth visiting.

HISTORIC SPOTS IN CALIFORNIA

Mission San Jose, Fremont

Alameda County

Alameda County was created in 1853 from portions of Contra Costa and Santa Clara Counties. The county seat was originally at Alvarado. It was moved to San Leandro in 1856, and from there in 1873 to Oakland, where it has remained.

The poplar or cottonwood tree (*alamo* in Spanish) is the basis for the word *alameda*, which means "a place where poplar trees grow"; it was also used to describe a tree-lined road. The county's name came from El Arroyo de la Alameda (Alameda Creek), lined with willow and silver-barked sycamore trees, giving it the appearance of a tree-lined roadway.

THE EMERYVILLE SHELL MOUND

From the 1850s the shell mounds found along the shores of San Francisco Bay excited the curiosity of the incoming new settlers. In 1902 these mounds were studied by Professors John C. Merriam and Max Uhle of the University of California. They made careful excavations on the site of the prominent Emeryville mound and published the results of their work. In 1908, N. C. Nelson completed a survey of the entire San Francisco Bay region, where he located, numbered, and mapped nearly 425 shell heaps, analyzing them in detail and publishing a summary of his observations and conclusions.

The Emeryville Mound, designated number 329 in the Nelson survey, was situated on the eastern shore of San Francisco Bay almost due east of the Golden Gate. It lay on the western side of the Peralta grant, or that part of Rancho San Antonio apportioned to Vicente Peralta by his father, Luís María Peralta. This section later became known as Emeryville, an incorporated city lying between Oakland and Berkeley. The shell mound (SRL 335) was located between the bay and the railroad tracks. Shellmound Street identifies the site; no official marker has been placed there. As W. Egbert Schenck explained:

> The first people who came to this area camped just above the shoreline, possibly on little hummocks at the edge of the marsh. As shellfish were obtained, the shells were thrown aside, and these with the by-products of daily life increased the campground and gradually crept out into the marsh. . . . As the shell area increased, subsequent people utilized it because it was drier, placing camps, perhaps over what had previously been marsh. . . . This shell area grew until it covered some hundreds of thousands of square feet.

The Emeryville mound was located at a point that was favorable for use as a camping ground by native peoples. Lying on the narrow alluvial plain that stretches along the Contra Costa ("opposite coast") between the foothills and the bay, it was bordered on the north by open, almost treeless plains, and on the south by a willow thicket some twenty acres in extent. Further south the thicket merged into a marsh extending about one and one-half miles along the shore and gradually increasing in width until at its southern end it was three-quarters of a mile wide. Beyond the marshes stretched a mile of rolling, oak-studded fields, the Encinal de Temescal.

In prehistoric times, Temescal Creek supplied fresh water to the nomadic people who visited its banks, and the abundant shellfish beds at its mouth supplied food. The quiet reaches of the bay were full of sea otter, perhaps hunted from tule rafts. Waterfowl filled the marshes, and deer were plentiful in the willow thicket and the oak grove to the south; acorns, seeds, and other vegetable foods were abundant, as the numerous mortars found in the vicinity indicate. The willow thicket also supplied ample firewood.

To this choice spot groups of Indians came yearly from the surrounding country, perhaps from long distances. They may have spent six months out of each year at this site, fishing and hunting, drying and pounding the shellfish for future food supplies, and taking the otter skins for clothing.

The Emeryville shell mound may be as old as 1,000 years, but it is impossible to determine this accurately. There is no certain evidence on when the place was last used as a rendezvous for nomadic tribes. Schenck says that it was apparently unoccupied when Fages passed that way in 1772, for no mention of it is made in the chronicles of that expedition. Anza, in 1776, and Gabriel Moraga, in the early 1800s, also failed to mention having seen Indians in the Oakland-Berkeley neighborhood, although they did note their presence both to the south and to the north. Yet even if these early explorers did not see Indians there, and even though there were no fogs concealing their whereabouts, the oak groves of which Father Crespí wrote, together with the willow thicket near the mouth of Temescal Creek, may well have formed an effectual screen behind which the Indians at the Emeryville mound were encamped—or perhaps took refuge—when the first white travelers passed that way.

Around the year 1836, Vicente Peralta built his adobe house not far from Temescal Creek and about one and a half miles east of the Emeryville mound. At the mouth of the creek was the Temescal embarcadero ("pier"), and the ancient mound was a landmark known to travelers along the old creek road during those days.

In 1857 the Peralta grant was surveyed and mapped by Julius Kellersberger, and in 1859 Edward Wiard purchased that portion of it on which the mound lay. Contemporary maps show buildings on both the eastern and western parts; in 1871 Wiard leveled a section of the eastern side and laid out the mile racetrack that became known as the Oakland Trotting Park. On the western side in 1876 he opened Shellmound Park, a popular holiday resort and picnic grounds; the Emeryville shell mound in those days was a picturesque landmark. On its low, truncated summit were a circle of trees, some windmills, and the round dance pavilion surrounded by a high cypress hedge. An atlas of 1878 shows this mound with the residence of J. S. Emery in the foreground.

The shores of San Francisco Bay were too valuable to be left undeveloped, and over the years virtually all the shell mounds were leveled and their contents dis-

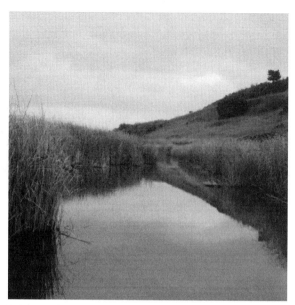

Tulare Marsh, Coyote Hills Regional Park, Fremont

persed. In 1924 the Emeryville mound was leveled in order to convert the area into a factory site. John Hubert Mee, president of the Mee Estate, which owned the property, made known his intentions and permitted the University of California to explore the site, with much assistance from Captain Ludwig Siebe, proprietor of Shellmound Park. The mound was razed by steam shovel; careful observations were made and collections were taken during the process. After the leveling operations were completed, controlled excavations of its lower levels were made by hand. Many skeletal and artifact materials were collected. The pile was found to be composed principally of shells—mostly clams, mussels, and oysters, with a plentiful mixture of cockleshells. Certain other kinds, found only in small quantities, had been treated in the manner of possessions. Besides human burials, the accumulation disclosed the skeletal remains of birds, quadrupeds, sea mammals, and fish. Many of these bone remains were placed in the Museum of Vertebrate Zoology at the University of California at Berkeley. One shell mound in Alameda County remains pretty much undisturbed, in Coyote Hills Regional Park in Fremont.

But the Emeryville shell mounds were not totally gone. In 1999 and 2000 renovations along the shoreline revealed substantial remains from these old sites, discovered as old buildings and lots were pulled down. Here, and across the bay in South San Francisco, efforts are being made to keep intact some traces of these long-dispersed sites, something very difficult to achieve in areas of high population and commercial density.

THE LINCOLN PARK SHELL MOUND

One shell mound of the 425 mapped by Nelson in 1906–8 has been memorialized. The site of this mound, located in the city of Alameda and now covered by streets and residences, extended over three acres of ground bounded roughly by what are now Central, Johnson, and Santa Clara Avenues and Court Street. The mound was removed by the city authorities in the summer of 1908, and the earth, combined with tons of shells, was used for the making of roads on Bay Farm Island.

The lower levels of this ground were examined by Captain W. A. Clark, who, working the ground carefully with a hand trowel, was able to save a number of fine relics. They were placed in the Alameda Public Library, where they are still on display.

Near the site of the old Indian mound in Lincoln Park is a stone monument with a bronze tablet inscribed: "One thousand feet due west was a prehistoric mound, 400 feet long, 150 feet wide, 14 feet high. The remains of 450 Indians, with stone implements and shell ornaments, were found when the mound was opened in 1908. Erected by Copa de Oro Chapter, D.A.R., 1914."

OTHER INDIAN SITES

From Albany in the north to Mowry's Landing in the south, there were at least twenty shell mounds scattered along the shore of the bay in Alameda County when they were cataloged and mapped by Nelson in 1906–8. Nelson in his report states that the 425 mounds found in the greater Bay Area probably did not include all of them, and that some doubtless had been obliterated in past years.

At the curve of Indian Rock Avenue where it meets the south end of San Diego Road in north Berkeley, a huge, irregular rock mass looms above the roadway. From its level summit there is a commanding view of the city and of the bay beyond. At the base of the main boulders are a number of smaller rocks with deeply worn holes or mortars where the Indians once ground acorns for meal. Nearby, the city of Berkeley has planted a garden in Mortar Rock Park. A few hundred feet lower down on Indian Rock Avenue at the head of San Mateo Road is Indian Rock Park, another prehistoric landmark set among small live oak and tall eucalyptus trees.

In the Trestle Glen neighborhood of Oakland there is a level spot where an Indian village once stood. It was originally called Indian Gulch because Indians still lived there when the first Americans came to that region. Nothing remains today as a reminder of the Indians, and Trestle Glen Road winds through a narrow canyon still shaded by immense live oaks and other trees.

TEMESCAL

Temescal, a name of Aztec origin meaning "sweat house," was brought to California by the Franciscan Fathers. A. L. Kroeber describes the *temescal* thus:

> From the outside its appearance is that of a small mound. The ground has been excavated to the depth of a foot or a foot and a half, over a space of about twelve by seven or eight feet. In the center of this area two heavy posts are set up three or four feet apart. These are connected at the top by a log laid in their forks. Upon this log, and in the two forks, are laid some fifty or more logs and sticks of various dimensions, their ends sloping down to the edge of the excavation. It is probable that brush covers these timbers. The whole is thoroughly covered with earth. There is no smoke hole. The entrance is on one of the long sides, directly facing the space between the two center posts, and only a few feet from them. The fireplace is between the entrance and the posts. It is just possible to stand upright in the center of the house. In Northern California, the sweat house is of larger dimensions, and was preeminently a ceremonial or assembly chamber.

Dr. L. H. Bunnell, in his history published in 1880 of his discoveries in the Yosemite Valley, noted some interesting details about the use of the sweat house:

> It . . . was used as a curative for disease, and as a convenience for cleansing the skin, when necessity demanded it. . . . I have seen a half-dozen or more enter one of these rudely constructed sweathouses through the small aperture left for the purpose. Hot stones are taken in, the aperture is closed until suffocation would seem impending, when they would crawl out, reeking with perspiration, and with a shout, spring like acrobats into the cold waters of the stream. As a remedial agent for disease, the same course is pursued.

Through what is now a busy part of Oakland, Temescal Creek wandered down from the Piedmont hills to San Francisco Bay. When Americans first came to this section of the country, it is said that they found an old Indian sweat house in the arroyo and that because of this circumstance they named it Temescal Creek. W. E. Schenck, however, believes that the name may have arisen not from the presence of a native Indian village and sweat house but because the Indian retainers on the Peralta rancho doubtless set up a *temescal* on the bank of the creek near their cabins. The Vicente Peralta adobe was built about two blocks north of where Telegraph Avenue crosses the creek, near 51st Street. Around this nucleus the settlement of Temescal grew up. The name first appears on the Kellersberger survey map of 1857 as "Temesconta," which, Schenck says, "may or may not be Temescal."

Temescal Creek flowed about 450 feet southeast of the center of the Emeryville shell mound and discharged into the bay some 800 feet southwest of the center of the mound. The creek seems to have been the determining physiographical feature of the region in prehistoric as well as in pioneer times, tending to focus population by its supply of fresh water and food; until about the 1880s, for instance, it had salmon runs. With the coming of the Spaniards to the eastern side of the bay, Mission San José was settled, and later the great ranchos of San Antonio, San Leandro, San Lorenzo, San Pablo, and others were granted. Gradually embarcaderos sprang up along the eastern shore of the bay. Among others, the Temescal landing at the mouth of Temescal Creek near the old Emeryville shell mound became a landing place for occasional parties from San Francisco. The old Temescal Creek Road probably followed the creek as far east as Telegraph Avenue, and perhaps beyond.

During this period, visitors landing in boats at the mouth of Temescal Creek continued to the ranchos or to the mission by way of the Vicente Peralta Adobe one and a half miles inland. It was said that all visitors were hospitably greeted. From there they would proceed close to the foothills to Antonio Peralta's adobe near what is now Fruitvale Avenue, and thence to Ignacio Peralta's on the bank of San Leandro Creek. The next stop was the Estudillo rancho on the south side of the creek, and from there they went to Guillermo Castro's adobe at the site of the present city of Hayward. Here roads led east to Amador's and Livermore's ranchos and south to Mission San José.

The old Temescal Creek Road no longer exists (though a portion of SR 24 follows the creek bed in some places), and the free flow of the stream was stopped in 1866 when it was dammed up in the hills to form the reservoir still known as Lake Temescal. At that time it furnished the principal water supply for several thousand inhabitants. The course of the arroyo itself is still plainly indicated in some places by a winding lane

of native oak, willow, bay, alder, buckeye, and cottonwood trees. The creek itself runs through culverts underground and in places runs freely; it forms part of the boundary between Emeryville and Oakland.

ORTEGA'S DISCOVERY OF THE "CONTRA COSTA"

In the fall of 1769, while he was encamped on San Francisquito Creek (on the San Mateo–Santa Clara county line), after his discovery of the great Bay of San Francisco, Gaspar de Portolá sent out a reconnoitering party. Commanded by José Francisco de Ortega, the expedition's purpose was to find a land route up the eastern shore of the newly discovered bay to Point Reyes in Marin County and Cermeño's harbor. It seems to have been anticipated that a settlement to be named San Francisco would be established on that harbor and there would be founded the mission dedicated to St. Francis.

Passing around the southern end of San Francisco Bay, Ortega and his men forded the Guadalupe River (in Santa Clara County). From there, wrote Father Juan Crespí, chronicler and chaplain to Portolá, "they went forward on the other side of the estuary eight or ten leagues, but there was still a long distance for them to go. [A league would be 2.633 miles today.] At this distance of ten leagues, they came upon another very large stream with a very strong current, and its bed was also wooded and its course was through a great plain which was also quite well wooded." Professor Herbert E. Bolton wrote that they must have gone as far north as Niles or farther, and the second "very large stream" with wooded arroyo was doubtless Alameda Creek, from which the county takes its name.

According to Father Crespí, on the evening of November 10, 1769

> the explorers returned [to Portolá's encampment] very sad. . . . They said that all the territory which they had examined to the northeast and north was impassable because of the scarcity of pasture and especially because of the ferocity and ill-temper of the heathen, who received them angrily and tried to stop their passage. They said also that they had seen another estuary [San Pablo Bay] of equal magnitude and extent with the one we had in sight and with which it communicated, but that in order to round it one would have to travel many leagues . . . and that the mountains were rough and difficult.

The austere aspect of what the Spaniards came to call the Contra Costa ("coast opposite" San Francisco) on that November day discouraged Portolá's weary, half-starved soldiers. They had gone far enough north to sight San Pablo Bay, but the view had only made further passage seem an impossible undertaking. Already disheartened because the long-sought port of Monterey had not been found, they voted unanimously to return to the Point of Pines in Monterey County.

FAGES, TRAILBLAZER OF THE CONTRA COSTA

Alameda County was again visited by the Spaniards in the autumn of 1770, when Pedro Fages, one of Portolá's men left by him in command at Monterey, decided on his own initiative to make another attempt to reach Point Reyes by land. It was on this trip that Fages opened the first inland route from Monterey to the future site of San Jose. From there he continued over the trail opened the year before as far as Niles and on to a point "seven leagues beyond the point reached by Ortega."

During this time, in Bolton's words, the party had "skirted the Contra Costa for two days. . . . From the Berkeley hills they looked west through the Golden Gate and to the north they beheld San Pablo Bay cutting across their route to Point Reyes."

Fages made a second attempt in the spring of 1772 to reach Cermeño's bay. Accompanied by Father Juan Crespí, "six Catalonian volunteers, six leather-jackets, a muleteer, and an Indian servant," he followed the trail that he had opened more than a year before. Northwest toward what is now Hayward the party retraced the ground already twice covered by Ortega and Fages.

Crespí's chronicle for March 25 reads:

> On this day of the Incarnation, after Mass had been said, we set out . . . in the direction of the north-northwest. At the start we traveled about a league from the estuary at the foot of a bare mountain range, and after traveling a short distance we were three leagues from the estuary. All the land is level, black, and very well covered with good grass, mallows, and other herbs. . . . We passed five villages of heathen, which are all on the banks of the arroyos with running water. . . . We halted on the bank of a large arroyo close to the mountains skirting the broad plain. The bed of the arroyo is very full of alders, cottonwoods, and willows.

Their route, like that of the long line of travelers who were to follow in their steps, lay close to the hills, and camp was made at San Lorenzo Creek, called San Salvador de Horta by Crespí.

Advancing as far as the site of Fruitvale on March 26, they pitched camp about where Mills College is today. During the day they had their first view of elk, which Crespí thought were buffalo but which the soldiers called mule deer. Five arroyos of running water had been crossed, their banks green with alder, cottonwood, live oak, and bay trees. At the end of five leagues, Fages and his men saw the Alameda peninsula, now an island, and the intervening *encinal* or live-oak groves. "The site," wrote Crespí, "is very suitable for a good settlement . . . on account of the proximity of the forest. . . . This place was called Arroyo del Bosque [Wooded Creek]"—probably Fruitvale Creek.

From here the march, as described by Bolton, crossed country now thoroughly urbanized, but then only a pleasant wilderness:

> On the 27th they turned inland to round the estuary and the adjacent marshes, and emerged from the hills near the site of Lake Merritt. Near the [Oakland] Technical High School Father Crespí made his observations of the Golden Gate. The islands which he describes in the gate are Alcatraz Island, Goat (Yerba Buena) Island, and Angel Island. The arroyo where they camped, a league north of the point of observation, was probably Strawberry Creek, and the campsite [was probably] near the western side of the campus of the University of California. On the 28th they continued past the sites of Berkeley and Albany to eastern Richmond in Contra Costa County.

In 1977, the Alameda County Historical Society placed a plaque on the campus of the California College of Arts and Crafts at 5200 Broadway in Oakland at what is believed to be the actual vantage point from which the 1770 Fages expedition first looked at the Golden Gate.

On the return trip in 1772, the first stop made in Alameda County was on April 1 at what are now the grounds of the Castlewood Country Club in Pleasanton. On April 2 "they descended Arroyo de la Laguna, crossing it near Suñol. Leaving Suñol Valley they crossed Alameda Creek, ascended Mission Pass, reentered the valley of San Francisco Bay, and continued past the head of the bay at a point near Milpitas" (in Santa Clara County).

The second Fages expedition seems to have been decisive in determining the location of San Francisco. Clearly Point Reyes was less attractive a site than the newly discovered bay. A settlement south of the Golden Gate would be accessible from Monterey both over land and by sea.

In the summer of 1775, an official Spanish expedition entered San Francisco Bay. The background of this trip is told in the San Francisco County chapter. Commander José Manuel de Ayala and his men spent more than seven weeks exploring the shores of the great bay. They noted the mud flats at what are now Oakland and Berkeley and poles driven into the mud, which they believed the Indians used as markers for fishing. Soundings were made, with the shallower depths of the south bay markedly different from the deep, swift tidal waters of the north. The report and maps resulting from this expedition encouraged the authorities to pursue their plan for a settlement on the shore of the bay, and that was put into effect the following year.

ANZA FOLLOWS THE CONTRA COSTA TRAIL

In 1776, after he had explored the sites for the presidio and the mission to be established at the port of San Francisco, Captain Juan Bautista de Anza, accompanied by Lieutenant José Moraga, his second in command, and by Father Pedro Font, chronicler and chaplain of the second overland expedition from Sonora to California, passed around the southern extremity of San Francisco Bay into Alameda County. With eleven soldiers, six muleteers, and servants, Anza and his companions were on their way to explore the "Rio Grande de San Francisco"—Carquinez Strait and the waters above it.

On the frosty Sunday morning of March 31, after Father Font had said Mass, the travelers left their camp on the Guadalupe River and, meeting with a network of sloughs and marshes along Coyote Creek, where it runs west, were forced to make their way for about three leagues until they emerged on higher ground at the foot of the hills. From this point forward, the line of march followed "far away from the water . . . through very level country, green and flower-covered all the way to the estuary, but with no other timber or firewood than that afforded by the trees in the arroyos which we encountered."

Font's map showed that the line of march was now close to the hills all the way, and Bolton identifies it as the route that passed by way of the Arroyo de la Encarnación, probably Scott Creek, and from there into what is now Fremont. The arroyo "about half way on the road" was apparently Alameda Creek, with its "very deep pools, many sycamores, cottonwoods, and some live oaks and other trees." It was here that a band of

about 30 armed but peaceful Indians ran out to greet them with shouts of "Au, au, au, au," which seemed to Father Font "like something infernal."

Passing three arroyos and two deserted Indian villages, Anza and his men crossed the fifth stream, San Lorenzo Creek, near which they pitched their tents. Here they met a lone Indian, who appeared frightened by their sudden appearance. This is the last mention of Indians until Wildcat and San Pablo Creeks were reached in Contra Costa County.

Mass was said in a thick and "very damp" fog April 1, and a small army of mosquitoes pursued the travelers. Continuing along the foothills, the route was much the same as that followed by Foothill Boulevard today. Professor Bolton has identified and sketched the way for us:

> The arroyo where they saw the bears was San Leandro Creek. Two leagues beyond they crossed the creek at Mills College. Just beyond they climbed the hill and from there Font drew the sketch of the Oakland Estuary and oak-covered Alameda Peninsula, now Alameda Island. . . . Descending the hill they crossed Arroyo del Bosque, a stream in eastern Fruitvale. Continuing northwest they crossed the site of Oakland. It was from Berkeley that Font sighted through Lime Point and Point Bonita to determine the trend of the north shore of the Golden Gate. It was in Berkeley, too, that the elk were chased, "at the Arroyo de la Bocana" of Crespí, a place of "very little water" and "a small growth of trees." Farther down this arroyo there was "a grove or growth of not very large timber."

Leaving the stream, now known as Strawberry Creek, and its brushy coverts behind them, the explorers passed over a level plain and low hills into Contra Costa County. Following Suisun Bay as far as Antioch, they turned south on April 4. After a tiring struggle with impassable tulares and the blinding, wind-driven ash of burned tules, they proceeded some six leagues "along the general course of the Old River." At a point just south of Bethany, Anza decided to give up his attempt to approach the Sierra Nevada, because of the apparently limitless and unfriendly countryside, and to return to Monterey.

Continuing south, the party entered the Lomas de las Tuzas, evidently by Midway Valley. Ascending Patterson Grade to the vicinity of the pass, they looked down into Livermore Valley and "descried in the distance the range of redwoods on San Francisco Peninsula. . . . Continuing southeast along the northeastern edge of Crane Ridge for seven or eight miles, about to the San Joaquin County line, they climbed to the top of Crane Ridge, perhaps up Sulphur Springs Canyon, reaching the summit west of Eagle Mountain. Continuing south they descended to Arroyo Mocho, striking it about at Callahan Gulch, some two miles north of the Santa Clara County line."

THE FOUNDING OF MISSION SAN JOSÉ

"In 1794," Bancroft writes, "the eastern shores of San Francisco Bay was almost a tierra incognita to the Spaniards." For nearly twenty years after the coming of Anza in 1776, there is no record of any exploring expedition until 1795, when Sergeant Pedro Amador visited the southern part of Alameda County some time before June. In his report, acknowledged by Governor Diego de Borica, on June 2, 1795, Amador used the name of Alameda, the first known official use of that designation, for the creek, resembling a tree-lined roadway. "The Alameda" was again visited in November 1795, when, in accordance with the governor's orders, Hermenegildo Sal and Father Antonio Danti set out from Monterey to search for suitable mission sites.

"Having arrived at Santa Clara on the 21st," says Bancroft, "they were joined by Alférez Raimundo Carrillo, and started the next day to examine the Alameda previously explored by Amador, whose diary they had." The party journeyed northward nearly to the site of modern Oakland, then returned to Alameda Creek, and continued to the south. At the base of what is now called Mission Peak, a suitable site was found. The place was twelve miles north of Mission Santa Clara, in an area that proved to have fertile soil and a healthy climate.

It took some time before official permission was forthcoming to establish Mission San José. In June 1797 Padre Presidente Fermín Francisco de Lasuén and a few soldiers set out for the new site, called Oroysom by the natives. An *enramada*, or temporary chapel, was erected, and on June 11, Trinity Sunday, Father Lasuén celebrated the first Mass at the site.

Five days after the founding, temporary buildings were begun, and on June 28 Fathers Isidoro Barcenilla and Agustín Merino arrived to take charge of the new mission. Barcenilla served until 1802, when Father Luís Gil y Taboada succeeded him, and Merino was replaced by Father José Antonio Uría in 1799. Of the various fathers who served Mission San José, Narciso Durán, a native of Catalonia who came to California from Mexico in 1806, was the most prominent. He went to Mission San José and, with Father Buenaventura Fortuni, began

his long ministry, which continued until 1833, when he moved to Santa Barbara. Father Fortuni left the mission in 1825, and from then on Father Durán served alone, being also *padre presidente* of the missions during the years 1825–27, 1831–38, and 1844–46. Throughout the troubled years of secularization, he managed the affairs of the mission with marked ability, attaining something close to what would today be called popularity with most people with whom he came in contact. An accomplished musician, he taught the Indians to read music and trained an orchestra of thirty Indians, with flutes, violins, trumpets, and drums.

The German explorer Georg Heinrich von Langsdorff, who came to California on the Russian ship *Nadeshda* in 1806, visited Mission San José early in May. He was the first non-Spanish foreigner to tread the southeastern bay shores. He received a warm reception from Father Pedro de la Cueva, then in charge of the mission, and a great Indian dance was given for his entertainment. Since he was particularly interested in the manners and customs of the natives, he devoted much space to them in his account of the trip. Langsdorff said of the mission that "the kitchen garden is extremely well laid out, and kept in very good order; the soil is everywhere rich and fertile, and yields ample returns. . . . A small rivulet runs through the garden, which preserves a constant moisture. . . . The situation of the establishment is admirably chosen, and according to the universal opinion the mission will in a few years be the richest and best in New California."

Langsdorff's prophecy was fulfilled to a large degree, for Mission San José grew and prospered throughout the years of its service, before the inevitable decline following secularization at last set in about 1841. Bancroft provides some statistics: "By the end of 1797 there were 33 converts, and in 1800 the number had increased to 286, the baptisms having been 364. . . . Meanwhile the large stock came to number 367, and there were 1,600 sheep and goats. Crops in 1800 were about 1,500 bushels, chiefly wheat."

Ten years later the number of neophytes had increased to 545. There were 1,806 people at the mission in 1824, when it was second only to Mission San Luis Rey in population, and in the number of baptisms San José greatly exceeded any other mission. It was fourth in the number of cattle and sheep raised, as well as in the average production of grain crops.

The highest population attained at Mission San José was 1,877 in 1831; the number fell to 1,400 in 1834, and to 580 in 1840. However, for the entire decade of the

1830s it maintained a remarkable record and was probably the most prosperous of all the California missions both before and after secularization, which was effected in Alta California between 1834 and 1837. Crops were good, and the livestock increased steadily. Engelhardt gives the last available official report (1832) as 12,000 cattle, 13,000 sheep, and 13,000 horses.

San José was the last mission but one to be secularized. In November 1836 the property was turned over to José de Jesús Vallejo, *comisionado* ("chief military officer," also "commissioner" or "trustee" of mission lands), and the transfer was completed in December. Vallejo remained in charge until April 1840, when José María Amador succeeded him. Temporary management of twelve missions, including San José, was restored to the padres in March 1843, but in May 1846 Mission San José was finally sold by Governor Pío Pico to Andrés Pico and J. B. Alvarado for $12,000.

Mission San José was a center for the social life of the ranchos on the east side of San Francisco Bay during the 1830s and 1840s. It was also a stopping place for expeditions sent against the Indians in the years when Spanish and Indian peoples were often at odds with each other. During 1849 and 1850 it provided a wayside station for those gold seekers who used the land route from San Francisco to the mines by way of Mission Pass and Livermore. At this time Henry C. Smith, a member of Frémont's California Battalion in 1846, had a trading post in the old adobe mission building.

Of the original buildings at Mission San José (SRL 334), only a part of the padres' living quarters remains today. It has been incorporated into the museum at the mission. To the north is the reconstructed church, completed in 1985, one of the most ambitious historical reconstructions in California. While the project was under way, archaeologists found the grave marker of Robert Livermore underneath the old church site. A leader in this restoration project was the late Father William N. Abeloe, who revised and edited the third edition of *Historic Spots in California*. Nearby is the Dominican Convent cemetery, with its background of cypress and olive trees. Ohlone College lies at the southern edge of the mission. A mile west on Washington Boulevard is the Ohlone Indian burial ground.

Although it is not located near the Guadalupe River, Mission San José is often referred to as "San José de Guadalupe." Guadalupe was not a part of its original name, and was probably acquired somehow through association with the Pueblo de San José de Guadalupe, now the city of San Jose, some fifteen miles away.

U.S.S. Hornet, Alameda Point

In 1956, the new city of Fremont was created by joining together the towns of Mission San José, Centerville, Irvington, Niles, and Warm Springs. Its area of almost a hundred square miles makes Fremont one of the state's largest municipalities.

MISSION PASS (SUNOL GRADE)

Mission Pass, the starting point of an old Spanish and pioneer American trail, cuts through the Mount Hamilton range just northeast of Mission San José. The winding SR 21 once followed its path approximately. Today it is a principal corridor into Silicon Valley; a freeway, I-680, crosses the widened pass, and the route is now called the Sunol Grade. It has the dubious distinction of being one of the most heavily traveled commuter routes in California.

Crossing over the lower hills, the old trail dropped down into Sunol Valley, where it went in two directions. One route, largely that of I-680 today, skirted the western edge of Livermore Valley along the Arroyo de la Laguna and proceeded up the Amador and San Ramon Valleys to the site of Concord, and from there on to the San Joaquin Valley. The other branch, in old days the more traveled one, went straight across Livermore Valley through the hills into the San Joaquin Valley.

In 1772 Pedro Fages and Father Juan Crespí came over the first of these trails by way of Concord on their return from the north, after having discovered the mouth of the San Joaquin River. Many later expeditions went through the same pass, among them the one led by Gabriel Moraga that opened up the Sacramento Valley region. Various expeditions against the Indians, made by Moraga, Vallejo, and others, started from the mission through this pass, as did later gold-seekers.

Little Brown Church of Sunol, built 1885

JEDEDIAH STRONG SMITH AT MISSION SAN JOSÉ

In May 1827, while Father Narciso Durán was in charge of Mission San José, Jedediah Strong Smith, the pioneer pathfinder, wrote a letter to the padre. Durán was suspicious of the strangers. Four hundred neophytes had run away from the mission on May 15 and 16, and the fur hunters were unjustly suspected of having been the instigators of the desertion. Low on supplies and far from home, Smith was writing to Durán for help. Durán, however, did not read the letter but forwarded it to Monterey for translation. Smith and his men managed to cross the Sierra and arrive at their base near the Great Salt Lake by early July, but soon returned to California. Hoping to get assistance from the mission, Smith, three of his men, and some Indian guides arrived at the mission in October, where Durán had them locked in the guardhouse.

Smith's plight improved with the visit from Captain J. B. Cooper, an influential citizen of Monterey, who offered to aid Smith in every way within his power. Within twelve or fourteen days, the governor sent a letter to Smith and a guard to escort him to Monterey. There on November 12, Cooper signed a bond in favor of Smith.

Smith returned to Mission San José on November 24, and for two weeks he and his men were busy preparing for the journey out of California—rounding up their horses, drying meat, repairing their guns, and baling the goods allowed them by Governor Echeandía's orders. On Sundays and holy days they attended services at the mission and there listened to the father address his people in Latin or in Spanish. Smith makes note in his journal of the music, which "consisted of 12 or 15 violins, 5 base viols and one flute." Having obtained permission from Father Durán, Smith removed

his group on December 24 "to a sheep farm belonging to the mission called St. Lorenzo, where there was plenty of grass and a pen in which I could shut up my horses and mules."

Impatient at continued delays and fearing further obstacles to an immediate departure, Smith finally negotiated his party's release to move elsewhere for better pasture. On December 30, in rain and mud, the band began its march northward, not by way of Bodega and Fort Ross, as officially planned, but through Mission Pass across the Livermore Valley to the Old River branch of the San Joaquin (sometimes called the Pescadero by the Spanish), and from there up the Sacramento Valley as far as Tehama, where Smith blazed a new trail out of California through Trinity, Humboldt, and Del Norte Counties.

RANCHO SAN ANTONIO

The present cities of Alameda, Albany, Berkeley, Emeryville, Oakland, Piedmont, and a part of San Leandro are located on what was once Rancho San Antonio (SRL 246). This vast estate extended five leagues along the eastern shore of San Francisco Bay, from San Leandro Creek on the south to El Cerrito Creek, now part of the boundary between Alameda and Contra Costa Counties, on the north. It comprised all of the land between the bay on the west and the crest of the Contra Costa hills on the east, a total of about ten square leagues, or about 44,000 acres.

In August 1820, Pablo Vicente de Solá, the last Spanish governor of Alta California, ordered the grant of Rancho San Antonio made to Luís María Peralta. Peralta was thereby rewarded for his loyalty, dedication, and service of almost forty years in the Army, and for valuable assistance in establishing the missions of Santa Cruz and San José. A native of Tubac, Sonora (now in Arizona), Peralta was born in 1759. He came to California with the Anza expedition in 1775–76, and enlisted at the San Francisco presidio about five years later. He commanded the guard at Mission San José from 1798 to 1800, and from 1807 to 1822 he was *comisionado* of the Pueblo de San José. In 1784 he married María Loreto Alviso, with whom he had seventeen children, of which four sons and five daughters lived to adulthood. Don Luís never made his home on Rancho San Antonio but maintained his residence in San Jose, where part of his adobe dwelling still stands at 184 West St. John Street.

Rancho San Antonio was occupied by the four living sons of Don Luís—Hermenegildo Ignacio, José

Domingo, Antonio María, and José Vicente—and the original adobe home was located in what is now the Fruitvale district of Oakland. Built in the 1820s, it was the second permanent settlement on the east side of San Francisco Bay after Mission San José. For a number of years the four brothers stayed there whenever they visited the rancho.

The site of this adobe is at 2511 34th Avenue at the northwest corner of Paxton Avenue, near the north bank of Peralta Creek (SRL 925). The adobe was torn down in 1897. Some of the adobe bricks were used to construct a small house in Dimond Park. This building, overshadowed by the gnarled branches of a gigantic evergreen oak, was used for years by the Boy Scouts, and was finally destroyed by fire. Part of the adobe construction was saved, however, and incorporated into the present building under the old oak. A few of the bricks from the original Peralta adobe were also used in a home built by a descendant of Ignacio Peralta at 384 West Estudillo Avenue in San Leandro, where they may be seen today near the front entrance.

Soon each of the Peralta brothers began to build his own adobe on the section of the rancho later apportioned to him. With their wives and children, and flocks of cattle grazing among the oak trees, they lived a patriarchal life. Sometimes Luís Peralta's former companions in arms from the Presidio de San Francisco would cross in small boats to participate in rodeos and to enjoy the festivities of the Contra Costa. To the north (in Contra Costa County) the Castros held Rancho San Pablo, while to the south there were the Estudillos, the Higueras, the José de Jesús Vallejos, and the Guillermo Castros, all living on vast estates of their own before 1842.

The legal division of the lands of Rancho San Antonio took place in 1842, when Don Luís Peralta came up from San Jose to divide the estate among his four sons. As they rode over the land together, the father parceled it out among them, marking out the boundaries by natural objects, as was then the custom. As nearly as possible, the land was divided into four equal parts, each running from the hills to the shore of the bay.

Ignacio, the oldest, was given the southern end of the grant, bordering on the north bank of San Lorenzo Creek. Domingo was given the northern end, where the cities of Berkeley and Albany now stand. Antonio received what is now East Oakland (where the original house stood) and the Encinal de San Antonio, now the city of Alameda. To Vicente fell the Encinal de Temescal, the portion that is now occupied by Emeryville, Piedmont, and central and north Oakland.

South of the original adobe, on what is now 34th Avenue, Antonio Peralta built a second adobe in 1840, with an eight-foot wall enclosing an area of about three acres. Two additional structures were made that year on the same plat, one of which was a guest house. These later buildings were all leveled in 1870, when Antonio built a frame structure on Paxton Avenue. In 1897 this was moved nearby to 2465 34th Avenue. The house was restored in the years 1999–2001, and is now the center of the Peralta Hacienda Historical Park.

Ignacio built his first house on the north bank of San Leandro Creek about 1835, after his term as *alcalde* (mayor) of San Jose. The site is at the end of 105th Avenue, near I-880; the house and a second adobe built nearby in 1842 disappeared in the 1870s.

Around 1860 William Toler built a brick house (SRL 285), said to be the first in Alameda County, for his father-in-law Ignacio Peralta. It is now the Alta Mira Club House and stands at 561 Lafayette Avenue in San Leandro. The furnishings are all from the twentieth century, but the old walls and exteriors remain as they were.

The adobe of Domingo Peralta was built in 1841 on the site of what is now 1304 Albina Avenue in Berkeley, just off Hopkins Street and on the south bank of Codornices ("quail") Creek. Neither this home nor a frame dwelling house later built on Hopkins Street is still standing.

None of Vicente Peralta's houses in what is now Oakland still stand. The first, an adobe (1836), was at 5527 Vicente Street; a later adobe was at 486 55th Street, and a frame structure on Vicente Street, later moved to Claremont Avenue, is gone. A section of the old roadway of Rancho San Antonio (SRL 299, an unmarked site) that led from Temescal south to San Leandro is closely followed by Santa Clara Avenue. The MacArthur Freeway, I-580, parallels this road.

The quiescent years of the 1830s and the early 1840s on the old ranchos of the Contra Costa were but a brief episode in the history of California. Americans began to visit the region as early as 1846. Soon the Peraltas found that their fertile lands were very attractive to these newcomers, who saw that they could be made valuable for other than pastoral purposes. In 1850, when the greater portion of the lands of Domingo and Vicente Peralta was sold, the first encroachment upon Rancho San Antonio was made. Don Luís Peralta, the grantee of the original princely estate, died on August 25, 1851, on or about his ninety-second birthday, having lived to realize that what he had given to his sons was one of the most valuable tracts of land in

California and that it was gradually melting away before their eyes.

A series of bitterly contested lawsuits helped destroy the Peralta patrimony. Daughters of the family and their husbands claimed a share of the lands; it was alleged that the father was mentally incompetent when he made his will; and American squatters brought continual legal problems before the courts.

The rancho and the four Peralta brothers are jointly commemorated by a bronze tablet set in a boulder and placed in Lakeside Park in Oakland by eleven Bay Area chapters of the Daughters of the American Revolution. The spot is just above the boathouse on the northern shore of Lake Merritt.

RANCHO SAN RAMÓN (DUBLIN AND CONTRA COSTA COUNTY)

José María Amador, the first settler of what would later be Murray Township, arrived there before 1830, according to local tradition. He brought with him a rich heritage of ingenuity and industry from his father, Pedro Amador, the Mexican soldier who had come to California with Portolá in 1769. Don José, himself a soldier, had been born in San Francisco in 1794, and had served as a private in the San Francisco Company from 1810 to 1827, being stationed in the military guard at Sonoma from 1824 to 1827. He took part in the expedition of Luís Argüello to the Sacramento Valley in 1821 and went with Gabriel Moraga to Fort Ross and Bodega that same year. After his discharge in 1827 he was mayordomo at Mission San José, and in 1834 and 1835 he was granted more than four square leagues of the rancho later known as San Ramón, the greater part of which lay in Contra Costa County.

The economy of Alta California did not rely entirely upon the sale of hides and tallow. Some domestic manufacturing was begun in the nineteenth century. Amador was one of the first manufacturers and farmers in Alameda County, herding vast numbers of cattle over his broad, unfenced acres and making leather, soap, saddles, harnesses, blankets, shoes, and even wagons in the adobe workshops on his rancho with the use of Mexican labor. At one time 300 to 400 horses, 13,000 to 14,000 head of cattle, and 3,000 to 4,000 sheep grazed on his lands. In 1848 the lure of gold drew Amador, along with thousands of others, to the Mother Lode country. According to Theodore H. Hittell, he mined in the county that was later named for him, assisted by a number of Indian laborers.

The site of Amador's two-story adobe is on the northwest corner of Dublin Boulevard and San Ramon Road in Dublin. Alamillo Spring still flows nearby. Robert Livermore helped Amador to build another adobe, and Amador reciprocated by assisting Livermore at his Rancho Las Positas, located to the east.

Natural landmarks usually designated the boundary lines between the Mexican land grants, although later surveys often varied from the original, less precise ones; the first surveys that marked out the confines of Rancho San Ramón may still be identified. To the west, the Pita Navaja ("knife point"), a sharp knob above the summit of Bulmer Hill Grade, indicated the division between Rancho San Ramón and Rancho San Lorenzo. It is mentioned frequently in early deeds. The southern boundary was a large oak tree in the small gulch running up the hillside opposite the site of the old Fallon House at 6035 Foothill Road. This tree once bore the marks of early surveyors, who used it as a landmark from which the boundary line between Ranchos San Ramón and Santa Rita was drawn.

In financial straits, Amador gradually sold portions of his estate to various newcomers. Michael Murray and Jeremiah Fallon, natives of Ireland, had come west together in 1846 and settled for a short time at Mission San José. Sometime before 1852, they bought sections of the Amador holdings south of the present Dublin Boulevard. Murray Township, organized in 1853, was named for Michael Murray, the first county supervisor from the district. The old homes of Fallon and Murphy survived into the 1960s, only to be pulled down.

John Green, another Irishman, was an active pioneer in the area. He was the storekeeper, postmaster, and supervisor for Murray Township, and also a large-scale rancher who owned lands both at Dublin and in the Livermore hills to the east. The settlement of Greenville, four miles east of Livermore at the entrance to Altamont Pass, was named for him, since he started the first store there. Greenville Road marks the end of the Livermore Valley. In spite of his busy days, Green spent his evenings studying law, especially the land-tenure laws pertaining to the Spanish and Mexican land grants. He had learned Spanish during his apprenticeship to a New York drug firm that had trade relations with South America. Thus it was natural that Green became a friend and adviser to the native Californians of the Amador and Livermore Valleys, and the old ranchers often drove to Dublin to discuss their increasingly complex land problems with their Irish neighbor.

Around the Amador adobes a town gradually grew

up, known until 1860 as Amador's or Amador Valley. The portion of the settlement south of the road to Stockton was called Dublin. It was said that Mississippi-born settler James Witt Dougherty first called it that when a traveler asked him the name of the community. Dougherty replied that the post office was called Dougherty's Station but that, since there were so many Irish living south of the road, they might as well call that part Dublin. The name stuck, although no post office bore that name until 1963.

The first business house in Dublin was the two-story Amador adobe, a wayside station until its destruction in the 1860s. The oldest business building still standing in Dublin is the old John Green store (1864), now a restaurant, at Donlon Way and Dublin Boulevard. Stucco covers the old resawed siding, and the building is much altered from its original appearance.

St. Raymond's Church, built in 1859, was the first church in the township. Land for the church and the adjoining Catholic cemetery was donated by Michael Murry and Jeremiah Fallon, both of whom are buried there. The first interment, in 1859, was of Tom Donlon, who was killed in an accident during construction of the church. The street on which the church stands is called Donlon Way. The nonsectarian portion of the cemetery was given by James W. Dougherty.

The old church gradually fell out of use and was nearly demolished, but in 1966 it was acquired by the Amador–Livermore Valley Historical Society for restoration, which was largely accomplished by 1980. The nearby Murray School is the museum of the Dublin Historic Preservation Association and is open at regular hours.

RANCHO AGUA CALIENTE (FREMONT)

Warm Springs, now part of the city of Fremont, is located on what was once Rancho Agua Caliente. This rancho was granted to Fulgencio Higuera in 1839, having been released by its earlier grantee, Antonio Suñol. Higuera's reconstructed adobe stands about two miles south of Mission San José in Rancho Higuera Historical Park, owned by the city of Fremont. Somewhat weather-beaten now, it is not open to the public. Another Higuera adobe is two miles further south, in a park in Milpitas (Santa Clara County).

The springs, known to the Indians, became something of a meeting place for the Californians before 1848, with rodeos occasionally held there. The area of the rancho including the springs was purchased by Clemente Columbet in 1850, and buildings for a resort were put up. Columbet moved a house all the way from San Jose to serve as a hotel; in 1858 he leased the place to Alexander Beaty. Until the earthquake of 1868, which did considerable damage to the buildings at Mission San José, Warm Springs was a fashionable watering place, where invalids and leisurely visitors alike partook of the sulfur waters.

Around 1869, the estate was sold to Governor Leland Stanford, who had the land planted with orchards and vineyards. His brother Josiah managed a winery there, one of the first in Alameda County. Until 1990 Wiebel Vineyards operated a winery here, but now the area is given over to large new houses, and only the state marker (SRL 642, "Leland Stanford Winery") stands at the north side of Stanford Avenue to mark the spot.

RANCHO LAS POSITAS (LIVERMORE)

A young English sailor named Robert Livermore entered California in 1821 on the trading ship *Colonel Young*. Deciding to stay, he worked at various places, apparently gaining the good will of most people wherever he went. In the valley that would later bear his name, he and his partner José Noriega applied for the easternmost rancho, Las Positas ("little watering holes"). It was on the frontier between the coastal settlements and the Indian territory of the hills and the great central valley and was therefore a place of some danger. By 1835, he was living in a house on the property. In 1838 he married the widow Josefa Higuera Molina, whose father owned Rancho Tularcitos in Santa Clara County, and began to raise a family. In 1839 Governor Juan B. Alvarado granted the land to Livermore and Noriega; Livermore later bought out Noriega's interest.

In 1844, Livermore became a Mexican citizen. Two years later he purchased Rancho Cañada de los Vaqueros, most of which lay in Contra Costa County but which skirted the northern portion of Livermore Valley. Under American rule, the two ranchos were confirmed to him, and Livermore became a wealthy man. The rancho was soon well stocked with cattle, but Livermore was more interested in horticulture and viticulture than he was in cows or sheep. After the fathers at Mission San José, he was the first man to plant a vineyard and an orchard of pears and olives in this section of California. He died in 1858, before the birth of the town named for him.

One of the first houses on Rancho Las Positas was an adobe built by Livermore, assisted by José María

Amador, his nearest neighbor in the valley. Amador did not forget that Livermore had given him help in a similar situation several years before. At times, too, Livermore's troubles with the Indians became so heated that he and his family took refuge with Amador for a while. Livermore's home became a popular stopping place for travelers on the road to Stockton. In March 1850, when Nathaniel Greene Patterson (a member of the California Battalion in 1846–47 and a gold-seeker of 1848) hired the adobe for a hotel, it became the first place of public entertainment in the valley. This house, which stood near the source of Las Positas Creek at a point about one and a half miles north of the center of Livermore, was partly in ruins by 1876 and was later torn down.

Livermore built a large frame dwelling near the adobe in 1849, the first wooden building in Livermore Valley. A part of the original structure, the timbers of which had been shipped around the Horn, stood until the 1950s. In Portola Park is a monument in honor of Robert Livermore (SRL 241); an arrow on top of the monument points to Livermore's homesite, about one-third of a mile to the north.

The first house within the present city limits of Livermore was built by Alphonso Ladd, who came to California from New Orleans in 1850. The following year he settled with his wife near the Suñol adobe, then the only dwelling in Sunol Valley. A few years later he took up 160 acres of government land in what was called the Livermore Extension, and in 1855 he built a hotel on the Stockton road at the site of what was to become known as Laddsville, a forerunner of Livermore. The Ladd Hotel, built of lumber hauled across the hills from Mowry's Landing, was a prosperous enterprise, but after it burned in 1876 the settlement of Laddsville never recovered.

The tracks of the Central Pacific Railroad were laid through the Livermore Valley in 1869. William Mendenhall, who had traveled overland to California from Pennsylvania in 1845, laid out a town that he named in memory of Robert Livermore; this was on what had been part of the gigantic Rancho El Valle de San José. The fire at Laddsville brought an end to the rivalry between the two neighboring towns. Livermore was incorporated in 1876.

The Livermore Collegiate Institute was founded by Dr. and Mrs. W. B. Kingsbury in 1870. For several years it was used as a sanatorium by J. W. Robertson, before becoming a private residence, which was ultimately destroyed by fire. The site is at 1615 College Avenue. Other health facilities still in use include the Arroyo del Valle Sanitarium and the grand United States Veterans Hospital, both on Arroyo Road. North of the veterans hospital at 2647 Arroyo Road is Ravenswood, the country home of Christopher A. Buckley, boss of San Francisco political life in the late nineteenth century. Buckley's Queen Anne home has been restored and is open to the public.

The Livermore Heritage Guild has restored the old Highway Garage on Portola Avenue. This was on the Lincoln Highway, the first transcontinental paved highway in the United States, begun in the early 1920s. The restored garage is now a museum of the Lincoln Highway. The Duarte family, builders and longtime operators of the garage, lived next door, and their home has also been preserved. In the old Carnegie Library at the center of town is the Livermore History Center, with excellent displays of the city's life over the years.

In 1942, a large tract of land east of the city became the Livermore Naval Air Base. In 1952, the University of California established the Lawrence Livermore Laboratory at the former base site for nuclear weapons research. It has also become an important center for electrical engineering and electronics research.

The Livermore Valley is one of California's famous wine-producing areas. Charles Wetmore's Cresta Blanca wine won the grand prize in the Paris Exhibition of 1889, creating international recognition for California's wine-producing quality. The Cresta Blanca Winery (SRL 586), founded in 1882, is now an operation of Wente Brothers Estate winery; it is located at 5050 Arroyo Road. The original Wente winery (SRL 957) at 5565 Tesla Road goes back to 1883. The Wentes are proud to be the oldest family-owned, continuously operating winery in California. Also established in 1883 was the Concannon Winery (SRL 641) at 4590 Tesla Road, still managed by Concannon family members, although the winery has been sold.

RANCHO SAN LEANDRO

José Joaquín Estudillo, the first settler in Eden Township, petitioned for a grant of the land known as the Arroyo de San Leandro in 1837 "with the object of securing subsistence for and supporting a large family, consisting of his wife and ten children, after having been in the military service for a period of seventeen years, four months, and seven days." The son of José María Estudillo and brother of José Antonio Estudillo of San Diego, he was born at the Presidio of Monterey in 1800. He held several positions of honor in the military service and in the government. William Heath Davis, a son-in-law, said that José Joaquín moved to San Leandro early in 1836 after he had first obtained a written permit from Governor Alvarado to occupy the land. He brought with him 300 heifers, by which he increased his herd until, on his death in 1852, he left to his heirs about three thousand head of cattle. His specialty and pride was "white cattle," because he said their color enabled him "to see his flock at a great distance."

Squatters first encroached upon Rancho San Leandro in 1851, when Americans began to settle there against the wishes of the legal owner. The intruders first made their appearance on the banks of San Lorenzo Creek, at a place subsequently known as Squattersville, now San Lorenzo. They soon overran the rancho, but Estudillo, "an educated, intelligent, and upright man," with the aid of his sons and sons-in-law consistently "opposed the evil-doers in seizing the land." A malicious element did much damage, shooting and wounding horses and cattle under cover of darkness, and fencing Estudillo's stock away from the creek.

Through the instrumentality of John B. Ward and William Heath Davis, the squatters were finally brought to terms. Some of the property was deeded to an alien, Clement Boyreau, in order to bring the case into federal courts. Judges Ogden Hoffman and Matthew Hall McAllister rendered a decision in favor of the Estudillo family. As a result, the squatters took leases from the family pending the final decision of the United States Supreme Court, and eventually they purchased the land from the original owners.

The town of San Leandro was founded for the purpose of being the seat of Alameda County. In 1854 Estudillo's two sons-in-law, Ward and Davis, submitted a plan to José Joaquín's widow, Juana Martínez de Estudillo, and her children for laying out a town. The family gave land for county buildings and reserved 200 acres for the town, which was surveyed early in 1855. A popular election in December 1854 brought the county seat to San Leandro from Alvarado. "The family mansion," wrote Davis, "was surrendered to the county for a temporary court house." It was damaged in 1855 by fire, probably set by an incendiary who wished the county seat returned to Alvarado. The election of 1854 was declared invalid, since it had not been authorized by the state Legislature, and the center of justice went back to Alvarado. By action of the Legislature, however, it was again in San Leandro in 1856, where it remained until 1873, when it was moved to Oakland.

The first adobe home built by José Joaquín Estudillo, about 1836–37, was located near the south bank of San Leandro Creek, roughly opposite the home of Ignacio Peralta. Some ten years later he moved to what is now the block bounded by Estudillo Avenue, San Leandro Boulevard, and Davis and Carpentier Streets. There he built a second home, possibly occupied by the spring of 1850. A wooden house, thought to be substantially the same as this second home, stood on that block until about 1947–48, when it was razed for the construction of the priests' residence of St. Leander's Church. The site of this house (SRL 279) was marked on the West Estudillo Avenue side on June 7, 1964, coincidentally the 112th anniversary of the death of José Joaquín Estudillo. The dedication was part of the festivities celebrating the centennial of St. Leander's Parish; the present church (1957) and rectory (1948) stand on the site of the old home. The Estudillo family gave land for the original St. Leander's Church, built in 1864 directly opposite the present church, where the primary school now stands. The venerable Gothic structure was demolished in 1957.

A permanent brick courthouse of two stories was built in 1856–57 in the central part of the block bounded by West Estudillo Avenue and Carpentier, Davis, and Clarke Streets, the main entrance being on the latter. It collapsed in the 1868 earthquake but was repaired and used until the county seat was moved to Oakland in 1873. In 1881 it became the first convent and school of St. Leander's Parish. Later a three-story wooden building was erected around it, and it stood until 1926, when it was replaced by the present convent and school, constructed on either side of it.

María de Jesús Estudillo married William Heath Davis at Mission Dolores in 1847. After her father's death in 1852, she inherited the portion of Rancho San Leandro near the original homesite. The street that now runs west from San Leandro to the Bay and crosses what was once the Davis ranch is called Davis Street.

Casa Peralta at 384 West Estudillo Avenue was built in 1897 for N. G. Sturdivant and bought and remodeled by Mrs. Herminia Dargie of the Peralta family in 1924. Adobe bricks from the first Peralta home are built into the house, now owned by the city of San Leandro and open to the public.

The oyster industry at what is now the San Leandro Marina (SRL 824) prospered during the 1890s, becoming the single most important fishery in California. Moses Wicks is credited with having been the first person to bring seed oysters around the Horn and implant them in the San Leandro oyster beds. The industry diminished after 1911 because of pollution in San Francisco Bay.

RANCHO EL VALLE DE SAN JOSÉ (PLEASANTON AND SUNOL)

The mission fathers early recognized the advantages of the fertile Arroyo Valle and pastured their herds among the great sycamores there. For many years after Mission San José was secularized, mission Indians still lived in the valley. The original name of the locality was Alisal, from *aliso*, which in Alta California could mean either "alder tree" or "sycamore grove." Rancho El Valle de San José was granted to four relatives, Antonio María Pico, his brothers-in-law Agustín Bernal and Juan Pablo Bernal, and his sister-in-law María Dolores Bernal de Suñol, in 1839. It was patented to the Bernals and to Antonio María Suñol in 1865.

Antonio María Pico, son of José Dolores Pico, was born in Monterey in 1808. He held various public and military offices throughout his career. He was stationed at San Jose from 1833 to 1839 and took part in the revolt against Micheltorena in 1845. After having been a member of the Constitutional Convention, he was appointed by President Lincoln as registrar of the United States land office at Los Angeles in 1861. He was a grantee of Rancho Pescadero (San Joaquin County) in 1843 and co-purchaser of the San Rafael Mission estate in 1846. Don Antonio married Pilar Bernal and sold his fourth of Rancho El Valle de San José to Juan Pablo Bernal.

Antonio María Suñol, a native of Spain, came to California in 1818 as a sailor on the French ship *Bordelais*, which he left. He married María Dolores Bernal, lived at the Pueblo de San José, and never took up residence on the Rancho El Valle de San José. A man "of excellent reputation," he held a few public offices but was mainly a stock raiser and trader. He was owner of Rancho Los Coches in Santa Clara County after 1847 and purchaser of San Rafael Mission in 1846 with Pico.

His son of the same name, Antonio Suñol, had an adobe on the rancho in the pleasant valley of the sycamores and alder trees, where he lived in the late 1840s and early 1850s. The site of this adobe is near the Sunol Water Temple of the San Francisco water system, which stands near the intersection of three old valley roads, one from Sunol, one from Pleasanton, and a third through Mission Pass.

Agustín and Juan Pablo Bernal, sons of Joaquín Bernal, were presidio soldiers who had served at San Francisco and San Jose. Agustín was in 1853 a claimant for Rancho Santa Teresa in Santa Clara County, of which his father had been grantee in 1834. In April 1850 he moved to his section of Rancho El Valle de San José and built an adobe home near the foothills at the western rim of Livermore Valley. The adobe still stands in a beautiful rancho setting west of Pleasanton on the west side of Foothill Road, about a mile south of the Alviso adobe of Rancho Santa Rita. In 1852 Juan Pablo Bernal, settling near Alisal, constructed an adobe building, no longer standing, on the north bank of Arroyo Valle.

The Bernals were good business managers. Consequently, they were able to secure their large holdings from the aggressive encroachments of newcomers and to maintain possession of their lands better than most California families.

The settlement of Alisal was renamed Pleasanton by John W. Kottinger, an Austrian who came to California in 1849 and married a daughter of J. P. Bernal in 1850. Late in 1852 Kottinger went to live at Rancho El Valle de San José, and built at Alisal an adobe and frame dwelling on the south bank of Arroyo Valle opposite Bernal's house. In 1867 he was one of the founders of a new town just south of Arroyo Valle that took the name of Pleasonton for General Alfred Pleasonton, who served in both the Mexican and Civil Wars. A clerical error changed the name to Pleasanton when the post office was later established, and that spelling became the accepted usage. Kottinger's old house was long ago destroyed, but its barn, also of adobe, still stands at the rear of the residence at 218 Ray Street in Pleasanton. The Amador–Livermore Valley Historical Society Museum is located in the Old Town Hall of Pleasanton at 603 Main Street, built in 1914.

Castlewood Country Club stands on part of the Rancho El Valley de San José about three miles southwest of Pleasanton. Here Phoebe Apperson Hearst, wife of Senator George Hearst and mother of the publisher William Randolph Hearst, lived in her beautiful Hacienda del Pozo de Verona from 1891 until her death in 1919. The building, formerly the clubhouse, burned in 1969, but it is still fondly recalled by many past visitors.

RANCHO POTRERO DE LOS CERRITOS (UNION CITY)

The Alvarado district of Union City is on what was once a part of the Rancho Potrero de los Cerritos, granted to Agustín Alviso and Tomás Pacheco in 1844. Alviso, a prosperous ranchero, married María Antonia Pacheco in 1830; he was mayordomo at Mission San José in 1840–41. Tomás Pacheco was a soldier of the San Francisco Company from 1826 to 1832 and later held various offices at the Pueblo de San José from 1834 to 1843. Both men built adobe houses, neither of which stand today.

In 1850 John M. Horner purchased from Alviso 110 acres in the tract that had been the mission grazing lands. He plotted a town site that covered the whole of his purchase, and the first lots were sold on September 9, 1850, the day that California joined the Union and became a state (although no one in California knew until later of the official act performed in Washington, D.C.). The town, Union City, was a success; it drew the trade of Mission San José from the more southerly sloughs and also provided a more direct outlet for the area east of the hills.

Henry C. Smith bought 465 acres from Alviso and Pacheco late in 1850 and had the town of New Haven laid out at the upper embarcadero adjoining Union City. In these communities, wrote J. N. Bowman, "grain, vegetable, and fruit ranching were proven feasible; . . . flour and sugar factories were later erected, and people and investors were even attracted from San Francisco." The success of these two towns, Bowman further noted, encouraged the development of a third adjacent to them, named for the former Mexican governor Juan Bautista Alvarado. In March 1853 Smith introduced a bill in the state Legislature, then meeting in Benicia, creating a new county of Alameda from parts of Contra Costa and Santa Clara Counties and designating New Haven as the county seat and Alvarado as the seat of justice. By the time the new county was organized in April, New Haven had discarded its name and was also known as Alvarado. In 1959, the towns of Alvarado, Decoto, and Union City were incorporated into the city of Union City.

The site of the New Haven embarcadero and of the building used as a county courthouse (SRL 503) is at Union City Boulevard near Smith Street; some old wooden buildings still stand in the vicinity. Northeast on Dyer Street is the site of the nation's first successful sugar beet factory (SRL 768), established in 1870 by E. H. Dyer. For many years, the Holly Sugar Company operated at the site.

Along the shore of the Bay, the Don Edwards San Francisco Bay National Wildlife Refuge is the largest urban wildlife refuge in the United States.

RANCHO SAN LORENZO (CASTRO VALLEY, HAYWARD)

There were two divisions of Rancho San Lorenzo. That portion on which the cities of Castro Valley and Hayward are located was granted to Guillermo Castro in 1841 by Governor Juan B. Alvarado and in 1843 by Governor Manuel Micheltorena. The portion west of Hayward and south of San Lorenzo Creek was granted to Francisco Soto in 1842 and 1844.

Guillermo Castro's adobe house was located on Mission Boulevard between C and D Streets, for many years the site of the Hayward City Hall. The adobe was one of the buildings in the area badly damaged by the 1868 earthquake. Located on the seismically active Hayward Fault, the City Hall is no longer open to the public. A landmark still standing in downtown Hayward is the Odd Fellows Hall on B Street, built in 1868.

One of the first Americans to come to Rancho San Lorenzo was William Hayward from Massachusetts. In the fall of 1851 he pitched a tent in Palomares Canyon under the impression that it was government land and that he would obtain there a homestead of 160 acres. Before long, however, he was visited by Guillermo Castro, who informed him that he was a trespasser. However, an agreement was made between Castro and Hayward so that the latter remained, and the relations between the two men continued to be friendly. Hayward soon removed his tent to the location of the hotel that would later become famous as a resort, on the hill north of A Street and east of Mission Boulevard; the hotel was destroyed by fire in 1923. In 1854 Castro laid out the plat of the town that he called San Lorenzo but instead took the name Haywards, later Hayward. A bust of the pioneer is on display in the Hayward Area Historical Society Museum at 22701 Main Street, where other artifacts from the region's past can be seen.

The relations of Castro with another American, Faxon D. Atherton, illustrate how shrewd Yankees often bested native Californians. Atherton lent money to Castro from time to time so that he might gamble. When the latter was unable to repay, Atherton took possession of a piece of land. Finally, Castro and all of his family except a daughter and one son, Luís, later surveyor of Alameda County, moved to South America.

Several large old ranch houses still stand in the Hayward area. Outstanding among these is the beautiful Victorian mansion of William Meek at 240 Hampton Road in San Lorenzo. Meek was one of California's pioneer orchardists. He came West prior to the Gold

Rush, bringing to Oregon, on one trip, a wagon load of grafted trees. There, with John Lewelling, he entered the nursery business, which they later moved to Alameda County. By 1866 he had clear title to 2,100 acres, most of which had originally belonged to the Soto portion of Rancho San Lorenzo. Much of this he planted with almond, cherry, and plum orchards. Meek was generous with his time and talent in public service. He was a member of the first board of trustees of Mills College and served four terms as an Alameda County supervisor. His home, surrounded by magnificent trees and gardens, was built in the late 1860s. The estate was threatened with destruction in 1963, when it was sold to a subdivider for an apartment project. The efforts of citizens and groups, including the Hayward Area Historical Society, however, led to its purchase by the Hayward Area Recreational District for preservation and development of the grounds.

The McConaghy Estate at 18701 Hesperian Boulevard is another project maintained by the society. This twelve-room farmhouse built in 1886 has been restored to its early appearance; the property also contains a tank house and a carriage house with many displays.

Another old house built about the same time is the former residence of Cornelius Mohr, still owned by the family, at 24985 Hesperian Boulevard in the Mount Eden district of Hayward. Here, as at the Meek home, the old carriage house also stands. Most of the Mohr ranch is now the campus of Chabot College. California State University at Hayward, east of Mission Boulevard, is built on what was once the ranch of Timm Hauschildt. Beyond lived Ahapius Honcharenko, Ukrainian patriot and Orthodox priest, from the 1870s to his death in 1916. He published the *Alaska Herald-Svoboda*, a bilingual newspaper, and translated the U.S. Constitution for the Russian-speaking people of Alaska. "Ukraina," the Honcharenko estate, is now owned by the East Bay Regional Park District.

One of the early settlers of Castro Valley was James Harvey Strobridge. He came to California from New England in the Gold Rush and stayed to work on the transcontinental railroad. He came to the Hayward area in 1869 to construct the Southern Pacific Railroad from Niles to Oakland. Liking the area, he purchased 500 acres along Redwood Road. The home of his son, Senator E. K. Strobridge, once surrounded by pear and apricot orchards, is now an apartment house next to the Castro Valley BART station. In 1866 Josiah Grover Brickell gave the land for the first public school in Castro Valley (SRL 776). The site is now Redwood

McConaghy Estate, Hayward

School, on Redwood Road between James and Alma Avenues.

Another landmark of Castro Valley history is the Stanton House. William Mattox built this house in 1860; he sold it and the surrounding 365 acres to Michael Stanton, who had followed his friend J. H. Strobridge to California, in 1871. Stanton grew fruit, vegetables, and grain, and raised chickens. In time Castro Valley became the second largest egg-producing area in California. The Stanton House was moved to Norbridge Avenue and is now a remodeled office building.

RANCHO ARROYO DE LA ALAMEDA (SOUTHWESTERN COUNTY)

Rancho Arroyo de la Alameda, taking its name from the stream that flows through the open plains that drain to the Bay, was granted to José de Jesús Vallejo in 1842. It consisted of 17,705 acres of fertile valley land. Don José, one of thirteen children of Ignacio Vallejo, a Spanish soldier of Alta California, was an elder brother of General Mariano G. Vallejo. He himself was active in military and governmental affairs from 1818 to 1847; among other offices he was *comisionado* and administrator at Mission San José from 1836 to 1840 and military commander at the Pueblo de San José from 1841 to 1842. In 1850 he was appointed postmaster at Mission San José, where his home stood just west of the highway and opposite the mission. Affairs on the rancho were left primarily in the hands of overseers, and an expensive flour mill, built about 1850, became the most famous asset of the estate.

Where tree-lined Alameda Creek issues from Niles Canyon and passes into the flatland that slopes away to the Bay, the old settlement of Vallejo Mills, now known as Niles, grew up in the 1850s. Historic landmarks may still be found in the neighborhood. The stone foundations of a second flour mill (SRL 46), erected here by Vallejo in 1856, remain in a Fremont city park at the northeast corner of Mission Boulevard and Niles Canyon Road. A mile up the canyon the stone aqueduct, which he built to conduct water to the mill, still parallels the road for some distance. The site of one of the several adobes built by Vallejo for his overseers is located at the entrance of the canyon.

Perhaps the most picturesque reminder of adobe days in this vicinity is the little building in the gardens of the California Nursery Company northwest of Niles off Niles Boulevard. This adobe, the first of the Vallejo adobes built in the vicinity, has been restored as a guest house.

Shinn's Nurseries was established in Niles in the 1860s and was operated by the Shinn family for three generations. Four and a half acres of the Shinn ranch were acquired by the city of Fremont in 1962; the Shinn Historical Park includes the family home begun in 1876, a barn and packing shed, a bungalow from 1910, and a walled Japanese garden. The park, at 1251 Peralta Avenue, is open on a regular basis.

The town of Niles, now part of the city of Fremont, was named in 1869 for Judge Addison C. Niles, an executive of the Central Pacific Railroad. Here, for several years ending in 1916, was located one of the first motion picture studios in the West. The Essanay Company ("S" for Spoor, "A" for Anderson) had been founded in Chicago by George K. Spoor and Gilbert M. "Broncho Billy" Anderson. The latter decided to move his base of operations to California and selected Niles as a suitable location. He made the first pictures at Niles in a barn, at the rear of 37467 Second Street, but soon built a block-long, story-and-a-half studio at Niles Boulevard and G Street (it has been razed, but the site is marked). Anderson starred himself in Westerns, frequently using photogenic Niles Canyon as a setting. Other actors who pioneered at Niles included Wallace Beery, Ben Turpin, and Charles Chaplin. Here Chaplin made his great film *The Tramp*. Some of the cottages built by the company along Second Street behind the main studio are still standing and occupied.

George Washington Patterson arrived in California to mine gold, but instead found wealth in the marshy lands near the Bay south of Alameda Creek. He arrived here around 1854 with his family, and set out to drain and clear the land. His white frame farmhouse, built in 1856, was the center of what was eventually a 3,000-acre farm named Ardenwood, apparently a reference to the

Mountain View Cemetery, Oakland

Forest of Arden in Shakespeare's *As You Like It*. The house was enlarged around 1880 and presents two different aspects, depending upon where the viewer is standing. Some 205 acres of the property were acquired in the 1970s by the East Bay Regional Park District and in 1985 were formally opened to the public as Ardenwood Historic Farm. The farm has producing fields that can be harvested in season, a working blacksmith's shed, and a replica of a short-line horse-drawn railroad that operated nearby in the late nineteenth century. Two old neighboring farmhouses were moved to the property and saved from razing.

Nearby is Coyote Hills, another East Bay Regional Park, part of which lies on the old Patterson Ranch, at 8000 Patterson Road in Fremont. Although primarily a natural preserve, the park contains a rare intact Indian shell mound. The park includes the lower estuary of Alameda Creek down to the Bay. The sloughs and tulares in the park demonstrate the challenging landscape that confronted early explorers into the San Joaquin Valley, the Delta region, and the marshlands around San Francisco Bay.

RANCHO SANTA RITA

Rancho Santa Rita was at the western edge of Livermore Valley and adjoined Rancho El Valle de San José to the east. It was granted to José Dolores Pacheco in 1839, and included more than 8,800 acres of excellent grazing land. Pacheco was often mentioned in the local annals of San Jose, where he held a number of public offices between 1838 and 1846. He died in 1852.

Samuel and J. West Martin purchased about five thousand acres of Rancho Santa Rita in 1854; there were enough cattle included in the sale to provide the purchase money. The little adobe (SRL 510, unmarked) that still stands beneath a giant oak tree at 3465 Old Foothill Road was built in 1845 by Francisco Solano Alviso, a year after he became mayordomo of Rancho Santa Rita. It is now owned by the city of Pleasanton, but not open to the public, although the grounds may be visited.

OAKLAND

The coastal portions of Rancho San Antonio were largely untended until the late 1840s. Then came the American invasion following the discovery of gold. Three men who separately had sailed around the Horn were responsible for the beginnings of Oakland: Edson Adams, Andrew Moon, and Horace W. Carpentier. The latter was a sharp attorney, who after service in the California militia was known as General Carpentier.

After a short time in the gold fields, the three determined to settle and lay out a town on the Contra Costa, the eastern shore of San Francisco Bay. In May 1850 they landed at what is now Jack London Square at the foot of Broadway in Oakland and built a cabin on Vicente Peralta's property. Challenged by Peralta, they asserted that the land was public domain.

Lawrence Kinnaird continues the story:

> Other squatters quickly followed their lead and the rightful owner found his property overrun by squatters who killed or stole his cattle and cut his timber. All the East Bay rancheros had troubles with squatters but Vicente Peralta suffered most. He finally got a writ of ejectment against Carpentier, Adams, and Moon from the county court at Martinez and Deputy Sheriff Kelly with about twelve men was sent to enforce the order. They found Moon alone at his cabin in a grove of live oaks. He pretended to be much astonished at the action taken against him and explained that he and his associates had no intention of damaging Peralta, for whom they had the highest regard. Taken in by Moon's smooth talk, Peralta finally agreed to lease the land. Moon and his partners had no intention to comply with the terms of the lease. Instead they took over the land as if they owned it and laid out the town of Oakland.

Julius Kellersberger was employed to lay out the area now bounded by First, Fourteenth, Market, and Fallon Streets. Streets eighty feet wide were planned; Main Street (now Broadway) was even wider, at 110 feet. In 1852 a bill sponsored by Carpentier, who had become enrolling clerk of the state Senate, was approved by the Legislature incorporating the town of Oakland. This came as a great surprise to the 150 or so inhabitants of the settlement, who learned of the bill only after the legislation had been enacted. Two years later the Legislature recognized Oakland's status as a city.

The trustees of the town granted to Carpentier the rights to the entire waterfront. In a series of intricate financial transactions, the general (who soon would become the first mayor of the city of Oakland) passed control to other members of his family, ultimately selling to the Central Pacific Railroad. Not until 1911 was the city of Oakland able to assert jurisdiction over its entire waterfront, which was subsequently developed into one of the most prosperous on the Pacific coast.

The original city of Oakland lay on the west side of San Antonio Slough. Several men had settled there before the arrival of Adams, Moon, and Carpentier in May 1850. The first, in the winter of 1849, was Moses Chase. He was followed by the Patten brothers, Edward, Robert, and William, in February 1850. These four men turned their attention to the east side of the slough and leased land there from Antonio Peralta. They laid out the town of Clinton on a tract of 480 acres in 1853, and in the same year a bridge was built across the slough to connect Clinton with Oakland. The area included in Clinton lay, approximately, between East Eighth and East Twenty-fourth Streets and Lake Merritt and Fourteenth Avenue, which was then a small creek. On the other side of this creek the town of San Antonio was surveyed on a tract of 200 acres in 1854. A flurry of excitement over a small gold discovery passed through the San Antonio region in 1856; hundreds of claims were staked out, but not enough gold was found to keep the enthusiasm high. Small traces of gold were found at the site of Merritt College, in the hills between Redwood Road and Skyline Boulevard, but not enough to support further activity.

By 1856 Clinton and San Antonio constituted a single town called Brooklyn. In 1870 Brooklyn was incorporated, and two years later it was annexed to the city of Oakland. For some time it had been under consideration as a possible county seat to replace San Leandro, where the courthouse had been devastated by the earthquake of 1868. In 1873 the people of Alameda County voted to move the seat of government to Oakland, and the site chosen was in what had been Brooklyn. The old wooden courthouse stood into the 1960s at 1952 East Fourteenth Street, and behind it, at 1417 Twentieth Avenue, was the building that housed the hall of records and the jail. Clinton Square, San Antonio Park, and Brooklyn Avenue in East Oakland commemorate these early towns.

By 1874 it was decided to move the county offices to a downtown location. When Julius Kellersberger mapped the town in 1853, he had set aside two squares, Washington and Franklin, for a civic center. They were used instead as parks until the city of Oakland gave them to the county of Alameda for the new county buildings. The courthouse was opened in 1875 on Washington Square (bounded by Fourth, Fifth, and Washington Streets and Broadway), and the hall of records about a year later on Franklin Square (bounded by Fourth, Fifth, and Franklin Streets and Broadway). The old courthouse stood until 1950 and the hall of records until 1964. The Oakland City Hall was built in 1914; it sustained a good deal of damage, as did the neighborhood, in the earthquake of 1989, but was repaired and strengthened and was back to work within a few years.

On November 8, 1869, the first train to arrive in Oakland over the newly completed transcontinental railroad pulled up to the station on Seventh Street. A salute of thirty-seven guns was fired and a grand celebration was held at which notables addressed the enthusiastic citizens. Actually, Oakland had been preceded by Alameda as the western terminal about two months earlier. While construction of the line continued, a temporary connection had been made with the San Francisco, Alameda, San Leandro and Haywards Railroad, opened in 1865, and the first transcontinental train arrived in Alameda on September 6, 1869. The terminal (SRL 440) where festivities took place that day was located at the wharf at the foot of Pacific Avenue in Alameda. This site was until recently part of the Alameda Naval Air Station, now known as Alameda Point.

Lake Merritt, covering 160 acres, is unique in that it is a wildfowl sanctuary in the middle of a large city. It was named in honor of Samuel B. Merritt, a graduate of the medical department of Bowdoin College, who came to California in 1850 and practiced medicine for a while before becoming engaged in business activities in Oakland. He served as mayor in 1868–69 and furthered many projects favorable to the development of the young city. Merritt Hospital was founded by his bequest, and Merritt College bears his name. He is one of many city fathers to be buried in Mountain View Cemetery in the Oakland hills. The large 226-acre cemetery, laid out in 1863, was the work of the great landscape architect Frederick Law Olmsted.

San Antonio Slough once spread over a large region at the head of the San Antonio Estuary. Into it flowed salt tides from San Francisco Bay as well as several creeks carrying the freshwater drainage from the out-lying foothills of the Coast Range. Dr. Merritt was instrumental in having a dam built to impound these waters—the first step in the formation of Lake Merritt as it is today, a saltwater lake with a broad causeway and a moveable floodgate. Lake Merritt was set aside by the state in 1869 as a wildfowl refuge, the oldest one in the United States. In 1909 the city of Oakland completed acquisition of the entire lake frontage and began to develop Lakeside Park. Organized feeding of birds began in 1915, and in 1926 banding of ducks was inaugurated.

The lake is a major attraction of the city, and in the 1930s was further embellished by a "necklace of lights" that lined the 3.18 miles of its shore. Terminated as a wartime economy measure in 1942, the long string of lights was restored as a civic project only in 1987.

St. Mary's Catholic Church, at Eighth and Jefferson Streets, was established as a mission in 1853 and a parish in 1858. The foundations of the present building were laid in 1868 and it was dedicated in 1872. The wooden structure has been extensively remodeled through the years, including a partial brick facing. St. James Episcopal Church (SRL 694), at Twelfth Avenue and Foothill Boulevard, was founded in 1858; the structure built the following year still stands next to the present church and is now used as a social hall. The First Unitarian Church (SRL 896) at Castro and Fourteenth Streets dates from 1890; its Romanesque design is embellished with remarkable stained-glass windows.

Along Broadway and Seventeenth Street are perhaps California's most extensive grouping of Art Deco buildings from the 1920s and early 1930s. The Paramount Theater (SRL 884) at 2025 Broadway opened in 1931, and was a movie palace until 1970. Its opulent decoration has made it famous. It is now a center for the performing arts.

A number of interesting old houses are still to be seen in Oakland, open to the public. The gabled house of J. Mora Moss, built in 1864, stands in Mosswood Park at MacArthur Boulevard and Broadway. The twenty-four-room home of James DeFremery, a native of Holland, was built in 1868 and is preserved in DeFremery Park at Eighteenth and Adeline Streets. The Cohen-Bray House at 1440 East Twenty-fourth Street (1884) was in the family for many years; it is a rare "Stick" Victorian home, more common in San Francisco. The home of John and James Treadwell, owners of the Tesla coal mine in eastern Alameda County, stands on the campus of the California College of Arts and Crafts at 5212 Broadway. The Camron-Stanford House, at 1426 Lakeside Drive, was built in 1876 as the home of William Camron, who married Alice Marsh, daughter of Contra Costa County pioneer Dr. John Marsh. Four rooms have been restored to their appearance when, on the first trip to California made by an incumbent president of the United States, Mr. and Mrs. Rutherford B. Hayes took tea in 1880 with the David Hewes family, who then owned the home. Josiah Stanford, brother of Governor Leland Stanford, was the third owner.

Dunsmuir House, a handsome Colonial Revival mansion at 2960 Peralta Oaks Court, was built in 1899. Acquired by the city of Oakland in 1961, it stands on forty acres of hills and gardens and has been used for many films and television programs. The residence of George C. Pardee (SRL 1027) is located at 672 Eleventh Street. Pardee was a physician, mayor of Oakland (like his father before him) from 1893 to 1897, and governor of California from 1903 to 1907. The Pardee Home Museum has been open to the public since 1991, following the death of the last, unmarried daughter of the family. Across Twelfth Street behind the Pardee Home is nearly a full city block, Preservation Park, where sixteen interesting old houses and buildings from the East Bay have been relocated and restored, many doing new duty as offices. Started in 1985, this park is a striking contrast to the new federal buildings nearby, built about the same time.

Among Oakland's several historic preservation districts is the Bret Harte Boardwalk on Fifth Street between Jefferson and Clay, honoring the writer who lived here (in a house no longer standing) with his sister Margaret and his stepfather, Colonel Andrew Williams, in 1854. Williams became Oakland's fourth mayor three years later. Victorian Row on Ninth Street is a group of old buildings, mostly commercial.

The Oakland Free Library was established in 1878 with Ina Coolbrith, later California's first poet laureate, as the first librarian. She encouraged the literary career of young Jack London, who was born in San Francisco but raised in Oakland. In 1893, upon his return from his first ocean voyage, Jack London entered a prize-winning manuscript, "The Story of a Typhoon off the Coast of Japan," in a contest sponsored by the *San Francisco Morning Call* newspaper. He lived with his first wife, whom he married in 1900, at 1130 East Fifteenth Street, and the following year they moved to a house of the Italian-villa type, the former home of sculptor Felix Peano, at First Avenue and East Twelfth Street near the shore of Lake Merritt. Scenes from the windows of this house, which looked toward the bridge at Eighth Street, are described in London's *Martin Eden*. While he wrote

The Call of the Wild, he was living with his family in a bungalow on Blair Avenue in Piedmont. The most familiar Oakland landmark associated with Jack London is Heinold's First and Last Chance Saloon at 50 Webster Street, where he spent many hours. The tavern was near the Webster Street bridge to Alameda, then a dry town, and travelers would get their first or last drink there, depending on whether they were going to or coming from Alameda. Nearby is a wooden one-room cabin brought here from the Klondike region, where London lived in 1898 during the gold rush there. Jack London Square, at the foot of Broadway, is now an area of fine restaurants and shops.

Robert Louis Stevenson lived off and on in Oakland before leaving for his last voyage to the South Seas. The poet Edwin Markham called Oakland home from 1892 to 1899. After his famous "The Man with the Hoe" was published in 1899, he and his family moved to New York.

Gertrude Stein grew up in East Oakland, where her playmates included Isadora and Raymond Duncan; all three found their careers in Europe. Of her childhood home, she wrote: "It was wonderful there in the summer with the dry heat and the sun burning and the hot earth for sleeping; and then in the winter with the rain and the north wind blowing that would bend the trees." On a visit to California in 1934, Gertrude Stein was disappointed to see that her childhood home was gone and the neighborhood was changed; in her cryptic style, she lamented that "there was no there there."

Dr. Cyrus Mills and his wife conducted the Benicia Seminary in Benicia from 1865 to 1871. Then they moved to what is now East Oakland, where they hoped to make their school the Mount Holyoke of the Pacific. Mills College, originally Mills Seminary, has been a prominent institution of higher education ever since; after many years as a women's college, it now has a coeducational graduate program. Mills Hall (SRL 849), one of the original buildings from 1871, is still in use. The long, four-story wooden structure was once considered to be the most beautiful educational building in California.

Julia Morgan's architectural work is much in evidence on the Mills College campus. Miss Morgan was the first woman to graduate from the École des Beaux-Arts in Paris and is perhaps best remembered for her work on William Randolph Hearst's San Simeon estate. At Mills, the campanile she designed and whose installation she supervised was her first independent commission (1904), and it triumphantly survived the earthquake two years later that laid waste to so many Bay Area structures. The library is largely her work. In 1923 she designed the charming Quong Ming orphanage for Oakland's Chinese community. The building was then far from downtown Oakland, and in 1938 it was sold by its patrons to Mills College, which acquired title to the grounds on which it stands. Renamed Alderwood Hall (but still with its decorative Oriental embellishments), it is the official guest house for the college and a frequent meeting center.

A tiny cemetery of the Mills family called Sunnyside is at the eastern edge of the campus, and it is said that it was responsible for preserving much of the Mills College grounds in the 1950s when the freeway (now I-580) was pushing through the district. The state might override the claims of a college, but a cemetery could not be moved.

St. Mary's College, founded in San Francisco in 1863, moved to Oakland in 1889. The site of the old building (SRL 676) at Broadway and Hawthorne has been marked by a tablet on the structure at 3093 Broadway. In 1928 the college moved from Oakland to its present campus at Moraga in Contra Costa County.

The College of California began as the Contra Costa Academy in Oakland in 1853. It was founded by the Rev. Henry Durant, a Yale graduate, and the Rev. Samuel H. Willey, one of the four commissioned Protestant missionaries sent to California by the American Home Missionary Society. The college was first located on Broadway and Fifth Street, but eventually settled at what is now the corner of Thirteenth and Franklin Streets (SRL 45), adjacent to the *Oakland Tribune* building. The site was abandoned in 1873 when the college, by then the University of California, moved to Berkeley.

Martin Luther King Jr. Plaza, on Martin Luther King Jr. Way in north Oakland, is a recent development, highlighted by the Children's Hospital Oakland Research Institute near the buildings of the former Merritt College, and before that, University High School.

The Oakland Museum at 1000 Oak Street includes a history gallery within its complex, superbly capped by a garden area. It offers a range of exhibits about California history, one of which is the old assay office from Nevada City. The African American Museum and Library at Oakland is in the historic Charles Greene building at 659 Fourteenth Street, on the edge of Preservation Park. Its collections include materials going back to the mid-nineteenth century.

"The Hights" was the estate of Cincinnatus Heine ("Joaquin") Miller, "Poet of the Sierra," who lived his last years here from 1870 to 1914. Situated on the hills overlooking San Francisco Bay and the Golden Gate, it is now Oakland's Joaquin Miller Park. The Abbey, his small home (SRL 107), is not open to the public. On the extensive grounds are stone monuments he built: the "Sanctuary to Memory," the "Funeral Pyre," the "Tower to Robert Browning," and the "Tower to General John C. Frémont." The latter was placed at the spot where Frémont, who named the Golden Gate, is said to have stood when he first saw the San Francisco Bay opening out into the Pacific.

Redwood Regional Park, a part of the East Bay Regional Park District, contains two historic landmarks. A short distance above The Abbey in the Roberts Recreational Area is SRL 962. Here stood the tall redwoods called the Blossom Rock Navigational Trees. Mariners entering San Francisco Bay, upon sighting these trees, were able to plot a course that would avoid the submerged menace called Blossom Rock. The Army Corps of Engineers destroyed the rock in 1870.

At the Fishway by the Redwood Regional Park office a plaque (SRL 970) commemorates the identification of the rainbow trout, *Salmo irideus*. At nearby San Leandro Creek (now known as Redwood Creek and Upper San Leandro Creek), three specimens were taken in 1855. Dr. W. P. Gibbons, the founder of the California Academy of Natural Sciences, identified these as a new species, but closely related to the steelhead, *Salmo gairdneri*, previously classified. The rainbow trout was successfully introduced into rivers and streams throughout the world.

BERKELEY

Ocean View was the name of the community north of Oakland, originally Jacobs' Landing on the Bay shore. Two miles inland, the first telegraph line to the rest of the Union was put up in 1861, along what are now Telegraph and Claremont Avenues. As the Telegraph Road branched out northward from downtown Oakland, development began along its path. The State Asylum for the Deaf, Dumb, and Blind attracted many newcomers. By 1865 Samuel Willey built the first house in the area at what is now 2709 Dwight Way. He was among those who thought that the emerging community ought to have an inspiring name. The name of Berkeley was first discussed as being appropriate for the new college town. Bishop George Berkeley, the renowned English philosopher and seer of what he believed to be the westward march of civilization, wrote the line "Westward the course of Empire takes its way" in his poem "On the Prospect of Planting Arts and Learning in America" in 1752. Berkeley's name, although not his pronunciation, was thus given to the city that began around the University of California at Berkeley (SRL 946). Ocean View was annexed in 1878.

Chartered in Oakland in 1868, the University of California moved to Berkeley in 1873. The one original building still standing is South Hall, just west of the Campanile. At the site of the old North Hall is the Bancroft Library, one of the most valuable collections of books and materials on the history of California, located in the library annex. The nucleus of this collection is the personal library of the great bibliophile and historical patron Hubert Howe Bancroft. Phoebe Apperson Hearst was the great benefactress of the university; the Hearst Memorial Mining Museum, built in 1907 in memory of her husband, and the Greek Theater are among the structures she endowed.

The University of California has been the scene of some of the most notable discoveries in the field of atomic physics and chemistry. Here Ernest O. Lawrence invented the cyclotron. In Room 307 of Gilman Hall, on the night of February 23–24, 1941, the man-made element plutonium was first identified by Professors Joseph W. Kennedy, Glenn T. Seaborg, and Arthur C. Wahl. Number 94 on the periodic table, plutonium is used in nuclear reactors and atomic explosives. The small laboratory where this history-making discovery took place has been registered as a National Historic Landmark by the Department of the Interior.

The First Church of Christ, Scientist, at 2619 Dwight Way, built in 1910, is considered a masterpiece of Bernard Maybeck, the renowned California architect of the early twentieth century. Its style includes elements of Japanese, Byzantine, Gothic, and Romanesque architecture. The church has been registered as a National Historic Landmark.

Across Bowditch Street from the church is an open area owned by the university but since the 1960s occupied by a motley crowd of people and unofficially known as "People's Park." This is one visible reminder that the area near the university was the scene of great protest in that decade of the Free Speech Movement and antiwar demonstrations.

The Berkeley City Club (SRL 908) at 2315 Durant Avenue represents one of the finest works of Julia Morgan; it was constructed in 1929–30. The Judah L. Magnes Memorial Museum at 2911 Russell Street is the home of the Western Jewish History Center.

The view from the Berkeley hills across San Francisco Bay to Marin County, the islands of the Bay, the Golden Gate, and the San Francisco skyline is among the most famous in California. Over the years the hills have been covered by homes in a remarkable variety of styles, with those of Maybeck, Morgan, and John Galen Howard among the most numerous from the days before the outbreak of World War II. Guides to historic buildings are available in bookstores and make Berkeley a living architectural treasury to walk through.

ALAMEDA

The island city of Alameda is locally famous for the preservation and restoration of its old homes and public buildings. The red brick City Hall, at Santa Clara Avenue and Oak Street, was built in 1896 in the fashionable Romanesque style. The nearby area bounded by Oak and Park Streets and Lincoln and Encinal Avenues is the Park Street Historic Commercial District. Nearby, in the old Masonic Temple at 2324 Alameda Avenue, is the Alameda Historical Museum. The Meyers House and Garden, at 2021 Alameda Avenue, is an 1897 Colonial Revival home built by prominent Bay Area architect Henry H. Meyers for his father, Joseph Meyers. Since 1993, it has been operated by the city and maintained as it was when the family lived there.

The Croll Building (SRL 954), at 1400 Webster Street, was first put up as a hotel in 1883. It has since been converted into offices and stores. The "Gold Coast" area, centered on St. Charles Avenue, has dozens of well-preserved Victorian houses in an area that is also a favorite for walking tours.

The *China Clipper* made the first transpacific air flight. On November 22, 1935, the first plane on this route took off from Alameda Naval Air Station, at the westernmost edge of the island. It put down at Pearl Harbor in the Hawaiian Islands, touched at the islands of Wake, Midway, and Guam, and finally, six days after it left Alameda, put down in Manila in the Philippine Islands. A marker (SRL 968) at what was the main gate of the Alameda Naval Air Station commemorates that first flight.

In the 1990s, military stations throughout the country were greatly reduced, and California lost a significant one with the closing of the Alameda Naval Air Station. The site is now known as Alameda Point. Since 1997, the USS *Hornet* has been berthed at Pier 3 there. In World War II, Alameda was the main home port for the aircraft carrier, which had an impressive military record. It saw service again in the Vietnam war and finished its career with the retrieval of the Apollo 11 astronauts in 1969. "After walking on the moon, Neil Armstrong and Buzz Aldrin's first steps back on Earth were on the decks of the *Hornet*," an Alamedan noted. The ship (SRL 1012) is now a museum with many activities; it is the only aircraft carrier to be converted to a museum on the West Coast. It is the eighth in a series of proud U.S. Navy ships to bear the name *Hornet*, the first being a sloop-of-war that, in two separate engagements in the War of 1812, defeated larger British vessels.

PIEDMONT

The springs in what is now Piedmont Park first attracted visitors to this area in the hills above Oakland, where a resort hotel was built in 1870. The spectacular view from here across San Francisco Bay to the city and the Golden Gate beyond was an early inducement for settlers. They put up small houses, such as the Wetmore House at 342 Bonita Avenue, built in 1879 in the distinctive Galveston style once popular on the Texas coast; this privately owned dwelling is now on the National Register of Historic Places. Jack London and his friends were part of a bohemian colony in the Piedmont hills for a short time early in the twentieth century, living in scattered "bungalows."

After the 1906 earthquake, there was a rush from San Francisco to the East Bay. Many new and very large houses were built on the splendid avenues that today make Piedmont one of the most attractive residential communities in the Bay Area. Piedmont Community Church began its ministry in the charming Romanesque structure it now occupies at 400 Highland Avenue in 1918, having been organized nine years before. Piedmont Park is now a city-owned area in one of the many canyons running from the hills down to the flatlands adjacent to San Francisco Bay. Incorporated as a city in 1907, Piedmont is entirely surrounded by Oakland.

ALTAMONT PASS

At the eastern edge of Alameda County a few miles west of the San Joaquin County line, Altamont Pass on I-580 is a low (1,009 feet) declivity in the hills separating the San Joaquin Valley from the San Francisco Bay Area. This area is subject to very high winds at certain times of the year, and on the slopes of Altamont Pass thousands of wind turbines have been erected to derive electrical energy from winds that have been clocked at more than eighty miles per hour. The first of these modern windmills was installed in 1982. The turbines may be as important in the state's future as the oil fields were in California's past.

Alpine County

Alpine County, named for its similarity to the alpine country of Europe, was created March 16, 1864, from parts of Amador, Calaveras, El Dorado, Mono, and Tuolumne Counties. The county seat was at first located at Silver Mountain but was transferred to Markleeville in 1875. Until 1863 the region was thought to be a part of Nevada, to which it is more closely united geographically; even today, many of its social and economic ties are with Nevada.

FRÉMONT'S CROSSING OF THE SIERRA

Among the few government explorers who came to the Pacific Coast before the Mexican War was John C. Frémont. In his company were French trappers familiar with the Western trails. Kit Carson, almost as famous as his noted leader, was the chief guide.

Fired by a desire to see Klamath Lake, Mary's Lake, and the fabled Buenaventura River, Frémont left Oregon for St. Louis in November 1843. Following a circuitous route through Oregon and western Nevada, he finally reached the Carson River. By this time supplies had been greatly depleted, and the horses and mules were in no condition to negotiate the rough Rocky Mountains. Frémont therefore made the bold decision to find a pass through the Sierra into California.

Perhaps no part of the entire journey was more difficult than that through the rugged region that is now Alpine County. The trail necessarily followed along the ridges, where the wind had cleared away a little of the snow and sometimes exposed grass and brush on which the half-starved animals could feed. Because of the difficulty of beating a path through the deep snows, the party had to make camp every few miles. On February 2 or 3, 1844, a halt was made at a spot one and one-half miles northeast of where Markleeville is today, near the confluence of Markleeville Creek and the East Fork of the Carson River. On the following night, camp was made near today's Grover's Hot Springs, five miles farther west.

On February 6, Frémont had his first view of the great Sacramento Valley lying in the dim distance far below him. From the top of a high peak Kit Carson, who had gone to California with Ewing Young fifteen years before, recognized the low mountains of the Coast Range 100 miles to the west.

On February 14, in company with Charles Preuss, Frémont climbed to the summit of another peak, for many years assumed to have been Stevens Peak, although Red Lake Peak was probably the one in question. From this height Frémont beheld a great sheet of water, which his first map designated merely as the Mountain Lake, but which he later named Lake Bonpland, after Aimé Jacques Alexandre Bonpland (1773–1859), the noted French botanist and companion of Baron von Humboldt. Maps of the 1850s designated it Lake Bigler, but today it is known as Lake Tahoe.

At last, on February 20, they reached the summit at the granite ridge immediately north of Elephant's Back, about three-quarters of a mile south of what was later known as Kit Carson Pass, at an elevation of about 8,600 feet. Here on the 21st Frémont and his companions looked out across the magnificent panoramas of snowy ridges and towering peaks interspersed with deep canyons. Far in the distance they saw the Sutter Buttes, the Sacramento Valley, and the Coast Range. They proceeded to the American River along a ridge that runs from Red Lake Peak to the river in the vicinity of Strawberry.

At the summit of Carson Pass a bronze memorial plate (SRL 315) commemorates this strenuous passage of the Sierra, giving special honor to the man for whom the pass was named. A portion of the tree that once stood here, on which Carson carved his name in 1844, was removed when the tree was felled in 1888 and is now in the museum at Sutter's Fort in Sacramento. (Another dating for Carson's carving is a later trip across the pass, in 1853, under much more leisurely conditions than a snowy Sierra winter journey.)

THE OVERLAND EMIGRANT TRAIL

Each year after 1844 saw more and more pioneers setting out for California from their homes east of the Mississippi River. The "California" or "Overland Emigrant" Trail was really several routes across the Sierra Nevada, and in recent years efforts have been made to mark these various passages. The Nevada Emigrant Trail Marking Committee, under the auspices of the Nevada Historical Society, has marked that portion of the Overland Emigrant Trail passing through Alpine County with seven distinctive yellow-painted iron markers and plaques, the easternmost of which is at SR 88 and the emigrant trail about one mile north of Woodfords. Others are in or near Snowshoe Springs Campground, Hope Valley, Red Lake, Kit Carson Pass, Caples Lake, and Emigrant Pass.

Three miles west of Carson Pass on SR 88, a monument (SRL 661) has been placed at the point where the old emigrant road of 1848 swung down across a meadow now covered by Caples Lake. A quarter of a mile east of the summit of Carson Pass are some large rocks on which a party of pioneers in 1849 inscribed their names and the emblem of the Independent Order of Odd Fellows. Some of the names are still legible. In 1941 the

Monument to "Snow-Shoe" Thompson, Carson Pass

Grand Lodge of California, IOOF, placed a plaque nearby and dedicated the spot as a memorial to the pioneer Odd Fellows (SRL 378). At the crest of Carson Pass is a striking obelisk dedicated to the memory of "Snow-Shoe" Thompson, the top portion of which is broken off and embedded in the base, symbolizing a life cut off at its prime.

"SNOW-SHOE" THOMPSON

From 1856 to 1876, John A. "Snow-Shoe" Thompson braved the winter storms of the High Sierra to deliver the United States mail to early pioneers. His courage, stamina, and reliability made him almost a legendary figure.

Early in January 1856, while on his ranch at Putah Creek, Thompson read in the papers of the difficulties experienced in getting the mails across the summit of the Sierra Nevada in winter. He made himself a pair of "snow skates," or skis, such as he had used in Norway when he was young Jon Tostensen, and began the arduous and heroic work that he carried on for two decades. His first trip was made in January 1856, from Placerville to Carson Valley, Nevada, a distance of ninety miles

over the old emigrant road on which Placerville was the principal town. Not only was Thompson "the father of all the race of snowshoers in the Sierra Nevada," but he was also the forerunner of the stagecoach and the locomotive over the High Sierra.

Thompson made his home until 1876 on a ranch in Diamond Valley, at the head of Carson Valley, close to the Nevada boundary line. This was near Woodfords, and Thompson was taken from that point to the deep snow line by sleigh or saddle horse. He had two general routes. One went from Woodfords to Placerville, following approximately the course of the present state highway along the West Fork of the Carson River to a point near the mouth of Horse Thief Canyon, four and one-half miles from Woodfords. There, he bore directly west in the direction of Thompson Peak. The other route was from Woodfords to Murphys, by way of Indian Valley and sometimes by way of the Border Ruffian Pass and Blue Lakes. On a few occasions he took the trail through Ebbetts Pass, stopping at Silver Mountain. These three routes to Murphys converged in Hermit Valley.

"Snow-Shoe" Thompson died at his ranch on May 15, 1876, not yet fifty years of age. He is buried at Genoa, Nevada; a pair of skis is incised on his marble tombstone. A monument was placed near the site of his home in Diamond Valley by the social and historical society E Clampus Vitus in 1956. A pair of his "snow-shoes" are on display at the visitor center of the Plumas-Eureka State Park at Johnsville in Plumas County.

ALPINE HIGHWAYS

The surface of Alpine County is elevated and rugged and on every side the view is grandly picturesque. The summit of the Sierra Nevada bisects the county. All but a small portion of the county lies within three National Forests: El Dorado, Humboldt-Toiyabe, and Stanislaus. A road, said to have been the first surveyed route of the High Sierra, was constructed as early as 1857, from Hermit Valley to Hope Valley by way of Twin Lakes Pass. Hope Valley was named by members of the Mormon Battalion on their return to Salt Lake City in the summer of 1848. The emigrant trail through Ebbetts Pass (SRL 318) to Angels Camp was opened up in the early 1850s, but no road went that way until 1864, when, as a result of the opening up of the Comstock Lode in Nevada, a toll road was completed under the name of the Carson Valley and Big Tree Road. It was over this trail, in September 1861, that a little group of Bactrian camels from the Gobi Desert in Mongolia was driven from San

Alpine Hotel, Markleeville

Webster School in Alpine Historical Complex, Markleeville

Francisco to Nevada, where they were used for transportation in the mines. The experiment was not a success, it seems, for the Nevada state legislature in 1875 passed "an act to prohibit camels and dromedaries from running at large on or about the public highways."

ALPINE GHOST TOWNS

Silver Mountain, founded as Kongsberg (Königsberg) in 1858 by Scandinavian miners, existed until 1886. The county seat was located there from 1864 to 1875. A ghost of Alpine's once thriving silver camps, it is marked today only by the crumbling walls of the old stone jail, the first in the county, near the site of the old courthouse. Silver Mountain is located on SR 4 a few miles southwest of its junction with SR 89, a junction that was once the location of the town of Mt. Bullion or Bulliona. En route to the jail ruins at Silver Mountain a tall brick chimney is passed on the right. This was part of the reduction plant of "Lord" Chalmers, an Englishman who came to Alpine County in 1867. Here, next to the chimney and by Silver Creek, is his home, called the Chalmers Mansion, and still containing some furnishings from the past.

Of Silver King, located on the headwaters of the East Fork of the Carson River west of US 395, only a little wreckage of old buildings remains to mark the site. Monitor, flourishing from 1858 to 1886 and entirely deserted by 1893, showed some return to activity (under the name of Loope) from 1898 to 1911, when it was again deserted until 1930, at which time there was a brief revival of mining for a few years.

Although silver predominates in the Alpine region, in large low-grade ledges gold is encountered in nearly every mineralized district. The "Uncle Billy Rogers" Copper Mine, situated in Hope Valley in the northwest angle of the county, is said to have been the first deposit (1855) of this ore ever opened in California or anywhere on the Pacific Coast, antedating the Comstock discovery by several years.

WOODFORDS

In 1847 Sam Brannan, on his way to Salt Lake City, stopped at the present site of Woodfords and left two men to establish an outpost—the first white settlement in this area. The project was abandoned, but other settlers arrived at what had come to be called Brannan Springs. Daniel Woodford, who came in 1849, put up a hotel, the first building of any permanence. About 1851 a man named Cary, whose first name seems to have been lost to history, built a sawmill, and the growing town became known as Cary's Mills, yielding in 1869 to Woodfords. Cary built a house, still standing but now generally called the Wade house, in 1852–53, from lumber milled at his own establishment. During the initial five weeks of its operation in 1860, the Pony Express was routed through Woodfords and maintained a remount station (SRL 805) at Cary's barn, the site of which is across the road from the present Woodfords store.

MARKLEEVILLE

The town of Markleeville is California's smallest county seat and the seat of its least populous county, which has neither a high school nor a hospital within its borders. The picturesque settlement had its beginning in the cabin of Jacob J. Marklee, who settled there in 1861, only to be shot and killed during a quarrel two years later. On the site of his dwelling (SRL 240) stands Alpine County's beautiful little courthouse, built of native stone in 1928.

By 1864 Markleeville had a population of over 2,500, but in 1875, when it succeeded Silver Mountain as the county seat, the entire county could boast only a few more than 1,200; such was the effect of the decline of silver mining. Although a fire about 1886 destroyed much of Markleeville, a few interesting old buildings still stand. The tall Alpine Hotel was originally built in Silver Mountain as the Fisk Hotel and was moved to its present location in 1885.

On the hill above the town is the Alpine County Historical Complex, an interesting group of buildings. The old wooden jail is open to visitors. Nearby the Webster School, in use from 1882 to 1929, was completely restored in 1968 by the Historical Society of Alpine County. Two years later a new museum building was completed, housing a collection of mining and domestic artifacts.

ALPINE COUNTY RESORTS

Three miles west of Markleeville is Grover Hot Springs State Park. The springs here boasted a hotel for many years, operated by the Grover family; the state acquired the property in 1959. The water that emerges from the earth at a temperature of 140 degrees is channeled into a pool where it cools somewhat and refreshes bikers, hikers, skiers, and other visitors to the area. The park's campgrounds are open throughout the year.

Western Alpine County, at the crest of the Sierras, has become a favorite winter playground as ski resorts, some of them more than sixty years old, have developed. Going from north to south near the county line, these resorts are at Hope Valley, Kirkwood, Meiss Meadow, and Bear Valley, and have helped bring the county from its natural isolation into closer contact with the rest of the state.

Amador County

Amador County was created in 1854 when the Legislature allowed the voters of Calaveras County to decide whether to divide the county at the Mokelumne River. Although the actual results were contested and never certified by Calaveras officials, organizers formed the new county nevertheless. Voters chose Jackson as the county seat and it remains so today. Amador's Creek, later Amador City, which gave its name to the county, was itself named for miner and settler José Maria Amador, a trader at the creek in 1848–49 and formerly a mayordomo of Mission San José. The county's first northern boundary was Dry Creek, but it was later extended to the Cosumnes River. In 1864, Amador lost its easternmost territory when Alpine County was formed.

THE MORAGA EXPEDITION

Gabriel Moraga's expedition of 1806 through the Sierra foothills in all probability passed through part of Amador County. The evidence lies not in documents or in diaries but in the fact that about fifty years later, miners near Mokelumne Hill found a bullet or slug embedded in a pine tree with some fifty growth rings around it. No gun-toting people are known to have been there at the appropriate time except Moraga and his company. There may have been solitary trappers in the foothills in later years, but no documentary evidence proves this.

SUTTER'S PINE WOODS

More certain is the fact that in the fall of 1844 or the spring of 1845 John A. Sutter sent employees out from New Helvetia (now Sutter's Fort), his estate in what is now Sacramento, to search the mountain lowlands for a good supply of cedar and pine trees for lumber. A logging project was established at Pine Woods, of which no trace remains today, although it is thought that it lay on the ridge five miles east of the later town of Sutter Creek, between Amador and Sutter Creeks. The distance from Pine Woods to New Helvetia (where Sutter planned to bring his Sierra lumber) was estimated in 1845 by John Bidwell, then in Sutter's employ, to be some forty miles. A reliable sawmill was needed at a site closer to Sutter's Fort, and so James Marshall, another of Sutter's men, was sent in the fall of 1847 to look for a better location. Neither of the two creeks below the ridge at Pine Woods had enough year-round flow of water to power a sawmill, so Marshall moved on. He found his better location on the South Fork of the American River. At what is now Coloma in El Dorado County Marshall began to build a sawmill for Sutter and there in January 1848 he discovered gold in the streambed.

THE EMIGRANT TRAIL, THE "CARSON EMIGRANT ROAD"

The Emigrant Trail of the 1840s descended from the Sierra into the foothills around Volcano and branches split off from there. One went through Jackson. A later stage road to Virginia City, Nevada, and today's SR 88 have followed its general course. On this trail, near the El Dorado–Amador county line, the Tragedy Springs massacre occurred on June 27, 1848. While members of the Mormon Battalion were returning to Utah, three advance scouts of the party were killed by Indians. An account of the event and the names of the scouts were carved on a tree at the spot; the carved section of the tree is preserved in the museum at Sutter's Fort.

Near Tragedy Springs, a monument (SRL 662) indicates where the emigrant road crosses SR 88. Less than two miles west of this point, beside the highway, is the last resting place (SRL 28) of one of the many emigrants who did not have the stamina to complete the long trek. The text of the plaque reads: "MAIDEN'S GRAVE. It is said that in 1850 a young girl, Rachel Melton, native of Iowa, was accompanying her parents on a journey West via covered wagon train when she became violently ill. Camp was made and every effort was made to cure her, as she was the joy of the party; but she passed away and was buried on this spot."

Kirkwood's stage station and inn (SRL 40), built in 1863 by Zack Kirkwood, still stands on SR 88, eight miles northeast of Tragedy Springs. Looking as sturdy as the day it was built, the place serves as a bar and restaurant. Kirkwood's log cabin, built around 1858, has been incorporated into the main building. When Alpine County was created in 1864, the division left the barn and milk house belonging to the Kirkwoods in Alpine, while the county line went directly through the barroom of the inn.

The Volcano Cutoff of the Carson Emigrant Road brought overland traffic into the central part of what is now Amador County in 1852, when Stockton and Volcano merchants paid a contractor to construct a wagon road from Volcano to the Emigrant Trail near Corral Flat. About this time, the name of Kit Carson was attached to the Emigrant Trail, although he had never been on it. The Volcano Cutoff is now followed by the Shake Mill Road, formerly the Fiddletown–Silver Lake Road, which joins SR 88 at Dewdrop Station.

PLASSE'S RESORT

Raymond Peter Plasse followed the Volcano Cutoff in 1852. Born in France, he had arrived in San Francisco in 1850 and had headed for the mines to try his luck. At the south end of Silver Lake he established a trading post near the roadway and placed a claim for 160 acres in the neighborhood. The log cabin he built in 1852 is now used as a generator house, and it is believed to be the oldest building still standing in the length of the Sierra Nevada. The Plasse family ultimately lived on a ranch south of Jackson but retained the mountain property as a summer place and pasturage, and in time other buildings joined the first log cabin on the property. Around 1900 the family opened a summer resort that is still in operation. Historian Larry Cenotto observes that this property has been in the hands of the same family for nearly a century and a half, something of a record for the gold country of California.

The first gold found in Amador County may have been discovered somewhere along the Mokelumne River, in the spring of 1848, by Captain Charles M. Weber, the founder of the city of Stockton. During the summer of the same year, within two months' time, a company of eight men headed by James P. Martin took out several thousand dollars' worth of gold each. In the autumn a mining expedition of one hundred men recently mustered out of the army came to the river. In the recently concluded war between the United States and Mexico, a few men had seen service under Colonel J. D. Stevenson, but most of the others had been stationed in California during the course of the war.

From all over the world thousands of eager miners flocked to the gulches and rivers of the Sierra in 1849, and during the first years of the 1850s they continued to swarm up and down the rivers, building small towns overnight at all of the rich river bars. Within the two decades that followed, an almost unbelievable change took place. Historian J. D. Mason, writing in 1881, described the transformation even then evident to one walking along the banks of the Mokelumne River. Hardly could one realize, he said, "that the stillness, broken only by the murmur of the river, was ever otherwise." Today, scarcely a fragment remains of the numerous cabins where "the miner fried his flapjacks or dried his wet clothing after a day's toil under a broiling sun in the ice-cold water."

Big Bar (SRL 41) was one of the prominent camps along the Mokelumne. An old inn, Gardella's, is at the Amador end of the bridge where SR 49 crosses the river; it is now a private residence. After the placers on the bars had been depleted, the center of trade moved across the river to Mokelumne Hill, in Calaveras County. The rushing river and the rugged canyon remain at Big Bar.

Middle Bar (SRL 36), two miles below Big Bar, was a larger community than its neighbor, and in the 1920s it had a brief lode mining revival. The old homesteads, however, were soon purchased by the East Bay Municipal Utility District, which built the Pardee Dam across the Mokelumne River six miles below Middle Bar. This district was formed when eleven cities in Alameda and Contra Costa Counties joined forces to secure water and power, and selected the Mokelumne River as the source of the purest water. Former governor George Pardee was president of the company when the dam was completed in 1929. This region, where hundreds of busy miners with pans or cradles once washed the gold from the river, is now covered with water. The old lode mines included the Big Tunnel or Mammoth, the Hardenburg, the Marlette, and the St. Julian or Caminetti, successors of the earlier placers and all big producers in the past.

LANCHA PLANA

Farther down the Mokelumne River, in the southwestern part of the county, many mining camps centered about Lancha Plana, among them Poverty Bar (in Calaveras County), Winter's Bar, Oregon Bar, and Put's Bar. This area is now inundated by the Camanche Reservoir of the East Bay Municipal Utility District. Lancha Plana ("flatboat"), just across the river from the exceedingly rich gravels of Poverty Bar, came into existence as the mooring place for the flatboat ferry, which carried miners from the north side of the river across to Poverty Bar and the mines of Calaveras County. Lancha Plana (SRL 30) reached the height of its prosperity after 1856, when hill and bluff mining were bringing greater returns than mining in the river had ever brought.

Buena Vista ("beautiful view") was the name applied to a settlement about six miles north of Lancha Plana, as well as to a mountain and a valley in the vicinity. Buena Vista, over the years, was a more important settlement than Lancha Plana. The old store at the intersection of the Pardee-Ione Road and the Jackson Valley Road still serves the public in its "new" location. It was originally built in Lancha Plana by William Cook in 1859. When the miners moved away to other fields, all business languished in Lancha Plana. Cook decided to set up in the more promising town and had the sandstone blocks of the Lancha Plana store taken down and rebuilt at Buena Vista in 1877.

BUTTE CITY

The Ginocchio Store (SRL 39), on SR 49 about one and one-half miles south of Jackson, is all that remains of what was once Butte City, a thriving mining camp in the 1850s. An old graveyard on the hill overlooks the place.

DRYTOWN

At Drytown (SRL 31), a mining camp on Dry Creek nine miles north of Jackson, mining for gold was first begun in the spring of 1848. It was not unusual, in 1849, to wash as much as $100 in gold from a single pan in the surrounding canyons. These canyons had an unpleasant collection of names—Blood Gulch, Murder-er's Gulch, and Rattlesnake Gulch among them. Although there were doubtless plenty of steady, industrious miners at Drytown, there were also desperate characters who left their mark. The town prospered until 1857, when fire swept the place. It never recovered from this disaster, for gold was already becoming worked out there. Two old brick buildings still stand, one a house claimed to have been owned by members of the same family since it was built, probably after 1857, and the other a store associated with the name of George Hearst, then beginning his mining career in San Francisco, who is said to have kept his mining records there in the late 1850s. The old town hall was in use by a popular little theater group when it burned down in 1987; the building was afterward restored but is no longer used for showing melodramas.

RANCHERIA

Mining at Rancheria, two miles east of Drytown, began in 1848. A mixed population, in which Mexicans and Chileans predominated, gathered there to the number of five or six hundred. From that year, the new American rulers of California became increasingly antagonistic to the Mexicans and Chileans moving into the state seeking wealth; the state Legislature imposed the Foreign Miners Tax (1851) in a blatant attempt to drive them out of the state. Law enforcement officials reflected this anti-Hispanic bias, the Mexicans and Chileans said, and violence against the "greasers" (an ugly term often used by the Americans of that time for all Spanish-speakers) resulted in a kind of ethnic civil war in some parts of California. One result of this conflict was a Mexican backlash. On the night of August 6, 1855, Rancheria was assaulted by a gang of Mexican horsemen, who sacked the town and killed nine people, five in one family. The retaliation was as brutal as the offense, and it is not certain how many Mexicans were lynched or otherwise killed by vigilantes. It is certain that the Spanish-speaking population of most of the Mother Lode nearly disappeared after 1855, driven out by American hostility. A monument on the mass grave of the slain Dynan family stands near the road from Amador City to Rancheria Creek.

VOLCANO

Volcano (SRL 29) is located at the bottom of a deep cup in the mountains, hence its name. It was a pros-pective mining town like many others, with the accident of geography thrown in: it lay between the Emigrant Road at the northern border of the county and the more populated region around Jackson and Sutter Creek. In 1852, the Volcano Cutoff (also called the Pennsylvania Cutoff in early accounts) was made by the merchants of Stockton and Amador County to bring wagons down from the trans-Sierra route into the settled region of the county. Volcano was thus on the highway of its day. It never became a ghost town, although the authors of the third (1966) edition of *Historic Spots in California* described it in romantic, eerie words: "Volcano's population has dwindled considerably since the 1850s, and its isolation, together with the weirdness of the gray rocks washed out by miners of long ago, make it a veritable 'Sleepy Hollow' of the West. Almost one looks for goblins among the ghost rocks, or for a headless horseman to come galloping down the steep wooded mountain road."

This was a very rich hydraulic mining district in early days, a million dollars in gold having been taken out of one mine alone, which was worked for over thirty years. Some gold is still found in the region, but activity of other sorts is more evident. The town of Volcano, nearby Daffodil Hill in springtime bloom, and Indian Grinding Rock (Chaw-Se) State Historic Park are popular tourist attractions. Retirement communities, vacation homes, and the commercial activities necessary for their support have changed the region, like many other places in the Sierra foothills.

Volcano today is a curious combination of modern-day activities and old surroundings. Several old stores on Main Street have only their stone facades left. Other buildings are open for business. The old General Store is claimed to have been serving the public continuously since 1852, when what is now a part of the store was built. The Odd Fellows and Masonic Hall, still in use, dates from 1856, as does the old Bavarian Brewery, now a private residence. Behind the Masonic Hall is the site (SRL 715) of the first known amateur astronomical observatory in California, built around 1860. The state marker here is missing. The most grandiose structure in Volcano is the St. George Hotel, three stories high. Built in 1863, the St. George is the fourth hotel built on the site since the early 1850s, and still accommodates guests. An E Clampus Vitus plaque on the hotel celebrates its history. Another "Clamper" plaque in the center of town notes that in 1934 plans were afoot to build a dam and to flood Volcano, but, in the words of the plaque, "Geology and water rights negated plan so Volcano didn't drown. Not by a dam site."

An interesting relic is "Old Abe," the six-pound bronze cannon on display next to the old Sing Kee Store. The cannon was cast in Massachusetts in 1837 and brought to California some time after the end of the Mexican War. In 1861, as the Civil War broke out, it was brought to its present site by the Volcano Blues, a pro–Northern state militia unit, and local tradition says that although it never fired a shot in anger, the presence of the Union cannon was enough to discourage Confederate sympathizers in the region. Since virtually all the six-pound bronze cannons in the United States were melted down in the early months of the war to make twelve-pound pieces, "Old Abe," far off in the West, is the oldest remaining six-pound bronze cannon in the nation.

Another relic from Civil War days is the bell presented to the town by Reverend Thomas Starr King, whose eloquent speech here on behalf of the Union in 1861 elicited generous contributions from the community. The bell was given by Union sympathizers in Boston to replace the one lost when Volcano's Methodist church burned. California had relatively few men in arms during the Civil War, but her contribution in gold was crucial to the ultimate victory of the Union. The bell is now displayed in the center of town.

Volcano is three miles from SR 88 at Pine Grove. Between the two towns is Indian Grinding Rock (Chaw-Se) State Historic Park, where the remarkable grinding rock, 173 feet by 82 feet, contains 1,185 *chaw-se*s, or mortar cups, and some 363 rock carvings. A Northern Miwok center, the park also contains replicas of native buildings, including a ceremonial roundhouse (SRL 1001). The visitors' center has good displays of local artifacts and natural history.

PINE GROVE

Pine Grove, on SR 88, has the appearance of a fairly new town, and indeed it has attracted many residents since the 1950s. The place began as an inn, the Pine Grove House, built in 1855 by Albert Leonard on the road between Volcano and Jackson. A restaurant now stands on the site of the inn. The town hall (1897), originally the Dance and Temperance Hall, has been the community center for over a century. The public school built in the 1890s is now a small museum and open to the public.

PLYMOUTH

In the northern part of Amador County numerous mining camps were once located on the Cosumnes River and its branches. Most of these camps have long since vanished. The richest location in the district was situated on the river at the main forks of the Cosumnes, and was called by the Indian name Yeomet. Several stores and a somewhat pretentious hotel were standing there in 1853, but the miners gradually took over the town, one building after another giving way to the diggings, until nothing was left except the old toll bridge.

On the stage road to Sacramento, four or five miles south of the site of Yeomet, was Plymouth, established in 1871, whose history is largely bound up with the quartz lodes of the region. Until the 1940s, the town was kept busy by the Plymouth Division of the Argonaut Mine. On the south side of Plymouth's main street is a brick structure (SRL 470) built in 1857 and at one time used as the office and commissary of the mining company. At the southwest end of the flat on which Plymouth is located was the hamlet of Pokerville, or Puckerville, at the site of which a unique building remains. The Old China Store, built around 1880, has sidewalls of local fieldstone, but the front and back are of brick, which is also used around the corners in a series of zigzag steps; a brick front was often thought to be a status symbol in the late nineteenth century. The original proprietor was a Mr. Ming, whose nationality probably led to the present-day name of the building.

FIDDLETOWN

A few miles east of Plymouth is the picturesque settlement of Fiddletown (SRL 35), scene of Bret Harte's story "An Episode of Fiddletown." It was first settled in 1849 by a party of Missourians. "They are always fiddling," said a Missouri patriarch; "call it Fiddletown." And Fiddletown it was until 1878, when the name was changed to Oleta. It is said that the change was made by the state Legislature upon a petition signed by, among others, "Judge" Columbus Allen Purinton, a prominent citizen who on frequent business trips to Sacramento and San Francisco had been embarrassed at being known as "the man from Fiddletown." Another petition in 1932 from, among others, the Committee on Historic Landmarks of the California Historical Society, resulted in the post office's restoring the name Fiddletown. Some buildings dating from the 1850s can be seen on the main street; the rammed-earth adobe built for a Chinese doctor and his family later was a general store and home until its owner, Chow Fong You, died in 1965. Chow's store and home was preserved and opened to the public by the Fiddletown Preservation Society and Amador County in 1988.

Across from Chow's store is another building from the 1850s, known locally as the Chinese Gambling House. The forge next door is also from the 1850s, as is the general store a few doors east. The general store is one of the oldest such places in California still doing business in its original location. The tall Schallhorn building was a smithy and wagon shop when it was built in 1870; it serves now as a garage. Fiddletown is an exceptionally charming town for a stroll on a summer's afternoon.

In the 1850s and 1860s Fiddletown was the trading center for a number of rich mining camps, American Flat and American Hill, French Flat, Loafer Flat, and Lone Hill among them. The entire region, including the ridge between Bridgeport and Slate Creek, is within an area of extensive old river deposits.

Central House, a popular stage station that stood on the road between Plymouth and Drytown where SRs 16 and 49 now join, was built of timbers brought around the Horn. Another much-frequented hostelry on this route was at Willow Springs, a few miles west of Drytown on the way to Sacramento. Forest Home, Arkansas Creek, and Yankee Hill were neighboring camps farther west.

The region around Fiddletown and Plymouth is now a prosperous dry-farming community, growing grapes, walnuts, pears, and various farm products. Shenandoah Valley, north of Plymouth, has been a rich farming section since the early 1850s, and descendants of pioneer settlers still occupy many of the old homesteads. Eight miles northeast of Plymouth at 14430 Shenandoah Road is the Shenandoah Valley Museum. The first winery here was established in 1856; the state marker (SRL 762) identifies the site as that of the D'Agostini Winery, which was neither its original nor its present name, which is Sobon Estate. The winery's original stone cellar is still in use. More than sixteen wineries can now be visited in the Shenandoah Valley, one of the state's important wine-making districts.

SUTTER CREEK

Sutter Creek (SRL 322) was named for John A. Sutter, who mined there with his Kanaka workforce in the

Monteverde Store Museum, Sutter Creek

summer of 1848. There was little activity at Sutter Creek until 1851, when quartz gold was discovered. Quartz mining was a very hazardous occupation in the early days. Timbering of shafts and tunnels was all too often inadequate and poorly constructed, resulting in many cave-ins. Large amounts of capital were needed to construct these shafts and tunnels before any return could be made from the project. Alvinza Hayward was one of the few to make millions from his investments. Some properties were incredibly productive: the Central Eureka continued in operation even after most of the mines were closed down by World War II. The shaft reached almost the 5,000-foot level and the mine produced about $17 million in gold.

In the late 1850s Leland Stanford, then a Sacramento merchant, became involved with the Lincoln Mine, between Sutter Creek and Amador City, when stockholders gave him a controlling interest in payment for their debts. By the time he had sold his interest in 1872, he had realized many thousands of dollars in profits since 1859.

Many visitors to the Mother Lode pass through Sutter Creek. The town had an industrial base as well as being a mining center. The first foundry and furniture manufacturing establishment in the gold country was built here. The Knight Foundry, started in 1872, still operates on Eureka Street (SRL 1007); it is believed to be the only water-powered foundry in the United States. Educational and religious activities also thrived here, making Sutter Creek a cultural center distinct from the wilder mining camps of the region. Some old buildings survived the fires that hit the town in its early days. The Methodist church at the south end of town was built in several portions, the earliest in 1862; the spire was added to the church tower in 1976. The Sutter Creek Grammar School was first used in 1871 and has been refurbished by the Sutter Creek Woman's Club. One downtown building, now a bed-and-breakfast, was built in 1857; on the same side of the main street nearby, an inn includes a two-story brick wing erected in 1859. As in many California cities of historical interest, walking guides may be obtained in the town that describe these and other old structures and sites. Several deep though inactive quartz mines, not open to the public, remain in the vicinity of Sutter Creek.

AMADOR CITY

Amador City, located on Amador Creek three miles north of Sutter Creek where it intercepts the Mother Lode ledge, had its beginnings as a mining center in 1848. But the placers were never very rich and, like Sutter Creek, the history of Amador City has been connected chiefly with quartz mining. The first quartz discovery in Amador County was made there in February 1851 by S. A. Davidson, a Tennessee Baptist preacher. Since three other ministers were associated with him, the mine was called the "Ministers' Claim." Soon thereafter the vein was discovered on the north side of the creek, and became known as the "Original Amador Mine."

The Keystone Mine at Amador was the result of the consolidation of the Original Amador with the Spring Hill, Granite State, and Walnut Hill mines in 1853. But the enterprise was not a success until the discovery of the Bonanza in 1869, when the first month's crushing paid $40,000. This high production continued for over a decade. The Keystone has been closed since before World War I, but there are people who believe that millions of dollars in gold still lie hidden within the earth thereabouts.

Amador City, a thriving community with many visitors, has a cluster of old buildings along SR 49, most of which are still in use. A beautiful brick building, the office and residence of former Keystone Mine superintendents, built in 1881, is now a motel with period furnishings. The Amador Hotel, recently restored, includes some walls built in 1855; the Imperial Hotel, with a renowned dining room, dates from 1879. Since a fire in 1878 destroyed most of its wooden structures, the city's older places are constructed of brick. A building that escaped the fire is the old schoolhouse on the hill behind the cemetery, with its old bell in place in the belfry. Although it has never been a very populous place, Amador City has been an incorporated city since 1915, and was once the smallest incorporated city in California both in population and in area.

JACKSON

Jackson, county seat of Amador County, is rich in old brick buildings from the mining days. A few of these retain such features as iron-shuttered windows, upper-story balconies, and heavy doors. For many years, it was a town with a diversified population: its people came from French, German, Italian, Mexican, Serbian, and Slavonian backgrounds, as well as from pioneer American families.

After a disastrous fire destroyed the town in 1862, construction immediately began on many of the stone and brick buildings on Main and Court Streets, which stand today. One of them is the two-story National Hotel. Nearby is the redbrick Independent Order of Odd Fellows Hall, whose three stories give it the claim to be one of the tallest three-story buildings ever put up. An earlier structure is the former drug store (1855) on Main Street, which in Civil War days housed the *Amador Dispatch*. The authorities came to believe that this newspaper was pro-Confederate and unpatriotic. When the news of President Lincoln's assassination arrived in California in April 1865, U.S. cavalrymen arrested the publisher and editor of the paper, put them in Alcatraz Prison (then a military station) in San Francisco Bay, and closed down the paper.

At 113–115 Main Street is the Pioneer Hall (SRL 34), where the Native Daughters of the Golden West were organized in 1886. At the corner of Water Street and Broadway is the Masonic Building (1854), one of the oldest in town. Jackson's most picturesque building is the little white Serbian Orthodox Church of St. Sava, on Jackson Gate Road, in the northern part of the city. Built in 1894, this is the mother church for the denomination in North America.

Commemorative plaques have been placed at several places in Jackson. One along Main Street identifies the site of Jackson's "Hanging Tree," where ten men were executed between 1851 and 1855. In front of handsome St. Patrick's Catholic Church (1868), another marker, placed by the Knights of Columbus, honors Jackson-born Angelo Noce (1848–1922), "Father of Columbus Day," who "devoted his life to the memory of Christopher Columbus . . . [and] through whose efforts were founded the national holiday which now bears his name." In the schoolyard at the corner of Church and North Streets another marker (SRL 865) commemorates the first Jewish synagogue in the Mother Lode, begun on the spot in 1857 but no longer in existence.

The Amador County Museum is housed in the A. C.

Brown House, at 225 Church Street, which was built of brick in 1859. The entire block, including wrought-iron fences, a Victorian carriage house, and the two-story residence itself, is maintained in excellent condition. Models of some of the mine structures from various parts of the county are among the many displays in the museum.

Jackson was named in 1849 by early miners for Alden M. Jackson, a capable New England–born lawyer who was often given the honorific "Colonel," although the rank was never awarded him. The location had formerly been known as Bottileas ("bottles" is one translation), apparently because of the debris scattered about by transients on their way to the mountains.

As is told in the Calaveras County chapter, what is now Amador County was part of Calaveras County when that became one of the original twenty-seven counties in 1850. Although Double Springs was named the first seat of justice in Calaveras County, some enterprising men from Jackson were able in July 1851 to remove the county archives from Double Springs to Jackson, which until the following April served as the county seat. An election on April 16, 1852, made Mokelumne Hill the Calaveras County seat, and not until Amador County was created in 1854 did Jackson officially become a county seat.

The diggings in the immediate vicinity of Jackson were not rich but, being the logical center for a large mining area and a convenient stopping place on the road from Sacramento to the southern mines, Jackson grew and prospered in the 1850s. The flats and gulches in the vicinity of Tunnel Hill, a mile and a half south of Jackson, at Scottsville, were good producers, as was the hill itself. A number of tunnels sunk into its sides gave rise to the name. This very rich deposit was worked to bedrock; the scarred hills are now grass-grown and serve as pasturelands.

Another rich gravel digging was at Jackson Gate (SRL 118), a mile north of town. A deep, narrow fissure in the rocks through which the creek flows gave the place its name. Here is Chichizola's Store, built in the 1850s. Ohio Hill and nearby Squaw Gulch were also very rich producers. At two sites in the Jackson Gate area, Marie Suize, a Frenchwoman locally known as Madame Pantalons ("pants"), dressed as a man and, working like the men, accumulated a hundred thousand dollars and then sold her claim for twenty thousand more, only to lose it in speculation.

Quartz mining continued to bring prosperity to Jackson after other forms of mining had ceased to be remunerative. Several deep quartz veins in the hills above the town were worked until World War II. The famous Argonaut and Kennedy mines (SRL 786), among the deepest in the world, are located here. The Argonaut, discovered in the 1850s, had many failures as well as successes, but it operated continuously from 1893 to 1942 and reached a vertical depth of 5,570 feet. Here, in August 1922, forty-seven miners lost their lives when they were trapped by fire in the lower levels, the greatest loss of life in a mine accident in California history. The total production of this mine has been estimated at over $25 million. The Argonaut can be located many miles away by its lofty water tower.

Across SR 49 from the Argonaut is the Kennedy, opened in the 1850s. It, too, had its ups and downs, vast sums being expended with little returns. Later, however, it became a record producer, yielding an estimated $35 million in gold. After 1900 modern equipment was installed, including a second hoist at the 4,600-foot level of its vertical shaft, which reached an ultimate depth of 5,912 feet before mining was stopped. A half mile east of the Kennedy Mine were four huge tailing wheels, used to raise the tailings, or mill waste, to the summit of a small hill, beyond which lay the disposal dump. Two of these still stand, and work is being done to restore a third. Built in 1902, these wheels are among the most photographed landmarks in the Mother Lode country; they are located in Kennedy Tailing Wheels Park, operated by the city of Jackson on North Main Street.

North and east of Jackson, remnants of several smaller mining camps may still be found among the hills. Clinton (SRL 37), eight miles east of Jackson, with its Catholic church built in 1877, is now surrounded by small ranches. Many miners were attracted to the region after water had been brought in through canals in the 1850s, but the diggings were never rich; this was a center for quartz mining as late as the 1880s.

Irishtown (SRL 38), seven miles northeast of Jackson at the junction of SR 88 and the Clinton Road, has vanished. The first American settlers on this spot found it "a city of wigwams," and hundreds of mortars in the rocks testify that this was an established Indian encampment. Pine Grove lies two miles beyond.

IONE VALLEY

Ione was variously known in the Gold Rush days as "Bed Bug" and "Freeze Out." But the place grew, and the more euphonious name of Ione replaced the older ones. Ione is a heroine in the 1834 novel *The Last Days of Pompeii* by Edward Bulwer-Lytton, and some believe this is the source of the town's name. Others cite Ione in Illinois, perhaps the home of an early pioneer. Then there is the story of William Hicks, who came to California with the Chiles-Walker party in 1843, and for a while settled in the area. He was the first to prospect the valley, which he left in 1850. When asked by visitors who owned all the land, Hicks is said to have replied, "I own it."

Ione was a supply center, not a gold town, and as agriculture gradually made headway throughout the state, the town prospered. The town's first school and its Methodist Episcopal church were both started here in 1852. When a larger church structure was needed, Bishop Matthew Simpson laid the cornerstone in 1862 for a striking brick building of Gothic design (SRL 506), which was completed in 1866. Among the old business buildings lining the streets of Ione, the Daniel Stewart Store (SRL 788) is the oldest; it was operated by the Stewart family until they sold the business in 1973. A double structure across Main Street houses the Masonic Lodge Hall on the second-floor west and the Native Sons of the Golden West Hall on the second-floor east. The Scully home on West Marlette Street dates from the 1850s and has been lived in by the Scully family since 1882. Charles Howard Park has been the scene of Ione's homecoming picnic since 1876; held on the first weekend in May, this is one of California's longest-established community events.

The Preston School of Industry was completed in 1894 as a school for juveniles referred by the courts; it is now a facility of the California Youth Authority. The principal building (SRL 867), known locally as "The Castle," is the leading example of Romanesque architecture in the Mother Lode. The old building no longer houses inmates, although it is still part of the large institution. The California Division of Forestry Fire Academy was established at Ione in 1967 and is another major state facility in the town.

Muletown, about two miles north of Ione, was a lively camp in the 1850s, and stories are told of the strikes in its rich foothill ravines: an Argentinean washed out $100 a day there; a Chinese miner, picking up a piece of gold weighing 36 ounces, was so elated that he immediately left for his homeland. After the ravines had been worked out, the surrounding hills were attacked by hydraulic power and produced even more wealth. Some claims paid as high as $1,000 per week per man. During its palmy days Muletown claimed several hundred inhabitants, a large proportion of them Irish. There is nothing left of the place today.

Nor does anything remain of the Q Ranch, Irish Hill, or Quincy, all of which were important for a while and then vanished; their sites are to the north and west of Ione in the vicinity of SR 104. Mule Creek State Prison now stands in this area.

Butte County

California State University Chico Administration Building

Butte County is one of the original twenty-seven counties of the state, at first encompassing an area much larger than it does today. The county seat was first at Hamilton; in 1853 it was moved to Bidwell's Bar. Since 1856, it has been in Oroville. "Butte" was used by early pioneers to name a high place, a mountain, or even a range of mountains. The "butte" in this name came from the Sutter Buttes, high hills to the south, now in Sutter County.

JOHN BIDWELL'S RANCHO CHICO

John Bidwell was born in Chautauqua County, New York, in 1819, and moved as a young man to Missouri in 1839. There he joined the first group of settlers going to California overland by covered wagon, in 1841. John Bartleson had organized the party but Bidwell became its leader. Among the company in this Bidwell-Bartleson party were men who would be prominent in the settlement of California: Josiah Belden, Joseph Chiles, Pierson B. Reading, Robert H. Thomes, and Charles M. Weber. For a time Bidwell worked at John A. Sutter's properties at New Helvetia ("Sutter's Fort") and the "Hock Farm" in what is now Sutter County, and explored the Sacramento River Valley. Although he was not at the Bear Flag raising in Sonoma on June 14, 1846, he helped draw up the resolution of independence for the "California Republic" and served with Colonel John C. Frémont when the latter took command and marched south to Monterey. Bidwell was one of the first civil magistrates of the recently captured pueblo of Los Angeles in 1846–47.

At the end of hostilities in the Mexican War, Bidwell like many others was excited by the news of the discovery of gold, and in June 1848 made his own gold strike on the Middle Fork of the Feather River, at a place thereafter known as Bidwell's Bar. In 1849 he purchased Rancho Chico, a large tract of land, from its grantees, William Dickey and Edward Farwell, and settled down to become one of California's greatest ranchers. On his ranch he founded the town of Chico in 1860, later donating land for public schools, setting aside a plot of ground for each church, and designating a large section for the Northern Branch State Normal School, started in 1887, which is today California State University at Chico. In 1868, he built the handsome two-story brick house that today is Bidwell Mansion State Historic Park (SRL 329).

John Bidwell was one of the foremost builders of the commonwealth of California. He was a member of the state Senate, and served in the state militia during the Civil War, where he attained the rank of general, by which title he was often known in later years. He was a pioneer agriculturist and horticulturist, and a man interested in humanitarian, educational, and reform movements. He was three times nominated for gover-

Bidwell Mansion, Chico

nor and in 1892 won the nomination for president of the United States on the Prohibition ticket, receiving the largest number of votes of anyone ever nominated by that party. But after serving a single term in Congress from 1865 to 1867, he was never again elected to public office. During his term in Washington he met Annie E. Kennedy, a member of an old Washington family. They were married in a wedding attended by President Andrew Johnson and many prominent persons of the day before going to California, where they spent the remainder of their long lives.

As manager for Sutter's Hock Farm, Bidwell had learned to work with and to like the Indian people; he had a reputation for being friendly to the Indians, treating them fairly, providing rancheria lands, hiring them to work on his estate, settling disputes, and providing both cultural and material advantages. He and his wife maintained a school and a church for the use of the Indians. One of the eighteen treaties between the United States government and the Indians of California was drawn up and signed at Rancho Chico on August 1, 1851. These treaties, made in 1851–52 during the administration of President Millard Fillmore, were never approved by the Senate, and remain as one of the grievances the Indian peoples experienced in these years.

Bidwell maintained a large experimental orchard near his house. It contained at least one specimen of over four hundred varieties of fruit and at the time of his death in 1900 included 1,800 acres of every species and variety adapted to the locality. He was the father of the raisin industry in that region as well as a pioneer in the manufacture of olive oil. He began wine making in 1864 or 1865, but after his marriage to the ardently prohibitionist Annie Kennedy, the vineyard was dug up and no wine grape was ever again planted on his land.

In 1886 Bidwell presented some thirty acres of land to the state as a forestry experiment station. The gift was neglected by the State Forestry Commission and in time came to be owned by the city of Chico. The site has been marked by a plaque (SRL 840.2) at Cedar Grove and East Eighth Streets in Bidwell Park.

Rancho Chico was remarkable for its splendid trees, both native and exotic. On July 10, 1905, five years after the general's death, Mrs. Bidwell donated a tract of the most desirable land along Big Chico Creek to the city of Chico. Named Bidwell Park, the grant was for more than 1,900 acres and included such beautiful areas as Oak Forest and Iron Canyon. In 1911 Mrs. Bidwell added another 301 acres to the gift, making Bidwell Park the second-largest city park in California, after Los Angeles's Griffith Park. She also donated an area along Lindo Channel to the state of California; this is now held by Butte County as an undeveloped park area. Two miles southeast of the city are 240 acres owned by the United States Department of Agriculture and used as an experimental station.

Four miles northeast of downtown Chico, off Manzanita Avenue near Hooker Oak Avenue, is the site of the mammoth Hooker Oak (SRL 313), perhaps the most famous of California's valley oaks (*Quercus lobata*, the largest of all the American oaks). The tree was named in honor of the great English botanist Sir Joseph Hooker, who visited Rancho Chico in 1877. Exactly one hundred years after Sir Joseph's visit, the tree (badly damaged by a storm in 1962) finally toppled. In its prime, the Hooker Oak was calculated to be over 100 feet tall and twenty-eight feet around its base. The valley oaks were discovered in 1792 by Spanish naval officers and were often mentioned in the narratives of Vancouver, Frémont, and other early explorers.

CHICO

Chico, named for the creek and the rancho (*chico* being Spanish for "little"), now is a bustling city centered on the university and surrounded by prosperous farmlands. The older district of the city, shaded by fine trees, contains some interesting old buildings. The Gage house at 410 Normal Avenue, built in 1861, is the oldest in town. Nearby is the Stansbury House at 307 West Fifth Street, built in 1883 for Dr. Oscar Stansbury of Mississippi. Dr. Stansbury practiced medicine for many years in Chico; his daughter Angelina's will bequeathed the home to the city of Chico when she died in 1974. It is open to the public and maintained by a preservation association. The Masonic Hall at 131 West First Street is the oldest (1871) public building still standing, although a portion of the Bidwell Building, ten years older, is still extant within the structure at 100 Broadway. The city plaza bounded by Broadway, Main, Third, and Fourth Streets was General Bidwell's gift to the new city at the time of its incorporation in 1872. Plans for a county courthouse on the square never materialized, since Oroville held onto its position as the seat of government. Local tradition has it that the elms shading the plaza today were planted by Bidwell himself. The handsome Main Post Office (1915) on the plaza is now on the National Register of Historic Places.

Two old cemeteries are of particular interest. The Mechoopda Indian Tribal Cemetery on West Sacramento Avenue at Mechoopda Street is close to the site of the old Mechoopda Indian village. Annie Bidwell established a church near the site in the early 1870s, and the cemetery was begun about that time. The Mechoopda Tribal Association still maintains and uses the old cemetery. Unfortunately, many of the older graves are no longer marked. At 700 Camellia Way is the Chico Cemetery, dating from 1860. It was begun as a Bidwell family plot (both the general and Mrs. Bidwell are buried there); relatives and family servants were also interred there, and in time it became the city burial ground, some thirty-five acres in extent.

The Chico Museum at Salem and Second Streets has, among other displays, parts of a Chinese temple reconstructed from the days when a large Chinese community ("Chinatown") was part of many northern California towns. The state university campus is a particularly attractive one to visit. The administration building (1929) is the oldest part of the campus; it replaced the Normal School Building of 1887, which was destroyed by fire in 1927.

RANCHO ESQUÓN AND CHICO LANDING

The headquarters of Rancho Esquón, granted to John A. Sutter and Samuel Neal in 1844, were located on Butte Creek seven miles south of Chico. Neal, a native of Pennsylvania, had come to California with Frémont earlier in 1844. With Frémont's permission, he remained at Sutter's Fort as a blacksmith. In April 1846, he entertained the colonel's forces on their way north to Oregon. Soon afterward, Neal began to export hides and tallow from his ranch down the river to Suisun Bay.

Chico Landing, first known as Bidwell's Landing, where steamers plying the Sacramento River unloaded, was an important place in the 1850s. It was located on nearby Rancho de Farwell, about five miles west of the present city of Chico.

HAMILTON

Hamilton was a mining town situated on a bend in the Feather River above Marysville. Its story is typical of many ghost towns in other old mining regions. The first mining was done here in the early spring of 1848 by John Bidwell and others. By 1849, there was enough mining for gold in the river that a town grew up.

Hamilton won out over Bidwell's Bar in the contest for county seat in 1850, but as the latter town (twenty-five miles further up the river) became richer and more prosperous, people left Hamilton and Bidwell's Bar became the county seat in 1853. Within the old cemetery, largely of the Moore family, is a monument erected in 1917 to mark the first county seat of Butte County. Since gold dredging in the river destroyed the town site, there is nothing left of it today. Just above the site was a settlement of Chinese miners, who worked in the same red hills that over a century later were the source of clay for the impervious layer in the construction of the Oroville Dam.

BIDWELL'S BAR, THE OROVILLE DAM, AND LAKE OROVILLE

Bidwell's Bar (SRL 330) was one of the many flourishing mining camps along the Feather River in the Sierra Nevada in the 1850s. Gold was discovered there by John Bidwell in July 1848. The camp was located on the Middle Fork of the Feather River, thirty-nine miles above the town of Marysville. In 1853 three daily stages ran to Bidwell's Bar directly from Marysville. As the mines at Bidwell's Bar became more or less exhausted, the inhabitants moved down the river to Ophir City, later called Oroville, where rich deposits were found. Oroville became the county seat in 1856, succeeding Bidwell's Bar, where the seat of government had been located since 1853.

The Oroville Dam is called the keystone of the California Water Project, authorized by legislative action in the 1950s. The project's purpose is to impound and distribute water, to create sources of electrical energy, and to make new recreational facilities. The Oroville Dam on the Feather River was completed in 1968. At 770 feet, it is the highest earth-fill dam in the world and the highest dam of any kind in the United States. The waters of

Bidwell Bar Suspension Bridge and Tollhouse (1856), Lake Oroville

Lake Oroville, which the dam has created, cover an area of 24 square miles with over 160 miles of shoreline.

Three relics of Bidwell's Bar, which now lies beneath the waters of the lake, have been preserved. The "Mother Orange Tree," planted at Bidwell's Bar in 1856 by Judge Joseph Lewis, is probably the oldest living orange tree in California. It still bears fruit. From its seeds developed the pioneer orange industry of nearby Oroville, still a large producer of navels and mandarins. The tree was carefully moved and successfully replanted at the State Division of Water Resources headquarters on Glen Drive off Oroville Dam Boulevard about a mile east of Oroville proper. The suspension bridge (SRL 314) and brick tollhouse that once were at Bidwell's Bar have been relocated to the Bidwell Canyon Marina on Lake Oroville. The bridge, the first of its kind in California, was shipped around the Horn from New York in 1853 and installed in 1856.

OROVILLE

The first miners came to the site of Oroville on the Feather River in 1849, and in 1850 a mining camp was formed there, Ophir City. By 1856 the town had been renamed Oroville, and its importance had increased so much that it had ambitions of being chosen as the county seat. Since Bidwell's Bar, then the county seat, was waning as a mining center, Oroville received the honor by popular election. The new county seat soon became a trading center for the mining towns in the surrounding hills, along Table Mountain, and up the Feather River.

Immediately east of Oroville were important river mining operations in the 1850s and for some years afterward. The river was diverted from its course so that the gravel of the bed might be mined. From Oroville to the junction of the North and Middle Forks of the Feather River the most extensive activities of this kind in California were carried on, but all evidence of this is under Lake Oroville now.

Several miles above Oroville was Long's Bar, founded in 1849 with the establishment of a store by the Long brothers. The first pan of gold washed out at Long's Bar netted $400. It became one of the principal settlements of the region during the 1850s. A marker was placed at Long's Bar in 1982 by the Butte County Historical Society, the Masons, and E Clampus Vitus. At the Cape Claim, in 1855, the mining of the river with flumes is said to have netted $1 million in sixty days. Lynchburg, another thriving camp with rich surface diggings, was located in the vicinity. It was a rival of Oroville in the contest for county seat, putting forth the claim of a superior climate. Thompson's Flat, first called Rich Gulch and mined as early as 1848, had so increased in population by 1854 that the town, then called New Philadelphia, was moved to the top of the hill, which still bears the name of Thompson. The pioneer cemetery at Thompson's Flat still exists near the shores of the Feather River, just above the Thermalito Diversion Dam. Morris Ravine, near Thompson's Flat, also saw some of the earliest mining in the county.

Because of all this activity up and down the river, Oroville had become a stage center of some importance by 1856, as indicated by an article in Oroville's weekly *North Californian* in November of that year: "Coaches are rattling through our streets at all hours of the day and night. We have ten, semi-daily, connecting this place with different parts of the world. There are six daily stages to Marysville, three for Spanishtown, one for Shasta, one for Bidwell, one for Forbestown, one for Bangor." Numerous pack animals also traveled up and down the highways and along the narrow trails into the higher mountains where no trails yet led.

In February 1857, the *Gazelle* arrived at Oroville, the first of the river steamers to penetrate that far. The last steamboats arrived there during the flood of 1862.

Beginning in the late 1850s and continuing through the 1880s, hydraulic mining was the chief activity at Oroville and Cherokee and in the surrounding country. Evidence of extensive hydraulic operations may still be seen in the form of canals, ditches, old flumes, and deeply scarred hills.

The decline of hydraulic mining was followed by the development of the gold-dredging industry, which originated at Oroville and from there spread around the world. The great gravel fields about the city give some idea of the extent of the industry, which gleaned many millions in gold from the land. One dredging company offered to move the entire town of Oroville and rebuild it at the company's expense if it was allowed to dredge beneath the town and remove the great treasure trove over which the city had been built. Oroville is nurtured by the rich agricultural region nearby and by tourism and vacation activities generated by the Lake Oroville State Recreational Area, but some mining is still carried on in neighboring towns in the hills. When the Oroville Dam was built, much of the material for its construction came from the tailings left by the gold dredgers.

Oroville's Chinatown, said to have housed 10,000 people, was one of California's largest, second only to San Francisco at one time. The Chinese Temple (SRL 770), dedicated in the spring of 1863, is now open as a museum, having been restored by Oroville's women's clubs; it is located at 1500 Broderick Street. A few blocks away is the Lott House in Sank Park, 1067 Montgomery Street, owned and maintained by the city of Oroville. The restored Victorian Gothic house, built in 1856, was lived in by the same family until 1961 and is open to the public on a regular basis. The gardens are maintained in a formal Victorian style. The Ehmann Home, built in 1911 at 1480 Lincoln Street, is preserved in memory of Freda Ehmann, who founded California's canned ripe olive industry, and is now the headquarters of the Butte County Historical Society. The Butte County Pioneer Memorial Museum at 2300 Montgomery Street contains material relating to early days in a building fashioned like a miner's cabin.

About two miles east of Oroville, on the Oroville-Quincy Highway just north of its junction with SR 162 (Olive Highway), is the site (SRL 809) of the discovery of Ishi, last of the Yahi tribe and the last known California Indian to have lived without contact with white settlers. On August 29, 1911, this emaciated survivor of years of wandering and persecution stumbled into the corral of a slaughterhouse at this location. He was at first lodged in jail but fortunately was put into the hands of two University of California anthropologists, Thomas T. Waterman and Alfred L. Kroeber, who provided a home for him until his death in 1916. Ishi made an extremely valuable contribution to our knowledge of California Indian languages, history, and customs.

CHEROKEE

The old town of Cherokee is ten miles north of Oroville and one mile west of that stretch of Lake Oroville that was formerly the West Branch of the Feather River. The Spring Valley Gold Mine here was the largest hydraulic gold mine in California at one time. Diamonds were found in the diggings around Cherokee as early as 1853. Over three hundred diamonds, many of gem quality, have been discovered there; at no other place in North America has an equal number been found. Stone walls and a vault mark the site of the Spring Valley Mine and Assay Office, a picturesque remnant of former days. Overlooking the well-kept Pioneer Cemetery at Cherokee is the massive bulk of Table Mountain, a remarkable picture in the spring when wildflowers cover its flanks. The Cherokee Museum is situated in what was once a boarding house for miners, and is one of the many small, attractive, and informative museums one encounters throughout California.

OREGON CITY AND ITS NEIGHBORS

Scores of mining camps were once located in the hill region north of Oroville. The early locations on the river bars were followed by those on the flats somewhat back from the streams, and finally the ridges and hills were worked. In some instances, the names of these camps remain to mark their location, but often even the name has been forgotten. Throughout the Feather River district the remains of crudely constructed fireplaces, sometimes found in isolated spots, are the only evidence of pioneer habitation.

By the autumn of 1848 gold-seekers from Oregon began to arrive, among the first from outside California. Their presence in the mining regions is evidenced by the names of Oregon City and Oregon Gulch, halfway between Oroville and Cherokee on Derrick Road. Oregon City (SRL 807) no longer has many inhabitants, but there are impressive restorations there. The 1877 schoolhouse was in service until 1922, when it became a community hall. In 1981 it was acquired by the Butte County Historical Society, and it has been restored as a historical museum. The covered bridge one crosses to reach the school ground is not a cherished relic from the past, as is everywhere else the case in California, but a modern (1982) structure, a replica of a previous one.

Perhaps the liveliest of these North Feather River camps was Spanishtown, so named because the rich diggings in the vicinity had been discovered in 1855 by Spanish-speaking Chileans and Mexicans. By 1856 a town had sprung up, twenty miles north of Oroville

Oregon City School Museum

and one mile from Frenchtown, that in turn became the chief town of the region, Yankee Hill.

MAGALIA, PARADISE, AND INSKIP

Twenty-five miles north of Oroville on the West Branch of the Feather River was Dogtown, now the thriving community of Magalia. An old French woman, so one story goes, lived in the area with a kennel of hounds, poodles, and mastiffs that were known all over the countryside. (The E Clampus Vitus plaque at the center of town says she was Mrs. Basset, with no reference to her nationality.) The name Dogtown was applied not only to the town but to the entire ridge as well. Two miles east of the town a gold nugget was discovered in 1859 that is said to be the largest ever found in Butte County. This "Dogtown Nugget" weighed fifty-four pounds in the rough and was valued at $10,690. On the Skyway near Magalia a marker points to the site of the discovery of the Dogtown Nugget (SRL 771). The old brown-shingled church at Magalia, also a community center, is on the National Register of Historic Places.

About five miles southwest of Dogtown is Paradise, the only one of the old communities that is a major town today. It began to grow rapidly after the completion of the Butte County Railroad from Chico to Stirling City in 1902. Then it was a center of the apple industry; today its population has grown primarily because of the influx of retired people who enjoy its clear air and wooded hills. A few miles west of Paradise on Honey Run Road from Chico, the Honey Run Covered Bridge spans Butte Creek. Built in 1894, the bridge is a local landmark, well restored today and in a county park.

Honey Run Covered Bridge over Butte Creek, near Chico

Bangor, ten miles southeast of Oroville, was settled in 1855 by the Lambert brothers from Bangor, Maine. With the discovery of the Blue Lead Mine it became quite important, consisting of 50 buildings. A one-room frame church built there in 1882 has been acquired by the Butte County Historical Society and is now a local history museum. Northwest of Bangor was Wyandotte, named after a company of Wyandotte Indians who mined there in 1850. It reached its greatest prosperity around 1853; in 1857 its "magnificent brick fireproof hotel" was cited as the only of its kind in the county. Bangor and Wyandotte are today centers of the orange and olive industries, and the old mining ditches are used for irrigation.

FORBESTOWN

On the South Fork of the Feather River were other mining camps. Stringtown, about four miles east of Bidwell's Bar, was so called because its buildings were strung out in a narrow, rambling line along the canyon. Within a year of its beginning in 1849, it had become very populous. But in July 1856 the *Butte Record* published its obituary in the following words: "The string of Stringtown has been pulled out." Nothing remains at the site today.

About seven miles east of Stringtown on the river was Forbestown, founded in September 1850 by B. F. Forbes. It was a center of mining activities for thirty to forty years. It was a town of some cultural importance also, with a private academy and a general assembly hall, where lectures were given during the week and where large congregations met for services on Sunday. This once bustling camp was described about 1930 as "a derelict town lost in a mountain cove where a second growth of timber is fast replacing a virgin forest. Heaps of debris and old foundations mark the sites of large buildings that have collapsed or been torn down. Other structures with crumbling roofs and gaping doors are verging on dissolution."

Forbestown today boasts the excellent Yuba Feather Historical Museum, centered around an abandoned school house acquired by the Yuba Feather Historical Association in 1980. Around it is a demonstration village, "Gold Trader Flat," with replicas of buildings dating from the late nineteenth century. The restored Masonic Hall, built in 1855, is another highlight of the community. Old Forbestown is now reached by a side

Exceptionally rich diggings were found in the late 1850s at Lovelock, nine miles north of Dogtown, and at Inskip, twelve miles north of Lovelock. These communities are all linked today by the Skyway, a good highway leading from SR 99 south of Chico north to Inskip. Today Inskip is a very small town, but its hotel is still in operation and is listed on the National Register of Historic Places. The E Clampus Vitus plaque on the hotel notes that this structure, built in 1869, is now the only one of the five hotels that once served the district.

Two other "Clamper" plaques on the Skyway south of Inskip commemorate Stirling City and DeSabla. The former was established by the Diamond Match Company, which in 1902 built the railroad to the town, named for the Stirling boilers used to heat the first workers' quarters. Eugene J. DeSabla Jr. was the engineer who is sometimes called the "Father of the Pacific Gas and Electric Company." The DeSabla Reservoir nearby is part of the huge power project that DeSabla began around 1900 and that ultimately became absorbed into the present-day corporation.

Dogtown was only one of a number of mining camps and stage stations on the road from Oroville to Susanville in Lassen County. Twelve miles north of Oroville, Manoah Pence and several partners started the Lyon ranch in 1850, opening a store and an eating place in a tent. The place grew and by 1864 a post office, under the name of Pentz, had been established there, with Pence as postmaster. Butte Community College, founded in 1968, is on SR 191 three miles west of Pentz; its present campus opened in 1974.

Historic Bangor Church

rises some 3,600 feet over the Grand Gorge of the Middle Fork of the Feather River near where Fall River empties into the larger stream. Devoid of vegetation, its white granite majesty resembles that of El Capitan in Yosemite Valley.

The entire region is one of spectacular beauty and is so wild and rugged that Indians, early white explorers, and prospecting miners either avoided or failed to penetrate it. In 1889 Emery Oliver, later a great railroad engineer, ran a survey through the entire Middle Fork Canyon, including that portion now known as Bald Rock Canyon. In 1908 two Geological Survey men also passed through it. There are immense granite boulders, deep caverns, and, above all, the superb beauty of Feather Falls, one of the most imposing of Sierra waterfalls. The falls drop a sheer 500 feet, with an additional 200 feet of cascades, and fill the canyon with heavy mist and iridescent lights for half a mile. The area is now Feather Falls Scenic Area within Plumas National Forest; Bald Rock Canyon on the Middle Fork of the Feather River has been designated a Wild River. Feather Falls can be reached by trail from the village of Feather Falls about three miles to the east; another way to see the falls is by boat from the surface of Lake Oroville.

road, a mile or so to the north. Near Forbestown is Clipper Mills, an early lumber camp, on the La Porte Road.

BALD ROCK AND FEATHER FALLS

Bald Rock, called U-I-No by the Maidu people, was believed by them to be the home of a giant evil spirit. It

Calaveras County

Calaveras County took its name from the river named by Gabriel Moraga on his expedition of 1808. Moraga had noticed exposed skulls (in Spanish, *calaveras*) along the banks of the river. Calaveras was one of the original twenty-seven counties. Pleasant Valley, later known as Double Springs, was designated by the Legislature as the first county seat on February 18, 1850, and was followed successively by Jackson, Mokelumne Hill, and finally San Andreas in 1866.

Double Springs (SRL 264) grew after it became the county seat in 1850. Other towns, however, were also growing and also aspired to be the county seat. One of these was Jackson (then in Calaveras County), north of the Mokelumne River. The story of the contest for the position of county seat is typical of what took place in various parts of California in the 1850s, after statehood made the state self-governing. In July 1851, a few young men of Jackson drove over to Double Springs, where some of their company treated the county clerk quite liberally at the tavern bar. Meanwhile the others went to the building used as a courthouse, loaded the archives into their wagon, and hurried back across the river to Jackson. Although this high-handed action was illegal, Jackson retained its position until April 16, 1852, when by popular election Mokelumne Hill became the Calaveras County seat. It is said that the votes cast were "out of all proportion to the number of voters."

In 1854 Amador County was separated from Calaveras County, and Jackson became the county seat of the new county. In 1866 San Andreas was given that honor in Calaveras County, in place of Mokelumne Hill, and it remains the county seat today.

Double Springs lies at the junction of SR 12 and SR 26, about four miles east of Valley Springs. The two springs for which the town was named still keep green the meadow that lies between the low hills. Here, surrounded by oleanders, orange trees, and aged locust trees, stands the lovely old mansion of squared sandstone built in 1860 by Alexander R. Wheat. On the hill across the road, under the shadow of a great live oak, is the family cemetery where he lies. The building that was the county courthouse when Double Springs was the county seat is behind the Wheat house and is no longer open to the public.

ANGELS CAMP

Angels Camp (SRL 287), named for its founder, Henry Angel, retains several iron-shuttered stone buildings from the Gold Rush days. Some of the most noteworthy landmarks are Angels Hotel (SRL 734) on Main Street, the Stickels Store built in 1856, and the famous Utica Mine, which originally sold for a song and which later produced millions during its great period from 1893 to 1916. Utica Park stands over the site of the mine; the Utica Mansion nearby, built in 1882, is on the National Register of Historic Places.

The Angels Camp Museum at 753 South Main Street has an extraordinary collection begun by local resident Dan Daniels, "who collected anything that wasn't nailed down." At the north edge of town stands St. Vasilije Serbian Orthodox Church (1910), one of the first of that denomination to be built in California.

Angels Hotel was built on the site of the Lake Hotel, which was destroyed in the disastrous fire of 1855 that wiped out much of the center of the town. In January 1865 Samuel L. Clemens stayed at the hotel, where he obtained the source for his story "The Celebrated Jumping Frog of Calaveras County" from a yarn told to him by hotel bartender Ben Coon. The story, set in Angels Camp, was published in the *New York Saturday Press* on November 18, 1865, under Clemens's pen name, Mark Twain, and was reprinted as the title piece of Mark Twain's first book in 1867. Now famous, he left California in 1868 for a brilliant international career. In front of the hotel is a marker surmounted by a bronze frog. Since 1928, a jumping frog contest has been held annually at Angels Camp; in recent years, it has been combined with the Calaveras County Fair, held on the third weekend in May in nearby Frogtown.

ALTAVILLE

Altaville (SRL 288) dates from 1852 and was formerly known as Cherokee Flat. It is located only one mile north of Angels Camp, and the two communities have grown to meet each other. D. D. Demarest established a foundry at Altaville in 1854, producing most of the stamp mills and a large part of the mining machinery installed in Calaveras and Tuolumne Counties. After many years, the foundry closed and its buildings were pulled down in 1985 to make room for a shopping center. The outstanding landmark at Altaville is the Prince and Garibardi Store (SRL 735), built in 1857 and still a strikingly handsome stone building. The old redbrick grammar school (SRL 499) was built in 1858 and was in use until 1950; it has been restored by the Calaveras County Historical Society.

North of Murphy's Grade Road about half a mile east of Altaville is Bald Hill, on the slope of which is the virtually hidden shaft of the old Mattison Mine. Here, at a depth of 150 feet, the famous Calaveras Skull was allegedly found by Mr. James Mattison of Angels Camp, in February 1866. It was pronounced a genuine relic of prehistoric man by Professor J. D. Whitney, then state geologist of California, at a public meeting later that year. Many were unconvinced of the skull's real antiquity (Bret Harte's mocking poem "To the Pliocene Skull" expressed this sentiment), and modern research has placed the skull's origin in a less ancient cave burial.

Five miles northwest of Altaville and just west of SR 49 is Fourth Crossing (SRL 258). The old stone bridge, built in 1857, may be the oldest bridge still standing in California. Between Altaville and Fourth Crossing is the site of Hawkeye.

CARSON HILL

Carson Hill (SRL 274), about four miles south of Angels Camp, has been called "the classic mining ground of California," for it was considered to be the richest camp in all the Mother Lode. There in November 1854 a mass of gold was found at Morgan Mine weighing 195 pounds and valued at $43,534, said to be the largest nugget in the United States. (It was really a pocket weathered out of a quartz vein, and not a nugget at all.)

Between Carson Hill and Hanselman's Hill at Albany Flat, about two miles south of Angels Camp on SR 49, is the elaborate James Romaggi stone house, built before 1856. It was located on the old road to Los Muertos, that wild camp on Arroyo de los Muertos ("creek of the dead") where the Battle of Six Mile Creek was waged between American and Mexican miners in the autumn of 1852. Los Muertos, with its predominant Mexican and Chilean population, is one of the many spots in California said to be a haunt of the bandit Joaquín Murieta.

The Morgan Mine on the north slope of Carson Hill produced some $26 million in gold, yielding a million dollars in a year as late as 1925. There are plans to revive mining in this region, which was unusually productive even by Mother Lode standards. James H. Carson, for whom Carson Hill and nearby Carson Flat on Carson Creek were all named, discovered gold on the flat as early as August 1848 and, according to his own report, panned 180 ounces of gold in a period of ten days.

On a two-ton mine car at Carson Hill a plaque has been mounted in honor of Archie Stevenot (SRL 769), member of a pioneer Carson Hill family, who was born half a mile to the west in 1882. One-time manager of the Carson Hill Mining Company, Stevenot in his retirement helped publicize the attractions of California's gold country and became affectionately known as "Mr. Mother Lode."

On the south slope of Carson Hill on the Stanislaus River is Melones (Spanish for "melons"). Originally

Hotel Leger, Mokelumne Hill

called Robinson's Ferry (SRL 276), the name Melones (from the shape of the gold found in the vicinity by Mexican miners) was borrowed in 1902 from a former camp midway between Carson Hill and the present town of that name. In the summer of 1849, within six weeks' time, $10,000 in tolls was collected at Robinson's Ferry. The settlement of Melones today is on the shores of New Melones Lake, the Stanislaus River having been impounded by the New Melones Dam a few miles to the south.

THE MOKELUMNE HILL REGION

Mokelumne Hill (SRL 269), perched above the Mokelumne River, is one of the most picturesque towns in the mining region. It was the county seat from 1852 to 1866 and also the commercial center of the central Mother Lode at that time.

Several interesting old buildings remain from mining days, as well as some ruins. Outstanding among the buildings is the International Order of Odd Fellows Hall (SRL 256), which formerly housed the Wells Fargo office; its two lower floors were built in 1854, and the third story was added in 1861. The Leger Hotel includes the building that served as the courthouse of Calaveras County (SRL 663) from 1852 to 1866. When the county seat was moved to San Andreas, George W. Leger, whose hotel was next door, acquired the building and combined it with his hotel, which had also been built in 1854; a second story was added in 1874. The Congregational church (SRL 261) was built in 1856 and is believed to be the oldest church building of that denomination in the state. "Mokelumne," spelled and pronounced in various ways, is a Miwok Indian word. It is the name of a tribe of people, or a village near Lockeford in San Joaquin County, or a term for "fish net," "red paint," or "manzanita berry," according to different references.

Overlooking the town of Mokelumne Hill is French Hill, the scene of one of the skirmishes in the so-called "French War" of 1851. American envy had been aroused by the good fortune of French miners throughout the region. A band of Americans attacked the Frenchmen on the pretext that they had hoisted the French flag and defied the American government. The defenders put up a temporary fort on French Hill, but the Yankee power prevailed and the French were expelled.

A mile and a half east of Mokelumne Hill a deteriorating stone building can be seen on the south side of SR 26; this was the winery of the Louis Baudin family, who lived across the road in a settlement, now gone, called Happy Valley. Just one-tenth of a mile east of this building a road branches to the right and leads 3.5 miles to the settlement of Jesus Maria (SRL 284), on the creek of the same name. Nearby a road sign indicates the junction of Jesus Maria Road with Whiskey Slide Road, this writer's favorite California intersection. Nothing remains of Whiskey Slide, later called Clear View, nor of McDonald or Poverty Flat in this region, which is still sparsely populated.

A road going southwest from Mokelumne Hill leads to Campo Seco (SRL 257), a rich placer camp in early days. After the 1860s it was the site of the rich Penn Copper Mine. Although its heyday was the first two decades of the twentieth century, the Penn Mine was still producing copper after World War II. One of the state's oldest and largest cork oaks (*Quercus suber*) grows at Campo Seco. Stone ruins and the pioneer cemetery are reminders of the past. The road from Mokelumne Hill to Campo Seco passes through Paloma, an old mining town formerly called Fostoria (SRL 295). Beyond Campo Seco was Camanche (SRL 254), once a picturesque community with old stone buildings. The East Bay Municipal Utility District leveled it in 1964 for the construction of Camanche Reservoir. The graves from the cemetery of nearby Poverty Bar, now like Camanche under the water of the reservoir, were moved to the old Pioneer Cemetery near San Andreas and the People's Cemetery in San Andreas.

At Chili Gulch (SRL 265), two miles south of Mokelumne Hill on SR 49, a little group of Americans were driven from their claim by a superior force of Chileans in December 1849. Later American retaliation drove the Chileans out, but not before many diplomatic protests had been exchanged by the governments of Chile and the United States. There are several places named "Rich Gulch" in Calaveras County. On the Lower Rich Gulch, which leads from Paloma to the Mokelumne River, is the famous Gwin Mine, once owned by State Senator William Gwin Jr., whose father and John C. Frémont were the first two United States senators from California. The mine was an excellent producer for many decades. To the east of Mokelumne Hill is another Rich Gulch, once a populous camp but now deserted; six miles beyond that is Railroad Flat (SRL 286), once a placer and quartz-mining center, where a store, a post office, and a few old homes can be seen. A near neighbor was Independence Point (SRL 268), where numerous small but rich quartz ledges were once worked. It is now a quiet mountain community with many homes of retired people. A few old buildings in the business district can be seen among newer ones. Two and one-half miles southeast of West Point on SR 26 is Sandy Gulch (SRL 253), where not much more than an old cemetery remains. About nine miles northwest of Mokelumne Hill, where the road forks to West Point and Railroad Flat, is Glencoe (SRL 280), once called Mosquito Gulch. Near West Point (formerly Bummerville), the Blazing Star Mine is in operation once more, producing both gold and tungsten.

MURPHYS

The country around Murphys (SRL 275) was first mined in July 1848 by two brothers, Daniel and John Murphy, who came to California in the same company with Henry Angel and James Carson. Like others of the group, the Murphys struck out for themselves on reaching the diggings and set up camp at a site on Angels Creek, which was soon known as Murphy's Diggings, later Murphy's Camp, and ultimately Murphys.

The town is one of the most photographed and painted in all the gold country; tree-shadowed Main Street is lined with historic old buildings, most of which are very much in operation today. The Peter L. Traver Building (SRL 466) was constructed in 1856; this, the oldest stone building in town, was the sole survivor of a disastrous fire in 1859. Today it houses the Old-Timers Museum, filled with artifacts from the town's past. The original portion of the Traver house on Jones Street was built before 1862. What is now the Murphys Hotel was originally Sperry and Perry's Hotel when it was built in 1856; damaged in the 1859 fire, it was restored and still serves as a hostelry. On Main Street may also be seen the Compere Trading Post (1860), now a private home; the Jones Apothecary Shop (1860); and the Thompson Building (1862). On the western exterior

Murphys Hotel, Murphy

wall of the Thompson Building is the Wall of Comparative Ovations of E Clampus Vitus, which bears more than seventy plaques commemorating men, women, and events of California's history—certainly one of the most colorful and amusing historical commemorations in the state.

At 350 Main Street stands the Chase House (1862), where Albert A. Michelson lived as a child; he went on to become the first American scientist to be awarded the Nobel prize (1907) for his pioneering work on the velocity of light. An E Clampus Vitus plaque commemorates him.

Two blocks north of Main Street, where it was missed by the great fire of 1859, stands St. Patrick's Catholic Church, built in 1858 with gold, contributions, and labor from the miners of Murphys. The present Congregational church stands in a building completed in 1895 next to the original (now gone) church building of 1853, in use until 1896. The restored Masonic Temple on the next block of Church Street, on the site of an earlier temple constructed in 1862, dates from 1902. Near the eastern edge of town, by SR 4, the old Murphys School stands. Built in 1860, it was used for many years as an elementary school and now serves as an adult educational center. Murphys makes good use of its historical buildings.

West of Murphys is the site of French Gulch. One mile east of Murphys on Pennsylvanian Gulch Road was Brownsville (SRL 465), a thriving mining camp in the 1850s and 1860s. About one mile northwest of Murphys are Mercer's Caverns, notable limestone formations in several successive "rooms" discovered by Walter Mercer of Murphys in 1885; the caverns are open as a commercial attraction.

From Murphys, SR 4 climbs northeast up the Sierra Nevada about twenty miles to the famous Calaveras Big Trees State Park, a beautiful stand of the *Sequoia gigantea*, the larger of the two species of California sequoias. While on a scouting expedition in 1841, John Bidwell came upon one of the fallen giants of the Calaveras, the first American known to have seen this grove. This reserve actually contains both the North Grove and a South Grove, acquired by the state in 1931 and 1954, respectively. The park now contains 5,437 acres of forest and meadow.

SAN ANDREAS

In most of the present-day Mother Lode towns one finds old and new structures within a neighborhood, and townspeople daily pass in the shadow of historic buildings. San Andreas (SRL 252) is an exception; the older area remains a small enclave. The Calaveras County Museum and Archives Building at 30 North Main Street was once the county Hall of Records. It stands next to the old two-story brick county courthouse; both of these buildings are now part of the county Historic Center. The Odd Fellows Building dates from 1856, and the Cassinelli adobe (now disguised as a white wood-framed apartment house) is nearly as old.

About eight miles east of San Andreas is El Dorado (SRL 282) or Mountain Ranch, where some of the old adobe buildings from mining days are still standing. The Domenghini family has operated a general store here since 1901, in the building that was the Domenghini Saloon, built in the 1850s. This was the location of an early sawmill. The original Mountain Ranch post office was located about a mile west of here but was moved to the town of El Dorado in 1868. Southeast of here was Cave City (SRL 956), the first cave in California to be operated as a commercial attraction. When the mines there gave out, its school was moved to El Dorado, but the district retained the name of Cave City. Between Mountain Ranch and Murphys is Sheep Ranch, one of several profitable investments made by Senator George Hearst. By the time the mine closed in 1942, it had produced more than $8 million in gold and reached 3,100 feet in depth. A plaque placed by E Clampus Vitus commemorates the Sheep Ranch Mine.

Six miles southeast of San Andreas are Old Gulch and Calaveritas (SRL 255), where one old adobe building stands and the ruins of others are to be seen. The

Calaveras County Museum and Archives, San Andreas

region is one of great tranquillity, showing no trace of modern times beyond the rather worn road.

Three miles northwest of San Andreas is Cottage Spring, and three miles west are North Branch and Central Hill, noted for their once productive gravel mines. Farther west is Valley Springs (SRL 251), founded in 1884 when the railroad entered this area. The large stone Late Ranch House was constructed in 1862 by the Scottish stonemason William Watt, who built several other homes in the vicinity, including the Wheat home in Double Springs. The town of Valley Springs was laid out on property formerly belonging to the Late Ranch.

On SR 12 about two miles west of San Andreas on the south bank of the North Fork of the Calaveras River is the old Pioneer Cemetery (SRL 271), the oldest in the county and, sadly, much vandalized.

VALLECITO

Vallecito ("Little Valley," SRL 273) is about five miles east of Angels Camp. A few landmarks from mining days remain, among them the Dinkelspiel Store, originally Cohen and Levy's Store, still in operation after more than a century. There is also an old church bell, which was brought up from San Francisco by an itinerant preacher in the early days. The bell was mounted on a large oak tree, and every Sunday morning scores of miners answered its summons. The bell is now mounted on top of a stone monument (SRL 370).

To the north, between Vallecito and Murphys, is Douglas Flat (SRL 272), on the Central Hill Channel, an ancient river deposit extending through the middle of the county from which vast quantities of gold have been taken. The old Gagliardo Building (1862), once a store and bank, is a roadside landmark here; the identifying sign is misspelled "Gilleado."

JENNY LIND AND COPPEROPOLIS

Jenny Lind (SRL 266), on the north bank of the Calaveras River, was once the center of most of the mining operations on the lower Calaveras; today it is a pleasant community of new and old homes. In the years 1850–52, the Swedish soprano Jenny Lind toured the eastern United States, performing before huge audiences. Promoted by P. T. Barnum, Lind became familiar when no telegraph crossed the United States and communication was very primitive. The naming of the place for her was not, as is sometimes asserted, in memory of her performance there, for she never visited California. Six miles south of Jenny Lind is Milton (SRL 262), the first town in Calaveras County to be connected to the railroad. The Southern Pacific arrived in 1871, and Milton was born. From here freight and passengers were conveyed by wagon and stage to other parts of the county.

Prior to the discovery of the large copper deposits in the northern part of the state, Copperopolis (SRL 296), in the southwestern part of Calaveras County, was the principal copper-producing center in California. In 1867 it boasted a population of nearly two thousand and had three schools, two churches, four hotels, and stores and workshops of all kinds. A fire in September 1867 destroyed much of the town, and it was never rebuilt, the mines having closed in the same discouraging year. The town today retains memories of its one-time importance in the disintegrating smelters, chutes, and shafts of the old mines, in the handful of brick stores flanking the highway, and in the pioneer Congregational church, which has been the community center since the 1950s. The neighboring Copperopolis Armory, an imposing brick structure, was built in 1861 to train troops in the days of the Civil War; it is now part of the community center. Near Copperopolis, at Funk Hill, Black Bart, the "gentleman bandit," committed his last stage robbery in 1883.

On the road from Copperopolis to Mountain Pass was O'Byrne's (or Byrne's) Ferry (SRL 281). The ferry of pioneer days was supplanted by a covered bridge, which spanned the Stanislaus River for almost a century. The structure, 210 feet in length, was removed in 1957 when Tulloch Dam was constructed. The little triangular valley, shared with neighboring Tuolumne County, hemmed in by steep and rugged mountain slopes covered with chaparral, is now filled with the waters of Tulloch Reservoir. Above it, "like the ruins of a Rhineland castle," as one writer described it, tower the lava-topped crags of Table Mountain.

Along the old Mokelumne Hill road from Stockton by way of Linden, now SR 26, many wayside inns refreshed the traveler in Gold Rush days. One-third of a mile east of the San Joaquin–Calaveras county line was the famous Red House, a two-story inn, no longer standing. Its stone corral (SRL 263), however, is intact today. Beyond Stone Corral, on the old river road to Jenny Lind, was the Pleasant Valley House, a two-story building since destroyed by fire. Halfway between Jenny Lind and Valley Springs on the north side of the road and across from the headquarters of present-day Rancho Calaveras was the North America House, where the stage horses were changed; these old hostelries vanished long ago.

The Kentucky House, about two miles south of San Andreas and the center of mining activities on the South Fork of the Calaveras River, was a stage stop between Sonora and Sacramento. The Calaveras Cement Company now has a plant there. The original Kentucky House was destroyed by fire, but a later building was erected on the same site and has been remodeled by the cement company as a clubhouse.

BRET HARTE

Francis Brett Harte (1836–1902) made a sizable reputation for himself as a storyteller of the Mother Lode. His actual connection with the area was rather tenuous, limited to about two months late in 1855, but from this visit he gathered impressions that he reworked for many years to come, both in California and in England, where he spent his last years. His popularity was greater in places such as London, where few people had any knowledge of actual conditions in the West, than in California, where critics agreed that his stories showed little intimate knowledge of mines or miners. Among the locations in Calaveras County that are believed to have influenced him are Angels Camp, McLean's Bar (a now-vanished spot on the Stanislaus River), and Fourth Crossing.

Colusa County

Colusa County was one of the original twenty-seven counties. The name comes from the Ko-ru Indians, and the county was originally known as Colusi, the present usage being adopted in 1854. Gudde and Bright's *California Place Names* gives some etymological background on the name: "The rancheria named Coru is mentioned by Padre Blas Ordaz on October 28, 1821, obviously in Patwin territory. The name was applied to two land grants: Coluses or Colusas (July 24, 1844) and Colus (October 2, 1845). Although simpler than other Indian names, it seems to set the record for spelling variants, ranging from Corusies to Colouse."

Monroeville, now in Glenn County, was the first county seat, but it was superseded by Colusa in 1854. A portion of Tehama County and all of Glenn County to the north were included in the original area of the county.

Colusa was built on the site of the old Indian village Ko-ru, tribal capital of the Ko-ru (or Ko-ru-si). In 1850, there were a thousand or more of these Indians living in villages in the Sacramento River valley within the present boundary of the county. As early as 1846 Americans began to settle along this part of the river, and by the close of the nineteenth century only two of the Indian villages remained: Tat-no, four miles above the town of Colusa, on what was at that time the Colonel Hagar Ranch, and Wyterre, on the upper end of the Rancho Jimeno.

There were at least thirteen of these villages. Loch-loch, at the head of Sycamore Slough, was where the town of Sycamore now stands. To the north was Coo-Coo, then Doc-doc; Colusa lies on the site of Ko-ru, the head village of the tribe. Across the river from Ko-ru was Cow-peck; Tat-no was north of Ko-ru on the same side of the river. This is today the Colusa Indian Reservation, where the remnants of the tribe now live, about five miles north of the town of Colusa. Si-cope occupied the bend of the river east of the site of the old Five Mile House, while at the Seven Mile House was Cahcheal. At the bend of the river, on the upper end of what became the Judge Hastings Ranch, was Si-ee ("view"), where there were no trees. On the Rancho Jimeno was Wyterre ("turn to the north"). Cha was at the Senator Boggs Ranch and Ket-tee was where the present town of Princeton now stands; north of Princeton, at what is now the Colusa-Glenn county line, was Tu-tu.

THE LARKIN CHILDREN'S GRANT

John Bidwell was the first recorded explorer of Colusa County, in the years 1843–44, while in the employ of John A. Sutter. In July 1844, Bidwell mapped out a grant of land that extended along the west bank of the Sacramento River north of what is now the town of Colusa and into the present Glenn County. This was the first land grant made in Colusa County and was known as the Larkin Children's Grant, having been secured for the children of Thomas O. Larkin, American consul at Monterey.

John S. Williams, brother of Isaac Williams, owner of Rancho Chino in southern California, was the first white settler in Colusa County. In 1847 he was employed to look after the Larkin property, and on it he built the first house in the county. Senator John Boggs later bought that part of the Larkin Children's Grant

Carnegie Library, now Colusa Police Department

on which Williams lived, just below the present town of Princeton. The town of Williams, incidentally, is named not for John S. Williams but for W. H. Williams, who laid out the town site on the route of the Southern Pacific Railroad.

The Sacramento Valley Museum has displays of shops and activities from the pioneer days of Colusa County and the Sacramento Valley as well as an interesting exhibit of farm machinery. It is at 1491 E Street in Williams.

COLUSA

On the spot where Ko-ru, chief settlement of the Ko-ru people, had been located only a few years before, Colusa was founded in 1850. The short-lived first name for the town was Salmon Bend. The land on which the new town was laid out and land beyond it were included in the grant made to John Bidwell in 1845. When Dr. Robert Semple, the founder of Benicia in Solano County, visited the country in 1847, he was impressed with its beauty, fertility, and access to the great river, and saw possibilities of a future city there.

Colonel Charles D. Semple, a brother of Dr. Semple, came to California in 1849. The doctor immediately told him of the fine country to the north, and Charles was favorably impressed. He purchased the land from Bidwell the same year, and in a small launch started up the river the following spring to found a new city. Mistaking the site originally chosen by his brother, the colonel landed seven miles to the north, at a place afterward known as the Seven Mile House, but a visit by the doctor soon rectified the error. Barges came up the

IOOF Hall, Colusa

Grand Island Shrine

river from Sacramento, and trade from the northern mines was good; Semple's hopes seemed justified, and the new town prospered.

In 1853 Dr. Semple and his nephew, Will S. Green, purchased Rancho Alamo on Freshwater Creek, six miles from Williams. Dr. Semple died there the following year and was buried on the ranch; later his body was removed to the Williams Cemetery, where a bronze tablet and monument stand at his grave. Another marker has been placed at the Semple ranch west of Williams on SR 20. Green became known as the crusading editor of the *Colusa Sun.*

Although Colusa did not become a great city, it flourished and in 1854 was made the county seat. Today it is the center of a thriving agricultural region. The courthouse (SRL 890) was built in 1861. Its neoclassical architecture reflects the taste of early settlers who came from the South; during the Civil War Colusa County was notorious for its pro-Confederate sympathies. The IOOF (Oddfellows) Building nearby dates from 1892, its top story faithful to the time of its construction, the ground floor modernized into stores and offices. Whereas old Carnegie Library buildings throughout California are being abandoned and turned into museums and the like, Colusa has taken its 1906 library, in use until 1964, and made it the headquarters for the police department. There are many Civil War veterans buried in the Colusa Cemetery.

THE GRAND ISLAND SHRINE

The brick shrine a mile and a half south of Sycamore on SR 45 commemorates the first Roman Catholic service

in Colusa County, a Mass celebrated on May 1, 1856, by Father Peter Magagnotto, C.P., of Marysville. According to Father Henry Walsh, the service was held in the home of Jacob Meyers on the Sacramento River, an area known as Grand Island. In September 1864 a mission was preached to the people of Grand Island by Father P. G. Laufhuber, S.J., and land was donated for a church. On September 14, at the close of the mission, a 27-foot wooden cross was erected on this property. No church was ever built, but in 1883 Father Michael Walrath put up the shrine, whose official name is the Shrine of Our Lady of Sorrows. The tiny structure will hold no more than four people at one time. Mass is celebrated there on Easter Sunday and occasionally at other times, and the little house of worship is a constant attraction for tourists. The wooden cross was later replaced by a concrete one.

THE RIVER ROAD

The old River Road, following the west bank of the Sacramento River from Colusa to Shasta City, was the only road in Colusa County in the early 1850s. Its popularity rivaled that of the river steamers, which plied as far north as Red Bluff. The volume of traffic over the road to the northern mines resulted in the building of many inns or stage stations along its course. From Wilkins' Slough in southern Colusa County to the mouth of Stony Creek in what is now Glenn County, a fringe of farms bordered the river, many with facilities to refresh travelers and their pack animals on the long trip to the gold fields.

The most important center on the route was Colusa,

from which as many as 50 freight wagons often started for the north in one day. Distances and names were often calculated from Colusa. Among the several stations on the River Road were the Five Mile House, where the Maxwell road branches off to the west; the Seven Mile House, where Colonel Semple made his first Colusa settlement; the Ten Mile House, built by L. H. Helphenstine and owned by the family for over seventy years; the Sterling Ranch, or Fourteen Mile House, where John S. Williams built the first house (an adobe) in Colusa County in 1847, and where Charles B. Sterling, the second settler, succeeded him in 1849; the Sixteen Mile House, two miles above the Sterling Ranch, where Princeton now is; and the Seventeen Mile House, owned by Hiram Willits, later founder of Willits in Mendocino County.

The small town of Princeton had a special celebrity for many years, since the only remaining ferry on the Sacramento River crossed from here to Glenn County, a journey usually lasting two minutes. After its closure in 1986, the Princeton Ferry was sporadically revived, but now appears to be entirely a thing of the past.

COLLEGE CITY AND ARBUCKLE

Pierce Christian College at College City was named after Andrew Pierce, who at his death in 1874 left a large amount of land to the Christian Church for religious and educational advancement. In 1876 a board of trustees established a college on the land and laid out a town about it. For years, this was the only school of higher rank in that part of California, and at one time most of the teachers of Colusa County had been educated there.

In 1896 the Pierce College grounds and buildings were given to the Union High School District of College City. This happened likewise in many districts in northern California during the last years of the nineteenth century, when denominational and other private schools gave their lands and buildings for the use of the newly established high schools. The colleges had been discontinued because the Christian Church had decided to consolidate its colleges scattered throughout the state into one adequately endowed institution, finally established at Los Angeles. In March 1937 Pierce Union High School was moved to its new campus in Arbuckle, and in the three years following, the college buildings at College City were razed.

In 1859 Tacitus Ryland Arbuckle established a homestead in the valley plain about a dozen miles southwest of Colusa. When the railroad came through in 1875 he helped plat the new town that developed. The E Clampus Vitus plaque in the town center honors the man who "founded the town, deeded the town lots, furnished the nails, and helped build the first houses in what since has become the city of Arbuckle. Known far and wide as 'The Home of the Almond.'"

WILBUR HOT SPRINGS

California's mountain hot springs attracted many visitors in the years after the Civil War. In 1868, the settlement of Wilbur Springs (named for its developer) was established in the southwestern part of the county. The small resort is still in operation as Wilbur Hot Springs, twenty-two miles west of Williams and five miles north of SR 20, and its oldest standing structure is about a century old.

STONE CORRAL

Six miles west of Maxwell is a hollow hemmed in on three sides by high hills, forming a natural site for a corral. The place may have been used by vaqueros as early as 1848, but the construction of the stone fence is generally attributed to Granville P. Swift, whose cattle operations covered a vast area of the Sacramento Valley in the early 1850s. After 1855 it was used by John Steele, who made further improvements. Settlers afterward carried away many of the stones. The Old Stone Corral (SRL 238), as it was long known, has been restored by the Colusa Parlor, Native Sons of the Golden West. It is located on the ranch at the south side of the Maxwell-Sites Road, where it crosses Stone Corral Creek.

LETTS VALLEY

Jack and David Lett settled in a small valley near the northwest corner of Colusa County in 1855. Letts Valley (SRL 736) is now the site of a lake and a campground within the Mendocino National Forest. The spillway is built on the site of a tunnel constructed by the brothers to facilitate drainage. The campground is located where the brothers met their death in 1877 while trying to prevent squatters from settling on their land. The area is southwest of Stonyford via Fouts Springs, discovered by John F. Fouts in 1873.

Rose Hill Cemetery, Black Diamond Mines Regional Preserve

Contra Costa County

Contra Costa County was one of the original twenty-seven counties of California. From San Francisco, it was first seen by the Spaniards, and thus was given the name "opposite coast." The significance of the name Contra Costa was lost when that portion directly across the Bay from San Francisco became part of Alameda County, created in 1853. Martinez has always been the county seat.

MOUNT DIABLO

Perhaps no other place name in California has gathered about itself so many legends as that of Mount Diablo, in Spanish *Monte del Diablo* or "Mountain of the Devil." Standing out above the flatland and foothills, in the center of Contra Costa County, its isolation makes it one of the most conspicuous landmarks in the state. There are actually two peaks on this eminence, Mount Diablo proper at 3,849 feet and North Peak about a mile to the north at 3,563 feet. A ridge connects the two summits. On a clear, windy day, it is still possible from the higher point to see over 60 percent of California's area; Professor Josiah D. Whitney estimated in 1862 that from this vantage point one could see an area of land equal to that of the six states of New England. The California State Parks bulletin states: "You can probably see more from its peak than from any other place in the United States." Air pollution and the haziness brought on in part by intensive irrigation in the Central Valley have reduced the number of such viewing days.

General Mariano G. Vallejo, in his report to the Legislature in April 1850, gave the following story of the derivation of the name in its Spanish form:

In 1806 a military expedition from San Francisco marched against the tribe "Bolgones," who were encamped at the foot of the mount; the Indians were prepared to receive the expedition, and a hot engagement ensued in the large hollow fronting the western side of the mount. As the victory was about to be decided in favor of the Indians, an unknown personage, decorated with the most extraordinary plumage and making divers movements, suddenly appeared near the combatants. The Indians were victorious and the incognito, *Puy*, departed toward the mount. The defeated soldiers, on ascertaining that the spirit went through the same ceremony daily and at all hours, named the mount "Diablo," in allusion to its mysterious habitant, who continued to make his appearance until the tribe was subdued by the troops in command of Lieutenant Gabriel Moraga, in a second campaign of that same year. In the aboriginal tongue *Puy* signifies "Evil Spirit"; in Spanish it means "Diablo," and doubtless it signifies "Devil" in the Anglo-American language.

Erwin G. Gudde, on the other hand, states that "Monte Diablo" referred originally to an Indian village at the present site of Concord, with *monte* used in the sense of "woods" or "thicket" rather than "mountain"; apparently early American settlers misunderstood the term and applied the name to the mountain.

An unsuccessful attempt was made by the state Legislature in 1865–66 to change the name of Mount Diablo. Although the Legislature might say "Coal Hill," the people continued to say "Mount Diablo," and Diablo it has remained.

The mountain was a landmark for explorers and pioneers. In the spring of 1772 Pedro Fages and his trailblazers skirted the western side of the mountain. During the spring of 1776, Juan Bautista de Anza also passed

Contra Costa County Court House, Martinez

that way, after retracing Fages's steps as far as the junction of the Sacramento and San Joaquin Rivers. Dr. John Marsh established his rancho at the base of the great mountain in 1836. The Bidwell-Bartleson company, the first overland emigrant train to enter California by way of the Sierra Nevada, was guided by the peak in 1841 to Dr. Marsh's estate.

A government cabin and telescope were placed on the summit of Mount Diablo in 1851, when it was chosen as the base point for United States surveys in California. With the exception of southern California and the Humboldt district, the locations of all lands in the state are determined by their situation with reference to the Mount Diablo "base and meridian" lines. The summit is at 37°52'54" north latitude and 121°54'49" west longitude. Between 1860 and 1864 much of California was surveyed by an official geological survey party headed by Professor Josiah D. Whitney. William H. Brewer, principal assistant to Whitney, made a series of notes and observations on the work of the party, from which some of his observations on the Mount Diablo region are taken. They noted the magnificent white oaks (*Quercus hindsu hindsii*) that studded the fields, "their great spreading branches often forming a head a hundred feet in diameter." Camp was pitched on May 6, 1862, "in one of the loveliest localities, a pure rippling stream for water, plenty of wood, fine oaks around"; and behind it Mount Diablo rose grandly, its summit "burning with the Tyrian fire of evening." The town of Clayton, with its store, tavern, and other buildings, stood a short distance from the campsite. The discovery of coal in the region had caused the settlement to spring up only a few months before. Early on the morning of May 7, five of the Whitney party, with their guests who had arrived the previous evening from San Francisco, climbed the mountain. The day was one of those rare, crystal-clear

days when the view from the summit stretched for hundreds of miles. "Probably but few views in North America are more extensive—certainly nothing in Europe," Brewer wrote. The Whitney party remained in the region until May 28, making investigations and measurements of the natural phenomena.

The superb beauty of Mount Diablo, the loveliness of its wildflowers, and the profuse scattering of juniper, piñon, oak, sycamore, and other trees very early attracted nature lovers as well as scientific explorers to its craggy summits. Two good wagon roads were laid out by 1874, one from Concord on the northwest and the other from Danville on the south side of the mountain, and two stages ran daily to the Mountain House. This hostelry was built some distance below the summit because the last part of the trail was too steep for vehicles. The Mountain House enjoyed some years of popularity in the 1870s and 1880s, but it was abandoned in the following decade when the government cabin burned and local ranchers shut off access to the summit.

Mount Diablo was again made accessible to the public when Mount Diablo State Park was created in 1931. In 1939, work was begun on an observatory and museum at the crest of Mount Diablo, which was completed in 1941. Except in very dry weather, when fire is a constant threat, and during severe storms, when roads become difficult to access, the park and the top of the mountain are open on a regular basis and campers and hikers make year-round use of the slopes. The beacon placed at the summit in 1928 by the U.S. Commerce Department and the Standard Oil Company of California is now lit only on December 7, a memorial to the men killed at Pearl Harbor when that base was attacked by the Japanese in 1941.

INDIAN SHELL MOUNDS

One of the largest of the more than four hundred shell mounds or kitchen middens that existed in the San Francisco Bay region when the first white men came to its shores was located within the present city limits of Richmond at what is now the foot of Eleventh Street. Twelfth Street intersects the site of the old mound as it extended across the marsh.

A large part of the Ellis Landing shell mound, as it was long called, was removed for grading purposes in 1907, and the final leveling took place in 1924. Like the one at Emeryville in Alameda County, this mound was of particular significance because of its unusual size and because of the extensive scientific explorations by the department of archaeology of the University of California. During the years 1906–8, a detailed study and report of this and other mounds was made by N. C. Nelson, and for two weeks in 1907 extensive scientific excavations were made. At that time about 67,500 cubic feet of material was removed, while 265 artifacts and 126 human skeletons were uncovered.

Before the ancient pile was torn down, it measured 460 feet in length, 250 feet in width, and about 30 feet in height, and its volume approximated 1,260,000 cubic feet. Scientists estimate that the process of accumulation extended over three to four thousand years. It consisted largely of broken shells, principally from common clams and mussels mixed sparingly with oyster, cockle, and abalone shells. Many broken rocks, pebbles, and ashes were also found, as well as fifteen house pits.

The Ellis Landing campsite seems to have afforded few of the advantages usually sought by the mound dwellers. In summer there was no fresh water for drinking, and except for drift there was no firewood, while at all times the location was exposed to strong winds. Since it lay on the shore edge directly north of Brooks Island with 600 yards of marshland at its back, access to it was difficult, and at high tide on stormy winter days it became an island completely surrounded by water.

The natural barriers around the shell heap long served to protect it from the plow, which has ruined many of these deposits. A Mr. Ellis, who lived at the landing for about forty years, stated that as late as 1890 the mound was still intact. His father ran a small canal from one of the marsh creeks up close to the mound on the landward side and began hauling away its rich soil.

Before humans began its destruction, however, nature had already made inroads upon the mound. Because the base of the pile was from eleven to eighteen feet below sea level before the leveling, the encroaching tides were yearly undermining the steep sea wall and were fast destroying the deposit itself. Since it rested upon solid gravel but was more than half buried in fine silt, Nelson estimated that "the region has sunk at least eighteen feet since the ancient inhabitants began to accumulate the refuse deposit."

THE DISCOVERY OF THE GREAT CENTRAL VALLEY

The Pedro Fages expedition continued in the latter part of March 1772 up the Contra Costa in search of a land route to Point Reyes. Leaving their camp on Strawberry Creek in Alameda County and continuing past the sites of Berkeley and Albany on March 28, the little band turned into the Contra Costa County hills and descended past them into the arroyo later known as Wildcat Creek. At the Indian village on its banks, the strangers were met in a most friendly manner by the natives, who presented them with generous gifts of native foods and "two dead geese, dried and stuffed with grass to use as decoys." The travelers reciprocated by offering colored beads, which were "eagerly received" by the Indians.

Four more arroyos "with running water" were passed before Fages at length halted his men on the bank of a fifth stream "at the foot of some hills." Before them "lay a large, round bay, which resembles a great lake," wrote Father Juan Crespí. This was San Pablo Bay, and in it they saw Mare Island close to the opposite shore. Camp was made at or near the present town of Pinole.

On the following day the explorers climbed the hills that come down close to the shore of San Pablo Bay, still confident that they could reach Point Reyes from this place. To their disappointment they found the passage completely shut off by Carquinez Strait. All day they roamed over the hills and gullies of the rough regions above the strait, passing "five large villages of very mild heathen . . . [where they] were well received . . . and presented with some of their wild food." Many other villages could be made out on the opposite shore.

"According to scientists," writes Nellie Van de Grift Sanchez, "the name Carquinez is derived from Karkin, the name of an Indian village in that region. . . . Fray José Viader, diarist of the Moraga expedition of 1810 . . . [and] other diarists speak of this Indian village and tribe under the name of the Carquines, making it fairly certain that the origin of the name is Indian." Crespí called the strait the Río de San Francisco.

Breaking camp near Martinez on March 30, the party crossed a deep arroyo "well grown with oaks, cottonwoods, alders, and laurels," which, says Professor Bolton, was probably Pacheco Creek. The expedition then entered the broad, oak-studded Concord Valley, which Crespí thought would be an excellent place for a settlement. Two native villages were seen in this neighborhood.

Leaving the valley behind them, the little cavalcade pressed forward over the western spur of Mount Diablo. From one of the high hills of the range they gazed out upon a vast new territory. Before them lay the great central valley of California and the Sacramento and San Joaquin Rivers, which converge at the head of Suisun Bay, and, far away to the southeast, "some high mountains," which probably were the Sierra Nevada.

A trail had been made through the Contra Costa, and although the specific goal of the expedition was never attained, a discovery of great magnitude had been made. The vast inland valley of Alta California with its great intersecting watercourses had been revealed for future exploration.

Camp on this evening was probably pitched between Pittsburg and Antioch. "From this place," wrote Crespí, "we decided to return to . . . Monterey, in view of the fact that our passage to Point Reyes . . . was cut off by these rivers." Before turning back, however, the expedition, wrote Bolton, "went ten leagues from Pacheco Creek, reaching an Indian village near Antioch."

Camp near the San Joaquin River was broken early the next morning. The range was crossed north of Mount Diablo, and Concord Valley was reentered north of Clayton. Continuing west toward Walnut Creek, the party turned southeast and proceeded past the site of Danville through the San Ramon Valley. Camp was made just south of Danville. The trail of Pedro Fages through this area has been commemorated by a plaque (SRL 853) at 856 Danville Boulevard, placed by the San Ramon Valley Historical Society.

Early on the first day of April Fages and his men traveled south through the San Ramon Valley and on into Livermore Valley, passing "many and good arroyos, and with numerous villages of very gentle and peaceful heathen. . . . It is a very suitable place," Crespí's diary records, "for a good mission, having good lands, much water, firewood, and many heathen."

IN THE FOOTSTEPS OF PEDRO FAGES

On April 1, 1776, from his position east of Richmond, Father Pedro Font mapped the Richmond Peninsula, which he took to be an island. Juan Bautista de Anza was the leader of that march up the Contra Costa. On the banks of Wildcat Creek, a "rather deep arroyo with a growth of trees and little water," the party came upon an abandoned Indian village. Crossing the creek near San Pablo, they came to a second arroyo with a very deep bed and a "heavy growth of live oaks, sycamores, and other trees." Here they found a native village where they were greeted by twenty-three men and seven women, who presented the travelers with a feast of roasted cacomites (a species of iris) in exchange for the glass beads that Anza gave them.

More hills and two or three small arroyos were passed, and another village of friendly Indians greeted them. At nightfall the travelers came to a "high hill"

from which they could see a wide expanse of the Bay and hear the waves on the shore. Bolton wrote that this was evidently one of the hills at the edge of Rodeo. Camp was made at Rodeo Creek.

At sunrise on the morning of April 2 the camp was visited by a delegation of Indians from a village nearby. They sang and danced and bore gifts of cacomites and chuchupate roots. After Mass had been said, Anza accepted his visitors' invitation to go to their village. Still singing and dancing, they led the way, the padre now and then interrupting them by chanting the Alabado, the morning hymn.

The village, which they soon reached, stood in a valley on the bank of a small arroyo about where the town of Rodeo now stands. The Indians welcomed the strangers "with an indescribable hullabaloo," and, with "banners made of feathers" and the skins of rabbits, they led the visitors to a level spot in the center of the village, where the singers resumed the dance of welcome accompanied by "much clatter and yelling." After an exchange of gifts, Anza and his men continued their journey, apparently to the sorrow of the villagers.

The next halt was made just west of today's Carquinez Bridge. Here at the edge of the water longitudinal measurements were taken. At this point, too, they found Indians fishing with nets from rafts, on which the fishermen afterward crossed to the opposite shore.

Continuing on to the Martinez Valley, where the Indians from across the strait joined them, the little band continued south along the route of today's I-680 toward Walnut Creek. Camp was made near Pacheco on the edge of the Concord Valley. Father Crespí had thought that this pretty wooded spot would be an attractive place for a mission but the arroyo lacked enough permanent water.

Following east along the edge of the strait, the party in the next two days passed Suisun Bay and the site of Antioch and entered a marshy region, the delta of the San Joaquin River. Anza proposed to cross the great valley and explore east toward the Sierra Nevada, but the tule swamps were impenetrable. South of Bethany (in San Joaquin County) the commander decided to halt the frustrated effort and return to Monterey.

RANCHO SAN PABLO

Rancho San Pablo, at first called Rancho Cochiyumes, consisted of four leagues of land bordered on the west and north by the bays of San Francisco and San Pablo, and on the east by low, verdant hills. There were no fences at all on the rancho, and likewise no roads. Divergent trails twisted through the grasses that stretched like a vast sea on all sides. Here and there the tract was dotted by islands of huge oak trees. It was home to numerous wild creatures: bears, coyotes, deer, and elk.

Into this wilderness Francisco Castro drove the first herd of cattle north of Rancho San Antonio (the property in Alameda County of the Peralta family). Like the herds of the Peraltas, Castro's soon multiplied into roving bands of untamed animals that supplied the rancho with food and the Yankee traders with hides and tallow. Here, too, the first fruit trees in the county and grape cuttings from the mission were set out.

Francisco María Castro, a native of Mexico, was a settler at San Francisco in 1800. For thirteen years he served as a soldier. In 1822 he was a member of the *diputacíon*, the governor's council. In June 1823 he acted as *diputado*, or official representative, of the exploring expedition led by Father José Altamira north of San Francisco Bay, and in that year he obtained, provisionally, the grant of Rancho San Pablo in the Contra Costa. Castro took up residence on this land in 1826, and there he lived until his death in 1831, three years before the official confirmation of the grant in 1834. The estate was left half to his widow and half to his eleven children. Through years of litigation, during which, says Bancroft, the whole Castro family was "kept in a state of landed poverty," the vast grant gradually dwindled to a few acres around the adobes at El Cerrito and San Pablo.

The venerable Castro adobe (SRL 356) stood until it was destroyed by fire in 1956; the site is now the El Cerrito Plaza shopping center. It is on the north bank of El Cerrito Creek, which here forms the boundary between Contra Costa and Alameda Counties. To the west rises El Cerrito ("the little hill"), a landmark for travelers and settlers along the northwest shore of the Contra Costa. It was one of the more substantial and permanent designations of the boundary line between Rancho San Pablo and its neighbor to the south, Rancho San Antonio.

About 1842, Jesús María Castro, one of the sons of Don Francisco, built an adobe house on what is now the west corner of San Pablo Avenue and Church Lane in the city of San Pablo. Martina, daughter of Francisco Castro, married Governor Juan Bautista Alvarado in 1839, and the governor thus came into possession of the portion of the estate that Martina inherited on her mother's death in 1851. This included the adobe at San Pablo, to which the governor had retired in 1848, re-

Alvarado Adobe, El Cerrito Civic Center

maining there until his death in 1882. Gradually, the vast acreage had been diminished until, at the time of his death, only about fifty acres remained in the vicinity of the adobe.

The Alvarado adobe (SRL 512) stood for many years behind a grocery store at the corner, and, covered with a wooden superstructure, was used as a storeroom. In 1954, despite the efforts of local residents and organizations to preserve it, the adobe was razed to build a motel.

In 1976 a replica of the Alvarado adobe was built on its original site, now named Alvarado Square and part of the San Pablo civic center; this is now a museum of the San Pablo Museum and Historical Society. Next to the Alvarado Square complex, which also houses the city offices of San Pablo, is the Blume House Museum. The ranch house and the bunkhouse of the Blume family, built elsewhere in 1905, were moved to this site in 1971 when the original site was purchased by the Chevron Land and Development Corporation. The buildings are open to the public.

The pastoral lands once occupied by the great Rancho San Pablo are now covered by miles of residences, commercial buildings, and paved highways; the cities of Richmond, El Cerrito, and San Pablo have grown up around the pioneer settlements.

RANCHO SAN RAMÓN

The vast acreage of Rancho San Ramón lay mostly within Contra Costa County after Alameda County was created in 1853. Two square leagues of this rancho were granted to Bartolomé Pachecho and Mariano Castro by Governor José Figueroa in 1833. Four leagues were granted by the same governor to José María Amador in 1834 and 1835. Leo Norris, a native of Kentucky who had come across the plains to California from Missouri in 1846, filed claim for one square league, which he purchased from Amador, and this was confirmed and later patented to him.

Pacheco and Castro divided their grant, Pacheco taking the southern half and Castro the northern. Castro lived at Rancho Pastoria de las Borregas in Santa Clara County and sold his share of the San Ramón to his brother-in-law, Domingo Peralta of Rancho San Antonio in Alameda County, in 1852. Pacheco died in 1839, and his land came into the hands of his son Lorenzo, who himself died in 1846. Lorenzo's widow, Rafaela Soto de Pacheco, eventually deeded part of this southern league to Horace W. Carpentier, who had also acquired much of Domingo Peralta's land. Early American settlers on the rancho, including John M. Jones, Daniel Inman, Albert W. Stone, and James Tice, had to pay Carpentier in order to get clear title to their land.

Leo Norris lived at Mission San José from June 1847 until the early autumn of 1850, when he and his son William migrated to the San Ramon Valley. With them went their relative, William Lynch, a native of New York, who had landed in San Francisco in June 1849. Lynch was a journeyman carpenter and practiced his trade in San Francisco before going out to the fertile valley of San Ramon, where he helped Norris build his house, the first frame dwelling in the valley, from lumber hauled from the San Antonio redwoods. According to J. P. Munro-Fraser, when Norris came to the ranch in 1850, he found a branch of the Soto family living in an adobe house then standing about 150 yards from the site of his residence. Apparently these were brothers of Rafaela Soto de Pacheco who planned to settle there, but they moved elsewhere when Indians stole all their horses. The old Norris dwelling, which stood on Norris Canyon Road at the mouth of the canyon, about half a mile west of San Ramon Valley Boulevard, was destroyed by fire around 1950.

Other American pioneers purchased portions of Rancho San Ramón. Joel Harlin, a native of Indiana, came to California with his parents in the spring of 1846. After a trip to the mines, followed by his marriage in April 1849, Harlan lived at different times in Napa, San Francisco, Sacramento, San Jose, and San Lorenzo (in Alameda County), where he was one of the first settlers at Squattersville.

In 1852, Harlan purchased a tract of land on Rancho San Ramón in Contra Costa County. There he built a dwelling, which, when Alameda County was created the next year, was one of the points defining the boundary line. Notwithstanding the unique, if somewhat indefinite, position of his house, Harlan always maintained that it stood on the Contra Costa side of the line. A huge oak tree in the corner of the original Harlan yard long served as a landmark. The spot is just west of the junction of Alcosta and San Ramon Valley boulevards north of Dublin.

Approximately two thousand acres purchased from the Norris tract were added to the Harlan estate in 1856. The following year the house at the county boundary line was moved north to a site three miles south of the town of San Ramon, and there in 1858 Harlan built the fine old country mansion now known as El Nido ("the nest"). The original dwelling was incorporated into a wing of the two-story building, which is set back from the road at 19521 San Ramon Valley Boulevard.

Christian Wiedemann, who came to San Francisco from Germany in 1852, settled on Rancho San Ramón in 1855. He built his home, which is still owned by his descendants, in 1865 on a 400-acre tract. It is located about one-half mile south of Norris Canyon Road at a point two and one-half miles west of San Ramon Valley Boulevard.

ALAMO

The towns of Alamo, Danville, Diablo, and San Ramon are located on the northern (Castro-Pacheco) portion of Rancho San Ramón. The name Alamo (Spanish for "poplar") was given to the town because poplar or cottonwood trees once grew abundantly in the valley and along the streams. Most of the old buildings of the place have been leveled to make way for newer structures. The Union Academy was built in 1859, with the Reverend David McClure as master; he had conducted the first services of the Presbyterian Church in the San Ramon Valley in 1857. When the building (about where El Portal Road meets Danville Boulevard, on the western side) burned in 1868, it was not rebuilt. Two houses built by German-born pioneer Frederick L. Harburg stand in Diablo, both moved from original sites and privately owned.

DANVILLE

It has been said that Danville was named for Daniel Inman, the pioneer who formerly owned the land on which the town now stands. In a story told in the *Danville Sentinel* in 1898, Inman noted that settlers wanted to name the new post office Inmanville, "but my brother Andrew and I objected to that. Finally, 'Grandma' Young, my brother's mother-in-law, said: 'Call it Danville,' and as much or more out of respect to her, as she was born and raised near Danville, Kentucky, it took that name."

In 1858, S. Wolf, M. Cohen, and Henry Hoffman dissolved the firm of Wolf and Company at Alamo and opened a store in Danville. About the same year H. W. Davis opened a hotel at the junction of the road from Tassajara and the highway through Danville. It burned in 1873, but a new Danville Hotel (first known as the Railroad Hotel) was built on the same spot in 1891. This hotel was moved in 1928 to its present location on Hartz Avenue, and still serves as a bar and restaurant, with specialty shops.

The Museum of the San Ramon Valley is located at West Prospect and Railroad Avenue in Danville, open on a regular basis. In nearby Blackhawk is a museum complex, part of which is operated by the University of California at Berkeley and part of which contains the superb vintage automobile collection of Kenneth Behring. In 2000, the Blackhawk Museum became an affiliate of the Smithsonian Institution.

SAN RAMON, OR LIMERICK

The northern boundary of the Norris division of Rancho San Ramón is just south of the town of San Ramon. Originally known as Lynchville, this town, like Dublin to the south, long retained the name of Limerick because the settlers of the vicinity were primarily Irish. When the population in the neighborhood justified establishing a post office in 1873, it was given the name San Ramon, although the settlement continued to be known popularly as Limerick for some time. An earlier post office named San Ramon had existed in the vicinity from 1852 to 1859. The Catholic church dedicated to St. Raymond was built in 1859 at Dublin, where it still stands.

RANCHO EL SOBRANTE DE SAN RAMÓN (TICE AND STONE VALLEYS)

In 1844 Inocencio Romero and his brother José claimed Rancho El Sobrante de San Ramón of five leagues. This was the *sobrante* ("leftover" or "excess") of land lying between the ranchos of "Moraga, Pacheco, and Welch." Some six or seven years before the Romeros petitioned for the grant, the tract had been claimed by Francisco Soto but had never been used or cultivated by him.

The large adobe residence of the Romeros, in Tice Valley southwest of Walnut Creek, was razed in 1900, but a small stone and mud house remained for some years afterward. El Sobrante de San Ramón was never confirmed to the brothers because of certain legal complications and vagaries, and James Tice, for whom the valley was named, later came into ownership of the property. Joseph Napthaly began to acquire land in the valley in 1874. He built a winery where Del Valle High School now stands. The former station of Saranap on the Sacramento Northern Railroad was a contraction of Sara Napthaly. In 1930 the Napthaly Rancho was sold to Stanley Dollar, the steamship magnate, and in 1960 it became Rossmoor Leisure World, a retirement community. About 1965 some children from Tice Valley School discovered in the hills a large sandstone rock with the chiseled inscription "J. W. Tice 1855."

The portion of San Ramón Sobrante that lies immediately east of Alamo was long known as the Stone Ranch and is still called Stone Valley. Albert W. Stone, a native of Pennsylvania and a blacksmith by trade, had come to California from Iowa in 1852. After returning to Iowa the following year, he again crossed the plains to California, this time with his family. For a while he lived in Colusa County on land later occupied by Dr. Hugh J. Glenn, but in 1858 he moved to Contra Costa County, where he purchased the farm of 800 acres adjoining Alamo. The two houses built by his family on or near today's Stone Valley Road have long since disappeared.

RANCHO ACALANES (LAFAYETTE)

Rancho Acalanes, lying among the fertile little valleys west of Lafayette, was granted in 1834 to Candelario Valencia, a soldier of the San Francisco Company. The name probably derived from Sakalan or Akalan, a Costonoan Indian village in the vicinity, which was called by the Spaniard the Acalanes "tribe." Like many another Californian, Valencia eventually became indebted to a foreigner and, unable to clear himself of entanglements, was forced to sell his land. Thus Rancho Acalanes fell into the hands of William A. Leidesdorff of Yerba Buena, who put it up for sale.

Meanwhile, Elam Brown, a native of New York, had arrived in California in October 1846 as captain of a company of fourteen families and sixteen wagons that apparently had crossed the mountains in company with the Boggs and Cooper parties. Brown spent his first summer in California whipsawing lumber in the San

Antonio redwoods and hauling it to the San Antonio Landing, where it was shipped across the Bay to San Francisco. Learning that Rancho Acalanes was for sale, Brown purchased it from Leidesdorff, together with 300 cows the latter had obtained from the Vásquez rancho at Half Moon Bay.

Brown took his family through the Moraga Valley to their new home, where they arrived in February 1848. They were the second American family to settle in Contra Costa County. The Browns' first two settlements had to be abandoned for lack of adequate water. They finally settled in a redwood house on the site of the present La Fiesta shopping center in Lafayette; a plaque placed by the Lafayette Historical Society marks the approximate location.

At first Brown had to make long, tedious trips on horseback or by ox team via the San Ramon Valley in order to carry his wheat and barley to Sansevain's mill in San Jose, where it was turned into flour. In 1853 he purchased a horse-powered mill in Benicia and set it up near his house. The millstone was placed in the Lafayette plaza in 1955 as a memorial to Elam Brown. The gristmill was located beside Lafayette Creek south of this monument, next to the Park Theater. Brown, who died in 1889, was for many years a respected and prosperous citizen of Contra Costa County. He was a member of the convention that framed the state constitution in 1849 and also of the first two Legislatures after its adoption.

Nathaniel Jones, a native of Tennessee, had started for Oregon from Missouri in April 1846 in company with fifteen or twenty other families. Circumstances diverted the immigrants to California, and at Sutter's Fort Joseph Chiles induced Jones to go to Rancho Catacula in Napa County. With three or four other families the Joneses arrived in Chiles Valley in November 1846. After volunteering and participating in the Battle of Santa Clara, Jones returned to Rancho Catacula. In 1847, Jones took his wife and small son to the San Antonio redwoods in Alameda County, and with the proceeds of the work that he did that summer he purchased a part of Rancho Acalanes from Elam Brown for $100.

Nathaniel Jones and Elam Brown moved to their new homes about the same time, and early in 1848 Jones built his house. In the spring of the following year he began to set out black locust trees, which gave the name Locust Farm to his ranch. The seeds for these trees had been brought to California by Major Stephen Cooper in 1846 and subsequently presented to Jones. A few of the

trees, now very old, may still be seen on Happy Valley Road, north of Lafayette's business district.

The settlement was named in 1853 in honor of the French hero of the War of American Independence; it is one of several Lafayettes in the United States, and a statue of the Marquis stands in Lafayette Plaza. Benjamin Shreve, who arrived at the Brown residence in 1852, taught school in the community during the winter of 1852–53, and later opened a store and built a home. The store building (1855) still stands at 3535 Plaza Way. Shreve is credited with naming the town—the first name suggested was Centerville, but because there was another town of that name in California, the post office refused it—as well as being the first post master. Of the first three schools in Lafayette, the first, near the plaza, no longer stands; the second is now a tavern at 3535 Mount Diablo Boulevard; and the third has been incorporated into the Lafayette Methodist Church at 955 Moraga Road.

A Lafayette Hotel stood near the plaza as early as 1853; the last of three buildings of the same name on the site burned down in 1925. A blacksmith shop established by Jack Elston in the 1850s continued for many years at 3530 Mount Diablo Boulevard. By 1913 Lafayette was linked to Oakland by a train powered by electricity, and a few residents commuted to their offices as far away as San Francisco.

RANCHO SOBRANTE (EL SOBRANTE, ORINDA)

The *sobrante* granted to Juan José and Victor Castro in 1841 was entirely surrounded by other grants, in a day when boundaries everywhere were uncertain. Governor Alvarado in making the grant stipulated that its boundaries should be determined by the boundaries of the surrounding grants—Ranchos San Antonio, San Pablo, El Pinole, La Boca de la Cañada del Pinole, Acalanes, and La Laguna de los Palos Colorados. The effect of this proviso was to throw the boundaries of the new *sobrante* into legal conflicts that lasted for forty years. When a grant of over 20,000 acres was confirmed to the Castro brothers in 1883, thousands of acres had already gone to pay attorney's fees. A survey map of 1893 showed Victor Castro, who survived his brother, as the owner of 549 acres. The family still lives in the area on Castro Ranch Road.

In 1980 the Orinda Historical Society placed a marker at the spot where the boundaries of Ranchos Sobrante, Acalanes, and Boca de la Cañada del Pinole converged, at the end of Dalewood Drive in Orinda.

RANCHO LA BOCA DE LA CAÑADA DEL PINOLE (BEAR CREEK VALLEY)

Around 1824, Ignacio Martínez occupied the area that he called Rancho El Pinole. Five years later he invited Felipe Briones, who had been a *regidor* or pueblo councilman in San Jose, to live on the ranch in exchange for various services rendered. In 1839, while Martínez's petition for Rancho El Pinole was still pending, Briones filed for a grant of land that apparently included El Pinole. When it was pointed out that Martínez had long been a resident there and that Briones's house was really at El Corral de Galindo, Briones changed his petition to request the area called La Boca de la Cañada de Pinole, which bordered on but did not include El Pinole.

In 1840 Briones was killed while trying to recover horses stolen by Indians. His widow continued the petition and received the grant in 1842, about the same time that Martínez, who had supported her claim, received his grant at El Pinole.

RANCHO EL PINOLE (PINOLE, MARTINEZ)

Ignacio Martínez was born in Mexico City in 1774, and, coming to California, entered military service as a cadet at Santa Barbara in 1799. He became an officer in the San Diego Company in 1806 and in 1817 he was recommended for promotion, this time to return to Santa Barbara. To his chagrin, a clerical error sent him to San Francisco instead. He was retired in 1831, after having been *comandante* at San Francisco during the last four years of his military service. He was a civilian official at San Jose in 1834–35, but then settled on his claim in Contra Costa, granted to him in 1842. One of his daughters married the English-born pioneer William A. Richardson.

The town of Pinole ("toasted grain") carries the name of this rancho, and the city of Martinez at the edge of his land is named for his family. The site of the Ignacio Martínez adobe is where Pinole Valley Road jogs while crossing the creek twice in a short distance. Two of the old El Pinole Rancho houses may still be seen in the vicinity of Martinez. One is on the John Muir Ranch in Franklin Canyon about two miles south of the center of Martinez, and the other is farther south on the John Swett Ranch in the Alhambra Valley.

The home of the great naturalist John Muir (SRL 312) is located at Alhambra Avenue and Franklin Canyon Road. The large house where Muir lived from 1890 until his death in 1914 stands on a knoll overlooking

Vicente Martínez Adobe, John Muir National Historical Site, Martinez

the orchards and homes below and the hills that surround them. The house was built by Dr. John Strentzel, Muir's father-in-law.

John Muir was born in 1838 in Dunbar, Scotland. He came to the United States in 1849 and went on to California while still a young man. Most of his life was spent exploring, studying, and writing about the great mountains of California and Alaska, their valleys, glaciers, and wildlife. Many of the mountain peaks and glaciers up and down the Pacific Coast were discovered and named by him. He was one of the foremost advocates of national parks, and his books have done much to cause people to know and cherish the natural wonders of the Pacific Coast states. More California sites have been named for him than for any other person. In 1892, the Sierra Club was founded in San Francisco, with Muir as its first president, "to explore, enjoy, and render accessible the mountain regions of the Pacific Coast; to publish authentic information concerning them; to enlist the support and cooperation of the people and the government in preserving the forests and other natural features of the Sierra Nevada." Perhaps the best known of his writings is *The Mountains of California* (1894).

The property is now the John Muir National Historic Site, operated by the National Park Service. The site, at 4202 Alhambra Avenue, also includes the Vicente Martínez adobe (SRL 511), which was the home of ranch employees during Muir's time. Vicente, a son of Ignacio Martínez, built the adobe in 1849. Four years later he sold it to Edward Franklin, who lived there a short time and for whom Franklin Canyon is named.

John Swett has been called "the father of the California public schools" because of his untiring efforts on their behalf while he was superintendent of public instruction from 1863 to 1867. He was born in New

John Muir House, Martinez

Hampshire and came to San Francisco in 1853, where he was at once employed as a teacher. Throughout his long career as a teacher and administrator he worked to build up the public school system of California.

The John Swett Ranch, at the end of Millthwait Drive off Alhambra Valley Road, lies in the heart of the Alhambra Valley in the midst of residential developments and the remains of some old orchards. The big old house itself is hidden among the trees along a stream. Beside it is a little white adobe built by Abilino Altamirano around 1849 and carefully preserved by Swett and his descendants.

Bernardo Fernandez settled near the mouth of Pinole Creek in the 1850s; he became a merchant and an early developer of Pinole. The two-story mansion he built on Tennant Avenue in 1894 is now owned and maintained as a public facility by the city of Pinole and is on the National Register of Historic Places.

RANCHO LOS MEDANOS (MARSH CREEK AND EASTWARD)

Captain Luís Antonio Argüello, accompanied by Fathers Narciso Durán and Ramón Abella, made a voyage up the Sacramento River in May 1817. It was on this expedition, according to Chapman, that the sandbanks or dunes that lie along Carquinez Strait between Pittsburg and Antioch were mentioned as *Los Medanos* ("the sandbanks"). During the late 1830s two adjoining ranchos were granted, both of which, according to Bancroft, received the name of Los Medanos, apparently because of the sand dunes lying along the left bank of the San Joaquin River in their vicinity. Later writers, however, have tried somewhat ambiguously to distinguish the two by calling the rancho originally granted to José Noriega and later purchased by Dr. John Marsh "Los Meganos" and the New York Ranch (where Pittsburg now stands) "Los Medanos." (The two names are variants of the same term, which means "sand dunes.")

José Noriega, who was aboard the *Natalia*, wrecked at Monterey in 1834, became *depositario*, or receiver, at Mission San José the following year. In October 1835 he also became grantee of a rancho in Contra Costa County, where he built some corrals and a few outbuildings. In 1837, Noriega sold his rancho to John Marsh, who settled upon it the same year and occupied it until his death in 1856.

Marsh, a native of Massachusetts, graduated from Harvard University with the bachelor's degree. After spending some time in Wisconsin, he left the United States for New Mexico in 1835. He traveled through a portion of Old Mexico and entered southern California early in 1836. He displayed his Harvard diploma to the *ayuntamiento* (town council) of Los Angeles, who received it as a medical diploma, and Marsh was given a license to practice medicine. A sympathetic biographer, John W. Winkley, noted that Marsh had in fact completed his medical education and had practiced for some years, although he lacked a formal medical degree, and that he was well qualified as a physician and surgeon.

By December 1837 Marsh had come north and acquired the rancho in the shadow of Mount Diablo. The local Indians became the doctor's friends and helpers, and he called his estate the Farm of Pulpones (evidently a corruption of Bolbones or Bolgones), from the name of a nearby tribe or village. Marsh maintained good relations with his Indian neighbors—healing their sick, purchasing their pelts, and leaving their ancient *ranchería* ("settlement") undisturbed. In return, the Indians helped the "Señor Doctor" to build a four-room adobe with an attic on the bank of the stream opposite their village. They brought grape cuttings from Mission San José to this first house and his grander mansion and helped him to plant a vineyard and an orchard of pears, figs, and olives. They plowed his field for him and helped him to sow it with wheat. When he died, it was said that the Indians watched beside his bier and mourned his passing.

Disappointment and tragedy experienced during his sojourn among the Indians in Wisconsin before he came to California had left their stamp upon the life and character of John Marsh. To all but his Indian neighbors he was notoriously parsimonious and often unkind. When the Bidwell-Bartleson party, the first party to cross the Sierra Nevada into California, reached his rancho in 1841, he received them but made them pay well for his services. (Even the Yankee traders complained about his sharp methods when he tried to beat them at their own game.) His treatment of the 1841 party is understandable because several of the members had killed some of Marsh's trained work oxen for food.

There were others, however, who admired the seemingly hard and tightfisted doctor, and several Californians, including General Mariano Vallejo, warmly praised him. Dr. Marsh was the first and for several years the only man to practice medicine in the San Joaquin Valley. He often traveled many leagues to minister to the sick, his services usually being paid in cattle. "The greater the distance," George Lyman writes, "the more cows he expected, but it was generally agreed that he brought comfort and relief to the households he visited. His reputation spread. Cows or no cows, his services were in demand."

Although naturalized as a Mexican citizen in 1844, Dr. Marsh joined Sutter's forces against the Californians in 1844–45 but took little part in the troubles of 1846–47. Nevertheless, he increasingly hoped for United States annexation of California, and almost every wagon train to the East carried letters from him to his friends praising the glories and possibilities of the land. Most of these communications were to Missourians and were published in Missouri newspapers.

These letters, written from direct observation, exerted a far-reaching influence on immigration to California, especially from Missouri. The Marsh letters are still a valuable source of information on the life and times of pioneer California.

In June 1851 Dr. Marsh married Abbie Tuck, the daughter of a minister in Chelmsford, Massachusetts, a beautiful and accomplished lady who had come to California in 1850 for her health. John Marsh dreamed of something better than his crude adobe for his wife and planned a stone mansion with a library, marble fireplaces, a tower, and a suite of room for Abbie and himself. She selected the site almost directly opposite the adobe but never lived in the mansion. About three years after the birth of their daughter, Alice, Abbie sickened

and died. The peak of John Marsh's happiness and prosperity passed quickly. His relationships with his Mexican neighbors deteriorated; it was claimed that he was parsimonious and overbearing, ignoring the rights of others. On September 3, 1856, he was murdered by three young Californians on the lonely road between his rancho and Martinez. The site of the murder is marked (SRL 722) on Pacheco Boulevard two miles north of Pacheco. In 1866 one of the murderers was apprehended and sent to prison for life. After twenty-five years he was pardoned.

Marsh's stone house, or at least its exterior walls, still stands in a wide, open field about four miles southwest of Brentwood via Walnut Boulevard and Marsh Creek Road. Here Alice Marsh, orphaned at an early age, was to experience poverty and hardship before she finally came into her inheritance. The Marsh estate was divided between Alice and Charles, the doctor's son by his first wife in Wisconsin, at whose death John began his travels to California. It was largely through the efforts of Charles that the property was finally freed from the hands of unscrupulous persons and given to the doctor's two heirs.

The fate of the Marsh home has been a sorry one. Abandoned for years, it deteriorated until little was left except for the walls, rising three stories above the fields. A long effort on the part of local historians resulted in the state's acquiring the property in 1979, but little has been done to retard the deterioration. As late as 1999 the Legislature included funds for its renovation in the state budget, but the funds fell victim to the governor's line-item veto.

RANCHO MONTE DEL DIABLO (CONCORD)

Salvio Pacheco, having held high offices in the government of Mexican California, was granted the Rancho Monte del Diablo, of 18,000 acres, in 1834. About ten years later he moved to it and soon built the adobe house (SRL 515) still standing in the present city of Concord, originally called by him Todos Santos, which was surveyed in 1868. The adobe is located at 2050 Adobe Street between Salvio and Central Streets, and is now modernized as an office building.

The adobe home of Salvio's son Fernando Pacheco (SRL 455) stands at 3119 Grant Street in Concord. It was built in the 1840s on a 1,500-acre tract given him by his father. Long neglected, it was restored by the Contra Costa County Horsemen's Association in 1941 and serves as their headquarters.

RANCHO LAGUNA DE LOS PALOS COLORADOS
(CANYON, MORAGA, ORINDA)

This rancho was granted to Joaquín Moraga and Juan Bernal in 1835. Moraga was the grandson of José Joaquín Moraga, founder and first *comandante* of the Presidio of San Francisco, and Bernal was the younger Moraga's cousin. The redwoods for which the rancho was named were in the canyons between Moraga's home and Rancho San Antonio of the Peraltas. The small community of Canyon lies in a deep redwood canyon between Moraga and Oakland. The laguna, or lake, was located at the present site of Campolindo High School on Moraga Road in Moraga.

The adobe built by Joaquín Moraga (SRL 509) and completed in 1841 was acquired and restored a century later by Katheryn Brown White Irvine. A private home, it stands at 24 Adobe Lane in Orinda.

ORINDA AND THE EAST BAY CONNECTION

William Camron, a cousin of Elam Brown of Lafayette, came to California in 1849 with his family and was orphaned five years later when he was eleven years old. Raised by his uncle, Judge Thomas A. Brown, he became a speculator in East Bay real estate. In 1871, he married Alice Marsh, daughter and heiress of John Marsh. "After the marriage," Muir Sorrick writes, "William managed her estate, eventually with disastrous results." He also acquired property on the eastern slope of the Berkeley hills, which he named Orinda Park in 1876. "Orinda" was the pen name of Katherine Philips, an English poet of the seventeenth century, and it is thought that Alice Marsh Camron derived the name from the copy of Dr. Samuel Johnson's *Lives of the Poets* that she had inherited from her father. It probably was a name more euphonious and pleasing to the ear than anything else, and in time would become (without the "Park") associated with a community naturally endowed with a beautiful landscape and climate. In 1985, Orinda became an organized city.

Orinda has historically been the connection between Contra Costa County and Oakland via various routes across the steep range of hills. William Camron was highly interested in building a toll road from Berkeley to Orinda, but he was financially strapped and unable to undertake the project. Theodore Wagner, who had a ranch in the lower Bear Creek Valley (part of which is a nature preserve today), undertook to build a road in 1889; it was ultimately paid for by official stipends and private contributions. Its course is today approximately followed by Wildcat Canyon Road, which runs from the San Pablo Dam Road in Orinda west through the Berkeley hills into Tilden Regional Park.

A more direct but more difficult route between the shoreline communities and those of the interior was the Telegraph Road, which was built in 1861 along the new telegraph line extending from Oakland to Nevada. The route followed what is today Telegraph Avenue in Oakland, then Claremont Avenue in Oakland passing into Berkeley, and from there over the summit (of 1,315 feet) and down what is now Fish Ranch Road to Orinda. The distance was short but the climb and descent were formidable. Most traffic between San Francisco or Oakland and Contra Costa came slowly by roads and later by railways along the shores of the Bay. Without better access, Contra Costa entrepreneurs feared their region would become a backwater.

After considerable prodding of their boards of supervisors, Contra Costa and Alameda County boosters rejoiced in the opening of a tunnel under the summit in 1903. It was narrow and dark and had a deceptive bend in the middle where the counties met but their road crews had not. Vehicles passed through it only with difficulty, and it was subject to occasional earth slides. Around 1915 the tunnel had to be closed for a year for repairs and cleaning.

In 1928, after considerable pressure had been put on the state Legislature, a special highway district was formed for the purpose of creating a new "low-level" tunnel (that is, at a lower elevation). Ground was broken in June 1934, with President Franklin D. Roosevelt and Governor Frank F. Merriam in attendance on the Oakland side. The two-bore tunnel was opened to traffic in 1937. It was named for Thomas E. Caldecott, an Alameda County supervisor and president of the highway district. Since then a third bore has been added, and it was announced in 1998 that traffic congestion would soon necessitate a fourth bore, although as of 2001 this remains conjectural.

Under the highway tunnel, a 3.5-mile-long train tunnel, one of the longest in California, connects the Rockridge and Orinda stations of the Bay Area Rapid Transit (BART) System, an extensive rail line that connects San Francisco and Oakland with communities as far away as Richmond, Pittsburg, Pleasanton, Fremont, and Colma. The system went into operation in 1972 after extensive planning and developments, and was one of the technological innovations of its day. Both BART and the Caldecott Tunnel have greatly increased movement between Contra Costa County and the Bay Area, so that Orinda, once an idyllic country retreat, is today only a short journey from the city scene.

RANCHO ARROYO DE LAS NUECES Y BOLBONES (WALNUT CREEK)

In the central part of the county is Rancho Arroyo de las Nueces y Bolbones, whose 17,782 acres were granted to Juana Sánchez de Pacheco in 1834. This rancho, located on the western flank of Mount Diablo, was patented to her heirs in 1866. Bolbones was the name of a tribe of Indians in the vicinity of Mount Diablo. Arroyo de las Nueces is now called Walnut Creek and has given its name to a thriving city. The original name for the city was The Corners, because roads converged here from Lafayette and Oakland to the west, from Martinez and Concord to the north, and from Livermore and the then-called Haywards to the south.

One of the early American settlers on this rancho was James T. Walker, who acquired some 1,400 acres in the 1850s, and in 1868 built a home that is still standing as a private residence on North Gate Road between Walnut Creek and Mount Diablo State Park. In 1867 Walker's uncle came to live with him. Joseph R. Walker was a trapper, trail maker, guide, and stock buyer of the 1830s and 1840s, for whom Walker Pass is named. The elder Walker moved into the new house with his nephew and lived there until his death in 1876 at the age of seventy-seven. He is buried in Alhambra Cemetery in Martinez, where his headstone recounts highlights of his career.

Near the Walker home, on Castle Rock Road, is the Borges Ranch, which was placed on the National Register of Historic Places in 1981. It has been acquired along with 2,300 acres of meadow and woodland by Contra Costa County and designated an Open Space Area. Built around 1900, the ranch home is still the center of a working farm. The county is planning to expand the farm and to develop museum and display facilities.

The Shadelands Museum at 2660 Ygnacio Valley Road is lodged in the 1902 farmhouse of Hiram Penniman. The Colonial Revival two-story building has many of the original family possessions and is maintained as a Walnut Creek museum of history. The farmhouse is on the National Register of Historic Places.

MARTINEZ

Contra Costa's county seat was incorporated in 1876; county government had been in operation there since 1850. A center for wheat shipping until the railroad came through in 1879, Martinez was also the southern terminus for the busy ferries that crossed Carquinez Strait from Benicia until the Benicia-Martinez Bridge was opened in 1960. Two disastrous fires in 1894 and 1904 all but destroyed the downtown area, which centered on Main and Ferry Streets, today the heart of the Martinez Historical District. Two buildings from 1904 serve as restaurants today. At 825 Main Street a marker commemorates the site of the *Contra Costa Gazette*, a paper founded there in 1858; it moved to Pacheco in 1863 and returned to Martinez in 1873, where it is now the *Martinez News Gazette*. The Contra Costa History Center, operated by the Contra Costa County Historical Society, was moved in 2000 to the old Hilson's Department Store building at 610 Main Street. The large facility has archives, books, maps, and pictures of life in the county for more than a century. It is open to the public on a regular basis.

The north-south streets in downtown Martinez are named for the old California families into which the daughters of Don Ignacio Martínez married: Castro, Richardson, Estudillo, and Berrellessa. At 1005 Escobar Street is the cottage built by Dr. J. S. Moore as his residence and dental office. It is now the home of the Martinez Historical Society and houses a vast collection of city memorabilia. Martinez has proven to its satisfaction over the years that the martini cocktail originated in this city and that the present name is a corruption.

PITTSBURG, "THE NEW YORK OF THE PACIFIC"

Colonel Jonathan D. Stevenson brought the First Regiment of New York Volunteers to California by sea, arriving in three transports in March 1847 to take part in the American occupation. In 1849 he purchased Rancho Los Medanos from the original grantees, José Antonio Mesa and José Miguel Garcia.

On this ranch, Stevenson laid out the site for a city about where Pittsburg now stands. He called it New York of the Pacific, after his home city, and the rancho was called the New York Ranch. The colonel hoped that his new city would become a large and prosperous seaport, and to that end he attempted to locate the state capital there in 1850, but the city of Vallejo won the honor by popular election.

When the Mount Diablo coal mines began operation in the 1860s, Pittsburg Landing was the coal shipping point. The industry was short-lived, however, because of the coal's inferior quality, and the town was not

"The Day the River Closed" by Frank J. Vitale, at Pittsburg Marina

of real importance until the twentieth century, when it became a manufacturing center. The name was officially changed to Pittsburg in 1911, although New York had long ceased to be used. Los Medanos College recalls the name of the old rancho. At the Pittsburg Marina, statues and markers celebrate the fishing activities along the New York Slough, an arm of the Sacramento River.

CONTRA COSTA'S MINING TOWNS

South of Antioch and Pittsburg, the lingering ghosts of coal-mining days remind one of the brief excitements that took place there from the middle 1850s to the middle 1880s. Nortonville and Somersville, Stewartsville and Empire, West Hartley and Judsonville, with their shipping counterparts at New York and Pittsburg landings, dominated the affairs of the county for a period of thirty years; in the case of Somersville, limited mining continued as late as 1905. High-quality sand was also mined between 1920 and 1949.

A unique population found its way into the Mount Diablo coal district from the coal fields of Wales and Cornwall. In 1882 about two hundred men and boys were employed in the mines at Nortonville, while the entire population of the place registered about nine hundred.

Bancroft states that coal was discovered in Contra Costa County as early as 1848. George W. Hawxhurst settled in 1855 at the place where the town of Somersville later grew up, and after prospecting for coal he discovered the Union vein in March of that year. Four years later, in December 1859, Francis Somers and James T. Cruikshank discovered the famous Black Diamond vein. With his associates, H. S. Hawxhurst and Samuel Adams, Somers located the lands afterward known as the Manhattan and Eureka coal mines, which comprised, with

the Union and Independent, the mines forming the basin that held the town of Somersville. In the 1880s the Pittsburg Railroad connected the district with Pittsburg Landing at the mouth of the San Joaquin River.

The Black Diamond, Cumberland, and Mount Hope Mines, located about a mile west of Somersville on the same vein, were opened by Somers and another group of men. Since they were unable to finance the building of necessary roads, they never secured title to those lands. Very soon, however, Noah Norton, from whom Nortonville received its name, came upon the scene and took over the Black Diamond, while Frank Luch and others undertook to develop the Cumberland. Luch soon sold his share to a group of men from Martinez, who took hold of the Cumberland diggings and made a success of the enterprise and also helped Noah Norton in getting the Black Diamond under way. Roads were opened to Clayton and to Pittsburg Landing, and in the 1880s a railroad connected the landing with the Nortonville mines.

The first slump in coal mining in the Mount Diablo district occurred in 1878, when the Somersville mines were closed temporarily, with the hope that they would soon reopen. Meanwhile, new locations were being made. One of these was the Empire Mine, opened near Judsonville in 1878, five miles south of Antioch and about three and one-half miles east of Somersville. A lavish outlay of capital was made, but competition demanded a cut in production costs, and this, in turn, brought the inevitable dispute between capital and labor over wages. Work was suspended early in 1880, to be continued with new men later that year.

Activities speeded up in 1881, when the railroad was extended from Judsonville to the Central Mine. Fifteen new houses and a large hotel were built, and the town of Stewartsville came into existence one mile east of Somersville. Nevertheless, competition was still strangling the industry. Since the newer mines were able to pay relatively low wages for a short time and the cost of production at Nortonville was increasing, coal mining there was doomed by 1883. In 1885 the Black Diamond Mine found that it could no longer stand the heavy expense of keeping the shaft clear of water, and by March the mines were permanently closed. Nortonville was deserted overnight. Lodges, churches, and schools were closed or moved to Martinez. Many of the houses were taken apart by their owners and moved to other places. Nothing remains of any of these little short-lived mining towns today except for the cemetery and a few place names.

Activity in Mount Diablo's sandstone belt has been

temporarily resumed at various times. For nearly three decades sand was mined at Somersville. In 1932 the coal mines at Nortonville were briefly reopened and worked again. The coal taken out then was given to the poor and unemployed in the vicinity.

While ranching took over the surface, the uncovered mine shafts were a menace that claimed the lives of several youthful and inexperienced explorers in the following years. In 1972 the East Bay Regional Park District acquired 2,763 acres of land in the area, including the Black Diamond Mine, and created Black Diamond Mines Regional Preserve. In the spring, the mine is opened to the public on a restricted basis. The preserve can be reached from Antioch by way of Somersville Road. A short road connects the parking area with the restored Rose Hill Cemetery, marked by five stately cypress trees. Many of the gravestones are of Welsh and Cornish miners. In 1934 a plaque was placed here by the Native Daughters and the Native Sons of the Golden West in memory of the pioneers of Nortonville and Somersville.

Clayton, southwest of Nortonville and southeast of Concord, was an important center in coal-mining days. It had a more diversified economy than the mining towns and survived to become an incorporated town in 1964. Joel Clayton ran a dairy farm when he was not a part-time coal miner. He wanted to name the settlement after the Italian patriot Garibaldi, but residents preferred the name of their neighbor.

Clayton's Main Street has some interesting old buildings, including the much-remodeled Pioneer Saloon from the 1860s; the Christian Endeavour Hall just off Main Street at Oak and Center, built in 1867 and now a community center; and the charming Clayton Museum at 6101 Main Street. The DeMartini or Clayton Winery building on the north side of Main Street at the western edge of town still stands, now serving as the City Hall. The Old Mount Diablo Winery on the east side of Marsh Creek Road is having a resurgence as a soft-drink bottling warehouse.

ANTIOCH

The story of Antioch begins with twin brothers William Wiggin Smith and Joseph Horton Smith, who were born in New Hampshire in 1811. Both brothers were carpenters and ordained ministers in the Christian Church, and both took their families to California to seek their fortunes in 1849.

Since carpenters were in demand, the Smith brothers agreed to work at a place called New York of the Pacific. Arriving there in July 1849, they were welcomed by Dr. John Marsh and were able to obtain the two quarter-sections of land where Antioch now stands. Here in December they broke ground and set up tents. Working their lands enough to hold them, the Smiths continued their carpentry work at New York of the Pacific, often going to Smith's Landing, as it was known at first, to cut firewood for the New York House, the hotel and eating establishment the brothers founded.

Joseph Smith died of malaria at New York of the Pacific in February 1850. The following summer, a shipload of settlers arrived in San Francisco aboard the *California Packet* from Maine. This group of New Englanders had sailed to California to establish a colony. Hearing of the new arrivals and their wish to settle in California, William Smith hastened to San Francisco to meet them. He invited them to come to Smith's Landing; although the gold mines proved too enticing for some of the company, a number accepted the invitation.

At what is now 600–604 Second Street, a picnic was held on July 4, 1851, at Smith's home. "What shall we name our town?" was the question of the day. One proposal was Minton, the name of a riverboat, in the hope that it might be induced to stop at the landing. Another proposed Paradise, which was rejected because of the uncertainty of land titles in California, a circumstance that might result in "Paradise Lost" for the holders. At length Smith proposed that, inasmuch as the first settlers on the spot were Disciples of Christ and one of them, his brother, had died and was buried on the land, it be given a biblical name in his honor. He suggested that they adopt the name of Antioch for their town, because "at Antioch, the followers of Christ were first called Christians." The name was accepted at once.

Although many of Antioch's old buildings have succumbed to fire or the ravages of time, an area known as Old Town can still be seen, bounded by E, I, and Sixth Streets and the San Joaquin River. The home of Stephen McKellips, the first engineer on the Empire Railroad that ran to the Empire Mine, was built in 1882 and still stands at 504 Sixth Street. At 302 and 308 I Street are the old McGuire and DeWitt homes; the Hard Home at 815 First Street was built about 1870 by Roswell B. Hard, first mayor of Antioch. Here the first city council met in 1872 when Antioch was incorporated.

CROCKETT

On the site of an old Indian village, Thomas Edwards Sr. built a home in 1867, the nucleus of the town of

Crockett. He had purchased land the previous year from Judge Joseph B. Crockett, who had acquired 1,800 acres in the area. As other settlers arrived, Edwards opened the first store. "The Old Homestead" (SRL 731), as the Edwards residence is called, stands with its tall palm trees on the south side of Loring Avenue. The timbers, some of which came around the Horn, are well preserved. For years Crockett has been the company town of the California and Hawaiian (C&H) Sugar Refinery.

PORT CHICAGO AND CLYDE

Port Chicago, where the Sacramento River meets Suisun Bay, began as Bay Point, built by the C. J. Smith Lumber Company of Minneapolis. The name was changed in 1931 to Chicago and changed again at the request of the U.S. Post Office to Port Chicago. In 1942 the U.S. Navy took over the riverfront area and created an ammunition loading dock, which became an important part of the military supply system in the Pacific Theater during World War II.

Here on the night of July 17–18, 1944, one of the great disasters in California's history occurred when an explosion destroyed the ammunition ships SS *Quinault Victory* and SS *E.A. Bryan*, killing 322 stevedores and servicemen instantly and wounding 390 more. The blast broke windows as far away as the St. Francis Hotel in San Francisco. Incredibly, no one was killed in the town of Port Chicago. Of the men killed, 202 were African-American, 15 percent of all African-American casualties during World War II. Two hundred and fifty survivors, members of the ordnance loading battalion, refused to return to work and were subject to courts-martial. Many were later given clemency, but not until 1999 was a presidential pardon given to one of the last survivors of those convicted by the military. After World War II ended, the Navy was determined to move civilians out of a hazardous area. Not until 1969 were the last residents evicted. The site was incorporated into the United States Naval Magazine, Port Chicago, which is now known as the United States Army Military Ocean Terminal, Concord. Port Chicago Naval Magazine Memorial, near the waterfront, honors the victims and survivors of the explosion.

The nearby town of Clyde owes its origin to the contract drawn up during World War I by the federal government with the Pacific Coast Shipbuilding Company to build ships at Bay Point. The town of Clyde—named for the River Clyde in Scotland, a center of the British shipbuilding industry—was to be the residence for the workers. The government did not want flimsy temporary homes and commissioned Bay Area architect Bernard Maybeck to design permanent buildings.

Although the war was soon over, building continued at Clyde until 1922, by which time a large 176-room hotel and 103 houses had been constructed in the distinctive Maybeck style. The hotel burned in 1969; in the same year the Navy closed down Port Chicago, some of whose houses were moved to Clyde. Some of the inhabitants of Port Chicago moved to an area west of Pittsburg, now known by the name of Bay Point.

BYRON HOT SPRINGS

Before white settlers came, Miwok and Costonoan Indians had known of the bubbling mud pots and mineral springs in eastern Contra Costa County. In 1868, after an unproductive attempt to produce salt from the region, Orange Risdon Jr. and his nephew Lewis Risdon Mead saw the possibility of creating a health resort, such as were springing up all over California. In 1888, Mead replaced the early cottages with a hotel. This burned in 1901 and was replaced by a second hotel, which met a like fate in 1912. The third hotel on the spot—by now known as Byron Hot Springs after the town of Byron, three miles to the north, from which the springs were reached—was put up in 1914 along with other structures. One of these structures, known as the Mead Memorial, built by Lewis Mead's widow in memory of her husband, was said to be the only building in the world equipped with natural hot and cold springs.

The resort's mineral waters were famous and often prescribed for their therapeutic value, but as the fashion for such watering spots waned during the 1930s, the place declined. In World War II the government used it for the internment of high-ranking German and Japanese prisoners of war. Many attempts were made after 1945 to revive the place, none successfully as of 2001. The old Byron Inn, a late-nineteenth century structure, was undergoing renovation when it burned in 2000.

OTHER HISTORIC SPOTS IN CONTRA COSTA COUNTY

During the eighteen months of its existence in the years 1860 and 1861, the Pony Express riders on some twenty-one occasions missed their connection at Sacramento and had to ride overland to Oakland to complete their journey. Their route passed through Contra Costa County, and markers to this enterprise have been placed at Martinez, Lafayette, and Orinda by the Contra Costa County Historical Society.

Tao House, in the hills about one and one-half miles west of Danville, was the home of Eugene O'Neill and his wife, Carlotta Monterey, from 1937 to 1944. Here the playwright, winner of the Nobel Prize for literature in 1936, wrote some of his greatest works, including *The Iceman Cometh*. The house is a National Historic Landmark and is owned and administered by the National Park Service. After many years of isolation, it is now open to the public on a restricted basis.

Point Richmond, at the eastern end of the Richmond–San Rafael Bridge, overlooks San Francisco Bay. Like Sausalito in Marin County, it is both an artist colony and a residential area. The business district contains a number of buildings from the early 1900s, when the Standard Oil Company and the Santa Fe Railroad developed their facilities nearby. A local landmark is Our Lady of Mercy Catholic Church on West Richmond Avenue, built in 1903. The community, part of the city of Richmond, is on the National Register of Historic Places. At nearby Point Molate, now a U.S.

Naval Fuel Depot, stood a building called Winehaven. It was said to be the largest winery not only in the United States but, from 1911 to 1917, in the world. It was a victim of Prohibition and never reopened.

The Richmond Museum at 400 Nevin Avenue in Richmond has many displays about the maritime and commercial history of the city. In October 2000, President Clinton signed legislation establishing the Rosie the Riveter World War II Home Front National Historic Park, to be located on the south shoreline of the city at the site of the Kaiser Shipyards of World War II. This is the first site dedicated to telling the story of the "civilian home front" in World War II. ("Rosie the Riveter" was a popular song telling of a young woman who worked at a shipyard, and the term became a symbol of the domestic war effort.)

East Brother Lighthouse, established in March 1874 on a tiny island off the Contra Costa shore at Point San Pablo, was one of a series of small lighthouses put up in inland waters in the late nineteenth century. Despite government attempts to shut it down in 1934 and again in 1968, local protests kept the station in operation. The principal building of the station is now a bed-and-breakfast inn, and the lighthouse is maintained by the Coast Guard (SRL 951, no plaque).

Del Norte County

Del Norte County was organized from a portion of Klamath County in 1857, and Crescent City was made the county seat. Del Norte is Spanish for "of the north"; the county is in the extreme northwestern corner of California.

Klamath County, which had been established in 1851, extended from the Pacific Coast to the summit of the Coast Range and from the Oregon boundary to the mouth of the Mad River. The first county seat was at Trinidad; it was moved to Crescent City in 1854 and to

Orleans Bar in 1855. A small population and low assessed values made county government burdensome, and in 1874 the Legislature was petitioned by referendum to divide the remainder of the county between Siskiyou and Humboldt Counties. This was done in 1876. Klamath is the only California county to have been disestablished. Between 1851 and 1857, all of what is now Del Norte County was part of Klamath County.

TRAILBREAKERS

The northwest corner of California was somewhat isolated from the outside world. Heavily forested, the land supported a small Indian population, who made use of the bounty of the rivers and the sea. The first non-natives to penetrate what is now Del Norte County were probably a party of American frontiersmen led by Jedediah Strong Smith in 1828. As will be seen in other chapters of this book, Smith's visit to Alta California aroused deep suspicion on the part of Mexican authorities in Los Angeles, who ordered the men out of the province. Smith headed toward the Oregon Country, to which both the United States and Britain had a tenuous claim.

Taking a northwest course across the Coast Range through what are now Trinity and Humboldt Counties to the sea, Smith and his group moved northward up the coast toward Oregon, which by treaty began at the 42° parallel. Following the Klamath River canyon, the pathfinder and his party traversed the region slowly and with difficulty. Trails had to be blazed over steep and rugged mountains, while heavy fogs often impeded progress. The scarcity of wild game, which was almost their only food, added to their hardships. On June 1, 1828, they entered what is now Del Norte County.

A level, grassy plain near the mouth of the Klamath River on Hunter's Creek was reached on June 5, and camp was pitched at a spot along the present US 101 near Requa. Here, the exhausted and half-starved men and animals of the party rested for two days and nights. Their food supply was rapidly diminishing, and the last dog and a horse had to be killed for meat. Then, on June 7, a dozen or so Indians visited camp, "bringing with them a few Muscles and Lemprey Eels and some raspberries [thimbleberries]." In a brisk trade, the travelers exchanged for these delicacies the glass beads they carried for such occasions.

From the Hunter's Creek camp, Smith's party crossed over to Wilson Creek on June 8. "We were weary and very hungry," wrote Smith; again, several Indian lodges near the camp supplied them with mussels and small fish in exchange for the prized beads. They also brought

> dried sea grass mixed with weeds and a few muscles. They were great speculators and never sold their things without dividing them into several small parcels asking more for each than the whole were worth. They also brought us some Blubber not bad tasted but dear as gold dust. But all these things served but to aggravate our hunger and having been long accustomed to living on meat and eating it in no moderate quantities nothing else could satisfy our appetites.

That afternoon Smith killed three elk, "thanks to the great Benefactor." The camp was changed from "the moody silence of hunger to the busy bustle of preparation for cooking and feasting." At the Wilson Creek camp, the explorers occupied the time making salt and cutting and drying the meat. The unblazed trail that they cut from June 11 to 16 through the wilderness of Del Norte County was rough and difficult. The prairie south and east of what is now Crescent City was reached on June 16. Although there were no mountains on this lap of the journey, the dense redwood forest, the thick brush, and swamps made travel difficult.

They made camp near the coast in the vicinity of Crescent City on June 17, and on June 18 Earl Lake was discovered by a reconnoitering party. On June 19 Smith himself discovered the river that in later years bore his name. On the north bank of the Smith River, tents were set up on June 20. The next day Smith pushed on northward, and soon he and his men were in Oregon.

Alexander Roderick McLeod, at the head of the trapping expedition of the Hudson's Bay Company, entered California from the north in 1829, trying vainly to follow Smith's trail but finally coming southward via the Umpqua Valley and Klamath Lake.

THE KLAMATH, RIVER OF MYSTERY

Early explorers and mapmakers found the Klamath River to be a mystery. Its source in the Klamath lakes and its upper course were known almost a quarter of a century before it was determined that its mouth was in what is now Del Norte County.

In the fall of 1826 a trapper of the Hudson's Bay Company, Peter Skene Ogden, set out from Fort Vancouver on the Columbia River for the region of the "Clamitte." His diary gives the earliest account of the visit of travelers into the country north of Mount Shasta. Between 1827 and 1850, British and American trappers continued to trap for beaver on the upper Klamath River and its tributaries, but no expedition followed the river to its mouth. Thus the westward-flowing lower course of the river was unknown, and the spot where it emptied into the sea was for a long time a matter of conjecture. Most maps represented the Klamath as entering the ocean north of the present California-Oregon boundary line, and the (actual) lower Klamath was represented as a continuation of the present Trinity River. These two rivers, together with the South Fork of the Trinity, extended from the southeast to the northwest and on some early maps were represented as one river, named Smith's River.

As related above, the Klamath was the river course traveled by Jedediah Strong Smith and his men in 1828 when he blazed a northwest trail from the Sacramento Valley into Oregon. The first Indian agent, who arrived on the Klamath in 1851, was familiar with the maps of the region that indicated its chief waterway by the name of Smith's River, and he sought to locate that stream. But by 1851 "Smith's River" had become a lost river. The true course of the Klamath had been determined late in 1850 by a party of miners who traversed its whole length from the mouth to the junction with the Shasta River, prospecting every bar for gold. Later the name "Smith's River" was given to an unnamed stream in Del Norte County also discovered by Smith.

The early miners in northwestern California had never known of a river called Smith's but were familiar with the Trinity River, first named by Major Pierson B. Reading in 1845. Reading had discovered gold in this stream, and as a consequence the upper course of the river with its tributaries was teeming with miners in the years 1849 and 1850. The approach was from the Sacramento Valley. More direct access to the sea was desirable, and soon vessels left San Francisco to explore the northern coast with the hope of finding the mouth of the Trinity River at Trinidad Bay. No river was found at Trinidad Bay, but farther north a large river was discovered (the Klamath) that many believed to be the Trinity River.

Soon all the streams of the region were being prospected for gold, and the Klamath, crossed and recrossed, was mistaken at first for the Trinity or the Salmon. Gradually, however, the true course of the Klamath was determined, and its tributaries were identified.

CRESCENT CITY

Settlers flocked to the northwest coast of California in 1850 as a result of the discovery of gold on the Trinity.

Eureka, Arcata, and Trinidad were established as trade centers. Klamath City, near the mouth of the Klamath River, directly opposite the present village of Requa, was established in 1851. This short-lived city arose with great expectations of becoming the port of entry for the gold-rich backcountry. But, because of the shifting sandbars at the mouth of the river, navigation was uncertain, and the place was deserted soon after 1852.

No coastal settlement was made north of the Klamath River until 1853, although some ships—the *Paragon*, the *Cameo*, and the *Laura Virginia*—had anchored in a crescent-shaped bay as early as 1850. The site of Crescent City was first observed from the landward side in the spring of 1851, when searchers looking for a legendary "Lost Cabin," and led by Captain McDermott, looked westward from the top of French Hill toward the ocean and saw in the far distance an indentation like a bay. Reports of this discovery spread to the interior, where miners were eager to make a shorter communication line to the sea. In September 1852 another party set out from Althouse Creek (now in Oregon) and after a perilous and fatiguing journey they cut their way to the coast. Elk Valley, located northeast of Crescent City, was named at this time for large herds of elk seen there by the miners.

Setting up camp on the beach, the party dispatched one of their number to San Francisco to charter a ship. In time the schooner *Pomona* arrived with prospective settlers, and in February 1853 the town of Crescent City was laid out. By the summer of 1854, 300 buildings had been erected. The business activity and social life of that early time in Crescent City were feverish in the extreme. Every day saw some new project for improvement. New hotels and businesses were opening continually. Soon the town was encroaching on the forest and even covered the beach. Fraternal societies were established and a fire department was organized.

Crescent City was the chief port of entry and the supply center for the gold miners of southern Oregon, Siskiyou to the east, and a part of Trinity County, as well as for the camp in the vicinity of Crescent Bay. It was made the county seat of Klamath County in 1854, but in December of 1855 lost this position to Orleans Bar.

Meanwhile, rich diggings were being uncovered in the hills immediately adjacent to Crescent City. In 1854 and 1855 the miners on Myrtle Creek twelve miles to the northeast were making from five to fifteen dollars a day. New diggings were also found on the South Fork of the Smith River, where individual miners were making from ten to twenty dollars a day.

Del Norte County Historical Society, Crescent City

Diggings were also found closer at hand. In November 1854 discoveries were made six miles from the city, on a creek that emptied into Smith River at the White and Miller Ferry, later known as Peacock's Ferry. Even the beach in front of the city was staked off into mining claims. In the Bald Hills six miles to the east gold mines were founded in 1856. Here Villardville, named for A. Villard, a Frenchman, was laid out. Many other mining camps and districts in the neighboring hills about Crescent Bay lived their brief life and then vanished, Redwood Diggins, Big Flat, Growler Gulch, Hurdy Gurdy Creek, Blacks Ferry, Altaville, and Low Divide among them.

Altaville was a center for copper and chrome mining during the 1860s, and was full of life and activity. By the 1880s, "its glory had departed, and it lay surrounded by peace and quiet. Black mouths of tunnels appeared on the hillsides, and heaps of bluish rock showed the location of mines."

A landmark at Crescent City is the site of an old Indian village (SRL 649) on Pebble Beach between Pacific Avenue and Freeman Street. For many years Tolowa Indians lived near the beach, and this site was occupied as late as the latter part of the nineteenth century. At this spot were redwood huts, a *temescal* or sweat house, a ceremonial dancing pit, and a burial place. Requa, south of Crescent City at the mouth of the Klamath River, is still an Indian settlement (the name comes from the Yurok *re'kwoi* or "creek mouth"). The old Indian "Family House" was restored there in the 1950s.

Crescent City figures, too, in modern history. A 10,745-ton General Petroleum Corporation tanker, SS *Emidio*, was the first ship torpedoed and shelled by a Japanese submarine off the Pacific Coast in World War II. The attack took place on December 20, 1941, at a point about 200 miles north of San Francisco. Five lives were lost. The disabled vessel drifted north and foundered on the rocks off Crescent City. Some pieces of the hull, salvaged in 1950–1, are preserved on the waterfront at Front and H Streets; E Clampus Vitus has marked the site (SRL 497).

On March 27, 1964, the town was devastated by a tsunami, a great wave engendered by Alaskan earthquakes. Over twenty-four blocks of the downtown business district were inundated, and much property was destroyed, although miraculously no lives were lost.

Two other points of historical interest in the vicinity of Crescent City are Whale Island, where in June 1855 a company engaged in the whaling business was located, and Battery Point, where three brass cannons were placed in 1855. They had been salvaged from the steamer *America*, which was wrecked and burned on June 24, 1855.

A lighthouse (SRL 951) was established at Battery Point in 1856. Made of huge stone blocks with a masonry tower, it survived the 1964 tsunami. By that time the station had been automated and was no longer in service; the main floor of the lighthouse had been taken over by the Del Norte County Historical Society as a museum. Later the tower was opened to the public. Since 1982, it has once again been a working lighthouse, a Private Aid to Navigation, with a light shining from dusk to dawn every night. The Battery Point Lighthouse Museum is offshore on an island at the foot of A Street and can be reached at low tide by a causeway.

The Del Norte County Historical Society Museum is located in the former County Hall of Records at Sixth and H Streets in Crescent City. The building was first used in 1926 and was acquired for a museum in 1963; it has been open since 1965. The Indian Room features an exceptionally fine collection of Yurok and Tolowa Indian artifacts and baskets.

A SEACOAST CEMETERY: THE TRAGEDY OF
ST. GEORGE REEF

On the bluff overlooking the sea to the west of Crescent City is an old cemetery, in which many of the headstones recall the terrible event that occurred in the summer of 1865. On July 30 the *Brother Jonathan*, owned and operated by the California Steam Naviga-

Battery Point Lighthouse and Museum, Crescent City

Old House in Kings Valley Road

tion Company, plying off the coast west of Point St. George, was overtaken by a severe storm. Attempting to seek a port of safety, the ship struck St. George Reef with such force that her foremast went through the hull. There was very little time to get passengers and crew off the doomed ship; between eighty and ninety drowned, and only one boatload was saved. The *Brother Jonathan* Cemetery (SRL 541) on Pebble Beach Road has been converted into a park. Some of the old headstones are to be seen in the Del Norte County Historical Society Museum in Crescent City.

THE LIGHTHOUSE OF ST. GEORGE REEF

The St. George Reef Light has guided scores of vessels away from the treacherous hidden reefs that lie at its base. The lighthouse is on a small island seven miles off the coast and thirteen miles from Crescent City. The keepers of the lighthouse were virtual prisoners the year round; the men could barely step out of doors, and in stormy periods, even this was impossible. During moderate weather, however, they were permitted to take turns ashore.

The St. George Reef Lighthouse is one of the greatest structures of its kind ever built by the federal government. Costing $750,000, it took four years to build, because work could be carried on only in fair weather. It was completed in 1891. The tower is of rock transported by barge to the lonely island. The base covers 6,000 square feet, described as "the enclosure within which men must work and exist and have all that is necessary to their labor."

The U.S. Coast Guard closed this unique outpost in May 1975, when the beacon light was replaced by a computerized buoy. While the lighthouse stands as

it did in the past, the Coast Guard has removed the eighteen-foot-high Fresnel lens from the tower. In 1982 it presented the 5,000-pound lens to the Del Norte County Historical Society Museum in Crescent City, where it is handsomely displayed today.

FORT TER-WER

Six miles from the mouth of the Klamath River, and to the east of the present town of Klamath on SR 169, Fort Ter-Wer (SRL 544) was established by First Lieutenant George Crook in October 1857 as an outpost to guard the Klamath River Indian Reservation and to encourage peace between the Indians and the incoming settlers. The name seems to be a variant of the Yurok name that was first applied to a native village and later given to nearby Terwah Creek. The fort was abandoned in 1862, and today the area is one of mobile homes and small houses.

CAMP LINCOLN

The early Gold Rush years produced conflict between Indians on their ancestral lands and incoming prospectors and settlers, and Del Norte County was one area of conflict. There were destructive floods throughout this part of the state in 1862, which only exacerbated settlement problems. In September of that year, a military post was established at Camp Lincoln, in Elk Valley on what is now Kings Valley Road, about 1.3 miles northeast of US 199 (SRL 545). Company G, 2nd Regiment, Infantry, California Volunteers, established the post. The original officers' quarters, now a private residence, can be seen from the road. All the other buildings of Camp Lincoln, which was abandoned in May 1870, are gone. Some interesting artifacts from the days of Camp Lincoln are on display at the Del Norte County Historical Society Museum in Crescent City.

GOLD CAMPS OF SOUTHERN OREGON

Mining camps along the Klamath River, of which Happy Camp (now in Siskiyou County) was the trade center, as well as the gold camps of southern Oregon, were long tributary to Crescent City in Del Norte County. These regions were populated and flourishing one or two years before the city itself was laid out. The Klamath section was mined and settled as early as 1851, in the wake of the party of miners who had prospected their way up the Klamath River from its mouth to its source. Happy Camp, Wingate Bar, Woods Bar, and Indian Creek Diggings were among the prosperous camps established as the result of the discovery of rich gold mines.

In the territory now included in southern Josephine and Jackson Counties in Oregon, the first discovery was made at Kirbyville in 1851. Another discovery made by a group of seafaring men led to the founding of Sailor Diggings, later called Waldo after a prominent California politician. Discoveries were made in Jackson Creek in 1852, and Jacksonville became the chief center of activities. Soon a thousand and more miners rushed to the scene of these discoveries and numerous mining companies sprang up.

The first port of entry to this region was Scottsburg, in Oregon, but more direct access to the sea became desirable after the experience of high prices and famine in the winter of 1851–52. Consequently, the trail to Crescent City was opened up in the spring of 1853, and pack trains soon brought in the necessary supplies. Agitation for a wagon road was started in 1854, the surveys being made by T. P. Robinson, who in June 1854 determined the Oregon-California boundary line. Work was finally begun in 1857 by the "Crescent City and Yreka Plank and Turnpike Company," and in 1860 the wagon road between Waldo (Sailor Diggings) and Crescent City was completed. A monument commemorating this old road (SRL 645) stands on US 101 at Elk Valley Road in Crescent City.

As the surface gold was depleted, most of the population departed. Hydraulic mining was introduced in the 1860s, and some localities were producing as late as the 1880s. The road to Crescent City was closed for many years because of the heavy cost of keeping it in repair. The modern highway from Crescent City into this region is US 199; just before the Oregon line is the Randolph Collier Tunnel, one of California's longest highway tunnels at one-third of a mile. It was named for longtime state senator Randolph Collier, the "father of the California freeway system." In Oregon, US 199 bypasses the deserted site of Waldo; the location can be reached from the town of O'Brien.

During the height of mining activity, southwestern Oregon was always connected more closely with California than with Oregon. Indeed, before the boundary line was determined, the miners considered themselves Californians. Regarding this boundary, A. J. Bledsoe says: "The decision caused some excitement . . . as the miners did not like to be so suddenly transported from California to Oregon. They had before voted in both California and Oregon Territory and had refused to pay taxes to either."

A half-serious movement on the part of some residents of Del Norte, Siskiyou, and Modoc Counties in California and of Josephine County in Oregon made headlines in late November 1941; angered by what was said to be neglect of highway and public works projects in their remote areas, these people proposed to secede from their respective states and form "the sovereign state of Jefferson." The attack on Pearl Harbor the following week diverted attention from the idea. In the 1980s and 1990s, citizens arguing that Sacramento continued to ignore the region's needs threatened to revive the state of Jefferson idea, although to date it has not gained the support it had in 1941.

THE REDWOOD REGION

Del Norte County and Alpine County in the high Sierra were for many decades California's most inaccessible counties. These are two of the four counties in California that the railroads could not penetrate; the others are Lake and Mariposa. US 101 is the principal access into the county today. From Humboldt County in the south, one drives north through Redwood National Park, established in 1968 and subsequently expanded. This corridor of coastal forestland extends from Orick in Humboldt County to Crescent City. The preserve surrounds Del Norte Coast Redwoods State Park to the south of Crescent City and Jedediah Smith Redwoods State Park to the east. Most of the eastern half of Del Norte County is now the Smith River National Recreation Area.

El Dorado County was one of the original twenty-seven counties. The first county seat was at Coloma, but it was superseded by Placerville in 1857.

The Spanish term *El Dorado* means "the gilded man" and was given to the county because gold was discovered there. The name arose from legend. Andean Indians, perhaps hoping to persuade their Spanish conquerors to go elsewhere, told of a land ruled by a king. So rich in gold was this land that the king's body was gilded every morning with a fresh coating of gold dust, which was washed away every night. The Land of the Gilded Man ("El Dorado") thus became a term for a fabulously rich region waiting to be discovered by the Spaniards.

COLOMA

In the fall of 1847, John A. Sutter, founder of "New Helvetia," later Sacramento, sent foreman James W. Marshall into the foothills to find a suitable site for a sawmill. Marshall chose a stretch along the South Fork of the American River, about forty-five miles northeast of Sutter's Fort at New Helvetia, and work soon began on the mill.

On the morning of January 24, 1848, while inspecting the site, Marshall noticed shining particles in the stream bed. These were tested and found to be gold. Marshall reported his discovery to Sutter, who immediately realized its significance and attempted to keep the news from leaking to the outside world. But the secret could not be kept, and although work went ahead and the sawmill was completed in March, the gold fever was already at work. History's greatest rush was on, and within a year California would be world famous.

Coloma, the earliest of California's mining towns, was founded on the site of Marshall's discovery early in 1849. Like most of these towns, its initial prosperity soon peaked, and it settled into a quiet village with a few old houses and sporadic mining activity in the vicinity. Its name came from a nearby Southern Maidu Indian village.

As the site of Marshall's discovery of gold, however, Coloma has been of special interest to Californians. In time, therefore, the state established the Marshall Gold Discovery State Historic Park, which includes the stretch of the river where the discovery was made and about three-quarters of the town of Coloma, nearly 300 acres all told.

The discovery site (SRL 530) on the bank of the river is marked by a stone monument where the original mill stood. Nearby, an electrically operated replica of the mill is run by park rangers from time to time. Half a mile up the hill behind Coloma is the huge monument placed by the state to Marshall (SRL 143); it was completed at the cost of $9,000 in 1890, five years after Marshall died in poverty. He lies beneath the granite pile, which is surmounted by his bronze statue, with his right hand pointing downward to the site of the gold discovery.

This was not the first discovery of gold in California; that honor belongs to Placerita Canyon, described in the Los Angeles County chapter, where gold was found in 1842. The Coloma discovery, however, was followed by hundreds of other strikes in a short time, touching off a population rush never equaled in American history.

Coloma, briefly El Dorado's county seat, has few old buildings left today. The Wah Hop Store, one of two nearly identical stone buildings, is a remnant of the days when a large Chinese population lived in the foothills; it is today a state museum. The Emmanuel Episcopal

Replica of Marshall's Sawmill, Gold Discovery State Park, Coloma

Church, also used by Methodists and Presbyterians over the years, has stood on High Street since 1856. Nearly as old is St. John's Catholic Church, a block farther up the hill. The Protestant cemetery on the hill is one of the oldest in the Sierra country. Near it is the reconstructed cabin that Marshall, who grew grapes in his later years, built and lived in until 1868.

The museum of the Marshall Gold Discovery State Historic Park has displays on early mining and on the lives of Marshall and Sutter; it is located on SR 49, which passes through the park, across from the gold discovery site. Coloma, a National Historic Landmark, is seven miles northwest of Placerville, nineteen miles southeast of Auburn, and fourteen miles southwest of Georgetown.

THE COLOMA ROAD

The earliest roads in the mining regions, in reality mere pack trails, were developed in El Dorado County. The first of these was marked out in 1847–48 by Sutter and his men, Marshall among them, as a way to his new sawmill on the American River's South Fork. Running along the south side of the river from Sacramento to where Folsom now is, this first trail followed approximately the same line taken later by the railroad and by US 50. From Folsom it passed into El Dorado County by way of Mormon Island, Green Valley (modern Rescue), Rose Springs, and Uniontown (modern Lotus) to Sutter's Mill, an early name for Coloma—the present route of a country road along which a few old landmarks still stand. The Pleasant Grove House (SRL 703) is at the left of Green Valley Road, nine and a half

miles east of Folsom. This was a changing station for the Pony Express when it used this route in 1860–61. It contains the only original horse barn from Pony Express days still standing in California, for which it has received national landmark status. A mile and a half northwest of Rescue, where the Green Valley Road turns toward Placerville, the old Coloma Road continues north to Lotus. On the right, three-quarters of a mile from this point, stands the Gordon House, the material for which was brought around the Horn.

The Coloma Road evolved from a narrow pack trail into a well-beaten, crowded highway soon after Marshall's discovery of gold in 1848. Over it thousands of gold-seekers directed their footsteps toward Coloma. Soon after the arrival of a ship at San Francisco, the Coloma Road became thronged with men on foot or on horseback, making their way to the diggings. Mexicans with long trails of pack mules loaded with freight and miners' supplies joined the procession. Oregonians very early brought in the first wagons. A mail business developed of such magnitude that wagon loads of letters never reached their destination and had to be sent to the dead-letter office. In 1849 the Coloma Road became the route of California's first stage line, which was established by James E. Birch.

Soon all available land around Coloma was staked out in claims, and newcomers were forced to seek other locations. Thus the mining area quickly expanded in all directions, with numerous trails opening up fresh diggings and newer El Dorados for the onward-moving Argonauts.

The first, and for a long time the principal, branch of the Coloma Road turned north at New York Ravine three miles east of Mormon Island. Crossing the South Fork at Salmon Falls (at first by ferry and later, in 1853, by toll bridge), this road proceeded, as it still does (although realigned around Folsom Lake), to Centerville (modern Pilot Hill), where it branched again, one fork going through Greenwood to Georgetown. From Georgetown a road led northwest to Spanish Bar on the Middle Fork of the American River, where it crossed over into Placer County. Continuing by way of Paradise and the North Star House, this trail to Todd's Valley and Forest Hill was much traveled during the 1850s and 1860s. Another crossing farther up the Middle Fork at Volcano Bar led to Michigan Bluff, in Placer County.

Another branch road starting at Centerville took a more direct route to Forest Hill by way of Murderer's Bar, located a few miles above the confluence of the

South Fork of the American River at Marshall Gold Discovery State Historic Park, Coloma

Middle and North Forks of the American River. The present SR 49 follows this road, but instead of crossing the Middle Fork at Murderer's Bar it now proceeds directly to Auburn via Lyon's Bridge.

Crossing the South Fork at Mormon Island, still another branch of the Coloma Road paralleled the North Fork, connecting the populous river-bar camps. Along the fifteen miles of the North Fork above its confluence with the South Fork, crossings were made at Beal's, Condemned, Whiskey, Rattlesnake, and Oregon Bars.

At first crude ferries were used—ships' boats brought up from Sacramento, flimsy rafts, and sometimes even the beds of abandoned emigrant wagons. Soon, regular ferry boats, or scows, large enough to carry a wagon were constructed, only to be supplanted by rough bridges, which were usually washed away by the next winter's flood. Structures of a more substantial and permanent character ultimately replaced these first primitive ones. All, however, were built by private capital for profit. So great was the traffic to and from the mines that many fortunes were made from tolls collected by the owners of pioneer ferries and bridges.

At Whiskey and Rattlesnake Bars, wire-rope bridges were constructed in 1854, and in 1856 W. C. Lyon built the Condemned Bar bridge, later torn down when he moved farther up the river.

The first regular ferry in El Dorado County was operated at Coloma early in 1849. In February 1851 this was superseded by a bridge, also the first in the county. All along the South Fork numerous bridges were established to take the place of the ferries of an earlier date. At the old Uniontown Bridge it was not uncommon to

collect from $600 to $800 monthly during the early 1850s, and the Rock Bridge a few miles farther downstream was almost as well patronized.

Of the maze of roads and branch roads radiating from Coloma to the scores of camps that sprang up, fewer than half a dozen are maintained today: the Georgetown Road through Garden Valley (now SR 193), the Gold Hill Road to Cold Springs and Placerville, and SR 49, the Mother Lode Highway, from Placerville via Coloma and Pilot Hill to Auburn. These old roads are rich in reminders of the historic past. Monuments commemorating the importance of the Coloma Road have been placed at Sutter's Fort, Nimbus Dam, Rescue (SRL 747), and Coloma (SRL 748).

THE CARSON EMIGRANT ROAD

The main route to Coloma and the gold diggings in 1849 and the early 1850s was the Carson Emigrant Road by way of the Kit Carson Pass. John C. Frémont and a few picked men, including Kit Carson himself, were the first to cross the Sierra Nevada by a route close to this pass, in 1844, and also the first to cross the length of what is now El Dorado County. Crossing the summit at the granite ridge immediately north of Elephant's Back, they proceeded along a ridge that runs from Red Lake Peak to the South Fork of the American River near Strawberry. They forded the river and climbed the opposite wall of the canyon to the southern edge of the Georgetown Divide, down which they proceeded to the Sacramento Valley and Sutter's Fort.

In the summer of 1848 members of the Mormon Battalion, on the way to rejoin their group in Salt Lake City, were the first known Americans to use Carson Pass. In the spring of 1849, Jefferson Hunt, a captain in the Mormon Battalion and later founder of San Bernardino, brought the first wagon that way, thus opening the Carson Emigrant Road to the host of Argonauts who entered California by this route in 1849 and afterward.

Winding its way over a pass 8,573 feet high, the Carson Emigrant Road was long and difficult, but, according to Bancroft, "the immigrants . . . in order to avoid the sharper hills and deeper gulches of a possibly lower pass, had preferred to climb to an elevation of nine thousand feet to secure a road less broken. As they arrived at the pass late in summer when the snow was off the ground this would do very well."

The course of the old road through El Dorado County may be traced on modern maps by the names of campsites, once important places along the divide between the Cosumnes River and the South Fork of the American River: Tragedy Springs (on the Amador County line), Leek Spring, Camp Springs, Sly Park, Pleasant Valley, Diamond Springs, Mud Springs (now El Dorado), Shingle Springs, Clarksville, and White Rock Springs (in Sacramento County). From White Rock Springs to El Dorado, US 50 follows roughly the same route today, but from El Dorado to Silver Lake in the High Sierra no through travel goes over the old road, the Carson Emigrant Road having been superseded by the Placerville Road, now part of US 50.

Traffic over the Carson Road was enormous during the early 1850s, and a chain of wayside stations was established along its entire length between Mormon Station (later Genoa, Nevada) and Hangtown (Placerville). Every mile had its inn or hotel. Few remnants of these early taverns remain, and even the sites of many would be difficult to determine exactly.

From the main road a number of branches diverged at various points, chiefly at Diamond Springs, where the stream of emigrants turned off to Coloma by way of Hangtown and (as new diggings were discovered) to Salmon Falls, Pilot Hill, Georgetown, Kelsey's Diggings, and numerous other camps. Two main branches led to the southern mines, one by way of Grizzly Flats to Brownsville (Mendon), Indian Diggings, and Fiddletown (in Amador County), and another via Mud Springs to Logtown, Quartzburg (Nashville), Saratoga, and Drytown (in Amador County). At Clarksville still another fork of the Carson Road went to Folsom, and thence to Auburn and the river-bar camps on the North Fork of the American River. Many of these arms of the old Emigrant Road may be traveled today over good county roads, with historic reminders of the past visible on every hand.

Although the Carson Emigrant Road continued to be used for twenty years or more, increased transportation necessitated the development of easier routes. As an all-year road, the Carson Pass Road, subject to deep snows, was impassible, and a road over a lower pass became imperative. This need led to the survey and construction of the Placerville Road over Echo Summit and down the canyon of the South Fork of the American River to Hangtown.

THE PLACERVILLE ROAD

Deviations from the Carson Emigrant Road began very early. Gold-seekers, impatient to reach their destination

quickly, often took great risks in trying new routes. The most popular of these shorter trails took the so-called Johnson's Cutoff, later the Placerville Road. With the construction of Bartlett's Bridge on the South Fork of the American River near the Pacific House, this route was made passable for wagons before 1854, and a large proportion of the overland emigration was early diverted to it.

The tremendous growth of population in California during the early 1850s and a corresponding increase in overland transportation hastened the demand for improved, all-year highways to take the place of those first long and precipitous trails over the higher passes of the Sierra. After much agitation, the state Legislature in 1855 passed a bill authorizing the survey and construction of such a road, the cost of which was not to exceed $105,000. No appropriation was made for the work, however, and the expense of preliminary surveys had to be met by private subscription.

Keeping to the southern exposures of the ridges and canyons, and avoiding, as much as possible, the higher altitudes in order to chart a route that could be kept open throughout the winter, Surveyor General H. S. Marlette and his assistant, Sherman Day, finally recommended the part of the Johnson's Cutoff route that followed the canyon of the South Fork of the American River as far as Echo Summit and from there through Luther's Pass, Hope Valley, and the canyon of the West Carson River to the state line. This path avoided the steep eastern declivity over the western summit of the Sierra negotiated by the Carson and Johnson routes.

The Placerville Road was actually being used by some emigrants, and toll companies had been constructing it piece by piece when in 1858 it became the joint project of El Dorado, Sacramento, and Yolo Counties, which together appropriated $50,000 for construction. Before the road was graded or leveled, J. B. Crandall's Pioneer Stage Company began to operate between Placerville and Genoa, Nevada, making the trip in twenty-four hours. Meanwhile, George Chorpenning had obtained a government contract to carry the weekly mails between Placerville and Salt Lake City, with an annual stipend of $136,000, and the first overland mail via this central route arrived in California at 11 P.M. on July 19, 1858. With this demonstration it was proved once and for all that "a highway over the 'terrible' Sierra was both possible and practicable."

State and county governments, however, continued to be lethargic. Failing to make appropriations for further improvements or maintenance of the road, the whole enterprise, so nicely started in 1858, would have collapsed, and the Placerville Road would soon have become impassable but for the timely discovery of the rich silver deposits of the Comstock Lode in Nevada. Private companies immediately obtained charters to establish toll roads, and immense sums were expended on the four or five detours routed by these new companies. So great was the traffic over the Placerville turnpikes that the promoters not only cleared all expenses but made vast fortunes from the toll collections.

During the years 1859 to 1866, this "grand artery of travel" witnessed a great era of staging and freighting by horse-drawn vehicles. By day continuous streams of one-to-eight-span teams moved in both directions, while at night from four to six Concord coaches rumbled in and out of Placerville loaded with bullion, passengers, and mail. Mule trains, filling the canyons with the music of their bells; cumbersome freight schooners, rumbling over the rough roads; aristocratic Concord coaches, rattling at breakneck speed over the narrow, tortuous thread of road; Pony Express riders, filling the night with the clop of galloping hooves—all passed over this great thoroughfare through country once traversed only by Indians.

An actual check made of this overland commerce as it passed by Swan's tollhouse during three months in 1864 revealed that 6,667 foot travelers, 833 travelers on horseback, 3,164 stage passengers, 5,000 pack animals, 2,564 teams, and 4,649 head of cattle had gone that way. During the years 1864 and 1865, 320 tons of freight passed through Placerville daily, while the combined freight charges of 1863 could not have been less than $12 million. William H. Brewer, who camped at Slippery Ford in August 1863, says that 5,000 teams were then employed steadily in the Virginia City trade. Mark Twain's humorous version of Horace Greeley's stage ride over the old Placerville road in the summer of 1859 is one of the choice passages of *Roughing It*.

LANDMARKS OF THE STAGECOACH TRAIL

Placerville Road is now US 50 and has been converted to freeway, thus missing most of the historic sites. Many years ago, rangers of the El Dorado National Forest placed a chain of "Pioneer Days" markers designating the sites of the old landmarks, but most of these signs have disappeared as a result of vandalism or the ravages of time. A number of the old stone mileposts designating the distance from Placerville can still be found along the parallel road through Camino and Pollock

Pines. During the centennial of the Pony Express in 1960, the state of California placed markers at the sites of the remount stations along the route. These markers indicated that US 50 actually touches and uses bits of the older road from Placerville to Meyers at the southern end of Lake Tahoe and beyond.

Leaving Placerville going east, one may take the road through Smith Flat, a former mining town, before joining US 50. The old Smith Flat House, built in 1852, still stands by the roadside. The site of the Three Mile House, later known as the Home Ranch and eventually one of 93 mile-marker houses on this road, marks the beginning of the actual ascent of the high mountains.

In Cedar Grove is the site of the original Sportsman's Hall (SRL 704), also known as Twelve Mile House. The plaque notes that it was both a stage stop and "a relay station of the Central Overland Pony Express. Here, at 4:40 A.M., April 4, 1860, pony rider William (Sam) Hamilton rode in from Placerville and handed the express mail to Warren Upson, who two minutes later sped on his way eastward." The present building is of a later date. In the mid-1860s stable room for 500 horses was maintained here.

A stone monument, placed by the Native Sons and Native Daughters of the Golden West in honor of the pioneer officers of the law, is at Bullion Bend high above the great canyon of the South Fork of the American River. This is now on a bypassed stretch of road below the highway and about a mile beyond Pollock Pines. At this point two coaches of the Pioneer Stage Line running between Virginia City and Sacramento were held up and robbed by a gang of fourteen men on the night of June 30, 1869. Eight sacks of bullion and a money chest were taken. An attempt was made to capture the bandits, resulting in an encounter at the Somerset House (in the southern part of El Dorado County) in which one deputy sheriff, Joseph Staples, lost his life, and another, George C. Ranney, was badly wounded. Later, one of the bandits, Thomas Poole, was captured and executed at Placerville.

Near here the first glimpse is had of the South Fork of the American River, a narrow silver ribbon gleaming amid the pines more than a thousand feet below, while far to the east Pyramid Peak stands silhouetted against the sky. Here the road begins to drop slowly into the canyon, passing Fresh Pond and the Pacific Ranger Station before reaching the Pacific House one mile beyond Fresh Pond. Built in 1859, the original hostelry at this site housed many a famous wanderer in the early days of statehood. Here Horace Greeley, Thomas Starr

King, and Mark Twain, among others, stopped on their way to Sacramento over the old emigrant trail.

Continuing east along US 50 and its parallel roads, one will find the site of Moore's Station (SRL 705), where the highway follows the north bank of the stream for several miles. The Sugar Loaf House (SRL 706) is a mile west of Kyburz, from which trails into the Silver Lake country lead into the magnificent scenic highlands of the region. One of the most interesting points along the Placerville Road is reached at Strawberry Flat, to the right of which the perpendicular walls of Lover's Leap rise more than 1,000 feet above the floor of the little valley. To the left the rocky summit of Pyramid Peak towers 4,000 feet above the river, with Horsetail Falls gleaming white against the gray and barren crags far up the mountainside.

In a beautiful Sierra meadow, surrounded by river and canyon and meadow, is Strawberry Lodge, once a popular teamsters' stopover. The original Strawberry Valley House (SRL 707) has been replaced by a newer building, itself recently renovated, which stands above the older site, above the river and closer to the road. An annual profusion of wild strawberries appears here.

Turning up the canyon toward Echo Summit, the highway passes by or near several more historic sites. Toll House Flat, with modern houses among the pines and meadows, is the site of George Swan's Upper Toll House. Next the traveler comes to the sites of the Snow Slide House of pioneer days and of Phillips Station, where modern rest-stop facilities are located. Audrain Station is next, then the beginning of the old Hawley Grade into Alpine County, over Luther Pass, used from 1859 to 1861. Hawley Grade is now a National Historic Trail for hiking. Finally, at 7,382 feet, the road reaches Echo Summit, where in pioneer days the Sixty Mile House was located. Here a magnificent panoramic view may be had of Lake Valley, the Upper Truckee River, the southern end of Lake Tahoe, and the barren mountains of Nevada on the horizon beyond.

From Echo Summit the highway drops quickly to the floor of Lake Valley. The road from Woodfords (in Alpine County) joins US 50 near Meyers, located on the site of Yank's Station (SRL 708). Following around the southern end of Lake Tahoe, the old Placerville Road continued on into Nevada by one of two routes, the Carson Valley route via Daggett Pass, and the later road along the eastern side of the lake by way of the old Glenbrook station in Nevada. Friday's Station, the easternmost remount station of the California division of the Pony Express (SRL 728), lay about three-quarters of a mile east of the California-Nevada state line, although the landmark site is on the west side of the line on US 50. In October, 1861, the Pony Express gave way to the transcontinental telegraph; the extraordinary enterprise acknowledged by the markers on the Placerville Road lasted just eighteen months.

RIVER BARS

In the summer of 1848, after Marshall's gold discovery, other discoveries followed, and soon mining was being carried on along the river bars above and below Coloma. Prospectors also pushed out across the Georgetown Divide to the Middle Fork of the American River, where many stopped to pan. By 1849, thousands of newcomers were working every foot of the Middle and South Forks of the American River, as well as the various branches of the Cosumnes River.

Practically nothing remains today to mark the exact site of these old river camps. Some are inundated by Folsom Lake. The bars themselves have changed location, and all of the buildings have disappeared. In El Dorado County there were scores of such camps, for the Middle Fork of the American River was generally considered to be the richest river-mining region in California. At least 10,000 men worked on this fork during the late summer and autumn of 1849, extracting something like ten million dollars worth of gold dust from the river sands.

Along the junction of the North and South Forks on the El Dorado side of the river were the following bars: Condemned, Long, Granite, Whiskey, and Oregon. East of the confluence of the North and Middle Forks were numerous other bars: Louisiana, New York, Murderer's, Wild Cat, Willow, Hoosier, Green Mountain, Maine, Poverty, Spanish, Ford's, Volcano, Big, Rocky, Sandy, Grey Eagle, Yankee Slide, Eureka, Boston, and Alabama. About three miles up the Middle Fork from its junction with the North Fork, Murderer's Bar in the spring of 1849 was the scene of the massacre of five miners by Indians in revenge for the murder of some Indians there by these very men several days before. Spanish Bar, mined as early as 1848 by men who came from Coloma, was one of several bars that produced more than a million dollars worth of gold.

Among the hundreds of claims along the South Fork were the following bars: Dutch, Kanaka, Red, Stony, Ledge, Missouri, Michigan, and Chili. Along the Cosumnes River and its branches were a dozen or more river camps, among them Big Bar, Michigan Bar, Diving Bell Bar, Wisconsin Bar, Nashville Bar, Yeomet Bar, Pittsburg Bar, and Buck's Bar.

PLACERVILLE

Placerville (SRL 475), at first known as Old Dry Diggins, and then as Hangtown, was founded in 1848. James Marshall states that in the summer of that year he had located the Old Dry Diggins. Usually, however, this discovery has been credited to William Daylor, owner of a ranch on the Cosumnes River not far from New Helvetia (Sacramento). Daylor did pan for gold on Hangtown Creek during that spring, in company with Perry McCoon and Jared Sheldon. With the help of a number of Indians, they took out from one small ravine, "not more than a hundred yards long by four feet wide and two or three feet deep," as much as $17,000 in one week's time. Governor R. B. Mason, who had the spot pointed out to him that July, included it in his report to the federal government and mentioned Daylor and McCoon as the men who had worked it.

The Old Dry Diggins had become quite a camp by the autumn of 1848. At first it was practically free from crime, but the motley society that began pouring in by 1849 brought with it "the criminal element of all nations." When robberies and murders became prevalent without an organized government, there was a popular reaction—a phenomenon found elsewhere in the state at this time. By the fall of 1849, three men had been flogged and hanged, thus giving rise to the name of Hangtown. The site of one of these hangman's trees is at 305 Main Street (SRL 141). By 1850, Hangtown had become a well-ordered community, and in May 1854 the town was incorporated under the name of Placerville.

The dry diggings on Hangtown Creek fluctuated with the seasons—in winter there was "water and prosperity," in summer "dullness and departures." But with the building of the South Fork Ditch, prosperity increased, and the place grew to be one of the leading mining centers of the county and one of the most populous of all the early mining camps. Its voting population in 1854 was the third largest in the state, and in 1857 it was made the county seat. As early as 1856, however, a decline had begun, with two severe fires and a diminution of activity in the nearby gold fields. A revival followed the discovery of the fabulously rich Comstock Lode in Nevada and the subsequent building of the Placerville Road. From 1859 until the building of the Central Pacific Railroad, Placerville witnessed an even greater period of activity, marked by the construction of

permanent church buildings, an academy, hotels, and business houses. Placerville was a relay station of the Central Overland Pony Express from April 4, 1860, to June 30, 1861; on July 1, 1861, it became the western terminus of the route, and remained so until the Pony Express ran its final course on October 26, 1861. A marker (SRL 701) in honor of this brief episode of Western history is located at Main and Sacramento Streets.

Much of the charm of present-day Placerville comes from its streets conforming to the topography. Following the courses of the streams and gulches and the contours of the surrounding hills, the earliest settlers pitched their tents or built their first log cabins along these meandering paths. Later the builders of the permanent town were content to emulate the early example set them. As the traditional cow paths set the pattern for the streets of Boston, so the pack-mule trails of the miners to the diggings are responsible for the intriguing course of Placerville's Main Street along Hangtown Creek, as well as for the direction of the side streets and alleyways that penetrate the ravines and steep hillsides, many now covered with old-fashioned homes and shaded gardens.

Placerville's central area was swept by fire in 1856, but the brick and greenstone John Fountain (or Nuss) Building at 524 Main Street, put up four years before, survived the fire and still stands today. It is now the Fountain-Tollman City Museum, operated by the El Dorado County Historical Society. Among its interesting collections is material from the city's once-thriving Chinese community, long since dispersed. The nearby Placerville Hardware Store was constructed after the 1856 fire and is one of the oldest continuously operating hardware businesses in California. The old City Hall at 487 Main Street was originally built in 1860 as the house for Confidence Engine Company No. 1, in the days of volunteer fire companies. It became Placerville's seat of government in 1902. Next door, at 489 Main Street, a plaque placed by the Native Daughters of the Golden West on a two-story balconied structure honors "Emigrant Jane [Shrovers Johnson, who] drove a band of horses across the plains and from the proceeds of that sale erected this building in 1861." A fire tower (1898) at the plaza in the center of Main Street still carries alarms to the community.

At 300 Main Street is the Cary House, built in 1857. It was a stage stop for the Wells Fargo and Pioneer Lines. Mark Twain was one of its early guests, as was Horace Greeley, who stayed there in 1859 on his overland journey to San Francisco in the interest of a

El Dorado County Court House, Placerville

transcontinental railway. It is reported that he addressed the town's residents from the veranda (no longer in existence). In the Comstock silver bonanza, Wells Fargo passed $90 million in bullion through this office alone. For many years known as the Raffles Hotel, it has been considerably remodeled and once again receives guests to the Cary House.

Among other residents of early Placerville were the merchants Mark Hopkins and Collis P. Huntington, two of the "Big Four" entrepreneurs who brought the first railroad to California (the other two being Charles Crocker and Leland Stanford); Philip Armour, a Placerville ditching contractor who became the meatpacking king of Chicago; and the poet and educator Edwin Markham, who also lived briefly in Coloma. John M. Studebaker, a wheelwright and blacksmith, worked from 1853 to 1858 in a shop (SRL 142) at 543 Main Street, where he made wheelbarrows for the miners and amassed the capital for the factory that he later started with his brothers in South Bend, Indiana. There, instead of wheelbarrows, they manufactured wagons and buggies. With the advent of the automobile, the Studebakers became distributors of the car that they later brought out and manufactured under their own name. In the decade of the 1900s, the elderly J. M. Studebaker revisited Placerville, the scene of his initial success, keeping a promise made when he left that he would return in fifty years. A little group of pioneers banqueted with him on this occasion.

In 1986, the Native Sons of the Golden West marked the Bee-Bennett Mansion at 643 Bee Street as a historic site. Now the Elks Hall, it was built in 1853 by Colonel Frederick A. Bee, who founded the Bee Telegraph Company, one of the first telegraph companies in California and a parent of Western Union. For many years after 1889, Judge Marcus Bennett and his family lived in the remodeled mansion.

The old Hangtown bell, used in the early days to call out the vigilantes as well as for fire alarms, has been removed from the plaza where it stood for many years and is now at the park on Bedford Avenue.

At the intersection of Main Street and Cedar Ravine stands the Druid Monument, commemorating the organization in 1859 of the first Grove of the Ancient Order of Druids to be established west of the Rocky Mountains.

Placerville's historic churches began with the building of the Methodist church in 1851, which has been moved to Thompson Way near Cedar Ravine and reconstructed as a pioneer memorial (SRL 767). The Episcopal Church of Our Savior at Coloma and Conrad Streets dates from 1865. It is architecturally interesting for its vaulted ceiling, an inverted clipper ship frame with joints and bracing following the shipbuilding practices of the day; Mother Lode churches often employed former shipwrights from San Francisco.

The Gold Bug Mine is a unique walk-through museum owned and operated by the city of Placerville. On Bedford Avenue about a mile from the center of town, the mine is part of a park, and visitors can go through its shafts and tunnels and see just how a mine looks. A huge stamping mill stands across from the mine entrance. The El Dorado County Historical Museum is located on the west side of town at the County Fairgrounds on Placerville Drive.

PLACERVILLE'S NEIGHBORS

Almost the entire region around Placerville for miles in all directions was very rich in gold, particularly along the ravines and in the depressions of the hills. Yields here averaged an ounce per day per man during the early days of the Gold Rush. Several ancient auriferous (gold-bearing) river channels run throughout the Mother Lode. These drained the region in prehistoric times and added to the wealth of later streams, creating immense deposits of gold. Placerville was always the supply center for this part of the Mother Lode, and dozens of little camps appeared in its neighborhood.

One of the richest spots in the vicinity was Diamond Springs (SRL 487), three miles south of Placerville. It was named for the crystal-clear springs on the north side of Main Street on what is now mined-out ground. A camp on the old Carson Emigrant Trail and then for a time on the later Placerville Road, Diamond Springs grew rapidly as a mining center. The little town was once noted for its fine sandstone buildings, a few of which have survived the devastating fires that have swept it.

Weber Creek bears many signs of early mining operations. It was named for Captain Charles M. Weber, founder of Stockton. Weber mined along this stream in the spring of 1848, at about the same time that William Daylor discovered the rich dry diggings on Hangtown Creek. Antonio María Suñol, owner of Rancho El Valle de San José (in Alameda County), was also mining farther downstream at this time. Weber had organized the Stockton Mining Company at Tuleburg (soon to be renamed Stockton) and was working the placers at Weber Creek, assisted by a large number of Indians. A store was established on the creek by Weber and his company in the summer of 1848, chiefly as a place where goods attractive to the Indians could be exchanged for the gold they dug. The Stockton Company was disbanded in September 1848, Weber having decided to give his attention wholly to the building up of the city of Stockton. The Weber trading post, however, continued to be a center for miners, and other camps soon grew up around it. Weberville, long vanished, was two miles southwest of Placerville.

Coon Hollow, about a mile south of Placerville, was one of the most prosperous of the early camps, with no less than $25 million in gold having been mined there from an area five acres in extent, the property of the Excelsior Mine. Other productive mines were on the Placerville side of the same ridge, at Spanish Hill and Tennessee Hill.

Cold Springs, beyond the confluence of Hangtown and Weber Creeks about five miles northwest of Placerville, was one of the liveliest of the early mining camps of El Dorado County. During its short heyday it had a population of 3,000 and enjoyed a direct stage connection with Sacramento as well as with Coloma and Placerville. From the fall of 1852 to the spring of 1853 Leland Stanford, with his partner, N. T. Smith, kept a store at Cold Springs, but as business began to decline, they moved to Michigan Bluff in Placer County. As mining activities slackened in the vicinity and no new locations were found, the miners gradually left for other fields. Stores had to close, the stage took another route, and before long the camp was left isolated and deserted on an unfrequented road. The name persists today in Cold Springs Road, and the grass-grown cemetery on the hill is the only remnant of the town.

On the summit of Gold Hill north of the site of Cold Springs and seven miles northwest of Placerville, ruins of the old town of Gold Hill may be seen at the crossroads. The roofless walls of a sandstone building bearing the date 1859 mark the site of this one time mining camp. The Wakamatsu Tea and Silk Farm was a colony of two dozen or so Japanese, the first to come to America, who settled here in 1869 under the leadership of a Dutchman, John Henry Schnell, who had married a Japanese woman. Japanese agricultural methods and crops had no success, and the colony broke up after the death of its leader two years later. The site (SRL 815) is about where Gold Hill and Cold Springs Roads meet. The area today is a flourishing region of orchards and gardens.

EL DORADO

Mud Springs, later known as El Dorado (SRL 486), was an important camp on the old Carson Emigrant Trail, subsequently becoming a mining center and crossroads station for freight and stage lines. It was a remount station of the Pony Express (SRL 700) in 1860–61. The name Mud Springs was bestowed on the camp because the ground around the springs where the emigrants watered their stock was always muddy—a name applied likewise to a number of other old California campsites. This was changed to El Dorado when the town was incorporated during the height of the gold fever. At that time the population was counted in the thousands, and the place was by all accounts thriving. By 1930 a traveler described El Dorado as "little more than a wide place in the road . . . ruined buildings, roofless, with gaping windows and doors half concealed by rank vegetation." A fire in 1923 had demolished most of what remained of the town; Nathan Rhine's store, built in the mid-nineteenth century, was repaired and still stands.

With El Dorado as its center, a rich placer-mining district spread out in 1849 and 1850 to include new diggings at Loafer's Hollow, Deadman's Hollow, Slate Creek, Empire Ravine, Dry Creek, and Missouri Flat. The last place, about one mile to the north, was a camp of some importance during the 1850s. To the north and south of El Dorado, several rich Mother Lode quartz leads were also uncovered, Logtown being a particularly active area around 1851.

Continuing south from El Dorado two miles on Union Mine Road, one passes the site of King's Store on the North Fork of the Cosumnes River, an important trading station in the early days.

About two miles farther is Nashville, originally called Quartzburg, one of the earliest quartz-mining districts in the state. Here the first stamp mill, brought around the Horn from Cincinnati, was used at the old Tennessee Mine, later called the Nashville. The town of Quartzburg was established on the site of an Indian camping ground, and a large rancheria still existed there when the first miners arrived. Less than a mile south of Nashville and one mile north of the forks of the Cosumnes River is a flat, east of SR 49 and across the North Fork. Here one of the eighteen unratified Indian treaties with the United States of America was drawn up and signed by O. M. Wozencraft, U.S. Indian agent, and representatives of the Cu-lu, the Yas-si, the Loc-lum-ne, and the Wo-pum-nes tribes, on September 18, 1851.

SHINGLE SPRINGS AND CLARKSVILLE

Several refreshing springs on the overland Emigrant Road and a shingle mill built in 1849 gave Shingle Springs (SRL 456) its name. A well-made building of native stone, once the Phelps Store, survives from the 1880s, its roof and doorways gone, and a sturdy locust tree growing up through its foundations. Half a mile west of Clarksville on the old Clarksville–White Rock Emigrant Road was Mormon Tavern (SRL 699), first opened in 1849 and a Pony Express stop in 1860–61.

LATROBE

Latrobe, named in honor of Benjamin H. Latrobe, the civil engineer who constructed the Thomas Viaduct over the Patapsco River for the Baltimore and Ohio Railroad in the 1830s, was laid out in the southwestern part of the county in 1864 as the terminus of the Placerville–Sacramento Valley Railroad. The Odd Fellows Hall is one of the old buildings still standing in this farming community.

PLEASANT VALLEY

Pleasant Valley, ten miles southeast of Placerville, was named by a group of Mormons who camped there en route to Salt Lake City in the summer of 1848. At the northern end of the valley a large corral was built for some of the cattle, and a second one was placed on the south fork of Weber Creek, one-half mile farther north. Gold was discovered while the pilgrims were at this spot, but even gold could not detain them from the real purpose of their journey, and after a three weeks'

rest they resumed their march up the divide and over the Sierra Nevada.

When some of these same Mormons returned to California in 1849, news of their discovery at Pleasant Valley the year before spread quickly, and many miners were soon panning out the yellow dust in the vicinity of the corrals, making an average of eight dollars a day. By July hundreds of Argonauts were pouring into California over what would later be called the Carson Emigrant Trail. Coming by way of Stonebreaker Hill, some of these wayfarers stayed on at Pleasant Valley. Several camps of rude tents and cabins sprang up: Iowaville, on the low divide between the forks of Weber Creek; Dogtown, at the first of the Mormon corrals; and Newtown, one-half mile southwest of Dogtown. With the building of ditches to carry water to the mines, Newtown grew rapidly. Later on, hydraulic operations were carried on there, but in 1872 the town was destroyed by fire. One old stone store marks the site of this settlement, on the Newtown Road northwest of Pleasant Valley.

With the revival of quartz mining at Grizzly Flats in the 1880s, Pleasant Valley took on new life; Tiger Lily, Hanks Exchange, and Cook's were three wayside stations on the road between Diamond Springs and Pleasant Valley.

OLD CAMPS ON THE UPPER COSUMNES

Grizzly Flats is located twenty-seven miles southeast of Placerville in a wild and rugged region on the ridge between the North and Middle Forks of the Cosumnes River. A company of miners who camped here in the fall of 1850 gave the place its name: while preparing their evening meal over a glowing campfire, the young men were surprised by the visit of a large grizzly bear attracted by the savory odors of the coffee pot and the frying pan.

Extensive placers were worked for miles around Grizzly Flats during the spring of 1851, and by 1852 the town had grown to such an extent that it polled 600 votes. Hydraulic mining here was of some importance during the 1870s, and a number of quartz mines were also developed, among them the Eagle, the Steely, and the very rich Mount Pleasant. Lumbering, still an important industry in this neighborhood, had its beginning in 1856, when sawmills were first built there.

Grizzly Flats today has only a few dozen inhabitants. Several wooden buildings date back to more prosperous days, and indelible scars of old mines mark the surrounding landscape.

Brownsville, Indian Diggins, Fair Play, Henry's Diggings, and Coyoteville were also located in the Cosumnes River region, where hydraulic mining was extensively carried out. Brownsville was renamed Mendon when a post office was established (there being another Brownsville, in Yuba County), but its original name was restored after the post office was discontinued. Brownsville is distinguished as the site of the rich Volcano Claim, discovered by Henry Brown and his companions, which is said to have produced hundreds of thousands of dollars worth of gold up to the year 1867.

Crossing the South Fork of the Cosumnes River from Fiddletown (in Amador County) in 1849, a party of prospectors located near an old Indian village in Telegraph Gulch. A lively camp, known as Indian Diggins by 1855, and three stage lines connected the mines with the outside world. The rich gravel beds of the region were gradually worked out by tunneling and hydraulic processes, fires swept the town in 1857 and 1860, and by 1890 only a hundred people remained in the place. Today it is a ghost town, marked only by an old cemetery and an abandoned farm. The nearest settlement is Omo Ranch, whose school preserves the name of Indian Diggins.

Fair Play, an old camp five miles northwest of Indian Diggins, was described as late as 1890 as "a neat little village prettily situated on a sort of table-land shelving from the slope of a large mountain to the southeast." Since the late 1970s, Fair Play has been the center of a flourishing wine-producing area, with no less than eight wineries in operation. The present Fair Play store is about a mile and a half from the original site of the town.

Coyoteville, south of Fair Play on Cedar Creek, received its name from the peculiar type of mining employed there, known as drift mining or coyoteing. Theodore Hittell explains the origins of the word "coyoteing" thus:

> Each miner had his separate hole, in which he delved. The men, while at work, were entirely out of sight of a person looking over the bar, flat, or slope in which they were operating, but the approach of night or any alarm or unusual noise would cause them to pop out of their holes; and their supposed resemblance under such circumstances to the Californian animal corresponding with the prairie wolf of the Mississippi states caused these pits, shafts, or tunnels to be called coyote-holes and the character of mining done in them coyote-mining. . . . While it was in vogue, many places were completely honeycombed by so-called coyote-holes.

FOLSOM LAKE'S BURIED CAMPS

When Folsom Dam, part of the Central Valley Project, was completed in 1955, the impounded waters of the American River rose and flooded an area extending into El Dorado County. Among the old towns now beneath the water are Negro Hill (SRL 570), a settlement of black miners; Chile Hill, Condemned Bar (SRL 572), Long Bar, and Salmon Falls (SRL 571). State markers are in Folsom Lake State Recreation Area, along with a marker for Mormon Island (SRL 569), on Green Valley Road just east of the El Dorado County line. Across the road is Mormon Island Memorial Cemetery, to which the remains of many pioneers were moved before their original resting places were flooded.

PILOT HILL

Standing up boldly above a wide expanse of hills and forested ravines, Pilot Hill's conical promontory has long been a landmark. John C. Frémont and his men passed this way when, early in March 1844, they followed the well-defined Indian trails leading out of the High Sierra and down over the foothills into the Sacramento Valley.

Mining first began in the vicinity of Pilot Hill in the summer of 1849. During the following winter scores of prospectors from the river bars and higher mountains congregated at this point, and a town bearing the name of Pilot Hill grew up near the northern base of the mountain. Not far away, Centerville and Pittsfield developed simultaneously, but the three camps soon consolidated under the name of Centerville, a title that clung to the place even after the establishment of a post office officially designated Pilot Hill. The small community of today has been bypassed by a realignment of SR 49, and the few businesses have relocated on the new road. On the old highway, now designated Pedro Hill Road, a decrepit hotel, a relic of 1854, stands among a handful of old cottages and newer homes. The hotel, now cut down to one story, long served as post office, store, and service station. On the slope above the old highway one mile east of Pilot Hill is a small pioneer cemetery, where many graves of the 1850s lie beneath the locust trees.

A quarter of a mile north of the Pilot Hill Hotel stands a grand old relic of the early 1860s, the Bayley House. It was built by Alcandor A. Bayley, a native of Vermont, who came to California in 1849. From 1851 to 1861 Bayley owned the Oak Valley House at Pilot Hill.

After it was destroyed by fire, he built the large three-story brick structure still known by his name. Believing that the overland railroad would pass that way, Bayley expended over $20,000 in the construction of a splendid hostelry. But the dreams he cherished at the grand opening in 1862 never materialized. Abandoned for many years, the Bayley House is now owned by developers who have plans for its restoration. The first grange in California, Pilot Hill Grange No. 1, was organized in 1870 on the Bayley property. A monument (SRL 551) stands at the site of the old Grange Hall.

LOTUS

Uniontown, one and a half miles down the river from Coloma, has had a succession of names. In 1849, it was called Marshall, after James W. Marshall; in 1850 the name was changed to Uniontown, in honor of California's admission to the Union; finally, with the establishment of a post office, the town was assigned the exotic and poetic designation of Lotus, its former name having been preempted by Uniontown (now Arcata) in Humboldt County. Gudde says that "the first postmaster, George E. Gallaner, suggested the name because, in his opinion, the inhabitants were as easygoing as the lotus-eaters in the *Odyssey*." Lotus it remains today.

In the 1850s, when Uniontown's population was over two thousand, Adam Lohry built a sturdy brick store with iron doors and a fine old brick mansion next to it. With its pleasant garden, this is a charming Gold Rush relic.

KELSEY

The mining area rapidly grew outward from Coloma, soon reaching across the river and up into the higher ridges. Among other rich claims was Kelsey's Diggings, located by Benjamin Kelsey, brother of Andrew Kelsey, for whom Kelseyville in Lake County was named. The two brothers had come overland with the Bidwell-Bartleson party in 1841, and early in 1848 Benjamin had come to this part of El Dorado County, discovering the diggings that took his name. Within a year the place had become a large camp, its prosperity continuing into the 1850s.

Kelsey was the last home of gold discoverer James Marshall, whose declining years were on the whole unhappy and full of disappointment. His blacksmith shop (SRL 319), built in 1872, was restored and carefully preserved inside the walls of a little fireproof building con-

structed by the state in 1921. A short distance up the road is the site of the Union Hotel, where Marshall's body was laid out for public viewing after he died at his home in 1885. On the hill is the cemetery, with many pioneer graves. The first slate quarries in the state, working a large deposit of blue-black slate, of which almost the entire mountain seems to be composed, operated there from the 1890s to 1915.

GREENWOOD

John Greenwood, an old trapper, established a trading post in Long Valley late in 1848. Soon other stores were built, and in 1850 the new town was christened Lewisville after the first white child born there. When the town attained the dignity of a post office, the name was changed to Greenwood. The town had social advantages not enjoyed by many of its neighbors, notably a well-patronized community theater. In the cemetery a small slab of stone bearing the initials J. A. S. and the date January 24, 1863, marks the grave of John A. Stone, a pioneer songwriter of the 1850s, who lived, sang, and died at Greenwood.

Situated in the midst of an old orchard community, Greenwood is still a trading center for a township of several hundred people. The historical marker (SRL 521) in the center of town is surmounted by a fire bell.

GEORGETOWN

The first mining operations near Georgetown (SRL 484) were carried on along Oregon Creek and Hudson's Gulch by a party of Oregonians in 1849. A company of sailors under the leadership of George Phipps followed, and in 1850 motley camps of tents and shanties grew up along the creek at the foot of what is now Main Street. Known first as Growlersburg, it was destroyed by fire, and the old site was deserted in 1852 for the present location on the hill. The name, too, was changed to Georgetown in honor of its nautical founder. To keep further fire damage at a minimum, the new town had unusually wide streets: Main Street is a hundred feet across, and side streets sixty feet wide are not uncommon.

Georgetown rivaled Placerville in the number and quality of its early social and cultural institutions. By 1855 it included in its list of attractions a school, a church, a theater, a town hall, a Sons of Temperance Hall, a Masonic Hall, and three hotels, as well as many stores. The cultural advantages of the little town, the beauty of its hill setting among the pines, oaks, and cedars of the Georgetown Divide, and the mild and tonic air of its 2,650-foot elevation won for it the title "Pride of the Mountains."

Along Georgetown's broad Main Street, beneath a double row of giant locust trees, stand stores with fronts of brick and stone. The former U.S. Armory, constructed in 1862, is especially attractive. It is now a commercial office. The Wells Fargo office dates from 1852. The imposing Georgetown Hotel is the third structure of that name on that site since 1856; the present building dates from 1896. The Shannon Knox residence, built in 1864 and marked with an E Clampus Vitus plaque, is now a handsome group of offices. The Odd Fellows Hall stands opposite.

The gardens and orchards of Georgetown were remarkable for their variety of flowers, shrubs, and fruits, all grown from stock obtained from a pioneer nursery established by a Scotsman in the 1860s. Scotch broom from the same nursery has grown wild all over the hills, glorifying the countryside each spring with golden blooms.

Seam mines, a formation of slate interspersed with quartz seams largely decomposed and varying in thickness from that of a knife blade to several feet, are characteristic of the Georgetown district. The Nagler or French Claim at Greenwood Valley is a seam mine that produced more than $4 million from 1872 to 1885. There are other seam mines at Georgia Slide, two miles northwest of Georgetown. Here an open perpendicular bank of slate rock was found with sheets of gold-bearing quartz coursing through it. George Slide, however, dates back to 1849, when a group of miners from Georgia first worked the spot for its placer gold. The camp was called Georgia Flat at first, but a big mountain slide occasioned the change in name. For years it was a wild, rough place with no outside communication except by pack trail. A few shells of houses mark the former camp at the end of Georgia Slide Road.

The old gravel beds of Kentucky Flat, six miles northeast of Georgetown, and of Volcanoville, three miles northwest of Kentucky Flat, once made production records. Among the many old hill camps dating back to 1851 and 1852 were Mameluke Hill, Bottle Hill, Cement Hill, and Jones Hill.

Johntown, five miles south of Georgetown, was named after a sailor who discovered its gold-bearing deposits. Later, when it became more profitable to raise vegetables there than to mine, the name was changed to Garden Valley. An old store stands there. The Empire

and Manhattan creeks join at this point to form Johntown Creek. Below their confluence miners have taken out between two and three million dollars in gold.

LAKE TAHOE

One of California's favorite resorts for more than a century has been Lake Tahoe, a fuller history of which is recorded in the Placer County chapter. First officially named Lake Bigler, after the governor of the state in 1852, the present name was introduced about the time of the Civil War. In 1859, the first lakefront hotel was built near what are now Lakeview and Lily Avenues in South Lake Tahoe. By all accounts, this was not a luxurious or even a comfortable resort: J. Ross Browne, visiting Lake House in the early 1860s, reported that its eight rooms sometimes held as many as 300 guests a night. When the hotel burned in 1865, it was not rebuilt. In the early twentieth century, as resort hotels began to spread across California, the Al Tahoe Hotel was constructed close to the site of the old Lake House. The hotel closed in 1968, but some of its cottages still stand.

California's first state highway was built in El Dorado County, connecting Placerville with Lake Tahoe in 1896. Paved road, however, had to wait for several decades.

For many years, well-to-do families maintained summer lodges along the shore of Lake Tahoe, traditionally open between Memorial Day and Labor Day. A magnificent example of this rustic splendor is to be seen at the Tallac estate, now maintained by the U.S. Forest Service. The visitor center is on SR 89 about a mile north and west of Camp Richardson. The summer homes of the Heller, McGonagle, and Pope families may be visited (between Memorial Day and Labor Day) in the pine forest by the water, a rare open space on the lakeshore. The grounds are open to the public on a year-round basis. The Tallac estate was once the site of a beautiful hotel put up by Elias J. ("Lucky") Baldwin, a San Francisco–based financier who also had extensive interests in Los Angeles County. The hotel was razed in 1927 and some of the area is now a public picnic area.

Farther north, a distinctive private home stands on the shore of Emerald Bay in the state park of that name. Vikingsholm was built in Scandinavian style in 1928 for Mrs. Laura Knight. A strikingly handsome building that is open to the public during the summer, Vikingsholm can be reached by trail from the highway above or by boat. Still farther north on SR 89 is the

Ehrman Mansion, now part of Sugar Pine Point State Park; this beautifully preserved home was built in the Queen Anne style greatly admired around 1900. There are many newer private estates and large houses on the shore of Lake Tahoe today, on both the California and the Nevada sides.

Since World War II, the popularity of winter sports and the casinos of Nevada have brought increasing numbers of people to live permanently along the south shore, and in 1965 the town of South Lake Tahoe was incorporated. The Lake Tahoe Historical Society Museum at 3058 Highway 50 displays relics from the transportation, lumbering, and resort and entertainment life of Lake Tahoe. A log cabin from the 1930s and the original 1859 Osgood Toll House have been relocated to the museum complex.

Fresno County

Fresno County was organized in 1856 from Mariposa, Merced, and Tulare Counties. On eight subsequent occasions its boundaries were altered, the last time in 1903. Fresno is Spanish for "ash tree" and was first applied to the Fresno River, often spelled "Frezno" on early maps. Millerton was the first county seat; Fresno became the county seat in 1874.

EL RÍO DE LOS SANTOS REYES (KINGS RIVER)

The Kings River rises in the High Sierra and flows through Fresno, Tulare, and Kings Counties, forming the boundary between Fresno and Kings for a short distance. Spanish explorer Gabriel Moraga discovered the river on January 6, 1805, the Feast of the Three Kings or Wise Men, and named the river in their honor. Moraga's was one of several expeditions made by the Spanish into the San Joaquin Valley in the early years of the nineteenth century. Some of these were made to pursue Indian renegades or deserters from the missions, some to explore for purposes that included extending mission activity into the Great Valley. Nothing permanent came of these expeditions, although the discovery in 1852 of a huge pile of adobe bricks near Laton on the banks of the Kings River has been taken by some historians to mean that they were intended for some kind of mission structure.

Caleb Strong Merrill, a stonemason who had come to San Diego in 1831 aboard a Boston hide drogher (a coastal craft for transporting cattle hides), worked at Mission San Diego and then at Monterey. Accompanying an expedition into the valley near Laton in the 1830s, he described the region, in the paraphrase made by F. F. Latta, "as a vast jungle or swamp. The party was never able to approach Tulare Lake. After climbing the highest trees, all they could see in all directions was more trees and a sea of tules."

PUEBLO DE LAS JUNTAS

Pueblo de las Juntas, a rendezvous for adventurers, refugees, and a few pioneers from the Spanish settlements to the west, was one of the first places in the San Joaquin Valley to be settled by Spaniards and Mexicans, although exactly when this happened is unclear. Much of the history of the San Joaquin Valley in these years was never written down and was only recalled by elderly people who were questioned a long time after events had taken place.

Las Juntas ("junction," or "meeting place") was located at the confluence of the San Joaquin River and Fresno Slough, but the name may have referred to the fact that it was a meeting place for fugitives. In the 1850s and 1860s it had a bad reputation of long standing. Horse stealing, gambling, and drinking went on unchecked, and murder was not uncommon. It was said that bandits Joaquín Murieta and Tiburcio Vásquez and their gangs obtained supplies here, where they were safe from the pursuit of American officers. Despite the town's tough reputation, a number of Hispanic families lived at Las Juntas, and in the 1870s the population numbered about 250. The Butterfield Overland Stage passed this way and often stopped at the old pueblo.

Ash trees, abundant along the banks of the slough, gave the name Fresno to the locality. Two large specimens of this tree grew on the banks of the San Joaquin River at Las Juntas, so it too was sometimes called Fresno. When a settlement (near the present Tranquillity) grew up about eighteen miles farther south at the head of Fresno Slough, it too was frequently called Fresno City. However, Las Juntas was the first Fresno.

In 1879, when a canal company bought the town site, most of the inhabitants of Las Juntas moved to Firebaugh. Soon after, the Miller and Lux ranching empire acquired the land, and the remaining settlers were forced to leave. The tule-thatched houses of brush and mudbrick at Las Juntas have long since disappeared and today the Delta-Mendota Canal runs through the site.

THE OLD LOS ANGELES TRAIL, EL CAMINO VIEJO

The oldest north-south trail to traverse the entire length of the San Joaquin Valley was known as the Los Angeles Trail, or El Camino Viejo ("the old highway"). It led from San Pedro on the coast to San Antonio, now East Oakland. Following a route identical with that later known as the Stockton–Los Angeles Road as far as the later Chandler Station (in Los Angeles County, between Gorman and Lebec), the road descended San Emigdio Canyon to its mouth in the extreme southwestern corner of the San Joaquin Valley. From there the trail skirted the eastern slope of the Coast Range foothills, finally passing out of the valley through Corral Hollow and Patterson Pass southwest of Tracy.

Early in the nineteenth century the Spaniards drove oxcarts over this route between San Pedro and San Antonio. Some of the old water holes along its course developed into historic places: San Emigdio in the present Kern County; Los Carneros, where there is a spectacular outcropping of Vaqueros sandstone, which composes also Tres Piedras ("three rocks"), Joaquín Murieta's stronghold; and Posa de Chiné, six miles east of the present Coalinga.

On the site of an Indian village, Posa ("pool") de Chiné, a small agricultural community made up of a dozen or so Hispanic families, was long the only Spanish settlement in what is now Fresno County. Later, American pioneers came and established stores and built houses. They also continued the practice begun by the Hispanics of cutting down the neighboring trees for firewood and shelter, gradually rendering the place barren and inhospitable. Today nothing marks the spot where Posa de Chiné stood, the pool itself having been obliterated in the flood of 1862.

Approaching Posa de Chiné from the south, El Camino Viejo crossed El Arroyo de las Polvarduras ("dust clouds"); El Arroyo de las Canoas ("troughs"); El Arroyo de Zapato Chino ("Chinese shoe"); and El Arroyo de Jacelitos, "so named by the Spanish," says F. F. Latta, "because they found there many 'Indian huts' from which the inhabitants had fled in terror." Continuing north from Posa de Chiné, the road passed other campsites on the Arroyo de Cantua (named for a prominent local family), Arroyo de Panoche Grande ("big sugar loaf"), and Arroyo de Panochita ("little sugar loaf.")

To the northeast on an eastern branch of El Camino Viejo there was another very early settlement, La Libertad, about five miles east and a half-mile south of the present Burrel. Largely Mexican in population as late as 1870, it was later dominated by English-speakers and was called Liberty; the community was in decline by 1890.

Continuing northward, other settlements were passed either on the main road or on laterals branching from it, among them Pueblo de las Juntas north of the present Mendota, and Rancho de los Californios on the south bank of the San Joaquin River several miles east of Fresno Slough, a settlement nearly gone by 1870.

AMERICAN EXPLORERS IN FRESNO COUNTY

Jedediah Strong Smith was the first American to arrive overland in California, in 1826. He was detained by suspicious Mexican officials at Mission San Gabriel but eventually was permitted to leave the province by a northern route. On the way, he came to the river that Moraga, two decades before, had named the San Joaquin, having come upon it on March 20, the feast day of St. Joachim. In his journal, Smith wrote that the Indians called the river Peticutry. Smith soon departed for the Rockies, from whence he had come to California. The men of his party, enthusiastically trapping the streams leading down from the Sierra Nevada, made a fortune in beaver and otter furs, which were sold to officials of the Hudson's Bay Company at their "factory" or trading post at Vancouver, now in the state of Washington. The British-owned company in turn sent trappers into California from 1827 to 1846, when Britain and the United States jointly occupied the Oregon Country.

The Hudson's Bay trappers, led by Peter Skene Ogden, soon encountered American adventurers such as Kit Carson, as the outside world became aware of the riches of California. Fresno County was in the line of march of several American expeditions, from the one led by Ewing Young in 1829 (Kit Carson's first visit to California) to John C. Frémont's in 1845. The accounts of these expeditions, particularly the one led by Joseph R. Walker in 1833–34, contain interesting descriptions of the San Joaquin Valley and the Sierra foothills on the eve of the American conquest. They also note that the Indian population seemed to be in a decline, an ominous foreshadowing of the wholesale destruction of the valley's Indian population in the mid-nineteenth century, a destruction due in large part to the Indians' susceptibility to the diseases of the white people.

OLD STAGE ROADS

In early pioneer days the Stockton–Los Angeles Road followed the base of the Sierra Nevada, with many trails branching off to the mines in the foothills. The route through Fresno County passed by the sites of the present towns of Reedley, Sanger, and Friant. Today only fragments remain of the old road where pack trains traced the first dim course and the lumbering prairie schooner later beat out a well-worn trail.

The principal streams along this road were crossed by privately owned bridges or ferries. Two detours, lower and upper, ran parallel a few miles apart. The Lower Detour crossed the Kings River at Pool's Ferry, settled as early as 1851, and designated one of the two voting precincts when Tulare County was organized in 1852. John Pool was running the ferry there as late as 1857, after which the records are silent. The ferry was

north of Reedley and eight-tenths of a mile southeast of the intersection of Adams and LacJac Avenues; the site has been marked on private property by E Clampus Vitus.

Smith's Ferry, established by James Smith in 1855, superseded Pool's and for nineteen years was the most important crossing on the Kings River. Because a crossing could be made at no other point along the river during high water, Smith's Ferry remained open to the public after all the others had ceased to operate. Only after the railroad was completed twelve miles to the west did business slacken, and in 1874 Smith's Ferry was likewise abandoned. This once prosperous place was located approximately one-quarter mile south of the intersection of Dinuba and Reed Avenues, less than one-tenth of a mile north of the Reedley Cemetery and of the highway bridge that crosses the river at this point. The site may be identified by a large grove of eucalyptus trees on the west side of Reed Avenue.

Scottsburg was established at the ferry on the Upper Detour in 1854. It stood on a knoll in the bottomlands of the Kings River east of the present town of Sanger. Following the devastating flood of the winter of 1861–62, when the whole town was washed away, a new site was chosen at the foot of the bluff to the northeast. Here again, in the winter of 1867, floods engulfed the settlement. Soon after, however, the town was established on the bluff and renamed Centerville, the name it still bears.

The old Stockton–Los Angeles Road also made two crossings of the San Joaquin River, one at Brackman's on the Lower Detour, and the other at Jones's Ferry on the Upper Detour.

The route usually followed by the Butterfield stages during the years 1858–61 turned off from the Stockton–Los Angeles Road east of Visalia in Tulare County and, passing through Visalia, crossed the country to Kingston, located on the south bank of the Kings River in what is now Kings County. From there, the route ran through Fresno County to Firebaugh's Ferry, operated by Andrew Firebaugh from 1853 to 1856, and the site of the modern town of Firebaugh. Hawthorn's Station, established by the Butterfield Company, and Elkhorn Station were stopovers between Firebaugh on the San Joaquin and Kingston on the Kings.

During very wet weather, when the river was too high to cross at Kingston, the Butterfield stagecoaches followed the old Stockton–Los Angeles Road along the base of the hills to Smith's Ferry; from there they took the road marked out by James Smith especially for the

Butterfield stages, crossing the valley fifty miles to Fresno City.

FRESNO CITY

At certain times of the year, and particularly in years of heavy rain and flooding, many of which occurred in the years after the declaration of statehood in 1850, the San Joaquin River could be navigated far into the valley by vessels of very shallow draft.

Fresno City was established about 1858 at the head of navigation on Fresno Slough, sometimes called the South or Fresno branch of the San Joaquin River. A pier was built for unloading freight from flatboats and barges. There were a few warehouses, several homes, and a hotel, the Casa Blanca, something of a landmark on the west side until it was destroyed by fire.

Fresno City was expected to become an important town because of its steamboat commerce, its station on the Butterfield line, and its location on the transcontinental telegraph line being built through the San Joaquin Valley. The expectation was not fulfilled, and Fresno City had been abandoned by the end of the Civil War. The name Fresno was given to another settlement, one that had much less promise but, as it turned out, a far greater future. The site of Fresno City is marked (SRL 488) near the present town of Tranquillity, at SR 180 and James Road.

MILLERTON

A mining town begun under the name of Rootville in 1851, Millerton became the county seat when Fresno County was organized in 1856. It was located on the south bank of the San Joaquin River in the Sierra Nevada foothills, near the southernmost part of the Mother Lode gold region. The Stockton–Los Angeles Road crossed the river at this point.

The rainy winter of 1861–62 caused flooding on the river that washed away nearly half the town. An even more destructive flood late in 1867 was so catastrophic that few inhabitants stayed to rebuild. In 1870 fire swept the community, which by now was shabby, disheartened, and an embarrassment as the county seat.

The new vigor in the county lay in the valley, where the Central Pacific Railroad was being constructed through the developing agricultural regions and where the station of Fresno had been created. In 1874 the burgeoning town replaced Millerton as the county seat.

Millerton remained a sleeping ghost town until the twentieth century. Friant Dam, part of the Central Valley Project, impounded the waters of the San Joaquin River and the town now lies at the bottom of Millerton Lake. The old two-story brick courthouse was carefully taken down and preserved in 1941, thanks to the Native Sons and Native Daughters of the Golden West, and the remains were kept until reconstruction became possible in a project completed in 1970. The result is one of the most impressive anywhere in California. The old courthouse now stands on Mariner Point, overlooking Millerton Lake and Friant Dam, about two miles from its original site. The brick and granite structure stands out against the landscape like a monument. Inside are a small museum, replicas of early county offices, and some modern commercial offices.

FORT MILLER

In 1850 the discovery of gold in the Millerton region of the Sierra Nevada foothills attracted a large number of miners. The Indian population in the surrounding hills vigorously opposed the invasion of their lands, and the United States government decided to place a detachment of soldiers there in order to hold the Indians in check. The first post established was known as Camp Barbour, after Federal Indian Commissioner George Barbour. It was here on April 29, 1853, that Barbour and his fellow commissioners Redick McKee and Oliver M. Wozencraft concluded one of the eighteen unratified treaties with the Indians.

The following month, a more permanent fortification was erected at Camp Barbour and named Camp Miller (in 1852 changed to Fort Miller), after Major Albert S. Miller, commander of the Army station at Benicia in Solano County. A marker (SRL 584) at Millerton Lake State Recreation Area commemorates the fort, the site of which is now beneath the waters of the lake. About this time, the settlement of Rootville changed its name to Millerton in honor of the fort. The fort was partly evacuated in 1856, and the last troops departed in 1864.

The first school in Fresno County was conducted in the hospital building at Fort Miller early in 1860. This building, along with all of the other buildings of the fort except the blockhouse, eventually fell into decay. Judge Charles A. Hart purchased the fort after the military left it for good, and the property remained in the hands of his family until it was inundated by Millerton Lake, created by the building of Friant Dam.

In 1944, as soon as it was known that the water would

cover the site, the blockhouse was carefully moved, piece by piece, and re-erected in Roeding Park in the city of Fresno. There it remained until the late 1990s, when it was again moved, this time to the site of the Table Mountain Rancheria Cultural Center.

So much fiction has been written concerning the young bandit Joaquín Murieta, and so little has been published of an authoritative nature, that historical facts and popular legends are hopelessly intermixed. A native of Sonora in Mexico, Murieta was said to have come to California about 1849, trying his luck at mining near Murphys in Calaveras County. Here he encountered the vicious racism that often developed as Americans swarmed into the gold country. Murieta's claim was jumped, he was beaten, and his wife was raped, or in some versions killed outright. A second tale, also from Calaveras County, has Joaquín swearing vengeance after his brother had been lynched by a "gringo" mob and Joaquín suffered the humiliation of being horsewhipped. He tracked down his assailants and put a dozen or more of them to death by dragging them behind his horse. The legend says that henceforth his life was dedicated to violence against the American invaders, who in a short period of time had taken California away from the Mexican people.

In 1851, the name of a bandit named Joaquín began to resound throughout central California and the southern Mother Lode. Some historians believe that as many as five different gangs, each calling itself the followers of "Joaquín," made raids on highways, farms, and mining towns alike. No one man could have been at all the locations in California traditionally associated with his name, often on the same date.

Murieta's chief stronghold was said to be in the Arroyo de Cantua, a place of numerous rocks and caves, some sixteen miles north of the present town of Coalinga. The massive buttes known as Tres Piedras, visible from the valley, protected the hiding place, and from this point the lookout could see for miles in all directions across the surrounding treeless plains. The Murieta Rocks, as they are popularly known, are on private property four miles by foot from the end of Monterey Avenue (locally known as Repeated Station Road). There is a monument (SRL 344) with a bronze plaque nine miles north of Coalinga on SR 198, just west of I-5. Fourteen miles farther north, another marker indicates a view of the rocks.

By the spring of 1853, Joaquín's depredations had caused the state to offer a reward of $1,000 for his capture. In addition, a special company of rangers was raised to bring Murieta and his gang to justice. Random killings all over the central part of California had stirred up a popular frenzy over the whereabouts of the outlaws. On July 25, 1853, the rangers surprised a group of Mexicans in the Arroyo de Cantua; a gunfight broke out, and six men were either killed or captured. The head of one was cut off and exhibited throughout the state for many years as the head of Joaquín himself; a severed hand that purportedly belonged to Three-Fingered Jack, one of Murieta's henchmen, was also displayed.

There is reason to believe that the grisly relics came from innocent men whom the overeager rangers murdered deliberately. Murieta, it was said, lived on, eventually succumbing to his wounds received at the Cantua. But when the site in Niles Canyon, in Alameda County, locally believed to be Murieta's grave was excavated in 1986, no trace of a burial could be found. State officials were satisfied that their quest had been fulfilled when they paid Captain Harry Love and rangers the promised reward for destroying the Murieta band. Although other bandits appeared in later years, Joaquín and his men seem to have vanished after the battle at the Cantua.

The Arroyo de Cantua was also a haven for the notorious (and real) Tiburcio Vásquez, who in the early 1870s had much of the San Joaquin Valley and the adjacent Coastal Range in an uproar. Firebaugh's Ferry and Kingston in Kings County were among the sites of Vásquez's raids, which were usually profitable and marked by senseless killings. Once more the state offered a bounty, and Vásquez was captured in 1874 and executed the following year.

Fresno is today the largest city in the San Joaquin Valley. It pioneered the development of gravity irrigation, which changed arid land into fertile farms, and it has used its location in the geographical center of the valley to become one of the largest wholesale trade centers in California. Fresno County is one of the nation's leading producers of grapes, raisins, figs, and cotton.

During the last decades of the nineteenth century, when Fresno was beginning its rise to agricultural prominence, one of the wealthiest landowners in the county was Martin Theo Kearney, whose estate, called "Fruit

Vale," lay west of Fresno. Of either English or Irish ancestry, Kearney arrived in California from Boston around 1880 and became a great landowner over the next twenty years. While he subdivided and leased much of his land, he retained a part for his own use and built a beautiful tree-lined avenue of three lanes from Fresno to the entrance of his home grounds, seven miles from town, and continuing eight miles beyond to Kerman. To avoid the monotony of an arrow-straight drive through the level valley land, he planned the road to include two graceful curves. On both sides of the wide center he alternated plantings of fan palms, eucalyptus, and oleanders. He lined other picturesque roads with such trees as orange, olive, and Monterey cypress. Huge and impressive, Kearney's trees still line Kearney Avenue, one of the most striking drives in all of California.

Kearney, who was president of the first California Raisin Growers Association from 1898 to 1904, planted sufficient acreage with fruit trees and crops to make the entire estate more than self-sustaining. In 1903 he constructed a two-story residence, largely of adobe, where he lived while he was in the area. This was to be superseded by a grandiose "Chateau Fresno," modeled after the Château de Chenonceaux in France; the two-story building was to become the home of his superintendent. Chateau Fresno was never built: in 1906, just as he was about to commence the project, Kearney died of a heart attack in mid-ocean while sailing to Europe.

By the terms of his will his entire estate was given to the University of California, which gradually divested itself of the property until by 1949 all of the land except the grounds around the house had been sold. The beautifully planted acreage surrounding the residence is now Kearney Park, a recreation area operated by the county of Fresno. The building itself, now called the Kearney Mansion, is open as a museum of the Fresno County Historical Society. Many of Kearney's original furnishings have been preserved.

Dr. Thomas Richard Meux practiced medicine in Fresno from his arrival from Tennessee in 1887 until his retirement about thirty years later. He and his family lived in the home he built at Tulare and R Streets, described by a local paper upon its completion in 1889 as "probably the most elaborate residence in Fresno," until the death of his daughter Anne Prenetta Meux in 1970. The two-story Victorian structure is noteworthy for its unusual combination of architectural forms, which include an octagonal master bedroom with a turreted roof, a sweeping veranda, many windows with batwing shutters, and highly ornamental gingerbread

Kearney Mansion, Fresno

scrollwork on the porches. Now on the National Register of Historic Places, the Meux home was acquired by the city of Fresno in 1973 and has been beautifully restored and maintained as a museum.

The Fresno Metropolitan Museum at 1555 Van Ness Avenue has displays of decorative arts as well as materials relating to local history. The attractive building in which it is housed was formerly the home of the prominent newspaper, the *Fresno Bee*. The Discovery Center at 1944 North Winery Avenue is primarily designed for young visitors but contains Indian baskets and artifacts of interest to all ages.

Fresno, with many ethnic groups, is a very cosmopolitan place. The Federal Census of 1990 showed that it has the world's largest population of Hmong (refugees from Southeast Asia). An unusual reference library and museum is that of the American Historical Society of Germans from Russia Museum at 3233 West Street. With the arrival in 1881 of Hagop and Garabed Seropian, the prominent Armenian community began. The Armenians found Fresno to have climate and soil similar to their homeland, and became famous for their crops of figs, melons, pistachio nuts, and raisins. The community commissioned a statue of David of Sassoon, "Epic Armenian Folk Hero," which was placed in 1970 on the lawn of the Fresno County Courthouse at Tulare and M Streets.

Fresno is the site of the first fight for free speech in California and the first attempt to organize the unskilled workers of the San Joaquin Valley. The Industrial Workers of the World demonstrated at the corner of Mariposa and I Streets from October 1910 to March 1911; the episode is commemorated by a plaque (SRL 873) at the Fulton Clock Mall Tower nearby at Van Ness Avenue and Fresno Street.

David of Sassoon Statue, Fresno

CALIFORNIA'S FIRST JUNIOR COLLEGE

Fresno can claim an important place in the educational history of California, since it was the home of the first junior college in the state. Institutions of this rank, in which California leads the nation, had their beginnings as postgraduate extensions of high school. Fresno Junior College, the oldest two-year college in California, opened in 1910 in the fifteen-year-old Fresno High School building, with three teachers and an enrollment of twenty-eight students. The original site of the junior college (SRL 803) is the block bounded by Stanislaus, O, Tuolumne, and P Streets. A fountain and plaque at the corner of O and Tuolumne memorialize this pioneer educational endeavor. The college was first maintained at local expense, but within several years junior colleges were made an integral part of the state school system. Fresno City College, at it is called today, is located at 1101 East University Avenue.

CALIFORNIA STATE UNIVERSITY AT FRESNO

Another important educational institution in the city is California State University at Fresno. It began as Fresno State Normal School in 1911, changing to a teaching college in 1921. By 1949 it was offering advanced degrees.

Located at 5241 Maple Avenue, it is now one of two dozen state universities.

THE UNDERGROUND GARDENS

One of California's most unusual landmarks is the Forestiere Underground Gardens (SRL 916), located about six miles north of downtown Fresno, at 5021 West Shaw Avenue near SR 99. An underground home of some sixty-five rooms, gardens, and grottos, it is the creation of one man, Baldassare Forestiere, who tunneled and burrowed there with only the simplest of tools from 1908 until his death in 1946. Born in Sicily in 1879, he relied on his experience gained as a "sandhog" in the eastern United States, which also taught him a way of escaping the high summer temperatures of the Fresno area. One of the most interesting features is a tree growing more than twenty feet below the surface of the earth and grafted to bear seven different kinds of citrus fruit. The catacombs, nearly a mile in length and covering an underground area of about seven acres, display the marvelous architectural, engineering, and horticultural skills of a man with "no formal education." The family opened it as a commercial enterprise in 1954.

WATER DEVELOPMENT AND AGRICULTURAL COLONIES

Intensive agriculture would not be possible in the San Joaquin Valley's long, hot, arid summers without a regular supply of water. It is believed that Indians at Posa de Chiné were the first people in what is now Fresno County to use irrigation canals. After California became a state in 1850, cattle ranching was the dominant activity in the valley. With the coming of the railroad in 1872 and new state laws requiring ranchers to fence in their livestock, cultivation of crops became the principal economic interest in the region, and schemes to build irrigation systems were manifest throughout the San Joaquin Valley. The Miller and Lux interests encouraged the development of a San Joaquin and Kings River Canal that would extend from Kern County to the Sacramento River delta. As Henry Miller anticipated, this project was too big to be completed; what was completed was the San Joaquin Canal, which extended north from the San Joaquin River just west of its junction with Fresno Slough into Stanislaus County, and benefited Miller and Lux more than any other consumer. The Kings River was repeatedly tapped by these new canals, which made possible, among other things, the settlement of the west side of Fresno County. According to Clough and Secrest's *Fresno County: The Pioneer Years*, by 1887 the county had canals that irrigated 610,000 acres of land and carried 3,500 cubic feet of water per second.

Also contributing to the growth of population in Fresno County after 1872 were agricultural colonies, communities of settlers initially dedicated to fruit growing. The first of these seems to have been the Central California Colony, begun in 1875 southwest of Fresno. Today's Cherry and Fig Avenues were some of the early roads of the community. Vineyards were also planted, and when the scorching summer of 1875 dried the grapes on the vine at the colony, the Fresno raisin industry began. The raisins were well received in San Francisco, and a major Fresno County endeavor was launched. The Sun-Maid raisin cooperative was founded in 1913, one of the most successful in American agricultural history.

Alternating periods of drought and flood ravaged rural California well into the twentieth century. A federal project to build great dams for water storage, flood control, and hydroelectric power, like the projects in the Tennessee River and Missouri River valleys, was begun in California in 1935. The Central Valley Project was mostly completed within the next twenty years. The Friant Dam created Millerton Lake and made possible the Friant-Kern and Madera canals, which irrigate the eastern side of the San Joaquin Valley to the southeast and to the northwest, respectively.

THE VALLEY TOWNS: FOWLER, KINGSBURG, REEDLEY, SELMA

The Central Pacific Railroad created a switch from its main line south of Fresno to the ranches of cattle baron and state senator Thomas Fowler in 1872; Fowler's Switch was the name given to the site, commemorated by an E Clampus Vitus plaque at Seventh and Merced Streets in downtown Fowler. By 1882, the town of Fowler had been established at the spot, then as now a processing and shipping center for valley crops.

Northeast of Kingston on the Kings River, the Central Pacific also established a switch initially called King's River in 1873. In the next three years, the location was renamed Wheatbury, then Kingsbury, then Kingsburgh; the terminal *h* was dropped in 1894. The town received a population boost with the arrival in 1886 of some fifty Swedish families from Michigan.

Some disastrous fires in the late 1890s damaged but did not destroy the well-established town, and Kingsburg continues to serve as an agricultural and transportation center, with an annual Swedish festival.

Reedley was begun as another railroad way station. The 76 Land and Water Company, an important enterprise in northeastern Fresno County, needed a shipping place for its products, and the site selected was on the Kings River close to old Smith's Ferry. Thomas Law ("T. L.") Reed, a prosperous local wheat farmer, encouraged the railroad to come into the area by granting it a half-interest in a town site, which was named for him. It was a successful settlement once the railroad arrived. Soon it had several substantial commercial enterprises, as well as a number of churches and schools, one of which is Reedley College. The Reedley Museum, housed in the former city hall building (1913) at 1752 Tenth Street, contains local Indian artifacts and memorabilia from the turn of the century.

Selma, lying on the railroad line between Fowler and Kingsburg, dates from 1880. There is uncertainty about the source of the name. Selma's history is much like that of neighboring towns. It began as a shipping center for crops, followed by the establishment of local businesses, schools, and churches, some destructive fires, and eventual restoration. In 1895, a strong Prohibitionist movement in the community resulted in the first city ordinance in California forbidding the sale or consumption of alcoholic beverages. Opponents were able to get the measure rescinded within a couple of months. By and large, California was not receptive to Prohibitionist measures. A plaque commemorating the founding of Selma was placed by E Clampus Vitus in front of Fire Station Number One, on West Front Street. North of Selma, adjacent to SR 99, is the Pioneer Village Museum, opened in 1980. Among the buildings that were moved to the site are the Apple House (built in 1904), the Lincoln School, St. Ansgar's Lutheran Church, the Unger Opera House, and the Southern Pacific Depot from downtown Selma, built in 1887. All are well maintained and worth a visit.

COALINGA

It is reported that peddlers in Millerton were selling gallon cans of crude oil as early as 1865. The oil was collected from seepages in the hills on the west side of the San Joaquin Valley. Some commercial efforts at oil drilling were made in the area over the next twenty-

Wooden Derrick Piece from Chevron Oil Field, Coalinga

five years, none successful enough to warrant further development.

In 1890, the Coast Range Company of Los Angeles sunk a well 135 feet deep in the Oil City field, northeast of present-day Coalinga. Although this well had but a small yield, it foreshadowed a larger strike that was made in 1896 in the same location. Within a year, a significant oil boom was on.

Meanwhile, a coal mine had been opened on the west side of Pleasant Valley. In 1887 the Southern Pacific Railroad opened a line from its station at Huron westward to Alcalde; the three loading sites on the route were called Coaling Stations A, B, and C. Coaling Station A—soon shortened to Coalinga—became a center for the oil boom, and as the coal business died out, petroleum took over. The boomtown became renowned for nothing but "hell and jackrabbits" around 1900; the barren fields nearby gave little encouragement to agriculture on any extensive scale.

Coalinga is still an oil-producing community. The R. C. Baker Memorial Museum at 297 West Elm Avenue offers a superb display of local history, including a great deal of equipment used in the petroleum industry. Baker was a pioneer developer in the field, and the building now housing the museum was once his office. On the east side of town, a wooden derrick stands as a memorial to the people who worked in the oil fields. The derrick was in use until 1979, when Chevron donated it to the city. Farther east, along SR 198, a few painted oil booms remain from a project of the 1980s, when the industrious little machines were fancifully painted, some decorated as cartoon characters, or whimsical animals, or futuristic designs; it was locally known as the "Iron Zoo." Coalinga, located a few miles east of the San Andreas Fault, suffered a particularly destructive earthquake on May 2, 1983.

EXPLORATION OF FRESNO COUNTY'S SIERRA NEVADA

Although the expeditions of Joseph R. Walker and John C. Frémont passed through Fresno County, the first expedition to make an extensive survey of the mountains that constitute the eastern third of the county was that led by William H. Brewer in 1864. Four years earlier, the California Legislature had established a geological survey of the state, and in the summer of 1864 Brewer's group turned its attention to this region of the Sierra Nevada. Some of this expedition's discoveries are discussed in other chapters of this book. The principal discovery in Fresno County was of the great canyon of the South Fork of the Kings River. Brewer wrote:

> Next to Yosemite this is the grandest canyon I have ever seen. It much resembles Yosemite and almost rivals it. A pretty valley or flat half a mile wide lies along the river, in places rough and strewn with bowlders, and in others level and covered with trees. . . . The river swarmed with trout; I never saw them thicker. . . . On both sides rise tremendous granite precipices, of every shape, often nearly perpendicular, rising from 2,500 feet to above 4,000 feet. . . . The whole scene was sublime—the valley below, the swift river roaring by, the stupendous cliffs standing against a sky of intensest blue, the forests through which we rode.

Today this canyon is enclosed within Kings Canyon National Park, established in 1940. Also within this park is the Tehipite Valley along the Middle Fork of the Kings River, discovered by Frank Dusy in 1869. On a later expedition, Dusy took his bulky camera equipment into the highest mountains; he seems to have been the first to photograph Tehipite Dome, in 1879.

LUMBER AND BIG TREES

The mountains attracted miners, sheepherders, and lumbermen. The first sawmills in the timber country began operation in 1852. Almost at once they faced the problem of getting the finished lumber to market in the emerging valley towns. Early roads were difficult to build and to maintain, and flumes, whereby water was funneled through wood or metal conduits, carrying lumber down to the valley, proved equally difficult to keep in operation. In 1867 the Tollhouse Road was built up the steep incline to the mills in the vicinity of Shaver Lake. The road was named for the building put up, at the place still called Tollhouse, to collect a toll from all vehicles being driven up or down the ten-mile road. The steep grade was sometimes called "Beast Killer." The modern Tollhouse Road largely follows its course. The small town of Academy on the road is named for a private secondary school established there in 1872; the place is marked by an E Clampus Vitus plaque. Pine Ridge and Swanson Meadow were important early lumber centers.

Fresno is one of seven counties in the state in which the *Sequoia gigantea* is found. A small stand of magnificent trees is contained in the General Grant Grove section of Kings Canyon National Park on the southern boundary of the county. The southern portion of the park is in northern Tulare County. The General Grant, 264 feet in height and more than 40 feet in diameter at its base, for which the grove is named, is one of the most noted of its trees. General Grant National Park was created in 1890 to preserve the grove and was ab-

sorbed by Kings Canyon National Park when that was created in 1940. There are seven smaller groves in Fresno County, besides the Evans Grove, east of Hume Lake, which contains 500 trees.

What surely saved these redwoods is the fact that, unlike their cousins on the Pacific Coast, their lumber is almost useless for commercial purposes. Before this was known, massive logging operations cleared out thousands of sequoias in the Converse Basin, said by some to have been finer than those of the Giant Forest in Sequoia National Park in Tulare County. In the Converse Mountain Grove, one monarch survives. This is the Boole Tree, a close competitor of the General Sherman as the largest of all the Big Trees. It was saved by Frank Boole, foreman, for whom it is named. An estimate made in 1985 declared that about two-thirds of the Sierra *Sequoia gigantea* still stood in primeval conditions, while some 90 percent of the coast redwoods had been logged.

Glenn County

Glenn County, named after Dr. Hugh James Glenn, was organized in 1891, when it was separated from Colusa County. Willows is the county seat.

THE SWIFT ADOBE

The adobe home built by Granville P. Swift stood for many years on Hambright Creek, about a mile north of Orland. This pioneer settler crossed the plains in 1843 and entered California from Oregon with the Kelsey party. He served in Sutter's campaign in 1845, participated in the Bear Flag Revolt, and in 1846–47 served

as captain in Frémont's California Battalion. Subsequently he settled near the confluence of Hambright and Stony Creeks and made his adobe the headquarters for cattle operations extending as far south as the present Woodland. In 1849, in partnership with his brother-in-law, Frank Sears, he purchased from John S. Williams the cattle and brand of the Larkin Children's Grant. Swift soon had vast droves of cattle, herded annually by Indian vaqueros, and extensive rodeos were held at the adobe on Hambright Creek and at a corral, no longer existing, on what later became the Murdock Ranch west of Willows. Swift also is credited with planting the first barley in the northern Sacramento Valley.

When John Bidwell discovered gold at Bidwell Bar, Swift amassed a fortune, it is claimed, by working large numbers of Stony Creek Indians on the Feather River. Legend has it that he buried his gold dust about his adobe; many have dug in the area over the years, but no fortune has yet been found.

Swift moved to Sonoma County in 1854, but his name is perpetuated in Glenn County in Swift's Point, near Hamilton City, a place on the Sacramento River once fordable at low water. The river road from Red Bluff and Shasta City crossed here to points east of the Sacramento.

The site of Swift's long-vanished adobe (SRL 345) is on the south bank of Hambright Creek about a hundred yards east of the railway north of Orland; the marker is on SR 99-W one mile north of Orland.

MONROEVILLE

Monroeville, at the mouth of Stony Creek (formerly called Capay River) in what is now northeastern Glenn County, was situated on the Capay Rancho, a grant made to María Josefa Soto, later the wife of Dr. James Stokes of Monterey. Out of this estate Mrs. Stokes gave a portion at the mouth of Stony Creek to a man named McGee in return for his aid in making the grant official. The first settler on the land, in 1846, was a man known only to history as Mr. Bryant, who also built the first house there.

After the discovery of gold in 1848 other settlers located there, among them Uriah P. Monroe, whose ranch and hotel became a popular stopping place on the old River Road. The hotel, which was to double as courthouse, was largely built from the remains of the *California*, one of the first steamers to ascend the Sacramento River. It was wrecked at the right-angle turn in the river on Monroeville Island, about a mile above the mouth of Stony Creek.

The Colusa County boundary had scarcely been defined when a quarrel began over the location of the county seat, a phenomenon seen elsewhere in California and the West. Monroe, an ambitious, aggressive man, was determined that the county seat should be established on his land and named for him. Colusa, however, also wanted to be the county seat. Monroe presented a petition to Moses Bean, a judge in Butte County, requesting that the county seat be organized and that Monroe's Ranch be designated as the only polling place

for the election of county officers. Bean complied, though he had no lawful authority to act, and this high-handed procedure seemingly carried the day. Monroeville assumed the role of the first county seat of Colusi County, as it was originally called, in 1851.

Little interest was shown in becoming an officeholder in the new county. The mines were too attractive and the opportunity to acquire princely farmlands was too great to tempt anyone to give his time to the irksome and unremunerative task of running the government. There was one notable exception, however: William B. Ide, primary leader of the Bear Flag Revolt in 1846. For a time, Ide performed the duties of judge, county clerk, auditor, treasurer, coroner, and surveyor. Death cut short his useful life on December 20, 1852; a victim of smallpox, Ide died at Monroeville and was buried in the local cemetery. The only remnant of Monroeville, the cemetery was beautifully restored in 1998. A stone monument has been put up in Ide's memory on SR 45 five miles south of Hamilton City, near the rice field and orchards that were once the site of Monroeville.

In 1853, Colusa won the fight to be named county seat, and Monroeville was soon deserted, even by its founder. South of Monroeville, equally ambitious contemporary "paper cities" arose, among them Placer City, about three-quarters of a mile north of Jacinto, and Butte, on the east bank of the Sacramento and formerly in Butte County. All traces of Placer City have long been obliterated, but Butte City is now an agricultural center for that portion of Glenn County east of the river.

WILLOWS

Standing out in bold relief from a vast expanse of treeless plains, a clump of willows bordering on a large water hole fed by several springs was the only landmark in early days between the settlements on the river and those in the western foothills. Travelers guided their course by "the Willows." The Native Daughters of the Golden West have placed a marker on SR 162 one mile east of the city of Willows at the site of the water hole, which has since been filled in. This place on Willow Creek, the only live watering place between Cache Creek in Yolo County to the south and Stony Creek to the north, was taken over in the late 1840s by Granville Swift and was used by all the cattlemen of the area for a fee.

When the Central Pacific pushed its rail lines northward to Oregon in the late 1870s, the town of Willows

Glenn County Courthouse, Willows

was formed, about a mile west of the old landmark. The post office was known as "Willow" from 1876 until the terminal *s* was officially added in 1916. Willows became the shipping point for many large wheat and barley ranches, and when Glenn County was formed in 1891 from the northern half of Colusa County, Willows became the county seat. The Willows post office, in the majestic turn-of-the-century Federal style, is on the National Register of Historic Places.

Five miles east of Willows the Beehive Bend gas fields were discovered in the 1930s, the largest in the northern part of the state. The fields are scattered over a large area. To the north and extending into Colusa County is the Sacramento National Wildlife Refuge, the largest of several wildlife refuges in the valley and one of many in California.

JACINTO AND DR. HUGH GLENN

Now little more than a wide space in the River Road (SR 45), which runs from Hamilton City to Colusa, Jacinto was once the busiest river town in the upper Sacramento Valley. This was at the time Dr. Hugh J. Glenn, for whom Glenn County was named, farmed 55,000 acres of wheat land in all directions except eastward from his headquarters at Jacinto.

Glenn, a Missouri physician, came to California in 1849 and worked for a time on a gold claim he had taken up at Murderer's Bar on the American River. He made a number of trips across the plains driving herds of cattle, horses, and mules from Missouri, but finally returned to settle permanently in California. After a few years spent farming in Yolo County, he purchased land in what is now Glenn County in 1867, to which he moved his family in 1869.

Dr. Glenn began the cultivation of wheat on a large

scale in the 1870s, purchasing large tracts of land in Rancho Jacinto (so named for the original grantee, Jacinto Rodríguez, who obtained the land from the Mexican government in 1844), Rancho Capay, and the Larkin Children's Grant. The town of Jacinto, twenty-seven miles above Colusa, was the supply center for the huge Glenn operations and the residence of the two to three hundred men he employed. In the 1880s it included a hotel, a large general store, several blacksmith shops, a butcher shop, a post office (1858–1910), and several immense grain warehouses. The first school in the present county was established there. The Glenn home stood for years in a tangle of trees and shrubbery until it was torn down about 1960. The site of Jacinto is twelve miles south of Hamilton City at the junction of SR 45 and Bayliss Road (County Road 39).

Glenn was nominated for governor of California by the New Constitution and Democratic Parties in 1879 but was defeated by George C. Perkins, a Republican. The man once called the world's "Wheat King" did not live to see the county named for him; he was shot to death on his Jacinto property by an employee on February 17, 1883. His great holdings have since been subdivided into small farms, now all under irrigation.

ELK CREEK

Located at the base of the steep Coast Range in an open valley bisected by Stony Creek is the mountain town of Elk Creek, established in the late 1860s as a trading center for the valleys drained by Stony Creek and its tributaries. The post office was opened in 1872, and the town was the stopping place for stages from Colusa, thirty-five miles to the southeast, to Newville, thirteen miles to the north. Elk Creek today is at the entrance to the far-flung Mendocino National Forest.

A conical hill of historical significance lies one mile east across Stony Creek from the little town. A large redwood monument has been placed on "Bidwell Hill" by the Willows chapter of the Daughters of the American Revolution to mark the encampment of John Bidwell on July 4, 1844, while on an exploratory trip in search of a suitable land grant for the children of Thomas O. Larkin. The trip was unsuccessful, but a year later Bidwell located desirable lands bordering on the Sacramento River, south of the mouth of Stony Creek and north of Colusa.

W. C. Moon and Ezekiel Merritt, both of whom were members of the Bear Flag Party, and Peter Lassen quarried and manufactured a large number of grind-

Alta Schmidt House Museum, Orland

stones in 1845 on Grindstone Creek, a branch of Stony Creek several miles north of the town of Elk Creek, and packed them on mules over twenty miles to the Sacramento River. Here they loaded them into fragile canoes and drifted with them down the river, selling a number at Sutter's Fort and the rest in San Francisco. These grindstones, Bidwell concluded, were doubtless the first "civilized" manufacture in Colusa County, if not in the entire northern part of the state. On the Grindstone Indian reservation at the confluence of Grindstone and Stony Creeks may be seen an excellent example of an Indian roundhouse.

ORLAND

A child of the railroad, Orland was founded in the early 1870s and became one of the larger grain shipping points in northern California. Three pioneer settlers met to select a name for the town. One urged Comstock, another Leland, and the third Orland, "after a town in England," according to one version of the story. Unable to agree, they placed the names in a hat, and a child at the meeting drew out the slip marked Orland.

Just east of the city on SR 32, Orland College, a private school for students above the ninth grade, was founded in the 1880s. Professor J. B. Patch, who became its first president, solicited funds from wealthy farmers throughout Colusa County for the two-story building. One of the few institutions of higher learning in the North Valley, it closed in the 1890s, following the opening of the Northern Branch State Normal School, now California State University at Chico.

Orland is the center of the Orland Federal Irrigation Project, an area of 20,000 acres watered by East Park Reservoir (in Colusa County) behind East Park Dam on Little Stony Creek. Formed in 1906, it was the

first irrigation project in the West installed and operated entirely by the newly formed United States Reclamation Bureau. It was a pilot project for federal irrigation in the state and was the forerunner of the statewide Central Valley Project, which was developed in the 1930s and 1940s. Eight miles northwest of Orland on the main channel of Stony Creek is the $13 million Black Butte Dam (in Tehama County), constructed by the U.S. Army Corps of Engineers as a flood control project, and completed in 1963. Black Butte Lake (mostly in Glenn County) contains 150,000 acre-feet of water and is a popular recreational area.

Orland today is a major processing center for almonds, olives, and oranges. Haigh Field, now Orland's airport, was first used as an auxiliary training field in World War II. The ladino clover crop of the Orland area furnishes much of the seed used in the nation; it is processed at a plant in Artois, nine miles south of Orland on I-5. Artois was originally known as Germantown; in 1918, after the United States declared war on Germany in the previous year, the name was changed to that of a battlefield region in France, an American ally during World War I.

ST. JOHN AND HAMILTON CITY

Hamilton City, Glenn County's newest town, might well be considered the legitimate descendant of the two pioneer towns that have passed into oblivion: Monroeville, about five miles south, and St. John.

St. John, two miles north of Monroeville, was founded by Aden C. St. John about 1856 on the banks of Stony Creek, about where it is crossed by the present SR 45. St. John was the home of the first large general merchandise store in Colusa County and boasted also a hotel and large warehouses and barns, built to handle the overnight oxen and mule traffic bound up the west side of the river to the mines at Shasta and Weaverville.

As Monroeville was superseded by St. John, so did St. John fade when Hamilton City was founded in 1905 as the site of a large sugar beet factory, no longer in operation. The place was named for J. G. Hamilton, president of the original sugar company.

Three and a half miles north of Hamilton City on the west bank of the Sacramento River, a marker (SRL 831) commemorates Will S. Green, guiding spirit of irrigation in the North Valley and for years editor of the *Colusa Sun*. On December 18, 1883, Green posted the first water notice in California on a nearby oak tree. The notice stated that 500,000 inches of river water were being diverted for irrigation of lands on the west side of the Sacramento Valley. The domination of northern California by the exploitative mining inter- ests, with their appalling hydraulic mining that wasted soil and water alike, was coming to an end. The area's future would be with those who farmed the land.

Trinidad Harbor and Trinidad Head

Humboldt County

Humboldt County was organized in 1853, with Uniontown, now Arcata, as its county seat. Like Humboldt Bay, it was named for the famous German scientist and traveler, Baron Alexander von Humboldt, who however never set foot in this area. It was formerly a part of Trinity County, and what is now its northern third was included within Klamath County from 1851 to 1876. When Klamath County was disestablished in 1876, its territory was divided among Humboldt, Del Norte, and Siskiyou Counties.

CAPE MENDOCINO

Cape Mendocino, the westernmost point of California, has been for centuries a landmark for mariners along the Pacific Coast. The name appeared on a map drawn in 1587, when accurate geographical knowledge of the coast was still scarce. It may have been named in honor of the viceroy of New Spain, Antonio de Mendoza. The monumental rock may first have been seen in 1542 by Juan Rodríguez Cabrillo, the discoverer of Alta California, but few writers agree on the exact route of his voyage, and it is more generally believed that he went only as far as the Northwest Cape in what is now Sonoma County. The real discoverer may have been Alonso de Arellano, a deserter from the expedition commanded by Father Andrés de Urdaneta in 1565. Before taking his vows as a monk, Father Urdaneta had been a noteworthy navigator, and his expertise was such that he was put in charge of this secular expedition.

In 1565 Urdaneta had opened up the route for the Manila galleon from Asia across the Pacific to New Spain, and in 1566 the galleon made its first trading voyage. For 250 years the Spaniards followed this route, sailing across the Pacific with rich cargoes of spices and other commodities from the Orient, and often sighting the coast of California as far north as Cape Mendocino.

Some of the explorers of the coast did sight Cape Mendocino and chart their course by it. Among them were Francis Drake in 1579, on his voyage around the world; Sebastián Rodríguez Cermeño, in 1595, while seeking a northern port for the Manila galleon; Sebastián Vizcaíno, during 1602–3, while exploring the coast from Cape San Lucas to Cape Mendocino; and George Vancouver, sent out by England in 1792 to investigate the extent of the Spanish possessions on the Pacific Coast. Each of these men, and perhaps others, passed by Cape Mendocino, or turned back southward from that point.

Cape Mendocino Lighthouse, no longer in service, was a forty-three-foot tower standing on the 422-foot high cliff, making its light one of the highest along the coast. In 1860, the steamer *Northerner*, one day out of San Francisco, struck a submerged rock off the cape and foundered at Centerville Beach to the north; thirty-eight people were drowned. A concrete cross (SRL 173) was placed by the Native Daughters of the Golden West at Centerville Beach, five miles west of Ferndale on Centerville Road, in memory of the victims. The tragedy resulted in the building of the lighthouse, completed in 1868. The Fresnel lens, made in France at a cost of $79,000, was visible for twenty-eight miles. The lens and the mechanism that operated it have been removed to a replica of the lighthouse on the Humboldt County Fairgrounds at Ferndale.

INDIAN WARS

After 1848, Americans flocked to California in large numbers and explored both the easily accessible regions and those more remote, such as the northern Pacific Coast. Soon these newcomers began to settle on lands that the Indian people had always regarded as their own; conflict was the predictable result. Trouble between Indians and whites was prevalent throughout California between 1850 and 1865. The coastal Indians of the Humboldt region were generally friendly and peaceable. But the mountain dwellers were less willing to coexist with the newcomers, and they set fire to grass, drove off livestock, and killed or drove out, one by one, the white settlers along the Mad River, Redwood Creek, and in the Bald Hills, until there were none left between Humboldt Bay and Trinity River.

A. J. Bledsoe, in his 1885 history of the Indian Wars, says:

> During the year of 1851 the trouble between the Indians and the whites became acute. The packers and miners used little caution in their treatment of the Indians, many regarding the latter as their natural enemies, to be shot down whenever opportunity offered. The Indians were unable to discriminate between these vicious white men and the more peaceful ones, and as a result when an Indian was killed some white man paid the penalty, and unfortunately it was seldom the man who had committed the wrong. Nor were the whites themselves at all times above this practice, for seldom was the effort made to apprehend the real offender among the Indians, but rather a general attack followed on the nearest rancheria.

The need for military protection for the new settlement caused the establishment of a post at Fort Humboldt (SRL 154), on Humboldt Heights in what is today the southwestern part of Eureka. Brevet-Lieutenant Colonel Robert C. Buchanan was entrusted with establishing the fort in January 1853, and within a year or so some fourteen buildings stood on the bluff around a 260-foot-square parade ground. Isolated from the rest of the world, fogbound for days at a time, and confronted with constant strife between Indians and settlers, the garrison was not a happy one. The four dreary and half-drunken months he spent there in 1854 convinced Captain Ulysses S. Grant to resign from the Army and to return to his family in Illinois.

For ten years after the establishment of Fort Humboldt, the United States Army sought, without success, to pacify the Indians of Humboldt County. In 1863 the Mountain Battalion of the state militia, composed of six companies of volunteers, was organized. Almost ceaseless warfare ensued during the next two years.

The unsettling wars took their toll on the Indians, as did the diseases of the white settlers. In 1864 the Hoopa Valley Indian Reservation was established, and the Indian wars came to an end in Humboldt County. Fort Humboldt was abandoned in 1870. In 1893 its land and the one remaining building on the property, the hospital, were sold to W. S. Cooper. Upon his death, his wife gave the property to the city of Eureka, which transferred it to the state in 1955. Now it is Fort Humboldt State Historic Park, overlooking US 101 at Highland Avenue in Eureka. In addition to the museum, visitors will see a remarkable display of lumbering that traces the history of redwood logging from its beginnings in 1850, highlighted by nineteenth-century "Gypsy" logging locomotives, to a Washington slack-line steam donkey of 1926, which was capable of hauling immense redwood logs as much as half a mile.

The Mattole Valley, Hydesville, Yager Creek, and Van Duzen districts were scenes of Indian conflicts. Many military posts were scattered throughout the region, among them Fort Baker (1862–63), twenty-eight miles east of Hydesville; Fort Lyons (1862) at Brehmer's Ranch on the Mad River, twenty-five miles southeast of Eureka; Fort Iaqua (1863–66) on Yager Creek, eight miles south of Brehmer's; Martin's Ferry, on the Klamath River about three miles west of Weitchpec; Camp Grant (1863) on the Eel River, about three miles east of Dyerville; Fort Seward (1861–63) on the Eel River, twenty miles southeast of Camp Grant; Camp Anderson (1862–66), near Minor's Ranch, where the road to Hoopa crosses Redwood Creek; and Fawn Prairie (1863) on the Hoopa Trail. One and one-half miles north of Arcata was Camp Curtis (SRL 215), the fort of the volunteer Mountain Battalion from 1863 to 1865.

THE "ARROW TREE"

One mile east of Korbel there is a redwood tree, now dead, that is the subject of an Indian legend. When white men first passed by the ancient tree, they found it stuck full of arrows for thirty or forty feet above the ground. It was like a mammoth porcupine. The Indians of the region had a tradition about the "Arrow Tree" (SRL 164) that went back to the time when it was young.

The Wiyots of the coast were at war with the Chilulas of the hill country, and the two met in battle. The hill tribes were defeated and peace was made near the great redwood tree, which was afterward looked upon as a boundary marker between the two nations. Both Chilulas and Wiyots passed the old tree from time to time, and, because it was sacred, they never failed to leave an arrow in its soft bark. "At one time," says one account, "the arrows may have been real war arrows, but within the memory of living Indians, they have been merely sharpened sticks. Gradually, the original significance of the tree was partially lost sight of, and it became more and more an altar for worship and a place of prayer."

Korbel is about seven miles east of Arcata off SR 299. The Arrow Tree is on Maple Creek Road, one mile east of Korbel, but it is not easy to spot, being on the slope of a steep hill where the road climbs at that point.

THE RAIN ROCK

Near the fishing place on the Trinity River in Sugarbowl Valley and four miles from Hoopa is a boulder, not over four feet in diameter and not at all conspicuous, called by the white people the "Rain Rock" and by the Hoopa the Mi, or Thunder's Rock. Near this rock, the Indians believed, dwells a spirit who, when he is displeased, sends killing frosts, or prolongs the rains to create floods, or brings drought and famine. Many legends are connected to the nearby Sugar Loaf Mountain, and other mountains, as well as rocks, trees, and rivers throughout the region, have similar legends connected with them.

THE HOOPA VALLEY INDIAN RESERVATION

The Hoopa Valley Indian Reservation is California's largest in area, covering some 93,000 acres. It may be reached by SR 96 from Willow Creek, fifty-six miles northeast of Eureka. The Trinity River flows through the center of the reservation and joins the Klamath at Weitchpec, and a corridor of the reservation follows on either side of the Klamath into Del Norte County all the way to the coast. At Weitchpec, representatives of thirteen local Indian tribes gathered in 1851 to arrange a treaty with the United States government concerning their lands. This document, signed on October 6 of that year, is now included among the eighteen unratified California Indian treaties on file in Washington, D.C. A military post, Fort Gaston, was established in the Hoopa Valley in 1855, and in 1864 Superintendent Austin Wiley selected the valley and surrounding hills for an Indian reservation. Indian ceremonial dances are still held on ancient grounds at Hoopa, Pecwan, near Somes Bar, and elsewhere. The Brush Dance, Jump Dance, and White Deerskin Dance feature beautiful and distinctive regalia and are traditions maintained with much pride. Some of the typical regalia can be seen at the Hoopa Tribal Museum. Half a mile north of the museum is an old village site with a family sweat house and other rebuilt cedar-slab structures.

HUMBOLDT BAY

The first recorded discovery of Humboldt Bay was made in 1806 by Captain Jonathan Winship, an American employed by the Russian-American Fur Company to hunt seals along the coast of California. With over forty small boats manned by Aleut Indians, Captain Winship in the *O'Cain* anchored twenty-five miles north of Eureka. While searching along the shore for sea otter, some of his men discovered the bay. Winship named the harbor the Bay of Indians because of the numerous native villages found along its shore. To the entrance he gave the name Rezanov after Count Nikolai Rezanov.

In 1827, Jedediah Strong Smith, trapper and pathfinder, penetrated into Humboldt County, but did not see the bay. It remained for Dr. Josiah Gregg to rediscover the bay that Winship had seen and named forty-three years earlier. Gregg had undertaken to trace the Trinity River from its source to its mouth. With his companions, he started from Rich Bar, in the vicinity of Weaverville, on November 5, 1849, and reached Trinidad Head on December 7. Here the expedition turned south and on December 20 reached the bay that Dr. Gregg named Trinity Bay. In April of the following year, Lieutenant Douglass Ottinger, in command of the *Laura Virginia*, anchored in the bay and named it Humboldt Bay.

Humboldt Bay lies halfway between Cape Trinidad to the north and Cape Mendocino to the south, a dis-

Sweat House from Sumeg (Yurok) Indian Village, Patrick's Point State Park, Trinidad

Memorial Lighthouse, Trinidad

tance of forty-five miles. It is very capacious, being almost the only good harbor between San Francisco and Puget Sound. It is a timber port with a small fleet of commercial fishing boats and several oyster farms. As elusive as the entrance to San Francisco Bay, it was passed and repassed for centuries by navigators unaware of its presence.

TRINIDAD

Trinidad is on US 101 twenty miles north of Eureka. Founded in 1850, it is California's smallest incorporated city. It was once in Klamath County (later abolished), where it was the county seat from 1851 to 1854.

Sebastián Rodríguez Cermeño probably sighted Trinidad's rocky headland on November 4, 1595, when the *San Agustin*, laden with silks and porcelain from the Orient, first sighted the coast of New Spain a little above 41° latitude. Trinidad was so named by the Spanish mariners Juan Francisco de la Bodega and Bruno Heceta on Trinity Sunday, June 9, 1775. Trinidad was next visited in 1793 by British Captain George Vancouver, who found the roughly hewn cross left by the Spaniards, with the inscription CAROLUS III DEI G HYSPANIARUM REX (Charles III by the Grace of God King of Spain). At the Coast Guard station south of town, a monument (SRL 146) in the form of a granite cross was placed by the women's clubs of Humboldt County. The town's early history is memorialized by a monument (SRL 216) at the corner of Edwards and Hector Streets. The Indian village of Tsurai, occupied until 1916, dated from very early times. It was visited by Captains Bodega and Heceta, the first outsiders, in 1775. A monument (SRL 838) stands at Ocean and Edwards Streets in Trinidad, overlooking the village site. The

Sumeg Indian village, scene of Yurok tribal gatherings since its construction in 1990, is in Patrick's Point State Park. The oldest building in the charming town is Holy Trinity Catholic Church (1873). The Trinidad Museum is at 529-B Trinity Street.

The Trinidad lighthouse, now automated, stands on the ocean side of Trinidad Head, and is not visible from the town. A replica of that structure, however, was put up in 1949 by the harbor and is known as the Memorial Lighthouse, in honor of those who perished at sea.

HUMBOLDT CITY

This settlement was begun in April 1850, immediately opposite the entrance to Humboldt Bay. Soon the rival settlements of Bucksport, Eureka, and Uniontown were also founded to the north. Despite the efforts of promoters to attract settlers, the town was situated on a low-lying beach and was subject to frequent flooding. A marker (SRL 882) at Harold Larsen Vista Point on Humboldt Hill Road just above US 101 commemorates the Humboldt Harbor Historical District. Bucksport to the north was named for David A. Buck, an early settler and a member of the Gregg party. This community was ultimately absorbed into Eureka and now lies within the southwestern corner of modern Eureka.

INDIAN (GUNTHER'S) ISLAND

Gunther's Island was a Wiyot Indian ceremonial center in Humboldt Bay. As the region became more populated, one night in 1860 a group of whites slaughtered between sixty and eighty of these people on what has since been known as Indian Island. Bret Harte, who was temporarily in charge of the Uniontown paper, the *Northern Californian*, denounced the massacre, and his editorial was approved by the majority of the community. The reaction of a "violent minority," however, was so threatening that Harte was compelled to return to San Francisco. The massacre was only one instance of many Indian-white conflicts in these years. A vigil in memory of their departed is held annually by the Wiyots on nearby Woodley Island.

The sites of two shell mounds are on Indian Island, which is registered as a National Historic Landmark by the Department of the Interior.

EUREKA

Eureka (SRL 477), destined to be the metropolis of Humboldt Bay, was the last of the towns to be established there. When the Mendocino Exploring Company arrived in May 1850, they found that the Union Company, located at Uniontown, already claimed the land. An agreement was made to share the establishment of the town, and lots were surveyed the same year under the supervision of James Ryan.

Development was slow at first, since the new settlement was farther away from the Klamath mines than Uniontown. When business shifted from the Klamath to the Trinity mining district, a road was cut to the Trinity area from Eureka, and the latter's position was improved. By 1860, lumbering was the dominant industry at Humboldt Bay, and Eureka, alongside the deepest natural channel of the bay and with good docks, grew rapidly. It became the county seat in 1856.

Eureka's outstanding landmark is the imposing Carson mansion near the bay at Second and M Streets. It is probably the best-preserved and most photographed Victorian home in California. Built in the 1880s by lumber magnate William Carson, it consists of three stories and an ornamented tower, with some of the most elaborate wooden scrollwork and embellishment to be seen anywhere in the state. The redwood house remained in the Carson family until the late 1940s and is now the Ingomar Club, a private organization, and is not open to the public.

The blocks west of the Carson mansion by the waterfront, between C and G Streets and Third Street and the harbor, have been designated the Eureka Old Town area. Within this area are the old Eureka Public Library (now a cultural center), a Carnegie bequest from 1902 at 636 F Street, and the Clarke Memorial Museum at Third and E Streets. The museum is housed in the former Bank of Eureka building, a handsome example of the Roman Renaissance style. Founded with a grant

Carson Mansion, Eureka

from Cecile Clarke in 1960, the museum has a special wing, Nealis Hall, that contains the largest collection extant (some 1,200 pieces) of northwestern California Indian basketry. The museum also has displays of regalia and materials relating to the Hoopa, Karuk, and Yurok tribes. Other parts of the museum display materials from the history of Eureka and Humboldt County.

The Humboldt Bay Maritime Museum on First Street between E and F Streets contains artifacts from the nautical activities of the bay, including relics from the wreck of the USS *Milwaukee* in 1917.

THE SAMOA COOKHOUSE

At Samoa, on SR 255 across the bay from Eureka, stands the Samoa Cookhouse, which has been serving gigantic meals since 1900. It was built for the workers of the Hammond Lumber Company. Most of the surrounding bunkhouses and other buildings of the lumber company are gone; one survivor is used as a museum. Cookhouses of this kind were once common throughout the lumbering country; the Samoa Cookhouse, now in business as a public eating place, is the last such establishment in the West. The Native Sons of the Golden West placed a plaque here in 1999.

ARCATA

Arcata, on Arcata Bay eight miles northeast of Eureka, was founded in 1850 by a group of San Franciscans under the leadership of L. K. Wood. Wood was one of the Josiah Gregg party, which discovered Arcata Bay and adjoining Humboldt Bay in 1849, at the point where Arcata now stands. On April 19, 1850, Wood and his men founded their town, which they named Uniontown.

When Humboldt County was organized in 1853,

Uniontown became the county seat. It was the center of activity in the days of pack trains, when goods were carried to the mines over the mountain trails that began at Uniontown and followed the Trinity and Klamath Rivers. When the lumbering industry superseded mining, the lumber mills centered at Eureka, which was on deep water, making it the natural shipping point of the bay. In 1860 Uniontown was renamed Arcata, the original Indian name for the spot, which is beautifully situated by the bay and surrounded by redwood forests. The Humboldt State Normal School was established at Arcata in 1913. In later years it became the Humboldt State Teachers College and Humboldt State College; today it is Humboldt State University. Its Natural History Museum at 1315 G Street contains the extraordinary Maloney Fossil Collection with some 2,000 specimens of plant and animal fossils. Perhaps the oldest house in Arcata (1850) has recently become the Phillips House Museum at Seventh and Union Streets, a restored farmhouse emphasizing domestic life in the 1880s.

At Eighth and H Streets is the Jacoby Building (SRL 783), a pioneer business house of Arcata. Augustus Jacoby built the basement and first story in 1857, and during its early years the structure served periodically as a place of refuge in time of Indian troubles. Various firms supplying the Klamath-Trinity mines were located here for many years.

The Arcata and Mad River Rail Road is the oldest line on the north coast. Established in 1854, it served as a link between Humboldt Bay and the Trinity River mines. A marker (SRL 842) commemorates the pioneer railroad at the depot, 330 Railroad Avenue in Blue Lake, the eastern terminus of the line, six miles east of Arcata on SR 299.

FERNDALE

The city of Ferndale (SRL 883) began as an agricultural community as early as 1852; dairying is still a principal industry. Dozens of ornate commercial and residential buildings (most from the 1890s) still stand, drawing tourists in increasing numbers and making Ferndale one of the best-preserved towns in California. The five blocks along the center of Main Street are listed on the National Register of Historic Places. A walking-tour map is available from the chamber of commerce or at the charming Ferndale Museum at Third and Shaw Streets. The Ferndale Cemetery and adjacent St. Mary's Cemetery on the brow of a hill to the south of town are large and well maintained.

FORTUNA

Springville was founded in 1875 and named for the numerous springs in the neighboring hills. It was subsequently renamed Slide and then Fortuna by its "fortunate" citizens. The Northwestern Pacific Railroad station, built in 1893 at the foot of Seventh Street, was purchased by the city and moved to 4 Park Street, where it now serves as the Fortuna Depot Museum. In addition to its displays on local history, it also serves as a research library.

SCOTIA

Scotia is a town entirely owned by the Pacific Lumber Company, whose giant mill was closed in December 2001. The old Scotia Inn was first opened in 1888; the present structure was completed in 1924. It still attracts guests and diners. The Pacific Lumber Company Museum is in the 1920 building that once housed the First National Bank of Scotia. Across the street is the rustic Winema Theater from the same era. Company towns once abounded throughout the logging areas of the West, and Scotia is one of the last of them.

ORLEANS

Orleans Bar was once a thriving mining center on the Klamath River, along which many rich mines of northern California were located. This was the county seat of Klamath County from 1855 to 1876, when the county was disestablished. Today it is a small village simply called Orleans, on SR 96 about fifteen miles northeast of the junction with SR 169 at Weitchpec.

WILLOW CREEK

The high mountains and steep valleys of northwestern California were never easily penetrated, and their remoteness gave rise to legends of mysterious creatures. One which has received much attention is the Sasquatch, also known as Big Foot, described as a very large shaggy biped, extremely shy and reclusive but capable of great feats of strength. Tales of near encounters with the creature are "documented" by blurred photographs and films and unusual piles of debris found in odd places. At Willow Creek, on SR 299, which follows the old road from Weaverville to the coast, there is a carved wooden statue of Big Foot in the center of town, near the Willow Creek–China Flat Museum. The mu-

Fortuna Depot Museum

seum itself focuses mostly on local farming and lumbering history.

MAIL RIDGE

Mail Ridge was once a part of the old mail stage route from San Francisco into the northwestern part of California before the advent of the railroad. It is about 3,500 feet above sea level with extensive views over the whole southern part of Humboldt County.

To reach the ridge, SR 36 leaves the Redwood Highway (US 101) at Fortuna, eighteen miles south of Eureka, and follows the Van Duzen River to Bridgeville. From Bridgeville, Alderpoint Road runs south through high mountain country to Blocksburg, and on to Alderpoint. The route leads uphill for eight miles to the town of Harris, then turns north again and follows along Mail Ridge, the old stage road.

PETROLIA

Humboldt County claims the honor of California's first drilled oil wells, and a quiet little town in the Mattole Valley remembers the brief boom in its name, Petrolia. Prior to 1865 the area was mapped by A. J. Doolittle as "New Jerusalem," but the shipment of the first crude oil to a San Francisco refinery by the Union Mattole Oil Company in June 1865 was the occasion for the bestowal of a permanent name. A monument in the town commemorates the oil wells (SRL 543), which are on private property about three miles east on the North Fork of the Mattole River.

The town is located near the most seismically active portion of the California coast. In 1992 a sharp earthquake created a fire that destroyed the historic store and post office that were the nucleus of the community.

COVERED BRIDGES

Humboldt County contains two of California's eleven remaining covered bridges. Both are located on the Elk River five to six miles south of Eureka, not far from Fields Landing, and both are fifty-two feet in length. The Berta's Ranch bridge, built in 1936, is the westernmost covered bridge in the United States. The Zane's Ranch bridge, farther upstream, was completed in 1937. When these bridges were built there were twelve covered bridges in Humboldt County alone.

THE REDWOOD GROVES

One of the great attractions of this area are the magnificent stands of *Sequoia sempervirens*, the coast redwood. Although this has been an area of intensive lumbering, groups such as Save-the-Redwoods League have been active in preserving groves and stands of virgin timber. Prairie Creek Redwoods State Park, along the coast at the northern edge of the county, is noteworthy for being a refuge for the Roosevelt elk that were once numerous in the region. Adjacent to it and extending south for many miles is the Humboldt County area of Redwood National Park, which was established in 1968. Grizzly Creek Redwoods State Park is a small jewel along SR 36 between Carlotta and Bridgeville. Richardson Grove State Park is another small redwood preserve bisected by US 101 at the southern edge of the county. The largest preserve is Humboldt Redwoods State Park, which contains the spectacular Avenue of the Giants. This road runs parallel to US 101, which passes the many groves set aside as memorials to families and organizations.

The title of the world's tallest tree has long remained among the Humboldt County sequoias. Until 1957 the honor belonged to the Founders Tree in Humboldt Redwoods State Park (height 352.6 feet). Then it was discovered that the nearby Rockefeller Tree in the same park was a few feet taller. In 1963, Dr. Paul A. Zahl, senior naturalist of the National Geographic Society, found a redwood over eleven feet taller than the Rockefeller. This 367.8-foot giant stands in a privately owned grove on Redwood Creek southeast of Orick. In the same grove two other trees were discovered that also exceed the Rockefeller Tree in height. It is quite likely that an even taller tree remains to be found.

The Humboldt Redwoods State Park visitors' center is two miles south of Weott on the Avenue of the Giants.

Imperial County

De Anza Hotel, Calexico

Imperial County was organized in 1907 from that part of San Diego County known as Imperial Valley, and is consequently the newest of California's fifty-eight counties. El Centro is the county seat.

A PREHISTORIC WONDERLAND

Imperial Valley is remarkable for the vast range of prehistoric and geologic relics to be found within its borders. Outlining and in a sense explaining these is the ancient beachline extending from north to south and plainly visible at 260 feet above the surface of the Salton Sea. Professor William P. Blake of the Williamson survey first observed the old beachline and examined its shells while engaged in making the first governmental survey of Imperial Valley in 1853.

Extending southward from Indio in Riverside County, past the Travertine Rock at the county line and on through western Imperial County to the Fish Creek Mountains, this ancient shoreline there turns east and south, skirting Superstition Mountain and crossing I-8 about three miles west of Dixieland. Continuing south along the West Side Canal and down into Mexico as far as Black Butte, it again turns northward, reentering Imperial County eight miles east of Calexico. Here the waterline follows the East Highline Canal northward, passing east of the Salton Sea into Riverside County, where the circuit is completed at a point slightly north of Indio.

This beachline, approximately 30 feet above sea level, is that of an ancient fresh-water lake that covered Imperial and Coachella Valleys. Indications are that in past ages it was filled many times by waters from the Colorado River and stood at this elevation for long periods before the river shifted course again and directed its flow into the Gulf of California. Along the entire length of this beach, or within a short distance from its sands, may be found relics of bygone ages: vast coral reefs, millions of fossils and shells, and even pottery made by a long-vanished people. The beachline is not always visible south of the international border. Presumably it is buried beneath silt from the Colorado River.

Travertine Rock is a landmark near SR 86 on the western shore of the Salton Sea. It is actually not true travertine but is covered by a calcareous rock called tufa, left there by receding waters at least a thousand years ago. The chalk-like surface is made even more interesting by the Indian rock carvings (petroglyphs) of a prehistoric age. Twelve miles to the south lies a petrified forest.

A group of prehistoric animal tracks, reached by a drive over rough roads and a short hike, can be seen in a small canyon north of the Fish Creek Mountains. Presumably a water hole where great prehistoric animals came to drink, the canyon is covered by hundreds of huge tracks that geologists believe to be the footprints of mastodons, solidified and preserved by succeeding geological epochs.

Painted Gorge, with its rugged walls tinted in a patchwork of colors like the design of an old-fashioned quilt, is seven miles north of I-8 and thirty miles west of El Centro. At the upper end of the gorge are high coral reefs and well-preserved oyster shells.

The best and most extensive coral formations are found in Shell Canyon across the Coyote Mountains from Painted Gorge. These deposits are reached only by a very difficult desert road followed by three miles of hiking. Two magnificent coral canyons may also be reached from Barrett Well with less difficulty: Barrett

Canyon in the Fish Creek Mountains to the north and Garnet Canyon in the Coyote Mountains to the south.

South of I-8 stretches the Yuha plain, with its myriad fish fossils, its beds of oyster shells, and what has been called "the most amazing rock concretions ever discovered in the United States." The latter were first mentioned by Juan Bautista de Anza in 1774 and first described over 125 years later by George Wharton James in his *Wonders of the Colorado Desert.* They consist of "detached rocks of various shapes and sizes, chiefly spherical . . . and resembling petrified fruits, vegetables, and flowers."

THE EXPLORATIONS OF ALARCÓN AND DIAZ

Just east of Pilot Knob, on SR 186 one mile south of I-8, is the marker (SRL 568) for what may be called California's first historic spot. The text reads: "Hernando de Alarcón Expedition, 1540. Alarcón's mission was to provide supplies for Francisco Coronado's expedition in search of the fabled Seven Cities of Cibola. The Spaniards led by Hernando de Alarcón ascended the Colorado River by boat from the Gulf of California past this point, thereby becoming the first non-Indians to sight Alta California on September 5, 1540." Eugene Chamberlin notes that the Coronado expedition "turned northeast from Culiacan and had no contact with Alarcón. The most northerly penetration of Alarcón's river boats was some fifteen miles northeast of present day Yuma. Here he left a message carved on a cross in case anyone from Coronado's group reached that point. Alarcón returned to the ships, made a second upriver trip, and then the ships returned southward."

The next Spaniard to walk upon California soil was Melchior Diaz, who had left Coronado's expedition near the present site of Ures, Mexico, in October 1540, with instructions to make contact with Alarcón if possible. Diaz proceeded up the Colorado River as far as the Gila, where his party crossed over on rafts, touching California soil at about the same point as Alarcón. His group continued inland several miles, still looking for Alarcón, who had only preceded him to the river by a few weeks. His group encountered "geothermal explosions" (perhaps near Lago de los Volcanes, some twenty miles south-southeast of the present Mexicali in Baja California) and turned back to the lower Colorado. En route, Diaz tried to spear a dog that was threatening them; he was himself impaled by the spear shaft and mortally wounded. The rest of his group escaped to Sonora, in which flight, apparently, the papers compiled by Diaz were lost. The accounts of the expedition are the recollections of the survivors; the actual route of the Diaz party probably can never be determined.

FIRST PASSAGE OF THE COLORADO DESERT

A trail from Mexico to the junction of the Colorado and Gila Rivers had been blazed as early as 1700 by Father Eusebio Kino, a Jesuit priest, whose purpose was to find an overland route from Sonora to the missions of Baja California. Kino was one of the great missionaries of New Spain. He was in Lower California from 1683 to 1685; the remainder of his life was spent in Pimería Alta (now southern Arizona and northern Sonora), where he founded some fifty missions and chapels.

The desire to find a way to connect the missions of Pimería Alta with those of Baja California led to numerous exploring expeditions. In 1701 Kino descended the Colorado River from its junction with the Gila, nearly to the mouth of the Colorado; in a longer descent of that river the following year Kino went as far as the Gulf. These explorations led him to believe that California was a peninsula and not an island, as had previously been supposed. Furthermore, the way had been opened to the great Colorado Desert, a trail followed over seventy years later by Garcés and Anza.

Father Francisco Garcés, famous priest-explorer, was the first Spaniard to enter the Colorado Desert. In 1771, believing that he was crossing the Gila River, he crossed the Colorado instead. During his wanderings, he skirted the Cocopah Range to its terminus at Signal Mountain near present-day Calexico. To the northwest he saw two great gaps in the mountain range, which he believed could be followed into Alta California without difficulty.

On this journey, Garcés gained information that influenced the decision of the government, which eventually supported Anza's plan to go overland to California. It was also this journey, more than any other, that helped to determine the path taken by the subsequent expedition.

In 1774, Juan Bautista de Anza, one of the great figures in the history of California, volunteered to find an overland route to the coast missions in order to avoid the perils and uncertainty of communication by sea, and to ensure the settlement of Alta California. Antonio María Bucareli, then viceroy of Mexico, accepted Anza's offer.

Accompanied by Fathers Francisco Garcés and Juan Díaz and twenty soldiers, Anza reached the junction of the Colorado and Gila Rivers on February 7, 1774. Two days later he crossed the Colorado at the ford above the Gila, camping on the California side.

On the following day, the party went four leagues along the river, passing the geological formation known later as Pilot Knob, which Anza named the Cerro de San Pablo, where the river turns south. Proceeding another league, they stopped for the night at the Ranchería de San Pablo, a Yuma Indian village. This was just above the present international boundary line, and from here the expedition continued southwest until they reached a lake that Anza called Laguna de Santa Olaya, twelve miles south of the boundary line and eight miles west of the Colorado, "the end of the known land." Beyond lay hostile Indians and uncounted miles of sand dunes blocking the way into what is now southeastern Imperial County.

Undaunted, Anza set forth to cross this forbidding waste, but the dunes proved impassable, and he was forced to retreat to Santa Olaya, which the party reached again on February 19. Having rested for several days among the friendly Indians at this oasis, the party resumed its journey on March 2, and finally reentered California on March 7, camping three or four miles southwest of the Yuha Well and about two miles north of the international boundary line. The next morning, they reached a little group of refreshing wells, "which, on being opened, distilled an abundant supply of most beautiful water." Here Anza rested for a day, refreshing both the footsore men and the starved horses. These life-giving springs were named by Anza the Pozas de Santa Rosa de las Lajas (the Wells of St. Rose of the Flat Rocks), because of the great number of peculiar rock formations. How the less poetic name of Yuha Well later came to be attached to them is not known. The site (SRL 1008) is marked by an E Clampus Vitus plaque at the eastbound Sunbeam Roadside Area on I-8 near Seely.

Anza's last important camp in Imperial County was reached on March 10. It was made at the junction or sink of the San Felipe and Carrizo Creeks, called by Anza the San Sebastián, in honor of Sebastián Tarabal, his Indian guide. Sebastián was a Baja Californian who had been Christianized by the Jesuits. He chafed under Franciscan discipline at San Gabriel, and with his wife and parents fled the mission eastward; he alone survived the desert. He joined up with Anza early in 1774. The campsite is now known as Harper's Well, at the base of the Fish Creek Mountains and at the western edge of the Colorado Desert. The next day the expedition entered San Diego County by way of San Felipe Canyon and San Carlos Pass.

On his return to Mexico in May, Anza again crossed the desert, camping at San Sebastián on May 7, and from there making a shortcut directly across the desert. On December 11, 1775, he again stopped at the Wells of Santa Rosa, this time to rest and refresh the first caravan of emigrants to enter California, the party destined to be also the first settlers of San Francisco. This caravan, which left Tubac on October 23, 1775, was made up of 240 persons, of whom more than thirty were women and 136 were boys and girls. Only one life was lost on the entire journey of 1,000 miles, and three babies were born en route. Over a thousand animals also began the journey, but many perished in the deserts.

On his final return to Mexico in 1776, Anza again made a direct cut across the desert, paralleling SR 86 past Kane Spring as far as Westmoreland, and camping on May 8 east of Imperial.

THE DESERT TRAIL

The old desert trail across Imperial Valley, first opened by Anza and followed later by generations of explorers and trappers, traders and Argonauts, and finally by a long line of home-seekers, has been variously known as the Sonora Road, the Colorado Road, the Emigrant Trail, and the Butterfield Stage Route. That part of the route from the San Felipe Sink via San Carlos Pass was closed after 1782 and has never been used since. In July 1781 the two missions established on the Colorado River the previous year were destroyed by Indians, and in 1781 and 1782 Pedro Fages carried dispatches to Mission San Gabriel concerning these Indian troubles. On the first of these trips he followed Anza's trail all the way, but on the second he traversed it only across the desert to the San Felipe watering place, where he turned up Carrizo Creek into the unexplored territory to the southwest, thus opening the road that now goes by way of Warner's Ranch, a trail followed by the southern emigrant trains of 1849 and the 1850s and known as the old Emigrant Trail.

The David E. Jackson party in 1831 followed Anza's trail across the desert to Carrizo Creek, where they crossed the mountains via Warner's Pass, probably the first Americans to journey that way. In 1834 Rafael Amador, a messenger for President Santa Anna of Mexico, made the trip in forty-eight days—record time—and in 1846 Stephen W. Kearney conducted the advance guard of the "Army of the West" across the old desert trail and over the mountains through Warner's Pass.

The Butterfield Stage used approximately the same

Section of Old Plank Road

road from 1858 to 1861, probably the first well-defined trail across the Imperial Valley. The ruined walls of the old Pilot Knob station could be seen for many years at Araz on I-8 a few miles west of Yuma. Except for the station at Indian Wells (also known as Sunset Springs and by various other names), the trail through the shifting dunes from Araz westward is uncertain until Carrizo Creek is reached. It led south of the international boundary line by way of the stations at Cook's Well and Alamo Mocho (both of which have disappeared) and then northwest into the present Imperial County by way of the station at Indian Wells, halfway to the Carrizo station (San Diego County). Indian Wells was located approximately eight miles south and a little west of Seely. The adobe building stood there until it was washed away by a flood in 1906.

Seventeen miles west of Yuma in the sand dunes can be seen what is left of the old plank road built in 1916–17, one of the first automobile roads through this part of the desert (SRL 845). It was wide enough for only one car, with turnouts provided for passing. Nearby is a bypassed stretch of US 80 (Gray's Well Road), built in 1927, which seems like a superhighway next to the plank road. Providing the greatest contrast of all, the I-8 freeway carries one through the dunes in a few minutes. Recreational vehicles today swarm over the area, now viewed as a major dune-buggy park instead of a formidable and impassable region. Some sections of the plank road have been reinstalled by volunteer organizations.

THE YUMA MASSACRE

Mission La Purísima Concepción and Mission San Pedro y San Pablo de Bicuñer once stood twelve miles apart in the southeastern corner of what would become Imperial County. The two were established in the autumn of 1780 by four Franciscan padres from Mexico, Fathers Díaz, Morena, Barreneche, and Garcés. The purpose of these missions was twofold: to convert the Yuma Indians living at this point along the Colorado River, and to make a way station on the overland emigrant trail from Mexico to the California missions.

The plan followed at Purísima and at San Pedro y San Pablo was different from that followed in other parts of California. The Indians were allowed to remain on their own rancherías, and the padres visited them there, ministering to their spiritual needs alone.

But this plan was not successful. The fathers had neither the means to visit the Indians often nor the necessary goods to allure them. Moreover, the soldiers, and the few white settlers who came with them, used for themselves the scant patches of ground on which the Indians raised their melons, beans, and corn, and the white settlers' cattle ate up the precious pasturage that the Indians' stock needed.

Naturally, the Indians soon looked on the white people as invaders, and in July 1781 one of the most tragic occurrences in the history of California took place. Captain Fernando Rivera y Moncada, lieutenant-governor of Baja California, was bringing a party of settlers from Mexico to establish the proposed pueblo of Los Angeles in Alta California. On reaching the Colorado River, the soldiers and settlers, over whom Rivera exercised little discipline, harassed the Yuma Indians. The families in the train were sent ahead with some of the soldiers, while Rivera remained behind to refresh his exhausted animals. From July 17 to July 19, the Indians struck back. Rivera and his soldiers, Father Garcés and the other priests at the two missions, and all other males were killed, thirty-four casualties all told. The women and children were made captive, being subsequently ransomed by Pedro Fages.

The missions and settlements were not established again on the Colorado, and the route that had been opened with such great effort by Juan Bautista de Anza in 1774 and 1775 became more dangerous to travelers than ever before. The colonists of Rivera's expedition did go on to establish the great city of Los Angeles, but the importance of the Yuma Massacre should not be underestimated. With Anza's land route effectively closed, the only means of supply from and contact with Mexico was the long sea route. The Californians soon saw the necessity of development from within and began to draw from California's abundant natural

Site of Mission San Pedro y San Pablo de Bicuñer, near Bard

Crossing and historic buildings on both sides of the Colorado River, such as the remains of Fort Yuma on the California side and the Territorial Prison on the Arizona side, have been registered as a National Historic Landmark.

In 1977 the site of Mission San Pedro y San Pablo de Bicuñer was determined by historian Phil Porretta, long after it was believed that the site had been lost. The excavations for the All-American Canal many years earlier had contributed to the problem. Porretta found that the site of the mission was about one-quarter mile west of the California bank of the Colorado River, some ten miles northeast of Yuma and one mile west of the Laguna Dam of the Colorado River. Close by is the state historical marker (SRL 921) on County Road 24, just west of the intersection of Levee and Mehring Roads, 4.4 miles northeast of Bard.

EARLY COLORADO RIVER FERRIES

Several ferries were established on the Colorado below its junction with the Gila in 1849 and 1850. The first of these was built by General Alexander Anderson, from Tennessee, in order to transport his party to the California side at a point several miles south of the Gila. Anderson afterward presented his boat to the Indians with a certificate of title, the terms of which seem to have been faithfully lived up to by the latter.

Another ferry, started in September 1849 by Lieutenant Cave J. Couts at Camp Calhoun on the California side, aided gold-seekers across the river. In December Couts sold his ferry to Dr. G. W. Lincoln, later reputed to have been a distant relative of Abraham Lincoln. This ferry came to a violent end. When John Glanton, a villainous character, purchased a half share in Lincoln's ferry, the enterprise quickly degenerated. Lincoln was secretly done away with and the neighboring Indian ferry was destroyed to rid Glanton's ferry of competition. The indignant Indians retaliated by surprising and killing Glanton and his henchmen and destroying their boat.

In the summer of 1850 the ferry was reestablished by L. J. F. Jaeger and others at a point several miles below the present site of Yuma near the Hall Hanlon ranch. Lumber for Jaeger's ferry was transported across the desert from San Diego by pack train. A ferry was operated at this point until the present old highway bridge was built in 1915. A marker commemorating these pioneer ferries stands at the old landing on the Arizona side near the Territorial Prison.

resources. At the same time dependence upon Mexico, both economic and political, was lessening, and contact was being established instead with the foreigners who came by land and sea, paving the way for an early and easy American occupation. The Yuma Massacre therefore had a major impact on the next half-century of California history.

After declaring independence from Spain, Mexico attempted to reopen the overland road from Sonora into California in 1822. In 1825 Lieutenant Romualdo Pacheco and his soldiers built an adobe fort here, the only Mexican fort in Alta California. On April 26, 1826, Kumeyaay Indians attacked the fort, killing three soldiers and wounding three others, and the discouraged Pacheco abandoned it, taking the soldiers to San Diego. The site of Fort Romualdo Pacheco (SRL 944) is on the west bank of the New River south of Worthington Road, six and one-half miles west of the town of Imperial.

In the early 1850s, Fort Yuma was established near where Mission Purísima had stood, and American troops were stationed there for several years. It was besieged by Indians in 1851. Today a Catholic chapel for the Indians stands on what is thought to be the site of Mission La Purísima Concepción (SRL 350). Next to the monument is a statue of the martyred Father Garcés. Some of the old buildings of Fort Yuma still stand nearby (SRL 806). These landmarks are on a hill just across the Colorado River from the Arizona Territorial Prison in Yuma, and like the prison they are reached from the former route of the main highway, which crosses the river by an old, narrow bridge. The Yuma

On the southwest bank of the Colorado River, twenty-five miles north of Yuma, is the site of Picacho, an early gold-mining camp, where gold was said to have been discovered by an Indian in 1860. It was first located by Mexican prospectors in 1862 and was one of the richest placers in California. The population of Picacho was almost entirely Hispanic during its first few years. The Americans came in later and found rich lodes in the neighboring hills, put up large stamp mills, and soon had a payroll amounting to $40,000 a month. As with most gold sites, the pay dirt in time gave out and the people moved away. Picacho today is being developed as the Picacho State Recreational Area. It is reached only by a dirt road from the south or by the river itself; few buildings are left. The site of the mines (SRL 193) is four miles south of the area on private land.

TUMCO

Tumco, known first as Hedges and then as Gold Rock, was once a mining town of some importance. Nine miles north of I-8 and slightly east of County Road 34, it lies in a narrow desert valley hemmed in on either side by two barren mountain ranges. Its name is an acronym for The United Mines Company that purchased the property. Once inhabited by 2,000 people, Tumco is today a desolate wasteland of ruined adobe walls and stone foundations; it has been marked by an E Clampus Vitus plaque. The Tumco mines (SRL 182), originally staked as a claim in 1884, operated until 1914. The most famous of them were the Golden Queen, the Golden Cross, and the Golden Crown. Five miles northeast of Ogilby, farther south on Road 34, was the American Girl Mine, developed later than Tumco and worked by fewer than two hundred men. Ogilby is itself now a ghost town, with an abandoned cemetery by the roadside.

WATER FROM THE COLORADO

The first diversion of water from the Colorado River to Imperial Valley was made through a temporary wooden gate, known as the Chaffey Gate, located several thousand feet back from the river a short distance above the Mexican border. The gate was too small and the sill too high; it was replaced in 1905 by a concrete gate, known as Hanlon Heading, which was located at the last place where rock formations are found on the lower Colorado River. This also was connected to the river by an open canal. This canal became filled with silt during flood periods, and in 1918 it was replaced by another concrete gate, Rockwood Heading, several thousand feet upstream and adjacent to the Colorado River. It was through these structures that every drop of water used by the people of Imperial Valley was diverted from 1901 until 1942, when the All-American Canal was completed.

It is this water from the Colorado River, conveyed through a vast system of canals and ditches to be deposited upon the rich soil of the Salton Sink, that makes Imperial Valley today's prosperous agricultural community. It is appropriate that around this spot should cluster the memories of three pioneers of the idea of reclaiming the Colorado Desert: Dr. Oliver Meredith Wozencraft, Charles Robinson Rockwood, and Charles Chaffey.

Dr. Wozencraft is considered the real father of Imperial Valley, "the first man to actually plan the reclamation of the desert sink for agricultural purposes by bringing the waters of the Colorado to the arid area to the west." He came to California in 1849, and immediately after his arrival in San Francisco he set out on an expedition to the little-known Colorado Desert. It was there, in 1849, that he first conceived the idea of reclamation. The project so possessed him that he devoted the rest of his life to making his dream a reality.

Obtaining favorable action from the state Legislature in 1859, Wozencraft was given all state rights in the Salton Sink. The next step was to get a patent or title from the federal government, but in spite of many attempts he never obtained this; the attention of Congress on the Civil War and the problems of Reconstruction were perhaps one reason. Dr. Wozencraft died in Washington in 1887 while making a final effort to obtain congressional action. His repeated attempts to interest investors in his project had been of no avail. However, an appeal made to George Chaffey for support in 1882, although not obtaining results at the time, was no doubt a factor leading to the final accomplishment of the reclamation under the latter's direction from April 1900 to February 1902.

Meanwhile, there was no one to continue the work begun by Dr. Wozencraft until Charles Robinson Rockwood, a civil engineer, in 1892 rediscovered the agricultural potential of Imperial Valley. The Salton Sink, Rockwood believed, would flourish with the water of the Colorado River. But it would take him several years to find the person with capital to finance the work. The investor was George Chaffey.

Desert View Tower, off I-8

Chaffey had begun his career of founding agricultural colonies based on irrigation at Etiwanda (in San Bernardino County) in 1881. Here he originated the idea of a mutual water company and set up the first dynamo for developing hydroelectric power on the Pacific slope. The next year he laid out the Ontario Colony, also in southwestern San Bernardino County. In 1886 he and his brother William began their work of establishing colonies in the arid regions of Australia. There he learned that it was possible for Britons to colonize hot and arid regions, provided that sufficient water could be brought to them. With this experience, Chaffey was ready, when approached by Rockwood in 1899, to undertake the very thing he had refused to do in 1882 when Wozencraft made his appeal.

Chaffey now became the chief factor in the reclamation of the desert. Entering into the work under his own terms, he built the project from its beginning, planning and directing the construction of vast canals and ditches. It was he who gave the name Imperial to the valley.

Water from the Colorado was first turned through the intake gate at Pilot Knob on May 14, 1901. This first heading was located about 500 feet south of the present Rockwood Gate. The construction of the canals was completed in February 1902.

Bringing water to Imperial Valley by a canal partly in Mexico was necessary but full of problems. Moreover, it was necessary in most years to build either brush or sand dams across the river in low-flood periods in an endeavor to divert a sufficient supply of water for the valley. It became apparent that a new diversion point would have to be found and a canal routed wholly within the United Sates was also needed.

Bills toward this end were introduced in Congress beginning in 1918. Ten years later, Congress approved the Swing-Johnson Bill, which provided for the construction of Boulder (now Hoover) Dam and the All-American Canal. Imperial Dam, the diversion point for the canal, is located about twenty miles north of Yuma. The headworks for the canal have very large gates through which the water is diverted and a system of desilting that is one of the largest in this country. Along the canal are many large concrete structures, including three power plants. At Pilot Knob the Imperial Irrigation District has built a power plant where surplus water is discharged into the river through the old Rockwood Heading. Where the All-American Canal emerges from the sand dunes, a branch canal flows northward for 120 miles on the east side of Salton Sea and around Coachella Valley to provide supplemental water for that valley.

There are now 3,000 miles of irrigation and drainage canals serving 500,000 acres of cultivated land in Imperial Valley and its cities and towns. A vast desert waste has become one of the world's most fruitful gardens.

THE SALTON SEA

In 1905–7 unusual rainfalls caused the whole flow of the Colorado River to break through the intake gates, threatening to fill the entire valley, a phenomenon that had happened before in prehistoric times. The flow of the river was finally turned back into its normal course by February 10, 1907, thus saving most of the valley. Most of this necessary work was done by the Southern Pacific Railroad, and ultimately the federal government reimbursed the company for the millions of dollars it had spent in the damming project.

In two years the runaway river left its mark in the newly formed Salton Sea, which had previously been dry land. Two streams from the Colorado, the Alamo and the New Rivers, flow northward from Mexico and empty into the Salton Sea. This body of water is about thirty-five miles long and from nine to fifteen miles wide. The elevation varies from year to year but averages about 230 feet below sea level. The recreational activities of the Salton Sea have been severely impaired by pollution in recent years, and its future is uncertain.

OTHER LANDMARKS OF IMPERIAL COUNTY

At the present site of Calexico, adjacent to and immediately north of the international boundary, Lieutenant Cave J. Couts, escort commander with the International Boundary Commission, established Camp Salvation (SRL 808) on September 23, 1849. Until the first of December the camp served as a refuge center for the distressed emigrants who were attempting to reach the gold fields over the southern emigrant trail.

An interesting treasury of Imperial Valley life can be seen at the Pioneers' Museum at 373 East Aten Road in the town of Imperial. The Imperial Valley Pioneers Society was formed in 1928 "to preserve the life histories of early settlers," and from its beginning sought to find artifacts to explain the life of people born in such different places as Korea, Lebanon, or Switzerland, who came to live in far-off California. The life of the Native American people of the Imperial Valley is also well presented.

At the western border of the county and only a hundred or so feet within the county line are two historical landmarks. Both lie within Imperial County, but by road must be reached via a spur from I-8 through San Diego County. The Desert View Tower was built in 1922–23 by Bert Vaughn of Jacumba (San Diego County) to commemorate the pioneers and road and railroad builders who opened the area. The tower (SRL 939) has a splendid view from its lofty top story. In the 1930s, W. T. Ratcliffe carved stone animal figures within the rocks surrounding the tower, creating a fantasy world of surprise and strange beauty. Adjacent to the tower is the plaque for Mountain Springs Station (SRL 194), a stone house about a mile to the north used as a store in 1862–70, and a toll road station for the San Diego and Fort Yuma Turnpike Company until 1876.

Palm Grove at Furnace Creek Ranch, Death Valley National Park

Inyo County

Inyo County was organized in 1866 from territory that had been set aside two years earlier from Mono and Tulare Counties and called Coso County. Coso County was never organized, however, and Inyo took its place. Inyo is a Paiute Indian word meaning "dwelling place of a great spirit," their name for the high mountains that lie east of the Sierra Nevada. Independence has always been the county seat.

Second largest of California's counties at 10,130 square miles, Inyo contains within its borders an extraordinarily varied topography. On its western boundary stands Mount Whitney, the highest peak in the continental United States; to the east is Death Valley, which contains the lowest spot in the Western Hemisphere. Death Valley abounds in scenic as well as historic interest, with places named Marble Canyon, Mosaic Canyon, the Sand Dunes, Grotto Canyon, Stovepipe Wells, Furnace Creek (a veritable oasis in the desert), Golden Canyon, Mushroom Rock, Pluto's Salt Pools, Badwater, and the Devil's Golf Course.

Mount Whitney is the highest peak in the United States outside of Alaska. It is one of a group of splendid mountains more than 13,000 feet in elevation situated in the High Sierra at the headwaters of the Kern and Kings Rivers. For many years it was thought that Mount Shasta was the highest mountain in California, but in 1864 the Whitney Geological Survey discovered that the summit of Mount Whitney was the highest point in the Sierra and higher than Shasta. The latest official measurements of their altitudes are 14,495 for Mount Whitney and 14,126 feet for Mount Shasta.

The mountain was named in 1864 in honor of Josiah Dwight Whitney, state geologist and leader of the Geological Survey, by the survey party led by William Henry Brewer. Clarence King, a member of the party and a leading geologist of the West, wrote: "For years our Chief, Professor Whitney, has made brave campaigns into the unknown realm of Nature. There stand for him two monuments: one a great report, made by his own hand; another the loftiest peak in the Union, begun . . . in the planet's youth and sculptured of enduring granite by the slow hand of time."

King, attempting to climb the peak in 1871, missed it on account of obscuring storm clouds and climbed Mount Langley by mistake. Learning of his error in 1873, he hastened west to climb the actual Mount Whitney on September 19. He was too late, however, for on August 18 the first ascent of the great mountain had been made by C. D. Begole, A. H. Johnson, and John Lucas.

Since 1881 Mount Whitney has been the base of operations for many scientific astronomical observations, the expedition under Professor Samuel P. Langley that year being the first. A frequently used approach to the mountain is from the eastern side, where a good road runs west from Lone Pine into the mountains to Whitney Portal, from which trails lead through the high country to the summit. The longer western approach is in Tulare County, through Sequoia National Park.

WINNEDUMAH

Directly east of Independence on the crest of the Inyo Mountains is a remarkable granite monolith commonly known as the Winnedumah Paiute Monument. Eighty feet high, it is visible on the skyline for many miles. A legend connected with it tells of Winnedumah, a medicine man, who was transformed into this great rock while calling for spiritual help in the course of a battle.

THE BISHOP PETROGLYPHS

Indian petroglyphs, or rock art, may be found throughout much of the arid West. Those of one area are unlike those of others, and so it is thought that different tribes made them. All, however, are similar in their simplicity of design. They are generally made in soft tufa by chipping, and are usually found near springs or streams on natural roads of travel. Sometimes these pictures are discovered in secluded mountain caves and protected spots.

A few miles north of Bishop, and extending into southern Mono County, the largest group of markings in this part of the state are found in the courses of stream beds or near long-used springs. Among these petroglyphs are crude pictures of what appear to be deer, footprints of humans and of animals, snakes, many-legged insects, and numerous geometrical designs. At Deep Springs Valley on the Midland Trail is a great round boulder covered with these carved pictures: sun symbols, snakes, a bird, what is possibly a rabbit, and concentric circles, which some think may be representations of sweat houses. At Little Lake, Coso Hot Springs, and Keeler are rocks on which animal figures predominate. Other petroglyphs are at the granite base of the Inyo Mountains near Swansea.

Similar carvings have been found from Alaska to South America. There is no positive proof of their respective ages, and their meaning is enigmatic. Everywhere, they are threatened by vandalism and exposure to the elements.

Big and Little Petroglyph Canyons, in the southern part of the county on the grounds of the U.S. Naval Weapons Center, have been registered as a National Historic Landmark by the Department of the Interior. Permission to visit them must be obtained from the authorities at the Weapons Center in China Lake in neighboring Kern County.

THE BRISTLECONE PINES

High in the White Mountains and straddling the borders of Inyo and Mono Counties is the Ancient Bristlecone Pine Forest, a region of Inyo National Forest. The bristlecone pine (*pinus arustata*) has a good claim to be the oldest living thing on earth. Thriving at an altitude averaging some ten thousand feet above sea level, these trees are also found in some other parts of the American Southwest. Dr. Edmund Schulman of the University of Arizona discovered that some of the group in the Inyo

Forest were over 4,000 years old, one or more proving to be at least 4,600 years old. It is likely that many old trees were cut down in the heyday of mining activity in the region to provide charcoal for the kilns of the mines.

The bristlecone pine is a survivor, existing in thin, rocky soil at high altitudes with long intervals of freezing winters and waterless summers. It is a botanical curiosity in that a good part of the visible tree is in fact dead; a thin strand of living bark keeps part of the tree alive for long periods of time.

OWENS VALLEY

Although trappers may have penetrated Owens Valley south to what is now Inyo County as early as 1826, the first authentic record we have is that of Joseph R. Walker, who led a party through near Owens Valley in 1834. He entered the valley again in 1843, this time from the north. Following his old trail, he led the Chiles emigrant party, the second wagon train to enter California from the east, south through the pass that was later named for him. In 1845 Walker accompanied the main body of John C. Frémont's second expedition to California over the same route. Frémont himself went by way of Donner Pass with Kit Carson, Richard Owens, and twelve others. Frémont considered Owens to be "cool, brave, and of good judgement," and he gave Owens's name to the river, the valley, and the lake that still bear it, although the man for whom they are named never saw this region.

William H. Brewer, of the Whitney Geological Survey, and his party crossed the Sierra from the west and descended the eastern slope. He gave an appreciative description of the region in his journal in 1864:

> Yesterday in the snow and ice—today in this heat! The thermometer [measured] 96 degrees in the shade, 156 degrees in the sun. . . . Owens Valley is over a hundred miles long and from ten to fifteen wide. It lies four to five thousand feet above the sea and is entirely closed in by mountains. On the west the Sierra Nevada rises to over fourteen thousand feet; on the east the Inyo Mountains to twelve or thirteen thousand feet. The Owens River is fed by streams from the Sierra Nevada, runs through a crooked channel through this valley, and empties into Owens Lake, twenty-five miles below our camp. The lake is the color of coffee, has no outlet, and is a nearly saturated solution of salt and alkali.
>
> The Sierra Nevada catches all the rains and clouds from the west—to the east are deserts—so, of course this valley sees but little rain, but where streams come out of the Sierra they spread out and great meadows of green grass occur. Tens of thousands of the starving cattle of the state have been driven in here this year [one of unusually prolonged drought], and there is feed for twice as many more. Yet these meadows comprise not over one-tenth of the valley—the rest is desert.

Early in the twentieth century, the city of Los Angeles began to acquire land and water rights in the Owens Valley and by 1913 was pumping water out of the valley for the use of the city. The drained valley of today bears little resemblance to the great meadows that Brewer saw many years ago. However, new concerns about environmental matters, translated into legislation as well as court cases, have since 1983 compelled the city of Los Angeles to take less water from the Owens Valley and the watershed around Mono Lake (told in the Mono County chapter) than before. What historian Norris Hundley has called "The Great Thirst"—the need for more and more water for California's burgeoning population—continues to be a significant issue in Inyo County.

DEATH VALLEY NATIONAL PARK

Death Valley, on the southeastern border of California, is a long, sunken desert basin, surrounded by high mountains. It includes Badwater, the lowest spot in the Western Hemisphere, 282 feet below sea level. Its grim name is believed to have been given after the William Lewis Manly and Jayhawker parties attempted to cross the valley into California in 1849, tragic episodes in California's history. Manly wrote in 1894, forty-five years after the event, that "we took off our hats, and then overlooking the scene of so much trial, suffering and death spoke the thought uppermost in our minds, saying: 'Goodbye, Death Valley!' . . . Many accounts have been given to the world as to the origin of the name, but ours were the first visible footsteps, and we the party which gave it the saddest and most dreadful name that came to us from our memories."

During Christmas week of 1849 more than a hundred half-starved emigrants, seeking a shortcut to the California gold fields, entered what some called the Valley of Burning Silence at the mouth of what was later known as Furnace Creek. This gateway on SR 190 at the eastern entrance to Death Valley National Park is now commemorated by a stone monument and a bronze plaque (SRL 442). From this point the Manly party proceeded south, while the Jayhawkers and other groups turned to the northwest. Manly's group crossed the salt flats and found water at what was probably Tule Spring. The site is marked (SRL 444) on the West Side Road. They called this place the Last Camp, for their situation was so critical that is was decided that the party should remain in camp while Manly and John Rogers set out over the mountains to seek help. After much suffering and many difficulties, these two brave men finally reached help and returned to Death Valley after almost a month to rescue their friends. At Last Camp it was found that only the Bennett and Arcane families remained, the others having attempted to go on alone. (A local name for this spot is the Bennett-Arcane Long Camp.) One Captain Culverwell, who had joined the last party out, died not far from camp. He is the only one of the Manly party known to have perished in Death Valley, but the fate of the others is unknown, and it is likely that they too died somewhere in the wilderness.

The story of the Jayhawkers, a high-spirited group of young bachelors who set out from Galesburg, Illinois, in the spring of 1849 with other emigrants, is even more tragic. Traveling by themselves for the most part, the Jayhawkers were often closely associated with the Manly-Bennett-Arcane party in their grim march across the desert, being together at some camps and apart at others. Accounts of the journey by participants in these two main parties differ, but the best authority seems to be that nine of the Jayhawkers perished to the east of Death Valley and four died after leaving it but while still in the desert. One of these, a man named Robinson, died within sight of deliverance not far from the base of the Sierra Nevada. Having separated from Manly's party at what is now Furnace Creek, the Jayhawkers and some others proceeded northwest to a place close to what is now Stovepipe Wells. This place has become known as Burned Wagons Point (SRL 441) for here the emigrants abandoned and burned most of their equipment before they continued westward on foot and, after suffering many hardships, reached safety.

Stovepipe Wells (SRL 826) was the only water hole among the sand dunes in the northwest part of Death Valley. It derives its name from the length of stovepipe inserted in the hole to mark it during times when drifting sand might obscure its location. A plaque has been placed on the Sand Dunes Access Road, one-quarter of a mile north on SR 190. In 1926 H. E. Eichbaum opened a toll road from Darwin Falls to Stovepipe Wells, the first maintained road into Death Valley from the west. A marker (SRL 848) at Stovepipe Wells commemorates

Eichbaum's toll road. As a result of this road, tourism gradually replaced mining as the economic base of the area, and in 1933 Death Valley National Monument was established. In 1994, it became a national park. A small triangular portion of the park extends into Nevada, and a portion of it lies in San Bernardino County to the south; the rest of its roughly three thousand square miles lies within Inyo County.

Manly's route lay over the mountain barrier to the south, through Red Rock Canyon, into the Mojave Desert, and on to the San Gabriel Mountains. There the party passed through Soledad Canyon and Newhall Pass into the San Fernando Valley.

Some contingents of Forty-niners, suffering from the thirst of Death Valley, which they had just left, attempted to secure water from Searles Lake. Finding it unpotable, they despaired and turned northward and westward across the Argus Range and other mountains in their search for civilization. This bitter disappointment is commemorated by a marker (SRL 443) about six miles north of Trona and just north of the Trona Airport.

This trek across Death Valley is the first recorded tragedy to be associated with it, but it is highly probable that lone wanderers before and since have entered the valley, many never to come out. Wandering miners in the 1850s found isolated skeletons at several places.

One of the earliest expeditions from the west was a mining company headed by Dr. Darwin French in the spring of 1860. These men discovered and named Furnace Creek after a crude furnace at the stream. It is not known whether this had been built by a Mormon party or by a group of Mexican miners.

The first scientific expedition was made by the State Boundary Commission in 1861. In 1871 the Wheeler Survey (Geographical Surveys West of the One Hundredth Meridian), conducted by Lieutenant George M. Wheeler of the U.S. Army Engineers, mapped this area of California east of the Sierra.

The ruins of the Harmony Borax Works (SRL 773) may still be seen in Death Valley just north of Furnace Creek Ranch and west of the highway. There, in 1880, large deposits of borate were discovered by Aaron Winters and his wife Rosie. A short while before this, Isidore Daunet, a prospector, had discovered white marshes in Death Valley a few miles north of Bennett's Well and twenty miles southwest of Furnace Creek. On hearing of the Winters' find, Daunet opened up the Eagle Borax Works, the first borax corporation in the valley. Borax is an efficient cleaning agent, widely sold in late-nineteenth century America. The product, however, proved to be

"Old Dinah" Steam Tractor and Wagons, Borax Museum

Gold Arrastra at the Borax Museum

impure and the plant was closed. Its ruins may be seen from the West Side Road between Shorty's Well and Bennett's Well.

The Winters' deposits of borate were finally acquired by Francis M. ("Borax") Smith and his partner, W. T. Coleman, who started the Harmony Borax Works. In 1889, after the marshes had been thoroughly worked out, Coleman assigned his property to the Pacific Coast Borax Company, and work at the Harmony plant ceased. Smith then entered the picture in earnest, working his way to the head of the company. A deposit at the base of Monte Blanco, a thousand-foot peak southeast of Furnace Creek, proved to be in a purer state than that previously worked and so rich that even today the mountain seems to be composed of almost solid colemanite, as the deposit was called. The miles of tunnels and drifts into the mountain did not begin to exhaust the supply. A picture of the twenty-mule team used to haul the borates 200 miles across the desert to Mojave became the trademark of the company and is used to this day, although the teams were replaced by the Tonopah and Tidewater Railroad in 1907. New borax deposits as rich as those of Death Valley, and far more accessible, were found in Nevada and Oregon and at Trona near Searles Lake in adjacent San Bernardino County. Borax is still present in Death Valley in great quantities, but the difficulties of transportation are too great and the mines are no longer worked.

The Borax Museum at Furnace Creek has an outdoor exhibit of some of the wagons used in the borax trade and indoor displays that show the processes whereby borax was extracted from the mined ores. Furnace Creek is a remarkable flow of water in the midst of a desert; from its emergence behind the Furnace Creek Inn, the creek passes the Visitors Center and waters the oasis of Furnace Creek Ranch, where a splendid grove of date palms provides cool shade.

In the extreme northern part of Death Valley National Park is the fabulous Scotty's Castle, built in the 1920s by Albert M. Johnson, a Chicago financier. Originally named the Death Valley Ranch, this rambling Spanish-style hacienda was made famous by the stories and newsworthy antics of Walter Scott. Scotty and Johnson had become acquainted in the early 1900s when Johnson grubstaked Scotty for his prospecting ventures in Death Valley. Albert Johnson and his wife Bessie came to Death Valley frequently, and the Johnsons ensured Scotty's residence at the Castle until the old prospector's death in 1954. The hacienda, which is administered by the National Park Service, is open to the public for guided tours. A few miles to the west is impressive Ubehebe Crater, half a mile wide and 800 feet deep, believed to be the result of a volcanic explosion 3,000 years ago.

EARLY SETTLEMENTS: LAWS AND BISHOP

Prior to 1861, the only white population in Owens Valley was composed of transient prospectors, mountain men, and travelers to the West Coast who took a shortcut through the valley or who used this route to reach the gold fields without going over the high Sierra Nevada. In August 1861 A. Van Fleet with three other men drove cattle into the northern end of Owens Valley from Nevada Territory. A cabin of sod and stone was built, the site (SRL 230) of which is at the big bend of the Owens River about four miles northwest of Bishop, not far from the community of Laws. In the same month Charles Putnam built a stone cabin on Little Pine Creek (now Independence Creek) and started a trading post. These were the first American buildings in Owens Valley.

Laws prospered due to its position on the narrow-gauge Carson & Colorado Railroad, which ran from

Mound House near Carson City, Nevada, to Keeler in California. The Laws railroad station (SRL 953) was built in 1863. When the line was sold to the Southern Pacific Railroad in 1900, the station was named for superintendent R. J. Laws. The line worked by the Slim Princess, as the narrow-gauge engines were affectionately called, ceased to operate in 1960. In the following year the Southern Pacific donated the railroad station and surrounding installations, together with Locomotive Number 9 and a string of cars, to the city of Bishop and Inyo County for the establishment of the Laws Railroad Museum. This attraction also features exhibits of domestic and commercial life in Inyo County around the turn of the century.

Samuel A. Bishop, for whom the town of Bishop was named, came to California in 1849. He was associated with General Edward F. Beale at Rancho Tejón before going to Inyo County and later, in 1866, he became one of Kern County's first supervisors.

Bishop and his wife came to Inyo from Rancho Tejón in 1861, settling on the creek that now bears his name. Here, where the stream leaves the foothills and enters the valley, about three miles southwest of the present town of Bishop, two small cabins of rough pine slabs were put up on August 22, and the new settlement was named the San Francis Ranch (SRL 208). The site is on Red Hill Road west of Bishop via SR 168. Bishop did not remain long in the area, moving in 1864 to the abandoned fort at Tejón.

Settlers were in and around the area from the time Bishop arrived. The town of Bishop, now the largest in the county, prospered mainly because of the rich farming land surrounding it, but early mining in the White-Inyo Range also contributed to its growth. The Paiute Shoshone Cultural Center at 2300 West Line Street features exhibits of Indian life in Owens Valley and is maintained by the tribes.

The early history of Indian-white relations in Owens Valley was one of war and conflict. The settlers at San Francis Ranch were alarmed by a large party of Indians in the autumn of 1861, the result of which was a treaty signed between settlers and chiefs on January 31, 1862. Whatever peace this brought soon ended, and Warren Wasson, Nevada Indian agent, fearing that real war would erupt, asked for federal troops the following March, in the second year of the Civil War.

On April 6, between fifty and sixty men under John T. Kellogg and a settler named Mayfield engaged in battle with 500 to 1,000 Paiutes lined up from a small black butte in the valley across Bishop Creek to the foothills in the south. Three settlers were killed, and after the moon had set, the pioneers retreated to the town of Big Pine. A marker has been placed on the Bishop Creek battleground (SRL 811) on Bishop Creek Road, about five miles southwest of Bishop on SR 168.

Troops had arrived at Owens Lake on April 2, and on April 8 they joined with the settlers in a second engagement with the Indians. Mayfield and Trooper Christopher Gillespie were killed. The site of this battle (SRL 211) is at the mouth of what was later named Mayfield Canyon, about one-half mile north of the former Wells Meadow Ranger Station, northwest of Bishop off Round Valley Road near Rovana. Temporary peace followed, but by May the valley was in almost undisputed possession of the Paiutes and many of the white settlers left the region. In July, Camp Independence was established. By the fall of 1863, emigrants in increasing numbers were coming into the valley and new settlements were springing up. Not until 1866, however, was the valley declared safe from Indian attacks, and troops were maintained at the post until 1877.

INDEPENDENCE

On July 4, 1862, Lieutenant Colonel George S. Evans with 201 men of the Second Cavalry California Volunteers arrived on Oak Creek, raised the Stars and Stripes, and established a military post, naming it Camp Independence in honor of the day. The post's purpose was to protect the few Americans in Owens Valley and to act as a fortification in case of invasion by secessionists from the territories of Nevada and Arizona. With the exception of the year 1864, troops were maintained at Camp Independence until July 1877, when the post was abandoned. The site (SRL 349) is about two miles north of the town of Independence, off US 395. The caves occupied by soldiers and the old cemetery are all that remain. They are on private land and difficult to reach.

A remnant of the old post may be seen, however, at the corner of Edwards and Main Streets in Independence. In 1872, an earthquake destroyed the adobe buildings at Camp Independence. The Army rebuilt the camp, this time with wood frame structures. The post was abandoned in 1877 and in 1883 these buildings were auctioned off. The "Captain's Quarters" was purchased by V. G. Thompson. Then in 1886, a fire in the town of Independence destroyed all the buildings on Edwards Street. Soon thereafter, the Dunsmore family acquired the Captain's Quarters at the site of the old post and rebuilt it at its present site. Renovated in 1963, the

Commander's House is open to the public. Its contents predate 1900, and include some furniture built by soldiers at Camp Independence. Also open to the public is the oldest house in Inyo County, the Edwards House built in 1865, on nearby Market Street. Both buildings are operated by the Eastern California Museum (also known as the Inyo County Museum) at Grant and Center Streets. This museum has a remarkable collection of artifacts from early times through the World War II internment camp at nearby Manzanar.

The town of Independence was started with the building of a stone trading post by Charles Putnam in August 1861. It was first called "Putnam's" or "Little Pine," the name of the nearby creek. Town and creek then took their new name from the adjacent Army post. The stone cabin was used as a residence, store, hospital, and fort, and stood on a site (SRL 223) southwest of the present courthouse until it was torn down in 1876. Gold was discovered in 1862 in the Inyo Mountains to the east, and for some years Independence was the center of a rich mining area. The platting of the town site was completed in 1866, the first to be found in the county records. Upon the organization of Inyo County that year, Independence became the county seat.

The home of Mary Austin (SRL 229), said to have been designed and supervised by the author herself, is on Market Street in Independence. There she wrote *The Land of Little Rain* and other works that portray the beauty of the Owens Valley and the Inyo desert regions. The plaque at the site bears a quotation from the book:

> But if ever you come beyond the borders as far as the town that lies in a hill dimple at the foot of Kearsarge, never leave it until you have knocked at the door of the brown house under the willow-tree at the end of the village street, and there you shall have such news of the land, of its trails and what is astir in them, as one lover of it can give to another.

Bell's Mill was the first flour mill in Owens Valley and served a vast, sparsely settled territory. Its wooden ruins may still be seen on Oak Creek, northwest of Independence, about half a mile west of US 395, by a road that branches from the road leading to the Mount Whitney Fish Hatchery. An E Clampus Vitus plaque placed there in 1991 is informative:

> In 1916, the citizens of Independence purchased a 40 acre tract of land and donated it to the State of California for the building of a fish hatchery. This structure was the result. The first trout were produced in 1918, and since

Cemetary Monument at Manzanar National Historic Site

that time, the California Department of Fish & Game has produced an average of 2 million fingerling trout per year to stock the lakes and streams of California.

About midway between Independence and Big Pine, Harry Wright's stage station on Taboose Creek, one and one-half miles north of Aberdeen and a mile west of the highway, was a popular gathering place in the 1860s and 1870s. A few black locust and willow trees mark the site, which is now a public campground.

MANZANAR NATIONAL HISTORIC SITE

The settlement of Manzanar, also known as the Orchard Community, grew up on the site of the Shepherd Ranch about seven miles south of Independence. The place was abandoned in 1935 when the city of Los Angeles bought the land. On February 19, 1942, in the early days of World War II, Executive Order 9066 went into effect, calling for the internment of people of Japanese ancestry. The Manzanar site (SRL 850) was one of ten Japanese War Relocation Centers created in the western United States for that purpose. Ten thousand people, the majority of whom were American citizens, were interned here. The inscription on the state marker at the gates off US 395 contains a passage like that found on the Tule Lake relocation center in Modoc County (SRL 850.2): "May the injustices and humiliation suffered here as a result of hysteria, racism and economic exploitation never emerge again."

Manzanar National Historic Site was established by an Act of Congress in 1992 with over 800 acres of land, the last of which was acquired by 1997. On the dusty Manzanar plain, not much remains today of the camp, which was here from 1942 to the end of 1945: the auditorium, some small stone guard buildings, and a striking monument in the cemetery completed in 1943 by internee R. F. Kado, a landscape architect and stonemason. A gravel road traverses the property; wooden plaques mark the site of long-vanished buildings. The National Park Service administers the site, which receives many visitors.

LONE PINE

Late in the year 1861, the first cabin was built at Lone Pine. A large pine tree standing at the confluence of Tuttle and Lone Pine Creeks gave the place its name; the shade of the tree provided a meeting place for early settlers, as it did for the Indians before them, it was said. The tree blew down in a storm in 1876.

On March 26, 1872, a sharp earthquake shook the Owens Valley, opening a great fault twelve miles long running north from Lone Pine, paralleling today's US 395. Along this crevice, land dropped from four to twenty-one feet, and in Lone Pine, twenty-seven persons were killed and dozens injured in a town of adobe buildings. Sixteen of the victims were buried in a single large grave (SRL 507) on the edge of the fault at the north end of the town.

Lone Pine is now a thriving community, the seat of the Interagency Visitor Center, where fourteen public agencies have displays and materials on their activities in the region. Some 90 percent of the Mono Basin–Owens Valley region is owned by the federal government or by the city of Los Angeles.

THE ALABAMA HILLS AND KEARSARGE

The Alabama Hills run generally north and south and are just west of Lone Pine and east of the alluvial basin at the base of the Sierra Nevada. The name comes from the days of the Civil War. Southern sympathizers, mining in a gulch at the north end of this picturesque stretch of hills in 1863, heard of the damage that the Confederate raider *Alabama* was inflicting on Northern shipping. In their elation over the news, they named the hills for the ship. These hills, with their attractive topography and comparative ease of access, have been the location for the making of many Western films. The visitor today may drive on the Alabama Hills Scenic Road and Movie Road, keeping alert for cinematographic stampedes.

Kearsarge Peak, a few miles to the northwest, and the town that followed the strike made in the Sierra Nevada in 1864 were named for the USS *Kearsarge*, which sank the CSS *Alabama* off the coast of France the same year. These miners were Northern sympathizers and jubilant over the sinking. They named their mine the Kearsarge, and soon the peak, a pass, and the town that grew up in the boom took the same name.

The town of Kearsarge was built at the southern base of the mountain's highest crest and had developed into a considerable camp by the end of 1865. Violent storms raged about the peak in February 1867, bringing rain, snow, freezing, and a sudden thaw. An avalanche swept down the side of the mountain, almost wiping out the settlement, killing a woman and injuring several men. Despite such setbacks, the Kearsarge, Silver Sprout, Virginia Consolidated, and other mines on the slopes of the mountain continued to be worked for a number of years. The town moved to another location, three miles east of Independence, but there are few remains today.

Close by are the ruins of Bend City (SRL 209), a mining camp established in the early 1860s, and designated to be the seat of Coso County (which, however, was never organized).

THE WHITE MOUNTAINS REGION

From the earliest coming of settlers into Inyo County, more than one aspiring city was staked out in the White Mountains east of Bishop, only to be forgotten. Just over the summit of the range from Owens Valley, town plots were actually surveyed for two would-be mining centers, which figured in an attempted election fraud in the fall of 1861. The "Big Springs precinct," with its alleged polling place at what is now known as Deep Springs, was created less than two weeks before the election. Although almost no one lived in the region, election returns showed that 521 votes had been cast. Investigation revealed that the names had been copied from the passenger list of a steamer at San Francisco. White Mountain City, neatly laid out on Wyman Creek on the Deep Springs slope, and nearby Roachville on Cottonwood Creek were only paper cities in 1864 and never became anything else.

Settlements were made near Big Pine in 1861, and the rich farming land fed by the creek was an early attraction to those wanting to locate in the new area. The town of Big Pine on US 395 is near Palisade Glacier, the southernmost glacier in the United States. A road leads westward from Big Pine to Glacier Lodge, near the base of the glacier. Eastward from Big Pine, other roads lead into Death Valley National Park and the Ancient Bristlecone Pine Forest.

THE CERRO GORDO MINES

THE CERRO GORDO MINES

Twenty miles northeast of Olancha, on the ridge of the Inyo Mountains, are the famous Cerro Gordo Mines, believed to have been discovered in 1865 by a Mexican prospector, Pablo Flores, and two companions, who later in the same year located the Ygnacio, the San Felipe, and the San Francisco claims. The Cerro Gordo ("fat hill") Mines produced silver, lead, and zinc, and were the most productive mines in Inyo County. During the 1870s the region had a population of several thousand. It is estimated that the mines yielded $28 million before ceasing operation in 1915. The site is on private property, and the buildings are reported to be in good condition. Cerro Gordo is reached only by a tortuous road from Keeler on the east side of Owens Lake.

LANDMARKS AROUND OWENS LAKE

Ore from Cerro Gordo was hauled to the foot of the Inyo Mountains, where a town named Keeler grew up on the eastern shore of Owens Lake, now dry. From here it was taken across the lake by the steamboats *Bessie Brady* and *Molly Stevens* to Cartago on the far shore, and thence to San Pedro. The trip cost more than $50 a ton, necessitating the building of smelters in the area. One of these was constructed at Cerro Gordo itself and another at what became known as Swansea, a short distance northwest of Keeler. This place was named for the smelter town of Swansea in Wales. At California's Swansea, all that remains of the furnace of the Owens Lake Silver-Lead Company is the old firebox (SRL 752). Across the highway stands part of the adobe house of James Brady, a superintendent of the company and the town's founder. The furnace operated from 1869 to 1874, and together with the one at Cerro Gordo, produced about 150 bars of silver a day, each bar weighing eighty-three pounds. Relics of the old steamboats can be seen in the Eastern California Museum in Independence.

From Keeler to Laws, near Bishop, a distance of 71 miles, the last remnant of the narrow-gauge Carson & Colorado Railroad operated until 1960. Some of the equipment is exhibited at the Laws Railroad Museum.

On the western shore of Owens Lake, fifteen miles south of Lone Pine and east of US 395, stand two of the Cottonwood charcoal kilns (SRL 537). Here wood was turned into charcoal and taken across the lake by steamboat to the Cerro Gordo furnaces. These kilns were vital to the smelting process, for all the available wood in the Cerro Gordo area had been used. These are the only documented adobe kilns in the western United States.

The town of Olancha is near the southern tip of Owens Lake. Near here M. H. Farley, working for the Silver Mountain Mining Company in the Coso Mountains, completed the first mill and furnace in the Owens Valley in December 1862. Two years earlier he had explored and named Olancha Pass and had conceived the idea for his mill. The site (SRL 796) is on Olancha Creek, about a mile west of the historical marker that stands on US 395 at Williams Road. East of Olancha and southeast of Keeler is the interesting old town of Darwin, named for Darwin French, an early explorer of Death Valley.

PANAMINT CITY

The Panamint Valley lies at the western edge of the Panamint Mountains, a desolate region so remote from the rest of the world that outlaws flourished openly and Wells Fargo, it was said, refused to send a stagecoach through it. High in the mountains at the end of Surprise Canyon, Panamint City was a fast-growing mining town equaled in reputation only by Bodie in Mono County to the north. By 1875, the Panamint Mining Company and the Surprise Valley Mill and Mining Company were in full operation, and the town boasted some 1,500 people. A torrential downpour in 1876 generated a flash flood so devastating that it is said 200 people were drowned and the loss in buildings was very great. The entire episode was over in less than an hour; Panamint City never recovered.

The road to Panamint City is not easy, but it is highly picturesque. Through Randsburg, by the edge of Searles Lake with its vast depths of potash and borax, up over the Silate Range, and down into the Panamint Valley, the road leads past the adobe ruins of Ballarat. From here the road leads on to the site of Panamint City, entering the gateway to the mighty chasm four miles from Ballarat. Where the canyon widens to several hundred feet is the site of Panamint City, now wrecked by cloudbursts, floods, vandals, and the ravages of time. A tall brick chimney rises from a smelter, and nearby are a few skeleton houses of wood among the juniper and mesquite bushes, while the thick stone walls of former saloons and gambling houses cluster along the base of the cliffs. Over all hangs the stillness, the grandeur, and the desolation of the wilderness.

Two later boom camps, Greenwater and Skidoo, had their start in the 1880s. The former, founded in 1884 on the eastern side of the Funeral Mountains and just over the summit from where the slope into Death Valley begins, has had few parallels in the "sudden rise, great outlays, small returns, and quick decline" that have attended its brief periods of excitement. Gold, silver, and copper finds each had their day, the latter as late as 1906, when the population increased from seventy to 1,000 within a month. Over a thirty-mile stretch of mountain range some 2,500 claims were staked within four months' time, and from them the "copper kings" reaped a rich harvest. But the camps were surrounded by hundreds of miles of barren mountain and desert, and their inaccessibility ultimately caused all claims to be abandoned. A cheerful miner from somewhere in the locality wrote in a letter that he was employed on the "graveyard shift in the Coffin Mine, Tombstone Mountains, Funeral Ridge, overlooking Death Valley."

Skidoo, located on the summit of the mountain on the western edge of Death Valley, was Greenwater's nearest neighbor. It had the luxury of pure mountain water piped many miles from a spring near the top of Telescope Peak. (This aqueduct was twenty-three miles long, and the term "twenty-three Skidoo," popular in the early years of the twentieth century, may refer to the satisfaction that comes from the completion of a difficult task.) Skidoo continued to produce gold and silver ores years after its sister mine was deserted.

Although it was not a wide-open, brawling town like others in the Eastern Sierra country, Skidoo had its moment of notoriety. On Sunday, April 19, 1908, Joe Simpson shot and killed Jim Arnold, the manager of the local store. Simpson was immediately jailed. On the following Wednesday night, while most of the town slept or refused to be aroused by stealthy footsteps, Simpson was taken out of jail and hanged, his swaying body found the next morning. The headlines of the next *Skidoo News*, a weekly paper, read in bold letters: "Murder in Camp, Murderer Lynched with General Approval." As if this did not create enough excitement, when reporters from daily newspapers arrived shortly thereafter, the body of Joe Simpson was dug up and hanged for a second time, with appropriate pictures made of the event.

Apart from this episode, Skidoo was a rather peaceful town until, its mines worked out, it was abandoned. A few buildings still stand in the town, now on the National Register of Historic Places; it lies within the border of Death Valley National Park at the top of a steep road branching off from Wildrose Road.

Kern County

Kern County was organized in 1866 from parts of Los Angeles and Tulare Counties. In 1845–46 an expedition into this region was led by John C. Frémont. Edward Meyer Kern, an artist from Philadelphia, was the company's topographer, and nearly drowned while crossing a great stream. Frémont named the river for his colleague. Kern died at the age of forty, two years before his name was given to California's third-largest county. The first county seat was located at Havilah in the mountains. Bakersfield, with a more central location, replaced it in 1874.

GRIZZLY GULCH

Grizzly Gulch, in northeastern Kern County and close to the Tulare county line, was noted in early days for its large number of grizzly bears. Several prospectors were reported killed or crippled by them, and active mining operations could not be carried on until they had been eliminated.

The prevalence of fossil bones of prehistoric animals and of archaeological remains of the Yokut Indians adds greatly to the interest of the region. South of Grizzly Gulch, and particularly in Rag Gulch and north of the Kern River, marks of an ancient shoreline are plainly visible, showing that this was once the eastern margin of a great body of water. For miles, the waterline may be traced by the remains of shellfish and other sea life, and at Shark Tooth Mountain, north of the Kern River, the bones and teeth of prehistoric sharks exist in great numbers.

An Indian rancheria once existed in Grizzly Gulch a little less than half a mile east of Blue Mountain Road. Hundreds of Indian mortars, many of them deeply worn into the granite through the grinding of acorns and seeds for generations, may still be seen in the bedrock and outcropping granite surrounding the little valley.

THE SOUTHERN PASSES

Lying between the southern end of the Sierra Nevada to the east and the Coast Range to the west at about the 35th parallel are the Tehachapi Mountains. To the north they fall away into the San Joaquin Valley and the basins into which the rivers flow from the Sierra. Six passes, all of historical interest, cut through this mountain barrier: from east to west they are Walker Pass, Tehachapi Pass, Oak Creek Road, the original Tejón Pass, the present Tejón Pass or Cañada de las Uvas, and San Emidio Pass.

One of the pioneer trails to California followed the Owens River Valley down through what is now western Inyo County, passing by Owens Lake, and thence through Walker Pass to the South Fork of the Kern River, and down the South Fork to its junction with the North Fork at Isabella, a town now under the waters of Lake Isabella.

There the trail divided. One branch went south by way of Bodfish, Havilah, and Walker's Basin, and then west by several routes to the ferry on the Kern River (called Gordon's Ferry for many years) about five miles northeast of Bakersfield. The other branch crossed the Kern River near Isabella, passing over the Greenhorn Mountains either to Poso Flat or to Linn's Valley (near Glennville), and then turning north to the White River and Visalia.

In 1834, Joseph R. Walker, captain of an exploring party, left California by the latter route, via the White River and the Greenhorn Mountains, and in 1843 he followed the same trail in, while leading the Chiles emigrant party, the second wagon train to enter California from the east. In 1845, John C. Frémont, on his second expedition into California, sent his main party, accompanied by Walker, via this route, while he and a few others crossed the Sierra at Donner Pass. It was on this expedition that Edward Kern mapped the river that Frémont subsequently named for him. Kern's campsite (SRL 742) at the junction of the North and South Forks is now inundated by Lake Isabella, but a monument has been placed on SR 178 on the east side of the lake. The summit of Walker Pass on the same highway had been marked (SRL 99) and in 1963 it was designated as a National Historic Landmark by the Department of the Interior.

A marker has been placed at Freeman Junction (SRL 766), a meeting place of old Indian trails that was found by Walker in 1834 after his discovery of the pass to the northwest. At this point the Death Valley Forty-niner parties diverged west and south after their escapes from that unhappy place. Later the place became a favorite haunt of the bandit Tiburcio Vásquez. It is now the junction of SR 14 and SR 178. A few miles north of this point on SR 14 is Indian Wells (SRL 457), a station on the Walker Trail and later on the freight line from Los Angeles to the Cerro Gordo Mines in Inyo County. It derives its name from a rock-walled spring, still in existence, at the former location of an Indian village.

THE TEJÓN PASSES

The pass that is today named Tejón ("badger") was first penetrated by Pedro Fages, then acting governor of Alta California, in 1772 while he was pursuing deserters from the Spanish army. A manuscript penned by Fages himself, discovered a long time afterward and published in 1937, describes his inland expedition from

San Diego to San Luis Obispo. Concerning this document, the eminent California historian Professor Herbert E. Bolton wrote:

> It is a surprising story of an entirely unknown California expedition, ahead of Anza, from the Imperial Valley, thence through Cajón Pass, along the edge of the Mojave Desert, through Antelope Valley, through a pass into the southern end of San Joaquin Valley, northwest across it to Buena Vista Hills and Lake, and through the mountains to San Luis Obispo, four years before Garcés entered the valley. . . . It gives Captain Pedro Fages a distinctive position, hitherto unrecognized, as far-travelling trail blazer, and as pioneer in the South San Joaquin.

The pass and canyon through which Fages blazed this trail have had various names. Fages himself called the canyon Buena Vista ("beautiful view"). The Spaniards who came later designated it La Cañada de las Uvas ("the canyon of the grapes"), and it is known today as Grapevine Canyon. The route over the summit, however, is designated on modern maps as Tejon Pass. A monument (SRL 283) has been placed at Lebec, near the summit, in memory of Pedro Fages, the first explorer to cross the Tehachapi Mountains by this pass and the first to enter the San Joaquin Valley from the south.

Leaving Grapevine Canyon, Fages traveled thirty miles northwest across the southwestern corner of the San Joaquin Valley to the Buena Vista Hills in the Coast Range, perhaps taking a shortcut by way of the low gap at the neck of Wheeler Ridge. A marker on SR 166, about seven miles west of SR 99, indicates the point (SRL 291) at which Fages's trail was crossed in 1806 by the expedition, in search of mission sites, that included Father José Maria Zalvidea. This party traveled from Santa Barbara Mission to San Gabriel Mission, passing the site of modern Bakersfield.

Reaching the foot of the hills on the southwestern shore of Buena Vista Lake, Fages found an Indian village, the existence of which is still attested by vast kitchen middens. Across the floor of the valley and about the lake itself Fages found "a labyrinth of lakes and tulares." The name Buena Vista has been given to the nearby hills and the village at their foot, and is the oldest Spanish place name in the San Joaquin Valley.

The site of the principal Tulamniu Indians encampment (SRL 374) is on Tupman Road, south SR 119, on the west side of Buena Vista Lake. This was the scene of excavation work done in 1933–34 under the auspices of the Smithsonian Institution.

The second Spaniard to enter the San Joaquin Valley from the south was a Franciscan friar, Francisco Garcés, in 1776. Garcés left San Gabriel in April of that year and, ascending the San Fernando Valley, crossed over the Newhall grade to the vicinity of the present town of Castaic, in Los Angeles County, where he passed northeast over the mountains by a trail running east of the present I-5. Near Hughes Lake on the edge of Antelope Valley he crossed Fages's trail of 1772 and then proceeded north across the valley to Cottonwood Creek, up which he climbed to the pass above. From there he descended into the San Joaquin Valley by way of Tejón Creek. To this pass, fifteen miles east of the pass over which Fages had entered the great central valley four years before, rightly belongs the name Tejón.

On April 30, 1776, Garcés visited the locality of the present Arvin, a fact commemorated by a statue of him (SRL 371) in front of St. Thomas Church on Bear Mountain Boulevard at the eastern limit of the town. On May 1 he crossed the Kern River, which he named Río de San Felipe, at a point (SRL 278) about one mile north of the marker on SR 178, eight miles east of Bakersfield. Since the priest could not swim, friendly Indians carried him across the river.

The padre traversed the valley as far north as the White River, near which on May 3 he baptized a dying Indian boy. This site of the first baptism in the south San Joaquin Valley (SRL 631) is marked by a cross on private property three miles north of the monument that stands on Garces Highway, seven miles east of SR 65 and sixteen miles east of Delano. Outdoor pageants dramatizing the visit of the pioneer Franciscan have been held in a natural amphitheater on the ranch property. On his return trip, Father Garcés visited, on May 7, an Indian rancheria at or near the site of the present city of Bakersfield. This city has commemorated him by a statue (SRL 277) in the traffic circle at Chester and Golden State avenues. A Catholic high school in Bakersfield has been named in Garcés's honor. The explorer returned by way of Arvin on May 10 and 11 en route to the Tehachapi region and the Mojave Desert.

Hudson's Bay Company trappers came as far south as the Tejón region in the 1830s, and in the name of the town of Lebec is preserved the memory of Peter Lebeck, possibly one of these trappers, who was killed on October 17, 1837, by a grizzly bear that he had shot and wounded near the site of Fort Tejón. Authentication is doubtful here, but it is believed that Lebeck was buried under a tree standing at the northeast corner of the old Fort Tejón parade grounds, a couple of miles north of Lebec.

RANCHO EL TEJÓN

Rancho El Tejón is one of the most interesting and important historic spots in the San Joaquin Valley. Here are the sites of several Indian villages that date back to prehistoric times. They were occupied until the last quarter of the nineteenth century.

The first record of the region was made by Father Francisco Garcés, who, on his expedition in April 1776, visited and named the Indian village of San Pascual, probably the one located at the mouth of Tejón Creek, later the site of the Los Alamos Butterfield Stage station. For many years this village was the center for traditional Indian ceremonies such as that described by Bishop William Kip, who visited the place in 1855: "It was a wild scene as the glare of the fire fell upon the dancers and a thousand Indians gathered in a circle around them."

General Edward Beale, while Superintendent of Indian Affairs, established a government Indian reservation on Rancho Tejón in the early 1850s, erecting stone and adobe buildings as headquarters for the agency on the site later occupied by the headquarters of the rancho on Arroyo del Paso. One of these buildings, built in 1856 and formerly used as a store, still stands, in part, although it has been extensively modernized. The thickness of its adobe walls is evident, and the old front doors, bearing the symbol of the Tejón brand, are still in use, having been replaced on the building after its original front portion was torn down. Most of the old buildings were razed following serious damage by the Tehachapi earthquake of 1952. At this location there were also later adobe buildings constructed from bricks salvaged from some of the old structures at Fort Tejón after its abandonment, but these too are gone. After the earthquake new ranch headquarters were built on the east side of I-5 three miles north of Lebec, opposite Fort Tejón State Historical Monument and on a portion of the old fort site. The old rancho headquarters are fifteen miles east of the highway. Entrance to Tejón Ranch properties requires a written permit from the headquarters near Fort Tejón. A marker beside the highway north of the Grapevine (together with the Rose Station marker) commemorates the government reservation, originally called Tejón but later renamed Sebastian Indian Reservation (SRL 133) in honor of William King Sebastian of Arkansas, chairman of the Senate Committee on Indian Affairs in 1853. Although the res-

ervation failed, General Beale, as owner of Rancho Tejón, encouraged the Indians to remain on the land, employing them as vaqueros and laborers. It is said that when the rancho was finally sold, it was stipulated that the Indian residents should be allowed to remain and that they should be well treated. For many years Indians lived in the little adobe houses scattered up and down Arroyo del Tejón for a distance of several miles, but the adobe houses did not survive the 1952 earthquake.

On the old road between Fort Tejón and Lebec is an adobe building known as "The Dairy." It is owned by the Tejón Ranch Corporation and was built in 1886 of adobe bricks salvaged from disintegrating buildings at the fort. Its circular gable windows are said to have been removed from the original guardhouse.

Rancho El Tejón was a grant made in 1843 to José Antonio Aguirre, a Spanish Basque who was a wealthy trader, and to Ignacio del Valle. The largest Mexican grant in the San Joaquin Valley, it included 97,616 acres of land. It lay in the extreme southeastern corner of the valley, a section of rolling hills and mountains. After the failure of the Indian reservation, General Beale purchased the rancho in 1865 from del Valle and Juan Temple (who had acquired Aguirre's share) and retired to it at the end of his term as United States Surveyor General. The irregularity of the boundary lines of the rancho is due to the fact that an attempt was made to include sufficient water facilities to support the land.

Rancho Tejón today is one of several combined ranchos owned by the Tejón Ranch Company, incorporated in 1936, totaling over a quarter of a million acres of cattle range. Other old Mexican land grants, each with an interesting history, are included in this vast domain: Rancho de los Alamos y Agua Caliente (partly in Los Angeles County), Rancho de Castac, and Rancho de la Liebre (also partly in Los Angeles County).

Rancho de los Alamos y Agua Caliente was purchased by Beale in 1865 from Agustín Olvera, Cristobal Aguilar, and James L. Gibbens. It had been granted in 1843 and 1846 to Francisco López, Luís Jordan, and Vicente Botello. Rancho de Castac, named for an Indian rancheria, is traversed throughout nearly its entire length by I-5, and extends northward from Castaic Lake, near Lebec, to a distance of two miles beyond Grapevine Station. It was granted in 1843 to José Maria Covarrubias, a French citizen of Mexico, who came to California as a teacher in 1834 and later took a prominent part in public affairs. He served as secretary to Governor Pío Pico, and in the autumn of 1849 became

Restored Barracks, Fort Tejón State Historic Park

a member of the first State Constitutional Convention and later of the state Legislature.

Rancho de la Liebre ("jackrabbit") was the first of General Beale's acquisitions in the area, in 1855. His old adobe still stands in Los Angeles County on property of the Tejón Ranch Company. The rancho had been granted to José Maria Flores in 1846.

In a description of historic Rancho Tejón one cannot omit mention of the vast wildflower gardens that each spring display their gorgeous colors along the upland canyons and mountain meadows. The broad valley floor, too, was once covered with miles of blooms, but now the huge acreages under cultivation have caused the wildflowers to become restricted largely to the foothills.

FORT TEJÓN

Old Fort Tejón (SRL 129) is located in a grove of old oaks and sycamores in an exceptionally attractive setting beside the mountain stream known on modern maps as Grapevine Creek (Arroyo de las Uvas). It was established in 1854 as the headquarters of the United States Army's First Dragoons, to protect the Indians from extermination and to deter cattle and horse stealing. It was important in the early years of American rule in California.

In 1858 the fort became a station on the Butterfield Overland Mail route, when six-horse stages covered the distance between St. Louis and San Francisco in twenty-three days. Soldiers from the fort went out to meet the stages and escorted them through the pass, where protection from Indians and bandits was needed. At its peak, the fort was one of the largest settlements in Southern California and the principal military, social,

and political center between Visalia and Los Angeles. The men at Fort Tejón traveled on duty to the Colorado River and Owens River valleys, escorted groups to Salt Lake City, policed the area, and brought some rule and order into a region that was sometimes a battlefield for miners, Indians, and land claimants. Fifteen officers who served at Fort Tejón later achieved the rank of general in the Civil War; eight served with the forces of the Union and seven with the Confederacy.

After the Army abandoned the fort in 1864, the land became part of General Beale's Rancho Tejón and the buildings on the post were used as residences, stables, and sheds. In 1939, five acres around the ruins of the buildings were granted by the Tejón Ranch to the state of California, which purchased an additional 200 acres from the Tejón Ranch Corporation in 1954.

Today, Fort Tejón State Historic Park is easily visited from I-5, which passes directly in front of the visitors' center. Principal structures are the orderlies' quarters, which have been preserved since 1854, reconstructed officers' quarters, and a barracks building. The park today still conveys a sense of a more tranquil past, and (unless one is there on a Civil War Reenactment Day) the modern visitor might well agree with the description written in the 1850s by an admiring visitor:

> The post of Tejón is on a little plain, entirely surrounded by high mountains, beautifully situated in a grove of old oak . . . most romantic and beautiful. On the plains and mountain sides, Mother Nature has almost excelled herself, carpeting them with flowers of every hue, giving to the eye one of the most beautiful prospects imaginable; and the air is bracing and exhilirating and inspiring. An oasis in the desert where all is freshness and life.

EDWARD F. BEALE

Edward F. Beale was born in a Maryland suburb of Washington, D.C. in 1822 and received a commission in the United States Navy at the personal intervention of President Andrew Jackson. He came to California in 1846 as a young officer under Commodore Stockton in the early days of the Mexican War, and was detached to serve with the land forces under General Kearny. He and Kit Carson carried the news of the Battle of San Pasqual to Stockton at San Diego in 1846 and stayed on in California in various capacities—he was the first to carry California gold to the east after the discovery of 1848, and made surveying and exploration trips throughout the West. Beale was made Superintendent of Indian Affairs for California in 1852 and initiated a policy of honest and humane dealings with the Indians. He established a government reservation and later employed them on his ranch.

Beale was an enthusiastic advocate of the camel as a means of transportation across the Southwest deserts, and brought the first caravan to California from Texas (the animals were originally from Tunis), a trying journey of 1,200 miles, taking from June 1857 to the following January. This feat proved to Americans beyond a doubt the great endurance of the animals. After crossing the Colorado River (where Beale proved that camels could swim), the caravan was driven to Fort Tejón, where some of the camels remained for more than a year. The camel experiment was a failure and was abandoned by 1861, when the corps was sent to the Benicia Arsenal in Solano County and ultimately sold off. A skeleton of one of the animals is preserved in the Smithsonian Institution in Washington.

Beale was appointed Surveyor General of California and Nevada in 1861 and later acquired Rancho El Tejón and adjacent properties, and until his death in 1893 he was a leader in the development of Kern County. A strong Republican, he returned to Washington in the Grant administration and served as American minister to the Austro-Hungarian Empire.

THE TEHACHAPI PASSES

From Bakersfield, SR 58 leads across the Sierra Nevada to the Mojave Desert by way of Tehachapi Pass, a comfortable drive on an excellent multilane freeway. Tehachapi is an Indian word that means something like "hard climbing"; it was spelled in many different ways until the Southern Pacific Railroad established a station there in 1876 and fixed the spelling. A tradition says that the real meaning of the term is the improbable "land of plenty of acorns and good water," but the abundance of sturdy oaks and artesian well water might justify the interpretation.

The summit of the Sierra is reached just east of the town of Tehachapi, and from there the road descends into the Mojave Desert. The first explorer to go through the Tehachapi was Father Garcés in 1776. On this expedition Garcés crossed the mountains from the south via Cottonwood and Tejón Creeks and penetrated into the San Joaquin Valley as far north as the White River, passing en route the site of Bakersfield. Retracing his steps, he crossed the Sierra into the Mojave Desert. His route varied considerably from that followed by the

present state highway and the railroad. Instead of going up Tehachapi Creek, Garcés reached Tehachapi Valley via Rancho Tejón and Cummings Valley, where he turned south into the desert, probably by way of Oak Creek Pass. A monument (SRL 97) has been placed at the summit of this pass, seven miles southeast of Tehachapi on the road to Willow Springs.

It is not possible to determine which of the passes through the Tehachapi Mountains Jedediah Strong Smith traversed in finding his way into the San Joaquin Valley in 1827. Kern County has remembered Smith with a monument (SRL 660) on SR 58 about twelve miles east of Bakersfield. Smith traveled where water was obtainable for his party; being primarily a trapper, he investigated the possibility of fur animals on the several watercourses emerging from the mountains, and so kept to the foothills. Considering the topography of the area, there is little doubt that he passed at or very near the site of the monument.

Other trappers and hunters went this way from time to time. John C. Frémont, on his way out of California in 1844, went into the Mojave Desert by way of Tehachapi Creek and Oak Creek Pass, called Tehachapi Pass until the building of the railroad in 1876, when the name was transferred to the present Tehachapi Pass. Later the old trail and wagon road used by the early emigrants followed closely along Frémont's trail through the original Tehachapi Pass. Frémont added to the confusion of subsequent historians by calling this Walker's Pass.

When the Kern River mines were centers of activity in the 1860s, this became an important stage road from Havilah to Los Angeles. Its importance continued during the 1870s, since it was the route between San Fernando and Caliente, which was at that time the southern terminus of the railroad under construction down the San Joaquin Valley from Stockton.

The first permanent settlers came to Tehachapi, in Tehachapi Valley, about 1854. Gold in the China Hill placers brought a large number of miners to the region, but it was not until 1869 that a post office was established there. Before this, the settlers had to get their mail from Los Angeles, a hundred miles away, whenever they or their neighbors went there for provisions.

The original town of Tehachapi was about three and one-half miles west of the present town, originally called Greenwich, which supplanted it when the railroad was built in 1876. At the first location, still known as Old Town (SRL 643), no buildings remain, but a monument indicates the site. The entire countryside is made fragrant each spring with the scent of millions of fruit blossoms, for in hidden nooks and upon sunny plateaus, often lying more than 3,000 feet above sea level, orchards of prizewinning apples and pears flourish.

Signs of modern industry are also to be seen in the area. The Monolith Portland Cement Company quarry and processing plant at Monolith, four miles east of Tehachapi, was originally developed to build the first Owens Valley–Los Angeles aqueduct. The aqueduct, which crossed Antelope Valley, was completed in 1913. The plant is one of the largest in California and is easily seen from the highway. Farther east on SR 58, where the air of the Mojave Desert mingles with that of the mountains, a veritable forest of gigantic wind machines generates electrical energy from the strong winds that rush through this pass and Oak Creek Pass to the south. This remarkable sight is much like that at Altamont Pass on the eastern edge of Alameda County, where similar wind conditions prevail. It is likely that in time such machines as these will become part of the story of California's endless quest for additional sources of power.

BUTTERFIELD STAGE STATIONS

The Butterfield stages rumbled back and forth through the Cañada de las Uvas and up the southern San Joaquin Valley on their periodic trips between Los Angeles and San Francisco during the years 1858 to 1861. Most of the stations along the way have long since disappeared. Although little remains today to indicate their sites, one may trace the trail through Kern County by the following names: Fort Tejón, Sinks of the Tejón, Kern River Slough, Gordon's Ferry, Posey, and Mountain House.

The Sinks of the Tejón, or Alamo, was located at the mouth of Tejón Creek. Here, where the water of the arroyo sinks into the dry sands, there was a perpetual spring, long a gathering place of the Indians. It was an important station for the Butterfield stages, and a barn and a hostlers' quarters were put up, along with a combined general store, post office, and drug store. This site on the property of the Tejón Ranch Corporation is now under cultivation, but a monument with bronze plaque (SRL 540) stands six miles west at the intersection of David and Wheeler Ridge Roads.

The old stage road continued north past the station at Kern River Slough, where horses were changed. This location is now marked (SRL 588) two miles east of Greenfield on Panama Road. The stage road then crossed the Kern River at Gordon's Ferry (the Kern River Station), about four miles northeast of Bakersfield near the China Grade. No remnant of the Kern River Station can be seen today, but there is a marker (SRL 137) at the south end of the bridge. Major A. B. Gordon operated a ferry here for several years before the establishment of the Butterfield route.

Going north, the next station was located at Posey (Poso) Creek, two and a half miles east of the marker (SRL 539) at the junction of Round Mountain Road and the Bakersfield-Glennville Highway. The plaque on this marker is missing. To the north was Mountain House, sometimes called Willow Springs (not to be confused with the Willow Springs near Rosamond in southeastern Kern County). Mountain House had a bad reputation because of several murders that had been committed there, and weird tales developed around it. Among them was the tale of the white ox that came to the spring to drink and then mysteriously disappeared, and that of the possum that hid at the watering trough, strangely disturbing the flow of water. The site of the Mountain House Station is on private property about a mile and a half north of the marker (SRL 589), which stands on the Bakersfield-Glennville Highway eight miles southwest of Woody.

OTHER LANDMARKS OF STAGECOACH DAYS

Rose Station, about four miles north of the present Grapevine Station and one mile east of I-5, was an important stopping place for travel between Bakersfield and Los Angeles during the late 1860s and early 1870s. A monument (SRL 300) stands on the highway at a point from which the site, on Tejón Ranch Company property, can be seen in the distance. This plot of land was first known as the Kanawha Ranch, operated by James V. Rosemyre and William W. Hudson. The latter was a native of West Virginia, born on the banks of the Kanawha River. When José J. López and William B. Rose bought the property in 1872, they seem to have recorded their purchase as the Canoa Ranch. *Canoa*, Spanish for "trough," is pronounced much like "Kanawha," thus creating some historical confusion about the name of the place that, under Rose's ownership, finally became Rose's Station. The adobe structure built in 1876 was still standing in good condition in 1933 when this section of the first edition of *Historic Spots in California* was published. Only a portion of one wall remained standing, according to the second edition in 1946. In the summer of 1963, Father William N. Abeloe could find only the bare spot where the building had stood, and he noted in the third edition of this book: "So pass our California landmarks."

Willow Springs (SRL 130), about eight miles west of Rosamond, was once an important watering place on the trail connecting the southern San Joaquin Valley and the desert. The springs were used by Indians from ancient times and numerous artifacts have been found there. The site was visited by Father Garcés in 1776, John C. Frémont in 1844, and the Death Valley Forty-Niners. On the old Tehachapi Pass route (Oak Creek Pass), it was a stage and freight station until the coming of the railroad in 1876. It was the dividing place for the ordinary stage travel to the Kern River mines by way of Oak Creek and the heavier ox-team traffic by way of Red Rock Canyon, Jaw-bone Canyon, and the South Fork of the Kern River. Ox teams bound for Inyo County also turned northeast at Willow Springs. Ezra T. Hamilton bought the property from the Beale estate in 1894 and established a resort. Little remains there today except some crumbling ruins and a few old houses. Another Death Valley Forty-niner water hole that later became a freight station is Desert Spring (SRL 476), one and three-quarters miles southeast of Cantil, which is east of SR 14 and a mile and a half south of the Red Rock–Randsburg Road.

North of the junction with the Randsburg Road, SR 14 passes through beautiful Red Rock Canyon State Park, an area of highly colored cliffs that have been eroded into what seem to be pillars, temples, and other fantastic formations. Some of the formations have been given names, including the Great Temple and the Phantom City. The coloration appears more vivid in early morning and late afternoon.

GLENNVILLE, GRANITE STATION, AND WOODY

The oldest known residence in Kern County is the Glennville Adobe (SRL 495). It was built by Thomas Fitzgerald, who ran a trading post at the intersection of two established Indian trails in the mountains. The Glenn brothers, for whom the community was named, arrived after Fitzgerald, in the early 1850s. The Kern County Museum has restored the building, which has its original ceiling rafters and a hand-hewn oak door hung on hand-forged hinges. Glennville is forty-two miles northeast of Bakersfield.

One mile from Glennville on the White River Road a marker (SRL 672) indicates the site of Lavers Crossing, community center for the settlers in Linn's Valley.

Glennville Adobe

Here miners and emigrants stopped en route across the Greenhorn Mountains to the gold strike of 1854 at Keyesville on the Kern River.

Granite Station and Woody lie on parallel routes leading from Bakersfield up to Glennville. The Kern County Historical Society has marked both places. The Granite Station marker, dedicated in 1981, notes that the place (now virtually deserted) was once known as Five Dogs and was established as a stage route stopover by John Elden in 1873. Woody is still a small town with its own post office; its marker, dedicated in 1982, notes that this early mining center and supply town was named for the pioneer rancher Dr. Sparrell W. Woody, who settled in the area in 1862. A hamlet near Woody's ranch developed about 1889 and was named for the doctor, who by that time was fully engaged in his farming career. In 1891 Joseph Weringer discovered copper nearby and operated the Greenback Copper Mine and the Weringer Hotel. In the same year the town was renamed Weringdale for its new booster, although by the time Dr. Woody died in 1909 the original name had been restored to the town.

KEYESVILLE

California historian Robert Glass Cleland said of the discovery of gold on the Kern River and of its importance to Los Angeles and southern California:

> Perhaps the most serious drawback to the material development of the south was its deplorable lack of money . . . and under such a handicap economic progress was necessarily slow. . . . In 1855 gold was discovered in considerable quantities on the Kern River.

This at once attracted miners from the entire State, and led to a rush of no mean proportions. The southern California merchants were naturally jubilant over this event in which they saw an opportunity of reaping some of the rich harvest their San Francisco, Stockton and Sacramento rivals had previously monopolized.

The first town to spring up in this new field was Keyesville (SRL 98), after Richard Keyes, who had opened up a mine likewise named for him. The town was situated in a semicircular cove of the Greenhorn Mountains at the edge of a rocky gulch, and its few stores were scattered about the middle of this flat. There were no streets and the houses went straying up the slope quite informally.

Keyesville was the scene of gambling dens and gunmen as wild as in any of the larger camps in the north. The town site is at the end of Keyesville Road four miles west of Lake Isabella. The passage of time and the depredations of vandals have almost obliterated old Keyesville; few of the old roughly hewn board houses, with their shake roofs, remain. The Kern River, with towering granite walls, banks lined with brilliant green, and "deep-throated roar," is the gateway to one of California's most stupendous mountain regions.

QUARTZBURG AND WHISKEY FLAT (KERNVILLE)

In 1860, Lovely Rogers (this was indeed his first name), a miner from Keyesville, was out looking for a lost mule. In a gulch eight miles north of his home, he found his mule and also a magnificent piece of quartz where the famous Big Blue Mine was later located. That was the beginning of Quartzburg and of its rival, Whiskey Flat, later known as Kernville. The rush to the gulches and mountainsides around Rogers's mine soon resulted in the opening of a dozen quartz mills, and the region became the richest in the state for several years.

On a small ledge above the river the town of Quartzburg sprang up. Water from the mine pumps irrigated the trees and gardens and alfalfa patches, and a homey atmosphere clung about the place from the beginning. Moreover, the influential citizens of Quartzburg believed in local option, and when an attempt was made to start a saloon in town, that unwelcome feature was forced to move a mile down the river to a place thereafter known as Whiskey Flat.

Kernville (SRL 132) eventually became the most important town in the Kern River mining district, but for several years it had a rival in the little town up the river.

By 1879 the Kern River region had reached the height of its prosperity, and most of the mines around Quartzburg had been acquired by Senator John P. Jones, who consolidated them into the Big Blue. Soon after this, the senator met with reverses and the mine closed down, thus shutting off the water supply for Quartzburg's houses and gardens. The former were gradually torn down and carted away, while the latter were left to run wild or die. Nothing remains at Quartzburg today to remind one of its past.

Kernville remained until the early 1950s a pleasant town of quaint houses and tree-shaded streets. Now it lies beneath the waters of Lake Isabella, created when two dams were completed in 1953. A new Kernville was begun in 1951 on the bank of the Kern River several miles north of the original site. Some of the old houses were moved to the new community. The old Kernville Cemetery, however, was not inundated by the lake, and may be seen bordering the highway to new Kernville near the site of vanished Quartzburg. The state landmark marker is located in front of the cemetery in Wofford Heights.

HAVILAH

Havilah (SRL 100) was named for the Biblical land "where there is gold" by Asbury Harpending, a man with a career almost as exotic as his name. The Kentucky-born adventurer joined William Walker's filibustering expedition to Nicaragua in the 1850s; when that collapsed, he came to California, about 1856. A Confederate sympathizer during the Civil War, he hatched all manner of plots against the Union, for which he was briefly jailed. He made a fortune in gold mining and in real estate and in 1864 learned of a rich quartz deposit just south of Clear Creek, a tributary of the Kern River.

Havilah became the chief settlement of the Clear Creek mining district; Harpending laid out its main street and did a land-office business in selling lots, beginning in July 1864. The region was soon thick with prospectors, and miners from all over the state made it a boomtown, aided by favorable publicity from the developers. When Kern County was created in 1866, the flourishing town was made its first county seat.

It was soon found that the ore-bearing deposits lay in deeper veins than had been anticipated, and that the cost of bringing the ore to the surface and refining it was almost prohibitive. Gradually, the mines began to shut down and their developers looked elsewhere. By

Havilah Courthouse

1879, mining activity in the region had been abandoned altogether.

Meanwhile, the agricultural future of the San Joaquin Valley was attracting settlers to towns such as Bakersfield, which soon challenged remote Havilah to be the county seat. After disputed elections, court hearings, and much bad feelings, it was declared in 1874 that a majority of eligible Kern County voters approved the change to Bakersfield.

Today it is difficult to imagine Havilah as a place where more than five hundred people lived in the summer of 1866 or where the business of Kern County was transacted for the next eight years. The courthouse, a one-story frame structure, was restored as a bicentennial project in 1976, and a small display area within is a museum of the palmy days of the settlement, which is now almost deserted. The site is on the Caliente-Bodfish Road, about eight miles south of Bodfish; the state marker is at the Bodfish post office, about eight miles north of Havilah.

OTHER MOUNTAIN MINING CAMPS

Several other almost-vanished mining towns are to be found in Kern County's mountains. Due east of Havilah in Kelso Valley in the Piute Mountains is Sageland, a brief mining center of the 1860s. Loraine in Caliente Canyon was not developed until the early years of the twentieth century; originally named Paris, which the post office said was already being used elsewhere in the state, its name was changed in 1912. Its decline is attributed to the enactment of Prohibition in 1919 more than to the inevitable falling-off of the mines; having the only saloon for miles around, Loraine was a much-

needed social center. It and nearby Twin Pines continue as small settlements today.

Frazier Park, on the border with Ventura County just west of Lebec and I-5, was a center for borax mining from about 1899 to 1908. Here as elsewhere in Kern County the prodigious labor and expense necessary to get the ore out was ultimately too burdensome to make it a profitable undertaking, although some lumbering activity also occurred. Frazier Park is enjoying a second life today as a mountain recreational and retirement community.

BAKERSFIELD

Thomas Baker was born in Muskingum, Ohio, in 1810, the son of a soldier in the War of 1812 and grandson of a Revolutionary War colonel. Baker himself was made a colonel in the Ohio State Militia when he was nineteen and, having completed his legal studies, was admitted to the Ohio bar. He moved westward first to Illinois and then to Iowa, where he was elected to the first Iowa state legislature, in 1846. A widower by then, Baker caught gold fever and journeyed to California; after brief sojourns in Benicia and Stockton, he moved to the San Joaquin Valley in 1852. That year his name was listed among the pioneer settlers in Visalia, Tulare County. He became active in public affairs, serving as assemblyman, Federal Land Office receiver, and state senator. He married a second time, and in 1863 moved to the banks of the Kern River, where disastrous floods in 1862 had swept away the settlement made there in 1860 by Christian Bohna, a German-born settler, and his family.

The swampy, forested area proved to be productive when reclaimed and drained. Its agricultural potential seemed better than that of the mining ventures that hitherto had been the primary attraction in this part of the state. Soon Baker built an adobe house that became a community center for the incoming population, and planted ten acres of his reclamation land with alfalfa. The place that had been called "Kern Island" for its location on the channels and sloughs of the Kern River was now becoming known as "Baker's Field."

One of the first visitors the Bakers had received after their arrival was Captain Elisha Stevens of the Murphy-Townsend-Stevens overland party of 1844, who made his final home in the area and is buried in Bakersfield. (The original spelling of the name is "Stephens," but this spelling is found in conjunction with his name throughout the state, and will be used here.) He brought the colonel and his family a welcoming gift of some hogs and chickens from the ranch he had established below the China Grade Bluff. Stevens's homesite is just east of the Greater Bakersfield Memorial Hospital on 34th Street; the marker (SRL 732) is north on Union Avenue at Columbus Street, just west of Garces High School.

By 1870 Bakersfield, with a population of 600, was fast becoming the principal town of Kern County. In 1873 it was officially incorporated as a city, an event that Colonel Baker, who had planned and mapped the town site, did not live to see, for he died in the typhoid epidemic of the previous year. Baker's insistence on wide streets and even wider avenues and a regular grid pattern for the city was sensible and wise; the city has grown around this nucleus with little change in streets since then. By 1874 Bakersfield had replaced the dying town of Havilah as the county seat. Railroads, agriculture, cattle ranching, oil, and highway transportation have continued the boom down to the present; Bakersfield is one of the major cities of California.

Alexis Godey, explorer with the Frémont expeditions, made his last home in Bakersfield, having acquired about sixty-six acres there in 1873. He disposed of much of this land but retained a favorite spot of high ground as his home. The site (SRL 690), facing Nineteenth Street, is now occupied partly by Central Park and partly by business and residential property.

PIONEER VILLAGE OF KERN COUNTY MUSEUM

The outstanding historical attraction of present-day Bakersfield is the Pioneer Village of the Kern County Museum at 3801 Chester Avenue. Begun in 1950 as an outdoor expansion of the museum's work, the Pioneer Village quickly became the principal repository of buildings and artifacts from Kern County's past. A superb collection of Californiana, this park became the model for others in the state. Its theme is early settlement in Kern County, from about 1860 to about 1900. Most of the buildings are authentic structures that have been moved to the site from various parts of Kern County to be preserved from inevitable destruction in the name of progress. Among these are the Thomas Barnes log cabin, built in 1868, the one-room Norris School from 1882, the modest William Pinckney residence from 1900, the elaborate W. A. Howell house from 1891, and the general store established in Woody in 1899. Specialized buildings include a doctor's office, a dentist's office, a barber shop, an undertaker's parlor,

a fire station, a newspaper office, a blacksmith shop, and a bank. The ranching, agricultural, railroad, and oil eras of Kern County history are also represented; a landmark of the village is the wood-framed oil drilling rig from 1910, the oldest known to exist in the United States.

The Kern County Museum, housed in a sturdy two-story building, has detailed exhibits of materials from Kern County's past, from Yokut Indian artifacts to modern machinery. The Harry D. West Vehicle Collection contains sixteen vintage horse-drawn vehicles, from freight wagons to surreys.

Next to the museum stands a replica of the famous Beale Clock Tower, which stood at the intersection of Seventeenth Street and Chester Avenue for almost half a century until it was razed following the earthquakes of 1952. The original had been given to the city in honor of his mother by Truxtun Beale in 1904. The son of pioneer General Beale had been the United States ambassador to Spain, and the tower was based on one he had seen and admired in that country. The replica was installed in 1964.

Bakersfield boasts a fine set of modern public buildings housing the city and county offices. These were constructed following the earthquake of August 22, 1952, which wrecked the city hall and courthouse beyond repair. This shock followed the earthquake of July 21 that devastated the town of Tehachapi. In front of the Bakersfield City Hall, at Truxtun and Chester Avenues, stands a statue of Colonel Thomas Baker (SRL 382).

THE RAILROAD

Construction had started in the spring of 1870 on the San Joaquin Valley branch of the Central Pacific Railroad, later Southern Pacific, but the tracks did not reach Kern County until 1873. The first station, at the northern boundary, was called Delano for Columbus Delano, then Secretary of the Interior. The railroad bypassed Bakersfield, since its citizens had refused to give the customary subsidy, and established a station called Sumner, a mile and a half east of town. This place, later called Kern, was consolidated with Bakersfield in 1909, and by that time the Santa Fe Railroad had already established itself in Bakersfield.

The Tehachapi Mountains presented a major engineering obstacle to the continuation of the railroad to Los Angeles County. Construction reached Caliente in April 1875, and here the engineers were faced with the task of raising the railroad 2,734 feet in sixteen miles to scale the pass at a height of 4,025 feet. Caliente (SRL 757) thus became the terminal for about sixteen months, while a force of up to three thousand men, mostly Chinese, labored in the mountains. A station just beyond Caliente was named Bealeville (SRL 741) for Edward F. Beale, on whose Rancho El Tejón it was located. (A shortcut from SR 58 to Caliente crosses the railroad at this point.)

The Tehachapis were conquered in twenty-eight miles of track laid on gradual curves and through eighteen tunnels. At one point the track is looped over itself, an engineering marvel directed by William Hood, who later became the chief engineer for the entire Southern Pacific system. A portion of the famous "Tehachapi Loop" (SRL 508) may be glimpsed from the Woodford-Tehachapi Road at a point about two miles south of Woodford (Keene). A monument has been placed on the spot, and with luck one may see the locomotive of a long Union Pacific train at the top of the loop and the last car or caboose just entering the tunnel below.

A station called Greenwich was established near the summit of the pass, but this soon developed into a town and stole the name and the population of nearby Tehachapi, now called Old Town. At this time also the name "Tehachapi Pass" was transferred from the pioneer Oak Creek route to the new railroad pass. The railroad was opened through the Tehachapis and across the desert to Mojave on August 8, 1876. With the coming of the railroad to Kern County, the modern era began and agriculture and livestock raising quickly replaced mining as the principal industry.

The desert town of Mojave, child of the railroad, was the rail terminus for the twenty-mule-team borax wagons that operated from Death Valley, Inyo County, to the railroad loading dock in Mojave. A round trip required twenty days. A monument (SRL 652) has been placed on the west side of the 16200 block of the Sierra Highway (SR 14) in Mojave.

The United States Borax and Chemical Company, formerly the Pacific Coast Borax Company, began to develop sodium borate mining at Boron, just north of modern Edwards Air Force Base and at the eastern edge of the county. As the Death Valley deposits were gradually exhausted, those at Boron were developed, beginning in 1925. In 1957 this became an open-pit operation and today is one of the largest open-pit mining operations in the world. The Twenty Mule Team Museum is at 26962 Twenty Mule Team Road in Boron, located in a renovated house from the old Baker Mine campsite.

MINING IN THE MOJAVE

A mining boom was inaugurated at the eastern edge of Kern County with the discovery of gold in 1895 in a group of rounded hills rising out of the Mojave Desert. The mine became known as the Rand, after the prosperous mining district of that name in the Transvaal, South Africa, and a town called Randsburg sprang up nearby. Randsburg soon became the center of several camps, including Johannesburg, Red Mountain, and Atolia, the latter two being in San Bernardino County. Tungsten and silver were later discovered in the area, and there is still some mining activity amid the remnants of boom days. The Rand Mining District is commemorated by a monument (SRL 938) on the eastern side of the junction of Randsburg Road with US 395. The Desert Museum at 161 Butte Street in Randsburg is a branch of the Kern County Museum, featuring mining tools and displays on the history of Randsburg, one of the most picturesque old mining towns in California.

On Garlock Road, one mile north of the Red Rock–Randsburg Road and ten miles west of Randsburg, a marker indicates the ghost town of Garlock (SRL 671), the one-time location of four stamping mills serving the Rand Mining District. Eugene Garlock set up the first of these near a water hole known as Cow Wells. The post office established there in the following year took his name. The Randsburg area was supplied by freight wagons hauling from the railroad town of Mojave, and Garlock became a regular stopping place. The town quickly grew to a population of 300 and promised further growth, but the completion of a railroad to the Rand area and the establishment of a stamp mill at the Yellow Aster (formerly the Rand) Mine caused Garlock to dwindle in importance, and its people gradually moved elsewhere.

On Black Mountain, about five miles northwest of Garlock, are the remains of a prehistoric Indian village, discovered in the 1880s. The ruins are fragmentary and there is not much agreement about the builders of the place, except to say that it is very old. In neighboring mountains and valleys there is much evidence of more recent tribes, among the most notable being the painted rocks or pictographs on the Kern River near Lake Isabella.

ROSAMOND MINING DISTRICT

Ezra M. Hamilton discovered gold northwest of Rosamond in 1896, after prospecting for two years. His enterprise was successful; it was purchased in 1909 by the Tropico Mining and Milling Company and its name was changed to Tropico. For a number of years after 1958, Tropico Mine was opened as a public attraction, but it is now closed. North of Rosamond, Standard Hill is the site of a gold discovery in 1894 by George E. Bowers. Subsequent bonanzas were made in both gold and silver, and the Cactus Queen Mine in the nearby Middle Buttes was the most productive silver mine in California until World War II.

BLACK GOLD

The story of oil in Kern County is essential to a complete picture of the modern era. The county today contributes about one-fourth of the oil produced in California. Even before the county was organized in 1866, oil was being refined in the area. The Buena Vista Petroleum Company was organized and incorporated in 1864, and soon thereafter a refinery was built at the foot of the Temblor Range, eight miles west of the marker at the intersection of SR 33 and Lokern Road, about seven miles north of McKittrick (SRL 504). The refinery operated until April 1867, producing 3,000 gallons of refined oil, but work ceased when freight charges were found to be prohibitive.

There were a number of relatively early discoveries in the McKittrick Field. The California Standard Oil Well No. 1 (SRL 376), not completed until 1899, has been incorrectly designated as the discovery well of that field. The McKittrick area is more famous for the refining of asphalt, the original name of the settlement being Asphalto. About one-half mile south of McKittrick on SR 58 a marker (SRL 498) stands near the location of a brea pit of the Pleistocene period (15,000 to 50,000 years ago), from which the bones of many animals and birds, trapped in the sticky asphalt, have been recovered. These relics, first brought to the attention of scientists in 1929, may be seen in the Kern County Museum in Bakersfield. The pit has now been filled in.

The west side of the county is generally associated with Kern's oil industry, with its thriving towns of Maricopa, Taft, and Ford City (the last deriving its name from the preponderance of Model-Ts there in 1921). The West Kern Oil Museum in Taft, at Wood Street and SR 33, has good displays on the oil industry there, and a newer section on transportation, featuring antique trucks.

In was in the Bakersfield area, however, that the discovery was made in 1899 that zoomed the county to prominence as an oil producer. Several miles northeast of the city on Round Mountain Road (not far from the site of Gordon's Ferry but on the northern bank of the Kern River), a marker (SRL 290) indicates the discovery well of the Kern River oil field, dug by hand in the summer of 1899. The first commercial well of the area was drilled a few hundred feet away several weeks later, and soon the towns of Oil City, Oil Center, and Oildale came into existence, communicating their prosperity to nearby Bakersfield.

Fellows was a railroad terminal in 1908 but experienced its greatest boom when the Midway Gusher, Well 2-6, blew on November 27, 1909, with a production of 2,000 barrels a day. The marker (SRL 581) is located a quarter of a mile west of Fellows on Broadway Road.

Although the Midway Gusher started the West Side oil rush, it was eclipsed a few months later when Lakeview Gusher Number One blew on the evening of March 14, 1910. This is the greatest gusher in the history of the world, producing an unprecedented 18,000 barrels in the first twenty-four hours. This Union Oil Company well flowed for eighteen months, producing nine million barrels. It presented a major control problem and fire danger, forcing residents of the nearby camp to leave their homes for a time. The output reached 68,000 barrels a day at its peak production. It is said that the tremendous flow of this gusher brought down the price of oil. Its location is marked (SRL 485) one and one-half miles north of Maricopa on Division Road off SR 33.

The town of Buttonwillow, also on the west side of the county, antedates the oil boom. It derives its name from a lone buttonwillow tree (SRL 492), still standing and marked one mile north of town on Buttonwillow Avenue; the tree was a landmark for early cowboys in the area and the location of their spring rodeos. It had been an old Indian campsite. Henry Miller established offices of the Miller and Lux enterprises at this town and bestowed the name of the tree on the railroad station and the post office, started in 1895.

TULE ELK STATE RESERVE

California's Great Central Valley was home to herds of tule elk, so numerous in the fertile floodplains and lowlands of the northern San Joaquin Valley that they were sometimes observed in groups of one or two thousand. Although the coming of the Spanish missions and ranchos had little immediate effect on the tule elk, the aggressive European grasses they introduced spread into the valley and overran the elk's grazing lands. The elk nearly vanished when hunters began a systematic slaughter of the animals after 1848. The state Legislature made elk hunting illegal throughout the state in 1854, but little seems to have been done to enforce the law. A state fish and game warden could find only a single pair of elk in the state around 1875, in the tule marshes near Buena Vista Lake.

Henry Miller (of the Miller and Lux firm) was determined to preserve the elk. He gave stern instructions to his employees to protect the animals and offered a generous reward for information about anyone disturbing them. Thus he was able to preserve a herd. Although they did thousands of dollars of damage to his crops each year, Miller nonetheless protected the elk. In 1930 Miller and Lux provided 600 acres as a temporary enclosure for the tule elk until a state refuge could be established.

In 1932 the State Park Commission purchased 953 acres near Tupman to be completely fenced and maintained as a tule elk sanctuary. Those elk that could be rounded up were maintained here, while wild and free-ranging herds of tule elk were established in Colusa County's Cache Creek area and in the Owens Valley, where they still exist today.

The Tule Elk State Reserve is located four miles west of I-5 and 27 miles west of Bakersfield and can be visited year-round. In recent years, changing water conditions have rendered this a less desirable retreat than it formerly was, and the state is considering the establishment of another reservation for the tule elk.

THE DESERT TORTOISE NATURAL AREA

The California State Reptile is the desert tortoise (*Gopherus agassizi*). The Bureau of Land Management set aside thirty-eight square miles of natural habitat for these animals in 1977, on the western edge of the Rand Mountains. This refuge is fenced off to prevent larger animals from entering and to keep the few, reclusive tortoises as protected as possible. The visitors center is located on the Randsburg Road five miles from California City Boulevard. Some of the area bounded by the fence is still privately owned, although plans are in effect to purchase all of the enclosed area for the reserve.

EDWARDS AND CHINA LAKE, SHAFTER

The largest dry lake in the United States is sixty-five-square-mile Rogers Dry Lake, named after a gold-and silver-mining company that operated there early in the twentieth century. Once called Muroc Dry Lake, that name is the reversed spelling of the name of Ralph and Clifford Corum, pioneer settlers. The hard lake bed has been used in the past for sports car racing. Its first use by the military was in 1933 as a bombing and gunnery range operating out of March Field near Riverside. In 1942, shortly after the outbreak of World War II, the north end of the lake was used for testing the XP-59, the first jet plane developed in the United States. Muroc Army Air Field became Muroc Air Force Base in 1948. It was established to include the dry lake bed, and since then most of the testing of experimental and production aircraft by the Air Force has been done here, and a number of world speed records have been set. Here, on October 14, 1947, Air Force Captain Charles E. Yeager, at the controls of a Bell X-1 Rocket plane, was the first man in history to fly faster than the speed of sound.

The base was renamed three years later in memory of Air Force Captain Glen W. Edwards, who died in the crash of his test plane in 1948. Edwards Air Force Base has been the scene of many aviation triumphs since then; one memorable one was in 1981, with the safe landing of the first manned space shuttle, *Columbia*. The Air Force Test Flight Museum on the base is open to the public on a regular basis and includes more than fifty aircraft.

North of Edwards Air Force Base, but also on the eastern border of the county and also extending into San Bernardino County, is China Lake, site of the United States Naval Weapons Center. The dry lake nearby derives its name from the Chinese who searched Indian Wells Valley for borax in the years following their construction work on the Central Pacific Railroad. The station was established in November 1943 for the development and testing of rockets. The Michelson Laboratory there is named for Albert A. Michelson, who in 1907 was the first American to receive the Nobel Prize in physics.

At Shafter Airport, fifteen miles north of Bakersfield, another aviation landmark was achieved on August 23, 1977, when a manpowered aircraft first completed a mile-long figure-eight flight (the "Kremer Circuit"). Dr. Paul B. McCready Jr. designed the aircraft, called the Gossamer Condor. It was operated by Bryan Allan, who won a prize of 50,000 pounds offered by the Royal Aeronautical Society of London for the feat. The flight of the Gossamer Condor is memorialized at the airport (SRL 923).

Kings County

"Bastille" Restaurant, Hanford

Kings County was named for the river called El Rio de los Santos Reyes ("the River of the Holy Kings"), after the Three Wise Men of the Bible, by a Spanish explorer, probably Gabriel Moraga, in 1805. At the time of the American conquest, the name was changed to "Kings River." In 1893 Kings County was organized from territory split off from adjoining Tulare County. Two small additions from Fresno County were made in 1909. Hanford has always been the county seat.

TULARE LAKE

Tulare Lake was discovered in 1772 by Pedro Fages, who gave the vast marshlands of the San Joaquin Valley the name Los Tulares ("the place of the rushes"). Charles E. Chapman says that as early as 1804 Father Juan Martín of Mission San Miguel crossed the Coast Range into the valley, going as far as an Indian village on Lake Tulare. He says that "in October 1814 a fresh search for a mission site in the tulares was made. The commander of the expedition was a sergeant (Juan Ortega?) whose name does not appear. The account comes from Father Juan Cabot, who was a member of the party. They went from San Miguel to Lake Tulare." The fur-trapping "mountain men" also visited Tulare Lake as early as 1827.

Tulare Lake comprises the natural drainage area in the valley for the Kings and Tule Rivers and other smaller watercourses. According to government surveys, the lowest point in the bed of Tulare Lake is 175 feet above sea level; the highest water on record reached 220 feet above sea level. In 1865, when its waters covered the site of the present town of Corcoran, it was thirty-five miles wide and sixty miles long. Its maximum depth has never been more than forty-five feet. In times past commercial fishing boats as well as pleasure boats operated on the lake. Sloughs fed a swamp area much larger than the actual lake. In the twentieth century, streams that formerly flowed into the lake have gradually been drained for irrigation purposes, and in dry years the entire lake bed has been given over to cultivation. Wet years still make their appearance, however, and periodically Tulare Lake floods to an impressive extent, sometimes for two or more years at a time. The building of Pine Flat Dam, on the Kings River in Fresno County, has helped to control some of the worst flooding and irrigation problems.

STAGE STATIONS IN KINGS COUNTY

A stage station known as the Head of Cross Creek was established at Cross Creek in 1856. The site is in the extreme northeastern corner of the county, four miles northwest of Goshen in Tulare County, and in stagecoach days it was the halfway point between Visalia and the Kings River Station at Whitmore's Ferry. After the coming of the Butterfield stages in 1858, the station was called Cross Creek Station. Like the other stations of this section, the Cross Creek post, now vanished, consisted of a board-and-batten barn and a cabin of the same construction for use of the hostlers, generally two in number. During the drought of 1864, Peter Van Valer built a toll bridge over Cross Creek; it was said to have been the only bridge between Visalia and Stockton.

Kingston, on the south bank of the lower Kings River eight and one-half miles northwest of Hanford, was founded in 1856 at Whitmore's Ferry, which had been established in 1854 by L. A. Whitmore. After 1858 the town became a stopping place for the Butterfield stages, which established a regular route through the San Joaquin Valley by way of Kingston and Whitmore's

Ferry after leaving the old Stockton–Los Angeles Road east of Visalia.

A toll bridge superseded the ferry in 1873, and its piers remain near the riverbank, about a quarter of a mile below the Santa Fe Railroad bridge at Laton in Fresno County. On the evening of December 26, 1873, before the tollgates of the bridge were in place, Tiburcio Vásquez and his bandit gang made a bold raid on the little town of Kingston. They bound thirty-nine men and robbed three stores before the alarm was spread, when they fled across the new bridge to horses waiting in a corral on the north side of the river and escaped; two bandits and a horse were killed in the attack.

Kingston is now gone, but a marker (SRL 270) commemorating the town has been placed in the park on the south bank of the Kings River, one-quarter mile west on Douglas Avenue from its intersection with Avenue 12-3/4.

EL ADOBE DE LOS ROBLES RANCHO

One of the oldest houses still in use in the central San Joaquin Valley is a long, low adobe (SRL 206), with casement windows of Spanish design, that stands beneath the shade of immense oaks and blue gums on SR 41 five miles north of Lemoore. It was built in 1856 by Daniel Rhoads, who arrived in California in 1846, having come over the Oregon Trail with the caravan of pioneers from which the Donner party separated to take the fateful Hastings Cutoff, later becoming snowbound in the High Sierra. In February 1847 Dan Rhoads became a member of the first relief party, which in the face of untold hardships and even death left Johnson's Rancho to go to the rescue of the starving emigrants at Donner Lake. Much of the material used by Bancroft for his account of the Donner tragedy was drawn from an interview with Rhoads.

Carefully preserved, and containing relics of pioneer days, the old adobe is maintained as a home and not as a museum. The site is noteworthy for its great plantations of trees—stately tall Australian blue gums and tall cypress trees planted by Rhoads himself and a line of old black olive trees along the driveway—and the many native oaks from which the house derived the name of "El Adobe de los Robles."

HISTORIC SPOTS OF THE WEST SIDE

The town of Avenal takes its name from the Spanish word for "field of wild oats." Much older than the town is the Avenal Ranch, fourteen miles south of Avenal and six miles off SR 41 in the foothills of the Coast Range. The ranch headquarters stand on the site of a prehistoric Indian village. The mission padres from San Miguel passed this way in their search for a mission site in the tulares. An old adobe barn, probably built in the early 1850s by the original owners, Welch and Cahill from Missouri, still stands on the property. There is also the old ranch house, most of whose original lumber is redwood brought by oxen from the Santa Cruz Mountains.

On the west shore of Tulare Lake an adobe trading post was established in 1870 by Cox and Clark. Since it was then the only building on that side of the lake, it served as a landing place for lake boats and as a trading center for the Indians. The site of the old post is three miles south of Kettleman City on SR 41. About three miles north of Kettleman City is the site of another adobe known as the Vaca dugout, built in 1863 by Juan Perría and Pablo Vaca; this was a vaquero headquarters, never a boat landing.

Both buildings were on the eastern branch of El Camino Viejo, which left the main road at Alamo Solo, a campsite twenty miles to the south of the Cox and Clark adobe. Alamo Mocho ("trimmed cottonwood") was another campsite on this road, located just south of Kettleman Hills, within a short distance of SR 41. A camp on the western branch of El Camino Viejo was located at the mouth of El Arroyo de las Garzas ("the herons"). It was here that Dave Kettleman, a cattle rancher, first settled. His name is remembered in Kettleman City and Kettleman Hills, as well as in the Kettleman Oil Fields, which achieved prominence in 1928.

LEMOORE

Dr. Lavern Lee Moore proposed that a post office should be established at the small agricultural community of La Tache, which was growing up north of Tulare Lake. The Post Office Department approved his request in September 1875, but gave the new office a name coined from that of the petitioner. Two years later the center of population moved a short distance to the branch railroad built through the area and across the Kings River to the Huron Plains and the important sheep-shearing center at Posa Chiné trading post. In 1890 Lemoore was considered to be the largest wool-shipping center in the United States. The older, pre-railroad crossing of the river to the west side was at what is still called Murphy's Bridge, one-quarter mile south of Jackson Avenue.

Kings County Courthouse, Hanford

Bastille Restaurant, Hanford

Aaron Mooney and his wife Sarah were prominent in the civic affairs of Lemoore. Their 1893 home at 542 West D Street was acquired from their grandchildren in 1973 by the Lemoore District Chamber of Commerce and is now the Sarah A. Mooney Memorial Museum, focusing on the history of Lemoore and its commercial activities.

During World War II, the Army Air Corps established a field just west of Lemoore. The town's available land, good flying weather, and central location commended it to the Navy as a training site for carrier-based fighter planes in the Pacific. In 1958, construction began on Lemoore Naval Air Station, near the former army airfield, dedicated in July 1961. Although the military presence in California has sharply declined since 1990, this facility has been recognized as the premier master jet base on the West Coast.

HANFORD

The same branch railroad gave birth in 1877 to Hanford, named for James M. Hanford, a Southern Pacific official, and destined to become the county seat when Kings County was formed. The town's wooden buildings were frequently destroyed by fire; in 1887 the town's first brick building was put up. It still stands at 110–112 East Sixth Street, in the historic district of Hanford. The city boasted one of the largest Chinatowns in California for some years, with as many as 600 residents. A street known as China Alley still remains, and on it is a Taoist temple dating from 1893.

The old Kings County Courthouse is a beautiful structure on Courthouse Square, built in 1897 and expanded in 1914. Until 1979 it was the seat of county government; today the brick and granite building houses offices and commercial establishments. The most strik-

ing building is the neighboring sheriff's office and jail, built in 1897 and dominated by an octagonal tower and parapet that give it a neo-Gothic appearance. Locally known as "La Bastille," the building has housed a restaurant since the county offices were moved elsewhere in 1974.

On the north side of Court Street across from "La Bastille" is the Veterans' Memorial Building built in 1925 and still much used by the community. It is claimed to be the first veterans' building in California. The museum located in the old Carnegie Library at 109 East Eighth Street has exhibits on Kings County and on Hanford. At 870 West Davis Street at the Roosevelt Elementary School is "Fort Roosevelt," an outdoor museum of natural history and Indian artifacts; the site was formerly the Southern Pacific freight depot, established in 1893.

THE MUSSEL SLOUGH TRAGEDY

Mussel Slough is a branch of the Kings River north of Hanford. Here on May 11, 1880, a bloody shoot-out took place between settlers and agents of the Southern Pacific Railroad. The railroad's claim to extensive lands in the San Joaquin Valley was in dispute for some years, during which time the railroad invited settlers to farm some of the property. When its title was confirmed by the courts, the company offered land to buyers without consideration for the settlers already established there; the company also won a court order ejecting these settlers. When Southern Pacific agents, accompanied by a U.S. marshal, attempted to settle two new purchasers on the land, the newly formed Settlers League resisted. In a tense atmosphere, aggravated when a horse reared suddenly and struck the marshal, firing broke out. Five settlers and a railroad agent were killed in less than a minute; two others died of their wounds later. Five settlers eventually went to prison, and the others either accepted the railroad's terms or abandoned their lands. The novelist Frank Norris used the incident as a critical episode in *The Octopus* (1901), an attack on the railroad's treatment of California farmers. The historical marker (SRL 245)

commemorating the tragedy is at the roadside on Fourteenth Avenue, between Elaine and Everett Avenues, four miles north of Grangeville. In 1880 this spot was in Tulare County, but it became part of Kings County when it was formed in 1893. By that date, it was being called Lucerne Valley, although no significant settlement developed there.

Lake County

Lake County was part of Mendocino County at the time of California statehood in 1850. The county was named for a great body of fresh water, Clear Lake, which lies entirely within its confines. In 1852, when Napa County was created, the boundary line between Mendocino and Napa Counties went through the middle of Clear Lake. In 1855, what is now Lake County became part of Napa County. Lake County was established in 1861, with Lakeport as its county seat. When the wooden courthouse and all its records were destroyed by fire in 1867, Lower Lake became the temporary county seat until a new stone courthouse was completed at Lakeport in 1871.

INDIAN LEGENDS

Lake County was naturally rich in fish, fowl, game, nuts, and berries and supported perhaps the densest Indian population in California. It is so mountainous that it was one of four counties in the state where no railroad was ever built. Years after other Indian peoples had succumbed to the invasion of outsiders, the Pomos flourished in a more protected environment.

Tule roots grew abundantly on the lake shores, and here Indians camped in great numbers during the digging season. Bright birds' feathers were prized for decoration. George Gibbs, writing in his journal in 1851, noted: "At Clear Lake the women generally wear a small round bowl-shaped basket on their heads, and this is frequently interwoven with the red feathers of the woodpecker and edged with the plume tufts of the blue quail." The massive bodies of obsidian found in the county were also prized. Those found southwest of Mount Konocti were used for making knives and razors, while those found near the east and northeast shores of Lower Lake were used for making spearheads and arrowheads.

A legend of the area concerns Mount Konocti, the most prominent feature of the landscape. Lupiyomi, daughter of the proud and powerful Chief Konocti, was sought in marriage by a rival chieftain, Kahbel. Chief Konocti, refusing consent to the union, was challenged to battle. He took his stand on one side of the Narrows of Clear Lake, while his opponent took a position on the opposite side. The rocks hurled across the water by these warriors during the combat are the immense boulders that now cover the mountainside. The maiden's tears formed a pool—now Little Borax Lake—a lasting memorial of her grief. The lover Kahbel was killed; his blood is seen in the red splashes in the gashed side of Red Hill, rising on the north shore. Chief Konocti also succumbed and, sinking back, became the rugged mountain that now bears his name. Distraught, Lupiyomi threw herself into the lake; her unceasing tears bubble up in Omarocharbe, the Big Soda Spring, gushing out of the waters of Clear Lake at Soda Bay. The lake had two names, Hok-has-ha from one tribe and Ka-ba-tin from another.

CLEAR LAKE

Clear Lake is the largest natural body of fresh water lying wholly within the state and is near the geographical center of the county. Thousands of years ago it was a broad valley draining into the Russian River. When landslides blocked this western outlet, the water rose until it found a new outlet, Cache Creek, which drains eastward into the Sacramento River. Ewing Young and his party of trappers crossed the Coast Range in 1832 by way of this lake on their journey from the Sacramento River to the Pacific Ocean. James Clyman, in his diary for December 1845, wrote that he camped on the outlet of Clear Lake and feasted on bear ribs and liver. Edwin Bryant, a traveler in California in 1846–47, wrote:

> A lake not laid down in any map and known as the Laguna among the Californians, is situated about sixty miles north of the Bay of San Francisco. It is between forty and sixty miles in length. The valleys in its vicinity are highly fertile and romantically beautiful. In the vicinity of this lake there is a mountain of pure sulphur. There are also soda springs and a great variety of mineral waters and minerals.

Lieutenant Joseph Warren Revere, in command of the north district for some months after the raising of the United States flag at Sonoma, made a tour to Clear Lake and wrote up his experiences for publication, saying, "Few white men have visited this magnificent Laguna." About sunset one evening, he and his men arrived at the narrowest part of Clear Lake, "opposite a pretty islet" upon which was a native village. The Indians, at first fearful because of the many raids made upon them to carry off laborers, were finally persuaded to ferry the travelers across on tule rafts. The island village, protected by this natural moat, had between two and three hundred inhabitants.

Clear Lake is nineteen and one-half miles long. It is shaped like a double-tailed polliwog. The fat body part is Clear Lake proper. The two tails are called East Lake and Lower Lake, and are joined to the body at the Narrows. Clear Lake State Park, near Soda Bay, contains an Indian Nature Trail that displays living plants and explains how they were used by the Pomo and Lile'ek people.

Anderson Marsh State Historic Park preserves the sites of forty Indian villages, some of which go back 10,000 years. Established in 1982, this thousand-acre preserve was first settled in 1855 when two brothers, Achilles Fine Grigsby and John Melchisadeck Grigsby, arrived by ox team from Tennessee. The Grigsbys raised livestock and agricultural produce, and built the central portion of the ranch house, which was enlarged by John Still Anderson and his family after they acquired the property in 1885. Members of the Anderson family continued to live and to work there until the late 1960s. The home, still standing but somewhat modernized, is now the park visitors' center. The park is located on SR 53 between the towns of Clearlake and Lower Lake. Archaeological work is continually being done here, making it a demonstration of a working dig.

Mount Konocti rises to the southwest almost 3,000 feet above the level of the lake, a majestic, solitary presence. Settlement near the summit of the mountain was attempted in the 1870s by O. S. Morford, who built the first wagon road in 1878 with the intention of establishing a public summer resort far up the mountainside. On May 1, 1878, Morford and two companions ascended to the peak and there unfurled the Stars and Stripes. His plans for a summit resort were never carried out. The first permanent settlers near the summit were the Euvelle Howard family early in the twentieth century. Orchards now grace the slopes of the mountain. On the lake front, Konocti Harbor Resort is a modern development, noted for summer music shows. The shores of the lake have many permanent homes as well as vacation places, and at Lakeport and other locations annual water carnivals have been held for many years. Excursion boats have been crossing the lake since the early 1870s.

LAKE COUNTY INDIAN TRAGEDIES

Alta California was developed chiefly by forced Indian labor. Each new activity required someone to build it. Native peoples fled from this new rule, and the army was called on to bring them under control. As early as 1821, Luís Argüello led a band of soldiers into what is now Lake County. When Mexico took over Alta California in 1822, Argüello became the first native-born governor of the province. In 1824 the mission at Sonoma was established. Within the next decade, the Vallejo family became important in the Sonoma region, and in 1836 Salvador Vallejo and Ramón Carrillo led another expedition into the Lake County mountains. This and later forays seem to have been in search of Indians to press into a labor force on the ranchos. The Indian Island Massacre of 1842, when the Indians resisted an invading group, was one of several tragic incidents in these years.

Even before an official grant of land was made to him in 1844, Vallejo and his brother Antonio had begun pasturing cattle in the region now known as the Big, Scotts, Upper Lake, and Bachelor Valleys. The cattle multiplied and became "exceedingly wild," at what cost to the Indian inhabitants can only be imagined. A log cabin and corral were built in Big Valley near the present site of Kelseyville, with a mayordomo and ten vaqueros to look after the ranch.

In 1847, Vallejo drove some of his cattle out of the valley and sold the remainder to four men: Charles Stone, a man named Shirland, and two brothers, Andrew and Benjamin Kelsey, who had arrived in California with the Bidwell-Bartleson party in 1841. Stone and Andrew Kelsey took possession of the ranch and employed Indians to build an adobe house for them west across Kelsey Creek from where Kelseyville now stands. Apparently the Americans treated the Indian workers cruelly, and after some particularly brutal punishments, the Indians retaliated by killing Kelsey and Stone in the fall of 1849.

In January 1850 a military expedition came to punish the offenders, but they found that the Indians had taken refuge on various islands in Clear Lake and could not be reached. In May Captain Nathaniel Lyon and a detachment were sent from Benicia for the same purpose, bringing with them two whaleboats on the running gears of wagons and two mountain howitzers. The only Indians they found were gathered on an island in Upper Lake. By using the boats, cannon, and bayonets, the soldiers practically annihilated the group. About a hundred Indians were killed, none of whom, in all probability, had taken any part in the Stone and Kelsey incident (which occurred on the other side of the lake). There are differing versions of this massacre, although the outcome is in no doubt. Since that time the place has been called "Bloody Island," although later reclamation projects have eliminated its water boundaries and it appears to be a hill by the shore of

the lake today. A monument with bronze plaque (SRL 427) marks the site, about one and a half miles southeast of the town of Upper Lake, just west of SR 20.

The remains of Stone and Kelsey were moved in 1950 to a monument (SRL 426) near the site of their adobe home, west of Kelseyville at Main Street and Bell Hill Road. The adobe stood on the bluff one hundred yards west of the monument.

The town of Kelseyville began in 1857 with Denham's store and blacksmith shop. The oldest business building presently standing is a brick structure on Main Street, built in the 1870s.

A LOST TREATY

To adjust land disputes with the Indian tribes, a commission to negotiate treaties was appointed by President Millard Fillmore shortly after the admission of California into the Union in 1850.

Commissioner Redick McKee, representing the United States government, and the chiefs and headmen of eight local Indian tribes signed a Treaty of Peace and Friendship on August 20, 1851, at Camp Lu-Pi-Yu-Mi on the south shore of Clear Lake. This treaty consisted of eight articles setting forth details of the promises on both sides, and a description of the lands to be given, in perpetuity, to these tribes, as well as certain benefits to be derived by them in recompense for their renunciation. Article III of the treaty states: "The said tribes, or bands, hereby jointly and severally relinquish, cede, and forever quitclaim to the United States all their right, title, claim, or interest of any kind, which they, or either of them, hold to the lands or soil in California." One wonders what this language meant to the tribes. At this council a gift was made to the assembled Indians of "ten head of beef cattle, three sacks of bread, and sundry clothing."

This treaty, along with seventeen others, was sent to the Senate by President Fillmore in June 1852 for approval. Never acted on, it is now referred to as one of the "Eighteen Lost Treaties." Attempts have been made to secure compensation for the Indians of California from the United States in lieu of the property rights granted them in the treaties, and some reimbursement has been made.

MEXICAN LAND GRANTS IN LAKE COUNTY

Three grants of land were made by the Mexican government within the territory now included in Lake County.

Rancho Lupyomi, about which there was much litigation, was originally granted to Salvador and Juan Antonio Vallejo by Governor Micheltorena in 1844. The map accompanying this grant showed the territory of Laguna de Lu-Pi-Yo-Mi extending sixteen leagues and embracing Upper Lake, Bachelor, Scotts, and Big Valleys. In 1854 settlers began to arrive, and by 1861 many families had located on the land, although their titles to it could not be made valid until certain claims were decided. After many delays, Judge Ogden Hoffman rendered a decision that an account says "gave satisfaction," and the potential owners met for a "jollification" at Lakeport on October 6, 1866. Soon after this, the land was surveyed and each settler secured a home. Kelseyville is on part of this grant.

Rancho Callayomi, consisting of three leagues of land in Loconoma Valley, was given to Robert T. Ridley in 1844 by Governor Micheltorena. Ridley, an English sailor, became captain of the Port of San Francisco in 1846, a position that he held but a short time. He had been naturalized as a Mexican citizen in 1844 and married Presentacíon Briones. Within a few years, in 1852, the claim of Colonel A. A. Ritchie and Paul S. Forbes to this land was confirmed, and a patent was issued to them in 1863. This grant was divided in 1871 and dispersed to settlers.

Rancho Guenoc, containing six leagues in Coyote Valley, was ceded by Governor Pio Pico to George Rock (or Roch) in 1845. Coyote Valley extends for several miles along Putah Creek. According to Bancroft, George Rock came into the valley as early as 1837. For a time he was agent there for Jacob P. Leese, who kept cattle both there and in Loconoma Valley. Rock lived in a cabin on the north side of the valley before 1850. The stone house (SRL 450) now standing on the site of Rock's cabin was built in 1853–54 by Captain R. Steele and Robert Sterling, whose wife was the first white woman in the valley. Colonel Ritchie and his partner, Paul S. Forbes, who had acquired Rancho Callayomi, also received the United States patent for the Guenoc grant in 1865. The stone house was torn down and rebuilt of the same stone about 1894 by Charles M. Young. It stands on private property about six miles north of Middletown on SR 29 at its southern junction with Spruce Grove Road, which meets the highway again to the north.

RESORTS AND MINERAL SPRINGS

The Indians of Lake County made use of its many mineral springs. Most of the places that grew up around them bear the names of their developers. Harbin Hot Springs is four miles from Middletown, visited by Colonel Ritchie in 1852. James M. Harbin, who came west with the Stevens-Murphy party in 1844, settled at the spot in 1857 and the place bore his name. Dr. Winslow Anderson in 1889 extolled the medicinal qualities of its waters, and it became a very fashionable resort by the end of the century. Other Lake County vacation spots, Adams and Anderson Springs among them, are still in operation. In 1989, the French-owned Vittel Company purchased Bartlett Springs, founded in 1868 on the middle fork of Cache Creek, and has built a plant to bottle its waters at Bartlett Springs Road and SR 20.

The mountains between Middletown and Clear Lake have been the site of summer resorts since the founding of Hobergs in 1885. Hobergs, like many other places, is now owned by a private organization and not open to the public. Cobb and Loch Lomond are resorts of long standing that have many summer visitors.

OLD MILLS

The many streams of Lake County afforded power for two industries of great importance in a pioneer community: the grinding of grain for food, and, in a few instances, the sawing of lumber for houses. Thomas Boyd built the first mill in the county on the south shore of Boggs Lake. It was a steam gristmill and sawmill combined, and was put in operation in 1858. In 1866, H. C. Boggs purchased the mill, which from this date was known as the Boggs Mill, although its location was changed several times. A few remnants mark its last location, three miles north of Harbin Springs.

Another mill, originally known as Elliott's Mill, was built in Upper Lake Township in 1855 by William B. Elliott. He had come overland from North Carolina, arriving in California in 1845 with his wife and children. He and his sons became successful hunters of the grizzly bears then prevalent in the mountain regions. His mill was in operation until 1867. It was popularly called the "Whittle-Busy," because, since it ground very slowly, its patrons whiled away the time by whittling.

The old Brown Mill (earlier called the Allison Mill) stood on Kelsey Creek about three miles above Kelseyville. Joel Stoddard's mill, about three and one-half miles west of Middletown, was known in the 1880s as "one of the neatest and best mills in Lake County." A later mill at the same location was operated by the McKinley family until 1935. The site on SR 29 is marked by an old millstone and a plaque placed by the Native Daughters of the Golden West.

MINES

Although a great variety of minerals have been discovered in the county, the quantities usually have been too small for economic development. Mercury, sulphur, and borax have been mined. The Great Western, a cinnabar (mercury) deposit, first produced in 1873. It is four miles south of Middletown.

The old Sulphur Bank Mine (SRL 428) grew out of the works of the California Borax Company. This was the location of the mountain of sulphur referred to in the journal of Edwin Bryant. It was forty feet high and some 300 feet long, and was completely removed by mining in 1865–69, having produced two million pounds of sulphur. The first mercury was mined here in 1873, and the place became a steady and important producer. It has been idle since World War II. The Sulphur Bank Mine is on the eastern end of East Lake south and across the lake from the town of Clearlake Oaks. A monument of native obsidian stands on the highway about one and one-half miles from the town at the junction of the road leading to the mine. In the hills, about one mile east of the monument and on the same side of the highway, stands the Saint Anthony (or Sulphur Bank) Church, which was erected in 1909 as a place of worship for workers in the mine. There are several other old mercury mines in the county, including the Abbott, the Mirabel, and the Helen.

The Manhattan was an old mercury mine in the Knoxville District, where Lake, Napa, and Yolo Counties meet. In 1978, gold was discovered on the site. The McLaughlin deposit was so promising that a new operation, the Home Stake Gold Mine and extraction facility, was soon created. The site is on the Berryessa-Knoxville Road about eighteen miles southeast of the city of Clearlake.

The first source of borax in California was Borax Lake, the mineral having been discovered there in 1856 by Dr. John A. Veatch. The California Borax Company began operation in 1864. In 1868 all work was transferred to Little Borax Lake, where Dr. Veatch had found borax eight years earlier. Operations were carried on successfully until 1873.

The Mayacamas Mountains, which lie along the Lake-Sonoma county line, include an area of considerable geothermal activity, the best-known evidence of which is probably The Geysers in Sonoma County. In

Lower Lake Stone Jail

2001, the Calpine Corporation, which has been developing The Geysers, opened its Geothermal Visitor Center at 15500 Central Park Road in Middletown. The California Department of Water and Power has constructed the Bottle Rock Power Plant, which uses geothermal energy, on the Lake County side of the mountains, off Bottle Rock Road just west of Cobb and Pine Grove. This facility went into operation in 1983 and is designed to provide supplementary power for state water agencies.

LOWER LAKE

The first house in the town of Lower Lake, two miles southeast of Clear Lake, was built by E. Mitchell in 1858, although there had been settlers in the area as early as 1848. The town became important for its location at a crossroads and was the center of business activity for the surrounding agricultural interests, mountain resorts, and mercury mines. It was a station on the stage line running from Calistoga in later years and was the county seat while the Lakeport Courthouse was being rebuilt after the 1867 fire. The Lower Lake Historical Schoolhouse Museum at 16435 Morgan Valley Road has, among other attractions, pioneer family collections and exhibits. Still standing in town is a tiny stone jail (SRL 429), built in 1876 at the height of the quicksilver (mercury) mining boom. A plaque on the monument states that Stephen Nicolai, one of the first stonemasons in the area, built the jail from local materials with the help of Theodore and John Copsey: "Theodore and John commemorated the completion of the jail by over-celebrating, thereby becoming the jail's first occupants. Rumor has it they were also the jail's first escapees—as they had failed to bolt down the roof."

Frame House, site of Clear Lake College, Lakeport

LAKEPORT

Lakeport, on the western shore of Clear Lake, was first named Forbestown. William Forbes owned 160 acres here before the formation of the county in 1861 and deeded forty acres as a site for the county seat in the vicinity of his already completed house and blacksmith shop. Forbes Street preserves his name. The first place of business in the county was a short distance south of Lakeport, at Stony Point, where Dr. E. D. Boynton built a store and put in a stock of goods in 1856.

The Lake County Courthouse, in use from 1871 to 1968, is a solid two-story building at 255 North Main Street in Lakeport (SRL 897). It is now the home of the Lake County Museum. Of particular interest are the artifacts of the Pomo Indians, remarkable weavers and craftsmen. A two-story frame structure at 102 Clear Lake Avenue was once the home of Clear Lake College, which held classes here from 1876 to 1896. Like most of the private and local colleges in late nineteenth-century California, it was unable to compete with the University of California and closed its doors. The first boat landing at Lakeport, in 1873, is commemorated by a marker on the grounds of the grammar school on Main Street.

MIDDLETOWN

Middletown lies on SR 29, the principal route from Clear Lake into Napa County to the south, at the junction with roads leading to the resort and geothermal areas to the north and west and to the mines in the east. It is near the center of the Callayomi land grant and was first settled in 1868. The oldest building now standing in the town was the O. Armstrong house, built in 1870; it is on the left side of a stretch of road between the high school and the old bridge on the way to

Lower Lake, and is still occupied. In the same year, J. H. Berry built a house that was later used as a hotel on what is now SR 29, the main street through town. This was replaced in 1875 by the larger Lake County House, which burned in 1918. The present Herrick Hotel stands on the site, incorporating some of the brick walls from the former hotel.

The last years of the distinguished scholar Dr. James Blake were spent in Middletown. A native of England and a California pioneer in 1849, Dr. Blake was a writer of medical books and former president of the California Academy of Sciences. He retired to Lake County in 1876 because of impaired health. He took up his residence near a large spring, where he built a cottage east of Mount St. Helena and just south of the county line in Napa County, about two miles east of SR 29. Feeling his health vastly improved here, he put up simple buildings where others might be helped, and where he carried on his medical research until he finally moved to Middletown, where he died and was buried in 1893. The main building of Blake's sanatorium is still on a private estate, although the cottage no longer stands. Dr. Blake's house in Middletown also remains, at the southeast corner of Barnes and Young Streets.

At the edge of Middletown on SR 29 a stone monument with bronze plaque (SRL 467) commemorates the old toll road over Mount St. Helena, built in the 1860s by John Lawley, and the earlier and steeper "bull trail" that it replaced. The Lawley road passed out of existence as a toll road in 1924, but a fragment of it remains to the east of SR 29 just north of Calistoga in Napa County.

THE CACHE CREEK DAM

To increase water power for mills, the Clear Lake Water Company constructed a dam in 1866 across Cache Creek near the outlet of Clear Lake. The level of the lake was raised to such an extent that the rich farmland, the established orchards, and the houses within a large radius were flooded. Appeals to the water company were ignored, and no compensation for damages was allowed. (These were the years when hydraulic mining, unimpeded by legal restrictions, was filling and destroying river valleys in the Mother Lode.) On Sunday morning, November 15, 1868, after being led in prayer by the Baptist minister Reverend B. Ogle, a disciplined crowd began the demolition of the dam and the nearby mill after taking the sheriff and law enforcement officers into custody. By Tuesday morning, the work was completed, and although lawsuits ensued, the dam was never rebuilt on this spot. Another dam on Cache Creek, below the town of Lower Lake, was completed in 1914 and is still in use.

THE LANGTRY FARM AND THE GUENOC WINERY

Lillie Langtry, the celebrated English actress known as the "Jersey Lily," in 1888 became joint owner of a property in the southern part of the county. "Freddie" Gebhard, a wealthy New York clubman, was the co-partner in the purchase of this 7,500-acre portion of the old Guenoc grant. At the time of the purchase, a winery was in operation and a few dwellings were on the premises.

Extensive improvements were made, and large sums were invested in race horses by the new owners. Dr. Charles Aby, former manager of the Santa Anita ranch of "Lucky" Baldwin, was put in charge, and a one-mile race track was constructed. Mrs. Langtry visited the place only once, for about two weeks in May 1888. For some years all went well; then in 1897 the partnership was dissolved. Barns, race track, and general operations were concentrated on the Gebhard land, and a stout fence was built to define the two holdings.

The Langtry property was sold in 1906 to George H. Mastick. It had several subsequent owners, who used it primarily as a stock farm. In 1963 it became the property of the Magoon family, who became interested in reviving the vineyard and the wine-making activities that once flourished there. In 1982 the Guenoc Winery was launched on the property. The Langtry house, occupied through all the years, has been refurbished in the style of the late nineteenth century, together with outbuildings, and is part of the private estate, although it is open to the public from time to time. The winery is at 21000 Butts Canyon Road, about seven miles southeast of Middletown.

Lassen County

Lassen County, named for the pioneer Peter Lassen, was organized in 1864 from parts of Plumas and Shasta Counties. Susanville has been the county seat from the beginning. The eastern portion of Lassen Volcanic National Park is in Lassen County, but the greater part of the park, including Lassen Peak, is in Shasta County.

PETER LASSEN

Peter Lassen was born in Denmark in 1800 and came to America in 1829. After working in Boston as a blacksmith for ten years, he came west to the Willamette Valley of Oregon in 1839. The next year he moved to Alta California. After brief sojourns at Bodega Bay, Fort Ross, and San Jose, he made his way to the Sacramento Valley, where John A. Sutter befriended him. In 1844 he received the grant of Rancho Bosquejo in what is now Tehama County and began intensive cultivation of wheat and grapes. Ultimately, however, he lost the land because of poor management and overspeculation in emigrant projects. His name is linked with the Lassen Trail into California of 1848. In the 1850s he pioneered for a few years in Indian Valley in Plumas County, after which he developed an interest in the

Big Valley Museum of Lassen County, Bieber

Honey Lake region of what is now Lassen County. While prospecting in the Black Rock Desert, across the line into what was then the Utah Territory, now part of the state of Nevada, Lassen and a companion were shot and killed by Indians on the morning of April 26, 1859. A third man escaped to tell the story.

Lassen's body was brought back to California; his grave (SRL 565) is at the edge of a meadow six miles south of Susanville via Richmond and Wingfield Roads. It is marked by a monument placed there by the Masons in 1862. (In 1848, Lassen brought from Missouri the charter for California's first Masonic chapter.) The grave of Edward Clapper, who was killed with Lassen, is nearby, as is the grave marked "Joseph Lynch, friend of Peter Lassen," who died in December 1885. Lassen had a cabin not far from this spot in 1855; Lynch lived in it until his death, after which it burned down.

Lassen died in relative poverty, but his contemporaries seem to have thought well of him and his name was bestowed on a number of locations in northeastern California. One early account states that Lassen himself climbed the peak that now bears his name, but there seems to be no corroboration for this statement.

THE LASSEN TRAIL

In 1848 Peter Lassen returned to California from a trip to Missouri, joining a wagon party headed west. The wagons followed the Applegate Trail, first opened two years before, across the wastes of Nevada and the extreme northeastern corner of California. Near Goose Lake in Modoc County, Lassen persuaded the group to leave the trail and turn in a southerly direction, which he claimed would be easier. (It is thought that he hoped to induce these and subsequent migrants to settle on his lands along the Sacramento River once they arrived in California.) The journey was a series of blunders, ending up in the canyon of the Pit River and making a long detour around the base of Lassen Peak. A party of gold-seekers from Oregon, coming across the tracks of the party, joined them and rescued them, and they all arrived safely at the Lassen Ranch. This "Lassen Trail" was used again in 1849, but as more reliable trails opened, it gradually fell into disuse.

A volunteer association, Trails West, Inc., has placed markers along the routes of the Applegate, California, Lassen, and Nobles Trails in California and Nevada in recent years. Many of these are inaccessible to any but the most resolute and well-equipped adventurers; a guide with copious directions has been published by the organization, which is headquartered in Reno, Nevada. Fairly close to roads are markers in Little Valley on Lassen County Road 404, 2.2 miles west of its junction with Lassen County Road 407; at Round Barn in Little Valley; at Harvey Valley; and in Westwood at the Community Center on Third Street. Two and a half miles west of Westwood on SR 36 a marker (SRL 678) stands near the Lassen Trail where it passed into neighboring Plumas County.

Another marker (SRL 763) commemorating part of the Lassen Trail stands on the grounds of the Veterans Building in Clara Bieber Memorial Park, two blocks south of SR 299 in Bieber. Next door is the Big Valley Museum of Lassen County, begun in 1976 with collections on the development of the cattle and lumber industries of this corner of Lassen County. The museum also contains a useful reference library and some original documentary materials.

THE NOBLES TRAIL

The Nobles Trail was one of the northern cutoffs used by emigrants in the early 1850s. In 1851 William H. Nobles, member of a prospecting party, saw the value of an alternative to the Lassen Trail used by his party and enlisted the support of businessmen of the town of Shasta (in Shasta County). In 1852 he succeeded in raising $2,000 for surveying a wagon road over the new route, with its terminus at Shasta.

The Nobles Trail began at the Humboldt River in Nevada, branching off from the Applegate Trail at Rabbit Springs and continuing west into California toward Honey Lake. Trails West has placed a marker just east of Viewland, an old railroad station along US 395, where there is also a state marker (SRL 677) noting the course of the Nobles Trail. The present highway into Susanville is near the old route; Trails West markers can be seen at Honey Lake Valley, Shaffer Station, Litchfield (or Soldier's Bridge), Willow Creek Crossing (on Lassen County Road A-27), and Roop's Fort in Susanville; another state marker (SRL 675) is in the Susanville County Park. Trails West markers farther west that are fairly easily reached on paved roads are at Big Springs, on SR 44 about five miles west of its junction with SR 36; Feather Lake, where the Lassen Trail and the Nobles Trail intersected; Poison Lake; and Butte Creek, at the boundary with Lassen Volcanic National Park. The Nobles Trail was faster and less dangerous than the Lassen Trail, which seems to have been bypassed in the next few years. With the opening of the Sierra passes and the coming of the railroad within the next two decades, both roads became deserted and in places are nearly inaccessible today. But they are historically important because they signify the beginning of a new way of life in this underpopulated and isolated part of the West.

"NATAQUA" AND THE SAGEBRUSH WAR

Isaac Roop, the first American settler in Honey Lake Valley, was the founder of Lassen County and of the county seat, Susanville. Roop came to Honey Lake from Shasta City in 1853 and returned the next year to build a store on the Nobles Trail, which had recently been opened through that region. Early in 1855 Peter Lassen discovered gold in Honey Lake Valley, and news of the find brought in a number of men from the Feather River mining region. Several land claims were staked out at that time.

Honey Lake Valley was so isolated during the pioneer years that a local government was set up on the initiative of the people themselves. About twenty signers, all original settlers in Honey Lake Valley, met at the Roop cabin on April 26, 1856, and formed the "Territory of Nataqua" with Roop as secretary and recorder and Lassen as surveyor. With the eastern boundary of California not definitely determined, the organizers of the new territory included a good deal of land in the present state of Nevada in "Nataqua," which was said to be a Paiute Indian word for "woman." One account deprecates the endeavor: "they made a wild shot at their location; they didn't even live in the territory they had created. It was thirty-five miles from their place of meeting to the western line of Nataqua, and the settlers furthest down the lake were almost twenty miles west

of it." Moreover, the citizens of the Carson, Eagle, and Washoe Valleys were not even notified that they were included within the boundaries of the new political division. Actually, "Nataqua" existed for a short time only, and then merely in the minds of a few people.

In 1857 the citizens of "Nataqua" decided to cast their lot with those who were petitioning Congress for separation from the Utah Territory with its Mormon dominance. While awaiting congressional action on their petition for the formation of a new territory, the settlers met again in 1858 to set up a local government. As a result, a constitutional convention was held at Genoa, Nevada, on July 18, 1859, and in the following September, Isaac Roop was chosen provisional governor of the proposed territory.

On March 2, 1861, Congress passed the bill creating the Nevada Territory, which, only with California's consent, was to include the eastern slope of the Sierra Nevada from Inyo to Modoc Counties. In creating its first counties the same year, however, the Nevada Territory extended its new Lake County to include Honey Lake Valley. In 1862 both Plumas County in California and Lake County in the Nevada Territory held elections in the valley. In February 1863, a skirmish called the Sagebrush or Boundary Line War, waged by forty or fifty of the original settlers of Honey Lake Valley against Plumas County officials, resulted from the attempt of the Plumas County sheriff to uphold the authority of his county in the valley. Two men were wounded before a truce was made. The confusion was cleared up by the creation of a separate authority, Lassen County, on April 1, 1864.

SUSANVILLE

Susanville was named after the only daughter of Isaac Roop. Roop's old log cabin, called Fort Defiance when it was used as a fort during the Sagebrush War, still stands on the east side of Weatherlow Street in the Susanville city park. Next to it is the William H. Pratt Memorial Museum, which contains many exhibits on the history of Lassen County as well as the various economic developments in the life of Susanville, located where the forests, the brushlands, and the grasslands of Lassen Valley meet.

"THE POTATO WAR"

The blunders and atrocities of a few white men against the Indians triggered a bloody conflict by the shores of

Honey Lake in October 1857. Unable to distinguish between members of different tribes, a white raiding party mistook a Paiute for a Shoshone and in killing him turned the Paiutes and Washoes against the settlers of the valley. The plundering of settlers' vegetables and livestock earned the skirmish the name "The Potato War." The settlers barricaded themselves in a farmhouse close to what is now the state highway rest stop on US 395 about four miles south of Buntingville. In the exchange of shots, twelve Indians were killed and one rancher was wounded.

Another Lassen County fort was located three-quarters of a mile from Janesville; Fort Janesville (SRL 758), as it was called, was built by the people of Honey Lake Valley in preparation for an Indian attack that never materialized. The commemorative plaque is located just north of Janesville Elementary School on Main Street.

OTHER HISTORIC SPOTS IN LASSEN COUNTY

Jack's Valley, ten miles north of Susanville on SR 139, contains a cement water trough, the only one of its kind in northeastern California, which was built in 1913 for the benefit of travelers. The place was named for "Coyote Jack" Wright, who left the spot in 1869. By 1880, as the E Clampus Vitus plaque placed here notes, five wagon roads converged here; a number of varied establishments stood here over the years.

Milford, on US 395 about seventeen miles southeast of Buntingville, was settled in 1856 by R. J. Scott; the name was bestowed by Joseph C. Wemple in 1861. The first flour mill in northeastern California was built here the same year. E Clampus Vitus placed a marker here in 1985.

Honey Lake, now almost a dry basin, was named for the substance deposited on the wild grasses by honey-dew aphids and valued by the Indians as a food.

Los Angeles County

Casino and Harbor, Avalon, Catalina Island

Los Angeles County was one of the original twenty-seven counties. Its boundaries have been changed many times; at its largest, in 1852–55, it covered an area of 31,000 square miles. The city of Los Angeles has always been the county seat, and its archives contain many pre-statehood records in Spanish.

JUAN RODRÍGUEZ CABRILLO AND SANTA CATALINA

Juan Rodríguez Cabrillo first sighted the coast of Alta California at San Diego on September 28, 1542. Due to his injury and subsequent death, early the following January, Cabrillo's journals are unclear. It has been argued that Cabrillo died and was buried at an unknown site, not on San Miguel, in the Santa Barbara Channel Islands, as tradition holds, but rather at Santa Catalina Island. Cabrillo, sighting the island on October 7, 1542, named it San Salvador. Sebastián Vizcaíno, sighting it on November 20, 1603, St. Catherine's Day, named it Santa Catalina Island.

A memorial plaque to Cabrillo was placed in Exposition Park, Los Angeles, by the Daughters of the American Revolution in 1915. A replica of this tablet was placed at Avalon on Santa Catalina Island.

PORTOLÁ'S TRAIL

In 1769, Gaspar de Portolá left San Diego to make a trail up the coast to the port of Monterey, where the second mission was to be established. Traveling through what are now San Diego and Orange Counties, he entered Los Angeles County on July 30, making camp near modern La Puente. The following day the party moved west and made camp in an open space in the valley north of the Whittier Narrows, not far from where Mission San Gabriel was later established.

On August 2 the party reached a spot on the Los Angeles River occupied by the Indian village of Yang-Na, at the center of today's Los Angeles. Camp was probably made near what is now North Spring Street, at the juncture of the Los Angeles River and North Broadway. This site (SRL 655) was marked in 1930 in Elysian Park. The hill, around which the Los Angeles River turned to the south at the point where it is bridged by North Broadway, is mentioned in the journal written by Lieutenant Miguel Costansó of Portolá's expedition.

On the same day, Wednesday, August 2, 1769, the diary of Father Crespí tells how he named the campsite by the river Nuestra Señora la Reina de los Angeles de la Porciúncula ("Our Lady the Queen of the Angels of the Porciúncula"). *Porciúncula* ("little portion") refers to a small parcel of land adjacent to the once tiny church of Saint Mary of the Angels, which is in the valley below the hill town of Assisi in Italy. There St. Francis received a revelation on August 1, 1206, and subsequently a basilica was erected on the site; the date became a major event in the Franciscan liturgical calendar.

Leaving their camp and crossing to the west side of the river, Portolá and his party bypassed the La Brea tar pits, which were discovered by their scouts, and camped the night of August 3 at springs surrounded by sycamores. The approximate site has been marked on La Cienega Boulevard, between Olympic Boulevard and Gregory Way, in Beverly Hills (SRL 665). The next day they moved on to two hillside springs where friendly Indians made them welcome. This campsite was apparently on or near the grounds of the Veterans Administration Center in West Los Angeles. From there the scouts went as far as the beach west of Santa Monica. On the campus of University High School at 11800 Texas Avenue in West Los Angeles are springs that may be those at which Portolá camped on August 4. Many Indian artifacts have been found here. The springs are known as "Serra Springs" (SRL 522) because it is said that Father Serra said Mass nearby in 1770.

On August 5 the Portolá party followed Sepulveda Canyon (the route of today's San Diego Freeway) up to the mountaintop from which they viewed the San Fernando Valley; they descended to camp at the warm springs now included within Los Encinos State Historic Park at Encino. (The large Indian village here was revisited by Portolá's party on January 15 and April 27, 1770, when they established the east-west route along the south side of the valley and through Cahuenga Pass.) On August 7 they camped northwest of what would become the site of Mission San Fernando, and the next day they traveled over San Fernando Pass to Newhall, pitching camp at a large Indian rancheria on the Santa Clara River near Castaic. From here, they proceeded west down the Santa Clara Valley, so named by Father Crespí on the feast day of Saint Clare, into Ventura County.

MISSION SAN GABRIEL ARCÁNGEL

On August 6, 1771, a party set out from San Diego, consisting of ten soldiers and two friars, Pedro Benito Cambón and Angel Somera, to establish a mission forty leagues to the north. On September 8, 1771, Mission San Gabriel Arcángel was founded.

The new mission, being on the direct overland route from Mexico to Monterey, was the first stopping place and supply station after the desert and mountains had been crossed. The padres protected this location with special care, and the mission grew rich and prosperous. It survived the years of secularization and has continued its usefulness to the present time as a thriving parish church.

The original site of the mission was five miles south of its present location, on a bluff overlooking the Rio Hondo (then called the San Gabriel) at North San Gabriel Boulevard and Lincoln Avenue in Montebello, where a granite marker has been placed (SRL 161). Nothing remains of the old buildings of this "Mission Vieja."

Floods from the Rio Hondo eventually forced the fathers to seek another location for their mission, and the first site was abandoned about five years after its founding. The new land chosen was higher and dryer but no less fertile, and luxuriant gardens and orchards soon flourished about the new buildings. An extensive vineyard, olive groves, and orchards of fig, orange, and pear trees covered several acres of ground, and were protected from wild animals and marauders by a high, thick cactus hedge. Remnants of this old hedge, as well as of the mission orchard, may still be seen here and there in the town of San Gabriel. Other vineyards were

Church of Mission San Gabriel

planted with cuttings taken from the Mother Vineyard ("Viña Madre") at San Gabriel.

The first church building on the second site of California's fourth mission was dedicated in 1776. This turned out to be only a temporary location. The present church (SRL 158), at 537 West Mission Drive in San Gabriel, was started in 1791 and completed in 1803 under the supervision of Father José Maria Zalvidea. It was solidly constructed of stone and cement as far up as the windows, and of brick above that. The paintings of the fourteen Stations of the Cross in the church, painted by the Gabrieleño Indians, are probably the oldest Indian sacred pictorial art in California. The massive walls and buttresses, its outside stairway leading to choir and belfry, and the bell tower with its several arches built to correspond to the different sizes of the bells make San Gabriel one of the most unusual and interesting of all the missions. In the yard behind the church there are many reconstructed buildings, including a smithy and a kitchen. The museum is in a separate building.

In 1987 a severe earthquake, centered in the nearby Whittier Narrows, caused much damage to the church, and it was closed for a time. Extensive repairs were made and it reopened in 1993.

About two miles north of Mission San Gabriel near the site of the Ritz-Carlton Huntington Hotel, Claudio López, under supervision of Father Zalvidea, built between 1810 and 1812 the first water-operated gristmill in California. The old mill, "El Molino Viejo," was constructed of solid masonry and still stands at 1120 Old Mill Road in San Marino (SRL 302). In 1903, H. E. Huntington bought the building and restored it to its former proportions, retaining the picturesqueness of mission days. For a time after 1923 it was used as a real estate office and then for many years as a private residence. It is now the southern California headquarters of the California Historical Society.

Juan Bautista de Anza reached the Santa Ana River on March 20, 1774, crossing it by an improvised bridge the following morning. That night he camped in a wooded valley near San Antonio Creek a little west of the present city of Ontario. At sunset on March 22 the party reached Mission San Gabriel (then located at its original site), where they were given a warm welcome.

Anza remained at San Gabriel for nearly three weeks, awaiting necessary supplies for the journey to Monterey. On the morning of April 10 he proceeded to the Los Angeles River and followed it into the San Fernando Valley. Camp was made that night in Russell Valley, in what is now Ventura County.

Anza followed much the same route in 1776 with the band of emigrants who settled San Francisco, the first settlers to come overland to California. The caravan reached the San Antonio Creek campsite on January 2, and on January 3 they halted at the San Gabriel Wash, reaching Mission San Gabriel the next day. There they rested until February 21 when, refreshed by the welcome hospitality of the mission fathers, they set out once more. Swinging westward to the Los Angeles River, they followed it northwest to a campsite west of Glendale. Crossing the southern edge of the San Fernando Valley on February 22, the party entered the Simi Hills at Calabasas and continued to the vicinity of Las Virgenes Creek. There tents were pitched for the night, and on the following day the travelers continued beyond the Santa Clara River, camping near El Rio in Ventura County.

LAKE HUGHES AND ANTELOPE VALLEY

Early in 1772 Pedro Fages passed the site of Lake Hughes on his inland journey from San Diego to San Luis Obispo, in pursuit of deserters from the Spanish army.

In April 1776 friar Francisco Garcés crossed Fages's path at Lake Hughes. Leaving San Gabriel, he crossed the San Fernando Valley, went over Newhall Grade to the vicinity of Castaic, and swung northeast over the mountains. Just before he entered the plains, on the edge of Antelope Valley, he mentioned a lake, evidently Lake Hughes, "and near thereto a village where, according to the signs, Señor Capitan Faxes has been."

Antelope Valley, geographically a part of the Mojave Desert, was the hunting paradise of Andrés Pico and other Californios, lured there by the immense herds of antelope that roamed through it and from which it derived its name. In the heart of this valley one of California's most glorious poppy fields adds its flame to the spectacular carpet of wildflowers that each spring spreads out across the valley floor. The Antelope Valley Poppy Reserve is sixteen miles west of Lancaster, and receives many visitors each spring. It is located on Lancaster Road between 130th and 170th Streets West.

North of Fairmont there is a splendid forest of tree yuccas (*yucca arborensis*), with their spires of exquisite waxen lily bells. These striking and distinctive inhabitants of the desert, more commonly known as Joshua trees, were named by early emigrants to California for their resemblance to the praying prophet.

John C. Frémont, coming down from the north by way of Oak Creek Pass on April 15, 1844, crossed Antelope Valley to the base of the Sierra Madre, following Fages's trail as far as Cajón Pass, where he connected with the Spanish Trail near Victorville. Frémont wrote in his diary about the "strange and singular" yucca forests and the fields of California poppies, as well as other shrubs and flowers in Antelope Valley. The Antelope Valley Indian Museum, at 15701 East Avenue M, in Lancaster, has good displays on the native peoples of the region.

ST. ANN AND CIÉNEGA

One mile southeast of the junction of Palomares Avenue with San Dimas Canyon Road is the site of an Indian camping place. In early mission days, logs were hauled here from the San Bernardino Mountains for the building of San Gabriel Mission. The Spaniards called this Ciénega ("wet place, swamp") because of the natural springs that were perpetually seeping up out of the earth.

In 1826, Jedediah Strong Smith, the first American pathfinder to blaze an overland trail into California, camped at a spot designated by the expedition's diarist, Harrison Rogers, "St. Ann, an Indian farm house." George W. Beattie assumes that this was really San Antonio Rancho, one of "the seventeen ranchos for cattle and horses possessed by Mission San Gabriel. The Mexican grant of San José on which both Pomona and Claremont are situated was a combination of the San José and the San Antonio ranchos of Mission San Gabriel."

Before 1870 there was a stage station at the springs on the road from San Bernardino to Los Angeles. This station was probably located near the site of the pumping plant on Palomares Avenue. All that remains of the old San Bernardino Road is a short strip of road less than one-half mile east of the springs, where Palomares Avenue turns southeast at Grand Avenue for a short distance. The seeping springs were pumped dry years ago, and their water was diverted elsewhere.

THE OLD ADOBES OF SAN GABRIEL

San Gabriel once had many quaint and picturesque old adobe homes. Among the few that remain, perhaps the oldest is located between West Mission Drive and Orange Street, at the end of a short, curving lane. Part of it is said to have been built as a home for the mission friars three years before the mission church was built. In the garden there were once many old trees, doubtless a part of the mission orchard, which was walled in by a cactus hedge. It was from this hedge that the ranch derived its name, Las Tunas ("the cactus"). The history of Las Tunas Ranch is uncertain. It was occupied some time before 1852 by Henry Dalton when he was mission administrator. Hugo Reid may have been another owner. Reid, a Scotsman who married an Indian, is noted for his splendid account of the life and customs of California Indians, which has been much quoted by later writers.

The Ortega-Vigare Adobe (SRL 451) at 616 South Ramona Street is the second-oldest adobe in the region, "erected in mission days, 1792–1805" according to the text on the plaque. Originally L-shaped, it is now only half its original size. In 1859, the adobe became the property of Don Juan Vigare. In the early 1860s, as San Gabriel's first bakery, it was separated from the mission's lime orchard by a high cactus hedge.

La Casa López de Lowther at 330 North Santa Anita Avenue is surely one of the former mission buildings, being of the type of adobe construction used during mission days. It was restored in keeping with its past by Doña Maria López de Lowther, whose family lived there for many years.

EL PUEBLO DE LOS ANGELES
HISTORIC MONUMENT

El Pueblo de Nuestra Señora de los Angeles, second of the three pueblos to be established in Alta California, was officially founded on September 4, 1781, four years after El Pueblo de San José de Guadalupe (now San Jose) was established. A few settlers from Mexico had already arrived by the September date. A carved wooden cross, placed on the north side of the present plaza at the south entrance to Olvera Street, commemorates the founding. Close by, an idealized bronze statue portrays Felipe de Neve, governor of Alta California from 1775 to 1782, who ordered the establishment of the settlement; this statue was erected in 1931 by the Native Daughters of the Golden West on the 150th anniversary of the founding of Los Angeles. In 1976, a plaque was placed here noting the names of the forty-four Pobladores, the first settlers of the pueblo.

The first site of the settlement was a nearly dry summer stream that became a torrent in the winter. A second site was also flooded out, and what remains today is the third and final site of the pueblo of Los Angeles. The plaza (SRL 156) around which the settlement grew was established between 1825 and 1830. Homes were built around the plaza by such prominent families as the Avilas, the Carrillos, the Coronels, the Del Valles, and the Lugos. Gradually the settlement grew outward from the plaza, which remained the center of community life even after the coming of the Americans.

The oldest building on the plaza is the Church of Nuestra Señora la Reina de los Angeles, which was begun in 1818 and dedicated in 1822. It stands at 535 North Main Street, on the west side of the plaza, and is the only building in El Pueblo Park still used for its original purpose. From 1822 to 1844 the city's first cemetery, the Campo Santo, was located just south of the church. In 1981, an archaeological excavation unearthed Indian artifacts from the eighteenth century and the foundations of the old house of the padres (1822).

The oldest dwelling house in Los Angeles is the nearby Avila adobe (SRL 145) at 14 Olvera Street, which probably dates back to 1818. It is much reduced from its size of a century and more ago, when it was in the possession of the Avila and Rimpau families. In January 1847 Commodore Robert F. Stockton made his California headquarters there for five days.

The renovation of the Avila adobe and of Olvera Street was the beginning of historical preservation in Los Angeles. In the 1920s, Mrs. Christine Sterling began a campaign to bring to the public's attention the deterioration of the neighborhood, which had gone so far that the Avila adobe had been condemned by the city as unfit for human habitation. In 1930, restoration began when Olvera Street was opened to the public. In 1953, it became El Pueblo de Los Angeles State Historical Monument, later Historic Park, jointly operated by the state of California and the county and city of Los Angeles. In 1989 control passed entirely to the city of Los Angeles, thus the present name.

The Avila adobe is now a museum on Olvera Street, where many shops and restaurants are built into the old buildings. A diagonal line of brick in the paving of Olvera Street marks the course of the old *zanja madre* ("mother ditch") that brought water from the river to the pueblo. An exhibit of the "History of Water in Los Angeles," mounted by the Los Angeles Department of Water and Power, traces the history of water in the Los Angeles area and has a model of the plaza in 1860.

La Casa Pelanconi, at 33–35 Olvera Street, was built in 1855–57; it was one of Los Angeles's first brick houses and is presently a restaurant. The site of the Lugo House is on the east side of the plaza on Los Angeles Street (SRL 301). The house was a two-story adobe built before 1840 by Vicente Lugo, who later donated the building to St. Vincent's College (now Loyola University), the first college in Southern California, founded in 1865. The college moved shortly after 1867 to another downtown location, and St. Vincent's Place (SRL 567), off Seventh Street between Broadway and Hill Street, commemorates the site. When the original Lugo home was torn down in 1951, it was found to have been rebuilt of brick. A small park here is dedicated to Father Serra.

El Pueblo de Los Angeles Historic Monument is on the National Register of Historic Places. Of its twenty-seven historic buildings, sixteen are individually listed on the register. Most of these come from the American period.

The Pico House was built by Pío Pico, last Mexican governor of California, in 1869; its three stories made it the tallest building in Los Angeles for a time. Located at 430 North Main Street (SRL 159), the old hotel has been renovated but remains closed to the public. Next door, at 420–22, is the Merced Theatre (SRL 171), the first theater in Los Angeles. The Masonic Hall at 416 North Main Street is the oldest building (1858) on the south side of the plaza; the second floor contains a Masonic museum. The firehouse, built in 1884 on the southern corner of the plaza (SRL 730), was the city's first. It ceased being a firehouse in 1897 and was the first building to be restored (1960) in the monument. It is open as a museum and houses historic firefighting equipment and memorabilia. The Sepulveda House at 622 North Main Street dates from 1887; it was built by Señora Eloisa Martínez de Sepúlveda, and the visitors' center is located on the ground floor. Henry E. Huntington in 1903–4 built the Plaza Substation on a lot between Olvera and Los Angeles Streets to convert electricity from alternating to direct current to power his electric street cars.

Pico [Hotel] House, Plaza of El Pueblo de Los Angeles State Historic Park

The monument and the area where Union Station is now located, off Alameda Street across from the monument, are the site of Los Angeles's first Chinatown. This was the center of activity of the Chinese population of Los Angeles until the 1930s, when there was an exodus to "Old Sonoratown" a few blocks north.

RANCHO SAN RAFAEL (GLENDALE, EAGLE ROCK, LA CAÑADA FLINTRIDGE, VERDUGO CITY)

One of the first grants made in Alta California was the great Rancho San Rafael given to José Maria Verdugo in 1784 and 1798. It was one of the largest of all the grants, comprising 36,000 acres of pasturage from the Arroyo Seco to Mission San Fernando. Four modern cities lie within its area.

Don José died in 1831, leaving his estate to his son Julio and his daughter Catalina; thirty years later they divided it, Julio taking the southern portion while his sister took the more rugged and mountainous section in the north.

Doña Catalina, who had been blind from girlhood, never married, and as she grew old she tired of living here and there with her nephews and wished for a home of her own. In the 1830s her nephew Teodoro built for her what is now the last Verdugo adobe, one of the five that were at various times built by the Verdugos on Rancho San Rafael. The Catalina adobe is a modest but charming house (SRL 637) set back from the street at 2211 Bonita Drive in Glendale, surrounded by beautiful old trees. It is a private home.

Tomás Sánchez, who married María Sepúlveda, built an adobe home for his wife and their nineteen children in 1865. Now known as the Casa Adobe de San Rafael

(SRL 235) at 1330 Dorothy Drive, it is owned by the city of Glendale. The house and the well-kept grounds are open to the public.

The "Doctors' House," now located in Brand Park in Glendale, is the home of the Glendale Historical Society, a house museum so named because at least four doctors lived in it at its original location, 921 East Wilson Avenue. It is an excellent specimen of the popular Queen Anne–Eastlake style of the late nineteenth century.

Glendale's Alex Theatre at 216 North Brand Boulevard is a restored example of 1920s opulence, with neo-Greek and Egyptian concepts underlying its decoration. The splendid U.S. Post Office at 313 East Broadway was placed on the National Register of Historic Places in 1984, fifty years after it opened. It is noted for the quality of workmanship and materials used in its ornamentation.

The Descanso Gardens at 1418 Descanso Drive in La Cañada Flintridge is on 165 acres of land that were once part of Rancho San Rafael. A live-oak forest cut by streams, the tract was purchased in 1937 by E. Manchester Boddy, publisher of the *Los Angeles Daily News*, who gave his land the name of Rancho del Descanso ("rest"). His estate included the largest ornamental camellia garden in the world, along with thousands of other plants. Today the gardens are owned and operated by Los Angeles County; the mild climate enables a year-round series of floral and arboreal displays. The Hospitality House on the grounds was the Boddy residence, built in 1939.

Eagle Rock takes its name from a massive rock that resembles an eagle in flight. It was an important landmark in early California. The rock, located at the northern end of Figueroa Street, has been declared a historic-cultural monument by the city of Los Angeles.

GRANTS OF SOUTHEASTERN LOS ANGELES COUNTY

Another early grant in California was made to Manuel Nieto in 1784, just three years after the founding of the Pueblo de Los Angeles. At first it included all the land lying between the Santa Ana and San Gabriel Rivers from Coyote Hills to the ocean, but this vast tract was later divided among Don Manuel's heirs. The ranchos thus created were Los Alamitos, Los Cerritos, Santa Gertrudes, Los Coyotes, and Los Bolsas. Los Alamitos, Santa Gertrudes, and Los Coyotes lie partly in Orange County, and Los Bolsas is wholly within it. Old adobes still stand on Ranchos Los Alamitos and Los Cerritos.

Rancho Los Cerritos, Long Beach

RANCHO LOS ALAMITOS (LONG BEACH)

Abel Stearns, a native of Massachusetts and one of the first American settlers in California (1829), brought Yankee business methods into the largely bucolic life of the Pueblo de Los Angeles. He opened a general merchandise store, prospered, and was active in public affairs after the American conquest. He was a member of the first constitutional convention, a city councilman, state assemblyman, and county supervisor.

Stearns married Arcadia Bandini, beautiful daughter of a prominent Alta California family. Doña Arcadia reigned as social leader at El Palacio ("the palace"), Don Abel's home, built on the site of his general store. In 1858 he built the Arcadia Block at the rear of El Palacio, fronting on Los Angeles Street. It was a commercial center for many years. After Stearns's death, Doña Arcadia married Colonel R. S. Baker. The Baker Block was built about 1878 on the site of El Palacio and stood at the southeast corner of what used to be the intersection of Arcadia and Main Streets. Most of that area of Los Angeles has been completely razed and rebuilt for the freeway system.

In 1842, Stearns bought Rancho Los Alamitos, on a part of which the eastern section of the city of Long Beach now stands. His prosperity began to wane when he abandoned the cattle business after the great drought of 1863–64, in which cattle died by the thousands. Michael Reese, who held a mortgage on the ranch, foreclosed, and in 1878 Reese's heirs sold the Rancho Los Alamitos to the Bixby family, who had leased it for several years. The Los Alamitos ranch house has remained in the Bixby family ever since. Although it has undergone many alterations, and very little of the original adobe remains, the house retains much of its charm as an American farmhouse of the 1870s, with extensive

gardens and interesting barns. The house is located at 6400 Bixby Hill Road, five and one-half miles east of downtown Long Beach, and is open to the public.

The oil well "Alamitos 1" (SRL 580), discovery well of the important Signal Hill field, takes its name from the old rancho. Drilled to a depth of 3,114 feet in 1921, it is located at Hill Street and Temple Avenue in Signal Hill.

RANCHO LOS CERRITOS (WESTERN LONG BEACH)

The ranch house of Rancho Los Cerritos is a magnificent building. On one side is a beautiful garden dating from early days; the courtyard has another planted more recently. The shaded *corredores*, the many and varied rooms, and the hand-finished woodwork are among its sights.

This splendid adobe mansion was built in 1844 by John Temple, another energetic young native of Massachusetts, who found life in Alta California agreeable and profitable and married Rafaela Cota, a cousin of Guillermo Cota. Temple bought out the shares that the grandchildren of Manuel Nieto held in Rancho Los Cerritos. The mansion is at 4600 Virginia Road, about four miles north of the center of the present city of Long Beach, the main part of which stands within the confines of the old rancho. The Los Cerritos adobe (SRL 978), a National Historic Landmark, is now owned by the city of Long Beach and is open to the public. For years it was owned by the Bixby family and was rebuilt by Llewellyn Bixby, son of the pioneer Llewellyn, in 1930.

Everything Don Juan Temple did was successful. He opened the first general store in the Pueblo de Los Angeles, and in front of it he planted pepper trees. He and his brother built the Temple Block, Los Angeles's first office building. Temple's establishments were located in what is now the Civic Center. The Federal Building on Los Angeles Street stands on the site of his general store. The market later became the courthouse, and the Temple Block stood just to the north. The sites of these two buildings are now occupied by the Los Angeles City Hall.

RANCHO SAN ANTONIO (SOUTH AND EAST OF LOS ANGELES)

It was said by an admirer that there were "no horses so fast, no cattle so fine, no land so fertile, no rancho more famous that the Rancho San Antonio. No family more prominent, no hospitality more welcome or as freely partaken, no hacienda more lovely, happy or prosperous than that of the Lugos." Rancho San Antonio was granted to Antonio María Lugo in 1810, and for fifty years it remained in possession of the family. Its 29,513 acres of land adjoined the original pueblo grant of the city of Los Angeles on the southeast. Don Antonio and his bride lived at first in a tule house on the site of the present-day town of Bell. In 1819 he built an adobe dwelling in Los Angeles on what is now the east side of San Pedro Street between First and Second Streets, and here his four sons were born. Vicente Lugo, a son of Don Antonio, built a two-story house that was long a center of social life in the pueblo. Neither house still stands, nor does Vicente's country estate in what is now Bell Gardens. Henry T. Gage, who was governor of California from 1899 to 1903, lived in an adobe a few blocks away from the now-vanished Lugo house; the Gage residence, privately owned, still stands at 7000 East Gage Avenue in Bell Gardens.

Ultimately, the pressure of American business closed in on the great Rancho San Antonio until, bit by bit, it was lost to its original owners. Among the communities now on the old rancho grounds are Bell, Bell Gardens, Huntington Park, Lynwood, South Gate, Vernon, and Walnut Park.

RANCHO SANTA GERTRUDES (DOWNEY, SANTA FE SPRINGS)

Antonio María Nieto received Rancho Santa Gertrudes, and in 1834 the Mexican government confirmed the title to his widow, Doña Josefa Cota de Nieto. Later, the rancho was sold to Lemuel Carpenter, a Kentuckian who married the beautiful María de los Angeles Domínguez. Carpenter and his wife conveyed a portion of Rancho Santa Gertrudes to José M. Ramírez in 1855; this section became known as the Ramírez Tract. The Carpenters had prospered under Mexican rule, but they failed under the more challenging business methods of the Yankees. On November 14, 1859, the rancho was sold by the sheriff. John G. Downey and James P. McFarland were the fortunate bidders. Carpenter took his own life.

John Gately Downey had the sort of career that made others think of California as a golden land of opportunity. Born in Ireland in 1827, he came to America as a young man and learned the pharmacy business in Washington, D.C. He then worked as a druggist in Mississippi and Ohio before coming to California in 1849. He became a naturalized citizen of the United States in 1851; in the following year he married María Jesús Guirado and was elected to the Los Angeles City Council.

In 1850 he opened Los Angeles's second drugstore in partnership with Dr. James P. McFarland, and the two purchased Rancho Santa Gertrudes in 1859. Two months before the purchase, Downey had been elected lieutenant governor of California on the Democratic ticket, and when Governor Milton Latham resigned early in 1860 to fill an unexpired U.S. Senate seat, Downey became governor. A strong Union supporter in the Civil War, he raised five regiments of infantry and six companies of cavalry from California for the U.S. Army, and presided over the laying of the cornerstone for the state Capitol in Sacramento. After his term expired in 1862, he was a trustee of Phineas Banning's Pioneer Oil Company, the first oil company in California. He was also a trustee of the Farmer's and Merchant's Bank, one of the patrons contributing land for the University of Southern California, and a founder of the Historical Society of Southern California. The city of Downey was begun in 1873. The oil-rich community of Santa Fe Springs began on its eastern boundary.

Downey has four twentieth-century historic spots of note. Two houses are on the National Register of Historic Places: that of James C. Rives at Paramount Boulevard and Third Street (1911), and that of Parley Johnson at 7749 East Florence Avenue (1926). The former Rockwell International Plant as 12214 Lakewood Boulevard was the site of the design and much of the technology for the Apollo lunar craft and the space shuttle. This would become Boeing property in the early 1990s. In 1999 the National Aeronautics and Space Administration (NASA) declared the property excess, and its historic preservation and reuse are being studied. And the world's oldest McDonald's Drive-In has been with its two golden arches at 10207 Lakewood Boulevard since 1953. The place was restored by the McDonald's Corporation in 1996, and now incorporates a museum and gift shop in addition to its regular services.

RANCHO SAN PEDRO (COMPTON, GARDENA, WILMINGTON)

The rich grazing acres of Rancho San Pedro covered 43,119 acres, extending from the coast near Wilmington up the estuary of the Los Angeles River halfway to Los Angeles. Gardena and Compton are situated on the northern boundary of the grant. San Pedro is one of the earliest grants in California, and has continued in part in the hands of the descendants of the original grantee. First granted to Juan José Domínguez before 1799 and again to his heir, Sargento Cristobal Domínguez, Rancho San Pedro came into the possession of Manuel Domínguez in 1826. Don Manuel lived on the estate until his death in 1882, a good host and a capable manager of the rancho.

The Domínguez ranch house (SRL 152) was presented by a descendant of the family to the Claretian Order as a seminary for the training of priests. Today the Claretian fathers use it as a retreat. In the chapel of the adobe is a stained-glass window bearing the inscription "Domínguez 1826." The site is at 18127 South Alameda Street in Compton. Only the shaded eastern *corredor* of the adobe and the garden remain from earlier days; arches and stucco have made the west front decidedly modern.

Rancho San Pedro was the scene of a battle between Californians and Americans on October 9, 1846. After the citizens of Los Angeles had given their allegiance to the United States, Commodore Robert F. Stockton, acting commander of American forces in California, and Colonel John C. Frémont left the city early in September, leaving Captain Archibald Gillespie in charge of fifty men. Leaving so small a garrison proved to be a mistake. A revolt occurred among the Californians of the pueblo, and the garrison, forced to surrender on September 30, retreated to San Pedro. Meanwhile, Commodore Stockton in San Francisco had heard of the revolt and sent Captain William Mervine and 300 men to assist the American forces.

Gillespie arrived in San Pedro on October 7, and was about to embark when Captain Mervine and his reinforcements arrived on the *Savannah*. The two commanders then joined forces and marched toward Los Angeles. They were halted on October 9 at the Domínguez rancho by a force of 120 mounted Californians commanded by José Carrillo. Armed with a four-pound cannon, the Californians held off repeated American charges until Mervine, with six men killed and a number wounded, retreated to San Pedro on the coast.

The American dead were buried on a little island near the mouth of San Pedro Bay. Deadman's Island, as it was christened by the burial party of the American forces, long remained a landmark in the bay, but it has now been entirely removed by harbor construction work. As a result of their victory on the Domínguez rancho, the revolt of the Californians quickly spread, and the Americans were confronted with the semblance of a real war.

At this point, the resourceful José Carrillo played a trick on the Americans that temporarily kept them out of Los Angeles. Setting his troopers to rounding up all the wild horses of the neighboring ranchos, he herded them back and forth across a gap in the hills where they kicked up such a cloud of dust that Stockton, watching from San Pedro harbor three miles away, took them to be a great body of mounted Californians. Knowing their daring and marvelous horsemanship, he weighed anchor and sailed for San Diego.

The official state marker at the Claretian retreat recounts the history of the Domínguez ranch house and the battle that took place there in 1846.

The first air meet in the United States was held atop Domínguez Hills on the old rancho from January 10 to 20, 1910. The first competitive meeting of pioneer fliers was held at a time when aviation was considered by many to be a passing novelty. Glenn H. Curtiss set a new air speed record of 60 miles per hour. The site (SRL 718) was marked in 1941 by the Native Sons and Native Daughters of the Golden West, but the marker is relatively inaccessible. Another monument has been placed one-half mile to the northwest, on Wilmington Avenue, one mile north of Del Amo Boulevard.

Wilmington, near the southern edge of Rancho San Pedro, was founded in 1858 by General Phineas Banning, "Father of Los Angeles Transportation," and was named for his home town of Wilmington, Delaware. Banning was famous first as an operator of stage lines and later as the builder of the first local railroads, and was a pioneer in the oil industry as well. In 1864 he built his splendid two-story Greek Revival–style house at 401 East M Street (SRL 147). Now the Banning Residence Museum, beautifully restored and operated by the City of Los Angeles since 1927, it sits in twenty-acre Banning Park. Drum Barracks (SRL 169) at Wilmington was the central supply station for the Union Army in Southern California during the Civil War. It was named in honor of General Richard Coulter Drum, adjutant general of the Department of the Pacific. The post was abandoned in 1871 and its nearly sixty acres were subdivided and sold. The only remaining building is the junior officers' quarters, now the Drum Barracks Civil War Museum, at 1052 Banning Boulevard, also operated by the city of Los Angeles. The officers' quarters stood at the west side of the now-vanished Parade Ground, and at the southeast corner of that ground, one other structure remains, the Powder Magazine, at the corner of what is now Eubank Avenue and East Opp Street.

Three nineteenth-century buildings are still in use in Wilmington. The Memory Chapel, Calvary Presbyterian Church, at 1160 North Marine Avenue, was built in 1870; it is the oldest Protestant church in the harbor area. St.

John's Episcopal Church was built in 1883 and moved to its present location, 1537 Neptune Avenue, in 1943. The Masonic Temple was built in 1882 and moved to its present location, 227 North Avalon Boulevard, in 1912.

Heritage House (SRL 664), at 401 South Willowbrook Avenue, is the oldest house in Compton. The original two rooms were built in 1869 by A. R. Loomis. The house, which originally stood at 209 South Acacia Street, was purchased by the city of Compton and moved to its present site in 1957. It is a tribute to the founders of the community.

Redondo Beach is at the northwest corner of Rancho San Pedro. At this point it adjoins Rancho Sausal Redondo. Between Pacific and Francisca Avenues at the north end of Redondo Beach is the site of an old salt lake (SRL 373) from which the Indians of the area obtained salt. A flourishing salt works operated here in the last half of the nineteenth century.

RANCHO LOS PALOS VERDES (SAN PEDRO, PALOS VERDES)

The great Rancho Los Palos Verdes grant was given to the Sepúlveda family in 1827, and the grant was confirmed to José Loreto and Juan Sepúlveda in 1846. It contained 31,629 acres, extending from south of Redondo Beach to San Pedro. San Pedro is now part of the city of Los Angeles. Almost the entire district was carved out of Rancho Los Palos Verdes, not out of Rancho San Pedro, as is often thought.

Juan Rodríguez Cabrillo sailed into San Pedro Bay on October 8, 1542, and named it Bahía de los Fumos ("bay of smokes"), because of the dense smoke arising from burning grass during the Indians' periodic rabbit hunts. He did not linger long. Sixty years later, Vizcaíno entered the bay, and as early as 1793 San Pedro had become the port of entry for the Pueblo of Los Angeles, three missions, and several ranchos. In that year the English navigator George Vancouver, on his second voyage to California, named the two extremities of the bay Point Fermin and Point Lasuen, in honor of his friend, Father Fermín Francisco de Lasuén, successor to Junipero Serra as padre presidente of the missions. The names given by Vancouver were retained, although Point Lasuen has disappeared in the reconfiguration of the shoreline.

The first Yankee ship to anchor at San Pedro was the *Lelia Byrd* in 1805, with Captain William Shaler in command, on his return voyage from the Sandwich (Hawaiian) Islands to Boston. This was the beginning of a brisk trade between California and New England ships. After this, American brigs as well as ships from other nations called regularly at San Pedro, in quest first of sea otter skins and later of hides and tallow. This was officially contraband trade until 1821, when Mexico, now independent of Spain, made it legal. From then on the port of San Pedro grew in importance.

The first harbor improvements were made in 1877, and in 1892 steps were taken for the creation of a deepwater port. Scarcely any of the old landmarks remain today. From 1874 to 1945 a lighthouse operated on Point Fermin, now a museum. A pleasant park surrounds the structure, at Paseo del Mar and Gaffey Street. Timm's Point (SRL 384), mentioned by Richard Henry Dana in *Two Years Before the Mast* as the place down which cargoes of hides and tallow were lowered to Yankee ships below, has disappeared with harbor improvements. The point and landing were located off the south end of Beacon Street near present Fisherman's Dock. The state plaque is on Sampson Way by the waterfront.

A short distance north is a plaque placed in 1998 at Fourth and Beacon Streets. Two unoccupied lots here in 1923 were the site of rallies behind a longshoremen's union strike. The text on the plaque (SRL 1021) reads:

> Liberty Hill. In 1923 the Marine Transport Workers Industrial Union 510, a branch of the Industrial Workers of the World (IWW), called a strike that immobilized 90 ships here in San Pedro. The union protested low wages, bad working conditions, and the imprisonment of union activists under California's Criminal Syndicalism Law. Denied access to public property, strikers and their supporters rallied here at this site they called 'Liberty Hill.' Writer Upton Sinclair was arrested for reading from the Bill of Rights to a large gathering. The strike failed but laid a foundation for success in the 1930s. The Syndicalism Law was ruled unconstitutional in 1968. Plaque placed by the State Department of Parks and Recreation in cooperation with the San Pedro Bay Historical Society and the American labor movement.

The Los Angeles Maritime Museum, Berth 84 at the foot of Sixth Street, is a good place to see old photographs and models of the harbor over the years. The SS *Lane Victory*, a World War II Merchant Marine vessel built in San Pedro, is moored at Berth 94 off Harbor Boulevard. Still operational, it makes cruises in the summer months.

The Fort MacArthur military reservation, much reduced in area and now known as Angels Gate Park, once covered much of the land around Point Fermin.

The fort was named for General Arthur MacArthur, father of General Douglas MacArthur. The Fort MacArthur Military Museum at 3601 South Gaffey Street has displays on World War II coastal defenses. Two gun emplacements from the World War I coastal defenses, Batteries Farley and Osgood, can be seen nearby. Here also is the Bell of Friendship between the Korean and the American people, placed in an imposing belfry on a bluff as part of the 1976 Bicentennial celebration. The view from the platform takes in the entrance to Los Angeles Harbor and the ocean beyond it. The International Korean War Memorial was dedicated in Angels Gate Park in 1987.

The Palos Verdes Peninsula, with its beautiful homes and striking coastal scenery, occupies much of the old Rancho Los Palos Verdes. At the residential community of Portuguese Bend a whaling station was located from about 1864 to 1885 (SRL 381).

None of the old Sepúlveda adobes stand today. The home of Diego Sepúlveda (SRL 380) was located in the 700 block of Channel Street in San Pedro and faced on Gaffey Street. Built about 1853, it was the first two-story Monterey-type adobe in southern California. An even earlier adobe stood southeast of Walteria at the foot of the Palos Verdes Hills. The home of José Dolores Sepúlveda (SRL 383), father of Diego, is said to have been built in 1818. The exact site is unknown, but the general area is indicated by old pepper trees at the mouth of the canyon into which Madison Street runs. Don José Dolores had trouble getting his land title cleared, so he took a trip to Monterey to get the matter settled in 1824; on his return, he stopped off at Mission La Purísima and was killed in the Indian uprising that year.

MISSION SAN FERNANDO REY DE ESPAÑA

Mission San Fernando Rey de España was founded on September 8, 1797, by Father Fermín Francisco de Lasuén. The spot chosen had been provisionally granted to Alcalde Francisco Reyes of Los Angeles. The padres took over the adobe house the alcalde had built, and within two months put up the first small chapel. A church was completed in 1799, and another church in 1806. Heavily damaged by the earthquake of 1812, it was subsequently repaired and in use until 1971. The mission was secularized in October 1834.

The first European industry in the Los Angeles area was the burning of limestone to produce lime, a necessary component of the construction of the missions and other adobe structures. Lime was needed for foundation cement, for mortaring and plastering walls, and for whitewash to protect the adobe bricks. It is believed that the *calera*, or kiln, near the present Chatsworth Reservoir was used to obtain lime for the construction of Mission San Fernando. A plaque (SRL 911) has been placed at Woolsey Canyon Road and Valley Circle Boulevard in Chatsworth near the site.

The vast lands of Mission San Fernando were leased in 1845 to Andrés Pico, brother of Governor Pío Pico. In order to obtain money to defend California against the Americans, the governor sold Rancho Ex-Mission de San Fernando in June 1846 to Eugenio de Celís for $14,000. Celís recognized Andrés Pico's lease, and in 1854 Pico bought a half interest in the rancho. He continued to make the old mission his country home and to herd his cattle on its vast ranges. Romulo Pico, the son or adopted son of Andrés, also came to live on the rancho.

In 1874, state Senators Charles Maclay and George K. Porter purchased the northern half of the rancho; B. F. Porter became associated with them in 1879. The southern half had already been bought by a group headed by Isaac Lankershim and I. N. Van Nuys, and with these two purchases the era of small farms and the building up of the town of San Fernando began. The old mission days were ended.

For many years the only intact building of Mission San Fernando was the *convento*, often called simply the "long building," 243 feet in length with twenty-one arches. It is said that this is the largest original building in any of the California missions. The building has several rooms used to display paintings and relics, and also includes the kitchen, refectory, and underground wine vats. In 1938, under the leadership of Mark R. Harrington of the Southwest Museum, restoration of the other buildings began. The mission church had fallen into ruin, and very little remained of the workshops and living quarters.

The Sylmar temblor of 1971 further damaged the church, and the building had to be demolished. The church was fully restored with a steel retrofit, which helped it to withstand the 1994 Northridge earthquake, which however did severe damage to the convento. In 1997, restorations and repairs were completed and the mission, at 15151 San Fernando Mission Boulevard in Mission Hills, once more attracts many visitors. The Archival Center of the Archdiocese of Los Angeles is inside the entrance to the mission, by the West Garden.

LOS ANGELES COUNTY

The Campo Santo or burial ground is the resting place for at least 2,000 Indians; it is on the north side of the property.

In what is now Brand Park (SRL 150), across San Fernando Mission Boulevard from the mission complex, are the immense stone soap vats constructed by the mission fathers as well as two beautiful fountains. One of the fountains, a replica of one in Cordova, Spain, was moved 300 feet from its original location in the mission courtyard in 1922. Both of them were a part of the old mission water system.

The Andrés Pico adobe was built in two parts. The earliest part dates from 1834 and was built by Indians from the mission. Pico acquired the adobe and added the second story in 1873. It fell into neglect in later years but was purchased and saved by Dr. and Mrs. Mark Harrington in 1930, who restored the building to its earlier condition. The beautiful structure (SRL 362) stands a quarter of a mile southwest of the mission at 10940 Sepulveda Boulevard. It is the headquarters of the San Fernando Valley Historical Society, which maintains it and a small museum within for the city of Los Angeles. It is the oldest house in the San Fernando Valley and second in age only to the Avila adobe in the city of Los Angeles. The 1994 earthquake also did severe damage to this building, which has since been restored and repaired.

The town of San Fernando began to boom about 1874, when Don Gerónimo López, who had built an adobe home on Rancho San Fernando earlier, decided to move there. In 1883 his son Valentino built the house at 1100 Pico Street that still stands. The López adobe has been somewhat elaborately restored, but it retains its quaint and picturesque upper balcony and outside stairway, and a traditional garden. It is now owned by the city of San Fernando and operated by the San Fernando Landmarks and Historical Commission.

The oldest nonsectarian cemetery in the San Fernando Valley is the San Fernando Memorial Cemetery, first known as the Morningside Cemetery, on Foothill Boulevard and Bledsoe Street, in Sylmar (SRL 753). It is presently being restored by a local citizens' group.

On the Workman Ranch, now called the Shadow Ranch Park, at 22633 Vanowen Street in Canoga Park, there is an adobe-and-redwood ranch house built around 1870 and now owned by the city of Los Ange-

les. In the same area is "Rancho Sombra de Robles," the adobe house and estate of W. W. Orcutt, an early oil engineer and one of the founders of the Union Oil Company, at 23555 Justice Street. This is owned as a Los Angeles city facility and designated the Orcutt Ranch Horticultural Center.

At Chatsworth, the Homestead Acre and the Hill-Palmer House are at 10385 Shadow Oak Drive. This 1.3-acre plot is all that remains of the 230 acres homesteaded by James David Hill and his wife, Rhoda Jane, in the late 1880s. Their seventh child, Minnie, was born here in 1886, later married, and returned to the place to care for her mother. Minnie Hill Palmer continued to live in pioneer style on the remaining land until she reached the age of 90, raising vegetables and canning fruit. She bequeathed the home to the Chatsworth Historical Society for restoration as a monument to pioneers who homesteaded the valley. At Oakwood Memorial Park, the Chatsworth Memorial Church now stands at 22601 Lassen Street. This nondenominational Protestant church served the community since it was built in 1903 at 10051 Topanga Canyon Boulevard and moved later to its present site, where it is being restored by the Chatsworth Historical Society.

Los Encinos State Historic Park, at 16756 Moorpark Street, Encino, is the old headquarters of Rancho Los Encinos ("the oaks"). Father Juan Crespí, who went north with the Portolá party in 1769, gave what is now the San Fernando Valley a grand name, El Valle de Santa Catalina de Bononia de los Encinos ("the valley of Saint Catherine of Bologna of the Oaks"). The Shoshone word *zelzah* ("oasis" or "spring") seems to have been used to describe the springs and vegetation marking the beginning of the Los Angeles River; the name has been perpetuated in a local thoroughfare. The presence of the native oaks also inspired the name of Rancho El Encino, which was granted in 1845 to three Indians: Ramón, Francisco, and Roque. It was purchased by Don Vicente de Osa, who in 1849 built the long, low adobe house that became the ranch headquarters. James Thompson acquired the rancho in 1867 and sold it two years later to Eugène Garnier, a French Basque, who made of El Encino a great sheep ranch. The broad pool or reservoir in front of the old adobe was constructed around 1868 by Garnier, and just to the north of it in 1872 he built the two-story stone house, which still exists. Garnier eventually had to sell the rancho, which at one point was a stagecoach stop. Los Encinos State Historic Park includes the springs that feed the lake; the Portolá expedition camped here on August 5, 1769. In 1984, excavations for an Encino building complex on Ventura Boulevard near Balboa Boulevard turned up what is believed to be the Indian village of "Encino," first visited by the Portolá expedition. Artifacts from this excavation were placed on display at the park headquarters.

The Northridge earthquake of 1994 was particularly destructive here, and the major buildings are all closed as of 2000, until thorough reconstruction can be made.

RANCHO EL ESCORPIÓN (CALABASAS)

Besides Rancho Ex-Mission de San Fernando and Rancho El Encino, there were other Mexican grants in the San Fernando Valley. One was Rancho El Escorpión of 1,100 acres, granted in 1845 to Joaquín Romero and to three Indians: Manuel, Odon, and Urbano. It came into the hands of Miguel Leonis, a Basque who arrived in California about 1858. Leonis enlarged an adobe that was begun in 1844 and completed in 1846 on public lands outside the boundaries of his rancho. Owned and operated by the Leonis Adobe Association, and open to the public, it stands at 23537 Calabasas Road in Calabasas, a well-preserved two-story house of Monterey style.

FIRST DISCOVERY OF GOLD IN CALIFORNIA

Placerita Canyon State Park is located about four miles east of Newhall in the San Fernando Hills, and about forty miles northwest of Los Angeles. The first discovery of gold in commercial quantities in California was made by Francisco López at Placerita Canyon. The following year he found gold in San Feliciano Canyon. The story of the first discovery is as follows.

One day in March 1842, López rode into Placerita Canyon. While resting in the shade of an oak tree, he began to gather wild onions. He suddenly noticed some shining particles clinging to the roots of the plants. Picking up more of the roots, he found the same kind of pebbles on them. Later, in Los Angeles, he was informed that they were gold nuggets.

This discovery not only caused considerable excitement throughout the south but also brought numbers of prospectors from Sonora, Mexico. In 1842, Abel Stearns sent the first California gold from the mines at Placerita to the U.S. Mint at Philadelphia. For many years thereafter he continued to send gold dust and nuggets from this region to Philadelphia.

Near the old placers on the west side of the canyon, a boulder with a bronze plate was placed in 1930 to mark the site of the first discovery of gold in California. Near the marker, the old oak tree under which López rested is still to be seen, below the level of the present main park road. It has been styled the "Oak of the Golden Dream" (SRL 168). Also in the park is the Walker Cabin, built by Frank Evans Walker around 1900. This tiny board-and-batten home housed twelve children and is now a small museum of local history.

RANCHO LA BREA (HANCOCK PARK DISTRICT, LOS ANGELES)

Rancho La Brea, originally a part of the Los Angeles pueblo lands, was granted in 1828 to Antonio José Rocha and Nemicio Domínguez by José Antonio Carrillo, alcalde of Los Angeles and brother-in-law of Pío Pico. Later, the grant was confirmed by Governor Echeandia. The rancho derived its name from La Brea Pits, where *brea*, or crude tar, oozed out of the ground in great quantities. Early conveyances of this land all provided that the owners were to allow the inhabitants of Los Angeles to take from the pits as much brea as they needed for the roofs of their adobe houses.

Antonio José Rocha was a Portuguese who came to California in 1815, settled in Los Angeles, and became a citizen of Mexico in 1831. In 1860 his son José Jorge Rocha deeded Rancho La Brea to Major Henry Hancock. Parts of the estate were later conveyed to Cornelius Cole, James Thompson, and Arthur Gilmore, but much of it remained in the hands of the Hancocks. For years, the Hancocks extracted immense quantities of petroleum from the rancho lands, but the oil gradually decreased. Today the derricks of the once wealthy oil fields have been replaced by the beautiful homes of the Hancock Park District. The site of the old pits has become Hancock Park (SRL 170), and the pools are now confined within a parklike enclosure.

In the heavy crude oil that has oozed out of the ground at La Brea Pits since time immemorial, animals, once caught, were unable to free themselves. Thousands of skeletons of prehistoric creatures (and one human being) have been recovered, and more still turn up. The George C. Page Museum of La Brea Discoveries at 5801 Wilshire Boulevard in Hancock Park is an excellent source of information on these excavations.

Although Major Hancock began to recover some of

these bones in the 1870s, their importance was confirmed in 1906, when University of California professor J. C. Merriam investigated them. Merriam and other scientists made extensive studies at the rancho. On June 23, 1913, Major Hancock gave exclusive right to excavate the beds to the city of Los Angeles. The Hancock Room in the Natural History Museum of Los Angeles County in Exposition Park is a memorial to his parents, Major Henry Hancock and Ida Ross Hancock. Rancho La Brea (Hancock Park) has been registered as a National Natural Landmark by the Department of the Interior.

The adobe house that remains standing about ten blocks north of the pits was built by Antonio José Rocha about 1830. It is one of the rancho's original adobes, and was restored with great care by oil magnate Earl E. Gilmore, who was born in the house in the 1880s and died there on February 27, 1964. It stands at 6301 West Third Street, on a private drive between the Farmers Market and the CBS television studio.

RANCHO SAN PASQUAL (PASADENA, SOUTH PASADENA, ALTADENA)

At 1804 Foothill Boulevard in South Pasadena is the Adobe de las Flores, beautifully restored and now a private residence. Begun by Manuel Gárfias in 1839, it was the first house built on Rancho San Pasqual. This rancho was part of the extensive lands of Mission San Gabriel granted first in 1835 to Juan Mariné, husband of Eulalia Pérez de Guillén, reputedly the oldest white woman in California at that time. This land was a gift made in recompense for Doña Eulalia's long services at the mission as nurse, overseer of spinning and tailoring, cashier, and accountant. Today, the cities of Pasadena, South Pasadena, and Altadena cover the former rancho lands.

The rancho was re-granted provisionally to José Pérez, who died in 1840, and eventually came to be owned by Manuel Gárfias, who was a son-in-law of Doña Encarnación Avila.

The casa has come to be known as the Flores adobe because it was there that General José María Flores, provisional governor of California, took refuge in January 1847 after the Battle of La Mesa, while Kearny and Stockton took final possession of Los Angeles and Frémont held the San Fernando Valley. General Flores and his staff held their last council within this house on the night of January 9, while the California horsemen kept watch on the hills outside. Knowing that surrender was inevitable, they made final plans to leave Andrés Pico in command while Flores and Manuel Gárfias, both commissioned officers in the Mexican army, fled to Mexico under cover of darkness on the night of January 11. On January 13 the Cahuenga Capitulation Treaty was signed by Frémont and Andrés Pico, and hostilities came to an end.

PASADENA

Pasadena is one of the longest-established residential communities in Los Angeles County. The oldest house in the area was built in 1869, five years before the founding of Pasadena, and is a privately owned adobe, "The Hermitage," at 2121 Monte Vista Street. The Clapp house at 549 La Loma Road is the oldest frame building in the city (1874); Pasadena's first school was located in the parlor of the new home where it originally stood, at the corner of California and Orange Grove Boulevards. The city became known for its elegant mansions, one of the most imposing of which is the Wrigley Estate at 391 South Orange Grove Boulevard. Mr. & Mrs. William Wrigley Jr. acquired the new house in 1914 and lived there until 1958. In 1959 the Wrigley heirs donated the estate to the city of Pasadena. It became Tournament House, the headquarters of the Tournament of Roses Association; it is open to the public on a limited basis. The Tournament of Roses is a Pasadena tradition, a parade held on New Year's Day that features elaborate floats adorned with flowers. The Rose Bowl game is played later that day.

The Rose Bowl Stadium in Arroyo Seco Park was built in 1922, although the first Rose Bowl football game was played on New Year's Day, 1902. Since 1916 the Rose Bowl game has been played here, except in 1942, when it was played in Durham, North Carolina, at the beginning of World War II. From here, on January 1, 1927, radio stations across the nation were linked together for the first coast-to-coast broadcast. The first west-to-east color telecast on a nationwide hookup was of the Tournament of Roses parade and Rose Bowl game on January 1, 1954.

The David B. Gamble House (SRL 871) at 4 Westmoreland Place is the finest surviving example of the work of architects Charles Sumner Greene and Henry Mather Greene. Built in 1908, it exemplifies the Arts and Crafts movement of the early twentieth century. The beautiful house in California Bungalow style has

David B. Gamble House, Pasadena

been registered as a National Historic Landmark and is open to the public.

The Fenyes Estate, completed in 1905, is a large mansion that was once the Finnish Consulate. Since 1970 it has been headquarters for the Pasadena Historical Society, and the Pasadena Historical Museum occupies the ground floor. A recent addition to the site, at 470 West Walnut Street, is a Finnish folk-art museum. Two blocks to the south is the Norton Simon Museum at 411 West Colorado Boulevard. The quality of its art collections makes it a major world treasury.

The Pasadena Playhouse (SRL 887) opened in 1925. It served as the training ground and launching area for many of Hollywood's finest actors, directors, and technicians. Among those who received early training at the Playhouse are Robert Young, Victor Mature, William Holden, Charles Bronson, Lee J. Cobb, Kim Hunter, Sally Struthers, Raymond Burr, and Dustin Hoffman. The building, in Spanish Colonial Revival style, is considered by many to be the finest work of architect Elmer Grey. It is located at 39 South El Molino Avenue.

The Ritz-Carlton Huntington Hotel at 1401 South Oak Knoll Avenue is one of the showplaces of southern California. It was begun in 1907 by General Marshall C. Wentworth with the idea that every room in the reinforced-concrete structure would receive direct sunlight at some time of the day—an innovation in hotel building at the time. The Wentworth Hotel closed after one unprofitable season but was reopened as the Huntington by the railroad tycoon and art collector Henry E. Huntington in 1914. Its gardens and public rooms are noted for their beauty and spaciousness.

The Pasadena Freeway, originally the Arroyo Seco Parkway, is California's first freeway. A six-mile stretch was opened on December 30, 1940, and two days later California suffered its first freeway congestion—traffic to and from the Tournament of Roses parade and the Rose Bowl game.

ALTADENA

The lovely residential community of Altadena takes its name from a nursery established in 1875 north of Pasadena and at the edge of the San Gabriel Mountains. "Altadena" was intended to mean "upper Pasadena." From here, an electric railway into the mountains ran between 1893 and 1938. Power for the Mount Lowe Railway came from a substation at 2245 Lake Avenue, now converted into commercial spaces.

Three historic houses stand on East Mariposa Street. At 209 is Scripps Hall, built in 1905 for William A. Scripps, of the newspaper family; Waldorf School now occupies the building. The house at 396 was built in 1907 for Arthur Woodward; at his insistence it was made fireproof, the first of its kind in Altadena. In 1920, Western writer Zane Grey purchased the place and lived here until his death in 1939, and it has since been known as the Zane Grey House. The Andrew McNally House at 654 is the earliest of these, built in 1888 for a founder of the Rand-McNally Publishing Company. The Queen Anne–style house was added on to with part of the Turkish Pavilion at the 1893 Columbian exposition in Chicago, shipped in to become a smoking room at the southeast corner of the house.

John and Frederick Woodbury are known as the founders of Altadena, and the latter built his house at 2606 Madison Avenue in 1882. Santa Rosa Avenue is the site of Christmas Tree Lane (SRL 990), a one-mile boulevard of Deodar cedars planted by the brothers in 1885. Since 1920 the lane has been lighted at the Christmas season.

SAN MARINO

San Marino is another beautiful residential community, between Pasadena and San Gabriel. An old adobe house that was part of its history was at Los Robles, the 400-acre estate of George Stoneman, governor of California between 1883 and 1887. A monument (SRL 669) at the site of the house at 1912 Montrobles Place incorporates some of the old adobe bricks. The home of Edwin Hubble, the great astronomer, is at 1340 Woodstock Road, and has been registered as a National Historic Landmark. Among other accomplishments,

Hubble discovered extragalactic nebulae and their recession from one another.

California's greatest collection of art and history is at the Huntington, 1151 Oxford Road. Henry E. Huntington was born in Oneonta, New York, in 1850 and came to California in 1872 to work for his uncle. Collis P. Huntington was one of the "Big Four" who made California an important part of the Union with the transcontinental railroad in 1869. As a director of the Southern Pacific Railroad, H. E. Huntington traveled widely, and in 1892 visited "San Marino," the J. D. Shorb estate, which he later purchased. After the death of his uncle, "H. E." moved to Los Angeles and became involved in the development of that metropolis by creating an extensive interurban transit system. As a result of the railway linkages and the development of the property adjacent to the lines, the population of the Los Angeles region tripled between 1900 and 1910. Huntington's wealth and influence became extraordinary: at one time he served on sixty corporate boards throughout the United States. He retired in 1910 at the age of sixty in order to devote time to his collections of books and manuscripts, artworks, and the development of his 600-acre property. In that year the Beaux Arts mansion, now the Art Gallery, was completed. It would be the home of Huntington and his wife Arabella (who was the widow of his uncle) until their deaths. In 1920 the library building was completed to house his outstanding collection.

"The Huntington" is short for the Huntington Library, Art Collections, and Botanical Gardens. The Library has rare manuscripts and early works such as a Gutenberg Bible and much early material from Shakespeare's time. California history is another part of its repository. The Art Collections' eighteenth-century British paintings and furniture collection is probably the finest outside of the United Kingdom. The Virginia Steele Scott Gallery of American Art is a newer addition. The fifteen gardens extend over 130 acres. Each part of the institution has changing displays, which make it a very popular museum and place to visit, which Mr. and Mrs. Huntington clearly intended.

RANCHO PASO DE BARTOLO VIEJO (WHITTIER)

At first a part of the lands belonging to Mission San Gabriel, Rancho Paso de Bartolo was granted to Juan Crispín Pérez in 1835, in the time of secularization. Pérez was *alcalde auxiliar* of Rancho Santa Gertrudes from 1831 to 1836 and later mayordomo of the mission in its declining years. After years of contention between various claimants, patents to the rancho's 8,891 acres were granted to Pérez and to Pío Pico in 1881. Pico, last Mexican governor of California, called the 8,000-acre rancho "El Ranchito" because of its diminutive size in comparison with his vast ranchos of Las Flores and Santa Margarita. It was his favorite home place, and as he lost most of his lands in time, El Ranchito was his last possession in Los Angeles County.

It is uncertain just when the adobe house of Pío Pico was built; in the flood of 1867 the nearby San Gabriel River swept away a portion of the building, and in the winter of 1883–84 additional floods destroyed what was left. The second casa was a blend of Mexican and American styles and was built with a capacious series of rooms and courtyards for the entertaining of guests, which Pico loved. This house was saved by a later owner, Harriet Russell Strong, and is now Pío Pico State Historic Park (SRL 127) at 6003 Pioneer Boulevard in Whittier.

What is now the city of Whittier began as a Quaker colony. It was named for the famed Quaker poet John Greenleaf Whittier, who was still alive in 1887, when Aquilla H. Pickering of Chicago founded the Pickering Land and Water Company for the purpose of establishing Quakers on neighboring farms. John H. Thomas established a ranch there in 1880, and Jonathan and Rebecca Bailey moved into his ranch house in 1887. The house still stands at 13421 Camilla Street; owned by the city of Whittier, it is now the Jonathan Bailey House and Park, and the building is on the National Register of Historic Places.

Nearby is the Whittier Museum at 6755 Newlin Avenue, displaying historical artifacts connected with the early days of Whittier. A Whittier landmark is the huge paradox hybrid walnut tree (SRL 681) in the 600–800 block of West Whittier Boulevard, which divides around it. It was planted in 1907 as part of an agricultural experiment by the University of California.

A legislative act of March 11, 1889, provided for a state school for juvenile offenders, and this was established in Whittier two years later as the Whittier State School for Boys and Girls. Since 1970 it has been known as the Fred C. Nelles School, after a longtime superintendent. Located at 11850 Whittier Boulevard (SRL 947), the school has been in continuous use since 1891, although its inmates today are all young men, the women's facilities being elsewhere in the state.

In the beautiful valley of Pomona west of the Arroyo de San Antonio, the boundaries of the great Rancho San José were first laid out by Ygnacio Palomares and Ricardo Vejar on March 19, 1837, the feast of St. Joseph. Father Zalvidea, who accompanied the party from Mission San Gabriel, performed the first Christian religious service ever held in the valley when he pronounced a benediction upon the two families about to establish their homes in the wilderness of San José. The ceremony was held under an oak tree, the stump of which still stands in the city of Pomona at 458 Kenoak Place. A bronze tablet commemorating this event was placed here in 1922 by the Daughters of the American Revolution.

The rancho was split between Ygnacio Palomares, who was given the upper part, and Ricardo Vejar, who held the lower half. Four old adobe houses remain, in the city of Pomona and in the foothills to the west. La Casa Primera, built by Don Ygnacio after 1837, stands among the orange trees as 1569 North Park Avenue. The older part of it has been torn down, and the low roof of the little house projects over a broad *corredor* extending the full length of the side that faces the old-fashioned garden. This building is owned by the Historical Society of Pomona Valley, and is open to the public.

About 300 yards southwest, at 1469 Old Settlers' Lane, is the Alvarado house, once the home of Ygnacio Alvarado, close friend of Palomares. In those days when neighbors lived many miles apart, the hospitality of the Californians was famous, but in few other instances was it expressed in so friendly and intimate a manner as in the case of Ygnacio Palomares and Ygnacio Alvarado. At the invitation of the former, Alvarado came to Rancho San José and built his home within a stone's throw of his friend's, the only stipulation in the arrangement being that Alvarado should build a chapel in his house, which he did. According to the present owners, the altar in the chapel was so arranged that after religious services were held, it could be turned to the wall and the large room used for secular purposes. The Alvarado adobe is on the National Register of Historic Sites.

In 1854 Ygnacio Palomares built another adobe (SRL 372) at what is now 491 East Arrow Highway in Pomona. Leaving his old home to his son Francisco, Don Ygnacio made his new house and its huge fireplace a popular stage station and tavern on the road to Chino and San Bernardino. For many years the deserted adobe moldered among the roses and oranges, but in time it was restored, and since 1940 has been open to the public as a museum of the Historical Society of Pomona Valley.

At 919 Puddingstone Drive in La Verne, the Carrión adobe (SRL 386) stands on the lower reaches of the hills. Saturnino Carrión inherited a portion of the old rancho from his uncle, Ygnacio Palomares, and here, on the old San Bernardino road, built one of the most attractive adobes in southern California. The house decayed in later years, but was restored in 1951 by Paul E. Traweek. Substantial additions were made to the house as late as the 1980s.

The first American settlement in Pomona Valley was at Spadra, a stage station on the emigrant road from Chino in the 1850s. Here "Uncle Billy" Rubottom, the first American settler in the valley, built a tavern in the 1860s, and the place was named Spadra for his native home in Arkansas. The Spadra Cemetery on Pomona Boulevard is the only vestige of this settlement. About a mile east of Spadra at 2640 Pomona Boulevard is the two-story mansion built by Louis Phillips in the late 1860s. The first brick house in Pomona, it is still in good condition and is now operated as a Victorian museum by the Historical Society of Pomona Valley. Ricardo Vejar, easygoing and trustful, had lost his portion of Rancho San José by foreclosure in 1864. A year or two later it was purchased by Phillips, who proved to be an excellent manager, and in his hands and those of his descendants the great rancho prospered.

Pomona College, founded in 1887, held its first class on September 12, 1888, in a small cottage, the site of which is at the southwest corner of Fifth and White Avenues in Pomona (SRL 289). Five months later, the college moved to Claremont. Dr. Cyrus Grandison Baldwin, president of Pomona College, organized the San Antonio Light and Power Company, which in 1892 built the first hydroelectric installation in California for long-distance transmission of alternating current at high voltage. A monument to this pioneer power plant (SRL 514) stands on the upper road in San Antonio Canyon northeast of Pomona, while the foundations of the plant can still be found on San Antonio Creek near the lower road. Pomona College is now one of the Associated Colleges of Claremont, the others being Scripps College for women (founded in 1926) and the co-educational Claremont Graduate University (1925), Claremont McKenna College (1946), Harvey Mudd College (1955), and Pitzer College (1963). The Claremont School of Theology and some special institutes are also affiliated with the association.

RANCHO LA PUENTE (LA PUENTE, HACIENDA HEIGHTS, INDUSTRY, WALNUT)

On November 5, 1841, a group of twenty-five emigrants, recruited partly in Missouri and partly among the Americans in New Mexico, reached Los Angeles by way of the Gila and Colorado Rivers. Like other early companies, this group was known by the names of its leaders, and history records it as the Rowland-Workman party. Upon their arrival in Los Angeles, John Rowland and William Workman began almost immediately to look for a permanent home. Both had lived in New Mexico for more than ten years, were married to New Mexican women, and had become citizens of Mexico. This entitled them to petition for grants of land in California, which they did in the spring of 1842, receiving Rancho La Puente ("the bridge") formally in 1845.

At first the two friends seem to have owned the great ranges of La Puente jointly, their herds sharing the unfenced pastures and their adobe dwelling houses standing less than a mile apart. Later, the land was formally divided, with Workman taking the western half and Rowland the eastern.

The Workman-Temple Home (SRL 874) at 15415 East Don Julian Road in the City of Industry is a striking example of historic preservation and of different periods of California living. In 1843 William Workman had a simple adobe house built for his family on his portion of the ranch. A later remodeling, before 1872, enlarged the house with two parallel arms and a central patio. By the 1870s, the Workman family had acquired considerable wealth and remodeled the adobe "into an English manor house." Unfortunately, the bank that Workman owned with his son-in-law, Francisco P. F. Temple, collapsed, and the family fortune went with it. The rancho became the property of financier Elias Jackson ("Lucky") Baldwin, and only the old homestead, the acreage immediately around the house, stayed with the Workman and Temple families.

New life came in 1917 when Walter P. Temple Sr., grandson of William Workman, restored the family's fortune through oil and real estate investments. He and his wife, Laura Gonzalez, then set out to restore the homestead's grandeur. They had a Greek Revival mausoleum put up in El Campo Santo, site of an Indian rancheria from the previous century and of an Indian cemetery. The Workmans made this the first private cemetery in Los Angeles County, and brought the bodies of Pío Pico and his wife from a remote bur-

ial spot for entombment here. A new house, La Casa Nueva, was put up in the 1920s not far from the old house, this one exceptionally rich in the decorative arts. Fortune turned away from the Temples after the 1929 crash, and they were forced to sell the property upon which so much care and money had been lavished. The homestead was used as a convalescent home, among other purposes.

The City of Industry was incorporated in 1957 to provide an ideal environment for manufacturing, distribution, and industrial facilities within its boundaries, and proved remarkably successful. Not wishing to neglect the historic past of the area, the city took steps that in 1974 resulted in the purchase of the Workman-Temple Homestead, La Casa Nueva, and El Campo Santo. Painstaking restoration over a number of years is now complete, and the site is a much-visited Los Angeles County showplace.

John Rowland's adobe is long gone, but about 100 yards south of its site a two-story brick house built by him in 1855 still stands. It is located at 16021 Gale Avenue east of Hacienda Boulevard. At the rear of the stucco-covered brick house is its first kitchen, a separate adobe building. An old watering tank at the front of the property has been converted into a museum of local history. Rowland is buried in the cemetery at the Workman place. Workman himself was laid to rest beside his partner, but his remains have now been placed in the mausoleum.

RANCHO LA MERCED (MONTEBELLO)

Rancho La Merced lay west of Rancho La Puente. It was originally granted to Doña Casilda Soto in 1846. In 1850 she sold the ranch and her adobe house to William Workman, who in 1851 gave it to his son-in-law, Francisco P. F. Temple, and Juan Matías Sánchez. The Temple adobe stood near the corner of San Gabriel Boulevard and Durfee Avenue; it has vanished, as has the little settlement of Temple's Corners along the Rio Hondo. Upon Temple's death in 1888, the home tract at Temple's Corners became the property of his widow; this part of Rancho La Merced remained in the Temple family for many years, and escaped the grasp of "Lucky" Baldwin, who acquired much land in the area.

One spring day in 1914, nine-year-old Thomas Workman Temple II, a grandson of Francisco Temple, was looking for tall wild oats, which he used to snare lizards on the hillside across the Rio Hondo from his home at Temple's Corners. On the search he discovered an upwelling of natural gas in a pool of water on the property his father, Walter P. Temple, had purchased in 1912. Operations were begun there in 1917 by the Standard Oil Company. Thus was the famous Montebello oil field established.

About two miles southwest of the site of the home of Francisco Temple, at 946 Adobe Avenue, stands the Juan Matías Sánchez adobe on a pleasant hill above the Rio Hondo. The older wing, facing the river, was built by Casilda Soto in the late 1840s. Sánchez enlarged the house in the early 1850s and built the wing facing the hills. Although elaborately remodeled within, some it as recently at the 1970s, the adobe retains some of its original exterior lines and character. Sánchez had owned 2,200 acres of excellent land in the San Gabriel Valley; it is said that his "friendship for William Workman and Francisco Temple, however, caused him to sacrifice all his possessions in a heroic effort to save the honor of his friends. His last years were spent in poverty, while rich oil wells about his adobe made later owners wealthy and preserved the old adobe house."

RANCHO CIÉNEGA O PASO DE LA TIJERA (BALDWIN HILLS, LOS ANGELES)

There were many natural springs and marshlands (*ciénegas*) below the hills at Rancho Ciénega, and two narrow valleys between the Baldwin Hills formed a pass that to the imaginative Spaniards resembled a pair of open scissors (*paso de la tijera*). Thus originated the double name of the great Rancho Ciénega or Paso de la Tijera, granted to Vicente Sánchez, alcalde of Los Angeles, in 1843. Rancho Ciénega was a long day's journey into the country in those days, and Sánchez's official duties required him to live in Los Angeles. The vast ranges of his rancho were therefore mainly used for cattle grazing. After Don Vicente's death, about 1850, his landholdings were partitioned among his heirs, and Tomás A. Sánchez, sheriff of Los Angeles for nearly ten years, received Rancho Ciénega, while his sisters took the property on Calle de los Negros in Los Angeles.

Don Tomás married Maria Sepúlveda, who received a portion of Rancho San Rafael after Fernando Sepúlveda's death. Tomás Sánchez sold Rancho Ciénega and made his home on his wife's little estate in Glendale, where a handsome adobe, still standing, was built near the site of the original home.

"Lucky" Baldwin finally became the owner of Rancho Ciénega, and when the estate was settled after his death in 1909, the rancho was listed as one of the most valuable of his extensive holdings. His luck has held, it seems, for this continues to be very valuable land, no matter how often it is subdivided.

When the Sunset Golf Corporation leased the estate from the Baldwin heirs in the 1920s, a few old adobes were still standing. One of these, at 3725 Don Felipe Drive, was used as the clubhouse for a golf course that no longer exists, and now serves as a women's club.

It was in this Baldwin Hills or Angeles Mesa district that the world's greatest athletes were housed during the Olympic Games in 1932. The Olympic village, including over 600 two-room dwellings, was built in the hills west of Crenshaw Boulevard; Olympiad Drive and Athenian Way are local street names. The Los Angeles Memorial Coliseum (SRL 960), built in Exposition Park in 1923, was enlarged for this international event.

The 1984 Summer Olympic games were also held in Los Angeles. Many events took place in the Coliseum, but there are now so many activities in an Olympic festival that even in so well-provided a city as Los Angeles they had to be dispersed around the metropolis, as far west as Lake Casitas in Ventura County and as far east as Chino in San Bernardino County.

RANCHO AGUAJE DE CENTINELA (INGLEWOOD)

Ygnacio Antonio Machado first settled on the Rancho Aguaje de Centinela in the mid-1830s, but did not receive a formal title until 1844. The next year, Machado traded his estate to Bruno Avila for a small tract of land with a house, corrals, and a vineyard in the Pueblo of Los Angeles. Today most of the Centinela Rancho is covered by the thriving city of Inglewood.

The *aguaje* ("water hole") of the Centinela was located in what is now Inglewood's Edward Vincent Park. It was the principal water supply for early settlers, as it had been for Indian people before them. A drinking fountain and plaque (SRL 363) commemorate the Centinela Springs in the park below the pool.

Rancho Centinela had a varied history. Bruno Avila lost the land in 1857 through foreclosure, and the title passed through several owners. In 1860 it was acquired by Sir Robert Burnett of Crathes Castle, Banchory, Scotland, who came to California in the 1850s, presumably to raise and sell sheep. He also acquired the divided lands of the neighboring Rancho Sausal Redondo. In time he accumulated nearly 25,000 acres, which he named the Centinela Ranch, an area today covered by eight cities and Los Angeles International Airport.

In 1864 Burnett married Matilda Josephine Murphy of New York and brought his bride to the refurbished Centinela adobe. While specializing in the raising of premium wool-producing sheep, Burnett also planted extensive orchards in the 1870s. His improvements, and the rising value of land, brought the baronet $140,000 in gold coin when he sold the ranch in 1885 to Canadian barrister Daniel Freeman. During the real estate boom of 1886–88, Freeman sold the heart of the ranch lands for one of the most spectacular new subdivisions of the era, the town of Inglewood. The community was famous as a center for the raising of poultry, and in the 1920s the world's largest chinchilla farm was started here by M. F. Chapman.

With the location of the aircraft industry in southern California during World War II, the agricultural phase of Inglewood's history neared its end. The U.S. Air Force initiated the Intercontinental Ballistic Missile Program in 1954 at the old St. John's Catholic School; a bronze plaque at the corner of Manchester Boulevard and Locust Street marks the site where the nation's space exploration program began with the development of the Atlas missile. Ygnacio Machado's Centinela ranch house at 7634 Midfield Avenue remains one of the most beautifully preserved of the smaller adobes of Los Angeles County. Its simple lines, early Victorian furnishings, and well-kept gardens reflect the lifestyle of the later Burnett and Freeman families. Two other buildings stand on the same grounds, which the Historical Society of Centinela Valley operates.

The 1887 Centinela-Inglewood Land Company office was moved to this site in 1975; in this building Inglewood's first citizens purchased their lots during the great land boom. Complementing the adobe in style is the Centinela Valley Heritage and Research Center, built in 1980. When the 1889 Freeman-Howland mansion in Inglewood was razed in 1972, the Historical Society of Centinela Valley salvaged paneling, doors, stained glass, and other artifacts, which have been incorporated into the structure of the new center. All the buildings are open to the public.

RANCHO LOS FELIZ (GRIFFITH PARK)

Rancho Los Feliz was granted to María Ygnacia Verdugo in 1843, but was occupied by her as early as 1841. The United States government issued a patent in her name for 6,647 acres. The rancho passed successively through the hands of Antonio Coronel, a pioneer of Los Angeles; James Lick, a San Francisco pioneer and the founder of Lick Observatory; and Colonel Griffith Jenkins Griffith, who in 1898 deeded 3,015 acres of the rancho to the city of Los Angeles. This is now Griffith Park, said to be the largest urban park in the United States. The Los Feliz adobe still stands at 4730 Crystal Springs Drive, within the park. Also within the park are the Los Angeles Zoo, the Greek Theater, and the Griffith Planetarium and Observatory. The Gene Autry Western Heritage Museum is also within the park, at 4700 Western Heritage Way, with good displays showing the Wild West of films and legend as well as realistic presentations of life on the frontier.

RANCHO SANTA ANITA (ARCADIA, MONROVIA)

Rancho Santa Anita, comprising 13,319 acres, was granted to Hugo Reid in 1845. For a time it was in the hands of William Wolfskill, but in 1872 his son Lewis Wolfskill sold it to H. Newmark and Company for $85,000. In 1875 Elias Jackson ("Lucky") Baldwin, San Francisco mining operator and horseman, purchased it for three times the amount paid by Newmark. Baldwin had made millions, it was said, in the Ophir Mines of Nevada. He soon moved from San Francisco into the ranch house at Santa Anita. Here he continued to win fortunes not only by developing a world-famous breed of racing horses but also by acquiring and selling great landed estates.

Baldwin was a lover of trees as well as horses. All the roads within his rancho were lined with trees, and many of the eucalyptus trees he planted still can be seen along parts of Huntington Drive and Santa Anita Avenue.

The heart of the Baldwin estate is now the Los Angeles State and County Arboretum at Arcadia. Here, surrounded by beautiful trees, flowers, and lakes, stands the original Hugo Reid adobe (SRL 368), built in 1839 and later occupied by Baldwin as his home. It was restored by the state and dedicated in 1961. The "Queen Anne Cottage" (SRL 367) was built by Baldwin in 1881 as a guest house, and has been restored. Still another landmark is Baldwin's old carriage house. The name of the rancho is continued in Santa Anita Race Track, which adjoins the arboretum.

The neo-Mediterranean home of Upton Sinclair has been registered as a National Historic Landmark.

The famed social critic and political writer, an unsuccessful candidate for governor of California in 1934, moved into this house in 1942. It stands at 464 North Myrtle Avenue in Monrovia.

LANDMARKS OF THE MEXICAN WAR

The Battle of San Gabriel took place on January 8, 1847, ten miles southeast of Los Angeles at a place on the Rio Hondo in the southern part of the present city of Montebello. There was quicksand at this point and a high bluff opposite the ford, which the Americans were attempting to cross from the east. The defending Californians, under command of General José Flores, held the bluff with between five hundred and six hundred men. The six hundred Americans, under Commodore Robert Stockton and General Stephen Kearny, had the difficult task of fording the river with their heavy artillery under enemy fire. Within an hour and a half, however, the feat was accomplished and the Californians retired toward Los Angeles. The action is described on a monument (SRL 385) at the corner of Washington Boulevard and Bluff Road in Montebello.

On January 9 the two forces met again at La Mesa, the site of the present Union Stockyards in the great central manufacturing district of Los Angeles. La Mesa was of slight importance itself, merely repeating the American victory of the previous day. Like most of the "battles" of the Mexican War in California, it was little more than a skirmish. The Californians, realizing the futility of resistance, soon withdrew to Rancho San Pasqual, where their decision to surrender was made. Camping that night on the outskirts of Los Angeles, Stockton and Kearny marched their forces to the plaza the next day, the city having already surrendered. With this action, control passed from Mexico to the United States.

With the forces of Stockton and Kearny in control of Los Angeles and those of Frémont occupying the San Fernando Valley, the Californians offered no further resistance. Frémont at once sent Jesús Pico to persuade the Californians to lay down their arms, which they agreed to do. Ready to make peace if favorable terms were arranged, the two parties met on January 13, 1847, at the Cahuenga adobe, about a mile from the entrance to Cahuenga Pass. Here Andrés Pico and Frémont signed the Cahuenga Capitulation Treaty, which ended hostilities throughout California.

The site of the old treaty adobe (SRL 151) has been preserved by the city of Los Angeles as a memorial park called "Campo de Cahuenga." It is at 3919 Lankershim Boulevard in North Hollywood, directly across from Universal Studios. Not far from the site, below Lookout Mountain, at a place called Los Alamos, a skirmish took place on February 20–21, 1845, between a band of rebel Californians, under José Castro and Juan Bautista Alvarado, and Governor Manuel Micheltorena's *cholo* army. The governor was forced to retreat to Rancho Los Feliz, where he surrendered, and Pío Pico was made governor in his stead.

The site of Frémont's headquarters in Los Angeles in January 1847 was at the southeast corner of Aliso and Los Angeles Streets. There he established himself in the Alexander Bell adobe, after Commodore Stockton had appointed him military governor of the territory on January 19, an office he held for fifty days. The old Bell adobe was torn down long ago, and the site is occupied by a modern public building.

When Stockton and Kearny entered Los Angeles on January 10, 1847, after the Battle of La Mesa, their troops, some 600 men, were stationed on a hill west of the plaza. On January 11, Frémont and his men came down from Monterey, via Cahuenga Pass, and for several weeks a thousand American soldiers were quartered on the hill. At this time, work was begun on a temporary fort, but it was never completed. Later, in the summer of 1847, Fort Moore (named for Captain B. D. Moore, killed in the Battle of San Pasqual) was constructed on the same spot overlooking the pueblo. Nothing of the old fort remains today, and much of Fort Moore Hill was leveled for the construction of the Hollywood Freeway. What remains of the hill is occupied by the Los Angeles City Board of Education headquarters. At the base the Pioneer Memorial from the 1950s honors the troops "who helped win the Southwest."

EL MONTE

Many American pioneers came into California by the southern route, variously known as the Old Spanish Trail, the Santa Fe Trail, or in part of its last section, the Mormon Trail. For many of the covered-wagon emigrants, El Monte became the end of the trail, where water and wood and grass could be found. At first El Monte was only a place to camp before going onward, but as early as 1851 Ira Thompson had established a stage station at a place called "Willow Grove" by the San Gabriel River. Soon immigrants from Texas were making permanent homes here. SRL 975 in Pioneer Park, 3535 Santa Anita Avenue, commemorates the first settlement in Southern California to be established by immigrants from the United States.

Walnut ranching began in 1868 and soon became a profitable business. By the 1920s, more than 4,000 acres were in production in the vicinity of El Monte. Gay's Lion Farm, established in 1923, had a much different kind of production: Mr. & Mrs. Charles Gay, European-born circus performers, arrived with the idea of raising wild animals for use in the burgeoning motion picture industry. (The roaring lion that became the logo of MGM pictures was "Jackie," one of Gay's most famous stars.) The Lion Farm was a popular tourist attraction for many years. The teams from El Monte High School were "the Lions." With World War II's rationing of gasoline and meat, the Lion Farm closed and its animals were farmed out to zoos throughout the country. It never reopened, and all that remains of this unusual enterprise is the noble statue of a golden African lion, which guarded the entrance to the farm, now on the grounds of El Monte High School.

The El Monte Historical Society Museum at 3150 North Tyler Avenue has a large collection of artifacts relating to early settlement in the community.

GLENDORA

The Glendora Bougainvillea (SRL 912) is believed to be the largest growth of the vines in the continental United States. Planting was done by Ruben Hamlin between 1900 and 1903. It originally bordered an orange grove, which has been subdivided. The vines are at the corner of East Bennett and North Minnesota Avenues. The Glendora Historical Museum is in the old fire station building at 314 North Glendora Avenue. Two houses of local interest are the Shank home, one of the oldest in the community, at 316 West Alosta Avenue, now a restaurant, and the Memlin House at 201 West Bennett Avenue, now the California headquarters for the Daughters of the American Revolution.

HOLLYWOOD

The Hollywood district of Los Angeles became "the glamour capital of the world" when the motion picture industry located and flourished there. The first feature-length motion picture made in Hollywood was *The Squaw Man*, filmed in 1913–14 by Cecil B. DeMille,

Samuel Goldwyn, and Jesse Lasky Sr. The studio in which the picture was made was a barn at the corner of Selma Avenue and Vine Street. In 1927 the historic barn (SRL 554) was moved to the Paramount Studio lot and in 1983 to 2100 North Highland Avenue, across from Hollywood Bowl. The barn is now the Hollywood Studio Museum and preserves some of the artifacts connected with DeMille. Other film memorabilia can be seen at the Margaret Herrick Library and Motion Picture Academy Archives at 333 La Cienega Boulevard in Beverly Hills. The handsome building was originally the Beverly Hills Waterworks Building, built in 1928.

The first Motion Picture Academy Awards were presented in 1928. The event was held in the Hollywood Roosevelt Hotel, still an important landmark, at 7000 Hollywood Boulevard. Visitors enjoy tours of Hollywood, Beverly Hills, and Bel-Air to see the homes of entertainment celebrities. Some places have become famous.

The Griffith Ranch (SRL 716), now privately owned, was the home of the pioneer filmmaker David W. Griffith and the locale of many of his pictures. A marker stands one and one-half miles east of San Fernando at Foothill Boulevard and Vaughn Street. The Harold Lloyd estate, "Greenacres," is at 1740 Green Acres Place in Beverly Hills. At the peak of his career in 1928, Lloyd began construction of a lavish forty-four-room mansion on the estate. This and the beautifully landscaped grounds were left to the city on Lloyd's death in 1971.

The William S. Hart Ranch, at San Fernando Road and Newhall Avenue in Newhall, is now a Los Angeles County Park. Here stand the original ranch house, built about 1910 by an earlier owner, and the mansion completed by the cowboy actor in 1928. Both are open to the public, as are the extensive grounds.

Will Rogers State Historic Park, at 14253 Sunset Boulevard in Pacific Palisades, includes the home built by the famed humorist in the 1920s. The 190-acre park has extensive hiking trails into the Santa Monica Mountains.

The Museum of Television and Radio is a recent addition to the scene; this facility is a storehouse of programs, which are presented in two theaters and made available on computers for individual listening. It is at 465 North Beverly Drive in Beverly Hills. Some materials are nearly half a century old, restored and well maintained.

Barnsdall Park, on Olive Hill at 4800 Hollywood Boulevard, is owned by the city of Los Angeles and is a major cultural center. Here stands Hollyhock House, the first California residence designed by Frank Lloyd Wright. It was built for Aline Barnsdall in 1918–20. The Arts and Crafts Building, by the same architect, was constructed about the same time. In 1927 Miss Barnsdall deeded her property to the city, and in 1954 Wright was engaged to design another building, the Municipal Arts Gallery.

LANDMARKS OF THE LOS ANGELES COUNTY COAST

Point Dume (SRL 965) was named by the English explorer George Vancouver on November 24, 1793, during his second voyage to California. He named it in honor of Father Francisco Dumetz of Mission San Buenaventura. The marker is located at Point Dume State Beach at the corner of Cliffside Drive and Birdview Avenue in Malibu.

Frederick and May Rindge acquired the Malibu Rancho in 1881, and on this land their daughter Rhonda Adamson built an exquisite beach home (SRL 966) in 1929; it is located on Malibu Lagoon State Beach at 23200 West Pacific Coast Highway. An adjoining museum traces some of the Malibu coast's history. Both are open to the public on a limited basis.

The J. Paul Getty Museum at 17985 West Pacific Coast Highway in Malibu was opened to the public in 1974. It is a replica of the Villa of the Papyri in Herculaneum, Italy, which was buried in the eruption of Mount Vesuvius in 79 A.D. A few miles inland to the east is the Getty Center, at 1200 Getty Center Drive, just north of the intersection of I-405 (San Diego Freeway) and Sunset Boulevard, at the eastern edge of the Santa Monica Mountains. Opened late in 1997, this has a second Getty Museum, a Research Institute for the History of Art and Humanities, an auditorium, and administrative offices in a beautiful complex. The Getty collection, which will ultimately be shown at both facilities, is a major cultural resource for the state.

From 1872 to 1890 the Southern Pacific Railroad enjoyed a virtual monopoly on all shipping to and from Los Angeles through the port of San Pedro. As rival rail lines were opened, Collis P. Huntington, president of the Southern Pacific, seeing his power and profits dwindling, put into operation in 1892 a plan to make Santa Monica, rather than San Pedro, the main deep-water harbor for Los Angeles. At that time, the Southern Pacific was engaged in an extensive building program to improve the San Pedro facilities. Huntington directed

that this program be abandoned and that construction begin immediately on Port Los Angeles, as he called it, at Santa Monica. The Long Wharf there was completed in 1893. Controversy raged for almost a decade over the various advantages and disadvantages of San Pedro and Port Los Angeles. After Huntington's death in 1900, the Southern Pacific lost interest in the new port and ultimately leased the wharf to an electric trolley line. By 1920 the wharf had been completely dismantled. The site of Port Los Angeles (SRL 881) has been marked at 15100 West Pacific Coast Highway in Will Rogers Beach State Park in Pacific Palisades. San Pedro remains the harbor for the city of Los Angeles to this day.

MANHATTAN BEACH

Manhattan Beach was incorporated in 1912 on lands once part of Rancho Sausal Redondo. The name was decided in a toss of the coin between two landowners, and John Merrill's "Manhattan," named for his New York home, won. The oldest cement standing pier on the West Coast is here, built in 1920; the Roundhouse on the end of the pier was built the following year. The rounded end helped the structure withstand the tides and currents of the ocean. Closed in 1989, the pier was renovated and reopened in 1992. Manhattan Beach State Pier (SRL 1018) extends into the ocean at the end of Manhattan Beach Boulevard. The Manhattan Beach Historical Society and Museum is located at 1601 Manhattan Beach Boulevard in the city.

HERMOSA BEACH

This community along the coast between Manhattan Beach to the north and Redondo Beach to the south shares some history with its neighbors. Its chief historical feature is the Municipal Pier, which extends into the ocean at the end of Pier Avenue. According to Gudde, its name (from the Spanish *hermosa*, "beautiful") was created as an advertising name. The Hermosa Beach Land and Water Company subdivided the community in 1901. The Hermosa Beach Historical Society Museum is at 710 Pier Avenue in the community center, once the Pier Avenue School.

REDONDO BEACH

Redondo Beach was one of the coastal areas that Collis P. Huntington advocated as a substitute port for San

Pedro in the 1880s. Incorporated in 1892, the city was famous in the 1890s for its Carnation Gardens and its excellent transportation system. The Redondo Hotel was a sister to the Hotel Del Coronado in San Diego, but was torn down in 1926, while the latter still flourishes. The Redondo Beach Historical Museum is located in the Queen Anne Cottage in Heritage Court at 302 Flagler Lane in Dominguez Park. The Redondo Beach Historical Society is engaged in a program of restoration of some of the community's picturesque turn-of-the-century houses.

LONG BEACH HARBOR

Long Beach Harbor has two interesting tourist attractions. The *Queen Mary*, launched in Scotland in 1936, was one of the great passenger liners in the heyday of Atlantic crossings. After World War II, when it served as a troop transport, it returned to luxury travel. Phased out by the Cunard Line, it was acquired in 1967 by the city of Long Beach, and it is now operated as a hotel, restaurant, and museum complex. Although permanently moored in the harbor, it is still the largest passenger liner afloat, and certainly one of the most handsome. The Aquarium of the Pacific opened in 1998 at 100 Aquarium Way and is another of the many large and well-designed aquariums on the Pacific Coast.

SANTA CATALINA ISLAND

Santa Catalina Island is part of Los Angeles County and is about a one-hour boat trip away from San Pedro or Long Beach. After going through several owners, the island was acquired in 1892 by the Banning brothers (Judge J. B., William, and Hancock). They formed the Santa Catalina Island Company to develop "Catalina" as a vacation resort. The company was purchased in 1919 by William Wrigley Jr., who made many improvements. He built the SS *Catalina* as a passenger ferry. It was in operation from 1924 to 1976, when it was sold to foreign interests. A marker (SRL 894) commemorates the ship at the Catalina Island museum on the ground floor of the Casino at the west end of Avalon Bay. The Casino, a popular attraction since it opened in 1929, has a theater on the lower floor and a celebrated ballroom above it. Near it, at 100 St. Catherine Way, is the Tuna Club of Avalon (SRL 997), the birthplace of modern big game sportfishing in 1898. The handsome building houses a private club.

The Santa Catalina Island Company in 1975 gave 86 percent of the island to the Catalina Island Conservancy to protect the natural environment. Eight plants native to the island are not found anywhere else in the world. The Wrigley Institute for Environmental Studies at Two Harbors is the largest activity of the only settlement on the island beyond the port at Avalon.

LANDMARKS OF DOWNTOWN LOS ANGELES

The first commercial orange grove in California was planted in 1857 by William Wolfskill on his ranch near the Pueblo of Los Angeles. For a number of years it was the largest citrus grove in the United States and yielded very heavy crops. In 1885 the owners of the ranch ceded to the Southern Pacific Railroad the site for the Arcade depot, no longer in existence, at Fifth Street and Central Avenue. Soon after, with the city rapidly expanding, the remainder of the famous orchard was sold and subdivided.

The site of the Coronel ranch house, where Helen Hunt Jackson was hospitably entertained by Antonio Coronel in the winter of 1881–82, and where she worked on her novel *Ramona*, is at Seventh and Alameda Streets.

In 1950 a marker was placed on Temple Street at the Federal Building to commemorate the centennial of the establishment of the Los Angeles post office. Two markers have been placed on the bank building at Main and Commercial Streets. One honors Southern California's first newspaper, the *Los Angeles Star* (SRL 789), founded on May 17, 1851. The site of the newspaper office is where US 101 passes beneath Los Angeles Street today; the plaque has been placed nearby on the Commercial Street side of the bank. The other marker indicates the site of the Bella Union Hotel (SRL 656), Los Angeles's pioneer hostelry, where the first Butterfield stage arrived from St. Louis on October 7, 1858. The Butterfield Overland Mail Company soon acquired the property at 145 South Spring Street and built there its Los Angeles station, one of the best equipped on the route. A plaque (SRL 744) marks the site.

The Bunker Hill district, just west of the Civic Center, was once one of the most fashionable parts of Los Angeles. One old house, the Samuel C. Foy residence, was moved to 631 South Witmer Street and divided into offices. Los Angeles's most interesting old business building is the Bradbury Building at 304 Broadway. The exterior of the five-story structure, built in 1893, is

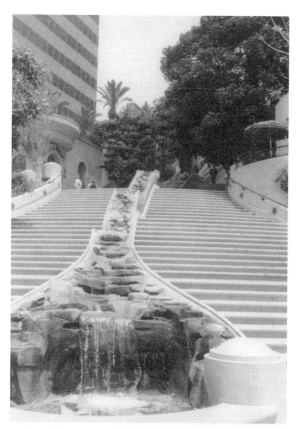
Bunker Hill Steps, Los Angeles

822) is near Lilac Terrace and Lookout Drive in the Chavez Ravine area, north of downtown.

Nearby, at 1700 Stadium Way, is the old Navy and Marine Corps Reserve Center (SRL 972); designed as the largest enclosed structure without walls in the world by California architects Robert Clements and Associates, this Art Deco building was constructed between 1938 and 1941 by the Works Projects Administration (WPA). For decades it served as the induction, training, and separation center for the Navy. It is now having a new life as the Frank Hotchkin Memorial Training Center of the Los Angeles Fire Department.

OTHER LANDMARKS IN THE CITY OF LOS ANGELES

The original building of the University of Southern California (SRL 536), opened in 1880, was moved in 1956 to Childs Way between Hoover Boulevard and University Avenue at the south end of the campus; it is now the Alumni House. In the same part of Los Angeles is the former mansion of oil magnate Edward L. Doheny, at 8 Chester Place, now part of the campus of Mount St. Mary's College. It was built in 1899–1900 and acquired by Doheny in 1901. Los Angeles was the birthplace of Adlai Stevenson, governor of Illinois, twice Democratic candidate for the presidency, and ambassador to the United Nations. He was born on February 5, 1900, at 2639 Monmouth Avenue, while his father was employed by the *Los Angeles Examiner*. The Doheny mansion and the Stevenson birthplace have been declared historic-cultural monuments by the Cultural Heritage Board.

The same board has officially recognized several old buildings at Sawtelle, the Veterans Administration Center in West Los Angeles, originally the Pacific branch of the National Home for Disabled Volunteer Soldiers. Among the oldest structures is the chapel, built about 1888.

In 1887 the State Board of Forestry established the first experimental forestry station in the United States in Rustic Canyon, Los Angeles. The station was operated by the board until 1893 and by the University of California until 1923. The site of the old Santa Monica Forestry Station (SRL 840) is near the intersection of Latimer and Hilltree Roads in Los Angeles.

El Alisal ("the place of the sycamore") was the home of Charles Fletcher Lummis from 1897 to his death in 1928. "Don Carlos" Lummis wrote and lectured vividly

undistinguished, but the interior is unique, with a covered court, open corridors, ornamental rails, and exposed elevator cages. Close by, the Grand Central Market at 317 Broadway, dating from 1917, is a thriving concern with an enormous variety of products for sale. On the Hill Street side of the market is "the world's shortest railway," the funicular Angels Flight, first erected on Bunker Hill in 1901, dismantled in 1969, and reinstalled and rebuilt in 1996, about half a block from its original location. The Bunker Hill steps begin on the north side of Sixth Street opposite the handsome Central Library, built in 1926. In the next block of Sixth Street, at the corner of Grand Avenue, is the renamed Millennium Biltmore Hotel, built in 1923.

"Little Tokyo" is a Japanese colony between Alameda and San Pedro Streets, with striking new buildings such as the Japanese American National Museum. The Latino Museum of History, Art, and Culture reflects another heritage, at 112 South Main Street. Many of the larger buildings in the downtown were built in the 1990s.

The first organized community effort by pioneer Jewish settlers of Los Angeles was the location of a burial ground from the city council in 1855. The site (SRL

174

on the Southwest, of which he was a lifelong student. From 1895 to 1910 he edited *The Land of Sunshine*, later changed to *Out West*, a magazine extolling the virtues of his adopted home. In 1894 he founded the Landmarks Club, which was largely responsible for the preservation of the old California missions at the turn of the century, and in 1902 he established the Sequoya League, which had as its goal "to make better Indians by treating them better." He and others founded the Southwest Museum in 1907, now located at 234 Museum Drive in the Highland Park section of Los Angeles, to house the collection of the Southwest Society of the Archaeological Institute of America. He was Los Angeles city librarian from 1905 to 1910. He died at El Alisal on November 25, 1928. This tribute was paid to him: "He was Southern California— he was the Great Southwest."

With his own hands, Lummis built his home of reinforced concrete, faced with river stones found on the site. Building took place from 1897 to 1910 around a giant sycamore. The original sycamores on the property have been replaced with new ones. El Alisal (SRL 531) is located at 200 East Avenue 43, near the Pasadena Freeway, and is open to the public. It is the headquarters of the Historical Society of Southern California.

La Casa de Adobe, at 4605 North Figueroa Street, part of the Southwest Museum, is a faithful and charming replica of an early California home. Built of adobe around a patio planted exclusively with shrubs and plants grown in early California gardens, it is furnished with genuine antiques of the period, most of which were provided by Hispanic and American pioneer families. It is open to the public.

Some miles south of here, at 1765 East 107th Street in the Watts district of Los Angeles, is one of California's most unusual landmarks, the Watts Towers (SRL 993). The three spires, the highest of which is 104 feet, were the work of one man from 1921 to 1954. Simon Rodia, an Italian immigrant, using only basic tools, constructed what has been called "a paramount achievement of twentieth-century folk art" of steel rods, wire mesh, seashells, broken dishes and bottles, and cement. He intended it as a tribute to his adopted land. In 1959 the towers were threatened with demolition, but a stress test proved their solidity and safety, and the city allowed them to remain. Since then, they have been declared a historic-cultural monument by the Cultural Heritage Board. Rodia left the area around 1954 and died in obscurity in Martinez in 1965 at the age of 90.

Watts, then a predominantly black area, was the site of one of the first major urban riots of the 1960s. On August 11, 1965, an angry crowd gathered as California Highway Patrol officers arrested a young black man on a drunk driving charge. After he was taken away, some members of the crowd began throwing rocks and bricks. Violence escalated over the next four days, with firebombing, looting, and much gunfire from the police and rioters. By the time the National Guard had restored order on August 15, thirty-five people had been killed, almost 1,000 seriously wounded, and more than 4,000 arrested. Damage in the fifty-square-mile area was estimated at some $46 million. Los Angeles was the scene of a second destructive outbreak, which was more widespread than the Watts one, in the spring of 1992. The news that a group of police officers who had been videotaped beating a defenseless black man, Rodney King, were cleared of all charges caused furious resentment and another outburst of destruction, some of it directed against Asian property owners and merchants, particularly in the South Central area of the city. This time the casualties amounted to more than fifty killed, over 4,000 injured, 12,000 arrests, and damage of over $1 billion.

The Los Angeles area is rich in historical museums. In addition to the ones already cited, there are the California Afro-American Museum at 600 State Drive in Exposition Park; the California Historical Society Museum at 6300 Wilshire Boulevard; the California State Museum of Science and Industry at 700 State Drive; the Wells Fargo History Museum at 444 South Flower Street; and the Santa Monica Heritage Museum at 2612 Main Street in Santa Monica.

ANGELES NATIONAL FOREST

Angeles National Forest in the San Gabriel Mountains of Los Angeles and San Bernardino counties was the first national forest in California and the second in the United States. President Benjamin Harrison set the area aside on December 20, 1892, and it was first called San Gabriel Timberland Reserve. In 1907 it became San Gabriel National Forest, and the following year it acquired its present name. The most scenic road in the forest is the Angeles Crest Highway from La Cañada to Big Pines. A historical monument commemorating the early forest preserve stands on this highway. The state marker (SRL 717) is at Angeles National Forest Headquarters at 1015 North Lake Avenue in Pasadena.

The side road to Mount Wilson and the observatory

branches from the Angeles Crest Highway at the Red Box ranger station. Just south of Red Box a dirt road leads east into the canyon of the West Fork of the San Gabriel River, where there was once a short-lived gold rush. About six miles along this road is "Old Short Cut" (SRL 632), the oldest building in the Angeles National Forest, built in 1900. The log structure was the original West Fork ranger station and is said to be the first U.S. Forest Service ranger station in the nation built with government funds. It takes its name from the Short Cut Canyon Trail, on which it is one of the main stopping points.

Several miles south and west of this spot is Tujunga, a community along Foothill Boulevard near the boundary of Angeles National Forest. This was once an incorporated city but is now a part of the city of Los Angeles. Bolton Hall, a unique building of native stone built in 1913 and at one time the Tujunga city hall, now houses the Little Landers Museum, devoted to the history of the region, at 10110 Commerce Avenue. The Little Landers were original settlers who had small holdings of property.

LANDMARKS OF SOUTHERN
LOS ANGELES COUNTY

Early in the twentieth century the city of Los Angeles acquired the water rights to the Owens Valley in Inyo County some 250 miles to the north. Under the direction of city engineer William Mulholland, an aqueduct was begun in 1905 and completed in 1913. The terminus of the aqueduct is about four miles north of San Fernando beside I-5. It is called The Cascades (SRL 653), and here water from the eastern slope of the Sierra Nevada may be seen coursing into reservoirs for the use of the metropolis. The Western Hotel in Lancaster was one place where crews were housed during the construction of the aqueduct. It was built in 1874 and still stands at 557 West Lancaster Boulevard in the Antelope Valley town (SRL 658).

The St. Francis Dam was built in 1926 as part of the same water project. Two years later, on March 12, 1928, the 185-foot-high dam broke, sending a wall of water down San Francisquito Creek and the valley of the Santa Clara River. Hundreds of homes were washed away, and nearly 500 persons were killed in one of California's worst disasters. Many had been asleep, for it was after midnight. The dam was not rebuilt. A heap of rubble marks the site (SRL 919), on the west side of

the road at 32300 San Francisquito Canyon Road outside Saugus.

On the east side of the Sierra Highway, about a mile north of its junction with I-5, is a parking area with several historical markers. Unfortunately, they have been vandalized and are nearly illegible. John C. Frémont went this way in January 1847 on his way from Santa Barbara to Los Angeles, and the crossing of the mountains became known as Frémont's Pass. In 1859 General Edward F. Beale and his men cut fifty feet of rock and earth from the gap to enable wagons to make the crossing more easily. One may still see Beale's Cut by hiking about a quarter of a mile east and north of the parking area, across a dry wash. Modern engineers consider it a remarkable feat of nineteenth-century engineering. As a passage, Frémont Pass was replaced by the Newhall Tunnel, directly west, and this, in turn, has been superseded by the present giant cut of the Antelope Valley Freeway, SR 14.

Today I-5 makes a smooth crossing of the high mountains between the Los Angeles basin and the San Joaquin Valley, but historically the Ridge Route has been a difficult one—far too steep for the railroads, and very taxing for motor vehicles. The first Ridge Route in 1915 had forty-eight miles of twisting, turning pavement between Castaic and the Grapevine in Kern County. US 99 superseded it in 1933. From time to time the motorist can see parts of the old road in driving over "The Ridge" today.

Several historic places are located in the vicinity of Newhall, in addition to the already-described "Oak of the Golden Dream" and the William S. Hart Ranch. On the Sierra Highway is the site of Lyons Station (SRL 688), an old stage stop. A small community grew up here in the 1860s; the pioneer cemetery has been expanded into Eternal Valley Memorial Park. The discovery well of the Newhall oil field, CSO-4 or Pico 4, is located in Pico Canyon west of Newhall beyond I-5 (SRL 516). It was spudded early in 1876, completed at 300 feet in September of the same year, and deepened to 600 feet still later in 1876, at which time it produced 150 barrels a day. It is the oldest continuously producing oil well in the world. The oldest oil refinery in the world and the first commercial one in California, also built in 1876, is on Pine Street just off the San Fernando Road (SRL 172).

Further down Pico Canyon is Mentryville (SRL 516.2), a town formed in the 1880s to support men working in the nearby oil fields and the Star Oil Refinery. The home of founder Charles A. Mentry still stands, along with a barn and a schoolhouse from 1885, but they are on private property and not open to the public.

The site of Lang Station is at Lang Station Road adjacent to the Union Pacific tracks, ten miles east of Saugus and at the Soledad Canyon exit of SR 14 (SRL 590). Here was driven the "last spike" that united the two sections of railroad, one coming north from Los Angeles and one coming south from San Francisco over Tehachapi Pass. With Crocker, Huntington, Stanford, and other officials in attendance, the last spike was driven on September 5, 1876. This ended the period of isolation that had kept Los Angeles "a sleepy and unprogressive town" and began the new era in which it would become one of the largest cities in the world. The old railroad station has been moved to Newhall, where it is adjacent to William S. Hart Park. It is the headquarters and museum for the Santa Clarita Valley Historical Society, and is open to the public.

The Newhall Chamber of Commerce is housed in a charming frame house at Market and Walnut Streets that goes back to 1889.

Robbers' Roost, better known as Vasquez Rocks, is an interesting geological formation on a high ridge between Soledad and Mint Canyons, northeast of Land and west of Acton. It is said that this was one of the hiding places of Tiburcio Vásquez, the most feared of all the outlaws of coastal California during the 1860s and early 1870s. He was captured in the Santa Monica foothills and taken to San Jose, where he was tried, convicted, and executed in 1875. The Vasquez Rocks lie on the great San Andreas Fault, which extends through California from the Mendocino coast to the Imperial Valley. Most of the great earthquakes in California history were centered at one spot or another along the length of this fault.

Rancho San Francisco (SRL 556), comprising 48,612 acres, was granted to Antonio del Valle in 1839. The marker stands near the junction of I-5 and SR 126, half a mile north of the site of the old rancho headquarters in Valencia. William Lewis Manly and John Rogers obtained supplies here in 1850, whereupon they returned to Death Valley to rescue their starving comrades. Rancho Camulos, to the west in Ventura County, is part of Rancho San Francisco, the site of Del Valle's beautiful adobe.

Several homes were built by Martin Ruíz and his sons in the Cañon del Buque, erroneously called "Bouquet Canyon" by General Beale and other early topographers, whose mistake persists on modern maps and road signs. It was in this region that Francisco ("Chico") López, nephew of the Francisco López who discovered gold in Placerita Canyon, pastured his cattle during the 1840s. Later one of his herdsmen, Francisco Chari, took up land here. Chari was a French sailor whom the Californians nicknamed *El Buque* ("the ship") for his many tales of the sea and the ships in which he sailed.

An old adobe stage station stood until the 1960s at 33839 San Francisquito Canyon Road, about two miles west of Green Valley. It has been torn down, but a later two-story adobe stands next to the site and is occupied. The older building may have been in use when the Butterfield stage line passed this way from 1858 to 1861.

On SR 138 in Antelope Valley is a small post office called Llano. It keeps the name of an ill-fated socialist colony, Llano del Rio, which existed in the area from 1914 to 1918 (SRL 933). The founder was Job Harriman, unsuccessful candidate for mayor of Los Angeles in 1910. He was associated with Clarence Darrow in the defense of the brothers James B. and John J. McNamara, arrested for the bombing of the *Los Angeles Times* building on October 1, 1910 during a tense period in the organization of labor. Harriman could well have been elected mayor if the McNamaras had been acquitted, but the brothers unexpectedly changed their pleas to guilty, and Harriman's political career was over. The desert colony he founded in 1914 moved to Louisiana four years later because of an insufficient water supply at the Antelope Valley site. A few ruins, notably the stone pillars and chimneys of the colony's hotel, badly vandalized, and two large cisterns stand along the highway half a mile west of the Llano post office.

La Casa del Rancho La Liebre stands on property of the Tejón Ranch Company in the northwestern corner of Los Angeles County. It is located about one-half mile south of SR 138 at a point about ten miles east of its junction with I-5 near Gorman. It stands on the floor of a small canyon known as the Cañon de las Osas ("canyon of the she-bears"). The adobe, which was built by General Edward Beale after he acquired the property in 1855, was the headquarters for his 48,000-acre Rancho La Liebre ("the jack rabbit"), a part of his vast estate of several ranchos that extended north well into Kern County. The house is strong and commodious, suggestive of the efficiency and thoroughness of its builder, and is said to have been his home for two or three years while he was Surveyor General. This region was another of the haunts of Tiburcio Vásquez.

Madera County

Wassama Roundhouse State Historic Park, Ahwahnee

Madera County contains the geographical center of California. It was organized from a part of Fresno County in 1853. Madera is Spanish for "wood" or "timber." It was given the same name as its principal town, Madera, which was made the county seat. Although most of the county's population is found in the San Joaquin Valley, the county extends far east and north into the High Sierra.

OLD TRAILS IN MADERA COUNTY

It is unlikely that many of the early Spanish expeditions entered the confines of Madera County, and no Spanish settlements were ever made there. This isolation was due, first of all, to the fact that it was practically impossible to penetrate the tulares from the west or to cross the sloughs that covered the whole central portion of the San Joaquin Valley at high water. In addition to this general inaccessibility, the streams throughout the area of the county were little more than dry, sandy washes except during and immediately after a heavy rainfall. Furthermore, the water holes along the foothills of Madera County were few compared with the broad, perennial streams to the north and south. For many years these conditions discouraged both exploration and settlement.

This natural barrier is described by F. F. Latta:

> Between Martinez on the north and San Emigdio, two hundred and fifty miles to the south, there were only two places where the San Joaquin Valley could be crossed from east to west except at time of low water. Throughout the course of the San Joaquin River and bordering the lakes to the south was an impenetrable sea of tule, sloughs, mud flats, and water, which, until as late as 1880, was passable only at these same places. When Tulare

Lake was below the extreme high water mark, the sand ridge which crossed it from east to west formed a bridge over which we know the Spanish crossed. The other point at which they were able to cross during time of high water was at the head of Fresno Slough near the present town of Tranquillity.

There is evidence, however, that the Pico expedition to the San Joaquin and Kings rivers in 1825–26 entered Madera County, crossing the rivers on tule rafts. Monte Redondo, a large grove of cottonwood trees near the Fresno River about seven miles west of Madera, seems to have been known to people on the coast as early as 1825.

Jedediah Strong Smith passed through what is now Madera County in 1827 and again in 1828. He was soon followed by Hudson's Bay Company trappers and later by Ewing Young, Kit Carson, and other Americans, who followed the trail of the beaver along the numerous streams that come down from the High Sierra on the eastern side of the valley.

The first definite record that we have of a trail across Madera County is that left by John C. Frémont on April 4–6, 1844. By means of rafts the party ferried Bear Creek (in Merced County) and then proceeded southward, their progress being greatly impeded by the numerous sloughs of this section. Continuing up the San Joaquin River, they passed "elk . . . running in bands over the prairie, and . . . along the left bank . . . immense droves of wild horses." Camp was made on the San Joaquin River on the 4th and 5th. On the 6th the party crossed the San Joaquin at Gravelly Ford, west of where SR 145 today crosses the river.

The Millerton or Stockton–Los Angeles Road, the only north and south route that passed through Madera County during the 1850s and 1860s, ran along the base of the foothills, crossing the Chowchilla River at the Home Ranch a little west of where the Merced-Mariposa county line intersects the Mariposa-Madera county line. The San Joaquin River was crossed at Millerton by means of the Converse Ferry, which fell into disuse after the building of the railroad.

Most of the miners at Coarsegold and other mining centers in Madera County migrated south from Mariposa County. Others came from Gilroy via Pacheco Pass, crossed the San Joaquin River just south of the mouth of the Fresno River, and from there proceeded to the Sierra Nevada mines. Alexis Godey, famous plainsman and guide to Frémont, operated a ferry at this point for a short time during the early 1850s.

In the late 1870s a stage road from Madera to the Yosemite Valley was constructed, passing through Bates Station, Kelshaw Corners, Coarsegold, Fresno Flats, Fish Camp, and Clark's Station (Wawona).

The Madera and Mammoth Trail is also known as the French Trail after its promoter, John French, who sought a better route to his mining interests in the Mammoth area. Biweekly trips from Fresno Flats (Oakhurst) to Mammoth City were started about 1880; the travelers were met at the stagecoach and continued the trip to Mammoth by saddle train. The French Trail proper began at the ranch of Jesse B. Ross, who settled there about 1858. Between 1910 and 1930 the property was owned by Samuel L. Hogue and has continued to be owned by the Foster family since then; the local name for it is Foster's Hogue Ranch. It is located on Mammoth Pool Road (Road 235), about four miles southeast of North Fork. The log house built by Jesse Ross in 1860 still stands. The property is famous for the apple orchards planted by consecutive owners. Four miles farther down Road 225 from the ranch is the marker on a hillside indicating the geographical center of the state of California. It is accessible by a short hike from the roadside.

HISTORIC INDIAN LOCATIONS IN MADERA COUNTY

About ten miles northeast of Madera on the River Road is the Adobe Ranch, the site of the old Fresno Indian Reservation established in the early 1850s. This was briefly in existence in the years when the presence of gold miners in the Sierra foothills caused great resentment among the local Indian tribes, who were for some time at war with the newcomers.

Wassama State Historic Park consists of several acres of land on SR 49 at the north edge of the town of Ah-wahnee. An Indian roundhouse was built here in 1893; subsequently burned, it was rebuilt by Miwok tribesmen in 1901. After many years of use, the house collapsed in 1978, the year in which the State Department of Parks and Recreation acquired the property. The newly reconstructed roundhouse (SRL 1001) was dedicated in 1985. The Indian school nearby is a visitors' center. A twenty-hole grinding rock is on display. The area remains an Indian communal and religious center.

The Sierra Mono Museum at North Fork is entirely operated by Mono Indians and is dedicated to the preservation of their heritage and culture; it is located where Roads 225, 228, and 274 converge in the middle of the village.

THE SAVAGE MONUMENT

Major James D. Savage arrived in California in 1846 and became active in the southern mines, where he operated at least four trading posts between 1848 and 1852. The first (SRL 527) was on the South Fork of the Merced River in Mariposa County; this was abandoned when war began with the Yosemite Indians in 1850. A second post was established at Agua Fria Creek, near the site of Buckeye, while a branch station was started on the Fresno River near Fresno Flats, now Oakhurst. The last post of Major Savage was near Fresno Crossing.

Savage was a colorful figure with a remarkable relationship with the Indians—tradition gives him as many as thirty-three concubines—and he became a local leader during the troubles known as the Mariposa War in 1851. Commissioned by the state to pacify warlike Indians in the foothills, he pursued them into the Yosemite Valley, thus becoming the second white leader (after Joseph R. Walker and his party) to visit the scenic valley. It was partly because of his efforts that the Mariposa War was ended by a treaty in 1851. Plans to settle recalcitrant Indians on the Fresno Reservation were largely ineffectual, however, and that institution ceased to exist in 1859. Meanwhile, Savage had been instrumental in the establishment of the new government of Tulare County in 1852; later that year, he was killed in a quarrel with a law-enforcement official whom he accused of attacking innocent Indians. A shaft of Vermont granite was placed above his gravesite at Fresno Crossing; the marker and Savage's remains were removed when the site was inundated in 1971 by the construction of Hidden Dam and Hensley Lake. The restored monument now overlooks the eastern shore of the lake, about eighteen miles northeast of Madera.

Extending from the northwest to the southeast throughout Madera County, the Mother Lode is marked by the shafts and tunnels of old mines and the sites of onetime mining camps. Before the quartz ledges were opened up in the 1870s and 1880s, however, placer mining began. As early as 1849 settlements sprang up in flats and ravines and along the bars of the San Joaquin and Fresno Rivers.

Among the early prosperous placer-mining camps, Coarsegold (at first known as Texas Flat) was the largest in Madera County. There in 1849 five Texans found diggings on the creek where sand yielded particles of gold so coarse that the stream was named Coarsegold Creek. Many fortunes were taken from the surrounding hills, and the settlement grew rapidly.

Other placer-mining centers quickly developed: Grub Gulch, six miles northwest, and Fresno Flats (now Oakhurst), seven miles northeast of Coarsegold; Fine Gold, about six miles southeast near Mountain View Peak; Temperance Flat, on the San Joaquin River four miles east of Fine Gold Gulch; Cassidy's Bar, also on the San Joaquin River in the vicinity of Fort Miller; Soldier Bar; and Rootville. These made up a round of lively little camps that, during the 1850s, comprised a small but rich mining district. However, little trace of them is left today.

Throughout this section of the Mother Lode a number of quartz mines likewise earned records as big producers during the 1870s and 1880s. The old mining camp of Coarsegold was located at the confluence of Coarsegold Gulch and Deadwood Gulch, thirty-two miles northeast of Madera. Radiating from it in all directions were quartz mines, traces of some of which remain today: the Texas Flat Mine, one mile to the northwest, and Topp's Mine (located in 1880), three miles north; the D'Or de Quartz, four and a half miles south; the Five Oaks, one and a half miles southeast; the Waterloo, a mile and a half farther on; and Last Chance, located in 1880, five miles by road from Coarsegold.

At the Grub Gulch camp the Josephine Mine (1880) and the Gambetta (which included the Arkansas Traveler Claim) were located, while two miles to the northeast was the Enterprise Mine.

Other mines located in the Potter Ridge District east of Grub Gulch included the Flying Dutchman, the Crystal Spring, the Rattlesnake, the King's Gulch, and the Victoria. The Potter Ridge Mine was two miles southwest of Fresno Flats.

The Hildreth Mining District was named after Tom Hildreth and his brother, who operated butcher shops in various Sierra mining camps and ranged their cattle on Madera County foothills. The district, extending ten miles or so northward from the mouth of Fine Gold Creek (which was three miles northeast of old Fort Miller and is now inundated by Millerton Lake), was located in the southern part of the county. Fine Gold Gulch was the western and northern boundary line of the section. Here were the Abbey Mine, a quarter of a mile east of the small camp of Hildreth; the Morrow Mine, located in 1881, in the same section and township as the Abbey Mine; the Hanover; the Golconda; and the Standard. One mile east of Fine Gold, too, was the Mountain View Mine, located in 1880 in the vicinity of Mountain View Peak.

During the 1860s, while copper excitement was at its height in California, a few copper mines were developed in the foothills of Madera County ten or so miles southwest of Raymond. Two located on the Daulton Ranch, the Ne Plus Ultra and the Jesse Bell, were especially productive, but after World War II the fall in copper prices brought an end to mining. There was a brief revival of activity around 1960.

OAKHURST

Oakhurst is the largest community in the mining area of Madera County today. It keeps alive memories of early days with an annual celebration and an outdoor museum, the Fresno Flats Historical Park. The exhibition contains old buildings from various parts of the county and an interesting display of old wagons; it is located on School Road (Road 427), just off Crane Valley Road (Road 426) near the center of the town. Oakhurst is also the southern terminus of one of California's principal highways, fittingly numbered SR 49, which goes north from here through the old towns of the mining days and ends at Vinton in Plumas County.

MADERA

With the construction of the railroad in 1870 an increasing demand came from the East for lumber from the great sugar pine forests of the Sierra Nevada. Some trade developed also in yellow pine, fir, cedar, and other woods. Quick transit from the mountains to the railroad was accomplished by the construction of a V-shaped flume sixty inches wide and sixty-three miles in length running from the Soquel Basin down into the

Laramore-Lyman House, Fresno Flats Historical Park, Oakhurst

Madera County Courthouse Museum

valley. This flume, built in 1874 at a cost of half a million dollars and later extended as far as Sugar Pine, carried countless millions of feet of lumber annually from the higher mountains to the railroad. The Sugar Pine Lumber Company and the Madera Sugar Pine Company, with a monthly payroll of $140,000, employed from 900 to 1,000 men. A section of the flume is displayed at the Fresno Flats Historical Park in Oakhurst.

A settlement grew up at the lower end of the flume where it terminated near the Central Pacific Railroad on the south side of the Fresno River. There in 1876 the California Lumber Company laid out the town of Madera. When the county was created in 1893, the same name was chosen for it, and the city of Madera became the county seat.

The majestic old Madera County courthouse, constructed in 1900 of granite blocks at 210 West Yosemite Avenue, is now the Museum of the Madera County Historical Society. A distinctive feature of the museum, which has many re-creations of rooms and activities from the past, is a photographic collection on the history of Madera County.

BORDEN

The little town of Borden (originally known as the "Alabama Settlement") was the center for a thriving agricultural community before the towns of Madera and Fresno even came into existence. Located about three miles southeast of where Madera would later be founded, it was the earliest farm center in this part of the valley, having been founded in 1868–69 by families from Alabama. It took its name from community leader Dr. James Borden. By 1873, Borden had become a promising settlement, with two hotels, two stores, and other buildings, as well as aspirations to become the county seat. A

decline set in within the next decade, however, and the only remnant of the town is the old Chinese cemetery, immediately to the west of the settlement, a reminder of the Chinese laborers who built the Central Pacific Railroad through the San Joaquin Valley.

THE BIG TREES

There is but one living group of *Sequoia gigantea* in Madera County, and that is the Nelder Grove Historic Area within the Sierra National Forest, about five miles south of the Mariposa Grove and just east of Sugar Pine. Partly cut over during the years 1888–90, it is now covered with a fine second growth. At first called the Fresno Grove, it was renamed for John A. Nelder, who had a cabin there in the 1870s. A Sierra National Forest campground is nearby.

DEVILS POSTPILE NATIONAL MONUMENT

Devils Postpile is a spectacular mass of basaltic columns like an immense pile of posts—one late nineteenth-century account refers to it as the Devil's Woodpile. These columns vary in size from ten to thirty inches in diameter and in some cases stand as high as sixty feet. In shape they are irregular polygons with from three to seven sides each but all closely and perfectly fitted together like a vast mosaic.

The group is located near the place where the old Mammoth or French Trail from Fresno Flats (Oakhurst) to Mammoth Lakes crosses the Middle Fork of the San Joaquin River. By car, it is accessible only from the eastern side of the Sierra, through Mammoth in Mono County, where SR 203 crosses Minaret Summit and continues west into the canyon of the Middle Fork of the San Joaquin. The Postpile is reached by a four-tenths-of-a-mile footpath from the parking area and ranger station.

Early Californians often regarded geological oddities as being of Satanic origin, and some 150 California place-names (such as Devil's Den in Kern County and the Devil's Cornfield in Death Valley) reflect this feeling. Virtually nothing is known to have been written about Devils Postpile before 1895, although the region was included in the original area of Yosemite National Park in 1890. In 1905, Congress returned some 500 square miles of land, including the Postpile, to the public domain. In 1910, a plan was made to dynamite the Postpile into the nearby San Joaquin River to form a rock-fill dam. Walter Huber of the U.S. Forest Service and members of the Sierra Club were alarmed at this proposal, and their efforts resulted in the creation of Devils Postpile National Monument, proclaimed by President William Howard Taft in 1911, under the authority of the Act for the Preservation of American Antiquities of 1906. It is a unique sight in California and a global rarity, of which perhaps only the Giant's Causeway, along the coast of Northern Ireland, is an equal.

Marin County

Golden Gate Bridge from Fort Baker

Marin County was one of the original twenty-seven counties. San Rafael has always been the county seat. "Marin" probably comes from the Spanish *Marinera* (variously translated as "mariners," "sailors," or "seafarers"). Lieutenant Juan de Ayala, who in 1775 led a reconnoitering expedition around the shores of San Francisco Bay, gave to present-day San Rafael Bay the name of La Bahia de Nuestra Señora Rosario de la Marinera ("Bay of Our Lady of the Mariner's Rosary"). Two small islands in the bay were listed on early maps as Ysla de la Marinera, and a map from 1850 called them the Marin Islands. It is also thought that the name may have come from "El Marinero," the name of a Christian Indian ferryman. Historian Jack Mason, however, writes that "the county is named for an Indian chief who gave California nothing but trouble. Chief Marin, captured by the Spaniards at Bodega in 1817, was sent to Yerba Buena for safekeeping, but escaped to harass the whites for nine more years, . . . [dying] in captivity in 1834."

THE INDIAN PAST

The Coast Miwok Indians lived in Marin County. Many shell mounds have been found by San Francisco and San Rafael Bays as well as on the shores of Bolinas and Tomales Bays—over two hundred throughout the county. Although all of the mounds have been leveled, their contents, such as arrow heads, beads, and utensils, have been placed in several Bay Area museums. When ground was leveled at Hamilton Air Force Base, the razing of two mounds revealed stone and shell ornaments and conical polished stones pierced at one end and believed to be ceremonial pieces used by a medicine man or possibly the insignia of a chief. An excavation at Fourth and Irwin Streets in San Rafael found the skeleton of a chief decorated with strings of stone beads and ornaments made of abalone and other shells.

In the Drakes Bay region, mounds going back to the sixteenth century that contain European and Oriental material from visiting or wrecked ships have been explored by University of California archaeologists and members of the Drake Navigators Guild.

The Miwok Archaeological Preserve at 2255 Las Gallinas Avenue in Marinwood includes the area where several shell mounds were found along Miller Creek. The Marin Museum of the American Indian at 2200 Novato Boulevard in Novato is at the site of a Coast Miwok settlement and contains displays of local artifacts.

FRANCIS DRAKE AND NOVA ALBION

Francis Drake set out from England late in 1577 in command of five ships; his purpose was to probe the defenses of the Spanish New World. The voyage turned into a plundering expedition, and Drake, having aroused the anger of the Spaniards, was compelled to round Cape Horn and enter the vast Pacific Ocean. His ship, the *Pelican*, renamed the *Golden Hind* later in the voyage, was the only one to return to England, in 1580, thus making the first known circumnavigation of the globe by one ship under the same commander. This much is agreed upon—what follows is conjectural.

The ship's log disappeared some time after 1580. The first published account of the voyage was an addition to an earlier work of 1589, Richard Hakluyt's *Principal Navigations, Voyages and Discoveries of the English Nation*, in which there was no mention of Drake. These pages included excerpts from the diary of Francis Fletcher, chaplain of the expedition; this diary no longer exists. Drake's nephew, also named Francis Drake, wrote *The World Encompassed by Sir Francis Drake*, published in 1628, which is full of material, some of which scholars think to be either contradictory or a fabrication. Nonetheless, it is a source of a persistent California legend.

Heading north along the California coast in 1579, the ship encountered thick fogs and severe cold, and turned back to the south, where "we fell with a convenient and fit harborough, and June 17 came to anchor therein, where we continued till the 23 day of July following." The dates are those of the Julian Calendar; June 17 would be June 28 by today's reckoning. At the landing the ship was reconditioned and contact was made with the local Indians, who were apparently impressed by their white visitors. Word of the strange arrival went through the countryside and each day more and more natives visited the harbor. About a week after their landing, the Englishmen saw on the beach a great number of people with their chieftain.

On this occasion the natives placed a kind of crown upon Drake's head. Drake's nephew reported that they

> in-riched his neck with all their chains, and offering unto him many other things, honored him by the name of 'Hyoh.' Adding thereunto (as it might seeme) a song and dance of triumph; because they were not onely visited of the gods (for so they judged us to be), but the great and chiefe God was now become their God, their king and patron, and themselves the onely happie and blessed people in the world.

Some days later, Drake with a large company of men journeyed on land and found "a goodly country and fruitfull soyle, stored with many blessings fit for the use of man." The account continues:

> This country our Generall named *Albion*, and that for two causes; the one is respect of the white bancks and cliffes, which lie toward the sea; the other, that it might have some affinity, even in name also, with our own country, which was sometimes so called. . . . Before we went from thence, our Generall caused to be set up a monument of our being there, and also of her maiesties and successors right and title to that kingdom; namely, a plate of brasse, fast nailed to a great firme post; whereon is engraven her graces name, and the day and yeare of our arrival there, and of the free giving up of the province and kingdom, both by the king and people, into her maiesties hands: together with her highnesse picture and armes, in a piece of sixpence currant English monie, shewing itselfe by a hole made of purpose through the plate; underneath was likewise engrven the name of our Generall, etc.

Just where did Drake make his anchorage? Probably no other question in California history has been so extensively debated. The Drake Navigators Guild has made an impressive case for Drakes Estero, an inlet just inside Point Reyes on Drakes Bay, and in 1916 the Sir Francis Drake Association of California placed a marker at that spot. E Clampus Vitus has also marked the place, now at the Visitors Center at Drakes Bay. The white cliffs in the citation above make a good case for Drakes Estero. Yet some other places fit the description made by Fletcher, who noted that the landing was close to the 38th parallel. Bodega Bay and San Francisco Bay have their champions. Partly because Fletcher took the trouble to transcribe some of the Indian words in his journal, many believe that the Indians in question were Coast Miwok.

In 1936 the riddle of Drake's sojourn received new attention when a plate like that described in the narrative was picked up by Beryle Shinn when he stopped his car near Greenbrae. The discovery was made public at a meeting of the California Historical Society in the Sir Francis Drake Hotel in San Francisco on April 6, 1937. Careful study of the plate was made by the eminent historian Herbert Eugene Bolton, of the University of California at Berkeley, and others, and after scientific tests the plate was declared to be authentic. The brass plate, now the property of the University of California, is displayed at the Bancroft Library on the Berkeley campus. It is eight inches wide, five inches high, and about one-eighths of an inch thick; there are square holes at top and bottom to admit the nails that presumably held it to the post. A jagged hole in the lower right corner is about the size of an Elizabethan sixpence. This is the text of the plate:

BEE IT KNOWNE VNTO ALL MEN BY THESE PRESENTS

IVNE 17 1579

BY THE GRACE OF GOD AND IN THE NAME OF HERR

MAIESTY QVEEN ELIZABETH OF ENGLAND AND HERR

SVCCESSORS FOREVER I TAKE POSSESSION OF THIS

KINGDOME WHOSE KING AND PEOPLE FREELY RESIGNE

THEIR RIGHT AND TITLE IN THE WHOLE LAND VNTO HERR

MAIESTIES KEEPING NOW NAMED BY ME AN TO BEE

KNOWN VNTO ALL MEN AS NOVA ALBION.

FRANCIS DRAKE

There continued to be skepticism about the authenticity of the plate, and as the quadricentennial of the Drake landing approached in the 1970s, further tests were ordered by the Bancroft Library authorities. Professor Thomas G. Barnes of the Department of History at the University of California at Berkeley had misgivings about the wording and lettering of the plate, as did colleagues from the Folger Shakespeare Library in Washington, D.C. Metallurgical tests were ordered from the Research Laboratory for Archaeology at Oxford University; the Chemistry Division of the Lawrence Berkeley Laboratory, under Dr. Helen V. Michel and Dr. Frank Asano; and Dr. Cyril Stanley Smith, professor emeritus of the Massachusetts Institute of Technology.

Meanwhile, another scholar, Harvard professor Samuel Eliot Morison, in *The European Discovery of America: The Southern Voyages* (1974), dismissed the plate as "a hoax perpetrated by some collegiate joker." In July 1977, James D. Hart, director of the Bancroft Library, presented the findings of the investigating groups to the public. The Lawrence Laboratory team declared that for the metal in the plate, "the most probable period is the late nineteenth and early twentieth centur-

ies," a finding more or less corroborated by the other scientists. Hart noted that not everyone would accept these findings as conclusive, and within a year a spirited defense of the authenticity of the plate by Drake scholar Robert H. Power appeared in *California History*. Since the perpetrator of the hoax, if hoax it is, has yet to appear, another puzzle has been added to the Drake story. (The ubiquitous "Sir" Francis Drake nomenclature in the Bay Area is a historical anomaly, by the way, since Drake was not knighted until after his return to England in September 1580.)

The Prayerbook Cross in San Francisco's Golden Gate Park commemorates the religious services held by Chaplain Fletcher on California soil in 1579. Fletcher's prayer book is a cherished possession of Grace Cathedral (Episcopal) in San Francisco.

SEBASTIÁN CERMEÑO

In 1594 King Philip II of Spain and Portugal ordered an exploration of the northwestern coast of North America. The viceroy of New Spain commissioned Sebastián Rodríguez Cermeño, a Portuguese, to take a ship to the Philippines, fill it with Oriental treasure, explore the northern coasts, and then return to Acapulco. On November 4, 1595, the *San Agustín*, a Manila galleon that Cermeño had filled with merchandise, arrived off the California coast at about 41° latitude. Three days later, the ship entered Drakes Bay, where it was wrecked by a storm; Cermeño and his men were forced to proceed in a launch they had constructed there as an auxiliary boat. They did not report any signs of Drake's visit there sixteen years before (if indeed this had been the site of Drake's landing). Before sailing, they explored inland a distance of four leagues and found several rancherias of Indians from whom they obtained acorns for food. Cermeño named the harbor the "Bay of San Francisco," a name that for many years caused great confusion among historians, since the name after 1769 was that of the great inland sea to the south.

MISSION SAN RAFAEL ARCÁNGEL

At Mission Dolores in San Francisco in the early nineteenth century, the mortality rate of the Indians became alarmingly high. It was suggested that some of the neophytes be sent across the bay to what was perhaps a healthier climate. A trial move proved the wisdom of the proposal, and it was decided to establish there a kind of rancho with chapel, baptistry, and cemetery.

Mission San Rafael

The name San Rafael Arcángel was chosen in order that the angel "who in his name expresses the 'healing of God' might care for bodies as well as souls." The mission was founded on December 14, 1817, on a spot called by the Indians "Nanaguani."

An adobe building seventy-nine feet long, thirty-eight feet wide, and sixteen feet high was built and divided by partitions into a chapel, padres' quarters, and other required apartments. San Rafael was at first only an *asistencia* to Mission Dolores, but by 1823 it had become self-supporting. Although there is no record that it was raised to the position of an independent mission, all the reports of the fathers refer to it as such, and it is so considered by historians. Father Juan Amorós, known for the zeal with which he undertook every task, served as missionary there from 1819 to his death in 1832. During this period the mission attained its maximum strength, although the French mariner August Duhaut-Cilly, passing within sight of it on his way to Sonoma in 1827, did not "deem this poor establishment worth stopping at for purposes of trade." Two years after the death of Father Amorós came secularization, and Ignacio Martínez, a distinguished military officer retired since 1831, was made *comisionado*. For two years he managed the affairs of San Rafael and established the boundaries of the pueblo that grew next to the mission.

The long, low adobe structure of San Rafael was much plainer and simpler than most of the mission structures. Old pictures show that the bells were hung in a wooden frame placed outside the chapel entrance. After secularization the neglected walls melted away, and no sign of them now remains. On the site of the chapel (SRL 220) at 1104 Fifth Avenue in San Rafael stands the present St. Raphael's Catholic Church. A replica of the mission was built nearby in 1949, one wing of which is used as the mission museum.

The Mission San Rafael rancho, consisting of sixteen square leagues, was sold by Governor Pico in 1846 to Antonio Suñol, of the San Jose Council, and Antonio María Pico, but they failed to get possession during the period of American takeover and their title was later declared invalid. In 1859 Bishop J. S. Alemany obtained patent for something over six acres of land for the church.

THE MISSION EMBARCADERO AND THE CITY OF SAN RAFAEL

The farthest inland meanderings of the Estero San Rafael are now lost beneath the streets of San Rafael. On A Street at Third is the probable site of the mission embarcadero. This was the scene of a tragic episode in the Bear Flag Rebellion. John C. Frémont and his men had arrived at the buildings of Mission San Rafael on June 26, 1846, just after the "battle" at Olompali (discussed in the Novato section of this chapter). Searching for the murderers of the Bear Flaggers, Frémont was advised that on the Contra Costa side of the Bay a Californian army under General Castro was planning further resistance to the American conquest. On June 28 a boat landed at the embarcadero, and three men climbed out and headed for the mission. Frémont seems to have assumed that they were Castro supporters carrying messages to Castro's aides in Marin County. He ordered Kit Carson to intercept the travelers and (according to one account) casually mentioned that "we have no time for prisoners." Carson and his men coolly shot the men down. Those killed were Don José de los Reyes Berryessa of Rancho San Vicente near Santa Clara (who was on his way to see his imprisoned son, the alcalde of Sonoma) and his twin sixteen-year-old nephews, Francisco and Ramón, sons of Don Francisco de Haro, former alcalde of San Francisco. For many years a white cross marked the site of this senseless murder.

The oldest part of the city of San Rafael lies west of a line drawn between the site of the mission and that of the mission embarcadero. At the northwest corner of Fourth and C Streets stood the adobe residence of Don Timoteo Murphy, started in 1839. Murphy had arrived in California in 1828 to supervise the packing and exporting of beef for Hartnell and Company in Monterey. General Mariano Vallejo befriended him (at one point he was being considered as a possible brother-in-law) and made him administrator of the secularized Mission San Rafael in 1837. The alcaldes transacted their official business in the old mission building until 1850, about the date when freight ceased to be landed at the embarcadero. The seat of justice was transferred to Murphy's house upon his death in 1853 and remained there until the Marin County Courthouse was built in 1872. The principal official functions of the county were transferred to the Marin County Civic Center (SRL 999) when the old courthouse burned in 1971. The Civic Center, designed by Frank Lloyd Wright, was the last principal work of the American master; its first unit was completed in 1962, the year after Wright's death.

The visually impressive Civic Center was the scene of a second bloodletting in San Rafael. On August 7, 1970, the courtroom of Judge Harold J. Haley was taken over by gunmen who forced the judge and four hostages from the courtroom in an attempt to liberate a San Quentin convict who was being tried before the judge for the stabbing of a prison guard. The escape van was fired on, and in the melee the judge, the defendant James McClain, and two gunmen, Arthur Christmas and Jonathan Jackson, were killed. Two hostages were wounded.

William T. Coleman, chosen leader of the San Francisco Vigilantes in 1856, had extensive interests in Marin County. He was one of the planners of the Mechanics Institute Library in San Rafael. His home, built in 1852, still stands at 1130 Mission Avenue, one of the first frame buildings in the city. The old mission spring is in Boyd Park, given by the shipping magnate Robert Dollar to the city of San Rafael. Dollar's mansion, built in 1879, at 1408 Mission Avenue is now the Falkirk Cultural Center. At the entrance to Boyd Park at 1125 B Street is the Marin County Historical Society Museum, housed in a building that began as a guest house on the Ira Cook estate in 1879 and was moved here in 1924.

Fifteen historic buildings on Fourth Street have been marked with appropriate plaques by the Downtown Art Center, the Marin County Historical Society, Marin Heritage, and the San Rafael Cultural Affairs Commission. Several houses were built in the city by convict labor in 1859 and 1860, when prisoners were hired under contract to the firm of Sims and McCauley. Two of these houses were on the public square; one was used as a pharmacy by Dr. Alfred Taliaferro and stands at 1221 Fourth Street. Across the street at 1222 is the other, the brick Marin Hotel, dating from 1859.

Just north of the center of modern San Rafael is the area that was once Rancho San Pedro, Santa Margarita y las Gallinas ("the hens"), granted in 1844 by Governor Micheltorena to Timoteo Murphy. On his deathbed in 1853 Don Timoteo deeded 317 acres of the rancho to Bishop Alemany for the foundation of a school. In 1855 the Sisters of Charity of St. Vincent de Paul established what is now St. Vincent's School for Boys (SRL 630). The beautifully landscaped grounds are approached on a long eucalyptus-lined avenue east of the Redwood Highway about one mile north of the Marin County Civic Center complex.

Dominican College occupies a large and beautiful tract northeast of the center of San Rafael. The Dominican Sisters, originally from Paris, first located on the West Coast at Monterey in 1851. From Monterey they moved to Benicia in Solano County, where Concepción Argüello became their first native-born novice. From Benicia they moved to San Rafael, where their convent was established in 1889. In 1950 the convent became a women's liberal arts college; it began to admit men in 1971. The old convent burned in 1990 and has been replaced by a modern structure. By gifts and by purchase the sisters acquired property that belonged to prominent early-day families. Forest Meadows, the outdoor auditorium, is on land that was owned by William T. Coleman; Meadowlands, the dormitory on Palm Avenue, was the country home of the M. H. de Young family of San Francisco. On the same avenue is the home formerly owned by William Babcock, also of San Francisco. His widow gave this completely furnished home to the college.

SAN QUENTIN

Point San Quentin is named for the Indian companion of Chief Marin. General Mariano Vallejo was impressed by the navigational skills of Quintin, as he was then known, and employed him to command his best lighter operating on Sonoma Creek. Vallejo, according to Jack Mason, "thought newcomers to California added the 'San' to Quintin's name theorizing that all local inhabitants were 'zealous Catholics.' The change in spelling to Quentin came at the same time." The Rancho Punta de Quentín took its name from this headland. It extended inland to Larkspur at its southern line and San Anselmo at its northern. The grant was first made in 1840 to Juan Bautista Cooper, who had owned other ranchos in the state, none of them for very long.

On the eastern part of this rancho at the edge of the bay stands San Quentin Prison, begun in 1853. Before it was built the state's convicted criminals were confined on hulks of ships anchored off Angel Island. It stands on the site of the projected but never-built Marion City. Until the Richmond–San Rafael Bridge was completed in 1956, ferry service was maintained between Point San Quentin and Richmond in Contra Costa County. Near the entrance to the prison is the San Quentin Museum, with displays tracing the history of the prison.

SAN ANSELMO AND FAIRFAX

These cities lie on the grounds of Rancho Cañada de Herrera ("vale of the blacksmith") or La Providencia, granted by acting governor Manuel Jimeno to Domingo Sais in 1839. Dr. Alfred Taliaferro, a skilled surgeon and physician, had come to Marin County in 1849 with a group of young men from Virginia. While wandering one day up San Anselmo Valley he "came upon a tract of parklike land, shaded by ancient trees with a sparkling stream of water running through it." He at once began negotiations for its purchase. When Don Diego learned that he wanted only forty acres, he said: "It is worth forty acres to us to have a good neighbor. Select your forty acres, we give it to you thankfully." The doctor fenced in his land and built a spacious house on the bank of the "sparkling stream" (Corte Madera Creek), cleared a considerable area of brush, built outbuildings, and settled into the life of a gentleman, as his forebears had done in Virginia. The abundance of wild game and his unstinting hospitality at once made the place popular with his sportsman friends.

Among the visitors in 1856 were Charles S. Fairfax and his wife. Fairfax was descended from English barons of that name, and his wife was famous for her wit and beauty. The couple became fascinated with the place. Some sort of arrangement was made; they took over the property, and Dr. Taliaferro remained as their permanent guest. Fairfax, in later years always called "Lord Fairfax" because of his ancestry, had come in 1849 at age twenty from Fairfax County in Virginia and had spent his first winter in a cabin near Grass Valley. A young man of good education and pleasant bearing, he became a member of the state Assembly from Yuba County in 1853 and in 1856 was clerk of the state Supreme Court, a position he held for five years.

The Fairfax home (SRL 679) was located not far from the present business district of Fairfax. Presided over by the gracious Mrs. Fairfax, it became a center of the social life of the period, where notables of the state and nation were entertained. Here also occurred the last politically motivated duel in California history.

A luncheon party had gathered at the house on May 21, 1861, the day following the close of the session of the state Legislature, where hot political debate had re-

sulted in a challenge to a duel. The prompt action of an official at that time had prevented the duel from taking place, and the principals, their seconds, and the surgeon had gone to the house of "Lord Fairfax," where their host attempted a reconciliation. The antagonists, Daniel Showalter of Kentucky and Charles W. Piercy of Illinois, had crossed the continent in the same small company some years before but on arriving in California had gone different ways. They had met again as members of the Legislature in the opposing Breckinridge and Douglas factions of the Democratic Party. After the luncheon, when all hope of preventing the conflict was abandoned, the hour of three o'clock was set for the duel. Following the first exchange of shots, in which neither man had been injured, Fairfax again attempted to pacify the hot-tempered men, but without success. On resuming their positions and firing, Piercy was killed instantly. Showalter, at once filled with remorse, begged the surgeon to save his opponent. Leaving California thereafter to join the Confederate Army, he was captured by the Union army and imprisoned.

In May 1868 the heirs of Domingo Sais deeded this forty-acre tract to the Fairfaxes. In that year Charles Fairfax was made chairman of the California delegation to the Democratic National Convention in New York. He attended the convention and died the following year in Baltimore. After his death the property became the restaurant of Madame Adele Pastori, who, on the decline of her career in Italian opera, came here with her husband, a theatrical director. Her attractive personality and the fine table set by her husband soon drew many artists from San Francisco. This wooded spot was for many years in the twentieth century the Marin Town and Country Club; it is now privately owned.

The San Francisco Theological Seminary, now located at 2 Kensington Court in San Anselmo, began as the dream of William Anderson Scott, D.D., who arrived in San Francisco in 1854 from Tennessee. He envisioned a training center on the coast for the Presbyterian ministry, and began his school in San Francisco. It moved three times, the last time, in 1877, to a building that still stands at 121 Haight Street. A generous citizen of San Rafael, A. W. Foster, donated the San Anselmo property to the school in 1891. The small hill on which the substantial buildings stand overlooks the town. The Montgomery Memorial Chapel, built at the foot of the hill, was the gift of the chief benefactor of the seminary, Alexander Montgomery, whose remains were interred there.

The attractive residential town of Ross was named for James Ross, who settled on this part of Rancho Punta de Quentin in 1859, the year of the death of the former owner of the rancho, Benjamin R. Buckelew. Kentfield is on land that passed from the estate of James Ross to Albert Emmet Kent when Kent came to California for his health in 1871. It was called Ross Landing in earlier days, when steamers came up Corte Madera Creek above the present US 101 bridge to load thousands of cords of wood, which they carried to San Francisco. Kent built a spacious house amid old-fashioned formal gardens, with vineyards and orchards at a distance. The Kent Estate is today subdivided into the Kent Woodlands subdivision.

RANCHO CORTE DE MADERA DEL PRESIDIO
(CORTE MADERA, GREENBRAE, LARKSPUR, MILL VALLEY, BELVEDERE, AND TIBURON)

Rancho Corte de Madera del Presidio was granted by Governor José Figueroa to John Reed in 1834. It lay on the peninsula northwest of Raccoon Strait and extended inland between the Punta de Quentín and Saucelito Ranchos. What are now Belvedere and the Corinthian Islands were also part of this property.

Reed, an Irish sailor, arrived in the area in 1826. As opportunity arose, he ran a boat for hire to Yerba Buena, antedating the regular ferry service by many years. He was naturalized as a Mexican citizen one month before receiving the grant of his rancho. For about five months between the Martínez and Murphy administrations of the secularized San Rafael Mission, he filled that position, beginning in November 1836. His rancho was named for the redwood timbers cut down for the use of the Presidio, and he built the first sawmill in Marin County in the mid 1830s. Some of the old timbers still stand (SRL 207) in Old Mill Park on Cascade Drive in Mill Valley, which was named for this early enterprise. A subsequent court case determined that this land was actually owned by Captain William Richardson.

One of the early settlements in this area was Blithedale. This sunny place, through which ran the Arroyo del Corte de Madera del Presidio, was chosen in 1873 by Dr. John Cushing and his wife as the location for a sanatorium. The idealistic agricultural community portrayed by Nathaniel Hawthorne in *The Blithedale Romance*, written twenty years earlier, inspired Dr. Cushing to give the name to this place. Dr. Cushing had not

been able to establish a sanatorium when he died in 1879, but his widow and son remained on the property and managed it as a summer resort for years afterward. The resort's extensive cement walks now surround private homes on the site in the 200 block of West Blithedale Avenue near the creek. The original Blithedale Glen, between Eldridge and Cottage Avenues, has been subdivided and built up as a part of the town of Mill Valley. The Mill Valley Outdoor Club (SRL 922) at 1 West Blithedale Avenue still has its headquarters in the building created for it in 1902, and still is concerned with the preservation of the local environment.

The town of Larkspur is located in the north corner of Rancho Corte de Madera del Presidio. Here an Indian shell mound formed a knoll, then practically surrounded by marshes, upon which Captain Frémont and some of his soldiers are said to have camped for a time in the summer of 1846. In 1850 a steamboat, plying by way of Corte Madera Creek between what is now Larkspur and San Francisco, made three or four trips a week to carry lumber, hides, beef, and other produce from the country and to return with goods purchased in the city. Today Larkspur is at the end of a regular ferry connecting it with San Francisco. A plaque placed by the Larkspur–Corte Madera Historical Society at the ferry terminal commemorates the maritime life of Larkspur and notes that it was once a busy terminal on the Northwest Pacific Railroad.

The Greenbrae brick kiln (SRL 917), last surviving structure of the Remillard Brick Company, is located at 125 East Sir Francis Drake Boulevard in Larkspur. The kiln operated from 1891 to 1915. The Remillard Brick Company was once the largest brick manufacturer on the Pacific Coast, with brickyards at several locations from 1865 until it closed in 1968. Such San Francisco landmarks as Ghirardelli Square and The Cannery are built of Remillard brick. The kiln has been converted into a restaurant.

Present-day Corte Madera began as a station on the Northwestern Pacific line. The site of the station is now a municipal park.

What is now Tiburon was part of the inheritance of Hilarita, daughter of John Reed and his wife Hilaria Sánchez Reed. In 1872 she married Dr. Benjamin F. Lyford, a Civil War surgeon who had arrived in San Francisco in 1866. He was interested in cleanliness and sanitation and was apparently an expert embalmer as well. The Lyfords planned to create a health resort to be called Hygeia, after the goddess of health. The plan never materialized. In 1884 a terminal where railroad passengers

Lyford House, Tiburon

could board a ferry for San Francisco created the beginning of Tiburon, and by 1888 new houses were being built. The picturesque Lyford home at 376 Greenwood Beach Road has been moved from an earlier site and is open to the public on a limited basis. Old St. Hilary's Church, now deconsecrated, was built in 1888, and is now a landmark museum at the junction of Esperanza and Alemany Streets on a hill overlooking the city.

SAUSALITO

William A. Richardson was born in England in 1795 and arrived in San Francisco as first mate on the whaling vessel *L'Orient* in 1822. He procured papers allowing him to remain on land and thereafter became active in the Bay Area. He was baptized at Mission Dolores in 1823, and two years later married María Antonia, daughter of Ignacio Martínez, at that time *comandante* of the Presidio. In 1830 he obtained naturalization as a citizen, his name being placed on record as pilot and shipbuilder with a knowledge of Spanish. From 1835 to 1844 he was the first captain of the Port of San Francisco, having been appointed by General Vallejo. In 1838 he was granted Rancho Saucelito by Governor Alvarado, and he made his home thereafter in Marin County. The final patent for 19,572 acres of the rancho was issued to his heirs in 1879, long after his death in 1856.

Richardson's private business was the collection of country produce by means of a launch that visited the various embarcaderos about the Bay. The shore of his own rancho was washed by the waters of Richardson's Bay, thus named at the time of his land ownership there. The site of Richardson's adobe home, built about 1841, is at the northeast corner of Bonita and Pine Streets in Sausalito.

Fine hillside springs on Rancho Saucelito gave life to the *sauces* or willows from which the name is derived, and in 1850 Captain Richardson piped water from these springs to a great cistern thirty feet square and fifteen feet deep that he had dug for the purpose. From this cistern, located on Richardson Street, Hurricane Gulch, Sausalito, pipes were run on a trestle to the waterfront and thence to a boat, the *Water Nixie*, equipped with tanks and casks for transporting the water to Meiggs' Wharf at San Francisco. From this point Marin County spring water was distributed to residents in the growing city by means of mule- and horse-drawn carts for the price of 50 cents a bucket. The mooring place of the *Water Nixie* is on Richardson Street near Bridgeway, not far from the place of first settlement of the town of Sausalito, where in 1862 there were a half dozen houses.

Richardson's last years were troubled with financial problems; three uninsured ships of his were lost at sea in 1856, forcing him into bankruptcy. He died in April of that year, and his remains were reburied some time later in a San Rafael cemetery where their precise location is no longer known. E Clampus Vitus placed a plaque in his honor in 1999 at Gabrielson Park, Sausalito, on the waterfront near the ferry terminal.

San Carlos Avenue in Sausalito is named for the first known ship to sail through the Golden Gate, on August 5, 1775, under command of Juan Manuel de Ayala. The *San Carlos*, after moving cautiously into the unknown strait, taking frequent soundings, first dropped anchor off Sausalito and later moved to Angel Island.

For many years the Sausalito waterfront was widely known as an anchorage and supply station for whaling vessels and men-of-war. Captain Beechey, in 1826, saw "seven whalers" anchored there. Sir George Simpson, governor-in-chief of the Hudson's Bay Company territories in North America, on entering San Francisco Bay in December 1841, wrote:

> We saw on our left in a deep bay known as 'Whaler's Harbor' two vessels, the Government schooner *California* and the Russian brig *Constantine*, now bound to Sitka with the last remnants of [the settlements at Fort] Ross and Bodega on board, . . . about a hundred souls, men, women, and children, all patriotically delighted to exchange the lovely climate of California for the uncongenial skies of Sitka, and that, too, at the expense of making a long voyage in an old, crazy, clumsy tub at the stormiest season of the year.

Captain Richardson sold a piece of property near Sausalito in 1855 to S. R. Throckmorton, who in turn sold it to the Sausalito Land and Ferry Company. This company built wharves, filled in marshy places, and put on a reliable boat for frequent rapid transit across the Bay to San Francisco. Their first boat, the *Princess*, made four round trips daily. It is in the vicinity of this wharf that the newer part of Sausalito has grown up. One of the largest working scale models in the world is the San Francisco Bay Delta Model at 2100 Bridgeway. Open to the public since it was built in 1956 by the U.S. Army Corps of Engineers, it is used to study the effects of tides and currents in the Bay complex from the Golden Gate to the Delta cities of Sacramento and Stockton.

On Bulkley Avenue, near Harrison Avenue, on the drive above the waterfront, a crescent-shaped cement seat honors the memory of Daniel O'Connell, grandnephew of the Irish patriot of the same name. O'Connell came to California after resigning from the British Navy and was a teacher at Santa Clara College in 1868; later he taught Greek at St. Ignatius College in San Francisco before devoting his time to journalism and other writing. A poet, he was one of the early members of the Bohemian Club of San Francisco. He lived in Wildwood Glen with his family in "the little house on the hill," which still stands, enlarged and modernized, at 41 Cazeneau Avenue.

In 1869, James H. Gardner, former state senator from Downieville and custom house broker, purchased from the Sausalito Land and Ferry Company a parcel of land where he built his house. "The Bower," as he named it, is the oldest house still standing in Sausalito, and is at 47 Girard Avenue. It is privately owned, as is the O'Connell house.

BOLINAS

Otter hunting, the first occupation engaged in by settlers in the vicinity of the town of Bolinas, was followed by lumbering in the 1850s, when many sawmills were operating in the tree-filled canyons back from the shore. The only evidence left is the few piles that mark the site of the lighter wharf (SRL 221, no plaque), about two miles north of Bolinas at the head of Bolinas Lagoon, not far from the junction with SR 1. It is estimated that thirteen million feet of lumber were shipped to San Francisco for building purposes from the lighter wharf at Bolinas before the supply was exhausted. After the large trees had been used for lumber, the smaller trees were felled for domestic fuel and sent to the same market.

Ocean gales raked the west shore of Bolinas Bay, and windbreaks in the form of cypress hedges had to be planted before the cottage gardens of the pioneer settlers could grow. In some parts of Bolinas, the roses, fuchsias, and lemon verbenas of early days have now attained tree-like proportions. Bolinas cherishes its privacy, to the point where highway signs are often torn down to discourage casual visitors, for whom there are few amenities, but who come to enjoy the beauty of the town.

NICASIO

Attempts were made to give three grants in the county to Christian Indians. Rancho Olómpali was successfully patented to Camilo Ynitia, but the other two, Ranchos Nicasio and Tenicasia, were not confirmed. Twenty square leagues of Nicasio had been granted to Teodosio Quilajuequi and others of his tribe in 1835 by Governor Figueroa, but this was rejected by the Land Commission in 1855. Tenicasia, given by General Mariano Vallejo to the San Rafael Mission Indians in 1841, was rejected by the commission in 1854 because of "failure of prosecution." Vallejo was a valiant friend of the neophytes, but he alone could not carry through the plan of obtaining farms for them where they could use the agricultural knowledge received at the mission. Timoteo Murphy, his friend and co-worker who held the confidence of the Indians and was furthering their interests, had died the year before the matter was settled, and no one else remained to intercede on behalf of the native claimants. "The history of land in Marin," Jack Mason observed, "is one of broken promises, litigation and injustice nurtured on political expediency."

In 1844, another part of Rancho Nicasio, containing ten square leagues, was granted by Governor Micheltorena to Pablo de la Guerra and Juan Bautista Cooper, men prominent in political and business affairs, who seem to have parted with the land before 1852. In that year a claim for it was filed by H. W. Halleck and James Black, and a supplementary claim was filed the following year by Benjamin R. Buckelew, Daniel Frink, and William Reynolds. The long and comparatively narrow stretch of this rancho reached from Keyes Creek, flowing into Tomales Bay, to the western boundary of Murphy's Rancho San Pedro, Santa Margarita y Las Gallinas. It was surveyed in 1859 and found to contain 56,621 acres, for which patent, signed by President Abraham Lincoln, was issued to all five claimants in 1861.

The extreme northwestern and northeastern ends

were claimed by and patented to Henry Wager Halleck, a West Point graduate, who had come in 1847 with a company of United States artillery to inspect Pacific Coast fortifications. He resigned his commission, was an active and influential member of the constitutional convention of 1849, acted as inspector of lighthouses on the coast, became the leading member of a San Francisco law firm, prepared a report on California land titles, and was the author of several law books. He was also one of the developers of the New Almaden quicksilver mining complex in Santa Clara County. Halleck resumed his military career and during most of the Civil War served as chief of staff of the Union Army. The southeastern corner of this large grant was patented to the heirs of Benjamin R. Buckelew, who was also the owner of Rancho Punta de San Quintín. The two middle tracts, along the eastern shore of Tomales Bay, were patented to the other three claimants, Frink and Reynolds owning the northern piece, and James Black, who also had Rancho Olómpali, the southern.

An interesting old building still standing in the town of Nicasio is the Church of Our Lady of Loretto, established in 1867.

THE PIONEER PAPER MILL (SAMUEL P. TAYLOR STATE PARK)

Samuel Penfield Taylor put up a paper mill in 1856 on what was then called Daniels Creek, afterward Paper Mill Creek, and today Lagunitas Creek. It was the first paper mill on the Pacific Coast and was run by water carried by a flume from a dam in the creek one-half mile above. The warehouse was situated at the end of Tomales Bay, where Point Reyes Station is now.

Rags to supply the mill were gathered by Chinese in San Francisco, made into great bales, and shipped by schooner to the head of Tomales Bay. They were then loaded on a scow and floated on the tide to Taylor's warehouse, from which a team of oxen completed the transportation to the factory. The finished paper was conveyed in reverse manner to San Francisco, where the product found a ready sale and was sent to all parts of the Pacific Coast. The undertaking was prosperous from the beginning and was especially so during the Civil War. By 1884 the demand for paper had become so great that a larger mill was built at a cost of $165,000 and employment there furnished a livelihood for about 100 families. Steam power was added, and the mill did a flourishing business until the depression of 1893.

After lying idle for over twenty years, the red-painted building with windows and doors outlined in white was destroyed by fire. Now only the damaged foundations remain; the columns that acted as supports for the water wheel are still standing, and crumbling bricks mark the site of the boiler. The site of the first paper mill (SRL 552) is marked by a stone monument with bronze plaque in Samuel P. Taylor State Park, off Sir Francis Drake Boulevard between Lagunitas and Olema. The ruins of the later mill are a few yards from the marker.

The Pacific Powder Mill was erected in 1866 about three miles upstream from the paper mill, but the exact site is now lost.

TOMALES BAY, INVERNESS, AND OLEMA

"Tomales" is a Coast Miwok word meaning "bay"; thus its present official name is redundant. In 1775, Lieutenant Juan Francisco de la Bodega y Cuadro, commander of the schooner *Sonora*, discovered Bodega Bay in Sonoma County by chance and "soon afterwards distinguished the mouth of a considerable river, and some way up a large port exactly resembling a dock," according to the Daines Barrington translation of the account of Don Antonio Mourelle. At first, members of the expedition thought that Tomales Bay was the harbor of San Francisco, but later they realized that it was not, because the Farallon Islands were not visible. Indians came in great numbers and rowed their tule rafts between Tomales Point (Punta del Cordon) and Sand Point (Punta de Arenas). They came alongside the ship to present gifts of "rosaries of bone, seeds, and plumes of feathers." Bodega in return gave "bugles, looking glasses, and pieces of cloth."

Bodega named today's Tomales Bay and Bodega Bay for himself—Puerto de la Bodega. The *Sonora* anchored in the mouth of Tomales Bay on October 3, 1775. After midnight, on the first flow of the tide, the full force of a northeast swell struck the ship and covered it with breaking water. The discovery boat on her side was shattered. By midmorning the *Sonora* set sail for Monterey. The following day, October 5, the expedition passed two miles from the Golden Gate, unaware that only a month before the *San Carlos* had departed for Monterey. Bodega was afraid to enter San Francisco Bay because of the loss of the discovery boat.

The town of Tomales, originally located at the head of Keyes Creek, which flows from the northeast into the bay, had its beginning in a store located here in 1852. The North Pacific Coast Railroad ran its first freight train from a warehouse there in 1874; its cargo of 300 sacks of potatoes was the forerunner of many trainloads of produce raised in the vicinity and shipped over this line to Sausalito and thence to San Francisco. The railroad has been discontinued for a long time.

When on December 28, 1841, the *Cowlitz* lay becalmed offshore at Drakes Bay after coming from the north, its passengers "began sensibly to feel the influence of a more congenial climate. The sails flapped listlessly against the mast, the vessel heaved reluctantly on the sluggish waters." Sir George Simpson, one of the passengers, continues:

> During the whole of the 29th we lay in this state of inactivity about five miles from shore which presented a level sward of about a mile in depth, backed by a high ridge of grassy slopes—the whole pastured by numerous herds of cattle and horses which, without a keeper and without a fold, were growing and fattening, whether their owners waked or slept, in the very middle of winter, and in the coldest nook of the province. Here, on the very threshold of the country, was California in a nutshell. Nature doing everything and man doing nothing. . . . While we lay like a log in the sea, we were glad to be surrounded by large flights of birds—ducks, pelicans, cormorants, gulls, etc.

The land Simpson described is that of Rancho Punta de los Reyes Sobrante, which after the advent of the American settlers became the first great dairy center of the state.

Rancho Punta de los Reyes, on the west side of Tomales Bay, was a 35,000-acre grant made in 1836 to a well-traveled Irish gentleman, James Richard Berry, who had spent much time in Spanish countries. He sold a portion of this land to Joseph Snook, an English-born citizen of Mexico, in 1839, who in turn sold his share to Antonio María Osio in 1843. Osio, a public official, meanwhile had made a successful application for the remaining 48,000 acres of Point Reyes, which was granted to him in 1840 as the Rancho Punta de los Reyes Sobrante ("surplus" or "leftover land"), surrounding the initial grant on three sides. The American takeover in 1846 brought rival claims to the property, complicated by the fact that here, as nearly everywhere in Alta California, no precise surveys had been made and much land was in dispute.

The two ranches became the property of Dr. Andrew Randall in the early 1850s. Randall, an American resident of Monterey, had been a member of the state Legislature and was the first president of the California Academy of Sciences in 1853. He overextended himself in land purchases and was murdered in San Francisco by Joseph Hetherington, one of his creditors. (Hetherington was lynched by the Vigilantes within the week.) Oscar L. Shafter, a Vermonter practicing law in California, took on Mrs. Randall's hopelessly debt-ridden inheritance, which finally passed to him and to his brother James. Both the Shafters became eminent in late-nineteenth-century California, Oscar on the bench of the state Supreme Court and James as a member of the Legislature.

James Shafter, who also held judicial office, was a regent of the University of California. At the time of the founding of Leland Stanford Junior University he delivered the dedicatory address and became a trustee of the new institution.

The Shafter brothers and Charles Webb Howard, president of the Spring Valley Water Company, jointly came to own both Point Reyes ranchos. To their large holdings was later added Rancho Tomales y Baulenes, which had been granted in 1836 by Governor Nicolás Gutiérrez to Rafael García. The combined property stretched south and east from the coast north of Point Reyes to include the top of Mount Tamalpais.

Dairying became the major activity in this part of Marin County. Almost the entire area was leased out by the grantees to dairy farmers, and houses were built for them near clear-flowing springs, of which there were a considerable number. Butter was shipped by schooners to San Francisco. Judge James Shafter was greatly interested in blooded stock, horses as well as cattle, and he frequently entertained friends at his private race track, where his fine horses were trained and shown.

At nearby Olema, a prominent landmark is Nelson's Hotel, built in 1877 and since then renovated and restored. Several other frame structures from around 1900 are preserved and occupied. Inverness, named after the city in Scotland from which the Shafter family emigrated, was begun by James Shafter in 1889 as a real estate development. In contrast to the lively, six-saloon neighboring town of Olema, Inverness was intended to be a model of sobriety "to the better class of citizens," according to one early announcement.

OLOMPALI STATE HISTORIC PARK AND NOVATO

Rancho Olompali consisted of two square leagues granted by Governor Manuel Micheltorena in 1843 to Camilo Ynitia, a Christianized Miwok and head of the village of Olompali. In 1862 Ynitia received the United States patent to the land. The rancheria was by San Antonio Creek and had an abundance of game and wild-fowl. Ynitia built himself an adobe house, about three miles north of Novato. With thirty-two-inch-thick walls and ceilings eight feet high, it was an impressive structure in the otherwise empty landscape. Nearby were corrals and outbuildings.

On June 24, 1846, there was a surprise skirmish, the Battle of Olompali, at this spot. The Bear Flag had been raised above nearby Sonoma ten days before, and the Americans were trying to secure their hold on the area. Led by Lieutenant Henry L. Ford, the Bear Flaggers made a raid on the horse corral at Olompali, unaware that a force of Californians under Joaquín de la Torre and Juan N. Padilla were at breakfast in the ranch house. Padilla was a wanted man in the eyes of the Bear Flaggers, since his force had murdered two Americans a couple of days before. Alerted to the raid, the Californians poured out of the ranch house, took to their mounts, and attacked the Americans, who took cover and sent volleys flying into the midst of the horsemen. Manuel Cantua fell to his death, and three other Californians were wounded; Padilla withdrew his men into the hills and then retreated to San Rafael. Ford's party retreated to Sonoma, and John C. Frémont moved onto the scene, with the tragic consequences recorded earlier in this chapter.

The greater part of this rancho was purchased in 1852 by James Black from Ynitia and his wife Susana who retained the southeast corner of the grant for themselves. Black, originally from Scotland, had become the assessor of Marin County and acquired many other tracts of land. He afterward gave this one to his daughter Mary.

In 1863 Mary Black and her husband, Dr. Galen Burdell, came to live at Olompali. Here the Burdells built their home, using Camilo Ynitia's adobe as its center (SRL 210). This is turn was enlarged by their son James Burdell in 1915, and it became one of the show-places of Marin County. Its garden was particularly admired, with its brick-lined walkways, conservatory, lily pond, and exotic plants. The estate remained in the Burdell family until it was sold in 1943, after which it had a remarkable series of owners: the University of San Francisco, who made a Jesuit retreat there; several purchasers who defaulted; the rock band The Grateful Dead; some leaseholders; and The Chosen Family, a utopian commune. It was in the time of the last of these, in 1969, that faulty wiring touched off a fire that destroyed the house and forced the evacuation of the group. The abandoned property was the site of an ex-

tensive archaeological excavation in 1974–75, during the course of which an Elizabethan sixpence was discovered, reviving interest in the "Drake plate of brass" at Bancroft Library, which holds the coin now. In 1977 the state of California, together with Marin County, purchased the property to preserve it as a state historic park. A feature of the park is a reconstructed Coast Miwok Indian village, a project begun in 1994.

Rancho Novato was granted in 1839 by Governor Alvarado to Fernando Feliz; it lay along the bay from Black Point to Rancho San José. The town of Novato lies in this district; rail service came through in 1879 and a subdivision made in 1888 marked the beginning of the city. The oldest building in Novato is believed to have been built around 1850, and was the home of postmaster Henry F. Jones for some time. It stood on South Novato Avenue until 1972, when it was given to the city by its owner, Fabian Bobo. The building was moved to its present location at 901 Sherman Avenue that year and was inaugurated as the Novato History Museum and Archives in 1976. One room of the museum is devoted to the history of the nearby inactive Hamilton Air Force Base. The building was marked by a plaque in 1985 placed by the Native Sons of the Golden West.

The Novato City Hall, nearby at Sherman and De Long Avenues, was built in 1893. It was once a Presbyterian church and is a good example of Victorian Gothic architecture. Joseph B. Sweetser and Francis De Long were largely responsible for Novato's early prosperity, planting orchards and vineyards and producing high-quality crops that were shipped from the landing on Novato Creek onto the bay and thence to San Francisco. The three-story home they built still stands at 50 Rica Vista Avenue; it is hemmed in by newer houses and almost unrecognizable from contemporary pictures, which show a majestic avenue of fig trees leading to its front veranda.

RANCHO SAN JOSÉ AND IGNACIO

Ignacio Pacheco, whose father, of the same name, was a Mexican soldier in San Francisco in 1790, was born in San Jose in 1808. When he was nineteen years old, he became a soldier in the San Francisco Company, and a sergeant ten years later. At the expiration of his military service in 1838 he settled on a tract of land bordering San Pablo Bay south of the Feliz grant of Rancho Novato, and in 1840 the tract was granted to him by Governor Alvarado. Don Ignacio's first wife, Josefa Higuera, named the rancho for her patron saint. The

China Camp State Park

family home still stands in the community of Ignacio and is still in the possession of the family; this is the second-longest occupancy by a single family in California, so far as is known.

The tall palms at 716 Lamone in Ignacio mark the site of the Reichardt villa, a country home of the late nineteenth century. Hamilton Air Force Base nearby was named for Lieutenant Lloyd Hamilton, the first American to fly with the Royal Air Corps in World War I. In operation between 1928 and 1975, it was a major bomber facility during World War II. In 1999, a very complex plan went into operation for the site, involving new homes, nature preserves, senior citizens buildings, and commercial space.

CHINA CAMP STATE PARK

Farther south along the bay is China Camp State Park (SRL 924). It is situated along Point San Pedro Road just outside the city limits of San Rafael. In the years after the Gold Rush, Chinese immigrants in California found many productive occupations. Along the shores of San Francisco and San Pablo Bays, shrimp fishing became a major industry after 1870; some twenty-six camps or fishing villages were recorded. Shrimping was an established trade in China, and the abundance of shrimp in the shallow waters of San Pablo Bay encouraged the start of this activity in California. The shrimp were caught, dried, and sent for export to Asian countries and to the Hawaiian Islands.

The China Camp site is all that remains of this once flourishing industry and community. Relatively isolated, it became a refuge for Chinese who were persecuted in the latter nineteenth century. Chinese families continued to live in the settlement long after its economic heyday had passed. The park itself consists of

1,476 acres of land, of which thirty-six acres constitute the shoreline village. Fishing is carried on off Point San Pedro as it has been for more than a century.

ISLANDS OF MARIN COUNTY

The eastern boundary of Marin County runs from Petaluma Point in San Pablo Bay south into San Francisco Bay far enough to include almost all of Angel Island. Within the water area lie several small islands; Belvedere, now joined to the mainland, was originally a separate island. The Sisters are a little to the northwest of Point San Pedro. The Marin Islands, upon which Chief Marin hid when escaping from his pursuers, lie midway between San Pedro Point and San Quentin Point; they are now the Marin Islands National Wildlife Refuge. Just south of the mouth of San Rafael Creek is San Rafael Rock. Directly northwest of California Point is Red Rock, an uninhabited area of an acre or so through which pass the boundary lines of Contra Costa, Marin, and San Francisco Counties, and about which cling traditions of buried treasure. The largest of all, Angel Island, opposite Tiburon Point, is separated from the mainland by Raccoon Strait. The strait took its name from the British 16-gun sloop of war *Raccoon*, which was laid up and repaired on the beach at Ayala Cove in the spring of 1814, after suffering damage on a Pacific voyage.

Early in August 1775, two Spanish ships entered San Francisco Bay under the command of Lieutenant Juan Manuel de Ayala. This was an exploring mission, to investigate the great inland sea, its inlets, harbors, and islands. On the 13th the expedition reached an island which Ayala named Nuestra Señora de los Angeles, today known as Angel Island. Finding good anchorage and plenty of wood and water, the explorers based at the island for several weeks while making careful surveys of the surrounding topography. The chaplain of the expedition, Father Santa María, and some of the officers landed several times on the mainland, where they visited a hospitable rancheria, undoubtedly that of Olompali.

It was the policy of the government of Mexico to see that these islands did not fall into foreign hands, particularly those of the Russians, who were trapping here as late as 1835. Angel Island (then called the Island of Los Angeles) was granted by Governor Juan Alvarado in 1838 to Antonio María Osio, who used it for raising horses and cattle. He did not live on it himself, but he subdivided it, built four houses, made a dam for the conservation of water for his stock, and placed part of the land under cultivation.

At the time of the American takeover, the United States government found Angel Island to be too important to national defense to be left in private hands, and despite Osio's protests, it passed into the public domain in 1852. It seems to have been notorious in the 1850s as a den of thieves and as a dueling ground. On August 21, 1858, before a large crowd, state Senator William I. Ferguson of Sacramento met San Francisco newspaper editor William Pen Johnson in a duel with pistols: the wounded Ferguson died 24 days later. A more respectable activity was the quarrying of sandstone on the eastern side, which continued into the 1920s. The island was fortified by the military during the Civil War, there being a persistent rumor of imminent attack by Confederate warships on San Francisco Bay. No marauders actually appeared, although a small Russian Imperial fleet visited San Francisco Bay between October 1863 and May 1864 on a peaceable mission; it was even permitted to use the Mare Island Navy Yard to overhaul one of its ships.

Between 1863 and 1946 the island was an Army base. Fort McDowell, the present East Garrison station, was a major induction facility. The house once occupied by the commanding officer, General William Rufus Shafter (later of Spanish-American War fame, and a cousin of the Point Reyes Shafter family), still stands, along with other military housing. During World War II some 87,000 soldiers passed through here on their way to the Pacific front. Prisoners of war were interned here as well.

A quarantine station was built in 1888 at Hospital Cove, and Angel Island became a major immigration and public health facility. Asian immigrants were interned here. This "Ellis Island of the West" was in operation until 1946. The island was turned over to Marin County at that time (except for two tiny points of shoreline that are in the city and county of San Francisco), and in turn it became a state property in 1955.

Today, Angel Island State Park (SRL 529) attracts many visitors; the old military and public health facilities, though deteriorating, can still be seen. Hospital Cove has been renamed Ayala Cove in honor of the Spanish explorer of 1775. Mount Ida, the 781-foot summit at the center of the island, was renamed Mount Caroline S. Livermore in honor of the pioneer Marin County conservationist in 1958. A Coast Guard facility is maintained at Point Blunt. Boat service to the island is available from Tiburon, Berkeley, and San Francisco, depending on the time of the year.

Golden Gate Bridge from Fort Baker

GOLDEN GATE NATIONAL RECREATIONAL AREA

This magnificent park was created by an Act of Congress, approved by President Richard M. Nixon, in 1972. It embraces most of the north and west coastal area of San Francisco and sizeable chunks of Marin County. Much of this was military property and closed to the public. Fort Baker, set aside as a military reservation in 1850, is the last military property in Marin County to be deactivated. Until recently it was occupied by army families in houses most of which were built between 1901 and 1904. It lies immediately to the east of the Golden Gate Bridge.

The Marin Headlands, along the northern side of the Golden Gate, are among the most breathtakingly beautiful spots in all of California. They were once part of the defense perimeter of San Francisco Bay. Originally called Lime Point Military Reservation, the region was divided into three posts named for commanding officers: Fort Baker (1897), Fort Barry (1904), and Fort Cronkhite (1937). Visitors can see the huge concrete emplacements for guns that were never used at several places along Conzelman Road leading west from Fort Barry. Battery Spencer, Battery 129, Battery Wallace, Battery Alexander, Battery Mendell, and Battery Smith-Guthrie can be seen along the drive.

A very interesting historic spot in California is the Nike Missile Site at Fort Barry. This is one of eleven created in 1954 during the Cold War to protect the San Francisco Bay Area, and their counterparts are to be found throughout the United States. Until 1974 these missiles, guided by electronic beams, were considered the last word in defense against attacks from the air. As new technology and a new political atmosphere changed, they became obsolete and were dismantled. This site has a most unusual visual element: once a month, the public can see an inactivated missile brought up from its underground chamber and raised to a firing position on the launch. It is a vivid reminder of the Cold War years.

Nearby Point Bonita Light Station, built in 1855, was the last to be automated, in 1980. The station had the first fog signal installed on the coast, an iron cannon transferred from the Benicia Arsenal. Sergeant Maloney, placed in charge at the point with instructions to "fire the gun every half hour during fogs," reported two months later that since there was almost constant fog and no one to relieve him "for even five minutes" he had been unable to get the "two hours' sleep necessary out of the twenty-four." He resigned shortly thereafter. The gun remained in use for two years before its expense and ineffectiveness caused it to be abandoned in favor of another kind of fog signal. The light station is open to visitors on a limited basis, where they can see the huge Fresnel lens that casts a beam that under favorable circumstances can be seen seventeen miles out to sea.

Tennessee Cove received its name after the disaster of March 6, 1853, when the steamer *Tennessee* went aground in a dense fog. There was no light station along the coast at that time. Fortunately, no lives were lost. The first light station on the coast was placed on Alcatraz Island in the following year.

Muir Woods National Monument has been incorporated into the Golden Gate National Recreational Area. This stand of *Sequoia sempervirens* on the western slope of Mount Tamalpais contains some trees estimated to be as much as 1,700 years old, with a diameter of twelve feet and a height of 240 feet. The forest area was made a national monument by presidential proclamation in 1908, a gift to the nation from William Kent of Kentfield, a member of the 62nd Congress, and his wife, Elizabeth Thatcher Kent. Although in accepting the gift President Theodore Roosevelt expressed his desire to name it for the donors, they wanted it named for John Muir, California's noted naturalist, who had long worked in the cause of forest conservation. Muir lived for six years to enjoy the honor conferred on him in the naming of Muir Woods.

MOUNT TAMALPAIS STATE PARK

Two Indian words, *tamal* (bay) and *pais* (mountain or country) form the name of the heavily wooded mountain that dominates the landscape on the north side of San Francisco Bay. West Peak is the highest of its three peaks, at 2,604 feet; East and Middle Peaks are just over 2,500 feet.

Pedestrian trails, some of which were originally made by Indians and others by American pioneers, are still used by hiking parties. These pathways begin at different places around the base of the mountain; a favorite one starts beneath the trees behind the old sawmill at Mill Valley. In 1896 the eight-mile Mount Tamalpais and Muir Woods Railroad was laid out, and after its completion a train drawn by a steam engine carried passengers over 283 curves, giving rise to the name "The Crookedest Railroad in the World." About halfway to the top the track became a double bowknot to accomplish a 100-foot rise within a distance of 1,000 feet. The railway has been a thing of the past since 1930, but a highway following another route displays an extensive panorama at every turn.

From the broad trail that circles the summit of East Peak one may see close at hand bays and islands, cities and bridges. If the atmospheric conditions are good, one can see to the north Mount St. Helena and Mount Shasta, to the east Mount Diablo and the distant peaks of the Sierra Nevada, to the south Mount Hamilton and Loma Prieta, and to the west the vast Pacific Ocean.

Mount Tamalpais State Park, a wooded area of about 2,000 acres, includes the East Peak. Below Rock Spring lies a natural amphitheater where performances are frequently given. The Dipsea Trail has been the site of an annual footrace since 1905. The Steep Ravine area in the park, gift of William Kent shortly before his death in 1928, is an abrupt descent, with redwoods, firs, and thickets of underbrush.

POINT REYES NATIONAL SEASHORE

After much negotiation between public officials and private landowners, Point Reyes National Seashore was created in 1962 when President John F. Kennedy signed the act of Congress bringing some 71,000 acres under federal control. Plans for such a park had been offered as early as 1935, but a persistent objection was raised by local property owners. The compromise worked out provided for extensive tracts of agricultural land to remain in private hands within the seashore, although such property can not be sold except to the federal government for inclusion in the park. A distinctive feature of Point Reyes is the lighthouse, built in 1870 and operated until 1975, in the midst of some of the foggiest territory in the United States.

Mariposa County

Mariposa County was one of the original twenty-seven counties. With an area of about 30,000 square miles, it covered one-fifth of the state. Stretching from the Coast Range to the present Nevada state line, and touching Los Angeles County on the south, it contained land now included within ten other counties. The county's present configuration dates from 1880, and its area is 1,455 square miles. Agua Fria was very briefly the first county seat, in 1850–51, after which Mariposa became the seat of government.

The name Mariposa ("butterfly" in Spanish) was first given in the plural form, Las Mariposas, to a spot in Merced County visited by the expedition led by Gabriel Moraga in 1806. The Mexican land grant conferred upon Juan Bautista Alvarado in 1844 and purchased for John C. Frémont by his agent, Thomas O. Larkin, likewise took the plural form of the name, while the singular form, Mariposa, was bestowed first upon the creek and later upon the town and the county.

Some have thought that this place name was derived from mariposa lily, the common name of the many-hued lilies (*Calochortus luteus* and other varieties) that in late spring and early summer give color to the region's hills. But the source of the place name must be traced to the butterfly, which at certain seasons is found here in countless numbers.

WALKER'S TRAIL OVER THE SIERRA

Joseph R. Walker, as early as 1833, came into California over the Sierra Nevada through what are now Mono, Mariposa, and Tuolumne Counties. "Reliable knowledge of the Sierra Nevada," wrote Francis P. Farquhar, "really begins with this expedition."

Passing down the Humboldt River Valley in Nevada and thence south by Carson Lake, Walker and his men struck westward across the Sierra, probably ascending its eastern slope by one of the southern tributaries of the East Walker River. After crossing the summit of the pass the party was lost for several days "in a maze of lakes and mountains." The description of this region given by Zenas Leonard, chronicler of the expedition, accords well with the character of the country in the vicinity of Virginia Canyon.

From this point, Farquhar says, "they would have crossed the Tuolumne, perhaps near Conness Creek. Passing Tenaya Lake, they probably followed the course of the present Tioga Road" (mostly in Tuolumne County) down the divide between the Tuolumne and Merced Rivers. On this stage of the journey the party saw either the Merced Grove or the Tuolumne Grove of *Sequoia gigantea*, the first Americans to see the Big Trees of the Sierra Nevada.

It is fairly certain that the Walker party saw Yosemite Valley in 1833, although they did not camp in the valley itself. Zenas Leonard recorded in his diary what is thought to be the first mention of Yosemite Valley by an American:

> We travelled a few miles every day, still on the top of the mountains, and our course continually obstructed with snow, hills, and rocks. Here we began to encounter in our path, many small streams which would shoot out from under these high snow-banks, and after running a short distance in deep chasms which they have through the ages cut in the rocks, precipitate themselves from one lofty precipice to another, until they are exhausted in rain below. Some of these precipices appeared to us to be more than a mile high. Some of the men thought that if we could succeed in descending one of these precipices to the bottom, we might thus work our way into the valley below—but on making several attempts we found it utterly impossible for a man to descend, to say nothing of our horses.

The diary of William Penn Abrams, a Gold Rush pioneer, reveals that he and his companion, U. N. Reamer, saw Yosemite Valley in October 1849. They were following the tracks of a grizzly bear when they came upon the spectacular scene. Bridal Veil Falls was described as it dropped "from a cliff below three jagged peaks into the valley." Half Dome looked to the men "as though it had been sliced with a knife as one would slice a loaf of bread." They called it "Rock of Ages."

Historical research may yet uncover other early accounts of Yosemite. However, it was not until 1851 that the valley can properly said to have been discovered and made widely known. The first effective discovery was made by Major James D. Savage and Captain John Boling, who, with a strong detachment of mounted volunteers and friendly Indian guides, entered the valley in March of that year to capture the resident Indians in order to put them on the Fresno Indian Reservation. One of this party of discoverers was Dr. Lafayette H. Bunnell, the first man to make the wonders of the Yosemite Valley known to the world.

Major Savage had come to the mines in 1848, enlisted Indian labor in his diggings in Tuolumne County, and soon developed extensive trading relations with the natives. His first post (SRL 527) was set up at or near the mouth of the South Fork of the Merced River in Mariposa County, but this was abandoned when conflict developed between the Yosemite Indians and the whites in 1850. Indians burned the building at the end of the year. The site of Savage's post is marked near a modern commercial establishment on SR 140 west of El Portal.

In 1851 and 1852 a number of punitive expeditions against the Indians entered the valley. The last, led by Army Lieutenant Tredwell Moore, finally drove the remnants of the tribe over the mountains, where they took refuge with the Monos.

The tourist history of Yosemite Valley began in 1855, when J. M. Hutchings, in company with three friends, formed the first tourist expedition to enter it. Five days of "scenic banqueting" were spent in exploring the region and sketching its wonders. The publicity given to Hutchings' writings and to the accompanying drawings of Thomas Ayers was considerable, and from then on Yosemite Valley attracted ever-increasing numbers of tourists.

The first improved pack trail into Yosemite Valley was made in 1856 by the Mann Brothers, a livery firm in Mariposa. The trail led from Mariposa to the valley by way of the South Fork of the Merced River, crossing at Wawona. Regular tourist travel to the valley began in 1857. The first house was built there in the autumn of 1856 and the first hotel in 1859. Until its destruction in 1940, the latter was a part of the Sentinel Hotel establishment known as Cedar Cottage.

Nearly all the early visitors to Yosemite were Californians, mostly campers. Only a few hundred came yearly until the completion of the transcontinental railroad in 1869. Today thousands come from all over the world. The Yosemite Valley Railroad from Merced to El Portal ceased operation in 1945, and the valley is today reached by four main automobile roads. SR 140, called the All-Year Highway when it opened in 1927, enters from the west via Merced, Mariposa, and El Portal, following the Merced River. SR 120, the Big Oak Flat Road, enters from the northwest, originating at Manteca in the San Joaquin Valley. The Tioga Pass Road, open only in the summer months, is an extension of SR 120 to the east, crossing to Lee Vining in Mono County. SR 41 enters from the south, beginning at Fresno, continuing through Oakhurst, and entering Yosemite National Park south of Wawona. Besides these, there are two old routes for the traveler with plenty of time and an indifference to steep, rough roads: the road that runs north and east of SR 49 over Chowchilla Mountain to Wawona, and the road that begins in Coulterville and, as the Old Yosemite Road (the first stagecoach road into Yosemite Valley), continues past Bower Cave and the Merced Grove of Big Trees.

Yosemite Valley (SRL 790) was made a state park on

June 30, 1864. A national park surrounding the valley was established in 1890, and the present Yosemite National Park was constituted in 1906, when the state of California ceded the Yosemite Valley and the Mariposa Grove of Big Trees to the federal government.

The name "Yosemite," spelled various ways in early accounts, seems to have first been given to the Indians living in the valley by the Mariposa Battalion invading the region in 1851. It is said that in one native dialect a similar word referred to the fierceness of the grizzly bear, and therefore was appropriate for the fierce defenders of their territory.

Yosemite Valley is only a small portion of the 1,189-square-mile national park, but it has always been the center of visitor interest. In the valley is the Visitors' Center, with a museum established in 1921 that includes departments of history, ethnology, botany, and zoology. The Indian Cultural Museum and the Indian Village are nearby. The Ahwahnee Hotel, named for the Ahwahneechee Indians who lived in the valley for several thousand years, is a world-famous luxury resort built in 1925. Camp Curry, built in 1899, features bungalows and tents. The wooden chapel was first built in 1879, and was moved to its present location in 1901.

WAWONA

At Wawona is the site of the log cabin built by Galen Clark in 1857, the same year in which he discovered the Mariposa Grove of Big Trees, only eight miles from his cabin and now within Yosemite National Park. Clark was a member of the first Board of Commissioners for the care of Yosemite Valley and the Mariposa Grove, and was for many years known as the "Guardian of the Valley." For more than fifty years he lived either in Yosemite or at Wawona. At the latter place his cabin was known to all travelers as Clark's Station, where kindly hospitality never failed to be extended.

At the age of ninety, in 1904, Galen Clark published his first book, *Indians of Yosemite*; in 1907, he published another, *Big Trees of California*. Clark finished his last book, *The Yosemite Valley*, just two weeks before his death on March 24, 1910, at the age of ninety-six.

Wawona is now the home of the Pioneer Yosemite History Center, a collection of the park's oldest structures, most of which were moved here from other areas for permanent preservation. Through this outdoor museum the history of Yosemite National Park is meaningfully interpreted for visitors. Among the buildings are a Wells Fargo office, a jail, a wagon shop, and several cab-

Covered Bridge over South Fork of Merced River at Pioneer Yosemite History Center, Wawona

ins, including one built by a trailblazer, another by a homesteader, a third by the U.S. Army, and a fourth by the National Park Service. The historical displays center on the old Wawona covered bridge, spanning the South Fork of the Merced River, begun about 1858 by Galen Clark, covered in 1875, and restored in 1956. A large collection of horse-drawn wagons is on the same grounds.

Nearby is the charming old Wawona Hotel, still in operation from April through November. The main building was constructed in 1879; one structure of the group, the Clark Cottage, dates from 1876.

HISTORIC SPOTS ALONG THE ALL-YEAR HIGHWAY, SR 140

The All-Year Highway (as it was called when completed in 1927), or SR 140 (as it is now known), runs from Merced to the Yosemite Valley. It passes through one of the most interesting and romantic of California's historic regions. Many of the landmarks of mining days have been obliterated, but here and there stark ruined walls of brick or stone marking the site of some ghost city of the hills may be seen, or an occasional hamlet invites the passerby to linger and picture the lively scenes enacted there in the heyday of its past.

About seven miles from the Merced county line the old Yosemite highway branches to the east. A little to the northwest is the site of Indian Gulch, while to the northeast is Guadalupe, both flourishing mining camps at one time. Stone fences built by Chinese labor are in evidence throughout much of this region. After traversing Cathey's Valley, first settled in the early 1850s and still claiming among its inhabitants descendants of original settlers, the road climbs into the lower mountains of Mariposa County. A few miles west of Mariposa, the Agua Fria Road swings to the north to Mount

Wawona Hotel, Yosemite National Park

Mariposa County Courthouse

Bullion. The marker (SRL 518) commemorating Agua Fria is on the north side of SR 140 at Carson, now deserted. Both Carson and sites at neighboring Arkansas Flat were operated as mining camps by hardscrabblers in the depression years of the 1930s.

Agua Fria, the exact site of which is just north of SR 140 on the road to Mount Bullion, was the first county seat of Mariposa County. Today scarcely a trace of the place is left except for a few foundation stones and abandoned diggings, and it is hard to believe that this was once the seat of government for one-fifth of California.

MARIPOSA

Mariposa, founded on John C. Frémont's Rancho Las Mariposas, a grant that occupied a unique position in the mining history of the state (discussed later in this chapter), became the county seat of Mariposa County in September 1851 and was long the center of trade for the mining area covered by the rancho. The town today has preserved some of the features of early mining camps—buildings with substantial walls of brick and stone supplemented by iron doors and shutters, with an occasional overhanging balcony.

Among the several buildings dating from early mining days the one of greatest interest is the courthouse (SRL 670). Lumber from neighboring forests was used in its construction and the timbers were fitted together with mortise and tenon and held in place by wooden pegs. Built in 1854, it is the oldest courthouse in California still in use. The clock on its tower has been running since 1866. The rear addition dates from 1900. In spite of their years of service the seats and the bar in the courtroom on the second floor remain unchanged. Adding to the building's historic interest are many documents and newspaper files of priceless value, which are kept in a fireproof vault. Court was conducted in rented quarters

in Mariposa from September 1851 until about May 1855, when it moved into the new courthouse. Three of the old houses facing the courthouse are more than a century old.

Other picturesque and historic buildings in Mariposa are St. Joseph's Catholic Church (1862, enlarged 1958), the Trabucco Warehouse (built before the fire of 1866, which it survived), the Schlageter Hotel (1866), the Trabucco Store, and the Odd Fellows Hall (1867), all of which, like the courthouse, are still in use, and the now-abandoned old stone jail. The Jones home on Jones Street (1858) is still a private residence, as is the Counts house (1865 or earlier) across the street. The weekly *Mariposa Gazette* boasts that it has not missed an issue since January 10, 1854; it is now located in a new building, but its old quarters may still be seen at Jones and Ninth Streets, a frame structure now housing the Chamber of Commerce.

The Mariposa County Library and History Center at Twelfth and Jessie Streets contains furniture belonging to the Frémont family, good displays of 1900s-era businesses, much Indian material, and outdoor exhibits connected with mining activities. Dedicated in 1971 and continually expanding, it is one of the most comprehensive collections in the Mother Lode country. The California State Mining and Mineral Museum, at 5007 Fairgrounds Road, displays collections begun in 1865 by the California State Geological Society and in 1880 by the California State Mining Bureau. E Clampus Vitus has placed a plaque "dedicated to the miners and founders for their foresight. Today's collection displays specimens from all over the world."

VANISHED TOWNS NEAR MARIPOSA

Mormon Bar (SRL 323), one and one-half miles southeast of Mariposa on Mariposa Creek, was first settled

Stamping Mill, Mariposa County History Center

in 1849 by Mormons, who, however, stayed only a short time. Their places were taken at once by other miners, while at a later period the same ground was worked over by thousands of Chinese. The site of Mormon Bar has been obliterated by the widening of the highway, but the Mariposa County Fairgrounds are today located close to the old town site. No longer to be seen is the old Chinese graveyard from which friends or relatives carried the bones of the dead back to ancestral burying grounds in China.

Buckeye to the west, where James Savage had one of his trading posts, Bootjack to the east, and Ben Hur, about ten miles to the north, all shared with Mormon Bar the prosperity of their neighbor, the town of Mariposa. Virtually nothing remains of these settlements today. The site of the last Ben Hur post office on the Quick Ranch is located about a mile southeast of the older site on the hill. (The first post office, established in 1890, was named for a then-popular novel; the post office was discontinued in 1951.) Not far away is the Quick ranch house, into which has been incorporated a portion of the original house built by Morgan W. Quick, who purchased the 160 acres of his ranch in 1859 from two men having squatters' rights. The garden and orchard around the present house are still watered from the perpetual spring that attracted the first settlers. The 4,000 acres that constitute the present ranch, still owned by the family, are fenced by a stone wall, built with great labor and remarkable skill by Chinese workmen in 1862. The old wall, which extends for five miles up hill and down, is a marvelous piece of workmanship, and appears to be as sound as it was when first laid.

MOUNT BULLION

Mount Bullion, located on the mountain of that name, on a part of the former Frémont estate, is some five miles northwest of Mariposa on SR 49. The peak was named in honor of Senator Thomas H. Benton, Frémont's father-in-law, whose nickname was "Old Bullion." Only a few buildings remain. The deserted Princeton Mine nearby produced almost $4.5 million from its ore. Originally one of Frémont's possessions, it has been closed since 1927; there persists a local belief that a fortune remains to be extracted some day.

MOUNT OPHIR

Another vanished town of the Mother Lode is Mount Ophir, located one and one-half miles northwest of Mount Bullion off SR 49. A historical marker stands by the road; the site is a few hundred feet to the west in a brush-covered area. Nothing remains of this once busy settlement except fragmentary ruins, long believed to be those of a privately owned mint from the early 1850s. Recent investigations indicate that no such enterprise existed. It has been suggested the marker was placed as part of an effort to attract tourists in the early 1900s. Just beyond Mount Ophir, on the way to Bear Valley, farther down SR 49, the walls of the Trabucco Store stand at the left of the road, "as pretty a ruin as most of the missions can show," as one traveler has described it. Louis Trabucco built his store here around 1853.

BEAR VALLEY

The present Mariposa County includes what was once Rancho Las Mariposas, the Frémont Grant, a vast estate constituting one of several "floating grants," and located originally in what is now Merced County. A "floating grant," the cause of endless litigation after the American conquest of California, was a grant of land for which the area was precisely given but the actual boundaries were left unspecified, usually because of inadequate surveys of the region in question. After gold was discovered in the Mariposa region in the spring of 1848, Frémont "floated" his rancho up into the hills. The new location proved to be very rich in gold, and for several years Frémont carried on large operations there.

The center of his activities was Bear Valley (SRL 331), on SR 49 about eleven miles northwest of Mariposa. At one time it was practically Frémont's own town, built, owned, and lived in by him. The site of his home is on a slight rise just southeast of Bear Valley to the east of the highway. Local Indians called the whitewashed frame structure "the little White House," probably without irony, although Frémont had been the unsuccessful presidential candidate of the new Republican Party in 1856, two years before the house was built. It was something of a rural showplace until it burned in 1866 and the site was leveled.

At Bear Valley one can see the iron framework of the Odd Fellows Hall, built in 1862 and now in ruins. The enterprising Trabucco family built yet another store here, the iron doors of which still stand. The Nicholas Pendola building and the Garbarius Store are other ruins.

Just beyond Bear Valley, continuing northwest on SR 49 toward Coulterville, stand the ruins of Bear Valley's once thriving Chinatown. The climb up the ridge road from this point is so gradual that one is startled, on making a sudden turn, to look down a thousand feet into "Hell's Hollow," a winding grade famous for its dangers even with modern roads. To the north, a vista overlooking the hills is of great beauty, particularly when the spring wildflowers are in bloom.

The winding grade down into the hollow passes the Pine Tree and Josephine mines, once big producers for Frémont. The next place of historic interest is Bagby, formerly Benton Mills, the site of one of Frémont's largest mills and river dams. Bagby was a station on the Yosemite Valley Railroad. When the New Exchequer Dam was completed in 1966 and the waters of the Merced River began to back up and create Lake McClure, Bagby was one of several locations inundated by the waters of the lake.

COULTERVILLE

The old mining town of Coulterville (SRL 332) is one of the most picturesque and interesting on the Mother Lode. Mexican miners were at work there when George W. Coulter and George Maxwell arrived in 1850 and set up stores. Coulter embellished his goods tent with a small American flag, and Banderita ("little flag") was the name first given to the settlement, although Coulterville soon became its official name.

Like most of the Mother Lode towns, Coulterville suffered a series of disastrous fires, and most of the remaining old buildings are of adobe, stone, or brick, many with iron doors and shutters. Among these are the Jeffrey Hotel (1851), still dispensing hospitality, and the picturesque Sun Sun Wo Company, like the Jeffrey Hotel an adobe structure dating back to 1851, but not in use since 1920. Both buildings are marked with informative E Clampus Vitus plaques. The Gazzola and Jaenecke Buildings have been restored and are in business, and the Canova House and Storehouse and the

Magnolia Saloon and Museum are standing in good shape. At the northern edge of town the old frame house associated with Coulter, built in 1857, remains a private residence.

Built around the ruins of the Coulter Hotel is the Northern Mariposa County History Center. The structure also includes the old Wells Fargo Building (1856) and McCarthy's Store. Nelson Cody, brother of "Buffalo Bill" Cody, was postmaster here in the 1870s. In front of the History Center (and under the town's Hanging Tree) is an eight-ton Porter narrow-gauge locomotive that did its duty on the tortuous line from the Mary Harrison Mine to the Black Creek Potosi stamping mill, one of several rail lines in California claiming to be "The Crookedest Railroad in the World." The locomotive was in service for many years, beginning in 1897.

EL PORTAL

This "gateway" on the west to Yosemite Valley was the terminus of the Yosemite Valley Railroad from Merced (1906–45). As the rising waters of Lake McClure filled some of the river valleys below, old equipment from the narrow-gauge railroad was brought to a site a half-mile west of El Portal and is now on display at the Yosemite Valley Railroad Center. El Portal is also a Park Service headquarters and contains housing for employees working in Yosemite National Park, which begins a half-mile east of El Portal. The settlement perches on a ledge above the Merced River and along SR 140.

UNUSUAL NAMES

In the early mining days millions of dollars in gold were washed from the gravel beds of Mariposa County's many streams. Quartz mining succeeded placer mining, and veins of fabulous wealth were located in the Mother Lode, which extends across the width of the county. Numerous camps sprang up all over the county, many of them with odd or unusual names, such as Texas Tent, Cow-and-Calf, Drunken Gulch, Red Cloud, Poison Springs, Hog Canyon, Fly Away, Boneyard, White Rock, Mariposita, Sherlock's Diggings, Whitlock, Pleasant Valley, Chamisal, and Hornitos. Only Hornitos can still be located and visited.

HORNITOS

Hornitos ("little ovens"), thirteen miles west of Mount Bullion, derived its name in all likelihood from the presence of many Mexican graves or tombs built of stone in the shape of little bake ovens and set on top of the ground. On the hillside just below the Catholic church and cemetery the ruins of two or three of these interesting relics may be seen. An alternative view is that the name Hornitos came rather from the outdoor ovens on which the Mexican families cooked. Some early settlers may have come from Los Hornitos in Sonora, Mexico, and bestowed a familiar name on the new location, a common practice throughout much of North America.

Hornitos was settled by Mexican miners and their associates, driven from the settlement of Quartzburg, four miles east on the highway, in 1850. The new place had a reputation for rowdiness and violence, with names like Dead Man's Alley, and a Chinese colony where gambling dens were run openly. Inevitably, local legends tell that the notorious bandit Joaquín Murieta was a denizen of Hornitos. "Blood was on nearly every doorstep and the sand was caked with it," says one account.

In time, however, a change came over the place. When the placers at Quartzburg (a short distance up the creek) gave out, many of its citizens came to Hornitos, where the diggings were very rich. In 1870 it became the first and remains the only incorporated town in Mariposa County. Ordinances were passed remedying many of the old social abuses, the gambling dens became stores, and children played on the streets. The "city" has never been officially disincorporated, but it has not exercised its municipal functions for many years.

Hornitos (SRL 333) has some interesting buildings from the mining days: the stout stone jail, the Cavagnaro and Gagliardo stores (parts of the interiors of which are on display in the County Historical Center in Mariposa), and two remaining walls of the store run by Domingo Ghirardelli, who left to open his chocolate factory in San Francisco "and has since become a household word," as one contemporary admirer says. The Masonic Hall, a single-story building from 1860 that is still in use, was once the only one in California with its meeting hall on the ground floor. A few bullet holes can be seen in the door casings. St. Catherine's Catholic Church, built in 1869, has not held regular services for many years, but it is periodically given a fresh coat of whitewash.

As for virtuous Quartzburg, at one time a populous center of placer mining in Mariposa County, with fraternal societies and all the organizations that made up the social life of the time but no tolerance for the Mexicans whom they called "rowdies," its last fragments were bulldozed when the highway was widened in 1979. Only the old cemetery on the hill to the north of Road J-16, about four miles east of Hornitos, survives as a reminder that in 1851 this place came close to being chosen the county seat of Mariposa County.

Mendocino County

Mendocino County was one of the original twenty-seven counties, but until 1859 the government was administered by Sonoma County officials. The name was first applied to Cape Mendocino, so named in honor of Antonio de Mendoza, the first viceroy of New Spain, although it is not known when the name was first used. Ukiah has always been the county seat.

POINT ARENA

Point Arena, or Punta de Arena ("Sandy Point"), is a prominent headland on the coast in the southwestern part of the county. Captain George Vancouver spent the night of November 10, 1792, offshore at this point in his ship *Discovery*, while on his way from Nootka, in what is now British Columbia, to San Francisco. Vancouver called the place Punta Barro de Arena ("sandy clay").

The land stretching back from this point was included in an unnamed and unconfirmed grant made in 1844 to Rafael García, an early soldier of the San Francisco Company and already owner of two grants in what is now Marin County. He stocked the land with cattle. The Garcia River flowing through the land bears his name. This grantee and Antonio Castro were reported to have been the leaders of a party of white men who raided the Indians in the vicinity of Ross in 1845 in search of laborers.

The Manchester Indian Rancheria is located on the Garcia River; the Point Arena Indian Rancheria is located about two miles to the west, off Windy Hollow Road, three miles south of Manchester.

Although a store was in operation on the site in 1859, the town of Point Arena was not incorporated until 1908. It is said that when the lumbering industry was at its height, Point Arena was the busiest town on the coast between San Francisco and Eureka. Asphalt, which exuded from the ocean bluff nearby in quantities insufficient for commercial exploitation—as was proved during the oil excitement of 1865—is used on the streets of the town and makes a satisfactory road surface.

In 1870 a light station was constructed near the edge of the point. The tower, built of brick, fell in the earthquake of 1906, and another, of reinforced concrete, was built subsequently a little distance back from the point. The present tower is 115 feet high; it and Pigeon Point Lighthouse in San Mateo County, of the same height, are the two loftiest on the Pacific Coast. Before the establishment of this light, many ships were lost here. In a disastrous storm on the night of November 20, 1865, ten vessels went ashore within a few miles of the point. In 1949, the British cargo ship *Pacific Enterprise* was wrecked near the lighthouse.

The light has been operated automatically since 1976. The tower is open to the public for tours. A museum is in the adjacent Fog Signal Building. The light station is located about three miles north of the town of Point Arena and about a mile and a half west of SR 1.

THE REDWOODS

The humid coastal belt in which this county lies is the natural habitat of the coast redwood (*Sequoia sempervirens*). The rugged shoreline, famous for its vistas of the Pacific Ocean, is cut by wooded canyons formed by the numerous mountain streams flowing seaward through fine stands of these and other native trees. The abundant redwood trees, and their superb, durable lumber, induced rapid settlement and exploitation in much the same way that gold brought settlers and adventurers into the Mother Lode and the Sierra Nevada. Fortunately, some of these forests escaped the axe and saw of the pioneer lumbermen. Efforts made by the Save the Redwoods League and other conservation groups have resulted in the creation of a series of parks and reserves throughout the Redwood Empire of northern coastal California.

Russian Gulch State Park just north of Mendocino covers 1,103 acres, some of which contain stands of second-growth redwoods. Other coastal preserves are Van Damme State Park to the south; along the coast north of Mendocino, the Jug Handle State Reserve; and, near the Humboldt county line, the large Sinkyone Wilderness State Park, containing a stand of old-growth redwoods, the Sally Bell Grove. North of Laytonville are the Smithe Redwoods State Reserve and the Standish-Hickey State Recreation Area. The Admiral William H. Standley State Recreation Area just south of Branscomb, fourteen miles west of Laytonville, is another redwood preserve, named for a naval officer born in the county. Montgomery Woods State Reserve and Mailliard Redwoods State Reserve are, respectively, northwest of Ukiah and west of SR 128 at Ornbaum Springs. The part of Hendy Woods State Park along the Navarro River contains two large redwood groves; the park is near Philo on SR 128.

COASTAL MILL TOWNS

During the height of the lumbering activity, between 1855 and 1915, a number of towns grew up along the coast, each one a shipping point. In almost every mile, along a creek or gulch or river, could be found a mill with its narrow-gauge railway built up a canyon a few miles for the purpose of bringing lumber or logs from the mountains down to the landing places. Ox teams dragged the logs from where they were felled to the railways. Most of these mills along the coast were operated with no loading facilities other than chutes from the cliffs, down which the lumber was slipped to the vessels lying at anchor below. A stationery device that was also used to pull logs was the "steam donkey," and one of these may be seen at the Jackson Demonstration State Forest on SR 20 about halfway between Fort Bragg and Willits. The Mendocino County Museum in Willits has a good display of various lumbering equipment.

From north to south these coast towns were Usal, Rockport, Hardy Creek, Westport, Cleone, Fort Bragg, Noyo, Caspar, Mendocino, Little River, Albion, Navarro, Greenwood, Elk River, and, at the very southern edge of the county, Gualala. With the decline of lumbering, many of these towns lost much of their population. Around 1960, a new influx of tourists headed for the Mendocino County coast; artists find the region stimulating, and hikers and naturalists enjoy the many nearby attractions.

Rockport is an almost abandoned place on a wild and inhospitable coast. Noyo, lying at the mouth of the Noyo River, is associated with fishing, another industry in decline. Little River contains two famous hostelries. The Little River Inn is located in the Silas W. Coombs House, built in 1853 and completely modernized. Nearby is Heritage House, whose first building was put up in 1877. For many years it was owned by the same family. The place enjoyed a varied past, and was said to be a rum-running center for bootleggers during Prohibition. Albion is another fishing town. The second mill in the county was erected there during the winter of 1852–53 under contract with Captain William Richardson of Marin County. In 1845 Richardson applied for a grant of land covering this area, which extended from the Albion River to the Garcia River. This Albion Grant was, however, never confirmed by the United States.

Navarro, set in a deep valley at the mouth of a broad, winding river, was in decline as early as 1913, when J. Smeaton Chase described it: "Most of the buildings were out of plumb; the church leaned at an alarming angle; and a loon, swimming leisurely in the middle of the stream, seemed to certify the solitude of the place." Today little remains of the old town of Navarro, but another community fourteen miles up the river preserves the name, now famous for its wineries. Greenwood is the location of the Elk post office. Gualala, at the mouth of the picturesque Gualala River, had its lumbering heyday in the 1860s and 1870s, and today is popular with artists.

Along this part of the Mendocino coast, many

Kelley House, Mendocino

houses and barns were built of the abundant lumber and painted red with white trim, a style said to be akin to that of the New England coast and described often as "State-of-Maine" architecture. While lumbering remained an important part of the coastal economy, agriculture also developed.

MENDOCINO

A ship on its way to San Francisco in 1851 with a cargo of silk and tea encountered a severe storm and was driven ashore at the mouth of the Noyo River. A party sent from Bodega to salvage the freight saw the timber along this part of the coast, with its readily available lumber supply, and carried the information to Alderman Harry Meiggs of San Francisco. Meiggs, in addition to his political interests, was a mill owner and lumberman, with his main depot at North Beach in San Francisco. With an eye on the opportunity to exploit the territory, Meiggs acquired special equipment to handle immense logs and in July 1852 brought his gear north on the chartered brig *Ontario* to the mouth of Big River. Here William Kasten, one of those who had been driven ashore by the storm, claimed the waterfront. Meiggs purchased Kasten's claim and set up the California Lumber Company, the first mill products of which went to build Kasten's new house on what is now Kasten Street in Mendocino.

Landmarks in the small town of Mendocino include the Mendocino Presbyterian Church (SRL 714), dedicated in 1868, the oldest of its denomination in continuous use in California, and the Masonic Hall at the corner of Lansing and Ukiah Streets. The carved redwood statuary atop the 1866 building are symbols of the Masonic Order. The Ford House Visitor Center at 724 Main Street was acquired by the State Depart-

Presbyterian Church, Mendocino

ment of Parks and Recreation as part of the Mendocino Headlands State Park in 1972. It has exhibits on the natural and cultural history of the area. The house was built by Jerome Ford for his bride, Martha, in 1854, and was in the family for many years; Ford was manager of the Mendocino operation of the California Lumber Company. William H. Kelley, who arrived with Meiggs at the mouth of Big River in 1852, stayed on to build his elegant two-story house at 45007 Albion Street in 1861. The Kelley House, preserved by Mendocino Historical Research, Inc., contains a useful reference library and is set in attractive grounds. The town of Mendocino is a Historic Preservation District listed on the National Register of Historic Places.

FORT BRAGG

U.S. Army Lieutenant Horatio Gates Gibson was ordered in June 1857 to establish a military post on the Mendocino Indian Reservation. The post was placed one and one-half miles north of the mouth of the Noyo River and was named Fort Bragg in honor of General Braxton Bragg of Mexican War fame. Lieutenant Gibson, who afterward attained the rank of brigadier general, remained there for one year. For some years before his death in his nineties he had the distinction of being the oldest living graduate of West Point.

Fort Bragg was located within the city limits of the thriving town that grew up on its site. A historical marker (SRL 615) at 321 Main Street stands upon land that was once part of the fort. The last building from the site, the Fort Building, once stood at 90 West Redwood Avenue, and was taken away. This location is now occupied by a large wooden structure, once the C. R. Johnson guest house and now known as the Guest House Museum (also known as the Fort Bragg Redwood Museum), which has displays on logging and lumbering.

Adjacent to the Guest House Museum is the Fort Bragg station of the California Western Railroad. Fort Bragg is the only coastal city in the county to have a railroad connection today. The route of the California Western is one of the most scenic in the state, passing along the Noyo River through magnificent forests to Willits on US 101, the Redwood Highway. The railroad, which ships lumber and freight, also offers a passenger service, the "Skunk Train," which has become very popular with tourists. Fort Bragg is also a shipping point for fish and farm and dairy products. From here the coast road (SR 1) runs north through several miles of sand dunes. At Ten Mile River the shore becomes rugged with high cliffs and surf-beaten rocks honeycombed with caves.

WILLITS

The town of Willits, forty miles east of Fort Bragg, had its origins in a store opened in 1856 by Kirk Brier from Petaluma. His venture was followed by a blacksmith shop and a saloon. Hiram Willits, who had come to the county in 1857, purchased the store; the town, which was incorporated in 1888, was named after him. The Mendocino County Museum is located at 400 East Commercial Street, an outstanding example of local historic preservation. Nearby is the eastern terminus of the California Western Railroad, popularly known as the Skunk Train. The name seems to have come from the diesel fumes encountered by passengers on the trip.

ROUND VALLEY

North of the town of Covelo is Round Valley (SRL 674), a circular valley about seven miles in diameter. This is the center of the large Round Valley Indian Reservation, established in 1858. Two years before, a farm called the Nome Cult Station (from *Nomcult*, the Wintun word for "West Tribe") was established by the

Guest House Museum, Fort Bragg

government to be a breeding and fattening station for beef to supply the reservation at Fort Bragg on the coast. In these years, there was a steady encroachment of settlers upon Indian lands, and "reservations" were made to bring Indians together away from areas of conflict with the white newcomers. At least nine tribes, some of them with legacies of enmity toward the others, were gathered together here beginning in 1858. With little interest from most government officials, tensions arose in this area of enforced settlement; in 1863 a military post was established there. Soon afterward a company of cavalry came as reinforcement. For some years, "hostile" Indians were sent here, where they were in relative isolation from their tribes. In the post–Civil War 1860s, the Army in the West was primarily concerned with Indian affairs, and General U. S. Grant turned over the post to the care of the Methodist Episcopal Church, in keeping with his more peaceable policy toward the Indians. Round Valley remains a sizeable community, now largely self-governing. The Round Valley historical monument is located at Inspiration Point on the main road between Dos Rios and Covelo.

Spy Rock Road extends eastward from US 101 two miles south of Twin Rocks Creek and thirty-three miles north of Willits, toward the Eel River Canyon and the western limits of the Round Valley Indian Reservation. About eight miles along this road is Spy Rock above the canyon, where it was said that Indians built smoke signal fires in the years when they were threatened by settlers.

THE SANEL GRANT, SANEL, AND HOPLAND

Most of the population and modern cities of inland Mendocino County lie in the upper valley of the Russ-

ian River. Fernando Felix or Feliz, a former *regidor* (town councilman) at the Pueblo San José and already owner of Rancho Novato, received in 1844 a large tract of land along the river in Sanel Valley. Just south of modern Hopland he built an adobe house and lived there with his family. He had been there for seven years when in 1860 he received the United States patent for his estate's 17,754 acres.

The settlement that grew up around the Felix home was known by 1859 as Sanel. Then a toll road was built down the east side of the river, which rerouted all the traffic that way, and the town gradually moved over to the road, leaving only a single brick store building behind. The new site was called Hopland. Later the building of a railroad drew business back to the original site, and eventually the two places consolidated as Hopland. The residents kept the memory of Old Hopland and New Hopland.

A populous Indian village once existed just south of Old Hopland on the south bank of McDowell Creek. It was called "Sanel," and from this village the grant, the township, and the town preceding Hopland all inherited the name Sanel. The first hops grown here were planted by Stephen Warren Knowles, who settled in Sanel Township in 1858, after arriving in San Francisco on the steamer *Northern Light* a few years earlier. Hop growing has now been replaced by extensive vineyards in this area.

Six miles south of Hopland on US 101 is Squaw Rock or Lover's Leap (SRL 549), which is associated with a Sanel Indian legend. Sotuka, an Indian maiden, is supposed to have jumped from the precipice upon her faithless lover and the girl for whom he had deserted her, as they lay sleeping below, bringing death to all three.

THE YOKOYA GRANT AND UKIAH

The Indian word *yokoya* has been translated to mean "deep valley between high hills" or "south valley." The Yokoya Grant of eleven square leagues lay in the fertile valley of the Russian River. It was given by Governor Pío Pico in 1845 to Cayetano Juárez, a native Californian who was a captain of militia and had engaged in many forays against the Indians. Captain Juárez was also the grantee of Rancho Tulocay in the Napa Valley four years earlier. He died in 1833, and his heirs received patent to this land from the United States in 1867. Later owners (Hastings, Curry, and Carpenter) surveyed the property and sold it in tracts.

The city of Ukiah, within the boundary of the grant and taking its name phonetically from Yokoya, had its origin in the 1850s. The first settler on the site, Sam Lowry, had established himself there by 1856, but sold out within a year to A. T. Perkins, who became a permanent resident. In 1859, when Sonoma County officials were relieved of the administration of Mendocino County affairs, the little town was chosen as the county seat. At that time only 100 people were dwelling in the Russian River Valley.

The Sun House (SRL 926) is an interesting and unusual building in Ukiah, at 431 South Main Street. This was constructed in 1911 in the California Craftsman style, featuring extensive use of redwood, and has the Hopi Indian sign for the sun deity placed over the front door. This was the home of John Hudson, M.D., and his wife, Grace Carpenter Hudson. He became one of the leading amateur anthropologists of his day, concentrating on the Pomo Indians. Grace Hudson was a well-known artist whose paintings—more than 600—document the life of the Pomo Indians, who were fast dying out in her lifetime. The Grace Hudson Museum, on the extensive grounds of the Sun House, is a showplace for many of her paintings and for Dr. Hudson's collections of basketry, manuscripts, and correspondence. Owned and operated by the city of Ukiah, the Sun House is listed on the National Register of Historic Places.

Another interesting building in Ukiah is Moore's Flour Mill at 400 South State Street. Still in operation, the water-powered mill employs grindstones well over 100 years old. The Held-Poage Memorial Home and Research Library at 603 West Perkins Street, built in 1903, contains some 4,500 volumes on American history, focusing on Mendocino County, as well as extensive historical photographs, maps, scrapbooks, and artifacts, including local native basketry. At the northern edge of Ukiah is the Parducci Winery, established in 1931, and for many years the northernmost winery in California.

MINERAL SPRINGS

Vichy Springs (SRL 980), known and used by the Indians before the arrival of white settlers, is three miles east of Ukiah. The resort opened in 1854 and is now the oldest continuously operating mineral-springs spa in California. The waters are said to be very similar to those of Vichy in France, which were known in Roman times. Another spa is at Orr Hot Springs, thirteen miles west of Ukiah on Orr Springs Road.

BLACK BART'S ROCK

South of Willits, at the bottom of a slope on the west side of US 101, is a huge boulder that once lay further up alongside the highway. This is Black Bart's Rock, said to be a haunt of the bandit Black Bart, who robbed the mail stage there. Between 1875 and 1883 Black Bart single-handedly robbed twenty-seven coaches, traveling on foot for thousands of miles in rough mountain country from the Coast Range to the Sierra. Once he was said to have robbed two coaches sixty miles apart within twenty-four hours in a rough mountain region. Never vicious and not a killer, he was immaculate in dress and polite.

For years this quiet, respectable-looking man lived in San Francisco; he even frequented a bakery on Kearny Street that was a favorite of San Francisco police officers, sometimes eating at the same table with them. Black Bart seemed to enjoy his cleverness and notoriety, and a decided sense of humor often expressed itself in facetious rhymes left on empty mail or express boxes for the baffled officers to read.

Black Bart's identity was unraveled through the combined efforts of Sheriff Thorne of San Andreas, Detective Harry Morse, and special agent James B. Hume of Wells Fargo Company, whose stages were most often robbed. The bandit's clean habits ironically proved his undoing. On November 3, 1883, at Funk Hill, on the stage run between Sonora and Milton in Calaveras County, near the scene of the first robbery of his career, he dropped a handkerchief while he was busily engaged in opening an express box containing $4,100 in coin. The mark "F.X.o.7." on this piece of linen led Detective Morse, hired by Hume, to a laundry in San Francisco to which the fastidious "Black Bart" had for years carried his little bundle. He lived in San Francisco under the name of Charles E. Bolton, ostensibly a mining man who made periodic trips to the mines. He was lodged in jail at San Andreas and was quickly sentenced to San Quentin Prison, where he began his term on November 21, 1883, and was released January 23, 1888. His whereabouts after that date are unknown.

ANDERSON VALLEY

About fifteen miles long and three miles wide, Anderson Valley is crossed by SR 128 halfway between US 101 and the coast. Settled in 1850, it has been a prosperous agricultural region ever since. In recent years wine making has been added to apple and hop growing.

"Boontling" is a dialect peculiar to Anderson Valley,

and is thought to have begun among the hop growers around the town of Boonville. The more than 1,200 special words of Boontling derive from Pomo Indian speech, Spanish, and the language of early Scotch-Irish settlers. It is still in use among many of the valley folk. Glossaries of Boontling have been compiled and can be purchased locally.

Boonville, the chief town of the valley, is also the site of the Mendocino County Fairgrounds and the charming Anderson Valley Historical Museum, located in the Little Red School House on the main thorough-fare through town. The Evergreen Cemetery, still in use, is a well-maintained historic spot on the outskirts of Boonville.

Merced County

Merced County was organized in 1855 from a part of Mariposa County. It was named for the river that Gabriel Moraga, in 1806, had called El Río de Nuestra Señora de la Merced, "The River of Our Lady of Mercy." The county seat was first located on the Turner and Osborn Ranch, but in 1857 it was moved to Snelling's Ranch, and in 1872 to the city of Merced.

RANCHERIA IN MENJOULET CANYON

Menjoulet Canyon, named for a French sheep herder of the late 1870s, is today under the waters of Los Banos Creek Reservoir. In 1925 the plateau adjacent to the canyon was excavated, revealing the site of a three- or four-hundred-year-old Indian rancheria. Well-defined outlines of six houses were discovered, one of them sixty-seven feet across and six feet deep. An old barn, fire pits, and the remains of some forty bodies were also discovered. A second excavation in 1964, just before inundation began, discovered the first cremations ever found in the region. This is the earliest known human habitation in Merced County.

FIRST EXPEDITIONS

Little was known of the great interior valleys of the San Joaquin and Sacramento Rivers until the beginning of the nineteenth century. During the second administration of Governor José Joaquín de Arrillaga (1802–14), active exploration of the interior began to check Indian raids on the coastal settlements and establish missions for Indian conversion. A number of minor expeditions were made into the tulares, or swamps, of the San Joaquin in 1805 and 1806, but little record is left of these. The first expeditions of which we have much knowledge, as well as the most important from the standpoint of accomplishments, were those made by Gabriel Moraga, called "the greatest pathfinder and Indian fighter of his day."

Moraga, with twenty-five men and Father Pedro Muñoz as chaplain and diarist, left San Juan Bautista on September 21, 1806, probably entering the valley of the tules by way of San Luis Creek in Merced County. Proceeding across the San Joaquin River, they reached a slough, the haunt of numerous butterflies, which Moraga named "Las Mariposas." Father Muñoz says that here one of the soldiers was sorely afflicted by a butterfly that lodged in his ear. The name, in the singular form, survives in Mariposa Slough, Mariposa Creek, and Mariposa County. The creek has its source in Mariposa County, which lay east of Moraga's march.

Traveling north and northwest, the party toiled for forty miles through a parched and treeless plain. Coming suddenly upon a clear, sparkling stream, they expressed their gratitude by naming it El Río de Nuestra Señora de la Merced, a name that was applied not only to the Merced River but later to the county and to the present city and county seat. The place seemed so beautiful to the tired travelers that Father Muñoz enthusiastically declared it to be an excellent site for a mission.

Moraga explored the lower course of the Merced River in the fall of 1808. He again touched the county in 1810 on his way down the west side of the San Joaquin River from the north. Turning west along San Luis Creek, he returned to San Juan Bautista by way of Pacheco Pass.

Neither Moraga nor the mission fathers seem to have appreciated his contribution to the knowledge of California geography. The mission fathers thought the project was a failure, since it had discovered no sites suitable for an inland chain of missions.

The first American to pass through the San Joaquin Valley, although he may not have entered what is now Merced County, was Jedediah Strong Smith, pathfinder and trailbreaker of the West. In 1827 he and his party camped on various rivers in the San Joaquin Valley while trapping beaver. Smith called one of these the Wimmulche or Wimilche after a tribe of Indians living there. Some historians identify this river with the present Kings River. Smith trapped at this spot for a time, and then, leaving some of his men encamped on the river, he crossed over the Sierra Nevada in an easterly direction, by a route that has not been definitely determined.

Following Smith's footsteps came other adventurers, and from 1828 until the American occupation, beaver skins may have been gathered along the rivers of Merced County by Hudson's Bay Company trappers and others, among them Peter Skene Ogden, Michel La Framboise, and Ewing Young.

John C. Frémont, on his way out of California in 1844, proceeded southward from Sutter's Fort, passing through what is now Merced County, and reached the Merced River on April 1. On the following day a raft was constructed, with which the party crossed the river somewhere near its junction with the San Joaquin.

Camp was made on the far bank. On April 3 the expedition stopped on the north bank of Bear Creek five miles from its mouth, and the next day they ferried the stream, continuing up the San Joaquin River into today's Madera County.

RANCHO PANOCHE DE SAN JUAN Y LOS CARRISALITOS

Throughout the southwestern portion of Merced County old Indian trails may be traced in the marshlands, and the remains of prehistoric Indian villages have been uncovered at various water holes. Early in the nineteenth century, Spanish settlers evidently had sought to live in the area. When the survey of Rancho Panoche de San Juan y los Carrisalitos ("raw sugar of St. John and the little patches of reeds"), granted early in 1844 to Julian Ursana, was completed in 1866 and its patent was approved by the United States, adobes, already of a considerable age, stood on the rancho. The rancho covered five square leagues, over 20,000 acres.

RANCHO LAS MARIPOSAS

In 1847 John C. Frémont again figured briefly in Merced County history when on February 14 he purchased the Rancho Las Mariposas from Juan B. Alvarado, who had received it from Governor Micheltorena in 1844. This grant, of ten leagues, stipulated that the land be located within the area bounded on the west by the San Joaquin River, on the east by the Sierra Nevada foothills, on the north by the Merced River, and on the south by the Chowchilla River. Alvarado never complied with the usual legal requirements by building a house on the grant and inhabiting it within a year. In fact, he never saw the land, but on account of the hostility of the Indians he did apply to the governor for a military force to enable him to take possession. In answer to this request General José Castro was sent to the region with a company of mounted Californians. Fortifications were begun on the east bank of the San Joaquin River about six miles south of the Merced River, at or near the place where the town of Dover was later located. In December 1844 the Indians stole most of the horses, and the Californios had to make it back to Monterey as best they could.

It is said that Frémont first attempted to locate his grant near the site of the present town of Stevinson; a place called Fremont's Ford exists at a point on the San Joaquin River near this town, just south of where SR

140 crosses the river. There is some evidence that Frémont tried to locate his ranch near the site of the present Le Grand on Mariposa Creek. Early surveyors' maps show a house called Fremont's Ranch south of Mariposa Creek, and it is possible that he lived there for a while in 1848. When gold was discovered in the foothills above this ranch, Frémont established himself in the hills of what is now Mariposa County. He was successful in securing confirmation of his grant as located by him in the mining regions, instead of the valley. The precedent thus set was to cost the United States government many thousand square miles of territory claimed in other grants of a similar nature.

San Luis Camp Adobe

THE OLD STAGE ROAD

The numerous rivers and streams running from the Sierra Nevada into the San Joaquin Valley made it necessary for the early roads to follow along the base of the foothills and thus avoid the tules or swamps of the lowlands. These foothill roads afforded solid foundation even in rainy seasons. Also, the streams were more easily forded before they spread out over the level valley floor. Population during the 1850s and 1860s was centered on the mines, and supplies had to be freighted into the southern Mother Lode from Stockton along the stage route at the base of the hills. At the time of the formation of Merced County in 1855, the Legislature placed the eastern boundary along this Stockton–Fort Miller Road, which was a part of the road between Stockton and Los Angeles.

WESTSIDE TRAILS AND PACHECO PASS

Where the foothills of the Mount Diablo Range meet the western edge of the San Joaquin Valley, El Camino Viejo, the westside trail from San Pedro to San Antonio (now in Oakland), crossed El Arroyo de Ortigalito ("little nettle"), a link in the long chain of arroyos and *aguajes* (water holes) where Indians had settled for ages. From the water holes at Ortigalito, El Camino Viejo proceeded northwest to El Arroyo de los Baños del Padre Arroyo, where fresh water was again found.

Still farther to the north the road crossed El Arroyo de San Luís Gonzaga at Rancho Centinela, where another water hole was found 50 yards to the north. Leaving Centinela, El Camino Viejo skirted the abrupt foothills that led to El Arroyo de Romero, named after a Spaniard from San Juan Bautista who was killed there by Indians. Finally, El Arroyo de Quinto ("fifth creek"),

the last watering place in Merced County, was reached. An adobe, perhaps built before 1840, stood on the plains among the cottonwoods of Quinto Creek as late as 1915.

With the coming of the Americans and the growth of transportation from Stockton to points south, the Stockton-Visalia Road was developed parallel to El Camino Viejo. It followed the west side of the San Joaquin River, the route varying according to the seasonal changes in the river country. The one-story adobe at San Luis Camp on Wolfson Road, seven and one-half miles north of Los Banos via Highway J-14, was once an important low-water station on this road. Neglected for many years, it has been protected from the elements by an overhanging roof. This adobe and other structures built in the early 1840s came under the control of Miller and Lux; Henry Miller customarily slept in the house whenever he visited this part of his property.

Joining the Stockton-Visalia Road eight miles northeast of Los Banos, the older Pacheco Pass stage road came in from the west. Long before the Americans came, Indians had worn a deep trail over the hills by way of Pacheco Pass, and Spanish explorers, as well as Spanish officers in pursuit of deserting soldiers or runaway mission Indians, made use of this old mountain path.

A toll road was built over the Pacheco Pass in 1856–57 by A. D. Firebaugh. Two miles west of the summit (in Santa Clara County), and a mile from where the Mountain House later stood, he built a toll station. Portions of the old rock walls of the tollhouse may still be seen in the narrow defile below the present highway.

The early stage road was used by the Butterfield overland stages from 1858 to 1861; on it San Luis Station was an important stopping place. It was eighteen miles from San Luis Ranch east to the Lone Willow Station, and from there the stages passed through a long stretch of desolate alkali wastes to Temple's Ranch and on to Firebaugh's Ferry in Fresno County. During the middle 1860s the loneliness of this part of the road was relieved by the cabin of David Mortimer Wood at Dos Palos. There, a lantern was placed in the window at night to guide the drivers of the Gilroy-Visalia stages. Water for the horses was available, too, and in return Wood received supplies and mail brought by the stagecoaches. The part of the old road that lay between Los Banos Creek and Santa Rita ran about one mile and a half north of the present highway SR 152, which was completed in 1923. Along it were the earliest pioneer American settlements of the Los Banos district. Very little remains to mark any of these places except an occasional black and gnarled tree or faint traces of the former roadbed.

Pacheco Pass is now SRL 829; the state marker is at the Romero Overlook above the San Luis Reservoir. A branch of the Pacheco Pass Road crossed El Camino Viejo at Rancho Centinela. From this point it continued northeast to the ford on the San Joaquin River where Hill's Ferry in Stanislaus County was established in the days of the Gold Rush.

THE FIRST "CATTLE KING OF MERCED"

The first American settlers in Merced County were John M. Montgomery and Colonel Samuel Scott, two young Kentuckians. In the fall of 1849 they camped under one of the large valley oaks on the banks of the Merced River a short distance north of the Cox Ferry Bridge on the left side of SR 59, about four miles west of the present town of Snelling.

John Montgomery became the richest man in Merced County and was known as the "Land and Cattle King of Merced," the predecessor of Henry Miller. Before 1852 he had established a permanent home on Bear Creek, on what later became the Wolfsen Ranch, six miles east of Merced.

OLD RIVER TOWNS

As early as 1850 settlers came to the rivers and streams of Merced County and established homes. The vast fertile areas along the streams were used for livestock raising and agriculture, and almost invariably the ranchhouses on the through roads became inns. Finally, centers of trade grew up around some of them. After the advent of the railroad, however, trade deserted the old river towns and they became little more than memories.

Located on the Merced River six miles below Snelling was Hopeton, at first known as "Forlorn Hope." It

boasted two churches before Snelling had any. Merced Falls was one of the principal crossings on the Merced River along the route of the Stockton–Fort Miller Road. A flour mill and a woolen mill, indicative of two of the county's most important early industries, were located there until they were destroyed by fire in 1893. The lumber mills of the Yosemite Lumber Company were later located there, but now Merced Falls is almost deserted. The falls themselves are now submerged by a dammed lake created for a Pacific Gas and Electric Company power plant.

Dover was a landing place on the San Joaquin River five miles above the mouth of the Merced. Freight was brought by water to this point. The first settlement at the site of Dover was made in the fall of 1844, when General José Castro attempted to build a fort there to facilitate the location of Alvarado's grant, Las Mariposas. Dover was occupied by American settlers in 1866. Better boating facilities led to the abandonment of the site in favor of Hill's Ferry in Stanislaus County, six miles down the San Joaquin River.

THE COURTHOUSE TREE

The first county seat of Merced was located on the Turner and Osborn Ranch on Mariposa Creek, a place that later became known as the Given Ranch. The Courthouse Tree, under which the first county meetings were held, stood on the bank of the old channel of Mariposa Creek, which was considerably to the south of the present channel. The spot is one and one-half miles to the west of SR 99 and about seven miles southeast of Merced. Floods killed the tree in the winter of 1868–69 and no trace of the site remains.

SNELLING'S RANCH

Early in the spring of 1851, John Montgomery, Colonel Samuel Scott, and Dr. David Wallace Lewis established a "house of entertainment," perhaps a *cantina*, which was the beginning of the town of Snelling. At first it was only a brush shelter, but Dr. Lewis very soon built what was later known as Snelling's Hotel. In the fall of 1851 the Snelling family arrived and purchased the property.

In 1857 Snelling's Ranch replaced the Turner and Osborn Ranch as the site of the county seat, but in 1872 it was in turn superseded by the new town of Merced, located in the valley fifteen miles to the south. By that time the mines in the mountain regions were giving out, while agriculture was steadily growing in importance. New towns sprung up in the fertile valley regions where railroads were being built, and the old hill towns soon became almost deserted.

Snelling, although not a mining town, was an overflow from the mining regions, and was of considerable importance at one time, being on the well-traveled road to the Mariposa mines. Settled largely by people from the South, it was noted for its spirit of hospitality. Today Snelling is a quiet place, picturesquely situated, where the visitor may find a link with the past in the old courthouse (SRL 409), erected in 1857. The lower story is of stone; the thick walls of that section, which was once used as a jail, are pierced by narrow, heavily barred windows. The upper story was used as a local court of justice until the early 1990s. The building is not in use at the present. A stone monument dedicated to the memory of the pioneers and commemorating the 75th anniversary of the organization of Merced County was placed in front of the courthouse by the Native Sons of the Golden West in 1930.

Merced County Courthouse Museum

MERCED

Merced owes its prominence to being on the line of the Central Pacific Railroad as it pushed south and east through the San Joaquin Valley and being the nearest valley town to the southern Mother Lode and Yosemite beyond it. It has always been an important shipping and exchange place, served by two railroads and the nexus of three busy highways, SRs 59, 99, and 140, all of which converge and pass through the city. The fertile farmlands nearby have made Merced a major agricultural center as well.

A highlight of the city is the charming Merced County Courthouse Museum, located in the Italianate Renaissance Revival building put up in 1875. Located in its own park at N and 21st Streets, the old courthouse was rededicated as the home of the county museum in 1983. Among the displays are some of the rooms used until 1975 as county offices. The museum is operated by the Merced County Historical Society.

ATWATER

The Central Pacific placed a station in 1872 on the property of Marshall D. Atwater, a leading wheat rancher, and named it for him. In 1888 a town by the same name was established by the Merced Land and Fruit Company. Atwater, John W. Mitchell, and George S.

Bloss, Jr., all of whom made important contributions to the towns of Atwater, Merced, and Turlock in Stanislaus County, were natives of Connecticut. The Bloss family was a benefactor of the town of Atwater, and their home on the block between First, Cedar, and Second Streets and Broadway is now the headquarters of the Atwater Historical Society and open to the public as a house museum. The Bloss Memorial Hospital, the Bloss Memorial Library, and many high school scholarships are among their endowments.

Atwater has one of California's most distinctive attractions, the Castle Air Museum, opened in 1981 next to the site of Castle Air Force Base, originally the Merced Army Air Field. It was renamed for Brigadier General Frederick A. Castle, posthumously awarded the Medal of Honor after the Boeing B-17 "Flying Fortress" in which he was leading a mission was shot down late in 1944. One of these planes is displayed on the grounds of the museum along with more than forty aircraft, from World War II to recent times. An interior museum displays Air Force uniforms, equipment, and all kinds of historical memorabilia. Inspired by the United States Air Force's Heritage Program, the Castle Air Museum Foundation established and maintains this facility, which is located just off SR 99 at the Buhach off-ramp at Atwater.

RANCHO SAN LUIS GONZAGA

Juan P. Pacheco and José María Mejía were granted Rancho San Luis Gonzaga in 1843. Captain Mejía's

Bloss Home, Atwater

name had been added to the petition to lend prestige, and by agreement he conveyed his interest to Pacheco. The rancho had previously been granted in 1841 to Francisco Rivera, but he had not met the conditions of the grant, having left the land unoccupied for two years. (Grants of land in Alta California were often made to prominent men, who in return were to help prevent roving Indians from raiding the stock at the coast missions.) The petitioners, Pacheco and Mejía, indicated that they were prepared to do this, and they received the grant. Juan Pacheco died in 1855, and his property reverted to his father, Francisco Peréz Pacheco, already the holder of much land in present San Benito County.

The Arroyo de San Luís Gonzaga, which had received its name very early in the nineteenth century from Spanish explorers, was chosen by Juan Pacheco as his homesite. He built his adobe on the water hole at the site of Lis-nay-yuk, an old Indian village. To it herds of antelope came to drink, and traveling tribes of Indians rested by its springs on their journeys over Pacheco Pass.

Until land was sold to federal and state agencies, the entire rancho was owned by direct descendants of the Pachecos. The one-story adobe built by the younger Pacheco soon after he took possession of the rancho stood in good condition at San Luis Station on SR 152 until 1962. Still displaying in its walls the loopholes through which guns could be fired, the adobe was used in various ways through the years, including as a roadside refreshment stand in the 1920s and 1930s. The rancho was chosen as the site of the San Luis Dam, and the old water hole was to be under several hundred feet of water in the new reservoir. Excavations (which disclosed prehistoric burials estimated to be between 1,000 and 1,500 years old) were begun, with President John F. Kennedy present at the inaugural ceremonies in August 1962. Since 1948 the adobe had been the home

of Miss Paula Fatjo, a fifth-generation direct descendant of Don Francisco Pérez Pacheco and owner of much of the old rancho. Rather than allow her adobe to disappear, Miss Fatjo decided to move it, at her own expense, to her new ranch headquarters on the western part of the old rancho, just across Pacheco Pass in Santa Clara County, ten miles down the highway. The building was only a mile from its destination when, on December 6, 1962, the oldest existing adobe in the San Joaquin Valley collapsed into the highway. Much of the material was saved, but it is unlikely that the very costly restoration will be undertaken.

Pacheco also built a two-story adobe at San Luis, but it was destroyed in the earthquake of 1868. From 1858 to 1861, it had served as a station on the Butterfield Overland Stage Line.

Rancho Centinela was originally a part of San Luis Gonzaga. No traces remain of its old buildings. Centinela, on the road to Gustine at the crossing of San Luis Creek, is one of many places in California where legends of buried treasure long persisted. The name of the current roadside stop at the old site has been corrupted to "Santa Nella."

RANCHO SANJÓN DE SANTA RITA

Santa Rita, as well as San Luís Gonzaga, was a place name known to Gabriel Moraga as early as 1806; they were both mentioned in the journal of his expedition of that year. Rancho Sanjón ("deep slough") de Santa Rita was granted to Francisco Soberanes in 1841. With the coming of the Americans the grant changed hands many times. In 1863, a portion of the land of the rancho came into the possession of Henry Miller, who thus secured his first foothold in the San Joaquin Valley.

By 1866 the remainder of Rancho Sanjón de Santa Rita had been purchased by Miller. From that year the firm of Miller and Lux gradually increased its holdings in this section, until by the 1890s they owned land extending for sixty-eight miles along the west side of the San Joaquin Valley, from Firebaugh's Ferry in Fresno County to Arroyo de Orestimba in Stanislaus County. In addition, they held thousands of acres in the Buena Vista Lake district of Kern County, 200,000 acres on the east side of the valley, as well as thousands of acres in other parts of California (including their original holdings in the Santa Clara Valley) and in Oregon and Nevada. At the time of Miller's death on October 14, 1916, it was estimated that the "Kingdom of Miller and Lux" included a million acres of land and control of a million and a half more through leases and grazing arrangements for Miller's herds.

Henry Miller was so dominant and ruthless in his activities that he was disliked and feared by nearly everyone who came his way. By means of irrigation, he turned many barren tracts into flourishing fields. He often seized waters and lands for this purpose, fighting those who tried to prevent him. Once he had acquired water rights by force, he made adjacent towns and ranches buy from him, and at his price. The immense Miller and Lux holdings are now divided into smaller farms.

The Miller and Lux headquarters were at the old Rancho Santa Rita. The site is north of SR 152 via Indiana Road, four miles west of the San Joaquin River, and thirteen miles east of Los Banos.

EL ARROYO DE LOS BAÑOS

Los Baños (SRL 550), a Spanish place name meaning "the baths," was applied to the deep, clear pool on El Arroyo de los Baños near its source. It is said that here Father Arroyo de la Cuesta refreshed himself when on missionary trips to the San Joaquin Valley. The name El Arroyo de los Baños del Padre Arroyo (now Los Banos Creek) was derived from this circumstance. Father Arroyo, who served Mission San Juan Bautista from 1808 to 1833, was an accomplished man. He invented a perpetual calendar and became familiar with as many as thirteen Indian languages, preaching in seven different Indian tongues. He also wrote an Indian grammar and recorded many facts concerning the Indians and their manner of life.

The present town of Los Banos, located about two miles from the creek, has its origins in the Lone Willow Stage Station, built in 1858 on the west bank of what is now called Mud Slough. This place, consisting of a small house for the station keeper and a large barn for the relays of horses, prospered until the Butterfield stages between San Francisco and St. Louis stopped running in 1861. It then became a mere way station on the San Francisco–Los Angeles route and later the shortened Gilroy-Visalia run. By 1865 the countryside was becoming sufficiently settled to require a store, and an enterprising German named Gustave Kreyenhagen opened one in the former residence of the station keeper. He soon realized, however, that he would have better trade if he moved to the junction of the stage road and the Stockton-Visalia freight road; he therefore moved three miles east, taking the store building

with him. This junction is eight miles northeast of present-day Los Banos.

Kreyenhagen would not remain there long. Miller and Lux fenced in their property and required that teamsters drive around it. In the summer of 1870, therefore, the storekeeper relocated his trading post twelve miles farther to the west on the Gilroy-Visalia Road, about two miles south of the present Volta. Kreyenhagen had long served as unofficial postmaster, bringing his customers' mail each week from Gilroy, and in 1873 an official post office was established in his store under the name of Los Banos. Other businesses followed, and soon there was a little town. Eventually Miller and Lux took over the settlement and, when the railroad came in 1889, moved post office and businesses five miles east to the tracks. The town is now the center of diversified industry, including fruit and dairy products, and a principal town on the west side of the San Joaquin Valley.

Beginning in 1873, the headquarters of Henry Miller for his Los Banos Division were at Canal Farm (SRL 548), just across the railroad east of the Los Banos business district. None of the original buildings remain at Canal Farm. In 1932 the present inn was constructed on the foundations of the old ranch superintendent's residence, which itself had been built on the ruins of the 1873 ranchhouse of Henry Miller. Canal Farm derived its name from an irrigation canal (not a Miller and Lux enterprise) built from Mendota Dam to Los Banos Creek in 1871. The orange and olive orchards planted by Miller at Canal Farm still exist. The Ralph Milliken Museum in Merced County Park in Los Banos holds local history materials as well as collections of Indian artifacts and military accoutrements dating back to the nineteenth century.

NATURAL PRESERVES

Merced County is near the center of the most populous state of the Union and yet enjoys many extraordinary natural areas under preservation on the western side of the county. The San Luis National Wildlife Refuge is the largest of these; others are the Merced National Wildlife Refuge, the Cottonwood Creek Wildlife Area, the Los Banos Wildlife Area, the Mud Slough Wildlife Area, and the Volta Wildlife Area. The Great Valley Grasslands State Park is an undeveloped park, preserving one of the last undisturbed native grasslands remaining in the San Joaquin Valley. It is on SR 165 about fifteen miles north of Los Banos.

Modoc County

odoc County was formed in 1874 from a part of Siskiyou County. Modoc means "people of the south" and was probably given to the inhabitants of this region by the Klamaths, their kin to the north. This northeastern corner of California was called "The Smiles of God" by the native Americans. The Modoc County Historical Society contributes a sympathetic explanation:

So intense was their love for this land of rugged lava plateaus, fertile valleys and towering mountains that many hundreds of these aboriginal inhabitants defended it to their death against the invasion of the white man. Because of those fierce Indian wars between 1848 and 1911 this area was once referred to as the Bloody Ground of the Pacific.

The Indians were the Modocs, Paiutes, and Pits. From time immemorial they lived, hunted and inhabited their sprawling generous kingdom. The Modocs, a break-away tribe of the Klamath Indians, chose the northwest section of the lava country; the Paiutes, nomadic horse people of the plains, preferred the eastern slopes of the craggy Warner Mountains (now Surprise Valley), and the Pits, the largest tribe and perhaps the most fierce and warlike people to occupy this land, enjoyed the far reaches of the Pit River.

Alturas, the first and only county seat, was originally called Dorris's Bridge, after the owner of the ranch on which it was located. The Dorris Ranch was purchased in 1960 by the U.S. Fish and Wildlife Service, and is now the Modoc National Wildlife Refuge.

THE TULE LAKE PETROGLYPHS

Most of the Lava Beds National Monument is in Siskiyou County to the west of Modoc County, but a small part of the area extends into Modoc County. Here, at the southeastern corner of Tule Lake, a high bluff of smooth sandstone projects into the dry lake bed, and a chain of petroglyphs, chiseled deep into the rock, extends for several hundred yards across its face.

Some authorities maintain that these carvings were made by the last of the Rock Indians, who antedated and were exterminated by the Modocs. The Indians living in the region in the early 1850s disclaimed all knowledge of them, regarding them with awe and surrounding them with legends. The elements have obliterated some of the carvings; others, however, remain clear, with accents of black and ochre. The petroglyphs are protected by a fence.

FRÉMONT IN MODOC COUNTY

In May 1846, John C. Frémont passed through Modoc County when he traveled from Sutter's Fort to Upper Klamath Lake over what was later known as the eastern branch of the Oregon to California Trail. Near what is today Newell, the party camped on May 1–4. Among the group were Kit Carson, Alexis Godey, and Richard Owens. Tule Lake is designated "Rhett Lake" on Frémont's map of the area. The campsite (SRL 6) is about eleven miles southeast of Tulelake, on the Old Alturas Highway about seven-tenths of a mile north of its junction with SR 139.

THE APPLEGATE CUTOFF AND LASSEN'S TRAIL

The Applegate Cutoff from Oregon across the northeast corner of California to the Humboldt River in Nevada was opened up by Jesse and Lindsay Applegate with the help of thirteen others in June and July 1846. In the following autumn, the Applegates piloted more than ninety wagons from Fort Hall into Oregon over the new road. In 1848 Peter Lassen followed this route, crossing Nevada and entering California by way of Surprise Valley. Passing between Upper Lake and Middle Alkali Lake and up the west side of the valley to Fandango Pass (SRL 546), the trail led down into Goose Lake Valley, where it followed the eastern shore of the lake to a narrow rock at the southern end of the basin, a few miles from Sugar Loaf Hill.

Across this neck at a point on the west shore of Goose Lake, the Applegate Road turned toward Oregon, passing around the north end of both Clear Lake and Tule Lake into the Klamath country. At this same point on Goose Lake, Lassen's Trail began. Running in an almost southerly direction across the Devil's Garden, and striking the Pit River near the mouth of Rattlesnake Creek four miles west of the present city of Alturas, it continued along the north side of the Pit, crossing the river near the mouth of a canyon below the site of Canby. Passing south and west, its course lay through Stone Coal Valley, where it went due west for a few miles and then turned south along the Pit River. Crossing and recrossing the stream several times, or following along the sides of the hills above it, the trail finally led across the river for the last time ten miles above the site of Lookout. From there it proceeded down the east side of the Pit River to Big Valley in Lassen County. Joseph B. Chiles with a company of twelve men, among whom was Pierson B. Reading, had followed much the same route into California, by way of Goose Lake and the Pit River, in October 1843.

Tradition has it that the Pit River was so named because of the many holes and pits that had been dug in the region by Indians for trapping game. In his journal, Reading mentions one of these treacherous pitfalls, into which one of his party fell. It should be noted, however, that Commodore Charles Wilkes, in his report and on his map of 1841, designated this stream as "Pitt's River" and Goose Lake as "Pitt's Lake," which suggests a different origin for the name. Hudson's Bay Company trappers had penetrated this region before 1830, a fact recorded by Peter Skene Ogden in his diary of 1829. In this record, also, we find mention of "Pitt's River" under the entries of May 21 and 28; the Englishmen of the Hudson's Bay Company might have had in mind former political leaders William Pitt the elder or his son William Pitt the younger, commemorated in such place names as Pittsburgh, Pennsylvania.

From 1846 on, the Applegate Cutoff was used by emigrants from Oregon, and in August 1848 the first wagon train to enter California from the north came in over the Applegate and Lassen roads. The Oregonians, captained by Peter Burnett (later the first American civil governor of California) and piloted by Thomas McKay, an old Hudson's Bay Company trapper, followed the Applegate Road to Clear Lake, where the party branched off, blazing a new road south to the Pit River. There, Burnett writes, "to our astonishment, we found a new wagon road. Who made this road we could not at first imagine." It was later found that this was the trail over which Peter Lassen and his band of emigrants had just passed, on their way to Lassen's Ranch in Tehama County. Southeast of Lassen Peak at the headwaters of the North Fork of the Feather River, the Oregonians came upon Lassen and his party, whom they found stranded and in distress, their provisions almost exhausted.

The general course of Burnett's trail was followed by gold-seekers in 1849 and the early 1850s, and the present highway from Klamath Falls in Oregon to Bieber in Lassen County follows closely the trail of the Forty-Niners. Trails West, a private volunteer trail-marking organization, has placed markers along these trails in Idaho, Nevada, and California.

A section of the old emigrant trail (SRL 111) may be seen near the Pit River–Happy Camp Road (Bushey Road), 5.5 miles west of SR 299; this road branches from the highway 4.2 miles southwest of Canby.

FANDANGO

The Wolverine Rangers, a company of gold-seekers from Michigan, entered California in 1849 through a valley west of the Warner Mountains and east of Goose Lake, to use modern names. "After camping one night the weather grew so terribly cold that the men had to dance to keep warm, and named their wild camping place 'Fandango Valley,'" a survivor recalled. (The fandango was a popular and lively dance in Mexican California.) The company disbanded there and burned some of their abandoned wagons; later emigrants, seeing the remains of the burned wagons, assumed that an Indian massacre had taken place.

Fandango (formerly Lassen's) Pass, over which the Applegate Cutoff and Lassen's Trail crossed the Warner Mountains, was apparently the scene of a tragedy in the early 1850s. The story is that a large emigrant train coming into California over this trail was encamped at a large spring at the edge of the valley beyond the mountains. Rejoicing over the arrival of much-needed supplies, the party was indulging in a fandango when the camp was suddenly attacked by Indians and almost all the company was killed. The name Fandango was given to the pass, the mountain, and the valley beyond. Today the Fandango Pass road is a twelve-mile-long good gravel drive between this valley and Surprise Valley to the east, through beautiful mountain country.

At the head of Fandango Valley in 1866 a battle took place between some settlers and soldiers from Surprise Valley and a band of Paiute Indians, in which the latter were badly defeated. Evidence of another early battle was found on the old Lassen Trail four miles west of Alturas on what was later known as Rattlesnake Ranch. Here in 1870 pioneers came upon a large circle of burned wagons on a flat on the north side of the Pit River close to the present Redding-Alturas highway, SR 299.

BLOODY POINT

One of the most terrible of the emigrant massacres in Modoc County took place in 1850 at Bloody Point (SRL 8), seven miles east of Tulelake on the Johnson Ranch and 3.5 miles south of the California-Oregon line. Passing over the old Oregon Trail, a band of more than ninety emigrants were attacked by Modoc Indians. All of the party were killed except one man who, badly wounded, escaped to the settlements of southern Oregon with his tragic tale. It is said that old wagon parts were picked up at the spot for many years.

Members of a second emigrant train narrowly escaped death at this point in 1851, and were rescued only by the timely arrival of the Oregon Volunteers. The spot apparently was a natural ambush; members of several other parties were killed there by the Modocs, who naturally saw the procession of wagon trains as a threat to them and to their existence.

THE MODOC WARS

The Battle of Infernal Caverns, one of the most famous Indian fights in California, took place on September 26 and 27, 1867, between 110 soldiers led by Lieutenant-Colonel George Crook and a band of seventy-five Paiutes, thirty Pit River Indians, and a few Modocs. For some time the Indians, well equipped with arms and ammunition, had been resisting the influx of settlers throughout southern Idaho, western Nevada, and northeastern California. Crook and his men had been sent to subdue them. The Indians were finally driven into a rough region on the South Fork of the Pit River. Here, before a seemingly impregnable fortress of caves

Modoc County Courthouse, Alturas

and rocks, a pitched battle took place. The Indians were eventually driven from their stronghold, leaving many of their number dead; eight of Crook's command were killed and fourteen were wounded.

The battleground of the Infernal Caverns (SRL 16), where the old fortifications may still be seen, is on the Ferry Ranch south of Alturas. Infernal Caverns is reached by going thirteen miles south from Alturas on US 395 and turning right for one mile on a good road leading to ranch homes. At the branch in the road, the right-hand road leads 3.5 miles to the Ferry Ranch house. The site of the battle and the graves are on private property, and permission should be obtained before proceeding further. The graves of six of the soldiers killed in action have been marked by regulation Army headstones at the foot of the slope. They are about a mile from the house and the caverns are above, in very difficult terrain.

The Modoc War of 1872–73 was a determined resistance mounted by the Modoc tribe against being taken from their homelands and placed on a reservation that they had been forced to share with the Klamaths, with whom they had bad relations. Although few in number, the Modocs were exceptionally effective guerrillas and they successfully defied the U.S. Army for several months.

An early engagement of the Modoc War took place on December 21, 1872, on what was then known as Land's Ranch (SRL 108), just south of the intersection of SR 139 and County Road 114, twelve miles southeast of Tule Lake. This was very close to the old Frémont campsite on the Oregon Trail. Army supply wagons, escorted by a detachment of cavalrymen, had reached camp in safety, but several of the soldiers who had dropped behind were suddenly attacked by Indians in hiding among the rocks above the road. Two soldiers were killed, and several more were wounded.

Soon after this event, the Modoc tribe retreated into the nearby lava beds in Siskiyou County, in which chapter their story is continued. Early in May 1873, the defeated Modocs broke out of their besieged stronghold, and in Modoc County, the last engagement of the Modoc War was fought at daybreak on May 10. Kientepoos ("Captain Jack"), the leader of the tribe, led a charge on the Army camp at Dry Lake. The soldiers awoke when their horses and mules stampeded, and were able to make a fierce and effective counterattack. Kientepoos was captured, the Modocs met their last defeat, and the Modoc War came to an end. The site of this battle is about a half-mile west of the Dry Lake guard station on SR 139.

SURPRISE VALLEY: CEDARVILLE AND FORT BIDWELL

Explaining how Surprise Valley got its name, William S. Brown wrote that the emigrants who had managed to cross the Black Rock Desert (in Nevada) were surprised to come from the arid sagebrush hills into a well-watered "smiling valley." Gudde says that the name was shown on maps "since about 1860." In Western history, the term *surprise* usually has two different connotations, one a pleasant one, as told above, and the other connected with ambush, tragedy, disaster, and unpleasantness.

Surprise Valley lies in the far northeastern corner of California, surely that part of the state as far removed from the rest as can be found. Here there still stand some of the first log cabins built by settlers, all provided with loopholes for defense. Among these is the trading post (SRL 14) that was operated by William T. Cressler and John H. Bonner. This, the oldest structure in Modoc County, was built in 1865 by James Townsend, who shortly afterward was killed by Indians. Townsend's widow sold the building to Cressler and Bonner, and here the partners set up the first mercantile establishment in Modoc County. A thriving trade was carried on, first with the overland emigrants, and later with the early settlers of Surprise Valley. This interesting relic stands in a park in the center of Cedarville, surrounded by a magnificent grove of trees planted by the original owners.

The first road from Cedarville to Alturas was constructed in 1869, passing over the Bonner Grade (SRL 15), named for John Bonner, who maintained the road

Southern Pacific Engine #2718 at Modoc County Museum, Alturas

until 1871 when Siskiyou County took it over. The road generally follows the course of the present scenic highway SR 299 over the Warner Mountains.

Fort Bidwell (SRL 430), at the head of Upper Lake in Surprise Valley, about thirty miles northeast of Alturas and ten miles south of the Oregon boundary, was named for General John Bidwell. It was established in 1865, and cavalrymen were stationed there against hostile Indians of northeastern California, southern Oregon, and northwestern Nevada. Fort Bidwell was abandoned as a military post in 1893, but until 1930 it was used as a government school for Indians. The boarding school was discontinued that year, and the military barracks, once used for dormitories, were torn down. The old military graveyard is about all that remains. Newer homes have taken over this peaceful spot, where life seems to revolve around the general store, built in 1876 and doing business continuously since then. An unusual feature of this building, but not a visible one, is the twelve inches of dirt layered between the main ceiling and the attic, providing both insulation and fireproofing.

The other prominent building in Fort Bidwell is the Community Church, built in 1885 and still in use.

ALTURAS

Originally named Dorris's Bridge for the pioneer ranching family on whose land the town was laid out, Alturas changed its name by community petition to the Legislature in 1876. Alturas is Spanish for "heights." Modoc County's largest settlement contains several interesting buildings, including the imposing County Courthouse (1914), the charming Sacred Heart Catholic Church (completed in 1910), and the NCO Office Building (1917), which, like the church, is on the National Register of Historic Buildings. NCO stands for the Nevada-California-Oregon Railroad, although local humorists say it also meant "Northern California Outrage" or

N.C.O. Building, now Alturas B.P.O.E. Elks' Club

"Never Come, and Overdue." The station, in Mission Revival style, was later sold to the Southern Pacific Railroad; today it houses the Elks Lodge. The Modoc County Museum at the south end of town has an impressive display of artifacts, particularly of local Indian peoples. On the property is the majestic Southern Pacific locomotive #2718 from 1904.

OTHER HISTORIC SITES

In July 1861, S. D. Evans Sr. and Joe Bailey were attacked and killed by Indians while they and their men were driving 900 head of beef cattle from Oregon to the mines at Virginia City, Nevada. The site (SRL 125) is on the Centerville Road to Alturas, 4.7 miles southeast of Canby. The Evans and Bailey fight is marked by a white obelisk on a hill near the road.

About seven miles north of Alturas near US 395 is Chimney Rock (SRL 109), the remains of the second building to be erected in the Pit River Valley. Thomas L. Denson, a California pioneer of 1852, built his cabin here in 1870, utilizing the rock as a chimney by cutting the fireplace and flue out of it.

On SR 139 at Newell, seven miles southeast of Tulelake in Siskiyou County, one building remains from the Tulelake relocation camp (SRL 859.2). The place where the camp once stood is now a county public works site and is usually closed to the public. In front of the surrounding fence a state marker has been placed, and its text is brief but eloquent:

> Tulelake was one of ten concentration camps established during World War II to incarcerate 110,000 persons of Japanese ancestry, of whom the majority were American citizens, behind barbed wire and guard towers, without charge or trial. These camps are reminders of how racism, economic and political exploitation, and expediency undermine constitutional guarantees of United States citizens and aliens alike. May the injustices and humiliation suffered here never recur.

Mono County

Boone Store and Warehouse, Bodie State Historic Park

Mono County was formed in 1861 of territory taken from Calaveras and Fresno Counties. The eastern boundary line of California was undetermined for several years, and in 1863 Aurora, the county seat, was found to be in Nevada. Since Aurora could not be the county seat, the honor was given to Bridgeport, which remains the center of Mono County's government. The northern and southern boundaries of the county were also uncertain. In 1864 Alpine County to the northwest and Inyo County to the south in 1870 were given pieces of land originally given to Mono County.

"Mono" seems to be a diminutive form of the Shoshonean Indian term "Monache," a name applied to those Shoshones living east of the Sierra and north of Owens Lake. "Monache" meant "fly people," and probably came from the fact that the chief food staple and trading article of this tribe were the pupae of the Ephydra fly, native to the shores of the lakes east of the Sierra. The name was given first to a lake and then to a Sierra pass before being used for the county. The Mono Indians, according to A. L. Kroeber, numbered some 4,000 in 1770 and 1,500 by 1910.

MONO LAKE

Mono Lake lies in the center of the county and is one of the most remarkable features of California's geography. It is estimated that the lake was formed 700,000 years ago. It has no visible outlet. The islands of Negrit and Paoha can be seen rising from the lake, along with towers of tufa, formations of calcium carbonate.

Throughout much of the twentieth century, the steady draining of water from the region by the City of Los Angeles's Department of Water and Power (DWP) caused the surface of the lake to fall. One result of this was to increase the salinity of the lake to the point that only the tiny brine shrimp and the pupae of the Ephydra fly could survive. Another result was to cause great exposure of the lake bottom, creating fierce dust storms and fouling the atmosphere. In 1978, conservationists began a campaign to force the DWP to cut back on its water diversion from the region. A ruling of the California State Supreme Court in 1983 cited the hazards to public health created at Mono Lake. The following year, Congress enacted the California Wilderness Act, part of which established the Mono Basin National Forest Scenic Area, the first National Forest Scenic Area to be created in the United States. The act also created a Comprehensive Management Plan, operated by the U.S. Forest Service and working with the DWP and conservation groups. An agreement was concluded in 1994 whereby the lake's surface would be maintained at 6,392 feet above sea level. Because the amount of water that could be taken from the basin by the City of Los Angeles was reduced, more water would flow into the lake from its tributaries. The agreement, which is subject to periodic renewal and revision, continues to keep concerns about Mono Lake very active. A visitors center

on US 395 two miles north of the town of Lee Vining has a great deal of information on the issue.

ROCK WRITINGS

The small town of Chalfont Valley lies on US 6 near the southern border of Mono County and about seven miles north of Laws in Inyo County. Facing the town on the west is a high volcanic tableland; cut into its eastern escarpment are the petroglyphs known as the Chalfont Valley Group. Near where gravel Fish Slough Road crosses Chidago Canyon, a towering wall nearly half a mile in length is covered with petroglyphs, or carvings on stone, and a few pictographs or paintings. The petroglyphs are principally circular in form and are believed to be the largest of this type found in the United States. Chidago Canyon at this point is a labyrinth of carvings and paintings in many interesting combinations. Some of the minor carvings represent such things as bears, bighorn sheep, deer, a dragonfly, lizards, snakes, human figures, and what may be chicken or bird tracks, as well as geometrical designs.

Here and elsewhere in the desert regions of California, Indian rock carvings have been vandalized, and the Bureau of Land Management has discouraged casual visits to these endangered areas. Therefore, the road west from Chalfont Valley has no signs marking the way to the petroglyphs.

THE SONORA TRAIL

The first party of Americans to come to California overland from the east was a group of fur trappers led by Jedediah Strong Smith. This "Pathfinder of the Sierra" and his men arrived from the Great Salt Lake at Mission San Gabriel late in 1826. Ordered out of the territory by Governor Echeandia, he and his men made the first known crossing of the Sierra Nevada, from west to east, the following year. It is not known for sure which of the mountain passes was used in this trip, but some historians have said that it was the Sonora Pass, which lies high up in the Sierra at the point where Mono, Alpine, and Tuolumne Counties meet. The Sonora Trail is the wagon road that later crossed the mountains over this pass.

In October 1841 the Bidwell-Bartleson overland emigrant party, weakened and disheartened after months of hardship, arrived in what is now Mono County and began the ascent of the Sierra on the north side of the Walker River. At last they came to a little stream that

Fuller Street, Bodie State Historic Park

Boone Store and Warehouse, Bodie State Historic Park

flowed west instead of east and realized that they had crossed the dividing ridge of the mountain range. This stream proved to be the headwaters of the Stanislaus River, one of the principal tributaries of the San Joaquin. The river's course through the mountains was rough and precipitous and terribly difficult to follow as the party struggled through what seemed to be endless gorges and canyons. Nearly exhausted and almost out of food, they stumbled through the Sierra foothills and came upon the great San Joaquin Valley.

Difficult as this passage was, the Sonora Trail had been opened, and within a decade or so the first faint trail left by the Bidwell-Bartleson party (which varied somewhat from the original route) had been beaten down and widened into a fairly well-defined road. It led through the heart of the Mother Lode country and was nearly as popular as the Truckee Road.

DOG TOWN AND MONOVILLE

Monoville was the first settlement of any consequence east of the Sierra and south of Lake Tahoe. Some mining had probably been carried on in the region from the time gold had been discovered there in 1852. Continued reports that the Mormons from Nevada were washing out gold in Dog Creek near Mono Lake brought a number of prospectors into the region in 1857, and Dog Town (SRL 792) quickly came into existence as a camp and trading center. "Dog Town" was a popular miner's term for a camp built of huts. The site of Dog Town is along US 395, seven miles south of Bridgeport. After 1859 Dog Town was deserted for its more promising neighbor, Monoville, which soon boasted a population of 700, made up mostly of arrivals from Tuolumne County, who came in via the Sonora Pass. Among the early arrivals were brothers Dick and Lee Vining. The nearby town of Lee Vining was named for the latter.

Monoville was different from most mining towns in that it left no notable record of crime. Although the town soon disappeared, it is noteworthy as the starting point from which the discoverers of other mining locations in the region set out. As late as 1864, Monoville was an ambitious contestant for the position of county seat. Nothing much remains from the brief bonanza days of Monoville except Sinnamon Cut, the result of a hydraulic mining operation that garnered James Sinnamon $90,000 and has scarred the landscape for a hundred and more years since he departed.

BODIE AND ITS "BAD MEN"

Bodie State Historic Park (SRL 341) is unlike any other in California. Its story begins in 1852, with the first discovery of gold ore in the Mono region. The discovery was made by members of Lieutenant Tredwell Moore's detachment of Second Infantry, who were in pursuit of Yosemite Valley Indians. This discovery led to a good deal of activity; Lee Vining and his party discovered gold in the canyon named for him through which the Tioga Pass Road (SR 120) now runs.

Knowledge of the Mono diggings reached the Tuolumne mines in 1857, resulting in a rush to the new field and the building of the Mono Trail from Big Oak Flat in Tuolumne County through the present Yosemite National Park. In 1859, William S. Bodey made a find, and the district was named for him. (The spelling was changed to Bodie to reflect the correct pronunciation of Bodey's name.) The sensational Aurora discovery made in 1860 affected Bodie, which was twelve miles southwest, and the Mono Trail became a much-traveled highway for pack trains and miners until the Sonora Pass wagon road was opened in 1864.

The Standard Mine, discovered in 1861, was the first of Bodie's mines to become famous. It is typical of the fluctuating fortunes of mining ventures. During Aurora's boom, the owners of the Standard found it hard to

Museum in Miners Union Hall, Bodie State Historic Park

create an interest in their project, then called the Bunker Hill Mine. In 1870, when the Aurora mines became exhausted, Bodie suffered a decline, which ended when a freak cave-in at the mine revealed, not far below the surface, a rich vein of ore. The adjacent Bodie Mine, at first considered a gamble, also rose in value, to the surprise of its owners. Between 1876 and 1880 Bodie was at the height of its success, with a population of more than ten thousand people. It was also known as one of the wildest mining camps in the West. "Good-bye, God! We are moving to Bodie!" a little girl is said to have written in her diary when she learned that her family was joining the bonanza. The "Bad Men from Bodie" acquired a widespread reputation for lawlessness. Legend has it that one murder occurred in every 24-hour period; the victims were almost always of the lawless sort, however, and thus the evildoers were somewhat thinned out by their own violent energies. The Reverend F. M. Warrington in 1861 saw Bodie, with its sixty-five saloons, as "a sea of sin, lashed by the tempests of lust and passion."

By 1883 all of the mines except the Bodie and the Standard had closed down, and in 1887 these were consolidated. Operations in later years were sporadic, ceasing altogether in the late 1950s. In 1962 the site became Bodie State Historic Park. It lies at the end of SR 270, which branches off from US 395 about seven miles south of Bridgeport. At the end of the paved road, three more miles of rough gravel must be driven before the visitor arrives at the site. When people left Bodie, the wooden buildings of their residences and shops remained abandoned and subject to the rough elements. Fires broke out from time to time, the most serious being on the windy day of June 23, 1932. Seventy per cent of the town was destroyed. There are still 150 buildings standing in various degrees of preservation.

It is the intention of the state Division of Parks and Recreation to maintain Bodie in a state of "arrested decay," whereas the buildings in Columbia State Historic Park in Tuolumne County are being restored to their original grandeur. Bodie is a complete ghost town, the only residents being the state park rangers and their families. There are none of the amenities, such as restaurants, service stations, or overnight facilities, found at other state parks in California. A museum is maintained in the Miners Union Hall, and there are several blocks of houses and stores as well as the Methodist Church that visitors can see. There are four cemeteries, and "Boot Hill," where burials were made without markers. The area where the stamp mill for the Standard Mine still stands is considered to be a hazardous area and is closed to the public. This unique town has also been registered as a National Historic Landmark by the Department of the Interior.

In the 1980s, there was a possibility that mining activities would be developed in the area adjacent to the town, and preservationists mobilized to prevent this from happening. A Bodie Protection Act introduced into Congress became law in 1994 as part of the larger Desert Protection Act. By 1997, 500 additional acres had been added to the site, with thirty buildings not previously part of the preserve.

The neighboring camps at Mono Lake, Masonic, Benton, Tioga, Lundy, and Mammoth City in California, and Aurora in Nevada, are also long deserted. At the settlement on the west shore of Mono Lake are two old wooden buildings that were moved from Bodie. Masonic, best reached by a nine-mile dirt road that leaves SR 182 three miles north of Bridgeport, is a photogenic conglomeration of old cabins lying close to the Nevada line. Here is an interesting tram system leading from the mines to the ruined stamp mill. At Benton, four miles west of US 6 on SR 120, are a jail, a schoolhouse, and a thick-walled general store with iron shutters, once the Wells Fargo office. The population of Benton once reached 6,000.

MINING TOWNS OF THE HIGH SIERRA

High in the Sierra east of Yosemite Valley relics of early silver-mining ventures may still be seen. One of the old camps in the region is Tioga (once Bennettville), a mile or two north of Tioga Pass. Here the Tioga Mine was located in 1860 as the Sheepherder Mine, and in 1874 William Brusky, a prospector, came upon the abandoned diggings and relocated the claims under the original name.

The Tioga Mining District was organized in 1878 by the Great Sierra Mining Company, made up of men from Sonora. The Sheepherder Mine was renamed the Tioga Mine, and Bennettville was made the company's headquarters. Great quantities of supplies and equipment were brought to the camp over very difficult roads from the east side of the mountain, an enormous expenditure of labor and money.

The pressing need for a good road over which to transport heavy machinery from the west side of the Sierra occasioned the expenditure of $64,000 for the Tioga Road, which was completed in 1883. Unfortunately, the total expenditure of $300,000 brought about the financial collapse of the company in 1884, and the project was abandoned before any of the ore had been milled.

Bennettville is off SR 120 about ten miles west of Lee Vining; a dirt road a half-mile past Ellery Lake leads to the site. The old livery stable and assayer's building are all that remain.

The Mount Dana Summit Mine (in Tuolumne County), opened in 1878, lay to the south of the Tioga Mine. Long-deserted rock cabins clustered about a deep mine shaft are the remains of a once-thriving camp. Hikers and fishermen from Yosemite Valley often come upon this interesting mountain ghost town, which is located within Yosemite National Park. The Gaylor Lakes trail, which begins at the Tioga entrance to the park, leads two miles to the remains, which are located on the slope above upper Gaylor Lake.

Lundy, another deserted mining camp a few miles north of Tioga, was established in 1879. Prior to that date, W. J. Lundy had a sawmill there from which he helped supply the enormous demand for lumber at treeless Bodie. Approximately $3 million was taken from the Lundy Mine, and the place remained a substantial town for several years. Lundy Lake was caused by the building of a dam that inundated part of the town site, which is today enjoying a revival as a resort and vacation site. It is located at the western end of Lundy Lake Road, about six miles west of the junction of US 395 and SR 167.

In the vicinity of Convict Lake and Convict Creek in southern Mono County a gun battle took place in 1871 between some desperate fugitives from the prison at Carson City, Nevada, and a posse from Benton. On September 17 of that year twenty-nine convicts—murderers, robbers, and horse thieves—had broken through the prison guard and escaped. Six of them headed south. On their way they met William A. Poor, a mail

carrier, whom they robbed and murdered. When news of the outrage reached Aurora and Benton, a posse was organized. The men from Benton followed the convicts into southern Mono County, the fugitives having been sighted by Robert Morrison, a Benton merchant, who saw them going up Monte Diable Creek, henceforth called Convict Creek.

On the following morning the posse followed up the canyon to the lake and its head. There, on September 24, they came upon three of the desperadoes, and in the gunfight that followed, Morrison (for whom Mount Morrison was afterward named) was killed. The convicts escaped toward Round Valley, where they were later captured. Taken to Bishop by irate citizens, the two men who had committed murder were hanged, and the third was returned to the Carson City prison.

BRIDGEPORT

Big Meadows was a grass-covered area that attracted farmers around 1855. A settlement grew up on the East Walker River, which lay across a footbridge from the road up the valley of the river. In time Bridgeport became the name of the settlement, the valley, and a nearby lake. The Mono County courthouse, erected in 1880, is the second-oldest courthouse in California still in use; it stands on US 395, which passes through the center of the small town. The Mono County Museum nearby is housed in a schoolhouse also built in 1880 and in operation until 1964. The collection has much of interest on the history of the county's many short-lived mining settlements. The Bridgeport Inn, established in 1877, stands opposite the courthouse on the main street and is still in operation.

MAMMOTH

About twenty miles south of Tioga Pass in the Lake District, a region of spectacular scenic grandeur, Mammoth flourished as a mining camp for a brief period. The first discoveries were made there in 1877; the greatest activity took place in 1879 and 1880. A mill was built and a trail constructed from Fresno Flats (now Oakhurst in Madera County, fifty-four miles to the west), but the expected ore was not forthcoming. Like many other camps in which enormous capital was expended, little or nothing was produced in return and the place was closed up by early 1881. Old Mammoth, as the 8,000-foot-high spot is now designated, lies just south of the Mammoth Lakes resort area on Old Mammoth Road.

Mammoth lies in the heart of one of the most superb recreational centers in the Sierra. It has become famous for its winter sports activities. At other seasons, interesting trips can be taken to the hot mineral springs at Whitmore Tubs, the ice-cold or the boiling springs of Casa Diablo, the Hot Creek Geyser, Mammoth Rock and the Old Mammoth Mill, the Devils Postpile National Monument (across the line in Madera County), the Earthquake Fault landmark, Minaret Pass, and Shohonk Pass. Pack trips may be taken to Shadow Lake, Thousand Island Lake, and the upper San Joaquin River, while good trails lead to splendid camping and fishing spots about the numerous lakes of the region.

Carmel Mission

Monterey County

Monterey County was one of the original twenty-seven counties. Monterey is Spanish for "hill or wood of the king." It was so named in honor of Gaspar de Zúñiga, count of Monterey and viceroy of Mexico. Monterey was the original county seat, but in 1873 the honor was given to Salinas. The county archives contain many pre-statehood records in Spanish.

THE DISCOVERY OF MONTEREY BAY

Juan Rodríguez Cabrillo, in command of the *San Salvador* and the frigate *Victoria*, discovered California in 1542 and sailed up the coast about to the Northwest Cape, near Fort Ross in Sonoma County. On the return voyage, the mariner noted that he had sighted for the second time a place that he had earlier called Cape San Martin, today called Point Pinos. This is the southern headland of Monterey Bay, and the evidence suggests that Cabrillo did not see the bay itself.

The Pacific Grove Lighthouse was established on Point Pinos in 1872, and the Daughters of the American Revolution have placed a marker there in honor of Cabrillo, the first European to see the coast of Alta California.

Probably the first explorer to see Monterey Bay itself was Sebastián Rodríguez Cermeño, a Portuguese in command of the Spanish galleon *San Agustín*, in 1595. Cermeño had been sent out to discover a port on the California coast where the Manila ships might find protection and supplies and receive warning of enemies. On November 30, the *San Agustín* was wrecked at Drakes Bay, but Cermeño continued his voyage in the *San Buenaventura*, a little launch or open sailboat that he had constructed. In this frail craft he saw Monterey Bay on December 10, 1595, and called it San Pedro Bay.

THE VIZCAÍNO-SERRA LANDING PLACE

Sebastián Vizcaíno was a merchant trader who had had much experience on the Spanish galleon route, and who had also been a shipmate of Rodríguez Cermeño on his voyage of discovery in 1595. In the flagship *San Diego*, Vizcaíno entered Monterey Bay on December 15,

1602, the second European to enter its waters and the first to make a landing there.

Vizcaíno was so enchanted with the beauty of this bay that "he wrote almost too enthusiastically to his Majesty concerning it." He spoke of it as a harbor "sheltered from all winds," and a legend grew up concerning this port that would influence all Spanish exploration along the coast for a century and a half to come. Later explorers, having only Vizcaíno's glowing descriptions to go on, failed to realize that Monterey Bay was in fact the San Pedro Bay of Cermeño and Vizcaíno.

The entrance into Monterey Bay and the act of taking possession of it were the principal events of Vizcaíno's voyage. The ceremony was performed close to the shore under a live oak tree, the same oak under which Padre Junipero Serra performed a similar ceremony in 1770, when Mission San Carlos and the Presidio of Monterey were founded. The site of the tree and the landing place (SRL 128), now within the Monterey State Historic Park, is marked by the Junipero Serra Cross, on the south side of the main gateway to the Monterey Presidio. On Presidio Hill, overlooking the bay, is the Junipero Serra Monument, dedicated by Mrs. Leland Stanford in 1891. A monument in honor of Gaspar de Portolá, founder of the presidio, has been erected at the landing place, near the Serra Cross, by the state of California. The Portolá Plaza at the foot of Calle Principal has a handsome statue of the soldier, the gift of King Juan Carlos of Spain, placed there in 1978.

PORTOLÁ'S TRAIL THROUGH MONTEREY

Leaving San Diego on July 14, 1769, Gaspar de Portolá started north with his men to search for the Bay of Monterey, described in such enthusiastic terms by Vizcaíno in 1602. Traveling up the coast by way of Gaviota Pass, the expedition entered what is now Monterey County and camped, September 21–23, on the banks of the Nacimiento River, near its source. The high ridges of the Coast Range had just been crossed with great difficulty, and the men were in need of rest.

After they had recuperated somewhat, the party pushed on and reached the San Antonio River at a point near Jolon, where they camped on September 24. The next day they camped in the upper Jolon Valley, and on September 26 they descended Quinado Canyon, reaching the Salinas River near King City. During the days following they camped successively near Metz, Camphora, and Chualar, and on September 30, below what is now Hill Town. From October 1 to

October 6 they camped near Blanco, and from this point they explored the Monterey Bay region and saw the river and bay at Carmel.

During all this week the party did not recognize Vizcaíno's wonderful harbor "sheltered from all winds" and described in Cabrero Bueno's sailing directions as a bay "round like an O." It was probably shrouded in gray fog, and not until a year later did they know what they had missed.

Leaving a cross planted upon the beach, near Monterey, the party continued the journey northward, camping on October 7 near Del Monte junction and then proceeding across the Pajaro River and camping near the present site of Watsonville, in Santa Cruz County.

MISSION SAN CARLOS BORROMEO (CARMEL MISSION)

The settlement of Monterey was at the point farthest north in the original plan for the colonization of California, and there the presidio and the mission were to be established. Portolá's party had failed to find the bay in 1769, but a second expedition was organized the following year, Portolá and Father Crespí going by land and Father Serra, who was ill, proceeding by boat.

Portolá reached the Bay of Monterey for the second time on May 24, 1770. He found the cross that he placed there the year before still standing near the beach, but curiously decorated, "with arrows stuck in the ground and sticks with many feathers, which the gentiles had placed there; suspended from a pole beside the cross was a string of small fish, all fairly fresh, while pieces of meat were deposited at the foot of the cross and a pile of mussels." The Indians later told the padres how, at night, the cross had become wonderfully illuminated, reaching far up into the heavens, and they were afraid and brought peace offerings to it. The day being calm and clear, the entire sweep of the bay was visible, and Crespí and others realized that this was indeed Vizcaíno's harbor.

Father Serra arrived in the San Antonio seven days later, and on June 3, 1770, under the same oak where Vizcaíno had held services 168 years before, the Mission San Carlos Borromeo and the Presidio of Monterey were dedicated.

The first mission building was constructed at the presidio on the site where the San Carlos Church stands today. The presence of the soldiers and the lack of good agricultural land caused Father Serra to look about for a more suitable location. This was found five miles to

Carmel Mission

the south in a fertile valley watered by the Rio Carmelo (so named for the Carmelite Fathers who accompanied Vizcaíno), which empties into the ocean at this point, and the formal transfer of the mission site was made in December 1771. Mission San Carlos Borromeo (SRL 135) became the favorite of Father Serra, where he spent most of his last days and where he died; he lies buried within the sanctuary today. Serra was beatified by the Vatican in 1988.

The present building at Carmel was begun in 1793 and dedicated in 1797. Being beautifully situated and prosperous, it was the headquarters for the padre presidente of the California missions until 1803. After secularization in 1836, it was not kept in repair and quickly fell into ruins. In 1882, through the efforts of Father Casanova, the graves of Presidentes Serra and Lasuén and Fathers Crespí and López were discovered within the church. Public interest was then aroused and funds were sought for the restoration, which was accomplished and the church rededicated in 1884. Restoration of the other buildings has continued to the present. Carmel Mission, as it is popularly known, is a National Historic Landmark. In 1960 it was raised to the rank of a minor basilica by the Vatican, and was visited by Pope John Paul II in 1987.

THE PRESIDIO OF MONTEREY

On the day the mission and presidio were dedicated, Gaspar de Portolá formally took possession of the land in the name of King Carlos III of Spain. A fort of rude palisades and a few huts were erected at once and the second presidio in Alta California was instituted.

Late in the eighteenth century, Spain placed a fort on the hill overlooking Monterey Bay, where the present presidio grounds are located. Count de la Pérouse,

who visited Monterey in September 1786, said that the guns of the Castillo ("fortress") greeted him; and in 1793, when George Vancouver sailed into the harbor, he also noted the battery on the hill. Vancouver's party was long and gratefully remembered by residents of the Monterey area (who numbered fewer than 500 by 1800), for they left "grains of the best quality" as well as fruit stones, or pits, which were planted and became productive trees. These added greatly to the variety of foods available in later years.

During the Spanish and Mexican periods, Monterey held first place as the military and social capital of Alta California. It was also the port of entry where American ships and whaling vessels came to trade with the colonists, finally breaking down the barriers placed by the reluctant Spanish government on foreign trade.

The little port, set like a jewel within pine-clad hills beside the blue bay, is described by Richard Henry Dana in *Two Years Before the Mast*. When Dana sailed into the harbor on the brig *Pilgrim* in the year 1834,

> The town lay directly before us, making a very pretty appearance, its houses being of whitewashed adobe. . . . The red tiles, too, on the roofs, contrasted well with the white sides and with the extreme greenness of the lawn upon which the houses—about a hundred in number— were dotted about, here and there, irregularly. . . . This, as they are of one story, and of the cottage form, gives them a pretty effect when seen from a little distance. . . . In the centre of it is an open square, surrounded by four lines of one-story buildings, with half a dozen cannon in the centre. . . . This is the Presidio, or fort.

In 1822 the Mexican government built a fort on the present presidio grounds on the hill overlooking Monterey Bay. In 1846, after the American occupation, a blockhouse was built there and ship guns were mounted. It was named Fort Stockton at first, but later in the same year the name was changed to Fort Mervine in honor of the officer in charge. The old fort is long gone, but the place where it stood has been marked.

The Sloat Monument, honoring Commodore John Sloat, commemorates the act of taking possession of California for the United States, July 7, 1846, and the raising of the Stars and Stripes over the Custom House at Monterey. The base of the monument was funded by popular subscription, and the superstructure was added by the federal government. It was dedicated and unveiled on the hilltop on the presidio grounds on June 14, 1910.

Fort Halleck was built at the presidio in 1847 and

named for Lieutenant Henry W. Halleck of the Corps of Engineers, which laid out the fort. Halleck later became secretary of state of California during Governor Bennett Riley's military rule, and was chief of staff of the Union army during the Civil War. He was a man of considerable influence during the period of transition from Mexican to American rule. In the early 1850s he was a prominent lawyer in San Francisco. Fort Halleck no longer exists, but the site is marked. The United States Army Museum, on Corporal Ewing Road in the presidio, has excellent displays on the history of Monterey.

The Defense Language Institute, an outgrowth of the Naval Postgraduate School, is now based at the Monterey Presidio.

ROYAL PRESIDIO CHAPEL

After the removal of Mission San Carlos Borromeo to Carmel, the mission building at the presidio of Monterey became the Presidio Chapel (SRL 105). The present building at 550 Church Street was built in 1794 and then called the Royal Chapel because the king's representative worshiped there. When the mission at Carmel was secularized in 1836, the chapel at Monterey became the parish church. The San Carlos Parish Church, as it is now known, was much restored, thanks to the efforts of Governor Romualdo Pacheco, and it is now a National Historic Landmark.

MISSION SAN ANTONIO DE PADUA

Father Junipero Serra, as soon as he had explored the Rio Carmel and had set his people to work building Mission San Carlos on the new site, set out for the Santa Lucia Mountains to found the third of the missions in Alta California. At length he came to a beautiful valley covered with oaks, which was named Las Robles, and which Portolá in 1769 had called La Hoya ("hollow") de la Sierra de Santa Lucia.

Close by the little river, which Father Serra named the San Antonio, the bells were hung from the branch of a live oak. The story is told that the padre grasped the rope and rang the bells long and loud: "Hear, O Gentiles! Come! Oh come to the holy Church of God! Come, oh come, and receive the Faith of Christ!" To his companion's plea that it was useless to ring the bells, he replied: "Let me give vent to my heart's desires; for I would that these bells were heard all over the world, or at least by all the pagan people who live in this sierra." In fact, after the rustic enramada had been raised and

Mission San Antonio

the simple altar placed, a single Indian hesitatingly approached to witness the celebration of the Mass. This was the first instance of a native inhabitant being present at the founding of a mission. By 1805 there were 1,296 neophytes from the neighboring rancherias.

Mission San Antonio de Padua was founded July 14, 1771, at a site one and one-half miles from the present church, which was begun in 1810. The latter is said to have been not only one of the largest but also one of the most picturesque and interesting of all the missions, unsurpassed in its artistic arrangement and the loveliness of its rural setting. The beautiful brick façade withstood the neglect of years and the stress of storm and earthquake, even after the body of the main building and the roofs of the long corridors had crumbled.

Standing in a well-watered valley through which the San Antonio flows southeast to join the Salinas River, the mission became famous for its excellent wheat and its fine horses. A stone mill for grinding the wheat was constructed and operated by water brought for many miles through a stone-walled ditch, or *zanja*. Remains of this feat of engineering still exist in the valley a few hundred yards from the mission, in what was once the garden, or orchard.

After the death of the Reverend Dorotéo Ambris, the last resident priest at San Antonio, the mission structures were deserted and from year to year became a more complete ruin. San Antonio never acquired a neighboring secular village, as did nearly all the missions, and it lay far off the highway that ultimately became US 101. The lands around it became part of the gigantic ranch of William Randolph Hearst. Within sight of the mission, on a nearby hill, Hearst had architect Julia Morgan design a delightful ranch house, still called the Hacienda, which was completed in 1930. Ten years later, the Army acquired 165,000 acres from Hearst and made the area into Fort Hunter Liggett. The Hacienda is now open to the public for meals and lodging.

In 1903, the California Historic Landmarks League and the Historic Landmarks Committee of the Native Sons of the Golden West, under the leadership of Joseph R. Knowland, made a plea for restoration of the mission, and in September of that year it was begun. In 1906 much of their effort was destroyed by the great earthquake, but the following year renovation of the church proper was completed. The mission stood in loneliness—a vacant but intact church and a long row of brick arches fronting heaps of adobe mud that were once the main wing—until 1949, when the Franciscan Order, aided by the Hearst Foundation, commenced restoration on a large scale.

Mission San Antonio (SRL 232) is twenty miles south of King City and five miles northwest of Jolon, in the Hunter Liggett Military Reservation. The padres' quarters and adjoining reconstructed rooms are now a museum of the life of the mission. Still one of the most tranquil historic spots in California, San Antonio is one of the four missions under the care of the founding order of the Franciscans.

Jolon was once a way station on the stage road between Los Angeles and San Francisco. Antonio Ramírez built a one-story adobe inn there, which was later expanded into a two-story hotel by George Dutton. At one point the property was claimed by Faxon Dean Atherton, whose son George (husband of the novelist Gertrude Atherton) chased out a nest of squatters on the land in 1877. Dutton's hotel is now in ruins, on the Jolon Road (county highway G14), just east of the settlement.

ANZA'S MARCH THROUGH MONTEREY

Juan Bautista de Anza and his band of settlers crossed the Rio del Nacimiento on March 5, 1776, and proceeded another mile to El Primo Vado ("the first ford") of the Rio de San Antonio, where Anza had made a brief stop on his previous journey in 1774 and where they now remained two days. The fathers welcomed them as royally as had their brothers at San Gabriel and San Luis Obispo.

On the morning of March 8, the expedition once more resumed its march, following up Sulphur Spring Canyon north to Upper Milpitas Road, east to the Jolon Road, northeast over the ridge, and down Kent Canyon to the valley of what was then known as the Rio de Monterey and is now called the Salinas River. Camp was made northward of the site of King City at

Los Ositos ("the little bears"), where Anza had stopped on April 17, 1774. On March 9 they rested at Los Correas (west and across the river from the present town of Gonzales), and the next day, in pouring rain, they reached the Presidio of Monterey.

Father Junipero Serra welcomed the travelers and escorted them to Carmel Mission. Anza was by now very ill. Before recovering fully, he insisted on fulfilling his mission and proceeded north to explore and to map out the site for the new settlement to be established at San Francisco, leaving his people at Monterey until arrangements could be made for their final migration to the new presidio.

On his way north, Anza followed the left of what is now the road to Salinas and San Juan Bautista. He made his final camp in Monterey County on March 23, at a place called La Natividad, near Sugar Loaf Mountain. A town and a rancho of that name were later located in the vicinity.

Having finished his work at San Francisco, Anza returned to Monterey on April 8. Governor Rivera was opposed to the settlement of San Francisco and refused to allow Anza to settle his people there. Greatly disappointed, Anza finally set out on his return march to Mexico on April 14, after bidding a sad farewell to his companions on the long and perilous journey from Sonora, who wept bitterly at his departure. On the return trip Anza had several unpleasant encounters with Rivera. The latter maintained his obstructionist policy until a letter from the viceroy forced him to proceed with the founding of a presidio and mission at San Francisco. Others led the settlers to the new outpost, but Anza was the founder in all but name.

Monterey has recognized Anza by a monument, dedicated by the California Centennials Commission, in El Estero Park.

THE MONTEREY CUSTOM HOUSE

The Custom House in Monterey (SRL 1) has a prominent place in California's history. This picturesque adobe and stone building was begun under Spanish rule in 1814. The roof was completed under Mexican rule in 1822, and the towers were added about the time the building came under American rule (1846).

The Monterey Custom House was the most important in the province of Alta California, and all trading vessels were required to enter their cargo on its records. To this quiet harbor came the hunters of sea otter and seal, the pioneers of trade on the Pacific coast, followed closely by whaling vessels, which came to be reconditioned after perilous voyages in far northern seas. Most important of all, ships from New England came early, seeking hides and tallow, and with their coming a new era on the coast of Alta California began.

The American flag was raised over the Custom House, temporarily, on October 19, 1842, by Commodore Thomas ap Catesby Jones, commander of the Pacific Squadron of the United States Navy. Relations between the United States and the republic of Mexico had been strained since Texas had declared its independence from Mexico in 1836, and there was some fear of British interest in acquiring land on the Pacific. Hearing rumors while at Callao, Peru, that the expected war between his country and Mexico had broken out, Jones brought his four-vessel squadron into the harbor of the capital of Alta California, where he quickly received the surrender of the hapless commander of the presidio. Upon learning from the United States consul in Monterey, Thomas O. Larkin, that he was in error, Jones apologized the next day, hauled down the flag, and sailed away—having demonstrated how easily California could be taken. On July 7, 1846, Commodore John Drake Sloat sent up the colors that announced the passing of California from Mexican rule.

For a while, the Custom House was the property of the U.S. government. In time it was sold to a group of private citizens, who in turn donated it to the state of California. It was restored by the state and marked by the Monterey History and Art Association. A museum of local relics is housed in it, and it is open to the public as a unit of the Monterey State Historic Park, at the corner of Alvarado and Waterford Streets. The Monterey Custom House has been registered by the Department of the Interior as a National Historic Landmark.

THE ADOBES OF OLD MONTEREY

Another National Historic Landmark is the Old Town Historic District of Monterey, in which forty-three structures from the nineteenth century are located. The Monterey History and Art Association has marked virtually all of the town's historic buildings. As late as the 1890s, Pacific Street, Alvarado Street, and Calle Principal were lined with old adobe buildings. Most have been demolished to make way for modern structures, and now few can be found on any one of these thoroughfares. Nevertheless, Monterey has done more than most California cities to preserve the tangible evidence of its past.

At the western entrance to Old Monterey stands one of the earliest of its historic buildings, the Casa Munras, one of the first homes to be built outside the original presidio grounds. It was erected by Estévan Munras, who came to California as a merchant. Considerably remodeled, it is now part of the Hotel Munras at 656 Munras Avenue, opposite what was once the southwest corner of the old presidio grounds.

Alvarado Street is the main street of old Monterey (although a parallel street is called Calle Principal); from the waterfront it leads up the hill to a group of dwellings rich in historic interest, centering on the Larkin House.

The Larkin House (SRL 106), located on the corner of Calle Principal and Jefferson Street, follows the type of architecture that prevailed throughout Alta California: softly tinted adobe walls, cool veranda and picturesque upper balcony, iron-barred windows and walled gardens, with rose and fig trees. It was built in 1834 by Thomas Oliver Larkin, who had come to Monterey as a merchant in 1832 and was appointed United States consul in 1843. Being thoroughly acquainted with conditions in the province, he rendered important service as consul and confidential agent, and his policies helped prepare the way for the American annexation of California. His house is now a unit of the Monterey State Historic Park and has been registered by the Department of the Interior as a National Historic Landmark.

The House of the Four Winds (SRL 353), built about 1830, stands at 540 Calle Principal. It was initially used as a residence; the first hall of records in the state of California was later housed there, and the first recorder in Monterey had his home as well as his office in the building. Monterey's first weathervane was installed on the building and gave the structure its unusual name.

Between the Larkin House and the House of the Four Winds is a small one-room adobe built by Larkin in 1834 and known as Sherman's Headquarters. It is an integral part of the architecture of the old Larkin garden, with its redwoods and palms and fig trees, and may be reached through the walled patio of the larger house. In 1847–49 Lt. William T. Sherman, later a famous Civil War general, had his civil and military headquarters here.

The Cooper-Molera adobe at 508 Munras Avenue is one of the largest adobes still standing in northern California. John Rogers Cooper, captain of the trading schooner *Rover*, came to Monterey from New England in 1823. He was British, born on Alderney in the Channel Islands. It was Cooper who influenced Thomas

Larkin, his half-brother by his mother's second marriage, to come to California and establish himself as a merchant. Cooper became a Mexican citizen, took the name of Juan Bautista Rogerio Cooper, and married Encarnación Vallejo, sister of General Mariano Vallejo. The home that he built for his wife in 1826 was divided in 1833, with five rooms being sold off. In 1902, Cooper's daughter Anna purchased these rooms, so that the complex of buildings was one again. Meanwhile, her sister Amelia had married Eusebio Molera, a native of Spain, and in time inherited the complex from her sister. The children of Eusebio and Amelia Molera became great patrons of California history and at various times lived briefly in the adobe. Andrew M. Molera never married and died in 1931; he is commemorated by a state park named for him along the Big Sur coast of Monterey County. His sister Frances also died unmarried, in 1968, and deeded the property to the National Trust for Historic Preservation. The California Department of Parks and Recreation, under a lease, is undertaking restoration of what is now a complex of buildings and courtyards. It is open to the public.

Adjoining this at 599 Polk Street is a separate adobe that was built about 1832 by Gabriel de la Torre, a Mexican alcalde, and would later be the first federal court building in California. Across the way at 516 Polk Street is Casa Amesti, a two-story balconied adobe built about 1825 by José Amesti, a Catalonian who had come to California and married Prudenciana Vallejo, another sister of the general, a few years later. The building is now a private men's club.

On the northwest corner of Webster and Abrego Streets is the one-story Abrego adobe, built by José Abrego in the 1830s. Bayard Taylor, in his book *Eldorado*, describes an evening party that he attended in this house in 1849, and also comments that José Abrego, having amassed a substantial fortune within a few years, was the most industrious Californian he had seen in the country. The building is now a private women's club.

The Francisco Pacheco House is a picturesque two-story adobe located on the southwest corner of Abrego and Webster Streets opposite the Abrego House. It was built around 1840 by Francisco Pérez Pacheco, a wealthy landowner who had come from Mexico in 1819. He is buried in the San Carlos Church directly in front of the main altar. The building, once used as a hospital, is now a private club.

At 530 Houston Street is the Robert Louis Stevenson House (SRL 352), where the gifted writer lived for a short time in the autumn of 1879. His attachment for Mrs. Fanny Van de Grift Osbourne, whom he had met in France, brought Stevenson to California. This proved to be the most decisive step he had ever taken, for both his character and the remaining years of his life were influenced by this visit to the West. The hills and beaches of the Monterey Peninsula gave Stevenson the landscape he made rich use of in *Treasure Island*. In Monterey some of his greatest friendships were matured; among them were those of Fanny Osbourne, who became his wife; her sister, Nellie Van de Grift Sanchez, his amanuensis and in her own right an important California historian; and Jules Simoneau, who provided the impoverished Stevenson with daily nourishing meals. Stevenson rented two airy rooms in the ell of the house, with five sunny windows opening on the balcony to the west. The place is now a unit of the Monterey State Historic Park and contains a collection of Stevenson memorabilia.

Directly behind Colton Hall on Dutra Street is one of Monterey's most picturesque adobes, Casa Vásquez (SRL 351), now a city office building. It was once the home of Dolores Vásquez, sister of Tiburcio Vásquez, California's most ruthless bandit, who terrorized the stage roads up and down the state in the 1870s.

On the northwest corner of Alvarado and Pearl Streets is a two-story adobe now used for stores. This was the home of Juan Bautista Alvarado, governor of Alta California from 1836 to 1842 and known to his contemporaries as "the silver-tongued orator" because of his brilliant eloquence and great personal magnetism. This Alvarado house is only one of several in various parts of the state in which Don Juan is said to have lived; another in Monterey is at 530 Dutra Street.

California's first theater (SRL 136), a long rectangular adobe built by Jack Swan in 1843, was originally a sailors' boardinghouse and saloon. It was first used for amateur dramas by four soldiers and a local group in 1847, and later by members of Colonel J. D. Stevenson's regiment of New York Volunteers. The building, which was restored in 1917, stands at the corner of Pacific and Scott Streets and was reopened as a theater in 1937.

The Pacific House (SRL 354), in the Custom House Plaza, was originally a hotel built for Thomas O. Larkin in 1847. It would over the years be a public tavern, an annex housing county offices, a church, and a ballroom. In 1880 it became one of the properties of Scottish-born David Jacks, who was a land developer in the region. Margaret Jacks gave the building to the state of California in 1954. Now it belongs to the Monterey State Historic Park; the first floor is a museum of California history, and the second floor houses the Monterey Museum of the American Indian. An exceptionally fine patio and garden are at the rear. Nearby, at Scott and Oliver Streets, is the Casa del Oro (SRL 532), recently renamed The Boston Store. This was also one of Thomas Larkin's buildings (1845), leased around 1849 to merchant Joseph Boston, who made it into Monterey's first mercantile store. It is said that gold dust was left here for safekeeping, hence the name "house of gold." It is operated as a concession by the Historic Garden League.

The Gutiérrez Adobe (SRL 713), adjoining buildings at 590 Calle Principal, is a well-preserved example of the domestic architecture of the 1840s. It is now a restaurant. One of the most beautiful adobes in Monterey is also part of the state park; this is the Soberanes adobe (SRL 712), the "House with the Blue Gate," at 336 Pacific Street. Built about 1830 by José Estrada, it is named for Feliciano Soberanes, who purchased it from him. In 1941 it became the home of the late Mayo Hayes O'Donnell, noted Monterey historian, and it is now open to the public.

The Casa Bonifacio once stood on Alvarado Street at Bonifacio Place, but it has been moved to Mesa Road. There is a legend about the place that is the source of its alternate name, "The House of the Sherman Rose." While Lieutenant William T. Sherman was stationed at Monterey in the late 1840s, he called several times at the home where Señorita María Ygnacia Bonifacio lived. On one of these visits, so the story goes, he unpinned a rose from his uniform (a most unlikely embellishment) and planted it in her garden, saying that if it took root and grew, their love would endure. The flower grew into a marvelous rose tree (or so the story goes) that almost covered the adobe and was admired by tourists for many years. Sherman never returned, and Señorita Bonifacio never married.

This house, however, has a more real association with the name of Robert Louis Stevenson, for it was here that his fiancée, Fanny Osbourne, and her sister, Nellie Sánchez, lived with Señorita Bonifacio. Stevenson was of course a frequent visitor, and there he began *The Amateur Emigrant*, gathered notes for "The Old Pacific Capital," and wrote *The Pavilion on the Links*, as well as the unfinished work "A Vendetta of the West."

COLTON HALL

Colton Hall (SRL 126) on Pacific Street between Jefferson and Madison Streets, was built in 1847–49 by Reverend Walter Colton, alcalde of the city. Colton came to

California as chaplain on the United States frigate *Congress* in 1846 and was named alcalde the same year by Commodore Robert Stockton. A man of great ability, he impaneled the first jury in California, and on August 15, 1846, in company with Robert Semple, established the *Californian*, the first newspaper to be published in California. His journal, *Three Years in California*, published in New York in 1850, is one of the most fascinating books on the early American period in California and a mine of information for the historian.

Colton Hall was "for many years the most useful building in the city, having been used as a constitutional hall, a schoolhouse, a courthouse, a public assembly hall, and a place of religious worship." California's first constitutional convention met here from September 1 to October 13, 1849. The forty-eight delegates held their sessions on the upper floor, which ran the length of the main building. The large room in which they met has been restored to look as it did in 1849. Robert Semple was chairman of the convention and William G. Marcy was secretary. While Monterey was county seat of Monterey County, from 1850 to 1873, Colton Hall was used as the county courthouse. The jail located at the rear of Colton Hall was constructed in 1854 and served as the city jail until 1956. No one ever escaped from its thick granite walls. Like Colton Hall, the Old Jail is now open to the public.

One of the first schools in California was held in this building, in 1849, by the Reverend Samuel H. Willey. Willey was later prominent in the founding of the College of California, predecessor of the University of California.

Unlike most of Monterey's early buildings, Colton Hall was distinctly of the old New England academy style. Rev. Willey, who was one of the chaplains of the constitutional convention, says in his reminiscences that when he landed from the steamship *California*, on February 3, 1849, he was struck by the contrast between the architecture of this plain white building and the many Spanish adobe buildings around it. "It might have dropped down from a New England village," was his comment.

The state of California made provisions in 1903 for its preservation, protection, and improvement, and it is now owned by the city of Monterey. The building itself is a two-story structure of stone and remains today in excellent condition; the ground floor houses some of the Monterey city offices. It was marked by a bronze tablet placed by the Native Sons of the Golden West in 1931.

CALIFORNIA'S FIRST CONVENT SCHOOL

The first convent school in California was established at Monterey in the spring of 1851 by three Dominican Sisters who had arrived in California the previous year. The old adobe building in which the school was held proved to be in very bad condition; further, the population in Monterey was diminishing while that around San Francisco Bay was rapidly increasing. The sisters, therefore, in 1854, decided to move to Benicia, a more central location at that time.

Concepción Argüello, the story of whose life is closely associated with San Francisco and Benicia, was the first novice to enter the Convent of St. Catherine at Monterey, and when the school was moved to its new location, she was transferred to Benicia.

After the removal of the convent to Benicia, the old building at Monterey was used as a chapel and parish house for a time. Later, it was rented to private parties and rapidly fell into decay; it was torn down soon after 1885. The site where it stood is on the northwest corner of Calle Principal and Franklin Street and is now occupied by the Doubletree Hotel.

OTHER OLD BUILDINGS OF MONTEREY

Many other old buildings are still standing in Monterey. At 177 Van Buren Street is the wood-frame Doud house. The Gordon house, another frame structure, is at 526 Pierce Street. Also on Pierce Street is the Casa de Jesús Soto at 460, and Casa de la Torre is at 502. On Pacific Street one finds the Merritt house at 386, and the Casa Serrano (headquarters of the Monterey History and Art Association) is at 412. At the south end of Friendly Plaza facing Pacific Street is the Underwood-Brown adobe. Hartnell Street has the Stokes house at 500 and Frémont's Headquarters at 539. Alvarado Street contains the Jacinto Rodríguez adobe at 378 and the Casa Sánchez at 412. The Estrada adobe, restored in the 1960s, is at 456 Tyler Street. The first French Consulate, an adobe originally standing at Fremont and Abrego Streets, was reconstructed in 1932 at the edge of Lake El Estero at the foot of Franklin Street. The Casa Madariaga stands on Abrego Street opposite the Casa Pacheco, and the Casa Buelna is on Mesa Road. Casa Joaquín Soto is at 5 Via Joaquin off of El Dorado Street.

Casa Boronda (1817), one of Monterey's oldest buildings, is at the end of Boronda Lane south of Fremont Street. Standing two miles southeast of downtown Monterey in the suburbs is the old Castro adobe of Rancho Aguajito, now restored by the Jacks family. It stands at 1224 Castro Road facing the Del Monte Golf Course.

THE MONTEREY MARITIME MUSEUM AND HISTORY CENTER

The Monterey Maritime Museum and History Center is located at the Custom House Plaza in a handsome facility completed in 1994. The center contains the holdings of the Allen Knight Maritime Museum, displayed elsewhere in the city from 1971 to 1994, with a good display on the era of sailing ships. From that collection comes the lens made in Paris by the Fresnel Company in 1887 for the lighthouse at Point Sur; so powerful was the nine-foot-high Fresnel lens that the beacon could be seen twenty-four miles out at sea. When the lighthouse was automated in 1972, the Coast Guard decided to present the complete light, lens, and rotating mechanism to the Knight Museum. The History Center is also known as the Stanton Center, begun with a gift from Virginia Stanton in 1988 in memory of her husband, architect Robert Stanton. This contains historical preservation materials and display halls.

CANNERY ROW

North of the presidio along the waterfront are some four blocks of buildings that remain from the days when Monterey was the third-largest port in fish tonnage in the world—Cannery Row. The commercial packing of fish in Monterey began modestly when Frank Booth, who had a cannery on the Sacramento River, set up a plant to process Monterey Bay salmon near Fisherman's Wharf. He noticed the large schools of sardines around the wharf and began a small sardine cannery nearby. After this burned, he built another plant at the foot of Alvarado Street and engaged Knute Hovden to develop it. Hovden was a Norwegian living in San Francisco for his health, and he became a major influence in the rising sardine industry. When World War I cut off supplies of European canned fish, the California product was in demand, and by 1918 there were twenty-seven canneries at work along the shores of the bay. Novelist John Steinbeck lived here in the 1920s and early 1930s and immortalized the place in *Cannery Row*. At 800 Cannery Row are the weathered clapboards of Doc Rickett's Western Biological Laboratory and across the street is Wing Chong's store, both of which appeared in the book under other names. Experts warned against overfishing, and in 1945 the dangers they had

Soledad Mission

warned of became evident. By 1948, the sardines were gone and the last canning plant had closed.

The area has been revived in recent years as a tourist attraction, highlighted by the superb Monterey Bay Aquarium, which began its operations in part of the old Hovden Cannery on the Monterey–Pacific Grove boundary line in 1984. The facility has expanded since then, and is today one of California's most treasured resources and most-visited sites.

MISSION NUESTRA SEÑORA DOLOROSÍSIMA DE LA SOLEDAD (SOLEDAD MISSION)

Soledad Mission (SRL 233) was founded by Father Lasuén on October 9, 1791, thirty miles southeast of Monterey and about a mile west of the Salinas River, with thousands of acres of bare, brown plains stretching away on every side. Although the property was enormous, soil and pasturage were only fairly good, and the growth in numbers of neophytes was very slow.

Gradually, however, the labors of the fathers surmounted these handicaps, until the Mission of Our Most Sorrowful Lady of Solitude was quite prosperous, and its occupants lived peacefully for about forty years. Governor Arrillaga died at Soledad in 1814 and was buried under the center of the church. In 1818 the secluded mission became a refuge for the coast missions during the appearance of the pirate Bouchard. In the 1820s the river twice flooded the mission, destroying first the church and then the chapel built to replace the church. After the decree of secularization, Soledad became impoverished, and Father Vicente Francisco de Sarría, who refused to forsake his flock, died there in 1835, destitute and enfeebled by age. The few remaining Indians carried his body forty miles to Mission San Antonio for burial. A mournful description of the site was left by the traveler J. Ross Browne in 1849: "A more desolate place cannot well be imagined.

The old church is in ruins, and the adobe huts built for the Indians are roofless, and the walls tumbled about in shapeless piles. Not a tree or shrub is to be seen anywhere in the vicinity."

This description of "the forgotten mission" was still appropriate a century later. In 1954, the Native Daughters of the Golden West began a project to restore the mission, of which only a few fragments remained. That year a chapel was built and in 1963 a connecting building. The University of California at Los Angeles is conducting an archaeological project there, which is well worth visiting.

The mission site is about four miles west of US 101 on Fort Romie Road, Soledad. Fort Romie, now vanished, was the site of an experimental Salvation Army farm in 1893.

LAND GRANTS

Mexico's Viceroy Antonio María Bucareli set forth in 1773 a plan for the colonization of Alta California. He authorized Captain Fernando Rivera y Moncada, who would succeed Pedro Fages as governor and *comandante* of Alta California in the following year, to distribute grants of land to worthy persons, either native or Spanish, who would devote themselves to farming and stock raising. Among those considered worthy persons were Spaniards who had married baptized Indian women. Such a man was Manuel Butron, a soldier, who married Margarita María of the San Carlos Mission and to whom Rivera gave a plot of land 140 varas square (less than five square miles), near the mission in 1775. This was the first Spanish land grant made in Alta California. The grantee, however, abandoned it later and was living in the Pueblo de San José in 1786.

After the Butron grant, pueblo lots were given to settlers, and by 1784 other tracts of land of larger dimensions were temporarily granted to individuals by Governor Fages in his second term of office. By 1786 grants of land up to three square leagues were authorized, provided that they did not overlap the boundaries of already established missions, pueblos, or rancherias. By 1793 a few had been granted provisionally to retired soldiers.

RANCHO BOLSA DE SAN CAYETANO (LOWER PAJARO RIVER VALLEY)

Ignacio Vicente Ferrer Vallejo, a Spaniard born in Jalisco, Mexico, came to Alta California in 1774 under

Lieutenant José Francisco Ortega's command. Records show that he was praised for bravery many times. After the termination of his enlistment he was employed at San Carlos Mission, where he directed agriculture and irrigation. He reenlisted in military service in the Monterey Company and held positions at Soledad, San Jose, and Branciforte. In 1824 he was at San Luis Obispo for the purpose of preventing an Indian revolt, and while there he received the grant of Rancho Bolsa de San Cayetano. The limit of this tract on the north was the Pajaro River; on the west, Monterey Bay; on the east, Rancho Vega del Rio del Pajaro; and on the south, an estuary separated it from the Carneros Rancho. Because it was the first land owned by the Vallejo family within the boundaries of California, the original house built on it has been termed the Casa Materna ("mother house") of the Vallejo family. Don Ignacio became the progenitor of the Vallejo family in the state.

This adobe was also known as the Glass House because of the many glass windows that once enclosed the upper porch. The house was occupied up to 1870; it then served as a barn, and finally fell into ruin. Although efforts were made by the Pajaro Valley Historical Association to renovate the old structure and make it a state park, these were in vain, and in 1962 a later owner removed the remains with a bulldozer. The loss of the "Glass House," the first permanent home of the eminent Vallejo family in California, is one of the most regrettable in the annals of the state's landmarks. The site (SRL 387) is at the junction of Salinas and Hillcrest Roads in the town of Pajaro.

In 1790 Don Ignacio married María Antonio, daughter of Francisco Lugo. Their family consisted of eight daughters and five sons. Five of the daughters married men of distinction in the county: Mariano Soberanes, José Amesti, J. B. R. Cooper, J. P. Leese, and José F. Alvarado, all of whom received large grants of land. Four of the sons survived their father, who died at Monterey in 1832 at the age of 83. The most distinguished of the sons was Mariano, a leading figure in the annals of California.

José de Jesús, probably the eldest son in the family (since his birthdate is ten years before that of Mariano), lived on his father's rancho and became the owner of it by grant from Governor Figueroa. It was confirmed to him as executor of his father's estate, and he received final patent to it in 1865. He apparently lived on this rancho only a few years after settling the estate, since he became the grantee of Rancho Arroyo de la Alameda in

1842. He spent the last years of his life at Mission San Jose, where he died in 1882 at the age of 84.

An adobe house of two stories, sometimes called the Hipólito adobe and sometimes the Pope adobe, originally constructed four miles from Watsonville on this rancho, was badly wrecked in the 1906 earthquake. Its material afterward was used in the construction of a small one-story cottage, now a private residence, at 514 Blackburn Street in Watsonville (Santa Cruz County). When in use on the rancho, the structure housed a gristmill in its northwest corner, with millstones on the second floor turned by ox power from the ground floor.

RANCHO EL ALISAL AND EL COLEGIO DE SAN JOSÉ (EAST OF SALINAS)

Rancho El Alisal ("alder tree"), consisting of one and one-third square leagues, was granted to Feliciano and Mariano Soberanes in 1834 by Governor Figueroa. Through this tract runs Alisal Creek, on the bank of which W. E. P. Hartnell had established a school of higher learning shortly before.

Hartnell, an Englishman who had married María Teresa de la Guerra in 1825, obtained a grant of land in this vicinity in 1834 for the purpose of building a summer home. Realizing how poor the educational facilities of Alta California were, he decided to establish an institute at his home. El Colegio de San José opened on January 1, 1834, with fifteen pupils. One of these was Pablo de la Guerra, later a member of the constitutional convention and afterward a state senator and chairman of the committee on counties and their boundaries. Two adobe buildings survived until 1960, when their owner, annoyed at the frequent intrusion of sightseers, had them destroyed. Hartnell College in Salinas commemorates the pioneer educator of El Alisal.

The grounds and site of the two adobes are now part of a private stock ranch at 955 Old Stage Road, five miles east of Salinas. The rancho, consisting of 2,971 acres, was patented to "M. T. de la Hartnell" in 1882, passing afterward from the Hartnell heirs to the Spreckels Sugar Company, which later disposed of the property.

The house of the original grantees, the Soberanes adobe, is in the same vicinity but to the west of the road. Hidden by trees, fences, and farm buildings, the place is still used as a family residence on the Silacci Ranch at 960 Old Stage Road.

John C. Frémont camped on the rancho on March

3, 1846. He approached it over the Salinas plain, where "the wild oats were three feet high and well headed." It was here that he received the peremptory order from General José Castro to "return with your people out of the limits of this territory," an order that Frémont ignored. He fortified his party on Gabilan Peak and raised the American flag in defiance.

RANCHO SAUSAL AND SALINAS

Although a large part of the city of Salinas lies on the Rancho Nacional, the northern part lies on the adjoining Rancho Sausal, which extends north and east of the city. Over this area the Natividad and Gabilan Creeks find their way into some of the sloughs that abound in this part of Monterey County.

The American pioneer Jacob P. Leese, who was a landholder in several parts of the state, acquired this property. He filed claim for a confirmation of his right on the basis of two earlier Mexican grants, and received a patent for 10,241 acres in September 1859.

Although the grant had been made to José Tiburcio Castro in 1834, he seems to have resided there much earlier, for his house, only a small part of which is still standing, is said to have been built in 1823. The remnant of the adobe building is in good condition, with leather thongs still binding the hand-hewn rafters. Now a private residence, it is located at 803 Sausal Drive, near the corner of Cambrian Drive.

World War II had a tragic impact on Salinas. Company C, 194th Battalion of the California National Guard, was called to duty in February 1941. Most of its 107 men came from Salinas. Their appointed place was in the Philippine Islands, and within a year these men and their American and Filipino comrades were battling for their lives as enemy forces closed in. Those who survived the Japanese attacks on Bataan and Corregidor were forced to make the Bataan Death March and were subsequently imprisoned. Only forty-six men returned. Salinas has commemorated its soldiers with Bataan Memorial Park, at the junction of Main, Market, and Monterey Streets.

NATIONAL STEINBECK CENTER

John Steinbeck was born in Salinas on February 27, 1902. The family home was built at 132 Central Avenue in 1897 and purchased by the Steinbecks in 1900, two years before he was born in the house. John lived there until he left to attend Stanford in 1919; he often spent

Steinbeck House, Salinas

time thereafter at the family cottage in Pacific Grove. The Steinbeck House has been beautifully restored by the Valley Guild, a volunteer organization that supports Salinas Valley charities and owns and maintains the residence.

The National Steinbeck Center at One Main Street in Salinas is one of California's newest historic museums, opened in 1998. By the time he died in 1968, Steinbeck had written several major novels and much shorter work and had garnered the Pulitzer prize for literature in the United States (1940, for *The Grapes of Wrath*) and in 1964 the Nobel prize for literature. The center has special sections on the background of two novels based on local history, *The Grapes of Wrath* and *Cannery Row*. Additional space is given to archives and reference material, available to qualified scholars.

RANCHO BOLSA NUEVA Y MORO COJO (CASTROVILLE)

Moro Cojo literally means "lame Moor"; but, since *moro* was used by Spaniards to mean anything black, tradition says that a lame black horse gave the name to this particular tract of land.

This eight-square-league rancho was granted to Simeon Castro in three parts. The first, Moro Cojo, was granted by Governor Luís Argüello in 1825; the second, Bolsa Nueva, by Governor Mariano Chico in 1836; and the third by Governor Juan B. Alvarado in 1837. The last one, according to Bancroft, had been given first to John Milligan, an Irishman who taught weaving at Mission San Juan Bautista. The whole was revalidated to the heirs of Castro by Governor Micheltorena in 1844. Irregular in shape, the rancho reached from the swamp near Monterey Bay to rolling, timbered hills. Its south-

Cooper Cabin, Andrew Molera State Park, Point Sur

eastern corner is Lagunita, a lake touched by three other ranchos: Bolsa de las Escarpinas, La Natividad, and Los Vergeles. The northwestern corner of this grant is near the Elkhorn Slough. The town of Castroville, founded in 1864 by Juan Castro, is situated within the bounds of this grant, and is famous for its artichoke crops.

RANCHO EL SUR (POINT SUR, ANDREW MOLERA STATE PARK)

In March 1852 Juan Bautista Rogerio Cooper, then harbormaster at Monterey, filed claim to two ranchos in Monterey County: Bolsa del Potrero y Moro Cojo, and El Sur on the seacoast south of Monterey. He received patents for these ranchos in 1859 and 1866, respectively. Cooper Point on the coast is the southernmost extension of this tract, and the mouth of the Little Sur River is the northern limit. His son, Juan Bautista Henry Cooper, inherited this property, which eventually came to his granddaughter Frances M. Molera. She had the land set aside to be kept in an undeveloped state, and asked that it be named for her brother. Today, Andrew Molera State Park is one of the finest natural properties on the California seacoast. The old wooden house that was the ranch headquarters, now called the Cooper Cabin, still stands about one-half mile southwest of SR 1 at the western side of the park.

RANCHO LA NATIVIDAD

Rancho La Natividad consisted of two square leagues of land south of a stretch of Gabilan Creek. The tract was granted to Manuel Butron and Nicolás Alviso by Governor Juan B. Alvarado in 1837, and their patent was confirmed by the United States in 1853.

One of the few battles that took place on California soil happened here on November 16, 1846. American rule over California had been proclaimed the previous July, but pockets of Californian resistance persisted. An American recruiting and foraging party of thirty-five men and 500 horses, led by Captains Charles D. Burrass and Bluford K. Thompson, was on its way to Monterey to join Frémont, who was preparing to go to Los Angeles to reinforce Stockton. Learning of this, a group of Californians under Manuel Castro decided to interfere. Making a night march from Monterey toward San Jose, Castro and his men met the American forces. In the skirmish that followed, both sides sustained a small number of killed and wounded men. The Americans were able to save their horses and continue southward to join Frémont. The Battle of Natividad was the only major engagement in the north during the revolt of the Californians against the American military occupation in 1846–47.

The site of the battle (SRL 651) is marked by a plaque near the junction of Old Stage Road and Crazy Horse Road, seven miles northeast of Salinas. Old Stage Road is the current name for the San Juan Grade; over it stagecoaches traveled between Monterey and San Juan Bautista in the 1850s. Natividad, the small town that grew up here, was a flourishing station on this line. When the line was discontinued and the main traffic was routed through Salinas, the town became deserted. The former schoolhouse has been remodeled and is now a private home, at 661 Old Stage Road.

RANCHO MILPITAS (JOLON)

Rancho Milpitas extended for many miles along the San Antonio River. In the fertile level areas by the river and along some of its tributaries were probably located those small plots cultivated by the Indians that gave rise to the name Milpitas ("little gardens"). Mission Creek was one of these tributary streams, which supplied water to nearby Mission San Antonio.

Ygnacio Pastor, a neophyte of the mission, received the grant of Rancho Milpitas from Governor Alvarado in 1838. Patent for 43,281 acres was issued to him in 1875. A small area of thirty-three acres around Mission San Antonio was patented to Archbishop J. S. Alemany in 1862. The southeast corner of the rancho is at Jolon (said to be an Indian word for "valley of dead oaks"). The property later passed to Faxon Dean Atherton and then to William Randolph Hearst. It is today part of the Hunter Liggett Military Reservation.

RANCHO LOS OJITOS (SAN ANTONIO RIVER VALLEY)

Rancho Los Ojitos (in free translation, "little springs ranch") is mostly today in the Lake San Antonio Recreational Area, created when San Antonio Dam was built across the San Antonio River. After the secularization of Mission San Antonio, the rancho was given to Mariano Soberanes by Governor Alvarado in 1835.

Because the grantee had resisted the American invaders, the place was pillaged by Frémont's men on their way to Los Angeles in 1846. Don Mariano's claim for damages gained him only a small patent of 8,900 acres, issued in 1871. The ruins of two old houses on the property can be seen from the Jolon-Pleyto Road about three and one-half miles southeast of Jolon.

RANCHES ALONG THE SALINAS RIVER

Of the thirty-two land grants in the Salinas Valley, twenty-six lie adjacent to the Salinas River. Near the mouth of the river was Rancho Rincón de las Salinas ("corner of the salt marshes"), extending just east of Twin Bridges (Neponset) to the ocean. No historic buildings remain from this rancho, or from Rancho la Sagrada Familia ("the Holy Family"), of nearly 7,000 acres, across the river.

Southeast of La Sagrada Familia was Rancho Rinconada del Sanjón ("deep ditch"), the southwestern boundary line of which was made by the curves of the river and the adjacent sloughs. This property of 2,230 acres was granted by Governor Alvarado to José Eusebio Boronda in 1840 and confirmed by United States patent in 1860. A second adobe home built by the family is just northwest of the city of Salinas at 333 Boronda Road. The Boronda adobe (SRL 870) is now owned by the Monterey County Historical Society, which maintains a small museum there. South of the Boronda estate along the river were Ranchos Las Salinas, El Chamisal, El Toro, and lands belonging to the city of Monterey.

Rancho Nacional lay northeast of the narrow ends of El Chamisal and El Toro on the east bank of the river. Its corner was at Hill Town, and it extended from the river into Salinas. The cattle, horses, and sheep belonging to Carmel Mission and the Presidio of Monterey were once pastured here. It was one of the *ranchos del rey*, land belonging to the King of Spain, to be used as directed by the government. The grazing was particularly good because of the rich bottomland and the many streams and sloughs. When the Argentine pirate Bouchard was a threat in 1818, people sought refuge here. The grant Vicente Cantua received in 1839 for this land was finally patented by American courts in 1866, for 6,633 acres. Hill Town is at the junction of SR 68 and the Spreckels Road, a few miles south of Salinas. In later years Hill Town was the site of one of the first ferries to cross the Salinas River. Operated by Hiram Cory, it was guided across the river by a cable and propelled by the force of the current. Hill Town Ferry operated until a bridge was built in 1889. A marker (SRL 560) on the banks of the river commemorates the pioneer ferry.

Up the river from Hill Town stretched two ranchos belonging to the Estrada family, Llano de Buena Vista and Buena Vista. Llano de Buena Vista was granted to José Mariano Estrada in 1823. Estrada had come to California in 1797 and retired from military service in 1829; the following year he was made executor of the Luis Argüello estate. His daughter Adelaide married David Spence, to whom this rancho of 8,446 acres was patented in 1860. On this grant was the town of Spreckels.

Rancho Buena Vista was granted to José Mariano Estrada and his son José Santiago Estrada by Governor Pablo Vicente de Sola in 1822. It consisted of two square leagues. José Santiago and his brothers received patent for this land in 1869.

Southeast of Llano de Buena Vista was Rancho Encinal y Buena Esperanza, also bordering on the Salinas River. It was granted to David Spence, the son-in-law of José Mariano Estrada, by Governor Figueroa in 1834. There were some conditions attached to this grant that are of interest. First, "within a year at least [the grantee] shall build a house thereon and it must be habitable." Then, when the property was confirmed, the corners should be marked not only by boundary stones but also by planting fruit trees, "either wild or tame, of some utility." Governor Juan B. Alvarado granted another square league to Spence in 1839, and his patent to 13,352 acres was issued in 1862. Spence was a Scotsman who came to California in 1824 and remained there until his death in 1875.

Another immigrant who became a large landholder in the area was Juan Malarin, a native of Peru, whose three ranchos—Chualar, Zanjones, and Guadalupe y Llanitos de los Correos, granted between 1831 and 1835 —were south of Spence's property. His son Mariano Malarin received patent to these ranchos by 1872. The town of Chualar stands on the western boundary of Rancho Chualar.

Along the river southeast of the Malarin estate was Rancho Rincón de la Puente del Monte, granted by Governor Gutiérrez to Teodoro Gonzales in 1836. A patent for 15,219 acres was issued to him in 1866. The town of Gonzales, named for the family, stands on this irregularly shaped rancho.

Southwest and across the river from the Gonzales property was Rancho Paraje de Sánchez ("Sanchez's place"). El Camino Real ran through this grant between Soledad Mission and the missions to the north. The 6,584 acres in this rancho were patented to C. Lugo and others in 1866. The reader will notice that it was not until many years after American possession in 1848 that these patents (land titles) were finally approved by American courts, here and elsewhere throughout the state.

The Salinas River curves in and out of the southwestern line of Rancho San Vicente. The town of Soledad is on the southern part of this nearly 20,000-acre grant made to Francisco Soto, Francisco Figueroa, and Estévan Munras. Munras was an early Spanish trader at Monterey. His wife was Catalina Manzanelli of Tepic, Mexico, under whose name Ranchos Laguna Seca and San Francisquito were held. Don Estévan, unlike many of his compatriots, was helpful to foreigners and quite ready for a change from the Mexican political intrigues of the 1830s and 1840s.

Across the river from Soledad and Rancho San Vicente lay the lands of Soledad Mission. On behalf of the church, Bishop J. S. Alemany was given patent in 1859 to 54 acres, containing orchards, vineyards, and springs. Feliciano Soberanes purchased 8,900 acres of the mission lands in 1846, reputedly for $800, and his title to them was confirmed. It was reported at that time that the mission was in ruins.

Part of an old adobe occupied by members of the Soberanes family is still standing, with other farm buildings at the far left of Fort Romie Road near a bend in the road three-quarters of a mile east of its junction with Foothill Road. Another mile or less down Fort Romie Road is Soledad Mission. The Richardson Adobe (SRL 494) still stands on Rancho Los Coches ("the pigs"), at the corner of US 101 and Arroyo Seco Road. Bancroft says that the grant of Los Coches was made in 1841 to María Josefa, daughter of Feliciano Soberanes. She was married to William Brunner Richardson, who built the adobe in 1843; the building, now neglected, has been a family residence, a stage station, and a post office over the years.

Rancho Arroyo Seco, which adjoined Los Coches on the south, consisted of 16,523 acres. Its northwest corner was near the junction of Clark and Paraiso Springs Roads. This was granted to Joaquin de la Torre by Governor Alvarado in 1840. Greenfield has grown up on the southeast boundary of this rancho.

Paraiso Springs is at the end of Paraiso Springs Road, in the foothills overlooking the Salinas Valley. The hot springs here have been known since mission times, when the padres dubbed the place Eternidad Paraiso ("eternal paradise"). In the 1890s a large resort hotel was built here, reached by stagecoaches from the Soledad railroad station. The privately owned Paraiso Springs resort today is open to the public.

Southeast of Arroyo Seco was Rancho Poza de los Ositos and across the river from it, Rancho San Lorenzo. Its owner was Feliciano Soberanes, who amassed much land in the Salinas Valley, including some of the lands once belonging to Mission Soledad. King City is located on the southern part of this grant. An important stopover on the journey between Los Angeles and San Francisco, the town has provided services for travelers for many years. In San Lorenzo Park, just off US 101 west of King City, is the Monterey County Agricultural and Rural Life Museum, displaying antique farm equipment, a working blacksmith shop, the Spreckels farmhouse, and the one-room schoolhouse from La Gloria, a nearby settlement.

Ranchos San Bernabe and San Benito lay farther south on the river; no buildings or landmarks remain. The southernmost rancho in the Salinas River region was San Bernardo, granted by Governor Alvarado in 1841 to Mariano and Juan Soberanes. At its northern line it joined Rancho San Lucas. San Ardo, a station on the railroad line that runs through the valley, is about midway on the long narrow tract, which includes 13,346 acres of rich bottomlands.

Much of the land of Rancho San Lucas is still owned by descendants of Alberto Trescony, who came to California from Italy in 1842 and purchased the estate in 1862. It had first been granted to Rafael Estrada in 1842. The headquarters of the ranch is six miles south and west of the town of San Lucas, one and one-half miles from the Paris Valley Road. The ranch house, built in 1865, consists of one story only. It has thick walls and is nearly surrounded by porches. The barn is of two stories, made of adobe bricks. The blacksmith shop is roofed with handmade tiles removed from a building on Rancho San Benito, also purchased by Alberto Trescony.

Rancho Punta de Pinos was a grant of 2,667 acres along the ocean side of the Monterey Peninsula, the northern limit of which was Point Pinos, the southwest headland of Monterey Bay and the site of the present light station. South of it was Rancho El Pescadero, extending from near Seal Rocks to Carmel. The shoreline is threaded by the Seventeen Mile Drive, of which Cypress Point is the westernmost limit and the most famous spot on the route. At this point on the rugged coast are found the picturesque Monterey cypress trees, whose branches have been bent and gnarled through long exposure to ocean winds. These trees (*Cupressus macrocarpa Hartweg*) have a restricted habitat and are native only to the coast adjacent to the mouth of the Carmel River. Because of early fishing activities carried on at the water's edge on the southern part of Monterey Peninsula, the name Pescadero ("place where fishing is done") was given to the rocks off the shore in Carmel Bay, to a point to the west of them, and to the rancho itself.

Both of these ranchos passed into the hands of David Jacks, who also owned Rancho Aguajito adjoining El Pescadero on the east. Jacks was more interested in developing these properties than in farming them. (Ironically, his name is preserved in one of California's most famous agricultural products, Monterey Jack cheese, first produced about 1892). He had come to California from Scotland in 1848 and put his business ability to work in the young city of San Francisco. In 1850 he began his lifelong interest in the Monterey region, acquiring the city lands in 1859 that were upheld by the courts but denounced by local citizens. In 1874 he was one of the capitalists who backed the Monterey and Salinas Valley Railroad as a challenge to the dominant and greedy Southern Pacific; the new railroad was to bring the grain of Salinas to the port of Monterey and avoid the high charges of the established railroad. Beset by difficulties of all kinds, the narrow-gauge Monterey and Salinas Valley was forced to sell out to the Southern Pacific in 1879.

In the same year, another Scotsman, Robert Louis Stevenson, wrote a sketch on Monterey that concluded with these words: "Alas for the little town! It is not strong enough to resist the influence of the flaunting caravanserai, and the poor, quaint, penniless native gentlemen of Monterey must perish, like a lower race, before the millionaire vulgarians of the Big Bonanza." Stevenson was referring to the fact that when the Southern Pacific Railroad bought out the Monterey

and Salinas Valley line, it built its own broad-gauge track to Monterey and began to plan a luxurious resort at its terminus, Charles Crocker of the Southern Pacific "Big Four" having become interested in the potential of the sleepy town of Monterey. The Del Monte Hotel, "the most elegant seaside establishment in the world," opened in 1880. Transforming Monterey almost overnight into a fashionable and highly successful watering place, the Del Monte Hotel became a California landmark. Twice destroyed by fire and twice rebuilt, since World War II it has housed the U.S. Naval Postgraduate School.

Jacks also developed a more sober and down-to-earth community, to the north of Monterey. The Pacific Grove Retreat began as a summer camp and setting for church meetings, patterned after an earlier undertaking at Ocean Grove, New Jersey. The Methodist Retreat Association developed this "haven for the gentle, the refined, the cultured, where carousing and dissipation are unknown." The community attracted many who sought intellectual and moral uplift. These were uniquely combined in the Chautauqua movement, an import from the East that first appeared in Pacific Grove in 1879. Lectures, concerts, and seminars in a setting that excluded outside distractions were a feature of the Chautauquas. In 1889, a hall was built at the corner of Sixteenth Street and Central Avenue to house these programs (SRL 839). At one time Pacific Grove was fenced off from its neighbors and imposed strict curfews on its members. Inevitably, the invigorating climate that first brought the Methodist elders into this pine forest attracted others as well, and Pacific Grove had become, by the early twentieth century, a more secular community. One connection with the old days has been preserved: the Asilomar (Spanish *asilo del mar*, "refuge by the sea") conference grounds, begun in 1913 under the sponsorship of Phoebe Apperson Hearst as a campground for the Young Women's Christian Association, are now owned and administered by the state of California. They are at the western edge of Pacific Grove.

THE CARMEL VALLEY

Los Tularcitos, the great triangular tract of 26,581 acres covering the Buckeye Ridge and Burnt Mountain, contains a short stretch of the upper part of the Carmel River. As the river flows through the southwestern corner of this rancho, Los Tularcitos Creek drains into it. This rancho was granted by Governor Figueroa to

Rafael Gómez in 1834. In 1852 his widow, Josefa Antonia Gómez de Walters, and his children filed claim for the property and received a patent for it in 1866.

Rancho los Tularcitos passed into the hands of Alberto Trescony, owner of Rancho San Lucas, in the late 1880s; gradually he sold off all but about 2,000 acres, which remain in the family. The main portion, however, which still bears the name Rancho Tularcitos, was acquired by the Marble family in 1924. On a hill south and across the road from the Marble residence is a fragment of adobe wall, all that is left of the original ranch house of Los Tularcitos. The Marble home overlooks a seven-acre tule-bordered lake, from which the ranch received its name of "the little tules." These landmarks are on Tularcitos Road, about two miles east of the junction with Carmel Valley Road.

There were two ranchos Los Laureles along the river; the larger one, through which the river flows, joined Los Tularcitos on the west; the smaller rancho lay to its west. The larger was patented to José Manuel Boronda and his son Juan de Mara, in 1866, based on their earlier grant of 1839. The original adobe home, with later additions, is still standing between Carmel Valley Road and the river to the east of Los Laureles Grade Junction. It is on the west side of Boronda Road one-tenth of a mile south of Carmel Valley Road and is occupied as a private residence. The old part of it is of unusual architectural interest. It is sixty-four feet long and nineteen feet wide. The thick-walled rooms are well preserved; roughly squared beams of the simple ceilings are carefully fitted. The ceiling of one room shows an interesting example of veneering done in softwood.

The smaller Laureles Rancho lay wholly north of the river, as did Rancho Cañada de la Segunda, which reached west to Carmel. On the south bank of the river was Rancho Potrero de San Carlos, which was patented in 1862 to Joaquín Gutiérrez and María Estefana del Real, daughter of the original grantee. This property was purchased in 1858 by Bradley V. Sargent, who also acquired adjoining lands. One of his purchases was Rancho San José y Sur Chiquito, stretching from the lower reaches of the Carmel River southward along the coast. In the northern part of this rancho near the river stood an adobe called "Los Virgenes" because tradition said that local Indians saw there apparitions of the Virgin Mary.

Bradley Sargent also purchased Rancho San Francisquito, lying to the southeast of Rancho Potrero de San Carlos. The San Francisquito ranch house is mentioned in the writings of Robert Louis Stevenson as the place he was taken by Captain Jonathan Wright to be revived after Wright discovered the writer lying, near death, within a short distance of the house. Stevenson had undertaken a solitary camping trip in the hope of strengthening his precarious health; Wright's kindness, he maintained, saved his life.

CARMEL-BY-THE-SEA

The community of Carmel-by-the-Sea began as a writers' and artists' colony in the early days of the twentieth century. Mary Austin and George Sterling were among the first to live there. The picturesque beauty of the area and its quiet isolation appealed to creative artists. Others would follow in time, and today Carmel is a much-visited tourist center and year-round community that yet retains some of the atmosphere of its earlier and simpler days. In addition to the mission, which lies near the mouth of the Carmel River on Rio Road, there are two other historic structures of note in Carmel. The oldest is the two-story stone studio built by artist Chris Jorgenson on Camino Real, now part of the La Playa Hotel. Nearby is the Tor House, built from native stone and capped by a striking tower of Viking aspect. The poet Robinson Jeffers and his wife, Una, built the Tor House in 1919, shortly after coming to Carmel. Jeffers lived there until his death in 1962. The house, at 26304 Ocean View Avenue, is still occupied by the family, and is open to visitors on a limited basis.

At the southern end of Carmel Bay is Point Lobos State Reserve, set aside by action of the Legislature in 1933. Here, where a whaling station operated from 1861 to 1884, 1,250 acres of coastal plans, sea lion rookeries, a stand of Monterey cypress, and tide pools and inlets have been preserved.

DEL MONTE FOREST

The Pacific Improvement Company was created in 1878 to control the financial interests of the "Big Four" of railroad fame: Charles Crocker, Mark Hopkins, Collis P. Huntington, and Leland Stanford. This group developed the Del Monte Hotel and held the land of the Ranchos Punta del Pinos and Pescadero. In 1915, the company was dissolved and began to sell off its properties in the Monterey area. Samuel F. B. Morse, who had been a classmate of Crocker's grandson at Yale, put together a new Del Monte Properties Company with the aid of Herbert Fleischhacker and other San Francisco financiers, and began the systematic development of the nearly uninhabited western side of the Monterey Peninsula.

The result is Del Monte Forest. One of the most carefully controlled areas of California, it was systematically developed for recreation and for privacy. It contains only two commercial establishments, the Pebble Beach Lodge and a small sand-mining company, and seven world-renowned golf courses. The Seventeen-Mile Drive winds through forests of Monterey cypress and pines and great estates; this privately owned road is open to the public upon payment of a toll.

FORT ORD

Fort Ord, on the southeastern shore of Monterey Bay, was a 28,000-acre site created as a cavalry post in 1917. With World War II, it became the headquarters of the Seventh Infantry Division of the United States Army, and a major training center for inductees. This continued for many years as an important Army base; the

nearby towns of Seaside and Marina grew up next to it. By the 1990s the military presence in California was being cut back, and the post was deactivated in 1993. Seven hundred and fifty acres were retained by the Defense Department and annexed to the Presidio of Monterey where they serve the Defense Language Institute, the Naval Postgraduate School, and the Coast Guard Station. Of the remainder, 1,500 acres were set aside for the campus of California State University at Monterey Bay, founded in 1994 and opened the following year. About 50 percent of Fort Ord's remaining property will be turned over to the Bureau of Land Management for use as open space. The coastal weapons range is undergoing clean-up work to become part of the California State Park System. The post's airfield was turned over to the city of Marina. The officers' club and several other buildings at Ford Ord will be taken over by the Monterey Institute of International Studies. Monterey still has a major role to play in the life of contemporary California.

Napa County

Napa County was one of the original twenty-seven counties. Gudde notes that "the meaning of the name Napa has never been satisfactorily explained, although there are probably more theories about it than about any other Indian name in California. . . . It is quite certain that the geographical term originated in Northern Patwin territory." The city of Napa has always been the county seat. The Napa River flows through the county from north to south, creating the Napa Valley, now famous for its viticulture.

THE INDIGENOUS PEOPLE OF NAPA COUNTY

The coming of strangers in the early nineteenth century was disastrous for the indigenous people of what is now Napa County. Spanish and Mexican officials tried to bring many of them under mission control. The first recorded expedition into the county was made in 1823, led by Francisco Castro, accompanied by José Sanchez and Father José Altamira; its purpose was to scout out potential mission sites. The last of the missions was founded in 1823 at Sonoma, and the Napa Valley was considered to be within its jurisdiction. When soldiers attempted to force the Indians into the mission, the native people resisted so strongly that the soldiers, backing off, called them *guapos*, a slang term we might today translate as "tough guys." Later, places identified with the Indians often had the name Wappo connected with them. Some think that this is also the source of the name Napa.

The newcomers killed the local game and brought in their own animals. The grizzly bear soon became extinct in the region, while prolific herds and flocks were introduced. The most devastating introduction (here and throughout North America) were the pathogens to which the indigenous people had no immunity. In 1838, smallpox raged across what is now Napa County, and by the end of the year, virtually all of the Indians were dead.

What remained of these people were their names, and as of 1838 some places and titles can be identified. Most of these terms come from documents in the Spanish or the English language. Beginning at the southern end of the Napa Valley, north of San Pablo Bay and where the city of Napa is today, were the Napa Indians. Living to the east of them were the Suscols, whose name is perpetuated in Suscol Creek and in Rancho Soscol, extending into Solano County. North of the Napas were the Ulucas, identified with Rancho Tulocay, then north of them, the Caymus. The Calajomanas lived in the upper Napa Valley, with the Mayacamas at the extreme northern end.

RANCHOS CAYMUS AND LA JOTA (YOUNTVILLE AND ANGWIN)

George Calvert Yount, a native of North Carolina, came to California from New Mexico with the Wolfskill party in 1831. He was soon engaged in hunting sea otter on the Santa Barbara Channel Islands and along the coast of the mainland. While at Santa Barbara, in 1833, he made what were probably the first shingles fashioned in California, for Captain A. B. Thompson. In the same year, Yount trapped beaver around San Francisco Bay and along the San Joaquin River. Toward the end of the year he proceeded to the missions at San Rafael and Sonoma, where his competence and ingenuity appealed to the padres, who engaged him to repair the mission buildings. General Mariano Vallejo had him make shingles for his house in Sonoma.

Mission life pleased Yount, and he stayed for almost three years. When in 1835 he was baptized into the Catholic faith at Mission San Rafael, his name (as was the custom in Alta California on such occasions) was rendered in the Spanish as Jorge Concepción Yount. In the same year he came to the Napa Valley. He lived there, with his family and a few Indian neighbors, until his death in 1865. Friendships with General Vallejo and the padres at Sonoma Mission determined his future.

In 1836, Yount received the first land grant in Napa County, a great estate of 11,814 acres, which he named Rancho Caymus for the neighboring Indian tribe. This lay in the heart of the Napa Valley, and included in its boundaries the northern fringe of the town of Yountville, named in his honor. Some of the Indians from the mission, which was now secularized, accompanied Yount to Rancho Caymus, where they helped him to build his first dwelling, a Kentucky blockhouse (probably the only one of its kind ever erected in California), as well as subsequent buildings. In 1837 the blockhouse was superseded by a low, narrow building with massive adobe walls, about a hundred feet long, that were pierced by portholes. This so-called adobe "fort" antedated Sutter's in Sacramento by two years. It is said that the fort was torn down in 1870, but a map of that year shows it standing just below the point where the old road to Chiles Valley crossed the Napa River. Charles L. Camp of the University of California, who made a study of some of California's earliest pioneers, says that after Yount moved into his new adobe house his daughter Mrs. Vines lived in the old fort.

A second grant, known as Rancho de la Jota, was made to Yount in 1843. It comprised 4,543 acres of timberland lying on Howell Mountain north of his first estate. A man of energy and enterprise, by 1845 Yount had a sawmill on this new property, as well as another sawmill and a flour mill on Rancho Caymus. The locations of Yount's blockhouse, adobe, and mills on the Napa River are indicated by a stone monument with bronze plaque (SRL 564) on Yount Mill Road about one and one-half miles east of SR 29, at a point about two miles northeast of Yountville. The hardy pioneer died in 1865, and his grave (SRL 693) is in the cemetery at the northern edge of Yountville.

The Veterans Home of California (SRL 828) at Yountville was founded in 1884 and has been under state ownership since 1897. The Veterans Home Museum, begun in 1974, is housed in the old Armistice Chapel of 1918, and has displays on the history of the home, the people who have lived there, and the wars of the United States. The newest museum in the county is the Napa Valley

Museum at 55 Presidents Circle, adjacent to the grounds of the Veterans Home, with among other things an outstanding collection of artifacts and materials concerning the wine industry.

Seventh-Day Adventists played a significant role in the subsequent life of Rancho de la Jota. In 1882 they founded Pacific Union College high on the western slope of Howell Mountain at the village of Angwin. About four miles west of this thriving institution is the St. Helena Hospital, also a Seventh-Day Adventist enterprise, located on the lower slopes of the mountain overlooking Napa Valley.

Just below the hospital is another important Seventh-Day Adventist building, Elmshaven, the home from 1900 until her death in 1915 of the writer and religious leader Ellen White. Open to visitors, the charming two-story house stands on three acres of grounds at 125 Glass Mountain Lane.

RANCHO CARNE HUMANA (UPPER NAPA VALLEY)

In the 1830s a young English surgeon, Edward Turner Bale, landed at Monterey, where he practiced medicine for five or six years. In the years 1840–43 he was surgeon of the California forces by appointment of General Vallejo. Dr. Bale married Carolina Soberanes, a niece of the general, and became a naturalized citizen of Alta California. He received the grant of Rancho Carne Humana in Napa County, to which he went in 1843. By the time of his death in 1849, he was able to leave a rich estate to his widow, two sons, and four daughters.

The name Carne Humana ("human flesh") is as peculiar a title as California history knows. Some authorities believe it to be no more than an attempt to express the name of the local Indian tribe (Calajomanas) phonetically in Spanish. Others explain it as the grotesque joke of Dr. Bale. (No evidence has ever turned up that the Napa Valley Indians were in any way cannibalistic.) Whatever its origin, the name that Bale submitted was accepted by the Mexican authorities and has been rather quickly passed over by later writers of American history.

Although Dr. Bale was a man of good education, hardy, bold, and adventurous, "his debts and personal quarrels," says Bancroft, got him into many difficulties. Resenting what he considered the too-friendly welcome given by his wife to her uncle Salvador Vallejo, the irate doctor quarreled with Don Salvador and challenged him to a duel. According to Bancroft, Vallejo, a skillful swordsman, "twisted his cumbersome opponent into ridiculous knots. Then sardonically, he beat the Eng-

lishman with his sword as though it were a whip. In a rage, Bale drew a revolver and fired. Luckily, the attempted murder was a failure. The intention, however, was counted more important than the deed. The doctor found himself in jail." It was rumored that the Kelseys and other foreigners planned to rescue Bale, and there was much excitement for a time. Narrowly escaping with his life, Bale was finally released.

Rancho Carne Humana comprised the whole of that part of Napa Valley lying north of Rancho Caymus. It consisted of two leagues of fertile land skirted on the west and east by wooded hills and overshadowed on the north by the purple crags of Mount St. Helena. In the 1850s the towns of St. Helena and Calistoga grew up within its bounds.

The Bale adobe was built around 1843 and collapsed in 1931, after which its ruins were cleared away. The site is one mile west of SR 29 on Whitehall Lane beside the small stream known as Bale Creek.

On his lands Dr. Bale had a sawmill and a gristmill; the former has long since disappeared. It was constructed by Ralph L. Kilburn in 1846 and stood on the banks of the Napa River just north of the present Charles Krug Winery. During the winter of 1847, lumber was shipped from here to Benicia and San Francisco. The mill also supplied the lumber for the first frame structure put up in the city of Napa. John York, who came to the valley in 1845, cut the first logs for Bale's sawmill.

The gristmill (SRL 359) is now the center of Bale Grist Mill State Historic Park, located on the west side of SR 29 three miles north of St. Helena. The gristmill was also put up in 1846, the ironwork and blacksmithing being done by F. E. Kellogg, who was paid for his services in land. While the Forty-Niners were eagerly searching for gold in the hills and ravines of the Sierra Nevada, the great water wheel of Bale's mill was daily grinding grain from the upper Napa Valley into flour for the settlers. The mill operated for twenty-five years. The lumber used in the building (ultimately of three stories with a false storefront) was cut from neighboring forests. The millstones were taken from the hill behind the mill, while the cogs in the great wheel, which made such a clatter when in operation, were all made of wood.

The mill's preservation is in part due to the care given it by the family of W. W. Lyman, owner of the mill for many years. In 1923, Mrs. Lyman presented the mill to the Native Sons of the Golden West, who found the task of maintenance against time and vandalism to be beyond their ability. In 1941, it became a Napa County Park and, in 1974, a State Historic Park. The water-powered grinding wheel resumed operation in 1988.

A number of American pioneers settled on Bale's rancho in the middle 1840s; among them in 1845 were John York, William and David Hudson, William Elliott and sons, William Fowler with sons William and Henry, William Hargrave, and Benjamin Dewell. They found Benjamin and Nancy Kelsey already living on what was soon to become the Kilburn place, owned in later years by Peter Teal and located one mile southeast of Calistoga at 4531 Foothill Boulevard. Here is the nearly buried hearthstone of the Kelsey house (SRL 686), on private property. Nancy Kelsey, the first woman to cross the plains, arrived in California in 1841 with the Bidwell-Bartleson party. Ralph Kilburn came to the Napa Valley in 1844. After Kilburn became established on the tract of land that he had received from Dr. Bale, Peter Storm, a Norwegian sailor, lived with him. Storm, in local lore, achieved brief fame as the designer of the Bear Flag that flew over Sonoma.

The incoming settlers of 1845 also found Samuel Kelsey living near Bale's Mill with his wife and children, while Elias Barnett already had a log cabin on what later became the George Tucker place. The Tucker house once stood across the highway from the Bothe–Napa Valley State Park. This park is the site of the first church in the valley, the Old White Church. Built in 1853, the Methodist Episcopal church was named for its organizer and minister, Rev. Asa White. Behind the marker identifying the site of the church is the oldest cemetery in the valley.

During the winter of 1845–46 John York built a log cabin for himself within the present city limits of Calistoga. The site (SRL 682) is at Foothill Boulevard and Lincoln Avenue. Diagonally across the intersection, where a service station now stands, was David Hudson's cabin (SRL 683), built about the same time as York's. The York cabin site is marked by the familiar bronze state-landmark plaque, but nothing marks the Hudson cabin site. York planted the first wheat crop in this section of Napa County. Both men moved in later years to larger quarters as their families grew.

It is interesting to note the number of women and children mentioned in the records of the pioneers. The experience of one mother and grandmother, who came early to the valley, is typical of the strenuous life. She was the wife of William B. Elliott, and with her came several grown children and grandchildren. For a time the family lived in a cloth tent, a frail protection against the elements and the wild animals. The entire family had to spend nights on a platform built in the forks of a mammoth oak tree, often watching helplessly while their uninvited guests plundered the tent for food. During the day the men frequently went on hunting expeditions; and in their absence Mrs. Elliott and the smaller children often had to take refuge in the trees to get away from prowling bears. Mrs. Elliott, however, was an excellent shot.

At the head of the valley one and one-half miles northwest of Calistoga on the road to Knight's Valley was the log cabin of Enoch Cyrus, who came to California with his wife and six children in 1846. Then came the Fowlers, who lived with William Hargrave in a log house at the foot of the Mayacamas Range west of Calistoga. Calvin Musgrove and his wife also lived on the Fowler ranch. Wells and Ralph Kilburn lived with their families one mile south of Calistoga.

In 1849 the Owsley family—husband, wife, and eight children—set up a log cabin, an orchard, and finally a frame house two miles south of what is now Calistoga. One-half mile farther south was the home of William Nash, who had come with his wife and fourteen children to California in 1846 in the original overland group from which the ill-fated Donner party separated. Nash and his party made it to California safely before the snows began in 1846. Purchasing 330 acres of land from Ralph Kilburn in 1847, Nash settled on his ranch in November 1848, naming it Walnut Grove. There he put up a house of boards cut at Bale's mill, and in January of the following year he planted an orchard from seedlings brought by Elias Barnett from Kentucky. Nash was among the first to inaugurate new and better methods of agriculture in California, practicing, among other things, deep plowing and cultivation. He sold Walnut Grove in 1868 and moved to his prosperous Magnolia Farm five and one-half miles north of the city of Napa.

The chain of pioneer homesteads continued southward to the log house of M. D. Ritchie, who lived with his wife and five children across the road from Reason P. Tucker. Tucker was another member of the historic 1846 overland crossing that the Donner party fatally abandoned, and, like Nash, he arrived safely in California. The Tucker family are still prominent residents of this area. F. E. Kellogg had a frame house one-half mile beyond. Having arrived in the valley in 1846 with a wife and seven children, he had obtained this land for services rendered in building Dr. Bale's gristmill. Kellogg's house still stands, just south of the mill, very much as it was when built in 1849 of lumber cut at Bale's sawmill. It is the oldest house in the upper Napa Valley and is now owned by the Lyman family, also important in the history of the old Bale mill.

Across the road from the gristmill Sarah Graves Fosdick opened the second American school in California in July 1847. The first had been established earlier that year by Olive Mann Isbell in the old mission buildings at Santa Clara. Mrs. Fosdick was a survivor of the Donner party who had been brought to the Napa Valley by Reason Tucker, one of the rescuers of that group. The school, a mere shelter of branches, could be used only in good weather. It was replaced in 1849 by a real building erected for Mrs. Fosdick by William Nash. This was used for about five years, until the first public school was opened.

RANCHOS YAJOME, NAPA, AND TULUCAY (NAPA)

Rancho Yajome, an estate of 6,652 acres of fertile land lying on the east side of the Napa River north of Rancho Tulucay, was granted to a soldier, Damaso Antonio Rodríguez, in 1841. It appears that he never lived on the land, however, and the claim to it was filed by Salvador Vallejo in 1852 and confirmed to him the following year. At what later became Longwood Ranch, north of Napa at 1006 Monticello Road, Vallejo built a handsome two-story adobe ranch house that stood until destroyed by fire in 1970. Now a vineyard, the property is also the site of recent archaeological diggings by the University of California, which have established Indian remains from at least 2000 B.C.

In March 1853, Don Salvador and his wife, María de la Cruz Carrillo, filed a claim for about three thousand acres of the much larger Rancho Napa granted to them in 1838 by Governor Alvarado. From time to time they had sold parts of their land that lay some distance back from the Napa River. The part retained and for which confirmation was now asked was called "Trancas and Jalapa," which can be translated to mean "Sticks and Morning-Glories." A Mexican settlement lay in the south end of this area between the road and the river. South of this community was Pueblo de Salvador, a piece of the original grant, where James Clyman purchased some land in 1850 shortly after his marriage to Hannah McComb, a member of the party he had guided across the plains and mountains in the autumn of 1848.

Rancho Tulucay, comprising two square leagues of land just east of the city of Napa, was granted to Cayetano Juárez in 1841. He had stocked the land as early as 1837 and became a permanent settler there before 1840, having built a small adobe house, no longer standing, and brought his family from Sonoma. About 1847 he built a second and larger adobe, which has been converted into a tavern and stands today at the junction of Soscol Avenue and Silverado Trail. Of all the adobes built in Napa County before 1848, this is one of only two remaining. E Clampus Vitus placed a plaque on the site in 1977.

Juárez, a native of California and a military man of some importance, had been a soldier of the San Francisco Company during the years 1828–31, had been promoted to the rank of corporal in 1832, and apparently served as sergeant in 1833. He had engaged in many Indian expeditions, was made mayordomo at Sonoma in 1836, and later served as captain of the militia. In 1845 he was appointed alcalde at Sonoma, the same year in which he received the grant of Rancho Yokoya (Ukiah, in Mendocino County). He distinguished himself in 1846 by his plans to rescue the prisoners held by the Americans after the Bear Flag Revolt and by a famous swim of nine miles that he made to escape capture. Juárez, who died in Napa in 1883, lies buried in Tulocay Cemetery, for which he had donated the land to the city as early as 1859. The cemetery is in the eastern part of the city and is surrounded by a high wall of exceptionally fine native stone.

Just south of the city of Napa stands the Napa State Hospital, on a site that once lay within the confines of Rancho Tulucay. The institution was initiated by the Legislature in 1869–70; in 1872 Napa was chosen by a commission as the site of the hospital, the cornerstone was laid the following year, and the first patient was admitted in 1875.

A few miles farther south, on Suscol Creek, where SR 12 and SR 29 turn briefly to the west and cross the Napa River, is the old Soscol House. Its history is told on an E Clampus Vitus marker placed on the building in 1983: "Soscol House, 1855. Built by Elijah True at the junction of the county road from Napa City and Old Ferry Road, now Soscol, which served the Soscol Ferry crossing at Napa River west of here.

"The thriving transportation center developed here from the stagecoach and wagon traffic was called Suscol; taking that name from the Patwin Indian village site located on the banks of Suscol Creek east of this place, at State Route 29.

"Moved March 1978 to this site, and refurbishing completed by H. & M. Carroll, December 1979." The old way station is now a thriving bar and restaurant, entered on Soscol Ferry Road. Rancho Soscol, in which it is located, lay mostly within present Solano County.

OTHER LAND GRANTS

Nicolás Higuera, a soldier in San Francisco from 1819 to 1823 and afterward *alcalde auxiliar* at Sonoma, received two grants from Governor Mariano Chico in 1836. One was Rancho Entre Napa, which lay to the west of the Napa River. The northeast section of this was bought by Nathan Coombs in 1848 and later patented to him; here he laid out plans for the present city of Napa. The other was Rancho Rincón de los Carneros, a tract of 2,558 acres lying to the north and west of the confluence of Carneros Creek and the Napa River. This afterward passed into the possession of Julius Martin, who received a United States patent for it in 1858.

Rancho Las Putas, on Putah Creek, covering most of the Berryessa Valley, consisted of eight square leagues. The rancho and the creek are named after a Patwin Indian tribe. It was granted by Governor Micheltorena in 1843 to two men, probably brothers, who had served as soldiers at San Francisco in the 1830s. The grantees were José de Jesús and Sisto Berryessa, whose wives, probably sisters, were María Anastasia and María Nicolasa Higuera. With the consent of their husbands, the wives filed claim for this tract in 1852 and received confirmation of their rights to 35,516 acres in 1863. Lake Berryessa, created by the construction of Monticello Dam in 1954, has inundated the sites of the old adobes, as well as the old stage-stop town of Monticello.

Joseph B. Chiles, who came to California first alone in 1841 and for the third time in 1848, bringing family and friends, received a grant of Rancho Catacula in 1844. The grant covered 8,877 acres along the Arroyo de Napa (Chiles Creek), east of Yount's Rancho La Jota. Near the arroyo, Chiles built a house and gristmill. The old mill stood unused for many years and has now collapsed. A bronze plaque has been mounted on a boulder (SRL 547) on the hillside across the road from the ruins. This location is in Chiles Valley, at the junction of the Chiles and Pope Valley Road with the Lower Chiles Valley Road, three and three-quarters miles north of SR 128, at a point seven miles east of Rutherford. On a ranch just north of the mill ruins on the road to Pope Valley stands, in excellent condition, the old adobe Chiles built in 1846. It has been restored by the Dollar family of San Francisco. Chiles's home at Rutherford is near the Niebaum-Coppola Winery; his

town house in St. Helena still stands at 1343 Spring Street, but it has been remodeled into a church.

In 1841 Manuel Jimeno granted Rancho Locoallomi, consisting of 8,872 acres, to Julian Pope, and Rancho Huichica, of two square leagues (or 18,704 acres), to Jacob P. Leese. Leese received an extension of his property three years later, when Governor Micheltorena gave him another three and a half leagues. The Huichica grant lay southeast of Pueblo de Sonoma and the Buena Vista tract of Colonel Haraszthy. Carneros Creek formed its northeastern boundary, with Ranchos Napa and Rincón de los Carneros as neighbors across the stream.

Pope Valley, which is named for pioneer Julian Pope, was thoroughly prospected in the 1860s, along with much of the northern part of Napa County. By 1880 the Aetna cinnabar mine was employing as many as 1,200 Chinese laborers. When this mine closed, many Chinese remained in the area as stonemasons; Napa County's roads are often lined with well-made stone fences dating from this period. The mine closed in 1887 because 102° mineral waters from Aetna Springs began filling the shafts.

By 1880, Aetna Springs was launched as a health resort, in time a very successful one. Some of its buildings were designed by the great California architect Bernard Maybeck and five are on the National Register of Historic Places. The Aetna Springs Golf Course, laid out in 1891, claims to be the oldest in California and is open to the public on a limited basis. Down into the 1960s it remained a popular resort. After many years of neglect, plans were made in the 1990s to revive and extend the property and golf course. Because this development would be in an agriculturally protected zone and have an environmental impact, the proposal was submitted to the voters in a referendum in 1999, which was defeated. The future of the property remains uncertain.

At 6654 Pope Valley Road, about halfway between the turnoff for Aetna Springs and the village of Pope Valley, is one of the most unusual "historic spots" in California—Litto's Hubcap Ranch (SRL 939). Emanuele "Litto" Damonte and his neighbors collected more than two thousand hubcaps in thirty years. All around Hubcap Ranch are constructions and arrangements of hubcaps, bottles, and pulltops; Litto Damonte died in 1985.

The village of Pope Valley is dominated by two structures, closed for some time, but still standing in good order. Henry Haus operated his blacksmith shop here from 1897 to 1950; since his death in 1955 the shop has been unused. An E Clampus Vitus marker was

First Presbyterian Church, Napa

placed here in 1982. Across the street, the Pope Valley Store was first opened in 1888; Thomas Neil added a saloon and a seven-room hotel, which were operated by him and later by his son, Elgy Neil. The place was closed when the latter died in 1970.

NAPA

The first Napa County courthouse, built in 1856, had to be condemned eight years later when large cracks appeared in the structure. A second building was completed in 1878; this impressive brick building has withstood the ravages of time and earthquakes and is still in use. Public buildings in Napa have often been kept up and refurbished rather than torn down. The Napa Opera House, built in 1880 at 1018–30 Main Street, is undergoing extensive restoration. Old office and business buildings still in use are the Semorile Building at 975 First Street, the Winship-Smernes Building at 948 Main Street, and the Hatt Building at Fifth and Main Streets; the latter is also undergoing a major restoration. The Chinese settlers of Napa are remembered in the Sam Kee Laundry building at 1245 Main Street. The Goodman Library building, a gift of George Goodman to the citizens of Napa in 1901, now houses the Napa County Historical Society Museum and Library. This beautiful two-story building of native stone is at 1219 First Street. The First Presbyterian Church (SRL 878)

has been in continuous use since its construction in 1874; it stands at 1333 Third Street. Although all of these buildings are close to the river, none was seriously damaged by the flood of February 1986, when the Napa River rose to its greatest recorded height during a prolonged rainstorm.

The building at 1711 Main Street was originally the Lisbon Winery, built of native stone in 1882 by Joseph Mathews (Mateus), a native of Portugal, who made prize-winning wines here for many years. It survived as a winery under various owners until the 1990s; now it is the Jarvis Conservatory, specializing in dance and musical performances. The building was marked by the Native Sons of the Golden West in 1978.

WHITE SULPHUR SPRINGS

The first mineral springs resort in California was White Sulphur Springs, located on a western extension of Spring Street in the foothills four miles west of St. Helena. Discovered in 1848, the place opened as a resort in 1852, with a wide array of activities for patrons. It is still in business today, with a small museum of artifacts and pictures of its long history.

CALISTOGA

Samuel Brannan, active in several parts of California, purchased in 1859 a tract of land in the region around the hot springs at the foot of Mount St. Helena, with the intention of establishing a summer resort. The story is often told that Brannan, at a promotional dinner, boasted that this great resort would be to California what Saratoga Hot Springs was to the state of New York; his toast to the "Saratoga of California" came out as the "Calistoga of Sarafornia." Some historians believe the origin of the name was less spontaneous and more calculated. Near the springs he built a hotel and twenty-five cottages and laid out elaborate grounds and a racecourse. The long row of elm trees on Lake Street originally led to the racetrack. The site of the resort is marked by a series of old palm trees at Indian Springs. One of the cabins (SRL 685) has been moved to 1311 Washington Street, where it is now a part of the Sharpsteen Museum, opened in 1976. Its benefactor, Ben Sharpsteen, a longtime producer for Walt Disney Studios, supervised the making of a remarkable diorama now on display, showing the grounds of the Calistoga resort as they were around 1876. This beautifully kept museum is a repository of Calistoga history.

Charles Krug Winery, St. Helena

Greystone Cellars, now Culinary Institute of America Facility

Another cottage from the resort stands on Cedar Street opposite Pioneer Park and is now a bed-and-breakfast inn. A third cottage, with two sentinel palm trees, is located on Wapoo Avenue just off Lincoln; this is a private residence. Across the street at the corner of Brannan Street and Wapoo Avenue is the store (SRL 684) in which Brannan made $50,000 one year; this is also a private home.

Sam Brannan was successful in getting financial support for a branch railroad to his resort. Its first trip brought some three thousand people from San Francisco and other parts of the state to the grand opening of Calistoga Hot Springs in October 1868. The Napa Valley Railroad Depot (SRL 687), built the same year, later became a Southern Pacific station when that line bought out its predecessor. Railroads no longer run to Calistoga; the station has been made over into shops and offices, and restored Pullman cars on the railroad siding have been transformed likewise.

Calistoga's mineral waters have been famous for over a century; they are bottled by plants here and in the northern part of the Napa Valley. On Tubbs Lane two miles north of the city an "Old Faithful" geyser is a tourist attraction.

Brannan also turned his attention to the adjacent hillsides. Encouraged by the example of Colonel Agoston Haraszthy in Sonoma County and by a few growers near Napa, he planted the slopes with cuttings of superior table and wine grapes. Today, the Napa Valley is a world-famous wine-producing region.

VINEYARDS AND WINERIES

On the wooded hillsides and in the valleys of Napa County, with its thousands of acres of vineyards, stand picturesque structures of stone and brick similar to those built long ago in France and Germany. These wineries, however, date back only to the 1860s, when it was realized that the climate and soil were favorable to the culture of the vine.

Both the Spanish and early American settlers had made wine from Napa County vineyards. A notable year, however, was 1859, when San Brannan planted his hillside. The previous autumn Charles Krug had made about 1,200 gallons for a Mr. Patchett at Napa. In the following year, Krug went to the Bale sawmill north of St. Helena and made wine for Louis Bruck, and in 1860 he made 5,000 gallons at Yount's place at Yountville. His reputation now established, in 1868 Krug began to build a stone wine cellar (SRL 563) north of St. Helena on the floor of the valley. Additions were made periodically to this winery until it was completed in 1884. Standing amid plantings of shrubbery in a large grove of oaks, and with newer buildings flanking it, it is still a major producer of the Napa Valley, under the ownership of the Mondavi family.

About four miles northwest of the Charles Krug winery on SR 29 and a short distance east of the highway on Larkmead Lane is the Hanns Kornell Champagne Cellars and the Frank-Rombaur Cellars. This operation is located in the buildings at "Larkmead," once the winery of Mrs. Howard Coit, better known in San Francisco as Lillie Hitchcock. In 1872, her father, Dr. Charles Hitchcock, bought a thousand acres of Rancho Carne Humana and built a country home, which he named "Lonely." By the time "Lonely" was destroyed by fire in 1929, the property west of the highway was owned by Reinhold Bothe, who made it into a commercial campground. Bothe's property was acquired by the state in 1960, and is now Bothe–Napa Valley State Park, adjacent to the Bale Grist Mill State Historic Park; the entrance is about a mile and a half north of the mill.

St. Helena is the center of Napa County's wine industry. The largest building from that activity is the for-

Rhine House, Beringer Winery, St. Helena

Schramsberg Winery, Calistoga

mer Greystone Cellars of the Christian Brothers, one mile north of St. Helena and almost directly across SR 29 from the Charles Krug winery. Built in 1889, this is one of the largest stone wineries in the world. It is now the Napa campus of the Culinary Institute of America, a premier cooking school. Closer to St. Helena on the west side of SR 29 is the interesting Beringer winery (SRL 814). Jacob L. Beringer, who had been foreman of the Charles Krug winery, selected this spot in 1875. The winery is built into the western hills, where the limestone formation is peculiarly adapted to the storing and aging of wines. The winery and 800 feet of cellars are cut into the stone, another feat of the Chinese stoneworkers whose activities are evident throughout this part of the Napa Valley. The tunnels running 250 feet directly into the hill are connected by several laterals, honeycombing the entire hill. This underground storage space is filled with oval oak casks, each with a capacity of about five hundred gallons. The lower floor of the Rhine House, the former Beringer family home, is now the tasting room for the winery; its beautiful colored glass windows are outstanding.

Chateau Montelena winery, on Tubbs Lane north of Calistoga, is in the huge stone cellar built in 1881 by Alfred L. Tubbs, who desired to copy Château Lafite in the Bordeaux region of France. Only the stone walls are reminders of the past; as in most California wineries, the interior and its workings are very up-to-date.

Three miles south of Calistoga on SRs 29 and 128 and a mile to the west of the highway is the historic Schramsberg Vineyard (SRL 561), begun by Jacob Schram in 1862. It was already something of a local attraction when Robert Louis Stevenson visited here in 1880. Today its focus is on champagnes and sparkling wines.

In 1870 Seneca Ewer came to live at St. Helena. In 1882 he and his partner, Atkinson, built a stone winery near Rutherford. The son, Fred S. Ewer, carried on his father's business and in 1915 sold the wine cellar to Georges de Latour, who enlarged the original stone building with an addition built of concrete. This is now the Beaulieu winery, on SR 29 at Rutherford.

In the foothills just west of Rutherford is a beautiful winery with an interesting history. The land for this vineyard, formerly the property of a sanatorium, was purchased by Gustav Niebaum in 1880 and planted with cuttings of European grapes. The three-story winery, built of stone quarried on the estate, was completed in 1887. Known for many years in the late twentieth century as Inglenook, the winery was purchased in 1994 by the noted filmmaker Francis Ford Coppola, who produces wine under the label of Niebaum-Coppola.

STEVENSON'S SILVERADO

In the spring of 1880, Robert Louis Stevenson and his bride, Fannie Van de Grift Osborne Stevenson, came to live at the abandoned mine camp of Silverado, on the south slope of Mount St. Helena on the road between Calistoga and Middletown in Lake County. Their honeymoon was in a deserted miner's cabin with its sashless windows "choked with the green and sweetly smelling foliage of a bay," and its three rooms "so plastered against the hill, that one room was right atop of another." More than a century later, the modern traveler can see just how the rolling morning fogs can seem to be "a great level ocean." *The Silverado Squatters*, a delightful collection of descriptive and narrative essays, is a rare description of late-nineteenth-century California by a first-rate artist. Completed in France, the book came from the memories of that health-giving summer on the slope of Mount St. Helena.

The Robert Louis Stevenson Memorial State Park

(SRL 710) has been established here, but it is undeveloped. The old cabin is gone; its place is marked by the Stevenson Monument, carved from polished granite in the form of an open book, on a base of ore taken from the Silverado Mine. This is not a landmark for the casual tourist; the Stevenson cabin site is up a steep slope.

On the east side of the city of St. Helena is the charming Silverado Museum at 1490 Library Lane, adjoining the St. Helena Library. The Silverado Museum is the creation of the Vailima Foundation, established in 1968 by Mr. and Mrs. Norman Strouse to collect materials associated with the career of Robert Louis Stevenson.

Nevada County

Nevada County was formed in 1851 from territory that had been originally a part of Yuba County. Nevada City was made the county seat. Situated in a region where the entire upper country wears a heavy mantle of snow during the winter months, the name "Nevada" (Spanish for "snow-covered") was appropriately chosen by its citizens for the town. The mountain range in which most of the county lies is named Sierra Nevada (Spanish for "saw-toothed mountains, covered with snow"), which is taken from a shorter range in southern Spain, near Granada. Later the name "Nevada" was also given to the county.

THE DONNER TRAGEDY

One of the routes into California most frequently used by the emigrants of the 1840s and 1850s was known as the California Trail, or the Truckee Pass Emigrant Road, which followed the Truckee River valley in Nevada up through Donner Pass in the High Sierra.

The first overland party of emigrants to follow the California Trail was the Stevens-Murphy party in the autumn of 1844. Caught in November snows, some members of the party were forced to winter by a lake just below the pass over the mountains. An eighteen-year-old man in this group, Moses Schallenberger, survived to write an account of the experience; with some difficulty, they succeeded in building a cabin and lived to reach California. In 1845, John C. Frémont, with a small detachment of his company, entered California by the same trail. But the most famous group to negotiate it was the Donner party, whose experiences in the High Sierra during the winter of 1846–47 are one of the most tragic episodes in the history of California.

In the spring of 1846 a party of emigrants, led by George and Jacob Donner and James F. Reed, was organized in Sangamon County, Illinois, and started its trek westward. When the party reached Independence, Missouri, the first week in May, it had grown to such proportions that between two and three hundred wagons were included in the train.

Upon arriving at Ford Bridger, the Donner-Reed party took the fatal step of breaking off from the larger group and following the Hastings Cutoff, a supposed shortcut that passed south of the Great Salt Lake. Instead of taking one week as expected, a whole month of valuable time was consumed in reaching Salt Lake. Struggling on over the great salt deserts west of the

Pioneer Monument, Donner Memorial State Historic Park

lake, where the party suffered many hardships, they finally reached the site of Reno, Nevada, entirely exhausted. Finding forage for their emaciated animals here, the party rested for three or four days. This delay, however, proved to be disastrous, for the storm clouds were already gathering when they reached the mountains. The little band hastened up the eastern side of the Sierra Nevada as fast as possible, but on October 28, 1846, before they could reach the summit, heavy snow began to fall—a month earlier than usual.

The emigrants, already weakened and spent, soon found it almost impossible to make progress through the rapidly deepening snow, which quickly obliterated all semblance of a trail. Several attempts to cross the mountain barrier ended in defeat. The party made what pitiful preparations they could for winter camp near the shores of what is now Donner Lake. The cabin where Schallenberger lived two winters before was discovered and occupied, and some cabins and shacks were quickly thrown together. The families of George and Jacob Donner, owing to an accident that delayed them, had been forced into camp at Alder Creek, about six miles below the lake. Here their only shelters were crude huts of canvas and boughs banked with snow. With such meager protection from the elements, during what proved to be the most severe winter in thirty years, and with actual famine impending, the members

of the unfortunate party would all have perished had no aid come to them.

Somewhere around December 16, a party of ten men and five women started out in a desperate attempt to get help. Struggling on for thirty-two days over the snow-covered mountains and enduring unbelievable hardships, forced to eat the flesh of their dead companions when nothing else was left, the five women and two of the men finally reached Johnson's Rancho, near the present site of Wheatland, some thirty-five miles north of Sutter's Fort.

With the aid of John A. Sutter and others, four relief parties were organized to attempt the rescue of those remaining in the mountains. With great courage and stamina, these parties succeeded in carrying in provisions, and brought out of their frightful camps of death the emaciated survivors, many of them children.

Of the eighty-nine persons who began the winter at Donner Lake and on Alder Creek, forty-two perished. Suffering, despair, and death stalked the camps, and human flesh was eaten here as well. The area at the eastern end of Donner Lake is now Donner Memorial State Park, provided, ironically, with campgrounds that are used in the summer and places where self-contained recreational vehicles may stay overnight in the winter.

The Pioneer Monument (SRL 134), erected by the Native Sons and Daughters of the Golden West, stands in the park near the entrance and near the site of the Breen cabin, one of the shelters used by the Donner party. The rock pedestal supports a group of four figures in bronze representing a pioneer family; the platform on which they stand, the top of the rock pedestal, is about twenty-two feet above the ground, approximately the level of the snow at this location in the winter of 1846–47. A nearby tablet identifies the site of Moses Schallenberger's cabin.

Where the Murphy cabin stood, a huge boulder bears a bronze tablet with the words "Donner Party, 1846–47. The face of this rock formed the north end of the fireplace of the Murphy Cabin. General Stephen W. Kearny, on June 22, 1847, buried under the middle of the cabin the bodies found in the vicinity." The tablet lists the names of the members of the Donner party, those who survived and those who perished. This boulder is 200 yards by trail from the Emigrant Trail Museum, a highlight of the park. The museum has good displays of the natural history of the region as well as its human history.

The area has been recognized also for its significance to the history of the nation and has been registered and marked by the Department of the Interior as a National Historic Landmark.

THE OLD EMIGRANT TRAIL

The old emigrant road, which the Donner-Reed party passed over, was first marked in the 1920s by P. M. Weddell, a San Jose high school teacher, with homemade signs, on some of which the picture of a covered wagon was traced. A few of these still exist. Permanent bronze plaques were later placed by the Native Sons of the Golden West and other groups. The tablet near the summit of Donner Pass on Donner Pass Road, the old Highway 40, bears the inscription "Donner Summit Bridge, dedicated to the pioneers who blazed the Overland Trail through these mountains."

One of the first permanent markers along the old emigrant trail was placed near Truckee and stands today in front of the Tahoe-Truckee High School, about a mile east of the Pioneer Monument on Donner Pass Road. The tablet contains the following inscription: "The emigrant trail in the pioneer days of California came through the low pass to the north facing this monument. The trail turned west at this point for a distance of approximately twenty-six hundred feet, where a tablet describes the route then followed. Placed by the Historic Landmarks Committee, Native Sons of the Golden West, September 14, 1929."

The second tablet, mentioned in the first and placed on the same day, stands on Coldstream Canyon Road about 150 yards south of its junction with Donner Pass Road. It reads: "The emigrant trail in the pioneer days of California turned to the south at this point for approximately three miles, then west across the summit of the Sierras about a mile south of the present railroad. It was here that the Donner party missed the trail, owing to the early snows, resulting in tragedy."

The Donner party and most of the other early emigrants who crossed the Sierra Nevada by way of the Truckee River and the Donner Pass traveled down the ridge north of the Bear River, entering the Sacramento Valley by using approximately the same trail as that opened by the Stevens-Murphy party in 1844–45.

The point at which the emigrant trail crossed present SR 49 has been marked (SRL 79) at Wolf Creek, halfway between Auburn and Grass Valley. Later a much-traveled emigrant road came down the San Juan Ridge between the Middle and South Forks of the Yuba River. This was used mostly by those who had come via the Henness Pass route in Sierra County. This trail followed the ridge over a soil formation and was preferable to the route over Donner Pass, which was extremely rough and rocky. During the 1860s this route became one of the stage and freight roads for the mines of the famous Comstock Lode in Nevada. In the 1920s a section of the road above Graniteville was rebuilt and used during construction of the Bowman Dam.

TOLL ROADS

During the 1850s and 1860s the rapid development of mines in the recesses of the mountains resulted in an imperative need for the construction of roads—a need that the counties could not meet because of the expense. Consequently, most of the roads and bridges that replaced the pack trails were constructed and owned by individuals or by turnpike companies, and were operated for profit.

The development of a system of state and national highways following roughly the early roads and trails has almost eliminated the toll-road system in the state (although all of the San Francisco Bay Area bridges are toll bridges, and toll roads have recently been introduced into Orange County). Nevada County bought the last of its toll roads and bridges around 1890.

Among the privately owned turnpikes leading from Nevada City were the following: the Nevada–Little York; the Nevada–Grass Valley; and the South Yuba Road, which went from Nevada City to North San Juan, crossing the South Fork of the Yuba River at what was known in 1853 as Robinson's Crossing, later as Black's and then as Purdon's Bridge.

Another important turnpike followed in part the route taken by the present SR 49 from Nevada City to Downieville. The first ten-mile stretch of the road, now bypassed on the west by several miles, was known as Purdon's Grade, and is today called Purdon Road. The bridge at the Middle Fork of the Yuba River is still known as Freeman's Crossing. Thomas Freeman, in 1854, purchased the property from Thomas Hess, who built the first bridge at this point in 1851. The winter floods carried it away, and a second structure, subsequently taken over by Freeman, was built in 1852. After the flood of 1862, Freeman built a substantial structure that he owned for some thirty years. Two of the old pilings of this bridge may still be seen in the river, less than half a mile west of the present bridge via Moonshine Road.

Just above the massive concrete bridge that carries the modern motorist across the river into Yuba County, Oregon Creek runs into the Middle Yuba. Here is the junction of three roads. One leads up Oregon Creek to Downieville; a second turns right across the creek through an old covered bridge to Alleghany, Forest, and Henness Pass in Sierra County; and a third goes left across Moonshine Creek to the Bullards Bar Dam in Yuba County—all are modern roads of superb scenic grandeur following the routes of historic trails and turnpikes. The covered bridge across Oregon Creek (in Yuba County) was built probably in 1862. A flood in 1883 swept it off its foundations and turned it around, depositing it on the bank 150 feet downstream. By means of ox teams it was inched back to its site on logs and planks, but since no way could be found to turn it around, what had been the south end is now the north. It was at this time, presumably, that the portals at either end of the bridge were curved to meet the road.

YUBA RIVER BARS

Early in 1849 John Rose, who gave his name to Rose's Bar in Yuba County, built a cattle corral at a spot in Pleasant Valley on the lower San Juan Ridge between the sites later occupied by the Anthony House on Deer Creek and Bridgeport on the South Yuba. Apparently Rose's original purpose was to trade with the Indians of the region, but during the early summer prospectors found their way up the South and Middle Forks of the Yuba River and Deer Creek, crevassing for gold and finding many rich gravel deposits on the bars along the margins of these streams. The news of these discoveries spread quickly, and by late summer and early fall of 1849 scores of miners were working the Deer Creek and Yuba River surface diggings. In order to accommodate the increasing trade, Rose established a trading post in a small adobe he had built.

As in practically all the mining regions of the Sierra Nevada, the first prospecting in Nevada County was confined to the gravel bars and the beds of running streams. Scores of river-bar camps sprang up almost overnight. Typical of these mining camps was Bridgeport, on the South Fork of the Yuba, about one and one-half miles from its mouth. For two years the town was exceedingly prosperous, but after river mining ceased to be profitable the camp declined. Today the name is preserved only in Bridgeport Township.

The present road to French Corral leaves SR 20 midway between Smartsville and Rough and Ready. The site of the old Anthony House is now buried beneath the waters of Lake Wildwood. After another five miles it crosses the river at Bridgeport near an old covered

Covered Bridge, Bridgeport State Historic Park, South Yuba River

bridge (SRL 390), built in 1862 by David I. Wood. It is the oldest housed span in the West, and, at 233 feet, the longest single-span covered bridge in the United States. The road continues to French Corral, less than three miles away, and in another five miles joins SR 49 near North San Juan.

Additional camps were established on the Middle Fork of the Yuba in 1850, among them Rice's Crossing (at first known by the rather dubious title of Liar's Flat and then as Lousy Level), Frenchman's Bar, and Condemned Bar in Yuba County. On the South Fork was Jones's Bar, which was once famous among the river camps.

Panning for gold was, of course, the first and most primitive method of washing the metal from the gravel. The first machine to be employed for the purpose was the rocker, which was introduced in the summer of 1848. This was, in turn, superseded by the long tom. Gradually the miners extended their activities to the gravel of the dry gulches, flats, and hillsides; then ground sluicing, introduced by William Elwell at Nevada City early in 1850, came into practice. With this innovation an elaborate system of ditches and sluice boxes was developed, out of which, in time, grew the more powerful and extensive hydraulic methods of the 1860s and 1870s. Many old mining ditches of today irrigate the orchards and gardens in the Sierra Nevada hill country.

ROUGH AND READY

Coming up from Marysville to Grass Valley on SR 20, the motorist passes near Timbuctoo and Smartsville in Yuba County and climbs wooded hills through a historically rich countryside. Here are deeply scarred gullies and gravelly hillocks marking abandoned diggings of the 1850s and 1860s.

A turn in the road brings one to a place of green upland meadows and a small town lying sheltered among aging shade and orchard trees. This peaceful spot belies its name, Rough and Ready, but in the feverish days of the 1850s, it was a busy mining town, one of the first to be established in Nevada County. A party of men calling themselves the Rough and Ready Company arrived in the vicinity on September 9, 1849, under the leadership of Captain A. A. Townsend, who had served under General Zachary Taylor ("Old Rough and Ready"), hero of the Mexican War, and in 1849 president of the United States. For several months the Rough and Readys were able to keep the richness of this region a secret, preempting all the surrounding land, but by 1850 the incoming tide of miners could not be held back and the place developed into a good-sized town (SRL 294).

One episode in the history of the town makes it unique. During the uncertain days of early 1850, while California's statehood was being debated by Congress, E. F. Brundage conceived the idea of a separate and independent government. Issuing a high-sounding manifesto, he called a mass meeting to organize the State of Rough and Ready. For a short period he had a following of about a hundred men, but the whole affair met with such ridicule that the State of Rough and Ready soon dissolved into thin air.

On June 28, 1850, Rough and Ready had its first devastating fire. In spite of this discouraging experience, in October it polled 1,000 votes and even aspired to become the county seat of the newly organized Nevada County. A committee to preserve law and order had been elected, a Christian Association was holding services in a little clapboard shanty, and the Masons and the Odd Fellows had joined in forming a benevolent association. The town continued to grow, and during the early 1850s there were more than three hundred substantial frame buildings.

Its decline began with the gradual exhaustion of the gold in the creeks and on the flats, and by 1870, after destructive fires in 1856 and 1859, only twenty-four houses were left in the town, a few of which are still standing. On the hill is the IOOF building, deeded by the society (now joined with the Grass Valley lodge) to the town of Rough and Ready as a community hall. As one leaves the town, the old Fippin blacksmith shop, deserted and dilapidated, stands on the left of the road. A little farther on the right is the Toll House, now an antique shop. Scars of old diggings are passed on either side of the road as one leaves Rough and Ready behind and climbs the hills toward Grass Valley, four miles away.

In 1865–66, during the copper-mining excitement, a boom occurred southwest of Rough and Ready, and the towns of Spenceville, Hacketville, Wilsonville, and Queen City were laid out. Only Spenceville endured, being the location of a post office from 1872 to 1932 and the center of a small agricultural community. It is said to have had a population of 150 in the 1920s. During World War II it was used by neighboring Camp Beale as a model German village for war maneuvers. The few remaining old buildings were posted with German signs and became targets for the soldiers' guns. Now the site is practically inaccessible, although a piece of the old road southwest of Rough and Ready is still called Spenceville Road.

About three and half miles northeast of Rough and Ready, via Beckman Hill Road and Newton Road, is Newtown, formerly Sailor Flat, while ten miles west and one mile north of SR 20 is Mooney Flat. Both were mining camps in the 1850s but now consist largely of newer homes. This has become a favored retirement area. The Mooney Flat Road continues past Englebright Reservoir to join the Pleasant Valley Road (to French Corral) above Lake Wildwood Dam.

GRASS VALLEY

The town of Grass Valley, full of memories of the colorful gold-mining days, received its name from the well-watered valley in which it lies. The valley was named by a company of emigrants who in 1849 found their way into the meadows kept green by perpetual springs, after toiling over the Truckee Pass Trail with their half-starved cattle. The gaunt beasts had strayed from the camp during the night and in the morning were found enjoying the abundant grass and water of the meadow.

In the previous summer, 1848, David Stump and two other prospectors came from Oregon to the diggings of El Dorado County, drifting northward into Grass Valley in October. Here they crevassed for gold near the sites of the Eureka and Idaho mines until approaching winter drove them from the mountains.

In August 1849 a party of five men headed by a Dr. Saunders built a cabin on Badger Hill near the eastern edge of what is now the city of Grass Valley. The Saunders party was soon joined by others, making a colony of twenty men who spent the winter in the valley. This became the nucleus of the present town.

Another settlement, which also became a part of the modern Grass Valley, was established in what came to be known as Boston Ravine, named after the company that arrived there in September 1849 under the leadership of the Rev. H. H. Cummings, its president. Four cabins were erected on the south side of the ravine, where the party spent the winter. For two years Boston Ravine, at the south end of present Mill Street, was the chief settlement in the vicinity, laying the foundation for the flourishing trade of the town that ultimately grew out from it.

Beneath the pines on Gold Hill, at Jenkins Street and Hocking Avenue, stands a monument (SRL 297) bearing the following inscription:

> This tablet commemorates the discovery of gold-bearing quartz and the beginning of quartz mining in California. The discovery was made on Gold Hill by George Knight, October 1850. The occurrence of gold-bearing quartz was undoubtedly noted here and elsewhere about the same time or previously, but the above discovery created the great excitement that started the development of quartz mining into a great industry. The Gold Hill Mine, 1850–57, is credited with a total production of $4 million. This monument dedicated by Quartz Parlor, N.S.G.W., and Manzanita Parlor, N.D.G.W., October 20, 1929.

This discovery aided the development of the city of Grass Valley, although its first prosperity came from the rich placer fields.

Other rich veins about Grass Valley were soon discovered, and crude mills for the reduction of the ore were built. Besides the Gold Hill Mine, where the discovery was first made, there were the Massachusetts Hill; the Eureka, located in 1851 on Wolf Creek; the Allison Ranch, located in 1853 two and a half miles south of the town and for a time one of the richest in the state; and the Idaho, located in 1863 just across Wolf Creek from the Eureka. Of special interest are the North Star, opened in 1851 on Lafayette Hill, and the Empire (SRL 298), located in 1850 on Ophir Hill one mile southeast of town, one of the world's major gold mines.

An incredible amount of tunneling has been done in this area. One vein alone extends for a distance of more than 9,000 feet—nearly two miles. The longest shaft, at the Empire Mine, has been sunk to an inclined depth of approximately 8,000 feet, the bottom of the shaft being 4,000 feet below the earth's surface and 1,500 feet below sea level. It is said that there are over 350 miles of tunnels, shafts, and stopes beneath the Empire Mine alone.

The Empire and the North Star were consolidated under one management in 1929, and continued to operate until the closing of the mines in 1942. In 1945, the Empire reopened, but operations were unprofitable because of the rigid limit set on the price of gold; this

Bourne Cottage, Empire Mine State Historic Park, Grass Valley

mine was permanently closed in 1956. The state acquired the property after this time and has gradually been opening sections of it to the public as the Empire Mine State Historic Park, located on East Empire Street, a mile east of town.

Although most of the mining equipment was sold off when the mine finally closed down, there is still much to see here. The park headquarters is in the old Retort Room of the mine. The hoist house at the head of the deep shaft still stands, and visitors can peer down many hundreds of feet into the shaft itself. An old stamping mill, sometimes in operation, can be seen. The grounds adjoining the Empire Mine were the summer home of its owner, William Bourn Jr., and his family. The Cottage is a well-preserved two-story structure built by Willis Polk for the Bourn family in 1898; adjacent to it is the greenhouse for the extensive gardens of roses and native California trees. The clubhouse (1905) contained facilities for tennis, bowling, dancing, and handball, plus kitchens and bedrooms; it is still used to a limited extent by a private club. The grounds are a delight to stroll through, under tall, stately pines.

The powerhouse (SRL 843) is the one remaining building of the North Star Mine; it too has been converted to public use, as the Nevada County Historical Mining Museum, also known as the Pelton Wheel Museum. Displayed here is the largest Pelton Wheel in the world, thirty feet in diameter, installed here in 1896; at its normal operating speed of sixty-five revolutions per minute, the rim moved at the rate of seventy miles an hour. Invented by Lester Pelton of Camptonville in neighboring Yuba County, the wheel was rimmed with a series of buckets divided into two chambers by a central barrier. A jet of water delivered from a high-pressure nozzle aimed at the center of the bucket was split by the barrier; the two streams thus formed were turned within the chambers of the bucket into two powerful reverse jets that drove the bucket forward. As a source of power that did not involve petroleum fuel, it was much in demand in mining operations, where asphyxiation was an ever-present danger. The museum also has extensive displays of other kinds of mining equipment; it is located at the south end of Mill Street at Allison Ranch Road, and operated by the city of Grass Valley.

The overwhelming majority of miners came to Grass Valley from Cornwall in England, where hardrock tin mining was a traditional activity. The Cornish pumps they brought were still in use many years later. According to one estimate, the population of Grass Valley in 1890 was 85 percent Cornish, and to this day distinctive Cornish dishes are to be found on Grass Valley restaurant menus. The Holbrooke Hotel (SRL 914) at 212 West Main Street was built in 1862 around the Golden Gate Saloon, originally built in 1852, and is the oldest continually operating saloon in the Mother Lode region.

The churches of Grass Valley reflect a significant historical background. Isaac Owen, the first commissioned Methodist minister in California and later the founder, at Santa Clara, of the University of the Pacific (now located in Stockton), preached his first sermon on California soil under the shade of an oak tree in Grass Valley on the north portion of Clark's Ranch in September 1849, having just come overland by ox team. In January 1852, while Owen was presiding elder of the district, a church was organized in Grass Valley in a building that had been used as a meeting place by the Presbyterians and as a schoolhouse. This building was superseded by a larger one in 1854 and by another in 1872; the present Grass Valley Methodist Church dates from 1937.

Opposite it on Church Street is the Emmanuel Episcopal Church. Bishop William Kip held the first Episcopal services in Grass Valley in April 1854 and the parish was organized the following year. The present building, built in 1858, has served the community since then. A few blocks up Church Street, old Mount St. Mary's Academy (SRL 853) still stands, but old St. Patrick's Catholic Church was replaced by a modern structure in 1949. The adjoining cemetery dates from 1853 and is commemorated by a marker placed in 1981 by the Native Daughters of the Golden West. The Congregationalists erected their first building in 1853 at the corner of Church and Neal Streets; it is now a commercial office. The first Women's Christian Temperance Union to be organized in California was formed here in 1874 by the women of the Congregational and Methodist churches.

A tablet placed in the public library in 1933 by the Harvard Club of San Francisco commemorates Josiah Royce, philosopher, historian of California, and noted Harvard professor, who was born in Grass Valley in 1855.

The house (SRL 292) now occupied by the Nevada County Chamber of Commerce, at 248 Mill Street, is a late-1970s replica of the home of Lola Montez. A beautiful woman with regal grace and lofty ambitions, Maria Dolores Eliza Rosanna Gilbert, professionally known as Lola Montez, dancer, was born in Ireland in 1818. In her brief, well-publicized career in Europe, she was a friend of George Sand, Alexandre Dumas, Victor Hugo, Franz Liszt, and, most notoriously, King Ludwig I of Bavaria, who made her Countess of Landsfeld and listened to her usually disastrous political advice. Exiled from Bavaria, Lola came to America in 1851, where her Spider Dance took San Francisco by storm. After a tour of the gold country, she settled briefly in Grass Valley and around 1852 built her house, where she kept a pet bear on a leash and was the sensation of the town for a couple of years.

Three doors down from Lola's home stands a two-story building (SRL 293) at 238 Mill Street that in 1853 was a boardinghouse. There a small, precocious child of six shyly admired the glamorous dancer, who became fond of little Lotta Crabtree and taught her the singing and dancing skills that would soon make the child one of the great entertainers of America. Unlike Lola Montez, who died at forty-two in New York in humble circumstances, Lotta Crabtree had a solid career that permitted her to retire comparatively young and to live graciously until she died at age seventy-seven, leaving $4 million to charity in her will. Lotta's Fountain still stands on Market Street in San Francisco as a gift to the city.

There are many ghost towns east and southeast of Grass Valley, with a roster of interesting names: You Bet, Red Dog, Gouge Eye, Little York, Walloupa, and Quaker Hill. Town Talk lay between Grass Valley and Nevada City.

NEVADA CITY

James W. Marshall, the discoverer of gold at Coloma, came to Deer Creek, a tributary of the Yuba River, in the summer of 1848 and panned for gold at this spot. Marshall did not prove that the stream contained phenomenal wealth, nor did he dream that just two years later more than ten thousand miners would be at work within a radius of three miles from the spot where he had found some grains.

Early in September 1849 Captain John Pennington and two companions built the first cabin on Gold Run above where that stream empties into Deer Creek, and just above the site of the bridge now known as the Gault Bridge. In October Dr. A. B. Caldwell put up a log cabin and a store on the slope of Aristocracy Hill, about where Trinity Episcopal Church now stands and close to the site of the first public school, built in 1854. For a time the place was known as Caldwell's Upper Store (or Dry Creek Diggings), since Dr. Caldwell had previously had a store seven miles below on Deer Creek at Pleasant Flat, where the town of Deer Creek grew up. Its inhabitants later removed to Newtown, where a number of springs furnished a good water supply.

In the same month the town's first family, the Stampses, settled in a ravine behind the present Coyote Street. Later in that autumn Madam Penn, an indefatigable worker who customarily took her turn at the rocker arrived. In the spring of 1850 this enterprising woman built a boardinghouse on a site that was continuously occupied by a hotel or a lodging house for the next 109 years, and on which the Union Hotel stood from 1863 to 1959.

In March 1850 the miners elected Stamps as alcalde of Caldwell's Upper Store, and at the same time they changed the name of the place. In the census of 1850 the name of the town is given as Nevada City, and the name was given to its post office, although it appears that some inhabitants used the name "Nevada" for the town itself. When a county was established in the eastern section of Yuba County in 1851, it was called Nevada, and Nevada City was made the county seat. Edwin Tyson makes the sensible observation that the term "Nevada City" was necessary to distinguish its jurisdiction from that of the new county. In 1864, when the Washoe Territory became the state of Nevada, protests came from California that it had first claim to the name. The matter was appealed to Congress, but no action was taken by that body. Thus there are three political jurisdictions extant from those days: Nevada City (named in 1850), which is the county seat of Nevada County (named in 1851) in the state of California, and the adjacent state of Nevada (named in 1864).

The region's phenomenal growth was due at first to surface placers. So eager were the miners to find rich strikes that even the streets of the town were not safe from invasion. Finally, it is told, one irate storekeeper approached a miner in the act of digging up the street and demanded that he stop. The miner refused, arguing that there was no law to prevent him from digging in the streets. "Then I'll make a law," replied the indignant merchant, producing a revolver, whereupon the miner beat a hasty retreat. Thereafter, the story concludes, the streets of Nevada City were not disturbed.

On the eastern end of Lost Hill gold was discovered early in 1850. The gravel ranges of this section proved extraordinarily rich, and news of the diggings spread rapidly, causing a city to mushroom almost overnight. It was not uncommon for the miners to take out a quart of gold, worth $6,000, in a single day in this region. Because the peculiar method of mining called "coyoteing," or tunneling, was adopted here, the town was called Coyoteville. During the two years of its existence, $8 million is said to have been taken from the surrounding gravel banks. The site of the old settlement constitutes the northwestern section of modern Nevada City.

Nevada City nestles at the foot of a panorama of mountains, and for many years it was said to be one of the most idyllic and attractive of all the gold rush towns: always busy, but still retaining much of the charm of the past. In the 1960s, a freeway was built through the very middle of the town despite a chorus of protests, an atrocity that unfortunately happened elsewhere in the state in those days. If one gets away from the bustle of the freeway and has the time to stroll through the streets of the town, some sense of its charming past will be found.

The town's back streets follow the old mule trains in a weblike pattern radiating from its center, by Broad Street and Deer Creek. Aged, steep-roofed houses of three or four stories climb to the precipitous walls of Deer Creek Canyon. One of them, a gabled structure of substantial brick at Clay and Prospect Streets, has long been known as the Red Castle. Here and there along the streets, brick and stone stores with iron doors and shutters still stand, doing business as they have for more than a century. At 211 Broad Street, the National Hotel (SRL 899) has been in operation since it opened in August 1856 as the National Exchange Hotel, within four adjoining brick buildings. It is today one of the oldest continuously operating hotels west of the Rockies. In a suite on the second floor, businessmen met in 1898 to create the Pacific Gas and Electric Company, which has since been a powerful element in the history of California.

Through the doors of J. J. Ott's first assay office, no longer standing, a miner from across the Sierra entered one day in 1859 with puzzling specimens from a new "strike" near Washoe Lake, now in the state of Nevada. The ore was examined, and the assayer's report proved to be the most sensational news since the announcement of Marshall's discovery of gold at Coloma in 1848, for it heralded the fabulous wealth of the Comstock silver mines, which within a few years produced almost one billion dollars. Some of the contents of the Ott Assay Office have been placed in the Oakland Museum in Alameda County.

Next door to the assayer's office on Coyote Street, the site of the 1853 Wells Fargo Express Office is commemorated by a plaque placed by Wells Fargo and the Native Sons. Another plaque commemorates Ott's Assay Office. The South Yuba Canal Office (SRL 832) at 134 Main Street is a two-story brick building that until 1880 housed the first incorporated company to supply water for hydraulic mining. This is now the office of the Nevada City Chamber of Commerce. Firehouse Number One on Main Street near Commercial, built in 1861 (the bell tower was added later), is now the Museum of the Nevada County Historical Society, a fascinating mixture of rare documents and the materials of everyday life. Firehouse Number Two, also built in 1861 to house another volunteer fire company, still stands on Broad Street.

Across the street from Firehouse Number Two stands the Nevada Theater (SRL 863), built in 1865, the oldest theater building in the state. It is now used as a playhouse and as a community center. Nearby at 325 Spring Street is the Miner's Foundry Building, built in 1856. The first Pelton Wheel was cast in this building in 1878. The building was used as a foundry until 1974; regrettably, by then none of the original equipment was still in operation or available for display purposes.

The first religious services in Nevada City, as in many other mining camps throughout the Sierra, were held under a tree. All the early churches were destroyed by the fires of 1856 and 1863. The Congregationalist structure erected in 1864 during the pastorate of Rev. H. H. Cummings is still standing at Main and Church Streets and is now a Baptist church.

The history of this Congregational church illustrates the broad influence that radiated from the pioneer ministries of many of these mountain towns. W. W. Ferrier says: "The movement out of which was to come the College of California [forerunner of the University of California] had its inception in May 1853, a few days after the arrival of Professor Henry Durant, in the little mountain town of Nevada City." There, on May 9, a joint session of the Congregational Associa-

Searls Historical Library, Nevada City

tion of California and the Presbytery of San Francisco (New School) was held, and on the 17th a plan was adopted for establishing an institution of higher learning in California.

Another pioneer church of Nevada City is St. Canice's Catholic Church, built in 1864 and still in use.

The distinctive Nevada City Courthouse on Church Street is the latest in a series of courthouses. The wooden courthouse and log jail that had stood on Broad Street since 1851 were replaced in 1856 by a building on Church Street. That building burned a few weeks after it was put up and was rebuilt at the same location. The new building was likewise destroyed by fire in 1863; the present courthouse was built on the same site in 1864. The courthouse was remodeled and enlarged in 1900 and again in 1936–37, as a result of which it has a somewhat anachronistic appearance in a neighborhood of older buildings.

Across the street from the courthouse at 214 Church Street is the Searls Historical Library. From 1872, this was the law office of Niles Searls, who served as chief justice of the California Supreme Court in 1887–88. His son and grandson followed him as attorneys and used this office until 1970. It is now a documentary repository for Nevada City history, and open to the public during regular visiting hours.

WASHINGTON AND ITS NEIGHBORS

Climbing the Washington Ridge over SR 20, one passes a solitary grave to the right, seven miles northeast of Nevada City. Here in 1858 an emigrant family buried their two-year-old boy, Julius Albert Apperson, and in 1971 the Native Sons of the Golden West placed a plaque above the site "in memory of all lone graves throughout the state of California." The State Highway Commission revised the original specifications for the road at this point so as to leave this lone grave undisturbed beneath its sentinel pine.

About seven miles further, the motorist suddenly comes upon a marvelous view of rugged mountain scenery dominated by the majestic Sierra Buttes, which rise above the pine-clad ridges to the north and are visible for 100 miles in every direction. From this point a road branches off to the north and winds down six miles through magnificent pines to the old mining town of Washington, picturesquely situated on the bank of the South Yuba River. Two old store buildings with massive stone walls are still at the center of the village; just beyond it are immense piles of huge granite boulders carried there stone by stone by Chinese miners of long ago, presumably for additional structures that were never built.

In the vicinity of Washington during the gold days, numerous mining camps were located at the wealth-producing bars and flats along the river, and some of these camps developed into trading centers of considerable activity. At the mouth of Canyon Creek about three miles up the river from the town was Canal Bar, from which the line of camps extended downstream past several bars to the Brass Wire Bar, across the river from Washington, which in 1880 was worked entirely by Chinese miners. Four miles east of Washington on SR 20, a monument has been placed near a viewpoint overlooking the diggings of Alpha and Omega, now ghost towns. Alpha (SRL 628) was the birthplace of Emma Wixom in 1859. As Emma Nevada, she went on to a brilliant operatic career in Europe and America. The Alpha mines became exhausted in 1880, but up to that time they produced no less than $1.5 million in gold. To the east was its sister camp, Omega (SRL 629), where the deep pit washed out by hydraulic mining reveals the old diggings from which $2.5 million was taken during the same period. This mine operated off and on until 1949. Across the river from the Washington bridge another road leads about three miles to the Spanish Mine, where Patrick Dillon first panned for gold on Poorman's Creek in 1851.

THE SAN JUAN RIDGE AND THE MALAKOFF DIGGINS

Hydraulic mining was extensively used on the San Juan Ridge to the north of Nevada City to extract gold from the enormous deposits in the higher mountains. Three companies owned vast mines in the region, which were operated at a tremendous outlay. High up in the Sierra, 6,000 feet above sea level, reservoirs were constructed from which the water supply for hundreds of mines along the ridge was obtained through a system of canals and flumes. Although constructed in 1850–80 merely with pick and shovel and carpenter's level, some are still intact in a few places and exhibit a remarkable workmanship.

The three companies were the Eureka Lake and Yuba Canal Company, with headquarters at North Columbia, which owned four reservoirs and a system of ditches 200 miles long; the North Bloomfield Mining Company, with forty-three miles of ditches; and the Milton Mining and Water Company, with offices at French Corral, which owned eighty miles of ditches. The total expenditure of these companies for construction and equipment amounted to $5,568,000.

In order to obtain the most effective management of the ditches and flumes along the ridge, the companies in 1878 built, cooperatively, the world's first long-distance telephone line, at a cost of $6,000. This line was sixty miles long and extended up the ridge from French Corral through Birchville, Sweetland, North San Juan, Cherokee, North Columbia, Lake City, North Bloomfield, Moore's Flat, Graniteville, Milton, and Bowman Lake. It was managed by the Ridge Telephone Company and owned jointly by the three mining companies. Edison instruments manufactured in Boston in 1876 were used.

Part of the area over which this line went is now Malakoff Diggins State Historic Park. Here hydraulic mining was carried on so extensively that tons of earth and gravel were washed away, leaving a deeply eroded landscape. The huge hole is second in size only to the LaGrange Mine near Weaverville in Trinity County. Enormous profits in gold were being washed out along San Juan Ridge when Lorenzo Sawyer, a U.S. circuit court judge, handed down the historic decision of January 7, 1884, that virtually outlawed all hydraulic operations in the state. (The Caminetti Act of 1893, a federal statute, permits very limited hydraulic mining and requires the impounding of all debris under the regulations of the California Debris Commission.)

More than a century has passed, and nature has gradually softened the harsh outlines of the Malakoff; trees now grow in the valleys and the place is a favored campground. The village of North Bloomfield is located within the park, and has an interesting museum and visitors center, open except for the winter months.

The office of the North Bloomfield Mining and Gravel Company (SRL 852) can still be seen.

St. Columncille's Catholic Church at the western edge of town has had a curious history. It was originally the Bridgeport Union Guard Hall, and was used as a training base for soldiers in the early days of the Civil War. In 1880 it was acquired as a house of worship for the Catholic community of the ridge towns. Later abandoned, it was purchased in 1969 by Mr. Babe Pinaglia and donated to the park, where it now stands. There was once a Catholic church on this site in North Bloomfield.

FRENCH CORRAL

French Corral was the earliest of the mining camps that sprang up along the old San Juan River channel. There in 1849 the first settler, a Frenchman, built a corral for his mules; very soon it was discovered that the locality was rich in placer gold, and a town grew up on the site of the Frenchman's corral. Later, as hydraulic mining developed, it became an important town, numbering its population in the thousands. Not much remains there today. The office of the Milton Mining and Water Company, in which one terminus of the first long-distance telephone line was located, has been torn down, but the site is marked (SRL 247). The brick walls of the old Wells Fargo Express Office, built in the 1850s and equipped with iron doors and window shutters that once guarded millions of dollars in gold, look as if they will stand for generations to come. A number of old homes are still occupied.

NORTH SAN JUAN

On SR 49 between Nevada City and Downieville lies North San Juan. San Juan Hill to the north was first mined in 1853 by Christian Kientz, who, according to tradition, was the originator of the name. Kientz had been with General Scott's army in Mexico, and saw in the California hill a strong resemblance to the hill on which San Juan de Ulloa in Mexico stands. Later, when the whole hill had been staked out to rich claims, the name was given to the promising camp that grew up close by. By 1857 San Juan was of sufficient importance to be assigned a post office; "North" was prefixed to the name in order to distinguish it from the much older San Juan in San Benito County.

North San Juan today consists of some old brick buildings, some modern houses, a few abandoned old places, and a cemetery. E Clampus Vitus has marked the Wells Fargo Office and the Masonic Hall, built in 1862 and now a general store for the community. Many houses had been built on the hill above town, but when these were found to be standing on "pay gravel" they were bought by mining companies and destroyed. A high cliff forms the southern wall of the chasm washed out by hydraulic operations, along the rim of which today a road winds, while in the distance rise the peaks of the Sierra.

CHEROKEE AND NORTH COLUMBIA

Passing along the scenic Ridge Road, now through groves of pine, now above them, one comes to Cherokee, five miles east of North San Juan. This remnant of the 1850s consists today of a little Catholic church and a handful of weatherworn houses that stand on the edge of the diggings. Just north of Cherokee is the old Badger Hill Mine, once a famous producer.

At North Columbia, originally known as Columbia Hill, three miles beyond Cherokee, a few old homes still stand, notably that of the Coughlan family. The old schoolhouse also remains. At North Columbia begins the Foote's Crossing Road to Alleghany in Sierra County.

North Columbia was originally built on the Pliocene gravel bed of the old river channel, but in 1878, when the site was found to contain rich gold deposits, the town was moved to its present location.

GRANITEVILLE

Graniteville, a town on the line of the old Ridge Telephone Company, lies in a beautiful forested region near the summit of the mountains twenty-six miles northeast of Nevada City. Gold was mined in the gulches here as early as 1850, and because the diggings were shallow a number of miners were attracted to the spot. The original name of the place was Eureka South, to distinguish it from Eureka in Humboldt County and Eureka North in Sierra County, but when the post office was established there in 1867, the present name was adopted.

Graniteville was threatened with extinction when the surface diggings became exhausted, but during the mid-1860s gold-bearing quartz was found in the vicinity and the town again became a thriving place. A severe fire swept through it in 1878, but because hydraulic-mining companies had reservoirs in the mountains above the town, Graniteville was rebuilt and until 1883 was an active distributing point for these companies. Afterward, however, its existence depended on quartz mining and lumbering. Now its schoolhouse and many of its old residences have been beautifully renovated as summer homes.

TRUCKEE

Off I-80, east of the summit of Donner Pass, lies the pioneer railroad town of Truckee. The transcontinental railroad reached Truckee from Sacramento on April 3, 1868, an event marked by a plaque (SRL 780.6) on the Amtrak depot in town; with this, the conquest of the Sierra by iron rails had been made. Thirteen months and seven days later the Central Pacific tracks met those of the Union Pacific at Promontory, Utah.

Truckee has some interesting old buildings, all very much in use today. Gray's Log Waystation, built in 1863, was moved to its present location at 10030 Church Street in 1907 and is marked with an E Clampus Vitus plaque. The Engelhardt Building at 10020, next door, dates from 1889. The White House was built in 1873 and became the home of banker C. B. White in 1903. It is now a restaurant with a Victorian museum on the second floor, and is listed in the National Register of Historic Places. Another museum is located in the old Truckee Jail, built out of native stone in 1875 and in use until 1964. The building is at 10144 Main Street.

Orange County

Mission San Juan Capistrano

Orange County was created in 1889 from a portion of Los Angeles County. Santa Ana has always been the county seat.

Although it is generally believed that the county was named for its orange groves, not everyone agrees. Most of the counties of southern California take their name from their county seats, but apparently "Santa Ana" did not find favor. The name "Orange" has been given to some fifty places in the United States, including the town founded here in 1873, before the creation of the separate county of Orange. Historian Jim Sleeper says that real estate promoters thought that "Orange" was reminiscent of the Mediterranean and its climate and would encourage immigration. William Wolfskill first introduced oranges as a commercial crop in Los Angeles in 1841. The first commercial crop in the county was forty acres planted by R. H. Gilman on the land that is now part of California State University at Fullerton in 1875. Oranges were an important product by 1889, particularly after the area's grape crop was killed by a devastating blight.

Orange County today is one of California's most heavily settled areas, and there are few orange groves left. Relentless urbanization here and elsewhere in California has often been made at the expense of the past; Orange County has an abundance of vanished landmarks. Fortunately, many historical societies are working to preserve sites and buildings and to establish museums of local history.

PORTOLÁ'S TRAIL

A little company of soldiers and priests led by Gaspar de Portolá entered what is now Orange County on July

22, 1769, on their way north to seek the port of Monterey. Passing through low, open mountain country, they made camp for the night near an Indian village north of San Onofre. Here the fathers baptized two little Indian girls who were very ill—the first baptism in Alta California. The soldiers named the place Los Cristianitos ("the little Christians"), and it is still called Cristianitos Canyon. The site of the first baptism (SRL 562) is the spring called Aguaje de la Piedra, now within the boundaries of Camp Joseph H. Pendleton and across the San Diego County line. A marker stands there, off Cristianitos Road, and another marker has been placed in the city hall in San Clemente.

On July 23, the Portolá party "came to a very pleasant green valley, full of willow, alders, live oaks, and other trees not known to us. It has a large arroyo, which at the point where we crossed it carried a good stream of fresh and good water, which, after running a little way, formed in pools in some large patches of tules. We halted there, calling it the valley of Santa Maria Magdalena."

Thus does Father Juan Crespí describe the valley of San Juan Capistrano, where Portolá and his men stopped. At the same spot, the explorers camped again on January 20 and April 21, 1770. Juan Bautista de Anza camped there on January 8, 1776, on his way from Mission San Gabriel to San Diego to lend aid to Governor Rivera during the Indian uprising.

From this point, Portolá's trail lay along the foothills east of the Santa Ana Valley and across the Puente Hills into Los Angeles County. On July 24, camp was made on Trabuco Creek, where there was a village of friendly Indians. The site is near the modern town of Rancho Santa Margarita. Here the party rested for two days, moving on a short distance to Tomato Spring on the Irvine Ranch on July 26. They pitched camp "near a dry lagoon on a slope, from which [they] examined the spacious plain, the end of which [they] could not see."

On the following day, after they crossed the plain, camp was made near a stream that is still called Santiago Creek. This campsite was close to the modern city of Orange, at a spot the Spaniards considered suitable for a city. Skirting the hills to the north, Portolá reached the Santa Ana River on July 28. There he pitched camp on the east bank opposite an Indian village. The site of this camp is due east of Anaheim. Anza camped here on January 7, 1776.

Crossing the swiftly flowing river with great difficulty on July 29, the party traveled northwest until they reached "a very green little valley, which has a small pool of water, on whose bank there is a very large vil-

At Mission San Juan Capistrano

lage of very friendly heathen." Camp was made on a hill near the pool and the place was called Santa Marta; the site is in Fullerton.

Descending the hill on July 30, the little band proceeded north across the valley and over the Puente Hills, coming into the spacious and fertile valley of the San Gabriel. The later main route, which came from Whittier to La Habra, and then through the hills where Harbor Boulevard runs today, was opened by the Portolá party on their return trips in January and April 1770.

MISSION SAN JUAN CAPISTRANO

Owing to the zeal of Father Junipero Serra, the founding of Mission San Juan Capistrano was first attempted as early as October 1775. Father Palou writes:

> The little troop, composed of Father Lasuén, Lieutenant Ortega, a sergeant, and the necessary soldiers, left San Diego toward the end of October. On arriving at the site, an enramada or arbor was hastily erected, near which a large cross was constructed, raised, blessed, and venerated by all. On an altar prepared in the arbor, Fr. Lasuén offered up the first holy Mass. This happened on October 30,1775, the last day of the octave after the feast of San Juan Capistrano, the patron of the mission. Formal possession was then taken of the lands and thus the beginning was made amid the rejoicings of the numerous pagans who had flocked thither. They proved their satisfaction by helping to cut and bring down the timber for the chapel and the dwelling.

St. John Capistrano was an Italian-born Franciscan theologian and preacher of the fifteenth century who participated in the Christian victory over the Turks at Belgrade in 1456.

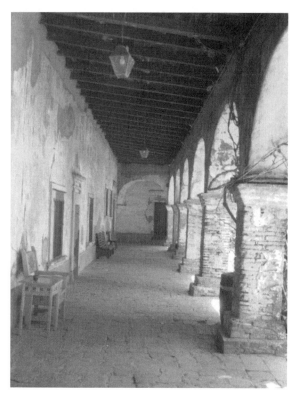

At Mission San Juan Capistrano

1806. Disaster struck just six years later with a powerful earthquake on December 8, 1812, which killed forty Indian neophytes and shattered the church.

Little was done to rebuild the fallen church until 1860, when some adobe restorations were made, only to be washed away by the first heavy rainstorms of winter. In later years, the Landmarks Club restored the beautiful arched corridors of the patio, the old kitchen with its quaint chimney, and Serra's church, the long building that still stands on the east side of the patio. Built in 1778, this is the oldest building now standing in California, and the only remaining church where Father Serra celebrated Mass. Extensive restorations were also carried out by the Catholic Church under the direction of Father St. John O'Sullivan.

San Juan Capistrano (SRL 200) was one of the grandest and most beautiful of all the missions. Today the great stone church is in magnificent ruins. The gardens are well kept, and the buildings probably attract more visitors than any other in the chain. There is also a special romance in the legend, celebrated in song, of the return of the swallows each year on St. Joseph's Day, March 19. This has become one of southern California's most cherished events, bringing in many visitors. (It is also believed that the swallows leave for the south with similar fidelity on the Day of St. John Capistrano, October 23.) A modern parish church, built in the 1980s, stands on the northwest corner of the mission grounds; it is based on a likeness of the Great Stone Church.

The town retains much of its charm and a few of its old buildings today. The original registration of San Juan Capistrano as a State Historical Landmark included, for this reason, the town as well as the mission. The restaurant known as El Adobe de Capistrano, often visited by President Nixon, incorporates two old adobes, the Miguel Yorba on the north (1778) and the *juzgado* or justice court and jail on the south (1812). The two buildings were originally remodeled as the Van der Leck residence in 1910. To the east across the street is the brick house of Judge Richard Egan, built in the 1880s on the site of an old Aguilar adobe. The Domingo Yorba adobe stands at 31871 Camino Capistrano; like most of these old houses, it is still privately owned. The Manuel García adobe dates from the 1840s and is the only surviving Monterey-style adobe in Orange County; it is located at 31851 Camino Capistrano. Part of the Juan Avilá adobe, once a huge structure, stands with a single floor at 31831 Camino Capistrano. The Blas Aguilar adobe is located at 31806 El Camino

Hardly had the first founding of San Juan Capistrano taken place than news of the Indian uprising at San Diego forced the fathers to give up the undertaking temporarily. It was not until October of the following year that they returned, this time in company with Father Serra himself. Palou relates that the cross put up by Father Lasuén the year before was still in place and that the two bells that had been left in hiding were disinterred, hung in position, and rung "joyously" to tell the Indians of the missionaries' return. An arbor was quickly built, and on November 1, 1776, the formal founding of Mission San Juan Capistrano took place.

The work of building and conversion was left in the care of Fathers Pablo Mugártegui and Gregório Amúrrio, both good and efficient men. The first site chosen for the mission apparently did not work out "because of water failure," in the words of Father Mugártegui's report for the year 1782. Whether his words refer to a flood or to a lack of water is unclear. Another site, the present one, was selected and the formal transfer made on October 4, 1778. A few buildings were put up. The heart of the mission was begun in 1796, and the Great Stone Church, as it was called, was nine years in the building. By this time Fathers Vicente Fuster and Juan Norberto de Santiago were in charge of the mission's activities. The consecration took place on September 8,

Real; part of it is said to have been built in 1794 and occupied by the mayordomos of the mission.

At Verdugo and Los Rios Streets, across the railroad tracks from the center of town, is the Ríos adobe, built in 1794. It stands near the tiny grant, just over seven acres, made to Santiago Ríos by Governor Manuel Micheltorena in 1843. The *ranchito* was located on San Juan Creek between the mission and the beach and was entirely surrounded by Rancho Boca de la Playa. The adobe is now an office; until recently, as the E Clampus Vitus plaque on it notes, it was famous for being the oldest single-family residence in California continuously occupied by the same family.

In Costa Mesa, half a mile east of the Santa Ana River at 1900 Adams Avenue, is the Diego Sepúlveda adobe (SRL 227), built about 1823–25 as an *estancia*, or station, of Mission San Juan Capistrano. An *estancia* was a less important outpost of a mission than an *asistencia*. The adobe was located on Rancho Santiago de Santa Ana, and, when the rancho was later subdivided, it became the home of Diego Sepúlveda, an auxiliary alcalde of Pueblo de los Angeles. The building is preserved and maintained by the Costa Mesa Historical Society in Estancia Park. The Costa Mesa Historical Society is at Anaheim and Plumer Streets; among its collections are memorabilia of the Santa Ana Army Air Base.

DANA'S COVE

On the coast four miles southwest of San Juan Capistrano and west of the outlet of San Juan Creek into the Pacific lies Dana's Cove. The promontory on the west is Dana Point (SRL 189). The San Juan Rocks are a short distance out in the ocean. In Spanish and Mexican days this cove was the site of the embarcadero, which played an important part in the material life of Mission San Juan Capistrano. Here, in 1818, the pirate Hippolyte de Bouchard landed to raid the mission.

This cove and the high cliff above it are described by Richard Henry Dana in *Two Years Before the Mast*, and they were later named in his honor. The name is also preserved by a modern seaside town, Dana Point. On May 5, 1986, 150 years after Dana's first landing, a marker was placed at the Dana Point Harbor by the Daughters of the American Revolution, honoring this distinguished young American writer.

Dana describes how cowhides were thrown from the edge of the cliff to the beach below and loaded onto the *Pilgrim*:

Replica of Brig *Pilgrim* at Dana Point Harbor

Down the height we pitched the hides, throwing them as far out into the air as we could; and as they were all large, stiff, and doubled, like the cover of a book, the wind took them, and they swayed and eddied about, plunging and rising in the air, like a kite when it has broken its string. As it was now low tide, there was no danger of their falling into the water; and, as fast as they came to ground, the men below picked them up, and, taking them on their heads, walked off with them to the boat. It was really a picturesque sight: the great height, the scaling of the hides, and the continual walking to and fro of the men, who looked like mites, on the beach. This was the romance of hide-droghing!

A replica of the two-masted brig *Pilgrim*, the ship on which Dana spent two years in the 1830s, is moored at the Orange County Marine Institute, 24200 Dana Point Harbor Drive.

RANCHO SANTIAGO DE SANTA ANA

Rancho Santiago de Santa Ana extended along the east bank of the Santa Ana River from the mountains to the sea. It was bounded on the east by a line extending from Red Hill to the sea and running parallel to the present Newport Boulevard one mile to the southwest. It is the only rancho lying entirely within Orange County whose history goes back to the Spanish period, some portion of it always having been in the hands of the Yorbas.

José Antonio Yorba first saw this land when he passed over it in 1769 as a corporal in Portolá's company. His father-in-law, Juan Pablo Grijalva, was awarded pasturage rights to the area in 1801, and built an adobe home. Grijalva had come to California with Anza in 1776. In 1810 the rancho of eleven leagues was formally granted to Yorba and his nephew Juan Pablo Peralta

(Grijalva's grandson), by the then King of Spain, French Emperor Napoleon's brother, born Joseph Bonaparte.

The site of the first adobe built on Rancho Santiago de Santa Ana is on Hoyt Hill, the westernmost point of El Modeno Hills, between El Modeno and Villa Park. Hoyt Hill is on the south side of Santiago Creek. Another adobe site was west of Orange. A cluster of adobes stood in the vicinity of the present town of Olive. The community became known as Santa Ana. A marker has been placed on the Orange-Olive Road north of Lincoln Avenue in Olive to commemorate Old Santa Ana (SRL 204). An old map designates an adobe just south of Olive as the "Casa de Yorba y tierras."

Red Hill (SRL 203), a prominent landmark three miles northeast of Tustin, near Browning Avenue and La Colina Drive, was known to Indians, padres, rancheros, and early mapmakers. Its name comes from the cinnabar ore that gives its soil a reddish color. It became the dividing point between ranchos. At its base was a swamp, La Ciénega de las Ranas ("the swamp of the frogs"), and some writings give this name to the hill with the erroneous Cerrito de las Ranas ("hill of the frogs").

The Ramón Peralta adobe built in 1871 stands in Santa Ana Canyon. This is one of the later and best preserved of the adobes of Orange County. It is situated in a shopping mall on the south side of Santa Ana Canyon Road, one and one-quarter miles east of the Imperial Highway Junction.

SANTA ANA

The city of Santa Ana was founded by William Henry Spurgeon, who settled in the area in 1869. He gave his town the name that had formerly been applied to a settlement near Olive. In 1913, two years before his death, Spurgeon built Orange County's first four-story building, the W. H. Spurgeon Block, at the southwest corner of Sycamore and Fourth Streets.

The Orange County Courthouse (SRL 837) at 211 West Santa Ana Boulevard is the oldest existing courthouse in southern California, in use from 1901 to 1979. The red Arizona sandstone used for its exterior makes this a striking building. Restored in recent years, the building is again in use for some county offices, including one courtroom and adjacent quarters. The Charles W. Bowers Memorial Museum is a Spanish Colonial–style building at 2002 North Main Street. Built in 1933, its newest emphasis is on the creative arts, but one area of the building focuses on artifacts and displays from Orange County history.

THE IRVINE RANCH

Rancho Santiago de Santa Ana was bounded on the east by Rancho Lomas de Santiago, toward the mountains, and Rancho San Joaquín, toward the sea. Lomas de Santiago, of 47,227 acres, was granted to Teodocio Yorba by Governor Pío Pico in 1846. San Joaquín was owned by José Sepúlveda, to whom it was granted by Governor Juan B. Alvarado in 1837 and 1842. When title was patented (confirmed) by the United States after 1855, its area was 48,803 acres. Sepúlveda's home once stood at the head of Newport Bay. Later he built another, "El Refugio," in southwestern Santa Ana, near Willits and Bristol Streets, where he lived during the 1850s and 1860s.

Ranchos Lomas de Santiago and San Joaquín, together with a strip along the southeast line of Rancho Santiago de Santa Ana, ultimately came into the hands of James Irvine, and most of this land—some 108,000 acres today—remains today as the Irvine Ranch, one of the last great landholdings in California. It covers almost one-fifth of Orange County and stretches from the mountains westward to the sea.

James Irvine, born in Belfast, Ireland, in 1827, came to California during the Gold Rush, but made his fortune in merchandising rather than mining. In the 1860s he entered into partnership with Flint, Bixby, and Company, and by 1876 was the sole owner of what became known as the Irvine Ranch. Irvine died in 1886, and management of the huge estate eventually passed to his son, James Irvine II, who formed the Irvine Company in 1894. This company holds title to the ranch today, but the lands are gradually being subdivided and converted to other uses. The University of California since 1965 has had a 1,500-acre campus on the ranch.

East Irvine, or Old Town Irvine, is the only intact original agricultural shipping center in southern California. Two buildings, the sack storage warehouse (1895) and the bean and grain warehouse (1946), are part of the Old Town Historic District, as are Irvine's General Store (1909), hotel (1913), and blacksmith's shop (1915). This area has undergone a great deal of development; the city of Irvine has a population of more than 114,000.

RANCHO SAN JUAN CAJÓN (PLACENTIA, YORBA LINDA)

The most important ranch house in Orange County during the Mexican period was that of Bernardo Yorba, one of California's greatest landowners. It was situated on Rancho San Juan Cajón on the north bank of the Santa Ana River. Don Bernardo, a son of José Antonio Yorba of Rancho Santiago, received his grant of 13,329 acres from Governor José Figueroa in 1834, and soon construction of the great hacienda began.

Decades later, the neglected, unoccupied old house was razed by its owner in 1927, and only a marker (SRL 226) at Esposito Road and Echo Hill Drive in Yorba Linda recalls one of the greatest Mexican ranch houses in California.

The lands of the ranch ultimately became part of the town of Placentia, which received its name in 1884 from Mrs. Sarah McFadden, who said, "Placentia means 'delightful situation.'" A. S. Bradford, from New England, arrived three years later and began a successful career as an orange grower and business leader. The home he built in 1902 at 136 Palm Circle is a "New England Colonial Revival, shingle, modified Queen Anne style house" and is now lovingly preserved by the Placentia Founders Society.

Another orange grower's house in Placentia is the historic George Key Ranch at 625 W. Bastanchury Road. This is an operation of the Orange County Department of Harbors, Beaches, and Parks. Here one can see displays of farm equipment and a one-acre grove of over one hundred Valencia orange trees. Placentia was a center for the production of these oranges, which had marketing advantages over other varieties.

HERITAGE HILL HISTORIC PARK

Rancho Cañada de los Alisos, an area of 10,668 acres, was granted to José Serrano by Governor Juan B. Alvarado in 1842 and by Governor Pío Pico in 1846. It was acquired in the 1880s by Dwight Whiting. One of Serrano's adobes (SRL 199) still stands at 25151 Serrano Road in El Toro. This parcel of land has been acquired by Orange County and is now known as Heritage Hill Historical Park. The Serrano adobe was built around 1862 and considerably added to by George Whiting, son of Dwight, in 1932. The extensive gardens are graced by two large peppertrees, one well over a century old.

On the same grounds are three historic buildings that have been moved from their original sites. The El Toro Grammar School is a one-room building that once stood on the corner of First Street and Olive Avenue in El Toro. This building was used until 1914, when a new two-room schoolhouse, still visible at that location, was constructed adjacent to it. After service as

St. Anthony's Catholic Church on El Toro Road from 1914 to 1968, the old schoolhouse suffered a period of neglect before being moved to Heritage Hill. The Bennett Ranch House originally stood at the corner of Second Street and Cherry Avenue in El Toro. It was built in 1908 as a caretaker's home for the Bennett navel orange ranch. St. George's Episcopal Mission was originally located on Whisler Drive in El Toro. It was built in 1891 for a colony of English settlers recruited by Dwight Whiting to become "gentlemen fruit farmers." Most of the interior furnishings are original. All three buildings are open to the public at regular hours.

ANAHEIM

Anaheim is the pioneer town of the American period in Orange County. It is antedated in the county only by the communities of San Juan Capistrano and Olive. It is also one of the oldest colony experiments in California, having been started in 1857 by a group of Germans, chiefly from San Francisco. Their plan was to buy a tract of land in common, lay it out in small farms and vineyards, and work it under the supervision of a general manager. Fifty charter members purchased a part of the Rancho San Juan Cajón de Santa Ana from the family of Don Juan Pacific Ontiveros, the original Mexican grantee.

This fertile tract of 1,165 acres on the west bank of the Santa Ana River and about twelve miles inland from the coast was divided into fifty twenty-acre lots for the little farms and vineyards, and fifty house lots that were to make up the nucleus of the community. Besides these, there was sufficient public land for schoolhouses and community buildings. A fence made of 40,000 willow poles, five and a half miles long, enclosed the entire colony. Most of the willows took root, forming a living wall about the settlement. Gates were erected at the north, south, east, and west ends of the two principal intersecting streets of the colony. The north gate, the site of which is marked (SRL 112) at the corner of Anaheim Boulevard and North Street, was the main entrance to the town, being on the road from Los Angeles. Lucile E. Dickson quotes a writer who says that "the colonists were a curious mixture . . . two or three carpenters, four blacksmiths, three watchmakers, a brewer, an engraver, a shoemaker, a poet, a miller, a bookbinder, two or three merchants, a hatter, and a musician." Dickson continues, "But in spite of this medley of professions, the colony flourished almost from the beginning, and for many years its name was almost a synonym for prosperity and industry throughout the south."

For many years the town was known as the "Campo Alemán" to its Spanish-speaking neighbors because of the continued predominance of Germans. Despite the many hardships and financial struggles of the colony's early years, only one of its fifty original settlers abandoned it.

Initially, supplies came to Anaheim through the port of San Pedro. By 1864, however, the colonists had organized the Anaheim Lighter Company and developed a port, with warehouse and dock, closer to the colony. Anaheim Landing (SRL 219), which served the entire Santa Ana Valley until the opening of the Southern Pacific Railroad in 1875, was located on the coast of what is now the town of Seal Beach. The marker is located at the corner of Electric Avenue and Seal Beach Boulevard. Electric Avenue follows the line of the Pacific Electric Railway, which operated between Los Angeles and the coast towns until after the end of World War II. The Pacific Electric Red Car Museum at 707 Electric Avenue in Seal Beach has a display of local transportation history in a converted work car.

The Pioneer House of the Mother Colony (SRL 201) is said to be the first frame house built in the Anaheim Colony. It was built in 1857 by George Hansen, a leader of the group. It has been moved from its original location on North Los Angeles Street and placed at 414 West Street. It contains an interesting collection of relics of pioneer days gathered in the neighborhood.

Anaheim has many buildings that reflect the successive fashions in domestic architecture in southern California from about 1870 to the early twentieth century. Italianate, Queen Anne, Greek Revival, and Neoclassical Revival houses are to be found in the area bounded by South, East, North, and West Streets. This quadrangle is in the process of becoming the Anaheim Colony Historic District. The Ferdinand Backs home at 225 North Claudina is an elegant Colonial Revival building adjacent to an older dwelling; the newer addition was begun in 1902. The remarkably unaltered Kroeger-Melrose Historic District contains more than seventy houses built between 1898 and 1916.

Anaheim is the home of Disneyland, which opened its 185 acres in 1955. The extensive orange groves that once surrounded the park are gone today. Another popular attraction is Knott's Berry Farm at nearby Buena Park, to which Walter Knott moved a number of old buildings from various Western towns. One of these is Maizeland School (SRL 729), the first school in the Pico Rivera district of Los Angeles County. It was originally on Shugg Lane, now Slauson Avenue. Knott also restored the ghost town of Calico in the Mojave Desert, noted in the San Bernardino County chapter. The Buena Park Historical Society Museum is in the home built in 1887 by Andrew Whittaker, moved from Whittaker Street to 6631 Beach Boulevard.

FULLERTON

The real estate boom of the 1880s in southern California led to the founding of several new communities. This city was founded in 1887; property developer George H. Fullerton, president of the Pacific Land and Improvement Company, was successful in getting the California Central Railroad (soon to be part of the Santa Fe) to route its line through the new settlement, which was named in his honor. The Amerigue Brothers, who were also land developers, ran an office that has been preserved in Amerigue Park at 349 West Commonwealth in Fullerton.

Fullerton College at 321 E. Chapman Avenue is the oldest community college in California in continuous use, founded in 1913. The residence of pioneer physician Dr. George C. Clark, built in 1894 on the original site of Fullerton, has been moved to the campus of California State University at Fullerton. Located at Yorba Linda Boulevard and Associated Road, this "Heritage House" also includes an arboretum of fruit trees and vines adaptable to growing conditions in southern California.

GARDEN GROVE

The story of Garden Grove resembles that of Orange County in many ways. The town was for many years noted for its agricultural produce and at one time had more Farm Bureau members than any comparable community in the United States. Dr. Alonzo Cook bought 160 acres of land in 1874 and named the community, which over the years first produced grain and grapes, then walnuts and sugar beets, and finally oranges and strawberries. The two-acre Stanley Ranch Museum at 12174 Euclid Street is an interesting collection of buildings from the community, and from other parts of southern California. Once located in North Hollywood, the Disney Garage was owned by Robert Disney; in 1923, using this as a studio, his nephew Walt perfected the animation machine used to make his motion picture cartoons. The center of the museum is the Ware-Stanley House, built in 1891 by Edward G. Ware and lived in as a comfortable ranch house by him and his descendants until 1971. It has been beautifully maintained and is open to the public, as are six of the other buildings on the property.

After World War II, the population of Garden Grove increased dramatically as the farms and orchards gave way to houses: today Garden Grove is the fourth largest city in the county.

THE RICHARD NIXON LIBRARY AND BIRTHPLACE

Richard Milhous Nixon was the first native Californian to reach the White House. He was born on January 9, 1913, in Yorba Linda, in a frame house completed by his father Frank the previous year. On the land immediately west of the house, at 18001 Yorba Linda Boulevard, admirers of the president, who served from 1969 to 1974, built the Richard Nixon Library and Birthplace. The large facility was dedicated on July 19, 1990, with Presidents Nixon, Ford, Reagan, and Bush and their wives in attendance. This is an outstanding treasury, both of Nixon's unique life and also of the United States and the rest of the world in the middle of the twentieth century. It is one of the newest and most interesting historic spots in California. The library includes fascinating visual material (Nixon's career owed much to television) and twenty-two galleries focusing on different aspects of Nixon's life and times. Mrs. Nixon died in 1993 and is buried on the grounds; her husband succumbed to a stroke in 1994 and is buried next to her, just a short distance from where he was born.

Following his resignation from the presidency in 1974, Nixon retired to his home in San Clemente. During his presidency it was known as the "Western White House." The building, now privately owned, is near the southern end of the city, on a bluff overlooking the ocean. San Clemente was one of California's planned communities, begun in 1925.

CARBON CANYON AND OLINDA

Carbon Canyon Regional Park, in Brea, contains an area that in the 1870s was used as grazing and cattle land. The arrival of the Santa Fe Railroad in the next decade initiated a land boom in the area that became frantic when Edward L. Doheny discovered oil in the region in 1897. Olinda (SRL 918) burgeoned immediately afterward, becoming a sizable but unincorporated town. At the close of World War II, as productivity

Richard Nixon's Birthplace, Yorba Linda

dropped in the oil fields, Olinda declined and finally vanished. Today it is remembered only by the plaque in the park, at 4442 Carbon Canyon Road.

NEWPORT BEACH

In 1870 Captain S. S. Dunnells of San Diego and D. M. Dorman established a small dock and warehouse that they called Newport Landing. In 1873 three brothers, James, John, and Robert McFadden, received a shipment of lumber at the landing for their personal use. Other settlers, however, prevailed upon them to sell their cargo, and the McFaddens decided to go into the lumber business. They purchased Newport Landing in the same year and made it their headquarters. It later became known as McFadden's Landing and Port Orange. It was located just below the bluff that divided upper and lower Newport Bay, or near the intersection of Dover Drive with SR 1 (the Pacific Coast Highway) at Newport Beach. A plaque (SRL 198) stands on Dover commemorating the Old Landing. The name was bestowed on the site when the McFaddens built a wharf on the ocean side of the peninsula at the present location of the Newport pier. The original wharf on this second site (SRL 794) was completed in 1888, and in 1892, the same year the town of Newport was laid out, it became the first line of the Santa Ana and Newport Railroad. Building material and rolling stock for the railroad were sent by sea to the pier, and from there used to construct the line. Until 1907 it was the major commercial port for Orange, Riverside, and San Bernardino Counties.

One of the most picturesque landmarks along the southern California coast is the Balboa Pavilion (SRL 959) at 400 Main Street in Balboa on Newport Bay. The Newport Bay Investment Company put up this striking building in 1905 to attract investors to the Balboa Bay Peninsula property development; the following year, it became the southern terminus for the Pacific Electric Company's Red Cars. The Balboa Ferry, which docks here, has been making runs several times a day every day since 1906, probably California's record in this field.

On May 12, 1912, Glenn L. Martin flew a hydroplane from Balboa on Newport Bay to Avalon on Catalina Island, the longest "water-to-water" flight made at that time. The event is commemorated by a plaque (SRL 775) on the Balboa pier.

ORANGE COUNTY DURING WORLD WAR II

The open fields of coastal Orange County underwent substantial development because of World War II. The largest lima-bean field in the world, some 17,000 acres, became the El Toro Marine Corps Air Station. At Tustin, one of three Lighter-Than-Air Stations on the West Coast (California had another at Moffett Field in Sunnyvale, Santa Clara County) was built to house the huge 14-ZPK-class airships, popularly called blimps. Each of the two remaining hangars could hold a squadron of six blimps; they are among the largest wooden buildings in the United States. The air base closed in 1999, and the future of these hangars is undetermined as of 2000.

Coastal defense consisted in part of huge gun batteries. The gigantic concrete pads for one emplacement may still be seen where Bolsa Chico and Warner Avenues meet in Huntington Beach.

LANDMARKS OF THE SANTA ANA MOUNTAINS

In the late 1870s and early 1880s Orange County (then still part of Los Angeles County) experienced a short-lived mining boom. Hank Smith and William Curry discovered silver in 1877 east of Santa Ana in an area that was to become known as Silverado Canyon. The mining camp of Silverado (SRL 202) sprang up the following year and prospered for three or four years. The Blue Light was the principal mine in the district, which is now filled with homes.

In 1878 Ramón Mesquida discovered coal nearby, and the town of Carbondale (SRL 228) was built on the flat at the intersection of Santiago and Silverado Canyons. The Southern Pacific Railroad operated a mine there for a few years. A marker is located at the Silverado Community Church at 8002 Silverado Canyon Road in Silverado Canyon. In 1879 August Witter also discovered

coal, this time in the Cañon de los Indios to the north. His mine was named the Black Star, and the canyon, a branch of Santiago Canyon, was soon known by the same name as the mine. Black Star Canyon was the scene of a battle in the early 1830s between William Wolfskill and other trappers and a band of Indian horse thieves. The site of the Indian village (SRL 217) is marked by mounds and grinding rocks, but no plaque has been placed. It is 6.2 miles up Black Star Canyon Road from the intersection of this road with Silverado Canyon and Santiago Canyon roads.

Rugged Santiago Canyon was chosen by the famous Polish tragedienne Helena Modjeska as the home to which she retired after a long dramatic career that took her all over the world. She had first come to California as a member of a small and short-lived Polish colony that attempted to establish itself at Anaheim; another member was Henryk Sienkiewicz, whose novel *Quo Vadis* was a best-seller in the 1890s. After the colony disbanded, Madame Modjeska returned to the stage for a few years. In 1883 she bought the canyon property from Joseph Edward Pleasants and named it for the Forest of Arden in Shakespeare's *As You Like It*. About four years later she began construction of a beautiful home designed by the New York architect Stanford White (who never saw the building or the site). She sold the property in 1906, three years before her death, and it was in private hands until the Orange County Department of Harbors, Beaches, and Parks acquired it in 1986. Arden (SRL 205), beautifully preserved in a secluded spot, is a National Historic Landmark. It is located in Modjeska Canyon at the edge of the Cleveland National Forest.

Across the creek from Modjeska's home is Flores Peak (SRL 225), scene of the capture of a group of bandits in January 1857 by a posse led by General Andrés Pico. Juan Flores, leader of the gang, escaped but was later captured by Pico. Pico's posse was organized after the killing of Sheriff James Barton of Los Angeles by the Flores gang. Flores had broken out of San Quentin Prison the previous October. The sheriff's posse of six encountered the outlaws at what became known as Barton Mound (SRL 218), and there Barton and three others met their deaths. The mound was leveled in the construction of the I-405 freeway, but the marker identifying the site may be found at the end of Sand Canyon Avenue near the junction of the freeway and SR 133 in East Irvine. The East Irvine Historic Area along Sand Canyon Avenue and Burt Lane contains several buildings from the early twentieth century that are being preserved.

Placer County

Placer County was organized in 1851 from parts of Sutter and Yuba Counties. Auburn was made the county seat. *Placer*, according to Gudde, is "a western American term of Spanish origin [and] designates alluvial or glacial deposits containing gold particles, which can be obtained by washing." At the time the name was adopted for the county, placer mining was the principal method employed there, and the placers of the region were among the richest in the state.

LAKE TAHOE

Lake Tahoe, located partly in Placer and El Dorado Counties and partly in the state of Nevada, lies 6,229 feet above the sea. It is remarkable for its great depth and the rare and exquisite color of its waters. The name "Tahoe" may be a corruption of a Washo Indian name, "Da-Aw-Aga," meaning "beside the lake" or "shores of the lake." The lake has also been known by other names for short periods.

Passing through Alpine County on his way to California in 1844, John C. Frémont climbed the ridge to the vicinity of Carson Pass. With Charles Preuss, he explored one of the highest peaks in the area, probably Red Lake Peak. From its summit on February 14, the explorers gained their first view of the lake. In his narrative of the expedition Frémont called the newly discovered sheet of water simply the "mountain lake," but on his later map of the expedition he labeled it Lake Bonpland. "I gave to the basin river the name Humboldt," Frémont wrote, "and to the mountain lake the name of his companion traveler [the noted French botanist Aimé] Bonpland, and so put it on the map of the expedition."

Frémont's name for the body of water he discovered has been forgotten. The official mapmaker of the state of California gave to it in 1853 the name Lake Bigler, after John Bigler, third governor of California, and people undoubtedly used this official designation for some years. A successful attempt to find a more appropriate name for this beautiful lake was made in 1862 through the efforts of William Henry Knight.

Knight had come overland to California from Missouri in 1859, and it was on this journey that he saw Lake Tahoe "from a projecting cliff 1,000 feet above its surface." The scene, wrote Knight

> embraced not only the entire outline of the Lake with its charming bays and rocky headlands but also the magnificent forest of giant pines and firs in which it was embosomed, and the dozen or more lofty mountain peaks thrusting their white summits into the sky at altitudes varying from 8,000 to 11,000 feet above sea level. No imagination can conceive the beauty, sublimity and inspiration of that scene, especially to one who had for weary months been traversing dusty, treeless, and barren plains. The contrast was overwhelming.

In 1861 Knight gathered data to compile the first map of the Pacific states, and in 1862 this map was published by the Bancroft Publishing House in San Francisco. On it the name of Lake Bigler had been changed to Lake Tahoe. Knight, who deliberately omitted the name of Bigler, urged John S. Hittell and Dr. Henry De Groot to support him in a change of names. At his request, also, De Groot had suggested "Tahoe, the Indian name for the lake" as a fit substitute. De Groot had heard the name for the first time in 1859 while on an exploring trip. Knight at once obtained the approval of the Land Office in Washington, D.C., and the new name appeared on all subsequent maps and in printed matter from the Department of the Interior. The California Legislature, oblivious to the popular acceptance of the name Tahoe, inexplicably legalized "Bigler" in 1870, and this act was not repealed until 1945.

Very early there were those who sensed the possibilities of the Lake Tahoe region as a pleasure and health resort. With increasing frequency pioneer vacationists from Nevada and elsewhere were lured to the place by the beauty of the lake, as well as by its fishing and hunting facilities. The earliest permanent settlements on the lakeshore were those at the mouth of McKinney Creek, at Ward Creek, at Tahoe City (all in Placer County), and at Glenbrook (in Nevada). In the summer of 1862 William Ferguson and Ward Rust built a cabin on the lake at the mouth of Ward Creek. Two other men, John W. McKinney and Thomas Wren, had located a hay ranch on the summit near the county line in 1861, and in 1862 McKinney moved down from his ranch and settled on the shore of Lake Tahoe near the creek that bears his name. There he established a hunting and fishing resort known as Hunter's Retreat. When the place was later acquired by David Chambers its name became Chambers Lodge.

The first survey for Tahoe City was made in 1863, and the Tahoe House was built by William Pomin the following year. While the nature lover and the tourist contributed to the early prosperity of Tahoe City, the town was at first essentially a lumbering center. After the completion of the Central Pacific Railroad as far as Truckee, a wagon road was constructed from that point to the lake. To accommodate the new influx of visitors, A. J. Bayley built his celebrated Grand Central Hotel at Tahoe City.

There are 159 inlets into Lake Tahoe, but its only outlet is the Truckee River. The outlet gates at Tahoe City (SRL 797) were first constructed in 1870; the present ones date from 1913. The gatekeeper's cabin nearby is a replica, built in 1981, of the earlier structure built in 1931 and destroyed by fire in 1978. It is now the museum of the North Lake Tahoe Historical Society and has an extensive collection of historic memorabilia and photographs of the lake, and a fine research library. Connected to the Gatekeeper's Museum is an annex, the Edmund S. Barnett Building, which houses the Marion Steinbach Indian Basket Museum, whose collection includes many other kinds of western Indian crafts. The museum is in William B. Layton Park, at 130 West Lake Tahoe Boulevard in Tahoe City. A monument nearby at the Truckee River Bridge on SR 89 commemorates the work of Dr. James E. Church Jr., who in 1910–11 made possible the accurate prediction and control of sea-

Gatekeeper's Museum and Marion Steinbach Indian Basket Museum, Tahoe City

sonal rise in the lake and river levels. This ended a long dispute between lakeshore owners and downstream Truckee River water users over control of the gates.

After the decline of the lumber industry, the fame of Lake Tahoe as a summer resort increased. Now it is an all-year playground with a substantial permanent population. But Lake Tahoe is in an ecologically fragile condition; pollution of the environment and what many believe to be overexpansion of commercial and residential lands make the place a continual concern.

Winter sports at nearby Squaw Valley and other resorts draw many visitors during the snowy months. At Squaw Valley (SRL 724), the VIII Olympic Winter Games of 1960 commemorated a century of sport skiing in California. The first organized ski clubs and competition in the Western Hemisphere were held in Sierra towns around 1860, mostly in Plumas County to the north. The first ski jump in Placer County was constructed at Granlibakken, about a mile south of Tahoe City, in 1931. Skiing became a major California activity after World War II.

EMIGRANT GAP AND THE OLD EMIGRANT TRAIL

Emigrant Gap, an old lumbering camp and a station on the Central Pacific Railroad, derives its name from a low opening in the mountains at the head of Bear River. A branch of the old California emigrant trail went down into Bear Valley by way of this pass, a region of wild and magnificent scenery.

Emigrant Gap is today a small settlement just south of I-80. West of the turnoff to the community, a monument at a viewpoint adjacent to the westbound lanes of the freeway commemorates Emigrant Gap (SRL 403). Here the covered wagons were lowered over the precipitous cliff to the floor of Bear Valley by means of rope and tackle held by iron spikes driven into the solid rock. It was first used by wagons in the spring of 1845 and continued as a part of the emigrant trail during and after the Gold Rush.

The early California emigrant trail over Donner Pass skirted the present boundary line between Placer and Nevada counties, following mainly along the Nevada County side. The easier route out of the mountains led north of the Bear River, since the narrow divide between that stream and the North Fork of the American River offered no roadway without improvements, which the emigrants were unable to make.

THE DUTCH FLAT—DONNER LAKE ROAD

It was not until the building of the Central Pacific Railroad up the divide between the Bear River and the North Fork of the American River in 1864–66 that a wagon road was constructed along its entire length. In 1849 the head of "wagon navigation" up this ridge was at Illinoistown, and within a few years vehicles had reached as far as Dutch Flat. By 1860, after the discovery of the rich Comstock Lode in Nevada, a great demand had developed for adequate means of transportation over the mountains, and the people of Placer County became anxious to have this very profitable traffic diverted their way. Several attempts made by groups of local citizens to build roads met with failure. Finally, in the fall of 1861, the "Big Four" and others who were building the Central Pacific Railroad over the mountains organized the Dutch Flat and Donner Lake Wagon Road Company, their purpose being to attract as much of the Nevada traffic as possible. This road was completed in June 1864.

By June 1865 the railroad had been constructed as far as Clipper Gap, and in July the California Stage Company began running coaches from that point to Virginia City, Nevada. As the railroad progressed up the ridge, stations were placed at various points, while the stages and forwarding houses moved on simultaneously, making connections at each terminus. By September 1865, the Central Pacific had acquired the greater part of the passenger and freight business between Nevada and California, most of which, up to that time, had gone largely to the Placerville Road in El Dorado County.

SICARD'S RANCH

The first settlement in Placer County was Sicard's Ranch, a Mexican grant on the south bank of the Bear River. This grant was given to Theodore Sicard, a French sailor, in 1844, and here in 1845 he built an adobe house about one-half mile above Johnson's Crossing.

Being located on the overland emigrant trail that crossed the valley via Sinclair's Ranch to Sutter's Fort, Sicard's Ranch became of some importance as a stopping place. A fellow countryman of Sicard, Claude Chana (also spelled Chané), arrived at the ranch in October 1846. That same fall, Chana and Sicard planted a few pits of dried peaches brought by an emigrant family and some almonds that Chana himself had; from this beginning came the pioneer commercial orchard of the Sacramento Valley. Chana was also the discoverer of gold in Placer County. After mining at Auburn Ravine, where the discovery was made, and later on the Yuba River, he purchased the Sicard Grant and sold the products of his orchard, vegetable garden, and vineyard to the miners at great profit. The site of Claude Chana's pioneer orchard now lies beneath the debris brought down the Bear River from the hydraulic diggings in the foothills.

Johnson's Crossing, on the Bear River about three miles east of Wheatland, received a post office in 1853, and for some years it was a lively settlement, a stopping place for emigrants and for many of the teams engaged in hauling freight from Sacramento to the northern mining camps. The great flood of 1862 nearly destroyed the place, but the real cause of its final desertion was the later avalanche of debris that poured down upon it from the hydraulic mines higher up the river.

ROGER'S "SHED" AND LINCOLN

About a half mile south of present Sheridan stood a very busy crossroads station during the days of the stagecoaches and freighters. It was situated on the Sacramento-Nevada road at a point where four other roads diverged: one running west to Nicolaus in Sutter County (13 miles), one running northwest to Marysville (15 miles) via Kempton's Crossing, a third going northeast toward Grass Valley (28 miles) via McCourtney's Crossing, and a fourth following east to Auburn (20 miles) via Danetown. At this location in 1857 a man named E. C. Rogers built a one-story house with a 150-foot shed in front. The "Shed" or "Union Shed," as it was called, soon became a place of importance. Here the long freight teams that thronged the roads received shelter from the heat in summer and the rain in winter, and here the farmers of the surrounding country brought hay and grain to supply the teams.

The bustling activity about the Shed did not last long, for the building of the California Central Railroad northward from Folsom did away with staging and teaming up and down the valley. In 1861 the railroad had been built as far as Lincoln, named for one of the promoters of the railroad, Charles Lincoln Wilson. From 1861 to 1866 Lincoln was a thriving stage and freight center; but when the terminus of the railroad was changed to Wheatland in 1866, the stage and teaming business was transferred also, and both Lincoln and Rogers's Shed lost their importance as stage centers. In 1868 the Shed, with all its buildings, was consumed by fire.

Manzanita Grove, situated on a wooded knoll in the middle of broad, open fields halfway between Lincoln and Sheridan and east of the highway between them, gained notoriety in early days as a stronghold for thieves. Here, hidden in the center of a thick grove of trees, was a corral where the bandits kept their stolen stock. The robbers were eventually cleared out, and by 1855 the grove had been made the cemetery for the countryside. Today there are only a few of the low-growing manzanitas left among the native oaks, which cast their shadows over the graves of the pioneers buried at this spot; it is a place of tranquil beauty. Manzanita Grove Cemetery is reached over Wise Road, which turns to the right from SR 65 about four miles north of Lincoln. Wise Road joins the Manzanita Cemetery Road in less than two miles, and from this point it is one mile to the cemetery.

RIVER BARS

Placer County, embracing several branches of the American River besides Bear River, included scores of river-bar camps. Beal's Bar was the first camp above the confluence of the North and South Forks of the river. As late as 1863 it polled ninety-six votes and was an active center of trade for the nearby mines. When the old bar immediately upon the river was worked out, the town was moved to a high bench adjoining, and the former site was dug out and its gravel washed for gold.

In this vicinity John Sinclair and some fifty Indian laborers, in the spring and summer of 1848, were among the first to mine on the North Fork of the American River. Governor Richard B. Mason, in his report to Washington in 1848, says: "He [Sinclair] had been engaged about five weeks when I saw him, and up to that time his Indians had used simply closely-woven willow

baskets. His net proceeds . . . were about $16,000 worth of gold."

Beal's Bar is now under Folsom Lake, but a marker near Beal's Point in Folsom Lake State Park recalls the old express trail (SRL 585) of 1849–54 that led to this and other camps. The Auburn-Folsom Road now parallels this route. Folsom Lake also covers the site of a number of settlements along the North Fork of the American River, chief among them Horseshoe Bar, Smith's Bar, and Rattlesnake Bar. Above the confluence of the North and Middle Forks of the river along the North Fork, old sites were washed away by the hydraulic mines of Gold Run and other places. A number of camps with a marvelous variety of names were located along the Middle Fork: Sailor Claim, Buckner's, Rocky Point Slide, Mammoth, Texas, Quail, Brown's, Kennebec, Buckeye, American, Sardine, Yankee, Dutch, African, Drunkard's, Horseshoe Number Two, and Stony bars among them. Humbug Bar was located in Humbug Canyon, a tributary of the south branch of the North Fork of the American River. The canyon, first known as Mississippi Canyon, was rechristened Humbug early in 1850 when a group of miners became disgusted with their luck at this place. Later these same prospectors returned with others and struck it rich, proving it to be no "humbug" after all.

AUBURN

Early in 1849, Auburn (SRL 404) was known as Woods Dry Diggings. It was one of the earliest mining camps in California, gold having been first discovered there in Auburn Ravine in May 1848 by Claude Chana and a party of Indians en route to Coloma from Sicard's Ranch on the Bear River. A prominent statue in downtown Auburn commemorates Chana's discovery. Chana was soon followed by Nicolaus Allgeier, who had come up from his ranch in Sutter County with his Indian retainers.

Hordes of prospectors and adventurers began to pour in by 1849 and camps sprang up everywhere. According to some authorities, Woods Dry Diggings was called for a time North Fork Dry Diggings. A large group of miners in the vicinity had come to California in 1846 in Stevenson's Volunteer Regiment from Auburn, New York. It is thought that they changed the name of North Fork Dry Diggings to Auburn in the summer of 1849. Records show that the early diggings here were very rich. During the peak of productiveness it was not unusual for a man to take out $1,000 to

Claude Chana Statue, Auburn

$1,500 a day. There is one instance of four cartloads of earth yielding as much as $16,000.

Auburn became the county seat of Sutter County in the spring of 1850. Its favorable location, as well as, in the ironic words of one observer, "its preponderance of population, and the inexhaustible powers of voting possessed by its citizens and partisans, decided the contest in its favor by a majority considerably exceeding the entire population of the county." On April 25, 1851, when Placer County was created from a portion of Sutter County, Auburn was made the seat of justice of the new county. The city was incorporated in 1860, disincorporated about 1866, and reincorporated in 1888. During the 1860s and 1870s, Auburn became a cultural and social center, having a private normal school and college, and enjoying a reputation as a health resort, the pure air of the lower Sierra being both mild and invigorating.

Devastating fires swept many of the mining camps several times during their early years. After Auburn's first experience, its citizens determined to rebuild the town with more substantial material. In the older section of town, adjacent to I-80, there are a number of solid brick structures dating from the 1850s and 1860s, with the heavy iron doors and iron-shuttered windows common to that period. As one writer has said:

> The Auburn of today is a city of contrasts. Entering it from the south, one descries a narrow street, flanked by old brick buildings, and overlooked by the high bell tower of a fire station. A half-mile beyond, upon the summit of a hill, is the modern portion of the community with up-to-date establishments and public buildings. It is plain to see that Auburn, like the chambered nautilus, outgrew the site upon which it was first located. But the shell that it left behind is still a part of its metropolitan area.

A distinctive sight in Old Auburn is the three-story Auburn Hook and Ladder Company Fire House Number Two, built in 1893 for a company that was organized in 1852 and that claims to be "the oldest volunteer fire department this side of Boston." The bell on the third floor is much older than the structure now housing it, and by custom it tolls the time of day at 8 A.M., noon, and 5 P.M. Nearby on "Main Street Island" is a cluster of buildings that escaped early fires, including Station A of the Auburn Post Office, once occupying a larger corner of the property. Dating from 1852, it is California's oldest operating post office. Three wooden buildings on Sacramento Street also date from 1852 and are collectively called the Chinese Merchants Section, a reminder of the lively commercial life of Auburn's Chinese pioneers. The Empire Livery Stable on Washington Street was built in 1864.

Dominating the skyline and overlooking the old part of town is the imposing Placer County courthouse, built in 1894. It is said that the building is made of bricks and lime from Auburn, marble from Colfax, granite from Rocklin, and slate from Slatington, all Placer County communities. The Placer County Museum is on the first floor of the courthouse, which is situated at 101 Maple Street. This part of the courthouse also houses the Pate Native American Collection of artifacts. Most of the county's official business is now transacted at the County Administrative Office, at 175 Fulweiler Avenue in Auburn.

The Bernhard Museum Complex at 291 Auburn-Folsom Road contains the Bernhard Residence, built around 1851 and one of the oldest wooden buildings in Placer County. The family lived here from 1868 to 1957. Also on the grounds are the Bernhard Winery (c. 1874) and the wine-processing building (c. 1881), and a reconstructed carriage barn. The Gold Country Museum is at the Gold Country Fairgrounds at 1273 High Street, with many displays on the various kinds of mining activities pursued in Placer County over the years.

AUBURN, A TURNPIKE CENTER

Auburn has always been the center of extensive staging and freighting operations. In its early days a network of trails radiated from it to the numerous camps springing up in all directions, and over these trails miners' supplies were carried by pack-mule trains. During the 1850s and 1860s most of these rough and narrow trails were gradually superseded by toll roads, which were not much better.

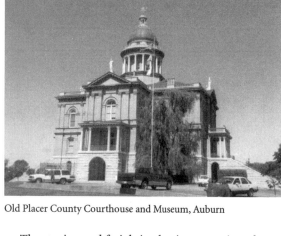

Old Placer County Courthouse and Museum, Auburn

The staging and freighting business continued over the many roads reaching out from Auburn even after the building of the Central Pacific Railroad up the ridge. The first passenger train arrived in Auburn on May 13, 1865, an event commemorated by a marker (SRL 780.4) at the train station at 639 Lincoln Way. The advent of the railroad created a demand for additional wagon traffic into Nevada County, and, in 1866, brought about the opening of a new and more direct stage route into El Dorado County, via Lyon's Bridge, where SR 49 now crosses the river. Today, buses and trucks still carry their quota of passengers, mail, and freight over the old mountain roads, most of them improved or reconstructed into modern highways leading to and from Auburn.

There were five main wagon roads centering in Auburn, while many laterals led out from these to all parts of Placer County. The highway from Sacramento up the ridge to Illinoistown went through Auburn, and a branch of this road was one of the main routes to Grass Valley and Nevada City, crossing the Bear River at a place later known as English Bridge and then at Gautier Bridge, ten miles north of Auburn on SR 49. A third road extended northeast to mining camps along the Forest Hill ridge, passing down Auburn Ravine to Ophir and Virginiatown. Still another ran south along the ridge above the American River to Folsom and Sacramento, and connected with roads coming from El Dorado County. On this road six and a half miles south of Auburn stood the Mountaineer House, on the site of which the stone mansion of J. J. Brennan was built, over the foundations of the old stage station. Near the Brennan ranch was Auburn Station, the final terminus of California's first passenger railroad, the Sacramento Valley, originally built from Sacramento to Folsom in 1855–56. It was to be extended to Auburn, but the Cen-

tral Pacific arrived first, and so the Sacramento Valley Railroad was discontinued. Auburn disincorporated to keep from paying the bonds on the railroad that never reached it.

Stupendous difficulties were encountered in transforming devious, threadlike pack trails into roads. The turnpike from Auburn to Forest Hill furnishes an excellent example of the problems met by the builders of these old "High Ways." Leading down into the canyon of the North Fork of the American River where the traveler crossed the stream by means of a crude ferry, the Auburn–Forest Hill trail climbed another steep and meandering path up the opposite canyon wall. Only by a great expenditure of money and labor could the obstacles presented by these mighty canyons be surmounted. Since the county government was unable to raise sufficient funds for the enterprise, the work was taken up by private turnpike companies, the new routes of travel thus becoming toll roads.

The grade of the North Fork Hill Road, as it was called, was improved in 1855 at a cost of $12,000, and in the early 1860s an additional $50,000 was expended upon it. Over a distance of more than twenty miles from Auburn to Yankee Jim's—winding up the deep gorge of the North Fork or clinging to the sides of a mountain far above the stream—this road was carved out of the canyon walls only through immense effort.

Over this old highland thoroughfare, a continuous stream of life from Auburn poured into the mining camps along the Forest Hill Divide, passing a number of stations and roadhouses along the way. They included the Junction House two and a half miles from Auburn, the Grizzly Bear House, Butcher's Ranch, Sheridan's, Mile Hill Toll House, and Spring Garden.

AUBURN RAVINE

Extending west from Auburn, down what was once the old Auburn Ravine turnpike, are a number of historic sites reminiscent of early mining activities. This is also a region of much modern development, and most of the historic sites are either lost or hard to locate. Ophir (SRL 463), three miles west of Auburn, was first known as Spanish Corral. Like the biblical land of Ophir whence came the gold to adorn the temple of Solomon, the region around Spanish Corral was found to be fabulously rich, and the name of the settlement was changed to Ophir. In 1852 it was, briefly, the most populous place in the county. Four miles to the west, Gold Hill was founded in 1852; most of it consists of

Griffith Building, Penryn

new homes today, although a small cemetery remains from earlier days.

Virginiatown, two miles west of Gold Hill, is commemorated by a marker (SRL 400) near the intersection of Virginiatown and Fowler Roads. In 1852 Captain John Brislow built California's first railroad here to carry pay dirt one mile to Auburn Ravine. Virginiatown no longer exists, but was the site of Philip Armour and George Aldrich's butcher shop, said to have led to the founding of the famous Armour meatpacking company in Chicago. In decline for many years, the region is today full of attractive modern homes.

SECRET RAVINE (NEWCASTLE, PENRYN, LOOMIS)

Secret Ravine, extending southwest from Auburn, was the scene of extensive placer mining operations during the 1850s and 1860s and of granite quarrying in the 1870s and 1880s. Commercial orchards were planted up and down the ridges as early as 1870, and these continue to be a source of income in the region today. Old mining camps that flourished in the ravine during the Gold Rush days were soon superseded after the coming of the railroad by other towns built along the ridge.

Newcastle, at the head of Secret Ravine, is a fruit-shipping center on the railroad. The arrival of the railroad at Newcastle on January 10, 1864, is commemorated by a marker (SRL 780.3) on the station. In 1865, construction pushed on to Auburn and eventually became part of the transcontinental railroad.

Penryn (also Penrhyn, after its patronym in Wales) was established and named in 1864 by Griffith Griffith, a Welshman, whose extensive granite quarries for a number of years supplied the building material for many structures in San Francisco, Stockton, and elsewhere. The quarry (SRL 885) is just off I-80 at the Pen-

ryn turnoff. A small museum, stoutly built of granite, is on the edge of Griffith Quarry Park, at the junction of Taylor and Rock Springs Roads. A two-story building of hewn granite blocks stands in nearby Penryn, built in 1878 by Griffith and containing the community's library and post office. David Griffith succeeded his uncle in 1889 and operated a much smaller granite works until his death in 1918.

About two and a half miles southwest of Penryn is Loomis, the successor of Pino. Pino took its name from the old mining camp of Pine Grove, which was established in Secret Ravine about a mile and a half from the site of Loomis, before the coming of the railroad.

ROSEVILLE AND ROCKLIN

The track of the Central Pacific Railroad reached Junction, now Roseville, on April 25, 1864, and Rocklin, four miles east, the following month. At Roseville a marker (SRL 780.1) in Depot Park at Washington and Church Streets commemorates the event. In 1908 the Southern Pacific Railroad moved its roundhouse from Rocklin to Roseville, making the latter a major railroad center, one of the largest in the western United States. The railroad's arrival at Rocklin is commemorated by a marker (SRL 780.2) on Taylor Street, where a small museum of railroad history is displayed in old railroad cars.

GOLD RUN

The Gold Run region, twenty-five miles northeast of Auburn, on the ridge south of Dutch Flat between Bear River and the North Fork of the American River, is a good example of early hydraulic mining. A vast bed of auriferous blue gravel two miles long, half a mile wide, and 250 feet deep, with pay dirt all the way down, it yielded immense profit until the early 1880s. O. W. Hollenbeck came to the region in 1854 and mined at a place called Mountain Springs. In 1859 hydraulic mining was begun on the Gold Run claim. In 1862 Hollenbeck laid out a town on Cold Spring Mountain, calling it Mountain Springs. A post office had been established in 1854 under that name, but the name was changed to Gold Run in 1863. The place developed into a mining center long after the other towns of the county and flourished during the 1860s and 1870s. Squire's Canyon, Canyon Creek, Goosling Ravine, Gold Run Canyon, Potato Ravine, and Indiana Canyon all had productive hydraulic mines. After 1884, when the courts outlawed hydraulic mining, the town became almost deserted. The original town of Gold Run (SRL 405) is near I-80 south of the present Gold Run railroad station.

DUTCH FLAT

Dutch Flat (SRL 397) is unique among the old camps of Placer County. Its main street, tree-lined, climbs abruptly from the hollow where the town had its beginning, to a narrow, sloping terrace, on which perches the settlement of later growth, and on up past summer and retirement homes.

Thousands of miners worked the ridges and hills about Dutch Flat, until the entire region was deeply torn by hydraulic operations. Aside from its prominence as a mining center, Dutch Flat was a stage station, making it one of the largest and most important towns of the county around 1865.

The town was first settled by a group of Germans, among them Joseph and Charles Dornbach. The name "Dutch" may have been derived from the nationality of these settlers (German/*Deutsch*), but one looks in vain for the "Flat." In 1856 the town was granted a post office under its present designation.

Past the town runs the old road, which from 1864 to 1866 was a much-traveled turnpike; over it the well-braced Concord coaches ran to the rich Washoe silver mines of Nevada, one branch going by way of Bear Valley, Bowman Lake, and Henness Pass, and the other via Donner Lake. The latter route, known as the Dutch Flat–Donner Lake Road, was built by the men who were at that time constructing the Central Pacific Railroad. The names of Governor Leland Stanford, Dr. D. W. Strong, and other promoters of the railway thus became linked with the history of this toll road and with the town. Strong, a resident of Dutch Flat, was the only one of the nine promoters of the railway who lived outside Sacramento. From the beginning he was an advocate for the Dutch Flat–Donner Pass route, even when others doubted its feasibility. In the fall of 1866, after the railway had reached Cisco about twenty miles farther up the ridge, Dutch Flat lost much of its importance as a stage center.

During the 1870s hydraulic mining operations at Dutch Flat reached their height. In 1872, the Cedar Creek Company of London purchased as many as thirty-two claims and worked them on a gigantic scale. Millions in gold were taken from the extensive placers of Dutch Flat, one nugget along being worth more than $5,000. It is estimated that $30 million more remains in this gravelly ridge.

Every old building in the block that forms the business section of Dutch Flat has a history. The old three-story hotel, built in 1852, now stands vacant. The IOOF Building (1858) is still in use, as is the stone store built in 1854. The Masonic Hall dates from 1856, and the Methodist Episcopal church from 1861. Good displays of mining activities in the community can be viewed in the summer months at the Golden Drift Museum at 32820 Main Street. Adjoining the American cemetery just above the town is the Chinese burial ground, almost lost in the pines. Most of the bodies were removed from the graves and taken back to China. The old site of Chinatown, with a population of 1,000, was on the railroad one mile above Dutch Flat.

COLFAX AND ILLINOISTOWN

Colfax is about fifteen miles northeast of Auburn in the center of a once-prosperous mining district. It began as a small settlement called Alder Cove in 1849; the name was soon changed to Illinoistown. The Central Pacific Railroad from Sacramento built its lines through here and at a place called Camp 20; the first train arrived on September 1, 1865. The event is commemorated by a plaque (SRL 780.5) on Main Street. The speaker at the celebration was none other than Schuyler Colfax, speaker of the House of Representatives, who delivered so rousing a speech that it was decided to name the place for him. Colfax went on to become vice president of the United States in the first term of President Ulysses Grant (1869–73). The town was an important business and trading center, with a narrow-gauge railroad extending north and west to the gold mines of Grass Valley and Nevada City (built in 1875). The old freight house through which millions of dollars of gold passed from these mines still stands on Main Street.

Perhaps the greatest challenge to the builders of the Central Pacific Railroad across the Sierra came five miles north of Colfax, at Cape Horn, a mammoth granite promontory rising 1,500 feet above the waters of the American River. More than ten thousand Chinese laborers, using only picks and shovels and lowered from the top by ropes, built a roadbed across this and similar locations further up the mountains. On SR 174 just outside Colfax on the road to Grass Valley, a monument placed in 1999 at a roadside vista of Cape Horn honors these workmen from China whose efforts made possible the completion of the first transcontinental railway across America.

From 1920 to 1960, the Colfax Fruit Exchange was a

major shipping point for local produce to markets in the East. The Fruit Exchange building is now used for modern offices and shops. Another interesting activity was a retreat for tuberculosis patients established in the nearby town of Weimar in 1919. The Weimar Medical Center was transformed into Hope Village in the early 1970s, as Vietnamese refugees who had supported the United States in the Vietnam War were housed here; most would become U.S. citizens. The Weimar Institute, a private college, now occupies the site.

IOWA HILL

The site of the little old town of Iowa Hill (SRL 401) is on the narrow neck of a high ridge between the North Fork of the American River on the north and Indian Canyon on the south. Nearly $20 million in gold was taken around this remote spot, all but deserted today. One of the most challenging roads in the Mother Lode is the Mineral Bar Bridge and Road linking Iowa Hill with Colfax across the canyon of the North Fork.

FOREST HILL

Forest Hill (SRL 399), a mining and lumbering camp of some importance in the 1850s and 1860s, is situated at an elevation of 3,400 feet, on the summit of the Forest Hill Divide between the Middle Fork of the American River and Shirt-Tail Canyon; the town is 2,500 feet above the river. Thousands of acres of pine forests surround it, and the canyon scenery is superb. The auriferous gravel of the Forest Hill Diggings is a part of the Blue Lead Channel, and the early claims, limited to fifty feet each, extended along the side of the hill. The tunnels penetrated the mountain to a distance of from 200 to 5,000 feet.

Early in the spring of 1850, a great rush of miners came to the Forest Hill Divide, lured by the news of rich diggings uncovered there. Coming from the south via Coloma and Greenwood Valley and from the west by way of Auburn, the two groups met about three miles northeast of Todd's store at a place that later became Forest Hill. The brush shanty set up at the latter site as a trading post in 1850 was replaced about 1858 by a substantial house and hotel. The Forest House, as it was known, became the nucleus of an important center of trade and travel to and from the numerous camps in all directions. The historic hostelry was destroyed by fire on Christmas Day, 1918, with the turkey dinner in the oven. Another hotel replaced it and bears the same name.

The height of activity began early in 1853, after the winter storms had brought down a great mass of loose gravel at the head of Jenny Lind Canyon, exposing many glistening chunks of gold. The Jenny Lind Mine alone yielded $1.1 million by 1880. The aggregate production of all the miners in the immediate vicinity of Forest Hill or within rifle shot of the express office was estimated at $10 million up to 1868. Rich mines in the region were the Dardanelles, New Jersey, Independence, Deidesheimer, Fast and Nortwood, Rough and Ready, Gore, and Alabama.

Forest Hill had already assumed a metropolitan air in the late 1850s, boasting a newspaper, "fireproof" hotels and stores, banks and elegant saloons, and neat homes surrounded by gardens and orchards. It was still one of the larger towns of Placer County in 1880, with about seven hundred inhabitants. The population later dwindled to about four hundred, but now the place is again beginning to prosper. Many of the buildings along the broad main street are new, but two old brick stores with iron shutters are still open for business. The Forest Hill Divide Museum, at 24601 Harrison Street in Leroy Botts Memorial Park, focuses on the history of the Forest Hill and the Iowa Hill Divides.

YANKEE JIM'S

A road from Forest Hill leads northwest three miles to Yankee Jim's (SRL 398), high up on the same ridge between the North and Middle Forks of the American River. A number of old weathered houses at Yankee Jim's are still standing, reminders of the days when it was one of the largest mining camps in Placer County; extensive diggings lie on its outskirts.

The origin of the name Yankee Jim's is one of those riddles often encountered in the mining regions. Some hold that the person from whom the camp derived its title was, indeed, a Yankee, but others say he was an Irishman or even an Australian. In any case, Yankee Jim appears to have been somewhat given to banditry, and when not stealing horses did some mining along the river bars of the North Fork. He sought to keep his discoveries a secret, but rumors spread quickly, and by 1850 miners swarmed over the entire ridge country. At the place of Yankee Jim's activities a town sprang up, was named for him, and became famous as a rich mining center.

Nearby is Shirt-Tail Canyon, along with its several branches—Brimstone Canyon, Brushy Canyon, Refuge Canyon, and Devil's Canyon—the scene of extensive gold excitement during the 1850s. The streambed in each of these canyons was worked, and numerous tunnels were dug into the rocky walls above. Shirt-Tail Canyon was so named when two prospectors discovered a solitary miner working the water's edge, wearing only a long shirt against the heat of the day and the icy stream.

MICHIGAN BLUFF

Looking over into El Dorado County to the south, Michigan Bluff (SRL 402), seven miles east of Forest Hill, clings to the steep slope of the Forest Hill Divide from 1,500 to 2,000 feet above the yawning gorges of the Middle and North Forks of the American River and El Dorado Canyon. The first town, commonly known as Michigan City, was located about half a mile below the present site, on the stretch of comparatively level ground once existing there and later mined out. Only an old well remains at Michigan City.

The first settlement on this ridge was made one mile to the west at Bird's Valley, where a party of sailors located in the summer of 1848. Later, these men reported at Sutter's Fort the rich diggings they had worked at Rector's Bar and other places below their camp. A second company, under the leadership of J. D. Hoppe, came up from Sutter's Fort the same fall. Following the trail made by the sailors up the mountainside, they too set up camp in Bird's Valley, crevassing for gold along the rivers in the canyons below. Working only upon and in the crevices of the bedrock, these first miners used the most primitive tools for their operations: butcher knives, iron spoons, a pan, and, on occasion, a steel bar. As the rainy season approached, the men returned to the valley, believing it to be impossible to winter in that wild country.

In the spring of 1849, hundreds of miners trekked over the rugged mountain trails to the new diggings, and a few stayed through the winter of 1849–50, among them two men at Bird's Valley. Rich discoveries had been found in El Dorado Canyon and along the bars of the Middle Fork during the summer of 1849, and with the coming of another spring a general stampede began in February 1850. Thousands of men climbed the trails from Hangtown, Coloma, Georgetown, Pilot Hill, and other places in El Dorado County already overrun with gold-seekers. Finding it impossible to mine along the streams, the rivers still being too high, they camped along the ridges, and Bird's store became an important rendezvous, with up to three thousand impatient argonauts gathered there to wait for the snow to recede and the water to subside.

A few ambitious men camped on the little flat to the east where Michigan City grew up. While grading out the mountainside for enough level ground for their cabins to stand upon, they struck a bed of auriferous gravel. Lack of water delayed the working of the find until 1853, when ditches were dug from the upper reaches of El Dorado and Volcano Canyons, twelve and fifteen miles to the north. Until 1858 the town enjoyed a period of great prosperity, shipping $100,000 worth of gold per month. The North American Mine alone yielded $300,000 up to 1868.

Michigan City had no sooner become established on the narrow shelf at the edge of the diggings than the shelf began to settle and to slip down the mountainside, cracking the walls of the houses and threatening to precipitate the entire settlement into the canyon. This was in 1858, and in 1859 the settlers moved en masse to the present site of Michigan Bluff higher up on the brow of the mountain. Hydraulic mining began in the vicinity in 1858, and during the 1860s and 1870s the town was one of the most prosperous centers on the Forest Hill Divide. By 1880 the numerous smaller claims had been bought up by the owners of the Big Gun Mine.

After 1884, when hydraulic mining was outlawed, Michigan Bluff went quickly into decline, until little of its former prosperity was apparent. Some of the old frame houses are empty and rotting on their foundations, while others have been attractively renovated. Leland Stanford kept a store here from 1853 to 1855, sleeping on the counter at night, for Mrs. Stanford had remained in the East. The business block of Michigan Bluff was destroyed by fire in 1857, in which year Elijah and Lyman Stanford and their families, cousins of Leland, lived in the community.

DEADWOOD

At the tip of a narrow mountain spur high above the chasms of El Dorado Canyon and the Middle Fork of the American River is the site of Deadwood, a one-time mining camp located seven miles from Michigan Bluff by pack trail. It is twenty-five miles by the long, circuitous route that winds around the head of El Dorado Canyon past the Forks House, continuing across the head of Indian Creek at Westville and thence down the Deadwood spur.

Gold was first found at Deadwood in 1852 by a group of miners who had previously experienced little success in the prospecting game. Encouraged by this sudden change for the better, the party remarked to all newcomers that they "now assuredly had the 'deadwood' upon securing a fortune"—in other words, it was a cinch. Thus Deadwood got its name.

The heartening news of the Deadwood discovery soon spread and a bustling camp sprang up, composed of more than 500 miners who had toiled over fearful canyon trails to this remote spot. It was a wild, austere habitat, to which only the most venturesome came. Deadwood was in a decline by 1855, although mining with moderate returns was carried on in the vicinity for many years. Only a small cemetery and an old well remain at the site.

A high bench or bar in the canyon of the north fork of the Middle Fork some two or three miles from Deadwood bears the delightful title of Bogus Thunder. A mile or more up the canyon from this place is a waterfall, the sound of which reverberates throughout the gorge with such a terrific roar that the first comers there thought they were hearing thunder. When they discovered the real cause of the noise, they named the place accordingly.

LAST CHANCE

Almost as difficult of access as Deadwood is Last Chance, above the canyon of the north fork of the Middle Fork, and the great network of narrow gorges and immense canyons that runs into it from the north. Perched at the tip of a promontory on the very brink of this tremendous drop-off, the Last Chance area seems like the jumping-off place.

The search for treasure had led a little group of prospectors into this remote region in 1850. Several rich deposits discovered in the vicinity caused them to linger until all the provisions were gone and starvation threatened. One of the company possessed a good rifle. Saying to his companions, "This is our last chance to make a grubstake," he went into the forest and returned with a large buck. Thus the miners were able to return to their diggings, and a new camp earned its name. This at least is one of several versions of its origin.

Last Chance had become a real town by 1852, and by 1859 the Masons, the Odd Fellows, and the Sons of Temperance had built halls. Only the cemetery remains today to show that it was once inhabited.

Across Peavine Canyon from Last Chance and about five miles to the southeast, the northernmost group of *Sequoia gigantea* in California stands on a well-watered vale on Duncan Ridge overlooking the Middle Fork of the American River. This grove, known as the Placer County Big Trees, consists of six living trees and two large fallen ones. They are within the Tahoe National Forest.

Plumas County

Plumas County was organized in 1854 from a portion of Butte County. The name was derived from El Río de las Plumas, "the river of feathers," so named by Captain Luís A. Argüello, who led an exploring party up the valley of the Feather River in 1820, and was impressed by the many feathers of wildfowl that he saw floating on the water. Quincy, originally American Ranch, has been the only county seat.

James Pierson Beckwith was born a slave in Virginia in 1798 and was freed by his father. In 1824 he joined a fur-trapping expedition up the Missouri River, and later became an explorer, trader, guide, scout, interpreter, and a chief of the Crow Indians of Montana. In 1854 Beckwith told the story of his life to Thomas D. Bonner, which was published two years later as *The Life and Adventures of James P. Beckwourth*. It is by the latter spelling that his name is remembered today.

Beckwourth Pass (SRL 336) over the High Sierra was discovered by Beckwourth in 1851, while on a prospecting expedition as he and his party crossed the mountains from American Valley to the Pit River Valley. This pass, at 5,212 feet, is the lowest over the summit of the Sierra. It is about two miles east of Chilcoot, on SR 70, which crosses the pass today. Beckwourth realized that the pass facilitated the transit of the Sierra for heavy emigrant wagons headed for the gold fields. He proposed to interested citizens at Bidwell Bar and Marysville to build a wagon road across the pass and down to American Valley and then to widen the existing pack trail between American Valley and Bidwell Bar, eventually reaching Marysville, the supply center for the northern mines. His plan was adopted, although money promised him at Marysville was never paid. As early as August 1851 the first emigrants reached Marysville by the Beckwourth Trail.

By 1852 there were more arrivals over the trail. One of them was an eleven-year-old girl named Ina Coolbrith, who had come with her family in ox-drawn schooners from St. Louis in Missouri. Speaking at a luncheon given in her honor in San Francisco on April 24, 1927, California poet laureate Ina Coolbrith gave this account of her trip:

> Ours was the first of the covered wagon trains to break the trail through Beckwourth Pass into California. We were guided by the famous scout, Jim Beckwourth, who was an historical figure, and to my mind one of the most beautiful creatures that ever lived. He was rather dark and wore his hair in two long braids, twisted with colored cord that gave him a picturesque appearance. He wore a leather coat and moccasins and rode a horse without a saddle.
>
> When we made that long journey toward the West over the deserts and mountains, our wagon train was driven over ground without a single mark of a wagon wheel until it was broken by ours. And when Jim Beckwourth said he would like to have my mother's little girls

Replica of Beckwourth's Cabin

ride into California on his horse in front of him, I was the happiest little girl in the world.

> After two or three days of heavy riding we came at last in sight of California and there on the boundary line he stopped, and pointing forward, said: "Here is California, little girls, here is your kingdom."

In that year of 1852, Beckwourth built a cabin on his "War Horse Ranch," just west of the present town of Beckwourth, fifteen miles west of the pass on SR 70. This, the first house in Sierra Valley, served as a trading post and hotel. It was said that Beckwourth's home "was the first the emigrant met in reaching the Golden State, and money or no money it was open to all who passed."

Beckwourth had renown, but also some bad luck. His first cabin was burned by Indians, as was a second built nearby. A third log cabin soon replaced the first two, and a part of this historic relic stood for many years on a ranch at Walker Mine Road and SR 70. In 1985, the cabin was transported to a new site a quarter of a mile away and is now maintained by Plumas County as a historic landmark. Traffic on the Beckwourth Trail began to fall off after 1855 as other routes were developed. Moreover, it was said that there were many plants along the way that were poisonous to stock. Discouraged, Beckwourth left California in the early 1860s and returned to Montana and the Crow Indians. He died in Montana in 1866 and is buried in an unmarked grave, the location of which is not known.

THE LASSEN TRAIL

The 1848 Lassen Emigrant Trail to California passed through Plumas County by way of Big Meadows, now the site of Lake Almanor. In 1849, over 8,000 emigrants to California passed this way, and Big Meadows became an important stopping place for food and water.

Trails West, Inc. has placed markers along many parts of this trail; one may be seen at Bunnel Point on the shore of Lake Almanor, another at Prattville just across the lake, others on less accessible sites as the trailheads west into the mountains. The Lassen Trail ended at the Sacramento River in Vina, Tehama County.

HUMBOLDT-HUMBUG ROADS

The Humboldt and Humbug Roads meet SR 89 approximately four miles south of the junction with SR 36. These two roads were the original stage and freight routes into the area from the Sacramento Valley. John Bidwell of Chico obtained the franchise to construct a toll road from Chico to the Honey Lake Valley in Lassen County in the early 1860s. The Chico and Humboldt Wagon Company was incorporated in 1864, and in 1865 stage and freight service was established between Chico and Ruby City, Idaho, the main purpose of the road being to supply the mines of Nevada and Idaho. The Humboldt Road, for the first several miles from the junction with SR 89, follows the route of the original Lassen Emigrant Trail. The Humbug Road, slightly older than the Humboldt, probably grew from early stock trails leading from the Oroville-Marysville area to Big Meadows.

THE GOLD LAKE EXCITEMENT

The higher regions of the Sierra Nevada were the last to be prospected during the early days of the Gold Rush. Several hundred argonauts in 1849 passed over the Lassen Trail through what is now northwestern Plumas County, but none stayed to work its streams. One man, however, was instrumental in opening up the country to a later influx of minters. This was J. R. Stoddard, about whom little is known before his arrival in California.

Stoddard claimed to have stumbled upon a lake in the high mountains somewhere between Downieville and Sierra Valley. The shores of this lake, he declared, were literally covered with chunks of gold. He did not reveal its exact location, and much of his story was garbled and unclear. But in these exciting days when strikes were being made all around, Stoddard's story attracted great attention. Soon Stoddard found himself the leader not only of the small group originally chosen to go with him to rediscover this fabled lake of gold, but also of several hundred others, all eager and determined to share in the riches. The number increased, as rumor

spread, until a thousand or more miners left their diggings on the lower reaches of the rivers to join the migration to the new El Dorado.

Gold Lake was never found. Nevertheless, the influx of prospectors into the highlands of the upper Feather River canyons resulted in the opening of the entire region, and many of the tributary streams were found to be very rich. The Gold Lake in Sierra County just across the line from Plumas County, and the much smaller Gold Lake just northwest of Spanish Peak in Plumas County, are reminders of this early excitement over the mythical lake with its gold-pebbled shores.

Intersected by the various forks of the Feather River, the land of the fabled "Gold Lake" is one of rugged scenic grandeur. The sculpturing waters have here chiseled the Sierra with canyons 2,000 feet deep; fertile valleys, watered by countless streams, nestle among giant hills and are made still lovelier by the mirrored beauty of numerous lakes. These valleys include Indian, American, Big Meadows, Buck's, Humbug, Sierra, Mohawk, Genesee, Long, Red Clover, Round, Last Chance, and Onion. Near the southern boundary of the county the South Fork of the Feather River rises in the neighborhood of Pilot Peak, while the Middle Fork, a much longer stream with many tributaries, has its headwaters in Sierra Valley. The North Fork rises in the northwestern corner of the county southeast of Lassen Peak. Flowing almost due south through Big Meadows, now largely occupied by Lake Almanor, it waters a considerable section of Plumas County before joining the Middle Fork of the Feather River at Lake Oroville.

Beginning with the gold excitement of the 1850s, mining, lumbering, and agriculture have played important roles in the history of Plumas County. With an increasing horde of gold-seekers pouring into every corner of the region in the early days, settlements of log cabins sprang up almost overnight. Soon there was a great demand for milled lumber with which to erect better buildings. Agriculture flourished, and ranches were established in the fertile valleys, where water and pasturelands were abundant. Some ranches are still farmed by descendants of the original owners.

Plumas County contains many mineral springs located in various parts of the county: in Humbug Valley, on the North Fork of the Feather River; at Soda Bar on the eastern branch of the North Fork; in Indian Valley near Greenville, where there are warm bathing springs; in Mohawk Valley at the Sulphur Springs Ranch, where both hot and cold water are found; and in many other places. Numerous jets of steam and hot mud accompanied by rumbling noises suggest volcanic activities in Hot Springs Valley near the northwestern corner of the county, as well as at Drakesbad, in the southeastern corner of Lassen Volcanic National Park, by Hot Springs Creek.

RICH BAR

Stragglers of the Gold Lake influence, some of whom worked briefly at the now-vanished camps of Onion Valley (a few miles north of Gibsonville on the Quincy Road) and Nelson's Point (where Nelson Creek meets the Middle Fork of the Feather River), made one of the major discoveries in Plumas County in July 1850 on the eastern branch of the North Fork of the Feather River at a place afterward called Rich Bar. Enormous production records were made at this point, where pans of dirt frequently yielded from $100 to $1,000. It is said that three Germans took out $36,000 in nuggets and gold dust during four days' time. Claims were so rich that they were limited to ten square feet. In the first two years after its discovery, Rich Bar yielded three to four million dollars in gold, thus earning its name. With the approach of the winter of 1850–51, most of the claims at Rich Bar were deserted, although a few log cabins were put up and occupied until the spring of 1851, when a host of miners again flocked to the region.

A vivid and colorful picture of life in this river camp has been preserved for us in the letters of a woman from New England, Mrs. Louise Amelia Knapp Smith Clappe, who lived at Rich Bar in 1851 and 1852. Written to her sister Molly, in the old home at Amherst, Massachusetts, these letters, playfully signed "Dame Shirley," were penned merely to give her sister "a true picture of mining life," with no thought of subsequent publication. However, two years later, they appeared in print, when a friend, Ferdinand C. Ewer of San Francisco, made use of them in *The Pioneer*, a monthly magazine of which he was the publisher and in which the twenty-three "Shirley Letters" appeared during the two years of its existence. These delightful descriptions, written on the spot and glossing nothing over, are the best firsthand account we have of life in the early gold camps, and are frequently quoted in California histories.

With her husband, Dr. Fayette Clappe, "Dame Shirley" came to Rich Bar in the fall of 1851. The journey from Marysville to Bidwell Bar was made in an "excruciatingly springless wagon," with the second stage of the trip negotiated on mule-back over winding mountain trails, passing, at long intervals, a rare and welcome farmhouse, where such things as fresh butter and cream might be obtained. Coming at length to the summit of the high ridge overlooking Rich Bar, she was enchanted with the exquisite beauty of the scene that lay before her: "shadowy nooks" and "far down valleys . . . half a dozen blue-bosomed lagoons. . . . It was worth the whole wearisome journey, danger from Indians, grizzly bears, sleeping under the stars, and all."

Mrs. Clappe soon found herself safely at "Barra Rica," as the Mexicans called it. The third in the series of letters describes it with great charm:

> Imagine a tiny valley, about eight hundred yards in length and, perhaps, thirty in width . . . apparently hemmed in by very lofty hills, almost perpendicular, draperied to their very summits with beautiful fir trees, the blue-bosomed "Plumas," or Feather River, I suppose I must call it, undulating along their base. . . . Through the middle of Rich Bar runs the street, thickly planted with about forty tenements, among which figure round tents, square tents, plank hovels, log cabins, etc.—the residences, varying in splendor from "the Empire" down to a "local habitation," formed of pine boughs, and covered with old calico shirts.

On the steep hillside behind the Empire Hotel lay the lonely graveyard where Nancy Ann Bailey, "the second 'Mrs. B.,'" one of the two women who preceded Mrs. Clappe at Rich Bar, was buried a week after "Dame Shirley"'s arrival. At the head of the bar was the little windowless log cabin in which this pioneer mother died on September 30, 1851, according to the date on the headstone. In 1994, a wooden fence was put up around her grave. Nothing else from the mining period remains at Rich Bar (SRL 337). Overlooking the river stands the Rich Bar monument dedicated by the Native Sons of the Golden West in 1915 in memory of the pioneers who settled at this spot, some of whom are buried on the hillside nearby, and in special honor of Nancy Ann Bailey. The town site is just across the river from SR 70, on the old Western Pacific (now Union Pacific) Railroad, about three miles east of Belden.

INDIAN BAR

In 1852 the Clappes moved to Indian Bar. Mrs. Clappe thus describes the river trail leading to her new home:

> The crossings are formed of logs, often moss-grown. . . . At every step, gold diggers or their operations greet your vision, sometimes in the form of a dam, sometimes in that of a river turned slightly from its channel, to aid the

indefatigable gold hunters in their mining projects. . . .
As we approached Indian Bar, the path led several times
fearfully near deep holes from which the laborers were
gathering their yellow harvest.

Just across from Indian Bar was Pea Soup Bar (not yet named when Mrs. Clappe wrote her letters), while opposite Rich Bar was a narrow diggings later known as Poverty Bar. It was on this bar that builders of the Feather River Highway, SR 70, established camp while blasting out a roadway from the cliffs of the gorge; the road reached the point opposite Rich Bar in the autumn of 1932. The Western Pacific Railroad was constructed up the canyon in 1909, under the leadership of Arthur Keddie (after whom a small town further up the valley is named). The Western Pacific line between Oroville and Chilcoot has thirty-four tunnels. Two are over a mile in length: Spring Garden is 7,344 feet in length and the Chilcoot tunnel is 6,002 feet. This is one of the great engineering projects in the history of California transportation.

SPANISH RANCH

In a part of Meadow Valley about six miles west of Quincy and just north of the old Oroville-Quincy Road, two Mexicans in July 1850 set up a camp. Miners would leave their horses and pack mules in care of these entrepreneurs, who also engaged in cattle raising and slaughtering. Soon names were given to the landmarks nearby: Spanish Creek, Spanish Peak, and Spanish Ranch.

The latter became a distributing center for surrounding camps. The first hotel, blacksmith shop, and store were erected there in 1852 by Lloyd and Snodgrass. A Wells Fargo express office was established in 1868. Millions of dollars in gold dust and nuggets passed through its doors. As late as 1881, the year's output in coin and bullion amounted to $114,076. Directly above the town site towers Spanish Peak (7,047 feet), pierced by the tunnel of the Monte Cristo Mine at an altitude of 6,288 feet, or within 759 feet of the summit.

Two miles southwest of Spanish Ranch is Meadow Valley, an old camp where J. S. Dean settled as early as 1852. A post office called Meadow Valley was established in 1855, but its name was changed to Spanish Ranch in 1861. A change of location may also have been involved. The present Meadow Valley post office was established in 1864. None of the old business buildings remain standing at Spanish Ranch and Meadow Valley (SRL 481). Two and a quarter miles west of Meadow Valley on the old stage road between Quincy and Oroville is the site of Toll Gate, where tolls were collected on one of the first turnpikes in Plumas County. The buildings here, too, have all disappeared.

Seven miles farther southwest the road passed Buck's Ranch, which was first occupied in the fall of 1850 by Horace Bucklin and Francis Walker. The Buck's Ranch Hotel served for years as a stage station and an express and post office. In the early days it was a haven for pioneers, where miners' pack trains stopped en route to the Feather River mines; later it became an important point in the passenger, express, and mail service to and from Quincy and other towns. The site is under the waters of Buck's Lake (SRL 197), which now covers most of Buck's Valley. The dam was constructed in 1925–27. In the rich Gravel Range District near Buck's Ranch, miners were known to have found gold, silver, and copper all in one ledge.

Beyond Grizzly Gulch, about 3.5 miles west of Buck's Lake, is a meadow amid the forest. Here, visible from the road, stands a granite monument (SRL 212) marking the grave of P. Linthiouh, a nineteen-year-old pioneer who was robbed and killed by bandits in September 1852. A comrade buried him under a pine tree, on which his name and age and fate were carved; the text is repeated on the monument, but the tree is gone.

LA PORTE

La Porte (SRL 213) is an old mining camp located on Rabbit Creek, a tributary of Slate Creek in the southwest corner of Plumas County. It was known as Rabbit Creek or Rabbit Town from 1850 to 1857. This area was part of Yuba County until 1852 and Sierra County until 1868. During the 1860s and 1870s it was a populous center for hydraulic mining. After 1884, when hydraulic mining became illegal, La Porte dwindled in population until it had only a few dozen inhabitants. Electricity, which most Californians had long enjoyed, belatedly came to La Porte in 1964. The area is having a revival as a sports, recreation, and retirement area, with winter and summer activities. It remains so out-of-the-way, however, that still there is no paved, all-year road linking the community to the county seat at Quincy, or any other part of the county. The Union Hotel, also known as the Rabbit Creek Hotel and begun in 1855 by the Coyot family, still stands but is not open. The family members are buried in the beautiful enclosed cemetery in the town.

Nearby stone walls are all that is left after a 1969 explosion destroyed the general store. The Frank C. Reilly

Union Hotel, La Porte

Museum, the creation of the local E Clampus Vitus branch, which also bears his name, opened in 1992. It is a modern building, filled with displays of old mining and lumber equipment. A stamp mill that was moved from the Oro Fino Mine on Hopkins Creek stands next to the museum; the mill was powered by a Pelton Wheel on one end and a steam engine on the other. The La Porte Pines Country Club is the site of what is claimed to be the world's first recorded ski race, in 1860.

ELIZABETHTOWN, OR BETSYBURG

Miners went to the region of Elizabethtown (SRL 231) in 1852 in search of gold. There being only one unmarried lady in the camp, Elizabeth Stark, the chivalrous miners named the new town in her honor. Elizabethtown, or Betsyburg as it was also humorously known, was a large camp by 1853, and within two years a post office was established there. But the surrounding gulches were soon exhausted. After Quincy was made the seat of Plumas County in 1854 the post office moved there, and Elizabethtown began a long decline. Today, only tailings from the old mines indicate its one-time activity. SR 70 passes through the Elizabethtown area two miles north of Quincy, near the campus of Feather River College.

QUINCY

The American Ranch was owned by James H. Bradley, one of the three commissioners who organized Plumas County. Owing to his influence, the seat of justice was decreed to be at the hotel on his ranch. With this as a nucleus, he laid out a town, calling it Quincy after his hometown in Illinois, and the people were induced to vote for Quincy as the county seat. The site of Bradley's American Hotel (SRL 479) is at Main and Fillmore Streets.

The part of Quincy bounded by Main, Church, Jackson, and Buchanan Streets is full of old buildings, some of which have been marked. The oldest building is the Masonic Hall on Harrison Avenue between Jackson and Main Streets, moved from Elizabethtown the year after it was built in 1854. Several homes still standing were constructed of lumber brought from abandoned houses in Elizabethtown.

The Methodist Episcopal church at Church and Jackson Streets dates from 1877. The memorial windows dated around 1912 are one of its special features. At Court and Main Streets is the site of the Plumas House (SRL 480), which was built in 1866, replacing an earlier log structure on the site. The hotel was destroyed by fire in 1923, and the Hotel Quincy built on the site met a like fate in 1966. The site is now a city park.

The pride of the town is the Plumas County Courthouse on Court Street, built in 1920 in Classic Revival style, replacing the earlier 1859 structure. The courthouse was criticized for its large size when it was put up—county supervisors insisted the architects provide "enough room"—but their foresight is appreciated today, county business having increased greatly since 1920. The interior is of Tuolumne County marble.

Quincy was one of the stations of Whiting and Company's Dog Express, which in the early days brought the mails over the Sierra. For stretches of twenty miles through snow-covered mountain country, Newfoundlands or St. Bernards, driven tandem, two or four to a team, pulled sledges often carrying loads of over six hundred pounds: passengers, express, and mail were all transported. This operation brought much-needed service to the community from 1858 until the invention of the horse snowshoe in 1865.

The Plumas County Museum at 500 Jackson Street has displays on the Maidu Indians and several changing exhibits on the commercial activities of the county's past. Across the street is the Coburn-Variel Home, built in 1878 by Indiana-born Joshua Variel and his son Will; it went through various owners and circumstances until acquired by the museum in 1996. At the Plumas County Fairgrounds, two miles east of downtown Quincy, the first schoolhouse in Plumas County (SRL 625) can be seen. It was built in 1857 by the residents of the eastern end of American Valley.

PLUMAS-EUREKA STATE PARK

A few miles to the west of Blairsden and Graeagle is Plumas-Eureka State Park, which includes or surrounds several important landmarks of mining days: Johnsville, Eureka Mills, and the Plumas-Eureka Mine (SRL 196.)

Operations started at the Plumas-Eureka Mine, situated on the east slope of Eureka Park, in the summer of 1851. A company of thirty-six men was formed, but instead of setting up stamp mills at once, they wisely mined with arrastras, or drag stones, until sufficient money had been made to warrant improvement. Chili wheels, heavy wheels rotated around a pivot, superseded the arrastras, and, finally, in 1856, a mill with twelve stamps was erected. In the vicinity of the Plumas-Eureka other quartz mines were opened at various times. To the northeast was the Mammoth Mine, worked by a company of eighty with the use of arrastras until they, too, erected a twelve-stamp mill. Two other mines in the vicinity, the Washington and the Rough-and-Ready, were not financially successful, because their promoters spent all their profits on equipment. The Washington Mine was owned by a company of seventy-six men, who laid out an ephemeral town on Jamison Creek, calling it the City of 76.

All of these claims—the Plumas-Eureka, Mammoth, Washington, and Rough-and-Ready—were bought by John Parrott, who sold them to the Sierra Buttes Company of London in 1872. This company represented a consolidated mining venture that had considerable success until the early 1890s, when productivity declined and the individual mines were sold off, the last ceasing activity in 1943.

Johnstown, now called Johnsville, was laid out in 1876 on Jamison Creek one-half mile east of the Plumas-Eureka Mine (it is not part of the state park and its buildings are private property). A few old buildings still stand in this village, notably the little firehouse built in 1908 and the rustic Catholic church. In this region of heavy snows, neglected buildings quickly deteriorate and even those of recent construction soon look very old. The "Johnsville Hotel" is now a private dwelling.

The headquarters of the Plumas-Eureka State Park are a short distance from Johnsville. The charming museum with its excellent displays of natural history, Maidu Indian artifacts, and mining activities is lodged in the former mine bunkhouse and office, and the massive fireplace still gets good use in the winter. A pair of skis (then called "snow-shoes") used by John A. ("Snow-Shoe") Thompson is displayed here. Johnsville is the pioneer ski area of America, attested by a monument (SRL 723) across the road from the museum. Winter sports events in the High Sierra were run annually as early as 1860. LaPorte, Onion Valley, Jamison City, and Johnsville, as well as the Sierra County towns of Whiskey Diggings, Poker Flat, Port Wine, and Howland Flat, organized the earliest ski clubs and held contests that resulted in some notable speed records. The VIII Olympic Winter Games, of 1960, held at Squaw Valley some sixty miles to the south, commemorated a century of sport skiing in California.

Across the parking lot from the museum stands the massive Eureka Mill, a wooden structure seventy-two feet high, where millions of dollars in gold were produced. The old forty-eight-stamp mill, once leaning precariously and falling into ruin, has been carefully restored. Mining equipment can be seen on exhibit in the grounds; a massive ore crusher is particularly striking.

A short distance from the park headquarters along the road to Gibsonville is a monument marking the old trail from Jamison City to Marysville. It consists of a stone taken from one of the early Jamison Creek arrastras and was dedicated in 1932 by the Native Sons and Daughters of the Golden West of Plumas County; a second marker was placed at Split Rock, now on an abandoned section of road between Johnsville and Mohawk. From this rock early miners obtained the arrastra stones that formed the primitive mills used to grind out the gold. The pioneer trail to Mohawk Valley passed near the site of this marker.

PORTOLA

Situated on the Middle Fork of the Feather River, in a region famous for its recreational facilities, the town of Portola is also a noted railroad center. Shortly after 1900, the Western Pacific Railroad came through here while completing a line from California to Salt Lake City. In 1985, the Feather River Rail Society, with the cooperation of the Union Pacific Railroad (which now owns the Western Pacific), opened the Portola Railroad Museum adjacent to the tracks of the main line. Here are locomotives and rolling stock from Western Pacific and some other lines, in good repair and taken out on the special tracks. The museum is open during the summer.

BLAIRSDEN, MOHAWK, AND GRAEAGLE

These three towns are clustered in the valley of the Middle Fork of the Feather River a few miles west of Portola. Blairsden is the site of the Feather River Inn, a luxurious resort built in 1915. "Virtually a small city," its historical brochure tells us, "the Inn generated its own electricity, raised its own cattle, operated its own dairy,

1864 Schoolhouse, Taylorsville

Indian Valley Museum, Taylorsville

ice plant, laundry, and dry cleaning facilities. In the 1950s, an airstrip was built west of the golf course so that guests could fly in." After being connected with the University of the Pacific as a school from 1977 to 1987, the resort was taken over by a group of UOP alumni who are now operating it as a conference and retreat facility. Mohawk was once a prosperous agricultural center for surrounding mines. All its early buildings have been destroyed by fire. It is now a popular resort.

Graeagle was once a lumber company town, and on the main street of the community one will see its distinctive red houses, large and small, all trimmed with white. These houses have been maintained for many years and are now all privately owned; some are used as commercial or professional buildings. Most of Graeagle today consists of new homes and resorts.

INDIAN VALLEY

Peter Lassen, the first pioneer to settle in Indian Valley, came there with Isadore Meyrowitz in the fall of 1850. Lassen called the spot Cache Valley, but later settlers gave it the name of Indian Valley because of the many Indians living there. Lassen and a man named Burton built a log cabin there in 1851, four and a half miles east of the town of Greenville, and developed a thriving trading post. Vegetables were raised and sold to the miners at high prices. The site (SRL 184) is on North Valley Road.

At Greenville, long a center of quartz mining, a bullion ledge was discovered in 1851 and first mined with profit by John W. Ellis in 1856. The Lone Star Mine was first worked there in 1857. At Round Valley, south of Greenville, John Ellis opened up the Ellis Mine in 1862, and a large camp grew up about the stamp mill. With the abandonment of the mine, the settlement faded out. Greenville is the largest town in Indian Valley to-

day. Southeast of Greenville at Crescent Mills quartz-mining and milling operations were carried on as late as 1926.

Two famous copper mines in the mountains east of Indian Valley made fine production records, and they continued to employ a large number of men until they were shut down. One was the Engel Mine, closed in 1930, fifteen miles northeast of Crescent Mills; the other was the Walker Mine, northwest of Portola and Beckwourth, which yielded $1,099,000 in copper in 1931 but was closed in 1941.

Between the broad meadows of Indian Valley and the dense evergreen forests of Mount Hough lies Taylorsville, founded by Jobe T. Taylor in 1852. A quiet charm pervades the town, with its great barns, shady streets, white-steepled community church, substantial and dignified old houses, and the burial ground of the pioneers, close against the hill in a tiny oak wood. A monument here marks the grave of Jobe Taylor. The present school stands on the site of the Taylor Hotel, which was built by the founder in 1859 and burned in 1949. A marker dedicated by the Native Sons of the Golden West stands in front of the school. Millstones from Taylor's gristmill, which was built in 1856 and destroyed by fire in 1918, were incorporated into the marker. At this site in 1852 Taylor built the first permanent residence in Indian Valley, later replaced by his hotel. The original one-room redbrick schoolhouse, built in 1864, still stands at the north edge of Taylorsville. It is now owned and maintained by the Native Sons of the Golden West, Plumas Parlor of Taylorsville.

The Indian Valley Museum, located in the Mount Jura Gem and Mineral Society Building next to the cemetery, contains extensive photographs and artifacts of the region and of the Maidu people. Outside, there is an interesting mining display around a mine tunnel entrance built into the adjoining hill.

BIG MEADOWS, PRATTVILLE, AND LAKE ALMANOR

Big Meadows, consisting of more than 30,000 acres along the North Fork of the Feather River, was an early stock-raising region in the middle of the surrounding mining and lumber country. The salubrious summer air led to the establishment of a resort, Prattville Springs, by Dr. Willard Pratt around 1880. Dr. Pratt, who was born in Pennsylvania and had practiced in Wisconsin, came overland in 1853 and practiced in mining communities. In 1859 he moved to the Sacramento Valley, first to Colusa and then to Chico, where his descendants still live. After retiring from the practice of medicine, he moved to Big Meadows; the town of Prattville developed around the two-story frame hotel he erected there. He died in 1888.

Big Meadows was bought out in 1907 by the Great Western Power Company, which in 1910–14 constructed a dam at the eastern end of the meadows. The lake thus created, Lake Almanor, was for two decades the largest man-made hydroelectric power reservoir in the United States. ("Almanor" was derived from the names of three daughters of Guy Earl, a founder of Great Western.) The cemetery at Prattville was relocated to a hillside where the modern community of Prattville now stands, and Dr. Willard Pratt's grave and monument now lie with others in a grove of tall, shadowing cedars. Now the property of the Pacific Gas and Electric Company, which bought out Great Western in 1930, Lake Almanor is a popular summer resort, and the permanent residents of the new Prattville still praise its salubrious air.

CHESTER

The western end of Big Meadows was a favored summer retreat from the heat of the Sacramento Valley. General and Mrs. John Bidwell of Chico had a campsite there and planned a more substantial home for their later years. A year after the general's death in 1900 the house was completed, and it was used by Mrs. Bidwell until her death in 1918. In 1926 it was hauled on skids to its present location on the northeast end of Main Street in Chester. Until the 1960s it was the summer headquarters for the Stover-McKenzie Cattle Company. The Bidwell House today is a restored Victorian-style bed-and-breakfast inn.

The Chester–Lake Almanor Museum adjoins the Chester Library on First Avenue. Opened in 1985, the museum's displays feature local Maidu Indian culture, nineteenth-century pioneer farming and dairying activities, and early twentieth-century hydroelectric and lumber industrial development.

Riverside County

Riverside County was created in 1893 from territory originally belonging to San Bernardino and San Diego Counties. The city of Riverside, founded in 1870 on a channel of the Santa Ana River, has always been the county seat, and gave its name to the county.

Riverside County is exceptionally rich in Indian rock carvings and paintings. The pictographs are painted in a vivid red pigment, while others combine the red with white and black colors. They are often found near a spring or watering place, or near traditional camping grounds, where these rock pictures may have been left as signboards. Only a few of these drawings have been deciphered, and modern Indian tribes do not know their origin or meaning.

There were once seven Indian villages in the San Jacinto Valley: Ivah; Soboba, near Soboba Hot Springs; Jusispah, at today's town of San Jacinto; Ararah, in Webster's Canyon on the road to Idyllwild; Pahsitnah, the largest in the valley, near Big Springs Ranch; Corova, the most northern, in Castle Canyon; and a small settlement of the Serranos from San Bernardino, near Eden Hot Springs. It is said that the tribes who lived here were among the most powerful of any in the Southwest, and this region with its great peaks of San Jacinto and Tahquitz has an abundance of Indian lore. There may be many carved and painted rocks in this region as yet undiscovered.

One of the finest of the Riverside group of pictographs is found in Indian Relic County Park in Fern Valley, on the northeast side of Idyllwild. Painted in vivid red on the face of a huge rock, the pictograph is apparently unfaded in spite of the action of the elements upon it. The design, too, is unusual and constitutes a remarkable piece of workmanship, conforming, so scientists say, to rock paintings and designs found among the early Aztecs of Mexico. In one interpretation, it tells the story of a great hunt: the long trail that the hunters follow, their encounter with a bear, the crossing of streams and the climbing of mountains, a skirmish with members of a hostile tribe, the trail again, the final kill, and the great feast.

The Maze Stone (SRL 557) is a remarkable petroglyph in Maze Stone County Park, three miles north of SR 74 and five miles west of Hemet. A huge swastika (a symbol associated with the Indians from ancient times) has been carved into a massive granite boulder. The larger figure is made up of four smaller swastikas, the whole being about four feet in diameter. A theory that surfaces from time to time notes that the design is very close to one found in Tibet or some part of Asia. There is an old story that some monks from China were cast ashore on a remote land, befriended by darker-skinned natives, brought to a region with plants resembling the agave, and eventually returned home, around the year 458 A.D. The Maze Stone is a mysterious artifact that invites speculation.

About seven-tenths of a mile east of the Ramona Bowl, on the southern edge of Hemet, is the site of the village of Pochea (SRL 104), one of the "seven villages of Pahsitnah." In the vicinity are a number of flat granite rocks whose surfaces are covered with grinding holes. The Ramona Bowl Museum displays Indian artifacts as well as the history of the Ramona Pageant, held here since 1923.

There are many other Indian rocks, both petroglyphs and pictographs, scatted throughout Riverside County. In Dawson Canyon is an interesting painted rock (SRL 190) that has been marked by the Corona Women's Improvement Club. This rock, found in the right-of-way of the Santa Fe Railroad, was saved from destruction by the club and placed in a cement base by the Santa Fe Railroad Company in 1927.

Chief Lafio of Temecula said the painted rock was the work of the Temecula (Luiseño) Indians, perhaps telling of a three-day fiesta or a religious celebration. It may have been, however, a flood warning, since the San Jacinto River formerly flowed beside the rock and on it are four water signs similar to those found on other rocks listed in the report of the United States Bureau of Ethnography. The painted rock is reached by the Dawson Canyon Fireroad, which turns to the east from the Temescal Canyon Road seven and a half miles south of Corona. A distance of only a quarter of a mile along the Dawson Canyon road brings one to the old Serrano tanning vats, immediately adjacent to the road on the right. From this point the painted rock may be seen across the field on the opposite side of the road. It stands next to the railroad track and is reached by an easy hike. In the vicinity there is also a carved rock (SRL 187), which is reached by the winding road through the clay pits that turns right from the Dawson Canyon Fireroad just one-tenth of a mile past the old tanning vats. A twisting mile or so along the clay pit road will bring one into clear view of a great natural amphitheater, in the midst of which stands the rock. Its top has been damaged, but many of the carvings are still intact.

In Mockingbird Canyon, between Riverside and Perris, there are two groups of painted rocks near the Mockingbird Springs. Other Indian rocks are located on private property throughout southwestern Riverside County.

The Coachella Valley was once a great inland lake,

the shoreline of which is still visible in places to the southwest of present-day Coachella. At the western end of Avenue 66, some ten miles south of Coachella, there is a remarkable group of circular depressions among a maze of boulders just below the ancient shoreline. Some authorities believe them to be vestiges of fish traps; others say they were foundations for primitive houses. Whatever the case, they were made by human hands a long time ago. The old shoreline extends down through the Imperial Valley into Mexico.

The ancient village of Ivah once thrived in the region of the present town of San Jacinto, near Massacre Canyon, on the Gilman Hot Springs Road. Many years ago a battle was fought there over a crop of chia, a grain that grew wild on nearly all the mesa lands. The story goes that a severe drought in southern California caused the total failure of the chia crop in Temecula Valley. The Temeculas, who were a tribe distinctly separate from the seven tribes at San Jacinto, and more warlike, came in search of seeds. Proceeding to gather the crop belonging to the village of Ivah, they precipitated a fierce battle. The Ivahs fought valiantly, but being outnumbered they were forced to flee into the narrow ravine now known as Massacre Canyon. There, with their backs against a vertical wall, they fought to their death. Long afterward Massacre Canyon received its name from the white settlers, who had heard the story from elderly Indians.

Perhaps the most inexplicable prehistoric relics in the county, both as to age and to purpose or meaning, are the giant desert figures (SRL 101) just west of the Colorado River. They represent both humans and animals and are best seen from the air, from which they were discovered. The largest of them is 167 feet long. The mesa is covered with sandstone pebbles that were moved by early people in such a way that bare earth was left to form the figures, the pebbles being placed in windrows about the edge as an outline. Now on the National Register of Historic Places, they have been fenced off by the Bureau of Land Management, which is attempting to protect these artifacts from further vandalism. Their location is about half a mile west of US 95, some seventeen miles north of Blythe.

PALM SPRINGS AND DESERT HOT SPRINGS

Palm Springs was once the exclusive domain of the Agua Caliente Indians. The world-famous resort is located on and around the Agua Caliente Indian Reservation. At the corner of Indian Canyon Drive and

Mission Inn, Riverside

Tahquitz Way is the Palm Springs Spa Hotel, on the grounds of which still flow the springs first discovered by the Indians. The first resort hotel was opened in the 1880s.

John Guthrie McCallum was the first American settler in the Palm Springs area; he arrived in 1884 and put up an adobe house. This has been moved from its original location on Palm Canyon Drive, once a rough dirt road, and now stands at 221 South Palm Canyon Drive, where it serves as the Palm Springs Historical Society Museum. The Village Green Heritage Center, where the museum is located, also has Miss Cornelia White's "Little House," built in 1893 by Welwood Murray, the city's first hotel operator. In the same center is Ruddy's General Store Museum, a re-creation of a village general store from earlier in the twentieth century. In 1991, the Agua Caliente Band of Cahuilla Indians established their Cultural Museum in the center. All of these are well displayed and amazingly diverse in their contents.

Two miles to the south of Palm Springs in the Palm, Murray, and Andreas Canyons are magnificent groves of native date palms, one of the grandest spectacles in all the Southwest. The Washingtonia palms are estimated to be from 1,500 to 2,000 years old. Here, too, in certain spring seasons after heavy rains may be witnessed the miracle of vast wildflower gardens springing as if by magic from the dry sands of the desert. The Palm Springs Aerial Tramway, two miles west of the city, has been called the "eighth engineering wonder of the world." Completed in 1963, the 13,200-foot line climbs from Valley Station in Chino Canyon (elevation 2,643 feet) to Mountain Station (elevation 8,516 feet) on the slopes of Mount San Jacinto.

Since World War II, Palm Springs and the adjacent region have been favorite vacation spots for such celebrities as Presidents Eisenhower, Ford, and Reagan, as well as many entertainers, after whom streets and local landmarks have been named.

Desert Hot Springs, about a dozen miles northeast of Palm Springs, was not discovered until early in the twentieth century. A remarkable structure at 67616 East Desert View Avenue is a thirty-five-room structure built by Cabot Yerxa, who settled in the area in 1913. Once operated as a museum of Western and Indian artifacts and many curiosities, it has been closed in recent years.

Indian Wells, seventeen miles southeast of Palm Springs on SR 111, is the site of an Indian ranchería where a life-giving well was in use until 1910. Mount Eisenhower on the south edge of the community honors a former part-time resident. The Living Desert Reserve in Palm Desert, three miles west, is a 1,200-acre park that preserves much of the desert life and atmosphere.

THE PECHANGA BURIAL GROUND

About five miles southeast of Temecula is the Pechanga Indian Reservation. A distinctive feature of the place is the old chapel and burial ground, where, it is supposed, Alessandro, hero of Helen Hunt Jackson's novel *Ramona*, buried his father after the massacre at Temecula. Mrs. Jackson's description of the cemetery is still accurate more than a century later: "The cemetery is quaint. . . . Broken pieces of pottery and household utensils are placed on the graves, whether in decoration or with the thought of possible need by those buried there, is debatable. . . . Small metates, bits of colored glass, parts of lamps, children's toys" can still be seen.

SAN CARLOS PASS AND ANZA'S TRAIL

San Carlos Pass, the first inland gateway to the coast of California, was discovered by Captain Juan Bautista de Anza in 1774 on the first continuous overland journey into the state. The trail and the pass were located by Professor Herbert E. Bolton of the University of California, and in 1924 the Native Sons of the Golden West marked them with a tablet bearing the following inscription:

> On March 6, 1774, Juan Bautista de Anza, Indian fighter, explorer and colonizer, led through this Pass (named by him, San Carlos) the first white explorers to cross the mountains into California. The party traveled from

Tubac, Arizona, to Monterey, California. On December 27, 1775, on a second expedition into California, Anza led through the Pass the party of Spaniards from Sonora who became the founders of San Francisco.

A marker (SRL 103) stands on the Anza Trail about eight miles southeast of the little town of Anza on the Cary Ranch. About a mile and half east of Anza the Terwilliger Road turns south from SR 71; at a point just under five miles along Terwilliger Road the Coyote Canyon Road turns east one and one-half miles to the Cary Ranch.

On March 16 the travelers marched through Cahuilla Valley to Laguna Principe, now known as Dry Lake and located on the Contreras Ranch. Another short march on the following day took them as far as San Patricio, at the head of Bautista Canyon. Following this canyon, the expedition descended the mountain to Rio de San Joseph, now the San Jacinto River. This was on March 18, and camp was pitched in a leafy cottonwood grove about three miles above the site of San Jacinto.

On March 19 Anza and his party passed San Jacinto Lake, now dry, camping at its western end. Turning west the next day, they proceeded past the site of Morena through Alessandro Valley, and descended the ridge, probably by way of Sycamore Canyon. Crossing the site of Riverside, the expedition stopped near an Indian village on the banks of the Santa Ana River about three miles southwest of Mount Rubidoux near the Union Pacific railroad bridge (SRL 787). Here, on March 20, a bridge of logs was thrown across the river, and the following day the party crossed the river. On the 22nd they entered San Bernardino County, and on the 24th they arrived at Mission San Gabriel.

Returning from Monterey in April 1774, Anza retraced his steps through Riverside County early in May, stopping again at some of his previous campsites. On May 10 he was once more at Yuma.

In December 1775, Anza again passed over this route as the leader of the band of pioneers who first settled San Francisco. On Christmas Eve, camp was made near the upper end of Coyote Canyon at Upper Willows, or Fig Tree Spring.

Here, shortly before midnight, a baby boy, Salvador Ignacio Linares, was born, the third and last birth after leaving Tubac. The colonists, forgetting their misery for a time, spent that first Christmas Eve in California singing and dancing and partaking a little too freely, perhaps, of the *aguardiente* that Anza had given them against the protests of Father Font. On Christmas morning, the travelers being detained in the canyon for another day on account of little Salvador, the priest took the opportunity to rebuke his now-repentant flock with a sermon, at the close of which he wished everybody a happy Christmas. In 1950 the California Centennials Commission put up a monument in Coyote Canyon near the San Diego County line to commemorate the birth of the first white child in California.

From here, the route was, with one variation, the same as on Anza's previous trip. After leaving Lake San Jacinto, the company went past the site of Lakeview, through Bernasconi Pass, and across Alessandro Valley by way of March Air Reserve Base to the old campsite on the Santa Ana River.

The route that Anza opened up at this time was used infrequently for a while. Along it came the colonists for Los Angeles, and the troops for the presidio at Santa Barbara, but after Fages's expedition in 1782 it was abandoned because of the hostility of the Yuma Indians. A statue of Anza stands at Fourteenth and Market Streets in Riverside.

THE OLD EMIGRANT TRAIL AND THE SAN BERNARDINO–SONORA ROAD

Anza's route across the mountains was superseded by another trail opened in 1782 by Pedro Fages, who, instead of following the older path back to San Gabriel after his expedition against the Yuma Indians, blazed a new one, coming into San Diego County by way of the Carrizo Creek, Vallecito, and over the Cuyamaca Mountains to Mission San Diego.

Santiago Argüello, while in pursuit of Indian horse thieves, rediscovered this trail in 1825. In January 1826 the Mexican government sent Romualdo Pacheco, lieutenant of engineers, to investigate it, and with his approval an official mail route was adopted via Carrizo Creek, Vallecito, San Felipe Valley, and Warner's Pass. A small detachment of soldiers was briefly garrisoned on the Colorado River to protect the road but apparently encountered no hostility. From then the road was occasionally used by mail carriers and traders from Sonora. Probably the first Americans to come this way were David E. Jackson and his party of fur traders, who had come overland from Santa Fe in 1831. Later it came to be known as the Emigrant Trail and formed a part of the Southern Emigrant Trail, a much-traveled route from the East into California during the 1840s and 1850s.

In Riverside and San Bernardino Counties there were two branches of the old Emigrant Trail. From the Colorado River to Warner's Ranch and continuing west to Aguanga there was one road. There the San Bernardino–Sonora Road branched north along the western base of the San Jacinto Mountains, while the Colorado Road went directly west and then northwest through the valley north of the Santa Ana Mountains. This section of the road through Riverside and San Bernardino Counties to San Gabriel was called the Canyon Road by the mission fathers, who opened it up immediately after Romualdo Pacheco had reestablished the overland route by way of Warner's. It was by the latter route that Jackson traversed Riverside County on his way to San Gabriel, going by way of Temecula, Elsinore, Temescal Canyon, and Corona.

The San Bernardino–Sonora Road passed through Riverside County west of modern Beaumont and turned south, passing through Lamb Canyon to San Jacinto and from there to what is now Hemet. It continued southward along what is now Sage Road to Aguanga, where it merged with another road from San Gabriel that was designated as the Colorado Road. From here the road continued into the desert and to Sonora. The well-traveled road was later used by Americans in their westward marches into California.

THE BUTTERFIELD OVERLAND STAGE ROUTE

The Butterfield route from St. Louis to Los Angeles passed through Riverside County on a route marked by the modern towns of Temecula, Lake Elsinore, and Corona. The long-vanished stage station at 20730 Temescal Canyon Road, four miles southeast of Corona, is marked by SRL 188. A short intact portion of the road lies in the Alberhill section of Elsinore Valley. To the southeast, on the old Machado ranch property, some vestiges of the stage route remain.

One of the old Machado adobes, possibly the one used as a Butterfield stage station, was at 32912 Macy Street near Grand Avenue on the southwest side of Lake Elsinore. It and a small adobe outbuilding have been razed, but the site is marked by three distinctive tall palm trees. Two rooms of another Machado adobe have been incorporated into the house at 15410 Grand Avenue. Agustín Machado acquired the Rancho La Laguna in 1858 from Abel Stearns, who had purchased it from the heirs of the original grantee, Julián Manríquez. The grant of over 13,000 acres was made by Governor Micheltorena in 1844.

The Bradshaw Road was a passage between the Colorado River and the Coachella Valley. Only two unconnected, unpaved pieces of the road remain. The easternmost extends twenty miles west from the end of 30th Avenue in the Palo Verde Valley. The other follows the Salt Creek Wash north of the Chocolate Mountains. At Wiley Well, named for the storekeeper and postmaster A. P. Wiley, nine miles west of Blythe at the junction of Bradshaw Trail and Wiley Well Road, E Clampus Vitus has placed a commemorative plaque. Another point marked by the society is at Shaver's Well, on Box Canyon Road. A third site commemorated by the Clampers is at Chiriaco Summit on I-10.

This point was crossed by US 60 of the new federal highway system in the early 1930s, the first modern road designed for automobiles and trucks in the region. In 1933, Joseph L. Chiriaco opened a gas station and general store at what was then called Shavers Summit, a little over forty miles east of Indio and twenty miles west of Desert Center. In the early months of World War II, a site next to Shavers Summit became Camp Young, headquarters of the Desert Training Center (SRL 985). The Colorado River Aqueduct passed by the campsite, providing the water necessary to maintain thousands of men. One of the first units transferred to the DTC, the 773rd Tank Destroyer Battalion, recorded in its official history: "Camp Young was the world's largest Army post and the greatest training maneuver area in U.S. military history, 18,000 square miles of nothing, in a desert designed in hell." Major General George S. Patton Jr. came to Camp Young in 1942 as the first commandant of the Desert Training Center. He established ten other camps in the Southwest deserts, where in the next two years twenty divisions consisting of more than one million men trained for combat. The camps were closed in 1944. Shortly after the end of the war in 1945, General Patton died from injuries sustained in an accident, and a memorial was planned for this celebrated Californian at the site of Camp Young. The Desert Training Center Museum was soon opened in one of the abandoned buildings from the camp. In 1958 Shavers was officially renamed Chiriaco Summit. The Chiriaco family later donated land for the building of a new facility, which was dedicated in 1988 as the General George S. Patton

Memorial Museum. The Bureau of Land Management has been a participant in this project and is attempting to preserve the remains of the sites, although they are very extensive in area. The Patton Museum has an interesting display of combat tanks from World War II, as well as much personal material from the general's career.

OLD TEMESCAL ROAD

A monument (SRL 638) has been placed at the junction of the Temescal Canyon Road and the road to Glen Ivy Hot Springs, 8.8 miles southeast of the intersection of Ontario Avenue and Main Street south of Corona. It commemorates the old Temescal Road, which has seen the transition from Indian trail to automobile highway, with many an explorer, argonaut, stagecoach, and military convoy in between. I-15 now passes through here, superseding SR 71, but old roads parallel the modern freeway, and along these historical landmarks are still to be found.

The first house in Riverside County was built by Leandro Serrano in 1824. Don Leandro was the son of a soldier who had come to San Diego with Father Junipero Serra in 1769. He became mayordomo of Pala Chapel, and in 1818, because of his long and faithful service and his influence over the Indians, the priest of Mission San Luís Rey sent him to settle on the mission lands in Temescal Valley, where many Indians were then living.

The valley contained groves of oak and sycamore, fields of wildflowers, and green marshes or *ciénegas*. A large Indian ranchería and sweat house or *temescal* were located nearby, and Serrano enlisted the natives in a drive against the bears and mountain lions of the region before bringing in his sheep and cattle.

The site of Serrano's adobe (SRL 185) is marked with a plaque on a boulder at the junction of Lawson Drive and Temescal Canyon Road, just north of Glen Ivy Hot Springs. Nearby, where Temescal Canyon Road meets Dawson Canyon Road, the site of the third Serrano adobe is marked (SRL 224). Also marked are the tanning vats (SRL 186), two of which are still visible, used for the preparation of hides on the rancho. Serrano lived in the area until his death in 1852; his family continued to live here until the end of the century.

The city of Corona, largely situated on the Rancho La Sierra of Bernardo Yorba, has honored its founders of 1886 by a monument (SRL 738) in the city park on

Sixth Street between Rimpau Avenue and East Grand Boulevard. Corona was formerly called South Riverside.

RANCHO JURUPA

Rancho Jurupa, a portion of which later became the Rubidoux Ranch, and on a part of which the city of Riverside now stands, was granted to Juan Bandini in 1838. Don Juan was a well-educated Peruvian gentleman of Italian descent who came to this part of California in 1828. A man of unusual ability, he was a member of the Territorial Assembly and at various times held many important offices in California. One of his daughters married Cave J. Couts and another wed Abel Stearns; thus Don Juan was identified with the emerging American political leadership as well.

Juan Bandini was one of the first white settlers in Riverside County, and in 1839 he built his first home on Rancho Jurupa. The site was on a high bluff along the northwest side of the Santa Ana River, about one thousand feet west of Hamner Boulevard at a point one-half mile north of the Santa Ana River bridge, five and one-half miles north of Corona. This site was three and one-half miles upstream from Bandini's later adobe (the Cota house). Rancho Jurupa consisted of over 32,000 acres of land, which extended for twenty miles along both sides of the Santa Ana River. The plains to the east of the river were considered worthless and were left wild and uncultivated or used for the pasturage of thousands of sheep. Today, the city of Riverside covers the old Jurupa "bench lands." Extensive orange groves replaced the sheep ranges, and these in turn have given way in large part to homes. The southeast corner of Rancho Jurupa is the prominent landmark of Pachappa Hill at the eastern end of Jurupa Avenue in Riverside. In 1859, the year of Don Juan's death, most of Rancho Jurupa was sold to his son-in-law Abel Stearns.

RUBIDOUX RANCH

On May 6, 1843, Juan Bandini sold one and a half leagues of Rancho Jurupa to Benjamin D. Wilson, a native of Tennessee. Wilson, affectionately known as "Don Benito" among the Californians, had been a trader in New Mexico. On coming to California he bought this property and settled down as a ranchero, marrying Ramona Yorba, daughter of Bernardo Yorba, his nearest neighbor. He was held in high regard by the Californians, and among the American pioneers he was a notable friend to the Indians. Robert Glass Cleland said of him: "A man of brave and adventurous spirit, who dealt justly and walked uprightly throughout the entire course of his romantic and richly varied life, B. D. Wilson might be selected as an example of the most admirable type of manhood bred on the western border in the period immediately preceding the Mexican War. He lived through stirring times in the history of California and contributed abundantly to the making of the state."

Wilson built for himself a fine adobe house, which he later sold to Louis Rubidoux. By 1850, Rubidoux had purchased the remainder of the land that Bandini had sold to Wilson in 1843, obtaining a deed from Wilson on May 3, 1848, for a half-interest in his land, and a deed from Isaac Williams for the other half-interest on December 13, 1849. Louis Rubidoux, a native of St. Louis, was of French descent, his family being prominent in the early history of Missouri. The name was originally Robidoux but was altered in Mexican California. His father was a pioneer merchant in St. Louis and his brother Joseph was the founder of the city of St. Joseph. Louis himself, as well as other members of the family, had been active in the trapping and fur-trading industry in the Southwest before coming to California. Louis Rubidoux exercised considerable influence in building up his community and served as local judge and supervisor. He was a well-educated, genial, kindly man, and his home became a haven for many pioneer families in southern California.

A tablet commemorating Rubidoux placed by the Daughters of the American Revolution is at the community center on Limonite Avenue in the town of Rubidoux, once known as West Riverside. The site of the old Rubidoux adobe (SRL 102) is now in a shopping center on the north side of Mission Boulevard in Rubidoux, about one hundred yards east of Bloomington Boulevard.

Rubidoux built one of the first gristmills in this part of California on the Rancho Jurupa in 1846–47. Being at that time the only mill of its kind in the region, it supplied a great need. It is said that the troops of the Mormon Battalion and Frémont's Battalion were the enthusiastic recipients of flour from the Jurupa Mill and beans from the rancho. One of the old millstones has been preserved at the Mission Inn, and another adorns the Rubidoux-Frémont Monument, which stands near the site of the mill (SRL 303) at the intersection of Fort

Drive and Molino Way, across Mission Boulevard from the site of the Rubidoux home. The tablet is missing from the marker, which has been vandalized. The monument, put up in 1926, honors two great figures of California history, but John C. Frémont had no direct connection with the Riverside area. Molino Way recalls Rubidoux's industry in the Spanish word for "mill," and Fort Drive commemorates a small military post that never deserved nor officially received the title of fort. A U.S. Army post was established at this spot on Rancho Jurupa in 1852 by Captain Lovell and Lieutenant Smith, and a small body of troops was kept there until 1854, chiefly as a protection against the Paiute and Mojave Indians. The site of the post is sometimes called "Fort Fremont," although Frémont himself never visited this spot.

Louis Rubidoux died in 1868, and in 1870 a brick house was built on former Rubidoux land—a house that still stands and is one of the Riverside area's oldest. Cornelius Jensen, a native of Denmark who married Mercedes Alvarado, became the storekeeper at Agua Mansa in San Bernardino County in 1854. His adobe house there was one of the few to survive the great flood of 1862. A few years later Jensen came to the Rubidoux ranch, purchased some of it, and built his fine brick home in Danish style. This restored place (SRL 943) is the heart of the Jensen-Alvarado Historic Ranch and Museum, at 4307 Briggs Street in Riverside. Produce is still grown on the property, now an operation of the Riverside County Regional Park and Open-Space District. Cornelius Jensen became a leading citizen of Riverside. He is buried in the old cemetery at Agua Mansa as also, reputedly, is Louis Rubidoux.

There were two settlements on the "Bandini Donation" of Rancho Jurupa—Agua Mansa on the northwest side of the Santa Ana River and San Salvador on the southeast—to which the New Mexican colonists moved from Politana on the Lugo rancho in the mid-1840s. These towns were devastated by flood in 1862, but both were rebuilt on higher ground. Of Agua Mansa only the cemetery remains. At San Salvador, better known as La Placita and called "Spanish Town" by the American pioneers, there remains the Trujillo adobe, preserved by Riverside County, a small, modest structure just a few hundred yards south of the San Bernardino County line, at the junction of North Orange and Center Streets. This was the home of Lorenzo Trujillo, leader of the New Mexicans who settled at Politana, Agua Mansa, and San Salvador.

When Trujillo's group left the Lugo rancho for the Bandini Donation, the Lugos replaced them at Politana with Juan Antonio and his band of Cahuilla Indians. This Indian leader had earlier founded the village of Saahatpa (SRL 749) in San Timoteo Canyon. The marker, at the Brookside rest area of westbound I-10, tells a terrible story:

> Saahatpa. Chief Juan Antonio and his band of Cahuilla Indians helped white settlers in the San Bernardino area defend their property livestock against outlaws during the 1840s and 1850s. In late 1851, Juan Antonio, his warriors and their families, settled at nearby Saahatpa. During the winter of 1862–63, a smallpox epidemic swept through southern California killing many Native Americans, including Juan Antonio. Cahuilla tradition asserts that the U.S. Government sent Army blankets that were contaminated with smallpox. After this disaster, Saahatpa was abandoned.

RIVERSIDE

In 1870, the town of Riverside was founded on the eastern portion of the Jurupa Grant by Judge J. W. North. North was born in New York in 1815 and became a lawyer. He took a prominent part in the material and cultural foundations of Minnesota, Nevada, and California. In Minnesota he was active in the territorial legislature, founded the town of Northfield, promoted the Minneapolis and Cedar Valley Railway, and helped to establish the University of Minnesota. He was active in the Republican national convention of 1860, which nominated Abraham Lincoln for the presidency; he was then appointed Surveyor General of the Territory of Nevada, and soon after became a territorial judge. He was president of the Nevada state constitutional convention in 1864.

Judge North went to Knoxville, Tennessee, to open up foundries after the Civil War. While there he became interested in organizing a colony in California. With men from Iowa, Massachusetts, Michigan, and New York, he went to California over the newly built Central Pacific Railroad. He examined sites in southern California and purchased a portion of Rancho Jurupa. In 1870, Riverside was founded on this land. Judge North later moved to Fresno County, where he had acquired land. His busy life ended there in 1890.

The old North residence once stood on the city block now bounded on the west by the Union Pacific depot, on the east by the Santa Fe depot, on the north by Mission Inn Avenue, and on the south by University Avenue. The site was set aside as a city park in 1927, and was named the Judge North Memorial Park in honor of the founder of Riverside.

The city of Riverside was incorporated in 1883, and ten years later it became the seat of a new county. The courthouse, the second built in the county, is a handsome beaux-arts structure at 3050 Main Street, designed by Franklin P. Burnham and built in 1904. Another handsome structure is the Riverside Municipal Museum at Mission Inn Avenue and Orange Street; originally built as the post office in 1912, it has housed the museum since 1945. The museum administers Heritage House at 8193 Magnolia Avenue, a restored Queen Anne mansion from 1891 containing much of its original décor and furnishings. Work is being done to restore some of Riverside's historic Chinatown. An active Chinese community was centered at Brockton and Tequesquite Avenues from 1880 to about 1930, the last building of which was removed in 1978.

Three old churches, all of them still active, display different architectural styles. The parish hall of the Magnolia United Presbyterian Church at 7200 Magnolia Avenue is in the Gothic style and was built in 1881. The First Unitarian Church at Mission Inn Avenue and Lemon Street was built in 1891 of red Arizona sandstone and suggests in its design a medieval English parish church. The First Church of Christ, Scientist, at Sixth and Lemon Streets, built in 1900, is the oldest Mission Revival structure in the city.

THE NAVEL ORANGE TREE AND THE TIBBETS MEMORIAL

The Tibbets Memorial in honor of Mrs. Eliza Tibbets, who raised the first navel orange trees in California, was placed by the Daughters of the American Revolution in a small park at the head of Magnolia and Arlington Avenues, Riverside, in 1920. Two young orange trees were sent to Mrs. Tibbets from Washington, D.C., around 1873 by Professor William A. Saunders, the husband of an old friend. Budlings had been sent to Professor Saunders from Bahia, Brazil. Two of these he sent to a friend in Florida, and two he sent to Mrs. Tibbets in Riverside.

The two budlings sent to Florida did not survive, but owing to Mrs. Tibbets's care and in spite of somewhat adverse circumstances, the two trees entrusted to her lived. From these two budlings grew the great navel orange industry of southern California, adding millions of dollars annually to the state's economy.

The trees were originally planted at the Tibbets home, the site of which is at Central Avenue and Navel Court. At this spot a marker was placed in honor of Eliza's husband, Luther C. Tibbets, in 1935. In 1903 one of the trees (SRL 20) was transplanted a short distance away, at Magnolia and Arlington, and in front of this tree, still producing fruit, is the memorial to Mrs. Tibbets. Offspring trees are on the same plot of land as the Mother Navel Orange, protected by a fence. The other tree was transplanted to the courtyard of the Mission Inn by President Theodore Roosevelt at the time of his visit here, also in 1903, but it died in the 1920s.

THE MISSION INN

Captain C. C. Miller came to southern California when it was first emerging from its hacienda days. In 1873 he was made engineer of the new colony of Riverside, which had been established on the old Rancho Jurupa in 1870. As his salary, he received a block of land in the new colony, and there, in 1875, he built an adobe cottage, one of the first solid-walled houses in town, which later became the nucleus of the famous Mission Inn.

The Miller family began to receive guests in the adobe as early as 1876, and the name Glenwood Cottage was given to it. The old-fashioned, homely hospitality of the Millers drew an increasing number of patrons, and a small group of frame buildings grew up around Glenwood Cottage. With this growth, the name was changed to Glenwood Inn, and later to Glenwood Hotel. Around 1900, Riverside, along with other places in southern California, began to attract the attention of Easterners in the winter months, and large numbers of them begin to visit the area for long visits.

Almost from the beginning, Frank A. Miller, son of the pioneer, was proprietor and manager at Glenwood. In 1902 he replaced the old wooden cottages with a new structure of concrete and brick, the building that now surrounds the Court of the Birds. The old adobe cottage stood on its original site in this court until 1948, when it gave way to the swimming pool. Around these two grew the Glenwood Mission Inn (now simply Mission Inn, SRL 761), inspired by the missions of California, and containing art treasures from all over the world. A National Historic Landmark, the inn has been extensively restored, reopening in 1992. It has had a

Giant Desert Figure "Indian Intaglios"

special appeal for many celebrities and for some who would later become famous, such as the young Pat and Richard Nixon, who were married there, and Nancy and Ronald Reagan, who honeymooned there. Still on display is the special oversized chair created for President William H. Taft on a 1909 visit. The Mission Inn Foundation operates the Mission Inn Museum within the hotel, featuring both permanent materials connected with the hotel's history and changing exhibits of a wide scope.

OTHER RIVERSIDE LANDMARKS

In 1907, the University of California established its Citrus Experiment Station on the eastern edge of Riverside, and for many years the development of various citrus crops was carried on there. In 1954, a campus of the university was created at the site, now a major educational facility. The California Museum of Photography is located at the University of California at Riverside.

The California Citrus State Historic Park at Van Buren Boulevard and Dufferin Avenue recalls Riverside's significance in the emerging citrus industry in Califor-

nia from the 1880s to the 1940s. The visitor center is a replica of a typical grower's house from around 1900. There are some eighty types of citrus trees planted on the grounds.

March Field, to the southeast of the city of Riverside, was one of the earliest air bases in the United States, established in 1918. The March Field Air Museum is dedicated to the history of the evolution of air power. Over thirty historic aircraft, ranging from the days of World War I to more recent times, are a feature of the exhibit. The museum is open to the public at what is now known as March Air Reserve Base.

MOUNT RUBIDOUX

In 1906 the Huntington Park Association acquired Mount Rubidoux and developed it as a public park. The mountain was named for Louis Rubidoux, who owned part of Rancho Jurupa, on which it is located. On April 26, 1907, the Serra Cross was raised on the highest point of the mountain and dedicated to Father Junipero Serra, founder of the California missions. The first annual sunrise pilgrimage to the top of Mount Rubidoux on Easter Sunday was held in 1909, and from that service have come all the subsequent Easter sunrise services of southern California. Thousands of worshippers climb the mountain every Easter morning for this annual event.

THE LAND OF "RAMONA"

Helen Hunt Jackson was a native of Amherst, Massachusetts. Like her childhood friend Emily Dickinson, she spent much time in writing—in her case, from the necessity to support herself after the death of her first husband. A crusader for the rights of Indians, she wrote a scathing account of their mistreatment at the hands of federal officials in *A Century of Dishonor* (1881). This book so impressed the Department of the Interior that she was invited to join Abbott Kinney in a survey of the condition of the Mission Indians of southern California.

Journeying through Orange, Riverside, and San Diego Counties, Mrs. Jackson developed both a love for a rather romanticized Californian past and a keen dismay at the wretched condition of the Mission Indians. Staying with the Wolf family on the Vail Ranch (about three and one-half miles east of Temecula), Mrs. Jackson investigated the condition of the Temecula Indians. The

RIVERSIDE COUNTY

countryside enchanted her, and the Pechanga Burial Ground, the Pala Chapel, and the Wolf Ranch all became vivid places to her. In 1883 she submitted an extensive report on the condition of the Mission Indians to federal authorities, who apparently paid little attention to it. Mrs. Jackson was determined that her investigations would produce some improvement in the living conditions of the Indians. "I'm going to write a novel in which will be set forth some Indian experiences in a way to move people's hearts," she wrote to friends later that year. "People will read a novel when they will not read serious books."

The result was *Ramona* (1884), which used the background of Temecula and Soboba and the San Jacinto Valley to tell the story of the tragedy of Ramona and Alessandro and their people. An instant best-seller, the book was viewed as a picturesque romance rather than a cry for action. Mrs. Jackson may have anticipated this disappointment in another private letter concerning the Soboba Indians: "It breaks my heart," she wrote, "to try to make them understand that all I can do is *tell* about them."

Throughout southern California for many years, tourists were shown aged women who were said to be the "original" Ramona and sites that were the "authentic" locales of the story. The work was really a combination of many stories Mrs. Jackson had gathered and sites she had visited. The Ramona Pageant is held each spring in the Ramona Bowl (SRL 1009), a natural amphitheater just south of Hemet. In the San Bernardino National Forest, between Sage and Anza, E Clampus Vitus has placed a plaque at Juan Diego Flats proclaiming: "In this valley a conflict between the culture of the Indian and the white man resulted in the death of Juan Diego (Alessandro in the play *Ramona*) by the hands of Sam Temple."

SAN JACINTO

San Jacinto is located on the lands of Rancho San Jacinto Viejo, an area of over 35,000 acres that was granted by Manuel Jimeno, governor pro tem, to José Antonio Estudillo in 1842. Estudillo was a member of the California family that also held land in San Diego and San Leandro in Alameda County. San Jacinto, now located on this old grant, is Riverside County's second-oldest city, having been incorporated in 1888.

At one time Rancho San Jacinto belonged to Mission San Luís Rey, and a survey of 1827 indicates that an adobe house for the mayordomo of the rancho then existed. Estudillo's petition for a portion of the grant noted the existence of the house, about five miles northwest of San Jacinto, and in time he came to live in the extended home he built around the adobe remains, called Casa Loma. The building still stands by the Ramona Expressway.

Two homes of the Estudillo family stand on the old grant. One is the substantial mansion located on Seventh Street in San Jacinto, with extensive grounds; the other, almost impossible to see from the road, is on the Althouse property on Soboba Road, close to the hot springs resort and formerly a part of it.

San Jacinto received national publicity on July 14, 1937, when a Russian plane that had flown nonstop over the polar route from Moscow missed March Field and landed in Earl Smith's cow pasture. A new world's nonstop distance flight record of 6,305 miles was established. The three aviators and the plane were safely returned to Russia. The marker (SRL 989) is near the intersection of Cottonwood and Sanderson Streets, west of San Jacinto.

The museum in this city has an attractive display dedicated to the work of Helen Hunt Jackson. At 181 East Main Street, it also has a wealth of material on the Cahuilla and Soboba Indians and on early ranching in the community.

BANNING

Originally a stop on the Southern Pacific Railroad, the town of Banning was named for General Phineas Banning, developer of Los Angeles County's transportation systems. The Malki Museum on the nearby Morongo Indian Reservation is a good source of information for the history of these people; it is open to the public on a regular basis.

The town was situated on Rancho San Gorgonio, the easternmost of the San Gabriel Mission ranches. An adobe building was put up in the canyon just north of the present town in 1854 by Jose Pope, mayordomo for Isaac Williams, a local landowner. After going through various hands, and becoming for a while a stage stop, the building and its surrounding property were sold in 1869 to James Marshall Gilman, originally from New Hampshire, who was looking for a cattle ranch to buy in the San Gorgonio Pass region. Although he was successful in his cattle ranching, Gilman eventually switched to fruit production, and his ranch became famous for its raisins, figs, prunes, apricots, peaches, almonds, and olives. The Gilman Ranch will also be remembered for what has been called

> the last [1909] great western manhunt, of Willie Boy, a Paiute Indian who wished to marry Lolita Boniface against her father's wishes. The young woman and her family were camped at the Gilman Ranch working on the fruit harvest when Willie Boy killed her father and escaped with Lolita, actions which outraged the Anglo community. A presidential visit to the Riverside area stoked the press into a frenzy, leading the public to believe that there was a danger to President Taft. The manhunt received national press coverage. Willie Boy avoided the posse for three weeks before he died by his own hand.

Gilman Historic Ranch and Wagon Museum, at Sixteenth and Wilson Streets in Banning, is operated by the Riverside County Parks Department. Extensive displays of covered wagons and ranch vehicles can be seen. The 1879 ranch house, destroyed in a fire in 1977, has been re-created on the original site.

LAKE ELSINORE

The discovery of hot sulfur springs at Lake Elsinore in the 1880s led to the establishment of an early resort. Riverside County has marked its site with a plaque at Graham and Springs Streets in the town of Lake Elsinore. At 201 Graham, a two-story wooden building from this period, called the Chimes House, still stands.

IDYLLWILD

A mile above sea level in the San Jacinto Mountains, Idyllwild was developed around 1900 as a sanitarium for tuberculosis patients; the clean, dry mountain air was considered to be very beneficial. A plaque near the center of the community commemorates Camp Emerson, an early resort. The community has a long tradition of artistic and cultural activities, with several schools and summer camps in the vicinity. Indian Relic Park is located near the base of imposing Tahquitz Peak.

On the road from Idyllwild to Palm Springs at Garner Valley, a plaque commemorates the Thomas-Garner Ranch, one of the oldest and largest cattle ranches in southern California. It is said that the couple who inspired Mrs. Jackson's Ramona and Alessandro actually lived and worked on the ranch in the late nineteenth century.

THE COACHELLA VALLEY, INDIO, AND DATE CULTURE

The dry climate of the Coachella Valley combined with sufficient groundwater produces the greatest amount of date culture in the United States. The first dates were imported from Algeria in the 1880s. Date cultivation was encouraged by the U.S. Department of Agriculture in cooperation with private enterprise in the 1920s, and today some 5,000 acres in the Coachella Valley are given over to magnificent groves of many varieties of date palms. Indio, the chief city of the Coachella Valley, began as a railroad center around 1875. It has hosted the annual Date Festival since the 1930s. The Coachella Valley Museum and Cultural Center at 82616 Miles Avenue in Indio is a repository of artifacts of the region from the days of the Cahuilla Indians to recent times, with special exhibits on the history of railroads and water resource development in the valley.

BLYTHE

The town of Blythe was named for financier Thomas H. Blythe of San Francisco, who in the 1870s developed the region known as the Palo Verde Valley, adjacent to the Colorado River. The site of the Blythe Intake (SRL 948) is twelve miles north of the town at the entrance to the Palo Verde Division Dam, and marks the first legally filed claim to the water of the Colorado River. The Palo Verde Historical Museum in Blythe is being developed to commemorate the history of the region.

PERRIS

The Orange Empire Railway Museum contains an operating railway, two and one-half miles long, on which are run railway and trolley cars that used to run on Western lines. Of particular interest are the municipal streetcars from the Los Angeles area. The museum is located at 2201 South A Street, just off I-215, south of Perris.

Lake Perris to the north is the southern terminus of the mammoth California State Water Project. Water brought from the northern parts of the state arrives here, 600 miles to the south, where it is impounded behind Perris Dam. Lake Perris has been a recreational center since 1974, but its greater importance is as a reservoir for the thirsty lands of southern California.

Sacramento County

Crocker Art Museum, Sacramento

Sacramento County was one of the original twenty-seven counties. It took its name from the river that forms its western boundary, named by Spanish explorers for the Holy Sacrament. The only changes made in its boundaries have been those necessitated by the shifting of the streambeds of the Mokelumne and Sacramento Rivers. Sacramento has always been the county seat.

AN INDIAN SITE

The Nisipowinan village site (SRL 900) near the confluence of the American and Sacramento Rivers in Discovery Park, Sacramento, is the most significant extant Indian village and cemetery site in the Sacramento region. Excavation of the mound—locally known as "Joe Mound," after a Portuguese farmer of the area who was called Joe—has shown evidence of habitation as early as 1000 B.C., and has produced artifacts from the encounters of the Indians with Captain John A. Sutter and his contemporaries around 1840.

OLD SPANISH TRAILS

Five Spanish expeditions had entered or seen the Sacramento–San Joaquin delta before 1800. In 1772 Pedro Fages, while exploring the "Port of San Francisco" for the purpose of finding a suitable mission site, went up the eastern shore of San Francisco Bay as far as the San Joaquin River and saw the great Sacramento River "from a point of vantage." In 1793 Francisco Eliza sailed into the Sacramento River and stated that this river had not yet been explored. Sometime before 1808 it was given the name Sacramento.

Long after the mission had been founded at San Francisco, and after nineteen of the twenty-one missions had been established along the coast of Alta California, several expeditions were organized and sent into the river country of the great interior valley to search for suitable sites for new missions. One of the most important of these expeditions was that commanded by Gabriel Moraga in 1808. On October 9 Moraga's party camped on the lower Feather River, which Moraga called the Sacramento, a name he applied also to the great river into which it flows further down, showing that he believed that the two composed the main stream. He considered the upper Sacramento, which he reached a little later, to be a branch of the main river and called it the Jesús María, a name long retained for that part of its course. It is easy to understand why Moraga reached this conclusion, for at the point where the Sacramento and the Feather come together, it is the Feather that makes a straight line north and south with the lower Sacramento, while the upper Sacramento flows at that point from the west.

An attempt to explore the river country by boat was made by José Antonio Sánchez in 1811, when he proceeded a little way up the Sacramento River. However, an expedition of more importance in the history of Sacramento took place in 1817, led by Luis Argüello, accompanied by Father Narciso Durán and Father Ramón Abella. Various channels that they followed, as well as a number of the places at which they camped, have been identified. At one time a fierce windstorm drove them behind the Montezuma Hills in the vicinity of the present town of Rio Vista (in Solano County), and again, from a vantage point on the site of Clarksburg, they had a fine view of the Sierra Nevada. Soon afterward they passed the site of what is now the city of Sacramento.

OPENING OF THE SACRAMENTO TRAIL

The Sacramento Trail was opened to trade and immigration by an American, Jedediah Strong Smith, who had made the first overland journey into California in 1826. Smith came again, in 1827, to rejoin that part of his company that he had left encamped on one of the rivers of the San Joaquin Valley. Although the Mexican government had demanded his departure from the province, he did not leave the region at once by the way he had come. Instead, he opened a new route that led north up the Sacramento River, called by Smith the Buenaventura.

After several unsuccessful attempts to find a pass through the Sierra Nevada from the river, the Smith party finally left the Sacramento about the middle of April 1828. Going northwest across the Coast Range through the wild regions now included in Trinity and Humboldt Counties, Smith and his men came to the seacoast and proceeded along it to Oregon. This route was soon followed by Hudson's Bay Company hunters and traders from Vancouver by way of Oregon.

A tablet in honor of Jedediah Strong Smith, placed by the Daughters of the American Revolution, is at the west end of the bridge over the American River on SR 160.

NEW HELVETIA

The first settlement in the Great Central Valley of California was made by John A. Sutter in 1839. Sutter, who was born in Baden, Germany, in 1803 of Swiss parents, came to the United States when still a young man. He eventually drifted to St. Louis and from there to the Pacific Coast by way of the Columbia River.

Slowly, the idea of founding a colony in California took form in the mind of this adventurer. Sailing from Fort Vancouver (in what is now Washington state) to the Sandwich Islands, he aroused the interest of a handful of Americans and Hawaiian natives (then often called Kanakas) in his project. With this as a nucleus for the future independent state of which he dreamed, Sutter reached Alta California early in July 1839. There he became a citizen of Mexico and obtained Governor Juan B. Alvarado's permission to establish his settlement inland.

The great Sacramento Valley at that time was Indian territory. A few Spanish expeditions had been made into the interior to search for mission sites or Indians who had run away from life in the missions. Jedediah Strong Smith had explored it in 1828, and Hudson's Bay Company trappers had hunted on its streams. The native peoples who inhabited the river country and the surrounding mountains frequently raided the scattered coastal settlements. Sutter's proposal to establish a frontier outpost that would act as a buffer against these raids was welcomed by the Mexican officials, especially since it meant no expense on their part, other than the granting of a few leagues of wilderness land for the proposed settlement.

With high hopes for the future, Sutter embarked in August 1839 from Yerba Buena up the Sacramento River to choose a location for his estate. About August 15 he landed at what was then the south bank of the American River, in modern Sacramento a place just north of B Street between 28th and 29th Streets. A marker (SRL 591) commemorates the landing place. Soon he moved to a site nearby, where he established a permanent camp and built his fort.

In 1841 Sutter was granted eleven leagues of land in the Sacramento Valley. The construction of a large adobe fort was begun in that year, with the outside walls being completed in 1844. In December 1841 Sutter acquired the equipment of the Russian settlement at Fort Ross in Sonoma County, then being disbanded. This purchase included a large number of horses and cattle, a small launch, and several pieces of artillery. The cannon was set up at Sutter's Fort, and armed guards and daily drill became a feature of the place, giving it a decidedly military aspect. Sutter named the little settlement New Helvetia (another name for Switzerland).

SUTTER'S FORT

Sutter's Fort, as it soon came to be known, was not merely a fort; it was a trading post and a place of refuge as well. Robert Glass Cleland writes:

> In addition to Sutter's military activities, he displayed a vast amount of energy in more peaceful endeavors. To care for the ever growing needs of his colony, and especially to meet the pressing demands of his Russian debt, he branched out into a great variety of pursuits and tried all sorts of experiments, most of which impoverished, rather than enriched him. He planted large areas to wheat; built a flour mill; diverted water from the American River for irrigation purposes; grazed large herds of cattle and horses; sent hunters into the mountains and

along the rivers for furs and elk skins; set up a distillery; began the weaving of coarse woolen blankets; ran a launch regularly for freight and passengers between his settlement and San Francisco Bay; employed nearly all foreigners who came to him for work, whether he needed them or not; trained the Indians to useful occupations; at times chastised the thieving, war-inclined tribes which the Spanish Californians could not subdue; administered justice as an official of the provincial government; and, in short, made his colony the nucleus of all activity, whether political or economic, in what was then the only settled portion of interior California.

In addition to these varied activities, with their decided local and personal interest, Sutter contributed in a much larger way to the making of California history through his aid to American immigration. Few people today realize how large a part this hospitable, visionary, improvident land baron of the Sacramento played in the American advance to California. His fort occupied the most strategic position in all northern California, so far as the overland trails were concerned, and became the natural objective for parties crossing the Sierras, by the central and northern routes, or coming into the province by way of Oregon.

At Sutter's, these immigrants, exhausted and half-starved as many of them were, found shelter, food and clothing, and an opportunity to learn something of the new land and people to which they had come. More than one company (the most famous of which was the Donner party), caught in the mountain snows, was saved from destruction by a rescue party sent from Sutter's Fort. The situation of the latter also made it impossible for the California authorities, had they been so inclined, to check or turn aside the stream of overland migration. The passes and trails of the northern Sierras lay open to American frontiersmen so long as Sutter maintained his position on the Sacramento.

Sutter's dream of New Helvetia was ruined by the discovery of gold at his mill at Coloma in 1848. His workers left him to go to the mines. The Gold Rush was a wave of humanity that swept over his lands. A bustling city grew up on the Sacramento. His splendid isolation was gone. Eventually Sutter, with his long-separated Swiss family, left California to spend his last years at Lititz, Pennsylvania. He died in 1880 in Washington, D.C., where he had gone to defend his land titles, and was buried at Lititz.

Sutter's Fort fell into the hands of other owners after 1850, and the buildings began to deteriorate. Final de-struction was threatened when in 1889 it was proposed to open 27th Street directly through the grounds from K to L Streets. This threat was checked by the efforts of General James G. Martine. The fort was restored by the state in 1891–93, and is now Sutter's Fort State Historic Park (SRL 525). It is located between K and L Streets on the north and south and 26th and 28th Streets on the east and west, two miles east of Old Sacramento. It has been registered as a National Historic Landmark by the Department of the Interior.

The original adobe bricks, made by Indians at Sutter's Fort, may be seen in the central building, which is all that remained of the original fort when reconstruction got under way following donation of the property to the state by the Native Sons of the Golden West. This two-story building, with basement, has walls about thirty inches thick, and the original hand-hewn oaken floor joists. Other walls within the fort were reconstructed of kiln-baked bricks, as were the outer walls. The fort was reproduced in its approximate original form and dimensions, with shops, storerooms, living quarters, and the like. About two dozen rooms or sections are devoted to museum purposes, for storage of reserve material, workshops, or displays of historical objects. Several cannon dating from Sutter's time preserve the military aspect of the place. A park, beautifully landscaped, is included in the grounds, which cover two city blocks.

Many interesting objects of pioneer days are housed in Sutter's Fort. These include a remarkable collection of Reed-Donner party items; firearms; stagecoaches and other vehicles; mining tools; costumes; objects made or used by James W. Marshall, the discoverer of gold at Coloma; equipment used by early fire departments; household furnishings; musical instruments; maps, documents, and diaries of Forty-niners; and paintings, prints, and rare photographs. The curator's office has files of information relating to California pioneers.

During the reconstruction of the fort, some of the workmen panned dirt near the east gate and recovered a quantity of gold dust that had been dropped years before by miners, or swept from gambling rooms and stores on the premises. Doubtless this was some of the first gold mined after the discovery at Sutter's sawmill in 1848.

A plaque has been placed at Sutter's Fort to mark the western end of the Coloma Road (SRL 745). The route was first used in 1847 to reach the site of Sutter's sawmill. In January 1848 James Marshall brought the first gold discovered at Coloma to Sutter's Fort by this road. In 1849 James E. Birch established California's first stage line along this route. Other markers on the Coloma Road have been placed near Alder Springs at Nimbus Dam (SRL 746), and at Rescue and Coloma in El Dorado County.

THE STATE INDIAN MUSEUM
AT SUTTER'S FORT

The California State Indian Museum is located at Sutter's Fort, with the entrance at 2618 K Street. Here is one of the finest and most complete collections of relics representing the workmanship of the indigenous Californians. Many artifacts were gathered from ancient campsites and burial grounds of the Sacramento and San Joaquin Valleys. In this splendid array one sees striking evidence that the California Indian was a skilled craftsman as well as an artist of rare ability. There are pipes, serrated arrow points, and bowls, scores of baskets from all over the state, ornaments and implements of stone, bone, and shell—all fashioned with a perfection of line and delicacy of detail found in the finest craftsmanship.

MEXICAN LAND GRANTS

John A. Sutter was not the first recipient of a land grant in the Sacramento Valley. In 1833 J. B. Cooper was granted the land "known by the name of Rio Ojotska," on the present American River three leagues east of the Sacramento. Cooper did not develop the property and renounced the grant in 1835. Four years later Sutter arrived at New Helvetia.

Sutter did not long remain the sole land baron in the Sacramento Valley. The beginning of the American occupation found him already surrounded by neighbors. Many of his former employees had occupied ranchos up and down the length of the valley.

John Sinclair, a Scotsman, settled on Rancho del Paso as early as 1841. On this estate of 44,000 acres, granted to Eliab Grimes in December 1844, Sinclair built a house on the right bank of the American River two and one-half miles east of Sutter's Fort. For a time this was the first recognizable settlement reached by the overland emigrant trains after crossing the Sierra Nevada. Sinclair was hospitable and kindly in his treatment of those in need, and as alcalde of the Sacramento district he was especially helpful in sending aid to the Donner party. Part of this rancho was homesteaded in the 1870s by a family named Gibson. This land is today Gibson

Ranch County Park on Elverta Road west of Watt Avenue, near the northern edge of the county.

Rancho Río de los Americanos, extending over 35,500 acres on the south side of the American River east of New Helvetia, was granted in 1844 to William A. Leidesdorff, vice-consul of the United States by appointment of Thomas O. Larkin. Leidesdorff died in 1848, leaving the rancho along with other valuable property in San Francisco. Captain Joseph L. Folsom, who had come to California as assistant quartermaster of Stevenson's New York Volunteers, purchased the vast Leidesdorff estate from the heirs for a song, thus becoming one of the wealthiest men in California. The town of Folsom was laid out on his rancho in 1855 and named for him. The site of the old Leidesdorff adobe, erected in 1846, is near Routier Road, just south of modern Rancho Cordova.

One summer evening in 1840, William Daylor, an employee of Sutter, climbed a hill southeast of New Helvetia and saw for the first time the rich valley of the Cosumnes River, then thickly populated with Indians. Daylor decided then and there that the lands bordering the north bank of the river were to be his. On returning to the fort he talked the matter over with his friend, Jared Sheldon, also an employee of Sutter. Sheldon, a native of Vermont, had become a naturalized Mexican citizen and held claims against the Mexican government for services in building the Custom House at Monterey. The two men formed a partnership whereby Sheldon was to obtain the grant of land through W. E. P. Hartnell in liquidation of his claim, and also to supply the cattle, while Daylor was to settle upon the land and look after the stock. The first grant, made in 1841, proved to be defective, and a second was drawn up and approved early in 1844 under the designation "Rancho Omochumnes."

MORMON ISLAND AND OTHER
AMERICAN RIVER MINING CAMPS

Mormon Island in the northeast corner of Sacramento County was the site of the second important gold discovery in California. Early in the spring of 1848 two Mormons, on their way to Sutter's Mill in Coloma, camped for the night at a bar on the South Fork near its confluence with the North Fork. One of the men remarked: "They are taking gold above us on the river. Let's see if we can find some at this place." Panning out a little dirt in one of their cooking utensils, they revealed a fine prospect. The two Mormons returned to the fort the next day and reported their find to Samuel Brannan, leader of the Mormons in California and associated with C. C. Smith, who kept a store at New Helvetia. Brannan immediately proceeded to the place where the discovery had been made and set up a pre-emptive claim, demanding a royalty of one-third on all the gold taken out at the bar. This fee continued to be paid to Brannan as long as the Mormons were in the majority. Later, when non-Mormons outnumbered those of the faith, the tithe could no longer be collected. Meanwhile, Brannan had accumulated thousands of dollars, which he invested in merchandising, becoming one of the wealthiest men in California.

Mormon Island by 1853 had become a city of over 2,500 inhabitants, but a fire in 1856 destroyed most of the town and it was never rebuilt. When it was inundated by Folsom Lake in 1955, a few rock cellars and locust trees were all that remained to locate the site of this historic gold town. At Green Valley Road just over the El Dorado county line the Mormon Island marker (SRL 569) was placed, but is now missing. The site is near the cemetery to which graves were moved from the Folsom Dam project area. In 1998 additional reinterments were made in the cemetery from the Prairie Creek Cemetery, discovered when a highway construction project uncovered them.

FOLSOM

Down the American River from Mormon Island were numerous camps, some of which were important towns in the early 1850s. In quick succession came Alabama Bar, on the north bank of the river; Slate Bar, opposite Folsom State Prison, where several stores were located; and Sailor Bar. Bean's Bar was one-half mile below Alabama Bar on the opposite side of the river.

Negro Bar was first mined by black people in 1849. By 1851 few blacks remained in a population of 700. The town of Folsom was laid out there in 1855. In the same year, at Sacramento, Theodore D. Judah began construction of California's first passenger railroad, the Sacramento Valley Railroad, which was completed as far as Folsom, a distance of twenty-two miles, in 1856. Historical markers have been placed at the Sacramento terminal at Third and R Streets (SRL 526), and at Folsom on the plaza at Sutter Street near Reading Street. The new town became an important center for stage and freight lines running to the northern mining camps and to Virginia City, Nevada. Great prosperity was enjoyed in the early 1860s, when many substantial hotels and business houses were established, as well as an academy and several churches. Some of these sturdy

Old Wells Fargo Office, Folsom

brick and stone buildings still stand. Prominent among them is the Wells Fargo Building, built in 1860, on Sutter Street. This was for one year the western terminus of the Pony Express. The building now houses the Folsom Historical Society's excellent museum. An addition to the building, completed in 1991, expanded the museum significantly.

The Folsom History Interpretive Center, at Wool and Leidesdorff Streets, is a recent addition to the city's commemoration of the past, as is the Folsom Railroad Museum, by the railroad tracks in the center of the Old Town.

The Folsom Powerhouse (SRL 633), a landmark in the history of long-distance high-voltage transmission of electricity, operated continuously from 1895 to 1952. It has been presented to the state by the Pacific Gas & Electric Company and can be toured. Below the powerhouse along the river are Maidu Indian grinding rocks. Sacramento Station A (SRL 633.2), built to receive power generated from the Powerhouse, is located at Sixth and H Streets in Sacramento.

Folsom has a "Nob Hill" of historic houses; the Cohn House at 305 Scott Street is a National Historic Landmark. The Burnham Mansion at 602 Figueroa Street and the Hyman House at 603 are also late-nineteenth century houses; all are privately occupied. At the eastern side of the city is Folsom Prison, established in 1880 and still a maximum-security prison. Early convicts did a great deal of stonecutting, which is still in evidence. A museum at the entrance to the facility is open to the public.

Earlier mining methods were replaced by giant dredges that created some of the most distinctive rock tailings seen anywhere in California. The largest area of these tailings was on the west side of town, between

Folsom Boulevard and the American River. The Natomas Company ceased operations in 1962, by which time millions of dollars of gold had been produced in this area; in the 1920s and 1930s the average annual production from gold dredging in Sacramento County was $1,300,000. In a remarkable development, most of these tailings, which had created a wilderness of desolation, have been rehabilitated and converted into foundations for light industrial sites and office complexes, and little remains to be seen of these historic grounds today.

On or near Alder Creek, two miles south of Folsom, was Prairie City (SRL 464), a mining camp that reached the height of its prosperity in 1853, after the Natoma Water and Mining Company's ditch was completed to that point. A large quartz mill was also built there, at a cost of $50,000. For a time, Prairie City was a city in fact as well as in name, being a center of trade for a number of other camps, including Rhoads' Diggings, Alder Creek, and Willow Springs Hill Diggings. This last-named place covered about two thousand acres and yielded several million dollars' worth of gold.

COSUMNES RIVER MINING CAMPS

Michigan Bar (SRL 468) was the most prominent of all the early gold camps on the Cosumnes River in Sacramento County. Founded in 1849 by two men from Michigan, it reached a population of 1,500 or more in the early 1850s. The original town site has since been washed out by hydraulic mining, destroying the last remaining landmarks, the old Heath store and the Wells Fargo Express office. The Addington Pottery Works at Michigan Bar was one of the earliest and largest in the state. The site of the town is on Michigan Bar Road about a mile north of its junction with SR 16; the state plaque is missing from the monument.

Fleeting towns developed in the vicinity of Michigan Bar during the early days of the Gold Rush. Cook's Bar, founded by Dennis Cook two miles below Michigan Bar, became a prominent town in the early 1850s, but by 1860 it had ceased to exist. Five miles southwest of Michigan Bar on the Ione Road was Sebastopol, named during the Crimean War, and a lively camp from 1854 to 1859. Katesville, near Cook's Bar, another mining center that arose in 1854, had several stores and saloons, a hotel, and a boardinghouse; by 1862 the place was deserted. Live Oak, north of Sebastopol, had rich returns from its diggings between 1854 and 1861.

Several roads to the southern mines passed through the Cosumnes River region, and ferries, succeeded by toll bridges, as well as a number of hotels, were established by enterprising men at a very early date. William Daylor and Jared Sheldon, as owners of the Omochumnes Mexican grant, were strategically situated and made great profits from mining, ranching, trading, and hotel keeping. In 1850 Sheldon built the Slough House (SRL 575) on Deer Creek (a branch of the Cosumnes River) where the Jackson Road crossed that stream. It was destroyed by fire in 1890 and rebuilt the same year on the old site. The second building still stands and the old cemetery is on a knoll just a few yards away.

Daylor established himself as a trader and hotelkeeper on the Cosumnes River about a mile east of Slough House. This place, which was at first known as Daylor's Ranch, later became the Cosumnes post office.

In 1846–47 Jared Sheldon built a gristmill on Rancho Omochumnes. Four years later he constructed a dam on the Cosumnes River to provide water to operate the mill. It caused flooding of the claims of miners working along the river below the dam. The miners threatened violence, and Sheldon placed a cannon there by way of warning. On July 11, 1851, the indignant miners began to tear down the dam. When Sheldon arrived with reinforcements two hours later, a battle ensued in which he and two of his men were killed. The dam was swept away by high water in the winter of 1851–52. The site of Sheldon's gristmill (SRL 439) is about one mile southeast of Slough House on Meiss Road.

ELK GROVE AND FRANKLIN

On the west side of SR 99, where it crosses the Cosumnes River between Elk Grove and Galt, was the ranch of Martin Murphy Jr. (SRL 680). Here the initial action took place in the conquest of California by the United States. On June 10, 1846, Ezekiel Merritt and a band of settlers overpowered the soldiers of Lieutenant Francisco Arce of the Mexican army and took their horses from the Murphy corral on the north side of the river. Four days later the Bear Flag was raised at Sonoma.

In the Masonic Cemetery at Elk Grove is the grave of Mrs. Benjamin W. Wilder, born Elitha Cumi Donner in 1832 (SRL 719). She came to California in 1846 in the ill-fated party in which her father, George Donner, was one of the leaders. She died in 1923. Elk Grove is the site of the first county free library branch in California (SRL 817), established in 1908. The pioneer effort has been commemorated by a plaque at 9125 Elk Grove Boulevard.

About two miles west of Elk Grove is the village of Franklin. In the Franklin Cemetery is the grave of Alex-

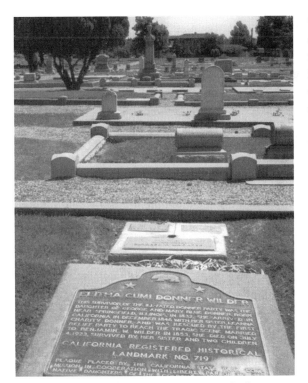

Grave of Elitha Donner Wilder (of the Donner Party), Elk Grove

ander Hamilton Willard (SRL 657), the next to last surviving member of the Lewis and Clark Expedition of 1804–6. Willard, who was born in New Hampshire in 1778, came overland in 1852 with his wife Eleanor and part of his family. He lived the rest of his life at Franklin. He died in 1865; his wife died three years later.

SUTTERVILLE

Sutter laid out a town site in 1844 on his ranch, about two miles below the Sacramento River embarcadero. Here, on high ground overlooking the river, he and his friends built a few dwellings and called the place Suttersville, later Sutterville. The location had one of the few elevations above the turbulent waters of the river, and the future of the little settlement seemed promising. It flourished until 1848 as the friendly rival of the fort and the embarcadero. George Zins built a brick building there in 1847, one of the first brick structures erected in California.

The discovery of gold by James W. Marshall in the tailrace of Sutter's Mill at Coloma in 1848 changed the course of events for Sutterville as it did for all California. Sutter's Fort became too small for the business demands that soon crowded in upon it from every side, a new town sprang up by the embarcadero, and Sutterville also became a settlement of some consequence. It

was eventually incorporated into Sacramento by an election in 1950. Its original site is now lost, but a marker (SRL 593) stands on Sutterville Road across from the zoo in the William Land Park. The site of the old brick brewery that stood nearby until it was pulled down in 1952 has been marked by E Clampus Vitus.

During the Civil War, Camp Union (SRL 666) of the California Volunteers was located for some months in 1861 and 1862 at Sutterville. A marker has been placed at Sutterville and Del Rio Roads.

THE FOUNDING OF SACRAMENTO

It was around the embarcadero at the foot of the long road leading to Sutter's Fort that the new city of Sacramento first grew up. Sutter had fallen heavily into debt, and finally, in order to evade his creditors, he turned his property over to his son John A. Sutter Jr., who had arrived at the fort in September 1848. By December, the younger Sutter, with Captain William A. Warner, had laid out a town at the embarcadero, naming it Sacramento after the river. By the first part of January 1849 two log cabins had been built, followed soon by the first frame building and a canvas house. In April there were thirty buildings, and by June over 100. On August 1 the first town election was held. Situated at the entrance to the gold fields, Sacramento profited tremendously from the mining trade. By October 1849 it had a resident population of about 2,000 and a floating population of 5,000. Sacramento was incorporated as a city in 1850.

Many home seekers arrived at Sacramento in 1849, expecting to take up homesteads there as they had done in Oregon and the Middle West. Sacramento was being built on the Sutter grant, but these settlers did not see why the laws of a foreign government should have more weight than the rights of free American citizens in the assigning of land. They claimed the right to at least one free city lot each. However, those men who had been buying from Sutter hotly contested this claim, and the Squatters' Riot was the result. The Sacramento River twice flooded the area early in 1850, adding to the uncertainty about what property belonged to whom.

A lot at the southeast corner of Second and N Streets was put to the test when Dr. Charles Robinson, a leader of the squatters, erected a shanty there, only to have it removed by the city authorities. In May 1850 a judgment was rendered in favor of Sutter's title, but on August 14 a body of about forty squatters contested this decision by attempting to gain possession of the lot from which Robinson had been ousted. When prevented from doing so, they retired up I Street to Third and thence to J near Fourth, where Mayor Hardin Bigelow met them with a small band of citizens. The squatters then threw a line across Fourth Street at J and fired upon the citizens' group.

In the fight that followed, Mayor Bigelow was seriously wounded, as was Dr. Robinson, while James Maloney and James Morgan, leaders of the squatters, were killed, along with another man and the city assessor. The mayor died of his wounds later that year. The insurgents dispersed, but the next day, when Sheriff Joseph McKinney was attempting to arrest some squatters who had fled to Brighton, he too was shot and killed. On August 19, troops having arrived from San Francisco, a proclamation was issued calling for law and order, and the Squatters' Riot was ended. For a number of years, however, property questions were put before the voters in city elections.

A plaque was placed by E Clampus Vitus in 1982 at the entrance of the California Fruit Express Building at 1006 Fourth Street, commemorating the event and listing the casualties.

THE CAPITOL

The state capital, after being located briefly in San Jose, Vallejo, Sacramento, and Benicia, was finally established at Sacramento in 1854. The county courthouse was offered for use as the state capitol, and the legislative sessions of 1852 and 1854 were held there. The site of the first courthouse, completed in December 1851, is on the north side of I Street between Sixth and Seventh. The building was destroyed by fire in 1854, but was immediately replaced by a second structure in which the state officials and the Legislature were housed until the late fall of 1869 (SRL 896).

The foundations of the state capitol buildings were laid on the present site (SRL 872) in the fall of 1860, only to be washed away by the flood of January 10, 1861. As a protection against recurring floods, two great terraces were constructed, and on this elevation the cornerstone was laid on May 15, 1861, under the auspices of the Masonic Grand Lodge of California. The unfinished structure was occupied by the government late in the fall of 1869, but the building was not completed until 1874. In 1951 an annex was completed on the eastern side that houses the offices of the governor and other executives. With the construction of the annex, the terraces were removed and the ground was graded to a gentle slope from the building to the street.

State Capitol

In the 1970s, new state legislation concerning the safety of public buildings in earthquakes caused throughout the state the demolition of old schools, courthouses, libraries, and the like and the erection of safer, but often less attractive, replacements. The state capitol was found to be unsafe according to the new criteria, and, after extensive consideration of other sites and new buildings, it was decided to gut the building, leaving the exterior walls, and replace the interior. Moreover, it was decided that the interior would be rebuilt as it had looked in 1905; the offices of the governor, the treasurer, and the secretary of state, all of which were lodged in the building then, would be restored as display rooms.

In 1975, an army of workers followed by droves of skilled craftspeople began the transformation of the state capitol. In January 1982, the renovated building was returned to use; the governor's office in the annex had remained unchanged, but the Legislature had to use temporary quarters. Some $67.8 million had been spent, making the project one of the most costly renovations in American history at that time. The verdict of nearly all who have seen the result is that it was worth every penny. Both as a museum and a working place, the state capitol is an exceptionally beautiful structure, which guides on regular tours describe in detail. Among the historic rooms is the state library as it was around 1900, with interesting bibliographical displays.

Surrounding the capitol buildings is Capitol Park. The park's thirty-three acres have been planted with thousands of varieties of trees and shrubs from all parts of the world, which seem to thrive in Sacramento's hospitable climate. Most of the specimens are labeled. Among the interesting plantings is the Memorial Grove, comprised of eastern North American trees transplanted as saplings from the most prominent battlefields of the Civil War by the women's auxiliary of the Grand Army of the Republic and dedicated by them to the state. A space of three acres at the southeast corner of the park is devoted entirely to California flora, where cactus, yucca, and desert willow are close neighbors of fern, azalea, huckleberry, and tiger lily, which thrive in the shade of sequoia and oak and pine, whose native habitat extends from the Coast Range to the Sierra Nevada.

Since nurseryman James Warren introduced them in 1852, camellias have been closely identified with Sacramento, "the Camellia City." There are over a million camellia bushes in the city and an annual camellia show is held in March.

Among the commemorative pieces in the park is a statue honoring the soldiers of the Spanish-American War of 1898 and the ship's bell from the USS *California*. The newest monument, at the east side of the park on 15th and L Streets, is the California Vietnam Veterans Memorial, whose panels are engraved with the names of the 5,822 dead and missing Californians from that conflict.

The California State Fair and Exposition has been held annually in Sacramento since 1859; earlier state fairs were held elsewhere. The extensive fairgrounds along the American River were developed in the late 1970s when the old Stockton Boulevard grounds became inadequate for what was becoming a larger event every year.

THE STATE LIBRARY

The California State Library was created on January 24, 1850, by act of the Legislature. By July it had acquired 135 volumes, the first donations being made by Colonel J. D. Stevenson, Senator Thomas Jefferson Green, and General John C. Frémont. The collection grew steadily, although little money was made available for the purchase of books. For many years the state library occupied the semicircular central wing of the capitol, additional rooms being assigned to it until it covered about 30 percent of the entire floor space of the building.

Today the state library is housed in a building of its own on Capitol Mall (M Street) between Ninth and Tenth Streets. A new annex was completed in 1993 to house the ever-increasing volume of material regarding California history. This has moved the California room from the Library and Courts building to the second floor of the new annex. Two adjoining rooms in the renovated capitol building commemorate the old library.

Nearby at the corner of Tenth and O Streets are the state archives, where historic documents are preserved and displayed. The oldest document of the collection is a 1798 Spanish-language census taken of the San Francisco Presidio. The archives are housed in a new building with expanded facilities, including the Golden State Museum (1020 O Street), with displays taken from the archival collection.

EARLY CHURCHES

The Pioneer Memorial Congregational Church, presently located facing Sutter's Fort, is recorded as having been the first church to be organized in Sacramento, in September 1849, and to hold regular services. Its first building went up in 1850 on a site (SRL 613) on Sixth Street at the southwest corner of the alley between I and J Streets. It was destroyed by fire in 1854, and another building was constructed the same year across the street almost opposite the first site. For over seventy years this historic edifice sheltered many significant gatherings. Its open forum, where some of the most distinguished orators of the day held forth, was a boon to the intellectual life of the city.

The founder of the First Congregational Church was the Rev. Joseph A. Benton, who began his long career in Sacramento in July 1849. His interests included education as well as religious activities. He taught at one of the first schools in Sacramento, and in 1849 he and Samuel Willey were among those already planning for public schools and a college in California. Benton was a founder of the College of California (forerunner of the University of California), and he later became a professor at the Pacific Theological Seminary in Oakland, now the Pacific School of Religion in Berkeley.

Other religious bodies also organized congregations early in the history of Sacramento. The first Roman Catholic parish was St. Rose of Lima; the church building, which stood at Seventh and K Streets, was opened in 1851, although Mass had been said at various locations in 1850. The Cathedral of the Blessed Sacrament, built on Eleventh Street in 1887, was the special project of Bishop Patrick Manogue, who persuaded the authorities in Rome to transfer the seat of the diocese from Grass Valley to Sacramento. The architectural design came from Paris, much of the stained glass came from Austria, and a huge painting was given to the cathedral by Mrs. Leland Stanford in remembrance of the care given by monks in Italy to her son during his last illness.

The Methodist Episcopal church was housed in a prefabricated building shipped around the Horn from Baltimore in 1849. It was located on the east side of Seventh Street between L and Capitol. In 1852 the Methodists sold the building to the local Jewish congregation and it became the first congregationally owned synagogue on the Pacific Coast (SRL 654).

OLD SACRAMENTO

Sacramento has more historic buildings dating from the American pioneer period than any other city in California. Most of them stand in the area bounded by Front, Third, H, and N Streets. This was the heart of the city for several decades. As the business center moved closer to the capitol and away from the riverfront, the old district declined and ultimately became a slum. Cheap hotels and stores occupied the solid old brick buildings where much of California's history was made; by the 1930s, they had been modernized beyond recognition by the addition of cement veneers and the removal of ornamentation of an earlier era.

For years, some proponents of slum clearance urged the complete demolition of the blighted area; other advocates, conscious of the architectural heritage of the area, said that the same end could be achieved by restoring the pioneer structures and attracting new businesses to occupy them. But little was done either way. The issue finally came to a head in the early 1960s when the State Division of Highways announced plans to build a freeway through the old district. The decision was welcomed by some as the answer to two of Sacramento's major problems—transportation and urban renewal—but historians and historically-minded persons insisted that the loss of Old Sacramento would be irreparable and urged an alternate freeway route along the Yolo County side of the Sacramento River. Inventories of the old structures were taken and plans drawn up for the renovation of the area as a historic district. At length a compromise was reached whereby the freeway, although routed through Old Sacramento, would be deflected to spare as many of the important buildings as possible. Their victory at least partly achieved, the historians began to plan in earnest for the careful recreation of pioneer Sacramento. Construction of the freeway began in the middle 1960s.

Old Sacramento State Historic Park (SRL 812) is now virtually complete. Front and Second Streets, and J and K Streets between Front and Second, have been restored to the appearance of earlier days, complete with high wooden sidewalks, reminiscent of the days when the river rose and flooded the area almost every year. Deep brick basements are still to be seen here and there, indicating how far above the surface of the soil most of these buildings stand. It is helpful to begin a tour of the area at the Sacramento History Center, which opened in 1985 at 101 I Street, in an exact reconstruction (costing $3.8 million) of the first public building in Sacramento, the City Hall and Waterworks Building of 1854. The exterior blends in with the mid-nineteenth-century look of Old Sacramento, while the interior uses the most modern methods of explaining and showing the history of the city, including extensive video displays.

The following is not a complete guide to Old Sacramento but an account of some of the buildings that have been designated state historic landmarks within Old Sacramento. One of the most important buildings was the two-story D. O. Mills bank (SRL 609) at 226 J Street, built in 1852. It replaced a small one-story frame building with a stone front that burned in 1852. The first bank's picture was used for many years on the bank's checks. In 1865 the bank was moved to the Heywood building (1857), still standing at the southeast corner of Second and J Streets. In 1912 the Mills bank found a new location at the northwest corner of Seventh and J.

Darius Ogden Mills came to Sacramento in 1849 and began his career as a merchant in the new, chaotic city. He was a man who saw a big opportunity and was quick to take it, and in October 1849 he opened the first banking house on the Pacific Coast. He became a leading figure in the financial life of California, building up the bank at Sacramento on a sound basis and becoming the first president of the Bank of California, established at San Francisco in 1864. He was also interested in educational and philanthropic movements and gave much of his wealth to these activities. Later, he became a prominent figure in the Bank of New York, and established the three Mills Hotels in New York City for the relief of poor, homeless men.

The B. F. Hastings bank building (SRL 606), built in 1852–53 at the southwestern corner of Second and J Streets, is better known as the western terminus of the Pony Express. Here began the first overland journey eastward on April 4, 1860.

The Central Overland Pony Express was inaugurated by the firm of Russell, Majors, and Waddell early in 1860, preceding the telegraph and the railroad in opening overland communication between the East and the West. Before this, mail had been carried by steamer via Panama, the official mail ship arriving at San Francisco once a month. The Butterfield stages had begun to carry the mail overland via the southern route in 1858, requiring from twenty to twenty-four days for the trip. In the same year George Chorpending operated over the central route between Placerville and Salt Lake City. The Pony Express inaugurated a special semiweekly mail service on horseback. Stations were established about every twenty-five miles, each rider spanning three stations at the rate of about eight miles an hour. Ten days from St. Joseph, Missouri, to Sacramento was the usual time required.

There were two Pony Express remount stations in Sacramento County. The first was at the Five Mile House (SRL 697), near the present California State University at Sacramento. The Fifteen Mile House (SRL 698), four miles east on White Rock Road, was next, followed by Mormon Tavern, just over the El Dorado county line. From July 1, 1860, to July 1, 1861, Folsom, rather than Sacramento, was the western terminus of the Pony Express (SRL 702). The mail was carried between the two places by the Sacramento Valley Railroad.

The ponies and their riders, who were picked with care from the hardiest of young Western men, kept the long trail open between the East and the West until October 26, 1861, when the service was discontinued with the completion of the overland telegraph. Tales of these courageous riders pursuing their path regardless of snow, storm, or hostile Indians were graphically and, except for a few minor details, accurately portrayed by Mark Twain in *Roughing It*. Although not a financial success for its promoters, the Pony Express was nevertheless a substantial aid to business and undoubtedly helped to hold California, isolated as it was, in the Union.

Another Sacramento building associated with the Pony Express is the stately three-story Adams and Company building (SRL 607) erected in 1853 at 1014 Second Street. Wells Fargo and Company occupied this structure at the time that it was the agent for the western portion of the Pony Express. Across the street at 1015 is the old telegraph building (SRL 366), long thought incorrectly to have been the Pony Express terminus. At Second and J Streets, by the pedestrian entrance to Old Sacramento State Historic Park, is a large, dashing statue of the Pony Express Rider, a modern contribution to the legend.

Sacramento's first major hotel was the City Hotel, built in 1849 at about 915–17 Front Street. Nearby, at

about 923–25, was the Eagle Theater (SRL 595), Sacramento's first, which opened in that year. The city's original buildings were not solidly constructed and fell victim to fire and flood. The theater has been reconstructed and is a performing stage. Another early hostelry was the Orleans Hotel (SRL 608), which stood from 1852 to the late 1870s at 1018 Second Street. Thousands of miners in the Gold Rush days thronged the What Cheer House (SRL 597) at the southeast corner of Front and K Streets, which has been rebuilt and now caters to the visitors who flock to the sights of Old Sacramento. Ebner's Hotel (SRL 602) at 116 K Street, and the Western Hotel (SRL 601), which is no longer standing, were among other taverns and stopping places in the area.

The Sacramento Theater was opened in March 1853 on Third Street between I and J Streets. Among the celebrities who played there were Ole Bull, Maurice Strakosh, Madame Anna Bishop, and the Robinson Family. A stock company, including Edwin Booth, took it over in 1855. The old building no longer stands, but nearby, at 917 Third, is the Pioneer Mutual Volunteer Firehouse (SRL 612), built in 1854 and occupied by Engine Company No. 1. The No. 3 firehouse is at 1112 Second Street. It is now a restaurant, having been restored in 1959 as one of the first efforts to rehabilitate Old Sacramento.

Newspapers have played an important role in the life of the state's capital city. The *Sacramento Union* issued its first edition on March 19, 1851, from a site (SRL 605) at 121 J Street; the building there has been restored. Although the *Union* is no longer published, another longtime paper, the *Sacramento Bee*, founded in 1857, continues. One of the early buildings occupied by the *Bee* (SRL 611) is a two-story brick structure at 1016 Third Street.

Sam Brannan's building is located at the southeast corner of Front and J Streets. The building now referred to as the Sam Brannan House (SRL 604) at 112 J was built on Brannan's property by Henry E. Robinson in 1853. Across the alley is the slim four-story City Market, a later building (from the 1870s) but one of Old Sacramento's most attractive. Newton Booth, elected governor of California in 1871 and later United States senator, maintained his home, headquarters, and wholesale grocery business (SRL 596) at 1015–17 Front Street. Part of his block still stands at 1019–21 Front. Booth also owned the beautiful three-story building at 1023. He entered business in Sacramento in 1851. Leland Stanford's wholesale warehouse, built in 1856, still stands at the southeast corner of Front and L. The Lady Adams building (SRL 603) is one of Sacramento's oldest. It was built in 1852 at 113–15 K Street and was named after a ship. The Overton-Read building (SRL 610), at the northwest corner of Third and J, was gone many years before the site was obliterated by the freeway; it housed the Sacramento Post Office from 1852 to 1859.

The structure popularly known as the "Big Four Building" has been moved from its original site on K Street (SRL 600), where the freeway was to be constructed, to the intersection of Front and I Streets at the Plaza in Old Sacramento. Built in 1852 and drastically altered through the years, it originally contained the Stanford store and the Huntington-Hopkins hardware store. From their offices here, Leland Stanford, Collis P. Huntington, Mark Hopkins, and Charles Crocker financed and built the Central Pacific Railroad, the western end of the first transcontinental railway, later gaining control of the political and financial affairs of California. The structure is now a bookstore and administrative center for the nearby railroad museum.

Not an old building at all, but a major attraction in Old Sacramento, is the spectacular California State Railroad Museum, at the northeast entrance to Old Sacramento at Second and I Streets. This was opened to the public in 1981, the result of years of planning. In 1937, a group of railroad enthusiasts in the San Francisco Bay Area formed the Pacific Coast chapter of the Railway and Locomotive Historical Society. The members had already begun to acquire historic locomotives and cars in the days when railroads were steadily being cut back, and by 1951 their collection numbered nearly twenty pieces. They hoped to build a museum in San Francisco, but neither funds nor adequate space could be found. In 1964, when the equipment had deteriorated badly because of weather and vandalism, the Bethlehem Shipyard of San Francisco contracted to refurbish and repair many of the more significant pieces.

In 1967, the proposal was made to build a state-sponsored railroad museum in Old Sacramento, birthplace of railroading in California; the State Department of Parks and Recreation soon became custodian of some of the locomotives and cars. In 1976 the Central Pacific Railroad Passenger Station, first phase of the California State Railroad Museum, was opened. In 1984, a steam-train excursion that runs from the station south along the banks of the river for four and a half miles was opened.

Among the many attractions within the museum are the Central Pacific Railroad Locomotive No. 1, "Governor Stanford," from 1862; the Virginia and Truc-kee Railroad Locomotive No. 12, "Genoa," from 1873; the private railroad car "Gold Coast," from about 1895, owned for many years by the authors and historians Lucius Beebe and Charles Clegg; and the Southern Pacific Railroad Locomotive No. 1, "C. P. Huntington," from 1893, which was used as the company's corporate symbol for decades. The museum has become one of the most popular places for Californians and their friends to learn something about the state's history.

THE FIRST TRANSCONTINENTAL RAILROAD

On January 12, 1864, President Abraham Lincoln signed a remarkable document attesting that the western base of the Sierra Nevada began where the Central Pacific Railroad crossed Arcade Creek in Sacramento. Government subsidies for railroad construction through mountainous terrain were considerably higher than those for construction through flatlands. The extra dollars provided by this decree contributed in no small measure to the completion of the transcontinental railroad. A plaque (SRL 780.8) has been placed on the west side of Arcade Creek in the Haggin Oaks Municipal Golf Course, 3645 Fulton Avenue in Sacramento.

On January 8, 1963, Governor Edmund G. Brown dedicated a bronze plaque (SRL 780) at Front and K Streets in Sacramento. It was 100 years to the day since Governor Leland Stanford, at the same spot, turned the first spade of earth to begin construction of the Central Pacific Railroad. An earlier plaque had been dedicated by retired railroad employees on the fiftieth anniversary, January 8, 1913.

Six years and four months after construction began, having conquered many obstacles, crews of the Central Pacific met with those of the Union Pacific, which had been building westward, at Promontory, a lonely spot in northern Utah. There, on May 10, 1869, the gold spike was driven to signify completion of the first transcontinental railroad. It also brought to an end the frontier era of California history, although it would be some time before that fact was generally recognized.

It should not be thought that the "Big Four" alone were responsible for this remarkable development. The man who planned the Central Pacific and who earlier had built the first passenger railroad in California did not live to see the last spike driven. In his memory a splendid monument of granite boulders stands in front of the Southern Pacific (Amtrak) depot at Fourth and I Streets. A bronze table on the face of the rock bears this inscription:

SACRAMENTO COUNTY

That the West may remember Theodore Dehone Judah, pioneer civil engineer and the tireless advocate of a great transcontinental railroad—America's first, this monument was erected by men and women of the Southern Pacific Company who, in 1930, were carrying on the work he began in 1860. He convinced four Sacramento merchants that his plan was practicable and enlisted their help. Ground was broken for the railroad January 8, 1861, at the foot of K Street nearby. Judah died November 2, 1863. The road was built past the site of this monument over the lofty Sierra—along the line of Judah's survey— to a junction with the Union Pacific at Promontory, Utah, where on May 10, 1869, the "last spike" was driven.

The Southern Pacific depot is built on what in Gold Rush days was China Slough (SRL 594).

Even before the Central Pacific was begun, the corner of Front and K Streets was a transportation center. In the early 1850s it was the terminus (SRL 598) for stagecoaches to various places in the Mother Lode country. At the same location, the first successful commercial fruit cannery in the Sacramento Valley, the Capitol Packing Company, was established in January 1882.

The California Almond Growers Exchange, founded in 1910, was the first successful grower-owned cooperative for the marketing of California almonds. The principal building (SRL 967), at 1809 C Street, is a shelling plant adjacent to the 1915 brick building that is now a visitors center, from which tours of the facility are conducted on a regular basis.

OLD SACRAMENTO HOMES

Under its avenues of fine trees, Sacramento has many early residences of brick or frame construction. The house at 800 N Street was built in 1857 for Sheldon C. Fogus, a Sacramento merchant; Seth Babson was the architect. It was purchased by Leland Stanford in 1861 and his name has been associated with the house ever since. Stanford and his wife, Jane Lathrop Stanford, lived there until 1874. Stanford served a single term as governor of California, 1862–63, and the story is told that on his inaugural day in 1862 the floodwaters of the Sacramento River had once again inundated the downtown district, so that the governor-elect and his lady had to climb through a ground-floor window and depart for the inaugural festivities at the nearby capitol in a rowboat. Leland Stanford Jr., their only child, was born in this house in 1868. The house was extensively remodeled by Stanford and presented by his widow to the Roman

Stanford Mansion State Historic Park

Catholic diocese of Sacramento in 1900, after which time it served as an orphanage for many years. Acquired by the state, it is now the Stanford Mansion State Historic Park (SRL 614) and is undergoing necessary renovations; it is open to the public on a limited basis.

The building known as the Governor's Mansion (SRL 823) is a stately white Victorian house at Sixteenth and H Streets. It was built in 1877 for Albert Gallatin, president of a pioneer Sacramento hardware firm. In 1887, Gallatin sold the house to Joseph Steffens, dry-goods merchant and father of the author Lincoln Steffens; in 1903, the state bought it for $32,500 unfurnished. This was the first official residence for California's chief executive; previous governors had had to rent houses, live in hotels, or, as in the case of Governor Stanford, purchase their own houses. Governor George C. Pardee was the first governor to bring his family to live in the mansion, in 1903. The State Fire Marshall declared the building unsuitable for occupancy in 1941, but no alternative residence being provided, Governors Earl Warren, Goodwin Knight, and Edmund G. Brown lived there throughout their terms of office. Governor Ronald Reagan was the last governor to live there; after a very short residence in 1967, he refused to remain in the house and sought other quarters. California's chief executives have gone back to renting houses, living in hotels, or purchasing their own homes. California is one of only six states that today has no official residence for its governor, the others being Arizona, Idaho, Massachusetts, Rhode Island, and Vermont. The Governor's Mansion is open to the public, and, whatever its shortcomings as a family residence, is a charming example of a Victorian home. The house has nine fireplaces, each of them fashioned from a different type of marble. The place is still used for some official functions.

The Crocker Art Gallery (SRL 599) stands at 216 O Street. Judge Edwin B. Crocker and his wife collected many fine paintings and drawings during their travels in Europe, especially during the Franco-Prussian War. In the early 1870s a building was erected at the southeast corner of Second and O Streets, next to their residence, to house their private collection. In 1884, Crocker's widow donated the building and its contents to the city of Sacramento, with the California Museum Association as co-tenant and administrator. After Mrs. Crocker's death, the old home at the southwest corner of Third and O, built by B. F. Hastings about 1868, was also acquired and converted into the gallery annex. Judge Crocker was a brother of Charles Crocker and was legal counsel for the Central Pacific Railroad. His acquisitions are beautifully displayed in the museum, which has many landscapes of California painted in the late nineteenth century, and a very interesting modern art gallery as well.

SACRAMENTO CEMETERIES

Sacramento's first cemetery (SRL 592) was established by John A. Sutter in 1849. It was located on Alhambra Boulevard between I and J Streets, and is now the campus of Sutter Junior High School. In the same year Sutter and H. A. Schoolcraft gave the land for the Sacramento City Cemetery (SRL 566), at Broadway and Riverside Boulevard. Many pioneers and important persons are buried here, including Governors John Bigler, Newton Booth, and William Irwin; Mark Hopkins; E. B. Crocker; and William S. Hamilton.

William Stephens Hamilton, youngest son of Alexander Hamilton, first secretary of the treasury and a prominent late-eighteenth-century statesman, came to California in 1849. Previous to that time he had served as surveyor of public lands in Illinois, pioneered in Wisconsin, where he served in the Territorial Legislature, and served with the rank of colonel in the Black Hawk War, distinguishing himself for "efficiency and bravery." In California he tried his hand at mining for a while, then went to Sacramento to trade. He died in that city on October 7, 1850. His remains lay in an unmarked grave for many years, but now, in another location, are entombed under a granite monument sent out from Massachusetts by his grandnephew.

Chevra Kaddish, or Home of Peace Cemetery (SRL 654.1), was the first Jewish cemetery in California. The land was acquired in 1850. The site is located at Thirty-third and K Streets in Sacramento.

MCCLELLAN AIR FORCE BASE

North and east of Sacramento is McClellan Air Force Base, established as the Sacramento Air Depot in 1936. The facility was renamed McClellan Field in memory of Major Hezekiah McClellan, a test pilot killed in a 1939 air crash. The base was identified with many historic flights: Col. Jimmy Doolittle brought his B-25s here for a final checkup before their historic bombing raid on Tokyo in 1942; C-47 transports used in the Berlin Airlift in 1948 were flown here for maintenance; and the F-117 Stealth was worked on here in secret in the 1980s, by which time it had also become a station for Coast Guard patrol planes. The base was selected for closing in 1995, and in 2000 the last military planes departed. The future of the site is uncertain.

THE DELTA REGION

The rich delta lands of the Sacramento and San Joaquin Rivers cover more than 425,000 acres of immensely productive country. It is a section suggestive of the dikes and canals of the Netherlands. First settled in the 1850s by gold-seekers who had failed to make a living in the mines and who had squatted on the river delta in order to raise enough food for their subsistence, the land early demonstrated its extraordinary fertility. After the completion of the Central Pacific Railroad thousands of Chinese workers were employed, for very low wages, in reclaiming the delta country for agriculture. They built the first systems of levees along the various islands, working laboriously with wheelbarrows. Agriculture is still the chief activity of the region, but fishing and pleasure boating are also important.

TOWNS OF THE LOWER SACRAMENTO VALLEY

South of Franklin and Hood is the unique town of Locke, which could easily pass for a Mother Lode mining camp or a Western movie set. It is neither. Locke is a community composed almost entirely of Chinese that was built as late as 1916, when fire destroyed the Chinatown of neighboring Walnut Grove. A number of displaced Chinese leased land from George and Clay Locke and began building their homes and shops. The town is centered on a twelve-foot-wide main street parallel to County Road E-13 (River Road); most of the buildings are two stories with overhanging balconies. An interesting feature of the town is the Dai Loy Gambling Hall, now a museum of the town's life. The community is on the National Register of Historic Places.

Walnut Grove nearby has a vigorous Japanese community; its Gakuen Hall, also known as the Walnut Grove Japanese Community Center, is on the National Register of Historic Places. The town, first settled in 1850, is divided by the Sacramento River. The bridge across the river was built in 1952, replacing an earlier one from 1916, which was the first cantilevered counterweight bascule bridge west of the Mississippi.

San Benito County

San Benito County derived its name from San Benito Creek, which was named by Father Juan Crespí in 1772; San Benito is Spanish for Saint Benedict. The county was formed in 1874 from a part of Monterey County, and the county seat has always been at Hollister. The area of the county was increased in 1887 by additions from the adjoining counties of Fresno and Merced.

MISSION SAN JUAN BAUTISTA

In the late eighteenth century, Spanish policy was to establish missions as fast as possible to fill gaps in the chain between San Diego and San Francisco. Soon after the dedication of Mission San José, Father Fermín Lasuén proceeded to the San Benito Valley, where on the feast day of St. John the Baptist, June 24, 1797, Mission San Juan Bautista was founded. Lasuén had chosen this spot over others suggested to him because this location "promised the most abundant harvest of souls."

Assisting in the ceremonies at the dedication were Father Magin Catalá from Mission Santa Clara and Father Manuel Martiarena, who was to be left in charge of the new establishment. The rites took place before a large assemblage of Indians from the nearby plains. These Indians were at peace with the Spanish, but there were others who inhabited the mountains to the east, including the warlike Asayames, with whom the mission was in conflict for several years.

The first temporary structure was replaced by a new church whose cornerstone was laid on June 13, 1803. Within this stone were placed coins and a sealed bottle containing a narrative of the proceedings at the celebration. Completed in 1812, the main structure was nearly 200 feet long and thirty feet wide, with a high roof about forty feet above the floor. The church and other buildings were of adobe brick, and made up two sides of a courtyard, the other two of which were completed by a wall. A corridor of twenty arches resting on brick pillars extended across the front of the church.

Father Estévan Tápis, who had succeeded to the office of padre presidente on the death of Father Lasuén, officiated at the 1812 dedication. Later that year, at the end of his term of office, Father Tápis went to live at San Juan Bautista, remaining there until his death in 1825 at the age of seventy-one. A man of considerable ability, he was familiar with several Indian languages and enjoyed teaching Indian boys to read and write.

Church of Mission San Juan Bautista

Furthermore, he seems to have gotten on well with the civil authorities who also lived at San Juan.

In 1831, the mission was visited by Captain Alfred Robinson, who wrote:

> It is conveniently located in the center of a large valley, with an abundance of rich land and large stocks of cattle. Padre Felipe Arroyo [de la Cuesta] was the missionary, whose infirm state of health kept him confined closely to his chamber. For amusement, when tired of study, he called in the children of the place and set them to dancing and playing their games. In his eccentric taste he had given them the names of all the renowned persons of antiquity, and Ciceros, Platos, and Alexanders were to be found in abundance.

In 1835, all the mission property in Alta California was secularized. José Tiburcio Castro, grantee of nearby Rancho Sausal, was made *mayordomo*. Sixty-three families of Indians were released from mission discipline at the time, and payments were made to them amounting to over $8,000. The value of the remaining mission property was estimated to be $138,973, with only a debt of $250 standing against it. The mayordomo's final report in 1836 listed 900 head of cattle and 4,000 sheep as the property of the mission and an account of $1,300 against the property.

Mission San Juan Bautista (SRL 195) has been in unbroken service since its founding: Mass has been said there every day since 1797. The church is the largest of all the mission churches in California, with three aisles. The statues, paintings, and sandstone baptismal font are all original, as is the colorful reredos for the statues behind the altar. This was painted by a stranded Boston sailor, Thomas Doak, in 1816, in exchange for room and board. The *convento* wing adjoining the church is today used as a museum.

The San Andreas Fault passes immediately to the east of the walled garden of the mission, and seismographic equipment is displayed on the east side of the plaza. The fault creates an abrupt drop of some twelve feet between the mission garden and the flatlands beyond.

SAN JUAN BAUTISTA STATE HISTORIC PARK

In Alta California, most of the missions attracted settlement, and towns arose nearby. San Juan Bautista was the name given to the mission; the town adjacent to it was first known as San Juan. The San Benito Valley was first called the San Juan Valley, and the mountains now known as the Gabilan Range were first called the San Juan Range. After statehood, the post office was established under the name San Juan. Since the name was widely used in California, some confusion developed. Around 1905 the post office was renamed San Juan Bautista, and since then the mission and the town have borne the same name.

In 1835 José Castro became interim governor of California, and in 1836 he and Juan B. Alvarado made San Juan their headquarters in the revolt that resulted in the exile of Governor Gutiérrez and his replacement by Alvarado. Castro petitioned for land in 1839: "Being the owner of a considerable quantity of cattle and horses without possessing any land of my own whereon to place them to increase and prosper, I have become acquainted with a suitable place in the neighborhood of this pueblo, known by the name of San Justo, which does not belong to any owner and is entirely unoccupied." The request was granted. In July 1844 Castro transferred the property to Francisco Pérez Pacheco.

In 1840–41 Castro built a two-story adobe house (SRL 179) on the south side of the plaza diagonally opposite the mission church. With its overhanging balcony, it is considered to be one of the finest examples of California adobe construction remaining from the Mexican era. In 1846, while interim *comandante general*, Castro again organized forces at San Juan; this time he wished to expel John C. Frémont from his temporary stronghold on Gabilan Peak, where the American captain maintained his forces from March 6 to March 9. On July 17, Frémont raised the American flag on the plaza at San Juan and there drilled his ten companies of volunteer troops before starting for Los Angeles to support Commodore Stockton in suppressing the revolt of General Flores.

Castro's house in the pueblo of San Juan was acquired by Patrick Breen and finally deeded to him in

Castro-Breen Adobe, San Juan Bautista State Historic Park

1854. Breen and his family, the first English-speaking settlers in San Juan, were among the members of the Reed-Donner party who survived the tragic winter of 1846–47 in the High Sierra. Their first home in California was the room in the convento wing of the mission now used as a gift shop. Breen purchased some of the mission property in addition to the Castro house and established an inn, which became famous as a stopping place for travelers between Monterey and the mines in 1849–50. Years later, Helen Hunt Jackson began to write *Ramona* while staying there.

In the 1850s and 1860s San Juan was the site of an exchange station on the route between San Francisco and Los Angeles; at one time eleven stage lines stopped at the Plaza Hotel (SRL 180), on the same side of the plaza as the Castro House. This building consists of two one-story adobes, which were combined, and a second story of wood. The larger of the adobes was built in 1813–14 as an armory and barracks for the soldiers of the mission guard. Angelo Zanetta added the second story in 1858 and opened the building as the Plaza Hotel. The old livery stable, built in the 1870s, is still standing and contains an interesting display of old vehicles. Next to it is the Zanetta house, the lower story of which was built by Angelo Zanetta in 1868 with bricks from the old mission nunnery (built in 1815, enlarged in 1832, and torn down in 1868). The upper story above the residence was a wood-frame public hall.

The Castro adobe, Plaza Hotel, stable, and Zanetta house are part of San Juan Bautista State Historic Park; these, with the plaza itself, have also been designated as a National Historic Landmark.

A few other old adobes stand along the streets of the old town, as well as several interesting wooden structures from the early American period. Notable among

the adobes are the Casa Juan de Anza at Third and Franklin Streets and the two-story building on Fourth Street near Washington; the latter was restored by the Native Daughters of the Golden West. Among the American wooden buildings, the Masonic Hall from 1864 is outstanding. San Juan Bautista State Historic Park, with its unspoiled central plaza, gives a unique impression of a mission town from earlier days. US 101 long ago bypassed the little community, and although it has many visitors throughout the year, it has been able to preserve its atmosphere of another time.

THE PACHECO RANCHOS

Francisco Pérez Pacheco was a Mexican carriage maker who came to California in 1819 with a company of artillery. His success in quelling Indian revolts won him promotion to junior officer's rank in 1824; afterward, he was commander of the Custom House guard and then of the military post at Monterey.

Since the padres at San Juan Bautista did not need all the land set aside for mission use, they allowed Pacheco to settle upon a part of it some time before 1833. This was the Bolsa de San Felipe, which came by the name Bolsa ("pocket") because it was nearly enclosed by a swamp, a willow grove, and a ravine called Sanjón de Tequisquite. Pacheco allowed the family of the mayordomo of the mission and some of the mission Indians who were living on it to remain. The formalities that attended the legal taking possession of land in that period included pulling up grass, cutting a few tree branches, throwing a few stones, and taking up a handful of earth. After taking possession, Pacheco built a large stone house, where he and José Maria Sánchez, owner of the adjoining Rancho Llano del Tequisquite, lived together for a time.

On petition to Governor Figueroa for adjoining property, the Ausaymas tract of two leagues was granted to Pacheco in 1833. In 1836 he petitioned for another two leagues, which he called Guadalaxarita but which the padres called San Felipe, and this tract was probably included in the grant of six leagues made by Governor Gutiérrez that year. Pacheco became an extensive landowner, eventually having in his possession the San Justo Rancho, conveyed to him by José Castro in 1844; the Bolsa de San Felipe near Hollister; the Ausaymas y San Felipe, extending into Santa Clara County; and the San Luis Gonzaga, lying in the counties of Santa Clara and Merced, including the Pacheco Pass and several miles of the Pacheco Pass Road. All of these ranchos were later patented to him by the United States.

In 1844 Don Francisco Pacheco was captain of militia and in 1846 tithe collector. Testimony given in 1852 states that he was then the owner of a house valued at between $15,000 and $20,000, ten cabins for laborers, and thousands of horses, cattle, and hogs, with pens and corrals, and that enough of his land was in cultivation to provide for all living upon it.

Rancho San Justo, through which the San Benito River runs, was sold by Pacheco in 1855, three years before his death, to W. W. Hollister and Flint, Bixby, and Company, men who brought two flocks of sheep from the East and turned the place into a sheep ranch. Some years later Colonel Hollister sold the eastern portion to the San Justo Homestead Association, a group of businessmen who established the town of Hollister. On the western part, Flint, Bixby, and Company built a three-family ranch house, which still stands as a part of St. Francis Retreat in the hills above San Juan Bautista. The old house and surrounding land were sold to the Franciscan Fathers in 1947.

RANCHO CIÉNEGA DE LOS PAICINES

Rancho Ciénega de los Paicines, named for a Costonoan village, was granted by Governor Alvarado to Angel Castro and José Antonio Rodríguez in 1842. Rodríguez died before 1853, when a claim to the property was filed by Angel Castro and Hilaria Castro de Rodríguez, widow of the co-grantee, and her three children. A patent for 8,918 acres was issued to these claimants in 1869. This grant covered the land extending from Tres Pinos Creek on the east to the Cienega Valley at the foot of the Gabilan Range on the west. Through it runs a stretch of the San Benito River and its tributary, Pescadero Creek.

Rancho Ciénega de los Paicines has passed through the hands of several owners since the days of Angel Castro. About one thousand acres were sold separately in a tract east of the stage road to San Benito and south of Tres Pinos Creek. Much of this acreage is now planted in wine grapes.

Cienega Road, south of Hollister, follows the main line of the San Andreas Fault for a distance of about fifteen miles. The fault is subject to sudden movements, such as caused the 1906 earthquake, as well as to gradual movement (also known as slow creep). Evidence of fault movement may be seen on the property of the Calera Wine Company, where the old winery is slowly being pulled apart and requires constant repair. The present

building, the Cienega Winery, is the third on the site. The San Andreas Fault at Cienega Winery has been registered by the Department of the Interior as a National Natural Landmark.

GABILAN OR FREMONT PEAK

The highest peak in the Gabilan Range on the border between San Benito and Monterey Counties is called Gabilan (or Gavilan) Peak, sometimes Hawk's Peak, *gavilán* being Spanish for "sparrow hawk." It is today more commonly called Fremont Peak (SRL 181). To this spot in 1846 Frémont took his band of followers, after being ordered by Mexican officials to leave the country. Taking possession of the peak, he erected an earthen fort there on March 6. He raised a flag (a modified version of the flag of the U.S. Army Corps of Engineers) over the fort, which his party held for four days. General José Castro prepared to dislodge the Americans, and Frémont, with his forces outnumbered five to one, slowly retreated north to Sutter's Fort.

The occupation of Gabilan Peak and the flying of a flag of defiance early in 1846 were the first of a series of increasingly serious hostilities, which would end in the American conquest within two years and a subsequent period of tension between the Hispanic and the American populations.

A memorial iron flagstaff was put up in 1908 atop the peak. There are no traces of the fort left. The site is now Fremont Peak State Park.

HOLLISTER

In the autumn of 1868 the San Justo Homestead Association was formed by a group of fifty farmers, who each held one share. They purchased from Colonel W. W. Hollister the eastern part of Rancho San Justo, containing 21,000 acres, for the sum of $400,000 and divided the best part of the land into fifty homestead lots, one for each member. One hundred acres in the middle was reserved for a town site and was laid out in blocks, lots, and streets. This is now the center of Hollister.

A man prominent in the association and the town was T. S. Hawkins, who came to California from Missouri in 1860. He settled first in Santa Clara County but came to what is now San Benito County in 1867, renting 1,000 acres of virgin soil and planting it with grain. In the following year, Hawkins helped to form the San Justo Homestead Association, of which he was made secretary and general manager in 1870. At that time he gave up farming and turned his attention wholly to the advancement of the town.

Because it seemed a waste of time to go all the way to the coast to transact legal business at the county seat in Monterey, the suggestion of forming a new county met with approval. San Benito County was organized on February 12, 1874, with the new town of Hollister as its seat.

Hawkins built the Hazel Hawkins Memorial Hospital, established in Hollister in 1907, in memory of his granddaughter, who had died in 1902. A new Hazel Hawkins Hospital at 911 Sunset Drive was built in 1962, and the original building is now part of a business complex. The San Benito County Historical Museum is at the corner of Ann Alley and West Street in Hollister.

TRES PINOS AND PAICINES

The settlement of Paicines, little more than a post office and general store, stands at the junction of SR 25 and the road to New Idria. This spot used to be called Tres Pinos, named for three stunted pine trees on the bank of Tres Pinos Creek. It was known as Tres Pinos when Tiburcio Vásquez made his last robbery, at Snyder's Store at this junction. The robbery occurred in August 1873. Three men were killed by the bandit: one a deaf man who did not hear the peremptory orders of Vásquez; one a Portuguese who did not understand the language; and the third the hotelkeeper across the street, who refused to open his door and was felled by a bullet fired through it. The residents of the area were so incensed at the callous crime that Vásquez and his gang sought safety in the south. Trailed by sheriffs and captured, they were brought back to Hollister in May 1874, and after trial in San Jose, Vásquez was executed there on March 19, 1875. The store burned in 1877, but was rebuilt and stands today on the spot where the crime occurred many years ago.

When the railroad was built out from Hollister to a point west of the original settlement of Tres Pinos, a town grew up at the station, and it also was called Tres Pinos. After a time, the older settlement came to be called Paicines, for Rancho Ciénega de los Paicines. The word itself is supposed to be the name of an Indian settlement. The main activity of the new Tres Pinos was handling freight for the New Idria Mines. The railroad was abandoned in 1944, but the town still prospers on SR 25. The San Benito County Historical and Recreational Park is located one mile south of Tres Pinos, just west of SR 25, on Bolando Road, and con-

tains interesting outdoor displays of farm equipment. The 1868 Sullivan house, oldest in Hollister, was moved here in the 1980s and is open to visitors.

THE ROAD FROM THE NEW IDRIA MINES

The New Idria Quicksilver Mine (SRL 324) lies on the slope below San Carlos Peak, in the remote and isolated southeastern corner of San Benito County. The date of the discovery of this ore deposit is unknown; local Indians were making use of its red pigment when the mission fathers arrived. Tradition says that the padres made assay of the ore and determined it to be cinnabar. Bret Harte, in his *Story of a Mine*, attributes the accidental discovery of the first quicksilver in the region to a group of prospectors who were burning specimens of rock to test it for silver and were surprised to find a pool of "liquid silver" in the ashes of their improvised furnace.

"New Idria" was taken from the name of the Idrija Mine in Austria, and the same square type of furnace used there was initially used here, but it was supplanted long ago by a more effective type. With records that go back to 1854, it ranks among the most famous quicksilver mines in the world.

In the 1850s and 1860s the town nearest the mine was San Juan, 68 miles away. The stage route between them became a well-traveled road livened by the jangle of bells on the freight teams. The road from the mine followed San Carlos Creek down to Griswold Creek, named for a local rancher. It passed several adobe houses, a few of which stand, vacant or in ruins, beside the road today, and cabins constructed of rough lumber, most of which have disappeared. Next it came to Panoche Creek and ran through Panoche Valley, excellent cattle pasturage, until it reached Tres Pinos Creek, which it crossed and recrossed by means of fords. That part of the road has long been called the "wiggletail." The roadbed of today has been somewhat improved and, for a part of the distance, is now cut out of the canyon side at a high level. Finally the settlement that was then called Tres Pinos, now called Paicines, was reached, and the remainder of the journey to San Juan was on a more even grade.

Between two hundred and three hundred men were employed at the New Idria mines when they were visited by William Brewer of the Whitney Geologic Survey in 1861, who left a description of three mines and their activities. In 1898 the mines were sold to the New Idria Quicksilver Mining Company. During World War

I the place was policed by a company of soldiers. The mines were operated by the New Idria Mining and Chemical Company until their closure in April 1972.

THE PINNACLES

On November 19, 1794, the English navigator George Vancouver, who had been ill for some time in Monterey, had sufficiently recovered to go on an exploring expedition. With a small party on horseback, he set out across the Salinas Valley and reached a point, possibly the southern end of the Gabilan Range, where he "was gratified with the sight of the most extraordinary mountains" that he had ever beheld. One side "presented the appearance of a sumptuous edifice fallen into decay; the columns, which looked as if they had been raised with much labor and industry, were of great magnitude, seemed to be of an excellent form, and seemed to be composed of . . . cream coloured stone." It is thought that Vancouver reached the Pinnacles; if so, his would be the earliest record of a visit to this region.

In *The Days of a Man*, David Starr Jordan wrote:

> From 1904 to 1908 it was my pleasure to assist an ardent mountain lover, Mr. C. S. Hain of Tres Pinos, in securing for the people as a Government Forest Reserve, a singular district known as the "Pinnacles" lying in the Gavilan Range on the line between San Benito and Monterey

Counties. There the mountain range of yellow Miocene sandstone has been scored into deep gulches by the long action of small streams unaided by frost or ice. The cuts are very narrow and regular, scarcely widened even at the top, and the cliffs assume varied fantastic and picturesque forms. The forests are of little consequence, being of scant oak and digger pines, but many rare flowers are found in the tract, and some of the precipitous walls bear nests of the great California Condor—*Gymnogyps*—a majestic vulture with wing spread of from nine to ten feet.

The area was set aside as a National Monument by proclamation of President Theodore Roosevelt on January 16, 1908. By grants made in 1923 and 1924, the area was increased to 2,980 acres. Further additions were made in subsequent years so that the present size of the monument is 16,222 acres. The spire-like formations of the Pinnacles rise to a height of 1,000 feet, and beneath them are caves and subterranean passages. An amphitheater enclosed by smaller pinnacles has been named in honor of Jordan.

Pinnacles National Monument is located in San Benito County, except for a small corner in Monterey County. The terrain is very rugged and can be entered only from either side; there is no connecting road. The east entrance leads to the Visitors Center and is about thirty-five miles south of Hollister. The less-used west entrance is about twelve miles from Soledad.

San Bernardino County

San Bernardino County was organized in 1853 from territory that was at first a part of Los Angeles and San Diego Counties. The name comes from the Spanish for St. Bernardine of Siena. The city of San Bernardino has always been the county seat.

The county is of extraordinary size. Its 20,094 square

miles make it by far the largest county in the United States and nearly twice the size of Inyo County, the next largest within California. Nine states of the United States are smaller, so much so that San Bernardino County could contain any two, at least, of the following states: Connecticut, Delaware, Hawaii, Maryland, Massachusetts, New Hampshire, New Jersey, Rhode Island, and Vermont.

In the southwestern corner of the county is the populous San Bernardino Valley, closely linked with neighboring Los Angeles, Orange, and Riverside Counties. North and east of the San Gabriel and San Bernardino mountains, beyond Cajon Pass, is the huge Mojave Desert, which rises into the mountains of Nevada. The Mojave region covers some 90 percent of the county's area and contains about one-fifth of its population. In 1988 its residents attempted to secede from San Bernardino County and form California's 59th county, to be named Mojave County, but the measure was voted down in the June election.

THE PLEISTOCENE LAND

When the most recent of the ice ages joined Alaska with Siberia in the Pleistocene era, people and animals moved eastward into North America. That era was generally wetter and cooler than modern times, and, according to geologists, some of the dry basins of today were once under water. Archaeologists have made many discoveries in the Mojave that indicate the presence of human society many thousands of years ago. Near the old silver-mining town of Calico is the Calico Early Man Archaeological Site. Since 1964, this dig has uncovered thousands of stone tools that are claimed to be as much as 50,000 years old, making it the earliest site in the Western Hemisphere where human artifacts have been found. Famed anthropologist Louis B. Leakey was a consultant on the location of this site, which is on an eroded Pleistocene alluvial fan. Excavations were conducted here by the National Geographic Society and the San Bernardino County Museum from 1964 to 1981. The Bureau of Land Management currently occupies the site, which is open to the public. Some of the finds from the site are on display at the San Bernardino County Museum in Redlands. The presence of so many artifacts in what is now a barren, sparsely populated region suggests a substantial climate change over the ages.

Another discovery, made in 1928–29 in the Turquoise Mountains east of Johannesburg, indicates that Indians were mining the turquoise lodes of the Mojave

sink region centuries ago; many traces of this activity have been obliterated by machinery in modern times. In an excavation of a cave east of Barstow in the Newberry Mountains in the 1950s, organic artifacts were found and were subjected to radiocarbon tests that proclaimed them to be at least 3,000 years old.

CAJON PASS AND THE MOJAVE INDIAN TRAIL

Professor Herbert E. Bolton of the University of California at Berkeley established that, as early as 1772, Pedro Fages traversed the region of the Cajon Pass, while on his way north into the San Joaquin Valley in pursuit of deserters from the Presidio at San Diego.

The first visitor to cross the San Bernardino Mountains into the San Bernardino Valley was Father Francisco Garcés, the famous Spanish priest and explorer, who came in 1776 from the Colorado River. Jedediah Strong Smith, the first American to enter California overland, traveled the same trail from the Colorado in 1826 and again in 1827.

At the eastern entrance to the town of Needles in a small parkway, a National Trails marker (SRL 781) has been placed, calling attention to an old Indian trail, still visible in some places, that ran roughly parallel to the Colorado River on the California side. It was over this route that Garcés and Smith traveled.

Study of the diaries of the Garcés and Smith expeditions has shown that the route taken by these two men did not lead directly through Cajon Pass, as had been supposed. Mojaves had served as guides from the Colorado on both occasions, and they used their ancient trail, which led across the desert and up the Mojave River to its western headwaters in the San Bernardino Mountains. Crossing the range eight miles east of the present Cajon Pass, it came down into San Bernardino Valley on the ridge between Devil and Cable Canyons, crossing Cajon Creek between Devore and Verdemont. From here it skirted the base of the foothills to Cucamonga, and led on to San Gabriel and, ultimately, to the coast. The old Mojave Indian Trail is therefore extremely important historically, since it antedates the Cajon as a mountain crossing for the white explorers.

Early in 1827, however, hostilities between the Mojaves and the white explorers broke out, with atrocities committed by both parties. Several alternative routes were developed over the next thirty years, as Indian relations heated and cooled. At the place where the Mojave Trail crossed the summit of the mountains, a marker (SRL 618) has been placed at Monument Peak

Mormon Trail Monument, Cajon Pass

commemorating both Garcés and Smith and their pioneering journeys across the area.

During the years 1830–31 three pioneer pack trains from New Mexico crossed the San Bernardino Mountains into the valley beyond. The first, forerunner of the Santa Fe caravans, was led by Antonio Armijo, a trader from New Mexico, who came in January 1830 by what he called "San Bernardino Canyon," probably the present Cajon pass. Ewing Young and his trappers came a little later in the same year, but the trail by which he crossed the mountains has not been determined. In the fall of 1830 William Wolfskill left Santa Fe with another band of trappers, and, according to J. J. Warner, went through the Cajon in February 1831. Certainly the last, and possibly all three, of these parties used the Cajon.

Seventeen miles north of San Bernardino, at the intersection of I-15 and SR 138, a marker (SRL 576) notes that this was part of the route extending into New Mexico once known as the Santa Fe Trail. North of Cajon Station on the railroad line another marker (SRL 578) notes that from here another road branched east and north to the Great Salt Lake in Utah. On SR 138 at West Cajon Canyon another marker (SRL 577) notes that the Mormons heading westward with their heavy wagons in 1851 passed through here rather than the "Narrows" at the top of the Cajon Pass. A mile and a half south of Devore, close to Glen Helen Regional Park, a monument (SRL 573) commemorates the campsite of the Mormon party in 1851 when they waited to move into the San Bernardino Valley itself.

The Wolfskill passage across the desert set the course for emigrants of the next thirty years. Depending on the destination of a traveler, it might be known as the Santa Fe Road, the Salt Lake Road, or, in more general terms,

the Spanish Road or the Mojave Road. Crowder Canyon, which extends into Cajon Canyon from Summit Valley, is reminiscent of the days (1830–60) when stolen animals were pastured in this region, before the long drive across the Mojave Desert. A brisk trade in California mules and horses was carried on with Santa Fe. Most of the mules were destined for Missouri, where there was a great demand for the superior animal then produced in California. While a large proportion of this trade was lawful, there was also much illegitimate and clandestine traffic carried on by Indians and whites alike. Hardly a year passed in which the mission fathers and the rancheros did not lose valuable livestock, which was driven off through Cajon Pass by raiding parties of outlaws. Even after the American occupation, these raids continued. One of the reasons settlement was deliberately encouraged in the San Bernardino Valley was the desire to discourage raiders from attacking the more densely settled areas.

FOUR OLD TRAILS ACROSS EUCLID AVENUE

Four historic trails once crossed what is now Euclid Avenue, the long, tree-lined drive that extends north and south through the modern cities of Ontario and Upland.

The first of these trails to be traversed by the newcomers was the Anza Trail, over which Juan Bautista de Anza in 1774 led the first overland party into California, and again in 1775 the first overland band of settlers, the founders of San Francisco. The Boy Scouts of America and service organizations of Ontario have placed a memorial boulder in honor of Anza in a small park on the corner of Euclid Avenue and Philips Street. On it a bronze tablet bears this inscription: "To the honor and glory of Juan Bautista D'Anza, Trailmarker, and his band of intrepid followers, who, on March 21, 1774, passed near this spot on their way to San Gabriel and Monterey, the first white men to break a trail overland to California."

The San Gabriel Mission fathers used this trail as far as the Santa Ana River in order to reach their mission in the San Bernardino Valley until a more direct route was cut shortly after 1822.

The second trail crossing Euclid Avenue, and the oldest of the four, was the Mojave Indian Trail, which was well established when Father Garcés traveled it in 1776. On this side of the Cajon Pass, the trail (also known by other names) descended south from the pass and followed the base of the mountains westward approximately where Foothill Boulevard runs today.

At the corner of Euclid and Foothill in Upland stands a striking monument, the "Madonna of the Trail." This is the westernmost of twelve such statues across the United States that mark the trail of the pioneers; the easternmost is at Bethesda, Maryland. The statues were dedicated simultaneously on February 1, 1929. Mrs. Carolyn Emily Cook, then eighty-one, who had made the trip from Iowa to California as a three-year-old child with her family in an oxcart, unveiled the heroic monument of a pioneer woman and her children. The two speakers at the dedication were Mildred Brooke Hoover and Judge Harry S. Truman from Missouri. Mrs. Hoover was the California State Regent of the Daughters of the American Revolution, which had undertaken the project. Shortly thereafter she began work on the first edition of *Historic Spots in California*, co-authoring one volume and entirely writing another. Her brother-in-law Herbert Clark Hoover was on that date president-elect of the United States. Judge Truman had assisted the DAR in the placement of the statues. Later he became a United States senator from Missouri, and in 1945 the thirty-third president of the United States. A memory box in the base of the statue containing coins, books, newspapers, and other printed matter was opened in 1979 on the fiftieth anniversary of the dedication.

The third trail crossing Euclid Avenue was the old Emigrant Trail. This trail, which followed Anza's route across the Colorado Desert as far as Carrizo Creek and crossed the mountains via Warner's Ranch, branched in two directions after leaving Aguanga; one branch, known as the San Bernardino–Sonora Road, followed north to San Gorgonio Pass and west through the San Bernardino Valley, while the other, known in mission days as the Canyon Road to the Colorado, and designed by the Los Angeles Court of Sessions in 1851 as the Colorado Road, took its course along the western mountains via Temecula, Elsinore, Temescal Canyon, Corona, and the Santa Ana River.

The San Bernardino–Sonora Road, the upper branch of the old Emigrant Trail, came from Warner's Ranch via Aguanga and passed down the San Jacinto Valley and across the hills to the site of what is now Beaumont in Riverside County. From there, it continued northward and west through San Bernardino County via Redlands and Old San Bernardino, or Gauchama, to what is now Colton. From that point the road went southwest past Slover Mountain to Agua Mansa, where it again proceeded westward to what is now Ontario, crossing Euclid Avenue one mile north of the Union Pacific Railroad. From there it continued west across San Bernar-

dino County to Los Angeles County via Ciénega (Mud Springs) near San Dimas.

The padres, after 1822 and before 1827, were the first to use this road on their way from San Gabriel to their mission outpost at Guachama. Smith took this route in 1827 on his journey out of California, camping at Jumuba Ranchería a few miles west of Guachama Mission Station. Here he awaited the much-needed supplies that Father Sánchez, of Mission San Gabriel, had ordered the mayordomo of Guachama to furnish him for his journey.

The last of the four trails crossing Euclid Avenue was the Colorado Road. This was opened from Carrizo Creek to Warner's in 1826 by Romualdo Pacheco, leader of a government expedition seeking an official mail route. Immediately thereafter the padres of San Gabriel opened up the road all the way to Warner's from San Gabriel via the canyon route. The first American to use this route was David E. Jackson in 1831, and it was used by other trappers and by those emigrants from Mexico and the East who followed the southern route via Santa Fe and the Gila River, of which the Colorado Road was a continuation. Since this southern trail was the only all-year route into California from the East, it was also used by the Butterfield stages from 1858 to 1861 for carrying passengers and mails.

The route of the Butterfield stages over this section of the Colorado Road may be traced by the adobes that it passed. After crossing the Santa Ana River near the Cota House, in what is now Riverside County, the road followed the base of the hills along Chino Creek, above which the highway from Chino to Santa Ana now runs. About three miles northwest of the Cota House, the stages passed the Raimundo Yorba adobe on Rancho Rincón, now in San Bernardino County. Although it was not one of the official stations along this route, doubtless stages did halt at the old adobe house, which still stands on the brow of the hill, beautifully restored. In 1868 Fenton M. Slaughter purchased this building from Yorba, and he lived in it until his death in 1897. His daughter, Julia Slaughter Fuqua, saved it from ruin and brought it back to its former beauty as a memorial to her father. The Yorba-Slaughter Adobe (SRL 191), built in the early 1850s, stands at 17127 Pomona-Rincon Road, a little over five miles south of Chino. This outstanding example of California adobe architecture is now administered as one of the San Bernardino County Museums.

At Rancho Rincón, the Butterfield route ran along the base of the hill, crossing the extreme southern terminus of Euclid Avenue at that point. From there it continued northwest along Chino Creek for seven miles to Rancho Chino, where a station was maintained on what is now the southern part of the California Institution for Men.

THE MOJAVE ROAD

Shortly after the admission of California to the Union in 1850, federal officials began to plan an overland railroad to make a closer link between the far-off Pacific state and her thirty sisters. The 1850s saw a massive program of exploration and mapping of all corners of the West. In 1854, a party headed by Army Lieutenant Amiel Weeks Whipple crossed the Mojave Desert and mapped it for a possible railroad line. They discovered a remarkable desert phenomenon, Piute (or Pah-Ute) Springs, a never-failing flow of some 150 gallons of water per minute that gives rise to Piute Creek. The creek flows for nearly a mile before disappearing into the desert and with the springs creates a remarkable oasis. It seems likely that the Paiute Indians had established some cultivated fields nearby. The springs, though located in a tangle of mountains and hills that were difficult for teams and wagons to negotiate, became a stopping point on the overland trail leading from Fort Mojave on the Arizona side of the Colorado River across the desert to Barstow and from there south over the Cajon Pass into the San Bernardino Valley. In 1867 the Army established a small post there, called Fort Piute, which is now in ruins; there are plans to restore the site, but even today it is as remote a spot as can be found anywhere within the state of California. The site is on the Piute Ridge overlooking the Lanfair Valley at the eastern edge of the East Mojave National Scenic Area, and some twelve miles by dirt road from US 95, about twenty-five miles northwest of Needles.

Until the coming of the railroads, the chief route across this part of California was the Mojave Road. Going west from Fort Piute, the Mojave Road crossed several vital sources of water. Rock Springs and "Government Hole" lay close together; the latter was dug in 1859 by teamsters in the employ of Phineas Banning. Marl Springs lay to the west, and further on, past an area of volcanic cinder cones, was Soda Springs, where a small Army post was put up in 1867.

Soda Springs got a new lease on life in the 1940s when Curtis Howe Springer homesteaded the property and used part of the old rock wall from the fort to build a religious resort with the distinctive name of "Zzyzx." Thirty years later the Bureau of Land Man-

agement succeeded in evicting Springer from the place, still shown on some maps as Zzyzx Springs. The Mojave River was first encountered at "The Caves" in Cave (now Afton) Canyon; sixteen miles further west was Camp Cady (SRL 963.1), where the old commissary and quartermaster store stood until they were destroyed by flood in 1938. The road proceeded along the valley of the Mojave River past modern-day Yermo, Daggett, and Barstow, by which time it had been joined by the Salt Lake Trail and turned south toward the Cajon Pass. Considerable efforts have been made to have the path of the Mojave Trail restored for the enjoyment of modern travelers, but the project is still largely undeveloped. The route of the Mojave Road, from Drum Barracks near Los Angeles Harbor through the Cajon Pass and across the Mojave Desert to the Nevada state line, has been designated as SRL 963. Its marker stands at the Midway Rest Area on the north side of I-15, thirty miles northeast of Barstow.

RANCHO AND ASISTENCIA SAN BERNARDINO

Mission San Gabriel Arcángel was established in 1771; what is now the San Bernardino Valley was intended to be one of the ranchos that supplied the mission. On May 20, 1810, Father Francisco Dumetz celebrated Mass in an enramada, or temporary chapel, just west of modern Redlands. The day being the feast day of St. Bernardine of Siena, the priest named the chapel "San Bernardino." The name was later to become that of a ranch, a branch mission, a city, a county, a valley, and a mountain range.

In 1819, Christianized Indians from the Guachama Ranchería asked the authorities at Mission San Gabriel to teach them to raise cattle and crops. When Father Mariano Payeras visited Guachama ("the place of plenty to eat" in the local language) in 1821, he found that there were mission cattle grazing in the valley and a number of old houses, probably for the herdsmen of the rancho, at Jumuba, a few miles west of the rancho headquarters. In 1827, Father Sánchez of Mission San Gabriel reported: "Rancho of San Bernardino. The house is of adobe. It consists of one long building. It has an enramada or structure of boughs that serves as a chapel. It has also a building with compartments for keeping grain. The walls of this structure are of adobe."

This was the Guachama Mission Station (SRL 95), or the rancho headquarters, on Rancho San Bernardino, which was owned by Mission San Gabriel. The little mission station was located north of what is now Mission Road and east of where it intersects Mountain View Avenue, while the site of the Guachama village was on the south side of this road. The marker is on Mission Road in the Bryn Mawr district of Loma Linda.

On what is now known as Barton Hill, one and one-half miles southeast of the old rancho buildings, and about two miles west of the present city of Redlands on Barton Road, an extensive adobe structure was begun about 1830. This was the Asistencia San Bernardino, a chapel under the supervision of Mission San Gabriel. The fathers had planned a chain of interior missions paralleling those near the coast, and San Bernardino, along with San Antonio de Pala and Santa Ysabel, was to have been part of this chain. The program never went beyond these three asistencias, for the secularization decree in the 1830s ended all mission activity in California.

After secularization, all work on the asistencia ceased and the buildings remained practically deserted until 1842, when a large section of the mission lands was granted to three sons and a nephew of Antonio María Lugo of Los Angeles. The cities of San Bernardino, Redlands, and Colton now stand on the Rancho San Bernardino of the Lugos. One of Don Antonio's sons, José del Carmen Lugo, came to live in the old asistencia buildings, thus saving them from complete disintegration for a time.

After the Rancho San Bernardino was sold to the Mormons by the Lugo brothers in 1851, Bishop Nathan C. Tenney, manager of agricultural operations on the lands formerly cultivated by the missions, occupied the old asistencia buildings. Upon the withdrawal of the Mormons in 1857, Dr. Ben Barton, a prominent pioneer settler, moved with his family into the buildings, occupying them until 1867. From this date the old adobes, untenanted and uncared for, gradually succumbed to the weather, until only a few mud walls remained.

The Asistencia San Bernardino (SRL 42) was meticulously rebuilt in the years 1928–37; wherever possible, materials salvaged from the original structure were incorporated into the replica. It stands at 26930 Barton Road, in the Bryn Mawr district. The striking whitewashed adobe bell tower is a landmark in the neighborhood. The building is used for religious services and also serves as one of the museums of San Bernardino County. This restoration project became a model for similar programs elsewhere in the state.

North of the asistencia, and just beyond the railroad tracks, may be seen the old *zanja*, or water ditch (SRL 43), built in 1819–20 by the Indians under the direction

of the Spaniards to bring water for irrigation from Mill Creek Canyon to the Guachama Rancheria. The ditch passes under the business district of Redlands. A little further north, at 11245 Nevada Street in Redlands, is the much altered home of Dr. Ben Barton, built for his family in 1866–67, to which they moved from the asistencia. The three-story brick building was one of the largest in the county at the time of its construction.

MISSION RANCHOS

Mission San Gabriel had three ranchos in the San Bernardino Valley: Rancho San Bernardino, already mentioned as the location of the mission station Guachama and later the asistencia; Rancho Agua Caliente, on which the present city of San Bernardino is located; and Rancho Jumuba, located between the present Loma Linda and Colton. Rancho Jumuba was named for an Indian rancheria that occupied the site beside a bubbling spring of water. It was here that Jedediah Strong Smith camped in 1827 while being outfitted by the mission fathers, just before starting on his return trip to Salt Lake via the San Joaquin Valley.

SAN BERNARDINO

The city of San Bernardino owes its beginnings to a colony of Mormons from Salt Lake City, who arrived in June 1851 and laid the foundation of a thriving community in the six years before their leader, Brigham Young, recalled them. Gradually, the lands purchased from the Lugo brothers were subdivided and sold to the individual members of the Mormon community, who established homes and farms. The town of San Bernardino was founded; in the San Bernardino Mountains, new sawmills were built; roads were constructed, the Mormons opening up the present Foothill Boulevard as far as Cucamonga; extensive agricultural activities were started; and churches and schools were founded.

Adobe and log houses were soon erected on a site originally known as "Agua Caliente," but the name of the neighboring Asistencia San Bernardino was transferred to the new town. Here, because of rumored Indian attacks, a fort and stockade enclosing eight acres of ground was put up in the form of a parallelogram, 300 feet wide and 720 feet long. The north and south ends were made of cottonwood and willow tree trunks closely fitted together and set three feet in the ground and twelve feet above, while the log houses were moved along the west side, forming a solid wall finished with logs in blockhouse fashion, with loopholes, bastions at the corners, and inset gateways. Within this stockade about a hundred families lived; a few, however, remained outside, camping at a spot now occupied by the Pioneer Memorial Cemetery at Seventh Street and Sierra Way.

The site of the old Mormon stockade (SRL 44) included the present Arrowhead Avenue from Third Street nearly to Fourth Street, and lands to the east, west, and south. Most of this area today is occupied by the striking San Bernardino County Government Center, completed in 1983, and the impressive county courthouse, dating from 1926. On the courthouse site also stood the José Maria Lugo adobe; the Native Sons of the Golden West placed a plaque there in 1927. A two-story adobe built by the Mormons stood at Third Street and Arrowhead Avenue until 1867, and was used as the first courthouse of San Bernardino County. Jefferson Hunt, an officer in the Mormon battalion, is sometimes called the "Father of San Bernardino County," for it was he, while a Los Angeles County legislator, who introduced legislation to create a separate San Bernardino County in 1853. The site of his home has been marked by the county on the south side of Fifth Street, between Arrowhead and Mountain View Avenues in San Bernardino.

In 1851, the year of their arrival, the Mormons built the first road from the San Bernardino Valley to the summit of the mountains, over which they hauled lumber from their sawmills to be sold in Los Angeles and other expanding communities of southern California. Much of the cost of their colony at San Bernardino was defrayed by the sale of lumber, and it was also needed for the construction of their own buildings. Where the Rim of the World Drive crosses the old Mormon lumber road at Crestline in the San Bernardino Mountains, a monument has been erected (SRL 96).

Although they were by and large a peaceable people, a quarrel arose between Mormon factions over land titles. The "Independent" group even put up an adobe fortification, Fort Benson (SRL 617), and maintained it for about a year. Its site is indicated by a monument east of Colton, on the west side of Hunt's Lane between I-10 and the railroad tracks. This was also the site of the Indian village of Jumuba.

In 1857, Mormon activity was halted by the decree of Brigham Young, the president of the Mormons. Young recalled his flock to Salt Lake City because of the threatened invasion of Utah by federal troops. The majority of the settlers obeyed the call and left their homes in the San Bernardino Valley, often selling them for very little. Over half the white population of the valley left in a short while, a unique event in the decade in which people were pouring into other parts of California at an unprecedented rate. Their departure seriously hindered the valley's prosperity for some time; the Mormons had been industrious citizens with great organizing ability, and they had been largely responsible for the development of the agricultural resources of the valley as well as for the sound basis of the city of San Bernardino.

CHINO

Rancho Santa Ana del Chino was another of the Mission San Gabriel ranchos. Soon after the secularization of the missions it was granted to Antonio María Lugo. The ranch house (SRL 942) stood about three miles south of the present-day town of Chino; the commemorative marker is at 4440 Eucalyptus Avenue. This adobe was built by Colonel Isaac Williams (known as Don Julián to the Californians), who came to California with Ewing Young in 1832 and became one of the leading citizens of Los Angeles. He married a daughter of Antonio María Lugo, who in 1841 deeded a half-interest in the Rancho Santa Ana del Chino to his son-in-law, and ten years later deeded the remainder to him.

The Williams adobe was the center of much activity, since it was near the well-traveled southern emigrant trail. Orchards and vineyards were planted; barns, shearing sheds, and adobe huts for many Indian and Mexican laborers were built, as was a gristmill, one of the earliest in southern California. The rancho was stocked with fine cattle, horses, and sheep, and an extensive trade in hides and tallow was carried on.

During the Mexican War the adobe was the scene of a battle between the Americans and the Californians. While Colonel Gillespie was shut up in Los Angeles in 1846, a score of Americans, commanded by B. D. Wilson, took refuge on Rancho del Chino, which was twenty-five miles east of Los Angeles. On September 27 the house was surrounded by a force of seventy mounted Californians; during the short skirmish that followed, one of the Californians, Carlos Ballesteros, was killed, and several Americans were wounded. The Californians, incensed by the death of their comrade, set fire to the *brea* roof of the adobe. At this point, Isaac Williams appeared with a white flag and his two little daughters, whom he insisted on placing in the hands of their uncle, Felipe Lugo, one of the attacking party, so they could be taken to their Grandfather Lugo in Los

Angeles. The leaders of the Californians, however, persuaded the Americans to surrender, promising them protection as prisoners of war. The success of the Californians in this encounter encouraged them in their attack upon Gillespie.

During the years 1858 to 1861, the Chino adobe assumed additional historical importance as a station on the Butterfield stage route, which passed its door. A marker has been placed by San Bernardino County at the corner of Eucalyptus Avenue and SR 71 in Chino.

Very soon after the death of Isaac Williams in 1856, his daughter Francisca married Robert Carlisle, a young Southerner, and Mercedes Williams married John Rains, who had been mayordomo at Chino. John Rains and his wife moved to Rancho Cucamonga, while the Carlisles remained at Chino. Robert Carlisle was an energetic, well-educated man and a good business manager; under his control the prosperity of Rancho del Chino continued until his death in 1865.

Francisca Williams Carlisle married again, and the Chino estate was managed by trustees. In 1881 it was sold to Richard Gird, a miner and engineer, one of the most picturesque characters of the early American period. On Rancho del Chino, Gird lived lavishly in a fine adobe built by Joseph Bridger (the site is on the grounds of the Los Serranos Country Club), and used his influence to persuade entrepreneurs to develop the region. A projected ironworks failed for lack of capital, but sugar beets, first planted on the rancho, had become a major industry in the region by 1900. Gird sold his property in 1894, and a short time later it was broken up into small tracts and sold; the Williams adobe disappeared long ago.

RANCHO CUCAMONGA

Rancho Cucamonga derived its name from an Indian village that was on the land when the first white men came there. It is said that the Cucamonga people were very intelligent and industrious and that they learned much from the padres at Mission San Gabriel. Gradually they acquired cattle and horses and raised good crops of corn and melons in the fertile hills and valleys of "Nuestra Señora del Pilar de Cucamonga," as the padres called the locality.

Tiburcio Tapia, a leading citizen of Los Angeles, petitioned for a grant to the Cucamonga lands in 1839 and received it in that year. Don Tiburcio immediately began the construction of an adobe house on the crest of Cucamonga's highest hill. "Massive as a fortress," its roof was covered with tar from Rancho La Brea near Los Angeles.

The Indians, who were employed in the building operations, rebelled when they realized that the newcomers were taking their rich grazing lands from them. Retreating to the foothills and canyons, they made occasional raids upon the stock of the white settlers. Desert Indians, too, frequently invaded the rancho lands, and many tales were told by old residents of raids and battles and even attacks upon the Tapia "fortress" on "Red Hill."

In the beginning, Don Tiburcio left his ranch largely in the care of his mayordomo, José María Valdez, who is said to have set out the "mother vineyard." This later developed into one of the large plantings of grapes in California, the first cuttings probably having been obtained at Mission San Gabriel. The history of the old rancho is closely associated with the development of its vineyard.

After Tiburcio Tapia's death in 1845, his daughter María Merced married Leon Victor Prudhomme, and moved with him to the adobe on Red Hill. In 1858, Prudhomme sold Rancho Cucamonga to John Rains and his wife, Mercedes Williams. An unpublished history of the 1890s says:

The coming of John Rains to this place marked not only a new but a progressive epoch in its history. The old Tapia residence on the hill was abandoned and a new one built at the highest point of the east bank of the arroyo, north of the vineyard. Labor and expense were not spared in its construction. . . . The walls were made of heavy brick made of the red clay dug from the hills and roofed with thatches covered with brea mixed with tallow. . . . A little to the east of the Valdez residence was built the store and nearby a blacksmith shop, stables, and several dwellings. . . . The rancho was stocked by Mr. Rains with sheep, horses, and cattle, and 160 acres were set to vines. The small still and winery were proportionately enlarged and improved. The road from Los Angeles to San Bernardino by way of Chino having been abandoned by the stage for the Arroyo San José routes to Bear Valley and the mines, this became a regular station, where the horses were changed and the traveler enabled to obtain refreshments.

With the vaqueros in charge of the flocks and herds, the laborers in the vineyards and winery, the stable hands in charge of stage relays, mechanics at work on buildings, teamsters, the blacksmiths and a trader and postmaster, the place became not only a hive of industry, but noted as the chief trading post and assembly point for all classes and nationalities east of Los Angeles. The Rains home was a center of social life, and, attracted by the hospitality of its master, the beauty of its mistress, the sparkling wines and festivities, here frequently gathered the representative wealthy and elite of the south.

This rather romantic account tells of what was actually only a short period of years. On November 17, 1862, John Rains was murdered, leaving his twenty-three-year-old widow with four small children and pregnant with a fifth. After a series of accusations, one Manuel Cerradel was arrested and confined to prison. Convicted not of Rains's murder but of an assault on a deputy sheriff, Cerradel was brutally lynched by a group of men while on his way to prison at San Quentin the following year. Ramón Carrillo, a family friend who had been accused by Robert Carlisle, Mercedes Williams Rains's brother-in-law, of the murder of John Rains, was shot to death in Mercedes' presence in 1864; Carlisle was killed in a shooting the following year. The distraught Mercedes married José Clemente Carrillo in 1864 and ultimately the couple became so indebted that they lost their estate. A daughter of John and Mercedes Rains, Francisca, married a young lawyer named Henry T. Gage in 1880. Gage became governor of California in 1899, and Mercedes attended his inaugural in Sacramento.

Meanwhile the Rains home, also known as Casa de Rancho Cucamonga, had become the property of I. W. Hellman through a mortgage foreclosure in 1871. In the following years the home became a private residence and later a hotel. From 1922 to 1948 Mr. and Mrs. Edwin Motsinger lived in the house, which they lovingly restored and to which they welcomed Francisca Rains Gage as a guest in 1946. In 1969 nearby Cucamonga Wash flooded and destroyed much of the surrounding area and the house had to be abandoned. After considerable legal difficulties, the property came into the possession of the San Bernardino Museum Association. The restored house is now on the National Register of Historic Landmarks and is open to the public at 7869 Vineyard Avenue, Rancho Cucamonga.

The old adobe winery (SRL 490) built by John Rains was at 8916 Foothill Boulevard nearby. Established in 1839 by Tiburcio Tapia, this was the first commercial winery in California. The winery was restored by H. H. Thomas, the eastern end being replaced after the 1969 flood. The Thomas Winery closed in 1995, but there are a few small wineries still in the neighborhood. The Cucamonga District was once among the major wine-producing regions, but urban encroachment has considerably restricted the acreage devoted to vines in recent years.

To the west of the winery, across Cucamonga Creek, is the site of the Tapia adobe (SRL 360) on the southeastern slope of Red Hill, which is now built up with homes and covered by the greens of the Red Hill Country Club.

YUCAIPA

Yucaipa is the site of an Indian rancheria from which it received its name. On the hillside just above the house at 33142 Avenue E, excavations by the San Bernardino Historical Society have revealed metates (grinding holes), fireplaces, and implements used by the peaceful Serrano Indians before and during the Spanish period. The place, well watered by springs and a creek, was a logical site for habitation. The marker (SRL 620) for the Yucaipa Rancheria is at the Yucaipa Adobe, described below.

The oldest dwelling still standing in San Bernardino County is located at 32183 Kentucky Street, near Dunlap Boulevard and Sixteenth Street, about four miles east of Redlands at the western outskirts of Yucaipa. The two-story Diego Sepúlveda adobe (SRL 528) was built in 1842 in the southeastern corner of the Rancho San Bernardino. Sepúlveda was a nephew of Antonio María Lugo, three of whose sons were co-grantees of the rancho with Sepúlveda. Later owners of the adobe included the Dunlap family, after whom the nearby street is named. In the early 1950s the old house, rapidly falling into ruin, was saved from demolition by a group of public-spirited citizens, who effected its purchase and restoration. Since 1955 it has been operated as one of the San Bernardino County museums, open to the public on a regular basis as the Yucaipa Adobe. The Mousley Museum of Natural History is at 35308 Panorama Drive in Yucaipa, with interesting anthropological displays as well as seashells and minerals.

AGUA MANSA AND SAN SALVADOR

These settlements on the "Bandini Donation" on Rancho Jurupa were composed of New Mexican colonists who had moved there in 1845 from the settlement of Politana on Rancho San Bernardino. It is thought that Politana lay somewhere in the vicinity of the modern city of Colton. Colonists were desirable at that time as protectors against the inroads of unfriendly Indians;

and when dissatisfaction with certain conditions at Politana arose, Juan Bandini invited the settlers to leave that place and locate on a parcel of land he donated. It lay on both sides of the Santa Ana River, and later formed part of San Salvador parish. Agua Mansa was on the north and west bank of the river, while the settlement on the south and east side was known as San Salvador. The original parish chapel in San Salvador collapsed before it was completed because it had been built on quicksand.

Agua Mansa ("gentle water") was the site of another chapel built in 1851 and in use until 1893. The Santa Ana River was anything but gentle in January 1862, when torrential rains caused a disastrous flood that washed away the homes of Agua Mansa and San Salvador on its banks. The chapel and the adjacent cemetery, on higher ground, were spared. The little burial ground is all that remains of Agua Mansa (SRL 121). The county's oldest cemetery, it is located about three miles southwest of Colton on Agua Mansa Road, east of its intersection with Riverside Avenue, and about half a mile north of the Riverside County line. The old chapel was restored in 1978 and is one of the San Bernardino County museums.

REDLANDS AND LOMA LINDA

Frank E. Brown and Edward G. Judson acquired land from the Southern Pacific Railroad in 1881 and added more to make a parcel of 4,000 acres. This was to be the planned community of Redlands, named for its reddish earth, and the town was incorporated in 1888. In order to find the water needed to make the community grow, Brown followed the recommendation of Dr. Ben Barton and investigated the nearby mountains. At Big Bear Valley he found a spot where a dam could be built, and in 1884 Big Bear Lake was created. This dam (SRL 725), built by the Bear Valley Irrigation Company, is still visible behind the present, higher dam, built in 1910. Citrus crops thrived in this portion of the valley, and the mild climate made Redlands attractive as a winter resort.

The Kimberly Crest Mansion at 1325 Prospect Drive is a reminder of this period of Redlands' history. Built in 1897 for an eastern industrialist, the French chateau-style building is open to the public with much of its original furnishings and decoration intact.

At 125 West Vine Street is the Smiley Public Library. The Smiley family developed Canyon Crest Park (popularly known as "Smiley Heights") on the southern edge of the city in the 1890s; beautifully landscaped, it

was a highly desirable area of elegant homes. The library was given to the city in 1898. On the grounds is the Lincoln Memorial Shrine, a repository of books and materials on the president and the Civil War.

The San Bernardino County Museum at 2024 Orange Tree Lane is one of the most spectacular in California. Opened in 1974, it is a large building worthy of a large county, with significant displays about natural history and the history of the people who have lived in the county.

The University of Redlands was the first four-year institution of higher learning in the county. It began as a Baptist institution in 1909; some of its oldest buildings date from that time. The Reverend Jasper Newton Field of the First Baptist Church of Redlands was the first president. It has developed into a distinguished liberal arts institution.

Nearby Loma Linda was the site of several unsuccessful attempts to establish a town, a resort, and a health center. When the only hotel closed for lack of patronage in 1904, "Lonesome Linda" was written off by many as a losing proposition. But the very next year, Seventh-Day Adventists purchased the property and began what turned out to be a highly successful revitalization of the place. The "vegetarian hotel and sanitarium" gradually attracted so many visitors that the facility expanded in 1909, becoming the College of Medical Evangelists. Its medical, nursing, and paramedical programs were consolidated in 1961 with the founding of Loma Linda University. In 1967 the university built a seven-story medical center, which today has an international reputation for its pioneering work in many surgical techniques. The university and the medical center are the heart of the worldwide Seventh-Day Adventist medical network.

FONTANA

Around 1900 the Fontana Development Company created small farms and houses on what had been part of Rancho San Bernardino. The settlement of Rosena was renamed Fontana in 1913. A. B. Miller, its chief promoter, encouraged the development of citrus, grain, and grape acreage as well as poultry and swine production. The location appealed to industrialist Henry J. Kaiser, who received important government contracts to construct ships on the West Coast as the United States entered World War II. In April 1942, ground was broken at Fontana for the largest steel mill in the western United States. Once a bucolic farm community,

Fontana became a major steel producer. Kaiser Steel continued to be an important industry for years after the end of the war. In the late 1970s, the company began cutting back its production and manpower and finally closed the mill in 1984. The California Steel Company took over the operation, on a greatly reduced scale.

The only experimental station in the United States devoted to the breeding and raising of rabbits was operated by the federal government at 8384 Cypress Avenue in Fontana between 1928 and 1965 (SRL 950). The site is now a senior citizens center operated by the city of Fontana.

THE SAN BERNARDINO MOUNTAINS

With the American conquest of California and the imposition of American law, it became urgent to have accurate land surveys. Three points in the state were selected to serve as the bases for the establishment of meridians and base lines. One was in Humboldt County; another was at the top of Mount Diablo in Contra Costa County; the third was established in 1852 by U.S. Deputy Surveyor Colonel Henry Washington on the west peak of Mount San Bernardino at 116° 55' 17" west longitude and 34° 07' 20" north latitude. Base Line Street follows this line for many miles.

High above the San Bernardino Valley the Rim of the World Drive takes motorists to the mountain resorts of Lake Arrowhead and Big Bear Lake, among many others. There are several historic spots in the region. On the east side of Waterman Canyon in the mountains north of the city of San Bernardino is the Arrowhead (SRL 977), a natural geological formation 1,376 feet in length and 479 feet across at its widest point. The unusual landmark can be seen from the city below and is the emblem for San Bernardino County.

About three miles north of Big Bear Lake, and roughly parallel to it, lies Holcomb Valley (SRL 619), now a peaceful, sheltered area but in the 1860s the scene of a full-scale gold rush, the largest in southern California. It derives its name from William Francis "Bill" Holcomb, who made the first strikes there in 1860. The area is crisscrossed with good dirt roads, along which Forest Service signs have been placed, indicating the principal landmarks. One of these is the site of Belleville, the valley's largest town, reputed to have reached a population of 10,000 and to have been a hotbed of Confederate sympathizers during the Civil War. By early 1862 Belleville was challenging the town of San Bernardino to become the county seat. San Bernardino kept its position in a close election, so a mountain story goes, only because a ballot box from Belleville was "accidentally" kicked into a bonfire on election night. The Holcomb Valley gold rush was short-lived, but it was responsible for bringing many new settlers into the county. Another contemporary gold rush occurred in the Lytle Creek–Glenn Ranch area far to the west.

There were a number of lumber roads between the mountains and the valley besides the one built by the Mormons in 1851. One of the most important was the Daley Toll Road (SRL 579), built in 1870 by Edward Daley & Co. from Del Rosa to the crest near Strawberry Peak. After twenty years as a toll road, it became a county road. A stretch of it can be seen where it crosses the Rim of the World Drive; the Native Sons and Daughters of the Golden West placed a marker there, one-half mile west of Rim of the World High School, in 1935.

CALICO

The Calico Mountains, "vivid with ever-changing colors, their wild and lofty grandeur wrought by age-old volcanic action," lie in the Mojave Desert five miles north of Daggett and two miles northwest of Yermo. At their base is the old mining town of Calico (SRL 782). In the 1880s the wealth of the silver mines discovered in this region brought 3,500 people to this place, and Calico became one of the most prosperous as well as one of the wildest camps of the great Southwest. A sensational drop in the price of silver was the cause of its abandonment, and the fury of desert storms caused its final desolation.

In 1952, Walter Knott of Knott's Berry Farm in Buena Park, Orange County, purchased the ruins of the old town and gave it a vigorous restoration. Knott's uncle had been sheriff at Calico in 1882. After several of its buildings had been restored, the town was eventually deeded to San Bernardino County. Calico Ghost Town Regional Park is located just off I-15 about four miles northwest of Yermo. To the east, three miles north of the intersection of I-15 and Mineola Road, is the Calico Early Man Archaeological Site, referred to in the beginning of this chapter.

NEEDLES

About ten miles below the place where the California-Nevada border line reaches the Colorado River some high pinnacles on both the California and the Arizona banks of the river were called by surveyors of the 1850s

"The Needles." When the Atlantic and Pacific (later the Santa Fe) Railroad was built across the Colorado in 1883, its station on the Arizona side was named Needles; later that year, a new station was built on the California side with the same name. In a rather isolated spot, served by both railroad and highway at the crossing of the Colorado River, Needles has long been an important rest or overnight stop for the traveler. On Front Street between G and H Streets stands the huge El Garces Hotel, once one of the Fred Harvey hotels associated with the Santa Fe line. The hotel is closed, with some plans for its future reopening. The Harvey House still serves meals. The Amtrak Train Depot is also in this complex, across the street from Santa Fe Park. The Needles Regional Museum is nearby at 923 Front Street.

HISTORIC SPOTS OF THE MOJAVE DESERT

Chimney Rock (SRL 737), at Rabbit Dry Lake in Lucerne Valley, is the site of the last Indian fight in southern California. In January 1867 Indians from this area raided a lumber camp in the San Bernardino Mountains, looting and burning a number of cabins and a sawmill. A retaliatory posse descended upon the Indians at their Chimney Rock camp and killed and wounded many of them.

The Joshua tree is a giant yucca native to the Southwest. Its twisted, distinctive shape was noted by Mormon pioneers, who, it is said, named the trees after a line from the Book of Joshua: "Thou shalt follow the way pointed to thee by the trees." Joshua Tree National Park was established in 1936; most of its 870 square miles lie within Riverside County, but the headquarters and visitors center for the reservation are at Twentynine Palms in San Bernardino County. This oasis was first explored in 1855 by Colonel Henry Washington, who noted that the neighboring Chemehuevi called the area "Marrah," or "land of little water." Its present name seems to have come from a slightly later exploration in 1858, when native palm trees were found at the oasis.

John Searles discovered borax in 1862 on the surface of the lake that now bears his name. In 1873 he and his brother Dennis formed the San Bernardino Borax Mining Company, which they operated until 1897. The now-dry lake today yields many other chemicals besides borax, and the significance of the Searles discovery is indicated by a historical marker (SRL 774) beside the highway at Trona. Borax mining near Calico maintained that old camp in existence for a few years after the end of the silver boom.

Not far from Trona the picturesque remains of the towns of Atolia and Red Mountain mark the Rand Mining District, which straddles the San Bernardino–Kern county line. Across the line, Johannesburg and Randsburg also contain much evidence of a flourishing past.

One of the argonauts trapped in Death Valley in 1849 led his family to safety by following the dry course of the Amargosa River south to Salt Spring, where they encountered the old Spanish Trail. Harry Wade is commemorated by a monument (SRL 622) thirty miles northwest of Baker at the junction of SR 127 and the graded dirt road into the southern part of Death Valley National Park.

Another marker of the desert is the Von Schmidt State Boundary Monument (SRL 859) on the east side of River Road about fifteen miles north of Needles. The cast-iron marker was placed by a surveyor, A. W. Von Schmidt, in 1873. Subsequent remeasuring put the actual boundary between California and Nevada about three-quarters of a mile to the north.

Wyatt Earp of Tombstone, Arizona, fame and now an almost legendary character via television, mined gold in the Whipple Mountains near the Colorado River from the early 1900s until his death in 1929. In his honor the little town of Drennan in the southeastern corner of the county renamed itself Earp. The house built by his brother Virgil Earp still stands at 528 West H Street in Colton.

The Stone Hotel at Daggett, built in the 1880s, is now closed while the San Bernardino County Museum plans restoration of the building where Death Valley Scotty was an occasional resident. The Walter Alf Blacksmith Shop in Daggett is still standing and contains the old tools and equipment used to repair the vehicles and machinery of miners and pioneers. The family-run private museum is open to the public.

Another private museum, also upon to the public, is the Roy Rogers–Dale Evans Museum at 15650 Seneca Road in Victorville. This museum contains extensive memorabilia of the career of this famous pair of entertainers; it is also a fascinating display of the changes in the motion picture industry over the years 1935–60.

The Spanish Colonial style was frequently used in the early twentieth century for public buildings in southern California. Two railway buildings still stand from this time. At Kelso, the 1906 Union Pacific depot stands in a grove of shade trees. At Barstow, the hotel built by Fred Harvey for the Santa Fe Railroad is commemorated (SRL 892) on the building "Casa del Desierto," erected on the site of the original structure, which burned in 1911. Some seventy-five Harvey Houses were built along the tracks of the Santa Fe Railroad in the late nineteenth century.

The Mojave River Museum at 270 East Virginia Way in Barstow has displays both outside and within on the many activities of the region over the years; this is an excellent example of the rather small but well-organized museums that are to be found extensively in California today.

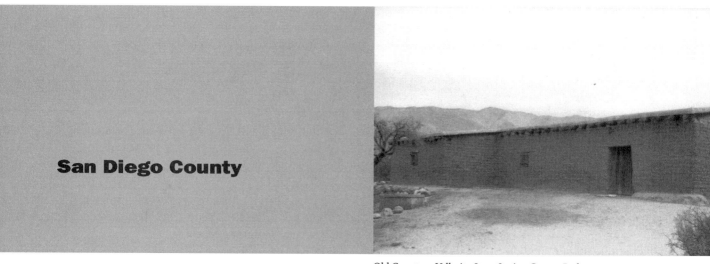

San Diego County

Old Cemetery, Vallecito Stage Station County Park

San Diego County was named after the harbor that Vizcaíno named in 1602. It was one of the original twenty-seven counties and the city of San Diego has always been the county seat. San Diego is Spanish for St. Didacus, a native of Spain and a Franciscan saint. Many pre-statehood records of deeds and wills in Spanish are housed in the courthouse.

THE DISCOVERY AND NAMING OF SAN DIEGO

On September 28, 1542, Juan Rodríguez Cabrillo and his chief pilot, Bartolomé Ferrelo, brought two small ships, *San Salvador* and *Victoria*, to anchor in a "port, closed and very good, which they named San Miguel." Cabrillo, an Iberian (Portuguese-Spanish) navigator, had been sent by Viceroy Antonio de Mendoza to explore the coast of New Spain and to discover, if possible, the elusive strait of Anián. Local historians believe that Ballast Point was the most likely place for Cabrillo to have landed. A half-acre of land within the Fort Rosecrans Military Reservation on Point Loma was set aside in 1913 as Cabrillo National Monument. It is near the end of Point Loma, south and slightly west of Ballast Point. The main feature of the little park is the old Point Loma lighthouse.

It was not until sixty years later that outsiders again visited the bay. On May 5, 1602, Sebastián Vizcaíno, with the two ships *San Diego* and *Santo Tomás* and the little frigate *Tres Reyes*, sailed north from Acapulco. He had been sent out by the new viceroy, the Conde de Monterey, to explore the coast of Alta California for safe and convenient harbors in which the Manila galleons might stop for repairs and the recuperation of scurvy-ridden crews, and from which observations on the whereabouts of English pirate ships might be made.

Early in November, Vizcaíno reached the port that Cabrillo had seen in 1542. In his diary this entry is found: "On the twelfth of [November], which was the day of the glorious San Diego, the general, admiral, religious, captains, ensigns, and almost all the men went on shore. A hut was built and mass was said in celebration of the feast of San Diego." Vizcaíno's name for the bay has been the established one since then.

THE SETTLEMENT OF SAN DIEGO

In the 1760s, rumors that the Russians were planning to extend their colonies from Alaska down the Pacific Coast in the direction of Alta California caused King

Carlos III of Spain to order the viceroy of New Spain to investigate the danger. The viceroy transmitted the order to José de Gálvez, visitador general, and Gálvez put into effect what had long been contemplated—the settlement of Alta California. His decision was influenced by personal ambition as well as by fear that the land might become the possession of Russia, or perhaps even England. In 1768, 226 years after the discovery of San Diego by Cabrillo, Gálvez organized the first colonizing project. Gaspar de Portolá was appointed military governor of Alta California and was placed in command of the expedition, and Father Junípero Serra was named padre presidente of the missions that were to be established in the new province. Officers, priests, soldiers, sailors, laborers, and southern Indian retainers, perhaps three hundred men in all, made up the personnel of this, the first band of settlers dispatched to California. The primary aim of the expedition was to find the harbor of Monterey, but a base was also to be established at San Diego. The Franciscan friars were to establish missions and convert the Indians, and the soldiers were to guard the country and protect the mission settlements.

The expedition was divided into five companies, three of which went by sea in the ships *San Carlos, San Antonio,* and *San José,* and two by land, one led by Portolá himself and the other under Fernando Rivera y Moncada, his second in command. The second of the sea expeditions to leave La Paz, under command of Juan Pérez in the ship *San Antonio,* was the first to arrive at San Diego, on April 11, 1769, after a voyage of fifty-five days. On April 19, the *San Carlos,* with Vicente Vila in command and Pedro Fages with his twenty-five Catalonian volunteers, arrived after a voyage "of great suffering" that lasted 110 days. Rivera, accompanied by Father Juan Crespí, whose diary is a primary source of California history, arrived on May 14, after a march of fifty-one days from Velicatá in Baja California. Governor Portolá and a few men of the second land expedition arrived on June 29. The rest of this division, with Father Serra, who had made the journey while suffering from an ulcerated leg, arrived last, on July 1. The *San José* and all aboard were lost at sea. Ninety-three Spaniards had died aboard the other ships; many of the Indians had died or deserted. Only 126 settlers were left at San Diego. The site of their landing (SRL 891) is at Spanish Landing Park on Harbor Drive.

Already advanced in years, Father Serra endured great hardship and privation with a cheerfulness that ignored physical ills and dangers for the cause to which he gave his life. His enthusiasm for the conversion of California's Indians was not dampened by suffering or discouragement.

With him were Father Juan Crespí (a fellow Majorcan who had studied under Serra at the university at Palma and had come with him to Mexico in 1749) and Fathers Gómez, Parrón, and Vizcaíno, besides Portolá and several other government officers. Portolá, with Captain Rivera and a band of soldiers, accompanied by Fathers Crespí and Gómez, and Miguel Costansó, geographer, engineer, and diarist, set out northward to search for the harbor of Monterey, where the first northern mission was to be established. Father Serra remained at San Diego to undertake the founding of the first of the Franciscan missions to be established in the wilderness of Alta California.

MISSION SAN DIEGO DE ALCALÁ

Immediately after the departure of Portolá and his men, Father Serra founded Mission San Diego de Alcalá on July 16, 1769, fifteen days after his arrival. The ceremony was performed in the presence of some thirty men, on what later came to be known as Presidio Hill. Here, overlooking the bay and the river, the first temporary chapel was erected, and the first cross was raised.

The order of ceremony followed at this first founding was much the same as that subsequently used in establishing all of the twenty other missions that finally comprised the chain. Helen Hunt Jackson described the procedure:

> A cross was set up; a booth of branches built; the ground and the booth were consecrated by holy water, and christened by the name of a saint; a mass was performed; the neighboring Indians, if there were any, were roused and summoned by the ringing of bells swung on limbs of trees; presents of cloth and trinkets were given them to inspire them with trust, and thus a Mission was founded. Two monks (never, at first, more) were appointed to take charge of the cross and booth, and to win, baptize, convert, and teach all the Indians to be reached in the region. They had for guard and help a few soldiers, and sometimes a few already partly civilized and Christianized Indians; several head of cattle, some tools and seeds, and holy vessels for the church service, completed their store of weapons . . . with which to conquer the wilderness and its savages.

The little settlement at San Diego had, perhaps, greater hardships to endure in the beginning than any of the missions that followed. For a whole year Father Serra labored in vain among the Indians before even one child was baptized. Supplies, too, were insufficient, and at the end of six months the whole enterprise was threatened with failure.

Meanwhile Portolá and his men, under great hardships, struggled northward on what proved to be an unsuccessful endeavor.

PORTOLÁ'S TRAIL TO MONTEREY

Leaving the port of San Diego on July 14, 1769, Portolá, with Father Juan Crespí as chronicler of the expedition, had started north on the long journey to Monterey, where the second mission was to be established.

Passing what is now called Mission Bay, the party came on an Indian village near the northeast point of the cove. Leaving the shore here, they passed into Rose Canyon and camped at some pools. The following day the route lay through Soledad Valley with its Indian villages. Camp was made in San Dieguito Canyon, near Del Mar, with another Indian village not too far distant.

On July 16 and 17 the trail led by way of the present county road called El Camino Real (the principal highway until the end of the nineteenth century) past San Elijo Lagoon, Batequitos Lagoon, Agua Hedionda Creek, and Buena Vista Creek, near Carlsbad. Many Indian villages were passed along the way, all of them friendly. On July 18, the verdant valley of San Juan Capistrano, the first name given to the valley of San Luís Rey, was reached and camp made. The location was pronounced by Father Crespí to be an excellent site for the placing of a mission, and several years later Mission San Luís Rey was indeed founded near this very spot.

From the valley of San Juan Capistrano northward Portolá passed valleys called by the explorers Santa Margarita and Santa Praxedis de los Rosales (because, it was said, of the numerous "Castilian roses and other flowers" growing there). These sites are commemorated in the name of the Rancho Santa Margarita y las Flores, north and west of Mission San Luís Rey.

Passing into the region of what is now Orange County on July 22, the party continued north. Six months later, returning from their fruitless search for the port of Monterey, sick and weary, their provisions nearly gone, the little company returned over much the same route, but the homeward marches were long, and several of the old camps were passed without stopping. On January 21, 1770, camp was made on San Onofre Creek, probably, and on January 24 the party rejoined the group anxiously awaiting their return at the newly established Mission of San Diego.

There, Portolá found that the supply ship, which had left for San Blas six months before, had not returned and that provisions were almost exhausted. In his discouragement he considered abandonment of the colony, but he would not yet admit defeat. Father Serra, although greatly concerned about the critical state of affairs, had no intention of giving up the enterprise, and, when the hour seemed darkest, his faith and determination were rewarded by the arrival of the *San Antonio*, and the settlement of Alta California was assured.

The search for the lost port of Monterey was renewed as soon as possible. Father Serra went north by sea, leaving Fathers Luís Jayme and Francisco Dumetz to carry on the work at San Diego. The land expedition under Portolá generally retraced its steps on the northerly route into what is now Orange County.

EL CAMINO REAL

El Camino Real, the King's Highway, stretched from San Diego north to San Francisco Bay in Hispanic days. In some places, as between San Diego and Los Angeles, the name was given to two or more parallel courses. US 101 approximately follows this route, which linked the missions and their settlements. In 1906, the El Camino Real Association and the historians Mr. and Mrs. A. S. C. Forbes began the project of marking the old road with several hundred mission-bell guideposts, each surmounted by a bell weighing 100 pounds or more. Through the years these disappeared, but a program to replace the missing bells was begun in the 1960s and the traveler on modern El Camino Real will often find these familiar markers. On November 24, 1963, the 250th anniversary of the birth of Father Serra, bronze plaques were dedicated at the southern and northern ends of El Camino Real (SRL 784) as he knew it and helped to blaze it. One was placed at Mission San Diego and the other at Mission Dolores in San Francisco.

THE SECOND MISSION SITE

The first site of the mission at San Diego proved to be unsatisfactory because of its proximity to the military post, and the fathers soon realized that it would be better for the Indian neophytes to be removed some distance from the influence of the soldiers. Furthermore, a location affording more water for agricultural purposes was desirable.

Mission buildings of wood were constructed in 1774 five miles up the valley from the presidio, and considerable progress had been made in the conversion of the Indians by October 1775. At that time, the number of neophytes totaled seventy-six, and sixty additional converts were baptized by the fathers on the day before the feast of St. Francis, October 4.

The hostility of the unconverted Indians, however, culminated in a fierce attack upon the unprotected mission on the night of November 4, 1775. Father Luís Jayme, who, "with the shining light of martyrdom in his eyes, and the fierce joy of fearlessness in his heart," sought to quiet the attackers by walking toward them, his hand extended in blessing and with his usual salutation, "Love God, my children!" was killed on the spot. Padre Jayme, the first Christian martyr in California, is buried in the mission sanctuary. The other inhabitants of the mission escaped to the garrison on Presidio Hill. The mission buildings were burned to the ground.

The next year, Father Serra returned to the gutted site and made plans to rebuild the mission. Adobe-covered walls and tiled roofs made the buildings more resistant to fire. By 1780 most of the reconstruction of the mission and its outbuildings had been completed. The church and other buildings were arranged in a quadrangle around a patio. In 1803 an earthquake damaged the church; the unique buttress-like structure in the front that was added in 1931 has helped the building to withstand subsequent shocks.

By 1797, San Diego was the most populous as well as one of the wealthiest of the California missions. Over 1,400 converts had been brought into the Church. The mission owned 20,000 sheep, 10,000 cattle, and 1,250 horses. Within a few years, extensive fields and vineyards were being irrigated by water brought over an aqueduct through Mission Valley. The old mission dam (SRL 52) built across the San Diego River gorge in 1807–16 and constructed of granite and cement twelve feet thick still stands, a remarkable testimony to the quality of California's first irrigation and engineering venture. The dam (and its accompanying flume, now mostly in ruins), a National Historic Landmark, is in Mission Trails Regional Park on Father Junipero Serra Trail, about five miles north of I-8 off Mission Gorge Road.

At the time of secularization, the mission was given over to Santiago Argüello. The United States Cavalry occupied the building from 1846 until 1862, when President Lincoln restored the mission lands to the Church. Decay set in, and by 1931 nothing remained of the buildings except the facade. In that year, restoration was be-

Mission San Diego

gun by the Native Sons of the Golden West under the scholarly supervision of J. Marshall Miller. The restoration is believed to be exact in every detail. In 1976, Pope Paul VI named the church a minor basilica. It stands at 10818 San Diego Mission Road (SRL 242).

THE SAN DIEGO PRESIDIO

Near the first cross in Alta California, raised on Presidio Hill on July 16, 1769, the first mission and the first military post were established. From this date to January 1, 1774, a mission guard was on Presidio Hill. The first presidio in Alta California was established at Monterey, in 1770, and not until the 1774 date did San Diego's post officially become a presidio. At this spot, on July 16, 1915, a group of San Diegans placed the Serra Cross, which stands on Presidio Hill today. From the heap of clay upon which it was raised, old tile from early buildings had been dug up and incorporated into the memorial cross. On it is a bronze tablet bearing this legend:

> HERE THE FIRST CITIZEN, FRAY JUNÍPERO SERRA,
> PLANTED CIVILIZATION IN CALIFORNIA.
> HERE HE FIRST RAISED THE CROSS,
> HERE BEGAN THE FIRST MISSION,
> HERE FOUNDED THE FIRST TOWN
> —SAN DIEGO, JULY 16, 1769.

Presidio Hill, being situated a little back from the river and the bay, afforded a good outlook over the surrounding country and made fortification easy as well. It was near the site of the old Indian village of Cosoy, ranchería of the Diegueños, and here, for over sixty years, San Diego was located within the adobe walls of the Spanish garrison.

The presidio, an essential feature of Spanish colonization, was usually a fortified square, constructed at first of wood and later of brick or stone. Inside the square the commandant's residence and the chapel formed the central points around which the garrison for the soldiers, the officers' quarters, and adobe houses for provisions and military supplies were located.

With the rest of California, San Diego peaceably passed from Spanish to Mexican rule in 1822. A more turbulent period followed, when frequent revolts occurred both between the Californians and the Mexican governors and between rival factions of the Californians themselves. José Maria Echeandía, the first governor sent from Mexico, established his headquarters at the Presidio of San Diego, which remained the capital of Alta California during the years of his administration, 1825–31.

It was during this time that the second overland party of Americans to enter California came by way of San Diego County under the leadership of Sylvester Pattie and his son, James Ohio Pattie. This expedition opened up a new overland route to the coast and added much to the knowledge of the Southwest.

Coming down the Gila and Colorado Rivers as far as the tidewaters of the Gulf of California, the party crossed the desert to the Spanish settlements on the northern coast of Baja California. At Mission Santa Catalina, they were arrested and conducted to San Diego in Alta California under heavy guard, arriving there on March 27, 1828.

In January of the previous year, Jedediah Strong Smith had led the first overland party of Americans to enter California; Smith's application for a passport was peremptorily refused and his party was made to leave the province. Thus Governor Echeandía was fearful and suspicious of this second party and treated the newcomers harshly, imprisoning them for several months. The elder Pattie, weakened by long privation, died under this treatment. Gradually, his son was able to soften the governor's attitude by serving as interpreter and by using his knowledge of vaccination to save the population in a smallpox epidemic. Eventually, in 1830, he was given passage to Mexico City, and from there made his way back to his native Kentucky.

After Echeandía's administration the presidio was gradually abandoned. Retired soldiers were often given grants of land and went to live on their ranchos, or built homes in the town at the foot of the hill. Within a decade the old garrison was deserted and dismantled. On December 25, 1838, earthworks were thrown up on Presidio Hill preparatory to an expected attack from José Castro, leader of a rebel faction from the northern part of the territory, then supposedly threatening the

San Diegans. Two cannon from Fort Guijarros were mounted, but the anticipated attack did not materialize.

The earthworks on Presidio Hill were never used by the Mexicans. On the coming of the Americans in 1846, they were improved by Commodore Robert F. Stockton, and United States troops, including Company B of the famous Mormon Battalion, were stationed there during the brief period of military rule before California's entrance into the Union (1850). The old American fort, of which scarcely a vestige remains, was called Fort Stockton during that period. An E Clampus Vitus plaque has been placed at the site (SRL 54), in Presidio Park, off Taylor Street, along with a flagstaff and bronze tablet from the Native Sons of the Golden West.

The presidio has been virtually obliterated by storms, earthquakes, and settlers, who used the materials for their houses. The walls of the presidio chapel, the old Spanish garrison, and the first civilian houses long ago crumbled into shapeless mounds of earth. Beginning in 1929, plans were developed for preserving the hill and marking some of its landmarks. George W. Marston's leadership was effective in eventually making this area a public park under the jurisdiction of the city of San Diego.

Here, on July 16, 1929 (the 160th anniversary of the founding of San Diego), the Junipero Serra Museum was dedicated. The museum focuses on activities in the area before 1848. The museum, the Serra Cross, the site of the first mission building, the site of the old Spanish garrison, and the site of Fort Stockton are all included within Presidio Park. Directly across Presidio Drive from the museum is the marker (SRL 59) noting the site of the presidio, which has been registered as a National Historic Landmark by the Department of the Interior. Nearby another marker (SRL 67) notes the site of the first date palms planted in California by, it is said, Father Serra himself. One stood here until 1957.

OLD TOWN SAN DIEGO

The tiny town that began at the foot of Presidio Hill as an overflow from the garrison grew and prospered as the tide of immigration into California increased. Old Town became a state historic park in 1968, when work was begun to restore and stabilize many of the buildings in the area. Since 1846, the American flag has flown over the plaza (SRL 63) on Washington Square. None of the buildings in Old Town are in their original condition, but several have been restored, most of them open to the public. The marker (SRL 830) for Old Town

San Diego is on the west side of the plaza at 4016 Wallace Street.

Casa de Carrillo (SRL 74) is the oldest restored home in Old Town; it was built before 1820. It is now the clubhouse for the Presidio Hills golf course, at 4136 Wallace Street. The Estudillo adobe (SRL 53) on the plaza was built about 1827 by Captain José Maria de Estudillo, commander of the presidio; when he died in 1830 it passed to his son José Antonio Estudillo. He and his wife, Doña María Victoria Domínguez, lived here with their twelve children, one of whom continued to live here with her husband until 1887. The house was restored in 1910 with funds provided by the Spreckels family, and is today beautifully furnished, with a lovely patio and well-tended trees and shrubs. For years this was popularly known as "Ramona's Marriage Place," though it is not the spot mentioned in Helen Hunt Jackson's novel *Ramona* (1884).

The Casa de Bandini (SRL 72) at 2660 Calhoun Street also dates from the late 1820s. It was built by Juan Bandini, who became the son-in-law of José Maria de Estudillo. Although he had held various offices under Mexican rule, Bandini invited Commodore Stockton to make his headquarters at Casa Bandini in 1846. On December 9 of that year, after a harrowing three nights' journey made in bare feet over country luxuriantly covered with prickly pears and guarded by mounted Californians, Lieutenant Edward Beale, with his Indian servant and Kit Carson, delivered the message from General Stephen W. Kearny to Commodore Stockton calling for needed reinforcements after the Battle of San Pasqual. The brave men's message got a quick response, and on December 12, Kearny and his soldiers, hungry, footsore, many of them wounded, arrived at Old Town. On the plaza opposite the Estudillo and Bandini houses is a granite boulder with a bronze marker placed by the Daughters of the American Revolution in 1920, marking the end of the Kearny trail from New Mexico to California.

The Bandini house acquired a second story in the 1860s, when Albert Seeley purchased the place and made it into the Cosmopolitan Hotel. It has since served as a store, a pickle factory, and a motel annex, and it is now a restaurant serving meals indoors and on the patio.

Casa de Pedrorena (SRL 70), at 2616 San Diego Avenue, was the home of Miguel de Pedrorena Jr. His father, a native of Madrid, was a man of good family and excellent education who came to San Diego in 1838. Courteous and polite in manner and of gracious bear-

Casa de Bandini, Old Town, San Diego

ing, it is said, he won the heart and hand of María Antonia Estudillo. Don Miguel was a member of the constitutional convention at Monterey in 1849, but he died the next year, before he could build on the lot he had acquired next to the home of his in-laws. Not until 1869 did his son, Miguel Junior, put up a building, now a bakery.

La Casa de Machado y Silvas (SRL 71), at 2741 San Diego Avenue, is now used for audiovisual programs and park volunteer activities. José Nicasio Silvas, who built this house between 1830 and 1843, lived here for many years with his wife, María Antonia Machado, and children. Their home stayed in the family for over a hundred years; it then became a boarding house, saloon, restaurant, art studio, souvenir shop, museum, and church. It was briefly pressed into service in 1846 as the headquarters of John C. Frémont.

La Casa de Machado y Stewart (SRL 73), at Congress and Mason Streets, was built by José Manuel Machado in the 1830s. Jack Stewart, a native of Maine who had visited San Diego in 1835, returned to stay in 1838. He served in the American army and later became a pilot on one of the pilot boats in San Diego Bay. In 1845 he married Machado's youngest daughter, Rosa, and the couple moved into the house to live with the Machados. Stewart had been a shipmate of Richard Henry Dana Jr., who describes a visit to the house in 1859 in *Two Years Before the Mast*. Descendants of the Stewarts lived in the house until 1966; it was acquired by the state in the following year.

Two adobes no longer standing are commemorated as registered state landmarks. The Casa de Cota (SRL 75) stood at Twiggs and Congress Streets until it was pulled down during World War II. The Casa de Lopez (SRL 60), at 3890 Twiggs Street, despite its name was actually built by Miguel Alvarez, in 1851.

Albert Seeley launched the San Diego–Los Angeles Stage Line; his Concord stages could make the trip in less than twenty-four hours if all went well. Soon he had acquired the Bandini house for his Cosmopolitan Hotel. By 1875 he was running daily stages, but gradually competition from the railroad, which reached San Diego in 1887, put the line out of business. The reconstructed Seeley stable and barns at 2648 Calhoun Street now house a collection of Western memorabilia and horse-drawn vehicles as well as Indian artifacts.

The Chapel of the Immaculate Conception (SRL 49), on Conde Street southwest of San Diego Avenue, is a replica of the adobe chapel that was originally built in the 1850s as the home of John Brown. José Antonio Aguirre bought it and presented it to the Catholic congregation, after restoring and altering it to fit the needs of a church. It was dedicated in 1858; the restoration dates from 1937.

The chapel was the special charge of Father Antonio D. Ubach, a native of Catalonia, who was educated in Missouri. He traveled thousands of miles as a missionary among the Indians, and came to San Diego in 1866, where he was placed in charge of the Catholic parish. He brought the first organ to San Diego, and also a football, which he tossed with the boys on the plaza. He had charge of many valuable relics and records of early Spanish days. The greater part of his work was among the Indians, with whom, it is said, he had much influence and by whom he was greatly beloved. Helen Hunt Jackson's *Ramona*, it is believed, used him as the original "Father Gaspara," and he claimed to have known originals of the characters in the story and their families.

OTHER OLD TOWN BUILDINGS AND SITES

In 1850 a public school was started in San Diego, and in 1865 a structure was built to house it. It still stands at 3960 Mason Street (SRL 538). The *San Diego Union* building at 2602 San Diego Avenue was prefabricated in Maine and shipped around the Horn in 1851. The wood-frame structure was the residence of José Antonio Altamirano and later the first home of the *San Diego Union*. It has been restored as nearly as possible to its appearance in 1868, when the newspaper's first edition came off the press.

The Whaley house (SRL 65), at 2482 San Diego Avenue, in which the San Diego County court met for about twenty years, was the first brick building to be built in the county. The white cedar woodwork and all of the hardware used in its construction were brought

around the Horn, but the bricks were made at Thomas Whaley's own kiln in Old Town in 1856, and the walls were finished with plaster made from ground seashells.

The Derby-Pendleton house at 4017 Harney Street was put up in 1852 by Juan Bandini for his daughter Dolores, the wife of Captain Charles Johnson. Captain George Allen Pendleton, a member of the state constitutional convention of 1849, purchased the place in the 1860s, and lived there with his wife, Concepción B. Estudillo. At that time the house was used as the office of the county recorder and the county clerk, both offices being held by Captain Pendleton himself until his death in 1871.

Lieutenant George Horatio Derby of the U.S. Corps of Topographical Engineers lived in the house during the years 1853–55 while engineering the first turning of the San Diego River into False Bay, now Mission Bay. Derby Dike (SRL 244), which can no longer be seen because of the development of the San Diego River Flood Control Channel, was a levee or earth embankment built west from Old Town 1,190 yards across the flats to the opposite high land. Deflection of the river was deemed necessary because of the silting of the harbor in San Diego Bay, imperiling Old Town itself. The marker commemorating this site is at the base of Presidio Hill, next to the Serra Palm Site. Derby had a secondary profession as a humorous writer, using about twenty pen names (like "Squibob"), and his columns for the *San Diego Herald*, written under the byline "John Phoenix" and collected by his friend J. Judson Ames under the title *Phoenixiana*, are classics of contemporary American writing.

El Desembarcadero, or the Old Landing (SRL 64) at the head of an inlet from San Diego Bay, was the usual landing place until at least 1870 for small boats carrying passengers or goods from the La Playa port to Old Town. The site, now filled in, is off the ends of Udall and Voltaire Streets, just below Rosecrans Street. Congress Hall (SRL 66), the site of which is at 4016 Wallace Street, was a two-story public house that lasted from 1867 to 1939. It was built on the site of the last Pony Express stop, when an adobe structure occupied the location. The old Catholic cemetery El Campo Santo ("the holy field") was used from 1850 to 1897 and is the resting place for such distinguished citizens of Old San Diego as Miguel de Pedrorena, José Antonio Estudillo, and Santiago Argüello. The cemetery (SRL 68) is on the northeast side of San Diego Avenue at Arista Street, although many of the 477 persons were buried under present streets, outside of the new walls of 1933, which are not on the earlier alignments. A marker at 2731 San Diego Avenue commemorates the Exchange Hotel (SRL 491), where the San Diego Lodge of the Masons was organized in 1851. In 1855 it became the first three-story building in the city, with two frame stores surmounting the adobe first floor, and was renamed the Franklin House. The hotel was destroyed by fire in 1872.

HISTORIC POINT LOMA

The ancient Playa trail of the Indians, later used by ox-carts and *carretas*, horse-back riders and walkers from the mission, followed the western shore of the bay. It may be roughly identified today as Rosecrans Street, which leads to the federal Military Reservation of Fort Rosecrans. A number of the landmarks on Point Loma (originally Punta de la Loma, "Point of the Hill") are located in restricted military areas. The trail, popularly known as "La Playa Trail," was continued to Mission Valley in the 1770s. During the 1930s it was marked by terra-cotta plaques on monuments at several points. Only four remain: at the mission, next to the Derby Dike plaque in Old Town, in the middle of Rosecrans Street south of Midway Drive, and at La Playa (SRL 61), just inside the main gate of the Naval Reserve. A bronze replica was placed next to it in 1989.

La Punta de Guijarros (Point of Cobblestones), probable landing place of Cabrillo in 1542, was named by Vizcaíno in 1602 and was so designated until early in the nineteenth century, when English-speaking men began to arrive at Old San Diego and La Playa. Captain George Vancouver, who anchored there in 1793, referred to it as "Punta de Guiranos." But it is the memory of long-vanished Boston ships steadied on their stormy homeward voyages around Cape Horn by cargoes of cobblestones within their holds that is preserved by the Yankee translation of the old Spanish name as Ballast Point (SRL 56). The point is within the Naval Base: Point Loma (the official name for the whole region, adopted in 1998) is at the end of Rosecrans Street, which terminates in a monument circle containing several State Registered Landmark plaques. The present lighthouse on Ballast Point operated from 1890 to World War II, but no longer displays a beacon.

It was on this small jutting headland that the Spanish castillo, Fort Guijarros (SRL 69), designed by Alberto de Cordobá, was begun about 1797, under the direction of Comandante Manuel Rodríguez. It was completed by the beginning of the nineteenth century and manned by Catalonian soldiers from the San Diego Presidio. Here was fought the so-called "Battle of San Diego" on March 22, 1803, when the American brig *Lelia Byrd*, commanded by Captain William Shaler, was fired on by the Spaniards under command of José Velásquez. The Yankees were attempting to carry on a barter in furs in defiance of Spanish laws forbidding foreign trade. "El Júpiter," a cannon cast in Manila in 1783 and used at Fort Guijarros in this early Spanish-American engagement, is now displayed at the Serra Museum. Fort Guijarros, built of Indian-made adobe bricks, stood at the foot of the short hill that runs down to the sea from the later Fort Rosecrans barracks (SRL 62). It was abandoned in 1838. Since 1980 the site has been intensively excavated by archaeologists of the Fort Guijarros Museum Foundation, and a wealth of artifacts has been recovered.

The first beacon to be placed by the United States government on this section of the California coast stood on a ridge about half a mile north of the tip of Point Loma. The lighthouse was built in 1854–55 and used for the first time at sunset on November 15, 1855. A few floor tiles from the ruins at Fort Guijarros were incorporated into the building. Because of the heavy fogs that obscured the beacon light at this point, the station was abandoned in 1891 for a lower and more suitable site located at the extreme southwestern tip of Point Loma; this facility is still in operation. The old Point Loma lighthouse (SRL 51) is now the central feature of Cabrillo National Monument.

In the years 1822–46, before the American conquest, the most flourishing hide-droghing (transporting hides in coastal craft) on the Pacific Coast was probably at La Playa, the eastern side of Point Loma. Here a cosmopolitan town of about eight hundred grew up around the ten or twelve great barnlike hide houses established there by the captains of Boston trading ships and named for the vessels they commanded. The most famous of these, the Brookline, under Captain James O. Locke, was the first to be erected and the last to disappear. Here the American flag was first raised over California, unofficially, in 1829. The Brookline was located near the seawall before the south buildings of the Quarantine Station, the place where ships inbound from foreign ports were examined for contagion. Vessels from almost every maritime nation in the world found anchorage in the little harbor. The colorful life of this place is described in two vivid accounts: Richard Henry Dana Jr.'s, in *Two Years Before the Mast*, and Alfred Robinson's, in *Life in California*. Old "Hide Park," as the Yankees called it, occupied the sandy tableland that extends from modern La Playa through the Quarantine Station and beyond, and that reaches back to the barren ridge on the west. The site is now within the Naval Base: Point Loma, at the south end of Rosecrans Street.

The site of the old Mexican customs house maintained on Point Loma during this period was probably identified by ruins at the former address, 1036 Bay Street, in the Roseville district, just north of modern La Playa. Don Juan Bandini was the first customs-house keeper.

About halfway out on the inner beach of Ballast Point, headquarters for two New England whaling companies (SRL 50), the Packard Brothers and the Johnson Brothers, were established during the middle of the nineteenth century. The remains of the try-pot fires, the sand still impregnated with oil and soot, could long be seen in this locality, which is also within the Naval Base: Point Loma.

Military reservation of the outermost three miles of Point Loma was ordered by the federal government in 1852. Possession of the property was not taken, however, until 1870. The post established in 1898 was named Fort Rosecrans (SRL 62) for General William S. Rosecrans, who died the same year; he had come to San Diego with Alonzo Horton in 1867. The last remnants of the old Fort Rosecrans are reached by driving to the south end of Rosecrans Street. The Fort Rosecrans National Cemetery (SRL 55), on the crest of Point Loma along the highway to Cabrillo National Monument, was originally designated Cemetery of San Diego Barracks in the late 1870s, although there had been earlier burials in the general area. Here, marked by a granite boulder from the battlefield of San Pasqual, are the graves of those who fell there on December 6, 1846. A granite obelisk memorializes the sixty sailors and Marines who lost their lives on July 21, 1905, in a boiler explosion aboard the gunboat USS *Bennington* at anchor in San Diego Bay, and most of them are buried here.

LANDMARKS OF NEW SAN DIEGO

Long before the establishment of New San Diego, La Punta de los Muertos, or Dead Man's Point (SRL 57), appeared on maps of the area. In 1782, several men from the coastal exploration ships *La Princesa* and *La Favorita* died of scurvy and were buried at this spot. The point is now at the corner of Pacific Highway and Market Street and is now surrounded by filled-in lands.

San Diego Barracks (SRL 523), of which no buildings remain, was located on the block bounded by Kettner Boulevard and Market, G, and California Streets. It was established in 1851 by Captain Nathaniel Lyon as a supply depot for frontier troops and was first called Post New San Diego. It became subject to Fort Rosecrans around the turn of the century and was abandoned in 1921. A marker is located on Market Street.

The incoming Yankees after 1846 soon saw that the old San Diego was unsuitable for a seaport town, and New San Diego, located on San Diego Bay, at length superseded it. William Heath Davis built the first wharf there in 1850, but his venture was a financial failure, and nothing more was attempted until 1867, when Alonzo E. Horton arrived and soon afterward laid out the nucleus of the present city. Further growth was made possible by the railroads of the 1880s. A plaque placed by the Daughters of the American Revolution on the Santa Fe Station at Broadway and Kentner Street in 1985 commemorated the linking of San Diego "to the rest of the United States."

The San Diego Maritime Museum at 1306 North Harbor Drive is a floating exhibit of three distinctive vessels. Largest and oldest, its masts silhouetted against the sky, is the sailing ship *Star of India* (SRL 1030). Built in England in 1863 and first named the *Euterpe*, she carried passengers and light cargo from Britain to the Antipodes for a number of years, later working the North American coastal trade. It has been berthed at San Diego since 1961. The *Berkeley* (SRL 1031) was a passenger ferry on San Francisco Bay from 1898 to 1958. The *Medea* was a luxurious steam yacht built in Scotland in 1904 to accommodate Captain MacAllister Hall's grouse- and deer-hunting parties.

The Gaslamp Quarter is a section of downtown San Diego built in the late nineteenth century and centered on Fifth Avenue and Market Street. The Horton Plaza honors the name of Alonzo Horton, a civic-minded entrepreneur who did much to develop the area. The blocks are small and without intervening alleys because Horton believed that corner real estate did best and that alleys served primarily to collect trash. John D. Spreckels's office building from the turn of the century occupies a whole block of Broadway between Sixth and Seventh Avenues.

San Diego State University was begun in 1897 in downtown San Diego as a two-year normal school. By 1935, it was San Diego State College, a four-year liberal arts college on Montezuma Mesa. In 1960 the California State Colleges were authorized to grant doctoral degrees jointly with the University of California, and honorary doctorates independently. On June 7, 1963, San Diego State College conferred upon President John F.

Kennedy the first doctorate to be granted by the California State College system. The event is commemorated by a marker (SRL 798) at the Aztec Bowl on the campus. In 1970 the institution, along with several others in the system, became a university.

The Villa Montezuma, at 1925 K Street, is operated as a museum by the San Diego Historical Society. Built by the author and musician Jesse Shepard in 1887, it is an eclectic medley of Victorian architecture, art-glass windows, and ornate woodwork, surmounted by cupolas and domes that add to its fantastic appearance. The society also operates the Marston House and its five acres of land with formal gardens at 3525 Seventh Avenue, on the northwest side of Balboa Park. This is a classic 1905 Arts and Crafts period home, built for the family of George Marston, a prominent merchant and civic leader.

Balboa Park, home of the Panama-California International Exposition in 1915–16 and the California-Pacific International Exposition in 1935–36, was set aside as a park in 1868. The first improvements were made in 1889 and three years later the city rented thirty-six acres in the northwest corner to Kate O. Sessions for a nursery. She paid the rent by landscaping the western portion of the park, and credit is due to her for much of the beauty of San Diego. A lovely park in Pacific Beach, north of Mission Bay, has been dedicated to the memory of Kate Sessions. Nearby, at Pico Street and Garnet Avenue, a plaque marks the site (SRL 764) of another of her nurseries.

The 1,400-acre Balboa Park is a treasury not only of horticulture but of human activities. The Museum of Man focuses on the history of Native American cultures. The Museum of San Diego History and the House of Pacific Relations have significant displays on the history of the region, while the San Diego Aerospace Museum highlights milestones in aviation history. The Botanical Building and the striking 200-foot-tall California Tower from 1915 are built in the attractive Spanish Colonial style that had so much influence on local architecture. The famous San Diego Zoo was founded in 1916 and has been a much-admired attraction ever since. Another operation of the zoo is the Wild Animal Park, begun in 1985, between Escondido and San Pasqual.

LA JOLLA

Now a northern coastal district of the huge city of San Diego, La Jolla began as a rustic, salubrious town. Its name came from the indentation where La Jolla Bay cuts into the coastline ("la jolla" is Spanish for "the hollow"; the name is also thought to have come from "la joya," "the jewel"). The La Jolla Caves at the shoreline have been continuously enlarged for over 200,000 years.

Ellen Browning Scripps, who lived here from 1897 to 1932, was, with her brother E. W. Scripps, a major benefactor of the area. The park named in her honor lies to the west of the caves. (Scripps College in Claremont, Los Angeles County, part of the Claremont Colleges, is another of her bequests.) The La Jolla Museum of Contemporary Art on Prospect Street is in the extensively remodeled house where Miss Scripps lived in her last years. The Scripps Institute of Oceanography, north along the coast, was founded in 1903 and in 1912 became a part of the University of California.

Further north, the Salk Institute for Biological Studies was founded in 1961 by Dr. Jonas Salk with support from the March of Dimes National Foundation. It overlooks the ocean at 11010 North Torrey Pines Road. The uplands just east of the Salk Institute were a U.S. Marines training base, Camp Calvin B. Matthews, from 1917 to 1964. The expanding University of California took over the site in 1964, and today it is the San Diego campus of the university. The architecture of the campus has a confidently late-twentieth-century assertiveness, which might be seen as descriptive of its age as are the Spanish colonial buildings of Old Town San Diego.

THE TORREY PINES

From La Jolla northward for several miles along the precipitous cliffs overlooking the Pacific Ocean, the Torrey pines grow in a few sheltered spots. These twisted, wind-blown trees are a very rare species, remainders of an ancient forest that was disrupted when glacial and geological movements separated what are now the Channel Islands from the California coast. The Torrey pines were recognized as a distinct species by Dr. Joseph L. LeConte in 1850. Dr. C. C. Parry, then engaged with the Mexican Boundary Survey, was told of the find, and the two men named the trees after their former instructor, Dr. John Torrey of Columbia University, who had reported on the plant collections of Frémont's first two expeditions and had visited California in 1865 and 1872. Torrey Pines State Park, south of Del Mar, encloses most of the trees on the mainland. The only other place where these trees are found is on Santa Rosa Island, one of the Channel Islands.

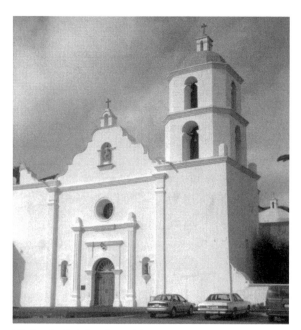
Mission San Luís Rey, Oceanside

MISSION SAN LUÍS REY DE FRANCIA

Four miles inland from Oceanside on SR 76, Mission San Luís Rey de Francia (SRL 239) stands on a slight rise overlooking a valley that is today populated and suburban. Local tradition holds that the Indian name for the area was Jacayme, or "pleasant view." It was named for King Louis IX of France, who was sanctified in 1279 for his crusades against the Saracens. On June 13, 1798, Father Fermín Francisco de Lasuén led the solemn ceremonies that celebrated the founding of the mission, on an eminence with great vistas in all directions. The location had already been noted by Father Juan Crespí in 1769 as a likely spot for a mission.

The first substantial church building, which was completed in 1802, was planned by Father Antonio Peyrí and erected under his direction. In 1811 the foundations for the present structure were laid, and on the feast of St. Francis, October 4, 1815, the completed church was dedicated. It was constructed of adobe and faced with burnt brick.

Under the efficient management of Father Peyrí, lasting over a period of thirty years, San Luís Rey prospered. The buildings covered an area of approximately six and one-half acres, with adobe walls 6.5 feet thick and thirty feet high. The "King of the Missions" was not only the largest of the missions but registered more baptisms, marriages, and funerals than any of the others. Its ranches were enormously productive of both cereal crops and livestock.

After secularization, the Indians at San Luís Rey were scattered and the property suffered many years of abuse and neglect—it is said that bullfights were held in the garden courts. On March 15, 1865, President Abraham Lincoln signed the document (a copy of which is on display in the mission museum) returning the missions to Church ownership. It was rededicated as a Franciscan seminary in 1893, and is one of the four missions still in the hands of the founding order. Perhaps because it is still a vital, active establishment, it remains one of the most attractive historic spots in California.

LAS FLORES ASISTENCIA

From 1823 to the 1840s, the tile-roofed chapel and hostel at Las Flores, built by Father Antonio Peyrí, served as the asistencia or outpost to Mission San Luís Rey and provided comfort to travelers on El Camino Real. The adobe structure and adjacent corral were the site of the April 1838 battle between Juan Bautista Alvarado and Carlos Antonio Carrillo contesting the provincial governorship of California. Alvarado won and continued as governor for a few more years. The site (SRL 616) is at the ruins inside Las Pulgas gate to Camp Pendleton. A roof protects the ruins.

ASISTENCIA DE SAN ANTONIO DE PALA

Among Father Peyrí's vigorous activities was the founding in 1816 of the Asistencia de San Antonio de Pala (SRL 243) as a branch of Mission San Luís Rey, located in the Valley of Pala about twenty miles from the missions. A thousand Indian neophytes were soon enrolled from the rancherias of the district.

Pala Chapel, often called Pala Mission today, is especially noted for its picturesque campanile and for its original Indian frescoes, for many years hidden by a coat of whitewash. The campanile stands apart from the main chapel building, in the old cemetery. It has been restored and is now joined to the main building by a little arched gateway. In its two graceful arches still hang the old bells that for generations have called the congregation to prayer.

Pala Chapel stands on the Pala Indian Reservation, where the Cupeño people were moved from Warner Springs in 1903. A resident priest has been there ever since; the Verona Fathers have been in charge of the mission's activities since 1948. This is the only one of the missions of California still serving what is primarily an Indian community. The chapel is about fifteen miles north of Escondido, six miles east of I-15. The highway up the mountain, SR 76, follows somewhat the same route that the old Emigrant Trail took to Warner's Ranch.

SANTA YSABEL

The Chapel of Santa Ysabel (SRL 369) was established by Father Fernando Martín in 1818 as an asistencia of the mission at San Diego. A permanent structure was built there at a later time, but it has since disappeared. Eugene Chamberlin has some information on later activities: "An archaeological 'dig' in August 1987 found that the site of 1818, about one-quarter mile north of the present structure, had been scraped during construction of a cattle reservoir. A second, Indian-built chapel had been used for many years, but it was burned in 1926; the foundations remain. The bells used until then were stolen, but the clappers were recovered in 1959." The present chapel was built in 1924, just south of the site of the old structure. Nearby is the picturesque old Indian cemetery. The Chapel of Santa Ysabel is on SR 79 one and one-half miles north of the town of the same name. A wooden St. Dominic's Church, with a separate wooden campanile, was built in 1897 about seven miles west of the Santa Ysabel site. It was used for many years by a small Indian band; there is an adjacent Indian cemetery still in use.

THE OLD EMIGRANT TRAIL

Pedro Fages, heading east from San Diego in search of army deserters, made the first entry by a European into Oriflamme Canyon on October 29, 1772. The party eventually reached Mission San Luis Obispo by traveling through Cajon Pass, the Mojave Desert, and the San Joaquin Valley. The Fages Trail (SRL 858) is commemorated by a plaque on county highway S1 about two miles southeast of its junction with SR 79.

Juan Bautista de Anza, who opened the route across the Colorado Desert into California in 1774, entered the mountains from the desert via San Felipe Creek. On March 12 and 13, 1774, he camped at San Gregorio (SRL 673) at the entrance to Borrego Valley, where welcome forage refreshed the half-starved animals. A jeep trail to the site proceeds east from the junction of Yaqui Pass Road and Rango Way, six-tenths of a mile north of the intersection of Yaqui Pass and Borrego Springs Roads.

Passing through the valley on March 14, Anza's party halted at Santa Catarina (SRL 785) in Coyote Canyon at Reed's Springs, or Lower Willows, just above Beatty's Ranch. The following day the party entered what is now Riverside County.

Anza's colonizing expedition of 1775–76 camped near San Felipe Creek on December 18, 1775. The next day they marched through the little pass called Los Puerticitos on SR 78, 1.7 miles east of Ocotillo Wells. From December 20 to 22 the party stopped at El Vado ("the ford") at the mouth of Coyote Canyon, and on the 23rd at Santa Catarina. These sites are within Anza-Borrego Desert State Park. El Vado (SRL 634) is about seven miles north of the town of Borrego Springs via Di Giorgio Road and its dirt continuation. Santa Catarina is several miles farther northwest by a jeep trail.

Anza's route was superseded by another trail opened by Pedro Fages on an expedition against the Yuma Indians in 1782. Instead of taking the old path back to San Gabriel, Fages blazed a new one by way of Carrizo Creek and Vallecito and over the Cuyamaca Mountains to San Diego. This route was rediscovered in 1825 by Santiago Argüello in pursuit of Indian horse thieves, and in January 1826 the Mexican government sent Romualdo Pacheco, lieutenant of engineers, to investigate it. As a result of his findings, an official mail route was adopted via Carrizo Creek, Vallecito, San Felipe Valley, and Warner's Pass, and from then on it was used occasionally by mail carriers and traders from Sonora. Probably the first Americans to come this way were David E. Jackson and his fur-trading party, who came overland from Santa Fe in 1831. This road, which came to be known as the Emigrant Trail, formed a part of the Southern Overland Trail and was a much-traveled path during the 1840s and 1850s. From September 1858 to the beginning of the Civil War it was also the route of the famous Butterfield Stage.

This trail, after crossing the deserts a little south of the international boundary line, entered what is now San Diego County via Carrizo Creek and Warner's Ranch. Passing down the mountain by the old Canyon Road to Sonora, the route proceeded by way of what is now Oak Grove in San Diego County to Temecula and Elsinore in Riverside County, and thence northwest to Mission San Gabriel and Los Angeles.

Another branch of the southern Emigrant Trail passed from Warner's down Palomar Mountain by the old Indian trail behind Pala Chapel to Mission San Luís Rey. Still another route, followed by General Stephen W. Kearny in 1846, led from Warner's to San Diego via Santa Ysabel and San Pasqual.

RANCHO SANTA MARGARITA Y LAS FLORES (CAMP PENDLETON)

Mission San Luís Rey possessed ranchos with thousands of head of cattle. North of the mission was Rancho Santa Margarita y Las Flores, one of the great estates of California. Since 1942 it has been Camp Joseph H. Pendleton of the U.S. Marine Corps. The 125,000 acres of land in this military reservation have been preserved almost intact within the heavily developed coastal area between Ventura and San Diego. Near the ruins of the Las Flores asistencia is the Las Flores Rancho house built by Marcos A. Forster, son of Don Juan Forster, who had purchased the large estate from Pio and Andrés Pico in 1864. It is today a Boy Scout headquarters and carefully preserved. Entrance to the area may be reached via the main gain to Camp Pendleton, where visitors may apply for admission.

Overlooking the valley of the Santa Margarita River stands the twenty-room Santa Margarita Rancho house (SRL 1026), now the residence of the commandant of Camp Pendleton. There is a museum in the old bunkhouse, built in 1864. The chapel nearby is open to the public for regular services; it is the oldest building on the base, said to have been built by mission Indians in 1810.

RANCHO LOS PEÑASQUITOS (RANCHO PENASQUITOS)

The first land grant in San Diego County was made to Francisco María Ruiz by Governor Luís Argüello in 1823. Rancho Los Peñasquitos ("small rocks") lies along the creek of the same name. Ownership was transferred to Francisco María Alvarado in 1837. The Alvarado adobe (possibly built by Ruiz as early as 1827) is mentioned in Major Emory's report of General Kearny's expedition of 1846. The soldiers reached the ranch house on the evening of December 11, after reinforcements from San Diego had enabled them to leave their forced camp on Mule Hill. Emory's report vividly describes the welcome abundance of food that the half-starved soldiers found at Los Peñasquitos. Much of this area is subdivided today. Ruins of the Alvarado adobe were uncovered in the late 1980s and early 1990s beneath the north wing of the much later Johnson-Taylor ranch house, accessible from Black Mountain Road into Peñasquitos Canyon Preserve. A view of the ruins can be seen from the freeway bridge where I-5 crosses Los Peñasquitos Canyon.

RANCHO GUAJOME (VISTA)

Although built after the Mexican period, one of the most typical of the adobe ranch houses still standing is that on Rancho Guajome ("the big frog"). Guajome was part of the original mission lands of San Luís Rey. In 1845 it was granted to two Indians, Andrés and José Manuel. A few years later they sold it to Abel Stearns, who gave it as a wedding gift to his sister-in-law, Ysidora Bandini, when she married an American, Colonel Cave J. Couts, in 1851. The house was built in 1852–53. The Guajome adobe was one of several Spanish-Californian homes in which Helen Hunt Jackson was a guest while gathering material for her novel *Ramona*. The adobe remained in the family for a long time; on July 15, 1943, Cave J. Couts Jr., son of Cave and Ysidora Couts, died in the same room and in the same bed in which he had been born in 1856. The beautifully restored adobe (SRL 940) and the surrounding land were acquired by San Diego County in 1973 and are today Guajome Regional Park. The park is located two miles southeast of SR 76 at 2210 North Santa Fe Avenue in Vista. On the same property is the Southwestern Antique Gas and Steam Engine Museum, an attractive display of farm machinery.

RANCHO EL CAJÓN (EL CAJON, LAKESIDE)

A few miles east of Mission San Diego, at the headwaters of the San Diego River, a large grant of eleven leagues of land was made by Governor Pío Pico in 1845 to Maria Antonio Estudillo de Pedrorena, wife of Miguel de Pedrorena. The property was named Rancho El Cajón ("the box") because its center was a box-like canyon surrounded by high hills and mountains. The large adobe ranch house stood in what is now the center of Lakeside; it is gone without a trace. The Lakeside Community Presbyterian Church, now the headquarters of the Lakeside Historical Society, was built in 1895, restored and rededicated in 1996; this civic landmark is at the corner of Parkside and Maine Avenue. The town is named for the county's only natural freshwater lake lying at its center, Lindo Lake, contained within a beautiful park.

The first commercial building in El Cajon Valley went up in 1876; this was Knox's Hotel, the project of Amaziah Knox, originally an employee of Isaac Lankershim, who owned the former Rancho El Cajon property in 1869. The two-story building now stands at the corner of Park and Magnolia Streets; the exterior is maintained by the City of El Cajon and the interior by the El Cajon Historical Society. Its focus is on the life of what has been until recently an agricultural community. Another museum in El Cajon is located on the campus of Cuyamaca College; this is the Heritage of the Americas Museum, and its coverage extends far beyond the boundaries of California.

OTHER RANCHOS OF SAN DIEGO COUNTY

A separate land grant lying within that of Rancho El Cajón but completely separate from it was Rancho La Cañada de los Coches ("glen of the pigs"), the smallest Mexican land grant in California, of 28 acres. It was granted to Apolinaria Lorenzana in 1843 by Governor Micheltorena. The marker (SRL 425) is missing from its site, the entrance to Los Coches Trailer Park on Olde Highway, just northeast of El Cajon and about a quarter of a mile from I-8. Rancho Monserate, near the junction of I-15 and SR 76, is today largely a mobile home park. The bunkhouse is the only building still standing from the Mexican era; it has been remodeled and is now the park's recreational center. In southern San Diego County, Rancho de la Nacíon gave its name to National City, in the northwest corner of the grant. Rancho Cuyamaca, 35,501 acres in eastern San Diego County, was the scene of a gold rush in 1870. Stonewall Mine, just south of Cuyamaca Lake, was active until 1892, having produced some $2 million in gold. In 1933, 25,000 acres became Cuyamaca Rancho State Park. Mr. and Mrs. Ralph M. Dyar, then owners of the property who made the bequest to the state, built a lovely stone house in 1923 that is now the park headquarters and museum.

WARNER'S RANCH

When the Spaniards first visited Agua Caliente (the "hot springs"), they found an Indian rancheria there. All of the land surrounding the springs, about 49,000 acres in all, later came under the joint control of Missions San Diego and San Luís Rey, remaining in their possession until the secularization and confiscation of mission property in 1836. At that time the whole valley, known as the Valle de San José, was granted to Silvestre de la Portilla, but his grant seems to have lapsed later, for when Jonathan Trumbull (Juan José) Warner, a Connecticut Yankee, applied for the land in 1844, the missions still laid claim to it.

Warner, who had come to California with the David E. Jackson party in 1831, was one of the first Americans

Warner's Ranch

to become an extensive landholder in California. He dispensed liberal hospitality on his estate, and Warner's Ranch became an objective for all those early wayfarers who entered California over the old Emigrant Trail, which crossed the Colorado Desert from Yuma. It was the camping place for various divisions of the Army of the West, notably Stephen W. Kearny's regiment and the Mormon Battalion, in 1846 and 1847. In 1853, explorers for a Pacific railroad passed and repassed it in search of a suitable route.

The old headquarters of Warner's Ranch (SRL 311) are located about four miles southwest of Warner Springs and just east of SR 79 on the road to Ranchita and Borrego Springs. The adobe ranch house and barn have been protected somewhat by corrugated-iron roofs, and the ranch has been designated a National Historic Landmark. The house served Warner both as a trading post and as a residence. Warner's Ranch became a stopping place for the Butterfield Overland stages in 1858.

At Warner Springs (the old Agua Caliente) is an adobe thought to have been built in the 1830s by an Indian named Cungalunga. This is the dwelling in which Warner is supposed to have lived when he first took possession of his ranch in 1844. It is now restored as Kupa House, a guest house of the resort. Also standing is the picturesque St. Francis Chapel, built about 1830.

THE KEARNY TRAIL

The trail that General Stephen W. Kearny and the Army of the West followed through Imperial and San Diego Counties, on their way to the fatal Battle of San Pasqual, has been traced by Arthur Woodward, one-time curator of history of the Los Angeles Museum, who went over this section of the old Kearny trail, tracing its route and locating the campsites one by one. He describes the route as follows:

On November 28, [1846,] they pressed on slowly and came to the large spring near which in later days the Carrizo stage station was erected. . . . From Carrizo, where they camped on the night of the 28th, they pushed on up the dry creek bed to Vallecito, where they camped on the nights of the 29th and 30th. . . .

Beyond Vallecito the road winds across the valley to the base of a small rocky ridge, 4.3 miles distant. On the other side of this low ridge lies Mason Valley. Up this valley marched the troops for a distance of 4.8 miles until they came to the entrance of Box Canyon, a narrow rocky defile through the hills. . . . Here the road emerges and swings west again and after passing over a low ridge of hills drops into San Felipe Valley. The troops marched for about twelve or thirteen miles along this route until they came to the Indian village of San Felipe, which was on the creek. They camped here on the night of December 1 and the next day pressed on up the valley, topped the divide and dropped down to Warner's Ranch. The present road to Vallecito from Warner's probably follows fairly accurately the old trail; indeed, in Box Canyon . . . it cannot have changed very much.

The army camped a trifle south of Warner's Ranch house. . . . The place upon which they camped is probably the rather level grassy flat a few hundred yards south of the house.

Here they remained recuperating during the days of December 2 and 3. They started for Santa Isabel the morning of December 4th and, after marching for thirteen and a half miles, they camped near the old Mission station of Santa Isabel (probably in the flats southeast of the present site of the chapel on the edge of the creek).

On the morning of the 5th, the army marched southsouthwest to the rancheria of Santa Maria. They were delayed en route by a parley with Captain Gillespie and the naval reinforcements from San Diego, probably at Ballena, about six miles from Santa Isabel. Thence through the hills they traveled southwest, skirting the western edge of what is now the Valley of Santa Maria (in which the town of Ramona is situated) and probably camping at the head of Clevenger's Canyon. . . . It is about eight or nine miles via the hill trail to the point where they probably emerged in the valley of San Pasqual at a point . . . [about half a mile from] the spot where the Santa Maria River empties into San Pasqual Valley.

THE BATTLE OF SAN PASQUAL

The battle of San Pasqual was fought in San Pasqual Valley near an Indian village of that name, east of the present-day city of Escondido. It was the bloodiest of all the battles fought on California soil not involving Indians, and took place on December 6, 1846. Kearny's army, as described above, marched toward San Diego through the narrow San Pasqual Valley. Suddenly they were met by a force of Californians under the command of Major Andrés Pico. In rain and fog, the mounted Californians carrying willow lances and sabers inflicted considerable damage on the Americans, eighteen of whom were killed in the first melee. By the time the Americans were able to bring their artillery into play, their gunpowder was damp and nearly useless. The Californians suffered a few wounds and at least one fatality; the Americans lost twenty-two all told, and several more sustained serious wounds, including General Kearny and Captain Gillespie.

Kearny rallied his men on a low, boulder-studded hill, from where Kit Carson and Lieutenant Edward Beale slipped out in the darkness to seek reinforcements from San Diego. The army remained on the hill until December 11, and the men were forced to eat their mules to keep from starvation. Mule Hill (SRL 452) is above Lake Hodges and near Kit Carson Park in Escondido. San Pasqual Battlefield State Historic Park is on SR 78, adjacent to the San Diego Wild Animal Park, an operation of the San Diego Zoo. A monument put up by the state of California in 1925 commemorates the American dead. A well-appointed visitors' center opened in 1987.

THE BUTTERFIELD STAGE ROUTE

On September 16, 1857, the Butterfield Overland Mail Company (closely affiliated with the Wells Fargo Express Company) was awarded the contract for the first transcontinental mail and passenger line to California, beating out eight other bidders.

A southern route through Yuma, Arizona, was selected because it was open all year round, and St. Louis was chosen as the central supply depot. Coaches or spring wagons were used, and they carried passengers as well as mail. Stations were created along the entire route at twenty-mile intervals, horses being changed at every station and drivers every two hundred or three hundred miles.

The first stage on the Butterfield line left St. Louis on September 15, 1858, and a second followed the next day. One of the chief remaining landmarks of the old route is at Vallecito ("Little Valley"). This section of the route goes northwest to Warner's Ranch and southeast through Carrizo Canyon, joining the highway from San Diego to Yuma a few miles west of El Centro. In 1847 the men of the Mormon Battalion, under the command of Lieutenant Colonel Philip St. George Cooke, passed this way on their journey to San Diego. Their wagons were the first vehicles to use this route.

The Vallecito stage station (SRL 304) was built of blocks of sod rather than adobe bricks. It stood deserted for a long time, prey to vandals and earthquakes, its walls rapidly crumbling before the elements. In 1934 it was rebuilt, and it is now Vallecito Stage Station County Park, within the borders of the Anza-Borrego Desert State Park, on the Overland Stage Route Highway (S2), about nineteen miles southwest of Scissors Crossing. This is one of the finest historical restorations in the state; fittingly, the old stage station is now surrounded by a series of campgrounds.

Vallecito was one of the six stations along the stretch of the Butterfield route through present San Diego County. The first was at Carrizo Creek, just west of the Imperial county line. The next was Palm Spring (SRL 639), about fourteen miles southeast of Vallecito by road and jeep trail. The third was Vallecito.

About ten miles northwest of Vallecito the Butterfield stages passed through Box Canyon (SRL 472), a narrow defile about a mile in length. Here, on January 19, 1847, Cooke's men of the Mormon Battalion had to use axes to hack a wagon road out of solid rock. A trail leads from the historical marker to the edge of Box Canyon. By climbing down into the canyon, one may see the cut made by the soldiers.

The Butterfield route (SRL 647) is still visible at the pass between Blair and Shelter Valleys, the latter known for many years as Earthquake Valley. The hill six miles south of Scissors Crossing on the road to Vallecito is the divide between the two valleys. On the south side, in Blair Valley, a dirt road branches from the main route and circles around to the pass, where a historical marker is located. In this area the Butterfield route passes through Anza-Borrego Desert State Park.

The fourth station was at San Felipe (SRL 793), where Kearny and his men had camped in 1846 on their march to San Diego and the battle of San Pasqual. The site is in San Felipe Valley about a mile northwest of Scissors Crossing. The fifth station was the Warner ranch house.

The last station before Aguanga in Riverside County still stands at Oak Grove on SR 79. It is a long, well-preserved adobe still in use as a store and bar—one of the few Butterfield stations still occupied (SRL 502). It is on the register of National Historic Landmarks. Across the road, from 1861 to 1866, was Camp Wright (SRL 482), established to guard communication between California and Arizona and to cut off traffic to the Confederate states. Troops from this post engaged in the only military action of the Civil War on California soil, the capture of a group of Southern sympathizers en route from El Monte to join the Confederate army. The Oak Grove stage station served as a hospital for Camp Wright.

JULIAN

Julian (SRL 412) is a town nestled among forests of oak and conifer. Today it is the center of an attractive agricultural community, where apples, pears, and honey supplant the gold of former days. The first discovery of gold in the region was made late in 1869; the first mine was named for George Washington. A small stampede followed, and several other mines with such names as the Cuyamaca, Golden Chariot, and Stonewall Jackson were put into operation. By the time the mines had played out in 1880, some $5 million in gold had been taken.

The Julian Hotel is one of the oldest operating hotels in southern California. It was begun in 1897 by a former slave and his wife, Albert and Margaret Robinson, and was originally named for them. After Mr. Robinson's death, his wife ran the hotel until 1921 when she sold it to Martin Jacobs, who changed the name to the Julian Hotel. It is now on the National Register of Historic Places. The Santa Ysabel School, built at Witch Creek ten miles west of Julian in 1888, was moved to its present site in the town in 1970 and is a museum of local artifacts. The Eagle and High Peak Mine at the end of C Street is open for tourists to get a taste of the gold-mining years.

OTHER LANDMARKS OF SAN DIEGO COUNTY

An adobe and frame ranch house, built in 1882 by Robert Kelly, then owner of Rancho Agua Hedionda, was restored in the 1930s by actor Leo Carrillo, a descendant of prominent early Californians. The Carrillo ranch is located off Palomar Airport Road (S12) two miles east of El Camino Real, and is now owned by the city of Carlsbad. Though once an extensive ranch of 2,538 acres, most of it has been sold to developers. A small remnant of less than twenty acres was dedicated in 1996 as Leo Carrillo Ranch (SRL 1020); it contains the central ranch buildings.

Nearby Mount Palomar is the location of the Palomar Observatory, where the largest telescope in the

Hotel Del Coronado, Coronado

United States, the 200-inch Hale Telescope, was installed in 1950. There is an interesting museum on the grounds.

Carlsbad has a Stagecoach Park, part of the Andrés Ybarra Rancho Encinitas. It has a marker at the remains of a stage station long used by coastal travelers. It was once the ranch house.

Olivenhain is the site of a small German colony that was started on Rancho Los Encinitas in 1884. Some old buildings still stand on Rancho Santa Fe Road in Rancho Santa Fe, including the meeting house of 1895.

Rancho Santa Fe (SRL 982) is a historic planned community. The land was granted to Juan María Osuña in 1845 as the 9,000-acre Rancho San Dieguito. It was used for growing thousands of eucalyptus trees for ties by the Santa Fe Railroad. The wood, however, proved to be unusable. In the 1920s the land was sold to become an attractive town of exclusive homes, unified by its Spanish Colonial Revival architecture, and has successfully held to this concept since then.

At Spring Valley, ten miles east of San Diego, is the Bancroft ranch house (SRL 626). The adobe was built in 1863 by A. S. Ensworth and came into the hands of the great California historian Hubert Howe Bancroft in 1885. Due to Bancroft's eminence, the house has been registered as a National Historic Landmark. It stands on Memory Lane off Bancroft Drive.

At Coronado, across the bay from San Diego, is the Hotel Del Coronado (SRL 844), a relic of the Victorian era that is still a showplace, with 399 rooms very much in use. It was designed by the famous architect Stanford White and was formally opened on February 14, 1888. It was the largest building outside New York City to have its own electrical power plant, which supplied the entire city of Coronado until 1922. The Naval Air Station, North Island, Coronado, is the site of the first military flying school in the United States (SRL 818), founded by Glenn Curtiss in 1911.

The National City Depot (SRL 1023) was the Pacific terminus for the Santa Fe Railroad. The depot was completed and opened when the first eastbound and westbound trains used it in 1885. Between 1885 and the 1960s the station served local passengers and freight when the Santa Fe moved its headquarters to San Bernardino and Los Angeles. Of the five stations originally built in the Italianate design on the transcontinental line, it is the only one surviving.

Eleven miles south of San Diego via National Avenue is Montgomery Memorial Park (SRL 711), set aside in honor of John Joseph Montgomery, whose glider flight at Otay Mesa in 1883, twenty years before the Wright brothers, was the first successful flight of a heavier-than-air craft. The marker for this site is no longer there. A monument in the shape of a wing has been erected near the site of the historic event. Montgomery died in a glider crash near Evergreen in Santa Clara County in 1911.

In Anza-Borrego Desert State Park, besides the numerous landmarks of Anza and the Butterfield Stage, there is a most unusual monument (SRL 750) in honor of Thomas L. "Peg Leg" Smith, who is supposed to have discovered gold in the vicinity about 1850. Many have sought the "lost" mine in vain. Legend has it that anyone who adds a stone to the monument will have good luck, while the removal of a stone will have the opposite result. The monument is located about seven miles northwest of Borrego Springs via Palm Canyon Drive and Peg Leg Road.

Campo is a small settlement along SR 94, a mile north of the international border. Here on December 5, 1875, a gunfight took place to rival the famous incident at the O.K. Corral in Tombstone, Arizona. The battle pitted Silas E. and Lumas H. Gaskill, the Campo storekeepers, against a gang of bandits from Tecate in Mexico. Several of the outlaws were killed or mortally wounded. The Gaskill brothers were injured but recovered. In 1885, they built the present stone store (SRL 411) about 1,500 feet east of the original wooden store of the 1875 gunfight. Operating commercially until 1925, it was closed until purchased in 1938 by E. M. Statler, given to San Diego County as a museum, and restored between 1943 and 1948.

Just north of Campo, on the shore of Lake Morena, is one of California's newest and most unusual monuments, commemorating the activities of Charles Mallory Hatfield. The wording on the plaque is as follows:

Hatfield the Rainmaker. Charles M. Hatfield agreed with the San Diego City Council members, after a four year drought, to "make it rain" sufficiently to fill Lake Morena reservoir for $10,000. His "rain enhancing" tower and pans were erected south of this monument. Hatfield and brother Paul worked diligently burning chemicals into the sky. Suddenly it began to rain, dumping 35 inches in one month on San Diego County. Two rainstorms in January 1916 caused great devastation, destroying Sweetwater Dam spillway, bursting Otay Dam, wiping out Otay Valley and Mission Valley, isolating San Diego and killing 14 people. Hatfield hurriedly left town and was never paid by the city for his services. Charles and Paul went on to "enhance moisture" around the world. Plaque placed in cooperation with the County of San Diego and the Ancient and Honorable Order of E Clampus Vitus, Squibob Chapter, April 24, 1999.

Hatfield lived until 1958.

In Border Field State Park a granite shaft marks the southernmost point of California and the southwestern corner of the continental United States. The monument was set up in 1851, later taken down and recut, and set back in place in 1894. Border Field State Park is reached from I-5 via Dairy Mart Road and Monument Road. The fence marking the international boundary straddles the border; the fence continues toward the ocean, whence the early voyagers came to explore San Diego County and Alta California.

San Francisco County

San Francisco County derived its name from Mission San Francisco de Asís, established within the present boundary lines of the city in 1776. San Francisco was one of the original twenty-seven counties.

Until 1856 the county included what is now San Mateo County, and the city of San Francisco was the county seat. After San Mateo County became a separate jurisdiction, the government was consolidated, operating as the City and County of San Francisco. Its forty-six square miles make it the smallest of California's counties in area. In the earthquake and fire of 1906, most of the city's records were destroyed, but fortunately, many pre-statehood records in Spanish were saved. Some of these are in the San Francisco History Room of the Main Public Library in San Francisco's Civic Center.

DISCOVERY OF THE GOLDEN GATE

The entrance to San Francisco Bay was discovered on November 1, 1769, by Sergeant José Ortega, pathfinder of Gaspar de Portolá's expedition who, a few days before, had seen the bay from the hills of what is now San Mateo County.

The expedition was searching for the "lost" bay of Monterey and had proceeded up the coast as far as San Pedro Valley. From this point, Portolá had commissioned Ortega to explore as far north as Point Reyes, which Portolá had seen from the summit of the Montara Mountains just east of Point San Pedro. The unexpected channel of the Golden Gate prevented Ortega and his party from reaching their objective. He accordingly proceeded along the south shore of the channel and climbed La Loma Alta (later called Telegraph Hill). From this vantage point, he could see the whole expanse of the bay, its islands, and the hills of the Contra Costa ("opposite coast") beyond.

Having made his observations, Ortega returned to camp to report. Portolá was bent on finding the putative bay of Monterey, however, and apparently did not realize that the expedition had made the great discovery of an enormous landlocked bay with access to the ocean. His expedition soon returned to the south.

In the next six years, Spanish expeditions along the California coast led to more discoveries, and on August 4, 1775, the ship *San Carlos*, commanded by Juan Manuel de Ayala, reached the entrance of San Francisco Bay. Ayala, suffering from an accidental head injury, sent his subordinate José Cañizares ahead to find an anchorage. The latter did not return all that day, for the currents and tides of the strait were too strong for the little launch in which he made the reconnoitering expedition. Therefore, on the evening of August 5, Ayala, in the *San Carlos*, passed through the strait and into the bay. Cañizares and Ayala thus are both recognized for leading the first recorded entrance into San Francisco Bay from the ocean.

For forty-four days Ayala and his men remained in the Bay, exploring every arm and inlet and going as far as the mouth of the San Joaquin River, at the same time taking soundings and making a map. Two of the names given at this time are in use today, in slightly different forms. The island just inside the strait was called Isla de Nuestra Señora de los Angeles, "Island of Our Lady of the Angels," and is known today as Angel Island. In a sheltered cove of this island, the *San Carlos* remained during most of its stay in the bay. Another island was named Isla de los Alcatraces, "Island of the Pelicans," and we have the name today as Alcatraz Island.

Ayala's exploration of San Francisco Bay established the suitability of its shores for settlement, and the location at San Francisco of the mission and the presidio was largely influenced by this expedition. A plaque (SRL 236) commemorating the entrance of the *San Carlos* into San Francisco Bay was placed at Fort Point in 1955 by the Daughters of the American Revolution.

The Spaniards had called the gateway to the newly discovered bay "La Boca del Puerto de San Francisco" but an American gave it the name of "Golden Gate." In his *Memoirs* General John C. Frémont says: "To this gate I gave the name of Chrysopylae, or Golden Gate, for the same reason that the harbor of Byzantium [afterward Constantinople] was called Chrysoceras, or Golden Horn." In a footnote he adds: "The form of the entrance of the bay of San Francisco and its advantages for commerce, Asiatic included, suggested to me that name which I gave to this entrance and which I put upon the map that accompanied a geographical Memoir addressed to the Senate of the United States in June 1848."

THE FOUNDING OF SAN FRANCISCO

No sooner were the first settlements made in Alta California than practical men such as Father Junipero Serra pointed out the great need for a dependable land route from New Spain. Furthermore, there was the possibility of foreign intervention in Alta California—Russia was becoming active along the northern Pacific Coast. Antonio María Bucareli, viceroy of New Spain, decided to send an expedition to find an overland route, and appointed Juan Bautista de Anza as commander.

Anza was a member of the aristocracy of New Spain, an officer of good character and ability. He led a successful overland journey to California in 1774, paving the way for further colonization of the province. An important concern here was the project of settling at San Francisco Bay and the region around what the Spaniards called the Río Grande de San Francisco, the delta of the Sacramento and the San Joaquin Rivers. These colonies were to be a base for further settlements to the north, as well as buffers against outside enemies.

Accordingly a second expedition was planned on which Anza was to take settlers and supplies with him to establish a presidio and a mission at San Francisco. After a difficult passage through desert and mountains, and needless delays caused by Governor Fernando Rivera, who was opposed to the settlement of San Francisco, this undertaking was accomplished. Anza himself reached San Francisco on March 27, 1776, but Rivera's lack of cooperation made it necessary for Anza to leave his settlers temporarily at Monterey.

The final lap of the journey had led along the hills, with "a good-sized lake of fresh water," now called Lake Merced, lying to the westward. From this point the company marched toward the Golden Gate, making camp at what the Spaniards called Laguna del Presidio and is now known as Mountain Lake. Arroyo del Puerto was the name given to the nearby stream known today as Lobos Creek, near the southwestern corner of the presidio military reservation. Anza made a thorough survey of the region, marking out sites for the presidio and mission. For the presidio fort he chose Cantil

Blanco ("white cliff"), above today's Fort Point along the water's edge. The cliff was destroyed later, during the American occupancy. He selected a place for the mission near a little rivulet that he named Nuestra Señora de los Dolores. The town was to lie on the plain between the presidio and the mission.

After exploring the Bay and the River of San Francisco up to the junction of the Sacramento and San Joaquin Rivers, Anza returned to Monterey. He was greatly disappointed not to be able to settle his colonists in San Francisco, but since he could not do so without the aid of Rivera, he left Monterey "amid the tears and lamentations of the settlers, who had learned to revere and love him in the course of their long march from Sonora." The colonists were settled at San Francisco by José Joaquín Moraga, Anza's capable lieutenant, and by Father Francisco Palou in the summer of 1776. Anza never returned to California, but he is remembered as a major pioneer in its history.

THE PRESIDIO OF SAN FRANCISCO

Anza chose the site of the Presidio of San Francisco (SRL 79) on March 28, 1776. On June 27 Lieutenant Moraga and the settlers who had traveled from Sonora to Monterey with Anza made temporary camp at the Laguna de Manantial, about where Dolores and Eighteenth Streets intersect today. The next day a shelter of branches was built to serve as a chapel, and on June 29, the first Mass was said. On July 26 most of the expedition moved to the presidio site, where shelters were put up and Mass was offered on July 28. On September 17 the presidio was dedicated, and Moraga took formal possession in the name of King Carlos III.

Neither the Spanish nor the later Mexican government had the ability to support the Presidio of San Francisco adequately. As John Phillip Langellier and Daniel B. Rosen point out, the location was exposed to the elements and often bitterly cold. Never fully garrisoned, it was thought of as what today would be called a hardship post. After 1835 regular troops were no longer stationed there, and by 1840 it was in ruins. However, with the American occupation on July 9, 1846, the Presidio became one of the principal United States Army establishments on the Pacific Coast. In 1963 the Presidio of San Francisco, headquarters of the Sixth Army, was registered as a National Historic Landmark. Congress established the Golden Gate National Recreational Area in 1972, at which time most of the coastal area of the Presidio was added to its jurisdic-

tion. In 1989 the closure of the post was announced. When the Army withdrew in the fall of 1994, the largest military reservation within an American city came under the jurisdiction of the Golden Gate National Recreational Area, although the future of the buildings and grounds within continues to be under considerable discussion with both federal and city agencies. Some buildings are still occupied by the Army.

When the United States took possession of the site in 1846, most of its 1,400 acres consisted of bare, windswept sand hills. In the 1880s, great plantings were made of eucalyptus, Monterey cypress, and pines, which have over the years suffered the ravages of time.

The sites of the old Spanish presidio buildings have been marked. At the southwest corner of the original presidio, a bronze tablet has been set in the wall of the Officers' Club and a marker placed by the Daughters of the American Revolution. At the northwest corner, a bronze tablet has been set in a stone in the parking lot adjacent to Building T-40 on Mesa Street. The southeast corner is marked by a chromium nail in the aisle of the Catholic chapel on Moraga Avenue. The only building remaining from the Spanish period is the *comandancia*, since 1848 the Officers' Club, on Moraga Avenue. The adobe incorporated into the walls was fashioned in the late eighteenth century.

Two Spanish cannon cast in 1673 stand in front of the Officers' Club. The touchhole of one contains the fragments of a file thrust there by John C. Frémont when he spiked the guns of the Castillo de San Joaquín during the Bear Flag revolt in 1846. Two other cannon from the castillo are located elsewhere on the grounds: one, cast in 1628, is at the Presidio Army Museum and the other, cast in 1684, is at Fort Point National Historic Site. Two more Spanish cannon, one cast in 1679 and the other cast in 1693, flank the post flagpole, four hundred feet northwest of the Officers' Club.

Many buildings remain from the early American period. One of the largest of these is the old post hospital, begun in 1857. In 1973, it became the Presidio Army Museum, offering many displays not only of military history but also of such San Francisco events as the earthquake and fire of 1906. The Army gave substantial aid to distressed citizens during that disaster, among other things putting up more than 5,000 one-room shacks for temporary shelter. Two of these shelters were saved from oblivion and in 1986 were refurbished and placed in the yard at the rear of the museum, which is located on Funston Avenue near Lincoln Boulevard.

The National Military Cemetery at the Presidio is

one of the largest in the state and is still used for burials. Like most of the Presidio grounds, it can be reached by car or by many of the hiking paths and foot trails that have been open to the public for many years.

CASTILLO DE SAN JOAQUÍN AND PORT POINT

Castillo de San Joaquín (SRL 82) was a Spanish fort located on the Punta de Cantil Blanco at the edge of the Golden Gate, near the old presidio but separate from it. Completed and dedicated on December 8, 1794, the Castillo de San Joaquín would never have withstood a siege, for "the structure rested mainly on sand; the brick-faced walls crumbled at the shock whenever a salute was fired; the guns were badly mounted, and, for the most part, worn out." The adobe-walled fort, frequently patched after heavy rainstorms, gradually became a ruin, and after 1835 no troops were stationed there.

On July 1, 1846, as an aftermath of the Bear Flag Revolt, John C. Frémont and twelve of his men crossed over from Sausalito in the launch *Moscow* and spiked the guns of the castillo. In his *Memoirs* Frémont says that the guns he spiked were large handsome pieces, but he fails to add that they were dismounted and lying on the ground.

With statehood, new plans were made for the defense of San Francisco Bay. In 1853, digging was begun to level the white cliff where the castillo stood, and by the following year that natural landmark was no more. At sea level, a new American fort was constructed, which was completed in 1861. The new fort stood about where the old Spanish fort had been and was customarily called Fort Point. In 1882 the Army gave it the name of Fort Winfield Scott, but the name did not catch on in common usage, and by the 1890s the name Fort Point was used again. In 1912 the adjacent area was given the name of Fort Winfield Scott, and it continued as a separate, independent post until 1946.

Fort Point was constructed to prevent the entrance of a hostile fleet into San Francisco Bay, though there is no record of anything of the sort having been attempted. The three-story fort, with walls between five and twelve feet thick, was designed to mount 126 cannon and to house 600 soldiers. With the advent of powerful rifled cannon, brick forts such as this became obsolete, and in 1886 Fort Point was abandoned. The building had a second life in 1933–37 as a base of operations during the construction of the Golden Gate Bridge, which is designed so that the bridge passes over

the fort but does not touch it. (More than one suicide from the Golden Gate Bridge has landed on the roof of Fort Point.) During World War II, the fort was garrisoned by about one hundred soldiers, who manned searchlights and rapid-fire cannon mounted on top of the fort as part of the protection for a submarine net stretched across the entrance to San Francisco Bay. In 1970, the fort was declared the Fort Point National Historic Site and was later incorporated into the Golden Gate National Recreational Area. Today it is open to the public, restored in part to its Civil War–era furnishings, and presents one of the most beautiful coastal views in all California.

MISSION SAN FRANCISCO DE ASÍS (DOLORES)

The first plans of the Visitador General of Mexico, José de Gálvez, did not call for a mission dedicated to St. Francis of Assisi, founder of the Franciscan order. The padre presidente, Junipero Serra, protested this omission, but Gálvez replied, "If Saint Francis wishes a mission, let him show you a good port, and then let it bear his name." Accordingly, when Portolá's party discovered the great bay, the Franciscan chroniclers in the group declared that this must be "the port to which the Visitador referred and to which the Saint has led us."

But it was not until seven years later, in 1776, that Mission San Francisco de Asís was founded. Juan Bautista de Anza had selected the site of the mission a short time before. This was on the bank of the little lake that Anza called Laguna de Manantial, now filled in. The stream that flowed into it he called Arroyo de Nuestra Señora de los Dolores, because it was on the Friday of Our Lady of Sorrows (Viernes de los Dolores) that he found it. The name of the mission itself in later years became popularized to "Mission Dolores."

Father Francisco Palou arrived at the lake on June 27, 1776, and two days later celebrated the first Mass in a temporary chapel. San Francisco celebrates its birthday each year on June 29, the anniversary of the first Mass at the mission site, and thus claims to be five days older than the Declaration of Independence.

The mission was not formally dedicated, however, until early October. The present mission church (SRL 327) was begun, a few hundred yards from the original site, on April 25, 1782 when the first stone was put in place, and dedicated on April 3, 1791. In contrast to other mission churches, it is a rather plain building,

Mission Dolores

Cemetery of Mission Dolores

unadorned by arches, towers, or arcades. It is, however, of an impressive size.

The shadow of a redwood cross in the enclosed cemetery beside the church falls across old graves. Here lie the remains of Don Luís Antonio Argüello, governor of Alta California from November 1822 to November 1825; he died in 1830. Don Francisco de Haro, first alcalde of San Francisco, is also buried here. Among other graves are those of James P. Casey and Charles Cora, both hanged by the Vigilantes. Within the church itself are buried Don José Joaquín Moraga, Anza's lieutenant and founder of the presidio, who died in 1795; the Noe family; and William Alexander Leidesdorff, the first black pioneer in San Francisco.

On the south wall of the mission is a memorial from the California Historical Society in honor of Father Francisco Palou, founder of Mission Dolores and California's first historian. On November 24, 1963, the 250th anniversary of the birth of Father Junipero Serra, a tablet was placed at Mission Dolores to mark the northern terminus of El Camino Real as Serra knew it and helped to blaze it (SRL 784). A similar tablet was placed at the southern terminus, Mission San Diego de Alcalá. Adjoining the mission is the larger parish church, rebuilt in 1918 after its destruction in the 1906 earthquake, and honored by the Vatican in 1952 with the title of minor basilica.

YERBA BUENA COVE

Captain George Vancouver, commanding the British sloop of war *Discovery*, brought his ship into San Francisco Bay on the night of November 14, 1792, and anchored "about a league below the presidio in a place they called Yerba Buena." This is apparently the first reference we have to the little cove that would later mark the beginning of the modern city.

Vancouver, the first English visitor to Alta California, was received hospitably by Father Antonio Danti, the priest at the mission, and by the presidio commander, Hermenegildo Sal. The captain has left an interesting description of the country, the bay, the presidio, and his trip to Mission Santa Clara. When Vancouver paid a second visit the next year, he was not received so warmly, for Don Hermenegildo had been reprimanded for letting a foreigner see the defenseless condition of the settlement.

THE RUSSIANS VISIT SAN FRANCISCO

At the same time that Spain was colonizing Alta California, far to the north the Russian Empire made a settlement in what is now Alaska. By 1806 the Russian colony was near starvation and in desperate need of assistance. Count Nikolai Rezanov was sent south to negotiate with Spanish officials in San Francisco, knowing that trade with foreigners was forbidden. On April 5, he brought his ship past the presidio and entered the harbor. Pleading the urgency of his mission, he made contact with José Darío Argüello, then commander of the presidio, and a good friend of Governor José Joaquín de Arrillaga. Count Rezanov was entertained in the Argüello household while he bartered the Russian goods he had brought for California food.

Here he met Concepción, the fifteen-year-old daughter of the Argüello family. Concha, as her family affectionately called her, was beautiful and lively, and she and the much older Rezanov fell in love. The Russian had won the favor of the authorities and was able to make an exchange of his cargo for food supplies. On May 21, six weeks after his arrival, Rezanov sailed back to the aid of his starving people in Alaska. From there, he returned to Russia, presumably to obtain royal and ecclesiastical permission for his marriage to Concepción. Fatally injured in a fall from his horse while crossing Siberia, he sent a last message to his betrothed, but the news did not arrive in California for several years.

The aftermath of this romance belongs to Benicia in Solano County, where Concepción spent the last years of her life and where she is buried. Its political significance concerns the Russian settlements at Bodega and Fort Ross, told in the Sonoma County chapter.

YERBA BUENA, THE FORERUNNER OF SAN FRANCISCO

Captain William A. Richardson was the founder of Yerba Buena ("good herb," Spanish for wild mint), which became the nucleus of the modern city of San Francisco. Born in England, Richardson came to San Francisco in 1822, when the Mexican flag was flying over the presidio and Governor Pablo Vicente de Solá, the last Spanish ruler, was just leaving California. Richardson gained permission from Solá to settle permanently at San Francisco, in return for which he was to teach the young Spaniards the arts of navigation and carpentry, two skills that were much needed. In 1825, Richardson married María Antonia, daughter of Don Ignacio Martínez, *comandante* of the presidio.

Richardson was a master mariner, and besides teaching the trades of carpentry and shipbuilding and the art of navigation to the presidio people, he was also the first to develop trade and communication by water on San Francisco Bay. For three years he managed the shipping that went back and forth between San Francisco and the embarcadero at Mission San José. He piloted vessels in and out of the bay, and later became captain of the port and Bay of San Francisco under the direction of Mariano Guadalupe Vallejo, commanding general in the north.

It was Richardson's plan to establish a port on San Francisco Bay at the best possible anchoring place, and he chose Yerba Buena Cove. Governor José Figueroa acted upon these plans and made Richardson the first harbormaster of San Francisco.

In 1835 Richardson moved to Yerba Buena with his family, living for three months in a tent. It is said that "this tent was the first habitation ever erected in Yerba Buena. At the time, Richardson's only neighbors were bears, coyotes, and wolves. The nearest people lived either at the Presidio or at Mission Dolores." The site where Richardson's tent stood is at 823–27 Grant Avenue, in the heart of today's Chinatown. By October 1835 he had put up a board house. He was the "solitary settler" described by Richard Henry Dana Jr. in *Two Years Before the Mast.*

In 1836 he built a more elaborate dwelling of adobe. This was the "Casa Grande" of Yerba Buena until 1848, the largest and most pretentious building there. It withstood several devastating fires, but was taken down in 1852 and replaced by the Adelphi Theater.

From the first, the settlement at Yerba Buena Cove was predominantly English-speaking, a group of foreigners in an area populated by Hispanic and Indian peoples.

The next settler there was Jacob Primer Leese, an American trader, who erected a substantial frame house in 1836. The site of his home is near the intersection of Grant Avenue and Clay Street. The first Fourth of July celebration in San Francisco was held in this house in 1836. Many prominent families from around San Francisco Bay attended the festivities, among them the Castro, De Haro, Estudillo, Guerrero, and Martínez families. General Vallejo himself was present, and several ships anchored in the cove took part in the celebration. This redwood house was the center for a large trading business that Leese and his partners, Spear and Hinckley, carried on with the ranchos bordering San Francisco Bay.

MEXICAN LAND GRANTS

Within the original boundary of San Francisco City lay private ranchos obtained through Mexican governors. When the county was divided in 1856, by far the greater part of the land thus granted was given to San Mateo County. The diminished county of San Francisco occupied the tip of the peninsula, where lands had been reserved for mission and presidio use and where little had been granted to private individuals. The line drawn to separate the two counties passed due west from a point on San Francisco Bay a little east of Visitacion Valley through the southern end of Lake Merced to the Pacific Ocean.

Two of the old ranchos were cut by this line. Rancho Laguna de la Merced, consisting of one-half a square league, was one of these. It was granted in 1835 to José Antonio Galindo, a corporal in the San Francisco militia. After holding it for two years, he sold it to Francisco de Haro for 100 cows and $25 in goods.

Francisco de Haro arrived in California with future governor Luís Argüello in 1819 as a sublieutenant in the San Blas infantry. In 1824 he helped suppress a revolt among Indian neophytes. In that year he married Josefa, daughter of José Antonio Sánchez, and thereafter lived in San Francisco, where they raised their family. In 1838, within a year of purchasing the rancho, he was made alcalde. In that office he was responsible for the guardianship of persons arrested for offenses against law and order. A problem arose when Galindo, former owner of the rancho, was taken into custody for the murder of José Peralta. Lack of a jail compelled Alcalde de Haro to order his fellow townsmen to act as guards. After holding the prisoner for three difficult months, he finally received Governor Alvarado's permission to send Galindo to the prison at San Jose.

Francisco de Haro held many important positions under the Mexican regime and is frequently mentioned in the annals of San Francisco. He died at a comparatively early age in 1849, his death hastened by grief over the senseless murder of his twin sons by Frémont's men in San Rafael three years before, a tale told in the Marin County chapter.

The second rancho cut by the new county boundary was the Cañada de Guadalupe, la Visitación y Rodeo Viejo, only a small portion of which was left in San Francisco County. It consisted of two leagues and was granted by Governor Alvarado in 1841 to Jacob Primer Leese. Since the grantee had a house in Yerba Buena, he and his family lived for only a short time on the rancho property, which he afterward sold. The United States patent for the tract was issued in 1865 to Henry R. Payson and William Pierce; the former possessed 5,473 acres and the latter 942 acres.

A tract of 12,643 acres of pueblo land was patented to the city of San Francisco in June 1884.

Other grants of land in the San Francisco area recognized by the United States government were few and small in extent. One of these was the Ojo de Agua de Figueroa, 100 varas, granted in 1833 to Apolinario Miranda, a soldier in the San Francisco Company. He constructed an adobe house to replace an earlier temporary structure in 1834. He was once brought before the alcalde for mistreating his wife, Juana Briones; her house in the North Beach section, about where Powell and Filbert Streets intersect, was the only dwelling between Yerba Buena and the presidio. She long outlived her husband, who was buried at Mission Dolores, and ended her days in Santa Clara County.

Among the other small grants were Las Camaritas, about nineteen acres, patented to Ferdinand Vassault; two lots in the pueblo land patented to J. P. Leese in 1858; the eight and one-half acres of Mission Dolores, patented to Bishop J. S. Alemany in 1858; and a few others, varying from half an acre to twenty-five acres, given to various persons.

In 1853 José Y. Limantour made a fantastic claim to the U.S. Land Commission that he had been granted four leagues of land within and adjoining what had become the city of San Francisco. The citizens were aroused and astounded, but the claims were proven to be fraudulent, and Limantour fled the country.

PORTSMOUTH PLAZA

Captain John B. Montgomery of the SS *Portsmouth* received orders from Commodore John Drake Sloat on July 8, 1846, to take possession of Yerba Buena and the northern frontier. On the morning of July 9 Montgomery and his men landed at what is now the corner of Clay and Leidesdorff Streets. Nearby, at the southeast corner of Clay and Montgomery Streets, is a tablet placed by the Native Sons of the Golden West in 1916. This plaque not only commemorates Montgomery's landing place (SRL 81) but also brings to the attention of all who view it the fact that the waters of San Francisco Bay once came up to the foot of Clay Street almost as far as Montgomery Street. On this site the Bank of Italy, later Bank of America, which had been founded in San Francisco by A. P. Giannini in 1904, built its first main office in 1908. For this reason, the *Portsmouth* was for many years pictured on the bank's official seal.

Montgomery Street was named for Captain Montgomery. The plaza, where the first American flag was raised in San Francisco and where the Custom House stood until 1851, was afterward called Portsmouth Square in honor of his ship; it is now officially Portsmouth Plaza (SRL 119).

In 1849 and the 1850s Portsmouth Square became the place where the principal gambling houses were situated. "Neither tree, nor shrub, nor grass adorned it, but it contained a rude platform for public speaking, a tall flag staff, and a cow pen enclosed by rough board." Today, Portsmouth Plaza, location of an underground parking garage since 1962, is planted with trees and grass. The pagoda roofs of Chinatown look down upon it, and it is a favorite gathering place for San Franciscans.

On the plaza, near the corner of Clay and Kearny Streets, is a monument commemorating the Clay Street Railroad Company (SRL 500), the first cable railway system in the world. Andrew S. Hallidie, English builder of aerial cables for use in Western mines, invented an arrangement whereby heavy cables could be laid underground to draw cars uphill. The first successful cars thus equipped ran on Clay Street between Kearny and Leavenworth Streets on August 1, 1873, and soon thereafter such lines were in general use. At one time San Francisco had eight lines, but for many years now, there have been only three. San Francisco's cable cars, among its most famous tourist attractions, have been registered as a National Historic Landmark by the Department of the Interior. At the corner of Mason and Washington Streets is the Cable Car Barn and Museum, where visitors may see some retired cable cars and learn about their peculiar operation.

Robert Louis Stevenson, while living in the Bay Area, spent a good many hours at Portsmouth Square, looking at the crowds of people and engaging in long conversations.

Scenes in *The Wrecker* are based on his rambles around the square. The first monument to him, planned and executed by Bruce Porter and Willis Polk, was put up here in 1897.

Much of the work that Stevenson began in Monterey was completed in San Francisco, notably *Across the Plains* and *The Amateur Emigrant*. He cherished the friends he made here, among them Judge John Boalt and Judge Timothy H. Reardon; Virgil Williams, painter and founder of the California School of Art, and his wife; and the author and professor Charles Warren Stoddard, who influenced Stevenson's move to the South Seas, where he spent his last years.

SAN FRANCISCO'S FIRST SCHOOLS

Soon after the American occupation in 1846, it was realized that a school was needed for the children of the rapidly growing town. In April 1847 the first private school was opened by J. D. Marston in a shanty on the west side of Grant Avenue between Pacific Avenue and Broadway. It was attended by some twenty or thirty children, but lasted only a few months.

The site of what has been called San Francisco's first public school (SRL 587) is on the southwest corner of Portsmouth Plaza, and has been marked by the Grand Lodge of Free and Accepted Masons. In the autumn of 1847 a committee met to plan the building, and on April 3, 1848, school was opened by Thomas Douglas, a graduate of Yale. The gold excitement took Douglas off to the mines six weeks later, but the school was resumed in 1849 by the Reverend Albert Williams, a Presbyterian. The small schoolhouse was used for various purposes, "town hall, court house, people's court for trial of culprits by the first vigilance committee, school,

church, and finally, jail. Owing to the range and variety of its uses, the building was dignified by the name of Public Institute." Like others of that time, the Public Institute School was not a public school in the modern sense, for it was obliged to charge some tuition and was not under complete government control.

In October 1849, John Cotter Pelton, a young New England schoolteacher and a Baptist layman, came to California to establish free public schools. On December 26 of that year he opened a school in the First Baptist Church at 878-A Washington Street; soon fifty children were in attendance. Pelton would accept no tuition in his school and worked indefatigably to arouse public interest and action on behalf of the free public school as an established institution.

As a result of Pelton's efforts, his school was adopted by the city in March 1850 and became the first public school in California. The first school ordinance in the state was enacted on April 8, 1850. The site on Washington Street has been marked by a bronze tablet placed by the Northern California Baptist Convention. Another early school was established in Happy Valley in 1850, as noted below.

St. Ignatius College was founded in San Francisco in 1855. On the south side of Market Street between Fourth and Fifth Streets is a plaque attesting that the college was first located there. The Jesuit school was moved to Van Ness Avenue and Hayes Street, near the present Civic Center, in 1880. It is now the University of San Francisco and is located west of the downtown area between Lone Mountain and the Panhandle of Golden Gate Park.

St. Mary's College (SRL 772) was founded in San Francisco in 1863 by Archbishop Joseph Sadoc Alemany, O.P. A marker at College and Crescent Avenues near Mission Street indicates the original site. The Christian Brothers took charge of the college in 1868, and in 1889 it was moved to Oakland. In 1928 it was moved to its present campus in Moraga, Contra Costa County.

THE FIRST CHURCHES

A party of Mormons, under Sam Brannan, held religious services in Captain Richardson's "Casa Grande" on Dupont Street soon after they arrived in San Francisco on the ship *Brooklyn*. In May 1847 a Sunday school was organized by a Methodist missionary, Rev. James H. Wilbur. The Mormon community moved inland by the end of 1847, and the Sunday school was soon disrupted by the gold stampede.

On July 25, 1847, Chaplain Chester Newell, of the United States frigate *Independence,* preached in the C. L. Ross store, on the northwest corner of Montgomery and Washington Streets. Although there were probably other services held by ships' chaplains, this is the first recorded Protestant religious service in San Francisco. Protestant worship was carried on in the Public Institute on an irregular basis for the next two years.

St. Francis Church at the northeast corner of Vallejo Street and Columbus Avenue is, after Mission Dolores, the oldest Roman Catholic parish in San Francisco, having been established in 1849. The present building was erected in 1859. Its interior was destroyed by the great fire of 1906, but the walls remained intact and it was fully restored. St. Patrick's Church was founded in 1851. The old wooden building that stood on Market Street about where the Palace Hotel now stands has been moved several times and now stands at the north side of Eddy Street east of Divisadero, where it is used as the parish hall of Holy Cross Church. It is one of the oldest frame buildings in the city. The present St. Patrick's at 756 Mission Street was rebuilt after the 1906 disaster but incorporates portions of the structure dating from about 1870.

Old St. Mary's Church (SRL 810), at California Street and Grant Avenue, San Francisco's first Catholic cathedral, was dedicated in 1854. The bricks came around the Horn, and some of the stone came from China. It was replaced in 1891 by a new cathedral at Van Ness Avenue and O'Farrell Street, and three years later was put in charge of the Paulist Fathers. Only the walls of Old St. Mary's survived the fire of 1906, but the church was rebuilt within them and rededicated in 1909. St. Mary's Cathedral on Van Ness Avenue was spared in 1906 but destroyed by fire in 1962. It has been replaced by a new cathedral, of striking design, on the block bounded by Gough, Ellis, Octavia, and Geary Streets.

Thomas Starr King, Unitarian preacher and vigorous advocate of the Union cause in the Civil War, came to San Francisco from Boston in 1860. Until his death, in 1864, he served as pastor of the First Unitarian Church, the initial site of which was on Stockton Street near Sacramento. Since the town was growing southward, a new church was built at 133 Geary Street near Stockton shortly after King's arrival. In this church he preached, and there he was buried. Later, the city's growth necessitated the removal of the church to its present site at Geary and Franklin Streets, where King's body lies in a white marble tomb (SRL 691) before the door of the church.

King used his eloquence to support the Union and the cause of the Sanitary Commission, a Civil War forerunner of the Red Cross. His portrait was hung in the state capitol with the inscription: "The man whose matchless oratory saved California to the Union." A bronze statue was erected in Golden Gate Park as an expression of San Francisco's admiration of his work. A statue of him done by Haig Patigian has been placed, along with one of Father Junipero Serra by Ettore Cadorin, to represent California in Statuary Hall in the Capitol Building in Washington, D.C.

On the west side of Montgomery Street near Columbus Avenue is a plaque that marks the site (SRL 462) of the first Jewish religious services in San Francisco. Here forty pioneers gathered to celebrate Yom Kippur on September 26, 1849.

The First Colored Baptist Church was founded by nine San Franciscans in 1852. Originally meeting in their homes, the congregation in 1854 purchased the building then housing the First Baptist Church and moved it to the corner of Grant Avenue and Greenwich Street, where a plaque (SRL 1010) commemorates the event. The church, later known as the Third Baptist, is now located at 1399 McAllister Street.

At the summit of Nob Hill stands Grace Cathedral, the seat of the Episcopal diocese of California. The cathedral is on the site of the Charles Crocker mansion. The Crocker family donated the land for the cathedral after the mansion was destroyed in the fire of 1906, and the cornerstone was laid by Bishop William F. Nichols in 1910. A distinctive feature of this prominent building are the doors for the east front, which are casts made from the doors of the celebrated Baptistry in Florence, Italy, the work of the fifteenth-century sculptor Lorenzo Ghiberti.

MONUMENTS ON MARKET STREET

Perhaps the most celebrated monument on Market Street is Lotta's Fountain, at the intersection of Geary and Kearney Streets. This was presented to the city in 1875 by Lotta Crabtree, famed entertainer who began her career as a child in Gold Rush days. In 1910 the great operatic soprano Luisa Tetrazzini sang at midnight on Christmas Eve before thousands massed around the fountain. In commemoration of this event a bas-relief portrait of Madame Tetrazzini by Haig Patigian was added to the fountain. A charming tradition was beginning in San Francisco: the survivors of the 1906 earthquake would gather at the fountain early on the morning of April 18 each year in memory of that event. As the years passed, the physical condition of the fountain became increasingly decrepit, and a windstorm in 1998 caused much damage. A restoration project was funded by the city's Board of Supervisors and by volunteer groups, and on September 9, 1999, the 124th anniversary of its original dedication, the fountain was rededicated.

At Market, Battery, and Bush Streets is the Mechanics Monument, dedicated about 1900 to the pioneer industrialist Peter Donahue. The sculptor was the deafmute Douglas Tilden. The Pioneer Monument, a gift of James Lick, was erected in 1894 at Market, Hyde, and Grove Streets.

The Native Sons Monument was given to the city by James D. Phelan to commemorate the admission of California to the Union. It was unveiled on Admission Day, September 9, 1897, and dedicated to the Native Sons of the Golden West. The monument was originally placed at Market, Turk, and Mason Streets. It was later moved to Golden Gate Park, and subsequently brought back downtown, where it now stands at Market, Montgomery, and Post Streets.

HAPPY VALLEY

Happy Valley was the name given to a small area between First, Second, Market, and Mission Streets. In the winter of 1849–50 about a thousand tents were pitched here, sheltered from the winds by the sand hills along Market Street. A successful school was opened here in 1850. One of its founders was Rev. Samuel H. Willey, pastor of the Howard Presbyterian Church in Happy Valley, and later one of the founders of the College of California in Oakland. W. D. M. Howard, a prominent merchant, and Thomas J. Nevins assisted Willey in building up this Happy Valley Public School. In November 1851 it became the first school operated under the city public school system.

THE CIVIC CENTER

San Francisco's handsome Civic Center owes much to the 1906 earthquake and fire, which destroyed nearly five hundred blocks of buildings, including the ramshackle City Hall on Larkin Street, about where the present City Library stands. The new City Hall, on the block bounded by Van Ness Avenue and Grove, Polk, and McAllister Streets, was completed in 1913 and boasts a dome more than eleven feet higher than that

of the Capitol in Washington, D.C. The City Hall was been the scene of many gala receptions, such as those connected with the creation of the United Nations in 1945. Tragedy struck here, too, on November 27, 1978, when Mayor George Moscone and Supervisor Harvey Milk were shot to death in their offices by Dan White, a former supervisor. Extensive renovations were begun in 1996, and the City Hall was reopened in 1999.

Across the intersection of Grove and Polk Streets from the City Hall is the Civic Auditorium (renamed the Bill Graham Civic Auditorium in 1996), completed in 1913 and used for numerous exhibitions, performances, and conventions. Here in 1920, the Democrats were the first major political party to hold a national convention in California. Across the Civic Center Plaza from the City Hall is the new Public Library, completed in 1998, next to the previous library, built in 1917 and in the process of becoming a new Asian Art Museum. The San Francisco Room in the library is a major repository for San Francisco history. Federal and state office buildings in the immediate vicinity add to the impressive quality of the Civic Center.

Across Van Ness Avenue from the City Hall are the complementary buildings of the War Memorial Opera House (SRL 964) and the Veterans Memorial Building. Both were inaugurated in 1932. The Opera House was the site of two of the most important diplomatic gatherings of the twentieth century. In the spring of 1945, delegates from forty-six countries met here to confer on ways to maintain peace once World War II, then raging in the Pacific, had come to an end. On June 26, the United Nations Charter was signed in the Veterans Memorial Building, and a new effort was begun toward achieving international amity. The conference ending the war with Japan (the armistice having been signed in September 1945) met here in 1951, and the treaty of peace was signed on September 8. Plaques commemorating these events are to be seen in the foyer of the Opera House. The Opera House suffered some damage in the 1989 Loma Prieta earthquake, and was closed for intensive repairs in 1996 and 1997. The Veterans Memorial Building houses many city offices, as well as the Herbst Theater for the performing arts.

THE SHORELINE MARKERS

The location of the shoreline on Market Street as it was in 1848 was marked by two bronze tablets (SRL 83) in 1921 by the Native Sons of the Golden West.

One of the tablets was placed at the corner of Market and First Streets and reads: "The shoreline of San Francisco reached a point twenty-five feet northeasterly from this spot at the time gold was discovered by James W. Marshall at Coloma, California, January 24, 1848." The other tablet was placed across the street at the base of the Mechanics Monument; on it is reproduced a map of the old shoreline from Howard Street to Pacific Avenue.

THE FIRST WHARVES

A little pier for the landing of small boats at high tide was built at the foot of Clay Street in 1846. The principal landing place, however, was at the Punta del Embarcadero, or Clark's Point, now the corner of Battery Street and Broadway. A small wharf was built there in 1847 by William W. Clark, replacing the town's first permanent wharf built there eight years earlier. Clark's Point was first known as the Punta de la Loma Alta. This land was granted in 1839 to Jacob Leese and Salvador Vallejo, who later transferred his interest to Leese. The grant was bounded by what are now Valley, Front, and Davis Streets and Pacific Avenue. All of San Francisco's present streets east of Montgomery between Broadway and California were originally wharves.

In the spring of 1848 the Central Wharf (also called Long Wharf, SRL 328) was built out from what is now Leidesdorff Street, between Clay and Sacramento Streets, some eight hundred feet into the Bay. The wharf was increased to two thousand feet in 1850, and Pacific Mail steamers and other large vessels anchored there. The success of Central Wharf (now Commercial Street) caused other wharves to be built, until the whole area was covered with wharves and alleyways. Gradually the entire cove was filled in, mostly with sand from the great dune extending to the ocean.

In 1853 Meiggs Wharf was built in the area between the foot of Mason Street and the foot of Powell Street. It was constructed by Harry ("Honest Harry") Meiggs, a prominent city official and businessman, who fled San Francisco to South America in 1859 to escape thousands of dollars of bad debts. Meiggs Wharf was enclosed by a seawall in 1881. The present Fisherman's Wharf is close by.

Running from Fisherman's Wharf to the east and south is The Embarcadero, along which piers extend into the Bay. In 1997, a pedestrian path along the thoroughfare was named "Herb Caen Way" in honor of the long-time San Francisco newspaper columnist who died shortly afterward.

THE BURIED SHIPS OF SAN FRANCISCO

The site of the Niantic Hotel (SRL 88) is on the northwest corner of Clay and Sansome Streets. Early in the spring of 1849 the ship *Niantic* was anchored on this spot, after it had brought 250 emigrants from Panama at $150 a head. Since it was impossible to obtain a crew for the return voyage because of the lure of the gold fields, the ship was simply left where it was. Storeroom and lodging accommodations were very scarce in San Francisco at that time, and any sort of space covered with a roof brought enormous rents. Thus in short order the ship was leased out to various occupants, who used it for stores and offices. The hull was used as a warehouse. The ship was connected to the land by the Clay Street wharf, which before long was lined with structures built on piles.

On May 4, 1851, the *Niantic* was burned to the water's edge in one of the great fires that devastated early San Francisco. On the hulk of the ship the Niantic Hotel was erected. Soon all the area was landlocked, and in 1872 this became the Niantic Block of buildings. In May 1978, workers excavating for the new Pacific Mutual Building at the corner of Clay and Sansome Streets struck the old hull of the *Niantic*, and the vessel became newsworthy once again.

Many other ships were abandoned in Yerba Buena Cove in 1849. While some of them were unseaworthy, even sound vessels often had to remain where they had been anchored, owing to the inability of their owners to obtain a crew for the return voyage.

Besides the *Niantic* there were the *General Harrison* (northwest corner of Clay and Battery Streets), the *Apollo* (northwest corner of Sacramento and Battery Streets), the *Georgian* (between Washington and Jackson Streets, west of Battery), and the *Euphemia* (near Battery and Sacramento). Most of them were used as warehouses until they were destroyed in the fire of May 1851. Before 1851 the *Euphemia* had been purchased by the city government and was used as a jail. Balance Street, off Jackson Square, received its name from the ship *Balance* buried there. Lower Market Street covers the remains of the sailing vessels *Bryan*, *Callao*, and *Galen*. At the southwest corner of Sacramento and Front Streets is the *Thomas Bennett*. The English brig *Hardie* and the ships *Inez* and *Noble* are in the block bounded by Pacific Avenue and Drumm, Davis, and Jackson Streets. The bark *Elizabeth* is under the Embarcadero between Clay and Merchant Streets, while the ship *Alida* is beneath Davis Street, between Washington and Jackson Streets. These are some of the Gold Rush ships buried beneath the streets of San Francisco. From time to time, as new construction replaces older buildings, other buried relics of the past turn up.

THE SAN FRANCISCO CUSTOMHOUSE

The first collector of United States customs at San Francisco was appointed in 1846, soon after the American flag had been raised over the city. An adobe structure on Portsmouth Square was used for a time; in 1854 a more permanent building was put up on a landfill at the corner of Washington and Battery Streets. This building was torn down in 1905, and a large, five-story granite building replaced it at the same location in 1911.

PIONEER BUILDINGS AND SITES

San Francisco is a small city, geographically limited. Throughout its history older buildings have been torn down to give way to newer, and usually larger, structures. Thus there are many plaques and markers throughout the downtown area commemorating long-gone buildings. At Jackson Square, historic preservation has taken place on a large scale. It began with the renovation by wholesale interior decorating firms of several old brick warehouses on what was once the waterfront. Cement veneers and other evidences of modernization were removed, and the buildings stood again as they had in the 1850s and 1860s. Before long, other businesses were attracted, and a once-shabby district was transformed into a handsome, useful center.

On the west side of Montgomery Street between Jackson and Washington Streets are several buildings erected in the 1850s, notably those at 722–28 Montgomery. At 722–24 is the building opened as a variety theater on December 15, 1857. A plaque at 728 indicates the site of the first recorded meeting of the Free and Accepted Masons in California (SRL 408) on October 17, 1849.

At the northeast corner of Montgomery and Jackson Streets is the building (SRL 453) to which William Tecumseh Sherman moved the branch bank of Lucas, Turner and Company in 1857. The corner buildings at Jackson Street and Hotaling Place were built about 1860 and served as the warehouses for the Hotaling

liquor business. The fact that they, like the other solid structures in the present Jackson Square area, escaped the great fire of 1906, inspired a popular jingle by Charles K. Field:

> "If, as they say, God spanked the town
> For being over-frisky,
> Why did He burn the churches down
> And save Hotaling's whisky?"

Remnants of the old Hotaling stables are in evidence in the building at 38 Hotaling Place, and in the basement of No. 42 is the entrance to a brick tunnel, said to have been used by smugglers to bring contraband from the wharf to downtown San Francisco.

The building at 432 Jackson Street has served in the past as the Tremont Hotel and as the French consulate. The Ghirardelli Chocolate Company was once located in the building at 415 Jackson. (This is not to be confused with Ghirardelli Square, another historic site, at 900 North Point Street near Fort Mason.) Close to Jackson Square, and now considered part of this historic district, is the old Barbary Coast on Pacific Avenue, a century ago one of the most infamous sections of any city in the world. A walking route of several miles in this part of the city is called the Barbary Coast Trail and is highlighted with appropriate markers.

The Montgomery Block (SRL 80) stood on the east side of Montgomery Street with sides on Washington and Merchant Streets. It was begun in July 1853 and was opened in December of that year. When the building was new, the owners, the law firm of Halleck, Peachy, and Billings, had their offices on the second floor. Among the tenants were other law firms and financiers. For thirty years a part of the Sutro Library was housed there. The old block, which survived the earthquake and fire of 1906, stood for more than a century before it was demolished in 1959. In its stead is a modern architectural wonder, the Transamerica Pyramid, completed in 1972.

On the southwest corner of Montgomery and Merchant Streets stood the western business headquarters of Russell, Majors, and Waddell (SRL 696), a Leavenworth, Kansas, firm that operated the Pony Express. On April 4, 1860, the first westbound rider arrived here carrying mail from St. Joseph, Missouri. The Pony Express ceased operation eighteen months later.

In the days of Spanish and Mexican rule, business in California had been transacted through barter. For a time after the American occupation and the discovery of great quantities of gold, payment was made in gold dust. This led to the coining of the metal. In 1849 and 1850 there were fifteen different operations making coins of various kinds in California. One of these establishments was situated on the south side of Portsmouth Plaza; O. P. Dutton was the director and F. D. Kohler was the assayer. Coins made here were stamped with the name of the Pacific Company and dated 1849.

Although private coins were legal tender until 1856, an act of congress in 1852 provided for a federal branch mint in San Francisco. This branch was established in 1854 at 608 Commercial Street (SRL 87); the first assayer was Agoston Haraszthy, later famous for his vineyards at Sonoma. Bret Harte was employed at the mint as a bookkeeper for a time. The building, still standing but reduced from three stories to one, was later the United States Subtreasury. Today it is the Bank of Canton Pacific Heritage Museum.

Another mint was constructed in 1870–74 at Fifth and Mission Streets. Designed by government architect A. B. Mullett, it is a fine example of the Greek Revival style typical of Federal buildings in Washington, D.C. It survived the 1906 fire, only to be supplanted by a new mint in 1937. The structure (SRL 875) is now a National Historic Landmark, registered by the Department of the Interior. It is now closed to the public, although proposals are made from time to time about some kind of restoration project. The present United States mint is operating at Buchanan Street and Duboce Avenue.

In the early 1840s the Hudson's Bay Company had an office on Montgomery Street between Clay and Sansome Streets. In 1846 this San Francisco operation was abandoned and the property was sold to Mellus and Howard. The building was afterward the United States Hotel. The Mellus and Howard Warehouse (SRL 459) once stood at the southwest corner of Montgomery and Clay Streets. Here, on August 31, 1850, the Society of California Pioneers, the oldest historical society in the state, was organized; W. D. M. Howard was the first president. The society's museum in Pioneer Hall at 456 McAllister Street has been moved to a new location at the Moscone Center Complex at 300 Fourth Street.

The office of the *California Star*, the first newspaper published in San Francisco (SRL 85), was on Brenham Place (now Walter U. Lum Place), at the southwest corner of Washington Street, just west of Portsmouth Plaza. It stood behind the house of its publisher, entrepreneur Sam Brannan. The first number was issued on January 9, 1847, with Elbert P. Jones as editor. From 1849 until it expired in 1891 the paper was called the *Alta California*. The site is now identifiable by the building at 743 Washington, the first structure in a purportedly Oriental style to be built in Chinatown. Built in 1908, it served for many years as the Chinese telephone exchange; today it is a branch office of the Bank of Canton.

At 405 Montgomery Street, at the corner of California Street, is the site of the Parrott Block (SRL 89), San Francisco's first fireproof building. Constructed in 1852 of granite blocks brought from China, the building was the headquarters for Wells Fargo Banking Express from 1855 to 1876. The three-story building came through the holocaust of 1906 relatively unscathed, but in 1926 it was demolished to make way for the Financial Center Building.

On the south side of Clay Street, between Kearny and Montgomery, is the site of the Portsmouth House, operated as California's first hotel in 1846.

The El Dorado and the Parker House (SRL 192), once on the east side of Portsmouth Plaza, were among the most famous of the saloons and gambling houses clustered about the center of the city's activity in 1849 and the early 1850s. Another hotel, the What Cheer House (SRL 650), opened in 1852, stood between Montgomery and Leidesdorff Streets on the south side of Sacramento Street. The Oriental Hotel (1854) stood on the southwest corner of Battery and Bush Streets. The Tehama House (1851), said to be frequented by "the elite of the town," stood at the northwest corner of California and Sansome Streets, where the Bank of California is now located.

The International Hotel (1854) stood on the north side of Jackson Street east of Kearny. The Russ Building on Montgomery Street between Bush and Pine today occupies the site of the Russ home and hotel owned by J. C. Christian Russ, who came to California with Company C, New York Volunteers, in 1847.

At 202 Green Street, a marker (SRL 941) notes that on this site, in a simple laboratory, Philo Taylor Farnsworth, 21, invented and patented the first all-electronic television system. The first successful transmission of a television image was made by the electronics pioneer on September 7, 1927.

The site of the old California Theater (SRL 86) is at 444 Bush Street. It was built by a syndicate headed by William C. Ralston, William Sharon, C. H. Fulton, and H. P. Wakelee. The architect, S. C. Bugbee, was ordered to design a building seating 1,600 and guaranteed to withstand earthquake and fire. It had its grand opening on January 15, 1869. The tablet marking the site was installed by the Commonwealth Club at the suggestion of Emelie Melville, the last surviving member of the cast of the inaugural performance. The California Theater was one of the many casualties of the fire of 1906.

In 1850 the Verdier brothers, immigrants from France, opened a store aboard the ship *Ville de Paris* to serve the argonauts passing through San Francisco. In 1871 they opened the City of Paris department store at the northeast corner of Montgomery and Sutter Streets. In 1896 the business moved into a handsome beaux-arts-style building at the corner of Geary and Stockton Streets (SRL 876); many older San Franciscans still think of it as the City of Paris Building, although Neiman-Marcus is now there.

Union Square (SRL 623), bounded by Post, Stockton, Geary, and Powell Streets, was set aside for public use on January 3, 1850, during the administration of San Francisco's last alcalde and its first mayor, John White Geary. Geary was a remarkable man. A veteran of the Mexican War, he had served for a short time as postmaster of San Francisco before becoming major; later, he became governor of the Kansas Territory and subsequently governor of the State of Pennsylvania. The square received its name in 1860 when pro-Union meetings were held there. The monument in the center of the square commemorates the victory of the American naval forces commanded by Admiral George Dewey at the Battle of Manila Bay (May 1, 1898) in the Spanish-American War. It was dedicated by President William McKinley in ceremonies held in 1901. An underground parking garage was built beneath the square in 1942. A massive reconstruction of the surface of the square was begun in 2001.

The main entrance to Woodward's Gardens (SRL 454), a pioneer amusement park, was on the west side of Mission Street between Duboce Avenue and Fourteenth Street. What Cheer House proprietor R. B. Woodward built his private home here about 1860 and filled it with works of art. Finding that his collections were appreciated by the public, he opened his grounds and built an octagonal pavilion with a seating capacity of more than five thousand, to be used for plays, dances, and skating. He added a zoological department across Fourteenth Street, with wild animals and an aquarium. A tunnel beneath the street connected the two parks. Nothing of them remains.

Hubert Howe Bancroft began to accumulate his ex-

traordinary collection in 1859. A successful dealer in books and manuscripts, the Ohio-born businessman decided to gather all the materials he could find for an encyclopedia of the history of the Pacific Coast. Soon he had a remarkable collection of material, which, in 1881, he placed in the first Bancroft Library (SRL 791) at 1538 Valencia Street. This treasury escaped the burning of Bancroft's bookstore on Market Street in 1886.

In 1905, the Bancroft collection was purchased by the University of California for $250,000, after a long debate in the Legislature, where many representatives balked at "paying good money for worthless old trash." Bancroft paid $100,000 of the price from his own pocket as an incentive to get the Legislature to act. The material was taken to Berkeley early in 1906, by the greatest good fortune escaping the San Francisco holocaust in April of that year. The collection is now housed in an annex of the main library on the Berkeley campus, and much material has been added to it over the years, so that it constitutes one of the major repositories of California historical material.

What is believed to be the oldest house now standing in San Francisco is the Phelps House at 1111 Oak Street. It is privately owned today. The house was shipped in sections and brought around the Horn from New Orleans. It was erected in 1850 on Abner Phelps's homestead at the foot of Buena Vista Hill, now near the Panhandle of Golden Gate Park. The first address of the house was 329 Divisadero Street, but over the years the house has been moved (on one occasion being turned around a full 180 degrees), always remaining near the corner of Divisadero and Oak Streets. At what is now 321–29 Divisadero is the site of Walter Phelps's haberdashery, built on the original foundation of the Phelps House.

The Haas-Lilienthal House at 2007 Franklin Street was built in 1886 for William Haas, a prosperous wholesale grocer who was born in Bavaria. Haas and his wife, the former Bertha Greenebaum, lived there with their two daughters, Alice and Florine. Both daughters were married in the parlor of the house. When Haas died in 1916, Alice and her husband, Samuel Lilienthal, moved in with her widowed mother. Upon Alice's death in 1972, the family gave the house to the city; today it is open to visitors under the aegis of the Foundation for San Francisco's Architectural Heritage. The unusual and distinctive wooden embellishments along the exterior make the Haas-Lilienthal House a favorite for photographers.

The site of old "Fort Gunnybags," or Fort Vigilance, the headquarters of the San Francisco Vigilance Committee of 1856, is located at 243 Sacramento Street. The city at that time was given over to a reign of terror. Many San Francisco residents believed that the municipal officials themselves were corrupt and in league with criminal elements.

The occasion for the formation of the Vigilance Committee in 1856—a previous vigilante group briefly appeared in 1851—was the murder of James King of William by James P. Casey. In his crusading newspaper, the *Bulletin*, King had attacked Casey's political corruption. A cry went up for the immediate punishment of the murderer. Later it was said that the officials of the city could not be depended on, and thus a committee of citizens undertook to see that justice was meted out. William T. Coleman became the chairman of this Vigilance Committee, and thousands of San Franciscans gave him their support. Casey was taken from the jail where he was being held in custody and was hanged along with another accused murderer, Charles Cora, on the evening of May 17, 1856, as King's funeral procession passed nearby. Hubert Howe Bancroft wrote that the work of the committee was "one of the grandest moral revolutions the world has ever witnessed." It appears that the crime rate of San Francisco decreased after this episode, although it cannot be said to have been permanent.

"Fort Gunnybags" (SRL 90) was first marked in 1903 by the California Landmarks League. In the 1906 fire the old building perished, and when the tablet was replaced in 1918 by the Native Sons of the Golden West, almost everyone who had taken part in the activities of 1856 had died. At the top of the table is a representation of the all-seeing eye that adorned official documents issued by the committee.

THE HILLS OF SAN FRANCISCO

The hills upon which San Francisco is built separated the three original settlements now lying within one municipality. These settlements were the presidio, the mission, and the commercial area of Yerba Buena. As the latter grew, it spread up and over the hills, so that some modern streets ascend and descend remarkably steep slopes, although the steepest parts have been somewhat lowered. It is said that there are forty-three hills in San Francisco.

Telegraph Hill (SRL 91), called by the Spaniards Loma Alta ("high hill"), with an elevation of 275 feet, is first in historic interest. From its top, on October 29, 1850, a fire signal was given to announce the news, brought by the steamer *Oregon*, of the admission of California as the thirty-first state of the Union. A battery built in 1846 under the direction of Captain John B. Montgomery on the east side of Telegraph Hill gave the name to Battery Street.

Many Chileans had homes near the base of the hill in the 1850s, and in later years Italian families predominated. The Irish lived on the slopes and on the summit. The part between Kearny and Montgomery and Green and Greenwich Streets housed what in the 1890s was called the Artist Colony. Since 1930, the hill has been the site of expensive homes and apartment houses.

As early as 1849, Loma Alta was used as a station from which to observe incoming vessels, and was sometimes called "Signal Hill." In September 1849, a twenty-five-by-eighteen-foot two-story house was built on the top, and this was soon purchased by George Sweeney and Theodore E. Baugh, founders of the Merchants' Exchange. The observers who lived here reported to the people of the city below information on incoming ships; upon the top of this house stood a kind of semaphore by which an elaborate system of signals could be given. The place was known as the Signal Station. The Outer Signal Station was then established near Point Lobos, where incoming craft were first seen and reported to the Inner Station. This was California's first telegraph line, opened in 1853. That same year the North Point Docks were constructed below the hill, and Sansome Street was cut through it. The house that had stood on top of the hill blew down in a storm in 1870 and was not replaced. Some of the oldest houses on the hill, and in the city, stand on Napier Lane, off the Filbert Street stairway.

In 1876 a group of citizens donated to San Francisco a tract 275 feet square between Kearny, Greenwich, and Filbert Streets, extending almost to Montgomery Street, as a park; later the city purchased an area of about the same size to extend the park to the summit. In the 1880s a castle-like building stood on the top and a funicular railway ran up Greenwich Street. In the early 1900s the top of the hill was cleared and the area was named Pioneer Park.

Today Telegraph Hill is capped by Coit Tower. The

structure, 210 feet tall, was the gift of Mrs. Lillie Hitchcock Coit for the beautification of the city. Lillie was brought to San Francisco by her parents at the age of eight in 1851 and became an enthusiastic supporter of the fire companies, all of which were manned by volunteers in those days. She was made an honorary member of the Knickerbocker No. 5 Company while still a girl, an accolade she never forgot. Although much of her adult life was spent in Paris, she returned to San Francisco before her death in 1929, and bequeathed $100,000 for a memorial to the volunteer firemen of San Francisco. The tower is shaped like a fire-hose nozzle. The interior is decorated with murals that were a Works Progress Administration project, depicting scenes of life in the city in the 1930s. On a clear day the view from Telegraph Hill is magnificent.

Among the writers who have lived on Telegraph Hill are Mark Twain, Joaquin Miller, Frank Norris, Ambrose Bierce, and Bret Harte, who complained that goats browsed on the geraniums in his second-story window boxes and tramped over the roof at night "like heavy hail-stones"; Harte's story "The Secret of Telegraph Hill" has some good local color. To Charles Warren Stoddard, the wandering goats were "the mascots of the hill." Robert Louis Stevenson called the summit the "Peak of the Wind."

Russian Hill, probably so named because of an early unenclosed Russian sailors' graveyard on its summit at the crest of Vallejo Street, also has superb views over the Bay. At the 360-foot summit an observatory stood about 1861, which was reached by means of a spiral staircase.

Among the writers who have lived on Russian Hill was Helen Hunt Jackson, who died there in 1886. Near her home on the eastern brow a mast was erected for use in the early days of wireless telegraphy. At Vallejo and Taylor Streets is the site of Ina Coolbrith's home, now a tiny park named in her honor. She and Bret Harte and Charles Warren Stoddard were known as the "Golden Gate Trinity" in the early days of the *Overland Monthly*, California's first literary journal (1868–1883). Much beloved, Ina Coolbrith was the first poet laureate of the state of California. Between Hyde and Larkin Streets Greenwich Street becomes a stairway, and here is another small park, this one dedicated to the poet George Sterling. Picturesque Macondray Lane attracted attention when writer Armistead Maupin used it as the model for "Barbary Lane" in his popular series *Tales of the City*, which first appeared in 1978.

On the 1000 block of Green Street are several houses that escaped the fire of 1906. The Feusier Octagon House at 1067 Green, built in 1855, is one of two octagonal houses in San Francisco. The former firehouse at 1088, now an elegant residence, was built two years after the great fire.

Rincon Hill (SRL 84) rose from Rincon ("corner") Point, shown on old maps of San Francisco. On the sheltered southern side of this point was a wooded area favored for picnic outings, and here George Gordon laid out South Park in 1852, patterning it after the squares then being created in London. Each purchaser of a lot there was required to build a fireproof house of brick.

Higher upon Rincon Hill grander homes were built, among them those of William C. Ralston, Milton Latham, General Henry W. Halleck, John Parrott, Peter Donahue, General Albert Sidney Johnston, Senator William M. Gwin, Mayor Thomas Selby, Joseph Donohoe, General William Tecumseh Sherman, H. W. Newhall, and the McAllister family. In 1852 the United States Marine Hospital was built on the eastern extremity, and in 1860 St. Mary's Hospital, the first Catholic hospital on the Pacific Coast (now located at the western end of Hayes Street), was built on the hill to the south.

In 1869 Rincon Hill was cut at Second Street, after which the social prestige of the place declined. By that time, the three military men mentioned above had gone east to fight in the Civil War; none returned to San Francisco. A few mansions were maintained by their owners until the fire of 1906, which devastated the area. In *The Wrecker*, Stevenson tells of seeing the hill in its decline in 1879, when he visited Charles Warren Stoddard's residence, then on Vernon (now Dow Place), off Second Street. The economic philosopher Henry George lived at 420 Second Street, just south of Harrison, from 1861 to 1880, and here he wrote *Progress and Poverty*. The "Battle of Rincon Hill" between striking longshoremen and strikebreakers took place on the nearby waterfront on "Bloody Thursday," July 5, 1934. Two maritime workers were killed, several hundred persons were injured, and a general strike followed.

The building of the San Francisco–Oakland Bay Bridge in the 1930s completed the demolition of Rincon Hill; what was left of it was leveled for ramps and the western anchorage of the bridge. Rincon Hill occupied the area that is today bounded by Spear, Second, Folsom, and Brannan Streets.

Nob Hill was originally called Fern Hill. Not until the cable car was put into operation was it possible to make this ascent in comfort and safety. Pretentious houses built on the hill by early nouveaux riches probably gave rise to the name "Nob Hill." The fire of 1906 destroyed most of these houses. The pillars of the Grecian doorway of the A. N. Towne residence were left standing among the ruins, and later these "Portals of the Past" were placed in Golden Gate Park, on the banks of Lloyd Lake near the main drive.

Nob Hill was the site of the great houses of the "Big Four" of the Central Pacific Railroad: directors Leland Stanford, Mark Hopkins, Charles Crocker, and Collis P. Huntington. The mansion of Governor (later Senator) Stanford was on the site now occupied by the Stanford Court Apartments at 901 California Street. The Mark Hopkins Hotel stands on the site of the Hopkins mansion; the carriage entrance and the retaining walls along Mason Street are from the original construction. In 1893 Edward Searles donated the mansion to the University of California, in trust for the San Francisco Art Institute, and it became San Francisco's first cultural center, the Mark Hopkins Institute of Art (SRL 754) "for instruction in and illustration of the fine arts, music and literature." (The San Francisco Art Institute is now located at Chestnut and Jones Streets on Russian Hill.) Charles Crocker's mansion stood at the present site of Grace Cathedral, now the crowning glory of Nob Hill. Across California Street is the stately Masonic Temple, dedicated in 1958. Collis P. Huntington lived in the mansion built by David D. Colton, now the location of Huntington Park, given to the city by Huntington's widow in 1915.

Among other notable residents on Nob Hill were the "Silver Kings" of Nevada's Comstock Lode, James G. Fair and James C. Flood. The Fairmont Hotel at 950 Mason Street is on the old Fair estate. The Flood residence is the only one of the great mansions remaining on Nob Hill. This brownstone structure is now the Pacific Union Club, at the northwest corner of California and Mason Streets.

Lone Mountain rises to an elevation of 468 feet between Golden Gate Park and the presidio. For years it was surmounted by a cross, first put up in 1862, which was removed to make room for the buildings of the San Francisco College for Women, a Catholic institution established in 1932, now part of the University of San Francisco. At the base of the mountain were four old cemeteries: to the north, Laurel Hill; to the east, Calvary; to the south, the Masonic; and to the west, the Odd Fellows. In 1937, the city voted to remove them.

Laurel Hill Cemetery was laid out in 1854 when earlier burial places in the city had been abandoned. Two earlier ones had been on Telegraph Hill, one on the southern slope near the corner of Sansome and Vallejo Streets and one on the North Beach slope in an area bounded by Grant Avenue and Powell, Chestnut, and Francisco Streets. Another small one had been near the top of Russian Hill and still another was at Fulton and Hyde Streets near the Civic Center. The oldest of these early cemeteries was the Catholic one at Mission Dolores, still intact. Most of San Francisco's cemeteries are located in Colma in San Mateo County. Laurel Hill Cemetery, the former burial place of many distinguished figures of California's early days, is commemorated by a marker (SRL 760) at 3333 California.

Twin Peaks has two distinct elevations at its top: a north one of 903 feet and a south one of 910 feet. Other names for them were Los Pechos de la Choca ("the breasts of the Indian maiden") and the Mission Peaks. The road to the summit was completed in 1916, and on a very clear day one can see the Farallon Islands in the ocean to the west and Mount Diablo in Contra Costa County to the east. A new viewing station on the peaks was completed in 1986.

With an elevation of 938 feet, Mount Davidson is the highest peak in San Francisco. It was surveyed in 1852 by the United States Geodetic Survey under George Davidson and was named Blue Mountain. It was included in Rancho San Miguel, later purchased by the public-spirited Adolph Sutro, who began the planting of the trees that now form Sutro Forest. Mount Sutro, with an elevation of 920 feet, is also in this grove. By 1911 the saplings had grown into trees and the highest peak was renamed Mount Davidson in honor of its first surveyor. In 1923 a cross was placed upon its summit and the first Easter sunrise service was held there, now an annual event.

Sponsored by the City and County Federation of Women's Clubs, twenty-six acres of land on the mountain were acquired by the city of San Francisco. This area was dedicated and named Mount Davidson Park on December 20, 1929, the ceremony being part of the celebration of the eighty-third birthday of John McLaren, creator of Golden Gate Park and superintendent of the city's parks for fifty-three years. The first two crosses erected on Mount Davidson were destroyed by fire. A third cross, 103 feet in height and made of concrete, was set up in March 1934. In 1997, yielding to protests that it was improper for a city government to own a specifically religious object, the city sold the cross and the 0.38-acre site to the Armenian Apostolic church for $26,000.

Some of San Francisco's finest old homes stand on Pacific Heights. One of the city's two remaining octagonal houses is located at 2648 Gough Street. It is owned by the National Society of Colonial Dames and is open to the public. It houses a collection of memorabilia connected with early United States history. Built in 1857, it was moved from its original site at 2645 Gough in 1953. In the same area, old houses are still standing at 1782 Pacific Avenue (built in 1869), 2439 Buchanan Street (1895), and 2209 Jackson Street (1861).

CHINATOWN

For more than a century, Chinatown in San Francisco was the most picturesque foreign enclave in the United States. The first Chinese immigrants arrived in 1848, and their number had grown to 20,000 within four years, according to Andrew Rolle. Most of these entered through the port of San Francisco, and a substantial number, after some time in the Mother Lode country, returned to the city. For many reasons, the Chinese population was not integrated with other social groups, and "Chinatowns" developed in many parts of California. By 1885, according to Bancroft, the Chinatown of San Francisco covered about ten blocks "closely packed with some 25,000 souls."

In the late 1870s, the presence of the Chinese in California became a political issue. Denis Kearney, the principal agitator in San Francisco, declared that low-paid coolie labor was undercutting American workmen. California congressmen took up the issue, and in 1882 the United States banned all further Chinese immigration, the first time such a law had been passed. In 1943 the law was repealed.

Much of the labyrinth of old Chinatown was destroyed in the 1906 fire. Gladys Hansen is one of the modern historians who believes that here thousands of victims perished in heat so intense that no remains were found, and that consequently the number of dead in the 1906 disaster may have been as many as 10,000, instead of the "official" toll of 498. The rebuilt area of Chinatown is still heavily populated, and continues to be one of San Francisco's principal tourist attractions. The Museum of the Chinese Historical Society of

America is at 644 Broadway. The Chinese Cultural Center is in the Holiday Inn at Portsmouth Plaza. The bodies of many of San Francisco's early Chinese settlers were returned for burial in their homeland, but there is a Chinese cemetery near Colma.

OTHER LANDMARKS

Golden Gate Park, one of the glories of San Francisco, is largely the creation of John McLaren, superintendent of parks from 1890 to his death in 1943. The land acquired by the city in 1868 was 1,017 acres of sand dunes. The original plan was for a gigantic park stretching from the ocean east to the City Hall!

The oldest building in the park is the Conservatory, modeled on that in London's Kew Gardens. James Lick, the eccentric San Francisco millionaire, had the building imported from England in sections for his San Jose property. At Lick's death in 1876 the building, still in crates, was offered to San Francisco; the thirty-three tons of glass and steel were purchased by a group of public-spirited citizens and put up in the park in 1879. Fire seriously damaged the building four years later, but it was rebuilt with generous funding from Charles Crocker. In January 1995, a severe gale struck the park, toppling many old trees and causing serious damage to the Conservatory. Very extensive repairs are being made.

The Children's House in Children's Playground dates from 1885. The gate and teahouse in the Japanese Tea Garden remain from the Midwinter Exposition of 1894. McLaren Lodge, the park's headquarters, was built in 1896. The California Academy of Sciences, founded in 1853, is the oldest scientific institution on the Pacific Coast; the present building was begun in 1924, with additions in 1970. Across the Music Concourse is the Michael H. DeYoung Memorial Museum, begun in 1916. Closed to the public since 2000, it will reopen after a thorough reconstruction is completed. In Lincoln Park is the California Palace of the Legion of Honor, a copy of the Paris building given to San Francisco in 1924 by Mr. and Mrs. Adolph Spreckels. Rodin's bronze statue "The Thinker" is in the atrium of the palace.

One of California's most interesting museums is the History Room of Wells Fargo Bank's main office at 420 Montgomery Street. Here are relics of the days when the Wells Fargo Bank and Express Company was one of the mainstays of California. The Museum of the City of San Francisco is located in the Cannery complex at

Ocean-going Tug *Hercules* at Hyde Street Pier, San Francisco National Maritime Historic Park

Ships *Balclutha* and *Eppleton Hall* at Hyde Street Pier, San Francisco National Maritime Historic Park

2801 Leavenworth Street. The headquarters of the California Historical Society is at 678 Mission Street; its gallery frequently displays items from the society's collection of California memorabilia.

The site of the Preparedness Day bombing of July 22, 1916, in which ten persons were killed and forty injured, is at 65 Market Street. Labor leaders Thomas J. Mooney and Warren K. Billings were falsely convicted of the bombing, and after many years in prison they were finally pardoned.

Harvey Milk, killed in a City Hall shooting in 1978, was the first openly gay elected public official in California. When elected to the Board of Supervisors he owned a camera shop at 575 Castro Street, where a plaque in his memory has been placed.

San Francisco has hosted two world fairs. The Panama-Pacific Exposition in 1915 was held in the Marina district. One of the major buildings, a temporary structure as they all were, was allowed to remain after the fair had ended, and it became a San Francisco landmark. This was the huge Palace of Fine Arts, designed by Bernard Maybeck. It deteriorated over the years, but thanks to a generous gift from Walter Johnson, the building has been renovated and now houses the San Francisco Exploratorium.

In San Francisco Bay, the Golden Gate International Exposition was held in 1939–1940 on Treasure Island, a landfill specially created for the event. The island was taken over by the United States Navy for many years until it left the site in 1997. A few structures from the exposition still stand, along with buildings built by the Navy. Treasure Island is connected to Yerba Buena Island (Goat Island), through which passes the traffic of the San Francisco–Oakland Bay Bridge. Like the Presidio, Treasure Island is in the process of transformation to civilian from military usage.

GOLDEN GATE NATIONAL RECREATIONAL AREA

By an act of Congress in 1972, 34,000 acres in San Francisco and Marin Counties became the Golden Gate National Recreational Area. Subsequently the area was dedicated to the memory of San Francisco congressman Philip Burton, who was a principal advocate of the project. The San Francisco portion includes most of the coast frontage of the presidio, highlighted by Fort Point. To the east of Fort Point is the San Francisco National Maritime Park. The building on the shore displays models and materials from the days of sail to the present. At the Hyde Street pier, several ships from early days are permanently moored and may be visited. One of these, the *Eureka*, was a commuter ferry on the Bay before the San Francisco–Oakland Bay Bridge rendered the ferry fleet obsolete, or so it was thought. The *Balclutha*, moved here in 1988 from its previous berth east of Fisherman's Wharf, is a tall British-built square rigger launched in 1886; it carried California grain around Cape Horn and returned with European cargoes for many years before ending its days in San Francisco. Since 1982 Pier 45 has been the home of the USS *Pampanito*, a World War II submarine with a valiant combat record.

Fort Mason, once the Army's port of embarkation, is the headquarters of the Golden Gate National Recreational Area. Several buildings from the 1850s still stand, among them McDowell Hall, the officers' club off the entrance from Bay Street and Van Ness Avenue, which was once the commanding general's quarters. The Haskell House (Quarters 3), east of the north end of Franklin Street, is where Senator David Broderick died in 1859 following his duel with Judge David Terry. The last Liberty ship from World War II, the *Jeremiah O'Brien*, is moored at Pier 32, but in the summer will be found at one of the Fort Mason piers. In 1994, in commemoration of the fiftieth anniversary of the Normandy invasion in World War II, the ship made the journey to the French coast and back under its own power. This vessel is also open to the public.

In addition to its historic sites, Fort Mason is home to the San Francisco African American Historical and Cultural Society, the Mexican Museum, and the Museo ItaloAmericano.

Alcatraz Island, in San Francisco Bay, is the location of the first lighthouse to be put to use on the California coast by the federal government, in 1854. Since the 1850s it has also been the site of fortified buildings first put up for defense of San Francisco Bay. It was occasionally used to detain prisoners, such as Confederate sympathizers during the Civil War or Indians en route to reservations, but it was not until 1908 that the Army began to send some prisoners there. Transferred from Army jurisdiction to the Justice Department in 1934, Alcatraz entered its most notorious period as a federal prison. The prison was closed in 1963. The deserted facility remained under federal jurisdiction for several years while its future was being debated. In 1969, a group of Native Americans took possession of the island as a protest against the losses of Indian lands to outsiders. After experiencing two years of increasing privations, the occupiers were driven off (1971) and the island became a tourist attraction, with regular sailings from Fisherman's Wharf.

FERRIES AND BRIDGES

As population increased in both San Francisco and the East Bay, the question of convenient transbay travel arose. Ferry lines increased in number, as did the docks along the Embarcadero. At the foot of Market Street, where a shed had stood since 1877, the Ferry Building was constructed of Colusa sandstone in 1896–1903. Through it poured the morning and evening throngs of local commuters as well as overland passengers to and from the Oakland terminal of the transcontinental trains. Ferry service to Oakland ended in 1959. Within a few years, however, ferry service was revived, first to Marin County, then across to Oakland and Alameda, and finally as far north as Vallejo.

Two famous bridges link San Francisco with her neighbors. The San Francisco–Oakland Bay Bridge was opened to traffic in a gala celebration on November 15, 1936. The San Francisco end of the bridge is a short way inland from Pier 26 on the Embarcadero. The eastern and western sections of this bridge are linked by a tunnel through Yerba Buena Island, midway between the two cities and just within the boundaries of the city and county of San Francisco. The earthquake of October 18, 1989, damaged the bridge so that it was out of service for several days. Fortunately, the damage was confined to the upper deck of the bridge. Just how the bridge will be strengthened to resist another earthquake remains a topic of much discussion.

The Golden Gate Bridge (SRL 975) crosses the channel between old Fort Point in San Francisco and Lime Point on the Marin County shore. Construction began in 1933 and the bridge was opened on May 27, 1937. Converging roadways at either end lead to the single suspension span, which is 4,200 feet long and at its center is 230 feet above the water.

THE FARALLONES

The seven Farallon Islands were probably discovered in 1543 by the Cabrillo-Ferrelo expedition, although no mention was made of them. In 1579 Francis Drake sent a party ashore to secure a supply of seal meat, birds, and eggs. He named them the Islands of St. James. In 1595 Cermeño called them simply "the islands." The Vizcaíno expedition in 1603 gave them the name of the "Frayles" in honor of the Carmelite fathers on board. In 1743 George Anson, a British naval commander, captured a Manila galleon on which there was a chart indicating the islands as "Los Farallones," but when or by whom they were so named is not known. In 1775 Bodega called them by a combination of two Spanish names, the "Farallones de los Frayles." *Farallón* is a Spanish term for a small, rocky island.

From 1809 to 1812 these islands were developed as a station for the Russian-American Fur Company, and a Russian settlement was made there. The Russians entered the harbor in canoes, hunting the plentiful sea otter under the very guns of the Spanish fort.

The Farallones have always been a natural rookery. In 1849, when fabulous prices were being asked for food in San Francisco, they became a profitable source of supply for egg hunters. This traffic continued for forty years, until the quarrels of rival egg companies caused United States marshals to interfere. Bird lovers were later aided by Admiral George Dewey in their efforts to have the islands declared a bird sanctuary, now one of several in California.

In 1855 a lighthouse was erected on the Farallon Islands. The place has a long history of disastrous shipwrecks; its bays and inlets bear the names of many lost steamers and sailing vessels.

San Joaquin County

San Joaquin County was one of the original twenty-seven counties. San Joaquin, Spanish for St. Joachim, was the name given by Gabriel Moraga in 1813 to the large river that flows from the south through this region, and was later used to designate the county. Stockton has always been the county seat.

INDIAN SITES

More than one hundred mounds, or kitchen middens, have been located in San Joaquin County. These mounds, many of which have been leveled, are the sites of aboriginal villages and burial places. They are found on relatively high ground along the banks of the numerous watercourses of the San Joaquin Delta region, such as the San Joaquin, Cosumnes, Mokelumne, and Calaveras Rivers, and the Mormon and French Camp Sloughs. For the native peoples, this was a plentiful and reliable hunting ground. According to W. Egbert Schenk, "it would be hard to exaggerate the number of water fowl that were formerly present in the marshy area of the Great Central Valley."

To inexperienced eyes, an Indian mound appeared much the same as the land around it. The archaeologist, however, perceived an appreciable difference. Schenck explains:

> Upon a mound's base, there is found a mass of earth essentially the same as the base and the surrounding land, but which has been acted upon by man until in color, texture, constituents, or all of these it is readily distinguishable from the base. . . . In color the mounds are characteristically blacker than the surrounding soil. . . . Presumably this darker color is due to the greater amount of organic matter which man has accumulated upon them.

James A. Barr, for many years superintendent of schools in Stockton, became interested in the archaeology of the Stockton region and during the years 1898–1901 made a large collection of specimens. His detailed field notes and catalogued specimens are an important source of information on the archaeology and ethnology of the Stockton region.

The principal aboriginal sites explored by Barr were the Stockton Channel, Walker Slough, Ott, Pool, and Island mounds. There were also three mounds on the Woods Ranch on Robert's Island; one on the Copperopolis road; and others on Martin's Ranch and the O. R. Smith Ranch, at Brandt's Ferry where Bowman Road now crosses the San Joaquin River, on the Lewis Ranch, and on French Camp Slough. The Stockton Channel mound, located in Stockton between Edison and Harrison Streets on the north bank of the Stockton Channel, is probably the site of the Passasimas village described by the 1817 Spanish expedition led by Luís Argüello and accompanied by Father Narciso Durán. It is possible, however, that this village may have been the one covered by the Walker Slough mound. The latter, being only an eighth of a mile from the Island mound, may be regarded as part of the same settlement.

The Ott mound (southeast of Stockton and north of French Camp Slough) and the Pool mound (nine miles southwest of Stockton) were undoubtedly inhabited when the Spanish visited the region in 1805, in 1810, and again in 1811. One of the most interesting localities worked by Barr was Union Island near Bethany, where the Spanish expeditions of 1810 and 1811 found the Yokut village of Pescadero ("fisherman"), so named because they saw Indians catching fish there. Rancho Pescadero, (35,446 acres), located north of Tracy, received its name from this settlement.

The Stanislaus River, which forms part of the boundary between San Joaquin County and Stanislaus County to the south, was the scene of a notable battle fought between the Indians and their Mexican rulers. In the spring of 1829, Estanislao, an Indian who had been baptized under the Spanish name for St. Stanislaus at Mission San José but who had run away from its rule, captained the defense of a riverside stronghold against Mexican troops. Twice in months past his forces had driven off their oppressors, but this third Mexican foray, led by young Ensign Mariano G. Vallejo, was successful. The outpost was taken, and the defenders were dispersed. This was one of the few instances in California in which cannons were used in battle. Long afterward, farmers in the vicinity from time to time plowed up cannon balls as relics of the Battle of the Stanislaus (the river having been named for the Indian leader). The site (SRL 214) is in Caswell Memorial State Park southwest of Ripon on the north side of the Stanislaus River within two miles of its junction with the San Joaquin River. Estanislao's story is told more fully in the Stanislaus County chapter.

FRENCH CAMP

French Camp lies a few miles south of Stockton and foreigners to California were first attracted here by fur-bearing animals, the beaver in particular. It is likely that Jedediah Strong Smith and his American companions trapped in the region in 1827. Around 1832 French-Canadian trappers employed by the Hudson's Bay Company were in the region. The site of the present town of French Camp (SRL 668) was along a route much used by trappers between 1832 and 1845. Michel La Framboise, leader of the fur hunters, came annually to French Camp, and James Alexander Forbes, agent for the company after 1836, likewise made many trips to it. As late as 1845 the place was occupied from spring to fall by the Canadians and their families, who had constructed shelters of tules and willow brush, many of which were plastered with mud.

As early as 1833, neighboring Indians began to sicken with the diseases brought in by the newcomers. The American trapper J. J. Warner "reported seeing skulls and bodies under every shade tree." This was bound to cause great hostility to the trappers on the part of the native people, and the ensuing years were not peaceful.

Charles M. Weber, a native of Germany, who was later to become the founder of Stockton, stopped at French Camp in the fall of 1841 while on his way into California with the Bidwell-Bartleson party. Weber was much impressed with the fertile, oak-studded lands that bordered on the San Joaquin River. Subsequently, in 1842, he settled in Pueblo de San José and soon after went into partnership with William Gulnac, a blacksmith. Gulnac came to California in 1833, perhaps with ican citizen. For a time the two men engaged in merchandising, manufacturing, and ranching at San Jose. In the spring of 1843 they organized a company of twelve men for the purpose of forming a colony at French Camp. In July, Gulnac, as a Mexican citizen, petitioned for a grant of land in the region, and in January 1844 he and others received a large tract, which included both French Camp and the site of the later Stockton. This was named Rancho del Campo de los Franceses. The company organized by Weber and Gulnac was the first colony of settlers to take up lands in the San Joaquin Valley.

In August 1844 the first settlers arrived at Rancho del Campo de los Franceses. One of the company, Thomas Lindsay, built a tule hut, the first dwelling (SRL 178) built by an American within the present city limits of French Camp. The site was what would later be the corner of Lindsay and El Dorado Streets, close to the city hall built there in 1927. In the spring of 1845, however, Lindsay was killed by Indians, his hut was burned, and his stock and tools were stolen.

To encourage other colonists, Gulnac offered a square mile of land at French Camp to any prospective settler. One of the first to accept the offer was David Kelsey, who with his wife and two children had traveled there from Oregon. Kelsey was soon stricken with smallpox and died; his eleven-year-old daughter, America, also sick, survived to nurse the remaining family back to health and settle with them in San Jose.

The task of inducing settlers to remain on Rancho del Campo de los Franceses was rather difficult, what with its hostile Indians, plagues, poor food, and primitive conditions. By April 1845 Gulnac was weary of the whole project and sold the entire estate to Weber for $60, the amount of a grocery bill he owed his partner. In order to persuade settlers to come to the region, Weber virtually gave away the major portion of his estate to those who would settle on it. The testimony and influence of dozens of these colonists ultimately persuaded the land commissioners to recognize Weber's claim to the grant, the whole of which may otherwise have been lost to him.

In 1847, Captain Weber (as he now was called after a brief stint as a soldier in the American takeover the previous year) laid out a new town on the south side of what became known as the Stockton Channel. There is dispute about the name Tuleburg, which some insist was never a serious name for the place, but referred to the dense tule swamps that bordered every watercourse in the region. Weber seems to have preferred Stockton, in honor of Commodore Robert F. Stockton, who had given Weber his commission in 1846. By 1849 that was the official name of the community. In the two years between 1847 and 1849, the United States had formally annexed California, gold was discovered at Coloma, and Weber had organized the Stockton Mining and Trading Company, which operated for some time on Weber Creek in El Dorado County. He soon realized that it would be in his interest to develop a city that would serve as a supply and shipping center for the southern mines. In September 1848 Weber sold his business and moved to the new city, where he would remain for the rest of his life.

On November 15, 1849, the first steamboat from San Francisco, the *John A. Sutter*, arrived and for a few months made weekly contact between that city and Stockton. By the winter of 1849 Stockton had a population of nearly one thousand, and in 1850 it became the county seat of San Joaquin County, having been incorporated on August 15 of that year.

Thousands of argonauts bound for the southern mines passed through Stockton in the early 1850s. Some came up the river by boat; others traveled over the Livermore Pass from San Jose and crossed the San Joaquin River at Doak and Bonsell's Ferry, located about where the Mossdale Wye on I-5 and SR 120 is today. From Stockton, this tide of humanity branched out over the various trails leading to the gold fields—the Mariposa, French Camp, Sonora, Mokelumne Hill, and Lockford Roads, all teeming with life and each one leading to a hoped-for El Dorado. Freighting and staging activities developed to enormous proportions, businesses multiplied, agriculture and stock raising in the vicinity increased, and Stockton soon became a flourishing center of trade and commerce.

The Stockton Channel was a deep-water slough that led into the San Joaquin River to the west. At the eastern end of the channel an embarcadero was created, about where Weber Avenue now parallels the water. The land immediately adjacent was called Weber Point, and here the first buildings of the town were erected.

Weber's house on Weber Point was of adobe and native redwood construction. To this house the captain brought his bride, Helen Murphy, daughter of Martin Murphy, a large landholder in Santa Clara County. Surrounded by gardens, the Weber house was a showplace in the 1850s and 1860s. After Weber's death in 1881 it deteriorated and was unoccupied; it ceased to exist some time after 1919. The foundation piers that supported the house, which were made of brick brought around the Horn, could long be seen at the original site on Weber Point. The place is now covered by a modern high-rise hotel, a restaurant, and a parking lot, although the spot is marked with a plaque (SRL 165). Weber's daughter built a two-story frame house on the southeast corner of the property facing Stockton Channel. This was moved in 1902 to West Lane, just north of the Calaveras River, and still stands. An outbuilding from this property was moved in 1984 to the San Joaquin County Museum in Micke Grove south of Lodi. The Stockton Channel, which borders the old homesite, has been largely cleared of the many old buildings that lined it for a century and more, and it now provides a clean pathway westward to the port of Stockton, which receives oceangoing vessels.

A few of Stockton's early buildings, dating from the 1850s, remained in the old business district until the 1960s, but most of these were destroyed by the redevelopment project encompassing the nine blocks bordered by Weber Avenue and Hunter, Washington, and Commerce Streets. Old St. Mary's Catholic Church at 203 East Washington Street was built in 1861 but includes later additions; the parish was established in 1851. There are several other old public buildings, all of which are on the National Register of Historic Places. The Weber Primary School at 55 West Flora Street (1873) is now a religious education center. The Sperry Union Mill Warehouse at 445 West Weber Avenue was also built in the 1870s. Nearby are the Sperry Building at 146 West Weber Avenue (1888), the Tretheway Building at 229 East Weber Avenue (1892), the Bank of Stockton at 301 East Main Street (1908), the El Dorado Elementary School at 1525 Pacific Avenue (1915), the one-time Commercial and Savings Bank Building at 343 East Main Street (1915), the California Building at 11 South San Joaquin Street (1917), the modest Nippon Hospital, built by the Japanese for their community at 25 South Commerce Street (1917), and the Federal Building at 401 North San Joaquin Street (1933). Private homes that have been placed on

Wong Mansion, Stockton

Faye Spanos Concert Hall, University of the Pacific, Stockton

the National Register include the home of Benjamin C. Holt at 921 South San Joaquin Street (1890) and the elegant Wong Mansion at 345 West Clay Street (1921).

Stockton's old cemeteries are interesting. Stockton Rural Cemetery, at the end of Cemetery Lane, was dedicated in August 1862. Among those buried here is David S. Terry, famed for the 1859 duel in San Mateo County in which he killed U.S. senator David C. Broderick. A few years before, both had sat on the California Supreme Court at the same time. Judge Terry's violent life came to an end in 1889 at the railroad station in Lathrop, south of Stockton, where he was shot by the bodyguard of U.S. Supreme Court justice Stephen J. Field. Terry had threatened Field because of the latter's decision against Terry's wife and client, Sarah Althea Hill, in her suit for a part of the fortune of her putative husband, William Sharon. Mrs. Terry went insane a few years later and died in the Stockton State Hospital in 1937.

The monument to Reuel Colt Gridley (SRL 801), erected in 1887, marks the grave of a man who raised $275,000 for the Sanitary Commission, the Civil War counterpart of the Red Cross, by selling and reselling a sack of flour. Stockton Rural Cemetery also contains the remains of persons originally buried in the city cemetery located on the block bounded by Weber Avenue and Pilgrim, Main, and Union Streets. When this cemetery was abandoned in the 1890s, the body of one John Brown was among those left at the old site, since he had no relatives to pay for the move. Brown, known as Juan Flaco ("Lean John"), was "California's Paul Revere." In September 1846 he rode 500 miles in five days on horseback to bring word of the siege of Los Angeles to Commodore Stockton in San Francisco. A marker (SRL 513) has been placed to honor the last resting place of this forgotten figure of California history, who died at Stockton in 1859.

Another early cemetery is the Temple Israel Cemetery (SRL 765), located on the block bounded by Acacia, Pilgrim, Poplar, and Union Streets. It was given to the Jewish community of Stockton by Captain Weber in 1851 and is the oldest Jewish cemetery in continuous use in California and west of the Rockies.

Even in pioneer days, cultural development in Stockton was not neglected. Churches and schools were established as early as 1850, and during the next two decades a number of private academies existed. Today it is the home of San Joaquin Delta College and of the University of the Pacific, which was transferred to Stockton from San Jose in 1924. The university has sponsored a good deal of California historical study and writing, and is home to the Conference of California Historical Societies.

The Haggin Museum and Art Gallery in Victory Park contains many interesting relics of the early days of San Joaquin County. Of particular interest are the displays relating to agricultural machinery, primarily the Holt Tractor Works, which ultimately became the Caterpillar Tractor Company (it moved out of Stockton in 1921), and the many aspects of the food canning industry.

THE MARIPOSA ROAD

Leading from Stockton to the southern mines are various roads that were first used during the days of the Gold Rush. Along these thoroughfares the first settlements outside the city were established; every house was a wayside inn for the accommodation of travelers. The cost of a meal was usually $1.50, the regular menu comprising pork and beans, with bread and coffee.

Dr. R. L. Chalmers, who settled at the site of Collegeville as early as 1850, persuaded the government teams en route to Fort Miller to pass alongside his ranch, thereby establishing the Mariposa Road, which became the main route to the southern mines. By 1851 the principal stopping places along this road were Chalmers' Ranch, George Kerr's House, the Fifteen Mile House, the Lone Tree House, and Heath and Emory's Ferry, on the Stanislaus River (since 1860 in Stanislaus County). A settlement grew up at Chalmers' Ranch, and because a college was located there from 1866 to 1874, the place was called Collegeville. The college was the project of the Cumberland Presbyterian Church; when the three-story frame structure housing it burned in 1874, it was not replaced. At the corner of Mariposa and Jack Tone Roads is a remnant of the Collegeville cemetery, no longer used but still cared for by the local Boy Scouts.

THE FRENCH CAMP ROAD

The Mariposa Road became impassable, a veritable mire of adobe, during the winter months as well as in flood years. The stagecoaches and wagons were then routed over the French Camp Road, which had a sandy loam base. This winter traffic made French Camp an important staging and freighting center during the early 1850s. Boats landed at the end of French Camp Slough, where goods destined for the mining camps were unloaded. In the summer of 1850 Major Richard P. Hammond laid out a town on the site for Charles Weber, calling it Castoria ("place of beavers"). Colonel P. W. Noble and A. Stevinson, who had come to French Camp in August 1849 and who had become agents for the sale of lots in the new town, built a two-story adobe structure in 1850, using it as a hotel and trading post. As late as 1880 the building was occupied as a home by Noble's widow. This hotel, with its broad fields for the pasturage of livestock, was thronged by travelers during the first years of its existence, but its patronage declined when a second hotel, owned by Le Barron and Company, was built, this hostelry likewise offering extensive pasturage facilities.

During the 1890s, the partnership of C. A. Bachmann and Charles H. W. Brandt was the largest supplier in the United States of chicory, a coffee additive and substitute. The partners had fine German equipment to roast and grind the chicory and their own vessel, the *Dora*, to ship their product to market. Formed in 1855, their California Chicory Works (SRL 935) operated until 1911 at 1672 West Bowman Road in French Camp.

The principal stopping place on the French Camp Road between French Camp and Heath and Emory's

Ferry, and almost the only one in 1852, was the Zinc House, the material for which had been brought around the Horn from New York early in 1850. The Zinc House consisted of one twelve-by-sixteen-foot room with a seven-foot ceiling. The first school in this part of the county was held in the Zinc House, and for many years the school district retained the name of the unique building in which it had its beginning.

On French Camp Road near Union Road stands the Dutch Point house, commemorated by a plaque placed by the Native Daughters of the Golden West. A public house was built here in 1849 and was well situated on a roadway with sandy soil that made travel possible in the winter. The two-story brick house is privately owned.

At Five Corners, the junction of the French Camp, Jack Tone, and Lone Tree Roads, stands the Atlanta Women's Club building, built by the Methodists in 1878 as their church. Nearby, on Lone Tree Road, is the old Protestant cemetery. A Catholic cemetery connected with the defunct St. Patrick's Church to the southeast, near Simms, is still in existence.

PIONEER FARMHOUSES

San Joaquin County is noteworthy for the number of pioneer farmhouses dating from the 1850s and 1860s still owned by descendants of the original builders. Many of these houses are in excellent condition and are occupied by their owners, while others, which have been abandoned for more modern structures, are being allowed to disintegrate. This is especially true of the frame structures built close to the ground without the protection of stone or brick foundations.

Among the historic homesteads found north of the Calaveras River, one of the most interesting is the Dodge house, situated on the bank of the river and the Waterloo Road to Lockeford, SR 88. A few giant oaks, all that are left of the hundreds that once flourished in the region, surround this fine old mansion. John C. Frémont camped near here on March 26, 1844, and noted that "this place is beautiful, with open groves of oak, and a grassy sward beneath, with many plants in bloom." The present Dodge house was built in 1866. Slight alterations have been made to the interior, while the exterior has assumed a rather modern appearance. It is still quite well preserved.

A two-story brick ranch house stands on the Jack Tone Road and the north bank of the Calaveras River about eleven miles northeast of Stockton. John H. (Jack) Tone and two associates came to California as

Dodge House

members of the Webb-Audubon party, under the leadership of Colonel Henry J. Webb and John Woodhouse Audubon, youngest son of the famous ornithologist. Most of the party was bound for the gold fields, but Aububon made the trip to gather specimens of birds and mammals. When Colonel Webb deserted his men in the Rio Grande Valley, Audubon was made leader of the party, which after many hardships reached Stockton in December 1849.

Jack Tone and his partners, in the autumn of 1850, settled on the Calaveras River, where they attempted to raise potatoes. Owing to their lack of skill in irrigating, their initial experiment in California ranching resulted in failure, so the three men tried their luck at mining for a time. In 1851, however, they returned to locate permanently on the Calaveras River, where they built a one-story adobe house on the high part of the riverbank about one-half mile west of the present brick house. The three partners were known thereafter as the "Dobey Boys" by the settlers who had meanwhile taken up land around them. This adobe stood for several years after the brick house was built in 1873. The homestead is today owned and occupied by descendants of Jack Tone, who treasure the stories of pioneer life on the ranch and are especially proud of that part of the *Audubon Journal* that mentioned their ancestor. Tone's wife, Alice Walsh Tone, daughter of Nicholas J. Walsh, another of the original Audubon party, aided Maria R. Audubon in the biographical sketch of her father. The house is marked by a plaque placed in front of it by the Native Daughters of the Golden West.

The J. H. Cole House, which stands just north of Eight Mile Road and a half mile east of SR 88, was built in 1863. The former McCall house, on the west side of SR 88 about 1.7 miles north of the Jonathan Dodge House, apparently stands on an old Indian mound, since many relics have been dug up in the garden from

time to time. The original house, which was built by Samuel Martin about 1858, has been incorporated into the present structure.

Many settlers came to the Mokelumne River in 1851 and took up homesteads along the rich river bottoms. Among these was B. F. Langford, a native of Tennessee, who became a California state senator in the 1880s. This enterprising pioneer built the one-story brick house that stands in the midst of orchards and vineyards on the north side of the river due west of Lockeford, on a segment of Woodbridge Road, just west of Tretheway Road. Beyond its walnut orchard on the opposite side of the river is the site of Staples' Ferry.

South of Lodi and back from the corner of Kettelman and Cherokee Lanes stands the ten-room David H. Kettelman house, built in 1858 of brick fired in a nearby kiln. Kettelman purchased the place soon after it was built and developed an extensive grain and cattle ranch before the town of Lodi came into existence with the railroad in 1869. He was treasurer and chief promoter of the Mokelumne Ditch and Irrigation Company in 1876.

The John Lyman Beecher house is located east of Stockton on Berne Road near the intersection of Alpine and Copperopolis Roads. It was built in 1860 and stands well preserved today, still in the Beecher family. Beecher crossed the plains from Massachusetts during the Gold Rush, but soon gave up mining in favor of teaming and freighting out of Stockton, and ultimately purchased the large ranch where he lived the rest of his life. His son John L. became a member of the California Legislature.

Seventeen miles east of Stockton was the "Oregon Ranch," first settled by George Theyer and David Wells, who built a tule house there in 1848. When traffic began to flow over the Sonora Road to the southern mines the partners opened the "Oregon Tent," the first stopping place along the road, on a site in what is now Farmington. In 1852 Nathaniel Siggons Harrold, a native of Pennsylvania, who had come by ox team to Woods' Creek, Tuolumne County, in November 1849, purchased the Oregon Ranch, and in 1868 he built a large brick house, still standing at the southern limits of Farmington. A town was laid out on the Oregon Ranch in 1858 by Dr. W. B. Stamper. It is said that he named the place Farmington because it was the center of an extensive and rich farming country.

In 1850, about three-fourths of a mile west of the Oregon Tent, James Wasley built the Wisconsin House, which later was moved to Peters, where it was used as a boardinghouse until about 1890. The Marietta House, three miles east, and the Texas Tent, four miles west, were other taverns on the Sonora Road in the 1850s. Harrold served as a cook at the latter establishment before purchasing the Oregon Ranch.

After passing Simms, the present French Camp Road becomes part of SR 120 and runs about one-half mile north of the course of the early thoroughfare. The original road can be traced, however, by the old-fashioned farmhouses surrounded by tall shade trees that stand south of the present highway. On the north side of the highway, three-fourths of a mile east of Simms, is the J. O'Malley homestead, in a thick grove of orange, olive, and walnut trees.

At Park and Pioneer Streets in Escalon is the John Jones house, a square, two-story mansion built in 1867 of bricks fired on the place. Jones, a native of North Carolina, came to California with his family in 1852, and at first kept the Blue Tent Tavern on the French Camp Road one mile east of the site of Escalon. In 1855 he purchased the ranch of 160 acres on which the brick mansion was later built. By 1875 Jones had increased the size of his ranch to 7,000 acres, and in addition he owned several thousand acres in other parts of the valley. In 1894 the town of Escalon was laid out on the home ranch by James W. Jones, son of the original owner.

Near the north bank of the Stanislaus River, about five miles southeast of Escalon, a picturesque two-story brick house stands at the bend of Burwood Road off the River Road. It was built in 1868 by Euphrates Monroe. Nearby, also on Burwood Road, is a two-story white frame house, built in 1862, in which Ishmael Monroe lived and kept the Burwood post office, which operated from 1859 to 1898.

MOKELUMNE RIVER FERRIES

John C. Frémont wrote that on March 25, 1844, his men "halted in a beautiful bottom at the ford of the Rio de los Mukelumnes," which received its name from an "Indian tribe living on the river." "The bottoms on the stream," he continued, "are broad, rich, and extremely fertile, and the uplands are shaded with oak groves." Most of these old woodlands have disappeared, having been supplanted by orchards and vineyards. The Indian rancheria, which existed at the ford when the first American settlers came, has likewise vanished, but relics unearthed at the spot have fixed the site on the Langford ranch some 200 yards east of the present brick house.

Among the early wayfarers and emigrants who made use of the ford mentioned by Frémont were Charles Weber, on his journeys between Sutter's Fort and Stockton, and the Murphy-Townsend-Stevens party, who in 1844 were the first to drive wagons along the trail and across the stream at this point. The next few years saw increased travel from Sutter's Fort to Pueblo de San José via this route, which soon came to be known as the Sutter's Fort–San Jose Trail. Later it was also known as the Upper Sacramento Road.

Although the first to settle at the ford was Thomas Pyle in November 1846, records show that in 1849 the place was known as Laird's Ferry. That year David J. Staples, J. F. Staples, and W. H. Nichols took up residence there. Organized as Staples, Nichols and Company, they acquired possession of the ferry in February 1850, which was thereafter known as Staples' Ferry. In the fall of 1850 the company built a toll bridge—perhaps the first in the county—across the river west of the ferry. The first to cross on the new bridge, so the story goes, was a grizzly bear, which was given free passage without question. A post office was established at Staples' Ferry in 1851, and until 1854 all stagecoach travel to Sacramento passed that way. After that date the route by way of Woods' Ferry (Woodbridge) was used except in times of flood. Staples' Ferry, however, continued to serve travelers for many years—even as late as 1880, although by that time it was known as Miller's Ferry. The site of the old Staples Hotel, built from lumber brought around the Horn in 1850, is on the south side of the river, about two miles west of Lockeford via Locke Road and Tretheway Road. In the former riverbed, just south of the present channel, the steamboat *Pert* lies buried under twelve feet of sand.

Benedict's Ferry, about halfway between Woods' and Staples' ferries, was established in 1850 by C. L. Benedict, who had a ranch on the north side of the Mokelumne River at this point. In 1852 the government opened a post office at Benedict's Ferry, and during the same year the Bramlett and Langford sawmill was built there.

Benson's Ferry (SRL 149), started in 1849 by Edward Stokes and A. M. Woods, was purchased by John A. Benson in 1850. After the murder of Benson in 1859 by Green C. Palmer, an employee, and the latter's subsequent suicide, E. P. Gayetty, Benson's son-in-law, took over the operation of the ferry. The two-story Gayetty house, built in the 1870s, still stands near the levee 300 yards west of the present bridge. During the flood of 1862 the earlier Benson house was lashed to a large tree that stood nearby, and was thus saved from being washed down the river.

Mokelumne City (SRL 162) was laid out at the junction of the Cosumnes and Mokelumne Rivers in 1854 shortly after the Snap brothers had opened a store there. High hopes were cherished that the place might be made the head of navigation and a center of trade for the mines. For a time the town grew and prospered: boats unloaded at the landing; lots were sold; hotels, stores, shops, warehouses, and dwellings were erected. Then came the flood of 1862. The town was submerged, and as many as nineteen houses were swept away by the rushing, swirling river. Mokelumne City never fully recovered from this disaster, although there was some business activity in the place and people continued to live there until 1878, when the town site was included in the property purchased by the Barber family for a ranch. The hotel was converted into a barn and stood until replaced by the present structure sometime in the 1890s. The site of the town is on an old stretch of road just east of Benson's Ferry, and three miles north of Thornton via the road to Franklin.

Some of the houses of Mokelumne City were removed to other localities, and a few still stand. One of these is the Jesse Thornton house, situated in a dense grove of oak trees at a beautiful spot on the Mokelumne River directly below the present bridge on the road from Thornton to Galt.

LODI

The town of Lodi was named in 1874, and has always been the heart of a productive agricultural region. In 1907 the town put up a ceremonial arch (SRL 931) at Pine and Sacramento Streets in the popular Mission Revival style (others can be seen at Modesto and at Orland) to celebrate the Tokay Carnival of that year. The word "Lodi" and a California bear were added to the arch in 1908, probably intended to be a temporary embellishment. But the arch is still standing and is now a state landmark.

South of town, in Micke Grove, is the San Joaquin County Historical Museum, which emphasizes in an outdoor location the history of agriculture in the county. It is also the depository for official county historic records.

LOCKEFORD

Dr. Dean J. Locke, a native of New Hampshire and a graduate of the Harvard Medical School, came to California in 1849 as physician for the Boston and Newton

Joint-Stock Association. For a few months he engaged in mining with his brother George at Mississippi Bar on the American River, but in December 1850 they both came to the Mokelumne River, where another brother, Elmer, had already become an enthusiastic settler. The Lockes purchased 360 acres of land from D. J. Staples for one dollar an acre, and in 1851 they built a log cabin, since destroyed, on a knoll thickly sprinkled with oaks. Grizzly bears were plentiful in those days, and when night came the hired men "roosted high in the trees like turkeys" for fear of them. The cabin site is now occupied by a modern farmhouse on La Lomita Rancho about a half mile northwest of Lockeford on Elliott Road. This is the site of the state historical marker for Lockeford (SRL 365).

Lockeford was laid out on the D. J. Locke ranch and named in 1859. Its founders envisioned the town as becoming the head of navigation on the Mokelumne River, an ambition that was strengthened when the little pioneer steamer *Pert* tied up to the Lockeford landing in April 1862. Eventually the Mokelumne Steam Navigation Company was organized, and for three or four years it carried on some business. After 1865, however, the mining population gradually scattered, and the coming of the railroad ultimately put an end to all navigation on the Mokelumne.

Dr. Locke was very influential in the development of the new town, and was especially active in organizing schools, churches, and temperance societies. Even before the town was officially laid out, Locke interested himself in the cultural life of the community. On the second floor of his adobe granary, built in 1858 just west of the site of the present brick house, he fitted up a hall for public gatherings, and here the Sons of Temperance was organized. The Congregationalists held services in this building as early as 1861; in 1869 they constructed the building on Elliott Road that is now the Grace Church. The first house on the site of Lockeford was a frame structure built in 1855, and to it Dr. Locke brought his bride that same year. This first house was outgrown in the succeeding years, and in 1865 the front part of the present two-story brick dwelling on Elliott Road was constructed on the same site. The old brick barn also remains.

Luther Locke, father of the Locke brothers, came to California when Dr. Locke returned with his bride. The following year he built himself a home, a frame structure, in which the first store in Lockeford was opened in 1862. The post office, established in 1861, was located in this building, with Luther Locke as the first postmaster. This landmark, long known as the "White House," stands, very much remodeled, at the northeast corner of Main Street and Elliott Road.

The Harmony Grove Church is a beautiful old brick church a mile and a half southwest of Lockeford on Locke Road. This oldest Protestant church in San Joaquin County was built in 1859. Abandoned in 1912, the building was handsomely restored by the Lockeford-Clements Women's Club and rededicated in 1973. Two old cemeteries flank the building. The site is now Harmony Grove County Park.

Four miles northeast of Lockeford is the little town of Clements. One mile north of here near what is now Stillman L. Magee County Park stood the Lone Star Mill (SRL 155) on the Mokelumne River. To this site the Bramlett and Langford sawmill, built near Benedict's Ferry in 1852, was removed by the new proprietors, David S. Terry and a man named Hodge. Terry (mentioned earlier in this chapter) was raised in Texas, and named the mill after the Lone Star state. In 1855 Terry and Hodge added a flour mill. The establishment was destroyed by fire in 1856 and rebuilt on the same site. S. L. Magee bought the Lone Star Mill in 1860 and continued to operate it until its abandonment around 1885. The present site of Clements was purchased from Terry by Thomas Clements in 1871.

WOODBRIDGE

The first permanent settlers in the vicinity of Woodbridge were George W. Emerson and Ross C. and J. P. Sargent, all from New England. When they arrived in 1850, it is said that they found huts of rived oak left by Hudson's Bay Company trappers. In 1852 Jeremiah H. Woods and Alexander McQueen established a ferry across the Mokelumne River at this point, about where the present bridge and dam span the stream, with the result that before long a new road from Stockton to Sacramento was routed by way of Woods' Ferry. After 1854 the stages that had formerly traveled via Staples' Ferry on the Upper Sacramento Road adopted this more direct route. In 1858 Woods, a very energetic and enterprising man, built a bridge at the site of the ferry (SRL 163), which for years was known as Woods' Bridge. From it the town, which was laid out on the south side of the river in 1859, took the name Woodbridge. For several years the place showed considerable activity, but with the death of Jeremiah Woods in 1864 Woodbridge lost its chief promoter.

Several of the early houses and business buildings are still to be found at Woodbridge (SRL 358); no markers have been placed for this and the previous landmark sites. On the main street is the IOOF building, a two-story brick structure, the lower part of which was built in the early 1860s, while the upper story dates from 1874. The older portion was at first the Lavinsky store; later, for a time, it served as a school. The Masonic Hall was built in 1882. A pioneer cemetery contains the grave of William Lewis Manly, who rescued the Death Valley '49ers, a story told in the Inyo County chapter.

The Woodbridge Academy, a two-story frame structure erected in the winter of 1878–79 under the leadership of Professor S. L. Morehead, was taken over by the United Brethren in 1881, when it became known as the San Joaquin Valley College (SRL 520). As such it continued to function until the beginning of the twentieth century, when it was superseded by a public school. Today another school building occupies the site on Lilac Street.

THE MOKELUMNE HILL ROAD

In 1850, seventeen public houses, all located within a distance of twenty-four miles from Stockton, lined Mokelumne Hill Road, now Linden Road (SR 26). None of them remain today. The town of Linden, which was laid out in 1862, had its beginnings in the little community that grew up around the Fifteen Mile House. This tavern had been established by Dr. W. D. Treblecock in the fall of 1849. Some years later, C. C. Rynerson built a flour mill in the vicinity. Soon after, John and James Wasley, cousins of Treblecock, and later brothers-in-law to Rynerson, joined the group and were founders of the town. John Wasley named the new settlement, presumably after his old home at Linden, Ohio. The Rynerson flour mill was destroyed by fire in 1865 and was replaced by a second structure, which met a like fate in 1868. A three-story brick mill, built in 1871 but no longer used as such, now occupies the site.

SAN JOAQUIN AND STANISLAUS RIVER CROSSINGS

In pioneer days river crossings were important points in the San Joaquin Valley, and it was on the various watercourses that the earliest settlements were planned. Among these first attempts at colonization was New Hope (SRL 436), later known as Stanislaus City, established on the Stanislaus River in November 1846 by a party of Mormons under the leadership of Samuel Brannan. About twenty colonists came up the San Joaquin River in the sailing launch *Comet*, landing on the east branch near the site at which John Doak and Jacob Bonsell established a ferry two years later. From this point the party proceeded overland to a spot previously selected by Brannan on the north bank of the Stanislaus River one and a half miles from the river's mouth.

By the beginning of 1847 a promising beginning had been made: three log houses had been put up, a crudely improvised sawmill was at work, and 80 acres of grain had been sown. But the stormy weather brought rains and floods, the colonists fell to quarreling among themselves, and by the summer of 1847 only one man remained; he too soon left. The discovery of gold brought an attempt to reestablish a settlement at Stanislaus City; its name is found on a map published in 1851, which also indicated that the road from Stockton to Tuolumne City crossed the Stanislaus River at that point. Nothing, however, came of Sam Brannan's "new hope." A monument commemorating New Hope stands at Ripon, six miles northeast of the site. A similar marker indicating the landing place of the *Comet* (SRL 437) is located on SR 120, west of Manteca near the San Joaquin River.

After attempts to establish Stanislaus City failed, a settlement was started on the west side of the San Joaquin River a little below the mouth of the Stanislaus. Hoping to become a rival of Stockton, San Joaquin City (SRL 777), as it was called, persisted for a number of years. As late as 1880 it had a hotel, a warehouse, and two saloons, as well as stores and homes. Nothing but a historic plaque marks the location today, on County Road J-3 1.4 miles north of the Stanislaus county line. North of this location a bridge crosses the river in the vicinity of the old Durham Ferry crossing, established by Titus and Manly in 1850 and later owned by Durham and Fisk. Durham Ferry State Recreational Area commemorates the name.

The first ferry to be operated on the San Joaquin River was that of John Doak and Jacob Bonsell, who in 1848 began to convey passengers in a small boat across the river at a spot located about where the railroad and I-5 cross today. It was here that the old Sutter's Fort–San Jose Trail crossed the river. Traffic to the mines soon grew so heavy that it became necessary to have a larger and more substantial ferryboat, so Doak went to Corte Madera in Marin County, where he built the new craft. With their increased carrying facilities, the partners did an enormous business, reaping equally

large returns, for charges on this pioneer ferry were high—one dollar for men on foot, three dollars for men on horseback, and eight dollars for horses and wagons. In 1852, however, Doak sold his share in the business to Hiram Scott, and later in the same year Bonsell died. With the subsequent marriage of Bonsell's widow to James A. Shepherd, the ferry became known as Shepherd's Ferry and was so called until 1856, when it was sold to William T. Moss. The place is still referred to as Mossdale.

The Mossdale area acquired additional historical importance with the construction of the railroad bridge (SRL 780.7) across the San Joaquin River in September 1869, thus completing the transcontinental railroad from the San Francisco Bay Area to Sacramento. Laying of track proceeded from either end until the two parties met at the river, making Mossdale a lesser counterpart of Promontory, Utah, where the Central Pacific and Union Pacific had met on May 10 of the same year.

CORRAL HOLLOW

Corral Hollow (SRL 755) may be reached over the Corral Hollow Road, County Road J-2, southwest of Tracy. Many Indian relics, including arrowheads, pestles, and beautifully shaped bowls, have been uncovered along the dry bed of the arroyo, indicating the probable existence of a former Indian encampment in the vicinity. Petrified cedar, as well as fossil leaves and shells, have been found in the arroyo and in the neighboring hills. In early days the hollow was known as El Arroyo de los Buenos Aires, through which an old Spanish trail, El Camino Viejo, ran. According to Bolton, Juan Bautista de Anza passed that way in April 1776. Later, Spanish and Mexican vaqueros made customary use of the trail, along which they drove their herds of cattle. Still later, during the Gold Rush, the old trail was much traveled as a road to the southern mines.

One of the first settlers in the hollow was Edward B. (Ned) Carrell, who in 1850 took up government land there. For many years it was believed that "Corral Hollow" was a corruption of "Carrell's Hollow," but Carrell's diaries prove this to be untrue. Probably the hollow was named for a corral built there in early days for captured wild horses.

Down on the arroyo among the cottonwoods, directly on the line of the old Spanish trail, Carrell and three associates, Horatio P. Wright, William Breyton, and John A. Stockholm, built, under Wright's leadership, a tavern called the "Zink House" where the buildings of the present sheep ranch stand. Here for several years food and drink was served to wayfarers. A famous visitor at Zink House was James Capen Adams, or, as he was popularly known, "Grizzly" Adams. With his two bears, "Lady Washington" and "Ben Franklin," and his dog "Rambler," famous actors in Adams's "Mountaineer Museum" in San Francisco, he spent several months in 1855 hunting in the region, his experiences afterward figuring in Theodore Hittell's biographical narrative.

In 1856 John O'Brien, a sheepman who had established his camp in Corral Hollow, discovered an outcropping of a black mineral at the upper end of the canyon about nine miles from the Zink House, which when tested proved to be coal. The Pacific Coal Mining Company was subsequently organized, and this became, in turn, the Commercial Mine and the Eureka Mine.

When Carrell, the only surviving owner of the Eureka Coal Company, died in 1880 at his homestead in the hollow, John and James Treadwell of the Bears' Nest Mine in Alaska purchased the Corral Hollow coal property. They named it the Tesla Mine in honor of Nikola Tesla, the great electrical inventor. During the early 1890s, under the management of the San Francisco and San Joaquin Coal Company, the yield from the Tesla Mine averaged 500 tons of coal daily. From six to ten carloads were shipped each day over the Alameda and San Joaquin, a branch railroad to Stockton, where the coal was transferred to riverboats bound for San Francisco.

About this time the Treadwells built a brick and pottery plant two miles down the gulch at Walden Spur on their railroad. Later they built a larger plant four miles down the gulch and organized it as the Carnegie Brick and Pottery Company to manufacture white glazed firebrick. Carnegie (SRL 740) became a town of some two thousand inhabitants and flourished until 1906, when the earthquake and failure of the California Safe Deposit Bank in San Francisco ruined the Treadwells financially and caused the abandonment of Carnegie. A great boiler explosion in 1907 and, finally, the floods of 1911, which washed out the railroad, sealed its doom.

The state marker at Carnegie has been vandalized. The area behind it is now Carnegie State Vehicular Recreation Area, which extends westward into a small area of Alameda County.

Southeast of Carnegie, just above the site of the former Camp Thomas of the Hetch Hetchy project, is a manganese mine, first developed by Aurelius Ladd in 1863. During World War I, interest again centered on this mine, when $80,000 was recovered from the tailings. It was worked again during World War II and the Korean War.

San Luis Obispo County

San Luis Obispo County is named for the Mission of San Luis, Obispo de Tolosa (St. Louis, Bishop of Toulouse). It is one of the original twenty-seven counties and was established on February 18, 1850. The city of San Luis Obispo, site of the mission, has always been the county seat.

UNAMUNO AND CERMEÑO

The coast of San Luis Obispo County was first seen by explorers in 1542, but there is no evidence that the Cabrillo expedition landed at any point within the present county. At least two Manila galleon captains, however, paid brief visits. In 1587 Pedro de Unamuno brought his ship into Morro Bay and, according to Henry R. Wagner, penetrated inland about to the present city of San Luis Obispo. Possession was taken in the name of the King of Spain, and a cross was erected. The first Indians encountered by this party were extremely timid, but later the Spaniards were caught off guard by an Indian attack in which two men were killed and several others wounded. Eight years later Sebastián Rodríguez Cermeño, returning to Mexico in an open launch after the loss of his galleon *San Agustín* at what is today called Drakes Bay in Marin County, put in at San Luis Obispo Bay. The hungry crew traded with the Indians, who, they recorded, shouted "Cristianos" and "Mexico," evidently memories of their contact with Unamuno. It is probable that Vizcaíno, who named the Santa Lucia Mountains, entered the same bay in 1602.

THE PORTOLÁ TRAIL

In 1769, Gaspar de Portolá led an expedition from San Diego northward to find the bay of Monterey. On September 3, the party entered what is now San Luis Obispo County, where a very lean bear was killed near their camp on the shore of a small lake. The Spaniards called the place Oso Flaco ("lean bear") Lake, and the lake and name are there today. On the 4th, a halt was made in Price Canyon north of Pismo Beach, and on the 5th, one in San Luis Canyon, where the party rested on the 6th. The tents were next pitched on the 7th, this time at the lower end of Los Osos Creek, where the soldiers spent the day replenishing their food supply with bear meat. The valley was thus named La Cañada de los Osos ("the canyon of the bears"), a name that it retains today.

Morro Rock (SRL 821), a navigational marker for centuries, stands just off the coast at Morro Bay. At a location within the present town of Morro Bay and in sight of Morro Rock, camp was made on September 8. Again the expedition was halted on the 9th, at Ellysly Creek just east of Point Estero. Continuing up Ellysly Creek and over Dawson Grade, the group stopped on the 10th somewhere south of Cambria, and on the 11th, at Little Pico Creek east of San Simeon Point. The following day the party went inland over the hills and

stopped above Arroyo de la Cruz. Reaching Ragged Point on San Carpojo Creek on September 13, Portolá found that further progress up the coast was barred by steep mountain precipices. The 14th and 15th were spent in preparing a trail over a most difficult pass by way of San Carpojo Creek to its junction with Dutra Creek, where camp was made on the 16th. On the 17th the march was resumed over very rough country to Wagner Creek, within today's Monterey County.

Three years later Pedro Fages, who had been a leader on Portolá's journey and was now commander of the Presidio of Monterey, had good reason to recall La Cañada de los Osos. The unpredictable supply ships had failed to reach the presidio, and near-famine conditions prevailed there and at Mission San Antonio de Padua. With thirteen soldiers, Fages organized California's greatest grizzly bear hunt and was able to supply the settlements for months.

THE ANZA TRAIL

In 1774 Juan Bautista de Anza led a party north through San Luis Obispo County on his way to Monterey. Stops were made at the mission on April 15 and at the Nacimiento River the following day. The group traveled north from the mission over Cuesta Pass, the same route followed by US 101 today. On a second trip, in 1776, Anza was leading a group that would become the first settlers of San Francisco. Camp was made at the following places: the Indian village of El Buchon, in Price Canyon two miles north of Pismo Beach, on March 1; at Mission San Luis Obispo on March 2 and 3; and at La Asunción, a short distance north of Atascadero, on March 4.

MISSION SAN LUIS OBISPO DE TOLOSA

St. Louis was a thirteenth-century bishop of the city of Toulouse, in southern France; his name was given to the fifth in the chain of Franciscan missions built in Alta California. Father Junipero Serra presided at the founding of the mission on September 1, 1772, while on his journey from Mexico to Monterey. Since no other priest was available at the time, Father José Cavaller was left in sole charge of the new mission, contrary to the rule that two priests must be stationed at each mission. He continued to serve there until his death in 1789.

The first church was roofed with tules, which burned three times. The first occasion was in 1776, when Indians shot burning arrows into the roof. The first at-

Mission San Luis Obispo

Sinsheimer Brothers Store, San Luis Obispo

tempt to manufacture tile in California was made at the mission and proved successful. After 1784, tile was used for the roofs of all the missions. At San Luis Obispo an adobe church, completed in 1794, replaced the original chapel.

The mission (SRL 325), at 782 Monterey Street, is an active parish church in the city of San Luis Obispo. It has taken on different appearances over the years; at one time the crumbling walls were concealed under boards and a steeple described as "incongruous" was added. Beginning in 1934, when a great deal of restoration work was being done on early California buildings, efforts were made to restore the mission and some adjoining buildings to their earlier aspect. In 1961 the city began work on preserving the creek area in front of the mission and making an open plaza. This has been achieved, and the mission today stands in one of the most attractive urban developments in California. A small historical museum is located in one of the adjoining buildings of the mission.

SAN LUIS OBISPO

San Luis Obispo was organized as a town in 1856 and incorporated as a city in 1876. Some beautiful old buildings have been preserved in the downtown area. Outstanding among them is the Pierre Hyppolite Dallidet adobe (SRL 720) on San Luis Obispo Creek at 1185 Pacific Street. This was the home of a French vineyardist who came to the area in 1853. His son Paul presented the old residence and gardens to the San Luis Obispo Historical Society in 1953, in memory of a family that had lived there for a century. The home and gardens are open to the public. Adjoining this is the Ramona Depot, an 1889 Southern Pacific structure moved here in 1980, with a display of old horse-drawn streetcars.

The name Ramona comes from an elegant hotel that stood on this spot until it burned in 1905. A marker at the nearby creek notes that this was the first source of water for the mission.

Among the other adobes in San Luis Obispo are the Hays home at 642 Monterey Street, the Murray adobe nearby at 747 Monterey, the Simmler adobe in a lovely garden at 466 Dana Street, and the Fisher adobe at 883 Nipomo Street. The Andrews adobe (Casa de Lobo), built for the mayordomo of the mission, is a wood-sided structure at 1451 Andrews Street. The old Sauer home at 964 Chorro Street and the neighboring art gallery at 970 are old adobes, wood-fronted today. At the end of Lizzie Street, somewhat isolated in a thicket of eucalyptus trees, is the two-story Quintana adobe.

San Luis Obispo's urban history has been rather leisurely, and perhaps as a result, several old downtown business buildings are still in use. These include the Sinsheimer Brothers Store at 849 Monterey Street, built in 1874 and with the only cast-iron storefront in the county. Kluver's Cigar Factory (1897) is now a restaurant at 726 Higuera Street. The Ah Louis Store (SRL 802) at 800 Palm Street was the first Chinese store in the county. It was established in 1874, and the present iron-shuttered brick store was completed ten years later. In addition to selling herbs and general merchandise, the place also served as a bank and post office for the numerous Chinese laborers employed in digging railroad tunnels through Cuesta Pass in the 1880s and 1890s. Ah Louis died in 1916 in his 99th year.

The San Luis Obispo County Historical Museum is located in the former City Public Library at 696 Monterey Street. The building was the result of a Carnegie grant in 1904. Among the museum's collections are materials relating to the local Chumash, the history of the coast, and the history of ranching in the county.

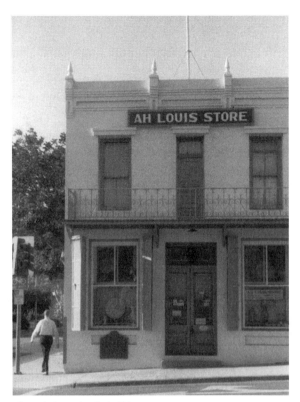

Ah Louis Store, San Luis Obispo

MISSION SAN MIGUEL ARCÁNGEL

Mission San Miguel Arcángel (SRL 326) was founded July 25, 1797, by Father Fermín Francisco de Lasuén, assisted by Father Buenaventura Sitjar. It was located at a beautiful spot on the Salinas River where there was plenty of water for irrigation. Some of the canals and dams built by the fathers for irrigating their orchards and crops may be seen around the mission.

The first temporary wooden buildings were gradually replaced, from 1799 to 1804, by adobe structures. Fire almost destroyed the entire establishment in 1806, and plans were made for reconstruction on a more spacious scale. The church building that was begun in 1816 and completed in 1818 still stands. Secularization took place in 1836, followed by confiscation and neglect. In 1859, the mission was returned to the church, and in 1878 a resident priest took up his office. The principal church building was restored, and the Franciscan Fathers, who maintain the old place as a novitiate, now hold services there. It is one of four California missions still in the hands of the Franciscan order.

San Miguel remains less spoiled by restoration than most of the missions, and contains perhaps the finest examples of original decorations done by the Indians under the supervision of the fathers, and, in this case,

under the particular direction of Estévan Munras of Monterey. Great rafters and corbels hewn from solid trees, carried by Indians forty miles from the mountains, support the ceiling, and all are colored in light green, pink, blue, and white. The walls are designed to represent fluted pillars tinted in blue, while between these are conventionalized designs of leaves and carved figures. A frieze in reddish brown represents a gallery with railings and pillars. The pulpit, also decorated and colored by the Indians, the confessional built into the adobe wall, the floor of burnt bricks laid in alternate rows of squares and oblongs, all remain as they were when first completed with such care by the padres and their charges. The monastery with its beautiful low-arched corridor, which extends from the side, is unique because its arches are of different sizes.

RIOS-CALEDONIA ADOBE AND
ESTRELLA CHURCH

At the south end of the town of San Miguel is the Rios-Caledonia adobe (SRL 936). Petronillo Ríos built this imposing two-story building with Indian labor in 1846. The roof was of handmade tiles and the rafters of pine poles tied in place with strips of rawhide. In time the place passed to George Butchart, who made the building into an inn and stage stop and gave it the name "Caledonia," which, he claimed, was a Scots word for "welcome." The coming of the railroad put the stagecoaches out of business, and eventually the Caledonia closed its doors, becoming a private home. Charles Dorries purchased it in 1923 and endeavored to preserve as much of it as he could, but illness and advancing age defeated him, and after his death in 1962 the abandoned structure became the prey of vandals and time. In 1968 a new group called the Friends of the Adobe was organized to save and preserve the building, and after great effort, the restored adobe was opened to the public in December 1972. It is an excellent example of how the dedication of a small group of people can have good results in historical preservation.

A few miles to the southeast, another old building has come under the care of the Friends of the Adobe. The Estrella Adobe Church (SRL 542) was the first Protestant church in northern San Luis Obispo County. It was built through the cooperation of members of several denominations in 1878. It was restored by the efforts of the Paso Robles Women's Club with the assistance of boys from the California Youth Authority and rededicated in 1952. Located on Airport Road just north

Rios-Caledonia Adobe, San Miguel

of the Paso Robles airport, it is about four miles northeast of Paso Robles.

THE ASISTENCIA OF SANTA MARGARITA

The Asistencia of Santa Margarita (SRL 364), belonging to Mission San Luis Obispo, was an outpost, or chapel and storehouse, located north of the mission across steep Cuesta Pass. It was built of stone on a knoll near Santa Margarita Creek, where there lived many Indians whom the padres hoped to enroll as converts. The few ruins of the building may be seen about one-quarter mile west of the town of Santa Margarita, between US 101 and SR 58. A visitor to this place in 1831, while the building was still intact, was Alfred Robinson, who wrote:

> We reached "El Rancho de Santa Rita," a place used for the cultivation of grain, where, on an eminence that overlooked the grounds, an extensive building was erected. It was divided into storerooms for different kinds of grain, and apartments for the accommodation of the mayordomo, servants, and wayfarers. At one end was a chapel, and snug lodging-rooms for the priest who, I was informed, frequently came and passed some weeks at the place during the time of harvest; and the holy friars of the two missions occasionally met there to acknowledge to each other their sins.

THE RANCHOS OF SENATOR HEARST (SAN SIMEON AND CAMBRIA)

The ranchos of Piedra Blanca, San Simeon, and Santa Rosa became the property of Senator George W. Hearst. The three stretch along the Pacific from the mouth of San Carpojo Creek southeast to the mouth of Villa Creek and extend far back into the hills.

Rancho Piedra Blanca is the farthest north. It was granted in 1840 to José de Jesús Pico, a former soldier at Monterey. Shortly after receiving this grant he became the administrator of Mission San Miguel. Although at one time he was arrested by Frémont and condemned to death, he was pardoned at the intercession of a band of women and children led by Doña Ramona Carrillo de Wilson, wife of Captain John Wilson. Pico afterward became a devoted friend of Frémont and assisted him in bringing about the Treaty of Cahuenga. In 1848 and again in 1849 he made successful trips to the gold mines but later spent his time on his rancho.

Mariano Pacheco purchased a portion of Rancho Piedra Blanca from Pico, and until the 1870s his family lived in the adobe house overlooking the ocean and located about three miles north of the town of San Simeon. Don Mariano was buried in the vicinity. After the departure of the Pacheco family, the extensive two-story adobe was used by tenants until about 1906. Its foundations, marked by a few old cypress trees, are hidden in a tangle of weeds on a hill in what is now a cattle pasture.

The town of San Simeon, which lies on this rancho, was for many years the center of an extensive whaling industry. As early as 1864 Captain Joseph Clark, still active in the 1880s, had a fleet of five boats outfitted for whaling. Many years ago a fire wiped out a large part of the little town, but a few old frame buildings still stand. Sebastian's store (SRL 726), built in the 1860s one-half mile to the west and moved to its present location in 1878, is the oldest store building along the northern coast of San Luis Obispo County. The store and the adjacent post office are still in business. There is also a warehouse built in 1878 by the Hearst interests and bearing the date of its construction. A little farther from the wharf are red-tiled, stucco residences built in more recent times by William Randolph Hearst for his employees.

Up the road behind the town is the large frame ranch house of Senator George Hearst, built soon after he purchased Rancho Piedra Blanca in 1865. It is still the headquarters for the Hearst cattle ranch. This building can be seen from the bus that transports tourists through the private ranch property to Hearst–San Simeon State Historical Monument (SRL 640) on a commanding height overlooking San Simeon Bay.

Here, from 1919 to 1947, William Randolph Hearst, son of Senator George and Phoebe Apperson Hearst, created La Cuesta Encantada ("the enchanted hill") at a cost of millions of dollars. Together with his architect,

Julia Morgan, he planned the Spanish Renaissance buildings where he lived and operated his vast empire, entertaining famous guests from far and near, including Calvin Coolidge, Winston Churchill, George Bernard Shaw, and a multitude of motion picture personalities. The main residence, La Casa Grande, has four floors with scores of rooms and twin towers housing carillon bells. The vast structure was never finished. There are also three guest cottages, each a mansion in itself with between ten and eighteen rooms. Casa del Mar faces the Pacific, Casa del Monte the ridges of the Santa Lucia Range, and Casa del Sol the setting sun. The building and the grounds are filled with the art objects collected by Hearst all over the world. The warehouses at San Simeon contain treasures destined for the castle but still in the packing crates in which they were shipped from European monasteries and palaces. Hearst transplanted exotic trees to his hilltop castle and even established a private zoo. There are both indoor and outdoor swimming pools. Hearst died in 1951 at the age of eighty-eight, and in 1958 the Hearst Corporation presented the castle and about one hundred and twenty-five acres of surrounding land to the state of California to be opened to the public as a memorial to William Randolph Hearst and his mother, Phoebe Apperson Hearst. The site is also listed as a National Historic Landmark.

Southeast of Rancho Piedra Blanca lies Rancho San Simeon, through which flows San Simeon Creek. This was a grant of one square league made to José Ramón Estrada, son of José Mariano Estrada, and patented to José Miguel Gómez in 1865, shortly before Senator Hearst acquired the property. The San Simeon adobe, gone long ago, was on San Simeon Creek about three-quarters of a mile back from the beach.

The farthest south of the three ranchos is Rancho Santa Rosa, a three-league grant made to Julián Estrada, son of José Ramón Estrada, and patented to him in 1865. The Estrada adobe stood on the road north of Swallow Rock at an elevation of 130 feet; nothing remains to indicate the site. The town of Cambria, first called Rosaville, was located on the property. It originated during the copper excitement of 1863 and was aided in its growth by the quicksilver prospecting of 1871 and by the activities of lumbermen.

RANCHO MORO Y CAYUCOS (CAYUCOS)

Cayuco is a nautical term applied to a small fishing boat that is like a canoe and often made of skins; it is the Spanish equivalent of the Eskimo word *kayak*. A point on the coast of San Luis Obispo County that was early used as a port was called by that name because the schooners, pausing offshore from the mouth of a small stream, had commerce with the land by means of these small boats. The creek, the little settlement that grew up near its mouth, and eventually the land nearby were all known by the name Cayucos.

In 1842, Rancho Moro y Cayucos was granted to Martin Olivera, from Rancho Sausal in Monterey County, and to Vicente Feliz, former mayordomo of another rancho. It was later owned by James McKinley, a Scottish sailor, who married Carmen Amesti, daughter of José Amesti of Rancho Corralitos. McKinley sold it in smaller tracts for dairy farms.

In 1867 this coastal region was served by a weekly stage running from San Luis Obispo to San Simeon. In this year James Cass came to the vicinity of Cayucos Landing and lived first in the hills just behind the settlement, but soon he built a large house that still stands on Ocean Avenue at Cayucos Drive in the town of Cayucos. He became a leader in the community; in 1870 he built a wharf, and soon afterward a store and warehouse. The broad streets of the town were laid out in 1875, and in the early 1880s a stage bringing passengers from San Miguel and way stations made connections with a weekly boat at Cayucos.

For many years considerable shipping was done from here, but finally a storm destroyed a large part of the pier and motor transportation eliminated the need of steamer calls. Only a small pleasure wharf is now on the site of the wharf built by Captain Cass.

RANCHO SAN BERNARDO (MORRO BAY)

Vicente Cané (Canet), a Spanish sailor, settled in Alta California before 1828. In 1840 he received a grant of one square league of land lying between San Bernardo and Morro Creeks, both of which empty into Morro Bay. The following year Don Vicente was a magistrate at Mission San Luis Obispo. His rancho home was built about that time on a hill above San Bernardo Creek two miles east of Morro Bay. Privately owned, it still stands on the north side of SR 1, to the east of a junction with San Bernardo Creek Road. One and one-quarter miles beyond the Canet adobe, toward San Luis Obispo, Canet Road leads half a mile to the old family cemetery.

Farther east on SR 1, one mile east of Cuesta College and on the outskirts of the city of San Luis Obispo, is Camp San Luis Obispo, the original home of the California National Guard.

John Wilson, Scottish shipmaster and captain of the *Ayacucho*, who had been trading for years on the coast, settled in California and married Ramona Carrillo de Pacheco. Señora Pacheco owned Rancho Suey and was a widow with two sons, one of whom, Romualdo Pacheco, afterward held many high offices in the state and is the only man of Hispanic origin to serve as governor (1875) since the American conquest. About 1839 Captain Wilson and James Scott, another native of Scotland, entered into a business partnership that continued for several years. Rancho Cañada del Chorro ("jet of water"), on the southwest side of the Santa Lucia Range, consisting of 3,167 acres, was granted to them. James Scott died in 1851 and Captain Wilson in 1860, so the patent to the rancho was issued to Wilson's heirs in 1861.

The Cañada de los Osos, so named by Portolá's men in 1769 because of the bears they killed here for food, was a part of the Rancho Cañada de los Osos y Peche y Islay. Once owned by Scott and Wilson (after some earlier and short-lived grants), this too became Wilson's property. Between Rancho El Chorro and Rancho Cañada de los Osos, an Indian named Romualdo cultivated a bit of level land at the base of Cerro Romualdo. This tract of 117 acres was purchased by Captain Wilson and called Huerta ("vegetable garden") de Romualdo.

Captain Wilson built an adobe house in the Cañada de los Osos and lived there from 1845 until his death. His widow continued to live there with her son, by then a rising figure in governmental affairs. The property later passed to her daughter. What is left of the old house is now a barn on a ranch to the east of Turri Road at a point half a mile north of Los Osos Road, about eight miles west of San Luis Obispo via Los Osos Road.

RANCHO SAN MIGUELITO (AVILA BEACH)

Rancho San Miguelito lay along the shore of San Luis Obispo Bay with a further shoreline extending northwest along the ocean almost to Pecho Creek. On this rancho an outpost of Mission San Luis Obispo was maintained for a time, and along the valley of the San Luis Obispo River the padres tended fields of corn and beans. The outpost stood near the present town of Avila Beach.

Miguel Avila, born in Santa Barbara and educated in San Francisco, was a soldier and copyist at Monterey; in 1824 he was corporal of the guard at Mission San Luis Obispo. One day at the mission, Father Luís Martínez (who appears in Helen Hunt Jackson's *Ramona*) harshly reproved him in the presence of a group of Indians for talking with an Indian at the rancheria. Both padre and corporal apparently became angry; this gave rise to curses and threats of excommunication. The corporal called the soldiers, and the padre rang the bell to call all his assistants and neophytes. "The two forces," so a tale goes, "faced each other in battle array, armed on one side with guns and lances, and on the other with book, holy water, and cross. Martínez began to read and Avila seized the book, thinking thus to escape damnation; but the padre went on, finished the rite in bad Latin from memory, and retired in triumph to the church." The matter was later sent to the *comandante*, and the excommunication of the corporal was annulled.

In 1826, two years after the trouble with the padre, Miguel Avila married María Inocenta, daughter of Dolores Pico, who was then in charge of Rancho Nacional. He lived in Monterey with his increasing family.

Don Miguel obtained the grant of San Miguelito in three pieces by 1846, and in 1845 he obtained the use of another part of the mission lands, Rancho Laguna, although this was patented in 1859 to Bishop J. S. Alemany. In 1849 Don Miguel was alcalde at San Luis Obispo. In his later years he became interested in the preservation of documents, but the large collection that he kept in his house was lost when that building was destroyed by fire. Avila Beach nearby is named in his honor.

CAVE LANDING

Cave Landing is situated on San Luis Obispo Bay about one-half mile east of Avila Beach, and can be reached from US 101 via Cave Landing Road off Avila Beach Road. The fathers used this landing place for shipping tallow and grain. A pathway leads down to the beach where one can see Arch Rock and the mouth of Robbers' Cave, named in the popular belief that it was a hiding place for contraband. Between Arch Rock and Robbers' Cave is tiny Moonstone Beach, so called from the moonstones among the pebbles and shells washed up by the waves.

From the white sands of Moonstone Beach one may climb over the rocks, ducking through tunnels made by the sea, until, rounding a corner, one comes suddenly upon an immense level rock that juts out 150 feet into deep water and beneath which the tide swirls. This is Cave Landing, an excellent natural pier for deep-sea fishermen. Here Indians fished for hundreds of years and buried their dead in crude graves along the rugged cliffs facing the east. After them came a romantic procession of smugglers and bandits, priests, and sea captains.

About 1860, David Mallagh, an Irish sea captain, erected a warehouse on the cliffs above the sea, with a long wooden chute leading down to the water. Huge iron spikes, with immense rings of iron fastened to them, were driven into the solid rock at the top of the cliff. Great ship cables were fastened to the rings. For a decade, Captain Mallagh handled all of the shipping at the cove and hauled passengers and freight to San Luis Obispo. After his death and the advent of the railroad, which reached San Luis Obispo in 1894, Cave Landing was abandoned. The place is still a haven for beach-lovers and hikers.

RANCHOS OF FRANCIS ZIBA BRANCH (PISMO BEACH, ARROYO GRANDE)

Francis Ziba Branch, a native of New York, arrived in California with the Wolfskill party in 1831. For a few years he made his home at Santa Barbara, where he kept a store and boardinghouse, leaving occasionally to hunt sea otters. In 1835 he married Manuela, daughter of Zefarino Carlón, a soldier of the Santa Barbara Company. In 1837 Branch received a grant of over sixteen thousand acres of land lying in the Arroyo Grande Valley about thirteen miles south of Mission San Luis Obispo, and named it Rancho Santa Manuela.

When Branch moved to his rancho, he found that the valley in front of his home was an impenetrable swamp—a thicket of willow and cottonwood trees where bobcats, mountain lions, and grizzly bears lived. His stock was often attacked by wild animals and sometimes by the Tulare Indians from the east.

Five years after Branch received his rancho, his father-in-law, Don Zefarino, obtained an adjoining grant of one square league named the Arroyo Grande but frequently called the Ranchita. It lay along the headwaters of the Arroyo Grande and was later patented to his son-in-law.

At the lower end of the Arroyo Grande Valley was Rancho Pismo, two leagues granted to José Ortega in 1840. This was purchased by Isaac Sparks, who resold it, half to John M. Price and half to Branch. To add further to his possessions, Branch bought a part of Rancho Bolsa de Chamisal adjoining the Pismo on the

south and a tract of land, Rancho Huerhuero (an uncertain name, according to Gudde, but it may be a reference to the "rotten egg" smell of sulfur water in the vicinity), lying several miles to the north of his earlier holdings in the vicinity of the present town of Creston.

The city of Arroyo Grande lies in the Arroyo Grande Valley on the boundary line between Ranchos Santa Manuela and Pismo. Many of its buildings on Branch Street from the early years of the twentieth century have been preserved and restored; the two-story Odd Fellows Hall on Bridge Street goes back to 1895. Near the town, at the mouth of Corralitos Canyon, long stood the remains of an old adobe believed by some to have been built by Mission San Luis Obispo as one of the buildings of an asistencia. It is known that farming was carried on by the mission fathers on the rich bottomlands of the Arroyo Grande as early as 1780.

The adobe that Branch built on Rancho Santa Manuela was for many years one of the most noted in the county. The unmarked site is located off the Huasna Road about three and one-half miles east of Arroyo Grande, near the Branch School. Nearby, old palms and cypresses indicate the site of the frame house where Branch's son Fred lived; the house has been destroyed by fire.

Another adobe built by the Branch family stands at 2878 Huasna Road, much disguised as a modern residence with Spanish-style arches. Yet another Branch adobe stands on a knoll to the left of the road leading to Biddle Regional County Park. It is half a mile beyond the junction of this road and the back road to San Luis Obispo, about five and one-half miles northeast of Arroyo Grande.

John M. Price, who held the half of the Pismo grant not purchased by F. Z. Branch, built an adobe house on the land. It still stands but is not occupied. Price also built an adobe schoolhouse nearby, which now is all but ruined. These buildings, together with the frame structure that was Price's last home, stand across the railroad tracks to the right of Price Canyon Road half a mile north of the junction of this road and Bello Street in Pismo Beach. The town of Pismo Beach lies on the coast about in the center of the grant.

Nearby Halcyon began as one of California's utopian colonies. Dr. William H. Dower and Mrs. Francia A. LaDue opened a sanatorium here in 1904. From this grew the theosophical, cooperative, quasi-socialistic colony of the Temple Home Association. On the edge of Halcyon, the old turn-of-the-century mansion in which the sanatorium was first located is still to be seen, its gleaming white wooden frame nearly engulfed in a mobile home park; it is at the corner of 25th Street and SR 1, at the east end of the town of Oceano.

RANCHO NIPOMO (NIPOMO)

One of the most famous old ranchos of California was the domain of almost 38,000 acres that constituted Rancho Nipomo (an Indian word said to mean "foot of the mountain"), for many years the first stopping place on El Camino Real south of Mission San Luis Obispo. Many of the early books on California mention Captain Dana, the owner of this rancho, his pleasant home at Nipomo, and his lavish hospitality. Among the travelers who were Dana's guests over the years were Colonel John C. Frémont, General Henry W. Halleck, and Edwin Bryant, author of *What I Saw in California*.

William Goodwin Dana, a cousin of Richard Henry Dana Jr. (who wrote *Two Years Before the Mast*), was born in Boston in 1797 and received his education there. While still a young man, he went to Canton in China and later to India in the service of his uncle, a Boston merchant. Returning home after three years, he soon reembarked, possibly on the *Waverly*, of which he was captain a few years later. In this capacity he engaged for several years in trade between China, the Sandwich (Hawaiian) Islands, California, and Boston.

In 1825 Captain Dana established his business in Santa Barbara, where he soon settled permanently. He became a prominent citizen, holding a number of important offices at various times. In 1828 he married María Josefa Carrillo, daughter of Carlos Antonio Carrillo, a resident of Santa Barbara and a short-term provisional governor of California in 1835. About this time Dana applied for Rancho Nipomo. The grant was not confirmed until 1837. In 1839 the captain moved into his rancho and built the large adobe house of thirteen rooms that still stands; until 1902, Federico Dana, one of his sons, lived there. The adobe, now owned and being restored by the San Luis Obispo County Historical Society, is located at 671 Oakglen Avenue at the south end of the town of Nipomo.

Frémont, on his way from Monterey to Los Angeles in December 1846, camped at Rancho Nipomo with his battalion of 430 hungry and footsore soldiers, soaked to the skin by the rain through which they had tramped on the long march from the north. The campsite was located in an oak grove at a point known as the Summit, not far from Casa de Dana; it is northwest of Nipomo on the west side of US 101.

RANCHO EL PASO DE LOS ROBLES (PASO ROBLES)

Rancho El Paso de los Robles received its name from the many large oaks that dotted the valley, and the name has survived in the modern town. Well known to the Indians, the hot springs on this rancho were also known to the Franciscan fathers who, possibly as early as 1797, placed a wall of logs around the edge of the main spring, forming a pool of water. Alfred Robinson, who visited Mission San Miguel in 1830, says that Father Juan Cabot "had erected a small house over the spot for the purpose of shelter and convenience for bathing, and it was resorted to by many persons."

At first an outpost of Mission San Miguel, Rancho El Paso de los Robles was granted to Pedro Narváez in 1844, and later confirmed to Petronillo Ríos. It was purchased in 1857 by Daniel and James Blackburn and Lazare Godchaux, and improvements were begun at once. James Blackburn built a frame house near the rancho adobe, said to have been put up by the mission fathers, and used the adobe for servants' quarters. Both stood six and one-half miles south of Paso Robles, near the entrance to the Crescent Dairy.

Drury James, a brother-in-law of the Blackburns, purchased the hot springs tract along the west bank of the river where the town of Paso Robles is now situated and built the first substantial house on the site, a duplicate of the James Blackburn house south of town. The site of the original hot springs and the first bathhouse built for it is the northwest corner of Tenth and Spring Streets, now a parking lot.

RANCHOS ASUNCIÓN AND ATASCADERO (ATASCADERO) AND RANCHO SANTA MARGARITA (SANTA MARGARITA)

Rancho Atascadero, granted to Trifon García in 1842, and Rancho Asunción, granted to Pedro Estrada in 1845, both of which lay between Ranchos Paso de Robles and Santa Margarita, became parts of the huge Murphy estate, with headquarters at Santa Margarita. The adobe house in which Pedro Estrada lived on Rancho Asunción is now a fragmentary ruin about two miles out of Atascadero on Traffic Way, a section of old El Camino Real that was left out of the construction of US 101.

Atascadero Administration Building, Atascadero

foundation of the settlement. Lewis's first building was The Printery, now the Masonic Temple on Olmeda at West Mall. The first rotogravure presses west of Chicago were installed to print supplements for major metropolitan newspapers and national magazines. The centerpiece of the community was the Atascadero Administration Building (SRL 958), built between 1914 and 1918 at 6500 Palma Avenue. The beautiful building and the nearby Veterans Memorial Building were made from locally produced brick and reinforced concrete. Their Italian Renaissance style is in homage of Thomas Jefferson's home Monticello in Virginia. Today it is the City Hall of Atascadero, which became an incorporated community in 1979. By that time, the Atascadero Colony had passed from the scene; Lewis's creditors forced him into bankruptcy in 1924. The Atascadero Museum is handsomely housed on the lower-floor rotunda of the City Hall, with excellent displays about a community whose dreams did not materialize. Looking at the surviving buildings, however, one is struck by their beauty and utility; today, nearing a century after they were put up, they remain impressive monuments to the hopes of Edward G. Lewis.

JAMES DEAN MEMORIAL

California is full of monuments, and one of the most unusual is at the little crossroads town of Cholame, where SR 41 meets SR 46. In the late afternoon of September 30, 1955, James Dean was killed in an automobile accident at this spot. Only twenty-four years old, Dean was a rising Hollywood actor who is best remembered for the film *Rebel Without a Cause* and was already attracting a good deal of attention as a symbol of a young and restless generation. His death was much lamented, and he became a hero for many young Americans.

Seita Ohnishi, a Japanese fan, decided to erect a monument to Dean on the site of his death, and on the twenty-second anniversary of the accident, September 30, 1977, the monument was placed in front of the tiny Cholame post office. It consists of a cast aluminum and stainless steel structure enclosing a tall ailanthus tree, the "tree of heaven," which is neither irrigated nor fertilized, receiving "only what heaven sends it." Mr. Ohnishi's inscription says that the monument "stands for James Dean and other American Rebels who taught us the importance of having a cause." The anniversary of Dean's death has annually brought carloads of fans to the memorial.

After secularization, Rancho Santa Margarita passed from the control of Mission San Luis Obispo and was granted to Joaquín Estrada, the brother of Pedro. In 1860 Martin Murphy Jr., who lived at Rancho Pastoria de las Borregas in Santa Clara County, came into possession of Rancho Santa Margarita; this, together with Ranchos Atascadero and Asunción and others that he owned, made up a magnificent landed estate totaling 70,000 acres. Martin Murphy's son Patrick took charge of the entire domain, making Santa Margarita his home and his business headquarters. As late as the 1880s, thousands of beef cattle were pastured upon this vast territory.

By 1913, Rancho Atascadero's 23,000 acres were owned by J. H. Henry. In that year, Edward Gardner Lewis came west from University City, Missouri, to found a model colony in California, already home to a number of idealistic communities. He was "a charismatic salesman, an investor of almost unlimited scope, a prolific writer, educator, publisher, ceramist, painter, city planner, developer and a gentlemen of intense drive and curiosity," according to the Atascadero Historical Society. Lewis acquired the rancho and set out to build his colony upon it, and a host of enthusiasts followed him. A complex of food-processing operations and business ventures was to be the economic

San Mateo County

Pulgas Water Temple, Upper Crystal Springs Lake

San Mateo County was organized in 1856 from the southern portion of San Francisco County. San Mateo is Spanish for St. Matthew. The county seat, located through fraudulent election at Belmont in May 1856, was changed within a year to Redwood City, where it has remained, although the question of its removal came up in 1861 and at other times.

In 1868, by an act of the state Legislature, the southern boundary of the county, which had been a line running due west from the source of the south branch of San Francisquito Creek and reaching the coast at San Gregorio, became an irregular line running southwest to the coast below Point Año Nuevo. This change transferred a large tract, including Pescadero, from Santa Cruz County to San Mateo County.

History and geography have tended to separate the county into coastal and bayside regions. As Alan Hynding noted:

> Beauty and isolation typified the San Mateo coast in the last century. Rugged, forested mountains and a rocky shoreline made access by both land and sea difficult. As a result, significantly fewer people settled there than on the bayside. As time passed, the coast became a backwater. . . . The first part of the county to be colonized by Europeans, the coast was the last to feel the impact of the twentieth century.

INDIAN MOUNDS

Indian villages were widely scattered along the shores of both ocean and bay. Near Point Año Nuevo, the southernmost corner of the county, are acres of dunes, where the shifting sands have revealed from time to time such evidences of Indian occupation as are usu-ally found in kitchen middens: broken shells, arrow points, bones of wild animals that were used for food, and occasional human skeletons that were buried near tribal dwellings. Farther north on the coast at Half Moon Bay are several mounds.

Perhaps the largest mounds in the county were in the vicinity of South San Francisco and Brisbane on the shore of the bay; while most of the material has been taken away, there are plans to keep two acres in South San Francisco free from development.

Many indications of early human habitation have been found on and near the banks of San Mateo Creek, once a favorite haunt of native tribes. During excavations for house foundations on Baywood Avenue west of SR 82, as many as six skeletons were taken out of one small area. The ground in this vicinity is largely impregnated with broken shell. Across the highway where the creek, for a little distance, is held within bounds by concrete walls, larger shell mounds were found. About two feet of surface shell, in which a few relics such as mortars were found, were removed before the construction of school buildings on the Civic Center site. It was probably from this village that the helpful visitors, mentioned by Anza, came to his camp on San Mateo Creek in March 1776.

In Redwood City the part of Main Street that runs between El Camino Real and the railroad track traverses the site of another Indian village. A small triangular park now marks the site.

LA PUNTA DE AÑO NUEVO

Sebastián Vizcaíno set sail from Mexico on May 5, 1602, to survey the California coast for a good harbor to be used by the Spanish galleons on their trips to and from the Philippines. He found a harbor that pleased him at Monterey and remained there at anchor for a few days. When he resumed his voyage on January 3, 1603, the first conspicuous point he sighted was a low headland to which the name La Punta de Año Nuevo ("New Year's Point") was given, the name that the southwesternmost point of San Mateo County still bears. It was the point that mariners following Vizcaíno described as the northwestern extremity of Monterey Bay.

The Mexican grant of land made in this vicinity in 1842 perpetuated the name. The westernmost tip of land is now an island frequented by sea lions. The point and beach are now part of Año Nuevo State Reserve, a protected breeding ground for northern elephant seals.

THE PORTOLÁ TRAIL

On Monday, October 23, 1769, Gaspar de Portolá and the members of his party, including Father Juan Crespí and Ensign Miguel Costansó, chroniclers of the expedition, having rested over Sunday in the Cañada de la Salud, which is now Waddell Creek in Santa Cruz County, resumed their march in search of the elusive bay of Monterey. Traveling two leagues that day, they entered the region now included in San Mateo County, passed La Punta de Año Nuevo without being sure of its identify, and camped for the night at an Indian village they called "La Casa Grande," because of an unusually large house in its center. This site was identified by Bolton as Gazos Creek (SRL 23), but later evidence seems to point to Whitehouse Creek as the location. Here they seem to have heard rumors of a port and a ship to the north, and were confirmed in their decision to continue.

They pursued their journey north, following the present Cloverdale Road inland to the site of Pescadero on Pescadero Creek, then over the hills near the shore to camp on San Gregorio Creek at the present town site of San Gregorio. They remained there for two days for the benefit of sick and tired soldiers. Father Crespí was impressed by the surroundings of the two Indian settlements, and proposed the place for a mission site. The explorers' stop is marked by a historical marker on the coast highway (SRL 26), close to where the Indians' permanent village was situated.

On October 27 they halted on the south bank of Purisima Creek (SRL 22), and the next night they pitched camp (SRL 21) near the town of Half Moon Bay. Pillar Point, probably first seen by the navigator Francisco de Gali in 1585, could be discerned from this place, lying to

the north-northwest. Here a halt was made over Sunday, October 29, because Portolá was ill. On October 30 they stopped on the bank of Martini Creek (SRL 25), just north of Montara Beach, having had to bridge some of the creeks on the way. Here the route was blocked by San Pedro Mountain, and Sergeant Ortega was sent to break a trail over the barrier.

Next morning the party ascended the mountain and looked down upon the Gulf of the Farallones. Some of the leaders identified this as the Bay of San Francisco of the ancient navigators, for Point Reyes was visible forty miles to the north-northwest. A base camp (SRL 24) was established on October 31 on the south side of Pedro Valley near a lagoon at its mouth. From this point Sergeant Ortega made an extended exploring trip, discovering not the long-sought bay of Monterey, but the inner or present-day Bay of San Francisco instead. A hunting party, which left camp on November 2 and returned at nightfall with news of an inland sea, was the first to report the discovery of the bay, since Ortega did not return until the night of November 3. He had been drawn inland by a report from the Indians of "a port and a ship therein" only two days distant from their camp. The site of the discovery (SRL 394) is on Sweeney Ridge, just east of Pacifica, and is reached by a trail. It is now in the southernmost part of the Golden Gate National Recreational Area and is also a National Historic Landmark.

On November 4, Portolá and his men crossed Sweeney Ridge just south of the present radar station behind San Bruno, paused beyond the summit to view the great arm of the sea drawing down far to the southeast on their right and disappearing on their left behind San Bruno Mountain. They then went down to camp by a pond now covered by the waters of San Andreas Lake, where a historical marker (SRL 27) now stands on Skyline Boulevard. The trail they followed on November 5 is today mostly covered by the Crystal Springs Lakes; camp was made near a lake later called the Laguna de Raymundo or Laguna Grande (SRL 94), now included in the upper reservoir, west of Ralston Avenue. Here the mountains on the right were covered with oak, redwood, and madrone trees. The party saw many herds of deer on the valley floor. This section is today the San Francisco Peninsula Watershed and State Fish and Game Refuge, where numerous deer may often be seen grazing.

On November 6 the party turned east over the low hills along the Redwood City–Woodside city limits and again established a base camp one league from the bay on San Francisquito Creek in Menlo Park (SRL 2), on the opposite bank from the huge redwood tree known as the "Palo Alto." From this point Ortega explored to the south and then up the east side of the bay, possibly as far as San Lorenzo in Alameda County. On November 10, he returned with the discouraging news that hostile Indians and another great arm of the sea barred further progress. After conferring with the other members of the party, Portolá decided to discontinue the search for the harbor of Monterey.

Retracing their steps, the little company returned to the unrecognized Monterey Bay over the route by which they had come, camping on November 11 north of Woodside (SRL 92), on the 12th again at San Andreas Lake, and on the 13th at Pedro Valley. From there they proceeded down the coast, stopping to relieve their hunger with shellfish at Martini Creek and with fowl at the "Plain of Wild Geese" at Half Moon Bay. Camping at Tunitas Creek (SRL 375), Butano Creek, and Año Nuevo Creek, they entered Santa Cruz County once more on November 20. On November 27 they were back at Monterey Bay, and again they did not realize that this was the harbor for which they were searching.

RIVERA'S TRAIL IN 1774

The Spanish viceroy in Mexico, Antonio María Bucareli, wanting to establish a mission at the port of San Francisco, ordered Fernando de Rivera y Moncada to go there to look for a suitable site. Rivera had been a member of the expedition led by Gaspar de Portolá, which had discovered that port.

Setting out from Monterey by Pedro Fages's inland route on November 23, 1774, the party of twenty reached San Francisquito Creek at the southern boundary of San Mateo County on November 28. Accompanying Captain Rivera on this journey was Father Francisco Palou, who, like the captain, kept a journal. Their camping place at the creek seemed to them suitable for a mission, since it met the requirements of wood, water, and native people to be Christianized. Therefore a cross made of two beams was put up to mark the spot for future consideration.

On the next day's march northward, they turned into the hills between present Redwood City and San Carlos, where they found friendly Indians; Father Palou, in his religious zeal, "embraced them" and made them gifts of beads, hoping to hold their friendship until the time for gathering them into the fold of the mission. As the day wore on, more and more natives

joined the travelers, pressing them to enter their villages, of which there were many along the route both in the hills and near the shore of the bay.

On November 30, the day of the feast of St. Andrew, Rivera and his party came to a pleasant valley (where Portolá had camped) that since that day has borne the name they gave, "San Andreas." On that day, too, friendly Indians seemed to enjoy the company and the food of the strangers, and again Father Palou intimated that he would return and would bring seeds for planting so that they could grow similar food for themselves.

For the next few days they explored in the territory now included in northern San Mateo County and San Francisco, being the first explorers to see the views from San Bruno Mountain and Mount Davidson. Then, deciding not to retrace their steps but to follow the coast as the Portolá expedition had done, they reached Pedro Valley, crossed Pedro Mountain, and on December 6 camped at Purisima Creek south of Half Moon Bay. Spending a day at an Indian village there, they continued south to Butano Creek on December 8. They crossed the present border of Santa Cruz County on December 10 and returned to Monterey on the 12th. Rivera and Palou recommended the establishment of Mission San Francisco on what later became known as San Francisquito Creek, but Father Serra decided instead in favor of the northern end of the peninsula, though the explorers had thought the place unsatisfactory.

ANZA'S TRAIL IN 1776

Juan Bautista de Anza, on his way from Monterey to the port of San Francisco with a party of thirteen, including Lieutenant José Joaquín Moraga and Father Pedro Font, entered what is now San Mateo County by crossing San Francisquito Creek on March 26, 1776. An Indian village of about twenty huts was near the creek, and on the north bank stood the cross erected by Father Palou two years before. Font's diary gives the information that along this arroyo were various trees: laurel, ash, and "a beautiful cypress called redwood."

After making gifts of beads to the women in this village, they proceeded through a plain of oak and soon were met by a group of shouting natives whose long-haired chief was recognized by Corporal Robles as being one of a group whom his companions of a former journey had called the "Shouters." Approaching the place where Redwood City now stands, they came to another village, where they saw a large heap of mussel shells. During the day's march, they passed four Indian villages. The last one was located on San Mateo Creek shortly before they made their camp for the night (SRL 48), in the present city of Burlingame, perhaps at Barroilhet Avenue, on one of the arroyos bordered with scented trees that they called laurel.

With an early start on March 27, the party's line of travel led past Millbrae, San Bruno, and Daly City, toward the port of San Francisco. Two days later half of the party with the camp equipment returned to await their commander at San Mateo Creek. Anza, accompanied by his chaplain and five soldiers, spent the day exploring the hills for timber for the new settlements. In the course of the afternoon, Corporal Robles shot an immense bear that appeared out of the woods near the Crystal Springs Lakes. The skin of this animal was preserved as a gift for the viceroy.

On reaching camp at the site of the city of San Mateo, they found most of the men from the Indian village congregated there. After a heavy rain during the night, they set out in the morning in a southeasterly direction. When San Francisquito Creek was reached, Father Font set the graphometer thirty-six varas from the foot of the tallest redwood tree there and found that its height was a little more than fifty varas, or about 138 feet, a vara being a measure of approximately thirty-three inches. The Indians watched this proceeding quietly. The tree that was measured has long been assumed to have been the famous Palo Alto beside the railroad tracks. It may, however, have been another redwood farther downstream.

From this point the party passed on into Santa Clara County. Soon the route thus established was again traveled, this time by Anza's company of settlers that, bound for San Francisco from Mexico, had rested for a time at Monterey while their leader went ahead. The colonists camped at San Mateo on June 24, 25, and 26, 1776; a historical marker (SRL 47) on Arroyo Court, north of Third Avenue and west of El Camino Real, commemorates the campsite.

EL CAMINO REAL, THE SAN JOSE ROAD

Although the Bayshore Freeway (US 101) has replaced it as the route of high-speed transportation, El Camino Real, the old road leading south from San Francisco, has an interesting story of its own, distinct from the histories of the ranches, estates, and large cities that have sprung up beside it.

When Mission San Francisco was founded in 1776, the trail from the south had already been established by Anza's exploration earlier that year. San Jose Avenue follows part of this route. Mission Street is part of the road built across the sand hills between downtown San Francisco and the mission in 1850 and extended southward by San Francisco County in 1851. The original San Jose road also remained open in the same period because it was a boundary between land grants. Its common Spanish designation as "camino real" was retained on title papers and property maps.

At the top of the hill in the Mission Street Gap, now the center of Daly City, Mission Street and San Jose Avenue come together, and the original trail to the presidio branched off to the northwest. South from this point the Spanish trail and the partly planked stage road of the early 1850s ran uphill and east of today's El Camino Real, which now begins in Daly City. Mission Street across the railroad tracks follows the old route, once famous for its taverns and roadhouses. One that remains is Molloy's Springs, or the Old Brooksville Hotel, at 1655 Mission Street in Colma. Built in 1883, it is commemorated by an E Clampus Vitus plaque. Through San Bruno and Millbrae the old Spanish trail and modern El Camino Real run parallel, skirting the edge of the bay marsh.

Just south of present Broadway in Burlingame, the road in Spanish times crossed a narrow neck of land between a natural salt pan and a lake (on present California Drive), and thence went over a grassy knoll to El Camino Real in a northward extension of its line south of Peninsula Avenue. From this point to San Mateo Creek, where a toll bridge was built at the present crossing in 1851, El Camino Real still follows its original route, with a shallow bend around the site of the adobe San Mateo outpost of Mission San Francisco.

At San Mateo the traveler left the summer fogs and entered a country of oak groves and natural clearings, spread between the hills and the sloughs. Somewhere south of here, Captain George Vancouver with his officers and an escort of seven Spanish soldiers stopped for a picnic on November 20, 1792, on their way to Santa Clara.

The great British navigator, the first foreign visitor to San Francisco, was impressed with the scene, particularly "a very pleasant and enchanting lawn, situated among a grove of trees at the foot of a small hill, by which flowed a very fine stream of excellent water. This delightful pasture was nearly inclosed on every side."

Leaving the steep south bank of San Mateo Creek, the road as traveled before the late spring of 1853 bore rapidly to the right of the present route, running nearly as far west as the present Alameda de las Pulgas in order to avoid the adobe soil north of Laurel Creek. South of present Hillsdale was a narrow pass and gap between the hills and marsh at Belmont, then called the Portezuelo de las Pulgas, very near the Old County Road. This road was bypassed when present El Camino Real was built west of the railroad tracks in 1917–18, through Belmont and San Carlos.

At San Carlos the wide oak plain begins. To Vancouver in 1792 it was

> a country I little expected to find in these regions. For about twenty miles it could only be compared to a park, which had originally been planted with the true old English oak; [with] the stately lords of the forest in complete possession of the soil, which was covered with luxuriant herbage, and beautifully diversified with pleasing eminences and valleys; which, with the range of lofty rugged mountains that bounded the prospect, required only to be adorned with the neat habitations of an industrious people, to produce a scene not inferior to the most studied effort of taste in the disposal of grounds.

In the White Oaks district the well-defined Spanish trail turned to the west, keeping in the edge of the trees, and crossed Cordilleras Creek into what is today's Redwood City, just east of Stanford Lane.

Turning sharply to the right to avoid the low-lying adobe lands, the original route (in a deed of 1851 called the Stage Route) went by the foot of Eagle Hill at Jefferson Avenue, thence to the Indian village near Union Cemetery, and diagonally across El Camino and the tracks south of Five Points to Semicircular Road and Fifth Avenue in Redwood City's North Fair Oaks neighborhood. This was the site of Steinberger's Woodlawn roadhouse, which was built early in 1852 and stood for many years.

From this point south the original Spanish highway is now called Middlefield Road. For the first half-mile the slight curve of the old trail is followed exactly by the modern street, but from Marsh Road through Menlo Park to the county line at San Francisquito Creek, the route was straightened by Steinberger's Middle Field Fence, the original trail having wandered slightly to the west in many places. The first bridge was built here in 1851, but it collapsed a few years later and was not replaced until around 1900.

Although Middlefield Road was considered the main highway in Spanish times, this crossing could be used only by horsemen and pedestrians. In 1784, we learn from a letter of Father Palou, high water still stopped communication between San Francisco and San Jose, but by the time of Vancouver's visit in 1792 horsemen could get through by an alternate route. By 1803 there was cart traffic, which followed a well-marked detour crossing San Francisquito Creek farther downstream. This route left Middlefield Road in North Fair Oaks and ran down toward the Bay to the Indian mound at Ninth and Fair Oaks Avenues and thence to Marsh Road. From that point the *camino carretero* is still in use as today's Bay Road, winding gently with the invisible contour of the land through two and a half miles of oaks and laurels. Just short of University Avenue in East Palo Alto the Spanish road bent away to the right, crossed an old channel of the San Francisquito, zigzagged through and around the mosquito-ridden willow swamps on both sides of the road just below the Bayshore Freeway crossing, and rejoined the main trail at the Mesa rancho in Palo Alto.

OLD LAND GRANTS ON THE SAN MATEO COUNTY COAST

The northern boundary line of the county runs through the Mexican grant of Rancho Laguna de la Merced, only a small portion of which extends from San Francisco County into San Mateo County. South of this, on the ocean side of the peninsula, are the lands of eight ranchos, each having one boundary line at the low-tide mark on the beach. The southernmost rancho reaches to the border of Santa Cruz County.

RANCHO SAN PEDRO (PACIFICA)

One of Father Palou's last plans for Mission San Francisco, before his retirement from California in 1784, was the removal of farming operations to a fertile valley on the ocean shore fifteen miles to the southwest, called by him the Cañada de las Almejas ("mussels"), in memory of the shellfish feast held by the Portolá expedition in 1769. The chief of Prúrstak, the largest Indian village, had been baptized in 1783, and a great harvest of souls was to be expected from the coast farther to the south. Accordingly, in 1786, Fathers Cambon and Noriega dedicated a chapel in the valley to Saints Peter and Paul, and work was pushed forward on a quadrangle of buildings with an entrance looking east up the valley. Half or more of the mission's eight hundred or so neophytes were moved to the new establishment, and for some years most of the new converts from the peninsula and down the coast were baptized—and buried—at the chapel, which in time became known simply as San Pedro. A devastating pestilence struck the settlement in the early 1790s. The newcomer's diseases wreaked havoc on the Indians of California, nowhere more murderously than in San Mateo County. It is estimated that there were at least fifteen hundred natives in the county in 1770; by 1860 there were fewer than fifty, most of whom had been brought in from elsewhere to supplement the dwindling labor force.

In 1834, shortly after secularization, Francisco de Haro, military *comandante* of San Francisco, petitioned the Mexican government for a grant of San Francisco Mission lands. The following year he specifically requested San Pedro, including a sketch map that showed the old building "in ruins." One of de Haro's company presented a similar petition the same year, but none of these petitions was granted. In 1836 de Haro's successor in command, Francisco Sánchez, copied his predecessor's map and petition, and in 1839 he was finally given a formal grant of the two leagues of land.

Don Francisco, son of José Antonio Sánchez, who owned Rancho Buriburi, was a native of San Francisco and a highly respected citizen. As a member of the San Francisco Company, he attained the rank of captain and finally that of acting commander. In 1846, when San Francisco was occupied by American forces, he moved to his ranch. In December 1846, annoyed by the depredations of the Americans, Sánchez headed the short-lived revolt in which Alcalde Bartlett of San Francisco was captured and held hostage. The revolt ended in surrender after the battle of Santa Clara. Sánchez lived largely at Mission Dolores until his death in 1862, by which time his country home had fallen into decay. The large two-story Sanchez adobe (SRL 391) now stands refurbished as a San Mateo County historical monument in Pedro Valley, a suburb of Pacifica, one mile east of the coast highway via Linda Mar Boulevard.

Rancho San Pedro, patented in 1858 with 8,926 acres, occupied very nearly the same bounds as the present city of Pacifica, incorporated in 1957; it includes the districts of Edgemar, Pacific Manor, Sharp Park, Vallemar, Rockaway Beach, Pedro Point, and Linda Mar. The Pedro Valley district, though now filled with modern homes, still has a few small houses from the 1850s and 1860s in the side canyons, witnesses to a century of large-scale irrigated truck gardening, an economic mainstay of coastal San Mateo County.

RANCHO EL CORRAL DE TIERRA (MONTARA, MOSS BEACH, PRINCETON, HALF MOON BAY)

This rancho, extending from the south face of San Pedro Mountain to Pilarcitos Creek, was first known as El Pilar or Los Pilares, from the rocks off Pillar Point, and was occupied by the horse and cattle ranches of Mission San Francisco as early as the 1790s. It very nearly became the location of the town of Branciforte, established instead at Santa Cruz in 1797.

Rancho Corral de Tierra contained one and three-quarter leagues, granted in two parts. The northern and larger grant was given in 1839 to Francisco Guerrero Palomares, whose widow, Josefa Haro de Guerrero Denniston, filed her claim in 1852 and received the patent for the land fourteen years later.

Point Montara is on the coast of this grant. Between 1875 and 1900 it was a fog signal station on the heavily traveled southern passage to San Francisco Bay. It became a light station in 1900. In 1928 the light was installed in a thirty-foot tower, seventy feet above the sea. The Point Montara lighthouse grounds were the first to be leased as a youth hostel, in 1980, a successful activity to be found at other lighthouses.

Two miles south from Point Montara is Princeton-by-the-Sea, on Pillar Point Harbor. Schooners once tied up at the pier here to collect produce for the markets of San Francisco. Like other coastal towns, it was said to have had a notorious rum-running career in the days of Prohibition. Today it attracts fishermen and vacationers.

Nearby Miramar began with the building of a wharf at Amesport Landing near the mouth of Arroyo de en Medio, a small stream dividing the property of the two owners of Rancho Corral de Tierra. Warehouses for the shipping of grain from this fertile region were built just south of the mouth of the creek. J. P. Ames, who headed this venture, came west with Stevenson's Regiment at the time of the Mexican War. Honorably discharged at Monterey in 1848, he came north to San Mateo County and became its treasurer in 1862. He represented the county in the state Legislature in 1876–77. Amesport Landing was afterward acquired by the Pacific Mail Steamship Company, which in 1917 sold the old warehouse site to the owner of a small hotel there.

The southern end of Rancho Corral de Tierra, granted to Tiburcio Vásquez in 1839, extended south from Arroyo de en Medio to Arroyo de los Pilarcitos, the latter name also used for the rancho. His claim was filed with the Land Commission in 1853, but the patent was not issued until 1873. The Vásquez adobe home was built on the north bank of Pilarcitos Creek a little west of the Main Street bridge, now at the northern edge of the city of Half Moon Bay. Don Tiburcio's youngest son, Pablo, built a one-story wooden house in 1869. Known today as the Pilarcitos House and still standing at 270 Main Street in Half Moon Bay, it is one of the oldest wooden structures in San Mateo County.

The Main Street bridge in Half Moon Bay, built in 1900, was the first in the county, and indeed one of the first anywhere, made of structurally reinforced concrete. A plaque on the bridge gives some of its history.

Near this bridge, a sign above the gateway of an enclosed cemetery on SR 92, the San Mateo highway, reads "Pilarcitos Cemetery 1820–1923," although the cemetery was actually established in 1857. Many of the graves within this Catholic cemetery are of old Spanishtown settlers. The International Order of Odd Fellows Cemetery, immediately to the east, was established by the IOOF and the Masons in 1856.

RANCHO MIRAMONTES (HALF MOON BAY)

This rancho, known also as San Benito, was granted to Candelario Miramontes by Governor Alvarado in 1841. When the first members of the Miramontes family, the sons Vicente and Rodolfo, took up residence there, grizzly bears and other predators native to the country were still present and proved destructive to the roaming herds of cattle. Miramontes built an adobe near the intersection of Johnston and Mill Streets in Half Moon Bay; it became his daughter's home, where all of her children were born, and survived until the twentieth century.

The Vásquez and Miramontes families were company—and protection—for each other. Around their houses the settlement called Spanishtown grew up. About 1860 the Yankees began to arrive, one of the first being Henry Bidwell, nephew of California pioneer John Bidwell, who ran a blacksmith shop and was the first postmaster. The town was platted in 1863 in the southwest angle formed by the confluence of Arroyo Leon and Pilarcitos Creek. The post office was named Half Moon Bay for the shape of the section of the adjacent coast, and in time replaced Spanishtown as the name of the settlement.

Half Moon Bay today is proud of its well-preserved downtown district. The Estanislao Zaballa house at 326 Main Street dates from 1863. Zaballa, a native of Spain, married Dolores, daughter of Candelario Miramontes, in 1853, and began the San Benito General Store and Sa-

loon. He platted Spanishtown in 1863. The oldest continuously operating place of business in town is Boitano's General Merchandise Store and Saloon at 527 Main Street, which has been in business since 1873. One of the oldest Protestant churches in the county is the handsome Methodist Episcopal church (1872) at the northeast corner of Johnston and Miramontes Streets.

James Johnston was an American pioneer who in 1853 purchased a half-league of land from the southern part of the Miramontes grant, and with his brothers went into cattle raising and farming. His house, begun around 1855, is a prominent saltbox built with mortise and tenon construction and wooden pegs. In its heyday the elegantly furnished house boasted a chapel on the second floor and an enclosed patio. Long abandoned, the house has been restored by a local foundation and is on the National Register of Historic Places. It stands on Higgins Purisima Road east of SR 1 about one-half mile south of Half Moon Bay. Across the road from James's house is the William Johnston house, built by his brother and still in use, although much modified since a second story was added in 1878. The property includes two original barns.

RANCHO CAÑADA VERDE Y ARROYO DE LA PURÍSIMA (PURISIMA AND TUNITAS)

This grant was made provisionally by Governor Alvarado in 1838 to José María Alviso, a military officer in San Jose. The following year Alviso transferred his claim to his brother José Antonio Alviso, who received the final grant from Prefect José Castro. In 1864 José Antonio Alviso received a United States patent for 8,906 acres lying between Purisima and Tunitas Creeks.

The town of Purisima was once flourishing, with a hotel, repair shops for wagons and farm machinery, a school, and a post office. Nothing remains of the town today except the old cemetery, marked by an E Clampus Vitus plaque on Verde Road, one-quarter mile east of its northern intersection with the coast highway.

Just before crossing Tunitas Creek by the long bridge at the southern edge of this rancho, one encounters the road from Kings Mountain, which leads on as a private road toward the beach and the site of Tunitas Glen, the terminal of the defunct Ocean Shore Railroad from San Francisco. Plans had been made by a group of San Franciscans to connect their city and Santa Cruz by train running through this scenic coastal region, but the line never got beyond this point. A stage service completed the journey, and the railroad, which struggled against constant landslides along the coast, was discontinued in 1920.

RANCHO SAN GREGORIO

Rancho San Gregorio, consisting of four square leagues, was granted by Governor Alvarado in 1839 to Antonino Buelna. The rancho included the whole of the lower San Gregorio Creek watershed and extended along the coast from Tunitas Creek to Pomponio Creek. When he received his grant, Don Antonino was in command of an expedition against Indians and foreigners in the San Joaquin Valley.

The settlement of San Gregorio is an old one. Early houses, not much more than shacks, quickly disappeared. When the La Honda road was completed, stores sprang up where the road intersected with the Stage Road paralleling the coast, about three-quarters of a mile east of SR 1 on SR 84 today. The "San Gregorio House," built in 1866, has been a summer resort, a stage stop, a hotel, a saloon, and a gas station. Today it is a private residence. A nearby general store built around 1900 still supplies tourists.

Pomponio Creek is named for Chief Pomponio, who ran away from a mission and was captured by Mexican authorities in Monterey in 1824. His mountain hideout had been at the headwaters of Pomponio Creek, a short stretch of which formed the southern line of Buelna's Rancho San Gregorio.

RANCHO EL PESCADERO, OR SAN ANTONIO (PESCADERO)

Rancho El Pescadero ("the fishery"), or San Antonio, was granted in 1833 by Governor José Figueroa to Juan José Gonzales, mayordomo of Santa Cruz Mission, and was patented to his descendants by the United States government in 1866. It consisted of 3,282 acres in the vicinity of the town of Pescadero on Pescadero Creek.

By 1842 Gonzales was living in a small adobe on the north bank of the creek one block east of the bridge over that stream at the north end of town. The Bartlett V. Wicks family, natives of Maine who came to California in 1859 via Nicaragua, purchased the 157-acre tract upon which this adobe stood in 1860. No vestige of it now remains; its site is at the south end of Goulson Street, formerly Pescadero Street, which was the original Spanish trail to the crossing of the creek.

The first American to take up permanent residence in this area was Alexander Moore, who after traveling

First Congregational Church, Pescadero

across the plains by covered wagon reached California in 1847 with his father and other members of the family. Alexander went to the mines on the Tuolumne River for a while. In 1853, attracted to the Pescadero region by the fertile soil, he put up a large L-shaped house north of Pescadero Creek, using lumber hauled by ox team from Santa Cruz. Two miles north of town, Thomas W. Moore founded the Willowside Farm, and the drive to the house, between gigantic eucalyptus trees, is now part of the public road.

Pescadero is an unusual San Mateo County coastal town in that its historical buildings are all American; indeed, it has been compared to a New England village. One manifestation of this is the white, steepled First Congregational Church (SRL 949) on San Gregorio Street. Now designated the Pescadero Community Church, the building dates from 1867 and is claimed to be "the oldest church building on its original site within the San Mateo–Santa Clara county region." The steeple was added in 1890, and the social hall dates from 1940. Services are still held regularly.

Across the street is the McCormick House, built in the late 1860s by James McCormick in the popular Classical Revival style, and now privately owned. St. Anthony's Catholic Church on North Street is also in the New England style.

RANCHO BÚTANO (SOUTH OF PESCADERO)

Rancho Bútano consisted of one square league lying along the ocean between Butano Creek and Arroyo de los Frijoles ("Bean Hollow"), south of Pescadero. It was given originally to Ramona Sánchez in 1838, confirmed by Governor Micheltorena six years later, and patented to Manuel Rodríguez by the United States government in 1866. The property was held for many years by Loren Coburn, who vainly tried to establish a resort along the coast. His hotel stood until it was demolished in the 1930s. Coburn faced frequent battles with other land-owners and with his own family, and was a leading pro-moter of the Ocean Shore Railroad from San Francisco to Santa Cruz that never was completed. On the coast south of Butano Creek is Pebble Beach, a deposit of varied, water-worn pebbles. They lie several feet deep over an area of approximately two acres; agate chal-cedony, jasper, moonstones, and sardonyx are found among them. Removal of pebbles is illegal today.

East of Rancho Bútano is Butano State Park, con-taining within its 2,100 acres the last small stand of vir-gin timber in this part of the mountains. Extensive log-ging was a principal economic activity here until the mid-twentieth century.

RANCHO PUNTA DE AÑO NUEVO

Rancho Punta de Año Nuevo was a vast tract of 17,753 acres granted in 1842 by Governor Alvarado to Simeón Castro, already the owner of two ranchos in Monterey County. The grant extended from Butano Creek, where an earlier grant was in dispute, to south of Point Año Nuevo. In 1866 the part of the ranch that lay between Butano Creek and Arroyo de los Frijoles was patented to Manuel Rodríguez as Rancho Bútano.

In 1851 Rancho Punta de Año Nuevo was sold to Isaac Graham of Santa Cruz, who leased parts of it. Van Houten, a tenant, built a prefabricated home (shipped around the Horn from the East) on what is now called Whitehouse Creek. Van Houten's white two-story resi-dence was said to be so conspicuous a landmark that mariners sailing north reckoned the distance to San Francisco by sighting it. Eventually hidden from view by a eucalyptus grove, it burned in 1976.

In 1862 Loren Coburn came into possession of the greater part of Simeón Castro's original rancho. In that year he leased it to a group of dairymen; in this group were Horace Gushee, Charles H. Willson, and three members of the Steele family: Edgar, Isaac, and Rensse-

laer. The Steeles were natives of Delaware County, New York, who arrived in California in the mid-1850s. Their first dairy was located north of San Francisco, where they made butter and cheese of superior quality and shipped it to the city. After moving to Rancho Punta de Año Nuevo, they continued the same line of work. A brother of Edgar and Isaac and cousin of Rensselaer was General Frederick Steele of the Union Army in the Civil War. As a donation to the Sanitary Fund (the forerunner of today's American Red Cross), the Steeles made a 3,850-pound cheese for display at the Mechan-ics' Fair in San Francisco. After the fair ended, slices of the cheese were sent to President Lincoln, General Grant, and General Steele, and the remainder sold for one dollar a pound. The project realized some $2,820 for the Sanitary Fund by January 1864.

In 1869 the Steeles purchased over seven thousand acres of the rancho lying south of Gazos Creek and es-tablished a chain of highly successful dairies. Important structures remaining from the dairies include the Cas-cade Rancho House and Dairy Building, the Ramsey-Steele House, the Año Nuevo Rancho House, and the Dickerman Barn. The enterprise is marked (SRL 906) on SR 1, "the Cabrillo Highway," about thirteen miles south of Pescadero and about two miles north of the Santa Cruz county line.

Just north of Gazos Creek is Pigeon Point Light-house, built in 1872. Its height of 115 feet is equaled on the Pacific Coast only by Point Arena Lighthouse in Mendocino County. The name comes from the clipper ship *Carrier Pigeon*, wrecked there on May 6, 1853; hap-pily, the captain and crew survived the ordeal. The worst disaster on the San Mateo County coast occurred here in dense fog in August 1929; at least seventy-seven lives were lost when the steamship *San Juan* collided with another vessel. Pigeon Point Lighthouse (SRL 930), still in operation, now shares its grounds with a youth hos-tel, and is one of the most photographed and painted spots on the California coast.

RANCHO FELIZ AND CRYSTAL SPRINGS

Three of the old land grants later recognized by the United States government lay entirely in the interior of the county, with no border on the coast. They are Ran-chos Feliz, Cañada de Raymundo, and Cañada del Corte de Madera.

The northernmost rancho of this group, Rancho Feliz, was granted in 1844 by Governor Manuel Michel-torena to Domingo Feliz, to whom 4,448 acres were

Pulgas Water Temple

confirmed by United States patent in 1873. Don Domingo built a house situated, according to a grant map of 1856, on the southern edge of his property west of a slough. Near it passed the road leading from San Mateo to the coast, converging near the location of his house with the road leading from Belmont to the coast. Skyline Boulevard coincides with the old San Mateo road where it crosses between Upper and Lower Crystal Springs Lakes on an earthen causeway.

The upper lakes of the San Andreas Valley (which gave its name to the great fault along which the 1906 earthquake occurred) lie on Rancho Feliz. The lakes were made by damming sloughs and lagoons to form reservoirs for the San Francisco water system. They hold the water brought from Hetch Hetchy Reservoir in Yosemite, two hundred miles away. The enormous project of providing water for San Francisco and the Peninsula began around 1900, but not until 1934 was Hetch Hetchy water actually brought to the lakes. At the south end of Upper Crystal Springs Lake is the Pulgas Water Temple, a Roman Renaissance–style structure, located at the outfall of the Hetch Hetchy tunnel. The inscription around the entablature reads: "I will give water in the wilderness and rivers in the desert to give drink to my people" (Isaiah 42:20). The present monument, built in 1938, replaced an earlier, temporary structure built for the ceremonies held in October 1934 when the first flow of Hetch Hetchy water poured into the San Francisco reservoirs. The Pulgas Water Temple is on the west side of Cañada Road, two miles south of its junction with SR 92.

Lower Crystal Springs Lake now covers the site of the settlement of Crystal Springs, near where Colonel Agoston Haraszthy made an experimental planting of European wine grapes in the early 1850s. Haraszthy, a Hungarian nobleman, was a naturalized American cit-

izen before he came to the West Coast and was a member of the state Assembly in the early days of California's statehood. After a test of his twenty-five-acre vineyard had proved that the fruit would not ripen properly in this location, he sold his property and removed the vines to Sonoma County, where soil and climate were more fitted to viticulture. There he established the Buena Vista Vineyard.

RANCHO CAÑADA DE RAYMUNDO (WOODSIDE)

Rancho Cañada de Raymundo was granted by Governor Alvarado in 1840 to John Copinger, "a man of ability and learning," once a British naval officer and later, in California, a lieutenant in charge of the artillery company that had brought about the success of Alvarado's revolution and put the governor in power. The rancho was bounded on the north by Rancho Feliz, on the south (at Arroyo Alambique) by Rancho Corte de Madera, and on the northeast by a line long in dispute with Rancho de las Pulgas.

John Copinger died in 1847, and in 1859 this property of 12,545 acres was patented to his widow, María Luisa (daughter of Rafael Soto), who in 1851 had married Captain John Greer, and to his daughter, Manuela Copinger, who afterward married José Antonio Miramontes and lived in a large house that long stood near present Woodside and Miramontes Roads.

The Mountain Home Ranch, on Portola Road just southeast of the junction with La Honda Road (SR 84), is a part of Rancho Cañada de Raymundo sold by John Copinger to Charles Brown, a Baltimorean who left his whaling vessel in San Francisco in 1833. Brown lived at Sonoma and around San Jose before coming to this region. He built an adobe house here, probably about 1838, and a sawmill in 1849 near Alambique Creek, southwest of the house. A historical marker (SRL 478) at the junction of Woodside and Portola Roads indicates the location of the first sawmill in San Mateo County.

At the time of the American occupation in 1846, there had been a settlement at Woodside for some ten years. As early as 1832, William Smith, an Englishman, came here to saw lumber for barter and sale. Other sawyers followed, and by 1849–50 sawmills were erected in the redwoods. Lumber was supplied to the incoming settlers of Santa Clara Valley and also shipped to San Francisco.

The old Woodside Store (SRL 93), the first store opened between San Francisco and Santa Clara, is the one surviving landmark of pioneer days in Woodside. Now owned by the county of San Mateo, it is open to the public as a museum of the pioneering lumbering days, at 471 Kings Mountain Road.

"Searsville" is commemorated by a marker (SRL 474) at the junction of Portola and Sand Hill Roads. John H. Sears emigrated to San Mateo County from New York via Cape Horn and in 1854 built a house later used as a hotel, known as the Sears House. A town grew up near this house, the location being a convenient stopping place for drivers of mule and ox teams hauling lumber from the mills east of La Honda ridge for loading on schooners at the Embarcadero in Redwood City. The little settlement was the scene of considerable activity on Sundays, when ox pulling, horse racing, and cockfighting were popular amusements. Searsville Lake covers a part of the old town; it now supplies water for the Stanford University campus and is included in the university's Jasper Ridge Biological Preserve.

The La Questa vineyard and house are located off Woodside Road at 240 La Questa Road. A vineyard was established here in the 1880s by Emmett H. Rixford with vines imported from France. The two-story winery was constructed by a Swiss mason of stones dug from the fields when the vineyard was laid out. The winery has been converted now into a private residence.

Filoli (SRL 907), now owned by the National Trust for Historic Preservation, is on the western side of Cañada Road. The great Georgian Revival mansion was designed by Willis Polk for William Bowers Bourn II and occupied by his family in 1917. The Bourn family motto ("Fight, love, live") inspired the name. It later passed into the hands of the William B. Roth family, Mrs. Roth being Lurline Matson of the famed navigation company. Surrounded by beautifully landscaped gardens, Filoli represents the high point of the era in which wealthy San Franciscans owned country estates.

RANCHO CAÑADA DEL CORTE DE MADERA (PORTOLA VALLEY)

This rancho, which lay above the confluence of Los Trancos and San Francisquito Creeks, covered a large tract between the streams. Portola Road runs across it, and Searsville, Coon, and Felt Lakes, which are named for owners of property near them, are within the boundaries of the old rancho.

Governor Figueroa gave one square league of land there to Domingo Peralta and Máximo Martínez in 1833. Peralta, who also had part of Rancho San Ramón

and a share of his father's great San Antonio Rancho across the bay, kept his part of the Corte de Madera grant for only a short time and divided it between his co-grantee, Martínez, and Cipriano Thurn in 1834. In 1879 some 3,566 acres of the rancho were patented to Thurn and Horace W. Carpentier.

More land appears to have been granted to Martínez at later dates, and the United States patent for 22,980 acres, of which a part extended across Los Trancos Creek, was given to him in 1858. His family lived in various houses on the property until 1901.

According to Gudde, Corte de Madera means "place where wood is cut," and in fact the redwoods in this area had been exploited from a very early date by the Pueblo of San José and Mission Santa Clara. In the 1830s a new draying road (arrastradero) was opened to get lumber to the southern markets. Following a trail made by wild cattle through the hills to the southeast, it crossed Los Trancos Creek at the present Arastradero Road bridge. Felix Buelna built a gambling retreat and meeting place for his friends here in the 1850s. In 1868, when a section of the never-completed Menlo Park and Santa Cruz Turnpike was opened, the building at the junction was taken over by an American; it still stands today as a wayside tavern (SRL 825). This place at the corner of Alpine and Arastradero Roads has for several generations been a favorite haunt of Stanford University students.

The name Portola Valley is a local shortening of the name "Portola-Crespi Valley," which a landowner and newspaper editor bestowed on the area from Crystal Springs to Searsville in 1886. The settlement of Portola grew up on land purchased in 1883 by Andrew S. Hallidie, inventor of San Francisco's cable cars. Here he later experimented with another approach by building an aerial tramway suspended from an overhead cable from bottom to top of the mountainside on his property.

Early Catholic residents of Portola Valley found that their first church, a reconditioned dance hall, was inadequate and set out to construct a new one. Many residents participated in the construction in some fashion. The Church of Our Lady of the Wayside (SRL 909) at 930 Portola Road, designed by Timothy L. Pflueger and dedicated in 1912, is a charming fusion of the Georgian and Mission Revival styles of architecture.

RANCHO CAÑADA DE GUADALUPE, LA VISITACIÓN Y RODEO VIEJO (BRISBANE)

Of all the old land grants in the county, those bordering on San Francisco Bay have become the most widely known and most thickly settled. In Hispanic days the area was crossed by El Camino Real, and today US 101 and I-280 lead south from San Francisco through this area.

The northernmost of these ranchos was Rancho Cañada de Guadalupe, la Visitación y Rodeo Viejo, consisting of two square leagues given in 1841 by Governor Alvarado to Jacob P. Leese. The grantee appears frequently in the early history of California because he engaged in commercial ventures in Monterey and in San Francisco and because he married Rosalia, sister of General Mariano Vallejo. Leese's ranch house was in the sheltered and oak-covered corner of the hill now occupied by the city of Brisbane, near Alvarado Street just west of Visitacion Avenue.

When in 1856 San Mateo County was formed by the division of San Francisco County, the dividing line ran through this rancho, placing most of its area in the new county.

RANCHO BURIBURI (SOUTH SAN FRANCISCO, SAN BRUNO, MILLBRAE)

Rancho Buriburi was granted to José Antonio Sánchez by the provincial government in 1835, confirming an earlier, tentative grant of 1827. The patent for the land was given to Sánchez's heirs in 1872 for 14,639 acres extending from the salt marshes on the bay to the Spring Valley lakes and including the modern cities of South San Francisco, San Bruno, Millbrae, and the northern part of Burlingame.

This land had hitherto been a government cattle ranch; in 1797 Governor Borica had sent 265 head of cattle to it to provide meat for the Presidio of San Francisco. Immediately upon the formal grant of the Buriburi tract in 1835 the Sánchez family constructed two identical adobe houses in the area now occupied by the city of Millbrae; the houses stood until 1871.

South San Francisco's first landholder was Charles Lux, partner of Henry Miller in the biggest cattle business in America, Miller and Lux. In 1856 Lux purchased 1,500 acres from the Sánchez family in 1856 and put up a stately home between what are now Oak and Chestnut Avenues. The land was used to hold cattle for grazing before they went to market, a forerunner of the "feedlot" common today. In time the meat-packing industry developed in the region and other industries followed, until South San Francisco, incorporated as a city in 1908, became known as "The Industrial City." This wording is on a prominent hill-

City Hall, South San Francisco

side sign, now on the National Register of Historic Sites. A notable feature is its city hall, a copy of Independence Hall in Philadelphia, constructed in the early 1920s. The South San Francisco Historical Society Museum is at the Magnolia [Senior] Center at 601 Grand Avenue, in a renovated school building. An interesting addition to the city is the Basque Cultural Center at 599 Railroad Avenue, serving a vigorous community with branches all over the state, and open to the public.

Darius Ogden ("D. O.") Mills, a New Yorker, was one of the country's most important bankers. In 1860 he became owner of the 1,100-acre headquarters tract of this rancho, and in 1866 built a three-story, towered wooden mansion that he named Millbrae. In 1872, by employing a large group of Chinese laborers to drain marshland, Mills reclaimed many acres that he used as pasturage for his fine dairy herd. After his death, his daughter, then the widow of Whitelaw Reid, former United States ambassador to the Court of St. James, erected the Mills Memorial Hospital in San Mateo as a tribute to her father.

During World War II the old Mills Mansion was used as a merchant marine convalescent home. In the 1950s the entire estate was razed for apartments and a shopping center; some doors, windows, and furnishings from the mansion were saved and incorporated into a building housing a restaurant on the south edge of St. Helena in Napa County. The mansion and grounds were located about where the block of apartments west of Ogden Drive now stands, and the entrance way is represented by Murchison Drive. The Millbrae railroad station, in Colonial Revival style, is listed on the National Register of Historic Places.

RANCHO SAN MATEO (BURLINGAME, HILLSBOROUGH)

Rancho San Mateo was given in 1846 by Governor Pío Pico to his secretary, Cayetano Arenas, as a reward for military service. The two leagues (confirmed for 6,438 acres) were taken from an old rancho of Mission Dolores and were the last parcel of land in San Mateo County to be granted by the Mexican government. The rancho lay along San Francisco Bay between Rancho Buriburi on the north and San Mateo Creek on the south and was bounded on the west by Rancho Feliz along the course of San Andreas Creek, which is now covered by Crystal Springs Lakes.

In November 1827, when some of the officers of the British ship *Blossom* passed through this region on their way to Monterey, they were impressed by its strong resemblance to

> a nobleman's park; herds of cattle and horses were grazing upon the rich pasture, and numerous fallow deer, startled at the approach of strangers, bounded off to seek protection among the hills. The resemblance, however, could not be traced farther. Instead of a noble mansion in character with so fine a country, the party arrived at a miserable hut dwelling before the door of which a number of half naked Indians were basking in the sun.

The litter scattered about the building "sadly disgraced the parklike scenery. This spot is named San Matheo, and belongs to the mission."

What the British sailors saw was the San Mateo outpost (SRL 393) of Mission San Francisco de Asís. There were two long adobe structures, located end to end on the north bank of San Mateo Creek, with one end in what is now the intersection of Baywood Avenue and El Camino Real. The ruined state of the outpost is mentioned in *Eldorado* by Bayard Taylor, who saw it in 1849. The earthquake of 1868 completely wrecked the walls, and in 1870 all that was left of them was leveled. Some of the tiles from the roof were preserved and, with tile from Mission San Antonio in Monterey County, were used to build the roof of the railroad station at Burlingame (SRL 846). This station, at California Drive and Burlingame Avenue, is an early example of Mission Revival architecture, and has served the community since it opened in 1894.

In 1848 this rancho passed into the hands of William Davis Merry Howard, a Bostonian who had first come to California as cabin boy of a hide-drogher (a ship that transported hides along the coast). Later, with Henry Mellus, he purchased the abandoned office buildings of the Hudson's Bay Company in San Francisco, where they carried on mercantile pursuits. Wishing to have property in whatever city might prove to be the metropolis of the new state, Howard bought large tracts of land in the towns of San Francisco, Sacramento, and Vallejo. Because of his philanthropic and commercial activities, Howard Street in San Francisco was named in his honor, and a memorial to him stands in St. Matthew's Episcopal Church in San Mateo, at the southern edge of his vast holdings. The church was organized in 1865 after preliminary services had been held in various locations, and was constructed of stone taken from a quarry on the Howard property on Crystal Springs Road. Situated at Baldwin Avenue and El Camino Real, the English Gothic church of today stands on the site of the 1865 structure, a victim of the 1906 earthquake. San Francisco architect Willis Polk designed the 1909 replacement, incorporating a small portion of the original building.

The city of San Mateo began with Nicholas de Peyster's roadhouse, situated in the old mission adobe in 1849 but moved the following year across the creek to a tall wooden structure called the San Mateo House. It stood until 1964, serving as a nurses' residence for the adjacent Mills Memorial Hospital.

In 1863, after the railroad had been built down the peninsula from San Francisco, a town was platted by C. B. Polhemus, and the San Mateo station became the northern terminus of the San Mateo, Pescadero, and Santa Cruz Stage Company lines owned by Taft and Garretson. Outlying places thus afforded communication with the railroad were Crystal Springs, San Feliz, Byrnes's Store, Eureka Gardens, Spanishtown, Purisima, Lobitos, San Gregorio, Pescadero, Pigeon Point, and, in Santa Cruz County, Seaside, Davenport, and Santa Cruz.

The town was eventually hedged around on three sides by large properties: that of W. D. M. Howard, who had purchased Rancho San Mateo on the north; that of Frederick Macondray, one of the first great merchants of San Francisco, who chose land just south of San Mateo Creek for a country home in 1854; and that of Alvinza Hayward, retired mine operator and financier, on the southeast.

The Macondray home in time became the property of John Parrott, identified with shipping and financial interests along the Pacific Coast. He developed the home and gave it the name Baywood; after its destruction in 1927 the site became the residential subdivision called Baywood. Hayward's home, afterward a hotel, stood near the tall palms on what is now Hayward Avenue.

Burlingame is named for Anson Burlingame, onetime U. S. minister to China and a purchaser of part of the Hayward property. The nearby community of Hillsborough, noted for its beautiful estates, has two mansions of particular historical interest. Willis Polk designed an Italian-style mansion in 1917 for Templeton Crocker that was one of the last great buildings of the Peninsula. It is now the Crystal Springs School at 400 Uplands Drive.

At 565 Remillard Road is Carolands (SRL 886), a huge French Renaissance–style mansion inspired by the Château of Vaux-le-Vicomte and designed by the French firm of E. Saint-Saëns. The name comes from its builder, Francis Carolan, whose wife, Harriet Pullman, heiress to the Pullman railroad car fortune, was determined to have a house that outshone all other California residences. It was purchased by Lillian Remillard Dandini in 1950, whose family ran a major California brick-making operation and indeed provided bricks for the original mansion. The countess, as she was known after her marriage to an Italian nobleman, died in 1973, leaving the place to the city of Hillsborough, but the city could not afford the upkeep, and for years the house was vacant and vandalized. It was finally purchased in 1998, but the future of the five and one-half acres of land and house is still uncertain.

RANCHO DE LAS PULGAS (SAN MATEO, BELMONT, SAN CARLOS, REDWOOD CITY, ATHERTON, MENLO PARK)

The Argüellos took a leading role in Spanish California, and the history of Rancho de las Pulgas is traced through the history of the children and grandchildren of this pioneer family.

José Darío Argüello arrived at San Gabriel with his bride in 1781. They had traveled overland from Mexico in the company that Rivera had formed for the Santa Barbara presidio, which was soon to be established. In June 1787 Argüello was promoted to lieutenant in the San Francisco Company, where he served as *comandante* until March 1791 and again for a ten-year period beginning in 1796. He held a similar position in Santa Barbara in 1814 when, at the death of Governor Arrillaga, he was made acting governor of Alta California. He continued to live at Santa Barbara during the year that he held the two offices simultaneously. Receiving a

commission as governor of Baja California in October 1815, he traveled overland with his wife and some of his children; although he would have liked to return to Alta California, he never did. His wife, Ignacia, niece of Lieutenant José Joaquín Moraga, first *comandante* of San Francisco, made both arduous journeys with him in those days when riding a horse or traveling in a creaking carreta were the only alternatives to walking.

The nine children of Don José Darío and Doña Ignacia Argüello were all born in California, and all were educated at home. The eldest son, José Ignacio Máximo, was sent to Mexico to be trained for the priesthood and in later years came back to California to officiate on special occasions. Gervasio, of some military importance, married Encarnación Bernal during the year that his father was acting governor in Santa Barbara and spent his last years in Mexico. Concepción, whose story is told in the chapter on San Francisco County, accompanied her parents to Baja California during the time she was awaiting word from her long-absent lover, Count Nikolai Rezanov. She stayed for a time before returning to Alta California to spend the rest of her life.

Santiago, one year younger than his sister Concepción and a cadet at the San Francisco Presidio when Rezanov made the acquaintance of the family, married Pilar, daughter of Francisco Ortega of Santa Barbara, when he was very young and became the father of twenty-two children. He became grantee of several tracts of land, held many important military positions, and left an honorable record when he died in 1862 at his Tijuana Rancho (San Diego County) at the age of seventy-one. The most prominent among the children of Don José Darío was Luís Antonio Argüello, born in San Francisco in 1784. Having been elected governor of California in 1822, a position he held until 1825, he was the first native-born governor of the territory. His was a controversy-filled administration and he did not win the wide approval that his father had enjoyed, but life was not easy for a Mexican governor in Alta California.

Two tracts of land appear to have been granted to Don José Darío Argüello before the year 1800. One, called "El Pilar," was, according to Hittell, an indefinite tract on the coast between Point San Pedro and Point Año Nuevo, and the grant was never confirmed. The other, known at the time as "Cachanígtac" but afterward called "Las Pulgas" (the fleas), contained about twelve square leagues and was situated on San Francisco Bay between San Mateo Creek on the north and San Francisquito Creek on the south. The western boundary line of this tract was the cause of much litigation. The Pulgas ranch house seems to have been a crude building, not an adobe, which stood on a little bend of Pulgas Creek on the south edge of present San Carlos Avenue in San Carlos.

This rancho consisted of very rich and accessible land, and the vague description of its western boundary, "back to the sierra or range of mountains," caused misunderstandings and disputes. The matter was finally settled in 1856 when a patent for 32,240 acres was issued to Doña María Argüello (widow of Don Luís Antonio), her two sons, and an attorney, Simón Monserrate Mezes, who had been given a part of the land in return for his services in defending the title against squatters. About this time Mezes built a frame house at present Cedar Street and Magnolia Avenue in San Carlos.

Since the 1850s the vast grant has been cut into many portions of varying sizes, and the land that comprised this rancho is now densely populated. El Camino Real, on whose borders the cities of San Mateo, Belmont, San Carlos, Redwood City, Atherton, and Menlo Park have clustered, runs through the grant from San Mateo Creek on the north to San Francisquito Creek on the south, and beyond into Santa Clara County. The close proximity of the cities makes the road for the entire distance like a city street. To carry the congested traffic, the parallel Bayshore Freeway (US 101) was constructed, and now the cities have stretched some of their streets over to the freeway and beyond. To the west, the Junipero Serra Freeway (I-280), extending from Daly City to San Jose, is another important artery.

The city of San Mateo has the largest population of the county's cities, and has to a great extent been taken over by new buildings. A block on Main Street between Second and Third Avenues has some buildings from about a century ago.

A bridge crossing the lower part of the Bay extends from San Mateo to Hayward in Alameda County. The San Mateo Bridge—twelve miles long, seven over water—was the longest highway bridge in the world when it opened in 1929. A new highway bridge replaced the old one in 1970. At the lower end of the rancho, a railroad bridge and the Dumbarton Toll Bridge cross the Bay from East Palo Alto to Newark. The Dumbarton Bridge, the first to span the Bay, opened in 1927; it too has been replaced by a more recent structure.

South of these bridges, at the very southeastern corner of the grant, the town of Ravenswood was platted. The John Beal Steinberger property at this point was purchased in 1852 by I. C. Woods, Rufus Rowe, D. H. Haskell, John K. Hackett, and C. D. Judah, who laid out the town. Promoters hoped that the Central Pacific Railroad would choose this spot for the end of a bridge across the Bay. When that plan did not materialize, the town was abandoned, and the temporary structures that had been put up soon disappeared. The site of the old Ravenswood wharf is known as Cooley's Landing. The Ravenswood area is now East Palo Alto, but the old name survives in the local elementary school district and in the Ravenswood Open Space Preserve, along the shore of the Bay.

BELMONT AND SAN CARLOS

The first permanent settler at present Belmont was Charles Aubrey Angelo, an Englishman, who in 1850 opened a stage station called the Angelo House on a spot now 1,200 feet south from Ralston Avenue between the railroad tracks and Old County Road. The town that grew up, which became the first county seat of San Mateo County in 1856, centered about the Ralston Avenue–Old County Road intersection in its early years. A store begun by Matthew J. O'Neill and Walter A. Emmett in 1880 still stands on the northwest corner of the intersection. Here, as elsewhere throughout the Peninsula, older buildings by the score have been pulled down to make room for newer and more commodious structures.

West of the town lies the Cañada del Diablo, chosen by S. M. Mezes, one of the patentees of the Pulgas rancho, for his home. There, too, lived Leonetto Cipriani, Mezes's one-time law partner, in a small villa set on the hillside. Cipriani returned to his native Italy in the excitement of the Risorgimento in the early 1860s, and William Chapman Ralston bought the villa and acreage. Ralston, a native of Ohio, had already gained experience in the shipping world before his arrival in San Francisco in 1854, where he soon became a powerful financier. He maintained a city as well as a country home, upon which he spent lavishly. From the modest villa of Count Cipriani he evolved a residence of great magnificence. With his wife, Elizabeth, he became "the perfect host," giving delightful weekend parties, banquets, and balls. From his stone-built, mahogany-stalled stables, he was able to provide mounts for a score of guests.

For the illumination of his country seat he built costly gas works that also benefited the town of Belmont; for his own use he built a wharf on the bay shore and generously shared it with the public. After his death by drowning in August 1875, the marvelously developed estate was taken over by his former business associate, William Sharon, of Comstock Lode fame. Sharon built a great dam and reservoir in the hills to provide irrigation for the plantings that have now grown to park-like proportions.

Following its occupancy by Sharon, the house at Belmont was used for a private school kept by the widow of Alpheus Bull, a business associate of both Ralston and Sharon. Between 1900 and 1921, the house was the Gardner Sanitarium.

In 1923 the place was taken over by the Sisters of Notre Dame, who removed to it their convent and college established in San Jose in 1851. The Ralston mansion is now Ralston Hall (SRL 856), restored somewhat to the style of the 1870s. The Cipriani villa is identifiable as one wing of the house, which is on the register of National Historic Landmarks. The building is part of the College of Notre Dame and the upper floors are used as administrative offices. The lower floor has facilities for public functions, concerts, and meetings.

Although San Carlos was the site of the original Pulgas ranch, the town dates only from 1887 and its name from the beginning of the following year; it is said to be called after the first ship to enter San Francisco Bay, the *San Carlos* (1775), which in turn had been named as a patriotic compliment to King Carlos III of Spain. In 1886 S. M. Mezes and others laid out the road called Alameda de las Pulgas, thereby preserving the original name of the area. The principal landmark of San Carlos is the railroad station, built in 1888 in an ornamental style of sandstone blocks and somewhat resembling the Stanford University architecture of the same period and material. Indeed, Italian stonemasons imported to build the Stanford quadrangle also worked on this building.

The Museum of San Carlos History is at 533 Laurel Street. A newer facility is the Hiller Aviation Museum at 601 Skyway Road. The Hiller firm was a pioneer in helicopters, and the museum has good displays on aircraft going back to 1908.

EMBARCADERO DE LAS PULGAS, REDWOOD CITY

A little creek, running through Rancho de las Pulgas where Redwood City, the county seat, now stands and emptying into a slough or arm of the bay, formed a natural shipping point or embarcadero.

Lumbering became an important industry wherever the redwoods grew, and there were many of these trees in the mountains within a few miles of this place. In 1850 the shipment of lumber from the Woodside and Searsville mills began, and the Embarcadero became a busy wharf. Several schooners were launched there that year. Wagon making and blacksmithing were important adjuncts to the business of hauling the product of the mills to the Embarcadero and were early established there. This was the nucleus around which the present Redwood City developed. Redwood Creek flows through the city today, in many places through underground pipes, and Redwood Slough is filled in.

William Carey Jones, who had come to the West Coast in 1849 as a special government agent to investigate the condition of land titles in California, acquired over two thousand acres near Redwood City from the Pulgas Ranch. It extended from Five Points to Whipple Avenue and from El Camino Real to the brow of the hill. This property was put up for sheriff's sale early in 1858, when it was purchased by Horace Hawes. He was a native of New York who had been named by President Polk to be American consul for the Society Islands and other South Sea islands in 1847. By an unanticipated routing of the ship on which he took passage, he arrived in San Francisco, where he remained and became prefect. He resided in San Francisco and at Redwood Farm, his country home, until his death in 1870. Hawes was a staunch supporter of the Union side during the Civil War. The western part of Redwood City stands on this property. If the original plans of the owner had been carried through, a seat of learning called "Mount Eagle University" would have been located in the area. On Woodside Road in this part of Redwood City is the Union Cemetery (SRL 816), which was created and named in 1859, reflecting, two years before the Civil War broke out, the patriotic sentiments of the community.

The first Protestant church in the county was organized in Redwood City in 1862. Land was purchased at the present corner of Middlefield Road and Jefferson Avenue for a building for the First Congregational Church, which had been meeting in the courthouse for some months.

Downtown Redwood City contains several interesting old buildings fairly close to one another. The oldest building in town, the Offerman House at 1018 Main Street, was built in 1857 and is now a café. The Lathrop House at 627 Hamilton Street is a handsome, restored two-story structure, whose establishment in 1863 is commemorated by a plaque placed by the Native Daughters of the Golden West. An interesting commercial structure is the old Bank of San Mateo County building from 1900, at the corner of Broadway and Main Street.

Dominating the Redwood City skyline is the impressive San Mateo County courthouse. This is the fourth courthouse in the county's history, and an unusual example of Roman-Renaissance architectural style. Designed in 1903, the building had been accepted by the board of supervisors but not yet occupied when the 1906 earthquake struck. The building was severely damaged, but the 116-foot-high dome and its massive panels of stained glass came through the earthquake unharmed. In 1910 the board of supervisors finally held its first meeting in the new courthouse. The courthouse, at Broadway and Hamilton, added a large annex in 1939, where much of the county's business is transacted. The "Old" (1906-10) Court House now houses the San Mateo County Museum; the address is 777 Hamilton Avenue.

MENLO PARK AND ATHERTON

The adjoining areas of Menlo Park and Atherton lie near the southern part of the county along El Camino Real. Their common boundaries are so irregular that it is difficult to distinguish the territory of the earlier-named Menlo Park from its newer neighbor.

Dennis J. Oliver and his brother-in-law, D. C. McGlynn, became owners of a 1,700-acre tract on the Pulgas rancho and in the 1850s erected a gate with a wooden arch across its top. This was at the corner of the present Middle Avenue and El Camino Real. The arch bore the inscription "Menlo Park" in memory of "the most beautiful spot in the world"—their former home in Menlough, County Galway, Ireland. This gate became weatherworn, but it was preserved while Camp Fremont, used for assembling troops during World War I, was in the area. The arch was destroyed in an automobile accident in 1922. The Camp Fremont buildings were gradually pulled down after the war, with the exception of one building designed by the noted California architect Julia Morgan. The building was the YWCA Hostess House at the camp during the war and was later moved across the county line to Palo Alto to a site near the intersection of University Avenue and El Camino Real (SRL 895) for use as a community center and veterans building. After significant restoration in the 1970s, it now houses a restaurant.

Upon the building of the San Francisco–San Jose Railroad down the Peninsula in 1863, a station called Menlo Park was placed a short distance from this old gate. The Victorian "gingerbread" station (SRL 955) built in 1867 still stands, now converted to other uses. Men

Church of the Nativity, Menlo Park

of wealth, many of them San Francisco businessmen, chose this locality for the luxurious country homes that they built on ample estates at convenient driving distances from the railroad station. A town of small houses, hotels, and stores grew up near the station, and in 1873 the first church in the town was organized by a group of Presbyterian residents. In the following year a house of worship was built on land donated for that purpose and in it Protestant families of the town and the surrounding countryside attended services. This frame structure was located on Santa Cruz Avenue a little west of El Camino Real. The Roman Catholic Church of the Nativity, built in the same period, still stands on Oak Grove Avenue east of El Camino.

Not far from the station a fine residence was built by Milton S. Latham, an Ohioan who had arrived in California in 1850 and had purchased land from John R. Doyle in 1871. He eventually bought several other small tracts adjoining his original purchase. He was elected governor of California in 1859, only to renounce that honor later in the same year to fill the unexpired term of United States senator David C. Broderick, who had been slain in a duel that took place within the county. Latham entertained extensively in this country home.

The house, with its stately pillars, costly interior, and elaborate fountains placed in well-landscaped grounds among large native oaks, became the property of Mary Hopkins, the widow of Mark Hopkins, who had arrived from New York in 1849 and was one of the "Big Four" who put together the Central Pacific Railroad. After her remarriage in 1888, the great house passed to their adopted son, Timothy, who followed in the footsteps of Mark Hopkins by becoming treasurer of the Central Pacific Railroad Company. The mansion was badly damaged in the earthquake of 1906, and eventually it was pulled down, having stood for decades at the end of a once well-kept drive far back in the grounds entered at the keeper's gate on Ravenswood Avenue. The Latham Gate House still stands at 555 Ravenswood, and is now occupied by the offices of community organizations as part of the Menlo Park Civic Center.

Besides the wealthy residents who came to the region of Menlo Park for rest and recreation on their large estates there were permanent residents who worked there. One such family was established by John and Margaret Murray, who came around the Horn from New York in 1854. They purchased various lands within the confines of the present county. From Menlo Park they shipped milk to San Francisco by stage, and there twin sons were born to them. In later years Margaret divided twenty-eight acres of land that she held on San Francisquito Creek among her four children. One son, John Jarvis, was given the part nearest the creek and on it built a house and barn around 1880. In 1930 the land was acquired from James, son of John Jarvis, by the Allied Arts Guild of California. On these three acres are ateliers, shops, and a restaurant; the proceeds of the latter help support the Lucile Salter Packard Children's Hospital at Stanford. The old Murray barn is part of this attractive philanthropic complex at Arbor Road and Creek Drive.

Atherton, incorporated in 1923, extends in its longest direction from Bay Road between Ringwood Avenue and Marsh Road, across Middlefield Road, the railroad, and El Camino Real, and to a little distance west of the Alameda de las Pulgas. Within this area are many large modern homes and the sites of older ones no longer standing.

Faxon Dean Atherton, originally from Massachusetts, first visited California in 1836 while a resident of Chile and a member of a firm engaged in the hide-and-tallow trade. In 1860 he acquired a tract of over four hundred acres, once owned by James King of William, and built a country mansion among the native oaks growing there. He named his estate "Valparaiso

Park," from the city in Chile where his wife had been born and where he had spent his early manhood. Life in this house was depicted by his daughter-in-law Gertrude Atherton, in her *Adventures of a Novelist*, written of the period when the country was sparsely settled and quiet afternoons on a comfortable veranda had few interruptions.

After the Atherton family left, the place was used as a school for boys by Ira G. Hoyt, a former state superintendent of public instruction, and during the occupancy of this school the mansion was destroyed by fire. The location, near the intersection of Elena and Isabella Avenues (names of two of the Atherton daughters), is now owned by the Menlo Circus Club, which was organized primarily for the purpose of raising funds for the Stanford Home for Convalescent Children. Valparaiso Avenue, not far off, carries the name of the old house, and the name of the former Fair Oaks station where a post office was established in 1867 has been replaced by the name Atherton.

John T. Doyle, a "scholar of rare culture and refinement" and one of the foremost lawyers of his day, in 1856 purchased land in the vicinity from Horace P. Jones and gradually added to the acreage until he owned a large tract. One of his accomplishments was the final disentangling of the affairs of the missions at the request of Archbishop Alemany. General William T. Sherman was one of the frequent honored visitors at the Doyle home, a palatial frame house. Although the old house no longer stands, the tall palms of the drive leading to its site still border Toyon Road off Ringwood Avenue. Not far from the Doyle house was the Joseph A. Donohoe residence on Middlefield Road, now the location of Menlo-Atherton High School.

Another man who had one of the early houses in the Menlo Park–Atherton vicinity was Charles N. Felton, who entertained there extensively. Originally from New York, he became subtreasurer at San Francisco and also served in the United States Senate in 1891–93, completing the term of George Hearst. He built his house in 1870 and lived in it until his death in 1913. The mansion is no longer standing, but the property, near Encinal Avenue and the railroad tracks, is now a residential subdivision called "Felton Gables."

James Clair Flood, who arrived in San Francisco in 1849 and became one of the "Bonanza Kings" of the Comstock Lode, bought a tract of land along Middlefield Road in 1876 and two years later began the construction of a great white mansion, Linden Towers. It was placed well back from the road and surrounded by lawn and fine trees. Eventually it passed to his son James L. Flood, who purchased neighboring land as well and enclosed the estate by placing a brick wall along the entire frontage on Middlefield Road. James L. Flood died in 1928 and the house was torn down in 1934; the brick wall still stands, now bordering a residential subdivision.

Until 1956 the oldest building in the Menlo Park–Atherton area was a unique structure that stood near the corner of Ringwood and Colby Avenues, probably the only surviving example in California of an early Spanish type of construction, the *encajonada* or "boxed-house." The walls were made of rammed earth columns tamped down inside a movable frame, in this case a lattice of redwood laths, rather than the usual wattle covering. It was probably built in the Mexican period to house herdsmen of the Rancho de las Pulgas. There is evidence that it was constructed before 1846; its redwood laths, therefore, must have been hand-sawed in the saw pits of Woodside.

After standing for over a century, the strange adobe found itself confronted with bulldozers clearing the land for a subdivision. The owner, John Wickett, a man with more than a passing interest in California history, could not bring himself to destroy it, and local authorities would not permit him to move the "substandard structure" to another site in the same area. He therefore had it raised on jacks and transported many miles over a winding mountain road to property he owned near Skyline Boulevard—no mean accomplishment, when it is remembered that what were moved were unframed, unsupported, foundationless walls held together only by their own compaction. The adobe stands on private grounds off Skyline Boulevard across from the Skeggs Point observation area.

LA HONDA

John H. Sears moved from Searsville in the winter of 1861–62 and settled seventeen miles from Redwood City in the mountains. The place eventually acquired the name La Honda, from the creek, Arroyo Honda ("deep"), so named for its deep and redwood-filled canyon. About 1877 Sears began the construction of a store, and in 1878 he became low bidder to build the present winding Old La Honda Road, the first road through the isolated region. The Sears store (SRL 343) was often called the "Bandit-Built Store," because the owner employed in its construction two newcomers to the vicinity who, after their departure, were believed to

have been the Younger brothers, Jim and Bob, outlaws from the Midwest, where the pair were jailed soon after they left California. The old store stood at the northwest corner of La Honda and Sears Ranch Roads until it was torn down early in 1960.

THE BRODERICK-TERRY DUEL

An aftermath of the bitter political campaign of 1859 in California was a duel that reverberated around the nation because of the prominence of the participants and the death of one. Both men were pioneers of 1849 and members of the same political party, although they espoused different factions.

David C. Broderick, born in Ireland in 1820, had lived in New York as a boy and had come from there to California, where he became a power in the Democratic Party. He was acting lieutenant governor in 1851 and became United States senator in 1857.

David C. Terry, born in Kentucky in 1823, had seen military service in Texas and Mexico before coming to the West Coast in 1849. He became chief justice of the California Supreme Court and was active in politics, first as a Whig, then as a leader in the American or Know-Nothing Party. In the campaign of 1859 he allied himself with the pro-Southern "Chivalry" faction of the Democratic party. Incensed by certain statements made by Senator Broderick of the opposing "Tammany" faction in his campaign speeches, Terry challenged him to a duel at a site outside the jurisdiction of San Francisco County.

A plaque in the parking lot at 1100 Lake Merced Boulevard in Daly City (SRL 19) is about one-quarter of a mile from the actual place of combat, which was located and marked in 1917 by the Landmarks Committee of the Native Sons of the Golden West. The site is in a small ravine just off a park that can be reached from the aforementioned parking lot or from El Portal Way between Cliffside and Lakeview drives. Two granite shafts were later placed where the principals stood, marked with their names. On the eminence nearby, where spectators witnessed the duel, there is a bronze tablet on a foundation of granite, stating the historic facts of the event. The text is as follows:

> U.S. Senator, David C. Broderick, and Chief Justice of the Supreme Court, David S. Terry, met here in the early morning of September 13, 1859, Senator Broderick receiving a mortal wound. This was the last of the great duels fought in California. With the exception of the

Burr-Hamilton affair, no duel has taken place in the United States where the principals were as well known or occupied as high official positions.

Broderick was carried back to San Francisco, where he died three days later. The story circulated that his pistol had misfired and that Terry had coolly shot him. Public opinion in California, disgusted by the rift in the dominant Democratic Party, began to favor the newly formed Republican Party. Abraham Lincoln, a Republican, was elected to the presidency in 1860 with the help of California's four electoral votes, and Leland Stanford, also a Republican, was elected governor of California the following year.

Terry, a combative man, soon joined the Confederate Army, where he became a brigadier general. After the war he spent some time in Mexico. He later returned to California, settling in Stockton, where his fiery temper embroiled him in many an altercation. In 1889 he was shot to death in the railway station at Lathrop (San Joaquin County) by United States Marshal David Neagle, bodyguard of United States Supreme Court Justice Stephen J. Field, whom he had attacked.

Santa Barbara County

Santa Barbara County took its name from the Santa Barbara Channel, so called by Vizcaíno when his ship entered it on December 4, 1602, the feast day of Saint Barbara. This was one of the original twenty-seven counties of the state, and the city of Santa Barbara has been the county seat from the beginning.

The first explorer to record a visit to the area was Juan Rodríguez Cabrillo, in the fall of 1542, who noted the numerous native peoples (the Chumash) and their extraordinary skill in building boats.

CHUMASH PAINTED CAVE
STATE HISTORIC PARK

In a canyon near the summit of San Marcos Pass, some 2,600 feet high and about twelve miles northwest of the city of Santa Barbara, is a remarkable cave filled with Chumash pictographs. This site is on Painted Cave Road, about two miles north of its junction with SR 154, the San Marcos Pass Road. Conventionalized pictures of human figures, trees, snakelike creatures, and the sun (including what may be a depiction of a solar eclipse) and circular designs and crosses, done in red, white, yellow, and black, cover the interior of the cavern. Modern research has come up with some tentative conclusions about these unusual paintings: they were made by some of the numerous Chumash family of Indians; they were probably shamanistic and used for rituals of some kind; and they were shown only to the initiates of a cult, for no more than two people can fit into the cave at the same time. The cave has been protected from defacement and injury by a locked gate.

In the early 1970s the land around the Painted Cave was purchased by a citizens' committee and the private, nonprofit California State Parks Foundation, which presented it to the state of California. Today, Chumash Painted Cave State Historic Park can be visited by permit from the local state park headquarters.

BURTON MOUND AND THE PUERTO DE SANTA BARBARA

Burton Mound (SRL 306), located within circular Burton Drive between Natoma Avenue and Mason Street in Santa Barbara, is today merely a gentle rise surrounded by city streets and dwellings, about a block and a half from Santa Barbara Harbor. It is thought that this mound is the site of the Chumash village of Syujtun, recorded by Cabrillo in 1542. In 1769 Portolá and Father Crespí also noted the existence of this Chumash village. Excavations conducted here by the Museum of the American Indian, Heye Foundation, of New York City in 1923 confirmed the antiquity of the site.

The old Puerto de Santa Barbara, an early landing place for the mission and presidio, was located at the foot of today's Chapala Street west of the mouth of Mission Creek and due east of and comprising Burton Mound. This land was owned by Mission Santa Barbara and was called El Rancho de la Playa ("the rancho of the beach"). After secularization it became the property of the Mexican government, which granted it to James (Santiago) Burke who, in turn, sold it to Joseph Chapman, the young New Englander who had escaped from Bouchard's pirate ship in 1818. Chapman, it is said, built a small adobe house on the mound, later conveying the land to Benjamin Foxen.

The large adobe that stood on the mound for over seventy years, long the most conspicuous landmark on the Santa Barbara waterfront, is thought to have been built by Thomas Robins. For about ten years, during the 1840s, it was the home of Captain George Nidever, who planted trees and gardens and added two outbuildings to the adobe house. The next owner, Santa Barbara attorney Augustus F. Hinchman, sold the property in 1860 to Lewis T. Burton. Burton had come to California with the Wolfskill party in 1831. He became a wealthy merchant and in 1839 married María Antonia Carrillo, daughter of Carlos Carrillo. Burton lived in the home until his death in 1879, by which time Santa Barbara had become famous as a resort. The Seaside Hotel Association acquired Burton's property with the intention of building a hotel on the site. Not until early in the next century, however, was the Potter (later the Ambassador) Hotel built, and beautifully landscaped gardens soon covered the historic Indian mound. The

hotel burned in 1921, and archaeological investigations were then started.

CARPINTERIA

On the east bank of Carpinteria Creek, about halfway between US 101 and the beach, is the site of an Indian shell mound. This was the location of the Chumash village of Mishopshnow (SRL 535), discovered by the Cabrillo expedition in 1542. One-half mile east of the mouth of the creek were asphalt pits, now excavated. The tar exuding from the banks along the shore was used by the Chumash people for caulking boats and lining baskets and vessels used for carrying liquids. Father Crespí's diary of the Portolá expedition in 1769 wrote: "Not very far from the town we saw some springs of asphaltum. These Indians have many canoes, and at that time were constructing one, for which reason the soldiers named the town Carpinteria [carpenter shop] but I baptized it with the name of San Roque."

Excavations have revealed the presence not only of human inhabitants over long periods of time, but also of prehistoric animals similar to those taken from the famous La Brea Pits in Los Angeles. At the far end of Carpinteria Beach State Park is the city Tar Pits Park, where in the early days of Santa Barbara County wharves were built at this spot and the asphalt was taken out for shipment to other parts of California.

The Carpinteria Valley Museum at 956 Maple Avenue has displays of artifacts both from the Chumash and more recent times.

THE SANTA BARBARA CHANNEL ISLANDS

Four islands lie in the Santa Barbara Channel off the coast of Santa Barbara County. San Miguel Island has long been thought to be the burial place of Juan Rodríguez Cabrillo, discoverer of Alta California. In 1542, Cabrillo's ships, the *San Salvador* and the *Victoria*, lay anchored for eight days in a bay at San Miguel awaiting the abatement of the autumn storms that delayed their passage north. During this time Cabrillo suffered a fall, breaking his arm near the shoulder or fracturing a shinbone, depending on which account one follows.

Despite his injury, which did not heal and gradually became infected, Cabrillo continued his voyage north, probably as far as the Sonoma County coast, where storms forced his ships to turn back south. Although tradition holds that he died and was buried on San Miguel on January 3, 1543, historian Harry Kelsey has argued that his final resting place was on Santa Catalina Island, in the southern Channel Islands group. A bronze tablet mounted on a granite boulder was placed in honor of Cabrillo by the Daughters of the American Revolution in 1919, in the palm garden along the waterfront on East Cabrillo Boulevard between Santa Barbara and Punta Gorda Streets.

Most of the Channel Islands are now part of Channel Islands National Park. Three of the islands within the jurisdiction of Santa Barbara County—San Miguel, Santa Barbara, and Santa Cruz—are also archaeological districts noted on the National Register of Historic Places.

POINT CONCEPTION

Point Conception was discovered by Cabrillo on October 18, 1542, to which he gave the name Cabo de Galera, because he thought the bluff resembled a seagoing galley. Many later explorers sighted the point, which marks a change in the direction of the California coastline. Vizcaíno passed and named the point on December 8, 1602, the feast day of Purisima Concepción ("immaculate conception"); the local post office uses the original spelling, but the anglicized one is now used to identify the cape.

The Point Conception Light Station, one of the most remote along the Pacific Coast, was built in 1855. The station was too high on the bluff for its light to pierce the coastal fog, and it was abandoned for a lower site in 1882, which is still in operation.

DISASTERS OF THE SANTA BARBARA COAST

Point Arguello, a rocky headland twenty miles southwest of Lompoc, forms, with Point Conception, the corner where the California coastline turns from a generally north-south outline to a line running east and west. Its historic interest is largely associated with the many ships that have been wrecked there.

The first of these was probably the *Edith*, wrecked in 1849. The story is told that the sailors aboard the *Edith*, being anxious to join the Gold Rush, deliberately ran the ship up on the beach, where it was broken up by the waves. Some of the crew and passengers stayed for a short time at Rancho Nipomo (in San Luis Obispo County), where the hospitable ranchero, Captain William Dana, gave them horses and money so they could continue to the mines. Afterward the ship was salvaged by Dana, the materials being used on his rancho. The smokestack over the forge in the blacksmith shop was part of the wreckage put to good use by this thrifty Bostonian. The side-wheel steamer *Yankee Blade* was wrecked in 1854, allegedly carrying $153,000 in gold bullion, none of which seems to have been recovered.

The greatest disaster along the California coast occurred here on September 8, 1923, when seven U.S. Navy destroyers, southward bound in a thick night fog, piled on the rocks at Point Honda, three miles north, one after the other. Twenty-two men were lost, and every ship was damaged beyond repair. The landward site can be visited on tours from Vandenberg Air Force Base, which extends along the forty-mile coastal stretch from Point Sal State Beach to Jalama State Beach.

Since 1923, the toll taken by the rocks from the procession of ships in these heavily traveled waters includes the passenger steamer *Harvard*, which went aground about one and one-half miles north of Point Arguello on May 30, 1931; the freighter *Iowan* in 1941; and the Greek freighter *Ionnes Kulkundous* in 1949. The first lighthouse at Point Arguello appeared fairly late, compared to others along the Pacific Coast; not until 1901 was a light station erected here. Another replaced it in 1934, and that in turn has been replaced by a fully automatic beacon.

PORTOLÁ'S TRAIL

In the summer of 1769, an expedition commanded by Gaspar de Portolá followed the coast of Alta California from San Diego to the bay of Monterey. Entering what is now Santa Barbara County just above Rincon Point on August 17, they passed the village already described as Carpinteria, and the next day reached a very large Chumash settlement, where downtown Santa Barbara now stands, and pitched camp there. Proceeding up the coast along the Santa Barbara Channel, the party passed many villages. The Chumash fishermen's boats were greatly admired.

The party's journey north took them to what are now Goleta, Dos Pueblos Canyon, Tajiguas Creek, Gaviota, Wild Horse Canyon by Point Arguello, Cañada Honda, and on August 30 the mouth of the Santa Ynez River at Surf. The next day camp was made near San Antonio Creek on what is now Vandenberg Air Force Base, and on September 1 the party traveled to Guadalupe Lake, beyond which lay today's San Luis Obispo County. Portolá's expedition returned south later in the year, mostly likely through Santa Barbara County by the same route they took northward.

Juan Bautista de Anza in 1774 followed a well-trodden path from San Gabriel to Monterey, broken first by Gaspar de Portolá and followed later a half-dozen times by Pedro Fages and also by Father Junipero Serra on his way from Monterey to Mexico in 1772. On his hurried trip in the spring of 1774, Anza made only three camps in Santa Barbara County: west of Goleta, April 12; east of Rocky Point, April 13; and on the south bank of the Santa Ynez River near its mouth, April 14. On April 15 Anza rode all the way from the Santa Ynez River to Mission San Luis Obispo, a distance of over 50 miles. On his return from Monterey, he camped on the north bank of the Santa Ynez River, April 26. On the 27th he met Father Serra on his way back from Mexico City. At the friar's urging, Anza recounted the story of his overland journey, and camped with him that night somewhere east of Point Conception and west of Goleta. On the 28th Anza continued, camping that night at Dos Pueblos Canyon.

The San Francisco colonists led by Anza in 1776 made camp at the following sites: Rincon Creek, west of Rincon Point, on February 24; near Carpinteria Landing at a Chumash village, February 25; west of Goleta, February 26; El Cojo Canyon, east of Point Conception, February 27; near Surf, at the mouth of the Santa Ynez River, February 28; near the mouth of San Antonio Creek, February 29. A tablet in honor of Anza has been placed in the courthouse grounds at Santa Barbara.

EL PRESIDIO DE SANTA BARBARA
STATE HISTORIC PARK

Founded on April 21, 1782, the Santa Barbara Royal Presidio was the last in a chain of four military fortresses built by Spain along the coast of Alta California; the others were at San Diego, Monterey, and San Francisco. The dedication was made by Father Junipero Serra in the presence of Governor Felipe de Neve and Lieutenant José Francisco Ortega and his 55 soldiers.

El Presidio de Santa Barbara State Historic Park (SRL 636) encompasses the original presidio site. It is located in downtown Santa Barbara at the intersection of Santa Barbara and Canon Perdido Streets. Two bronze markers in the sidewalk, placed by the Native Sons of the Golden West, indicate where the lines of the old presidio quadrangle crossed the streets. (Canon Perdido, "lost cannon," derived its name from an inci-

Presidio, Lieutenant's Quarters and Soldier's Quarters, Santa Barbara

dent that occurred during the American military occupation of Santa Barbara. In the spring of 1848, a six-pound brass gun from a wrecked American ship disappeared and was presumed to have been stolen. The military governor imposed a $500 fine upon the townspeople, to their outrage. Ten years later, a storm uncovered the cannon on a beach.)

Lieutenant Ortega, the first *comandante* of the presidio, directed construction of the temporary fortifications and living quarters for the first settlers, the fifty-five soldiers and their families. Construction of the permanent adobe presidio structure was directed by his successor, Lieutenant Felipe de Goycoechea, who served from 1784 to 1804. The buildings of the presidio formed a quadrangle enclosing a central parade ground, surrounded by an outer defense wall.

Two adobes of the original presidio quadrangle have survived, and work has begun on the reconstruction of the entire presidio. One of the two surviving adobes is known as El Cuartel ("the soldiers' quarters"), located at 122 East Canon Perdido Street. El Cuartel is the oldest building in Santa Barbara, and the second oldest in California (the Serra Chapel at Mission San Juan Capistrano is the oldest). El Cuartel houses a museum. The other surviving structure, the Canedo adobe, stands across the street at 123 East Canon Perdido. The reconstructed padre's quarters and the *Comandancia*, the commander's residence, adjoin the Canedo adobe, both of which have museum exhibits. The largest building of the quadrangle, the reconstructed presidio chapel, is adjacent to the padre's quarters.

El Presidio de Santa Barbara State Historic Park is operated and is being developed by the Santa Barbara Trust for Historic Preservation under an agreement with the state Department of Parks and Recreation.

Mission Santa Barbara (SRL 309) was not founded until four years after the establishment of the presidio. Father Serra had selected the site, and after his death in 1784, the work of building the mission was carried on by his successor, Father Fermín Francisco de Lasuén. Father Lasuén performed the ceremonies of consecration on December 4, 1786, the feast day of St. Barbara, and held a second ceremony upon the arrival of Governor Fages twelve days later.

The building of the first temporary chapel and adjoining dwellings and storehouses was begun the following year. Gradually the establishment grew in size and prosperity until, in 1807, there were over 1,700 neophytes living in the Indian village of 250 adobe huts that surrounded the mission.

In 1789 a new church of adobe roofed with tile replaced the temporary structure. In 1793 this church was replaced by a larger one, which was finished in 1794. This, in turn, was superseded by a more magnificent structure, the earthquake of 1812 having damaged the former building. The new structure, built on the same site, was dedicated in 1820. The massive walls, six feet thick, the stone steps and tile floors, two of the six chapels built into the solid walls, which are of double thickness at these points, all make it the most solidly built of any of the missions. The 1925 earthquake, however, necessitated a thorough rebuilding of the church. Another rebuilding of the towers and facade was done in 1950–53.

In the beautiful old tree-shaded cemetery are the graves of 4,000 Chumash and 500 white people. One grave is said to be that of Juana María, a Chumash woman reputed to have lived alone for eighteen years on San Nicolas Island in the Santa Barbara Channel. Juana María was found and brought to Santa Barbara by Captain George Nidever in 1853. She died in 1854, and it is thought that she was buried in the mission garden, although no record of the burial has been found in the mission archives, nor is there any document bearing testimony of her baptism and the bestowal of her Christian name after her rescue. Her story was told by Captain Nidever, who was greatly respected in the community where he lived for fifty years, and rests on his testimony. The Daughters of the American Revolution placed a bronze tablet at what is thought to be her grave site in 1928.

In front of the church is a stone fountain, and near it is a long stone trough, once used for washing clothes.

These were constructed in 1808. About 500 feet north of the mission church, in what is now Mission Historical Park of the city of Santa Barbara, is a square stone reservoir, constructed in 1806, part of the irrigation system to collect water for the mission orchards and gardens. This reservoir, still in good condition, forms part of the city's water system. Across Pedregoso Creek, about a mile and a half north of the mission in what is now called Mission Canyon, a dam was constructed in 1807. It may be seen in the Santa Barbara Botanic Garden.

Mission Santa Barbara has never suffered from the neglect and decay of the other missions after secularization. In 1842 the bishop's residence was changed from San Diego to Santa Barbara, and in 1853 a petition to Rome resulted in making the mission a hospice, the beginning of an apostolic college for the education of Franciscan students for the priesthood. St. Anthony's Seminary was completed in 1901 and adjoins the mission. Since its founding, Santa Barbara Mission has been used continuously for religious observances. It is the only one of all the missions that has remained in the hands of the Franciscan fathers since its founding, and it is one of four now under their administration. For its historical and architectural importance to the United States, Mission Santa Barbara has been registered as a National Historic Landmark by the Department of the Interior. The archive-library, added to the west wing, houses original documents of mission days and old and rare books about California's Hispanic period. The facility is open to qualified scholars and writers.

MISSION LA PURÍSIMA CONCEPCIÓN

Father Fermín Francisco de Lasuén founded the mission on December 8, 1787, the Feast of the Immaculate Conception of Mary. This, the eleventh in the chain of missions founded by the Franciscans in California, was in what is now the city of Lompoc. By 1812 an adobe structure roofed with tile was in place, but in that year a disastrous earthquake completely destroyed the building; a few ruins are left (SRL 928), at the corner of T Street and Locust Avenue. A new church, about four miles northeast of the first site, was promptly built by Father Mariano Payéras. The father died in 1823; in the next year, an Indian uprising spread from Mission Santa Inés down the Santa Ynez River valley. La Purísima was captured and held for several weeks, until soldiers from Monterey finally dispersed the Indians.

At one time La Purísima was very prosperous, but

the neglect that followed secularization and confiscation and the inroads of weather caused its steady disintegration. Finally it became a crumbling ruin, its roof gone, its walls fallen and half choked with wild mustard and elderberry bushes. Only a stately row of white pillars testified to its past. Such was its condition when, in the mid-1930s, the mission was restored and rebuilt by the Civilian Conservation Corps and the National Park Service. Now it is La Purisima Mission State Historic Park (SRL 340), one mile north of SR 246 and two miles northeast of Lompoc. It is one of two missions owned by the state, the other being San Francisco Solano at Sonoma. La Purísima, in its lovely rural setting, is the only one of California's twenty-one missions to be restored as a complete mission establishment. The state property consists of almost 1,000 acres, an area large enough to take in the water system in Purisima Valley. A self-guided round-trip hike of one mile enables the visitor to gain a complete picture of mission life at its height. Besides the main buildings—church, shops and quarters, and padres' residence—restoration has included numerous outbuildings, gardens, a soap factory, a tannery, and reservoirs. This is also a National Historic Landmark. A visit to Mission La Purísima Concepción is an educational experience unparalleled in California.

The Lompoc Museum is at 200 South H Street, in the 1910 Carnegie Library Building. Among its features are extensive Chumash artifacts and a collection of modern aerospace exhibits. The Lompoc Valley Historical Museum at 207 North L Street is in the Fabing-McKay-Spanne House from 1875, the first two-story house built in the Lompoc Valley.

MISSION SANTA INÉS

Mission Santa Inés was founded in order to reach the Chumash living inland. Father Estévan Tápis made a survey of the country in 1798, and from his report a site for the proposed mission was chosen in the beautiful valley of Calahuasa, forty-five miles northwest of Santa Barbara via Gaviota Pass. Thirteen Chumash rancherias in the vicinity, with an estimated population of over 1,100, gave promise of many converts.

After the death of Father Lasuén in 1803, Father Tápis succeeded him as padre presidente, and in 1804 he founded the new church at Santa Inés. A simple chapel was erected at first; this was replaced, after the earthquake of 1812, by a building of brick and adobe, roofed and floored with tile. This structure, completed

Mission Santa Inés, Solvang

in 1817, still stands in an open area with a background of rugged, purple mountains. There is an especially lovely garden with a fountain. Near the mission are the ruins of an old gristmill, built by Joseph Chapman in 1820.

The Indian uprising of 1824 started at Mission Santa Inés, as a result of their harsh treatment by the soldiers. The Indians revolted, burned a large number of the mission's buildings, but left the church unharmed, and escaped to La Purísima, where they were finally overcome by soldiers from Monterey.

After the secularization of the missions in the 1830s, Pope Gregory XVI took steps to establish California as a diocese with its own bishop. In 1840 one of the Franciscan friars, Francisco García Diego y Moreno, was appointed and consecrated Bishop of Both Californias, his territory including Baja California in Mexico as well as the present state of California. Bishop Diego established the first seminary for the training of priests in California at Mission Santa Inés in 1844. The seminaries of the several Roman Catholic dioceses of California can all trace their beginnings to Santa Inés.

Santa Inés suffered materially from the effects of secularization, as did nearly all of the missions. It was in a sad state of ruin until early in the twentieth century, when restoration was begun. The renovated mission retains much of its old charm: Indian frescoes and hand-carved doors, harmonious arcades and flower-filled patio, and a beautiful campanile, its plain wall pierced, as at Mission San Gabriel, by niches for the bells that ring for prayer.

Mission Santa Inés is located just south of SR 246 at the east end of the Danish community of Solvang. It is now administered by the Capuchin Fathers, a branch of the Franciscan order.

Santa Barbara, like Monterey, is a city of beautiful old adobe homes. Through the efforts of the Santa Barbara Trust for Historic Preservation and the Santa Barbara Historical Society, steps have been taken by the city to ensure the preservation of its architectural heritage. After a state law was passed in 1959 enabling cities to take such steps, an "El Pueblo Viejo" ordinance was enacted by Santa Barbara in 1960, setting aside the sixteen blocks bounded by State, Figueroa, Laguna, and Ortega Streets as a historic area. Within these boundaries no building of historical or architectural value is to be destroyed or altered, and no new construction is to be undertaken that does not conform to the style of architecture of the old adobes.

Casa de la Guerra (SRL 307) is, after the mission, perhaps the most interesting remaining landmark of the old Spanish days in Santa Barbara. It was built with Chumash labor by José Antonio Julián de la Guerra y Noriega during the years 1819–27. One of the adobe bricks in the front corridor still bears the date 1826 plainly marked on it.

Don José Antonio, a native of Spain, came from Mexico to California as a lieutenant in 1806. There he married María Antonia Juliana Carrillo, and in 1815 he was made *comandante* of the Presidio of Santa Barbara, an office he held until 1842. De la Guerra was a man of strong character and ability. His home was the center of social life in Santa Barbara and a stopping place for many distinguished visitors. Among others, Richard Henry Dana, author of *Two Years Before the Mast*, visited the adobe mansion in 1834 and again in 1859.

El Paseo, initially called "The Street in Spain," was designed by James Osborne Craig and built in 1923. The walkway passes by the De La Guerra adobe and the two adjacent Gaspar Ireña adobes (1849 and 1858). Taking its style and decorative motifs from Spanish architecture, El Paseo greatly influenced the rebuilding of Santa Barbara after the earthquake of June 29, 1925.

Across from the adobes is De La Guerra Plaza, one of the city's original parks, dedicated in 1855. Santa Barbara's first city hall was built in the center of the plaza in 1874 and demolished in 1924; the two tall palm trees that still stand there were located at the rear of the building. The current city hall, designed in Spanish Colonial Revival style, was built in 1923. Complementing it is the *News-Press* Building, from 1922.

The Hill-Carrillo adobe (SRL 721) at 11 East Carrillo Street was built about 1825 by Daniel Hill, a native of Massachusetts who came to California in 1823 and married Rafaela Ortega. In this house, in 1833, was born the first child of American parents in California, Isobel, daughter of Thomas Oliver Larkin, the first American consul in California, and Rachel Holmes Larkin. It became the home of Captain John Wilson and Doña Ramona Carrillo de Wilson and, later, of Guillermo Carrillo. The building was purchased in 1928 by philanthropist Max C. Fleischmann, and was given to the Santa Barbara Foundation to be preserved as one of the historic buildings of Santa Barbara.

The Covarrubias adobe (SRL 308), located at 715 Santa Barbara Street, was built in 1817 by Domingo Carrillo, whose daughter María married José María Covarrubias in 1838. This house is a fine example of California architecture. Owing to the fact that sunshine was permitted to enter the rooms through skylights, the building is in a remarkable state of preservation. Adjacent to this adobe is the so-called "Historic" (or Malo) adobe. It is supposed to have been built about 1836 near the present corner of State and Carrillo Streets for Concepción Pico de Carrillo, sister of Governor Pío Pico. In 1903 it was taken down brick by brick and reconstructed at Carrillo and Anacapa Streets. In 1922 it was again moved and rebuilt in the same fashion at its present location by John R. Southworth. In 1938 the Covarrubias and "Historic" adobes were acquired by Los Rancheros Visitadores, an equestrian organization. They are now the property of the Santa Barbara Historical Society, whose museum—of adobe, in authentic style—was built on the adjoining land at 136 De la Guerra Street in 1964.

The Gonzales-Ramirez adobe at 835 Laguna Street was built in 1825 and occupied by members of the Gonzales family for many years afterward. This building is a National Historic Landmark. The Rochin adobe at 820 Santa Barbara Street, built in 1856, is sheathed in shiplap siding and is still occupied by a descendant of the original owner. The Santiago de la Guerra adobe at 110 East De la Guerra Street (reputedly built about 1812 but now much altered) housed the lieutenant of a Spanish-speaking cavalry unit that was formed to join the Union forces in the Civil War. The Lugo adobe, built about 1830, was remodeled in 1922 into the Meridian Studios at 114 East De la Guerra Street. The little Pico adobe, built about 1820, was built for the family of a retired soldier, Santiago Pico, founder of the Pico family; still occupied, it stands at 920 Anacapa Street behind the Cota-Knox home at 914–916 Anacapa. The latter is a brick structure built in 1871. The Miranda adobe, built about

1840, and the old guardhouse have been incorporated into a restaurant and office complex at De la Guerra Street and Presidio Avenue. The two Cordero adobes stand at 304 East Carrillo Street and, at 906 Garden Street, behind a store. The two-story Botiller-Grand adobe is at 1023 Bath Street; the family retained ownership of the house for well over a century after it was built, about 1844. The Arellanes-Kirk adobe, built about 1860, is the most recent; it stands at 421 East Figueroa Street and has always been in residential use.

OTHER BUILDINGS OF SANTA BARBARA

Santa Barbara has many historic buildings that come from what might be called the "post-adobe" period. At the corner of State and De la Guerra Streets a bronze tablet was placed by the Native Sons of the Golden West in 1929, commemorating the first raising of the American flag in Santa Barbara. The Lobero Theatre, at 33 East Canon Perdido Street, stands on the site (SRL 361) of the old adobe theater and opera house operated by José Lobero, who in 1873 enlarged a wood and adobe school to make Santa Barbara's first theater. This was torn down in 1923 when renovation proved to be impossible. The present structure opened in August 1924, and Santa Barbara's annual Old Spanish Days Fiesta dates from the celebration of this opening. The Fox-Arlington Theater at 1317 State Street is on the site of the Arlington Hotel (1875) and a later hotel (1910) that was wrecked in the 1925 earthquake. When Fox West Coast Theaters planned to build a motion-picture theater on this site, the architect Joseph Plunkett conceived the building in the Spanish Colonial Revival style, and it was so created in 1930–31. In 1976 it became the Arlington Center for the Performing Arts.

The culmination of Santa Barbara's architectural renaissance is the county courthouse on the 1100 block of Anacapa Street, designed by William Mooser and dedicated on August 14, 1929. County oil revenues covered the $1.5 million cost of the building. It is one of the most beautiful adaptations of Spanish-California architecture in the entire state and one of the notable public buildings of the United States. It is listed on the National Register of Historic Places.

The Upham Hotel at 1404 De La Vina Street is the oldest Santa Barbara hotel in continuous operation. The name comes from Cyrus Upham, who owned and operated the hotel from 1898 through 1911. The two-story redwood structure, surmounted by a cupola, was built in 1871 in the Italianate style. Another Italianate

Lobero Theatre, Santa Barbara

structure stands at 925 De La Vina Street, the former St. Vincent's School, later the Knights of Columbus Hall. Built in 1874, it was completely renovated as an office building in 1983.

A small architectural-historical area centers on the Trussell-Winchester adobe (SRL 559) at 412 West Montecito Street. Captain Horatio Gates Trussell, a native of Maine, built it in 1854, shortly after his arrival in California. Into it he incorporated timbers from the SS *Winfield Scott*, wrecked in 1853 on Anacapa Island. The adobe was later acquired by the Winchester and Hastings families. It is an important example of the transition from adobe to frame construction in the early American period. The Judge Charles Fernald house, one of the best examples of the Victorian period in Santa Barbara, was moved to its present location at 414 West Montecito in 1959. Built in 1862, the house was lived in by the Fernald family until 1958, and like the Trussell-Winchester adobe, it is open to the public.

The Hunt-Stamback house is an Italianate structure that has been moved to three different locations since its erection in 1873 at State and Anacapa Streets. Its present location is at 821 Coronel Street. Peter J. Barber, who built many houses in Santa Barbara in the late nineteenth century, was the architect. "Crocker Row" is a series of five Mission Revival houses built for William H. Crocker of San Francisco in 1894–95 as exclusive rentals for winter visitors. Located at 2010–2050 Garden Street, each house is set back slightly from the next in order to provide ocean views.

A second historic district has been created by the city of Santa Barbara—the Brinkerhoff Avenue Landmark District. This block-long street and its environs were developed in the late nineteenth and early twentieth centuries. It was named for a local physician, Dr. Samuel Brinkerhoff, who owned the block but did not

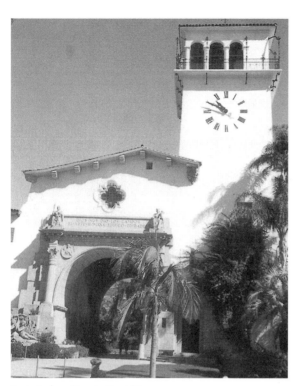

Santa Barbara County Court House

subdivide it. The district's earliest existing houses were built in 1887–88.

Stearns Wharf, extending from the foot of State Street, was built by John Stearn in 1872. It served the town as a port for cargo, passenger, and fishing ships. It was damaged by wind and waves and a waterspout, but was always rebuilt, until it was destroyed by fire in 1973; the pier was later rebuilt and opened to the public.

Nearby, just off US 101 at Chapala and Montecito Streets, is the gigantic Moreton Bay Fig Tree, one of the sights of the city. It arrived as a seedling from its native Australia and, in the belief that it was a rubber tree, was planted by a local family on this spot in 1877. It has become so enormous that is said that 10,000 people can stand in its shade at noon.

MONTECITO

Montecito, Santa Barbara's neighbor to the east, is a community of beautiful homes. Here, too, are relics of adobe days. The Pedro Masini house, the oldest two-story adobe in the Santa Barbara area, was reputedly built in 1820. Still occupied, it stands at the junction of Sheffield Drive, Ortega Hill Road, and North Jameson Lane, just north of US 101. The Hosmer adobe, at 461 Ysidro Road, is still occupied by members of the Hosmer family. The same road leads to the San Ysidro

Guest Ranch at 900 San Ysidro Lane, where one room of the old Casa San Ysidro (1829) still stands, incorporated into a building of this handsome resort hotel.

GOLETA

West of Santa Barbara is Goleta, location of the University of California at Santa Barbara. A campus landmark is 175-foot high Storke Tower, built in 1969 in honor of Thomas M. Storke, journalist, publisher and founder of the *Santa Barbara News-Press*. The tower contains a 61-bell carillon, said to be the most complete instrument of its kind in the United States.

An adobe built in the 1840s by Daniel Hill, who also built the Carrillo adobe in the city, is a private residence at 35 La Patera Lane in Goleta. Enlarged and modernized by James G. Williams early in the twentieth century, it is covered with wooden siding and not easily recognized as an adobe.

The La Patera ranch consisted of 1,043 acres in the eastern portion of the Dos Pueblos grant. In 1872 William Whitney Stow of San Francisco purchased this land; his 21-year-old son Sherman moved to La Patera immediately afterward and started planning his house. The house, begun the following year, was the home of Sherman and his heirs for the next ninety-five years. W. W. Stow became interested in the cultivation of lemons, and in 1874 3,000 lemon trees were planted on the ranch, probably the first commercial lemon planting in California. These early plantings were at the site of the present Crestview Oaks subdivision. In 1967, after many years of family use, the Stow House was given to the county of Santa Barbara. Since then the house has been looked after and opened to the public by the Goleta Valley Historical Society, by arrangement with the county. Stow House is located at 304 Los Carneros Road in Goleta.

On the grounds, in an old barn-warehouse, is the Horace A. Sexton Memorial Museum, named in honor of a native of the area who was a major contributor to the growth of the Goleta Valley Historical Society. The museum, which has many outdoor displays, focuses on farm equipment and early relics of the automobile in Santa Barbara County.

Adjacent to the Stow House is Los Carneros County Park, with the South Coast Railroad Museum, housed in a 1901 Southern Pacific depot relocated at this site in 1981.

The Ellwood Oil Field lies along the coast near Goleta. Early in World War II, on the night of February 23, 1942, the Japanese submarine *I-17* came to the surface

Stow House, Goleta

and shelled the oil field for twenty minutes without any significant American reprisal. There were no casualties, and the damage was minor; one oil well was hit and a pier was partially destroyed. Two large gasoline storage tanks, the primary target of the enemy, were untouched. The Tokyo press, however, reported that Santa Barbara had been devastated. Lumber from the damaged pier was subsequently sold as salvage and was later incorporated into a building on the north side of US 101.

EL REFUGIO AND GAVIOTA

About twenty miles west of the city of Santa Barbara, the Cañada del Refugio once marked the eastern boundary of the great Rancho Nuestra Señora del Refugio, which ran westward along the sea for twenty-five miles to the Cañada del Cojo. Here in the Cañada del Refugio the Ortega family lived for many years. José Francisco de Ortega, who had accompanied Portolá on his expedition to Monterey in 1769 and had assisted in the founding of the Presidio of Santa Barbara in 1782, was rewarded for his services with permission to occupy this land in 1794. After his death, it was granted to his son José María Ortega.

The coast of El Refugio has some romantic history, for here on the beach Don José had his embarcadero, where he engaged in genteel smuggling, and here the pirate Hippolyte Bouchard landed in 1818 and sacked and burned the adobe house that stood at the canyon's entrance facing the sea and El Camino Real. Here, too, the Yankee Joseph Chapman deserted from the pirate ship. He later married into the Ortega family and proved to be a very useful citizen.

Don José built his second adobe about three miles back in the Cañada del Refugio. It and the old vineyard, once famous in California, have disappeared. The road that winds through the canyon and up the mountain,

almost inaccessible toward the summit, leads down into the valley of Santa Ynez by way of Refugio Pass. Former president Ronald Reagan's Rancho del Cielo lies to the west of this road in a secluded portion of the Santa Ynez Mountains.

West of El Refugio two Ortega adobes still stand, one of them completely rebuilt. Two and a half miles west of Cañada del Refugio and Refugio Beach State Park a private road turns north from US 101 and turns north two miles up Tajiguas Creek to one of California's most beautiful adobe homes. It was built perhaps as early as 1800 and enlarged and improved in 1879. It later fell into ruin, and in 1924 was taken down and rebuilt by Kirk B. Johnson, with George Washington Smith as architect. It has since passed into other hands and has undergone further renovation.

The other Ortega adobe was built by Pedro and José Ortega about 1850. It is situated in Arroyo Hondo, about four miles east of Gaviota. Clarence Cullimore in his *Santa Barbara Adobes* (1948) wrote that when this adobe is seen from above, it is "a rare gem, in a perfect setting."

GAVIOTA AND SAN MARCOS PASSES

San Marcos Pass, about fifteen miles northwest of Santa Barbara, was one of the passes over which the early explorers and mission fathers crossed from the coast to the inland valleys. Gaviota Pass, the northernmost of these passes, is twenty-eight miles farther up the coast west of Santa Barbara.

North of Gaviota, US 101 crosses Gaviota Pass (SRL 248). This has long been the main route between the Santa Barbara coast and the inland Santa Ynez Valley. In 1846, on his way from Monterey to reinforce Commodore Stockton in Los Angeles in the first year of the war with Mexico, John C. Frémont eluded the Californian soldiers who were waiting to ambush his battalion in Gaviota Pass by taking the route over the San Marcos grade instead. The latter route was less known and presented many difficulties. Guided by Benjamin Foxen, the Americans succeeded in reaching the top after swinging artillery across the intervening chasms on ropes, a struggle that lasted all that Christmas Day. From the summit, Foxen's eldest son William led the invaders down the mountain and into Santa Barbara.

FOXEN CANYON

Located in Foxen Canyon about fifteen miles northwest of Los Olivos and twenty-five miles southeast of

Santa Maria is the site of the old Foxen home. Rancho Tinaquiac (a Chumash word, its meaning unclear), on which it was located, comprised two leagues of land and was granted in 1837 and 1842 to William Benjamin Foxen, an Englishman who had settled in California in 1828. He was baptized a Catholic as William Domingo Foxen, married Eduarda Osuna, and became a citizen of Mexico. The Californians often referred to him as Don Julián.

Here in December 1846 Frémont arrived with his force of 700 men on their way to Santa Barbara and Los Angeles. Frémont had been told by William Dana at Rancho Nipomo (San Luis Obispo County), where he had camped on December 18, that the Californians were waiting for him in ambush at Gaviota Pass. It was the main passage through the mountains, a narrow defile between towering walls of sandstone from which huge boulders could be rolled down upon a passing enemy. In an account published in 1931, William Dana's son Juan Francisco said that Frémont was advised to consult Foxen, a man familiar with the country to the south where an alternate and more difficult pass might be crossed. According to other accounts, it was Foxen himself who warned Frémont of the ambush.

Proceeding to Rancho Tinaquiac, Frémont camped on December 20 in the woods near the Foxen home. There, according to Dana's account, he sought the aid of Foxen, who, though "torn between loyalty to the Californians and the tie of English blood which bound him to the invaders," agreed and led the battalion on its difficult route over San Marcos Pass and into Santa Barbara, unharmed. Foxen for some time afterward suffered at the hands of his resentful Californian neighbors, who on more than one occasion set fire to his rancho buildings.

Foxen is commemorated by a memorial chapel (SRL 877) built in 1875 by his daughter and son-in-law, Ramona and Frederick Wickenden, at the head of Foxen Canyon, four miles east of Sisquoc at the junction of Foxen Canyon Road and Tepusquet Road. Foxen lies buried under a marble column in the family cemetery nearby.

From the chapel and the cemetery it is less than two miles southeast on Foxen Canyon Road to the Frederick Wickenden adobe. Wickenden married Ramona Foxen in 1860 and two years later built the central portion of the structure of adobe, making frame additions through the years. The house, now headquarters for Rancho Tinaquiac, served also as a store, post office, and stage station. Wickenden died in 1918 at the age of

ninety-three. Another mile and a half along the road brings one to the approximate site of Frémont's camp on the Foxen ranch, which has been marked by the Pioneers Section of the Minerva Literary Club of Santa Maria. Less than two miles southeast of this marker, on the right side of the road, is an adobe mound, all that remains of Benjamin Foxen's home; E Clampus Vitus placed a marker there in 1965.

SANTA YNEZ VALLEY

On the south side of the Santa Ynez River at Buellton, just west of US 101, is the adobe built in 1853 by Dr. Ramón de la Cuesta. It has thirteen rooms and remains much in its original condition. De la Cuesta came to California in 1849 and two years later purchased Rancho de la Vega, some 8,000 acres. The old adobe is a private residence.

Three miles east of Buellton is the Danish town of Solvang, neighbor of Mission Santa Inés. The old mission stood practically alone until the founding of the settlement in 1911. Solvang ("sunny field" in Danish) was founded by the Danish-American Corporation, which included Danish professors from Illinois, who established the now-defunct Atterdag College in 1914. Today the town is a major tourist center, a fusion of Danish and California life. The history of the town and the Danish experience in America is well shown in the Elverhoy Museum at 1624 Elverhoy Way. The museum's name comes from a Danish folk play ("elves on a hill"). In 1950 Viggo and Martha Brandt-Erichsen built their house here in the eighteenth-century style of northern Jutland, and it subsequently became the home of the museum.

Two miles east of Solvang is the town of Santa Ynez. The Santa Ynez Valley Historical Society Museum, begun in 1961, has a well-chosen display of the different cultures of the valley. There is a small research library in a room of this museum. Next door, the Parks-Janeway Carriage House, also operated by the historical society, has a splendid array of more than thirty carriages and stagecoaches, restored to prime condition. The exhibits come from all over the state. Saddles from various periods in California history are also displayed. These two facilities are excellent examples of how California history can be preserved and displayed even in areas of comparatively low population. They are located at Faraday and Sagunto Streets in Santa Ynez.

North of Solvang is Ballard, a former stagecoach stop. Santa Barbara County has granted landmark status to its old Presbyterian church and its one-room schoolhouse, built in 1883 and still used by students up to the third grade, at 2425 School Street. Two miles north of Ballard is the town of Los Olivos, in the middle of a small, choice area of vineyards. From early times a stage station was maintained at Los Olivos, and the narrow-gauge Pacific Coast Railway, coming through in 1887, increased the community's economic base. Mattei's Tavern was built here on Railway Avenue in 1886. The rail line shut down in 1934, but Mattei's still serves the public.

West of Buellton was Rancho Santa Rosa, a grant of some 17,000 acres made to Francisco Cota in 1839. The old adobe ranch house still stands on a knoll overlooking the property. Plans to make it a county park in 1938, when it had long been abandoned, did not materialize, but fortunately it has been extensively renovated and again serves as a private residence. It is located on Mail Road near Santos Road, less than a mile south of SR 246 six miles west of Buellton.

The Lompoc Oil Field lies in the Purisima Hills north of the old mission and the city of Lompoc. Here is a historic well, Hill 4 (SRL 582). It was the first oil well in which water was shut off by pumping cement through the tubing and behind the casing. The development of the modern cementing technique, of which this well was the forerunner, has increased the productive life of thousands of oil wells and made available millions of barrels of oil that might otherwise have remained underground. Hill 4, spudded in 1905 and completed the following year, was drilled to a final depth of 2,507 feet by the Union Oil Company of California. It produced for over forty-five years.

VANDENBERG AIR FORCE BASE

Vandenberg Air Force Base lies on the Santa Barbara County Coast west of Lompoc. The 86,000-acre territory has an interesting history. Rancho Jesús María, the heart of the reservation, was a 40,000-acre grant made in 1837 to Lucas Antonio and José A. Olivera. In 1941 this estate and portions of five neighboring ranches were acquired by the United States Army as a development and training ground for infantry and armored forces. Camp Cooke was activated on October 5, 1941, and was named for Major General Philip St. George Cooke, who in 1847 opened an early wagon trail into California. As war broke out in a couple of months, the camp saw much use: 400 units trained there, and it also served as a prisoner-of-war base and a maximum-security army

disciplinary barracks. In 1946 the post was virtually closed down, only to be reopened during the Korean War. The disciplinary barracks would be moved in the 1950s to house civilian offenders and today is known as the United States Penitentiary at Lompoc.

By the late 1950s the missile age and the Cold War had given urgency to the space program. In 1956 about half of Camp Cooke was transferred to the Air Force, which in the next few years developed a number of weapons and programs. Its remote location in an underpopulated area and proximity to the coast made it ideal for the safe launching of intermediate range ballistic missiles and intercontinental ballistic missiles, as well as for launching satellites into polar orbit without flight over populated land masses during missile take-off. In 1958 Cooke Air Force Base was renamed for the late General Hoyt S. Vandenberg, the second chief of staff of the Air Force. In December of that year, a Thor intermediate range ballistic missile was the first missile to be launched from the base.

In the ensuing years, many missiles and other space programs were tested here, among them the Space Shuttle program, which was moved to Cape Canaveral in Florida in 1989. Space Launch Complex 6 has since then been used by commercial launch firms. By the beginning of 2000, 1,790 orbital and ballistic missiles had lifted off from Vandenberg.

The old adobe ranch house still stands and is used as a guest house for the base. About four miles northwest of the Vandenberg main gate on the Lompoc-Casmalia Road, and not far from the San Antonio Creek Road junction, a turnoff to the left is marked "Marshallia Ranch." From this point it is about one mile to the adobe.

The base, which is a very active post, can be visited by the public on a regular basis. It is one of the most distinctive historic spots in California.

SANTA MARIA VALLEY

The first settlement in Santa Maria Valley was known as La Graciosa and was located a short distance southwest of Orcutt. It is on Bradley Road, off Clark Avenue, about two and one-half miles southeast of town. Six miles northwest of Orcutt, the old Elizalde adobe still serves as a private home on the Righetti Ranch, to the north side of SR 1.

The town of Guadalupe in the northwestern corner of Santa Barbara County was named for the old Mexican rancho on which it is located. Rancho Guadalupe, of 43,681 acres, was granted to Diego Olivera in 1840. A large one-story adobe built by the Arrellanes family about 1849 still stands on Tenth Street near Guadalupe Avenue, SR 1.

Santa Maria Valley, about thirty-five miles long and from three to ten miles wide, is known as the "Valley of the Gardens" because of its extensive agricultural development. The city of Santa Maria, first called Grangeville and then Central City, was founded in 1874. The Santa Maria Valley Historical Society and Museum at 626 South Broadway in Santa Maria has displays on the various people who have lived in the region. A more specialized institution is the Santa Maria Museum of Flight at 3015 Airpark Drive. There are several vintage planes displayed in an aircraft hanger, along with an extensive collection of model planes from throughout the twentieth century. An annual air show is held here in late summer.

Los Alamos, fifteen miles southeast of Santa Maria, became a stage stop in 1877; before that time it was part of Rancho Los Alamos, a 48,803-acre grant made in 1839 by Governor Alvarado to José Antonio de la Guerra y Carrillo, son of José Antonio de la Guerra y Noriega of Santa Barbara. Subsequently the rancho was acquired by Gaspar Orena, brother-in-law of the younger De la Guerra. The De la Guerra–Orena adobe, beautifully preserved, is now a National Historic Landmark. It is located three and one-half miles west of Los Alamos just off the road leading to Vandenberg Air Force Base. Part of Rancho Los Alamos eventually came into the hands of the oil magnate Edward L. Doheny.

Much of Santa Barbara County is rugged mountainous area included in Los Padres National Forest and penetrated by few roads. As early as 1925 Robert E. Easton led the efforts to establish a sanctuary in the upper Sisquoc River region for the vanishing California condor. It was an appropriate gesture in a county where the preservation of California's fast-disappearing past is so strongly pursued. The California condor, which has the longest wingspread of any North American bird, is an endangered species. In the late 1980s, with less than thirty left, all the condors were captured. A captive breeding program has increased their numbers substantially, and now some of them have been released in the wild, in Los Padres National Forest, near Big Sur, in Arizona, and elsewhere.

Santa Clara County

Santa Clara County was named for Mission Santa Clara, which was established in that region in 1777. It was one of the original twenty-seven counties. San Jose has always been the county seat, and was California's first state capital. Many pre-statehood records written in Spanish are filed in the county courthouse.

INDIAN MOUNDS

Indians in considerable numbers dwelt in the region of Santa Clara County when the first explorers came this way. Portolá's party reported in 1769 "many large villages" of natives at the lower end of San Francisco

Bay. Anza, in 1776, saw three large rancherias with many residents on the Guadalupe River and another about two miles to the north, possibly near the lower end of Moffett Field, where Chief Iñigo later had his ranch.

Even after homes had been established by the Spaniards, some of the old Indian villages were occupied at times, for the wife of Don Secundino Robles said that three groups of natives were within a short distance of their house, which had been built about where Alma Street meets San Antonio Avenue in Palo Alto. Nearby was the place known as the Castro Indian mound, which, until its destruction, was the largest mound in the lower Bay region. Spreading out to a width of 290 feet, it had a length of 450 feet and a height of ten feet or more. Excavations were made by archaeologists from Stanford University and the University of California at Berkeley, both of which have museum specimens from the place. The mound was reduced by scrapers and eventually leveled; much of the soil was hauled away for fertilizer, and a subdivision now covers the site.

The principal artifacts discovered were mortars, pestles, bone scraping blades, awls, needles, chains of small beads, and an occasional bowl of a soapstone pipe evidently obtained through barter. The few obsidian implements found suggest some kind of trade, since that material could only have come from what are now Lake or other counties to the north. This kitchen midden, unlike those further north along the bay shore, showed a scarcity of certain ordinary species of shell and a preponderance of a small species, less desirable for food, but common throughout the Bay Area. The almost exclusive appearance of this small species of shell throughout the mound's layers suggests that the salt marsh along the bay has been an effective barrier to more desirable species of edible shellfish from the time of the earliest habitation of the mound.

On the northeast side of Middlefield Road south of Marion Avenue in Palo Alto is the site of an Indian village, commemorated by a plaque placed at Marion and Webster Streets by the City of Palo Alto and the Palo Alto Historical Association.

Five miles west of Gilroy is the Chitactac-Adams Heritage County Park, located on the former Adams School grounds. Stationary mortars in large flat boulders may be seen. Arrowheads and stone implements have been plowed up in several neighboring fields. The E Clampus Vitus plaque says: "For over 3,000 years, this area supported large populations of ancestral Ohlone people. This locality is believed to be the ethno-historical village of Chitactac."

OLD TRAILS OF SANTA CLARA

In 1769, Gaspar de Portolá was sent by José de Gálvez, *visitador general* of New Spain, to take possession of and to fortify the ports of San Diego and Monterey in Alta California. Portolá failed to find Monterey on this expedition but discovered instead San Francisco Bay.

Leaving their camp on San Pedro Creek on November 4, Portolá's party journeyed down into the Santa Clara Valley, by way of what are now the Crystal Springs Lakes and Woodside, to the northwest bank of San Francisquito Creek at Menlo Park. Father Juan Crespí, chronicler of the expedition, wrote:

> We pitched camp in a plain some six leagues long, grown with good oaks and live oaks, and with much other timber in the neighborhood. This plain has two good arroyos with a good flow of water, and at the southern end of the estuary there is a good river, with plenty of water, which passes through the plain mentioned, well wooded on its banks [this was the Guadalupe River]. . . . This entire port is surrounded by many and large villages of barbarous heathen who are very affable, mild, and docile, and very generous.

The site of the camp under a tall redwood is generally thought to be across the creek from the lone redwood tree that still stands beside the railroad tracks at Palo Alto. Beneath this tree is a boulder on which is a bronze tablet carrying the following inscription:

> Under this giant redwood, The Palo Alto, November 6–11, 1769, camped Portolá and his men on the expedition that discovered San Francisco Bay. This was the assembling point for their reconnoitering parties. Here in 1774, Padre Palou erected a cross to mark the site of a proposed mission. The celebrated Pedro Font topographical map, of 1776, contained the drawing of the original double-trunked tree, making The Palo Alto the first official living California landmark. Placed by the Historic Landmarks Committee, NSGW, November 7, 1926.

This tree was long a landmark for the Indians and later for the Spanish explorers and the missionaries and soldiers traveling up and down the peninsula between San Francisco and the missions of Santa Clara and San José. The Spaniards called it the *palo alto* ("tall tree"), and the name passed on to the modern city that grew up beside it. Although the tree is now very old, and in weakened condition, efforts are being made to maintain it.

From this central camp at the tall redwood, José Francisco de Ortega went up the eastern shore of the Bay, and it is thought that he explored as far as Alameda Creek. On the return journey to Monterey, Portolá's party retraced its former trail through what are now San Mateo, Santa Cruz, and Monterey Counties.

Pedro Fages was the first explorer to go inland from Monterey Bay to San Francisco Bay. His first expedition was made in 1770. In 1772 he made a second trip, which was also recorded by Father Crespí. Fages left Monterey on March 20, 1772, and, passing through the Salinas River Valley, climbed the Gabilan Mountains, dropping down into the valley on the other side where Mission San Juan Bautista would be established in 1797 by Father Lasuén.

From there, continuing north, he entered the Santa Clara Valley north of Hudner in San Benito County, passed Tesquisquite Slough and San Felipe Lake, traveled the broad valley that he named San Bernardino de Siena, and on March 22 pitched camp on Llagas Creek a little north of modern Gilroy.

The next day the party followed the west side of the Santa Clara Valley and climbed the low hills that extend eastward into the valley near San Martin. Camp that night was made near Coyote Creek, on the shores of a lake named San Benvenuto by Crespí. On March 25 the party followed the edge of the eastern foothills and camped at San Lorenzo Creek in Alameda County.

After discovering the Sacramento Valley, Fages reentered the Santa Clara Valley by way of Mission Pass, continuing around the head of San Francisco Bay to a point near Milpitas. Retracing their old course, on April 3, the party made camp at the spur of hills near San Martin. On April 4 camp was pitched near the site of San Juan Bautista.

Juan Bautista de Anza, in 1775–76, made his second expedition from Sonora in Mexico to San Francisco. After stopping a few days in Monterey, he proceeded northward on March 23, 1776, by way of the Salinas River and the Gabilan Mountains to the "San Bernardino Valley," the southern end of what is now the Santa Clara Valley. There he camped at Llagas Creek. On March 24 he entered the valley through the low hills above the Coyote River and named the plain before him the Llano de los Robles del Puerto de San Francisco ("Plain of the Oaks of the Port of San Francisco"). The party kept to the western side of the valley

along the foothills, camping on the Arroyo de San José Cupertino on March 25, from which they had a broad view of San Francisco Bay.

On March 26 the little band reached the tall redwood tree on the banks of San Francisquito Creek and found the cross that Palou had placed there on November 28, 1774, five years after Portolá had passed that way. A plaque at the corner of Middlefield Road and Coleridge Avenue in Palo Alto was placed two hundred years later, during the celebration of the United States bicentennial, commemorating the passage of the Anza party through the region. From this point Anza proceeded northward up the peninsula, where he explored and located the sites for the Presidio and Mission of San Francisco.

Over this old trail up the Santa Clara Valley, marked out by Pedro Fages, the mission fathers came later. It became a part of El Camino Real, "the Royal Road," linking the missions of the south with the settlements in the San Francisco Bay area.

MISSION SANTA CLARA DE ASÍS

The founding of Mission Santa Clara de Asís took place on January 12, 1777, with Father Tomás de la Peña from Mission San Francisco de Asís officiating, and José Joaquín Moraga and his soldiers from the Presidio of San Francisco present at the ceremonies. The site chosen for the new mission was on the banks of Río Guadalupe, the chief camping and fishing grounds of the local Costonoan Indians and called by them So-co-is-u-ka, meaning "at (the) laurel." Another name for the place seems to have been Thamien. Here the mission cross was planted on the bank of a stream on a spot later forming part of Laurelwood Farm. The site of the original mission has been determined to be the west of now dry Mission Creek, about one-quarter mile south of the confluence of this creek and the Guadalupe River. The site (SRL 250) was marked at Central Expressway and De la Cruz Boulevard in Santa Clara but the bronze plaque is missing from the monument.

Twice within the next two years the Guadalupe River, swollen by winter rains, flooded the church, and in 1779 the padres moved a short distance south. This second location is now marked by a cross in a small city park at the northeast corner of Martin Avenue and De la Cruz Boulevard. The mission remained here until 1784, when a site on higher ground was selected as a better location. The third site was on Franklin Street, near the Santa Clara Caltrain station. The building erected here is said to have been one of the most elaborate and beautiful of all the mission structures in California. It was begun by Father José Antonio Murguía on November 19, 1781, and was dedicated by Father Junipero Serra, in one of his last public appearances, on May 15, 1784. The Indian name for this site was Juquensen, or "Valley of the Oaks." The cornerstone of the third Mission Santa Clara was unearthed during construction in 1911, and a cross was placed to mark the spot.

Earthquakes in 1812 and 1818 caused serious damage to the buildings at the third site, and the fathers were obliged to move again. This they did in 1819, to a point on the east side of the present campus drive (Alviso Street) of the University of Santa Clara, opposite the south half of the Jesuit residence. The mission remained here until the completion of the church at the fifth and last site (SRL 338), a stone's throw away, where the university chapel now stands. The fifth church was begun in 1822 and dedicated on August 11, 1825.

After the secularization of the California missions in 1835, the lands of Mission Santa Clara were confiscated and the buildings became sadly neglected. In 1850 the Rt. Rev. Joseph S. Alemany, O.P., bishop of the new Diocese of Monterey, invited the Society of Jesus to restore the church and to build a college. Accordingly, on March 19, 1851, Santa Clara College was established in the old mission buildings by Rev. John Nobili, S.J., who adapted what was left of the old adobe buildings to the requirements of a school. Changes necessitated by the growth of the school finally altered the mission buildings until little of the original remained. By 1855 frame structures had replaced many of the former adobes. The 1825 adobe church, used as the students' chapel and the parish church, was encased in wood and given two towers quite out of keeping with mission architecture.

In 1855 the state granted a university charter to the college, but it was fifty-seven years before it became the University of Santa Clara, on April 29, 1912. Since then, many fine buildings have been placed by the Jesuits around the site of the old mission. Fire destroyed the 1825 church on October 25, 1926, and in its place a concrete replica of the Franciscan adobe church was built in 1928–29 on the same site. Part of the altar end of the adobe church was saved after the fire and was incorporated into the replica; the bricks may be seen through glass in the sacristy. Many relics dating from the beginning of the mission's history were rescued and preserved. Part of the 1777 cross from the first site is encased in the large cross standing in front of the present

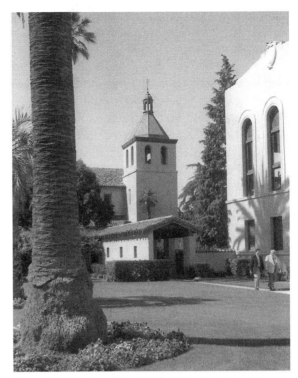

Tower of Mission Santa Clara Church, University of Santa Clara

church. To the right of the church is a gate leading into the old "Campo Santo" or cemetery. In the garden at the rear of the church one adobe building and an adobe wall from the original cloisters of 1822 still stand. In the arch south of this wall are grinding stones used in the mission period for making flour and olive oil.

The DeSaisset Museum at 500 El Camino Real, on the University of Santa Clara campus, has artifacts from the original mission and other materials on California history.

EL PUEBLO SAN JOSÉ DE GUADALUPE

Because the Spanish governors had difficulty in supplying provisions for the religious and military establishments in Alta California, Governor Felipe de Neve, during his journey in 1777, under orders from Viceroy Antonio María Bucareli, selected certain locations for the placing of agricultural establishments. One of these was near the newly established Mission Santa Clara. The governor appointed Lieutenant José Joaquín Moraga to found a settlement on the Guadalupe River two and one-quarter miles from the mission. Moraga was to take with him nine soldiers "of known skill in agriculture," two settlers, and three laborers.

On November 29, 1777, the new town was founded on the bank of the small river from which it derived its name. El Pueblo de San José de Guadalupe began at what is now the corner of Hobson and Vendome Streets in San Jose; the state marker (SRL 433) is at the city hall on Mission Street. The floods of March 1778 inundated the marshy land on which this first settlement had been started during the previous dry season and washed away the nearly completed dam built for irrigation purposes. In July a new dam was constructed farther upstream, and the small group of settlers moved to high ground. This move caused some confusion in land titles, and Moraga was instructed by Governor Pedro Fages in 1782 to clear up the tangled property claims, to make the allotments uniform and regular, and to designate vacant lands and common lands. The hastily constructed first houses were replaced by adobes.

San José de Guadalupe was visited by Captain George Vancouver in 1792, who praised the beauty of its broad, oak-studded fields and the fertility of the valley in which it was located. The yearly winter floods worked against this settlement, however, and a new town was established on higher ground in 1797, near what is now the corner of Market and San Fernando Streets; some buildings may have been built there at an earlier date.

In 1803 the mission fathers built a small adobe church on the new plaza. It was improved in 1835 and later encased in brick, but was ultimately destroyed by fire. In 1877 the present stone structure, St. Joseph's Church, was completed at the corner of Market and San Fernando Streets (SRL 910), on the site of the old adobe chapel. The park enclosed by South Market Street is a part of what was the plaza.

San Jose, as the city is known today, is California's oldest civil settlement. For over a century and a half the seat of municipal government was maintained at the second site of the pueblo, on or around the plaza. A new civic center was built in the 1960s on Mission at First Street near the Guadalupe River, practically within sight of the original pueblo location of 1777.

EL EMBARCADERO DE SANTA CLARA (ALVISO)

Mission Santa Clara had its embarcadero, or landing place, at the head of the navigable slough that extends south from San Francisco Bay and is known today as Alviso Slough. In early mission days it was called the Embarcadero de Santa Clara de Asís, and played a very important part in the life of the settlers at Mission Santa Clara and the pueblo of San José.

Yankee ship captains, from 1835 to 1850, opened up an extensive trade with the dons who owned the vast ranchos bordering on San Francisco Bay; every rancho had its embarcadero. The Embarcadero de Santa Clara was one of the principal landings, as noted by Richard Henry Dana Jr. in *Two Years Before the Mast*: "The Mission of Dolores, near the anchorage, has no trade at all, but those of San José, Santa Clara, and others situated on the large creeks or rivers which run into the bay . . . do a greater business in hides than any in California. Large boats, or launches, manned by Indians . . . are attached to the missions, and sent down to the vessels with hides, to bring away goods in return."

Ygnacio Alviso settled at the Embarcadero de Santa Clara in 1840, and shortly thereafter the name of the landing was changed to Alviso. He had been granted Rancho Rincón de los Esteros in 1838. Alviso was mayordomo at the mission and was engaged in construction work there at about the time the fifth and last church was built. Alviso prospered as a port with the development of the mercury mines at New Almaden, opened in 1845, and the discovery of gold in the Sierra three years later increased the flow of trade substantially. A steamer was run between Alviso and San Francisco, and the first warehouse was built there in 1849–50. It was during this time that the first state capital was located at nearby San Jose.

After 1865 the railroads began to divert trade from the embarcaderos on the Bay, and although a branch of the railroad was built through the town in 1876, Alviso went into a steep decline in the latter years of the nineteenth century. The old brick Wade warehouse is one of the few landmarks remaining from these days.

Thomas Foon Chew opened his successful Bayside Canning Company in Alviso in 1906, and by 1921 it was the third-largest cannery in the United States. The enterprise did not long survive Chew's death in 1931. Today Alviso is a historic district on the National Register of Historic Places, and the Department of the Interior has included parts of it in its 23,000-acre San Francisco Bay National Wildlife Refuge. The town was annexed to San Jose in 1968. The South Bay Yacht Club, organized in 1896, continues to function, and its 1906 clubhouse is in regular use. An E Clampus Vitus plaque on the clubhouse notes the historical importance of the small town.

THE ALAMEDA

The tree-lined avenue known as the Alameda was first planted by the padres for the benefit of wayfarers between Mission Santa Clara and the Pueblo de San José. The planting of trees was begun in 1799 by Father

Magín Catalá, who employed two hundred Indians to transplant common black willows from the riverbank. The young grove was watered and protected until the trees were large enough to withstand the roving herds of cattle that pastured in this unfenced territory. Bordering one side of this grove was a three-mile *acequia*, or ditch, taking waters from the Guadalupe to irrigate the mission garden and other land. Three rows of willows grew there in the early days, and they served as shade from the hot summer sun and as protection from the wild cattle that resented the intrusion of pedestrians.

Captain Alfred Robinson, who visited here several times before 1841, wrote of the road:

> It is frequented generally on the Sabbath or feast days when all the town repair[s] to the church at Santa Clara. On a Sunday may be seen hundreds of persons of both sexes, gaily attired in silks and satins, mounted on their finest horses, and proceeding leisurely up the road. No carriages are used, and, of course, the scene is divested of all the pomp and splendor which accompanies church-going in the larger places of the republic, yet in one respect it excells them all, that is, in the display of female beauty. No part of Mexico can show so large a share of bright eyes, fine teeth, fair proportions, and beautiful complexions.

For almost a century the grove remained untouched, but as the region was opened up and traffic grew heavier over this highway, it became evident that a more solid roadbed would be necessary. Although it was the most important road in the region, winter rains made travel difficult. In the winter of 1852 it became impassable, and all traffic was compelled to use a route to the west, making the journey from the mission to the town much longer. In 1856 Crandall Brothers established an omnibus line to carry passengers along the Alameda, but the roadbed was still far from satisfactory. In order to secure maintenance, a franchise to collect tolls was granted to the Alameda Turnpike Company in 1862 in return for making and maintaining a good road. Upon the expiration of this franchise in 1868, a railroad with horse-drawn cars began operations, two years later changing to steam locomotion and extending the line some miles at the southern end. When electrification of the line came in 1887, public opinion finally consented to the destruction of the center line of trees. One of the county papers on November 24, 1887, announced: "The last of the beautiful grove of trees which has stood for a century in the Alameda, San Jose's lovely drive, has been cut down to make room for the electric road to Santa

Luís María Peralta Adobe, San Jose

Clara." Tradition has it that three willows on the east side of the Alameda that survived until 1961 were of the original 1799 planting.

The Alameda is now a paved modern highway, much of it SR 82, and in 1984 it was designated by the San Jose City Council as a City Historic Landmark, taking in all the lots fronting the Alameda between SR 17 and Race Street.

ADOBES IN SAN JOSE

Many buildings in the old pueblo were constructed of adobe, but travelers writing of them as late as 1850 had little to say in their favor. One by one they were replaced by better structures. In later years, when the adobes of California had begun to be regarded as historical landmarks, only two remained.

The first of these adobes stands at 184 West St. John Street. This adobe is believed to have been built in 1799 by Manuel González, an Apache Indian, who died in the adobe in 1804. It was later owned by Luís María Peralta, *comisionado* of the pueblo from 1807 to 1822 and grantee of the huge Rancho San Antonio in Alameda County. Jacob Bowman believes this "Peralta Adobe" (SRL 866) is, after Mission Dolores, the second-oldest adobe in the nine Bay Area counties. In the days of the pueblo the adobe was at the extreme northern edge of the plaza.

Don Luís preferred to live here rather than at his land grant, which he gave to his four sons, and here he died in 1851 at the age of ninety-two. The adobe and fourteen acres of land were left to his unmarried daughters Josefa and Guadalupe. Today only two of the original rooms remain. In 1949 a concrete structure was built so close to it that the adobe lost part of a wall to accommodate the newer building. The adobe was acquired by the San Jose City Council in 1966, and through the efforts of the Peralta Restorations Fund Committee, it was restored to its original state. A park enclosed by adobe walls now surrounds the building. In August 1976 the park was dedicated as a part of the U.S. bicentennial festivities; the adobe is also listed on the National Register of Historic Places.

The second remaining adobe in San Jose stands at 770 Lincoln Avenue. Here on the grounds of Rancho Los Coches a low one-room adobe had been built by an Indian known as Roberto around 1836, eight years before he received the grant of the rancho. When Antonio María Suñol purchased the rancho from Roberto in 1847, he added three large brick rooms to the structure. A Dalmatian sea captain, Stefano Splivalo, purchased the building and fifty-five acres in 1853, and made major architectural changes, further enlarging the house and adding a complete second story and balcony. The deterioration that inevitably ensued was halted over a century later when John Bruzzone purchased the building and set out to restore it. Today, identified as the Suñol adobe (SRL 898), it has been converted into law offices and is open to the public. The nearby freeway, I-280, was rerouted to pass to the north of the building, sparing it and the garden with its 150-year-old fig tree, the branches of which form a canopy over a redwood arbor in the garden.

ADOBES IN SANTA CLARA

At 3260 The Alameda (SR 82 between Franklin and Benton Streets) is a one-story adobe building (SRL 249) that was part of José Peña's house, and may have been constructed as early as the 1790s as an Indian dwelling of the third Mission Santa Clara. It was preserved by the Santa Clara Women's Club and is used by the group as their clubhouse. It stands back from the street in an old garden of pear and apricot trees, succulents, and flowering shrubs. Nearby on the grounds of the University of Santa Clara an adobe remnant of the old mission has been converted into an administration building.

At 373 Jefferson Street stands a modest family residence of one and one-half stories now called the Berryessa adobe. A narrow porch runs along the north side; at the rear is a wooden stairway leading to the one-room upstairs attic. A large olive tree shades the front corner of the home, which is privately owned.

THE COURTHOUSE

The first tribunal of the region, the *juzgado*, was built within the original Pueblo de San José in 1783. After the

(Thomas) Fallon House, San Jose

removal of the pueblo to higher ground, a second *juzgado* was built about 1798 in what is now the center of Market Street at the intersection of Post Street. The second adobe structure, before it was torn down in 1850 and the brick removed for use elsewhere, saw the growth of the Spanish and Mexican pueblo into an American town. It was a low building with a sloping, tiled roof, and in front of it Thomas J. Fallon hoisted the United States flag on July 13, 1846. (Fallon later became mayor of San Jose, and his home, built about 1859, still stands at 173 West St. John Street.)

The first county court convened in March 1850 in an adobe building on the west side of South First Street opposite the passageway then known as Archer Alley, later Fountain Alley. Over the next few years the court met in several other buildings, including the former state capitol, none of which stand today. In 1866 work began on an imposing two-story domed building on North First Street opposite St. James Square, and this county courthouse was occupied by the authorities on January 1, 1868. It was still the seat of county government when fire destroyed the interior on May 18, 1931. The outer walls remained intact, and the restoration of the interior was completed by September 1932. In the process of restoration, a third story replaced the dome. Further restoration costing more than $700,000 was done to update the building, which was rededicated in 1973. More restoration was done in the 1990s.

THE MONTEREY ROAD

El Camino Real stretches southward from Santa Clara and San Jose toward Monterey. In Spanish times the road to the capital ran from the south end of the plaza between the double row of mud houses that was San Jose. To avoid the pueblo's reservoir (a pond eight hundred feet in length, lying just south of Duane Street and east of Almaden Avenue), the road skirted the Canoas marches on the right and continued south through the low bare hills called Las Lagrimas, approximately in the line of present South First Street. Continuing down the valley parallel to US 101 and the Union Pacific Railroad line, the road passed through the settlements of Coyote and Morgan Hill. A marker (SRL 259) at the northwest corner of Old US Highway 101 and Tennant Avenue in Morgan Hill commemorates the site of the Twenty-One Mile House, one of a chain of taverns catering to travelers in the mid-1850s, and the now-gone Vasquez Tree, inexplicably connected with the name of the bandit Tiburcio Vásquez. The southernmost settlements on the road in Santa Clara County were Gilroy and San Martin, after which the road headed through the low hills toward the Pajaro River, often turbulent and difficult to cross in those days, and from there into San Benito County. The first permanent span across the Pajaro was built in 1866.

THE SAN FRANCISCO ROAD

The first road north from San Jose led to Santa Clara Mission, and beyond that point it followed the trail opened by Juan Bautista de Anza on March 30, 1776. Beginning in the plaza between the church and the royal granary, the road ran close among the adobes, emerging on the west side of a pond at the intersection of present Santa Clara and Market Streets. The pueblo's main *acequia* ran parallel at some distance to the left, and a branch of it was crossed at today's St. James Street. Between Market and First Streets, at Julian Street, the highway to Mission San José (in Alameda County) and the Contra Costa forked off to the right, over a plain strewn with the bleached bones of slaughtered cattle, until it reached an immense sycamore grove near Coyote Creek and became one with the present Old Oakland Road. At the road fork began the *suertes* or farming lots of the residents of the pueblo. The first lot on the right was inhabited by the family of Plácido Californio, one of the first Baja California Indians brought north by the Franciscans, who retired from Mission Santa Clara and settled in the pueblo in 1796.

The road to San Francisco continued through the *suertes*, which were bordered by willow hedges and little alleys stretching to the riverbank, and went on past the area called the Pueblo Viejo, where the town had first been founded. As it reached the open country, the road bore more and more to the west of present North First Street, finally reaching the Guadalupe River near the place where Anza's men had opened a ford. At this point, near the original site of Mission Santa Clara, the river was crossed, at first by the bridge built by the missionaries. In 1797, when the crossing began to be used by travelers between Mission San José and the third Mission Santa Clara as well as between the Pueblo de San José and San Francisco, the authorities constructed a more satisfactory bridge. In its later state, this consisted of two tree trunks supporting a roadbed of five-foot squared timbers topped with planks, the whole suspended above bank level by a heavy chain anchored from four tall sycamores. The "Old Spanish Bridge" remained a landmark until the 1880s, and a piece of the chain, said to have come from a Portuguese ship, is preserved in the museum at the University of Santa Clara.

From the Guadalupe River northwest, the original trail became a boundary between ranchos, and for this reason the present Bayshore Freeway (US 101) still follows the same general line. Where Moffett Field now is, the trail swung first to the right of the freeway, then inland to the left. In records of 1836–53 this route is called the old or summer road, the lowlands by the bay being nearly impassable during the winter. Nevertheless, the first American squatters found the northern end of the trail useful; they fenced and improved it, and it is now the longer portion of Charleston Road in Palo Alto.

After Mission Santa Clara was moved to near its present site, a better if slightly longer road was opened. This road began at the plaza and ran slightly north and east of today's El Camino Real. Near the western side of Santa Clara the road passed to the north of the main ranchería inhabited after secularization by the mission Indians.

Where present El Camino Real runs due west along a section line to the Lawrence Expressway and Fremont Avenue, the main highway in use before the 1850s swung slowly to the right across what was known as the Baijo, an open area filled with mustard plants and intersected with sloughs; this is the site of the battle of Santa Clara, fought in 1847. Today's Lawrence Expressway passes over the railroad (site of the Lawrence post office from 1887 to 1935) at the easternmost point of the Roblar, a great forest of valley oaks and live oaks extending down the west side of the valley between the low adobe lands and the chaparral nearer the hills. In the 1830s and 1840s travelers coming from the north caught sight here of the white-walled mission church beside its bell tower.

Northward the main trail lay for several miles in the

edge of the woods, east of the present railroad. The oaks in this section succumbed first to charcoal burners, then to the insatiable wood-burning locomotives and the needs of mechanized large-scale wheat farmers, and finally to fruit orchards. In present Mountain View the oak woods and the road formed a semicircle extending three-fourths of a mile east of the railroad, around the alluvial fan of Stevens Creek, which was fringed with willow swamps. After swinging west again to the mission's Corral de Pastoria near present Central Expressway just south of Rengstorff Avenue, the Spanish road bore to the right across Adobe Creek with its dark adobe flats and continued north past what is now the Palo Alto Art Center to the Middlefield Road crossing of San Francisquito Creek. A plaque at the corner of Middlefield Road and Palo Alto Avenue, placed by the city of Palo Alto and the Palo Alto Historical Association in 1969, marks this crossing.

SPANISH AND MEXICAN LAND GRANTS IN SANTA CLARA COUNTY

Some fifty grants of land in what is now Santa Clara County were made by the Spanish and Mexican authorities before the official annexation of California to the United States in 1848. Virtually all of this territory was accessible, habitable, and productive land and thus became the site of most of the twentieth-century cities and towns in the county. Two land grants originate from the Spanish period: Rancho San Ysidro, in southern Santa Clara County, and Rancho Los Tularcitos.

RANCHO SAN YSIDRO (OLD GILROY)

According to Bancroft, Rancho San Ysidro, one of the finest in the district, was granted in 1810 to Ygnacio Ortega, son of Captain José F. Ortega, who probably came with his father from Mexico between 1769 and 1773. Don Ygnacio, whose wife was Gertrudis Arce, was a *soldado distinguido* of the San Diego Company in 1792.

After Don Ygnacio's death in 1833, Governor Figueroa granted the lands of this rancho to his heirs, divided approximately equally between Ysabel Ortega (the wife of Julian Cantua), Quentin Ortega, and María Clara de la Asunción (the wife of John Gilroy). Ysabel received the portion called Rancho La Polka, in the hills east of San Martin and northeast of Gilroy. Rancho San Ysidro was divided between Quentin Ortega and John and Clara Gilroy. Their houses lay close to each other, the

dividing line between the property roughly following present-day SR 152, the Pacheco Pass Road. The buildings on these properties have long ago vanished.

John Gilroy, the first non-Hispanic foreign settler in California, deserted the *Isaac Todd* in Monterey in 1814. He was of Scots descent, born John Cameron, and when he became ill with scurvy and left his ship, he adopted his mother's maiden name as his own, a successful ruse to avoid being retaken. By September of that year he had been baptized at Mission San Carlos as Juan Bautista María Gilroy. In 1821, he was married at Mission San Juan Bautista to Clara, daughter of Ygnacio Ortega.

Gilroy, a man of fine physique and pleasant manners, though possessed of little education, had much natural ability and became influential in his locality. When he became a naturalized Mexican citizen in 1833, he produced certificates to show that he was a soapmaker and a millwright of good character, with a wife and four children, and had also some livestock on Rancho San Ysidro. As the years passed, he lost all his property, and toward the end of his life he became dependent upon charity. He died in 1869 at age seventy-five. The little settlement of San Ysidro, over which he was alcalde for a time, stretched along the Pacheco Pass Road, and is now known as Old Gilroy.

While John Gilroy was still living, the first American to locate permanently in the vicinity came upon the scene. This was Julius Martin, born in North Carolina in 1804, who had come overland from his former home in Missouri with his wife and daughters and arrived at San Ysidro in 1843. For part of the overland journey the Martins had been with a larger group, most of whom proceeded to Oregon. Near Fort Laramie, they met Joseph R. Walker, who, returning to California as leader of the smaller group, brought them across Walker Pass. During the ensuing years Walker was a frequent and welcome visitor at the Martin home.

Julius Martin settled in San Ysidro, where he constructed a small horsepower flour mill with a capacity of twenty bushels a day, as well as three houses, none of which are still standing. He became a captain of the American Scouts under Frémont and saw the Bear Flag raised in Sonoma. When Charles Bennett, Sutter's messenger, paused in San Ysidro on his way to report the discovery of gold to government headquarters in Monterey, his story so interested the settlers that most of them left for the diggings. Julius Martin was among the number who went, and he did well enough that after he returned in 1850 he was able to pay cash for 1,220 acres of Rancho San Ysidro, which had 4,460 acres all told. Martin held this property until his death in 1891. Although blind for the last thirty years of his life, he was victorious in litigation that threatened to deprive him of his land. He was a man of good education, and had an excellent memory. From his reminiscences, told to interviewers during his last years, we know many of the details of the early history not only of the immediate vicinity but also of other parts of the state.

RANCHO LOS TULARCITOS (MILPITAS)

Rancho Los Tularcitos lay in the north part of Santa Clara County near the lower end of San Francisco Bay. It extended south from the confluence of Calera and Penitencia Creeks along the latter stream to present-day Calaveras Road in Milpitas, and east to include the mountains at the heads of Calera Creek and the Arroyo de los Coches. The southeastern point was marked by a live oak tree, which also denoted the northeastern point of the outlying lands of the Pueblo de San José.

This rancho was granted by Pablo Vicente de Solá, the last of the Spanish governors of Alta California, to José Higuera in 1821. The grant was renewed by the Mexican governor Juan B. Alvarado in 1839; patent for 4,394 acres was issued by the United States government to Higuera's heirs in 1870. The land was afterward purchased by Henry Curtner, a native of Vermont.

The old adobe built by Higuera on the rancho still stands in a well-landscaped Milpitas city park, at the end of Rancho Higuera Drive, and is open to the public.

RANCHO MILPITAS (MILPITAS)

Rancho Milpitas (from *milpa*, Spanish for "maize field") lay immediately to the south of Rancho Los Tularcitos. The right to the lands of the rancho was claimed by two men, Nicolás Berryessa and José María de Jesús Alviso. Both men were sons of Spanish pioneers in Alta California and soldiers of the military company in San Francisco, where they served together from 1819 to 1827. Both were leading men in the Pueblo de San José, Alviso being alcalde in 1836, at which time Berryessa was *regidor* (member of the pueblo council), and both were living in San Jose in 1841.

Berryessa was an unlucky man: his cattle were plundered by Frémont's battalion; his brother, José de los Reyes, was killed by Frémont's men; squatters settled on his land; and, as the last straw, his claim to Rancho Milpitas, based on a decree from Alcalde Pedro Cha-

boya, was rejected by the Land Commission in 1855. He died insane in 1863.

José María de Jesús Alviso, who received Rancho Milpitas, was the son of Francisco Javier Alviso, a member of the Anza expedition. (The name Alviso is of Basque origin, and was originally spelled "Albizu"; José María de Jesús Alviso signed his name "Albizu.") His claim to the rancho was based on a grant from Governor José Castro in 1835. His home on the rancho was about two miles from the center of Milpitas, near the intersection of present-day Calaveras and Piedmont Roads. One adobe of the hacienda remains, probably built in the 1830s. The second story of this adobe above the upper veranda is covered by weatherboarding to protect the original material. It is now owned by the city of Milpitas, and there are plans for its restoration.

Milpitas lies on the western boundary of the rancho. The Spanish originally named the town Penitencia, after the nearby creek. According to tradition, the creek was named for a "house of penitence" on its banks, a small adobe where priests from the missions came at stated intervals to hear confessions.

José María de Jesús Alviso's cousin Ygnacio owned the Rancho Rincón de los Esteros to the west; no buildings from the Hispanic past remain on this property.

RANCHO ULISTAC (AGNEW)

Lying between the Guadalupe River and Saratoga Creek, Rancho Ulistac was first granted by Governor Pío Pico in 1845 to Indian claimants; in 1857 the heirs of Jacob D. Hoppe were confirmed in his claim to the property. Hoppe, a native of Maryland, reached California in 1846 at the age of thrity-three. A year after his arrival on the West Coast, he became interested in the establishment of a weekly newspaper. The printing materials that he had were afterward turned over to the proprietors of the *Alta California*. He lived in San Jose, where he was the first American postmaster and a delegate to the constitutional convention. His life ended as one of the unfortunate victims of the explosion of the steamer *Jenny Lind* in San Francisco Bay on April 11, 1853.

On a portion of this property James Lick built his mansion. A native of Pennsylvania and a piano maker by trade, Lick arrived in California in 1848 and bought up land there and elsewhere at low prices. Later this property greatly increased in value until it was worth millions. Lick's mansion and gardens and the round brick warehouse from his water-powered flour mill still stand on the west bank of the Guadalupe River north of the present Montague Road, which was named after a neighbor of Lick. Today, the property is privately owned and not open to the public. Across the river is the town of Agnew, where Agnews State Hospital existed for many years; the town is gone now.

Lick began giving away his vast wealth in 1873; at his death in 1876 a board of trustees was still coping with the distribution of his fortune. The amount of $700,000 was allocated to the establishment of Lick Observatory. The site, on the summit of Mount Hamilton, about twenty miles east of San Jose, was granted by act of Congress in 1876, and, with additional grants of land, the reservation now totals 3,133 acres. The observatory was opened to the public by the University of California in 1888. Lick lies buried under the supporting pier of the 36-inch refracting telescope.

Mount Hamilton, 4,209 feet above sea level, was named in honor of the Rev. Laurentine Hamilton, a pioneer missionary preacher in San Jose and also superintendent of schools. With William H. Brewer and Josiah D. Whitney, Hamilton was one of the first Americans to climb the mountain, on August 26, 1861.

RANCHO POSOLMI AND MOFFETT FIELD

The land at the lower end of San Francisco Bay was the home of an Indian tribe whose chieftain, Lope Iñigo, was granted formal possession by Governor Micheltorena in 1844. This Rancho Posolmi, some 1,697 level acres of salt marsh, proved to be ideally suited for the West Coast's first lighter-than-air base. In 1931 President Herbert Hoover established the Sunnyvale Naval Air Station to house the navy's newest airship, the dirigible USS *Macon*. Eight days before the formal dedication of the base on April 12, 1933, tragedy struck when the *Macon*'s sister ship, the USS *Akron*, crashed off the coast of New Jersey with the loss of 73 lives, including that of Rear Admiral William A. Moffett. The Sunnyvale Naval Air Station was subsequently renamed Moffett Field. Shortly after the *Macon* itself crashed on the California coast near Point Sur in 1935, the Navy abandoned its dirigible program. After many years of activity at the field, the Navy withdrew in the late 1990s. Moffett Field remains a major aeronautical facility, housing the Ames Research Center, operated by the National Aeronautic and Space Administration. The Moffett Field Historical Museum is housed in Hangar One, displaying lighter-than-air balloons, blimps, dirigibles, and models of old craft, as well as newer heavier-than-air equipment.

RANCHO PASTORÍA DE LAS BORREGAS (MOUNTAIN VIEW AND SUNNYVALE)

Adjacent to Rancho Polsomi and lying mostly to the south of what is now the Bayshore Freeway is Rancho Pastoría de las Borregas ("pasture of the ewes"), also called Rancho Refugio. It was originally granted in 1842 to Francisco Estrada. A series of decrees by the Land Commission in the years between 1856 and 1881 divided the property into two tracts, with Permanente Creek as the dividing line. A city park at the corner of Rengstorff and Crisante Avenues in Mountain View is the site of the home of the Castro family, who owned the northern half of the old rancho. Mariano Castro was the father-in-law of Francisco Estrada and inherited his claim upon the early deaths of his daughter and her husband.

Henry Rengstorff Sr. came to California from Germany in 1850, was a prominent citizen of Mountain View, and helped to found the Whisman School. His Italianate-style house was built in 1867 and in 1990 was relocated from its original place at 1737 Stierlin Road to Mountain View Shoreline Park at 3070 North Shoreline Boulevard.

The Rengstorff home is open to the public. The southern half of the rancho was purchased by Martin Murphy Jr., who arrived with his father in California in 1844 in the Stevens-Murphy party. The Murphys came from Ireland and first settled in Canada. The family became prominent in the life of the community, particularly in the activities of the Catholic Church; Murphy had an important part in the establishment of Santa Clara College and the Convent of Notre Dame. The picturesque house they lived in was framed on the East Coast and brought around the Horn about 1851; it was occupied continuously for over a century by members of the same family. It was demolished in 1961, but the site is marked (SRL 644) in the Murphy Historic Park at 252 North Sunnyvale Avenue in Sunnyvale. The Sunnyvale Historical Museum, with a wide spread of displays, is on the same property.

RANCHO RINCÓN DE SAN FRANCISQUITO (PALO ALTO)

In 1824 José Peña built a wood house on what is now the Stanford University campus, then outlying land of Mission Santa Clara. His son, Narciso Antonio Peña, later justice of the peace in the area, built a small adobe some time later near the mission horse corral. In 1841, while teaching at Santa Clara, José Peña received a formal grant of the land from Governor Alvarado. The Rancho Rincón de San Francisquito, about two square leagues in area, lay between the creek of that name and San Antonio (Adobe) Creek, on the former mission cattle range.

Secundino Robles, born in Santa Cruz around 1812, was mayordomo at the mission in 1841. In 1846 he was commander of some of Francisco Sánchez's troops, when he was taken prisoner and distinguished himself by breaking his sword in two before surrendering to his American captors. Some years before his marriage in 1835 he had discovered the location of an outcrop of cinnabar on Alamitos Creek—the secret source of the red paint so long prized by the Indians for the decoration of their bodies. Afterward, when the cinnabar deposit proved to be rich in mercury, he and his brother Teodoro received a payment of $13,000 in cash and an interest in the company formed to develop the mine at New Almaden.

The brothers traded their interest in the mine to José Peña for his rancho and all the buildings upon it, "orchards, corrals, and all property he may have on said land." The deed was drawn up in September 1847; Secundino took immediate possession with his wife and four children and set about enlarging the small Peña adobe.

In its heyday the Robles home was famous for its hospitality; for a while it was even a stage stop between San Francisco and San Jose. Twenty-five more children were born to Secundino and María Antonia Robles after they took possession of the estate, making twenty-nine in all. By the end of the century, the house was unoccupied, and it collapsed in the April 18, 1906, earthquake. The site of the adobe has been marked by a plaque at the corner of Alma and Ferne Avenues placed by the city of Palo Alto and the Palo Alto Historical Association.

The rancho dwindled over the years. Jeremiah Clarke of San Francisco bought a portion of it from María Rosalía Robles, former wife of Teodoro Robles, in 1859. Clarke held a good deal of land in the area; his holdings extended to Mayfield Slough by the Bay. At the Clarke-Wilson landing, goods were shipped to San Francisco. The bayshore property belonging to Clarke was in time sold and developed; a wooden building that was a hammer factory in the late nineteenth century still stands at 2995 Middlefield Road at Matadero Creek.

RANCHO RINCONADA DEL ARROYO DE SAN FRANCISQUITO (PALO ALTO)

Don Rafael Soto, born in the Pueblo de San José, was the son of Ignacio Soto, a member of the Anza expedition. He had received a small piece of land in a bend (*rinconada*) of San Francisquito Creek on loan from Mission Santa Clara after its secularization, a place that had been the headquarters of the mission's sheep ranch. Soto petitioned for title to the Rancho Rinconada del Arroyo de San Francisquito in 1835, which was denied on a technicality.

Don Rafael had discovered the navigability of San Francisquito Creek up to the point at which he established an embarcadero for the loading and unloading of boats. The way between the embarcadero and El Camino Real, some three miles away, was not a properly defined road until 1874, when the present Embarcadero Road was opened by the county.

After the death of Don Rafael, his widow, Doña María Antonia, married into the Mesa family and received the grant for Rancho Rinconada del Arroyo de San Francisquito in 1841 from Governor Juan B. Alvarado. The 2,230 acres of the property bordered San Francisquito Creek from the Bay to the Palo Alto, the landmark tree that stands beside the railroad bridge in the city of that name. The house in which the Mesas and the large Soto family lived stood for many years at the corner of Middlefield Road and North California Avenue; the site is marked by a plaque placed by the city of Palo Alto and the Palo Alto Historical Association.

RANCHO SAN FRANCISQUITO (STANFORD UNIVERSITY)

Rancho San Francisquito lay along the eastern side of San Francisquito Creek to the south of Rancho Rinconada del Arroyo de San Francisquito. It was formally granted by Governor Alvarado to Antonino Buelna, who had been active in the revolt that put Alvarado into power, in 1839, two years after Don Antonino had begun building his adobe house near the northern edge of what is now the Stanford University golf course. In time this became known as El Paso del Arroyo ("the crossing of the creek") for the nearby and much-used ford at the creek. Ox teams, hauling logs and lumber from mills on the mountainside, could at this point take on a double load for the easy grade in the valley.

After American rule began, the rancho had a large number of squatters, whose claims caused much confusion in the 1850s. Most of the squatters were bought off by George Gordon, a wealthy San Francisco businessman, who in 1863 secured title to most of the original land. Before his death in 1869 he had built a country home on the property and laid out Eucalyptus Avenue and other drives.

Leland Stanford purchased the property from the executors of the estate and made the Gordon house the nucleus for his own grand residence, no longer standing. He greatly enlarged his holdings by the purchase of adjoining lands, so that he eventually possessed 9,200 acres, which in time became the site of Stanford University.

RANCHO SAN ANTONIO (LOS ALTOS)

This rancho was an oblong strip of land stretching from San Antonio (Adobe) Creek to Cupertino (Stevens) Creek along the foothills. It was granted to Juan Prado Mesa in 1839 by Governor Alvarado. Don Prado was a soldier stationed at the presidio in San Francisco who had become *alferez* (officer in command) in 1837. He built a large square adobe, which lasted long into the twentieth century as a crumbling ruin locally thought of as a fortification. The site today is on a hill on the southeast side of El Monte Avenue near Summerhill Avenue in Los Altos, most of which is situated on the territory of the rancho. The Los Altos History House Museum is located in the J. Gilbert Smith house, the home of an orchardist in the Depression years, recreating the life of the 1930s. The museum is at 51 South San Antonio Road in Los Altos.

RANCHO LA PURÍSIMA CONCEPCIÓN (LOS ALTOS HILLS)

Rancho La Purísima Concepción was granted in 1840 to José Gorgonio, an Indian who had been at Mission Santa Clara, by Governor Alvarado. He and another Indian, José Ramón, occupied the land for some years before the formal grant; their home was on a hill on the west side of Adobe Creek near present Fremont Avenue. The grant was sold to Juana Briones de Miranda in 1844. Juana was the daughter of a pioneer family that arrived in California in the 1790s. Her marriage to Apolinario Miranda, a soldier at the San Francisco Presidio, seems to have been unhappy—in 1843 he was sent before the subprefect for "not living harmoniously" with his wife, and the bishop gave her a legal separation.

In the North Beach district of San Francisco, where she had an adobe house, Juana frequently acted as doctor, nurse, or midwife. She continued this activity after moving with her seven children to the Rancho la Purísima Concepción, a hilly tract of land from which rise several small streams that join to form Adobe Creek. A glimpse of rancho life can be gained from a description of a shopping trip to San Francisco, which required a full week, three days going, and three days returning, and one day for the necessary errands in the city. The carreta, drawn by a team of oxen and piled with hides to be sold, got an early start and, jolting over the uneven road, reached the first night's destination at the Argüello rancho, Rancho de las Pulgas. The next day, a fresh team of oxen was supplied for the second lap of the journey, which ended at the Sánchez rancho, Rancho Buriburi (both ranchos are in what is now San Mateo County). There another exchange of oxen took place and Mission Dolores was reached on the third night. On the fourth day, the travelers greeted old friends and took the hides to Davis or to Leidesdorff, the two most successful merchant-ship owners of the time, exchanging them for supplies. The return journey saw all the oxen returned to their home corrals, and the travelers reached home with their own animals the night of the seventh day.

The Juana Briones de Miranda adobe (SRL 524) is actually made of rammed earth, but known by the generic term adobe nevertheless. It is located at 4255 Old Adobe Road on the border between Palo Alto and Los Altos Hills, just west of the intersection of Arastradero Road and the Foothill Expressway. Dr. Charles Palmer Nott, a botanist at Stanford University, purchased the place in 1900 and made many improvements to both the house and the grounds. The long and narrow building, found falling into decay, was protected by being covered with boards. Dr. Nott added rooms, including a second story, for his growing family. The property was acquired in 1925 by Dr. George Lee Easton of San Francisco and remains in the family.

RANCHO QUITO (SARATOGA)

Rancho Quito lay in the fertile country between the town of Saratoga and SR 82, watered by Saratoga and Calabasas Creeks, with the Arroyo San Tomás Aquino as its eastern boundary. The rancho was granted in 1841 by Governor Alvarado to José Noriega and José Zenon Fernández. Both men arrived in California as part of a colonizing expedition organized by José María Padrés and José María Híjar. They settled in San Jose, where Fernández taught for a time in nearby Santa Clara. At the time of the grant he was secretary to the council of the pueblo of San José. Both owners transferred the property to Manuel Alviso in 1844. Noriega continued to live in the vicinity. The American patent of 1866 was granted jointly to Alviso and the heirs of Fernández. Meanwhile, in 1839, Alviso had sold part of his interest in the property to José Ramón Argüello, son of Luís Argüello and grandson of José Darío Argüello. Argüello's Quito Farm was at the junction of modern-day Saratoga Avenue and Quito Road. There Argüello planted olive trees, a fruit orchard, and a small vineyard, which passed in 1882 into the possession of Edward E. Goodrich, who further developed the property by building a winery, an oil mill, and houses for his employees.

The city of Saratoga lies at the southwest corner of Rancho Quito on Saratoga Creek. The old settlement of Gubserville (SRL 447) was on the road from Santa Clara that extends through this rancho. The settlement was the first place on the stage route out of Santa Clara at which the driver paused to leave mail. The post office existed here from 1882 to 1899, and Frank Gubser was postmaster as well as saloonkeeper. Gubser's "Half-Way House" stood on the northwest side of Saratoga Avenue about opposite Los Felice Drive, where the state marker is located. Nearby, at Payne and Saratoga Avenues, is the site of the Moreland School (SRL 489), which, when it was marked by the state of California in 1953, was the center of the oldest known rural school district in the state.

RANCHO RINCONADA DE LOS GATOS (LOS GATOS)

Rancho Rinconada de los Gatos, consisting of one and one-half square leagues, was granted by Governor Alvarado in 1840 to Sebastián Peralta and José Hernández. The Arroyo San Tomás Aquino formed its western boundary and separated it from Rancho Quito. The rancho extended south of present-day Los Gatos into the broad lower end of the canyon, which is described by John C. Frémont in his *Memoirs* as a valley "openly wooded with groves of oak, free from underbrush, and after the spring rains covered with grass. On the west it is protected from the chilling influence of the northwest winds by the Cuesta de los Gatos [Wildcat Ridge], which separates it from the coast."

It is said that a fight took place there in 1831 between the Indians of the region and soldiers from Mission Santa Clara. Several legends, too, are connected with the naming of the place, all having to do with the number of large native cats. These seem to have been both plentiful and fierce, since the legends tell of several encounters with them. The ridge was known by the name of Los Gatos as early as 1831, and the rancho and the modern city of Los Gatos adopted the name from the ridge.

Sebastián Peralta sold 2,500 acres of the rancho to Claud Simond in 1852, and on this land Simond built an adobe home of one and one-half stories that is still standing at 14610 Quito Road. A private residence, the adobe has been remodeled over the years, but it still retains its Mexican charm, with its deep-set windows and doors. A commemorative bronze tablet was affixed to the outer wall of the old part in 1927 by the Colonial Dames of America.

RANCHO SANTA TERESA (SAN JOSE)

Rancho Santa Teresa originally consisted of 9,647 acres granted to Joaquín Bernal, a native of Mexico. The land he chose lies today within the southeastern part of the city of San Jose, bounded on the east by Coyote Creek. Much of the territory is now Santa Teresa County Park. On this rancho was signed the Treaty of Santa Teresa on November 29, 1844. Governor Manuel Micheltorena, who was opposed by Juan Bautista Alvarado and José Castro, agreed by its terms to send his army of *cholos*, an unpopular band of ex-convicts, out of California within three months. In fact he did not do so, and the "battle" of Cahuenga Pass, near Los Angeles, took place the following February; it resulted in Micheltorena's finally being unseated as governor.

RANCHO EL POTRERO DE SANTA CLARA (SAN JOSE)

One of the earliest boundary markers in California was placed between Mission Santa Clara and the Pueblo de San José to fix the extent of the mission pastures. The Potrero ("pasture lands") de Santa Clara was enclosed by a willow hedge and running ditch at its northwest end; the Alameda was built around its southern end. The ditch and the other early irrigation ditches were fed from the Posa de Santa Clara, a natural pond excavated into a shallow well, which had a perennial flow. This source is recognizably described in the early mission reports; its location has been identified as the middle of the block bounded by Mission Street, Park Avenue, and the Alameda.

After the secularization of the missions, this land reverted to the Mexican government, and in 1844 Governor Micheltorena granted Rancho El Potrero de Santa Clara, purportedly consisting of one square league, to James Alexander Forbes, who was then the British vice-consul for California. A native of Scotland, Forbes had arrived in California around 1830, had become a naturalized Mexican citizen, and in 1834 had married Ana María, daughter of Juan Crisóstomo Galinda, claimant of mission lands near Milpitas. According to some sources, El Potrero de Santa Clara was given as a marriage dower to the bride. A number of former mission Indians also claimed this property.

In 1847 Forbes sold the property to Commodore Robert Field Stockton, U.S.N. Born in 1795, Stockton had seen long service with the Navy, beginning with the War of 1812; he commanded the squadron that accepted the surrender of the Mexican garrisons at Santa Barbara and Los Angeles, and was military governor of California from the summer of 1846 until early in the following year. He did not spend much time in California (he represented his native New Jersey in the United States Senate in 1851–53, after his resignation from the Navy), but he is credited with three new business ventures that proved important for the region: a nursery for the propagation of fruit trees, a residential subdivision called Alameda Gardens, and the importation of houses from the East brought around the Horn. Agents established a nursery with stock imported from Massachusetts; it is said that the first strawberry plants in the Santa Clara Valley were brought in at this time, the beginnings of what was to become an important crop in the area. Stockton also imported bees from Italy; a marker (SRL 945) at the San Jose Airport, however, attributes the introduction of the honeybee in California to Christopher A. Shelton in 1853 at the Rancho El Potrero de Santa Clara.

For the Alameda Gardens subdivision, Stockton ordered houses to be made in New England ready to be erected in California after being shipped around the Horn. Ten houses were put up; a house now standing at another location on 968 Emory Street is thought to be one of these, the others all having disappeared.

RANCHO LOS COCHES (SAN JOSE)

The first case decided for property in Santa Clara County by the Federal Land Commission, following the terms of the Treaty of Guadalupe-Hidalgo, was that of Rancho Los Coches (called "the pigs" because it had been the mission's swine pasturage), consisting of one-half square league lying southwest of the Alameda. The boundary began on the Alameda at the Ciénega de Santa Clara and extended westward to the Roblar del Torotal, thence southeast along this forest to the Arroyo de los Gatos, thence to the Guadalupe River. This rancho had been granted in 1842 by Governor Micheltorena to Roberto, a Christianized Indian of Mission Santa Clara who had been living on the land with his wife and children before that date. The issue in this case was concerned with the legality of a grant to an Indian and further with his right to dispose of the property. The question being decided in the affirmative by the commission, a claim, based on Roberto's ownership, was filed in 1852 by Antonio Suñol, his daughter Paula Suñol de Sansevain, and Henry M. Naglee, and the claimants received the patent to the rancho in 1857.

Antonio María Suñol, a Spaniard once in the French naval service, left the *Bordelais* in Monterey Harbor in 1818. He settled in San Jose, where he kept a shop, and about 1824 married María Dolores Bernal. He was postmaster from 1826 to 1829, *sindico* (receiver) from 1839 to 1840, and subprefect from 1841 to 1844. In his ranch activities, he sold cattle to Captain John Sutter on credit and had difficulty in obtaining payment. The Suñol adobe, still standing, has been described earlier in this chapter.

Henry Morris Naglee, a distinguished officer in the Civil War and one of the three joint patentees of Rancho Los Coches, long held a portion of it in his name. Naglee Park, which extended from Eleventh Street to Coyote Creek in the city of San Jose, was once his property (although not on Los Coches), and here on a 140-acre tract stood his residence, reached by a driveway one and one-half miles long. Now remodeled as an apartment house, the building stands at the northwest corner of San Fernando and Fourteenth Streets. The redwood trees and the stately palms remaining from his planting, which line some of the streets in this vicinity, give some idea of the extent and beauty of the grounds laid out around his home in 1865.

RANCHO LAS ANIMAS (SOUTHERN SANTA CLARA COUNTY)

The first census of San Jose, taken in 1778, lists thirteen-year-old José Mariano Castro, eldest son of Joaquín Castro and his wife, María Botiller, both of whom came to California in 1776 with the Anza colonists. This boy, grown to manhood and married to Josefa Romero, journeyed back to Mexico in 1801 and obtained the grant of Rancho La Brea. The document, directly from the Spanish viceroy Marquinas, was dated August 17, 1802. Together with an addition to it granted in 1810 by Viceroy Lizano y Beaumont, it was the only rancho in California granted directly by a viceroy, according to Theodore Hittell. In later years some difficulty regarding the title was encountered, but in 1835 the matter was adjusted by the re-granting of it under the name of Rancho Las Animas by the Mexican governor, José Figueroa, to the widow of Don José Mariano, Doña Josefa.

In time this rancho passed into the possession of José María Sánchez. The 26,519 acres patented to his heirs in 1873 extend from the border with San Benito County across US 101 south of Gilroy to Mount Madonna County Park in the Santa Cruz Mountains. On this rancho, the Carnadero Creek flows for miles through a series of rolling hills, after it leaves the higher region near Mount Madonna. Excellent pasture lands are on these hills, and here around Miller's Station was the celebrated Bloomfield Ranch of Henry Miller, who climbed to success through his ability to raise and market cattle and sheep, and to pursue his goals with ruthless tenacity.

Heinrich Alfred Kreiser was the name of this young German in his native land, but in his journey from New York via the Isthmus of Panama he had used a ticket purchased from a chance acquaintance named Henry Miller. On March 30, 1858, eight years after he had reached California, he changed his name by legal procedure to Henry Miller. In that year he entered into partnership with Charles Lux, a partnership that lasted until the death of Lux twenty-five years later. As time passed, the firm of Miller and Lux became familiar throughout the West. Henry Miller seemed to succeed in all that he undertook; his ability to foresee the outcome of his plans was remarkable. The lands and herds of this firm stretched over the state; in several counties large feeding grounds and fields for cultivation were acquired. More than a dozen of the old ranchos were owned in whole or in part by Miller and Lux, and the number of their employees was huge. When the animals were driven to market in San Francisco, no matter how long the journey, there were always convenient feeding and resting places on their own property.

The Bloomfield Ranch is easily recognized by three large concrete silos, built relatively recently, along US 101 three and one-half miles south of Gilroy. It is said that one of the dwellings on the ranch, visible from the highway, is part of the old ranch house.

On Mount Madonna (elevation 1,897 feet) in the mountains on the northwest part of this rancho, Henry Miller built an elaborate country home overlooking the broad valley below. There he entertained his friends. After his death in 1916 the house, which had been purchased for rebuilding elsewhere, was removed piece by piece, and the fountains, terraces, and choice trees and shrubs that graced the grounds were left untended. The ruins of the estate may be seen in Mount Madonna County Park, marked by an E Clampus Vitus plaque.

RANCHO OJO DE AGUA DE LA COCHE (MORGAN HILL)

An epic of the westward movement might be written using as a theme the Martin Murphy family. Martin Murphy Sr., nearing the age of sixty, arrived in California in 1844 with his sons and daughters and several grandchildren. Murphy was born in 1785 in Ireland, where he married and where his older children were born. From unpromising Ireland, he took his family (with the exception of his eldest son and daughter, who joined him later) and moved in 1820 to Canada, where he settled and remained for twenty years.

Around 1840 another move was made, this time to a part of the United States west of the Mississippi River near St. Joseph. The new location proved unsatisfactory because of the lack of religious and educational opportunities and because of the presence of malaria, which killed his wife, Mary Foley, and three of his grandchildren. Once more he took up his family and moved on; this time his destination was chosen because of the influence of a priest who had visited California and described it with enthusiasm. Selling all his land, Murphy put the proceeds into provisions, wagons, oxen, and equipment for the long trek to the Far West in 1844. At a point on the Missouri River, the parties headed by Martin Murphy and Elisha Stevens joined forces for mutual protection and aid.

With the young men of the party on horseback accompanying the wagons drawn by oxen and containing the family and all their household goods, the long journey finally ended in safety around Sacramento. Here most of the men in the group enlisted at once under Sutter's leadership to go to the aid of Governor Micheltorena in putting down the Alvarado-Castro insurrection of 1845. When this episode was ended, the immigrants were free to settle where they chose, and the party disbanded. Martin Murphy Jr. bought land nearby on the Cosumnes River, where he lived until the Gold Rush of 1849 enabled him to sell his land and livestock at a considerable profit, when he again followed his father.

Martin Murphy Sr. had settled in Santa Clara County near the present town of Morgan Hill. Purchasing Rancho Ojo de Agua de la Coche ("sow spring"), which had been granted by Governor Figueroa to Juan María Hernández in 1835, he built an adobe residence between the town of Morgan Hill and the hill that rises to the west of the town, known as, among other names, Murphy's Peak or Twenty-One Mile Peak. Martin J. C. Murphy, a grandson, received the United States patent to the rancho in 1860. US 101 and the Union Pacific Railroad pass through the town, which was named for Hiram Morgan Hill, who married Martin Murphy's granddaughter Diana. Hill's home "Villa Mira Monte," built in the 1880s, has been restored by the Morgan Hill Historical Society in a community park at 350 North Monterey Street. E Clampus Vitus commemorated the town in a plaque at Monterey Highway and San Martin Avenue.

NEW ALMADEN

The Indians of the Santa Clara Valley often visited the hill of red earth (cinnabar) above the poplar-lined stream that the Spaniards later called the Arroyo de los Alamitos ("river of the little poplar trees"). The red earth made excellent pigment, which the Indians used for adornment.

As early as 1824 the Spanish settlers of the valley knew about the red hill and its pigments. In that year an attempt was made by the Robles brothers, Secundino and Teodoro, and by Don Antonio Suñol, to find silver or gold in the deposit; in time their excavation was called "La Mina Santa Clara."

In the year 1842 Governor Alvarado made grants of land in this vicinity: Rancho Cañada de los Capitancillos was granted to Justo Larios, and Rancho San Vicente was granted to José de los Reyes Berryessa. On November 22, 1845, Andrés Castillero, a deputy of the Mexican government, filed with Alcalde Pedro Chabolla in San Jose a document in which he claimed discovery of "silver with a ley of gold" on the rancho of José Berryessa. In conformity with the mining ordinances he asked that notices of his discovery and of his intention to develop it be affixed in public places. After making certain crude tests he filed a second document in the following month reporting the discovery of "liquid quicksilver" in the deposit, and shortly thereafter went back to Mexico.

Soon there began long-drawn-out litigation over the ownership of the mine. In 1846, Barron, Forbes and Company of Tepic, Mexico, owned the controlling interest in the project, and after the discovery of gold at Coloma in 1848, there was a tremendous increase in the demand for mercury, used in the reduction of gold ore. New Almaden, named for the great Almaden mine in Spain, became one of the most famous and most productive mercury mines in the world. The text on the state plaque (SRL 339, located on Monterey Road one-half mile south of Troy Road) says that a new purchaser in 1864 paid $1.7 million for the property. Mining operations ceased in 1975.

The Department of the Interior designated New Almaden a National Historic Landmark District in 1958. The district encompasses the Hacienda, or mining community, that evolved along the banks of the Alamitos Creek, and the Cinnabar Hills where the actual mining operation took place. Santa Clara County purchased 3,500 acres of Cinnabar Hills open space for the creation of Quicksilver Park in 1975. A highlight of the place is the Casa Grande, the home of the mine superintendent, with two-foot-thick walls and magnificent hand-carved fireplaces. The building dates back to 1854; the original formal landscaping was done by John McLaren, who developed Golden Gate Park in San Francisco. The building has been recently refurbished and is now the New Almaden Museum. An E Clampus Vitus marker on the building recounts its history.

The picturesque settlement continues up to the furnaces and reduction works. Small wooden houses, many marked with historic plaques, line the main street (SRL 339-1, marker at Bulmore Park). The Hacienda Cemetery has been restored and maintained by the California Pioneers of Santa Clara County and is located on Bertram Avenue in back of the hacienda.

The site of the Almaden Vineyards (SRL 505), planted by Charles Le Franc in 1852, is at 1530 Blossom Hill Road in San Jose. The winery is no longer in operation.

THE BATTLE OF SANTA CLARA

The American conquest of California was not unchallenged, but the so-called battles that took place were, on the whole, mere skirmishes with few casualties. On January 2, 1847, one such skirmish, known as the Battle of Santa Clara, was fought about two and one-half miles west of Mission Santa Clara at a spot marked at 2780 El Camino Real by E Clampus Vitus. The American leaders were captains Joseph Aram, John W. Murphy, and Charles M. Weber; Francisco Sánchez was the Mexican captain. Four Californios were killed and four wounded; two Americans suffered wounds. The site of the Armistice Oak (SRL 260), under which the battle is said to have ended, is in Civic Center Park, on El Camino Real at Lincoln Street. A five-day armistice followed the battle, during which time Sánchez and his forces retreated to the Santa Cruz Mountains and then surrendered to the American authorities.

CALIFORNIA'S FIRST STATE CAPITAL

San Jose became the first state capital of California after the adoption of the initial state constitution on November 13, 1849. The Legislature convened there on December 17, delayed by heavy rains, which kept many legislators from reaching the town for the announced December 15 opening. Nine months later Congress passed the act that formally admitted California to the Union. Although serious work was accomplished at San Jose, this session is known as "the Legislature of a Thousand Drinks" because of the freely imbibing Senator Thomas Jefferson Green and his advocacy of adjournment to the local saloon.

The capital was removed from San Jose to Vallejo by act of the second Legislature on February 14, 1851, and the removal took effect on May 1 of that year. The building that served as the first state capitol was a little two-story structure, adobe below and frame above, which stood on a site (SRL 461) directly across South Market Street from the spot now marked by a granite boulder and bronze plate on the east side of the old plaza. The tablet, placed by the Native Sons of the Golden West, bears an image of the old adobe capitol, which was destroyed by fire in 1853.

THE FIRST AMERICAN SCHOOL IN CALIFORNIA

The first American school in California was held in the crumbling buildings of Mission Santa Clara in the spring of 1847 by Mrs. Olive Mann Isbell. She and her husband, Dr. James C. Isbell, had just arrived from Ohio with other members of an overland emigrant party. While the men were called to do military duty, the women and children were left at the mission. Partly to relieve mothers of the constant care of their families, Mrs. Isbell began to give rudimentary instruction to the children with the slender means at her disposal, lacking books, paper, pencils, and chalk. One of the pupils later recounted that letters of the alphabet were drawn on the back of the hand with a stick of charcoal and thus made visible to the beginners. When the men

returned from their short period of military service and the reunited families went their separate ways, this unique school ended; Mrs. Isbell taught for many years in other parts of the state.

THE COLLEGE OF NOTRE DAME

Two sisters from the Order of Notre Dame de Namur established the College of Notre Dame in San Jose in 1851; the college was officially chartered as an institution of higher learning four years later. The flourishing establishment occupied a tract of land extending from West Santa Clara Street to West St. John Street and from Notre Dame Street to Santa Teresa Street. In 1923 the college was moved to the less urban atmosphere of Belmont in San Mateo County, some twenty-five miles to the north.

THE UNIVERSITY OF THE PACIFIC

The University of the Pacific, founded under Methodist auspices in San Jose, is the oldest incorporated educational institution in California, having received its charter on July 10, 1851, under the name California Wesleyan University. In 1870 the college, by then called the University of the Pacific, was moved to College Park, about halfway between Santa Clara and San Jose, and now within the San Jose city limits. In 1921 the name was changed to the College of the Pacific, and in 1924 the entire establishment was moved to Stockton, where in 1961 it once more took the name of the University of the Pacific. The site on the old College Park campus is now occupied by Bellarmine College Preparatory School, operated by the Jesuits and originally the high school department of the University of Santa Clara.

SAN JOSE STATE UNIVERSITY

The first normal school (an institution specifically designed for the training of teachers) in California began in San Francisco in 1857 as a private enterprise, Minns's Evening Normal School, taking its name from the first principal, George W. Minns. By act of the Legislature in 1862 it was made a public normal school. In 1870, after a spirited contest over the location, the school was moved to San Jose. In 1921 all the normal schools in California were changed into teachers' colleges. The institution became San Jose State College in 1935 and was raised to university status in 1972, along with many other state colleges. SRL 417, commemorating the original normal school, is located at Tower Hall, a structure dating from 1910.

OTHER HISTORIC SPOTS IN SAN JOSE

One of San Jose's finest old buildings began life in 1883 at 161–63 West Santa Clara Street as the LeFranc Block. Charles LeFranc, pioneer French vineyardist, became famous for his wines grown in the Santa Clara Valley, beginning in the 1850s. By 1880 another Frenchman, Paul Masson, had become part of his operation. The block contained a large wine cellar, many offices, including that of the Paul Masson Champagne Company, and the St. Nicholas Hotel. After LeFranc's death in 1887, Masson expanded his interests, developing his own winery and in 1930 putting a new façade on what was now called the Masson-LeFranc Building. In 1998 this was further remodeled into apartments, offices, and showrooms.

The French prune, one of Santa Clara Valley's best-known products, was introduced into California at San Jose in the winter of 1856–57 by Louis Pellier, aided by his brothers Pierre and Jean. A native of France, Pellier came to California in 1849, and the following year opened a nursery called City Gardens (SRL 434). On November 29, 1977, the two hundredth anniversary of the founding of the pueblo, Pellier Park was dedicated on the site at St. James and Terraine Streets by the city of San Jose.

At 432 South Eighth Street is the Edwin Markham Cottage (SRL 416), the house where the poet lived from 1869 to 1889 and wrote the first draft of his most celebrated work, "The Man with the Hoe." After a boyhood spent in Solano County, Markham attended the normal school at San Jose and upon graduation began teaching school at Evergreen.

The Hayes Mansion (SRL 888) at 200 Edenvale Avenue is a 1904 example of what is called Mission Revival–Italian Renaissance architecture, designed by George W. Page. The Hayes family was prominent in religious and political activities in San Jose for many years.

A larger building is the Winchester House (SRL 868) at 525 South Winchester Boulevard by the junction of I-280 and SR 17. Sarah Winchester was the heiress to the Winchester Repeating Arms Company fortune. Following the deaths of her husband and baby daughter, she came to California in 1880 and set out to enlarge a country house. A spiritualist, she became convinced that her life depended on constantly adding to her house; some 160 rooms had been completed at the time of her death in 1922. The Winchester Mystery House is a very popu-

Rosicrucian Egyptian Museum Entrance, San Jose

lar public attraction today, where visitors can see staircases ending in the ceiling, doors that open onto blank walls, and five fully equipped kitchens.

Another unusual building in San Jose is the Rosicrucian Egyptian Museum at Park and Naglee Avenues, containing remarkable displays of ancient artifacts collected by the Rosicrucian fellowship.

The San Jose Museum of Art at 110 South Market Street is located in the old post office (SRL 854), the first federal building in San Jose, constructed in 1892. Nearby are two churches that, like the post office building, are on the National Register of Historic Places. St. Joseph's Catholic Church (SRL 910) at Market and San Fernando Streets was completed in 1877 and has had a thorough renovation. The First Unitarian Church (SRL 902) at 160 North Third Street has been in continuous use since its completion in 1892. A third church, Trinity Episcopal, at Second and St. John Streets, is a redwood structure, built in 1863, and is the oldest church building still standing in San Jose.

A plaque at the northwest corner of First and San Fernando Streets (SRL 952) commemorates the site of the first broadcasting station in the world, established by Dr. Charles Herrold in 1909. It later became known as KQW and is now KCBS, with offices in Oakland, San Francisco, and San Jose. Another plaque, at 79 North Market Street, marks the birthplace of Amadeo Peter Giannini, born in what was then the Swiss Hotel in 1870. In 1904 Giannini founded the Bank of Italy, now Bank of America, in San Francisco, and in 1910 he opened the bank's first out-of-town branch, in San Jose at the corner of Santa Clara and Lightston Streets. The bank structure has been moved to the San Jose Historical Museum.

The San Jose Historical Museum, situated in Kelley Park at 635 Phelan Avenue, contains a number of his-

Old Post Office, now part of San Jose Museum of Art

Ainsley House, Campbell

toric buildings from the city and from the Santa Clara Valley, including the old Coyote Post Office, dating from 1862. Dominating the site is a replica of the San Jose Electric Tower; this was the inspiration of J. J. Owen, owner of the *San Jose Mercury*, who in 1881 printed an editorial suggesting that if the city provided one high and immense source of arc light, the night would become as day for the downtown area. The idea met with public approval, and the 237-foot tower was installed by the end of the year. Straddling the intersection of Santa Clara and Market Streets, the tower's 24,000 candle-power light failed to illuminate the area as expected; it was damaged in a windstorm in 1915 and collapsed later that year. The 115-foot replica is scaled to fit the streets around the museum.

MUSEUMS OF SANTA CLARA

The Santa Clara Historic Museum is located in the Headen-Inman House at 1509 Warburton Avenue and offers memorabilia and photographic collections relating to the city of Santa Clara. The Harris-Lass Historic Museum, which is called "Santa Clara's last farmstead," is located in a restored 1865 Italianate house with barn, tank house, and summer kitchen, at 1889 Market Street. Train buffs can visit the South Bay Historical Railroad Museum in the restored Santa Clara depot (1863) at 1005 Railroad Avenue; a theme of the institution is the influence of the railroad on California's history.

CAMPBELL

William Campbell, a native of Kentucky and a veteran of the War of 1812, arrived in Santa Clara County with his family in 1846, having traveled on the first part of the overland journey with the Donner party. The fol-

lowing year he assisted in the surveys of the towns of San Jose and Santa Clara, and in 1847–48 he built a sawmill, about three miles above present-day Saratoga near Long Bridge, on the creek now called by his name. His elder son, David, went to another county to live, but Benjamin, who was nineteen when his family arrived in California, purchased land some miles northeast of his father's mill, on which he raised wheat until 1887. In that year he subdivided the tract and sold lots for the town of Campbell.

The town was at one time the center of fruit-raising activities in the Santa Clara Valley. The Campbell Fruit Growers Union cooperative was taken over by the George W. Hyde Company, which operated one of the world's largest drying grounds. On a visit to the area in 1903 (in the course of which Mrs. Winchester refused to receive him in her home), President Theodore Roosevelt planted a redwood tree on the Campbell High School grounds, an offshoot of which still stands at the intersection of Winchester Boulevard and Campbell Avenue. By 1965, houses and apartments had entirely taken over the orchards and food-processing activities of the past.

That past may be relived in the newly refurbished Campbell Historical Museum at First Street and Civic Center Drive where the heyday of the fruit-canning industry is featured. The Ainsley House nearby at 51 North Central Avenue was moved from its original location in 1989. Built for Mr. & Mrs. J. C. Ainsley in 1925, the English Tudor house displays the gracious living of this canning entrepreneur; the English garden reflects the heritage of this couple.

LOS GATOS

Situated on the Arroyo de los Gatos after it flows from the canyon into the wider open space at the foot of the

Santa Cruz Mountains is the city of Los Gatos. It had its beginning in the Santa Rosa Flour Mill (SRL 458) built on the east side of Los Gatos Creek by James Alexander Forbes in 1854.

The mill had three stories of stone taken from the nearby canyon and a fourth story of redwood. A dam was built half a mile upstream and water was carried from it through a wooden flume to power the two water wheels that ran the totally automatic machinery. Forbes overextended himself in constructing the mill and by 1856 had declared bankruptcy. Other entrepreneurs followed, until the mill was closed in 1887. The earthquake of 1906 badly damaged the building, and in 1916 its owner, the Pacific Gas and Electric Company, had the four-story mill pulled down, leaving intact a two-story stone addition from 1880 to serve as an electrical substation. The building today serves as the Forbes Mill Regional History Museum, established by Eureka Federal Savings Company and now operated by the independent Los Gatos Museum Association. Its permanent displays focus on the history of the community; it also houses traveling exhibits from time to time. It is accessible from East Main and Church Streets in Los Gatos, on the east side of SR 17.

El Camino Real, from Mission Santa Clara to Mission Santa Cruz, passed just to the east of Forbes's Mill. A flood in 1862 demolished the road. Beginning in 1847, sawmills were operated in the canyons above the present town. The trail through the canyon was used for hauling the lumber down to a lumberyard where College and Main Streets now meet, so that teamsters from San Jose would not have to travel the dangerous one-lane road to the mills.

A good wagon road into the redwoods and over the mountains to Santa Cruz was needed. In 1857, the first meeting of the Santa Cruz Gap Turnpike Joint Stock Company was held in the tollhouse, which still stands at 142 South Santa Cruz Avenue, at the corner of Wood Road. In October 1858 the toll road was completed from Los Gatos, up the west side of Los Gatos Canyon to Lexington, and on to the summit. There it connected with the Santa Cruz Turnpike near the cabin of Charles Henry "Mountain Charley" McKiernan, the first permanent white settler in the Santa Cruz Mountains.

Royce Street in Los Gatos is named for Josiah Royce, historian, philosopher, and psychologist, who spent a part of his early years on that street in the house of his mother, Sarah Eleanor Royce.

At 17535 Santa Cruz Highway one can see the statues of two cats, eight feet high, flanking the entrance to the estate once owned by Colonel and Mrs. Erskin Scott Wood. The concrete felines are the work of sculptor Charles Paine and were put up when the estate was built in 1922. They are now regarded as the official symbol of the town, which is named for the wildcats in the area.

Kotani-En (SRL 903) at 15891 Ravine Road is a classical Japanese residence surrounded by gardens covering an acre and a half. It was commissioned in 1918 by San Francisco financier Max H. Cohn.

The Los Gatos Museum at 4 Tait Avenue is housed in the city's old firehouse. Its displays include changing art shows and a natural history museum.

HISTORIC SPOTS OF THE SANTA CRUZ MOUNTAINS IN SANTA CLARA COUNTY

Rising toward the ridge marking the Santa Cruz County boundary, the Santa Cruz Mountains south of Los Gatos contain a few remaining historical landmarks and some names of historical interest. When the Lexington Dam was completed in 1953, impounding the waters of Los Gatos Creek, the historic area of Lexington and Alma was inundated. Here the first sawmill in Santa Clara County was set up in 1848. As roads into the area were constructed, John Pennell Henning of Lexington, Missouri, laid out a "city of Lexington" in 1858. A number of commercial enterprises were in operation at its height in 1867, including the Lexington House Hotel, which catered to sportsmen who fished for trout in Los Gatos Creek or hunted bear and deer in the nearby mountains.

Alma originated in 1862 as the Forest House, a roadside hotel. The Lexington post office was moved there in 1873 and given the name Alma (Spanish for "soul"), for Alma was the soul of the redwood district. A mile up the canyon from Lexington, Alma prospered when James Fair's South Pacific Coast Railroad began its run from Alameda in 1878; the passengers left the narrow-gauge line at Alma and took stagecoaches over the mountains to Santa Cruz. The railroad to Santa Cruz was completed in 1880 and seven years later was taken over by the Southern Pacific Railroad, which converted the line to standard-gauge track in 1909. The last trains ran between Los Gatos and Santa Cruz on March 4, 1940.

The oldest building believed still to be standing in the Santa Cruz Mountains is at 22849 Summit Road, built in 1852 by the German cabinetmaker John Martin Schultheis for his family. Closer to the main road, at 22951 Summit, is the frame house built in 1880 by Vol-ney Averell, who married Alice Schultheis. The Summit Opera House, run by Averell and Charles Aitken, was at nearby Patchin (SRL 448), commemorated by a plaque at Mountain Charley Road and Old Santa Cruz Highway Road, east of today's SR 17.

"Bohemia" is a picturesque building at 241 Loma Prieta Road. It was built in the mid-1870s by Z. A. Catton to serve as both a private residence and an inn. In the latter capacity, it was a haven for writers such as Ambrose Bierce, Jack London, and George Sterling, whose patronage gave it a bohemian tone.

Austrian Dam stands at the junction of Austrian Gulch and Los Gatos Creek. Austro-German immigrants in the 1870s settled on these mountain slopes and with their industry and thrift soon made a prosperous settlement of orchards and vineyards. A terrific cloudburst in 1889 swept away their possessions; the foundations of their immense winery were so loosened that it collapsed and thousands of gallons of red wine poured down Los Gatos Creek. Although a few undaunted souls remained, most of the colony returned to Europe or sought employment elsewhere in California. A forest fire in 1923 destroyed the few wooden buildings left in Austrian Gulch.

Holy City is still marked on road maps, but no longer exists in fact. It was founded in 1918 by William E. "Father" Riker, the leader of a white-supremacist religious cult and perennial candidate for governor of the state. The colony became a tourist attraction on the highway between Santa Cruz and the Bay Area; its wooden buildings plastered with garish signs housed a print shop, a mineral water concern, a radio station, and tourist facilities for "the world's perfect government." After SR 17 was rerouted in the 1950s, Holy City began its terminal decline.

SARATOGA

William Campbell and his sons, David and Benjamin, began construction of a sawmill on Arroyo Quito late in 1847. Before the mill was finished, word reached them of the discovery of gold in the Sierra Nevada. They rushed to the mines in the Sierra, but soon returned to complete their mill, only to find that one was already in operation on Arroyo de los Gatos, even though it began a month later than their own. The Campbell mill was thus the second operating sawmill in Santa Clara County. It was located at or near Long Bridge (now Saratoga Springs Picnic Resort), about three miles west of Saratoga at the junction of SR 9 and Sanborn Road. In the early 1950s, Campbell Creek was officially renamed Saratoga Creek.

In 1850-51 Martin McCarty, another lumberman, built a toll road up the canyon to what had become known as Campbell's Redwoods. At the lower end of the road, a little settlement began to grow, known at first simply as Toll Gate. In 1855 a post office was established under the name of McCartysville. McCarty's tollgate crossed the present Big Basin Way (formerly Lumber Street) near the corner of Third Street, about where 14477 Big Basin Way is today.

Meanwhile, in 1854, William Haun and John Whisman had established a gristmill called Redwood Mills. It was later purchased by Charles Maclay, who added a tannery and changed the name to Bank Mills. The McCartysville post office was also renamed Bank Mills, but in 1865 it became Saratoga (SRL 435), because, like New York state's Saratoga, it was close to valuable and popular medicinal springs.

Pacific Congress Springs, a short distance west of Saratoga on SR 9, was one of the earliest and most fashionable recreational resorts in California. The mineral springs were discovered in the early 1850s by Jerd Caldwell. Wealthy men, including D. O. Mills and Alvinza Hayward, became interested in the place and formed a corporation, and in June 1866 Congress Hall opened to the public. The building stood about five minutes' walk from the springs. The company owned about seven hundred and twenty acres of wooded hillside, and eventually other buildings were added. The mineral water was proclaimed to be "a refreshing beverage and invigorating tonic." The resort was closed in 1942, and all the buildings are now gone.

Although efforts were made to establish manufacturing in Saratoga, it continued to be chiefly a hub of the lumbering industry and also pioneered in fruit raising, drying, and packing. Today Saratoga is a city of beautiful homes, some of them of considerable age. The James Springer house at 20770 Wildwood Way is the oldest (1851) in town, a prefabricated house brought around the Horn. Martin McCarty's widow, Hannah, lived in a house thought to have been built in 1877 that still stands at 20600 Lomita Avenue. Remodeled now as an office building, the John Henry home at 14630 Big Basin Way (1869) is also of interest. The earlier McWilliams house (1865) has been moved to 20460 Saratoga–Los Gatos Road, in the Saratoga Historical Park. Next door at 20450 Saratoga–Los Gatos Road stands the Saratoga Historical Museum, in what was a commercial building built in 1904. The Saratoga Foothill Clubhouse at 20399

Park Place was designed by Julia Morgan, and has been in continuous use since 1915. Welchhurst at 15808 Sanborn Road was built as a family retreat by Judge James R. Welch in 1914. It is interesting for its use of indigenous materials and now serves as a youth hostel. Both Welchhurst and the Saratoga Foothill Clubhouse are on the National Register of Historic Places.

In Madronia Cemetery, at Oak and Sixth Streets, are buried A. T. Dowd, discoverer of the Calaveras Big Trees; Riley Moutry, one of the heroic rescuers of the Donner party; and Mrs. Mary Ann Brown, the widow of John Brown, famous abolitionist of Harper's Ferry. Mrs. Brown came to California in 1864, five years after her husband's execution. She and her family settled at Red Bluff, where the home built for her by the townspeople is still standing. In 1870 the Browns moved to Humboldt County and eleven years later to Saratoga. Mrs. Brown's home from 1881 to 1883 was on the side of the mountain three miles above town, overlooking a wide sweep of the Santa Clara Valley. In 1883, before moving to San Francisco, Mrs. Brown sold the mountain farm and lived a short time in a rented house, no longer standing, on the site of the present Sacred Heart Church at 13915 Saratoga Avenue. Mary Ann Brown died in San Francisco in 1884, but her remains were returned to Saratoga for funeral services and burial.

Senator James Duval Phelan, philanthropist, statesman, and patron of the arts, named his Saratoga country place Villa Montalvo in honor of the Spanish writer Ordoñez de Montalvo, in whose *Las Sergas de Esplandian* ("The Exploits of Esplandian"), published in 1510, the name California appears for the first time. The house, built in 1912 on an estate of 175 acres, is situated in the foothills of the Santa Cruz Mountains in a region of great natural beauty with an extensive view over valley and mountains. In the nineteen-room mansion, which surrounds three sides of a colorful court, the owner placed priceless works of art gathered from many lands during a long period of years. Here this native son of San Francisco entertained his many friends in the social, political, commercial, and artistic circles in which he moved.

At the death of Senator Phelan in 1930, the place with all its previous furnishings was left to the San Francisco Art Association. It is now administered as an art gallery and cultural center by the Villa Montalvo Association, and is on the National Register of Historic Places. The gates at the beginning of a long driveway to the mansion are located at 15400 Montalvo Road, Saratoga, just southeast of the town's business district.

The Hakone Japanese Garden at 21000 Congress Springs Boulevard has been a city of Saratoga park since 1966. The fifteen-acre property was originally owned by Mr. & Mrs. Oliver C. Stine of San Francisco, who in 1917 constructed here a Japanese house in the old-country style, using neither adhesives nor nails. The extensive and exquisite gardens were completed by Naoharu Aihara, a relative of the court gardeners to the emperor of Japan, the following year. Mrs. Stine called the estate Hakone because, lying in the Congress Springs area, it reminded her of Fuju Hakone National Park, with its mineral springs, in Japan.

The Paul Masson Winery (SRL 733) is on Paul Masson Mountain Winery Road, reached from 13150 Saratoga Avenue. The number 1852 is prominently displayed above the entrance; the marking on the state plaque implies that this is the date of the winery, but local historians insist that no such building existed in that year.

STEVENS CREEK AND CUPERTINO

Stevens Creek was originally known as Arroyo de San José Cupertino. SRL 800, in the west parking lot of Monte Vista High School at 21840 McClellan Road in Cupertino, marks the approximate spot where on March 25, 1776, on the second Anza expedition, Father Font wrote in his diary the name that had been bestowed on the stream. The creek now bears the name of Captain Elisha Stevens, an early settler in the area, a South Carolinian who led the first successful passage of wagons over the Sierra Nevada in 1844. (It appears that the correct spelling of his name is "Stephens," but historical markers and street signs all over California use the other spelling.) He settled on the banks of the Arroyo de San Joseph Cupertino in 1859, but by 1864 headed south to the Kern River area, claiming there were too many people in the region for his liking. The oldest house still standing in the Stevens Creek area is that built by W. T. McClellan at 22221 McClellan Road, in the Cupertino city facility now called the McClellan Ranch Park.

The first millionaire in the region, Charles Baldwin, started a large estate in 1887, which he named "Beaulieu," with seventy acres of vineyards. Cupertino was then noted for its wine production. The estate is now the campus of De Anza College. The well-known San Francisco architect Willis Polk designed for Baldwin a large home, which has been moved to its present location at 21250 Stevens Creek Boulevard on the college campus; it is now the California History Center, and the location of the Louis Stocklmeir Regional History Library. Other reminders of the early estate are the stone winery and underground cellars, now used as the college bookstore and cafeteria.

"Woodhills" at 22800 Prospect Road, built in 1913, was the country home of Fremont Older, a distinguished San Francisco newspaper editor, and his wife, Cora, who was active in California historical work. An adjacent adobe tile structure was built in 1923 from materials Mrs. Older salvaged from an 1847 adobe in San Jose that was being dismantled. The Older home, restored, is open to the public on a very limited basis. The Cupertino Historical Museum at 10185 North Stelling Road focuses on the history of the town.

"THE FRENCHMAN," PETER COUTTS

An almost legendary character is the "Frenchman" of Frenchman's Tower and Frenchman's Road on the property now owned by Stanford University. Known as "Peter Coutts" during his residence in California, Jean-Baptiste Paulin Caperon was his real name. In France he was a wealthy banker and the publisher of the anti-royalist newspaper *La Liberté*. Leaving his homeland as a political exile, he lived for a while in Switzerland under the name of a cousin, Peter Coutts. Using a passport in this name, he came with his family to America, settling on the Matadero Ranch in the vicinity of Mayfield around 1874. "Ayrshire Farm," as he called it, soon became a showplace, with prizewinning Ayrshire cattle and extensive orchards and plantings of trees. Coutts spent much time and money in tunneling into the hillside in search of an adequate water supply. It is speculated but not proven that the round red brick tower standing on Old Page Mill Road was to house the tank for some portion of a hoped-for water supply. He laid out a racetrack between his house and El Camino Real, and his horses were among the noteworthy features of his estate. His house still stands at 859 Escondido Road on the Stanford campus. In 1891 this cottage was occupied by the young president of the newly founded Leland Stanford Junior University, Dr. David Starr Jordan, who gave it the name "Escondite," or "hiding place."

It was generally believed that this was only a temporary residence for Coutts until a more appropriate, grand structure was built. His many activities gave rise to wild rumors as to who he was, why had he settled in California, and what he was up to. Suddenly, one morning in 1880, the Coutts family disappeared almost as mysteriously as it had arrived. In time his true identify was revealed. The political situation in France had become favorable for his return, and his last years before his death in 1890 were spent in wealth and comfort.

Two other buildings remain from Coutt's ranch. At 860 Escondido is the two-story brick building that was Coutts's library, and at 830 Escondido is a much-remodeled Spanish-style adobe residence known as "the Hacienda." Leland Stanford purchased the Ayrshire Ranch in 1880, enlarging his extensive property holdings in the county.

STANFORD UNIVERSITY

Leland Stanford, a native of New York, came to California in 1852 at the height of the gold fever. Stanford, however, did not seek gold but with his three brothers went into extensive mercantile operations in and around Sacramento. He became wealthy in the following eight years. The first Republican governor of California, elected in 1862, he materially aided the Union cause in the Civil War. His considerable energies thereafter were devoted toward the building of the first transcontinental railroad. He was one of the "Big Four" Sacramento businessmen who built and owned the Central Pacific Railroad (the others were Charles Crocker, Mark Hopkins, and Collis P. Huntington). This railroad was subsequently merged with the Southern Pacific Railroad, a major force in the life of California in the last decades of the nineteenth century and the first decade of the twentieth. Stanford resumed his political career in 1885 as United States senator from California and was in that office when he died in 1893.

In 1870, Stanford purchased the land that had been the Rancho San Francisquito. The Stanfords remodeled and enlarged the house built by the previous owner, George Gordon. In time this became the Stanford Convalescent Home, which stood at 520 Sand Hill Road until 1965, when it was torn down to make room for expansions to the Stanford Medical Center.

Stanford University lies in large part on the Palo Alto Farm, which Stanford had used for the breeding and training of pedigreed racehorses. The Red Barn, still standing from this period on Junipero Serra Road, is on the National Register of Historic Places. Over the years, Stanford's horses held nineteen world records. Nearby is the grave of Palo Alto, the most famous of Stanford's horses, and a statue of Electioneer, the horse that sired nine world record holders. Of particular in-

Stanford Mausoleum, Stanford University Campus

terest is the plaque (SRL 834) noting that motion pictures were born here.

Did all four hooves of a running horse leave the ground at the same moment? The question had long interested Stanford and other horse fanciers. He made arrangements with San Francisco photographer Eadweard Muybridge to bring his cameras to the farm in 1878–79. According to the plaque on the site, "men and animals in motion" were photographed in "consecutive instantaneous exposures . . . provided by a battery of 24 cameras fitted with electro-shutters." The pictures reveal that a horse, while running rapidly, can have all four hooves off the ground at the same time.

Tragedy struck the Stanford family when Leland Jr., their only child, died in Florence, Italy, in 1884 at the age of sixteen. On November 11, 1886, the Stanfords founded the university that was to be "not only a memorial to their adored son but a gift of love to all the children of California." To provide an adequate campus, the senator purchased Coon Farm lying between San Francisquito and Los Trancos Creeks and Felt Farm or Rancho de Trancos lying along Los Trancos Creek. The university's cornerstone was laid on May 14, 1887, and in October 1891 its doors were opened to students.

Time has brought many changes to what was once the tranquil, secluded campus situated at the end of the impressive Palm Drive leading to nearby Palo Alto. The old center of the university is the Quadrangle,

built of native sandstone with archways and tile roofs reminiscent of California mission-style architecture. At the center of the inner quadrangle is the Stanford Memorial Church, dedicated by Jane Stanford to the memory of her husband. It was completed in 1901, four years before Mrs. Stanford's death. The campus was badly hit by the 1906 earthquake, and the church steeple was toppled into the midst of the ruins. The restored church was built without the architecturally incongruous steeple. The mosaics, inside and out, were built by Italian craftsmen who returned to the university to repair the damage. The later earthquake, in 1989, also did considerable damage to some of the university buildings, all of which were repaired. The style of the Quadrangle is reflected in the Thomas Welton Stanford Art Gallery, funded by a younger brother of the senator and opened in 1917.

Several other buildings on the campus are of historical interest. The oldest university building, constructed the same time as the Quadrangle, is Encina Hall on Serra Street, modeled after a Swiss hotel that the Stanfords once visited. Long a men's dormitory, it now houses university offices. "The Knoll" on Lomita Drive was built to be the home of the president of the university and was first occupied by Ray Lyman Wilbur and his family in 1916. The Hanna-Honeycomb House at 737 Frenchman's Road was designed by Frank Lloyd Wright for Professor and Mrs. Paul Hanna. Considered to be one of his most important buildings, it now belongs to the university.

The Stanfords, father, mother, and son, lie in a mausoleum on campus. Not far away is the former Leland Stanford Junior Museum, damaged in the 1989 earthquake and reopened a decade later as the Iris and B. Gerald Cantor Center for Visual Arts. The striking Rodin Sculpture Garden (1985) is another Cantor bequest to the university.

The first graduating class of 1895 included Herbert Hoover, president of the United States from 1929 to 1933. He received the news of his election at his home on the campus at 623 Mirada Avenue. The twenty-one-room house (SRL 913) was the work of Birge Clark, designer and architect, who worked closely with Mrs. Hoover in its creation. The official name of the place is the Lou Henry Hoover House; after her death in 1944 it became the home of the president of the university. A landmark since 1941 has been the 280-foot tower of the Hoover Institution on War, Revolution, and Peace. The nucleus of this library and research organization is a body of materials that Hoover began assembling in 1919 at the conclusion of World War I.

MAYFIELD, COLLEGE TERRACE, AND PALO ALTO

Mayfield and College Terrace are the oldest parts of the city of Palo Alto. A plaque placed by the city and the Palo Alto Historical Association at the corner of Sherman Avenue and Birch Street marks the site of the "Herring Box School" (so called for its small size), the first school in Mayfield, from 1855.

Mayfield became a town in 1867; its name came from Mayfield Farm, the home of Sarah Wallis (SRL 969). The site of her home, which no longer stands, is on the south side of La Selva Drive midway between Military Way and Magnolia Drive in Palo Alto. The house was destroyed by fire in 1936. Sarah Wallis was the first president of the California Suffrage Association in 1870; in 1873 she was the first president of the California State Woman Suffrage Education Association.

College Terrace is a somewhat later development lying between Mayfield and the Stanford campus. The Kee house at 2310 Yale Street, built in 1889, is probably the oldest house in the neighborhood.

Where Palo Alto now stands, only grain fields existed when the cornerstone of the university was laid in 1887. The Stanfords were unhappy that nearby Mayfield permitted the sale of alcohol. At their urging, Timothy Hopkins, a financial associate of Stanford, acquired some seven hundred and forty acres along El Camino Real south of Menlo Park, and a new town named University Park came into being. A distinctive feature of the Hopkins tract was the restriction prohibiting the sale of alcoholic beverages within its boundaries, a restriction not lifted until after World War II.

Palo Alto, the name of Stanford's stock farm, soon became the preferred name of the town, officially incorporated in 1894. Adjoining tracts were added to the city, largely to the south, Mayfield being annexed in 1925. In addition to the landmarks already mentioned, Palo Alto has a number of historic sites. Professorville Historic District comprises the blocks bounded by Lincoln, Waverley, Kingsley, and Emerson Streets. The neighborhood was the earliest off-campus residential area for professors at the university and their families. The university's policy of granting a long-term lease, rather than outright ownership, of campus property was an incentive for professors to build in town. One of the many historic homes in the area, at 345 Lincoln Avenue, is of interest as the home of Professor C. B. Wing, who with his neighbor, Professor C. D. Marx, helped develop Palo Alto's unique system of municipally owned utilities.

The Ramona Street Historic District is a block between University and Hamilton Avenues designed in the 1920s by Birge Clark and by Pedro de Lemos, director of the Stanford University Art Museum. A unifying theme of Mediterranean and California Colonial Revival styles characterizes the design of the buildings in the area.

The Squire House at 900 University Avenue (SRL 857) was designed in Classic Revival style by T. Paterson Ross of San Francisco for John A. Squire. The Hostess House at 27 University Avenue (SRL 895) was originally part of Camp Fremont, in nearby Menlo Park, San Mateo County. Designed by Julia Morgan in 1918, it was moved to its present location the following year and became the first municipally sponsored community center in the nation. In the 1970s, after many years of service as a community center, the building was leased by the city for commercial purposes; it currently houses a restaurant. A fairly new activity is the Museum of American Heritage, devoted to electrical and mechanical devices commonly in domestic or commercial use between 1800 and 1950. The museum is located in the Williams House and Gardens at 351 Homer Street.

The site of the laboratory of Dr. Lee De Forest (SRL 836) is at 913 Emerson Street. The two-story frame house was demolished in 1978; the landmark plaque reads: "Electronics Research Laboratory. Original site of the laboratory and factory of Federal Telegraph Company, founded in 1909 by Cyril F. Elwell. Here, with two assistants, Dr. Lee De Forest, investor of the three-element radio vacuum tube, devised in 1911–1913 the first vacuum tube amplifier and oscillator. World-wide developments based on this research led to modern radio communication, television, and the electronics age." Elwell's house at 1451 Cowper Street still stands; here in 1908 he transmitted radio signals to Mountain View and Los Altos, the first radio-telephone station on the West Coast. At 1044 Bryant Street is the childhood home of Russell and Sigurd Varian, who, with William Hansen, invented the Klystron tube, a key component of radar, and established the pioneer electronics firm of Varian Associates in Stanford Industrial Park after World War II.

At the rear of the driveway at 367 Addison Avenue

(SRL 976) is the one-car garage that William Hewlett and David Packard used as a laboratory in 1938. Newlyweds David and Lucile Packard occupied the two-story house, Hewlett the small shingle cottage behind it. In the garage they invented electric machines for the nearby Palo Alto Medical Clinic as well as other devices for other clients, notably an audio oscillator for which they began receiving orders in 1939 from, among others, the Walt Disney Studios. By the mid-1950s, the Hewlett-Packard Company they founded had become a world leader in electronics and computer design and manufacturing. This was the beginning of "Silicon Valley," the area around Palo Alto where these industries have since flourished. In October 2000 Hewlett-Packard purchased the property for $1.7 million, to guarantee that the buildings will be preserved.

MONTGOMERY HILL

John Joseph Montgomery, born in Yuba City in 1858, is remembered for flying a glider at Otay Mesa, south of San Diego, in 1883, thus becoming the first man to go aloft in a heavier-than-air craft. Montgomery Hill (SRL 813), on Yerba Buena Road in Evergreen, commemorates this aviation pioneer whose fifty-five successful flights demonstrated aerodynamic developments of great importance to aviation. Montgomery, a professor at Santa Clara College, was killed in a glider crash at the site in 1911.

GILROY

The chief town of southern Santa Clara County is named for pioneer settler John Gilroy, as described in the section on Rancho San Ysidro. John Gilroy is commemorated with a plaque placed by E Clampus Vitus at Christmas Hill Park on Miller Avenue in the city. Several buildings of historic interest still stand. The Christian Church at 160 Fifth Street originally stood on Third Street, but was moved to this location in 1887. The frame structure was built in 1857, making it the oldest church building in continuous use in Santa Clara County. Another old church, in the next block at 214 Fifth Street, is the Presbyterian church, much expanded since it was built in 1869.

Fifth Street is a gallery of fine old buildings. The Baxter House at 323 was built in 1875 for hardware merchant J. A. Baxter; it was later the home of Millie Lewis Sargeant, a great-granddaughter of Julius Martin, also

mentioned in the Rancho San Ysidro section of this chapter. The Ball House at 314 was saved from condemnation in 1973, its hundredth year, and completely restored. The Hoxett House at 338, begun in 1869, was the home of Gilroy benefactress Caroline Amelia Hoxett; it became the site of the Women's Civic Club after her death in 1927. She provided the clocks in the old city hall building at Sixth and Monterey Streets (built in 1905 and now housing a restaurant) and gave land for the IOOF Children's Home as well as for the Carnegie Library building. The latter, begun in 1910 at 195 Fifth, is now the location of the excellent Gilroy Historical Museum, which has a rich repository of materials on southern Santa Clara County. The Holloway House at 7539 Eigleberry Street is a Queen Anne home designed in 1903 for the Edgar Holloway family by William Weeks and is now on the National Register of Historic Places.

Gilroy has always been a farming center. Large acreages of garlic were planted near the town in the 1920s by Kiyoshi Hirasaki and by Joseph Gubser Sr. By 1955 Gilroy proclaimed itself the "Garlic Capital of America," with 90 percent of the U.S. garlic crop grown nearby. An annual Garlic Festival in July has attracted many visitors to Gilroy since the first celebration in 1979.

Near Redwood Retreat, ten miles west of Gilroy in the Mount Madonna region, is a log cabin built by novelist Frank Norris a short time before his death in 1902. He and his wife established themselves there near the forest cabin of their friend Fanny Stevenson, the widow of Robert Louis Stevenson. Here Norris planned to write *The Wolf*, which was to complete the trilogy begun by *The Octopus* and *The Pit*, but his sudden death following an appendectomy at the age of thirty-two intervened before the manuscript was finished. A semicircular seat, built of stones brought from the nearby stream, is a memorial created near the cabin by friends of the novelist. The cabin is on a private road reached from Gilroy by a route including the Hecker Pass Highway, Watsonville Road, Redwood Retreat Road, and Sanders Road. The cabin is about three-quarters of a mile from the site of the old Redwood Retreat Hotel.

Gilroy Yamato Hot Springs Resort (SRL 1017), about fifteen miles northeast of Gilroy, was built around a single hot spring discovered by a sheepherder, Francisco Cantua, in 1865. By 1874 a post office had been established and small cottages built to accommodate guests. The Gilroy Hot Springs Hotel was built in 1879, its three stories made entirely of redwood. Soon it was a popular retreat patronized by those who liked to fish and to hunt as well as to "take the waters." The waters flowing from the spring at 105 degrees contained soda, magnesium, iron, sulfur, and iodine, among other trace minerals; they were claimed to cure almost everything except consumption.

In 1938 the resort was purchased by H. K. Sakato, a successful Japanese-American farmer from Watsonville. Renamed the Gilroy Yamato Hot Springs, it was the only Japanese American–owned commercial hot springs in California. The resort served as a recreational and spiritual center for Japanese Americans before World War II and briefly as a hostel after the war for those returning from internment camps.

The resort declined thereafter to the point that, in 1963, all the buildings were condemned for public use. The property was up for sale in 1980 when fire destroyed the hotel, the clubhouse, and five of the nearby buildings. The place is presently closed to the public, and it is reported that 105-degree water still flows unceasingly from the spring.

Santa Cruz County

Santa Cruz County was named after the mission and the city ("holy cross") in its center and was one of the original twenty-seven counties. It was created on February 18, 1850, and was named Branciforte County; the name was changed to Santa Cruz the following month. The northwestern part of its original area, including the town of Pescadero, was annexed to San Mateo County in 1868. The county seat is the city of Santa Cruz. Pre-statehood documents are housed in the Special Collections of the McHenry Library on the campus of the University of California at Santa Cruz.

THE PORTOLÁ TRAIL

Leaving the region of Monterey County and proceeding northward, Gaspar de Portolá and his men crossed the Pajaro River on October 8, 1769, unaware that they were leaving behind the bay they sought. The Rio de Pajaro ("Bird River") was named by the soldiers for a very large stuffed bird that looked like an eagle set upon the riverbank, presumably an Indian totem. In this valley the Spaniards were amazed by gigantic trees, taller than any they had ever seen, which they called *palos colorados* because of the color of the wood. This is the first mention of a redwood tree in California's written history. The trees they saw were a stand of coast redwoods, *Sequoia sempervirens*, to be distinguished from their giant cousins of the High Sierra, the *Sequoia gigantea*.

During the following week the party traveled up Corralitos Creek, camping east of Corralitos Lagoon and again just east of modern Aptos. They then crossed Soquel Creek about three miles from the coast, their route having been close to the present SR 1 from Watsonville to Soquel.

On October 17 the party camped on the west bank of a large river, which they called the San Lorenzo, the name it still bears. Here they again saw many redwoods and "roses of Castile" but, much to the disappointment of Father Crespí, no Indians. The city of Santa Cruz is now located at this spot.

From October 17 to the end of the month, the expedition traversed the route now covered by SR 1, along the coast of Santa Cruz and San Mateo Counties. This route, for a few miles northwest of Santa Cruz, lies across the ancient sea beaches now raised to form fertile benches of land on which vegetable crops are grown. The region is well known to geologists because of the plainly pictured story of changes shown by the series of sea terraces between the hills and the present tide line.

The going was sometimes arduous in this region; at one arroyo a bridge of poles and earth had to be constructed before men and animals could get across. Seven gulches of varying difficulty were crossed in one day alone. On October 20 they arrived "at the mouth of a very deep stream that flowed out between very high hills of the mountain chain," and camped there for three nights.

On Sunday, October 22, Father Crespí wrote:

The day dawned, overcast and gloomy; the men were wet and wearied for want of sleep, as they had no tents, and it was necessary to let them rest. . . . What excited our wonder on this occasion was that all the sick, for whom we feared the wetting might prove exceedingly harmful, suddenly found their pains very much relieved. This was the reason for giving the canyon the name of La Salud.

La Salud ("health") is now known as Waddell Creek, and still becomes, after heavy rains, the "very deep stream" that the travelers found. From here the expedition proceeded northward, and its subsequent story belongs to the history of San Mateo County.

MISSION SANTA CRUZ

The Viceroy Condé de Revilla Gigedo and Father Matías de Noriega decided in 1789 to establish a mission on the spot called Santa Cruz between those missions already established at San Carlos (Carmel) and Santa Clara. Two years after this decision was made, Father Fermín Francisco de Lasuén consecrated a site at the lower end of the San Lorenzo Valley. Here, on St. Augustine's Day, August 28, 1791, he said Mass in the presence of many Indians and raised a cross.

The following month fathers Alonzo Salazar and Baldomero López, accompanied by Hermenegildo Sal, *comandante* of the San Francisco Presidio, and his military escort, arrived at the prospective site. Christian Indians brought along from Santa Clara were set to work at once cutting wood for the construction of a brush shelter, or *enramada*, for the fathers.

On Sunday morning, September 25, 1791, the formal ceremony for the founding of Mission la Exaltación de la Santa Cruz was celebrated. The fathers had brought with them as a nucleus for the mission a painting of Our Lady of Sorrows and an image of Saint Francis. From the neighboring missions at Carmel, Santa Clara, and San Francisco came donations of horses, cows, oxen, mules, sheep, and two bushels of barley for seed. At the end of three months eighty-seven Indians had been baptized. It is thought that the first church was constructed about where North Pacific Avenue and River Street now intersect, with the southern end of the spacious plaza at the present juncture of Pacific Avenue and Mission and Water Streets. Soon the establishment was found to be too near the river, and in the move to higher ground only the garden was left on the lower level.

The first stone of the new Mission Santa Cruz was laid on February 27, 1793, and the completed structure was dedicated in the spring of 1794, with Commander Sal and father Tomás de la Peña of Mission Santa Clara present. The church, built on the mesa above the river, was a substantial building—112.5 feet long, 29 feet wide, and 25.5 feet high, with walls five feet thick. The lower part of the walls was made of native rock and the upper part of adobe. The vaulted roof, at first covered with thatch, was later re-covered with tile.

Other buildings, built in succeeding years, formed an open square about where the present park is located, bounded by High, Emmet, Mission, and Sylvar Streets. The mission church and the priests' quarters were on what is now High Street. On the present Sylvar Street were storehouses and rooms for looms. Back from Emmet Street, along what is now known as School Street, were the women's quarters; and on the other side of School Street was the adobe building, still standing, that is believed to have been the guardhouse. This, the only building remaining from the mission of 1793-94, has been designated Santa Cruz Mission State Historical Monument. The building was divided into two residences around the time of secularization and is known as the Neary-Rodriguez adobe, after the early owners. The building is at 136 School Street and is marked by a plaque placed by the Daughters of the American Revolution.

All went well with the mission for more than twenty years; trouble then arose with the secular Villa de Branciforte nearby. To add to the troubles of the mission, the pirate Hippolyte Bouchard, flying the insurgent flag of Buenos Aires, threatened an attack in 1818. Because of a storm at sea the attack, fortunately, never took place, but in the frantic effort to save mission properties in this emergency, much damage was done to the church and its furnishings by misdirected zeal.

The mission was secularized by Governor Figueroa in 1834. In 1840 an earthquake weakened the walls; and on January 9, 1857, another tremor caused the final destruction, for a month later at three o'clock in the morning the southwestern corner fell with a loud crash.

On the site of the ruined mission (SRL 342), at 126 High Street, a wooden frame church, now called Holy Cross Church, was dedicated in 1858. This served the parish until the present English Gothic Holy Cross Church, designed by Thomas J. Welsh of San Francisco, was completed in 1889. In 1891, on the centennial of the founding of the original mission, a memorial arch of granite was erected in front of this brick church. The bell that rings out from the church was recast from the old bells salvaged from the earthquake-ruined mission.

In 1931 a half-sized concrete replica of the original mission was built on Emmet Street facing the upper plaza. It is approximately seventy-five yards from the original site. In this replica are housed many objects that were in the original mission, notably a chandelier now altered for electricity and hanging near the entrance. A statue of Our Lady of Sorrows occupies a niche in the front part of the little church, while in a room off the outer corridor are preserved richly ornamented vestments.

Holy Cross School was founded by the Sisters of Charity in 1862 in an adobe that stood next to the Neary-Rodriguez adobe. The school adobe is no more, but the kindergarten and grammar school occupy the site and the high school is diagonally across the plaza.

VILLA DE BRANCIFORTE

Three secular towns were established by the Spanish in California: San Jose, Los Angeles, and Branciforte. Whereas the first two were designated as *pueblos*, the latter, named for the Marquis of Branciforte, viceroy of Mexico, was called by the Spanish synonym for "town," *villa*. According to Gudde, this is the only instance in which the term was so used in Spanish California. The town was established in 1797 under the direction of Governor Diego de Borica and was located across the

San Lorenzo River from Mission Santa Cruz. Governor Borica showed his practical mind when he chose this place: good building material was close at hand, there was a plentiful supply of fish in the waters of the bay, and the facilities for shipping could easily be developed to handle the future produce of the town. His recommendations were likewise sensible: "An adobe house to be built for each settler so that the prevalent state of things at San Jose and Los Angeles, where the settlers still live in tule huts, being unable to build better buildings without neglecting their fields, may be avoided; the houses not to cost over $200." Each colonist was to receive from the government a musket, a plow, a few necessary animals, and a subsidy of 116 pesos on a plan of easy repayment. The observance of religious duties was to be enforced. He called for farmers, mechanics, artisans, and sailors as settlers. Gabriel Moraga was taken from his position as *comisionado* of San Jose and placed in charge of the new community.

On May 12, 1797, the schooner *Concepción* arrived in Monterey Bay with colonists from Guadalajara, but no houses were ready for them. Don Alberto Córdoba, lieutenant of engineers in the Spanish Army who had visited there the previous year, arrived in August with instructions to follow a plan that had been drawn up in Mexico. He began a canal for irrigation, erected a few temporary houses, and sent estimates for further work to the governor and the viceroy, before the work was suspended in October.

Among the passengers on the *Concepción* were three men who became alcaldes: José Vicente Mojica, who brought a wife and five children, was alcalde in 1802; José Antonio Robles, who married first Rosalía Merlopes and at her death her sister, Gertrudis, and reared several children, held a number of offices before becoming alcalde in 1842; and Agustín Narvaez, nineteen when he arrived, stayed at Branciforte only a few years before becoming alcalde in San Jose in 1821. Among the disabled soldiers sent there in 1798 were José Joaquin Castro and José Antonio Rodríguez, both of whom played an important part in the affairs of their time and whose descendants are now widely scattered throughout the state.

In 1799 Gabriel Moraga was succeeded by Ignacio Vallejo as *comisionado*, and the villa continued under the military jurisdiction of Monterey (except for two years under the civil jurisdiction of San Jose), until the time of its dissolution. The fathers at Mission Santa Cruz seem to have regarded the town and its easygoing ways as detrimental to their work of the salvation of the Indians, who greatly declined in number as the nineteenth century wore on. There was little incentive for new colonists to join the community, and while it was never entirely deserted, it did not flourish as did the pueblos.

After the American occupation and the coming of American pioneers, Branciforte became a community of attractive homes. By a special election in 1907, it became part of the city of Santa Cruz. The mile-long racetrack, laid out in 1797 by Córdoba, is now Branciforte Avenue. The intersection of this avenue with Water Street is the center of the old Villa de Branciforte (SRL 469), which occupied a rectangle one-half mile wide from east to west and one mile long from north to south. A bull-and-bear-fight arena was located on the flats near the Soquel Avenue Bridge, between the San Lorenzo River and Branciforte Creek. As late as July 13, 1867, four bulls "from the Gabilan and Taurian mountains" fought here, with lances, firecrackers, and red flags adding to the excitement. "Admission and seat— $1.00. Standing room on the sunny side—50 cents."

SANTA CRUZ

A period of disintegration followed the Mexican order to secularize the missions, but before the Gold Rush several industries had developed in the town of Santa Cruz, which had grown up around the plaza of the mission.

Thomas Fallon, who had arrived in Branciforte in 1845 and who had raised the flag of the United States in San Jose in 1846, put up a building on the plaza. This had an outside staircase and did double duty as a residence and saddlery shop. The county later purchased this property for use as the county courthouse, paying Fallon $3,500.

William Blackburn, a Virginia cabinetmaker who had come overland to California with the Swasey-Todd company in 1845, worked as a lumberman in the Santa Cruz Mountains before joining the California Artillery Battalion, Company A, as a second lieutenant. He was alcalde of Santa Cruz from 1847 to 1849 and became county judge in 1850. It is said that the decisions of his court became noted for their originality. His orchards were one of the attractions of Santa Cruz during his lifetime. His home grounds extended from Chestnut Avenue to Walnut Avenue and to the Neary Lagoon. The old Blackburn house still stands in the middle of a block with one address at 101 Cedar Street and another at 152 Center Street.

Richard C. Kirby, born in England in 1817, left a whaling boat in Oregon in 1845 and came by land to California, where he became associated with Paul Sweet in a tannery business on the San Agustín rancho shortly after his arrival. In the fall of 1850 he put up a small establishment for tanning leather in Squabble Hollow, now Glen Canyon. Kirby leather soon became famous; he tanned not only hides from local sources but also those shipped from South America. In 1852 he married Georgiana Bruce, who had been a member of the Brook Farm Colony near Boston in the 1840s and had come to California to establish a school. She too was English-born and had come to America as a governess; while teaching in the South, she had become an ardent abolitionist. Mrs. Kirby has left a vivid picture of life in Santa Cruz in the 1850s in her journal. She was much interested in the beautification of her home and surroundings and imported rare shrubs and trees. The Kirby home, a frame house, stood at 321 Mission Street, and now will be found at 117 Jordan Street.

The oldest wood-frame house in Santa Cruz is the Alzina house, at 109 Sylvar Street. Francisco Alzina was the first sheriff of Santa Cruz County, serving from 1850 to 1868. He and his wife, the former María González, built their little house at the corner of Mission and Sylvar Streets; it was later moved to its present location and the Willey house was erected in its place. The Willey house at 105 Sylvar Street is a late Eastlake-style mansion with stained-glass windows and handsome porch railings. Henry Willey had the redwood house built in 1893 for his bride. Like the Alzina house, this is a private residence today. Other old houses from this era are to be found on Green and Mission Streets.

The old commercial and public buildings of Santa Cruz are grouped along Pacific Avenue. In 1987, this area was placed on the National Register of Historic Places, with some thirty-six buildings qualifying for citation. Just two years later, in 1989, the earthquake centered a few miles to the southeast at Loma Prieta struck the city with great force. The area by the river was especially hard-hit; in the historic district alone twenty marked buildings were damaged beyond repair. The future of the district remains uncertain.

The Branciforte adobe is the name given to the one remaining structure from the Villa de Branciforte. E Clampus Vitus has marked the place, at Goss and North Branciforte Avenues. Not much is actually known about the early history of the house; the text of the plaque

Santa Cruz Boardwalk

suggests that it may have been the residence of the *comisionado* in the early nineteenth century.

The Cowell House at 1001 High Street goes back to about 1850, when it was the ranch house for the Cowell Ranch, north and west of the city of Santa Cruz. The property originally belonged to Albion P. Jordan, pioneer lime industrialist, who later established a partnership with Isaac E. Davis. In 1865 he sold his share and his home to Henry Cowell. Cowell and his brother John, originally from Massachusetts, worked limestone deposits and operated limekilns on the ranch. The family lived in this house from 1865 to 1897, when they moved to San Francisco. Father Henry feared fortune hunters and forbade his children to marry. One son, Ernest, married without parental blessing and was ostracized. He was later reinstated, however, when he broke with his wife. Ernest left $250,000 to the University of California for the establishment of Cowell Hospital.

The University of California also benefited from the Cowell family when, in 1961, the regents of the university announced that a new campus would be built on the 2,000-acre Cowell Ranch. One building that survives from the ranch days is the Cook House, put up about 1880, which stands on the first quarry on the property. It took on a new existence as the chancellor's office when the campus went into operation in 1965 and today houses the campus security services; it is located at the south end of the campus just north of High Street.

Since the late nineteenth century, Santa Cruz has been a resort city. In 1907 the Santa Cruz Beach Boardwalk was constructed along Beach Street between Cliff Street and the San Lorenzo River. It was one of California's first amusement parks (SRL 983), and today is the only oceanside amusement park operating on the West Coast. The Giant Dipper Roller Coaster was one of the first of its kind, installed in 1924, and is still running, along with many other attractions, including a charming carousel from 1911.

The Santa Cruz County Historical Museum, and with it the Art Museum of Santa Cruz County, is located in the octagonal County Hall of Records at Cooper and Front Streets, built in 1882. The unusual shape is said to have been inspired by a $50 gold piece minted in San Francisco in 1851–52. With the aid of a federal grant, the building was refurbished after its records were moved to the new County Governmental Center in 1968. Since 1972 it has presented changing displays of local historical interest as well as a fine photographic collection of county history. The Santa Cruz County Society for Historical Preservation, Inc., which operates the museum, also owns and operates the 1914 jail at Davenport.

The Mark Abbott Memorial Lighthouse has a museum open to visitors on a limited basis at Lighthouse Point at the western side of Santa Cruz Harbor. This lighthouse is one of the newest structures on the Pacific Coast. It was built in 1967 to replace an earlier structure that was being undermined by three large sea caverns.

The Santa Cruz City Museum, while emphasizing the natural history of the city and the coastal area, also has many displays connected with local history. The attractive building is along the shore at 1305 East Cliff Drive.

RANCHO SAN ANDRÉS (MONTEREY BAY COAST WEST OF WATSONVILLE)

Three grants, given to members of the Castro family in 1833, stretched along the shore of Monterey Bay from the mouth of Soquel Creek to the mouth of the Pajaro River and extended far inland. The southernmost of these three ranchos had been occupied for possibly ten years by a pensioned soldier, José Joaquín Castro. As a boy he had come to California in the company of Juan Bautista de Anza. He held several minor positions in the Villa de Branciforte and was alcalde in 1831. His Rancho San Andrés, consisting of two square leagues, was confirmed to his eldest son, Guadalupe, in 1854.

The first house of Don José Joaquín on the rancho was located not far from the beach, but when he built his large adobe house he chose a site on a hill above Larkin Valley, overlooking in the distance a great sweep of the Pajaro Valley. This house, at 184 Old Adobe Road, is one of the few large ones remaining from earlier times. After years of neglect, it was purchased in the 1950s and beautifully restored. The two-story adobe has an upper and a lower veranda across the whole length of the front, and a ballroom on the upper floor with extensive views of the property on all sides. The access road climbs a hill from the crossroads of Larkin Valley Road and Buena Vista Drive, a few miles northwest of Watsonville.

RANCHO APTOS

Rancho Aptos, of one square league, was granted by Governor José Figueroa in 1833 to Rafael Castro, an industrious and prosperous ranchero who had held a few minor official positions. The southeast line of this grant adjoined the larger Rancho San Andrés belonging to his father, José Joaquín Castro, and extended north along the bay to present-day Borregas Creek. In the early 1870s he donated property for a Catholic chapel, the Church of Our Lady of Mount Carmel, at the present corner of Seacliff Beach State Park Drive and Soquel Drive, the old Santa Cruz–Watsonville highway. Excessive deterioration caused it to be abandoned in 1925. A bell from this church is preserved at Mission Santa Cruz, and a statue of Our Lady of Mount Carmel, originally from Spain, is now in St. Joseph's Catholic Church in Capitola. A new church was built on the Aptos property in the 1960s.

In a niche in the tall marble monument that marks his grave in the cemetery near the church is a miniature bust of Don Rafael, who died in 1878. His wife, Soledad Cota, and other members of his family are buried in the family plot. In the outlying part of this churchyard but still within the confines of the old cypress hedge lie the bones of many Indians removed from an early Indian burying ground not far away when the property was taken over by Claus Spreckels.

On the coast of modern Aptos is Seacliff State Beach. At the end of a wooden pier about halfway along the beach is the 435-foot concrete supply ship *Palo Alto*. This was one of several concrete-hulled ships built during World War I, in a project that came to naught. The *Palo Alto* was purchased by promoters and brought to Seacliff, where it has been since 1929. For some time the moored ship was an amusement pier with a dance floor on deck. The inevitable ravages of time and surf have made it unsafe to venture onto the ship, and in

time it will probably crumble into Monterey Bay. Meanwhile, the fishing pier leading to it is a busy place most of the year.

RANCHOS SOQUEL AND SOQUEL AUGMENTACIÓN

Martina, a daughter of José Joaquín Castro, obtained the grant of Rancho Soquel, 1,668 acres, from Governor Figueroa in 1833. To her was given also the larger grant, Rancho Soquel Augmentación, of 32,702 acres, on which lies the greater part of the watershed of Soquel Creek, containing vast forests of redwood, live oak, and madrone. A good part of this today is the State Forest of Nisene Marks, which has been intentionally left undeveloped. The grant stretched over the mountaintops of the county boundary to Loma Prieta. Both of these grants were confirmed and patented to her in 1860.

Martina's second marriage was to Michael Lodge, a sailor from Dublin, and when her grant was confirmed, they built an adobe house on a point of high ground near a ravine and springs of pure water. The empty field where the Lodge adobe once stood is at the end of Hill Street beyond Capitola Avenue. On the property there was an ox-powered flour mill, no longer standing, and the millstones are now mounted in Pringle Grove, the property of the Soquel Pioneer Club, off north Main Street.

The Bay View Hotel in Aptos is the oldest such establishment operating in Santa Cruz County and is marked by an E Clampus Vitus plaque. It was built about 1870 by José Arano, said to be a French immigrant, who married María de la Augustia, youngest daughter of Don Rafael Castro. It is said that while the hotel was under construction, Arano personally inspected every bit of lumber that went into it, and every stick of furniture, much of which is still there today. The Bay View was a luxurious watering place for many years; its patrons included King Kalakaua of the Hawaiian Islands and the entertainer Lillian Russell, as well as local entrepreneur Claus Spreckels, who had bought a large part of Rancho Aptos. In 1944 the hotel was purchased and moved about 100 feet back from the railroad tracks; it is on Soquel Drive near Trout Gulch Road.

The First Congregational Church on Soquel Drive in the middle of Soquel was built in 1870. It was the creation of Samuel A. Hall, a ship's carpenter from Maine, who dreamed of creating a New England–style church for the Congregationalists of the area. Land was donated by Joshua Parrish, and the building was truly a congregation-wide effort. In the years since 1870 a social hall and steeple have been added.

RANCHO CORRALITOS

In the eastern part of the county lies Rancho Corralitos, which was granted in 1823, 1841, and 1844 to José Amesti, a native of Spain who came to California on the *Panther* in 1822 and became a prominent citizen and merchant in his adopted land. He married Prudenciana, daughter of Ignacio Vallejo, in 1824. The 15,000 acres of this property were patented to his heirs in 1861. The Amesti adobe is located at 162 Amesti Road, on a hill northwest of the Amesti schoolhouse.

The town of Corralitos in the northern part of the rancho was a place of bustling activity in the pioneer days of the 1860s. It was surrounded by forests in which sawmills were moved from place to place as each location became "sawed out." As early as 1865 several families living there had the luxury of water in their homes, running through pipes made by boring a hole lengthwise through redwood logs.

The first sawmill in this region was in Brown's Valley near Garcia's bridge three and a half miles above Corralitos and was owned and operated by Brown and Williamson from 1865 to 1867. The same company later built Gamecock Mill farther up the canyon. The narrow, rough logging roads, when abandoned by their original users, were improved for general travel by the settlers "working out" their taxes by filling chuckholes, hauling gravel, and widening the track.

In 1855 Benjamin Hames bought a site just above the present town and built a flour mill to which settlers as far away as Salinas hauled grain to be ground. The water from a dam in Eureka Canyon was brought through redwood flumes to operate the mill. In 1877 the site and buildings were bought by Peter and James Brown for a paper mill, where sun-dried straw board was made from straw grown on Pajaro Valley ranches. For a few years the binding boards used in making textbooks for the schools throughout the state were manufactured here.

The first school serving the settlement was built among oak trees one and a half miles south of the town on the road leading to Watsonville and was called Oak Grove. The oaks are now gone, but a redwood grove on the opposite side of the road identifies the spot. Other schools were subsequently built; the present school is about one mile south of Corralitos.

RANCHO SALSIPUEDES (EASTERN PAJARO VALLEY AND NORTHWARD)

Gudde writes that *Salsipuedes*, a "Spanish expression, meaning 'get out if you can,' was repeatedly used in geographical nomenclature, usually for narrow enclosures or for canyons where the terrain is very rough." The Salsipuedes grant of 31,201 acres was made to Francisco de Haro in 1834 and regranted to Manuel Jimeno in 1840, the final grant being for a total of eight leagues. These lands extended on the south from the Pajaro River north to the mountains at the county line, and a small part near Bodfish Canyon lay in Santa Clara County.

Don Manuel, who came to California from Mexico in 1830, was a man of great influence and was much respected in civil affairs. His wife, said to have been as vivacious as he was witty, was Agustías, daughter of José de la Guerra y Noriega. He was secretary of state for several years under Governors Alvarado and Micheltorena. Two of his sons, Antonio and Porfirio, went east with William T. Sherman for their education. After many years of poor health Don Manuel died in Mexico in 1853. The site of his adobe is on the Chittenden Pass Road, which runs for many miles through this rancho.

William F. White, who had come from Pennsylvania with his young wife in 1849, acquired land from Don Manuel five miles east of Watsonville, and in 1853 he built the first substantial American-owned house in the Pajaro Valley. The exterior lumber for this house, shipped from Maine, was of outstanding quality. White installed a pump, which was a great curiosity. The family residence was used as a place of worship one Sunday a month, the officiating priest coming from Mission San Juan Bautista. The house still stands, at 508 Riverside Road, and has been the property of the Silliman family for more than a century.

Associated with White in the purchase of this rancho were three other influential men: William T. Sherman, of Civil War fame; Montgomery Blair, postmaster-general in Abraham Lincoln's cabinet; and Edward D. Baker, an early United States senator from Oregon. A patent for this land was issued to "James Blair et al." on March 2, 1861, two days before Lincoln became president. White was a bank commissioner, appointed by Governor Irwin, and was a member of the constitu-

Bockius House, Watsonville

tional convention of 1878 before becoming a candidate for governor on the Workingman's ticket in 1879.

RANCHO BOLSA DEL PAJARO AND WATSONVILLE

Rancho Bolsa del Pajaro consisted of two separate grants that stretch along both sides of the Pajaro River northeast of its mouth. It was granted by Governor Alvarado in 1837 to Sebastián Rodríguez, who also claimed the Rincón de la Ballena in present San Mateo County, a claim that was rejected by United States authorities.

Don Sebastián, a sergeant of the Monterey Company and *comisionado* of Santa Cruz in 1831, died in 1855, leaving a large family and an estate on which many troublesome squatters had arrived. The litigation concerning Rancho Bolsa del Pajaro after American occupation was finally ended in 1860 when a patent was issued to the heirs for one of the grants.

D. S. Gregory and Judge John H. Watson, the latter a native of Georgia, obtained the other grant before the death of Don Sebastián and laid out the town of Watsonville in 1852. W. L. Thrift, one of its first settlers, put up a tent that served as a hotel; when a post office was established the following year, he became the town's first postmaster.

These riverine lands were once proclaimed to be "acre for acre the richest land on earth." Potatoes were the first principal crop, followed by mushrooms, strawberries, and flowers; Watsonville is also famous for its apple orchards. The Martinelli Cider plant at 227 E. Beach Street is a big producer. Stephen Martinelli came to California from Switzerland in 1859 and established the family business in 1868.

Watsonville's City Plaza was donated to the city in 1860 by Sebastián Rodríguez, son of Don Sebastián. Located on the plaza are two cannons, one a large field piece, made in 1899, and the other from the mail steamer *Oregon.* When the *Oregon* entered San Francisco harbor on October 18, 1850, this cannon fired the shots announcing that California had been admitted to the Union as the thirty-first state. The Mansion House building, put up in 1871 at the corner of East Beach and Main Streets, was a hotel for many years and was moved to its present location at 418 Main Street in 1914. Now it houses offices and is listed, along with the City Plaza, the Judge Lee house (1894) at 128 East Beach Street, and the Resetar house (1925) at Madison and East Lake Streets, on the National Register of Historic Places. The history of the Pajaro Valley is the theme of the William Volck Memorial Museum at 261 East Beach Street, named for the entomologist who made important contributions in combating the codling moth that had threatened the valley's apple industry.

Occupying half a city block is the splendid home at 332 East Beach Street built in 1870 for Godfrey Bockius, farmer, banker, judge, and member of the state Legislature. The Bockius House, designed by Alex Chalmers, is now the headquarters of the Pajaro Valley Historical Society, and is a fine example of a prosperous family home of a century ago, open to the public.

St. Patrick's Catholic Church is an imposing building on the northern edge of town at 721 Main Street. The first church on the site was a wooden one; the present stone building dates from 1903.

RANCHO ARROYO DEL RODEO (CAPITOLA AND SOQUEL)

This rancho consisted of one-quarter of a square league lying on the shore of Monterey Bay between Soquel and Rodeo creeks. Most of today's cities of Capitola and Soquel lie on its land. It was granted by Governor Figueroa in 1834 to Francisco Rodríguez, the early California poet. On Soquel Creek a dam and a flour mill were constructed in 1858; over the years the flour mill became a sawmill and later a paper mill, the name of which survives in Paper Mill Road today. Frémont and his party camped at the spot on March 1, 1846.

The name of the rancho was derived from the cattle roundups or rodeos of the herds of the Castro and Rodríguez families, which took place in a natural amphitheater a half-mile south of the present Soquel Avenue bridge across Rodeo Creek. The amphitheater is now covered by a huge freeway fill.

Capitola, an old California resort, has an interesting history. A tract of land along the shore of Monterey Bay at Soquel Landing was purchased in the late 1850s by a German immigrant, Frederick Augustus Hihn, who built a wharf there and then moved on to other projects that would make him the first millionaire in Santa Cruz County. Hihn gave a lease on the wharf and nearby property in 1869 to Samuel A. Hall, builder of the Congregational Church in Soquel, who in 1870 created a summer campground on the beach for vacationers. Hall's daughter Lulu Hall Wolbach, a Soquel teacher, suggested the name "Camp Capitola," which was first used in 1874. Capitola was a heroine in popular novels by the English author E. D. E. N. Southworth. The broad-gauged Santa Cruz–Watsonville Railroad brought in thousands of summer visitors from the sweltering interior of the state in 1883, by which time Hihn became interested in the place and soon ousted Hall from his lease with a heavy rent increase. The oldest commercial building in Capitola is the "Superintendent's Office" at 201 Monterey Avenue (SRL 860), which Hihn used as his headquarters from 1883 until his death in 1913. The Capitola Wharf, with "founded in 1857" on its marker, is now a fishing pier, completely rebuilt and modernized.

Katherine Hihn Henderson inherited the property from her father and sold it in 1919 to Henry Allen Rispin, a San Francisco entrepreneur who planned to modernize Capitola and make it appealing to San Francisco Bay Area vacationers. He went bankrupt about 1929 attempting to promote "Capitola-by-the-Sea," while some destructive fires damaged part of the town. Easily accessible, the beautiful site of Capitola continued to attract visitors, and in 1949 it became the third incorporated city in the county. It has a long history of being a favorite resort for San Francisco Bay Area residents.

RANCHO SAN AGUSTÍN AND SCOTTS VALLEY

An archaeological dig in 1983 at the site of the present Scotts Valley City Hall on Kings Drive unearthed an Indian cutting tool believed to be from eight thousand to ten thousand years old, perhaps the oldest artifact ever unearthed in northern California. More recent history begins with the granting of Rancho San Agustín in 1841 to Juan José Crisóstomo Majors, the name that Joseph

L. Majors of Tennessee had assumed when he became a Mexican citizen three years earlier. He received a United States patent for his land, in his original name, in 1866. (By this time the rancho had been sold to the Scotts.) In 1841 he also received a grant of the Zayante rancho, discussed below.

Hiram Daniel Scott came into Monterey Bay in 1846 as second mate on the *C. Whiting*, and in 1852 he purchased Rancho San Agustín. The father, also named Hiram, followed his son west and took the ranch over. The area is now known as Scotts Valley; it was incorporated as a city in 1964. The Scott home, built in 1853 and since moved a few hundred yards from its original site, has been restored and preserved. It serves as a meeting place for the Scotts Valley Historical Society, at 4603 Scotts Valley Drive.

RANCHO CARBONERA (SAN LORENZO RIVER VALLEY)

Rancho Carbonera, bordering the San Lorenzo River north of Santa Cruz, was granted by Governor Alvarado to José Guillermo Bocle in 1838. It was patented to him in 1873.

Bocle was a man of many aliases—Boc, Buckle, Mead, and Thompson being a few. He and his brother Samuel (who had come to California in 1823, according to his own statement, and who was naturalized in 1841) both took the name of Thompson after the American occupation. William Thompson or Guillermo Bocle was an English sailor who came in California in 1823, married María Antonia Castro, and became the father of a large family. At his death, unable to sign his own name, he left "to those now living with me" 15,000 acres of land along with horses, cattle, and money. Thompson's Flat, a section of his old holdings, includes the campsite of John C. Frémont, then lieutenant in the topographical engineering corps of the United States Army, and his sixty men on February 25–28, 1846. All this is now located on the Pasatiempo Golf Course.

Paradise Masonic Park, established and incorporated in August 1924, is also within the boundaries of this rancho. A sawmill was constructed here in 1855. James Waters, a carpenter from Maryland who was in charge of this mill, became a prominent builder in Santa Cruz and Monterey Counties and rose to a position of importance in the Pajaro Valley. Here in 1860 a paper mill was established with a reputed peak daily output of a ton of coarse brown paper, the first pulp

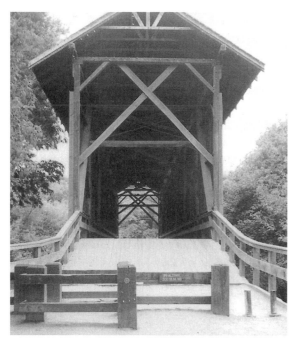

Felton Covered Bridge

mill on the West Coast. It survived only two years, until high water carried away the flume.

In 1865 the California Powder Works were constructed with an entrance about where the gates to Paradise Park now stand. A 1,300-foot tunnel through the mountain brought water from the San Lorenzo River to operate the grinding mills, the output of which was used for blasting in the construction of the Central Pacific Railroad. It was here that smokeless powder was first produced. Work continued at the plant until 1916.

Santa Cruz County is the only county in the state to have as many as three covered bridges still intact. Only the one in Paradise Park, however, still carries vehicular traffic. Constructed in 1872 from local wood, it is used daily by residents of the community. Built by the San Francisco Bridge Company to serve the California Powder Works, it is the only covered span in the West to be equipped with fire hoses at both ends. Other distinctive features are the diamond windows in its siding and the center doorway leading to an observation platform overlooking the San Lorenzo River. The 180-foot-long structure is in Paradise Park, about three miles northwest of Santa Cruz, on the east side of SR 9.

RANCHO ZAYANTE AND FELTON

Rancho Zayante was granted in 1834 to Joaquín Buelna, who had previously held the post of alcalde at Branci-

forte. It was granted in 1841 to Joseph L. Majors (who also held Rancho San Agustín), who immediately sold it to Isaac Graham, to whom it was patented in 1870, although Graham had died in 1867.

Graham, a hardy frontiersman, had come from Kentucky in 1833. Three years after his arrival he assisted Juan B. Alvarado in expelling Governor Gutiérrez, with the understanding that the country should be free from Mexican domination. However, shortly after Alvarado came into power, Graham and his associates were arrested as dangerous foreigners and placed in confinement on a boat in Monterey harbor. A few of the group were released before Don José Castro sailed with the prisoners for Mexico, and all were released by the Mexican authorities after their arrival. It was reported that Isaac Graham received $36,000 as compensation and that a part of this sum was used in the purchase of the rancho. Within a year after he came into possession of the land, he built the first power sawmill in California, on the west bank of the Zayante Creek opposite Bean Creek. This was in 1842, about two months before the one at Bodega Bay was established.

Both Mount Hermon and Felton in the southern part of this rancho are near the junction of Zayante Creek and the San Lorenzo River. Between these two settlements is another covered bridge (SRL 583), built across the river. Settlers had attempted to establish a bridge in place of the ford at this location and succeeded in having one built in 1879; it was replaced in 1892 by the covered bridge now standing. The Felton covered bridge is the tallest covered span in the nation. It was built of local redwood and is 186 feet long. It was replaced in 1938 by a concrete span nearby and is the first example in the West of a bypassed covered bridge that has been preserved.

The county's third remaining covered bridge once crossed Branciforte Creek on the Glen Canyon road after it leaves Santa Cruz via Market Street. Only eighty-three feet long, it was built in 1892 and used until 1939, when it was moved half a block into De Laveaga Park for preservation. Though not in use, it still graces the same creek and looks so much a part of the surroundings that one would think that it had been there from the beginning. It is said to be the most photographed of all the covered bridges in the nation, having been featured in several motion pictures and television productions. It is about two miles northeast of Santa Cruz.

Felton is named for Senator Charles N. Felton, attorney for one of the owners of Rancho Zayante. About 1878 Mr. and Mrs. George Day ran the first hotel in Felton, the Big Tree House. Supplies for the hotel had to be brought across the river, and when the river was in flood, a horse had to swim across, carrying both rider and food. In addition to his hotel, Day conducted a livery stable and ran a stage line. George U. Collins, brother of Mrs. Day, was a lumberman from Maine who was then operating a shingle mill on Bean Creek. He built a road from Felton to the Big Trees, placing a tollhouse at the point where the Toll House Resort would later be located. The buildings of the resort are still there, but the resort is no longer in operation.

RANCHO REFUGIO (WEST OF SANTA CRUZ)

This rancho was situated on the shore of Monterey Bay southwest of Rancho de la Cañada del Rincón. Its northwestern boundary was Laguna Creek. Similar creeks—Coja, Baldwin, and Meder—flow from the hills through this tract into the bay. The old coast road, successively used by the Portolá expedition, vaqueros, lumber wagons, and stagecoaches, extended across this rancho, as does SR 1 over the same route today.

In 1839 this land was apparently granted to María de los Angeles Castro and her three sisters, one of whom was the wife of José Antonio Bolcoff, to whom it was definitely granted by Governor Alvarado in 1841. It was later claimed by his sons, Francisco and Juan, as executors of the estate.

José Antonio Bolcoff was one of the earliest foreign settlers in Spanish California. A native of Kamchatka, he deserted a Russian sailing vessel when it visited Monterey Bay in 1815, settled in Santa Cruz, and in 1822 married Candida, one of the daughters of José Joaquín Castro. They raised a family of eleven children. After being naturalized as a Mexican citizen, he became alcalde at three different times and held that office when the American flag was raised over California.

Following the order of secularization, he was put in charge of the buildings and properties of Mission Santa Cruz, and assumed these duties in July 1839. To govern the little group of people over which he had control, he immediately promulgated twenty-two statutes. These laws, intended for a few Spanish families and about seventy Indians, dealt with precautions to be taken against fires spreading to grass and timber, the responsibility of each resident for keeping the street in front of his house clean, prohibition of the sale of liquor af-

ter eight o'clock, and an eight o'clock curfew, the hour later being changed to ten.

On receiving the grant of Rancho Refugio, he built an adobe house, part of which is still standing at the Wilder Ranch on Meder Creek, about four miles west of Santa Cruz on the coast road. The original tiles remain on one end of the long, low building now used as a storeroom, the other end of which fell years ago. Excavation for the foundation of the Wilder family home, a frame house now standing between the old adobe and the road, uncovered the base of the old fireplace, and in the earth about it were found old knives, spoons, and crockery.

This land passed from the Bolcoff heirs to Moses Meder, one of the Mormons brought by Sam Brannan to San Francisco on the ship *Brooklyn* in 1846. The place had been in the possession of the Delos Wilder family for nearly six generations when it was bought for a state park. One of the frame ranch houses at Wilder Ranch State Park standing within a few yards of the adobe and the later Wilder residence was built during the early pioneer days and shows on its roof the original hand-split and hand-planed shingles.

RANCHO ARROYO DE LA LAGUNA

Adjoining Rancho Refugio on the northwest at Arroyo de la Laguna, now Laguna Creek, was Rancho Arroyo de la Laguna, which extended along the coast as far as San Vicente Creek, just south of the present-day settlement of Davenport. This grant was made in 1840 by Governor Alvarado to Gil Sánchez, a tithe collector at Branciforte.

James Williams, a lumberman and blacksmith, who with his brother Isaac came overland to California with the Chiles-Walker party, settled near Santa Cruz. Another brother, Squire, a former member of Frémont's Battalion, died in the Yuba mines in 1848. In 1852 James and the heirs of Squire filed claim to the lands of this grant, and it was patented to them in 1881. On the edge of this rancho, at the mouth of San Vicente Creek, is the site of Williams Landing, where in the 1850s lumber from the hills was loaded on schooners.

RANCHO AGUA PUERCA Y LAS TRANCAS (DAVENPORT AND SWANTON)

This square league of land, given by Governor Micheltorena in 1843 to Ramón Rodríguez and Francisco Alviso, extends along the coast from the mouth of the Arroyo Agua Puerca ("Dirty Water Ravine") at the old

Jail, now a Santa Cruz Historical Museum, Davenport

Davenport landing on the east to the Cañada de las Trancas ("crossbars") on the west. Scott Creek, which flows almost the entire length of the rancho, enters it from the hills at its northeast corner and near the southwest corner joins the Pacific Ocean.

Near the confluence of Big Creek, Little Creek, and Scott Creek is a hamlet, once the stage station Laurel Grove, now called Swanton after one of the men who built a long-gone powerhouse further up Big Creek.

James Archibald purchased this rancho. He employed Ambrogio Gianone, who came from Switzerland via the dairies of Marin County in 1869, and the Gianone name since that time has been closely identified with this locality. The ranch headquarters at that date were on Archibald Creek, where now an old barn and other farm buildings stand beside the Swanton Road, one and a quarter miles north of its junction with SR 1. Across the road is a small, substantial "rock" house, which young Gianone built soon after his arrival. Set into the hillside, it was used for the making of cheese; it is now known simply as the Gianone storehouse.

The small settlement of Davenport on the coast has long been identified with the cement industry. The St. Vincent de Paul Catholic Church, a handsome structure built in 1915, was constructed mostly with volunteer labor from the factory workers. The Davenport Jail operated from 1914 to 1936, and is now displayed by the Santa Cruz County Historical Society. Local lore is that it was closed because it had virtually no tenants in its official life.

OTHER MEXICAN GRANTS

Stretching back from the coast between San Vicente and Molino creeks is Rancho San Vicente, granted in 1846 to Blas A. Escamilla and patented to him in 1870 (although Bancroft states that it was previously granted to Antonio Rodríguez in 1839.) On this tract was the Agua Puerca School which, although it changed location several times for the convenience of families with children of school age, always retained the name Agua Puerca because its earliest site was near the creek of that name.

In the northwestern part of the city of Santa Cruz a grant of less than 200 acres was given in 1844 to Nicolas Dodero, an Italian sailor who left the *María Ester* at San Francisco in 1827 and spent most of his life in San Jose and Branciforte. He received his patent in 1866 to this Rancho Tres Ojos de Agua ("three eyes of water"), referring to the springs near High Street south of the University of California campus, whence a stream flows down through the town. Nothing remains of several other small grants in the Santa Cruz region.

SCHOONER LANDINGS

Santa Cruz County lies along the northeastern shore of Monterey Bay. With few wagon roads and no railroads in the pioneer days, and with the products of its kilns, tanneries, and mills too great for local needs, the active residents of this region depended upon water transportation for a wider market. Inlets at the mouths of streams were used as landing places for schooners, and loading was sometimes done through the surf before wharves were built.

The southernmost landing was that of Pajaro at the mouth of the Pajaro River. A mile north of Pajaro a wharf was built in 1903 at a spot named Port Rogers, later Port Watsonville. A storm in 1912 destroyed the pier. The landing at the mouth of Soquel Creek was in use as early as 1849. Near Soquel Landing is the Capitola Pier, described above.

A wharf was built in 1849 near the mouth of the San Lorenzo River at Santa Cruz by Elihu Anthony. It was purchased later by Isaac E. Davis and Albion P. Jordan, who maintained a fleet of small schooners to haul lime to San Francisco and who, in 1855, had the $150,000 schooner *Santa Cruz* built in the East and brought around the Horn. Davis and Jordan had the largest industry in the town of Santa Cruz in the 1850s. Both Forty-niners from New England, they were engineers on a Sacramento River steamboat before coming to this region. Their original kiln was at the upper end of Bay Street; later they moved farther north to the Rincón rancho.

In the shale on the beach, about one-half mile north-west of Meder Creek, are some mooring irons used by schooners that once called there for the produce of the Cowell Lime Company. The old brick-built kilns are located about three miles up Meder Canyon behind the Wilder Ranch, and from the kilns ox teams hauled the burned lime to this natural wharf.

Williams Landing was at the mouth of San Vicente Creek. Lime from the kilns in the vicinity was shipped from there, and in 1851 W. W. Waddell shipped lumber from the mill he had established there, the first of four mills that he eventually operated within the county.

At the mouth of the Arroyo del Agua Puerca farther northwest, Davenport Landing was the site of extensive whaling operations. The French explorer La Pérouse, in 1786, wrote while in Monterey Bay, "it is impossible to conceive the number of whales by which we are surrounded." Captain John P. Davenport, an old whaling master, who fifty-five years later was living on the shore of the bay, also observed the great number of whales. According to Hittell's 1885 *History of California*, he devised a scheme whereby he could go out from shore in a whaling boat, capture a whale, and tow it to land, where the blubber could be removed and prepared in great pots, instead of completing the whole operation at sea. While directing this work, which began in the 1850s, Captain Davenport lived in a frame house on the west side of the arroyo overlooking the 450-foot wharf that he had built. His men lived in cabins or in the hotel that stood a little way up the arroyo and served as headquarters for the lumber and lime men of the region.

Despite the action of wind and wave, the captain's wharf outlasted a newer one built by the Reese Lime Works near their storehouse on the opposite side of the arroyo.

The hotel that housed the workers in these early industries and the few small houses of the time have all disappeared, along with the old wharves, giving way to a one-room country school, no longer in use, and a few scattered homes just west of SR 1. Old Davenport shows no trace of its former shipping or other activities, but a new Davenport, about one mile south on the hillside above San Vicente Creek, has grown up around a busy cement plant.

The landing farthest north and west in the county was between Punta de Año Nuevo and the mouth of Waddell Creek. Through the change of county line made in 1868, this spot in now in San Mateo County. But at the time of its operation it was a part of Santa Cruz County, and pickets, posts, and sawn lumber from the forests in the canyons for miles around were shipped from there. The landing was built by W. W. Waddell to transport lumber to the mill on the creek that bears his name.

WADDELL CREEK, CAÑADA DE LA SALUD

Waddell Creek, the perennial coast stream that rises in Big Basin Redwoods State Park, is fed by water trickling down from springs on the mountain slopes bordering its banks and continues downward to its lagoon on the Pacific. The valley through which this stream flows has a history paralleling, in miniature, that of the state.

Little is known of the earliest human inhabitants of this canyon. But the discovery, as late as 1920, of broken arrowheads and chips of flint on a knoll on the west side of the creek about a quarter of a mile back from the lagoon, and the unearthing, in 1916, of a large and perfectly made obsidian spearhead in the clearing out of a spring on the mountainside about five hundred feet west of this knoll, prove that at least a few Indians used this place as a camping ground.

The name "Cañada de la Salud," or "Canyon of Health," was bestowed on the valley by the Portolá expedition in 1769. The place is easily identified because the engineer of the party, Don Miguel Costansó, appended a note to his diary stating that Punta de Año Nuevo, which had been discovered and named by the Vizcaíno sea expedition of 1602–3, was in approximately the same latitude as their camping place.

After the establishment of the mission at Santa Cruz, the mission herds roamed the coast up to a point where they mingled with the cattle from the mission at San Francisco, according to August Duhaut-Cilly, who traveled along the coast in 1827. The land of this valley, however, was never included in any Spanish or Mexican grant but lay between Rancho Agua Puerca y las Trancas and Rancho Punta de Año Nuevo.

After the American annexation, the wooded sides of the canyon resounded with the blows of the woodsman's axe and the buzz of his saw. At this time the place became known and recorded on maps as "Big Gulch." There William W. Waddell, who was born in Kentucky in 1818 and arrived in California in 1851, established his fourth and last sawmill in 1862 (others were at Williams Landing, at Rincón, and at Branciforte). To transport lumber to the wharf built between the mouth of the creek and Punta de Año Nuevo, he constructed a five-mile horse tramway in as straight a line as possible, following the course of the stream, and built twelve bridges across the meandering channel. The mill was located on high ground between, and at the confluence of, the east and west forks of Waddell Creek.

After Waddell died in 1875 of an injury inflicted by a grizzly bear, lumbering and woodcutting in the valley gradually ceased. The wharf was finally destroyed in a storm. At the mill the huge boilers were left in place and are still there, although they are now hedged around by second-growth redwoods.

The lower part of the valley was owned at one time by the Ocean Shore Land and Investment Company. When it abandoned the prospect of building the Ocean Shore Railway from San Francisco to Santa Cruz, it sold the property in 1914 to Theodore J. Hoover, who had previously purchased the upper part of the valley. Hoover was the brother of President Herbert Hoover and dean of the Stanford School of Engineering, and was much interested in the conservation of natural resources.

An interesting note on this family comes from Santa Cruz historian Margaret Koch:

> Theodore Hoover spent his last years in the valley he loved and the large home he and his wife had planned. He died in 1955 and lies buried on Grateful Mountain, high in the Rancho range. Beside him is his wife, Mildred Brooke Hoover, who died in 1940. Mrs. Hoover became a well-known California historian with the publication of . . . *Historic Spots in California*, in 1933 and 1937. It was published in three volumes originally, and Mrs. Hoover collaborated on it with her brother-in-law and sister, Hero Eugene Rensch and Ethel Grace Rensch.

Much of the Waddell Creek Valley is now part of Big Basin Redwoods State Park. Theodore J. Hoover Natural Preserve, which includes Waddell Marsh, is located at the mouth of Waddell Creek at the ocean.

MOUNTAIN CHARLEY

Charles Henry McKiernan, formerly an Irish quartermaster in the British army, arrived in San Francisco during the Gold Rush and went directly to the mines. In 1850, coming with his wages as a miner into the Santa Cruz Mountains, he followed a rough trail through the Los Gatos region to a place near the Laguna del Sargento, where the Indians and Spanish had camped from time to time. Using whipsawed lumber from the redwood trees, which grew thickly around him, he built a

house near a spring and with redwood pickets enclosed corrals for the livestock. Grizzly bears, mountain lions, coyotes, and eagles took a heavy toll on the calves and lambs. However, he became so adept with his muzzle-loading blunderbuss that he won fame as a bear hunter. An attack by a wounded mother bear nearly cost him his life, and he ever after wore in his skull a plate made by a Santa Cruz physician from two Mexican silver dollars.

McKiernan was for two years the only resident of this region, and he was known to later arrivals as "Mountain Charley." He made many trails and roads through his property; one of them was a cutoff down the old Indian trail near his home through the Moody Gulch territory to Los Gatos Creek. When the Santa Clara turnpike was organized, he became a stockholder, and one of his roads became part of the route from Los Gatos to Santa Cruz. Leaving Los Gatos, this stage road curved to the west above the later site of Alma and climbed to the summit. A relic of it, designated by a sign reading "Mt. Charley Road," may be followed from Summit Road south to a junction on the Glenwood Highway at a point two and one-half miles southwest of Glenwood. Narrow and winding, the road is little changed since stagecoach days.

Mountain Charley, after settling down as stockman and stage owner, did not forget his experience as a miner but carried on investigations of the mineral possibilities of his property. Other parts of his story belong to Santa Clara County and are told in that chapter. He moved to San Jose in 1884 so that his children might be closer to schools, and died there in 1892. As a memorial to this pioneer, a redwood tree, one of the largest of its kind, has been named the Mountain Charley Big Tree. It stands three hundred feet back from the road and is one-half mile north of Glenwood.

STAGE LINES OUT OF SANTA CRUZ

After the close of Mexican rule in California, the former methods of travel—on foot, on horseback, and in bumping, creaking carts—became inadequate, and various kinds of omnibuses and stages were put to use as soon as roads connected the pivotal points.

A stage line was established between Santa Cruz and San Jose, via San Juan Bautista, in 1854. Passengers for San Francisco stopped overnight in San Jose and in the winter season proceeded by boat from Alviso the next morning; in summer it was possible to continue the journey on another stage line.

A driver on this line between Santa Cruz and San Jose was "Cock-eyed Charley," recorded in 1867 as Charley Darkey Parkhurst, aged fifty-five, a farmer and native of New Hampshire. A typical stage driver, Charley took a nip at roadhouses, carried the U.S. mail, swore at the horses, and voted as a good citizen. After giving up public driving, Cock-eyed Charley retired to a ranch near the Twelve Mile House out of Santa Cruz and began stock raising on a small scale. Not until death came in 1879 was it learned that Charley was a woman. Her grave is in the Watsonville Cemetery on the west side of Freedom Boulevard.

By 1858 a road over the mountains from Soquel had been completed through the efforts of German-born entrepreneur Frederick A. Hihn. A stage immediately put on between Santa Cruz and San Jose used this route, which today joins the old Los Gatos–Santa Cruz highway beyond Burrell at the site of Schultheis Lagoon in Santa Clara County.

Above the old Soquel–San Jose road in this same area is the community of Skyland, with a picturesque old Presbyterian church, built in 1887, standing with its detached bell tower under spreading oaks. This place had its own post office from 1884 to 1886 and from 1893 to 1910, and even boasted a small newspaper at one time. The economy was based on the vineyards and fruit orchards in the surrounding forests, most of which were owned by Frederick Hihn, who at one time paid one-tenth of all Santa Cruz County's taxes. A few old ranch houses still stand in the area.

In 1872 a horse-drawn stage was driven by "Billy" Bias up the coast from Santa Cruz to San Gregorio. Turning inland here, the stage followed a road winding over the mountains to Redwood City via La Honda, similar to the present SR 84. This route was a hazardous one, not only because of narrow and poorly built mountain roads but also because of the precipitous cliffs at Waddell Beach, which had to be passed by driving over the sand at low tide. A road has since been cut into the face of the cliff at this point; but even today, in wet weather, slides of crumbling rock sometimes block the road.

Nathan P. Ingalls, a native of New Hampshire, who had driven a four-yoke cow team across the plains in 1853, succeeded Bias as owner and driver on this line. Commencing July 1, 1874, he took the mail contract, in addition to others, from Santa Cruz to San Mateo and drove the route to Pescadero once a day for over twelve years, a distance of thirty-seven miles. A veteran stage driver, he had previously put on the first stage from Napa to Clear Lake and had driven a stage for Woody and Taft from San Mateo to Pescadero for three years before taking the Santa Cruz route. It was his boast that he had never been held up in his life. After becoming county supervisor in 1890, he again became interested in stage lines, this time in Monterey County.

GLENWOOD

Charles Christopher Martin, born in Nova Scotia, came around Cape Horn from Maine in the late 1840s. Arriving in California, he worked for a time as a teamster in the lumbering area of Lexington in Santa Clara County, and in 1851 he began homesteading land adjoining that of Mountain Charley McKiernan. He operated a tollgate and stage station on Mountain Charley Road at a point now called the "Station Ranch" and still owned by his descendants.

In the 1860s, while engaged in lumbering, Martin built a home in a quiet, sheltered valley below the stage route. There he and his wife, Hannah Carver Martin, raised their family. By 1873 he had built and opened a store. The place was at first called Martinville but soon became known as Glenwood (SRL 449, marker at 4175 Glenwood Drive). The post office was established in 1880, and Martin became the first postmaster.

That same year, 1880, saw the passage of the first train over the completed narrow-gauge South Pacific Coast Railroad of the James G. Fair interests. By 1877 it had been built from Alameda, along the eastern side of San Francisco Bay, to San Jose and Los Gatos. Then came the task of tunneling through the Santa Cruz Mountains to join the previously built Felton–Santa Cruz line. Two of the tunnels were over a mile long, and one of these emerged at Glenwood. Southern Pacific took over the line in 1887, and it was converted to broad gauge early in the twentieth century.

Many resorts were developing in the mountains, and they became even more popular now that there was rail service from the Bay Area. The railroad that passed through Glenwood became known as the "Picnic Line." Charles Martin himself built a hotel in the 1890s that became a social center for San Francisco millionaires. Perhaps the biggest boost to the economy came when the main automobile road to Santa Cruz was constructed through the settlement, a project Martin had been encouraging for some time. Not long after, the old pioneer died at the age of ninety.

But Glenwood's prosperity as a tourist stop on a main highway was to be short-lived. In 1934 the highway was realigned, and Glenwood was left off the beaten track. The store, which had been remodeled and to which had been added a gasoline station, was closed the same year, and it was razed in 1949. Another blow was dealt when the Southern Pacific discontinued its Los Gatos–Santa Cruz service and pulled up the tracks. The line had been failing for several years, and final abandonment was caused by storm damage during the severe winter of 1939–40. The last train passed through Glenwood on March 4, 1940. The town's post office was discontinued in 1954; the last postmaster was Margaret Koch, great-granddaughter of Charles C. Martin, who has written extensively on Santa Cruz County history.

BOULDER CREEK

One of the early post offices in the county was Boulder Creek, situated at the point where Boulder Creek from the northwest and Bear Creek from the east flow into the San Lorenzo River, a lumber center for many years. An older settlement, called Lorenzo in the 1870s, is now within its limits.

The timber from the site of the town had been cut out by James F. Cunningham, a man who had come West after considerable military service in the East and had taken up government land on the San Lorenzo River. After the early 1870s, he was identified with the lumber interests in the county. J. W. Peery was another mill proprietor. He had the Silver Lumber Mills and in connection with them opened a tannery. Peery's Toll Road ran up the San Lorenzo River across to Saratoga. The Bear Creek Toll Road also ran across the mountains to Lexington. Completed in 1875, it never even paid the wages of a toll keeper, and was finally sold to the county in 1891.

The lumber produced in the vicinity of Boulder Creek was sent over the V-flume built by the San Lorenzo Flume and Transportation Company. This V-flume originally extended from a point about five miles north of Boulder Creek to a point in the lower end of Felton. From Felton the lumber was shipped to the wharf at Santa Cruz over a narrow-gauge railroad. The "dump" at the end of the flume was at about the point where the Felton Bowl now stands in the lower end of the town and extended some three hundred or four hundred feet.

Around Boulder Creek during timber cutting, over fifty saw and shingle mills operated within a radius of seven miles. Because of the size of this operation, the Southern Pacific changed the railroad line to standard gauge in 1907. But in 1934, when the timber was exhausted and the mills were closed, the last train was run, and the rails between Felton and Boulder Creek were removed.

Boulder Creek has an interesting museum at 12788 State Highway 9, with much information on the floods that have caused such havoc in the region. Four country newspapers have been published at Boulder Creek, and their names suggest the tenor of their reportage. The first one was the *Boulder Creek Hatchet*, the second was the *Boulder Creek Blast*, the third was the *Mountain Echo*, and the fourth, which printed its last page in 1924, was the *Valley Echo*.

BEN LOMOND

Ben Lomond Mountain was named by Thomas Burns, a native of Scotland. The town that grew up in the 1880s on the river at the base of the mountain took on the name. James J. Pierce, of Santa Clara, owned much timberland there and operated a mill at a site between Mill Street and the river. He laid out the town, and two bridges, still located on the highway passing through the town, are built on the site of two early ones that he gave to the county in exchange for bringing the main road through his new town site.

At the confluence of Love Creek and the San Lorenzo River stood a waterpower sawmill first operated by Vardamon Bennett, a native of Georgia, who brought his large family to California in 1834. This mill was later owned by Harry Love, a former captain of spies appointed by General Zachary Taylor during the Mexican War. In 1853, when the California Legislature raised a special force to run down the bandit Joaquín Murieta, Harry Love was made its captain. Love and his rangers overtook and killed a man who they claimed was the outlaw at a place in Fresno County, in which chapter the story is told. In 1854, Love was rewarded for his services by an additional state appropriation of $5,000. With this money he began logging in the mountains, and, by marrying the widow of Vardamon Bennett, he came into possession of the mill. To get the logs to the mill, he built a road since known as the "Harry Love Grade," and the creek where the mill stood is Love Creek, over which one of the bridges on the main street of Ben Lomond extends.

The many coast redwoods, *Sequoia sempervirens*, throughout the Santa Cruz foothills and mountains have made the region famous. Because it was in this county that these trees were first glimpsed and named for posterity—by the Portolá expedition in October 1769 in Pajaro Valley—it is fitting that here the first state park was set aside for their preservation. A few virgin groves and many acres of second-growth trees became the inspiration for the California State Park system.

Big Basin Redwoods State Park (formerly called the California State Redwood Park), situated in the northwestern part of the county in the heart of the "Big Basin" in the Waddell Creek drainage area twenty-three miles from Santa Cruz, contains over fifteen thousand acres of redwoods and other native foliage in an extensive preserve that extends from the crest of the mountains to the Pacific shore. Apparently the first person to mention the desirability and necessity of acquiring redwood forests for posterity was Ralph Smith, whose editorials in the *Redwood City Times and Gazette* awakened general interest before his untimely death in 1887. The cause was then taken up by Captain Ferdinand Lee Clark and Andrew P. Hill. Hill, then living in San Jose, made many trips to photograph the trees in the Big Basin and was tireless in his efforts to bring the matter of their preservation before the public and to produce legislative action.

A group of interested persons was called together on May 1, 1900, in the library of Stanford University and a committee was appointed to visit and report upon this remote region. On the last evening of their inspection visit, May 18, 1900, sitting on the west bank of Sempervirens Creek, they organized the Sempervirens Club, the main object of which was the acquisition and preservation of the surrounding forest.

The idea of state parks was new. Parks hitherto had been the creation of communities or the bequest of local families. That the state should own and administer a huge area called a "park" was a disturbing idea to those who thought that the less the state or any government had to do with anything, the better it was for the private citizen.

Editors of newspapers in the two counties most interested united in giving publicity to the project of a state redwood park. Among these papers were the *Boulder Creek Mountain Echo*, the *Santa Cruz Surf*, the *Santa Cruz Sentinel*, and the *San Jose Mercury*.

In 1901 the California Legislature passed an enabling act whereby 3,800 acres were purchased by the state in the next year for a quarter of a million dollars. Subsequently, Governor Gage appointed the following men to the first state board of commissioners: Father Robert E. Kenna, S.J., president of Santa Clara University; Professor William Russell Dudley, botanist of Stanford University; A. W. Foster, regent of the University of California and president of the Northwestern Railway; and William H. Mills, land agent of the Southern Pacific Railway Company. The governor of the state was ex officio chairman.

Big Basin Redwoods State Park (SRL 827) was established in 1902, the first of the many state parks that have been created since then. Another group of redwoods twenty miles south of the Big Basin park is the Henry Cowell Redwoods State Park, formerly Santa Cruz Big Trees County Park. It became a state park in 1954. The largest tree in this group is the "Giant," 306 feet high.

WORLD WAR II'S STRANGEST NAVAL BATTLE

On the afternoon of December 20, 1941, off the California coast in view of the Santa Cruz Mountains, an incident took place that has been called "World War II's strangest naval battle." The opponents were the Japanese submarine *I-23*, under Commander Genishi Shibata, and the Richfield Oil Company tanker *Agwiworld*, commanded by Captain Federico B. Goncalves, bound for San Francisco from Los Angeles Harbor with a full cargo of oil. When the submarine surfaced and began to shell the unarmed tanker, Captain Goncalves, in a moment of audacity, headed his ship toward the Japanese vessel with the intention of ramming it. The submarine withdrew, but by this time the *Agwiworld*'s master realized the futility of counterattack and headed full speed for Santa Cruz. The *I-23* pursued and continued firing, but the tanker, by following a zigzag course and heading directly into a heavy wind and a rough sea, escaped being hit. Meanwhile, the sailors of the *Agwiworld* replied to the shots by hurling potatoes at the *I-23*. The submarine, her low deck awash in the turbulent seas, finally abandoned the attack, and the oil tanker reached Santa Cruz in safety.

The *I-23*, strangely, made no attempt to torpedo the defenseless *Agwiworld*. On the same day, several hundred miles to the north, another Japanese submarine successfully torpedoed the tanker *Emidio* with a loss of five lives; this story is told in the Del Norte County chapter.

Shasta County

Shasta County was one of the original twenty-seven counties and at first included within its boundaries all of the territory that later became Modoc and Lassen Counties, as well as parts of the present Siskiyou, Plumas, and Tehama Counties. The name "Shasta" probably came from a tribe of Indians living in the vicinity of Mount Shasta. The county seat was first placed at Reading's Ranch, then moved to Shasta in 1851. Redding became the county seat in 1888, and continues to be the principal city of Shasta County.

Newcomers to California geography and history can be understandably confused by the fact that Lassen Peak and more than half of the area of Lassen Volcanic National Park lie within Shasta County, not neighboring Lassen County, while Mount Shasta, the great landmark of northern California, lies within neighboring Siskiyou County.

LASSEN VOLCANIC NATIONAL PARK

Lassen Peak (10,453 feet) was called Monte San José by the padres who accompanied Luís Argüello on an exploring expedition in 1821 to seek for mission sites. Early maps of California note it as Mount St. Joseph. The Maidu Indians called it "La Lapham Yerman y'aidum," meaning "the long, high mountain that was broken." It was later named Lassen Buttes after Peter Lassen, the Danish-born pioneer of northern California, and finally (and officially) Lassen Peak. Nevertheless, the name most people give it today is Mount Lassen.

On May 30, 1914, after having been quiescent for more than 200 years, Lassen Peak began a series of about 300 eruptions, which continued with decreasing frequency for about seven years. B. F. Loomis took many remarkable photographs of the volcanic eruptions, and in the 1920s these were placed in a new museum named for him at the northwest entrance and visitors center of the park. Constructed of local rock, the Loomis Museum also has much interesting information on volcanic activity in general.

Lassen Peak and Cinder Cone were set aside as National Monuments in 1907. On August 9, 1916, the region was designated the Lassen Volcanic National Park, and in January 1929 it was enlarged to its present area of 163 square miles. The park contains other interesting volcanic cones, such as Prospect Peak and Harkness Peak, as well as numerous fumaroles, hot springs, mud pots, and boiling lakes, since the entire region is of volcanic origin. The park lies at the southern end of the Cascade Range (which includes the volcanically active Mount St. Helens in Washington) and at the northern end of the Sierra Nevada; it presents a magnificent skyline. Within the area are outstanding scenic features—multicolored lava crags of varied and fantastic forms rising to a height of over 8,500 feet above sea level, impressive canyons, and primeval forests.

Among the most beautiful of the individual wonders included in the park is Lake Tartarus, or Boiling Springs Lake, which has been described as lying "jade-green and ominous amid the encircling forest." Boiling Springs Lake is part of a group of volcanic phenomena to the south of Lassen Peak that includes the Devil's Kitchen, Willow Creek Geyser, Bumpass Hell, and many other mud pots and hot springs. Most of these are within Shasta County. The park extends eastward into Lassen County, and southward into small portions of Tehama and Plumas Counties, in the latter of which is the resort of Drakesbad.

A number of old trails crossed the Upper Sacramento Valley in the vicinity of Redding. The earliest to be blazed, known as the Trinity Trail, was made by Jedediah Strong Smith in the spring of 1828. Smith's route led across what are now Trinity and Humboldt Counties and on up the coast through the Del Norte region into southern Oregon. Learning of the new pathway from Smith, a party of Hudson's Bay Company trappers, led by Alexander Roderick McLeod, almost immediately set out for California, with John Turner, a former member of Smith's party, acting as guide. McLeod probably reached the Upper Sacramento Valley by this trail, and for a number of years trappers no doubt continued to follow it into California.

The Trinity River was discovered and named in 1845 by Pierson B. Reading, who was trapping in the Trinity country at that time. In 1848 he found the first gold in the region. Somewhere between Kennett (an old copper-mining town now inundated by Shasta Lake) and Castle Crags, Reading's earliest trail into the Trinity country crossed over the stretch of steep mountains separating the Sacramento and Shasta Valleys known as the "Devil's Backbone." On his way back he crossed the same mountains at a point between Castella and Delta. In 1848 he took a new route, this time over the mountains that lie at the head of the middle fork of Cottonwood Creek, and on his return he blazed the trail later known as the Shasta-Weaverville Road, followed by thousands of miners in 1849 and the 1850s. Supplies for the mines of the Trinity, Scott, and Salmon Rivers, brought in by way of the town of Shasta, were taken over this trail by muleback. In 1861 the main section of the trail, that going west from Shasta to Weaverville, was widened into a wagon road by Charles Camden. The Redding-Eureka highway, today's SR 299, roughly follows this early thoroughfare.

In 1859 a stage road to Oregon was opened up, which ran from Shasta to Yreka by way of French Gulch, Carrville in Trinity County, and Callahan and Fort Jones in Siskiyou County. Part of this is today's SR 3. During the 1860s it was the principal wagon road to the north. At the junction of this road and the Shasta-Weaverville Road formerly stood the Tower House, a landmark famous in the early days.

When Levi H. Tower and Charles Camden arrived at this spot in November 1850, they found a log cabin occupied by a man named Schneider. Here Tower built the Tower House Hotel with lumber hewn from the surrounding forests and split by hand. For many years after it was abandoned, remains of the old hostelry still stood near the highway. The residence of Charles Camden, erected some time later near the old hotel, now belongs to the National Park Service and has been restored. In its beautiful mountain setting, Tower House with its lands was the showplace of the county in early days, and it is still a magnificent estate.

The second oldest trail through the Upper Sacramento Valley may have been the east branch of the Oregon to California Trail, although no absolute proof of this has yet been found. It seems likely that McLeod took this route on his way out of the valley in 1829. It is known that he lost most of his supplies in the snowdrifts and was forced to cache his furs at the approach of winter. On his return the following spring he found them spoiled, a circumstance that led to his discharge from the Hudson's Bay Company. At the headwaters of the North Fork of the McCloud River on Bartle's Ranch in Siskiyou County, a wooden trough and some guns were uncovered in 1874. At that time it was believed that these were the remains of McLeod's cache. In any event this early trail was followed by explorers and trappers before 1829, for in Ogden's diary of that year "Pitt's River" is mentioned. In 1841 Pitt's Lake (now Goose Lake) and Pitt's River (since known as the Pit River) were accurately mapped by Charles Wilkes, whose source of information had been the Hudson's Bay Company, which indicated that its trappers had explored the region through which the trail passed.

The east branch of the Oregon to California Trail, after leaving the Sacramento Valley, crossed a ruggedly mountainous country before passing out of the state between Tule and Clear Lakes in the north. In crossing this difficult region, early travelers developed variations of the road. One such route was taken by Frémont and his men in the spring of 1846. In the latter part of April they had passed up the east bank of the Sacramento River as far as its confluence with Cottonwood Creek, opposite which they turned east and then northeast across what is now Shasta County. In Lassen County, some distance east of Fall River, Frémont's party forded the Pit River. Crossing the mountains to Big Valley (called by Frémont "Round Valley"), they spent the night of April 30 at its upper end. From there the party journeyed north over the route followed later by emigrants from Oregon.

In the fall of 1848 the first wagon train into California from Oregon followed the Applegate Road as far as Clear Lake in Modoc County. The lure of gold brought many Oregonians into California in 1849 and the early 1850s. From Big Valley, most of the argonauts bound for Shasta and the Trinity mines climbed the mountains to the west and crossed the Pit River west of Fall River Mills. Leaving the Pit at this point, they went south for some distance and then turned west through Burney Valley and thence southwest to Shasta, the trading center of the Trinity region. In 1856 a road to Yreka was built by way of the Pit River crossing, and shortly thereafter the California Stage Company inaugurated a daily schedule from Sacramento to Yreka, the first through stage service to that point. Because of Indian conflicts in Fall River Valley and attacks on the stage, this line was discontinued in January 1857 for a short time.

It is not known who first blazed the west branch of the Oregon to California Trail, which followed the Sacramento River canyon and around the west side of Mount Shasta, but it is certain that Hudson's Bay Company trappers used it annually from 1832 to 1845. Ewing Young, the trapper, making his way into Oregon to settle in 1834, followed this route, being the first to travel the entire length of the "Oregon Trail" from San Bernardino in southern California to the Methodist mission in northern Oregon. In 1837 the demand for cattle in the Willamette Valley led to Young's second expedition over the trail, when he accomplished the arduous task of driving 700 head of cattle and forty horses over the Devil's Backbone. Young's party included P. L. Edwards, the diarist of the company, and twenty others, among whom were settlers bound for Oregon.

In 1841 a contingent of the Wilkes Exploring Expedition, consisting of about eighteen persons under the command of Lieutenant George F. Emmons, came down the Oregon to California Trail across the Siskiyou Mountains and through what are now Siskiyou and Shasta Counties to New Helvetia and Yerba Buena. A number of Oregonians had joined the party, making a total of thirty-nine persons and about seventy-six animals. On his map Wilkes designated that part of the Sacramento River above its confluence with the Pit River as "Destruction River," a name that may have been given originally by Hudson's Bay Company trappers to the McLeod (now spelled "McCloud") River, on the banks of which McLeod met disaster in the winter of 1829. That part of the Pit River in Shasta County was called the Sacramento.

The largest early expedition to use the west branch of the Oregon to California Trail was led by Joseph Gale, who in May 1843, in company with forty-two settlers bound for Oregon, drove 250 head of cattle, 650 horses, and 3,000 sheep northward over this difficult path. On May 30 of the same year Lansford W. Hastings started for California with a party of discontented Oregonians. At the Rogue River they met Joseph Gale, who persuaded about two-thirds of the party to return to the Willamette Valley. With the remaining emigrants, Hastings continued to California over the route just traveled by Gale. In 1845 James Clyman, with thirty-five men, one woman, and three children, also passed over this trail on the way south.

All of these parties had to cross the Devil's Backbone, and over these lofty, barren mountains they struggled slowly and painfully. The Wilkes party, while traversing these precipitous slopes, which Clyman described as "almost too steep for brush to grow . . . and in many places too narrow for a rabbit to walk over," lost their way but were guided to safety by the Indian wife of one of the company.

Late in 1848 gold-seekers from the north began using the Oregon Trail; and after the Siskiyou region was opened up in 1850, miners poured over it from the south. Because of the mountainous character of the route, it remained a pack trail until 1860, when a wagon road was constructed from Upper Soda Springs to Yreka. Today I-5 and the Shasta Route of the Union Pacific Railroad follow the old Oregon to California Trail closely—many of the railroad stations are on the exact line of the trail—making this the oldest continuously used road in northern California.

Where the California-Oregon stage road crossed the present highway two miles north of Anderson, a marker (SRL 58) has been placed by the Native Sons of the Golden West. On the banks of the Sacramento River opposite this place was an early steamboat landing, the northernmost point on the Sacramento to be reached by riverboats.

At the Bridge Bay off-ramp on I-5 a marker (SRL 148) notes that nearby Bass Hill on the old stage road was a notorious spot for holdups. It memorializes W. L. (Williamson Lyncoya) Smith, division stage agent of the California and Oregon Stage Company, as well as the pioneer stage drivers along the road.

The McCloud River north of its junction with the Pit (now within Shasta Lake) was the site of a Wintun Indian settlement, and the home of Consalulu, the last

Wintun chief. About two miles above the mouth of the McCloud River, fossil remains of at least twenty-five species, including the mastodon, giant sloth, large extinct lion, and cave bear, were taken from the Potter Creek Cave. In the same area was a place known as Joaquin Miller's Pass, where the poet is said to have forded the McCloud River on mule back.

On the park highway in Lassen Volcanic National Park, a few hundred yards northwest of the checking station at Manzanita Lake, is a monument (SRL 11) marking the Nobles Pass Road followed by the pioneers of 1852. A large lava rock about five feet high, bearing a bronze plaque, stands at the junction of the two park highways, one going down to Lost Creek and Hat Creek to Burney, and the other turning west to Viola, Shingletown, and Redding. The latter was the route used by early emigrants who came over Nobles Pass. It was at this point that they caught their first glimpse of the Sacramento Valley. The summit of Nobles Pass is about three miles to the northeast.

SR 44 closely parallels Nobles Trail from Viola to Redding. Trails West, Inc., a private organization, has placed markers along this road at Deer Flats, Battle Creek, Shingletown, Charley's Place, Dersch Ranch, and Emigrant Ferry, in addition to others that are not easily accessible to the average motorist.

READING'S RANCHO BUENA VENTURA

Pierson Barton Reading, a native of New Jersey, came West with the Chiles-Walker party in 1843. He and twelve other men, one of whom was Joseph Chiles, separated from the main party at Fort Hall, coming into California by an uncharted trail, now known as the Yellowstone Cutoff. Passing through what is now Shasta County, Reading and his companions arrived at Sutter's Fort on November 10, 1843.

A comparison of Reading's descriptions of the trail followed by the Chiles party in 1843 with the geographical features of northern California clearly indicates the route traveled. Leaving Big Valley, in Lassen County, on October 25, the band of thirteen men followed the course of the Pit River through the mountains, camping on the stream eighteen miles to the southwest. The next day they continued over mountainous country above the Pit River canyon. "In some places," Reading writes, "the descent from the top of the bank to the water must have been 1,200 feet, the stream pitching over rocks and ledges, forming beauti-

ful cascades, one of which had an abrupt fall of about 150 feet." This was, without a doubt, Burney Falls, in McArthur–Burney Falls Memorial State Park, whose actual drop is 128 feet. Successive halts were made by Reading and his companions at Goose Valley on October 28, at the head of Hatchet Creek on the 29th, and on Cow Creek on the 31st. On the first day of November they traveled sixteen miles down Cow Creek, again pitching their tents on its banks. The next day, camp was made on Battle Creek, a part of the present boundary line between Shasta and Tehama Counties, and the day after, upon traveling eight miles, they passed through Iron Canyon, where they found the course of the stream "very crooked." Camp was made at the end of the day in the valley east of Red Bluff, whence the journey was continued to Sutter's Fort, on the American River near Sacramento.

Here Reading worked for a time in Captain Sutter's employ. In December 1844, through Sutter's friendship and influence, Reading obtained a grant of 26,000 acres from Governor Micheltorena, which he took over in August 1845. This was the northernmost land grant in California. It consisted of a three-mile-wide strip of land extending for nineteen miles along the west bank of the Sacramento River from the mouth of Cottonwood Creek at the head of Bloody Island in the south to Salt Creek in the north. A house was built for Reading's overseer on Rancho Buena Ventura, as Reading called his new estate, and the land was stocked with cattle. This first house was burned by Indians the following spring.

Reading participated in the Bear Flag Revolt at Sonoma in June 1846, and the next month he enlisted in Frémont's Battalion, serving first as lieutenant of artillery and then as paymaster with the rank of major, which office he held until May 1847. In June he returned to his rancho and erected a permanent adobe house (SRL 10), which stood for many years, seven miles east of Cottonwood via Balls Ferry Road and Adobe Lane.

Ranch life, however, did not claim all of Reading's attention this early. In April 1848 he was among the first to visit the scene of Marshall's discovery of gold at Coloma. An examination of the soil satisfied him that gold must be present on his own rancho, and he returned at once to investigate. In May he and his Indian laborers washed out the first gold to be found in Shasta County, at the mouth of Clear Creek Canyon on a spot later known as Reading's Bar. In July of the same year he found gold on the Trinity River. On his return jour-

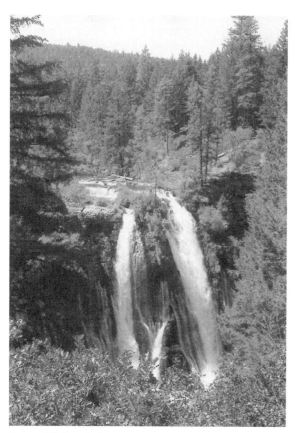

Burney Falls State Park

ney he camped on the site of the present town of Shasta, known for a time as Reading's Springs.

When Shasta County was established in 1850, Reading's Ranch, as Rancho Buena Ventura had come to be known, was designated as the county seat. But with the organization of the Court of Sessions at the major's adobe on February 10, 1851, the county seat was ordered to be removed to Shasta. "In the lonely still of the night," the tale is told, the court packed up the county records and carried them on horseback twenty-five miles to the new location, perhaps "the most quiet county-seat removal on record in California." No one rejoiced more heartily over the change than Major Reading.

In 1852 Reading was appointed United States special Indian agent, and for several years, without remuneration, he carried on work among the Indians. His kindliness is reported as one of Reading's outstanding characteristics. Going to Washington in 1855 to settle his land grant title, Reading met Miss Fannie Wallace Washington, whom he brought with him to California as his bride. The adobe on Rancho Buena Ventura was enlarged and became noted for its hospitality. About the great fireplace many celebrities gathered: Bidwell,

Frémont, Sutter, Lassen, and Joaquin Miller among others. Pierson B. Reading died at his home on May 29, 1868.

A simple granite slab bearing a bronze memorial plate marks his grave, on Adobe Lane a quarter of a mile from the site of the historic adobe, on a slight eminence overlooking the Sacramento River and the valley beyond. The old house, built with thick walls and high windows for protection from Indian arrows, has now eroded away to a shapeless mound. The Shasta Historical Society has given the site to the county of Shasta. Later the towns of Anderson and Redding were established on the rancho. (The town of Redding was named for B. B. Redding, land agent for the Central Pacific Railroad, and not, as may be thought, for Major Reading.)

MCARTHUR–BURNEY FALLS MEMORIAL STATE PARK

Samuel Burney, a Scotsman, was the first settler in Burney Valley. His name was bestowed on the local valley, mountain, town, and waterfalls. Burney came to the valley in 1858 and built a log cabin, barn, and corral a mile north of the present town of Burney. Although friendly with the Indians and speaking their language, he met death at their hands the following year. His grave is close beside the Redding-Alturas highway, SR 299, one-half mile east of Burney.

Burney Falls, one of the most beautiful natural phenomena in California, is the chief attraction of McArthur–Burney Falls Memorial State Park, a tract of 160 acres given to the state in 1920 by Frank McArthur as a memorial to his father and mother. Burney Creek wells up from the ground within the southern boundary of the park and falls 128 feet in two streams that water the ferns and mosses on the rocks. Although the creek goes dry in the summer between the park and the town of Burney, some ten miles to the south, the falls flow all year around with an unvarying temperature of 48 degrees.

SHASTA STATE HISTORIC PARK

Shasta (SRL 77), five miles west of Redding on SR 299, was a bustling place in the 1850s. It was called Reading's Springs by the first settlers who arrived in 1849, but by the following year the present name was adopted. Shasta was the main center of wagon transportation

Courthouse Museum, Shasta State Historic Park

for the Trinity mines and the roads north. As many as 100 freight teams stopped in Shasta on a single night. Its favored location soon made it the commercial shipping center of northern California, and its merchants did a thriving business.

The decline of the mining industry and the coming of the railroad along the banks of the Sacramento River both contributed to the decline of Shasta. By 1888 the county seat had been moved to Redding. Guidebooks written as late as 1948 described the place as a virtually abandoned town. Soon afterward, much of the property was acquired by McCloud Parlor No. 149 of Redding, Native Sons of the Golden West, and presented to the state of California, which in turn began the work of restoring the old site. Today it is Shasta State Historic Park.

The restored county courthouse has been renovated and is now a museum of the boom years. The Masonic Lodge nearby was the first to be established in the state, its charter having been brought to California by Peter Lassen in 1848. The lodge was first organized at Benton City on Lassen's Ranch (Tehama County), but in 1851 it was moved to Shasta. The present hall, which has been in use since 1853, is owned and carefully preserved by Western Star Lodge, No. 2. These buildings stand on the northeastern side of SR 299, Main Street of Shasta today.

Across the highway is a series of brick storefronts, the remnants of Brick Row. In its early days, the town of Shasta operated from rough lumber and canvas structures. Destructive fires in 1852 and the following year showed the need for a different kind of construction, and the "fireproof brick" building first introduced here around 1853 was the result. As the town of Shasta went into decline, so did most of its buildings; these

brick fronts still stand. The one to the furthest right, facing the block, is the remains of Jacobson and Company, Dry Goods and Clothiers.

At the eastern edge of Shasta a marker directs the visitor to the foundation of a Catholic church that was never built (SRL 483). Father Raphael Rinaldi, an Italian priest who arrived in the Shasta diggings in 1855, was dissatisfied with the small church in which the Catholics of the camp worshiped; he desired a magnificent, basilica-like cut stone edifice, modeled on the architecture of Italy. The cornerstone was laid in 1857 by Archbishop Joseph Sadoc Alemany, O.P., of San Francisco, but the church never rose above its foundation, which remains today in a cluster of brush and high grass. Unless one is looking very hard for it, this historical landmark can easily be missed. The nearest point of reference is the corner of High and Main Streets.

A little less than a mile west of town off SR 299 is the grave of a baby boy (SRL 377), all that remains of a pioneer Jewish cemetery. The original headstone has been replaced. The Hebrew inscription is followed in English with: "Charles, son of George and Helena Brownstein. Born May 4, 1864, died December 14, 1864."

SHASTA MINING CAMPS

Reading's Bar, where Major Reading in 1848 discovered the first gold in Shasta County, and where he washed out as much as fifty-two ounces daily, is now only a memory. On a flat adjoining the bar a camp grew up that was known at first as Clear Creek Diggings and later as Horse Town. By October 1849, over 300 miners had congregated at Clear Creek diggings, and considerable gold was taken out.

One of these prospectors, who had arrived in camp with one pack horse, settled there permanently and later built a hotel. As a result, so the story goes, the name of the place was changed to "One-Horse Town" in 1851. It did not remain a one-horse town, however, for before many years it boasted 1,000 inhabitants and had two hotels, stores, shops, a Catholic church, a newspaper (the *Northern Argus*, established in 1857), and fourteen saloons.

The site (SRL 32) of Reading's Bar and Horse Town is east of the Clear Creek bridge seven miles west of SR 273 on Clear Creek Road, which intersects the highway at a point four miles south of Redding and less than a mile north of Clear Creek itself. Horse Town was destroyed by fire in 1868, and the site has been thoroughly dredged out. Reading's discovery of gold at this place is also commemorated by a native boulder bearing a bronze tablet (SRL 78) on a now-bypassed stretch of SR 273 at the end of the Clear Creek Bridge.

In the vicinity of Horse Town were other early mining camps: Centerville to the north, Muletown to the northwest, and Piety Hill, Igo, and Ono to the west. The latter two still exist as small settlements, sharing the Igo-Ono School. There seems to be no single recognized source for their names, although it is said that the pioneer preacher Rev. William Kidder chose one from the biblical "plains of Ono."

Whiskeytown (SRL 131), on SR 299 between Shasta and Weaverville, was settled in 1849. It was a lively place, as its name might imply, where money was plentiful and freely spent. The U.S. Post Office Department refused to allow the name Whiskeytown as a postal designation until 1952. Prior to that, the post office had been called Blair, later Stella, and finally Schilling. The old town now lies beneath Whiskeytown Lake, created by the Whiskeytown Dam; a new Whiskeytown lies on higher ground on what is now the lakeshore. Whiskeytown Dam was dedicated by President John F. Kennedy on September 28, 1963, on what turned out to be his last trip to California.

At French Gulch (SRL 166), originally called Morrowville, the diggings were very rich. In their avid search for gold, some of the miners even tore down their cabins to follow the gold leads extending under them. This once wild camp is today a peaceful community, on Trinity Mountain Road three miles north of SR 299; the turn-off is five miles west of Whiskeytown.

SOUTHERN'S STATION

Simeon Fisher Southern arrived in Shasta in 1855, where at first he operated the Eagle Hotel, and later the St. Charles. In the next few years he ran hotels in French Gulch and Dog Creek on the Oregon to California Trail. In 1859 he built a cabin of shakes and hand-hewn logs at a spot forty-five miles north of Redding that would later be known as Southern's. This developed into a busy trading post for miners from Hazel Creek and the Upper Sacramento River. When stagecoaches replaced pack-mule teams on the Oregon Trail in 1871, Southern's became an important station. Gradually the place took on the aspect of a summer resort, and in 1882 a two-story extension was added to the original cabin. Eventually the old cabin was torn down and the two-

story addition was much enlarged to care for the increasing number of summer visitors.

After the death of Southern in 1892, changes crept in. With the sale of the property to lumber interests in 1902, the surrounding forests were cut and the old hotel disappeared, to be replaced by modern facilities. The spot on which the old hotel stood (SRL 33) is about eight miles south of Castella on Old Highway 99. The names of many famous people appear on the old hotel register, which is still treasured by the family; among them are President Rutherford B. Hayes, Generals William T. Sherman and Philip H. Sheridan, Robert Ingersoll, Mrs. Jay Gould, George Jay Gould, and the "Big Four" leaders of the Central Pacific Railroad: Charles Crocker, Mark Hopkins, C. P. Huntington, and Leland Stanford.

REDDING

Redding, named in honor of B. B. Redding, for many years land agent for the Central Pacific Railroad, was founded in the summer of 1872. It was the temporary railhead of the line until construction began up the Sacramento River gorge in 1883; the line was connected to Portland, Oregon, in 1887. The town was incorporated the same year, the first municipality in Shasta County. It became the county seat in 1888. Because of its central location, it has always been an active center of trade and transportation. At 1911 Rio Drive, in Caldwell Park on the riverside, is the excellent City Museum, with departments of ethnology, history, and the fine arts.

Shasta College was opened in Redding in 1950 and in 1967 moved to its present site. Its museum and research center at 11555 North Old Oregon Trail, housed in a modern-day replica of Major Reading's adobe, is open to the public on a limited basis; it contains extensive material on Upper Sacramento Valley history in the early twentieth century as well as displays on natural and Indian history. The Shasta Historical Society maintains a research facility at 1449 Market Street.

ANDERSON

Elias Anderson, one of Shasta County's first settlers, purchased the American Ranch in 1856, and on his land grew up the nucleus of what is now the town of Anderson. The ranch was also an early stopping place for teamsters and travelers on the Oregon to California Trail, and from here a trail branched off to the Trinity mines. The first buildings of the old stage, the site of which is near the highway across the creek from central Anderson, were of adobe.

BELL'S BRIDGE

Five miles south of Redding off SR 273, a few hundred yards above the Clear Creek Bridge, is the site of the Bell hostelry, built by J. J. Bell in 1851. During the Gold Rush the place teemed with activity, and thousands of men and animals found refreshment there on their way to the Shasta, Trinity, and Siskiyou gold fields. High prices were paid for food and lodging, and with the proceeds Bell was able to make extensive improvements on his property. He also operated a toll bridge across Clear Creek at this point; the marker (SRL 519) commemorating Bell's Bridge is at the junction of SR 273 and Clear Creek Road.

FORT READING

Fort Reading, named in honor of Major Pierson B. Reading, was established in May 1852 on Cow Creek on the Nobles Pass Road at a site six miles northeast of the present town of Anderson. It was abandoned in 1867 as part of the post–Civil War demobilization of the army. Nothing remains of the fort itself, but a marker (SRL 379) is at the site, 3.4 miles east of the junction of Dersch and Airport Roads.

THE DERSCH HOMESTEAD

Northeast of Anderson stood the Dersch homestead (SRL 120). In 1850 a Mr. Baker had set up a tent hotel there, making the place an emigrant station on the Nobles Pass Road. George Dersch followed him, using Indian labor from rancherias flourishing at Jelly's Ferry (Tehama County), Cottonwood, Reading's adobe, and Millville. Roving Indians raided the ranch in 1863, driving off the cattle, stealing the household provisions, and leaving the family destitute. In 1866 a second raid was made, in which Mrs. Dersch was killed. The soldiers at Fort Reading were appealed to, but with no results. The settlers took matters into their own hands and massacred most of the Indians in the surrounding rancherias. The old house stood until it burned in 1934. The state landmark was dedicated in 1999; there is also a Trails West marker on the site, on Dersch Road 7.8 miles east of its junction with Airport Road.

Dersch Homestead

MILLVILLE

Fourteen miles east of Redding on SR 44 is Millville, a thriving place with a distinctive atmosphere of pioneer days. It was settled in 1853 by S. E. and N. T. Stroud, who built the first house there on the banks of Clover Creek. The first gristmill in Shasta County was built in Millville in 1856 by D. D. Harrell and Russell Furman, who named the place Bunscombe Mills, after Harrell's birthplace in North Carolina. Eventually the name was changed to Millville.

SHINGLETOWN

Shingletown was established before 1860 as a lumber center. One pioneer family, the Ogburns, established themselves in the region as early as 1848. The Ogburn Ranch (since 1942 the Johnson Ranch), just off SR 44 near Charley's Place, has been in operation since that time; an E Clampus Vitus plaque commemorates the place. The Ogburn-Inwood Cemetery nearby is still in use; its earliest gravestones bear the date of 1860.

FALL RIVER VALLEY AND FORT CROOK

On July 1, 1857, a fort was established by Lieutenant George Crook on Fall River at the upper end of Fall River Valley to serve as a buffer against Indian attacks on the early settlers. The post consisted of some twenty log buildings placed in an oblong form. With the abandonment of Fort Crook in 1869 and the transfer of the soldiers to Fort Bidwell, the buildings were used for a time as a school, but were later moved to Burgettville, now Glenburn. The site of the fort (SRL 355) is now in a cultivated field on private property two miles northwest of Glenburn.

The first settlers in Fall River Valley were two men named Bowles and Rogers, who came there from Yreka in 1855. They brought heavy mill machinery with them by ox team and in 1856 set to work cutting trees, some of which still lie where they fell. In the autumn other settlers joined them, among whom were the Lockhart brothers, who located on the site of Fall River Mills. Bowles, Rogers, and William Lockhart spent the winter at this place but were killed by Indians early the following spring. When Sam Lockhart returned to the valley, he was saved from a similar fate only by the timely arrival of a company of men from Yreka. The remains of "Lockhart's Fort," in which he made a gallant five-day fight for life, may be seen today on the hill near Fall River Mills. Shortly after his arrival, Sam Lockhart established a ferry (SRL 555) where the Oregon-California stage road crossed the Pit River just below the mouth of the Fall River. There, also, he built a bridge across the Pit River in 1859, only to have it washed away in the flood of 1862.

The first school in Fall River Valley (SRL 759) was built in 1868 at a spot that is now three and one-half miles east of McArthur on the south side of SR 299. It was a simple log building, twenty by thirty feet, without floor or windows. About two years later the first sawmill in the valley was set up at Dana, and lumber from this mill was used to floor the school and to construct desks.

The Fort Crook Historical Society operates and maintains the handsome museum at Fall River Mills, on SR 299 at the edge of town. Both Indians and settlers are represented in this interesting collection. The building, dedicated in 1963, is twelve-sided, patterned after a twelve-sided "Round Barn" built in the valley in 1910 and now being renovated. Buildings from other places have been moved to the museum grounds; these include a one-room schoolhouse built in 1884, a very old log cabin built in 1860, and a building housing farm equipment, dating from the beginning of farming in the valley.

THE COPPER BOOM

Around the turn of the century Shasta County enjoyed a copper-mining boom. In 1906 five copper smelters were in operation, at Keswick, Coram, Kennett, Bully Hill, and Ingot. The copper-refining process produced sulfur fumes that killed surrounding vegetation, and some smelters were closed for this reason.

CASTLE CRAGS STATE PARK

Sharply outlined against the sky, the lofty gray turrets of Castle Crags offer a striking contrast to the dark green of the pine-covered mountains that surround them. This superb group rises more than 6,600 feet above sea level and includes among its towers the Cathedral Spires, Castle Dome, and Battle Rock. Hidden high up in the recesses of Castle Crags lies Castle Lake in Siskiyou County, discovered by Crook and his men while in pursuit of Indians.

Below these crags, at first known as Castle Rocks, lay historic Lower Soda Springs (called Castle Crag with the advent of the railroad in 1886) in a green meadow east of the Sacramento River at its confluence with Soda Creek. It was long the favorite camping ground of the Shastas and other Indian mountain tribes. It is known that Lansford Hastings and sixteen companions, who had started from Rogue River, Oregon, in May 1843, camped at the springs. It is said that Hastings was so taken with the magnificent location of Lower Soda Springs that he applied for a grant of land that would include both Castle Rocks and its snow-covered neighbor to the north, then known as Shasta Butte and now as Mount Shasta. The grant never materialized, since Hastings would not become a Mexican citizen.

The first permanent settler in the region of Lower Soda Springs was Joe Doblondy, "Mountain Joe," frontiersman and guide for Frémont. It is not known just when Mountain Joe came to this spot. On the Lower Soda Springs Ranch he tilled the soil, built houses, kept a sort of hotel, guided travelers up the Oregon to California Trail past Mount Shasta, and fought the Indians. He was also the friend of Joaquin Miller, who in 1854 ran away from school in Oregon and came to live with Mountain Joe under the shadow of the crags. "He was my ideal, my hero," wrote the poet in later years, and it was from Mountain Joe's seemingly inexhaustible store of tales, as well as from the majesty of the surroundings in which he lived, that Miller gained the inspiration for much of his poetry.

The first mining on Soda Creek was carried on in the early 1850s by Bill Fox, who had escaped from the Yreka jail and hid in this isolated spot. He took out a large amount of gold, but was discovered and had to leave the country. Mountain Joe's tales of the fabulous Lost Cabin Mine and other supposedly rich diggings lured a large number of miners to Soda Creek and the Upper Sacramento River in the spring of 1855.

According to one account, "the little valley was soon a white sea of tents. Every bar on the Sacramento was the scene of excitement. . . . The rivers ran dark and sullen with sand and slime. The fish turned on their sides and died, or hid under the muddy clouds that obscured the deepest pools."

But the tales of wealth told by Mountain Joe proved unfounded, and the army of angry, disgusted miners soon left the region. The results of their short sojourn, however, were not so easily removed. The fish and game on which the Indians depended had been killed or driven out, and the desire for vengeance stirred the warriors to action. One morning in June 1855, while Mountain Joe was absent, a band of Indians, descending from Castle Rocks, plundered and burned the settlement at Lower Soda Springs. On his return, Mountain Joe and Joaquin Miller traced the flight of the Indians up the rocks by the flour they had spilled. With recruits from the neighboring settlements of Portuguese Flat and Dog Creek, Mountain Joe soon gathered together a company to take revenge on the Indians. Judge R. P. Gibson, who had married the daughter of the chief of the Shastas, persuaded this tribe to join with the white settlers against the Pits, the Modocs, and other hostile tribes.

The Battle of the Crags, graphically described by Joaquin Miller, a young participant in the fight, took place on Battle Rock (SRL 116), the most prominent of all the spires and domes of the group. Directly under the highest crag in the northwest corner of the great mass, the settlers, led by Gibson and his Shasta allies, fought face to face with the Modocs. The settlers and Shastas were victorious, but many on both sides were killed or wounded; among the wounded was Miller, who afterward told how he was carried down the mountainside in a large buckskin bag tied to the back of a wrinkled old Indian woman. Camp was made on the riverbanks below the site of the later Soda Springs Hotel, and there Joaquin was cared for by Mountain Joe until he recovered from his wounds. The Battle of the Crags was one of a long series of conflicts between the Indians and the white settlers of northeastern California that culminated in the Modoc War nearly twenty years later.

After passing through several hands, Lower Soda Springs came into the possession of G. W. Bailey in 1858, who operated a ranch, a wayside inn, and a summer resort at this spot. In 1892 the new owners, the Pacific Improvement Company, built the Castle Crag Tavern, the largest summer hotel in Shasta County. It became famous and people from all parts of the world visited it, but it was destroyed by fire early in 1900 and never rebuilt. A number of log cabins were put up in its stead and the place was operated as a summer camp until 1930, when it was sold and closed to the public. It is now known as the Berry Estate.

SHASTA DAM AND SHASTA LAKE

On the Sacramento River, ten miles northwest of Redding, the U.S. Bureau of Reclamation constructed Shasta Dam between 1938 and 1944. This is the principal unit of the Central Valley Water Project. The 602-foot-high dam, the second highest in California, is open to the public for tours; there is also a visitors center and museum. The impounded waters of the Sacramento and its tributaries, among which are the Pit and McCloud rivers, now form Shasta Lake, 29,500 acres of water with 365 miles of shoreline. The lake is now a major recreational area, as well as a site of vital importance for water storage, flood control, and hydroelectric power.

The construction of the dam led to the founding of several small towns in the area: Pine Grove, Project City, Central Valley, Toyon, and Summit City. After the dam was completed, these towns continued to flourish, and have been incorporated as the city of Shasta Lake, at the north edge of Redding.

Lake Shasta Caverns, now a commercial enterprise, was discovered on November 3, 1878, by James A. Richardson, a federal fisheries employee, whose inscription, written in carbide from his miner's lamp, can still be seen within the caves. It is located on the northern side of Shasta Lake, off the O'Brien Recreation Area turnoff from I-5.

The Whiskeytown-Shasta-Trinity National Recreation Area now embraces Whiskeytown Lake and its environs, Shasta Lake and its environs, and Clair Engle Lake and Lewiston Lake and their environs in Trinity County. These are all man-made lakes with abundant camping and recreational facilities.

On June 17, 1950, during the Shasta Centennial celebration, the California Centennials Commission dedicated an official plaque on Shasta Dam. The tablet is inscribed: "If you seek their monument, look about you. To pioneer mothers and fathers of California— whose urge to envision what lay beyond the far horizon and whose courage to overcome hardship opened the unknown West, converting wilderness into empire."

Sierra County

Sierra County was organized from a part of Yuba County in 1852, and Downieville was made the county seat. The name Sierra Nevada ("saw-toothed mountains, covered with snow," originally given to those south of Granada, in Spain) is applied to the mountain range that extends from Tehachapi Pass north to Lassen Peak.

GOODYEARS BAR

Goodyears Bar, settled in the summer of 1849 by Andrew and Miles Goodyear and two companions, was one of the first mining camps on the North Fork of the Yuba River. Superb mountain peaks look down upon the old river camps here—Saddle Back, Monte Cristo, Fir Cap, Grizzly Peak, and others—where Goodyears Creek joins the river. By 1852 the place had become the center for a number of lively camps up and down the river as well as on the neighboring ridges. Nearby were the Ranse Doddler and Hoodoo Bars, with St. Joe's Bar two miles below and Woodville, at first known as Cutthroat Bar, farther up the river.

The diggings in the vicinity yielded rich returns. At Kennedy Ranch, located at the upper end of Goodyears Bar, Peter Yore's men cleaned up $2,000 in gold dust from a single wheelbarrow load of earth, a find that was kept secret from the other miners until a considerable harvest had been gathered.

Goodyears Bar prospered through the 1850s, but it declined in the early 1860s, with the gradual exhaustion of ore deposits along the river. A devastating fire swept through the town in 1864. The small triangular flat on which a horde of miners once lived and worked has less than 100 inhabitants today, with a scattering of houses that stand near the abandoned diggings. The old two-story-and-attic frame hotel built in 1864 is now enjoying a revival as a bed-and-breakfast inn. The community center is housed in the old school, built in 1862.

DOWNIEVILLE

Downieville, in one of the highest and most rugged regions of the state, is set in a magnificent wooded amphitheater surrounded by lofty, pine-clad mountains. Here the Downie River (also called the north fork of the North Fork of the Yuba River) flows into the larger stream of the North Yuba, a part of that network of forks and tributaries that descend through deep canyons from the higher altitudes of the Sierra.

William Downie (usually called "Major" Downie), a Scotsman, for whom the town was later named, arrived at "The Forks" in November 1849. With him were ten black sailors, an Indian, an Irish boy, and Jim Crow, a Kanaka, who later became a notorious character in the North Yuba River country and for whom Jim Crow Canyon was named. Putting up a few log cabins, the major and his men wintered at the flat just above the present town site. Some of the men spent their time digging into the rocky crevices under the snow, taking out $100 to $200 worth of gold each day.

There was a rush of miners into the area the following spring, accompanied by rich strikes on all the neighboring bars and flats. "The Forks" soon became the center of the wide circle of camps reaching up and down both rivers and their tributaries, and before long the name of the place was changed to Downieville. By 1851 the population of the town had increased to more than 5,000. Stories told of the miners and their life on the North Yuba indicate the phenomenal richness of the placers. On Durgan Flat, where the courthouse now

St. Charles Inn, Goodyears Bar

Sierra County Sheriff's Gallows, Downieville

stands, Frank Anderson and three companions in eleven days took out ore valued at $12,000 from a claim only sixty feet square. One day's return was valued at $4,300, while the total yield during the first six months that the location was worked brought over $80,000. Jersey Flat, just above the present town, at the spot where Downie and his party first made temporary camp, was a close second to Durgan Flat in production. According to the major, Jim Crow killed a salmon weighing fourteen pounds here, and after the fish had been cooked for supper gold was found at the bottom of the kettle. At Zumwalt Flat each man averaged five ounces a day for three and a half hours' labor, while at Tin Cup Diggings, opposite Zumwalt Flat, three men who worked there in 1850 were said to have made it a rule to fill a tin cup with gold before quitting work at night, which they had no trouble doing.

But the miners were not satisfied, and in order to get out the gold that still lay in the bedrock of the river, they flumed the entire North Yuba between Downieville and Goodyears Bar out of its channel. When the winter floods came, however, their flume was swept away like so much straw.

Other diggings in the canyon country brought vast wealth. At Gold Bluff, two miles above Downieville, in the fall of 1850 a nugget of pure gold was taken out that weighed twenty-five pounds, the largest ever found on the North Yuba. The black slate of this area continued to produce thousands of dollars in gold up to the time of World War I, when mining activities were discontinued. Below Slug Canyon, so called because of the coarse lump or slug gold found there, the Steamboat Company on Steamboat Bar took out an average of $5,000 a day for several weeks during 1851. At the head of this canyon and about three miles south of Downieville is the City of Six Quartz Mine, a famous producer in the

early days. Another famous mine, Monte Cristo, is located on the south slope of Monte Cristo, 1,000 feet above Goodyears Creek and three miles northwest of Downieville. It was opened in 1854, and at one time the adjoining camp had a population as large as that of Downieville.

Downieville remains much as it was in the gold days. Along the main street, which is still lined in part by boardwalks, stand many old buildings. Along the riverbanks and up the mountainsides the old-fashioned houses, set amid aged locust and fruit trees, line the shady streets and alleyways, making the residential part of Downieville one of the town's most charming features.

One of the first buildings in Downieville, thought to have been built in 1852, a stone structure with heavy iron doors and shuttered windows, was restored and presented to the town for use as a museum by the heirs of J. M. B. Meroux, a pioneer. The walls of this building are made entirely of flat rocks laid horizontally, a very early type of construction. The nucleus of the museum is a collection of valuable relics gathered by former sheriff George C. Bynon.

The Hirschfelder house, now a grocery store, is another stone structure that dates from 1852, as does the Craycroft Building across the main street. The frame Masonic Hall was built in 1864 to replace an earlier structure. The Catholic and Community Methodist churches, both built in the 1850s, have been marked by official state plaques, although neither has been assigned a registration number.

Across the Downie River from the business section stands the courthouse, a modern structure that was built after fire destroyed the old courthouse in 1947. Here there are two old cannon, an arrastra wheel used by the pioneers to grind the gold-impregnated quartz,

Downie River Bridge, Downieville

and at the rear of the building the gallows (SRL 971), which, the state plaque tells us, was used only once, in 1858. A more noteworthy hanging, which made Downieville notorious, took place in 1851, where the Jersey Bridge takes SR 49 across the Downie River eastward out of town. Jack Cannon, a popular Australian miner, was stabbed to death by Juanita (Josefa in some accounts), a Mexican woman who claimed that she had been mortally insulted by Cannon. Anti-Mexican feelings were high—Cannon's group had broken the door to Juanita's dwelling the night before the murder—and in short order Juanita was lynched, an event that aroused much criticism both in the United States and abroad.

Near the courthouse are the diggings, huge piles of granite boulders marking the rich river claims where miners in 1850 and 1851 averaged $100 to $200 daily. Here the Chinese came after others had ceased to consider the location worthwhile. Lifting the heavy stones one by one, they cleared out the bed of the North Yuba, leaving mammoth heaps as evidence of their great labors.

Heritage Park stands by the river on the town side, displaying old monitors (nozzles that forced water out at high pressure), mining equipment, and a stamping mill.

SIERRA CITY

The North Yuba River's canyon is the only passage eastward from Downieville over the crest of the Sierra. An old stage road in the last century and SR 49 today likewise follow the scenic canyon to Sierra City, thirteen miles further east. Almost a mile above the town rise the majestic Sierra Buttes, jagged granite peaks that can be seen from miles away. In Gold Rush days they witnessed feverish activity along the creeks de-

scending into the North Yuba, and even the almost perpendicular sides of the granite pile were climbed in the search for gold.

In the spring of 1850, P. A. Haven and Joseph Zumwalt located on the site of Sierra City, in a region thickly populated with Indians. In the same year a Mr. Murphy discovered the Sierra Buttes quartz ledge. By 1852 tunnels penetrated the craggy buttes in all directions, and the miners were using as many as twenty arrastras, run by mules, to pulverize the rock. During that winter a heavy blanket of snow and avalanches from the steep mountain above crushed every house in the mining camp. In the face of this disaster it was not until 1858 that a permanent settlement was established on the town site.

Another rich quartz deposit of the Sierra Buttes was opened up at the Monumental Quartz Mine, where in 1860 an immense gold nugget, 1,596 troy ounces in weight and valued at $25,500, was taken out, the second largest to be found in California.

One mile east of Sierra City on SR 49 is the Kentucky Mine, site of the Sierra County Historical Park and Museum. The mine was first worked in 1853, and continued with some interruptions until 1953. The large wooden structure dominating the site houses the stamp mill, which docents demonstrate during the summer months. The Historical Park and Museum was officially dedicated here in 1977. The museum also houses a good local reference library.

Sierra City is unusual among the gold towns in never having suffered a serious fire, owing in part to abundant supplies of water from its many mountain streams. These watercourses have been harnessed to furnish power not only for the mills at the mines (such as the Kentucky Mine, whose flume can still be seen), but to generate electricity and to supply the needs of the town.

Among the interesting historic structures of Sierra City are the Busch Building on Main Street, erected in 1871, the Catholic Church, and the Masonic Hall. The Busch Building at one time housed the Wells Fargo Express Office, and is currently being refurbished. Its lower two stories of brick survived a fire about 1948 that destroyed the third story of wood.

E CLAMPUS VITUS

E Clampus Vitus (the name is nonsensical) was in part a fraternal organization, charitable toward widows and orphans, and also a prankish group that mocked the solemn lodges of mid-nineteenth-century America. It

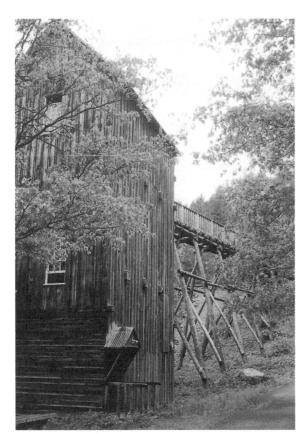

Stamping Mill at Kentucky Mine, Sierra County Historical Park and Museum, Sierra City

was organized in Sierra City in 1857, and until recently its ECV mark still could be found by a doorway in the Busch Building. Although the lodge died out, it was brilliantly reorganized in 1931 by a few members of California historical organizations who were interested in preserving the lore and fun of Gold Rush days. The organization today is a major participant in state commemorations. Plaques placed by the "Clampers," as members of E Clampus Vitus Redivivus are popularly known, are to be seen throughout California today, and are frequently cited in this book.

FOREST

Forest, fourteen miles south of Downieville via Goodyears Bar, was one of the liveliest camps in Sierra County during the middle 1850s. It was first called Brownsville, after an early settler; then Yomana, an Indian name said to designate the high bluff above the town, and finally Forest City; the latter part of the name was dropped in the 1890s.

Having worked out the streams, bars, and banks about Forest, the miners began to tunnel into the moun-

tains to the south. The name of one of these tunnels, the Alleghany, was given to a flourishing camp on the opposite side of the mountain, where pay dirt was struck in 1855. The town of Alleghany increased in importance so rapidly the following year that the entire population of Forest flocked to the new camp, leaving the older place an empty shell. When a rich strike was made in the Bald Mountain district in 1870, Forest awoke from its sleep, only to relapse after a short time into the quiet hamlet of today.

ALLEGHANY

The main road to Alleghany begins at SR 49, in the area of Freeman's Crossing on the Nevada-Yuba county line between North San Juan and Camptonville. The road crosses Oregon Creek and, a few miles beyond, enters Sierra County. At a point about six miles beyond the bridge over the creek a road leads north to what remains of Pike City, a few old cabins and foundations. About four miles beyond the Pike turnoff a handsome monument stands beside the main road at the site of the Plum Valley House (SRL 695), built in 1854 by John Bope. Deriving its name from the wild plums that grow in this area, it was a toll station on the Henness Pass Road (SRL 421) between Marysville and Virginia City, Nevada. This route had been in use as an emigrant trail as early as 1849. A dirt Forest Service road still follows its course across Henness Pass (6,806 feet) to join SR 89 nine miles southeast of Sierraville.

Alleghany is still essentially a "gold camp"—one of the few left in California—where most of the hundred or so citizens have some connection with the gold-mining industry. Almost every year, newspapers report some new gold strike in the Alleghany area. Clinging "like a cluster of cliff swallows' nests to the side of the mountain," the houses of the town are built on a series of terraces connected by streets. The most prominent house was built before 1910 by H. L. Johnson, who in 1903 leased the old Tightner Mine, thought to be pretty much worked out, and four years later he found rich ore in its shafts. In 1916, after Johnson had sold his lease, it was discovered that the Tightner Mine and the Original Sixteen-to-One were tapping the same vein. This discovery led to the consolidation of the two operations with the Twenty-One Mine, an adjacent property, and the claim was worked until December 1965. Most of the mining done around Alleghany since then has been on a smaller scale.

Fires, one as recently as 1987, have steadily reduced

the town; in the words of a citizen, "When we lose something now, nothing gets replaced." In the clearing before the Johnson house is the community fire bell, essential for a small town dependent upon its volunteer brigade. A general store and a tavern remain, together with many abandoned small buildings.

GOLD BEYOND THE MOUNTAINS

Towering thousands of feet above the North Yuba River canyon, a huge mass of mountains crowned with castellated peaks and knifelike crests, of which the Sierra Buttes are a part, forms an effective barrier to direct travel into the old mining district of northwestern Sierra County. In order to drive to this area one must turn north above Sierra City and follow a circuitous route by way of Gold Lake, Mohawk, and Johnsville to Gibsonville, or else retrace to Bullard's Bar in Yuba County and from there proceed northward via Challenge and Strawberry Valley, through La Porte in Plumas County, and thence to Gibsonville on the road to Quincy. Most of these roads are gravel at best and quite a few are dirt roads; this is adventuresome country for the motorist.

The northwest corner of Sierra County was first prospected in the spring of 1850, when gold was found along the ridge between the North Fork of the Yuba River and the South Fork of the Feather River by an old sea captain named Sears, whose name was later given to the ridge.

Returning to the Yuba, Sears prepared to lead a company of prospectors to the scene of his discovery. But the news that Sears had struck it rich spread, and before proceeding very far his party found that they were being followed by a group under the leadership of a man named Gibson. When ordered to turn back, Gibson's men refused, saying that the mountains of California were as free to them as to any man, and that if there was gold beyond those mountains they were going to get their share. A compromise was at length reached and the two parties proceeded to Sears' Ridge, where operations were begun at a place known afterward as Sears' Diggings.

Before long a number of other locations were staked out in the vicinity, some of which proved to be richer than the original strike. Gibson, an especially enterprising prospector, discovered very rich deposits on an adjoining ridge overlooking Little Slate Creek, a site later developed into the large and thriving camp of Gibsonville, which as late as 1870 was a busy place.

With the passing years Gibsonville, in windswept isolation, became more deserted, and now it has no permanent residents.

Gibson struck another rich deposit at a place that became known as Secret Ravine because he had kept the location a secret from his comrades, who charged him with playing them false. The resultant dissension among Gibson's followers and growing dissatisfaction among Sears's men caused a scattering of the two groups, resulting in new discoveries in all directions. Many new camps were established, among them Howland Flat (or Table Rock), Pine Grove, Potosi, St. Louis, Queen City, Poker Flat, Craig's Flat, Deadwood, Chandlerville, Port Wine, Scales, Poverty Hill, Brandy City, Hepsidam, Whiskey Diggings (or Newark), McMahon's, Morristown, and Eureka City at the source of Goodyears Creek.

At La Porte a good dirt road turns southeast across the Sierra county line and runs four miles to Queen City. At this point a road running northeast and southwest is intersected. The branch to the northeast goes to Howland Flat via St. Louis. St. Louis, staked out on the site of Sears' Diggings in the fall of 1852 by a party of Missourians, enjoyed a brief period of prosperity until it was swept by fire in 1857. Later, during the 1860s, a short-lived hydraulic boom revived the place. Howland Flat, where the post office (1857–1922) was always called Table Rock, is situated on the north side of Table Rock at an elevation of 6,000 feet. From here a trail leads three miles to Poker Flat on Canyon Creek. The road continues from Howland Flat to join the Johnsville Road east of Gibsonville.

The road southwest from Queen City goes to Port Wine, Poverty Hill, and Scales. Less than a mile from Queen City is a magnificent old stone building, a strange sight in this wilderness. This former store, with its iron doors, plus an old cemetery and piles of long-forgotten diggings, are all that remain of Port Wine, named by prospectors who found a cask of port wine hidden in a nearby canyon. The road continues past the turnoff to Poverty Hill to the little community of Scales. From here the motorist can follow the road west into Yuba County, joining the main road to La Porte about two and a half miles northeast of Strawberry Valley.

SIERRA VALLEY

Sierra Valley lies in the eastern part of the county, and its history is more involved with producing cattle and crops and lumber than it is with mining. Sierraville is on SR 49 east of Yuba Pass and some twenty-three miles east of Sierra City. Cut off from the rest of the county by winter snows, Sierraville made an unsuccessful bid in 1989 to replace Downieville as county seat. The town is also on SR 89, an all-weather route between Quincy and Truckee. The Globe Hotel is Sierraville's oldest building, now refurbished as a motel. Nearby Sattley and Calpine are towns connected with the lumber industry, the latter having been a company town for the Davis-Johnson Lumber Company since 1900.

Loyalton, near the northern terminus of SR 49, is the site of the Sierra Valley Museum, which has displays on the ranching and logging industries of Sierra Valley. An old school building, later used as a Catholic place of worship, has been moved onto the grounds, which are at the Loyalton City Park.

Captain Jack's Stronghold, Lava Beds National Monument

Siskiyou County was created in 1852 from the northern part of Shasta County and a part of Klamath County. In 1874, when Klamath County was dissolved, Siskiyou County received still more of its territory and a new Modoc County was created from territory in eastern Siskiyou County extending to the Nevada border.

The name Siskiyou, according to Erwin G. Gudde, meant "bobtailed horse" in the Cree language and was borrowed by the Chinook jargon, the trade language of the Oregon Territory. A mountain pass was given this name after Alexander McLeod of the Hudson's Bay Company lost a horse while going through it in 1828. The boundary between Oregon and California, along the 42nd parallel, follows the natural border formed by the Siskiyou Mountains, although the two men who made the boundary by treaty in 1819 (U.S. Secretary of State John Quincy Adams and the Spanish minister in Washington Don Luís Onís) had no reliable geographic knowledge of the area. The Siskiyou Pass is in southern Oregon, about four miles north of the California boundary, and is crossed today by I-5.

MOUNT SHASTA

"Lonely as God, and white as a winter moon, Mount Shasta starts sudden and solitary from the heart of the great black forests of Northern California," wrote poet Joaquin Miller, who as a young man spent several years near its base. The beautiful legend of how the Great Spirit "made this mountain first of all" was told to him by the native people among whom he lived. That story included the long-held Shasta Indian tradition that "before the white man came they could see the fire ascending from the mountain by night and the smoke by day, every time they looked in that direction."

"Shasta," wrote John Muir, "is a fire-mountain, an old volcano gradually accumulated and built up into the blue deep of the sky by successive eruptions of ashes and molten lava." Periods of quiescence intervened between eruptions. Then the glacial winter came on, "a down-crawling mantle of ice upon a foundation of smouldering fire, crushing and grinding its brown, flinty lavas, and thus degrading and remodeling the entire mountain." The summit was a mass of ruins, considerably lowered, and the sides deeply grooved and fluted. Beneath the snowy surface the fires still glowed, but the glaciers still flowed on, "sculpturing the mountain with stern, resistless energy."

Five of these glaciers—Bolam, Hotlum, Whitney, Wintun, and Konwakiton—still scour the sides of the great mountain, principally on the north and east slopes above the 10,000-foot level. Hundreds of streams are fed by these ice rivers; Big Spring, one source of the Sacramento River, gushes from the mountainside in a cold flood just one mile north of Mount Shasta City. John Muir describes the fountainhead of the McCloud River, to the east, thus: "Think of a spring giving rise to a river, a spring fifty yards wide at the mouth, issuing from the base of a lava cliff with wild songs—not gloomily from a dark cavey mouth, but from a world of ferns and mosses gold and green."

Shasta is undoubtedly a word of Indian origin, although both derivation and meaning are uncertain. Another Indian name for the mountain was "I-eka," from which the name of the town Yreka came. According to Stephen Powers, Shas-ti-ka was the tribal name of the people in this region. (Alleged Russian or French origins for the name—*tchastal*, "white," and *chaste*, "pure"—are now generally discredited.)

Shasta's snowy summit, at 14,162 feet, dominates the landscape for a hundred miles and is visible for almost twice that distance. The first recorded mention of it, as "Shatasla," was in 1814, in the journal of Alexander Henry, an early mountain man. It is possible that Spanish explorers in 1817 observed it from a distance when an expedition from San Francisco led by Luís Argüello, with Father Narciso Durán, traveled by boat up the Sacramento River, reaching as far north as the mouth of the Feather River. Durán made this entry in his journal on May 20: "At about ten leagues to the northwest of this place we saw the very high hill called by soldiers that went near its slope 'Jesus Maria.' It is entirely covered with snow." There is no way of knowing, however, whether this mountain was in fact Mount Shasta.

British and American explorers during the early part of the nineteenth century viewed the great mountain and placed it on their maps under variant spellings. Lieutenant George Emmons, of the Wilkes Exploring Expedition, who saw it on October 3, 1841, mentioned it in his report and on accompanying maps as "Mount Shaste"; Frémont, who five years later saw it on his third expedition, referred to it in his subsequent report as "Shastl" and on his map of 1848 as "Tsashtl"; Lieutenant

Robert S. Williamson, of the United States Topographical Engineers, in his report of the expedition that surveyed for a railroad route from Oregon to the Sacramento Valley in 1851 and 1855, designated the mountain "Shasta Butte," *butte* being a term freely used by American trappers in the West.

The first recorded ascent of Mount Shasta appears to have been made by Captain E. D. Pearce in August or September 1854. Shortly afterward, Pearce led a party of thirteen adventurous citizens from Yreka, Humbug, and Scott Valleys to the summit. Other ascents followed; Israel S. Diehl, of Yreka, climbed to the top alone on October 11, 1855. He was followed by a German, Anton Roman, in April 1856. Joaquin Miller, who ascended the mountain several times, climbed it for the last time in 1858 at the age of seventeen. It was his book, *Life Amongst the Modocs*, written in London in 1873, that made Mount Shasta known to the world.

The first scientific ascent of the mountain was made in September 1862 by Josiah Dwight Whitney, his chief assistant William H. Brewer, and Chester Averill. The glaciers on Mount Shasta were discovered by Clarence King in 1870. Captain A. F. Rodgers, of the United States Coast and Geodetic Survey, began a series of observations from the summit in 1875. In October of that year he erected a steel monument, some fourteen feet high and capped by a nickel reflector, on the highest point. This monument stood for many years. In the summer of 1877 John Muir visited Mount Shasta's forests and wild gardens with Sir Joseph Hooker, the great English botanist, and Professor Asa Gray, American's foremost botanist at that time. B. A. Colonna, of the Coast and Geodetic Survey, spent nine successive days and nights on the summit of Mount Shasta in July and August 1878. At the end of that period he succeeded in exchanging heliograph flashes with observers posted on Mount St. Helena, 192 miles to the south.

Mount Shasta is in the middle of the 29,260 acres of the Mount Shasta Wilderness, which lies entirely within Shasta National Forest. The Sierra Club erected the stone Shasta Alpine Lodge in 1922 at Horse Camp (7,992 feet), nine miles from Mount Shasta City. Although the mountain is a beloved and familiar sight to Californians, it is not easy to ascend; as late as 1999 an experienced hiker was lost near its summit.

SHEEP ROCK

At the foot of Shasta Pass twenty miles north of Sisson's Station (now Mount Shasta City), the first wagon road from the Sacramento Valley to Yreka led over a low divide from the eastern slopes of the mountain into Shasta Valley. There the bold and craggy summit of Sheep Rock rises 2,000 feet above the gray sagebrush and sand of the valley and 5,714 feet above sea level. The rock's several square miles of comparatively level surface, dotted with bunch grass, were one of the chief winter pastures of the wild mountain sheep. They came down from the high ridges of Mount Shasta to the warm lava crags and plateaus of Sheep Rock, where the snow never lies deep. Stockmen still follow the ruts of the old stage road at Sheep Rock. A marker (SRL 517) has been placed on US 97 about fifteen miles northeast of Weed at a point 600 feet south of the crossing of the old emigrant trail. The marker stands at the intersection of the old Military Pass Road from Fort Crook in Shasta County.

John Muir, who loved and explored Mount Shasta from summit to base, wrote with characteristic enthusiasm:

> Far better than climbing the mountain is going around its warm fertile base, enjoying its bounties like a bee circling a bank of flowers. The distance is about a hundred miles, [and] a good level road may be found all the way round, by Shasta Valley, Sheep Rock, Elk Flat, Huckleberry Valley, Squaw Valley, following for a considerable portion of the way the old Emigrant Road, which lies along the east disk of the mountain, and is deeply worn by the wagons of the early gold-seekers.

Portions of this old road are still used by the Forest Service, and it is possible during the summer months to drive around Mount Shasta, a distance of sixty-five miles from Weed or Mount Shasta City. The road takes one through aspen thickets and forests of Shasta fir, across glacial washes, and to points where superb views may be had, all within a few miles of the snowbelt.

MARBLE MOUNTAIN

The Marble Mountain Wilderness Area in the Klamath National Forest is a region of magnificent mountains and forests covering 237,527 acres. In it lies Marble Mountain, from which the area derives its name.

Lying between the Klamath River and its tributary, the Scott River, the Marble Mountain Range culminates in a castellated peak, 7,396 feet in elevation. Composed of limestone, a large proportion of which is marble of high commercial value, the rugged grandeur and the "monumental purity" of this massive upheaval in-spired the traditions and beliefs of the Indians, who knew the peak as the "White Mountain."

Owing to its striking appearance, Marble Mountain served as a landmark for early pioneers, and the Kelsey Trail, lying almost directly at its base, was one of the first paths ever blazed across these mountains into Scott Valley. Travelers over this rugged trail almost invariably halted to gaze upward with wonder and amazement at the beetling cliffs and towering domes of Marble Mountain lying above them. This route, at best a rough and dangerous one for man and beast, was long ago abandoned for more accessible passes through the mountains.

THE OREGON TO CALIFORNIA TRAIL

Lying halfway between San Francisco Bay and the Columbia River, the Siskiyou region, first crossed by trappers and settlers, was soon marked by a well-defined route. This trail was the principal thoroughfare during the gold period. Today's trade and commerce continue to flow over it. In general, Richard Silva notes, it has been called the Oregon to California Trail, but it should be noted that this and the similar term California-Oregon Trail have been applied from time to time to several other routes to and from Oregon through northern California. The earliest was the coast route, through what is now Del Norte County, blazed by Jedediah Strong Smith in 1828 and followed for a time by Hudson's Bay Company trappers. Alexander R. McLeod, for whom the Mc-Cloud River is named, was the first of these, in 1829.

In 1830 Peter Skene Ogden, another Hudson's Bay agent, opened up a route by way of the Pit River and Goose Lake, and in his footsteps came Michel La Framboise, the leader of trapping expeditions from the north from 1830 to 1845. The central route leading up the Sacramento River Canyon was first crossed in its entire length by Ewing Young in 1834. Young, on his way to settle in Oregon in 1834, was the first to follow the Oregon to California trail around the western base of Mount Shasta. A scarcity of cattle in the Willamette Valley led him to return to the San Francisco Bay region in 1837. Driving 700 Spanish longhorns, he and about twenty other men started for Oregon, and succeeded in bringing 680 of the animals over the rugged mountains of the Sacramento River Canyon into Shasta Valley. In 1843 the enterprising Joseph Gale, with a much larger herd of livestock, made the same arduous climb.

The old trail and the difficulties experienced by the many early travelers who passed over it are described in the journals of Philip l. Edwards, diarist of the Young party of 1837; in the George Emmons report of the Wilkes Expedition in 1841; in the account by Lansford W. Hastings of his trip in 1843; and in the diary of James Clyman, a vivid depiction of a journey in 1845. By 1840 California began to attract settlers, and every year of that decade saw an increasing number of emigrants passing over the trail from the Willamette Valley to the Sacramento Valley, the climax being reached during the Gold Rush years of 1848–53.

During the 1850s, when gold mining was the chief industry of the Siskiyou region, two variations of the route appeared, one of which led around the eastern base of Mount Shasta while the other crossed over Trinity and Scott Mountains into Scott Valley and thence to Yreka.

Lieutenant Emmons and his men of the Wilkes Expedition camped on September 28, 1841, at the foot of the Boundary Range (today's Siskiyou Mountains) within sight of what was then called the Boundary Mountain, which Emmons called

a singular, isolated rock, which stands like a tower on the top of the ridge, rising above the surrounding forest with a bare and apparently unbroken surface. . . . From its top an extensive country is overlooked, and as soon as the party came in sight of it a dense column of smoke arose, which was thought to be a signal made by the Klamet Indians, to the Shaste tribe, of the approach of our party.

Charles Wilkes, commander of the expedition, named this Emmons' Peak in honor of the leader of the California contingent of the expedition, but the name Pilot Rock has since been applied to it. Located in southern Oregon, it is visible for many miles on both sides of the mountains.

When the Wilkes Expedition passed through the Siskiyous they feared attacks by hostile Indians, who were determined to keep the white invaders out. The party avoided all contact with the natives and thereby frustrated one of the trip's main objectives—making detailed observations of the Indians in their natural habitat. Ascending the Siskiyou Mountains on September 29, the party was in constant fear of these so-called "Rogues." To the travelers the whole mountainside seemed "admirably adapted for an ambuscade." However, little opposition was encountered, and at the summit the men had their first glorious view of the "Klamet Valley," and of "Mount Shaste, a high, snowy peak, of a sugarloaf form, which rose through the distant haze."

Descending the southern slope of the Siskiyous, the expedition pitched their tents on "Otter Creek [now Cottonwood Creek] within a mile of the Klamet River," and on October 1 they camped on the Shasta River, probably near the present-day town of Montague. There they found Indians spearing abundant quantities of salmon. Not far from Sheep Rock, near the modern town of Gazelle, large herds of antelope and some long-horned mountain sheep were seen the next day. At midday the party left the Shasta Valley and camped on Parks Creek, near where Old Highway 99 crosses the stream. This place was the camping group of an Indian tribe whom Emmons observed closely and recorded as "a fine-looking race," very skillful in the making and use of the bow and arrow. Continuing their journey on October 3, the party "entered the forest on the slopes of the Shaste Range. . . . After passing this ridge, they soon met the head waters of the Sacramento, flowing to the southward, and their camp was pitched on the banks of another stream, that came from Shaste Peak." This camp would be on Cold Creek, just south of the Fish Hatchery in Strawberry Valley, Mount Shasta City.

With the Wilkes Expedition traveled Joel Walker and his wife, the first white woman to arrive in California on an overland trip.

James Clyman climbed the Siskiyous and made his way down the Sacramento River Canyon in 1845. His diary is full of vivid descriptions revealing the rugged character of the old trail. Like other early travelers he was constantly on guard against Indian attacks. Climbing the "Siskiew mountain" on June 23, the party neared the summit where there was "a bad thicket to pass whare nearly all the parties passing this Trail have been attacted." The Clyman company, however, met with no misadventure and soon came in sight of the vast wilderness lying to the south, "wild and awfully sublime." On June 24, the "Clamet" (Klamath) River was crossed, a few hundred feet east of the present bridge near the site of the now-gone lumbering town of Klamathon near the mouth of Willow Creek. Going around the north slope of Black Mountain, the emigrants passed over Little Shasta River, where they made camp and where Clyman noted the striking volcanic character of Shasta Valley.

Clyman's party traversed the valley on June 26; after crossing the Shasta River, they set up camp on a site near the present town of Edgewood. From this point Clyman describes Pilot Rock, plainly visible across the Oregon border to the north. They resumed their journey on June 28, and passed through what would later be known as Wagon Valley. To the east of the pass rose the snowy peaks of Mount Shasta, while on the west stood Mount Eddy, the whole region magnificently timbered.

The first wagon team (1855) and the first transportation by stage and freight team (the California Stage Company, 1856) from the Sacramento Valley crossed the Pit River at Fall River Mills in Shasta County. Continuing northwest, the road passed around the eastern base of Mount Shasta, down through Sheep Rock Pass into Shasta Valley, and then again northwest to Yreka. From there it continued northeast, crossing the Shasta River about five miles northwest of Montague. The Klamath River was ferried just north of its junction with Willow Creek, where the road became identical with the older trail followed by trappers on their way over the Siskiyou Mountains. The part of the road that passed east of Mount Shasta was used for about a year, until Indian conflict caused traffic to be transferred to the Yreka-Callahan-Shasta route in 1859. This route became known as the California-Oregon Stage Road and was operated until the advent of the railroad in 1887–88.

Henry Slicer had already opened a stage line to Callahan's in 1854. After abandoning the route around the eastern base of Mount Shasta, the California Stage Company bought out Greathouse and Slicer and began, at great expense, to complete the road to the town of Shasta (in early days sometimes called Shasta City). This road was pushed over Trinity Mountain in 1857, and in 1859 Scott Mountain was also crossed. Meanwhile the Oregon Stage Company had completed its turnpike over the Siskiyous. It connected with the California Stage Line at Yreka in 1858, and a through route was thus staged for the first time from Portland, Oregon, to Sacramento, California. It was over this route that the first telegraph line from California to Oregon was constructed.

After 1870 the route from Yreka to the Klamath River went by way of the Anderson Grade, crossing the Shasta River about four miles north of Yreka. On this road the Ten Mile House, a stage station of the 1870s, still stands. Ascending the mountain over a steep grade, the road descended to the Klamath River about six miles south of Cottonwood (now Henley), where the river was ferried. The trail of the trappers over the Siskiyous continued to be used from this point on. Pioneer Bridge on SR 263 was built over the Shasta River three miles north of Yreka in 1931 and dedicated to the memory of the early-day stage drivers who traveled this road.

STOPPING PLACES ON THE OREGON TO CALIFORNIA TRAIL

With the discovery of gold in California, the procession down the Oregon Trail became a flood of humanity. Hotels or inns were built on the early campgrounds and proved to be popular stopping places. With the coming of the first wagons a road was constructed, and soon the mule trains were superseded by freighters and stagecoaches. The wayside inns became stage stations, with towns growing up about them. When the Southern Pacific Railroad was constructed from Redding into Oregon in 1886–87, its route was practically identical with that of the Oregon to California Trail and portions of the early stage road. Many of the railroad stations are on the exact line of the first trail, or very close to it.

Upper Soda Springs, the southernmost Siskiyou County station on the Oregon Trail, is today in the northern part of Dunsmuir. The stage station is long gone. An important railroad center, Dunsmuir was first called "Pusher" because extra engines were added to northbound trains at this point to push them over the summit. When Alexander Dunsmuir passed through in 1886, he was so charmed by the place that he offered to give a fountain to the town if it were renamed after him, and the bargain was made. The central part of Dunsmuir, flanked by the large old brick railroad hotel, is on the National Register of Historic Places. The Dunsmuir Museum at 4101 Pine Street has an excellent collection on the history of the railroad and the community. Near Upper Soda Springs, in Railroad Park, Southern Pacific engine 1727, which was in service on the line over the summit, is on permanent display.

The next camp on the old trail, which here ran about half a mile west of today's I-5, was located in Strawberry Valley, where a settlement grew up in the early 1850s. A post office was established in 1870 under the name of Berryvale. For twelve years J. H. Sisson was postmaster and hotelkeeper. When the railroad came through in 1887 the station, one mile east of Berryvale, was named Sisson's, and the town that soon grew up on the new site was called Sisson. In 1924 the town was renamed Mount Shasta.

Sisson's Hotel at Berryvale was a favorite summer resort and outfitting point for early-day mountain climbers. From there, trails radiated in all directions:

Mount Shasta, with its glaciers and distant panoramas; Black Butte, an odd cinder cone that is on the western side of the mountain; Mount Eddy, with its lovely Shasta lilies and Castle Lake; and the flowery fringes and wooded streams of Strawberry Valley.

The Old Stage Road still exists in Mount Shasta and runs by the State Fish Hatchery on the west side of town. The hatchery was established in 1888 and can be visited by the public. At the time it was built it was the largest in the world. The building closest to the road, old Hatchery A (1909), is now the Sisson Hatchery Museum. The history of Mount Shasta (both the mountain and the town) is chronicled here. The museum houses many changing as well as permanent exhibits and much interesting material on the history of railroading in the area.

Sisson's Hotel stood from 1865 to 1916 almost at the top of the low hill just before the hatchery gate. Across the road is the site of the Strawberry Valley stage station (SRL 396). On the same side of the road as this site is a small white house with a red roof; this was the old post office and store kept by Mrs. S. J. Fellows, who followed J. S. Sisson as postmaster.

About fifteen miles north of Berryvale the old trail passed the site of Butteville, now Edgewood, a camping ground mentioned in most of the early journals. From Butteville the trail proceeded to Edson's, now Gazelle, and thence across the Shasta Valley. The Shasta River was forded near the site of Montague, where there was an important campsite, and continued to Willow Creek. After 1850 the trail, which had developed into a stage road, made a detour to Yreka and rejoined the old trail before it reached Willow Creek.

Near where Willow Creek runs into the Klamath River from the south, the next stopping place on the old emigrant trail was not far from the site of the later settlement of Klamathon. Proceeding downstream three miles to Cottonwood Creek, which runs into the Klamath from the north, the trail followed Cottonwood Creek Canyon and crossed the summit of the Siskiyous about where the present railroad passes over. The last camp before reaching Oregon was made in the canyon of Cottonwood Creek just before the trail began climbing over the mountain.

In 1870 the stage road into Oregon was rerouted over the so-called Anderson Grade. Cottonwood, later Henley, was the place where stagecoaches and freighters en route from Yreka to Oregon changed horses from 1860 to 1887, when completion of the railroad ended stage operations.

The first argonauts from Oregon passed through Siskiyou County without stopping to prospect its streams, and no mining was done there until the summer of 1850. In June of that year gold-seekers penetrated the wild and rugged Salmon Mountains. Crossing the ridge from the North Fork of the Trinity River, they came upon the South Fork of the Salmon River, which they followed downstream until they reached the mouth of the North Fork, where rich deposits were found. The camp established at that point came to be known as Forks of Salmon, and during the summer several hundred men gathered there. From here they spread up the North Fork of the Salmon River and over the divide into the Scott River Valley.

Meanwhile a party of miners had traveled up the Klamath River from its mouth to the Shasta River, panning for gold at every bar. "It was this group of miners," says David Rhys Jones, "that established the course of the Klamath River below the junction of the Shasta. From that time on, the river that had been variously known as the Clamitte, the Klamet, Indian Scalp River, and Smith River, has borne the name by which it was known near its source." A geographical puzzle was thereby solved, Jones says:

> Prior to 1850 all maps delineating the Klamath River represented its source and upper course correctly—as it had been observed by trappers. The course of the river below Shasta River was unexplored, but the mouth of a large stream in southern Oregon had been crossed by Jedediah S. Smith in 1828. This was the mouth of the Rogue [River]. So the Hudson's Bay Company map presented to Wilkes, and published as part of his travel records, shows the Klamath River turning back into Oregon through the Siskiyous, below the Shasta, and emptying into the ocean at the mouth of the Rogue.

When winter approached, the miners on the Klamath left for the settlements of the Sacramento Valley, following a southerly course and passing the future sites of Yreka and of Greenhorn, where gold was discovered on the creek. A few miles to the east they came upon the Oregon Trail, where they found a fresh wagon track. Camping that night at Edson's, they reached Wagon Valley the following day, and found an abandoned wagon recently transported across the Siskiyou Mountains. While there is a long-standing tale that this wagon was abandoned by Governor Joseph Lane of Oregon, modern scholars do not believe this was his doing.

In San Francisco two years before, while on his way to organize the Oregon Territory, Lane had resisted the gold fever; in the summer of 1850 it hit him. With the gold fields of the Sierra Nevada as an objective, he crossed the border into California. Lane's party did a little incidental prospecting on the Klamath River, and on the Shasta River at Joe Lane's Bar near the mouth of Yreka Creek. This is where his party met up with the first Klamath River miners described above. In 1851 Lane returned to Siskiyou County at the head of a large company of men bound for Scott Bar, where they did considerable mining.

Scott Valley was first explored in 1850 by a group of miners led by John Scott, who had crossed the Salmon Mountains from the North Fork of the Salmon River. These men panned for gold at a point on Scott River named Scott Bar for their leader. Indians soon drove them from this location. Returning to the Salmon River and crossing the mountains to the Trinity River, they spread the news of their discovery of gold at Scott Bar. Many parties started at once for the new location and the place was soon overcrowded with miners. As a result, prospecting parties spread over the entire region, and many new diggings, the scene of thriving camps in 1851, were uncovered.

One such find was the chance discovery of gold on the site later occupied by Yreka. This location attracted little attention at the time, for a rich bonanza was found at Ingall's Gulch on Greenhorn Creek soon afterward. Its discoverers came to Scott Bar for provisions, where they organized "as secretly as possible" and returned to Ingall's Gulch. They were followed, however, and while they lay asleep their claims were occupied by others. This was the beginning of mining on Greenhorn Creek, in January 1851.

SALMON RIVER CAMPS

The first mining camp up the Salmon River from its mouth is Somes Bar. Today a country store there serves a small, scattered population. Continuing up the river on SR 96, one finds it hard to realize that in the early 1850s every bar, creek, and gulch along the course of the river teemed with miners.

Forks of Salmon had a population of several hundred in the summer of 1850, although fewer than fifty spent the winter of 1850–51 there. Before winter had passed, the report of rich diggings attracted miners from all directions, many rushing to the spot without supplies. As a result, when late snows blocked the trails in March, thousands all up and down the Salmon River and its branches were on the verge of starvation, but supplies were somehow brought through the drifts. Forks of Salmon remains a small settlement, famous for its excellent fishing in the summer months.

Sawyer's Bar, on the North Fork of the Salmon River, has been hard hit by fires. The only historic building remaining there is St. Joseph's Catholic Church, built in the 1850s of whipsawed lumber. Paradise Flat, the little piece of ground on which the church stands, has never been mined and is popularly believed to contain a small fortune in gold. South of Sawyer's Bar are a number of quartz mines, chief among them the Black Bear Mine seven miles to the southwest. Material for the mill of this mine was carried over the mountains on muleback or dragged in on sleds by oxen.

SCOTT VALLEY

Scott Valley was named for John Scott, the discoverer of gold at Scott Bar. When William H. Brewer of the Whitney Geological Survey visited the region in the fall of 1863, he praised the beautiful valley's "rich bottom, with fertile ranches, surrounded with high and very steep mountains, rough and rugged, and furrowed into very deep canyons." Once famous for its gold production, the valley is now primarily agricultural.

The Scott Bar of 1850 was located a few hundred yards above and on the opposite bank of Scott River from the Scott Bar of 1851 and succeeding years. The old trail of the 1850s zigzagged for three miles through the precipitous canyon that lay between Scott Bar and the mouth of the Scott River, the canyon proper being at least 3,000 feet deep in many places. In the early 1850s this great gorge was teeming with life. Among the bustling camps of the region were French Bar, Johnson's Bar, Poorman's Bar, Lytle's Bar, Slapjack Bar, Michigan Bar, and Junction Bar. Governor Lane worked Lane's Gulch on Whitney Hill near Scott Bar in 1851.

Some of the old buildings in the vicinity of Scott Bar are still intact. The Quartz Hill Mine yielded millions and continued to operate into the twentieth century.

Etna Mills, now Etna, originally known as Rough and Ready Mills, grew up around the flour mill established there in 1856 in competition with a neighboring concern known as the Etna Mills, built in 1854. There was considerable rivalry between the two communities, but the newer place finally won out as a town in 1863, when the post office was shifted from Etna Mills to the more successful Rough and Ready. Since there was already a Rough and Ready in Nevada County, the name of its rival, Etna Mills, was given to the new post office.

Etna lies in the midst of a rich agricultural district shut in by the heavily forested Salmon Mountains to the west and the Scott Mountains on the south and east. Its Main Street has willow-shaded sidewalks and several charming old buildings; one of them, at 520, is the Eschscholtzia Parlor #112, Native Daughters of the Golden West Museum (*Eschscholtzia californica* is the state flower, the "California poppy").

CALLAHAN

Callahan's Rancho, or Callahan, near the junction of the East and South Forks of the Scott River, was the first stopping place after crossing Scott Mountain from the south. Here in the autumn of 1851 M. B. Callahan opened a public house and store. Soon after Callahan sold out in 1855, the place became the terminus of Greathouse and Slicer's stage line from Yreka, which used the two Concord coaches that Henry Slicer had brought over the Siskiyou Mountains from Oregon in 1854, the first in Siskiyou County. At Callahan's, passengers were transferred to mules for the difficult journey over Scott Mountain to the Trinity River and over the Trinity Mountains to French Gulch and the town of Shasta.

The Callahan Ranch Hotel, built in 1854, was originally a stage stop and later a hotel; it is now closed. Across the street is a general store, The Emporium, which has been in business at the same spot since the early 1900s.

FORT JONES

Fort Jones was established in 1852 as an Army station protecting settlers and miners against hostile Indians. It was named for Colonel Roger Jones, adjutant general of the Army from 1825 to 1852. The fort was abandoned in 1858, and the frame houses that had replaced the first log cabins were purchased and moved into town. The site of the fort (SRL 317) is one mile south of the town of Fort Jones on SR 3 and Scott Valley Road. Three of the men serving at Fort Jones, upon their discharge from the Army, became pioneer settlers of the valley. The town of Fort Jones was originally named Wheelock and was a stage station on the road from Yreka to Shasta. The Fort Jones House on East Main Street has been marked by E Clampus Vitus as the principal building of

Van Choate-Rosborough House, Yreka

the community since the 1850s. The Fort Jones Museum is at 11913 Main Street.

YREKA

In March 1851 a gold strike was made at Yreka Flats, an event that brought 2,000 men to the spot in less than six weeks. This discovery was made by Abraham Thompson in a ravine later known as Black Gulch. The camp that grew up was called Thompson's Dry Diggings and was located on a knoll near a spring at the intersection of today's Discovery and Yama Streets in Yreka.

Meanwhile, miner's cabins were built for three miles along Yreka Creek from Greenhorn to Hawkinsville, and business soon moved away from the flats and nearer to the creek. A town, at first called Shasta Butte City, was laid out in May 1851. To avoid confusion with the older Shasta City (in Shasta County), the name was changed to Yreka, which phoneticized the Indian name for Mount Shasta, I-eka. (Gudde says that the intended spelling was "Wyreka" and that the present name is due to a clerical error.) When Siskiyou County was formally organized by the state Legislature in 1852, Yreka was designated the county seat, and so it remains.

Among the episodes that enlivened the early history of Yreka, the Greenhorn War of 1855 was perhaps the most exciting. This was a contest over water rights waged by two mining factions, the Yreka Flats Ditch Association and the miners on Lower Greenhorn Creek. The latter precipitated the war when they cut the Yreka Flats Ditch because it was diverting water from their claims on the creek. The matter was taken before the local court, which supported the Yreka faction and enjoined against further cutting of the ditch. The injunction was disobeyed and the guilty party arrested. This was the signal for the Greenhorn miners to act. In a body they marched to the Yreka jail and got the prisoner released after an encounter with the law. Nevertheless, the decision of the court stood, and the Yreka Flats Ditch Association continued to use the water brought from Greenhorn Creek.

Law and order gradually emerged in Yreka, but only after the first excitement of gold fever died away and more sober industries such as lumbering became the basis of the town's economy. On July 4, 1871, one-third of the town burned within one terrifying hour. The brick structures downtown survived and today are part of the Historic District (SRL 901) of Yreka, centered on Third Street from Lane Street to Center Street and branching out along Miner Street from Main Street to Oregon Street. A walking-tour guide to the houses and buildings, most of which are marked with the date of their building, can be obtained in town. A walk through this district is a delightful experience, and the plaques on the old houses are clear and readable. The historic district was first identified and marked in 1972.

On Miner Street, then as now a commercial thoroughfare, one can see the City Meat Market at 319, built in 1854 and now a restaurant; the Livingston and Bro. building at 311–13, from either 1854 or 1855; and a dozen others, all well marked. The IOOF building at 107–11 Miner Street, built in 1859, is perhaps the most imposing of these structures.

Third Street is principally residential, and its many charming old buildings are all marked and all still lived in. At 310 Third is the Van Choate–Rosborough House (1858), a one-and-one-half story house with red siding and white trim; at 216 is the Ivy house (1899), with an elegant veranda on the two stories facing the street; and at 122 is the Cummins-Forest home (1855), a frame house with apple trees in the side yard. Walking through the old, preserved neighborhoods of California towns is one of the great pleasures for the historian and traveler.

At the south end of Yreka is the Siskiyou County Museum at 910 South Main Street, housed in a replica of the Callahan Ranch Hotel. On the museum's grounds are log cabins from mining and lumbering days and a remarkable, extensive collection of mining gear. Within the Siskiyou County courthouse on Fourth Street is a special adjunct of the county museum, a display focusing on the mining activities of the county, such as distinctions between the gold nuggets found in different regions.

The story of Indian Peggy comes from the 1850s when Peggy's people, the Klamaths, were preparing to

C. J. Fry House, Yreka

attack the encroaching white settlers at Yreka. Trying to avoid bloodshed, Peggy traveled twenty miles over rough mountains to warn the settlers. When the Klamath warriors approached the town, they found it strongly guarded by sentries and were forced to retreat. For years afterward, Peggy, fearing to associate with her kinfolk, lived among the people of Yreka, who never forgot the service she had rendered. When the remnants of her tribe were finally placed on the reservation four miles to the south of the town, Indian Peggy was pensioned and cared for until her death at the great age of 105 years. Her grave, on private property, memorializes her deed.

GREENHORN AND HAWKINSVILLE

Many mining camps formerly existed near Yreka. Greenhorn was a cluster of miners' cabins to the south. A company of miners had dug a ditch some distance back from the creek, but finding their claims unprofitable they had abandoned their location. A new arrival, called a "greenhorn" by his more experienced companions, asked where he could find a good place to work. Thinking to enjoy a joke at his expense, the miners directed the young fellow to the hill they had just vacated. The "greenhorn," setting to work on the abandoned ditch, was rewarded by a rich strike, which he kept a secret. When the jokers finally learned that the "green-

Abandoned Brick Catholic Church, Hawkinsville

horn" had been quietly working the richest ground in the area, there was a rush for claims on the new lead. To perpetuate the joke, so the story goes, the creek was called "Greenhorn," which passes through Greenhorn Park at the south edge of Yreka.

Two miles to the north was Frogtown, founded in 1851. The following year, when the Oregon to California Trail went through, Frogtown was moved to higher ground and renamed Hawkinsville. An E Clampus Vitus plaque commemorates Frogtown two miles north of Yreka on SR 263. The brick Catholic church stands in the center of Hawkinsville, remodeled from a structure originally built in 1858; it is no longer in use.

WEED

Lumberman Abner Weed founded the town that bears his name and was incorporated in 1901. The Weed Historic Lumber Town Museum on Gilman Avenue commemorates the industry that brought many people into this area. Like many California towns, Weed boasts a handsome decorative arch spanning its Main Street. The Living Memorial Sculpture Garden, the work of Dennis Smith, a Vietnam War veteran, is twelve miles northeast of the town on US 97 and is dedicated to all veterans. There is a magnificent view of Mount Shasta from the grounds.

MCCLOUD

McCloud, another lumber town, was built south of SR 89 at the site of Friday George Mill. Here in 1896 Scott and VanArsdale Inc. established the McCloud River Lumber Company and the McCloud River Railroad. There is a pleasant architectural harmony to the wood-framed buildings of the historic district, which is listed on the National Register of Historic Places. The McCloud Hotel, built in 1915, is still in business, as is the nearby Mercantile Building (1899) at 241 Main Street. The Heritage Junction Museum at 320 Main Street highlights the history of the town.

BUTTE VALLEY

Butte Valley lies in the eastern part of the county near the Oregon border. Its principal town is Dorris, originally a Southern Pacific Railroad station named in 1907 for Presley A. Dorris and his brother Carlos J. Dorris, stock raisers in Little Shasta in the 1860s. The town boasts the tallest flagpole in the United States, "rising 200 feet above the valley floor elevation of 4,200 feet." The Butte Valley Museum at 500 South Butte Street is gathering materials commemorating the life of the region, which still has a strong emphasis on stock raising.

LAVA BEDS NATIONAL MONUMENT

For the archaeologist and the student of early Western history, as well as for the lover of unique natural formations, the Modoc Lava Beds in the Lava Beds National Monument hold a great fascination. This region was once the domain of the Modoc Indians. Their name for the region is said to have meant "the land of burned-out fires," and its labyrinthine caves, seemingly bottomless fumaroles, and extinct craters demonstrate the fitness of that designation. This vast mesa-like formation is broken by buttes and cinder cones several hundred feet high; the harsh outlines of these volcanic masses are relieved by the contrast of blossoming shrubs, clumps of pine and juniper, and beautiful vari-colored rock.

Lava Beds National Monument, established in 1925, lies at the eastern edge of Siskiyou County, with a portion extending further east into Modoc County. A good road crosses the region, leaving SR 139 at Newell in

Living Memorial Sculpture

Old Cabin at Butte Valley Museum, Dorris

Modoc County in the north and returning to that road near Tionesta, also in Modoc County, to the south.

From the visitors' center near the southeast entrance to the monument, a short drive takes one past a series of remarkable natural phenomena. Indian Well, for instance, has two pools of crystal-clear ice water that never seem to diminish, even in the driest seasons. Near Indian Well are Labyrinth Cave, Skull Cave, Symbol Cave, and Symbol Bridge. Labyrinth Cave is a series of subterranean cells connected by a maze of tunnels running in all directions, the main gallery being almost two miles in length, with a part of the distance navigable only in a crouching position. Skull Cave, the largest cavern in the region yet explored, has three stories at its lower end. A river of ice covers the floor of the lower chamber and in it are embedded numerous skulls of Rocky Mountain sheep and pronghorn antelope, bones of now-extinct animals, and even scattered human remains. On the rocks and about one of the entrances to Symbol Cave are clear and unfaded Indian petroglyphs, described in the Modoc County chapter.

Beyond Symbol Bridge and Antelope Well, with its abundant clear, sweet water, is Bearpaw Cave, a series of rock and ice chambers connected by underground corridors. One of the chambers contains a river of ice that lasts throughout the year, while at the opposite end of the cave another immense cavity holds an unfailing water supply. Sentinel Cave, Crystal Cave, Chocolate Bridge, Painted Cave, Jove's Thunderbolt, and "The Chimneys" (large vents projecting twenty feet or more above the ground and extending straight down into the earth to a depth so great that a rock dropped from the top cannot be heard to strike bottom) are among the natural phenomena most accessible to the tourist. The Catacombs Cavern, the most beautiful of the entire group, resembles a medieval cathedral, its roof buttressed by massive columns and the walls and ceilings frescoed by a delicate coral-like formation traced in fanciful designs. About 150 caves in this interesting group have been discovered and explored.

THE MODOC WAR

The coming of American miners and settlers into the Klamath Basin threatened the existence of the Modoc Indians, who began retaliating against the invaders. Federal officials set aside a reservation in southern Oregon for both the Modocs and the Klamaths, but the arrangement did not work out. Attempts to force the tribe to return to the reservation met with armed resistance on November 29, 1872, and thus began the six-month Modoc War. The Modocs, under Kientepoos ("Captain Jack"), retreated into the lava beds, where the terrain gave them many advantages. An attempt in January 1873 to storm their stronghold ended in thirty-seven Army casualties and no Modoc losses.

To avoid further bloodshed, peace talks were arranged between the Army and the Modocs. Wi-ne-ma ("Toby") Riddle, Kientepoos's cousin and the wife of a white man, acted as interpreter. Meanwhile, the Army was bringing in reinforcements. Virtually compelled to assert his leadership by agreeing to an act of violence, Kientepoos had General Edward Canby and Reverend Eleazar Thomas shot from ambush as they came unarmed for a peace parley on April 12, 1873. With this act, any chance of a negotiated settlement was lost. Within three days, the Army had moved mortars and howitzers onto the field, and within three more days, the Modocs began a retreat that ultimately forced them to surrender. Kientepoos and three other leaders were hanged in October for the murders of Canby and Thomas, and the remainder of the tribe was exiled to far-off Oklahoma.

The battleground lies within Lava Beds National Monument. "Captain Jack's Stronghold" (SRL 9), at the southern end of Tule Lake, remains almost unchanged. Simple rock forts, used by Indians and soldiers alike, are now overgrown with sage and bitterbrush. Trails with signposts have been made through the area, and the visitor can understand how fewer than sixty fighters held off an army of over 600 men for nearly five months in this half-acre of lava outcroppings. Canby's Cross (SRL 110), three miles to the west, marks the site of his murder; the Native Daughters of the Golden West have placed a monument nearby. Just under a mile west of Canby's Cross is Guillem's Graveyard (SRL 13), where nearly 100 Army casualties of the war were buried in one location. Their remains were removed to the National Cemetery in Washington, D.C., in the 1890s, but the rock wall surrounding the old cemetery may still be seen. Hospital Rock, an Army refuge, and Captain Jack's Cave, the Modocs' headquarters, are also in the vicinity and well marked.

This is a haunted landscape; once visited, it is not forgotten.

TULELAKE

North of the lava beds is the Tule Lake National Wildlife Refuge. To the northwest and extending into Oregon is the Lower Klamath National Wildlife Refuge, which has been declared a National Historic Landmark. Established in 1908, this was one of the first major waterfowl reserves in the United States. The town of Tulelake was the location of three "relocation" camps during the Second World War, one each for German and Italian nationals within the town and a third for Japanese a few miles east, across the county line and actually within Modoc County. Only the site of the latter remains.

THE STATE OF JEFFERSON

Many residents of Siskiyou and the neighboring counties of Del Norte and Modoc long felt they were largely ignored by the state government far to the south in Sacramento. As early as 1852 a bill was introduced into the Legislature to create a State of Shasta; nothing came of this or of a State of Klamath bill, which failed the following year. A similar movement in the southern part of the Oregon Territory died with Oregon's statehood in 1859. As the northern tier of California counties became settled, demands for roads over the great distances of this region increased, with many complaints that the state of California did not sufficiently meet the needs of this remote area.

In 1941 a publicity stunt and another means of protest achieved the election of a "provisional government of the State of Jefferson." From their "Temporary State Capitol" in Yreka, a "Citizens Committee" issued a Proclamation of Independence that read:

> You are now entering Jefferson, the 49th State of the Union. Jefferson is now in patriotic rebellion against the states of California and Oregon. [In addition to the three aggrieved California counties, Josephine County, Oregon, joined the movement.] This state has seceded from California and Oregon this Thursday, November 27, 1941. Patriotic Jeffersonians intend to secede each Thursday until further notice. For the next hundred miles, as you drive along Highway 99, you are traveling parallel to the greatest copper belt in the far west, seventy-five miles from here. The United States government needs this vital mineral, but gross neglect by California and Oregon deprives us of necessary roads to bring out the copper ore. If you don't believe this, drive down the Klamath River Highway and see for yourself. Take your chains, shovel, and dynamite. Until California and Oregon build a road into the copper country, Jefferson, as a defense-minded state, will be forced to rebel each Thursday and act as a separate state.

A Great Seal of the State of Jefferson was created, depicting a gold pan with XX painted at the bottom, symbolizing how Jeffersonians had been double-crossed by their mother states. Journalists and radio reporters rushed to Yreka and newsreel photographers enjoyed filming scenes of armed men turning away "invaders" at the "frontier." A week after the Proclamation, December 4, 1941, Judge John L. Childs was inaugurated as governor in a ceremony held in Yreka. Signs were plastered around the new "Capitol City" which read: "Our roads are not passable, hardly jackassable, if our roads you would travel, bring your own gravel."

Three days later, the attack on Pearl Harbor quickly put all of these high jinks aside as the United States entered World War II. New roads were soon constructed in the region. Although no political separatist movement has been successful in California since statehood in 1850, similar efforts arise from time to time, and always find much publicity.

Solano County

St. Peter's Chapel, Mare Island, Vallejo

Solano County, named in honor of an Indian chief, was one of the original twenty-seven counties. The first county seat was at Benicia, but in 1858 it was removed to Fairfield.

SOLANO, CHIEF OF THE SUISUNS

The last of the missions established in California by the Franciscan friars was at Sonoma in 1823 and was called San Francisco Solano after an illustrious Franciscan missionary to the New World who died in Peru in 1610. Father José Altamira, founder of the mission, bestowed this name in baptism upon Sem Yeto, who was an exceptionally able chief over most of the rancherias between Petaluma Creek and the Sacramento River. The chief accepted the title and the new faith.

At Soscol Creek (Napa County) in 1835, a skirmish took place between Chief Solano's people and a force led by Mariano Vallejo, commandant at Sonoma. The Indians were defeated, but the two leaders became friends thereafter. One of the tribes over which Solano was chief was the Suisun ("west winds"), which occupied the valley east of the Soscol Hills, with a ranchería in present-day Rockville. When a county was formed in this area, General Vallejo suggested that it be named Solano County in honor of his friend.

Dr. Platon Vallejo, the general's son, described the relationship between the two men:

> The *comandante* always held Solano . . . as a personal friend and equal. He consulted him on all things. The chief was a most welcome guest at the hacienda when the *comandante* settled at Sonoma. He might be savage still in some things. When enemies opposed him he killed them if he could, but he also had the primitive virtues of truth, honor, and everlasting good faith, and

the trust placed in him was never betrayed. My father has often told me that he never came in contact with a finer mind. He was a keen, clear-headed thinker, readily grasped new ideas, learned to speak Spanish with ease and precision, and was so ready to debate that few cared to engage him in a contest of wit.

At the corner of Texas Street and Union Avenue in Fairfield, opposite the county courthouse, is a heroic bronze statue of the chief by sculptor William Gordon Huff. A plaque on the grounds of Solano Community College near Rockville, placed by the Native Sons of the Golden West in 1971, marks the vicinity of the chief's grave, the exact site of which is unknown.

RANCHOS SUISUN AND TOLENAS (FAIRFIELD)

Rancho Suisun was the first of five Mexican grants in this county that were confirmed with patents issued by the United States government after 1848. Francisco Solano made a petition in 1837 describing himself as the "principal chief of the unconverted Indians and born captain of the Suisun" and asked for four square leagues. The land, he said, belonged to him "by hereditary right from his ancestor," and he wished to "revalidate his right." The grant was temporarily made to him and confirmed by Governor Pío Pico in 1845. The land was afterward purchased by General Vallejo, who sold it to Archibald A. Ritchie, who received patent to its 17,754 acres in 1857. On the border of this grant is Fairfield, the county seat, which was established by Ritchie's partner, Captain Robert H. Waterman.

Rancho Tolenas was granted to José Francisco Armijo, "by birth a Mexican, having four sons of the same country without any lands to cultivate," in 1840, the year after he petitioned for three square leagues of land. Governor Alvarado made the grant with the proviso that Armijo should not in any manner molest the Indians already located there. The title to the 13,315 acres of the rancho was acquired by Antonio Armijo upon his father's death in 1850 and was confirmed by U.S. patent in 1868. The adobe home built on this rancho, five miles northwest of Fairfield, is long gone, but the name of Armijo lives on in a Fairfield high school.

RANCHO DE LOS PUTOS,
THE WOLFSKILL GRANT

John Reed Wolfskill, the first American settler in Solano County, arrived in California in 1838 and lived in the southern part of the province with his brother William, a trapper, who had reached California a few years earlier. In 1842 John drove ninety-six head of cattle north to a point near the bank of Putah Creek (named for a Patwin Indian tribe), where he put up a wattle hut. The Río de los Putos grant was made in 1842 to William Wolfskill, who had acquired Mexican citizenship; the patent of 1858 awarded him 17,754 acres on either side of the creek, partly in Solano County and partly in Yolo County. William's home, however, was in Los Angeles.

Three other brothers, Sarchel, Milton, and Mathus, eventually acquired this vast tract of land, along with John, and all four made homes along the fertile banks of Putah Creek, or Río de los Putos. John erected a house one and a half miles southeast of Sarchel's and farther from the creek, using smooth, white volcanic tufa, the native stone. A true horticulturist, he planted many acres of black walnuts, pecans, pomegranates, apricots, oranges, figs, and olives, which became the basis for Solano County's orchards. The stone house fell in the earthquake of 1892 and was replaced the following year by a seventeen-room frame house. This stood, as did the former one, at the end of a long driveway lined with olive trees. Emblazoned on this later house was the number "96," the Wolfskill cattle brand, a reference to the cattle John had driven north in 1842. This house, in which John Wolfskill lived until his death in his nineties in 1897, burned in 1948.

Over a hundred acres of this property, owned by John Wolfskill and after him by his daughter and then by his grandchildren, was willed to the University of California at Davis for an agricultural experimental station, with the provision that the old olive plantings be retained. The spot (SRL 804) is two miles southwest of Winters, off Putah Creek Road. It is easily identifi-able by the magnificent avenue of gnarled olive trees leading to two university buildings at the site of John Wolfskill's house.

RANCHO LOS PUTOS AND
THE VACA VALLEY

Among the names of immigrants arriving in Pueblo Los Angeles in November 1841 with the Rowland-Workman party appears "J. Manuel Vaca and families." Originally from New Mexico, Juan Manuel Vaca and Juan Felipe Peña then went north to Sonoma, where General Vallejo housed the women and children, and the men journeyed on to look for desirable land and to build homes. In June 1842 they petitioned for a grant of land, which was made the following year by Governor Micheltorena. The language of the grant was so vague that it appeared to include lands that were part of the earlier Wolfskill grant, and a heated controversy developed that was finally resolved by Micheltorena in Wolfskill's favor.

The settlers' adobe homes were built about two miles southwest of the present city of Vacaville in the lower end of Vaca Valley and its lateral Lagoon Valley. Vaca's house was razed before 1900. The Peña Adobe (SRL 534), still standing beside I-80, was occupied by descendants of the Peña family until 1918. Its restoration was begun in 1963 through the initial efforts of the Solano County Historical Society. The adobe structure, fifty by eighteen feet, was found to be in good condition, since it had been sheathed in frame about 1875. Replacement bricks have been made with adobe from the nearby lagoon. The Peña adobe and its grounds are now owned by the city of Vacaville; the Mowers-Goheen Museum, housed in an adjacent building, contains Indian artifacts and natural history exhibits. The Willis Linn Jepson Memorial Garden has an interesting collection of native plants.

Ulatis Creek, which flows through this rancho, was named for the Indian tribe sometimes designated the "Ooloolatis," who occupied the area and left many artifacts. The Ulatis were wiped out by the smallpox epidemic of 1837–39. The life of Chief Solano of the neighboring Suisuns was saved by vaccination.

RANCHO LOS ULPINOS AND
JOHN BIDWELL

John Bidwell, a naturalized Mexican citizen, petitioned in 1844 for the grant of Rancho Los Ulpinos, 17,726 acres in the eastern part of the county along the bank of the Sacramento River. Governor Micheltorena made the grant in the same year. After the American conquest of California, Bidwell sold parts of the grant to several persons, until the boundary lines were in a state of chaos. In 1855 these properties were all defined amicably when the entire rancho was divided into twenty equal tracts made by measurements along the riverfront extending back one league. The tracts were sold in Benicia, and the proceeds were allocated to the various claimants. The land was finally patented to Bidwell in 1866, thus making all titles valid.

UNPATENTED LAND GRANTS

The Soscol grant, eleven square leagues extending northward from Carquinez Strait, was claimed by General Vallejo, who said it had been given to him by Governor Micheltorena in 1843 in consideration of his services as an officer and of the large sums of money that he had furnished the Mexican government. Although the American courts ultimately declared his title to be invalid, purchases made under it were allowed when further small payments were made. Within the borders of the Soscol grant lies much of modern-day Benicia, Cordelia, and Vallejo.

The Sobrante grant came into the public domain when the courts rejected the claim of brothers José and Juan Luco. Within its fifty square leagues are present-day Birds Landing, Collinsville, Denverton, and most of the Montezuma Hills.

COLLINSVILLE

Lansford W. Hastings, a lawyer from Ohio, reached California by way of Oregon in 1843 in command of the emigrant party that bore his name. He was active in the early American settlement of the region, traveling extensively in his effort to attract new residents. Returning to the eastern part of the United States, he published there in 1844 *The Emigrant's Guide*. Coming back to California, he became agent for the Mormons and selected a site for the location of one of their colonies on the north side of the Sacramento River near its junction with the San Joaquin. There in 1846 he laid out a town and built an adobe for himself. This building was called "Montezuma House," and Bayard Taylor, in *Eldorado* (1849), mentions it thus: "'City of Montezuma,' a solitary house on a sort of headland, projecting into Suisun Bay, and fronting the rival three-house city, New-York-of-the-Pacific" (now Pittsburg,

in Contra Costa County). Hastings had hoped to obtain a large grant of land from the Mexican government, but after the American flag was officially raised over California on July 7, 1846, the Mormons lost interest in the site. During his stay, Hastings established a ferry across to the Contra Costa side. After leaving Montezuma, he became attorney for the northern district of California and was a member of the constitutional convention, where his geographical knowledge was useful in fixing boundaries.

The adobe built by Hastings stands at the end of Stratton Lane a little more than a mile east of Collinsville overlooking the place where California's two principal rivers meet. The building is gradually decaying and is fenced to keep visitors away; the adobe was sheathed in redwood many years ago. Numerous machines for fabricating and stamping coins were found in the house after the builder left it; it is thought that they were intended for the use of the Mormons.

Collinsville was named for C. J. Collins, who settled in the area in 1856. In the next decade, a planned city attracted much interest but few residents, since many of the lots were under water at high tide. F. E. Booth and Company built a salmon cannery here in 1873 and employed many Italian fishermen, who lived in homes built on stilts to allow free circulation of flood tides beneath them. Some called it "Little Venice." But the salmon decreased, and there were fires, and there was only one road to the outside world. Today only a few occupied houses remain, some elevated but not on stilts, in one of the strangest historic spots in California.

BENICIA

Benicia lies on the north side of Carquinez Strait, between San Pablo and Suisun bays. In 1850 it rivaled San Francisco as the metropolis of northern California. The town was a pioneer military, religious, and educational center. Benicia was laid out in 1847 by Dr. Robert Semple, who had taken part in the Bear Flag revolt in 1846 at Sonoma, in which General Vallejo was captured. Dr. Semple, impressed with Carquinez Strait as the possible site for a city, made a bargain with his prisoner (whose estate covered much of the present Solano, Napa, and Sonoma Counties) for a part of his Soscol grant, the land now occupied by the city of Benicia. The site was deeded to Dr. Semple and his friend Thomas O. Larkin after General Vallejo had been released from imprisonment at Sutter's Fort. The city covered 2,100 acres, according to the survey of 1847.

The name first selected for the city was Francisca, in honor of the wife of General Vallejo. For a while, Francisca's boosters expected it to become the chief city of the greater San Francisco Bay Area. When it was learned that the older town of Yerba Buena had changed its name to San Francisco in the same year, Francisca's name was changed to Benicia, one of Señora Vallejo's other names.

Dr. Semple established the first ferry across Carquinez Strait in 1847. It proved to be a very lucrative operation in the ensuing years of the Gold Rush. There was continuous ferry service between Benicia and Martinez in Contra Costa County for 115 years, until the present bridge carrying I-680 was completed in 1962.

Many noted men and women connected with the early history of California are associated with Benicia. General Vallejo was the donor of the land; Dr. Robert Semple founded the city and was president of the state constitutional convention at Monterey in 1849; Thomas O. Larkin was the first and only United States consul in California; General Persifer F. Smith was the commanding officer of the Pacific Division of the United States Army after California became a state; General Bennett Riley founded the Benicia Arsenal; and Concepción Argüello, whose romantic tragedy was unfortunately quite real, ended her days here.

On the west side of First Street between C and D Streets was the adobe built in 1847 and rented to Captain E. H. von Pfister. The captain was keeping a store in the building in May 1848, when Charles Bennett stopped by on his way to Monterey to have tests made on some gold nuggets picked up by James Marshall on the American River on January 24, 1848. Bennett told the story of Marshall's discovery, showed the nuggets, and thus helped to precipitate the rush to the gold fields. The site where the adobe once stood has been marked.

One of the first hotels in northern California was built in 1847 for Major Stephen Cooper. Here Cooper's daughter Frances married Dr. Semple soon after the opening of the hotel in the town's first wedding ceremony, performed by the former governor of Missouri, L. W. Boggs, then alcalde of Sonoma. Cooper's California House was sold in 1854 to John Rueger, who turned it into a brewery. The remodeled building stood at the south side of West H Street near First until it burned in 1945; the site is now occupied by "The Brewery," a tavern that contains interesting murals of Benicia's pioneer days.

Benicia's oldest hotel building still standing is the Washington House at 333 First Street. The frame structure was a hotel in the 1850s, remodeled in 1897, a speakeasy in Prohibition days, and until 1946, a Chinese lottery house. Today it is divided into several shops.

Dr. W. F. Peabody established a hospital in Benicia in 1849 and is said to have prospered from the patronage of miners returning from the Sierra. He served on the Benicia Seminary Board while mayor of the city, where he lived until 1864. The hospital at 245 West H Street has been completely rebuilt into a private residence; here as elsewhere in downtown Benicia, a marker on the sidewalk designates the site.

The first Masonic Hall in California (SRL 174) was formally dedicated at Benicia at the end of 1850. The two-story frame building is located at 106 West J Street. The lower floor was used as the county courthouse until 1852. About 1880 the Masons sold the hall, reacquiring it in 1950. Many of California's prominent pioneers received their degrees in this building, including George C. Yount, early settler of the Napa Valley. Still in use, the hall is one of three places in California where any Masonic lodge may hold meetings to confer degrees.

The first Pony Express relay rider from St. Joseph, Missouri, William Hamilton, reached Benicia on April 23, 1860, and was ferried across the strait. A bronze marker commemorating the event is set at the southeast corner of First and A Streets. The old railway station is nearby. From here the transcontinental railroad crossed to Contra Costa County by the steamboats *Port Costa* and *Solano*. The latter transported forty-eight cars and a locomotive on one trip and served until the completion of the Southern Pacific Railroad bridge in 1929.

Near the Pony Express marker is a plaque commemorating Jack London. The young writer frequented the Benicia waterfront while gathering firsthand impressions for his *Tales of the Fish Patrol* and *John Barleycorn*.

FIRST PROTESTANT CHURCH IN CALIFORNIA

On the site of what is now the Benicia City Park, the first Protestant church in California (SRL 175) was established on April 15, 1849, by Rev. Sylvester Woodbridge, a missionary sent to California by the Presbyterian Church of New York. Until 1854, it was the only Protestant church in Benicia. Reverend Woodbridge exerted considerable influence in the community, for he was the keeper of the town records in addition to being a successful farmer and a teacher. In the latter capacity, he established Benicia's first school, which was one of the first in California. The site is marked on the north side of West K Street. The church membership became divided over the question of secession and loyalty during the Civil War; the church declined and was closed in 1871, and Woodbridge moved to San Francisco.

THE BENICIA ARSENAL AND BARRACKS

The Benicia Barracks (SRL 177), one of the first United States military posts in California, was established in 1849 by Lieutenant General Silas Casey, commanding two companies of the Second U.S. Infantry. The first buildings were put up that year, since Benicia promised to become the central military post of the region. It was strategically located on Carquinez Strait, into which both the Sacramento and the San Joaquin Rivers empty, and thus stood at the gateway to the interior of California and the mining regions. However, San Francisco, instead of Benicia, became the metropolis of San Francisco Bay and the port of entry to central California; consequently, the Benicia military post was superseded in importance by the presidio at the Golden Gate. In 1908 the barracks was placed under the control of the Benicia Arsenal. A marker at the east end of Hillcrest Avenue indicates the site of the barracks.

In August 1851, the Army began setting up the first ordnance supply depot in California. A small wooden powder magazine was erected, soon followed by others of brick, frame, and stone. Benicia Arsenal (SRL 176) was officially designated as such in April 1852. The oldest stone magazine, built in 1857 at a cost of $35,000, has walls four and a half feet thick, with a vaulted ceiling and modified Corinthian pillars, constructed by French artisans recruited by the federal government. The beautiful interior makes it hard for one to realize that the building was intended for so prosaic a purpose as the storage of gunpowder. This and other structures of hand-hewn sandstone blocks from the surrounding hills are among the finest examples of the stonecutter's art in California. Some of the other structures, still standing in excellent condition, are the first hospital, built in 1856, which served as the post chapel during World War II (thus accounting for the small belfry on the roof); the famous clock-tower building of 1859; and two fine stone warehouses built in 1853–54 and today known as the Camel Barns. The sandstone clock-tower building, with fortress-like walls pierced by gun ports, overlooks the strait. It was originally a three-story building with two towers, but it was damaged by an explosion and fire in 1912 and reduced to two stories and the single massive tower housing the clock, which still keeps time.

The Camel Barns derive their name from a brief moment in their history. In 1856 a herd of camels was imported from the Near East by the Army as an experiment in the transportation of military supplies across the deserts of the Southwest. The experiment was unsuccessful, and in 1863 the camels were driven to Benicia and housed in the two stone warehouses on the arsenal grounds. In February 1864, the camels were sold at auction; it is believed that the last of these camels died in Los Angeles's Griffith Park in 1934. One of these buildings is now a museum of Benicia history. Between the two buildings is a small machine shop that is part of the museum complex. The Camel Barn museum, operated by the Benicia Historical Museum and Cultural Foundation, is open to the public.

In its first decade, the arsenal housed many soldiers, including the young Army lieutenants Ulysses S. Grant and William T. Sherman. Its facilities were continuously used for ammunition storage and ordnance repair, even after the last of the troops had moved out. Through the years more buildings were constructed, reflecting the architectural modes of different eras, until the arsenal grounds included structures from virtually every period of the state's history. World War II brought an increase of the arsenal's size from 345 acres to 2,192 acres. For the storage of high explosives, 109 concrete bunkers were built into the neighboring hills. Most of this ammunition was later removed inland to Utah, where it was thought to be safer from enemy attacks. The arsenal was never attacked, however, and it was a major shipping center of war materiel for the Pacific theater of operations.

For more than a century the arsenal and its magnificent buildings were closed to the general public. In 1961 the Army began deactivation of the post, which was completed in March 1964. Much of the property has been converted to commercial and industrial use, but most of the historic structures have been preserved.

Other landmarks at the arsenal include the cemetery, with burials as early as 1849 and as recently as World War II, when eight German prisoners of war were interred; the headquarters building from 1870; the guardhouse and the permanent barracks, both from 1872; three shop buildings erected in 1876, 1884, and 1887; and the commanding officer's residence, a two-story building with an imposing east entrance overlooking the strait, built in 1860. The commanding officer in 1906–11 was Colonel James W. Benét, father of the poets Stephen Vincent Benét and William Rose Benét.

The main entrance to the arsenal grounds is at the end of Military Road East.

THE OLD STATE CAPITOL BUILDING

The most prominent structure of early Benicia is the third state capitol building (SRL 153), located at the northwest corner of First and G Streets. The imposing two-story brick structure, built in 1852 at a cost of $24,800, was ostensibly intended for the city hall but was promptly offered for the use of the state. The offer was accepted, and Benicia became the third capital of the state of California, following San Jose and Vallejo. It held the honor from February 4, 1853, to February 25, 1854, three days after which the "capital on wheels" made its final journey to Sacramento.

The stately building was designed to resemble a Greek temple. Two fluted columns are set flush with the entranceway. Brick walls, plastered on the interior, support the iron-covered roof. Two angular staircases connect the Senate chamber on the lower floor with the Assembly room on the second story. The building has been restored and furnished as it was in 1853 when it was the center of California government.

Next to the capitol is the Fischer-Hanlon house (SRL 880) at 137 West G Street. This was once part of a hotel on First Street, begun in the Gold Rush era. Following a fire in 1856, the unburned half of the building was purchased by Joseph Fischer, a Benicia merchant of Swiss birth, who had the building moved to its present location and added a kitchen, porches, and servants' quarters. His descendants, having used it as a family home since 1856, donated it to the state in 1969. Completely renovated, it is now open to the public.

THE BENICIA SEMINARY

Benicia was home to a number of early educational institutions, most of them short-lived. The Benicia Seminary, established in 1852, was one of the first Protestant girls' schools in California. Miss Mary Atkins, who became its principal in 1854 and its owner the following year, gave the school fame and success. A strict disciplinarian, she insisted that "no student [was] to tarry before a mirror more than three seconds" and admonished parents against "over indulgence in spending money." Ill health forced her to sell the seminary in

1865 to Reverend Cyrus T. Mills and his wife, who conducted the school until 1871, when they moved to Oakland and there established Mills College. After a time, Miss Atkins, now Mrs. Lynch, repurchased her old school and led it from 1878 until her death in 1886. Many members of the faculty went on to teach elsewhere in the state, and several founded other seminaries. Some of Miss Atkins's pupils also became prominent teachers in public and private California schools.

The seminary site (SRL 795) is on the north side of I Street west of First. It is indicated by a small marker, but, for reasons of space, the state bronze plaque and monuments were placed in the Benicia City Park facing Military Road West.

ST. AUGUSTINE'S COLLEGE AND ST. PAUL'S EPISCOPAL CHURCH

When Dr. Robert Semple founded Benicia in 1847, he set aside some land for a college. A nondenominational boys' school was established in 1852, which in 1867 became a military school. The campus covered fifty-two acres and was adjacent to the entire block occupied from 1870 by its sister school, St. Mary's College of the Pacific. Gertrude Horn (later Atherton) was a pupil at St. Mary's, which closed in 1885; St. Augustine continued until 1889.

Bishop J. H. D. Wingfield of the Sacramento diocese supervised both schools for a time and had his residence on the campus from 1876 to 1898. The bishop's house, today a private residence at 36 Wingfield Way, is the only building remaining from either campus. The bishop now has his headquarters in Sacramento, and the campus has been subdivided.

St. Paul's Episcopal Church (SRL 862), in downtown Benicia, is a picturesque and significant landmark of early days. Its ceiling, like an inverted ship's hull, was designed by Captain Julian McAllister, commander of the Benicia Arsenal. The church was consecrated in January 1860, with Captain McAllister as lay reader until the arrival of Reverend James Cameron in October of that year. The church stands in excellent condition today at First and East J Streets. The rectory at 120 East J Street was originally a New England saltbox home, built in 1790 in Torrington, Connecticut. Captain McAllister purchased the house in 1864 and had it dismantled, shipped around the Horn, and reassembled at its present site in Benicia. The original fireplace and staircase remain, with a master bedroom and kitchen added in 1865.

ST. DOMINIC'S CHURCH AND PRIORY

Catholic families in Benicia at first drove by oxcart to Sonoma Mission for Mass. The first Catholic church in Benicia was built at the corner of Fourth and East I Streets in 1852. The present stone and concrete Church of St. Dominic, on the north side of East I Street between East Fourth and East Fifth Streets, was blessed in March 1890, shortly before the earlier building was demolished.

St. Dominic's parish was formally established on March 16, 1854, when the Very Reverend Francis Sadoc Villarasa, O.P., arrived from Monterey with his whole religious community and accepted the care of the parish in the name of the Order of the Preachers. Father Villarasa and the Most Reverend Joseph Sadoc Alemany, O.P., had arrived in San Francisco late in 1850. The latter, who became the first archbishop of San Francisco in 1853, gave to the former for the use of the order the church already built in Benicia. Near the church the first residence for the community was built in 1854. This was used until 1887, when a new priory was put up on Fifth Street East near East I Street.

The work most dear to Father Villarasa on his arrival in California was the establishment of a convent and a novitiate for the education of Dominican priests. These he had established in Monterey, but he had them moved to Benicia when he came there in 1854. The Dominican priory existed until 1935, when it became a vicariate. With this change valuable old books brought from Spain in early years and protected within these walls were made available to interested historians.

ST. CATHERINE'S CONVENT AND
SISTER MARY DOMINICA ARGÜELLO

The Dominican Sisters arrived in California in 1850. They settled first at Monterey, where in the spring of 1851 they established the first convent school in California. However, the old adobe building in which they were located was in bad condition, and since the population in Monterey was diminishing and that around San Francisco Bay was rapidly increasing, the sisters decided to move to Benicia, which seemed to be a more central point. Here they established St. Catherine's Convent in 1854. It was operated as a convent and school until 1959. Luisa and Maria Vallejo were among the young women who received their education here, and many orphan children were given shelter and schooling. In 1889 the Sisters moved to what is now the Dominican College of San Rafael, but they continued to operate St. Catherine's in Benicia until it was razed in 1966. The site, where First and L Streets meet, is now a commercial center.

One of the saddest romances of early California history is the story of Concepción Argüello and the Russian count Nikolai Rezanov. Bret Harte, Richard White, and Gertrude Atherton are among the writers who have given their versions of the story to the world. At the Presidio of San Francisco the two pledged their engagement in 1806. Rezanov returned to Alaska and thence to Russia to get imperial permission for his marriage. For years, Concepcíon waited for her lover, refusing all suitors. After several years, rumor reached California of the count's death while crossing Siberia; it was confirmed only in 1847, forty-one years after his departure.

Concepcíon at length joined the Third Order of St. Francis, giving her life to teaching the poor and caring for the sick. When the Dominican Sisters founded their convent school at Monterey in 1851, she became their first native-born novice, and when the convent was moved in 1854, she came to Benicia with the Sisters. Sister Mary Dominica Argüello died at the Convent of St. Catherine on December 23, 1857, at the age of sixty-six. She is buried in St. Dominic's Cemetery on Hillcrest Avenue at the northeastern corner of the town. Her simple tombstone is in the second row in the section reserved for sisters' graves; a modern memorial to her stands nearby.

OTHER BENICIA LANDMARKS

Benicia was of great importance as a port of entry for many years. It had the advantage of deep water at the shore, where seagoing vessels could discharge their cargoes directly on the land. Captain John Walsh, having led a seafaring life, settled there in 1849 and became collector of the port. His house is now a bed-and-breakfast inn, handsomely preserved, at 235 East L Street. The house is one of three almost identical houses prefabricated in Boston and brought around the Horn to California in 1849. The second house, now gone, ended up in San Francisco, and the third became Lachryma Montis, General Vallejo's home in Sonoma.

The site of the Pacific Mail and Steamship Company docks is at the end of East H Street. The company began operations here in 1850 with a fleet of six sidewheelers. California's first large industrial enterprise flourished here, as docks, foundries, machine shops,

Capt. John Walsh Bed and Breakfast, Benicia

and repair dry docks were established; here the great seagoing ships of that era were repaired and coaled.

At the foot of Eleventh, Twelfth, and Thirteenth Streets, along the waterfront, is the site (SRL 973) of the Turner-Robertson Shipyard, which operated here from 1883 to 1918.

The *California*, the first steamer of the line to make the journey around the Horn from New York, arrived in San Francisco on February 28, 1849, crowded with passengers. Coal for refueling for the return journey had to be brought to California by sea, and since the first shipload had not arrived, the steamer was forced to wait. Refueled, the *California*, with Captain Forbes in command, made an excursion to Benicia with a party of invited guests in April before setting off in May to return to New York. After the establishment of the docks, all the great ships of this company, the *California*, the *Oregon*, and the *Panama*, berthed in Benicia between regular trips until the company removed its headquarters to San Francisco in the early 1860s.

The competition of the overland railway, completed in 1869, was felt keenly by the Pacific Mail and Steamship Company, and by 1881 it had left Benicia altogether. Some of its waterfront property was taken over by the Benicia Agricultural Works. The area today is a thriving commercial center.

CORDELIA AND GREEN VALLEY

The town of Cordelia, next to Benicia the oldest in the county, was named in honor of the wife of Robert H. Waterman, founder of Fairfield. Situated at the lower end of Green Valley on the route from Benicia to Sacramento, it was a stopping place for stages, and a hotel for the accommodation of travelers was operated there in 1855 by John Charles Pitman, an Englishman. Stone

quarried near Cordelia was taken by barges through the Cordelia Slough and across the bay to San Francisco, where it was used in building and in paving the streets. The shipping point was then called Bridgeport; and when in 1868 the California Pacific Railroad was routed through there, the community of Cordelia was moved a short distance south to the newer site. The Pitman House was succeeded by the Cordelia Hotel, which years later became a family residence and survived until it burned in 1937. The Thompson Bar in Cordelia is said to be one of the oldest in the county. Cordelia is just south of the junction of highways I-80 and I-680.

North of Cordelia on the other side of I-80 stretches Cherry Valley, an area now more residential than agricultural. About three and one-half miles north along Green Valley Road, set back some distance to the west of the road, is the imposing stone residence started in 1860 by Granville P. Swift, Bear Flagger and the builder of Temelec Hall near Sonoma. After eighty years in the related Swift and Jones families, the building is now the clubhouse for the Green Valley Country Club.

ROCKVILLE AND THE ROCKVILLE
STONE CHAPEL

Rockville was a settlement on the old stage road between Benicia and Sacramento and today is a settled crossroads on Suisun Valley Road about two miles north of I-80. Through this area runs the northern boundary of the unconfirmed Soscol grant.

By 1852 summer camp meetings were being held regularly on Suisun Valley Creek, where baptism by total immersion was possible. The settlers gathered from afar with their tents and cookstoves and even the family milk cow, prepared to spend a week. Circuit riders preached at the meetings and services lasted into the night, with the aid of lanterns hung in the oak trees. At two such camp meetings, in 1854 and 1855, $5,000 was raised to build a permanent structure, the Rockville Stone Chapel. Landy and Sarah Alford, pioneers in the area, gave five acres for the site of the church and a cemetery. The cornerstone was laid on October 3, 1856, the stone coming from the adjacent hills; the church was built by volunteer labor.

Many pioneers were highly sensitive to the split in the Methodist Episcopal Church caused by the slavery question. One Sunday in 1863 the predominant Northerners sang "The Battle Cry of Freedom." Indignant Southerners in the congregation promptly installed a stone plaque, still visible, reading "M. E. Church South 1856," and the Northerners began to worship elsewhere.

Regular services were held in the chapel (SRL 779), just north of the Rockville crossroads, until 1895, and occasional services were held until 1919. The building gradually deteriorated except for the stone walls, which had withstood the 1906 earthquake. In 1929 the reunited Methodist Episcopal Church deeded it to the Rockville Public Cemetery District on condition that it be restored as a pioneer monument, and this was done in 1940.

SUISUN CITY

In October 1850, Dr. John Baker and Curtis Wilson sailed up the Suisun Slough to Suisun Island, a bit of hard upland rising from the marsh, and landed at the present site of Suisun City, where they discovered a herd of elk among the tules. In the same year Captain Josiah Wing began to run various watercraft to the island. In 1852 he put up a warehouse on this "embarcadero" (the name by which the place was then known), and his schooner, the *Ann Sophia*, transported the produce of the valley, beginning an industry that assumed vast proportions as the country became more populous. In 1854 the captain and John Owen, who later became a merchant in the place, laid out the town of Suisun west of the wharf and just below the southern boundary line of the Suisun grant. In 1857 the first church was built under Presbyterian auspices, the land and building being donated by the people of the vicinity. In 1858 Captain Wing built a residence for himself in the town. Suisun was incorporated as a city in 1868, when the railroad arrived.

The old plaza is formed by the broadening of Main Street between Solano and Morgan Streets. The Lawler house is the oldest surviving dwelling in the city; it was built in 1856 and moved to its present location, at 712 East Main Street, in 1982, where it is used as an office building. The Suisun Marsh nearby is the largest (84,000 acres) brackish marsh in the United States and the largest remaining coastal wetland in California; tours are available in different seasons.

THE "MOTHBALL FLEET"

At the end of World War II, some 300 seaworthy cargo vessels were moored in Suisun Bay just east of Vallejo. As they were needed, they were taken from reserve and put into service, as in the Korean and Vietnam wars. This Ready Reserve Force, popularly called the "Moth- ball Fleet," is administered by the Maritime Administration Division of the Federal Department of Transportation. The ships can be seen from I-680 just east of the Benicia-Martinez Bridge.

VALLEJO, CALIFORNIA'S SECOND CAPITAL

California's first state capital was at San Jose; at the urging of General Mariano Vallejo, it was moved in 1852. Vallejo promised to grant land on which to build a capital city and also promised to build a capitol building, lodgings, and such social institutions as schools and churches. As a compliment to their benefactor, the Legislature named the new city "Vallejo," although he himself had suggested "Eureka."

On January 5, 1852, the Legislature met for the first time in the new frame capitol building. But it was dissatisfied with the poor housing facilities, and, since Vallejo found himself unable to fulfill his promises of accessory buildings, the Legislature moved hastily to Sacramento on January 12. A devastating flood in Sacramento caused them to adjourn on May 4, 1852, to meet again in Vallejo on January 3, 1853. On February 4, this "Peripatetic Government," or "Capital on Wheels," as it has been variously designated, was carried to the neighboring town of Benicia, where it remained until February 25, 1854, when Sacramento finally won the contest for the state capital.

The site of the capitol building (SRL 574) is marked at 219 York Street near Sacramento Street, in downtown Vallejo. Nearby, in the old city hall at 734 Marin Street, is the Vallejo Naval and Historical Museum, exhibiting materials connected with the history of the city and of neighboring Mare Island Naval Shipyard.

A Methodist Episcopal church was organized in Vallejo in 1855, the outcome of a Sunday school that Mrs. David G. Farragut, wife of the first commandant of the Mare Island navy yard, and others had been conducting for some months. In 1856 General John B. Frisbie donated a site for the building, giving a deed to five men, one of them being Commander Farragut, "in trust for the Methodist Episcopal Church in the town of Vallejo." Upon this lot and largely through the exertion of Farragut, a small rough structure was built, which served for a time the double purpose of chapel and schoolhouse—the first record of a publicly supported school in Vallejo. The site is at 420 Virginia Street.

The California Maritime Academy is situated on Carquinez Strait in Vallejo, just west of the I-80 highway bridge. Established in 1929, it is now part of the

Shipyard Commander's House, Mare Island

California State University system, "a marine-oriented college of business and technology."

Vallejo was the site of one of California's earliest orphanages, built by the Good Templars of California and Nevada and operated until the early 1920s. The site of the large home and school is on the hilltop near the present intersection of La Crescenda and Rincon Way.

MARE ISLAND

The former United States Naval Shipyard (SRL 751) is located on Mare Island, just across the Napa River from Vallejo. The island was first named "Isla Plana" (Flat Island) in 1775 by Juan Manuel de Ayala of the *San Carlos*. The tale of its present name is connected with General Vallejo. One day a barge transporting horses and cattle across Carquinez Strait was caught in a sudden squall. The frightened animals stampeded, capsizing the frail craft. Some of them were lost, but one white mare, much prized by the General's wife, swam to a neighboring island, where she was rescued a few days later. General Vallejo named the island "La Isla de la Yegua" (Mare Island).

In 1851 Congress authorized a floating dry dock for the West Coast; in 1852 a naval commission headed by Commodore John D. Sloat was sent to the San Francisco Bay Area to investigate and recommend a site for a navy yard and depot. Mare Island was selected and purchased by the federal government for $83,401. The first commandant arrived on September 16, 1854, and immediately began construction of a shipyard. This young officer was David G. Farragut, who in the following decade became the hero of battles at New Orleans and Mobile Bay in the Civil War, and would be named the Navy's first full admiral.

Until its closure in 1996, the naval shipyard built over five hundred craft for the Navy, including the battleship *California*. It built the first warship on the coast (*Saginaw*, 1859), made the first conversion of a coal-burning ship to oil (*Wyoming*, 1908), built the first flight deck on any ship in the world (cruiser *Pennsylvania*, 1911), and built the hull of the world's first aircraft carrier (*Langley*, 1921–22). The nuclear-powered attack submarine *Drum* was the last vessel completed at Mare Island, in 1970.

Mare Island had the first radio station in the Pacific. The Navy's oldest chapel, St. Peter's, stands here. Mare Island's cemetery was established in 1856 and contains 900 graves, including those of sailors of eight nationalities and the daughter of Francis Scott Key, author of our national anthem. Mare Island's gun park includes the two forward guns of Farragut's flagship *Hartford*, which helped to silence the forts at the entrance to Mobile Bay, and the figurehead of the frigate *Independence*, built in 1812 and station ship at Mare Island from 1855 to 1913. Mare Island is joined to the mainland by an earthen causeway. Since the closing of the base, the site has been successfully developed for industry, research, and educational facilities. It remains somewhat restricted; visitors may apply to the City of Vallejo for permission to enter the grounds.

VACAVILLE

In 1850 Don Manuel Vaca deeded nine square miles of Rancho Los Putos to William McDaniel, who paid the sum of $3,000 in cash and agreed to lay out a town site on one of the square miles, to name it Vacaville, and to give to the former owner certain town lots. The streets were given Spanish names, which were not retained by the American settlers. The earliest occupation of the settlers here was cutting the rank growth of wild oats and transporting the hay to landings on the Sacramento River. The Vacaville Museum at 213 Buck Avenue has displays on the history of Solano County and of Vacaville.

A private school called Ulatis Academy was started in Vacaville in 1855 by a Professor Anderson from San Francisco. The academy was succeeded around 1861 by the Pacific Methodist College under the auspices of the Methodist Episcopal Church, South; the poet Edwin Markham was one of the students. The college was moved to Santa Rosa in 1871. The one surviving college building, at 312 East Main Street, is thought to have been a girls' dormitory.

The "Nut Tree" wayside place, now within Vacaville's

St. Peter's Chapel, Mare Island

city limits, was started with a black walnut planted in 1860 by Josiah Allison, a pioneer of 1854. His young niece, Sally Fox, had picked up the nut in Arizona on the westward journey. A huge tree grew beside the Western Wagon Road, now I-80, and became shelter for a fruit stand. The tree is gone, but from this beginning Allison's descendants developed the famous "Nut Tree" restaurant and market. Though it has been closed in recent years, plans are in the making for a revival of the place, one of the landmarks of the Sacramento Valley.

SILVEYVILLE AND DIXON

Silveyville, on the old route between Napa and Sacramento, was established by Elijah S. Silvey, who made two trips from Missouri to California, accompanied by his wife and two children, before settling permanently here.

On his second arrival, in 1852, he built a house for his family and a corral for the herd of 100 milk cows he had brought. His house became a country hotel, and the corral accommodated horses of the stagecoaches and freight wagons. It became his custom to place a red lantern aloft at night to guide travelers. A trading center called Silveyville developed there, only to be moved

five miles east to the new California Pacific Railroad in 1868. Thomas Dickson donated ten acres on the line of the railroad for a station, and at that spot a town grew up, taking the name of its benefactor but misspelling it Dixon. Silveyville gradually disappeared. Some of the frame buildings were moved intact, while the bricks of the merchandise store were hauled to the new town and used to construct the Capitol Hotel, which stood until 1920. The Old Methodist Episcopal Church was moved in the spring of 1870 to Dixon, where services are still held at its present location on the corner of North Jefferson and B Streets.

FAIRFIELD

The location of the county seat at Benicia provoked complaint because it was on the very edge of the county, a serious defect in those days of slow travel, when residents of outlying sections had business to transact. The agitation for a change became acute in 1857. Robert H. Waterman, a sea captain born in New York and once warden of the Port of San Francisco, who in 1848 had purchased with Archibald A. Ritchie four leagues of the Suisun grant, made a gift of a block of land and money to place the county buildings upon it. On September 2, 1858, a referendum chose the new location to replace Benicia, and Captain Waterman's offer was accepted. The name Fairfield, after Waterman's boyhood home in Connecticut, was given to the place. An effort in 1873 to move the county seat to Vallejo was unsuccessful.

The home in which Captain Waterman lived is one mile north of Fairfield off Mankas Corner Road. The well-built two-story frame house, standing at the end of a long drive between eucalyptus trees planted by him, is in excellent condition, as are the marble fireplaces, high ceilings, and curved staircase. Old fig trees planted by the captain grow near the house, which was begun in 1852. It is now a private residence, and is called Ten Gate Ranch.

Travis Air Force Base, a huge installation primarily involved with transpacific military air traffic, is located four miles northeast of Fairfield. Established in 1942, it is named in honor of Brigadier General Robert T. Travis, who was killed there in an airplane accident on August 5, 1950. This is one of the nation's largest Air Force bases; in the 1990s, when the military presence in California was greatly cut back, this remained one of the most important sites in the state. An Air Force Museum on the base is open to visitors by appointment.

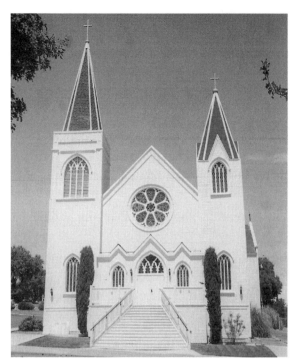

St. Joseph Catholic Church, Rio Vista

Shiloh Church

RIO VISTA

In the fall of 1857 a town called "Brazos del Rio" (Arms of the River) was laid out by Colonel N. H. Davis on his land at the upper end of the Ulpinos grant near the junction of Cache Slough and the Sacramento River. The wharf constructed by Colonel Davis in 1858 was sold the following year to the Steam Navigation Company, which doubled the size of the wharf to accommodate large steamers.

The name of the settlement was changed to Rio Vista, but on January 8, 1862, heavy rains swept the town away. The inhabitants began to look for a better location, and negotiations were entered into with Joseph Bruning for a location in the upper edge of the Montezuma Hills, in the northeast corner of his ranch. The new town plat was surveyed and recorded; part of the site was on the Bruning property and part on the adjoining ranch of T. J. McWorthy. The main street of the new Rio Vista now runs between the sites of these two old farms.

Saint Gertrude's and Saint Joseph's were academies begun in the 1870s; these two schools did not survive the 1920s, and no trace of them remains. The Catholic church built in 1862 at the northwest corner of California and Fourth Streets is still in use. The oldest residence, also built in 1862, is still occupied and is located at 198 Logan Street.

The Rio Vista Museum at 16 North Front Street has interesting displays on various events of the community's history, including the discovery of the largest gas field in northern California in 1936.

CALIFORNIA RAILWAY MUSEUM

Halfway between Rio Vista and Fairfield is the California Railway Museum, the creation of the Bay Area Electric Railroad Association, Inc. The purpose of the association is to preserve cars from the days of interurban electric rail transport. The site, acquired in 1960, is at 5848 State Highway 12 (Suisun City being the postal location). The museum is open to the public, and rides on a mile-and-a-quarter track are offered on weekends.

LANDINGS

Solano County, bordered on the south and east by the Sacramento River, Suisun and San Pablo Bays, and Carquinez Strait, began at an early date to make use of water transportation for freight and passengers. Embarcaderos were placed in many inland sloughs and landings along the river. Maine Prairie, at the head of navigation on the Maine Prairie Slough, shipped much of the wild oat hay and wheat from northern Solano County; 50,000 tons were said to have been transported in one season. The flood of 1862 swept the community away, and although some rebuilding occurred, the advent of the railroads decreased the prosperity of this community and others; beyond place names, virtually nothing remains of them.

Birds Landing, south of the California Railway Museum and on Montezuma Slough northwest of Collinsville, was originally a shipping point for John Bird, a New Yorker who arrived in California in 1859. He purchased 1,000 acres of land and started a storage and commission business; the building of the wharf around 1869 afforded an easy means of shipment of hay and wheat. Only a few piles remain today. At the crossroads about half a mile northeast of the embarcadero he built a general store and this site is today's Birds Landing. The long-closed store is undergoing extensive renovation. The post office at Birds Landing, which operated out of the general store until 1968, was officially cited in June 1988 as one of the three smallest post offices in the United States (the others being Ochopee in Florida and Salvo in North Carolina).

On the slough northwest of Collinsville were Mein's and Dutton's landings. At Mein's Landing, one mile due west of the Birds Landing crossroads, the house built about 1880 by Captain Mein is still standing. It is now used as the headquarters for a private duck club. Dutton's Landing, about two miles northwest of Collinsville, was once the site of a ferry; it can now be reached only by the Grizzly Island Road, across that island. Much of Grizzly Island, along with neighboring Hammond Island, is given over to the Grizzly Island Nature Area, a preserve designed to protect these wetlands.

On Miner Slough is berthed the old barge *Golden Gate*, which was built in the 1890s and last saw service in the building of the Golden Gate Bridge. The was acquired by John Stringer in 1970 and is now a tavern and restaurant under the name "The Golden Gate Island Resort."

Old Round Barn at Fountain Grove, Santa Rosa

Sonoma County

Sonoma County was one of the original twenty-seven counties. "Sonoma" is the name of an Indian tribe whose village site was taken over by Father Altamira in 1823 for Mission San Francisco Solano. The county seat was located at the town of Sonoma from 1850 to 1854; since 1854 it has been at Santa Rosa.

DISCOVERY AND NAMING OF BODEGA BAY

The Vizcaíno expedition of 1602–3 made a lengthy and perilous voyage along the coast of Alta California. Searching for harbors and suitable anchorages, the fleet of three ships put in at several places as far north as Cape Mendocino, and it was on the northern leg of the voyage that Bodega Bay was discovered. It remained for a later explorer to map the bay and give it the name by which it is now known.

On October 3, 1775, the Spanish explorer Juan Francisco Bodega y Cuadra entered the bay that now bears his name in the little schooner *Sonora*. Bodega's mission was to discover potential anchorages on the California coast. His careful observations and acts of possession were of importance to succeeding explorers and colonizers.

On October 20, 1793, Archibald Menzies, a naturalist of the expedition led by Captain George Vancouver of the British Navy, landed on the northwestern shore of Bodega Bay near an island (probably Bodega Rock), which the party named Gibson Island. His party was in search of botanical specimens. Partly because the ground had been burned recently by the Indians and partly because of the season of the year he found few plants, and, to his disappointment, these few were similar to those he had already found at Monterey and San Francisco. The party, which also encountered a small group of peaceful Indians, did find something of interest—described as "a cross formed from a piece of stave of a cask fastened to a pole by rope yarn." Its origins are unknown. The various landings made at Bodega Bay are commemorated by a marker (SRL 833) in Doran Regional Park by the harbor.

THE RUSSIAN PRESENCE

In 1741, Russian forces under the command of Admiral Vitus Bering discovered the sea and the strait that bear his name. On this voyage he also passed by Alaska, whose waters were alive with fur seals. Another expedition followed in 1765.

These activities on the part of the Russians undoubtedly had some influence in rousing Spain to the danger of losing California and led to the occupation of San Diego and Monterey. Subsequently, missions, military posts, and settlements north of San Francisco Bay were established to block Russian advances into California.

By the close of the eighteenth century, the Russian-American Fur Company had established itself on the Aleutian Islands and on the coast of Alaska. These colonies were rich in furs but lacked trade connections by which they could obtain food and necessary supplies. Russia began to look southward to California, with its warm climate and fertile soil, from which she might feed her needy colonists.

In 1806, the czar's chamberlain, Count Nikolai Rezanov, went to Sitka on official business. He found the colonists starving and stricken with fever and scurvy. Temporary relief was obtained from an American ship, but something more permanent was needed. Accordingly, Rezanov sailed south to open negotiations with the Spanish officials in San Francisco, well knowing that trade with foreigners was forbidden.

The advent of the Russians into California is associated with the names of two women, the young Concepción Argüello and the Russian princess Helena de Gagarin. The story of Concepción and her love for Count Rezanov is told in connection with the San Francisco Presidio, where the romance began, and with Benicia (Solano County), where Concepción spent the closing years of her life in the Convent of St. Catherine. The story of Princess Helena is told later in this chapter.

Nikolai Rezanov came to California in 1806 to promote Russian commercial interests. His courtship with Concepción seems to have been genuine, although surely mixed with diplomacy. Certainly, its result was propitious for his enterprise. The account of Doctor Georg von Langsdorff, his friend and companion, shows quite clearly that his ultimate purpose was to establish a Russian colony in northern California. Rezanov's untimely death on the steppes of Siberia prevented him from carrying out this plan himself. A few years later, however, his purpose was fulfilled by Ivan A. Kuskov, an agent of the Russian-American Fur Company.

FOUNDING OF BODEGA BAY, KUSKOV, AND FORT ROSS

Rezanov had taken observations all along the coast on his return voyage to Alaska in 1806, and his report was most favorable. In 1809, Kuskov came down from Siberia prepared to make temporary settlements. One was made at Bodega Bay and another in the Salmon Creek Valley six miles inland. Wheat was sown and harvested, and in August, with the precious store of food and 2,000 otter skins, Kuskov returned to Alaska.

In 1811 Kuskov came again, as governor of the Russian settlements to be established in California. Although he did not go through a ceremony of taking possession of the land for Russia, he made permanent settlements at Kuskov (in Salmon Creek Valley) and, in 1812, at Fort Ross, twelve miles north of the mouth of the Russian River on a high bluff overlooking the sea. These settlements were fortified and the Russian flag raised over them. Title to the territory for a considerable distance had been secured from the Indians who inhabited the region.

Today nothing remains to mark the site of the Salmon Creek Village. This location, where Stephen Smith later settled, is about a mile northwest of Bodega.

FORT ROSS

The Russian settlements flourished; the one at Fort Ross became the center of activities. Not only did the settlers gather rich fur harvests on land and sea, but they became a prosperous agricultural community, supplying food for the Alaskan colonies as well as for their own people. During the years 1810–22, they also carried on a considerable trade with their Spanish neighbors, who were eager to secure the finely made articles that the Russians exchanged for food supplies. This trade was carried on even though it was still officially forbidden; the Californians made opportunities for it, and almost no friction arose between the two peoples.

Nonetheless, it seems clear that fear of the Russian advance in northern California led the Spanish authorities to explore and settle the regions north of San Francisco Bay in what are now Marin, Solano, and Sonoma Counties.

In December 1823 President James Monroe asserted that the United States had a special interest in the Western Hemisphere. He admonished the Powers of Europe not to meddle in the internal affairs of an independent New World state nor to seek to extend their territorial claims in the Western Hemisphere. In this statement, later known as the Monroe Doctrine, Monroe was referring not only to the newly liberated colonies in Latin America but also to the growing presence of the Russian Empire in North America. The Russians recognized his warning in 1824 by agreeing to limit all future settlements to Alaska. For nearly twenty years, however, the colony at Fort Ross remained independent of Mexican control. Meanwhile, the sea otter had been almost exterminated, and the Russian-American Fur Company could no longer maintain American colonies. The political aspect was no longer significant, moreover, and by 1839 Russian officials had sent orders for the withdrawal of all colonists from California. In 1841 the entire property was sold to Captain John Sutter of New Helvetia (Sacramento), and the colonists returned to Alaska.

The original inhabitants of Fort Ross consisted of about one hundred Russians and eighty Aleuts, the maximum population never exceeding four hundred. The settlement stood on a bluff above a little cove in the sea. The land sloped gently upward to the base of a range of hills covered with pine, fir, cedar, and laurel.

The fort itself was enclosed by a palisade built of heavy redwood timbers and mounted with cannon. Two blockhouses, one octagonal and the other heptagonal, surmounted the corners of the palisade, facing the sea on the southwest and the land on the northwest corners. Within the enclosure were nine buildings, among them the commander's quarters and the chapel. Outside were fifty buildings, besides blacksmith, carpenter,

Mission San Francisco Solano, Sonoma

and cooper shops and a large stable for 200 milk cows. At the landing place on the beach below was the boathouse, where seagoing vessels were built.

Fort Ross State Historic Park (SRL 5) has been owned by the state since 1906 and is partially restored. The distinctive Russian Orthodox chapel with its hexagonal tower and round cupola, all of redwood, was destroyed by fire in 1970 and has been completely reconstructed. The commandant's house and the bastions, as well as the bastions surrounding the fort, have also been restored. SR 1, which formerly ran through the grounds, has been rerouted to pass east of the quadrangle. The visitors' center contains many interesting displays on Russian colonial life. Fort Ross is a registered National Historic Landmark, as is the separately designated commandant's house.

FOUNDING OF MISSION
SAN FRANCISCO SOLANO

In 1823, Governor Argüello became anxious to check the Russian advance into the interior north of San Francisco Bay, a region that Gabriel Moraga had already explored during 1812–14 and earlier. The governor advised Father José Altamira, a young priest newly stationed at San Francisco, to transfer the Mission of San Francisco de Asís and San Rafael Arcángel to Sonoma without delay. The Sonoma site was chosen for its proximity to the Russians and because its climate was more favorable for the Indian neophytes than that of the established missions. Without waiting for the final approval by the proper church authorities, the zealous Father Altamira set out at once to choose the site for the new missions, the foundations of which were laid perhaps as early as 1823.

So radical and unauthorized a step occasioned much dissatisfaction within the Church leadership. A compromise was ultimately arranged whereby Missions San Francisco de Asís and San Rafael Arcángel were to continue as before and approval was given for the establishment of a new mission. It was called Mission San Francisco Solano (SRL 3), in honor of St. Francis Solano, an illustrious Franciscan missionary to the New World who died in Peru in 1610, and was thus distinguished from Mission San Francisco de Asís at San Francisco, named in honor of St. Francis of Assisi.

In everyday usage, as it turned out, the mission in San Francisco was known as Mission Dolores, and the new one in the north has always been called Sonoma Mission. This, the last and northernmost of the twenty-one California missions, was a plain, low building with an overhanging roof covering the corridors of the wing. After secularization in 1834, the mission chapel was rebuilt by Mariano G. Vallejo, who was appointed *comisionado*, and then became the parish church. It was sold in 1881 to Solomon Schocken by Archbishop Alemany and subsequently was used for secular purposes. In 1903 a public fund was raised and the old mission was deeded to the state of California. Part of Sonoma State Historic Park today, it is located diagonally across from the northeast corner of Sonoma Plaza. The padres' house, built about 1825, is the oldest structure in Sonoma. The adobe church dates from about 1840, the earlier church having stood east of the padres' quarters.

FOUNDING OF THE PUEBLO OF SONOMA

In 1833 Governor José Figueroa directed the occupation and settlement of what are now Sonoma and Marin Counties. His primary object was to force the Russians out of California. The man who was entrusted with this task was Mariano Guadalupe Vallejo, then military commander and director of colonization on Mexico's northern frontier. In the summer of 1833 Vallejo made an official tour of the Russian settlements, where he made his mission clearly known to the Russian governor.

Mexican settlements were attempted at what are now the towns of Petaluma, Santa Rosa, and Fulton, but the hostility of the Indians caused their abandonment. Sonoma Valley was then chosen as the place of settlement, and there in 1835 General Vallejo founded the Pueblo de Sonoma next to Mission San Francisco Solano.

THE SONOMA PLAZA

General Vallejo himself laid out the new pueblo around a square or plaza, which was used as a drilling ground

for the soldiers who defended the town between 1835 and 1846. On the northeast corner of the plaza stood the mission church and next to it the padres' house. Adjoining the padres' house on the right was a larger adobe, in which Vallejo is said to have lived temporarily; this has long since disappeared. To the west of the church stood the barracks, a two-story building with a balcony. This house (SRL 316), which is still standing, was begun around 1837 by Vallejo for his soldiers and was occupied by American troops from 1846 to 1848. Now a part of Sonoma State Historic Park, it is used as a museum of local history.

The Toscano Hotel next door is the state park headquarters. First called the Eureka when it was built in the 1850s, it became the Toscano in the 1890s when many Italians immigrated into Sonoma. This is a wood-frame, two-story building.

Next to the barracks, a large two-story adobe mansion, known as the Casa Grande, was put up soon after the founding of Sonoma. Here General Vallejo lived during the years preceding California's annexation to the United States. The Vallejo adobe had a balcony extending across the front, and on the southwest corner there was a tall square tower, giving a view on all the surrounding country. Eleven of Vallejo's children were born here. Only the long, low adobe in the rear, used as a kitchen and as a servants' quarters, survived a fire in 1867; it can be seen today as one of the park buildings.

Other adobes were gradually built around the open plaza. A few of these remain today, some of them encased in wood but still retaining the picturesque Spanish balconies. One of these is the Leese-Fitch adobe at 487 First Street West. Jacob Leese was an Ohioan who came to California in 1834, did business in Yerba Buena, became a naturalized Mexican citizen, and married a sister of General Vallejo in 1837. A trader in hides and tallow, he was one of the first businessmen in Sonoma. He was taken prisoner along with the Vallejos at the time of the Bear Flag uprising in 1846; later he was the alcalde of Sonoma. The house was headquarters for General Persifer F. Smith during the American occupation, was briefly an academy for young ladies, and has been a private residence with a succession of owners for many years.

Salvador Vallejo, brother of the general, first lived in Sonoma due west of the Casa Grande. He built a new home at 411 First Street West in 1840 and moved in with his bride, María de la Luz Carrillo, sister of the general's wife. The home was torn down and replaced by the Sebastiani Apartments in 1938. Another building of Salvador Vallejo's is now the Swiss Hotel (SRL 496) at 18 West Spain Street. This has been a hotel since 1882. What is now called the Salvador Vallejo Adobe (SRL 501) is next to his first house, at 415–17 First Street West. Only the ground floor is adobe; what lies above is later wooden building. At one time (1858–64) it was a Presbyterian coeducational boarding school, and after that (1880s) a winery. All of these buildings face the plaza.

Since the raising of the Bear Flag here in 1846, the plaza has seen many changes. In the 1870s the plaza was a treeless open area crossed by paths, and its perimeter was flanked by buildings of one or two stories. In 1880, the Sonoma Valley Railroad laid tracks down Spain Street to the plaza, where the company built a depot and a roundhouse. By 1890, the railroad property had been removed north to what is now Depot Park, and the Ladies Improvement Club (later the Sonoma Valley Women's Club) began a successful campaign to make the plaza into a park-like area. The Sonoma City Hall was built in the center of the plaza in 1906–8; architect A. C. Lutgets of San Francisco designed the unusual Mission Revival building so that all four facades were identical. The Sonoma Plaza has been designated a National Historical Landmark.

The Blue Wing Inn (SRL 17) is opposite the mission at 133 East Spain Street. In the years after the American conquest, it was the principal hostelry of town, with Generals Grant, Sherman, Hooker, and Frémont among its guests. It houses retail merchandise today after a major restoration. The site of the Union Hotel and Union Hall (SRL 627) is marked by a plaque across from the southwest corner of the plaza.

Other old adobe buildings stand at some distance from Sonoma's plaza. The John G. Ray house, at 205 East Spain Street, was built around 1847. The Nash Adobe (SRL 667), at 579 First Street East, was built about the same year by H. A. Green. John H. Nash was the first American to be alcalde of Sonoma during the Mexican regime. He was living here in July 1847 when Lieutenant William T. Sherman of the U. S. Army arrested him because he refused to turn over his office to the American-appointed alcalde, Lilburn W. Boggs. Nancy Patton, a survivor of the Donner party, and her husband, San Francisco merchant Lewis Adler, purchased the house in 1848, and it was carefully restored in 1931 by Nancy's great-granddaughter Zolita Bates. Today this privately owned dwelling looks much as it originally did, as does another old adobe, "La Casita" at 143 West Spain Street.

The Vasquez house in the El Paseo Complex off East First Street is one of the first wooden frame houses in Sonoma. Built for General Joseph Hooker, it first stood across the plaza on West First Street and was moved to its present location to serve as the headquarters for the Sonoma League for Historic Preservation.

North on West First Street is the old Sonoma Valley Railway Depot in Depot Park. Relocated here from the plaza in 1890, it eventually became the Sonoma Valley Historical Society Museum, devoted to preserving the artifacts of the region.

In Sonoma's Mountain Cemetery is the grave of the only known veteran of the American Revolutionary War to be buried in California. Captain William Smith, who joined the Virginia Navy as a boy of eleven in 1779, died in Sonoma in 1846. A plaque on his grave was placed by the Daughters of the American Revolution in 1965.

THE BEAR FLAG REVOLT

As 1846 began, official relations between the governments of the United States of America and the Republic of Mexico were strained. The recent American acquisition of Texas, which had declared its independence from Mexico in 1836, reminded Mexican officials of the powerful American presence on its borders, and skirmishes had taken place between Mexican and American forces in the Rio Grande Valley. Early that year, Captain John C. Frémont and a party of soldiers appeared near the capital at Monterey and threatened Mexican rule there, a story told in the San Benito County chapter. Many American settlers in the Sacramento Valley and neighboring areas believed they were in danger of being driven from the country by the commander of the Mexican army, General José Castro. Although no one in California at the time could have known the precise timing of events, on May 13, 1846 Congress approved President James K. Polk's request for a formal declaration of war against Mexico. Frémont's small force was still within Alta California at the time, and would soon take over Sutter's Fort at Sacramento.

On June 14, 1846, a group of thirty-three men surprised General Vallejo at Sonoma and took possession of the town. Although Vallejo had always been friendly toward Americans, he, his brother Salvador, and a few others were taken to Sutter's Fort, where they were imprisoned for two months. William B. Ide was left in command of the rebel forces at Sonoma. Vallejo remained on good terms with the new regime, and in 1849 was a member of the Monterey convention to make a constitution for the new State of California.

Since the action of the insurgents did not represent

the United States government, the Stars and Stripes could not be raised in place of the Mexican flag. The Bear Flag of the California Republic was therefore created. "California Republic" was written in black above a red border along its base. The banner had a white field with emblems of a bear and a star. (Texas, the "Lone Star Republic," had been isolated between 1836 and 1845, an episode certainly fresh in American memories.) A slightly modified version of this flag was adopted as the California State Flag by the Legislature in 1911. The original Bear Flag, which was on display in San Francisco, was destroyed in the fire of 1906.

The Bear Flag Monument (SRL 7), a bronze statue representing a young pioneer holding the staff of the Bear Flag, which floats above him, was placed on the Sonoma plaza and dedicated on June 14, 1915. A bas-relief on the face of the pedestal shows the raising of the Bear Flag in 1846; nearby, the modern Bear Flag is flown daily.

MARIANO G. VALLEJO AND HIS LANDS

Mariano Guadalupe Vallejo, born on July 4, 1807, was the son of Ignacio Vallejo and his wife, María Antonia Lugo, who lived in Monterey County. His schoolmates at Monterey included Juan B. Alvarado and José Castro. A military career being his choice, he entered the Monterey Company in 1823 and was promoted to *alferez*, or ensign, in San Francisco in 1827. In 1830 he was elected to the *diputación*, and in 1832 he married Francisca Benicia, daughter of Joaquín Carrillo. José Figueroa, governor of Alta California from 1833 to 1835, chose Vallejo *comisionado* to secularize Mission San Francisco Solano and to establish the town of Sonoma. In compensation for his services, the governor gave him large tracts of land north of San Francisco Bay and in 1835 a plot of ground in the new town of Sonoma.

With his ability and experience, Vallejo was the outstanding native Californian of his day. Advanced to the rank of colonel in 1836, he assumed the position of commander general, and eventually persuaded the Mexican government to unite the military and civil leadership in the north into a single officer. In 1842 he turned over his command to Governor Micheltorena. Rancho Soscol, a large area in Solano County, was granted to him. His principal residence was at Rancho Petaluma, the ten leagues of which were granted to him by Governor Micheltorena in 1842; in the following year he received five additional leagues. The large holding was confirmed by U.S. patent in 1874.

Home of General Mariano Vallejo, Sonoma

Between 1834 and 1844 he built a house on the rancho that was the grandest in northern California. The adobe walls are three feet thick, and the framework is constructed of beams hewn from solid trees and bound together with strong rawhide thongs. The house is in a large U shape, with a patio open on the south side; it is two stories in height, with broad balconies around the second story. Now it is the Petaluma Adobe State Historic Park (SRL 18), given to the state in 1951 by the Native Daughters of the Golden West; they had acquired the property from the heirs of William D. Bliss, the second owner of the property after Vallejo sold it in 1857. The restoration of the building is deservedly praised for its authenticity, and it is frequently cited as the finest example of adobe building in the Mexican period in California.

General Vallejo purchased a part of Rancho Agua Caliente along Sonoma Creek west of the town of Sonoma. Thaddeus M. Leavenworth, who had come to California as chaplain of Stevenson's regiment of New York Volunteers in 1847, owned the part of the rancho that lay between the town and Vallejo's land. The general put up a frame house on his property (SRL 4) in 1850. It was prefabricated in the eastern United States and, with two others, was shipped around the Horn. Vallejo called his home Lachryma Montis ("tears of the mountain") because of the large hot and cold springs in the nearby hillside. He lived there many years before his death in 1890, and his burial place is on a hillside north of Sonoma very near his home. In the immediate vicinity of the home is a building called the Swiss Chalet. It is made of brick and wood, the lumber also having been brought around the Horn. Lachryma Montis and the Swiss Chalet, together with the surrounding seventeen acres of land, were purchased in 1933 by the State Parks Commission. The Vallejo Home is a part of Sonoma

State Historical Park and is at the northern end of Third Street West; there is a small museum in the Swiss Chalet.

One old adobe still stands on Rancho Agua Caliente, the Justi home, about three miles southwest of Kenwood on Dunbar Road. Built around 1850, it was at one time the Glen Ellen post office. It is wood-covered today. In the same area, at 13255 Sonoma Highway, is Glen Oaks, a beautiful stone mansion built in 1860.

TEMELEC

One of the Bear Flaggers later settled about four miles southwest of Sonoma. In 1858 Captain Granville Perry Swift constructed Temelec Hall (SRL 237), a magnificent stone mansion, using Indian labor. Its cost was estimated at $250,000, the most expensive in the county at that time. It was for many years a private home, with about twenty large rooms and nine fireplaces, all with marble mantles. Today it is the clubhouse of a retirement community off Arnold Drive.

SANTA ROSA

Several tracts of land in Sonoma County were granted to relatives of General Vallejo's wife, Francisca Benicia Carrillo. These tracts included Rancho Cabeza de Santa Rosa, given to her widowed mother in 1837; Rancho Sotoyome, to Henry Fitch, a brother-in-law; Rancho Los Guilicos, to John Wilson, another brother-in-law; and Rancho Llano de Santa Rosa, to Joaquín Carrillo, a brother.

Both Fitch and his mother-in-law were residents of San Diego. Fitch continued to live in the south. Señora María Ignacia López de Carrillo moved to her Rancho Cabeza de Santa Rosa with her unmarried children and lived there for the remainder of her life. The city of Santa Rosa is situated on part of her grant.

Her home was located on the south side of Santa Rosa Creek. One ruined building remains near the corner of Hartley Drive and Franquette Avenue, just north of Montgomery Drive, in eastern Santa Rosa. It is the oldest dwelling in Santa Rosa.

The name of Santa Rosa Creek was supposedly bestowed by Father Juan Amoros of San Rafael when he baptized an Indian girl there in honor of Saint Rose of Lima in the late 1820s. A marker along the highway on the north side of Santa Rosa Creek, roughly opposite the Carrillo adobe site, commemorates this event, but the baptism is not recorded either at San Rafael or Sonoma.

In 1853, the son Julio Carrillo filed a claim for part of his mother's property, two square leagues lying between Rancho San Miguel and Santa Rosa Creek. He built his house near the stream on a site that is now downtown Santa Rosa, on Second Street. He gave the land for the plaza where the old courthouse stood, between Third and Fourth Streets. The earthquakes of 1906 and 1989 did a great deal of damage to downtown Santa Rosa, the latter requiring the demolition and replacement of both the City Hall and the Courthouse. The county administrative center is now located north of the city, in a complex near Fountain Grove.

Santa Rosa benefited from the coming of the railroad in 1870. The first depot at Fourth and Wilson Streets was destroyed in a fire and rebuilt of local stone in 1904. It survived the 1906 quake. The Santa Rosa Bank was not so lucky, and its building at 37 Old Courthouse Square had to be pulled down and rebuilt. The Empire Building, which took its place, is a four-story building that has been identified with commerce and banking. The Sonoma County Museum is in the old post office building, now located at 425 Seventh Street, with changing and permanent displays on Sonoma County history.

A Santa Rosa landmark is the Church Built From One Tree. In 1873, a giant redwood near Guerneville was cut down, and the 78,000 board feet of lumber it produced went entirely into the construction of the First Baptist Church in Santa Rosa. The church was located for many years on B Street, but when the congregation moved to a new facility in 1957, the old building was moved to its present location at 492 Sonoma Avenue by Juilliard Park. Shortly thereafter, it became a museum devoted to the career of Robert L. Ripley, Santa Rosa's native son, whose "Believe It Or Not" was a newspaper feature for many years and who died in 1949. In addition to displays about Ripley and the old church, the museum has material on Santa Rosa and the neighborhood.

Ripley began his career as a cartoonist and died as a resident of New York state. Another great cartoonist was Charles M. Schulz, born in Minneapolis, who spent his later life in Santa Rosa, dying there in 1999. He is commemorated at several places in the city, often by his creations from "Peanuts": Charlie Brown, Lucy, and Snoopy.

LUTHER BURBANK HOME AND GARDENS

Luther Burbank, a brilliant botanist and agricultural pioneer, was born in Massachusetts in 1849. A student

Luther Burbank Home and Gardens, Santa Rosa

of nature from his earliest years, he desired a mild climate in which to work and purchased four acres of land in 1878 on the south edge of Santa Rosa. On this tract he grew specimens from many parts of the world and carried on extensive research in plant life. He developed marked improvements in certain fruits, vegetables, and flowers and, by hybridization, produced striking changes in size, form, and color. The Burbank potato first brought his name before the public. As time went on, more space was needed, and in 1885 he purchased eighteen acres near Sebastopol, where he established the Burbank Experimental Farm and where by planting large fields he was able to carry on more extensive experiments than before. He became known as "the Plant Wizard," and the results of his labors can be seen in orchards and gardens throughout the world. At his death in his late seventies, he left behind him an extraordinary record of accomplishment. He lies buried beneath a tree in his Santa Rosa garden.

After her husband's death in 1926, Mrs. Burbank, a woman many years younger than her husband, moved into the charming two-story cottage that, with its adjoining gardens, is now administered by the city of Santa Rosa at the corner of Sonoma and Santa Rosa Avenues (SRL 234). The Luther Burbank Home and Gardens have also been registered as a National Historic Landmark. There is a small museum of Burbank memorabilia in the old carriage house, and since Mrs. Burbank's death in 1977, the home has been open to the public for limited tours.

FOUNTAIN GROVE

At the northern edge of Santa Rosa, where Business Highway 101 joins the US 101 freeway, Fountain Grove stands as a memorial to one of the several utopian colonies that flourished in California in the late nineteenth century. Thomas Lake Harris, spiritualist leader of the Brotherhood of the New Life, moved some of his followers here from the East in 1875. Robert V. Hine writes that the Brotherhood of the New Life was "the product of ecclesiastical revolt, a deep feeling for social reform, Christianity, spiritualism, and Swedenborgianism mixed in the mind of Harris with later additions of Oriental mysticism and late nineteenth-century anti-monopoly socialism." Much of the 1,500 acres that Harris acquired was planted with vineyards. About thirty colonists, most of whom lived in a community house, thus supported themselves until 1891, at which time difficulties, including rumors of scandalous activities, caused the downfall of the colony. After the dispersal of the colonists, Kanaye Nagasawa, Harris's disciple, remained at Fountain Grove, of which he became the sole owner in the 1920s. Nagasawa managed the Fountain Grove Winery until his death in 1934. The community house burned long ago, but other buildings remain, including an interesting round barn. The area has been extensively developed in the 1990s as a light industry and recreational park as well as a large residential tract.

RANCHO SOTOYOME AND
ALEXANDER VALLEY

Henry Delano Fitch, a dashing young sea captain from Massachusetts, met Josefa Carrillo upon his arrival in San Diego in 1826. They planned on marriage three years later, but the groom's foreign status (despite the approval of the bride's parents) created such problems that the couple decided to elope. A document in the Bancroft Library gives the wedding date as January 18, 1831, in Valparaiso, Chile. The pair found difficulties when they eventually returned to California, and Fitch was asked to give "a bell of at least fifty pounds in weight for the church at Los Angeles," which he did. Thereafter he lived in San Diego, where he kept a store.

In 1841 Captain Fitch received a grant of three square leagues of land in Sonoma County, where his wife's sister and her husband, Mariano Vallejo, lived. Eight more leagues were added to Rancho Sotoyome in 1844. Instead of living on the property, Captain Fitch traveled north, inspected it, made arrangements for its upkeep, and returned to his business in the south. He sent an acquaintance, Cyrus Alexander, to live there and offered to give him, as remuneration, two leagues of land. Alexander, a trapper and trader, who had had reached San Diego in 1833, agreed. Alexander Valley, northeast

Watson School

of Healdsburg, is named for him. His old adobe was restored as a private home about 1970 and stands on the ranch at 8644 Highway 128, across the road from the old Alexander School, now also a private home. The Alexander Valley is famous today for some of the finest wines produced in California.

On the southwestern boundary of Rancho Sotoyome, six miles south and west of Healdsburg, is the hop kiln of the former Walters ranch, a tripartite structure dating from 1902–4 (SRL 893). Located at 6050 Westside Road, it remains as a monument to what was once a major hop-growing center of the United States. This area of the Russian River Valley is now an important vineyard region, and the building has been transformed into the Hop Kiln Winery.

RANCHOS OF THE RUSSIAN RIVER

In 1836 a tract of land along the Russian River was granted to Juan Bautista Cooper, who, after a seafaring life, settled in Monterey, where he met and married Encarnación Vallejo. When Mariano Vallejo, Cooper's brother-in-law, returned to Monterey from an official visit to Bodega and Fort Ross, he told Cooper of the productive region he had seen. The area lying between the Estero Americano on the coast and the Russian River was then inhabited by only a few Russians and Indians. Vallejo encouraged Cooper to make a tour of inspection. This Cooper did and obtained a grant of four leagues along the Russian River in exchange for two tracts previously held by him on the American River.

On his new grant he built a sawmill in 1834, and called the tract Rancho El Molino. The sawmill, believed to be the first power-operated commercial sawmill in California, was actually put up two years before the grant became official. The site (SRL 835) of Cooper's

mill is about two miles north of Forestville on Mark West Creek, where floods in the winter of 1840–41 destroyed the mill. The state marker is at the corner of Mirabel and River Roads, near Mirabel Park, eight miles west of Santa Rosa. No buildings or sites remain from three other ranchos established in the region between Estero Americano and the Russian River. Ranchos Estero Americano, Cañada de Pogolimi, and Cañada de Jonive were granted to Americans recommended by Cooper. In 1858, the latter was patented to Jasper O'Farrell, who is remembered for having laid out the streets of San Francisco.

RANCHO BODEGA

Rancho Bodega, consisting of eight square leagues on the coast between Estero Americano and the Russian River, was granted to Stephen Smith by Governor Micheltorena in 1844. When the land was confirmed in 1859 and patented to the heirs of the grantee, the more than 35,000 acres claimed were accepted by the court as being "the same land described in the grant to Stephen Smith (now deceased)."

Smith, a native of Maryland who visited California in 1841, came from Peru, where he had spent a little time. On this visit, he made plans to return to California after a trip east and to set up a sawmill. The mill machinery was brought from Baltimore and set up in the redwood region east of Bodega Head. Although confident that the country would eventually belong to the United States, Smith obtained Mexican citizenship in order to become a landowner. Within two years after receiving the grant of Rancho Bodega, he had the pleasure of raising the American flag over his property. The eastern boundary line of his rancho lay a little way to the east of his mill, which was placed to the north of Salmon Creek. His house stood near the creek and north of the Estero Americano, the boundary between Ranchos Bodega and Blucher, the latter of which lay partly in neighboring Marin County. To both of these tracts he laid claim, and both were awarded to his descendants.

A year after the death of Stephen Smith in 1855, his widow married another Southerner, Tyler Curtis. Squatters caused trouble, resulting in what is called the "Bodega War," and Curtis was forced to sell land, including an area that had been the site of the Russian settlement in 1811. The Curtis family moved to San Francisco, and in time Smith's adobe home succumbed to fire and erosion.

St. Teresa of Avila Catholic Church, Bodega

In the town of Bodega itself is the charming St. Teresa of Avila Catholic Church (SRL 820), built in 1859, a much-photographed white-painted frame building high on a hill.

RANCHOS LOS GUILICOS AND KENWOOD

John Wilson, who reached California in 1837 and married Ramona Carrillo, was the grantee of Rancho Los Guilicos (a fusion of Miwok and Spanish, which Gudde says means "dusty place"), containing 18,833 acres and given by Governor Alvarado. It was patented in the name of William Hood in 1866. Afterward it was owned jointly by Mrs. Wilson and Hood, who had purchased a part of it. Hood's old home (SRL 692), built of bricks fired on the property, still stands at 7501 Sonoma Highway, Santa Rosa. This rancho lies between Santa Rosa and Sonoma, the town of Glen Ellen being on its southern tip. The former railroad stations of Kenwood and Melita are on this old grant. In the old Pagani winery nearby, built in 1906, the Kenwood Vineyards Winery has been established.

RANCHO MALLACOMES AND KNIGHT'S VALLEY

This rancho, lying in the upper part of Knight's Valley, consisted of 17,742 acres granted in 1843 by Governor Mi-

cheltorena to José de los Santos Berryessa. The grantee was a soldier at Sonoma from 1840 to 1842 and alcalde there in 1846. Knight's Valley, in which the grant lay, was named for Thomas P. Knight, a native of Maine who came to California in 1845. After he reached the Sierra on his overland journey, an explosion of powder under his wagon destroyed all his possessions, including a stock of goods that he had planned to sell. He took part in the Bear Flag Revolt and then went to the mines before settling down as a farmer in Napa and Sonoma Counties.

Knight lived in the two-story adobe built by Berryessa and made additions to it. A small part of the house still stands beside a newer dwelling in Knight's Valley, about seven and one-half miles northeast of Calistoga (Napa County) on SR 128, on the east side of the highway three-tenths of a mile south of the intersection of Franz Valley Road.

RANCHO COTATI

Rancho Cotati, granted to Juan Castañeda in 1844, was patented to Thomas Page in 1858. "Cotati" recalls the name of a local Indian chieftain. Its 17,238 acres lay to the south of Santa Rosa. The Northwestern Pacific Railway passed through it early in the twentieth century, and the station of Cotati is in the southwestern corner of the rancho. Cotati's hexagonal town plan was designed in the 1890s by Newton Smyth as an alternative to the traditional grid. (Detroit, Michigan, is the only other American city known to have a hexagonal street pattern.) Each of the streets surrounding the six-sided town plaza (SRL 879), where Dr. Page's barn once stood, is named after one of his sons.

HEALDSBURG

The valley of the Russian River was home to thousands of the Pomo Indian people when the white settlers arrived. As elsewhere in California, diseases brought by the newcomers soon devastated the indigenous population, beginning with the smallpox epidemic of 1837. It has been estimated that upwards of ten thousand Pomo villagers lived in the area in the 1830; only twelve were recorded in 1916.

Much of this region became part of Rancho Sotoyome. As the quarrel between the squatters and the widow Fitch erupted following Captain Fitch's death in 1849, disputes over rightful ownership of land became frequent. Thanks to the support of a pioneer lawyer,

Colonel L. A. Norton, Mrs. Fitch was ultimately confirmed in her title to most of her property, and the squatters, many of whom had already settled and begun farming, bought and paid for their land.

One such settler was Ohio-born Harmon Heald, who had come to the area with his brothers in 1850 after a failed attempt at gold mining. Heald noted the advantageous location of that part of Rancho Sotoyome bordering the trail between San Francisco and the northern mines. In 1851 he built a cabin along this route at what is today the 300 block of Healdsburg Avenue. He added a store the following year and opened a post office in 1854. Buying up what land he could, he obtained title to it when the Fitch claim was cleared, and in 1857 he officially subdivided and laid out a town he named Healdsburg. He donated lots for a central park, a school, a cemetery, and churches; the remaining lots were sold for $15 apiece.

The town was incorporated in 1867, eight years after Heald's death. With the arrival of the Northwestern Pacific Railroad in 1871, Healdsburg began to flourish as an agricultural exporting center; winemaking is still a major activity of the city.

Healdsburg's plaza remains a center of activity. It is bordered by many well-preserved buildings, such as the old Schwab Brothers Store at 113 Plaza Street, built in 1883, and two structures from 1885, the Gobbi Building at 312 Center Street and the Cook Hardware Building next door at 318. Healdsburg also has some well-preserved homes, of which the John Hassett house (1853) at 239 Center is the oldest known. Two interesting Greek Revival homes, both built in 1871, are the Polly Reynolds house at 105 Fitch Street and the Samuel Meyer house at 308 Tucker Street. An earlier Greek Revival house (1854) is associated with the name of Lindsay Carson, brother of Kit Carson, who settled here in the 1850s and 1860s. The building is now a law office at 641 Healdsburg Avenue. The Healdsburg Museum is located at 221 Matheson Street, in a former Carnegie library building.

PETALUMA

The Petaluma River, actually a slough, runs northward from San Pablo Bay to the present-day city of Petaluma. It is thought that its first recorded ascent was by a Spanish expedition under Ferdinand Quiros in 1776. In 1819, Father Mariano Payéras visited what he called the Llano de los Petalumas ("Plain of the Petaluma people"). Mariano Vallejo began the construction of his impressive adobe nearby in 1834.

It was the river that determined the placement of the city of Petaluma. Hunters' camps and trading posts to supply the gold miners appeared on its banks in 1849. The valley became an important source of grain, exported to San Francisco. Waterborne commerce between San Francisco and Petaluma thrived until August 1950, when the last steamer, *Petaluma*, made her final mooring at Gold Landing in McNear Canal. In addition to cereal and vegetable crops, Petaluma became known for its poultry. In 1879 L. C. Byce won a gold medal at the California State Fair for his new incubator and soon thereafter began to make in Petaluma the brooders and incubators that made the mass production of poultry both possible and profitable. In 1918, Bert Kerrigan, secretary of the Petaluma Chamber of Commerce, dubbed the town "The Egg Basket of the World." "Chicken Is King" was a later publicity motto, around 1938. Such slogans nurtured the image of Petaluma as the Chicken Town.

Petaluma today is a more diversified place. Along North Petaluma Boulevard and Kentucky and Fourth Streets are a number of old commercial buildings. The "Iron Front" buildings from the 1880s and 1890s are outstanding examples of prefabrication; their factory-made fronts, usually of cast or sheet iron, were made in San Francisco and then shipped to Petaluma. The 1906 earthquake, so destructive to Santa Rosa and San Francisco, spared Petaluma, and consequently many of these buildings are unaltered from their original design. On the south side of Western Avenue, between Kentucky Street and North Petaluma Boulevard, is a matchless row of iron fronts, including the Masonic Hall, the former Arcade Saloon, the New Model Saloon, and the Mutual Relief Building. The smaller, graceful iron front of the McNear building (1886) can be seen where North Petaluma Boulevard bends at Center Park. Extending west for some blocks on D Street west of Fourth is an attractive row of houses from many different periods. The Petaluma Museum is housed in the old Carnegie library building at the corner of Fourth and B Streets.

THE VINEYARD OF COLONEL HARASZTHY

Wine grapes from Europe were first grown successfully in Sonoma County, which is now an area of exceptionally productive vineyards and wineries. Agoston Haraszthy, a Hungarian nobleman who has often been called "the father of wine making in California," attempted first to ripen grapes from his imported stock at Crystal Springs in San Mateo County in 1852, but this was a failure. Looking for a proper climate and soil for his purpose, he moved to the sheltered Sonoma Valley, where General Vallejo had already made one variety of wine from the ordinary mission grape.

In 1856 Colonel Haraszthy purchased a piece of land east of the town of Sonoma that became known as the Buena Vista Vineyard and placed his son Attila in charge. In 1857 he employed Chinese labor to dig a tunnel into the hillside, where he stored five thousand gallons of wine as an initial vintage. This tunnel was followed by another in 1858 and a third in 1862. In that year the first stone cellar was built of rock excavated from the tunnels. Another and larger cellar, also with three tunnels, was begun in 1864. In 1862 Haraszthy's winery was the first in the world to use California redwood for wine tanks. Redwood tanks are now standard storage for wines in many areas. The old cellars (SRL 392) may still be seen at the Buena Vista Winery at the end of Old Winery Road, two miles northeast of Sonoma.

In 1861, Governor Downey appointed a committee to report on the ways and means of improving viticulture in California. One member of the committee was Colonel Haraszthy, who went to Europe and brought home cuttings of every obtainable variety. One of these, the Zinfandel of much-disputed origin, later became a major California product. He lost most of his land through business reverses. His Palladian villa on the grounds of the Bartholomew Park Winery at 1000 Vineyard Lane, burned in a fire, has been recreated as the Wine Country Museum. In 1868, the colonel went to Nicaragua, where his mysterious disappearance was reported the following year; it is supposed that he met his death while crossing a river.

Arpad Haraszthy, his son, went to Europe in 1857 to be educated. After having spent two years in the study of wine making, particularly the making of champagne, and in visiting vineyards and wineries, he returned to California. Years of experimental work were necessary before he was satisfied with the champagne made under conditions in the West. Arpad Haraszthy was the first president of the California Viticultural Commission. Both he and his brother Attila Haraszthy married daughters of General Vallejo.

The Sebastiani Winery (SRL 739) at Fourth Street East near Spain Street is another interesting Sonoma winery. Around 1900, Samuele Sebastiani purchased the original vineyard of Mission San Francisco Solano, first planted in 1825. It was here that General Vallejo, af-

ter the secularization of the mission, produced many prizewinning wines. The Gundlach-Bundschu Winery at the end of Thornberry Road was begun in 1858.

THE ITALIAN SWISS COLONY AT ASTI

The Italian Swiss Agricultural Colony (SRL 621) was organized in 1881 under the leadership of Andrea Sbarboro. Its membership consisted of 100 immigrants living in San Francisco who had been thrown out of work by hard times. The colony settled at the Truett Ranch, 1,500 acres along the Russian River four miles south of Cloverdale. In 1887 a substantial concrete winery was built, which for decades produced inexpensive wine that was locally famous. It has not been in production for some time, but the large facility still stands at Asti, just east of US 101.

CLOVERDALE

Cloverdale, in the Russian River valley at the northern edge of the county, was famous early in the twentieth century for its citrus crops; it is the most northerly point in the state where citrus fruit is grown. Each February the town has a well-attended Citrus Festival. An interesting museum of local history is maintained by the Cloverdale Historical Society at 215 North Cloverdale Boulevard.

Three miles south of Cloverdale, on Bluxome Creek, the short-lived Icaria-Speranza Community (SRL 981) was established in 1881. This was the only French utopian ("Icarian") colony founded in California. Like other Icarian communities started in Iowa and in the Mississippi Valley in the 1870s, this one believed in liberty, brotherhood, and freedom, as well as the importance of marriage, family life, and education. By 1887 the colony was dissolved, thanks to unfavorable litigation and the impossibility of keeping it a French-speaking organization so far from home.

JACK LONDON STATE HISTORIC PARK

On a wooded hillside overlooking the orchards and vineyards of the Valley of the Moon is the ranch of Jack London, author of *The Call of the Wild*, *The Sea-Wolf*, and other tales of adventure, as well as of social criticism. Although he was often elsewhere for months at a time, London lived here from 1905 until his death in 1916 at the age of forty. His widow, Charmian, continued to live on the property, and in 1919 she built the

"House of Happy Walls" of native fieldstone as a memorial to her husband. Although the Sonoma Valley had been called the Valle de la Luna as early as 1841, Jack London's writings made the name "Valley of the Moon" world famous.

In 1959 Irving Shephard, nephew of Jack London and heir of Charmian London, gave forty acres of the ranch to the state of California. This includes Charmian's home, now a museum of Jack London artifacts, and the author's grave, marked by a red lava boulder and close to the graves of two pioneer children that were on the land when London bought it. By far the most unusual landmark, however, is the ruined "Wolf House," which was to have been the Londons' permanent home and was nearly completed when it burned on September 13, 1913. Although London hoped to rebuild, nothing was done except to clear away debris. The remaining four-story exterior, with its archways, chimneys, and staircases built of native volcanic stone, is one of California's most-photographed historic spots.

Jack London State Historic Park (SRL 743) has expanded to include the author's "Beauty Ranch," which is next to the forty acres of the original grant. At this ranch, London built experimental (and expensive) quarters for his livestock; the stallion barn and the circular "pig palace" can still be seen. "The Cottage" where London died on November 22, 1916, is also on the property. A short distance northwest of Glen Ellen, the park has been registered by the Department of the Interior as a National Historic Landmark.

MOUNT ST. HELENA

Mount St. Helena is at the point where Sonoma, Lake, and Napa Counties meet. On one of the northwest spurs of the mountain, seven miles in a straight line northeast of Geyserville, are the Geysers, while near its southern slope, partly in Napa County and partly in Sonoma, lies the Petrified Forest—indications of the mountain's volcanic origin.

The mountain was named in honor of the patron saint of Russia by Princess Helena de Gagarin. The princess, wife of Count Alexander Rotcheff, governor-general of Siberia and of the Russian colonies on the shores of the North Pacific, had read the fascinating descriptions of California made by the great navigator Otto Kotzebue. Arriving at Fort Ross in 1841, she organized an expedition into the interior of California that included the first recorded ascent of the peak, which she and her companions made on June 20 of that year.

In May 1853 a tablet placed on Mount St. Helena twelve years before was found by Dr. T. A. Hylton of Petaluma. It was later displayed in the museum of the Society of California Pioneers in San Francisco, only to be destroyed in the fire of 1906. Dr. Hylton had made a paper facsimile of the tablet, from which a replica was made in 1912. The replica was placed on the summit of Mount St. Helena in commemoration of the centenary of the founding of Fort Ross.

THE GEYSERS

The native peoples believed that the Great Spirit dwelling within the mountain worked miracles, and their sick went to the healing springs and hot-water jets that welled up in the vicinity of the Geysers. In April 1847 the pioneer hunter and trapper William B. Elliott came suddenly upon the region while tracking a wounded bear. Back in Sonoma, he told his friends that he had found the gates to the Inferno.

The Geysers became a tourist attraction, and in 1854 an inn was built nearby, which registered twenty visitors its first year. A larger hotel, built from lumber sawed on the spot, was put up in 1857–58. Its register displayed the signatures of Presidents Ulysses S. Grant, William McKinley, and Theodore Roosevelt, as well as those of Giuseppe Garibaldi, Horace Greeley, Mark Twain, J. Pierpont Morgan, and William Jennings Bryan. The hotel was destroyed by fire in 1937.

The Geysers are now closed to the public, and there is little to be seen at the end of the long roads twisting up the mountain. The region is operated as a source of geothermal power by the Calpine Corporation of San Jose and some other firms. In 2001, Calpine opened its Geothermal Visitor Center at Middletown in Lake County.

THE PETRIFIED FOREST

Surrounded by groves of living oak, fir, and redwood, the Petrified Forest lies across a small valley from the southwestern base of Mount St. Helena at an elevation of 1,000 feet. The petrified trees that form the group are mainly redwoods, silicified and opalized. They lie in two tiers in a parallelogram a mile in extent from east to west and about a quarter of a mile from north to south. The trees, measuring from three and one-half to twelve feet in diameter and as much as 126 feet in length, were buried millions of years ago by lava from the now-extinct volcano five miles to the north. The fact that the trees are lying with their tops pointing away from Mount St. Helena seems to indicate that lava streams from the cone caused their downfall and their ultimate preservation in forms of stone.

The forest was discovered in the 1850s, but excavation was not begun until 1870, when the prospector Charles Evans, "Petrified Charlie," homesteaded the land. Much of the brush, volcanic ashes, and deposits of silica that had pressed upon the trees for ages was removed by Evans, who enclosed the ground and charged a small fee to visitors, one of whom was Robert Louis Stevenson. In his book *The Silverado Squatters* (1880) Stevenson wrote a more detailed description of the proprietor than of the property, which is still a privately owned tourist attraction.

In all the specimens found in this ancient stone forest, the transmutation from wood to stone has been so perfect that texture and fiber are completely preserved, making it easy for scientists to determine species. Many of the trees are of great size and, though broken, retain the relative positions of the pieces. The largest tree in the group was uncovered in 1919 at a depth of ninety feet. It lies intact and is one of the most perfect specimens known. In 1930 Professor Erlingdorf of Princeton University found twelve varieties of prehistoric fossilized leaves on the property.

The Petrified Forest (SRL 915) can be reached by leaving US 101 at Santa Rosa on Mark West Springs Road and continuing twelve miles northeast on this road and its extensions, Porter Creek Road and Petrified Forest Road. It lies very close to the Napa county line, and is five miles west of Calistoga on Petrified Forest Road.

En route from Santa Rosa is Mark West Lodge, now a restaurant. Mineral hot springs were discovered here by William Travis in 1857, and the place was operated as a resort for many years.

Stanislaus County

Stanislaus County was named for the river that forms part of its border with San Joaquin County to the north. The river was named for an Indian chief who was baptized by the padres with the Spanish name Estanislao, for a Polish saint, either Stanislaus Kostka or Stanislaus of Krakow. The county was organized in 1854 from a part of Tuolumne County, and the first county seat was placed at Adamsville. Within a few months the seat of justice was moved to Empire City; in December 1855 it was transferred to La Grange; in 1862 to Knight's Ferry; and in 1871 it was finally located at Modesto.

THE STANISLAUS RIVER AND ESTANISLAO'S STORY

The Stanislaus is one of the major rivers flowing from the Sierra Nevada into the San Joaquin Valley. It is one of the few "wild" rivers in California, which means that for most of its length it is not barred by dams or reclamation projects. The first explorer to arrive at the Stanislaus was Gabriel Moraga, who discovered it in 1806 while on one of his expeditions through the river country of the north in search of mission sites. He explored it again in 1808 when he crossed, for the second time, all the Sierra rivers as far north as the upper Sacramento, and discovered the territory of at least ten additional counties. In 1810 he again passed through the country watered by the Stanislaus, in an unsuccessful attempt to capture runaway Indians.

Estanislao was such an Indian. Baptized at Mission San José, he was educated by Padre Narciso Durán, and one story says that he was especially proficient in music. In 1827 or 1828 he ran away from the mission and took refuge in the San Joaquin Valley, where he became a leader of the Indian people. The Mexican authorities believed that he and his followers were preparing a general uprising, and two military expeditions were sent out against them. Both were ineffective, but a third, led by twenty-one-year-old Ensign Mariano Vallejo in 1829, brought defeat to Estanislao and his people. The site of the battle (SRL 214) is in San Joaquin County, near Ripon, on the north bank of the Stanislaus River, which seems to have been named around this time for the fighting chieftain.

Estanislao somehow made peace with Father Durán and returned to the mission, which he soon left, but to which he again returned. In the late 1830s he died in an epidemic that nearly destroyed the remaining Indian community at Mission San José. For one who made an impact on California's history, Estanislao has not been well remembered. Richard J. Orsi notes that the E Clampus Vitus marker at Caswell Memorial State Park (San Joaquin County), "Estanislao's Stronghold," depicts him in the dress of a Great Plains warrior rather than that of a native Californian.

THE HISTORIC WEST SIDE OF THE SAN JOAQUIN VALLEY

El Camino Viejo, the old road of the Spanish and Mexican periods, followed the west side of the San Joaquin Valley and crossed many creeks that are known today by their Spanish names. Among those in Stanislaus County are Arroyo de las Garzas ("the herons"); Arroyo de Orestimba ("the meeting place," so called because the padres, when first gathering Indian neophytes in the region, made an agreement with the remaining natives to meet them there again the following year); Arroyo Salado Grande ("big salty creek," where the pioneer known as "Salty" Smith settled in 1855); Arroyo del Puerto ("the gate," so named because of the natural cut in the hills west of Patterson through which the creek flows in the rainy season); and Arroyo del Hospital (named for the experience of a party of Spaniards who,

overcome by sickness, rested beside this stream and were healed).

Spanish settlement on the west side seems to have had an early beginning, for at least one Spaniard, a deserter from the cavalry, settled on Arroyo de las Garzas as early as 1820. A battle took place in the vicinity that year, when a detachment of Spanish troops came to get both the fugitive soldier and some Indians who had run away from the missions. American pioneers in 1852 found the mestizo son of this former cavalryman living in an adobe on Arroyo de las Garzas just across the line in Merced County several miles west of the present town of Gustine.

Above the sycamore grove on Arroyo de Orestimba stood the ranch house of Rancho Orestimba y las Garzas, granted in 1844 to Sebastián Núñez, a son-in-law of Francisco Pacheco.

Jesse Hill, one of the owners of Hill's Ferry on the San Joaquin River, settled on the Arroyo de las Garzas in 1854, where he built a house from lumber brought around the Horn and hauled to Las Garzas by ox team. The site was later occupied by one of the Simon Newman Company sheep camps.

HILL'S FERRY

A ferry across the San Joaquin River at the site later known as Hill's Ferry was first operated in the autumn of 1849, when a man named Thompson carried emigrants from Mexico across the river at this point. Jesse Hill and John de Hart later purchased the ferry from Thompson. After De Hart's death, Hill became the sole owner, until in 1865 the ferry passed into the hands of C .G. Hubner.

By this date the town of Hill's Ferry had achieved some importance as a shipping center for grain. During the high-water season, from April to July, boats customarily came up the river this far to exchange their cargoes for grain and other farm produce. But during the rest of the year the isolation of the town was complete. There was no telegraph service, and the mails had to be brought in by stage from Banta, a day's journey away. Nevertheless, during its heyday, Hill's Ferry was a lively place. Its very isolation infused it with a decidedly "Wild West" spirit. Horse thieves and outlaws found it a convenient crossing place en route to mountain hideouts. The place became noted for its tough characters, and there was much drinking, gambling, and shooting.

In 1886–87, at the time the west side railroad was being constructed, Simon Newman, who was the chief

STANISLAUS COUNTY

517

merchant at Hill's Ferry, donated some land to the railroad. When the town of Newman was laid out on this land in 1887, the people of Hill's Ferry and those living at Dutch Corners, two miles away, were induced to move to the new town. With this change Hill's Ferry literally ceased to exist, since most of the houses were carted away to other locations. The site of Hill's Ferry is on the west bank of the San Joaquin River about five miles northeast of Newman.

KNIGHT'S FERRY

Knight's Ferry (SRL 347), an old mining town and trading post on the Stanislaus River forty miles southeast of Stockton, was founded in the spring of 1849 by William Knight, an Indianan who was educated as a physician but in the West was a hunter and trapper. He first came to California with the Workman-Rowland party in 1841. The following year he brought his family from New Mexico, and in 1843 they settled on the banks of the Sacramento in Yolo County at a place still called Knight's Landing.

The first ferry to be established on the Stanislaus River was the one at Knight's Ferry, on the old Sonora Road from Stockton to the southern mines. As early as 1850 thousands of miners passed this way, when ferry receipts could scarcely have been less than $500 a day. The importance and prosperity of Knight's Ferry were further enhanced by the fact that the river bars and banks, hills and gulches, were rich in gold for miles in all directions. Above the ferry was Two Mile Bar, and below it was Keeler's Flat, where Keeler's Ferry, in the shadow of what is now called Lover's Leap, was started later in 1849.

After the death of William Knight in a shoot-out on November 9, 1849, John and Lewis Dent came into possession of the ferry. In 1854 it was superseded by a bridge built on the site of the present structure. During the same year the Dents and David Locke put up a gristmill and a sawmill on the riverbank some 300 yards above the ferry. In 1856 a town was laid out on the north bank of the river. This was referred to by some as Dentville, since by now three Dent brothers and their families lived there, but the name was always officially Knight's Ferry. The place continued to grow and prosper, and from 1862 to 1871 it was the county seat of Stanislaus County.

Knight's Ferry is still one of the most picturesque of the old river towns. Perhaps its most striking feature is a wooden covered bridge, built in 1863 to replace the

General Store, Knight's Ferry

bridge from 1854, which was destroyed in the flood of 1862. Stanislaus County purchased the bridge from a private owner in 1884 and made it toll free. The National Historic Preservation Act made it possible for the U.S. Army Corps of Engineers to acquire title to the bridge in 1985. The Corps manages it as well as nine recreation areas along a fifty-nine-mile stretch of the Stanislaus River. At 330 feet it is the longest covered bridge in the western United States. It is now open only for pedestrian traffic. The house built in 1851 by Lewis Dent, the oldest building in town, still stands on Ellen Street. The Dent's brother-in-law, U.S. Army Captain Ulysses S. Grant, who was stationed on the Pacific Coast while his wife, Julia Dent Grant, remained at home in Indiana, visited the house on three occasions between 1852 and 1854.

The general store on Main Street has been doing business steadily since it was constructed in 1852, making it the oldest continuously operating general store in California. Excepting regular holidays, it has been closed only once, for three days in the flood of 1955. The Isaac Dakin home (1853) and a modern replica of Dakin's smithy are other sights of the town. The Village Church was built in 1900 on the foundations of the original building of 1860 and was first known as the Knight's Ferry Methodist Episcopal Church. Another old building that has seen much service is the Masonic Hall, built in 1870 and still in use. Knight's Ferry is an outstanding example of an old town that is very much alive today, still flourishing around its well-preserved buildings. About two miles southeast on Willms Road is the headquarters of the Willms Ranch (SRL 415). John R. Willms, a German-born Forty-niner, and his partner, John H. Kappelmann, began to acquire land here in 1852 and eventually had 3,600 acres. Kappelmann died in 1881, and Willms carried on alone until,

Covered Bridge, Knight's Ferry

La Grange

at his death in 1910, the ranch totaled 8,600 acres. The present ranch house, built in 1892, replaced an earlier one destroyed by fire. Members of the Willms family still own the ranch and live on it.

LA GRANGE

La Grange was first known as French Bar, French miners having come to that region to prospect as early as 1852. Later the settlement was moved higher up on the bank of the Tuolumne River away from the original bar. By 1855 La Grange had become a thriving center of trade, since the bulk of the population in the county had moved up into the mining regions. The county seat was transferred from Empire City to La Grange in December 1855, and there it remained until 1862, when another contest took it to Knight's Ferry by a majority of only twenty-nine votes.

At the height of its prosperity, La Grange had from four to five thousand inhabitants and was served daily by three or more stage lines. During the 1870s extensive hydraulic operations were carried on in the vicinity, when ditches were built at a cost of $5 million to convey water to the diggings. The La Grange Dam near the Tuolumne county line was built in 1891–92 and today is part of the system of Stanislaus County reservoirs that supplies the Modesto and Turlock irrigation districts. The Tuolumne River is the life force of the region.

For several miles along the banks of the Tuolumne, thousands of rock mounds and pyramids stand as monuments to the prodigious efforts of early miners to harvest gold from the river's bed. The tiny town of La Grange has a very attractive setting on the Tuolumne River. The National Register of Historic Places includes the entire town in its listing, and the Stanislaus County Historical Society has marked historic spots. Most of

these are congregated at the east end of Main Street, by the modern fire department.

Several deserted old stone buildings, with heavy iron doors, can be seen in town. Among them is the oldest remaining structure in La Grange, the trading post built in 1850–51 by John Inman. The old jail was marked with a plaque by E Clampus Vitus in 1976. Part of the old adobe post office has been incorporated into a barn. The deserted Odd Fellows Hall is another landmark. On a bluff east of the town stands St. Louis Mission and its adjacent picturesque cemetery. A plaque commemorating La Grange (SRL 414) was placed by the Native Daughters of the Golden West in 1984 at SR 132 and San Pedro Dam Road.

A ferry was operated at La Grange, first by Nathan McFarland and later by Anthony McMillan, from the early 1850s until about 1880, when a bridge was built across the Tuolumne at this point. Two miles below the town, where the present highway bridge spans the river, is the site of Branch's Ferry, which George C. Branch operated from 1851 to 1862; this is now a boat-launching spot in La Grange Regional Park.

ADAMSVILLE AND EMPIRE CITY

When Adamsville, which was founded in 1849, was made the first county seat of Stanislaus County in 1854, there were so few buildings in the place that the initial session of court was held out-of-doors, under a large tree. Before many months the county government was moved to nearby Empire City, and Adamsville, on the south bank of the Tuolumne River, ceased to exist. E Clampus Vitus placed a plaque in 1990 at the corner of Jennings and Service Roads, a few miles southwest of Modesto, about one-half mile east of the site of Adamsville.

Empire City was originally situated on the Tuolumne River twenty miles from its mouth. It was laid out on the south side of the river by John G. Marvin, a lawyer from Boston, who later became the first California state superintendent of schools. Because it was at the head of navigation on the river, Empire City was made the Army supply station in 1851 for outlying forts, including Fort Miller and Fort Tejón. Floods nearly destroyed the place in 1852, but it was rebuilt and became the county seat after a hard political fight, only to have the seat of justice moved to La Grange little more than a year later. Today the cemetery is all that remains of the first Empire City, which had lost its importance some time before the later Empire City was laid out as a trade center for a growing farm community. The pioneer burial ground has been incorporated into Lakewood Memorial Park, about one mile south of the present town of Empire on Highway J-7; a plaque placed by the Native Daughters of the Golden West is at the entrance to the park. A monument (SRL 418) has been placed by E Clampus Vitus to the memory of the citizens of old Empire City, at the turnoff from the highway to the park.

TUOLUMNE RIVER FERRIES

There were a number of ferries up and down the Tuolumne that served as crossings to the Mariposa mines in the 1850s. Dickenson's Ferry, located below the present Roberts' Ferry Road Bridge about eight miles east of Waterford, was established in the early 1850s by Gallant Duncan Dickenson and developed into one of the most important stopping places on the old Fort Miller Road. Dickenson, who came overland with his family from Missouri in 1846, was an active, energetic man who engaged in many pioneer enterprises. Shortly after his arrival in California he became a member of Joseph Aram's garrison at Santa Clara, and in 1847 he built at Monterey what is said to be California's first brick house. The following year he mined for gold at Dickenson's Gulch in Tuolumne County, and from there he went to Stockton, where he built and operated a hotel and served as prefect of the San Joaquin District in 1849–50.

In 1862 John W. Roberts, who had come from Boston in 1849, purchased the properties at Dickenson's Ferry, which now became known as Roberts' Ferry. When the original Dickenson Hotel was destroyed by fire in 1865, Roberts immediately replaced it with a two-story brick structure, the lower story of which still stands near the river.

At Horr's Ranch, near Roberts' Ferry, an unsuccessful attempt was made in the 1860s by Dr. B. D. Horr to found the town of Horrsville, a name that probably never stood a chance of public acceptance. A little pioneer cemetery located near the present highway a half-mile north of the river and a half-mile west of Roberts' Ferry Road Bridge marks the approximate site of the town.

Among other early ferries on the Tuolumne was Salter and Morley's Ferry. Calvin Salter and his partner, I. D. Morley, took up ranch land two miles east of Dickenson's Ferry and four miles below Branch's Ferry. There they established a ferry, stage station, and post office. Salter's farm was on the river near the ford, while Morley's land occupied the site on which the Turlock Reservoir now stands.

TUOLUMNE CITY

Many development schemes throughout California in the early American days, 1846–56, came to naught. Newcomers with no knowledge of California learned, to their grief, that water and weather and soil conditions in the region paid no heed to the plans of the new entrepreneurs.

Among the several towns founded with great expectations along the Tuolumne River was Tuolumne City, located about three miles from the mouth of the river where it joins the San Joaquin. Paxson McDowell, its promoter, dreamed of great wealth when he established the town in the spring of 1850. Lots were staked out on a plot of 160 acres and were sold at high prices. Unfortunately, when summer came it was found that the river was too low for navigation, and the place soon became deserted.

In the middle 1860s Tuolumne City was revived as the center for a small farming community, and navigation on the river during high water was resumed. When nearby Modesto became the county seat in 1871, however, virtually all the inhabitants of Tuolumne City moved there, along with the newspaper that became the *Modesto Bee*.

A rival of this town existed for a time in Paradise, laid out in 1867 by John Mitchell on his ranch in Paradise Valley five miles east of Tuolumne City. A flour mill, a warehouse, and a number of stores were built. During Paradise's several years of prosperity, regular weekly and tri-weekly boat service from Stockton was maintained. But with the founding of Modesto, Paradise also came to an end. At least two houses still standing in Modesto were first erected in Paradise and brought into the new city: they are the Church home at 302 Burney Street and the house at 1016 Franklin Street, which has been in Modesto since 1870.

A. J. Grayson, in 1850, established a ferry on the San Joaquin River eight miles above the mouth of the Tuolumne, and a settlement known as Grayson grew up there. After 1852 the place was practically deserted for several years, although the ferry was still operated. In 1868, after the development of grain farming in the region, the place was surveyed and a town was laid out by J. W. Van Benschotten, who had purchased the ferry. A brisk upriver trade caused the place to flourish until the building of the west side railroad in the middle 1880s. Grayson today is a small town two miles northeast of Westley.

LANGWORTH AND BURNEYVILLE, OAKDALE AND RIVERBANK

The present towns of Oakdale and Riverbank, which date from the 1870s, are the successors of Langworth and Burneyville, respectively, which had been established before the coming of the railroad. Langworth, plotted as a town in 1860 by Henry Langworthy, was located on the Mariposa Road on the hill above the ferry owned by James Burney. Burney was a former sheriff of Mariposa County and a member of the Mariposa Battalion under Major James D. Savage in 1851. He moved down the river to begin Burneyville in 1867. When the railroad was run east of this site in 1871, the post office moved to the new town of Oakdale, and Langworth was finished. A plaque commemorating the town was placed by E Clampus Vitus at the junction of Langworth Road and SR 108, about three miles west of Oakdale. Oakdale has been an agricultural processing and shipping center for many years, as well as a stopover for travelers on the way to Yosemite from the San Francisco Bay Area.

At the corner of First and High Streets in Riverbank, an E Clampus Vitus marker notes that Burneyville was founded on the riverbank below the bluff by Major James Burney in 1867. Burney operated a second ferry at this point for a few years. He then served with distinction, in the words of the plaque, as "public servant, school superintendent and justice of the peace; Burney lived a full life [and] died [in] 1901 at the age of 87 years." The small community of Burneyville has been absorbed by the expanding town of Riverbank.

MODESTO

Modesto was a creation of the railroad. The Central Pacific reached the site in 1870, and it was two years before the next thrust down the San Joaquin Valley carried the line farther south and east. Although early accounts seem to agree that the railroad terminus was not an attractive spot, it was clear to many people that the future of Stanislaus County lay along this central route. Within a year the new community was chosen to be the county seat, even though accommodations were so few that the county offices were scattered among boarding houses, the back rooms of commercial buildings, and similar improvised quarters.

The explanation most often given for the distinctive name of the town—Modesto is Spanish for "modesty" —goes as follows. The directors of the Central Pacific named railroad stops for officials of the company or members of their families. The name of William C. Ralston was proposed for the new town, but the San Francisco banker declined the honor. The chosen name reflects his unusual modesty in so doing.

Modesto's early history is full of stories of Wild West hell-raising in saloons and dens of iniquity. Vigilantes frequently purged the undesirable elements, who returned after a short while. At the same time, the undeniable progress in agriculture and the prosperity brought by the railroad ensured that a more serious, permanent quality would eventually take over in the community. In 1912, the energetic Modesto Business Men's Association received permission to erect an ornamental iron arch at the intersection of Ninth and I Streets in what was then the commercial heart of town. (Other towns in the Central Valley, such as Lodi and Orland, made similar constructions.) Although the slogan to be written on the arch was originally NOBODY'S GOT MODESTO'S GOAT, sanity mercifully prevailed and the runner-up in the competition for the slogan— MODESTO: WATER WEALTH CONTENTMENT HEALTH— was chosen. It can be seen to this day, smartly embellished with electric lights at night, as the planners intended.

The McHenry Museum at 1402 I Street is housed in what was once the city library building, given to the city in 1912 by the McHenry family. Among its treasures are reconstructed offices, a large collection of guns and cattle brands from Stanislaus County, and a research and archive center for Modesto and Stanislaus County history. The McHenry Mansion, in which this prominent family lived, is nearby at Fifteenth and I

Streets. It has been restored to its Victorian grandeur, including the distinctive cupola on top, visible, it was said, for miles around when it was constructed in 1883. The museum and the mansion are open to the public on a regular basis.

PATTERSON

An interesting example of a planned community, Patterson was founded in 1909. Thomas W. Patterson, one of the heirs to his uncle's Rancho del Puerto, was impressed by the colonization projects in other parts of the Central Valley, which had brought many settlers into the region. His town was laid out in the shape of a wagon wheel, the streets converging on a plaza where

the Hotel Del Puerto was built. The hotel, built in 1910, was the first building in town, along with the office of the Patterson Ranch Company, which stands in the center of the plaza and is now the home of the Patterson City Museum. The Hotel del Puerto burned down in 1996.

The handsome palm-lined thoroughfare of Las Palmas Avenue, leading into the town from the west, was planted by Patterson. It is said that Patterson's avenue was made in emulation of Kearney Avenue in Fresno.

A complex irrigation project, bringing water from the San Joaquin River to the town, ensured its success, and within a few months of its establishment, Patterson was on the way to becoming a principal town on the west side of the San Joaquin Valley.

Sutter County

Sutter County, named in honor of John Augustus Sutter, was one of the original twenty-seven counties. During the first two years of its existence the county seat went to four towns in succession: Oro, Nicolaus, Auburn, and Vernon. Auburn was later included in Placer County when that county was created. The county seat was finally located at Yuba City, where it has remained.

SPANISH EXPEDITIONS

Gabriel Moraga explored the great inland valley of California several times. On his second expedition, in 1808, he ventured further north than he had gone on the expedition of 1806. His habit of naming every geographical feature he encountered caused much confusion later

on in California's history, when names were mixed up owing to the sketchiness of his records and those of other travelers. Moraga declared that the Feather River was the principal stream of the great northern valley and that the Sacramento was its principal tributary. It is true that at the point where the Sacramento and Feather come together it is the latter that makes a straight course north and south with the lower Sacramento, whereas the upper Sacramento flows in at that point from the west. The Moraga expedition also saw "a mountain range, in the middle of the valley"—surely the Sutter Buttes.

Interest in the great river country lagged for several years, but in 1817 the founding of missions in the interior was again urged by padre presidente Mariano Payéras. As a result, in May of that year, a voyage was made by boat up the Sacramento, probably as far as the mouth of the Feather River, or within sight of the Sutter Buttes. This expedition was led by Luís Argüello, accompanied by Father Narciso Durán and Father Ramón Abella.

THE SUTTER BUTTES

The Sutter Buttes are a short range of volcanic hills that rise abruptly from the level floor of the valley in northern Sutter County. They bear within their rugged declivities the same marks and fossils found in the Coast Range to the west. In the spring their slopes blossom with many wildflowers and shrubs. First discovered by the Spaniards, the Buttes were seen by Jedediah Strong Smith, in 1828, and by a Hudson's Bay Company trapper, Michel La Framboise, as well as others who followed after him. In the various documents relating to Sutter's Grant, these peaks were designated simply as "*los tres picos*," and John C. Frémont, who camped there from May 30 to June 8, 1846, spoke of them as "the three Buttes." A monument in Frémont's honor was placed three miles northwest of Sutter City in the South Pass of the Buttes on the old stage road to Colusa in 1923 by the Bi-County Federation of Women's Clubs of Sutter and Yuba Counties.

As settlers began to appear in the upper Sacramento Valley, the Buttes began to attract a few newcomers. Between the years 1861 and 1887, settlers clustered around three small settlements, known as North Butte, West Butte, and South Butte. In 1887, P. D. Gardameyer, who had recently married a local widow, announced from San Francisco plans for the Sutter County Land and Improvement Company. Centered around South Butte, now renamed Sutter City, the area had 200 buildings and 800 residents by 1890. Orchards and farmlands were to be developed along with the town. Gardameyer's most ambitious plan, Walt Anderson writes, "was for the Buttes themselves. He envisioned them as more than a picturesque backdrop to the new Sutter City. He imagined the south face of South Butte, the highest peak in the range, neatly terraced and built up as a luxury resort hotel, where clients could step out into an extensive game reserve for the sport of shooting the elk, deer, antelope, and other animals." Gardameyer's financial status was unstable, and he eventually abandoned the idea (and California, moving to Texas). The community of Sutter remains a small rural center, with most of the lands of the Buttes in private owner-

ship. In 1990 the area was the scene of a referendum, echoed elsewhere in California, about the desirability of "open space" land preservation. To date, the preservationists have prevailed. Most of the county's urban growth has been to the north of Yuba City, away from the Buttes.

CAMP BETHEL

Though no trace of its existence is to be seen now, Camp Bethel was once one of the largest of the old religious camp meetings in northern California. It was founded by Reverend George Baker in 1862 on land donated by Gilbert Smith of East Butte, two miles north of what is now the town of Sutter. Methodist camp meetings were held in a board pavilion 100 feet square for three weeks in the summer. Families from all over the state lived in little wooden cabins, doing their own cooking or boarding with Mrs. Smith. When attendance dwindled in the 1880s, the land reverted by agreement to the Smith family, and later the site became the Lang Ranch. A mile south of Camp Bethel stood a house belonging to the Bland Ranch. Henry Meade Bland, California's second poet laureate, spent his boyhood here, at "Saint's Rest," as his father, a pastor, called it.

SUTTER'S HOCK FARM

One of General Sutter's several ranchos was Hock Farm (SRL 346), from the German word *hoch* or "upper." An Indian village nearby was called after the farm. On this rancho, which was located on the west side of the Feather River about eight miles below Yuba City, Sutter kept men to look after his cattle from 1841 to 1850. An adobe house was put up on the property in the winter of 1841–42, followed by other structures from time to time. Hock Farm, also referred to as Upper Farm, became Sutter's principal stock ranch, the animals ranging freely over the entire countryside between the Feather and Sacramento Rivers and south of the Buttes.

By 1850 gold-seekers had despoiled Sutter of the greater part of his lands at New Helvetia. It was at this time that he retired to a plot of ground at Hock Farm that he had reserved for his home. There he built a mansion one and a half miles above the site of the adobe house. The grounds were laid out with beautiful gardens, an orchard, and a vineyard, and there Sutter kept an open house for the many travelers and friends who called to pay their respects. Following the flood of 1862, debris from the mines gradually buried the best part of the gardens and orchard at Hock Farm. In 1868 Sutter left California and found a home among the Moravians at Lititz, Pennsylvania, where he is buried. He died in Washington, D.C., on June 18, 1880.

The old adobe and the later mansion have disappeared from Hock Farm. For many years the remnant of the garden and orchard was used as a picnic grounds. Today the site is marked by one wall of the old iron fort, which stands on the Garden Highway at the end of Messick Road, seven miles south of Yuba City. The memorial tablet on it was placed by the Bi-County Federation of Women's Clubs of Sutter and Yuba Counties in 1927.

NICOLAUS

Nicolaus, the ranch and trading post of Nicolaus Allgeier, was established on the road between New Helvetia and Hock Farm because of the need for ferry transportation at this point on the Feather River. Allgeier, a native of Germany and for a time a Hudson's Bay Company trapper, was employed by Sutter to help build the adobe at Hock Farm. In compensation for this work, as well as for anticipated services as ferryman, Allgeier was given a plot of land one mile square at the crossing. Here he put up a hut of mud-covered tules, and in 1843 he constructed a primitive ferry, which he maintained with Indian labor.

The ferry at Nicolaus was one of many places in California to come into the hands of land speculators. The arrival of a United States government barque in 1849, with supplies for Camp Far West, was the signal for a broadside issued by its promoters, in August 1850. The public was told that Nicolaus was "the head of navigation," and that it was "the only port of entry that has ever been established north of Sacramento—the only town north of that city that has ever had a full-rigged seagoing vessel lying at her landing." Its advantages were already "too manifest to be any longer denied and doubted. Furthermore, the close proximity of the town to the rich placers on the Feather and Yuba Rivers, Deer, Dry, and Bear Creeks, and the forks of the American ensures its continuance as a depot for the supplies for all the northern mines."

Allgeier, who had put up an adobe house at his landing place in 1847, built a two-story adobe hotel there in 1849. During the following year, as a result of advertising, over three hundred lots were sold, and three hotels, a dozen stores, and over one hundred dwellings were erected. For a time the little river town showed such business activity that it presented a more flourishing appearance than Marysville, twenty miles to the north.

Realization that Nicolaus was not at the head of navigation fell heavily upon that hopeful town in the winter of 1849–50. Boats could usually reach Marysville, but when the river was low they were compelled to unload at Vernon, nine miles below Nicolaus. By 1853 many of the houses had been torn down and carried away, and the town was almost deserted. Until the building of the railroad, however, the place served as a shipping point and center of trade for surrounding ranches.

Nicolaus was the second county seat of Sutter County, from 1850 to 1851; it lost that honor, first to Auburn and then, after Auburn had become the county seat of the newly created Placer County, to Vernon. The seat of justice was reestablished at Nicolaus in 1852, but in 1854 it was transferred to Yuba City for a few months. Returned again to Nicolaus for a period of two years, the county seat was permanently established at Yuba City after 1856. Nicolaus still exists as a small farming community in the southeastern part of the county. Some old residences remain as landmarks. The town lies under the levee protecting it from the Feather River.

ORO

Thomas Jefferson Green purchased a tract of land from General Sutter at the junction of the Bear River with the Feather River, just north of Nicolaus, and announced that the new city of Oro would be built on the spot. An influential state senator, Green got his paper city designated as county seat when the Legislature created Sutter County in 1850. In order to win over his rivals at Auburn, Nicolaus, Vernon, and Yuba City, each better fitted for the position than Oro, Green exercised to its full extent "the power of a shrewd, energetic, and imposing presence, a persuasive tongue, and a bluff, good-natured personality. The outcome was that the senator won the day."

Since there was not a house in town for any purpose, much less for the holding of a court, a zinc structure twenty by twenty feet was put up, we are told, "without glass or shutters at the windows, or doors for the entrances. Not a tree, or bush, or shrub grew near enough to give its shade to the building." Under a brilliant May sun the first court met in the zinc house, but "law and equity, lawyers and litigants, jurors and witnesses, with

Old Sutter County Courthouse, Yuba City

Sutter County Hall of Records, Yuba City

a spontaneity of action that would astonish nothing but a salamander, rushed out of and fled that building, never to return." Oro remained a paper city.

VERNON (VERONA)

In April 1849 Sutter sold a strip of land three miles in length and one mile wide along the Sacramento and Feather Rivers. The purchasers laid out a one-mile square town at the junction of the rivers. This was Vernon, another of the short-lived river towns of 1849–50.

The winter of 1848–49 was such a dry one that the Feather River could not be navigated. Vessels were compelled to unload at Vernon, thus arousing hopes that the place would become the head of navigation. Prospects for a glorious future seemed bright, and lots were sold rapidly. One hotel was built entirely of mahogany from a shipment bought in Chile; originally intended for New York, this expensive cargo had been brought to California because the ship's captain desired to reach the gold fields.

The heavy rains of 1849–50 caused the rivers to rise so that it was possible for ships to go as far as Marysville. This was a deadly blow to Vernon, as well as to most of the infant cities along the river. Former enthusiastic speculators transferred their interests to other towns further up the river. But Vernon did not expire without a struggle. E. O. Crosby, a property owner who was a member of the state Senate, succeeded in having the county seat transferred to Vernon from Auburn in 1851. The position was lost the next year, however, and by 1853 the hotel ceased to be a public house and the post office was closed. No vestige of Vernon remains today. Only its name is preserved in Vernon Township and Vernon Road. A settlement called Verona was later established not far from the site and still exists.

YUBA CITY

Samuel Brannan, Pierson B. Reading, and Henry Cheever laid out Yuba City in July 1849 on the site of the Maidu village found on this spot by explorers earlier in the century. Where the round earthen huts of the Indians once clustered on the riverbank at the foot of what is now Second Street, a levee and terraced lots now stand, and no vestige of the old mound is visible.

The Sutter County Courthouse stands at 446 Second Street, next to the Hall of Records, which has the date 1891 on its facade. Other county offices are across Second Street. A newer complex on the west side of town includes Yuba City's City Hall and the Community Memorial Museum of Sutter County. The museum is housed in a handsome building dedicated in 1975. Its displays range from Maidu Indian artifacts to souvenirs of the home front in World War II and the Korean War —a good introduction to the history of Sutter County.

Yuba City and Marysville, its "twin city" across the Feather River where it is joined by the Yuba River, are situated in a natural flood plain. In 1955 a large portion of the town was inundated. Dams on the mountain streams and higher levees have since then kept flood damage to a minimum, but 1986 saw considerable flooding in the lower part of Sutter County. Rich farmland has made the county, small in size and population, a major agricultural region. To this area immigrants have come ever since 1850. Among the most recent arrivals are Sikhs from India, the largest settlement of this group in the United States. Since 1970 they have erected two huge temples in the Yuba City area, Gurdwara on Tierra Buena Road, and Guru Nanak on Bogue Road. Their white walls, blue trim, and onion-shaped domes make these temples picturesque additions to the lower Feather River landscape. They are open to the public.

William Thompson, an Englishman, settled west of the town of Sutter in 1863 and began farming. In 1872 he sent to New York for three cuttings of "Lady de Coverly" grape vines. One cutting survived to produce the Thompson Seedless grape, first displayed in Marysville in 1875 and an instant success. Thousands of acres of this grape have been planted in California to produce raisins, wine, and table grapes. A marker (SRL 929) has been placed on SR 20 near Thompson's farm site at 9001 Colusa Highway near West Butte Road.

Tehama County

Tehama County was organized in 1856 from parts of Colusa, Butte, and Shasta Counties, and the county seat was located at the town of Tehama. In 1857 the county seat moved to Red Bluff, where it has remained to the present. Eugene Serr gives an insightful account of the origin of the county's name:

> The name Tehama is almost certainly an Indian name since a Nomlaki village called Tehemet was nearby. The meaning of the word is not clear, but most authorities agree it was probably "low land" or "high water," which is consistent with the frequent flooding of the town. However, an intriguing complication has arisen with the discovery that the Indians of the Sacramento area called that area Tehama, and that the first use of the name by whites was apparently in Sacramento (Tehama Block Building) and not in the town of Tehama. A possible explanation is that both the Tehama (Nomlaki) Indians and the Sacramento (Nisenan) Indians had the same word, Tehama, which seems possible because of its simplicity and melodious sound.

FIRST TRAILS

The first recorded expedition into Tehama County was that of Luís Argüello, who in 1821 probably pushed as far north as Cottonwood Creek. Then the American Jedediah Strong Smith passed through in 1828, and in his footsteps came a stream of hunters and traders from the south. Hudson's Bay Company trappers from the north followed much the same general course during the year 1830–45. This old Sacramento Valley route, known as the Oregon to California Trail, was soon beaten into a well-defined path by trappers and explorers, among them Ewing Young, Lieutenant George Emmons of the Wilkes expedition, and Joseph Gale. Sometimes proceeding all the way down the western side of the river, and at other times crossing over to the east side somewhere between Red Bluff and Tehama (a variation used most frequently by the gold-seekers of 1849 and the 1850s), this historic road has been used through the years by pack-mule trains, herds of cattle and sheep, stagecoaches, and finally the railway and modern cars, trucks, and buses.

In 1843 John Bidwell, accompanied by Peter Lassen and John Burheim, chased a band of horse thieves over this trail, pursuing them as far as Red Bluff, where the thieves were overtaken and the property was recovered. It was on this trip that Lassen selected the land that was later given to him by the Mexican government.

Returning to this region the following year, Bidwell

brought with him five other men who were destined to become the first settlers in the upper Sacramento Valley. Of them, Pierson B. Reading settled in what is now Shasta County, while Job Francis Dye, William George Chard, Robert Hasty Thomes, and Albert G. Toomes followed Lassen as the earliest American settlers in Tehama County. Each of them located on Mexican grants chosen on this trip with Bidwell in 1844. Also on this trip Bidwell mapped the valley, giving to its streams names by which they are now known.

"BLOODY ISLAND"

Samuel J. Hensley, who had accompanied Reading to California in 1843, while rafting logs on the Sacramento River in the northern part of Tehama County early in 1844, had an encounter with some Indians on an island that lies in the river just below the mouth of Cottonwood Creek. It is said that Hensley named the place "Bloody Island" because of this experience. During his stay in the region, Hensley noted the fine land north of Cottonwood Creek (in what is now Shasta County), and later recommended it to Reading as suitable for a ranch. This was the southernmost part of the grant made to Reading in 1844. A nearby spot is called Battle Creek for a similar reason; it is the site of Battle Creek National Fish Hatchery.

LASSEN'S RANCH

Through the influence of John A. Sutter, Rancho Bosquejo ("the wooded place"), comprising 26,000 acres of good farming land, was granted in 1844 to Peter Lassen. This pioneer blacksmith was a native of Denmark who came to America in 1829 and went westward to Oregon ten years later. He sailed on an English ship for California and landed at Fort Ross. From there he went to the Pueblo de San José, where he spent the winter of 1839–40. After ranching at Santa Cruz in 1841, he was at Sutter's Fort in 1842–43, where his blacksmithing abilities made him very welcome. In time Lassen received Mexican naturalization papers and was granted his property by Governor Micheltorena, a friend of Sutter's. High floodwaters in the valley forced Lassen to spend part of the winter of 1844–45 on the Sutter Buttes before he could occupy his land. With hundreds of Indians in the region, Lassen opened a trading post on his rancho near the mouth of Deer Creek on the east side of the Sacramento River. There is no trace left of any ranch buildings to-

day, but the site is near Vina, eighteen miles south of Red Bluff on SR 99.

Lassen entertained dreams of becoming an entrepreneur and in 1847, as Alta California was steadily coming under American control, planned "Benton City" (named for Missouri Senator Thomas H. Benton, John C. Frémont's influential father-in-law) to be laid out on his ranch. In the fall of that year, he returned to Missouri, where he had lived before coming to Oregon, to induce settlers to come to Benton City and, incidentally, to obtain a charter for the first Masonic lodge in the Far West.

THE LASSEN TRAIL

Lassen returned to California overland in the spring of 1848 with a party of emigrants. This trip was very difficult, but the party arrived at Lassen's Ranch by the fall. A considerable number of emigrants undertook to shorten their journey overland in 1849–50 using the same route. While it never became popular, since it proved to be a long cutoff, steep and precipitous, and passing through the territory of hostile Indians, the Lassen Trail did serve to introduce many emigrants to northern California, thus quickening an interest in that part of the state.

The Lassen Trail came into California from northwestern Nevada through Surprise Valley and over the Fandango Pass. It continued southwest, following the Pit River part of the way and on to Big Meadows, now covered by the waters of Lake Almanor. The trail entered Tehama County over Deer Creek Pass to Deer Creek Meadows before following the ridge between Mill Creek and Deer Creek over the once-precipitous "Narrows," now less risky since it has been widened for logging trucks. Other historic spots along the way include Bruff's Camp high in the forest belt, and Steep Hollow and Emigrant Springs in the rocky foothill slopes, before the trail emerges into the Sacramento Valley near Toomes Creek, at a point near the railroad two miles below Los Molinos and some four miles above Vina.

LATER HISTORY OF LASSEN'S RANCH

Lassen's party arrived in California in the fall of 1848 to learn of the discovery of gold, and at once the entire plan of settlement on Lassen's Ranch was abandoned as members of the party headed for the mountains. In May 1851 the Masonic chapter was moved from Benton City to Shasta in Shasta County. Benton City is completely gone, but the Masons of Tehama and Shasta

Counties have put up a monument on the site. It stands on the east side of SR 99 just north of Deer Creek.

In 1848 Lassen gave to Daniel Sill, a trapper, one league of land on which the latter built an adobe and on which the town of Danville was projected but never built. In 1852, Lassen conveyed his remaining lands to Henry Gerke, a German, who settled there in 1869. In 1881, former governor Leland Stanford (later a U.S. senator and founder of Stanford University) purchased from Gerke 9,000 acres of the original Lassen grant. Subsequently Stanford purchased additional lands, all of which were included in the famous Vina Ranch of 55,000 acres, which the senator conveyed to Stanford University by the Founding Grant, November 11, 1885. The name Vina was derived from the fact that here Senator Stanford planted a vast vineyard, one of the largest in the world. After the ranch became the property of the university, plans for developing the vineyard were abandoned. In 1955, 580 acres of the Lassen Grant, including the headquarters building of the original Stanford-Vina Ranch, were purchased by the Abbey of New Clairvaux, a Roman Catholic monastery of the Trappist-Cistercian Order, which now occupies the spot. Visitors may see the historic buildings on the site. Trails West, Inc., a private organization, has placed a marker near the stone cross at the entrance to the monastery, marking the end of the Lassen Trail.

FRÉMONT AT LASSEN'S RANCH

John C. Frémont, coming up from New Helvetia in March 1846 on his way to Oregon, spent a month at Lassen's Ranch, from which he made a local exploring trip through what is now Tehama County. Arriving at the ranch on March 30, he noted that Lassen had a vineyard, that he was experimenting with cotton, and that his wheat crop was large.

On April 5 Frémont and his men set out up the valley, camping that night "on a little creek on the Sacramento, where an emigrant 'from the states' was establishing himself and was already building a house." This was probably Albert Toomes on his Rancho de los Molinos. On April 6 the expedition crossed the river in canoes to another farm on the right bank, no doubt that of Toomes's friend and partner, Robert Thomes. There Frémont made camp on "a creek wooded principally with large oaks."

During the next few days the party crossed Red Bank Creek and Cottonwood Creek (later the boundary between Tehama and Shasta Counties), and on April 9 they crossed to the east side of the Sacramento River, camping on Cow Creek in what is now Shasta County. Two days later they were back at Lassen's Ranch, where they remained until April 24, when the march to Oregon was resumed. A month later, on May 24, when returning from Oregon to participate in the stirring events of the American occupation, Frémont again stopped at Lassen's Ranch on his way south.

FIRST SETTLERS

Robert Hasty Thomes (pronounced "Thomas"), a native of Maine, came to California with the Bidwell-Bartleson party in 1841. For a time he was engaged as a carpenter and builder in San Francisco and Monterey in partnership with Albert Toomes, as is evidenced by the frequent appearance of the firm name of Thomes and Toomes in Thomas O. Larkin's books and other records.

In the winter of 1844, Thomes received the Mexican land grant of Rancho de los Saúcos ("elder trees"), located south of Elder Creek in what is now Tehama County. Although he stocked the place in 1845, he did not settle there permanently for a year or two, when he built an adobe house on his property. This house burned in 1858. Sometime around the year 1870, Thomes erected the brick house that stood until its destruction by fire in 1945, on what was known as the Finnell Ranch, later as the El Camino Colony, and now as the Elder Creek Ranch. A hotel, known as the Tehama House, was built on the site of the old adobe at the corner of Fourth and C Streets in the town of Tehama.

Robert Thomes was a man of character and influence in his community. He died in 1878 and lies buried under the largest and most ornamental monument in the Tehama Cemetery, a monument composed of granite from the quarries of Penryn in Placer County.

William G. Chard, a native of New York, came to California from New Mexico in 1832. He was at Los Angeles until 1836 and at Santa Cruz from 1837 to 1841. During the years 1843–45 he was in partnership with Josiah Belden in a store and boardinghouse at Monterey. In 1844 Chard obtained a grant of land on the north side of Elder Creek (in Tehama County), naming it Rancho de las Flores ("the flowers"). In 1845, Chard took his cattle to Rancho de las Flores in 1845, and in the next year built a cabin on the Sacramento River at a site four miles north of the present town of Tehama. He did not go to his rancho to live until 1847 because he was employed at the New Almaden Mine (in Santa Clara County) from 1845 to 1847. The log house at Rancho de las Flores came to be known as Sacramento House, and it was a popular stopping place on the road to the northern mines. North of Chard's grant, Josiah Belden in 1844 obtained Rancho de la Barranca Colorada ("red ravine"), so called for a place on the river where the water had cut the soil some fifty feet, exposing sand and gravel of a reddish hue.

Across the river from Chard's rancho, Job Francis Dye built an adobe in 1847 on Rancho de los Berrendos ("the antelopes"). Dye, a Kentucky trapper who came from New Mexico with Ewing Young in 1831–32, for a time engaged in hunting sea otter along the coast. Later he ran a store and distillery at Santa Cruz, where he also had a ranch. Until the 1880s, Dye's adobe stood on the west bank of Antelope Creek on what later became known as the Cone Ranch. It was located on a spot not far from where the Cone Methodist Church now stands.

Albert G. Toomes, a native of Missouri who came to California with the Workman-Rowland party in 1841, was given the grant of Rancho Río de los Molinos ("river of the mills") in 1844. Toomes visited his property in 1845 and again in 1847, to stock it with cattle, and in 1846 he built an adobe near where the settlement of Los Molinos grew up. That Toomes did not go to live permanently on the estate until 1849 is evident from the fact that the firm of Thomes and Toomes is mentioned in records at Monterey until the end of 1848.

William C. Moon, who also came to California with the Workman-Rowland party in 1841, settled on the west side of the Sacramento River opposite the mouth of Deer Creek as early as 1845, and ran a ferry at this point during the Gold Rush. The ferry was located about where the present Squaw Hill Bridge crosses the Sacramento River on the road from Vina to Corning. Moon lived on his ranch until his death in 1878. The original post-office desk where mail was sorted at the Moon House may be seen at the Tehama County Museum in Tehama.

"THE WILLIAM B. IDE ADOBE"

William B. Ide, a native of Rutland, Massachusetts, came with his family from New Hampshire to what is now Tehama County in 1845. He built a log cabin on the R. H. Thomes ranch and spent the winter there. In the spring of 1846 he moved to the Belden ranch, where he put up another log house on Ide's Bottom south of what was later Red Bluff. In 1847 Ide purchased the Rancho de la Barranca Colorada from Belden. Ide had been commander during the Bear Flag Revolt at So-noma in 1846. After 1850 he lived much of the time at Monroeville, Colusa County, where he eventually held virtually all the county offices and where he died in 1852. The site of Monroeville is now in Glenn County.

One and one-half miles northeast of Red Bluff on the west bank of the Sacramento River stands an adobe house built in the late 1840s or early 1850s. Joe D. Hood, of the California Department of Parks and Recreation, has found that a claim for a parcel of land to the south of the house filed in 1852 by Kendall V. Bumpass identified the property as Ide's adobe. That building in fact stood eight miles further to the south, and the adobe in question was built by one Abraham Dibble, about whom nothing else is known. The error made by Bumpass (whose unusual name lives on in the geothermal region known as Bumpass Hell in Lassen Volcanic National Park) seems to have gone uncorrected and was used by Judge Edward J. Lewis in his book *Tehama County History* in 1880, by which time the only adobe standing in the region was the one built by Dibble but which was now identified by Lewis as Ide's.

When the state took over the property in 1960, the identification of Ide with the building was well established, although no one could provide any evidence that Ide was in any way connected with the building. So today's visitor will find the William B. Ide Adobe State Historic Park (SRL 12) three miles northeast of Red Bluff, misnamed but otherwise in good condition, with a restored adobe as its centerpiece.

TEHAMA

Robert Thomes's adobe was built on a spot later covered by Tehama, the first town in the county. It has been reliably established, however, that before Thomes settled on the site, he had given to his friend Albert Toomes a small tract of land where Tehama now stands, thus making Toomes the founder of the town. In 1849 Tehama (then known as Hall's Ranch), located on the west side of the Sacramento River twelve miles south of Red Bluff, was an important center of trade and freighting on the Oregon Road as well as the principal ferry crossing between Marysville and Shasta. (Other ferries were soon established at Moon's Ranch; the "Ide" Adobe, where it was known as the Adobe Ferry; and Red Bluff.) When the steamer *Orient* landed at Red Bluff in 1850, Tehama at once lost its prestige as a river town. As a stage center, however, it held its own for a number of years.

The first stage line from Colusa to Shasta was opened up by Baxter and Monroe in 1851. An opposition line

Tehama Museum, Tehama

Kelly-Griggs House Museum, Red Bluff

from Marysville, via Hamilton, Neal's Ranch, and Bidwell's Ranch, in Butte County, was started by Hall and Crandall in 1852. The two lines converged in Tehama, creating a prosperous activity that continued until the coming of the railroad.

Tehama, with its old buildings and tree-lined streets, is today a quiet settlement. The old Masonic Lodge building, erected in 1859, was used as a school for the first twenty years of the town's existence, and used by the Masons for over one hundred years; it stands at Third and C Streets. A museum is operated there by the Tehama County Museum Foundation, with interesting materials on the history of the county. A replica of the old Tehama County Jail, built in 1884, stands on the western side of the museum building. The first courtroom in Tehama, in a structure no longer standing, is commemorated by a plaque (SRL 183) at Second and D Streets.

THE NOME LACKEE INDIAN RESERVATION

The Nome Lackee Indian Reservation was established in 1854 by the United States government to provide a home for Indians who were displaced as white settlers moved onto the land. Grain was the major crop raised on the more than 25,000 acres of land that formed the reservation. From 300 to 2,500 Indians lived there until 1866, when they were moved to Round Valley in Mendocino County.

Colonel B. F. Washington, great-grandson of Lawrence Washington (brother of George Washington), came overland to California from Virginia in 1849, finally settling in Tehama County. He acquired title to a considerable tract of land near the Nome Lackee Indian Reservation. His home, located by a spring, was known for many years as Washington's Garden, but it has long since disappeared.

The nearby community of Paskenta is one of the oldest in the county, started by Samuel Jenison around 1856. "Paskenta" is a Nomlaki term for "under the bank" or "under the hills." In 1868–70 a major industry of the town was gambling; it was located on the road to the gold mines at Harrison Gulch in Shasta County. In more recent times it was a lumbering town.

William Nixon Henley also acquired land nearby; hence, the name Henleyville was given to the small community east of Paskenta and Flournoy. A monument with a descriptive plaque (SRL 357) marks the location of the Nome Lackee Indian Reservation four miles north of Flournoy on Osborn Road.

RED BLUFF

First mapped in 1851 as a settlement in southern Shasta County, Red Bluff began to prosper when the steamboat service reached it in the early 1850s. The railroads reached Red Bluff in 1871, and the city continued to grow as a transportation center. In 1876, the Centennial Bridge spanning the Sacramento River was built here. The first courthouse of 1860 gave way to the graceful pillars of the 1922 courthouse, with its modern brick addition of 1979. The Odd Fellows Building at 382 Oak Street was built in 1883 and is still in use; the cast-iron details around the ground-floor veranda are very distinctive. The Kelly-Griggs Museum at 311 Washington Street is located in the Griggs house, built in 1885, and contains a beautiful collection of Victorian furniture and glassware as well as Indian artifacts. A number of houses in the vicinity are listed on the locally available map of a walking tour.

Joseph C. Cone came to Tehama County in 1857 and eventually amassed a ranch of some 10,000 acres, becoming one of the "wheat kings" of California. Among his many business dealings was a partnership with Major Gorham G. Kimball forming the Cone and Kimball

Mrs. John Brown's House, Red Bluff

Company, a successful mercantile organization. In 1886 they built a large two-story brick building at the corner of Main and Walnut Streets in Red Bluff, including an ornate 100-foot clock tower. Although this building was destroyed by fire in 1984, the clock tower image is still replicated in the city's logo. A park is planned at the site that will include a reproduction of the famous old clock tower.

In 1864, near the close of the Civil War, Mary Ann Brown, the widow of abolitionist John Brown of Harper's Ferry, came to Red Bluff with some of her children. A sum of money was raised to provide the family with a home. The house (SRL 117) was built at what is now 135 Main Street, and there Mrs. Brown lived until 1870, when she and her three daughters moved to Humboldt County. The house, somewhat remodeled, continued to be used as a private dwelling until in 1988 the owner of the building let it be known that it was no longer economically feasible to make the necessary repairs and that he was about to tear the place down. Local historical groups protested. (Designation as a State Registered Landmark does not guarantee the preservation of a building; a number of landmarks in California commemorate structures no longer standing.) With the help of the Tehama County Genealogical and Historical Society and the California Housing Improvement Program, the historic house was renovated on the inside into a modern dwelling while the exterior retained the look of the simple frame house occupied by Mrs. Brown. The place is once more a private residence.

Andrew Jelly built a brick house northeast of Red Bluff in 1856. Jelly came to California in 1848 and gained title to his land by buying scrip that soldiers of the Mexican War had received instead of pay for military service. The scrip entitled the holder to 160 acres of frontier land. Jelly was a brick mason by trade. He built the house large enough to take care of his family and to accommodate travelers, using brick made and baked from the clay soil on the ranch. At one time a post office was established and maintained there. In the 1890s the Haakonson family purchased the Jelly Ranch; members of that family still live on the ranch in the remodeled ranch home. The location is on Jelly's Ferry Road, about six miles northeast of Red Bluff.

TUSCAN SPRINGS

Tuscan Springs is located near the head of Little Salt Creek, approximately nine miles east of Red Bluff. The springs were named after the similar sulfur-type springs of Tuscany in Italy by their first owner, Dr. John A. Veatch, who purchased the property in 1854. Two years later, in Lake County, he discovered the first borax ever found in California, but the quantities were insufficient for commercial development.

Tuscan Springs was developed as a health resort by several successive owners, one of whom was Ed Walbridge. In the years 1892–1912 he built a two-story hotel to accommodate 125 guests, ran a daily stagecoach from Red Bluff, and established a post office. Walbridge's first hotel was destroyed by fire in 1899 and was replaced with a three-story hotel. From the spring waters, he developed and sold bottled mineral salts for medical purposes. A second fire in 1916 ended the days of this popular health resort. The rise and fall of Tuscan Springs was closely paralleled in many places in California in the same years.

THE SIERRA LUMBER COMPANY

When lumbering operations were developed in the pine belt of the northern Sierra Nevada, a major problem in the early days was transporting the lumber to shipping points in the valley. C. F. Ellsworth designed and constructed the first V-flume in the state. His original Empire Flume was built in the early 1870s and was over forty miles in length, extending from Lyman Springs in the mountains east of Red Bluff to Sesma, a site near the present Los Molinos. The high-trestle flume followed Belle Mill Road, entering the valley near Antelope Flouring Mills. In 1881 the route was changed so that it ended along the east bank of the Sacramento opposite Red Bluff.

By 1878, several small lumber mills had combined to form a large corporation known as the Sierra Lumber Company, which operated mills at Lyonsville. Lumber was shipped to the large mill at the end of the flume in

Antelope, where it was finished and shipped by steamboat, barge, or rail. In 1907, the Diamond Match Company purchased Sierra Lumber's large timber holdings and its mills at Chico and Red Bluff, as well as the mill at Lyonsville, since torn down. Following severe flooding and fires, the mill at Antelope was closed, and Diamond moved west across the Sacramento. Its integrated forest products' plant south of Red Bluff was completed in 1958. By the late 1980s the plant was sold and shut down. Other lumber mills in the county and region have suffered similar fates.

CORNING AND GERBER

Corning, named for John Corning, a railroad superintendent for the Central Pacific Railroad, was founded in 1882. Like the Lindsay region in Tulare County, Corning is a center for the production of olives. Before 1920, the University of California planted test plots here, and their success started the olive industry. The Corning Museum is at 1110 Solano Street, with displays on local history. Five miles northwest of Corning on Davis Road is a two-story adobe house with a facing of cobblestones, built in 1852 by Henry Clay Wilson, later a state senator. It is believed to be the oldest house in the county, and is still occupied.

Gerber, named for a Sacramento family, became a center for the Southern Pacific Railroad, which moved its roundhouse from Red Bluff to Gerber in 1916. The South Shasta Model Railroad can be seen at the Humann Ranch, 8620 Holmes Road. This is a model display of the railroad's operations.

ISHI

In 1911, a man whom his biographer Theodora Kroeber called "the last wild Indian in North America" was discovered at a slaughterhouse near Oroville in Butte County. He was Ishi, the last survivor of the Yahi people, who lived in rugged Deer Creek canyon in the southeast part of Tehama County. He was brought into contact with Professor Alfred Kroeber, pioneer anthropologist of the University of California at Berkeley, where for five years he supplied valuable information on his tribe and history. Much of his story was recorded and can be seen on film and video today. He died in San Francisco in 1916. A plaque in the town of Vina is dedicated to his memory. An Ishi Wilderness Area was set aside in Lassen National Forest to include his hidden campsites. A few of his bows and arrows and other artifacts are on display at the Kelly-Griggs House Museum in Red Bluff.

Trinity County

Trinity County was one of the original twenty-seven counties, and Weaverville has always been the county seat. The Trinity River, which flows across the county, was named in the erroneous belief that it flowed into the ocean at Trinidad Bay in Humboldt County.

EARLY EXPLORATIONS

Jedediah Strong Smith and his party were probably the first Americans to explore Trinity County. In early April 1828 Smith came up the eastern side of the "Buenaventura" (the present Sacramento River) to the vicinity of Red Bluff. There he found "the rocky hills coming in so close to the river as to make it impossible to travel." After scouting parties had been sent north and northwest, it was decided that the most practicable route to Oregon, their destination, was to the northwest. He crossed the river on April 11, and, traveling in very rough country, passed over the divide made by the Trinity Mountains into the present Trinity County on April 17. So far Smith's route seems to have followed approximately that of the present Red Bluff–Eureka highway, SR 36.

The next day Smith's party followed down one of the tributaries of the South Fork of the Trinity River, probably Hayfork Creek. On April 21 they reached "a small valley on the river which turned in its course nearly North and . . . received a branch from the South." Smith states in his diary that he named the river he had been following Smith's River. Many of the early maps label as Smith's River the rivers now known as the Trinity and the Klamath, into which the Trinity flows. Later the name was transferred to the present Smith River in Del Norte County.

On April 24 he had to cross to the west bank because the mountain came so close to the east bank of the river that it was impossible to proceed. There he found the traveling to be rough; the ground was so rocky that the horses' feet were being mangled. Climbing the high ridge to the west of the river, the party crossed over into what is now Humboldt County. Jedediah Smith had opened up the coast route to Oregon on the first journey ever made by an American from California into Oregon. This route was followed in later years, at least in part, by agents of the Hudson's Bay Company from Oregon. The noted trapper Ewing Young made his first passage to the north this way in 1832.

THE OLD TRINITY TRAIL

SR 299, which crosses the mountains of Shasta and Trinity Counties between Redding and Weaverville, frequently follows the old Trinity Trail opened up by early trappers and gold-seekers. Trappers of the Hudson's Bay Company may have used this route to some extent in the 1830s and 1840s. The first trails were made by Indians, and the first white men to travel this country used these paths. The first definite knowledge (apart from Smith's recorded journey) comes from Major Pierson B. Reading, who says that in 1848 he had crossed the mountains "where the travel passed . . . from Shasta to Weaver." Reading had previously visited the area on a trapping expedition as early as 1845, and it was he who gave the Trinity River its present name, not realizing that the river flows into the Klamath, not into Trinidad Bay on the coast.

The Forty-niners also used the Trinity Trail on their way to the Trinity gold fields, and the need for safe transportation of gold in the early 1850s led to the establishment of express offices and what were known as "pony express" lines. Over these trails mail and bullion were carried on horseback. The mail route for Trinity County led from Red Bluff in Tehama County to Shasta and thence over the mountains to Weaverville, fifty miles to the northwest. These trails were for pack trains of horses and mules only. Such slow and laborious means of transportation delayed the development of the county and the coming of families.

THE WEAVERVILLE AND SHASTA TOLL ROAD

The route of the old Trinity Trail was followed until the first wagon road in the county was built. In 1857, the Weaverville and Shasta Road Company began work on a road connecting Weaverville, Shasta, and Redding; it was completed in 1858. The credit for the construction of this road is given to William Spencer Lowden of Lowden's Ranch, located on Grass Valley Creek. Lowden, a deputy United States surveyor, was an Adams & Company relay rider in the celebrated ride made in January 1854, when two express companies, Adams and Wells Fargo, raced the text of President Franklin Pierce's annual message to Congress from San Francisco to Portland, Oregon. Lowden was then a young man of twenty-four, and it is said that he rode his relay of sixty miles from Tehama to Shasta in two hours and thirty-seven minutes. While another rider took the bags and dashed on to Yreka, Lowden continued west forty miles farther to Weaverville. In his ride from Tehama to Shasta it is reported that he changed horses nineteen times, touching the ground only once.

During the early 1860s, the Lewiston Turnpike Road, a variation of the Weaverville and Shasta Road, was constructed from near the Tower House in Shasta County to Lewiston in Trinity County. This, like the Weaverville and Shasta Toll Road, was originally a private toll road.

THE HYAMPOM TRAIL

An important pioneer line of travel called the Hyampom Trail passed through the settlement of Hyampom.

According to Harvey Pitkin, the unusual name may have come from the Wintu Indian expression for "slippery place." A wagon road came from Humboldt Bay as far as Hydesville in Humboldt County, in the center of an agricultural region. From Hydesville the road became a trail that ran east through Carlotta and Yager. Beyond Yager the trail passed by the Redwood House and Fort Baker and over Coyote Flat. Crossing Mad River and climbing Hohn Ridge, it reached Pilot Creek, where it turned northeast over South Fork Mountain to Hyampom. Here the trail branched, one branch going to Big Bar and the other up Hayfork Creek to the Sacramento Valley.

The Hyampom Trail was always a pack trail. The country was rough, and the way often steep and dangerous. Parts of it are still used by ranchers to bring in winter supplies. In 1922 a road was completed between Hyampom Valley and Hayfork.

THE OREGON ROAD

Although a road had been built over the Trinity Mountains, Scott Mountain still had to be crossed by mule pack train. In 1860, however, this obstacle to travel to Oregon was overcome, when Scott Mountain Road was built at an expense of $25,000. The road went from Shasta and French Gulch in Shasta County over Trinity Mountain into Trinity County. From there it went through Trinity Center and Carrville, after which it climbed over Scott Mountain into Siskiyou County to Yreka. This road became the main artery for interstate commerce between California and Oregon until the railroad up the Sacramento Canyon was built in the 1880s. In spite of heavy snowfall, this road was kept open all winter. Oxen housed at the summit were driven back and forth over the road after a snowstorm to tramp down the loose snow. Because of difficulties, the stage to Jacksonville had been run only in the summertime up to the fall of 1859. That year the Oregon Company spent $10,000 in improving the road over the Siskiyous, and in 1860 a daily line of stages was established between Sacramento and Portland. When the railroad was built, this road did not pay as a toll road and was taken over by the county. Today SR 3, a state scenic highway, follows this old route over Scott Mountain.

THE FIRST DISCOVERY OF GOLD

In 1858 Major Pierson B. Reading described his discovery of gold at Reading's Bar ten years earlier:

In the month of July 1848, I crossed the mountains of the Coast Range at the head of Middle Cottonwood Creek, struck the Trinity at what is now called Reading's Bar; prospected for two days, and found the bars rich in gold; returned to my home on Cottonwood, and in ten days fitted out an expedition for mining purposes; and crossed the mountains where the travel passed about two years ago from Shasta to Weaver.

My party consisted of three white men, one Delaware, one Chinook, and about sixty Indians from the Sacramento Valley. With this force I worked the bar bearing my name. I had with me one hundred and twenty head of cattle with an abundant supply of other provisions. After about six weeks' work, parties came in from Oregon, who at once protested against my Indian labor. I then left the stream and returned to my home where I have since remained in the enjoyment of the tranquil life of a farmer.

The identity of the parties from Oregon who caused Reading to abandon his mining operations is not known. But Reading's Bar, on which the major and his men worked, is located on Trinity River at the mouth of Reading's Creek immediately below the Douglas City bridge.

RIVER AND CREEK MINING

The first settler in Trinity County is said to have been a Frenchman named Gross who came here from Oregon in 1849. After discovering gold at a place he named Rich Gulch, he settled at Evans' Bar on the Trinity River and built a cabin, perhaps the first of its kind in that part of the county. There was a rush of gold-seekers in 1850; by the end of 1851, contemporary accounts stated that all of the gold-bearing sections of the county had been explored and prospected.

The early mining was done on the river bars and along the creeks. On the Trinity River below Lowden's Ranch at the mouth of Grass Valley Creek were numerous river-bar camps; Ingrams, Union, Ferry, Trinity, and Texas Bars were all active before 1856. At the point on the Trinity where it was joined by Weaver Creek was the rich Kanaka Bar, renamed Douglas City for Stephen A. Douglas, Democratic candidate for president in 1860. Farther down were Reading's Bar and Cape Horn Bar, where German and Danish miners built "neat houses." Opposite Cape Horn Bar was Turner's Bar, from which six Danes and Germans took $32,000 in one year. One-half mile below Turner's was Buckeye

Bar, with a water dip-wheel forty-two feet in diameter. Steiner's Flat, four miles below Douglas City, is one of the few places worked intermittently from 1850 to the present day.

Eight miles downriver from Steiner's Flat is the site of the Arkansas Dam across the Trinity River, about four miles above Junction City. Some sixty miners made the first attempt to construct this dam during the summer and fall of 1850. The dam had been completed, turning the water from the bed of the river into a canal, and some work in the bed of the river was proving the gravels to be of high value when the first rain of the season came, swelling the waters of the river so much that the dam was washed away. The dam was again constructed in the following year, to be once more destroyed by the rise in the river at the first rainfall. It was not until three years later that a log dam placed across the river withstood the waters passing through it in the late fall and winter months.

Near Junction City were Hocker's Ranch, Ferry Bar, and Red Hill. In 1851 Joseph McGillivray, a Scotsman of wonderful resourcefulness, persistence, and ability, came to Cooper's Bar, five miles down the river from Junction City, and began to develop it into a home, ranch, orchard, and garden spot. He employed William Berber, a trained horticulturist from New York. All the leading varieties of fruit trees, flowering shrubs, and other plants were introduced, and before long he was supplying the whole county. McGillivray's Ranch became famous as a beautiful spot. Now it is a waste of heaped-up dredge tailings.

Cañon City, located above Junction City on Canyon Creek, was one of the first mining camps, originally known as Jackass Bar. It became one of the largest gold-producing settlements in the county. The last trading post there closed its doors in 1885.

At the mouth of the North Fork of the Trinity River was an important town called North Fork, later renamed Helena. Here Herbert Hoover worked for a time as a young mining engineer. Until 1926 this was the end of the road; from here the traveler west had to follow a trail. In that year the state highway was opened all the way down the Trinity River. Helena is listed on the National Register of Historic Places.

Big Bar, eight miles below Helena, was an important mining center in the 1850s. Weaver and Company, which mined there in 1850, spent $10,000 diverting water from Little Weaver Creek (now known as Big Bar Creek) and took out $100,000 in gold.

The canyon of the Trinity River between North Fork and Big Bar was once the scene of much mining activity in the bed of the river. Chinese miners were the last to work here. Manzanita Flat, worked for many years, had a twentieth-century revival with the use of the water of Manzanita Creek.

Cox's Bar was quite famous in the early days, but no evidence remains of the extensive mining done there except moss-covered tailing piles and scarred banks. Mosses have been taken from the rock there and burned, the ashes yielding fine "flour" gold. At Big Flat, near Cox's Bar, was a large settlement—450 people in 1856.

The largest gold nugget ever found in Trinity County, valued at $1,800, was discovered on Digger Creek by George Van Matre. Minersville, near the mouth of Stewart's Fork, was a center of rich pocket mines. In 1880 the noted Brown Bear Quartz Mines were discovered on Deadwood Creek; they have produced more than a million dollars' worth of ore. Crow's Bar, of eighty acres, was mined by water brought from Rush Creek through a ditch eight miles long, built at a cost of $20,000.

Since the 1850s much gold has been taken from the banks and bed of the Trinity River and its tributaries, but none of them has been worked completely. During the depression of the 1930s, a large number of men worked along the bars with equipment such as was used by the early miners: the pan, the rocker, the sluice. Many earned enough to live on. Today, one can see small dredging operations along the length of the river after the winter storms have abated.

LA GRANGE MINE

Mining in Trinity County goes back to 1851. In 1873 several mining claims were consolidated into the Weaverville Ditch and Hydraulic Mining Company. In 1879 the Trinity Gold Mining Company was formed and purchased the property in Oregon Gulch, four miles northwest of Weaverville. Five years later, Baron La Grange, a Frenchman, formed the La Grange Hydraulic Mining Company and purchased the mine for $250,000. The La Grange Mine (SRL 778) was for years one of the most important hydraulic mines in California.

Water for washing the gravel in this tremendous deposit was first obtained through ditches from West Weaver Creek. As this supply proved inadequate, a ditch was extended to Rush Creek in 1894. Finally a water right on Stewart's Fork was obtained in 1898. The total length of the ditch and flume was twenty-nine miles. The tailings of this mine were run into a narrow

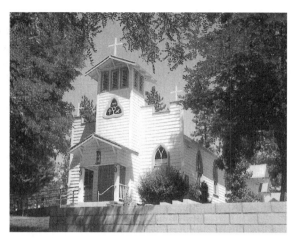

St. Patrick's Catholic Church, Weaverville

Weaverville Joss House State Historic Park

valley owned by the company and from this valley drained directly into the Trinity River. Since this stream is not navigable and the surrounding country is not farmland, this was considered an ideal dumping ground for mine waste.

For many years the La Grange Mine was known as the largest operating hydraulic mine in the world, but it has been closed since World War I. A vast quantity of low-grade gravel is left, but the cost of reopening the works would be considerable because of the necessity of creating tunnels and cuts.

THE BRIDGE GULCH MASSACRE

When the first settlers came to Trinity County, they were constantly annoyed by the depredations of the Indians, who resented the invasion of the settlers and the brutal destruction of the forests and countryside. A number of expeditions were organized to drive the Indians out. In 1852 the killing of a man named Anderson aroused high feeling among the white settlers. Anderson had gone alone to the range to bring in some of his cattle when he was attacked and killed by several Indians, who drove off the cattle. When Anderson failed to return to Weaverville and his riderless mule appeared at the corral, a search party was formed, which found his arrow-pierced body. A portion of the party set out after the Indians, while the remainder went back to Weaverville to spread the alarm. Soon afterward seventy men were ready to start. Joining the advance party, whose position was relayed by messengers sent back to Weaverville, they again picked up the Indians' trail. After tracking them to their camp at Bridge Gulch in Hayfork Valley, the whites surrounded the camp and, in an attack from four sides, massacred 153 Indians.

Only two little girls, who were overlooked, survived. These children were brought back to town and reared by white families. One of them, Ellen Clifford, was long a resident of Weaverville. At a later date "Indian Bob" of Douglas City claimed that he was a boy of nine at the time of the massacre and had hidden behind a log until the whites had left the scene. There is no one to verify or discredit his story.

The natural bridge where the massacre took place is on Hayfork Creek, about nine miles above the town of Hayfork and a mile from the Leach Ranch–Wildwood Road. Carved from limestone by the action of the water, it has a span of 150 feet and is thirty feet high. The highway to Hayfork makes this point easily accessible.

WEAVERVILLE

The mining town of Weaverville, named in 1850 for John Weaver, a gold prospector who arrived in the vicinity in 1849, is located in what was one of the wildest and most inaccessible regions of California. Now it is easily reached by SR 299 from Redding and Eureka. It was once the center of great mining activity, and in 1850 it became the county seat of Trinity County. Many old buildings, some with iron shutters and winding outside stairways, give charm to the narrow streets of Weaverville.

Like many other towns of the county, it has suffered heavily from fires. The first fire, in March 1853, destroyed thirty-five of the forty-one buildings in the town, but the inhabitants immediately started rebuilding, this time replacing the wooden and canvas buildings wherever possible with brick ones. During the summer of 1853, the first courthouse and jail were built; and the Masonic Lodge, chartered in the summer of

1852, was for a time housed on the second floor of the first courthouse building.

Early in the winter of 1855 fire once more swept the town, but again the citizens began rebuilding immediately. More brick buildings were constructed in 1855, some of red-burned brick and some of adobe, and by 1858 there were twenty-five brick buildings on Main Street. Some of these were two-story structures, and nearly all were equipped with iron doors and shutters. In old buildings throughout the gold country, one sees many of these iron doors, protection against fire and theft if properly secured.

In 1999, nineteen brick buildings erected between 1855 and 1859 were still in use in Weaverville. One of these, built in 1856 as a saloon, store, and office building, was purchased by Trinity County in 1865 and has been used continuously as a courthouse ever since. The community bandstand, a handsome gazebo dating from 1902, is across the street, commemorated by an E Clampus Vitus plaque. Three adobe buildings from this period also survive, but except for part of the old firehouse, they have been so extensively remodeled that a passerby might not recognize their original material. Three two-story brick buildings on Main Street have outside spiral staircases built from the sidewalks to the overhanging balconies of the second floors. These iron staircases were locally made, the newest in 1935. When these buildings were put up, they often had two owners, one for the lower floor, one for the upper. Since space was at a premium and all the buildings were wall to wall, the best solution was an outside front stairway. The Historic District of Weaverville is centered on four blocks on Main Street and is on the National Register of Historic Places. There are over thirty-five marked old buildings here; one, the Weaverville Drug Store, has been in business at the same location and under the same name since 1862, in a building built as a pharmacy in 1855.

Weaverville's Chinatown centered on two blocks of Main Street; by 1854, some 2,000 people lived in crowded shacks, often destroyed by fire. After the disastrous 1905 fire, most of the Chinese simply left the county. The adobe Sam Lee Ranch House on Lorenz Road was built in 1918 on part of the old Lorenz Ranch property by one of the first generation of the only pioneer Chinese family still living in Trinity County. It is a local cultural center. The Weaverville Joss House State Historic Park (SRL 709) is situated on the west side of Main Street on a knoll across the bridge from Sidney Gulch. The present building was built in 1874 to replace one that had

Store and Spiral Staircase, Weaverville

burned. It continues to be a place of worship and is open to the public. The furnishings, for the most part, are those saved from the fires and are the very ones brought from China in 1854. In a small room there is a sort of frieze near the ceiling with the names of hundreds of Chinese who once constituted a part of Weaverville's Chinatown.

The Chinese Tong War of 1854 occupies a place of note in the town's history. About six hundred combatants took part in a battle on a flat near Five Cent Gulch, about a mile east of the center of town, in the vicinity of today's Weaverville Elementary School. There is a marker at the school grounds on SR 3, one-quarter of a mile east of its junction with SR 299. The site of the battle has been mined, and little of the 1854 landscape remains. In the collections of the J. J. Jackson Memorial Museum at 508 Main Street one may see sword, pike, and spear relics of this war between the tongs.

The Jackson Museum is housed in a structure dedicated in 1968. On its two floors are excellent displays of materials tracing the history of Trinity County, including an outstanding photographic collection. The History Center, opened in 1995, makes a two-story addition to the museum. Its documents and photographs are the core of the Historical Society's collections. The adjacent property is the Trinity County Historical Park, like the museum administered by the Trinity County Historical Society. In the park are several interesting displays. A restored steam-powered two-stamp mill from the Paymaster Gold Mine near Lewiston is fully operable and is demonstrated from time to time. An old miner's cabin from the La Grange Mine region can also be seen here.

An 1849 hand-pump fire engine, which first saw service in San Francisco before being purchased by Weaverville in 1906, is on display at the Weaverville Fire Department Fire Museum on Main Street. The museum also shows the challenges of this terrain for firefighters a century ago.

HISTORIC TOWN SITES AND STOPPING PLACES

In the 1850s and 1860s, settlements equipped with homes, stores, sawmill, blacksmith shop, and meat market flourished at Big Bar, Burnt Ranch, Campbell Ranch, Cañon City, Carrville, Cox Bar, Douglas City, Evans' Bar, Hayfork, Indian Creek, Junction City, Lewiston, Logan Gulch, Minersville, North Fork, and Trinity Center. Much of the travel in those days was over trails on foot, requiring frequent stopping places and making them successful places of business. The long-gone Trinity House was a famous inn on the north bank of the Trinity River below the old Lowden Bridge; the present bridge is one mile above the site.

Carrville, formerly the ranch of Curry and Noyes, became one of the best-known resorts in northern California. James E. Carr was the founder of the family that owned the place, one mile south of Coffee Creek. The beautifully restored Carrville Inn is a two-story building, now a bed-and-breakfast, adjacent to the pioneer cemetery. The Bonanza King Quartz Mine, lying on the mountain east of Trinity River, has been one of the valuable mines of the county. There has been much gold dredging along the river here and below.

Trinity Center was a lively and populous place in the early 1850s and for over a century was the center of one of the principal mining sections of Trinity County. The water ditches built in 1853 leading from Swift Creek were still in use a hundred years later. The district was settled in 1851, and by 1853 it had become a famous mining center. Trinity Center and the old settlement of Minersville have been inundated by the Trinity Dam project, which was completed in 1962. A new town of Trinity Center has been built on the shore of Trinity Lake. Nine buildings from old Trinity Center were moved to the new town site and stand today as reminders of the town's origin. Trinity Lake is now part of the Whiskeytown-Shasta-Trinity National Recreation Area, as is Lewiston

Lake, created by the Lewiston Dam, part of the same project.

Lewiston, one of the oldest settlements in the county, was on the road taken by packhorses from Shasta to Weaverville. The route was from the Tower House to the summit of Trinity Mountain, thence down Hoadley Gulch to Lewiston, and along the Trinity River until it turned north over Brown's Mountain to Weaverville.

At the mouth of Rush Creek was Dutch John's Trading Post, later Jacob Paulsen's, a well-known spot. Logan Gulch, midway down the canyon from Helena to Big Flat, was a leading trade center in the 1850s. Rich returns were obtained from the bed of the river.

Burnt Ranch, or McWhorter's, was one of the oldest settlements of Trinity County, first occupied in 1853. The charred remains of the house, destroyed by Indians, caused the place to be named Burnt Ranch. In this section of the county, a choice fruit-growing region, are Salyer, Hawkins' Bar, Denny, and New River. Lake City was an important settlement but was destroyed in Indian wars in 1865 and never rebuilt. During early Gold Rush days, an average of four hundred to five hundred miners worked the mountainous New River area, and in the 1880s New River itself was the scene of a large quartz-mining boom. Heavy milling machinery was packed in by mules, and gold worth millions of dollars was taken out.

Hayfork is an important agricultural and mining area, the site of the Trinity County Fair. There, in the pioneer period, Bayles's flour mill supplied nearly all the flour used in Trinity County. Hyampom is another agricultural section, where ranching began in the 1850s.

THE NATIONAL FORESTS AND THE TRINITY ALPS WILDERNESS AREA

Although gold mining brought the pioneer population to Trinity County, the chief importance of this county is now as a recreational and lumbering center. The major part of the land area of the county lies within the Trinity portion of the Shasta-Trinity National Forest. This forest, covering approximately 77 percent of the county, comprises 1,780,960 acres of timberland, in which Douglas fir predominates, with ponderosa pine second. The Trinity Alps Wilderness Area, 500,000 acres, is a distinctive part of the forest, which is being preserved as nearly as possible in its original state. The Forest Service has constructed good trails through much of this forest, and the dirt and gravel roads are accessible to four-wheel drive vehicles.

Tulare County

Kaweah Post Office

Tulare County was created in 1852 from the southern part of Mariposa County and the northern part of Los Angeles County. Tulare is Spanish for "a place of tules, or rushes." The first county seat was at Wood's Cabin, afterward known as Woodsville, but in 1853 it was removed to Visalia, where it has remained.

HOG WALLOWS

Parts of the San Joaquin Valley were once covered by curious mounds called hog wallows. Fairly regular in shape, they were as much as fifty feet long, twenty feet wide, and six feet high; at their bases, water collected in the winter and encouraged the growth of tules. All kinds of theories have been advanced to explain them. The Yokut Indians believed they were leftover earth dumped from work baskets after the building of the great Sierra Nevada. Since hardpan underlies most of them, early theories held that pressure from gas and water escaping through cracks below caused the mounds. A modern theory, not accepted by all, is that the common pocket gopher is largely responsible.

Leveling the hog wallows was necessary to make the land suitable for agriculture, and over the years most of this area has been filled in and cultivated. In order to preserve a fragment of this land in its unplowed, natural state, the Buckman family of Exeter presented a plot of ten acres in 1979 to the Tulare County Historical Society. A marker has been placed on the northern edge of the preserve, which is located on Avenue 314 just west of Road 220, near Lindcove.

INDIAN MOUNDS

As in other areas of California, most sites of early Indian habitation in Tulare County have been all but obliterated.

The largest of a group of remarkable mounds, once surrounded at flood time by the waters of Tulare Lake, was situated fifteen miles due west of Tulare on what is known as the old Jacobs Ranch. This mound, about 150 yards long and six feet above the surrounding country, was composed of a solid mass of the common softshell clams of Tulare Lake, which were found in layers "as clean and closely packed as if they had been washed and stacked by hand." Wagon loads of these thin, white shells were gradually hauled away for chicken feed.

Locally known as the Paige Mound, one of the largest rancherías ever reported in that section of the San Joaquin Valley was located along an old channel of Cameron Creek about two miles east of the settlement of Paige, southwest of Tulare. Many years ago an irrigation ditch was cut along the top of this mound, disclosing old burials and Indian artifacts. Gradually, over a period of years, the mound was leveled.

Several miles from the eastern shore of Tulare Lake there was a long island or series of islands that remained unknown to American settlers for many years on account of the dense screen of tule swamps that stretched for miles along the lakeshore in both directions. These islands always escaped the winter floods. Said to have been discovered in 1853 by a cattleman, the land was acquired soon afterward by Judge J. J. Atwell of Visalia, who used it as a pasture for hogs. Atwell's Island, as it came to be known, formed at least two islands during the highest water. The one to the west was called Skull Island, because the remains of Indian houses and skeletons uncovered by wave action were found there by the first white settlers to visit it. Another was called Pelican Island. The present town of Alpaugh is located on what was once Atwell's Island, and a little to the south and west of town many artifacts and remains of Indian villages have been found along old streambeds.

The Derby Expedition, which entered the San Joaquin Valley in April 1850, a few weeks after the Wood Massacre on the Kaweah River, reported that there were two large rancherías at Outside, Cameron, and Deep Creeks; and that the two hundred inhabitants of these villages had treated them with great hospitality. The Broder family, which settled on Cameron Creek in the early 1850s, also found several hundred Indians living on what came to be known as Broder's Mound and along the ridge to the southwest. Successive epidemics, however, reduced this number to not more than twenty. The Broders built their first house in this region about two hundred yards from the old mound, but later a more pretentious house was erected on the mound itself. This house became a refuge for neighboring white settlers during the flood of 1862, when the mound was the only dry land for miles around. The Broder mount property finally came into the hands of a Visalia bank in 1927, when, owing to a series of delays in leveling and building operations, local archaeologists working under the supervision of F. F. Latta succeeded in making one of the most extensive studies of ancient Indian cultures in the San Joaquin Valley. Perhaps the most remarkable example of Yokut burial customs ever unearthed was found at this site, yielding more than eight hundred specimens within an area of not over forty-five by sixty feet. Three distinct cultures were uncovered, including that of what was probably the first migration into the valley, as well as that of later Indians found at the site by the first American settlers.

The Sweet mound, found on the west bank of Elk Bayou, four and a half miles south of Waukena, was the site of one of the most extensive permanent rancherías on the east shore of Tulare Lake. This mound was found by two boys on the property of Adolph Sweet on Thanksgiving Day, 1928, and it was subsequently excavated by local archaeologists. Early American settlers had noted that this site was occupied by Indians as late as 1860. The burials and house sites unearthed at the Sweet mound appeared to be very old, showing no signs of contact with later Indian cultures or with whites.

Many Indian petroglyphs may be seen along the western slope of the Sierra foothills throughout Tulare County. The most remarkable of these are located north and slightly east of Visalia and Woodlake, Dillon's Point, and Kaweah Caves.

THE OLD SPANISH TRAIL

Gabriel Moraga went into the river country on the western side of the San Joaquin Valley in 1806 to search for mission sites. On his return trip he ascended the Kings River a short distance, crossing what is now Tulare County seven miles east of Visalia at Venice Hills, known as Kaweah Hills to local Indians and early pioneers.

Another party, possibly under the leadership of Juan Ortega, accompanied by Father Juan Cabot, chronicler of the expedition, went into the tulares in 1814, also in search of mission sites. In 1815, Juan Ortega and Father Cabot led an expedition from Mission San Miguel to hunt for Indians who had run away from the mission. Proceeding up the Kings River, the party crossed over to the Kaweah River in Tulare County and from there went on to the area of Venice Hills.

These expeditions reported favorably on the region near the present city of Visalia. They considered it especially suitable for mission sites, and in the biennial report for the years 1815–16 Padre Presidente Mariano Payéras renewed his recommendation to found a mission and presidio in the valley. The site selected was approximately at the location of present-day Mooney Grove Park, which had the three requisites of water, timber, and receptive Indians. When Lieutenant José María Estudillo went into the valley in 1819 in an attempt to subdue uprisings among the Indians, his report emphasized that a presidio would be necessary in connection with any mission established in that country. To be sure, there were numerous Indians in the area, but, in his opinion, they were very unfriendly. Nothing was done in either the Spanish or the Mexican period to make permanent settlements in Tulare County.

AMERICAN PATHFINDERS

The first Americans to pass through Tulare County was the party led by Jedediah Strong Smith, in 1826 and 1827. Skirting the Sierra foothills along the eastern side of the San Joaquin Valley, he probably followed the same route as that taken later by the Stockton–Los Angeles Stage Road, and now approximately by modern highways SR 65 and SR 245 through Porterville, Lindsay, Exeter, and Woodlake. Smith was followed in 1834 by Joseph R. Walker, who led the Bonneville hunters out of California over the Sierra by the pass that now bears his name, which forms an outlet from the South Fork of the Kern River to the eastern side of the divide.

John C. Frémont, in 1844, followed the old trail out of California. In the winter of 1845–46, a second expedition under Frémont reached Walker's Lake in Nevada. There the company divided, Frémont himself crossing the mountains with a few men to Sutter's Fort, while the main body, under the leadership of Joseph Walker, went through Walker Pass and down the Kern River, where they camped for three weeks early in 1846. Frémont, who had hurried south to meet his men, and who had understood the Kings River to be their meeting place, waited for several weeks before returning to Sutter's Fort. During this time he ascended the Kings River along the right bank to its junction with the North Fork, up which he climbed to an altitude of 10,000 feet. Walker, with the main body, after waiting in vain at the Kern River camp for Frémont's arrival, pushed on northward through Tulare County, finally rejoining Frémont near Mission San José.

WOODSVILLE

Under the leadership of John Wood, a party that was said to have come from the Mariposa mines settled on the south bank of the Kaweah River either at the end of 1849 or early in 1850. A substantial log cabin was built a short distance south of the Kaweah River delta, seven miles east of the site of the present city of Visalia.

The group had been established only a few months when a band of Kaweah Indians arrived and, because of earlier mistreatment at the hands of the Wood party, demanded that they leave the region within ten days. The white men were slow in making preparation to leave and delayed beyond the allotted time; all but three were massacred.

Another settlement had been made at the same time, about half a mile distant, by Loomis St. Johns, after whom the St. Johns River was named. Although it was near the Wood cabin, the St. Johns settlement was left unmolested by the Indians. Also about the same time two brothers, A. A. and C. R. Wingfield, claimed squatter's rights on land along the Kaweah River from the Wood cabin south.

When Tulare County was created in April 1852, the Legislature provided that the seat of justice be placed at the cabin on the south side of Kaweah Creek, near the bridge built by Dr. Thomas Payne, and that it be called Woodsville.

The first election board, a party under the command of Major James D. Savage, opened its polls on July 10, 1852; instead of votes being cast in the cabin, the election was held out of doors under the shade of a great oak tree on the south side of Kaweah Creek. Many years later, markers were placed designating as the Election Tree or the Charter Oak (SRL 410) a tree on the north side of the St. Johns River, which was created in the flood of 1862 and is, in fact, slightly north of Kaweah Creek. In 1905 some surviving participants in that election claimed that the tree thus marked was the actual Election Tree. Modern travelers can understand the confusion when they try to find the Election Tree amid the magnificent stands of oak in the countryside east of Visalia. The marked tree is on Charter Oak Drive east of Road 168 and about eight and one-half miles from the city.

VISALIA

In 1852 a group of settlers from Iowa and Texas located a few miles to the southwest of the Wood cabin. In November they built a log fort on the north bank of Mill Creek for protection against the Indians. To this they gave the name of Fort Visalia, probably suggested by one of their number, Nathaniel Vise, whose family home was in Visalia, Kentucky. Visalia claims to be the oldest town in California between Stockton and Los Angeles. Fort Visalia stood in the area now bounded by Oak, Center, Garden, and Bridge Streets, and is commemorated by a marker placed there by the Boy Scouts and the Tulare County Historical Society.

An election in September 1853 resulted in the removal of the seat of justice from Woodsville to Visalia. The county board of supervisors subsequently decreed that the name of the county seat should be Buena Vista, but petitions and protests caused them to rescind this action, and since March 1854 Visalia has been the official name of the Tulare County seat. It was not incorporated until 1874, long after it was well established as the most important town in the San Joaquin Valley south of Stockton.

California was admitted as a free state in 1850, and officially remained loyal to the Union in the Civil War. Nonetheless, pockets of Confederate or "secesh" (from "secessionist") sympathies persisted, one of which was in Visalia. Officials felt it necessary to establish a military camp at the town, and in October 1862 a company of the Second California Cavalry arrived to establish Camp Babbitt, named for the quartermaster general of the Pacific. Within a month, violence broke out between the townspeople and the soldiers after one of the latter was shot and killed in a saloon brawl. The alarmed camp commander sent off to Army headquarters in San Francisco the warning that "this command does not number more than 100 men and the rebels can bring to it 250 men in 24 hours and 400 men in 2 days all of them well armed." Two additional companies were dispatched to join the garrison at Visalia. A pro-Confederate newspaper was shut down, prominent citizens (including the future founder of Bakersfield, state senator Thomas Baker) were arrested and released only after taking a loyalty oath, and another soldier was shot and killed. As the Confederate fortunes waned, so too did "secesh" sympathies, and at the war's end, Camp Babbitt was disbanded. The camp had been established in the 400 block of East Race Street and moved later to Ben Maddox Way and East Houston Avenue. It is said that resentment against the government continued in a quiet way for many years; not until twenty years after Appomattox did the Republican Party elect any office-holders in Visalia.

Visalia's early buildings are mostly gone. This "City of Beautiful Trees" is one of the most wooded in the state, and the ubiquitous valley oak is the official city symbol. The College of the Sequoias is the community college.

MOONEY GROVE AND TULARE COUNTY'S PIONEER PARK

About five miles south of the center of Visalia on SR 63 (Mooney Boulevard) is Mooney Grove County Park, 100 acres of virgin oak purchased from the heirs of Michael Mooney in 1909 and preserved as a remnant of the forest of valley oaks that formerly covered much of the Kaweah River delta. In the park is the Tulare County Museum, which was founded by a grant from Hugh Mooney. The museum is a repository of Tulare County's past, ranging from Yokut basketry and projectile points to life in the county during World War II. The museum's Pioneer Village is a collection of old and historically important buildings that have been moved from various parts of the county and reconstructed. Among them are a log cabin (1854), the Cramer residence and post office from a settlement in the North Tule River valley (around 1863), and the Surprise School (1908). One of the most interesting relics is the ornate Gothic facade from the Masonic and Odd Fellows Hall in Visalia, built in 1873 and torn down in 1963.

STONE CORRAL

The oldest man-made landmark in Tulare County is located on the southeast side of Stokes Mountain, east of Cutler, and north of Seville. James Smith built this fifty-foot square corral of large rocks as a hog pen, in 1853. Near here, on the night of June 11, 1893, occurred the fight between a sheriff's posse and the notorious out-

Log Cabin, now in Tulare County Museum

laws John Sontag and Chris Evans. Sontag was killed and his wounded companion was captured the next day. Cedar rails split by Evans are on display in Pioneer Village.

TULE RIVER INDIAN RESERVATION

In 1857, after hostilities between the Tule River Indians and the new settlers had ended, a reservation was established near the present city of Porterville. To it were brought Indians from several tribal groups of a widespread area. The reservation was placed near the rancherías of the Koyeti and Yaudanchi tribes, both of which were branches of the Yokuts, who occupied the San Joaquin Valley. The first Tule River Indian Reservation was located on both sides of the Old Springville Highway, where, for about a quarter of a mile, it runs south to join the later highway at the Alta Vista School. A marker (SRL 388) is on Reservation Road, two miles east of Porterville. The location did not prove satisfactory, and in 1873 the reservation was moved ten miles southeast, into the mountains, to its present location.

THE STOCKTON–LOS ANGELES ROAD

The Stockton–Los Angeles Stage Road crossed the Kaweah River delta at a place long known as Four Creeks, that portion of the delta lying south of the Venice Hills. Stages and freight teams used this road, which went from Los Angeles north to Fort Miller and the mines.

The route was divided into what were called the Upper and Lower Detours. These detours paralleled each other as they passed along the base of the hills a few miles apart, and the southern junction of the two was near the base of the Venice Hills and a little to the southwest, where the railroad now crosses the St. Johns River.

For a half mile it continued south and then turned to the southwest for a quarter of a mile, crossing the Kaweah River a half-mile south of the Election Tree.

BUTTERFIELD STAGE STATIONS

During dry weather the northbound Butterfield Overland Stages, in the years 1858–61, turned off from the Stockton–Los Angeles route east of Visalia (where one of the main stage stations was located at what is now the southeast corner of Main and Court Streets) and crossed the country to the Kings River Station (Whitmore's Ferry). When the river was too high to be crossed at Whitmore's, a route along the base of the hills was followed to Smith's Ferry near present Reedley in Fresno County.

Proceeding southeast from Visalia, one passed the following stations: the "Pike" Lawless Ranch, one mile south of the present Outside Creek Bridge; the Tule River Station, later Porterville; and Fountain Springs. At the Tule River Station, Peter Goodhue put up the first building, a shake house with a fireplace at each end and a porch on the south side. The site of this old overland station (SRL 473) is at the foot of Scenic Hill, Main, and Henderson Streets, at the northern city limits of Porterville.

PORTERVILLE

In 1859 Porter Putnam arrived at the Lawless Ranch, where he obtained a job caring for the stage horses. Soon afterward he went to the Tule River Station. Putnam was an enterprising young man, with an affable nature. He bought out Goodhue and developed the station into a popular stopping place and hotel, and the place came to be known as Porter's Station. The town that grew up around it was called Portersville, later Porterville. A marker commemorating the site of the Putnam House and Store was placed at the corner of Main and Oak Streets by the Historical Committee of the City of Porterville. Another historical marker, on East Putnam Avenue between Plano Street and Leggett Drive, commemorates the site of the Porterville Flour Mill, which operated there from 1868 until it closed in 1912. The buildings were deeded to the city along with several acres of land to form Murry Park in 1929, but they were torn down in 1938.

A charming relic of the past is the Zalud house at the corner of Hockett and Morton Streets. Built in 1891 for Bohemian-born John Zalud and his family, the two-story home with its distinctive mansard roof sits in a lovely garden, especially noted for its summer display of roses. Pearle Zalud, the last survivor of the six children of the family, bequeathed the house and its garden to the city of Porterville upon her death in 1970. The house is open to the public on a regular basis and contains articles brought back from the family's travels and furniture from the late nineteenth century.

Nearby, at 257 North D Street, in the building constructed in 1913 as the passenger depot for the Southern Pacific Railroad, is the Porterville Historical Museum. Begun in 1963, the museum emphasizes the highly successful citrus industry that from the beginning of the century has contributed to Porterville's prosperity. As urbanization has taken over more and more land along the southern coast, the superb oranges from this region have become a major California product.

OTHER POINTS ON THE BUTTERFIELD ROUTE

A monument (SRL 648) stands at the small crossroads community of Fountain Springs to commemorate the early stage station that stood one and one-half miles to the northwest at the junction of the Stockton–Los Angeles Road and the road to the Kern gold mines. The actual site of the station is on private rangeland half a mile from the road.

Ducor, originally Dutch Corners, lies west of Fountain Springs and is commemorated by a marker placed by E Clampus Vitus in 1980. The little settlement was a way station on a Southern Pacific route put through in 1888, a line parallel to the Butterfield route.

Another marker (SRL 473) has been placed just west of Lindsay on a portion of the old Butterfield Stage route where SR 65 meets SR 137. A nearby marker from 1928 commemorates John C. Frémont's passage through the area.

TAILHOLT, A GHOST OF THE WHITE RIVER

The present hamlet of White River, also known as Tailholt (SRL 413), a little over seven miles southeast of Fountain Springs, was at one time a mining camp almost as well known as Angel's, Columbia, or Sonora. It is a small residential community today.

It was first established about 1856, during the Kern River gold rush. Placer gold was discovered on a small tributary stream in Coarse Gold Gulch, about two miles east of the present town, and the original settlement called Dogtown grew up. When the first road into Linns

Valley was built, old Dogtown was left one and one-half miles to the east. A new settlement, for a short time also known as Dogtown, was established at the present site. An interesting happening gave it the curious name of Tailholt. The story, as told by F. F. Latta, is as follows:

"Yank" Booth, the old stage driver, while en route to Visalia, stopped at [Dogtown] to change horses. He had with him a society lady who was returning from the Kern River Mines after having visited her husband, a mine operator at that place. This lady seriously offended . . . Yank by effectively "high-hatting" him. She further aroused [his] ire by carrying with her in the stage a pet poodle.

As the horses were being changed at Dogtown, a large cat crossed the street ahead of them, leaving the restaurant of Mother Cummings and proceeding to the hotel of Levi Mitchell. The dog spied the cat and attempted to jump from a small window at the side of the stagecoach. The lady made one wild grab for the dog and succeeded in catching it by the tail as it was leaving the stage. Yelping at the top of its voice, the dog hung suspended from the window, and the lady screamed for help. Yank took in the situation at a glance and went on changing the horses. Mother Cummings came to the rescue. While lifting the dog through the window she remarked, "Well, ma'am, a tail-holt is better than no holt at all." When Yank reached Visalia he told the postmaster and keeper of the stage station that the name of the new place on White River was Tailholt.

Two old cemeteries at Tailholt are especially interesting. One, situated on the crest of a hill to the north of the river, was reserved for respectable people. The other, located on "Boot Hill," south of the river, was for the renegades—desperate characters who died with their boots on. Of the seven burials at Boot Hill, five were the result of gunfights.

TULARE

Throughout the West in the late nineteenth century, it was a common practice for agents representing a railroad-building project to approach the city fathers of a community and demand favors for the railroad. Without them, it was warned, the railroad would be constructed to serve another, rival, settlement, to the great economic disadvantage of the unfriendly city. When Visalia authorities refused to cooperate with the Southern Pacific, the railroad's officials deliberately routed the San Joaquin Valley line westward, founding the town of Tulare as the local station in 1872. Visalia was by then well-established enough to survive this deprivation, and in time it did become a way station on the Southern Pacific line.

Tulare never became a sizable city, as did other railroad-favored spots such as Bakersfield and Fresno, but it remains one of the principal towns of the county whose name it bears—a unique example of a town taking its name from the county and not the other way around.

The old Tulare Woman's Club House at West Tulare and I Streets, built in 1882, was constructed for its employees by the Southern Pacific Railroad. Its original name was Library Hall, since the railroad provided books for the employees and townspeople (most of whom worked for the railroad). It was also a social and recreational center for the town. After many of the railroad's operations were moved to Bakersfield in 1890—causing a considerable loss of revenue to Tulare—the building served as a public library. When the Carnegie Library was built in 1905, the building was abandoned; some time later, it was turned over to the Tulare Woman's Club rent free in return for maintenance. In time the burden of maintenance became too great, and the city of Tulare took over the building in 1969. It continues to be a social center for the town.

Zumwalt Park, at the corner of Tulare and Main Streets, was named in 1971 for an illustrious Tulare family. Dr. Elmo Zumwalt, son of Tulare pioneers, was for many years a practicing physician and public official of the city, twice its mayor, and administrator of the Tulare County Hospital. His son, Admiral Elmo Zumwalt Jr., a graduate of Annapolis, had a very distinguished career. In 1971 he was named Chief of Naval Operations; he was the youngest man to hold that honor.

TRAVER

The traveler through the mining districts of California often comes upon ghost towns, tiny settlements that thrived for a few months or years before meeting an early death. A rare example of such a place in an agricultural region is Traver, some sixteen miles north of Tulare on SR 99.

For intensive agriculture, it was realized, the San Joaquin Valley had to depend on irrigation. In 1882, Peter Y. Baker, a civil engineer, conceived the idea of a large irrigation project that would furnish water to some 130,000 acres of land on the south side of the Kings River in both Tulare and Fresno Counties. Enough investors participated in the project to allow the newly formed corporation to acquire 30,000 acres. The corporation was called the 76 Land and Water Company, after the cattle brand of Senator Thomas Fowler, owner of part of the new holding and a principal stockholder. The main settlement of the project was named in honor of Charles Traver, company director. The 76 or Alta Canal was built to bring water into this hitherto unplanted area, and the town site was platted while railroads offered excursion rates to bring prospective settlers into the area.

After some initial setbacks, Traver was soon in full swing. Annie Mitchell continues the story:

> When the first contingent of buyers arrived on April 4, 1884, water was flowing through the canal. On that auspicious day the depot was the only completely finished building, but by the end of the day buyers had invested $65,000. Two months later Traver had two general stores, a drug store, a hardware store, two lumber yards, two hotels, two barber shops, two livery stables, three saloons, a post office, a school, an express office, a large Chinatown and a lively red light district.
>
> Fruit, grapes, vegetables and alfalfa did well, but basically Traver was a storage and shipping point for grain. Each of three warehouses held 30,000 tons of sacked grain. Most of the time they were filled and sacks of grain were piled outside and along the railroad right of way. Teamsters waited hours and even days to unload their wagons. By 1886 Traver was one of the largest grain shipping towns in the nation.

Since the bonanza gold rush days, very few California towns had boasted such rapid growth and apparent prosperity.

By a terrible irony, Traver was already beginning to die in the middle of this boom; in Annie Mitchell's words, "Traver was ruined by the same thing that created it—water." The soil was highly alkaline, and as intensive irrigation brought the alkali to the surface, virtually all the plants were destroyed. Like a blight, the alkali spread until the fertile fields were a desert plain. At the same time, the railroad opened a new line on the eastern side of the valley, developing the new towns of Dinuba and Reedley. Then in 1887, Traver experienced the first of five fires that discouraged settlers from remaining.

Traver still exists, marked by the plaque E Clampus Vitus placed there in 1974. Better farming methods have restored some of the land, though it remains a rather bare patch in the luxuriant fields of Tulare County. On or about April 8 of every year, descendants of former Traver residents join the inhabitants of today in a homecoming festival.

ALLENSWORTH

The unsuspected alkali that wiped out Traver's hopes worked with equal destructiveness in the southwestern corner of the county, in another kind of promised land, the town of Allensworth.

Allen Allensworth was born into slavery in Kentucky in 1842. During the Civil War he escaped and served with the Union forces. After the war, he and his brother operated restaurants in St. Louis while he pursued a formal education, becoming a minister in 1871. In 1886, by then married, he returned to the military as chaplain of the all-black 24th Infantry, where his service took him as far away as the Philippine Islands. When he retired in 1906, Colonel Allensworth was the highest-ranking chaplain and the highest-ranking black U.S. Army officer of his time.

The colonel's dream was to find some place in the United States where black Americans might live and create "sentiment favorable to the intellectual and industrial liberty" of their people, a dream shared by Professor William Payne. In 1908 Allensworth and Payne and three other black men incorporated the California and Home Promotion Association and in the same year acquired several thousand acres by the Santa Fe Railroad tracks, a few miles east of Alpaugh. Proximity to the railroad was important for a community that hoped to send its produce to market easily and to provide a refreshment and rest stop.

The settlement grew rapidly, many of the newcomers arriving from parts of the United States where segregation was enforced by both custom and law. Allensworth became a remarkably self-sufficient community. The church and the school soon developed, as, in time, did the blacksmith shop and the livery stable, the barbershop, and the pharmacy. But the economic life of the community depended on agriculture, and the irrigation needed for Allensworth's crops brought to the surface the same alkaline poisons that destroyed Traver. The accounts of Allensworth's brief years of prosperity (1910–15) are bright with the promise of crops that seldom saw a third yield.

As with Traver, a series of mishaps doomed Allensworth. The colonel was killed in an automobile accident in southern California in 1914, just when the first evidence of alkali was being found in the wells of the town. Allensworth believed that the railroad's proxim-

Tulare County Public Library at Allensworth State Historic Park

Schoolhouse at Allensworth State Historic Park

ity would also benefit the community, but this was not to be, for after World War I the new highways and the growing trucking industry bypassed the town. Bereft of their leader, often made aware of being outsiders in a strange land, and confronted with the implacable alkalinity that killed most vegetation, the people of Allensworth gradually moved elsewhere.

Allensworth State Historic Park was established in 1976. Some visitors have described it as a ghost town, but unlike Bodie State Historic Park in Mono County, it has restored buildings, and about thirty inhabited houses, many of them of recent construction. It is easily accessible from SR 43 some eight miles west of Earlimart on SR 99. The home of Colonel and Mrs. Allensworth is among those still preserved, as is the schoolhouse, where a commemorative jubilee is held annually in the middle of May. Projects for further development can be seen in the park's visitors' center.

SEQUOIA NATIONAL FOREST AND PARK

Sequoia National Forest and Sequoia National Park (in which is the General Sherman Tree, the largest *Sequoia gigantea* of all) comprise the most extensive as well as the most remarkable group of trees in the entire Sierra Big Tree belt, numbering fifty-three individual groves in all. Within this vast assemblage some of the most magnificent of the Sierra groves are to be found, a few of the most notable being Little Boulder Grove; the General Grant Grove section of Kings Canyon National Park, containing the General Grant or the Nation's Christmas Tree, one of the three largest of the Big Trees; the Muir Grove; Giant Forest, generally considered to be the largest and finest of all the Sierra Big Tree forests, where scores of separate groves merge, one into another; Redwood Canyon, another magnificent stand of over three

thousand trees; Redwood Meadow; Atwell; Garfield; Dillon Wood; and Mountain Home or Balch Park.

Giant Forest, in what is now Sequoia National Park, was discovered by Hale Tharp, a stockman who in the summer of 1856 had located in the Three Rivers district at what became known as the Tharp Ranch, now inundated by Lake Kaweah, about two and one-half miles below the present town of Three Rivers. Friendly Indians told Tharp of the existence of a neighboring forest of "big trees," and in the summer of 1858, wanting to see for himself and needing summer pasture for his cattle, he made his first trip into the Giant Forest, accompanied by two Indians.

A huge hollow sequoia log still lying at Tharp's old camp in Log Meadow testifies to this first visit of a newcomer to the great forest. On this log Tharp carved his name and the year, 1858, on the day he arrived. The inscription has now been obliterated by vandals. In this log Tharp built a unique home, where he spent many summers. It was fitted with a door, a window, and a stone fireplace, and contained one large room 56.5 feet long. The tree itself is twenty-four feet in diameter at the base and is estimated to have been 311 feet high when it fell. It is now carefully preserved by the National Park Service and is reached by a paved road extending six-tenths of a mile from the Crescent Meadow parking area.

Tharp was the first visitor not only to enter the Sequoia National Park region but also to live there, and his discovery led to further search and discovery of other important groves: Kings River, Tule River, and Deer Creek. By the summer of 1862 all of the groves in the state had been discovered.

A movement for the protection of the groves of giant sequoias in the mountains of Tulare County for purposes of permanent drainage, lumber supply, recreation, and scenic beauty was begun in 1878. A long, hard fight followed with the private interests that were seeking to buy up the Big Trees for commercial purposes. The leader in the fight was Colonel George W. Stewart who, as publisher and editor of the *Visalia Delta* in 1890, was also the chief promoter of the campaign for the creation of the Sequoia and General Grant National Parks. The latter is now part of Kings Canyon National Park.

Because of his unselfish and persistent work in pushing the cause of the giant trees, George Stewart has been justly acclaimed the "Father of the Sequoia National Park." A mountain in the Great Western Divide, rising almost 13,000 feet above sea level and about 5,000 feet above the Big Trees of the park, has been named Mount George Stewart in his honor.

THE JOHN MUIR TRAIL

For years a ridge trail from Yosemite to the headwaters of the Kern River had been the dream of many lovers of the High Sierra. In 1914, on the annual trip of the Sierra Club, Meyer Lissner suggested that the state Legislature be requested to appropriate money to build such a trail. While plans were being made, John Muir, for many years the leader and president of the club, died. "In seeking a fitting memorial to the man who had done so much to explore and make known to the world the wonders and beauty of the High Sierra, it seemed but fitting that a trail to be constructed near the crest of his 'range of light' should bear his name."

The first appropriation of $10,000 was approved by Governor Hiram Johnson in 1915, and another $10,000 was made available in 1917. No further appropriations were secured until 1925, and work on the trail was then resumed.

Walter L. Huber described the trail thus:

> In its course the trail passes Thousand Island Lake and the Devil's Postpile National Monument, rounds the flanks of the loftiest and most famous mountain peaks, from Mt. Ritter and Banner Peak on the north to the Evolution Group, Mt. Goddard, the Palisades and Mt. Tyndall on the south, zigzags up a succession of the highest and most impregnable divides, and affords approach to the Tehepite Valley, Kings River Canyon, and the Canyon of the Kern. It is the gateway to the best fishing, the most ambitious mountaineering, the sublimest and most diversified scenery that the High Sierra has to offer.

The southern terminus of the trail is Mount Whitney, the highest point in the United States, exclusive of Alaska. Along the route are 148 peaks rising to elevations of more than thirteen thousand feet, including twelve of the fourteen summits in California which attain elevations of more than fourteen thousand feet. The crest of the Sierra is more than thirteen thousand feet in elevation for eight and a half miles continuously adjacent to Mount Whitney. Even these cold statistics give an inkling to the grandeur of the region which this trail has made accessible, but not *too* accessible; for here is, I am glad to say, one of the most extensive areas in any of our Western states yet remaining practically free from automobile invasion.

Huber added that with the John Muir Trail should be mentioned the High Sierra Trail, constructed by the National Park Service in Sequoia National Park from the Giant Forest to Mount Whitney. This trail opened some of the finest mountain scenery on the North American continent and, with the John Muir Trail, made a complete loop through one of the most scenic areas of the High Sierra.

THE KAWEAH COOPERATIVE COMMONWEALTH

Tulare County was the home, from 1886 to 1892, of a socialist utopian colony, the Kaweah Cooperative Commonwealth. Under the leadership of Burnette G. Haskell and James J. Martin, several dozen people established themselves on the banks of the Kaweah River "for the purpose of demonstrating the advantages of cooperation in social and industrial life." The population of the colony at its peak reached about three hundred, but at other times it averaged only fifty to seventy-five. One of the objectives of the colonists was to support themselves by cutting timber in what is now Sequoia National Park, and they did succeed in building a sawmill and an eighteen-mile lumber road. The colonists, however, recognized the value to scientists and tourists of the magnificent sequoias in the Giant Forest. What is now known as the General Sherman Tree was called by the colonists the Karl Marx Tree.

The dissolution of the colony was the result of internal troubles as well as external pressures—from the large timber interests, the press, and the federal government, which established Sequoia National Park on September 25, 1890, and a few days later declared the adjacent lands a national forest. The colonists were never able to secure title to their land and soon disbanded, but many of them remained residents of Tulare County. The road from Kaweah to Old Colony Mill, painstakingly built by hand in 1886–90, was completed to the Giant Forest by the government in 1903. It was the only road into the forest until the Generals Highway was completed in 1927. Today, the old road is maintained as a fire road. About three miles north of Three Rivers is another tangible reminder of the hopes of the colonists, the wood-frame Kaweah post office (SRL 389), one of the smallest public buildings in California.

Tuolumne County

Tuolumne County was one of the original twenty-seven counties, and Sonora has always been the county seat. In 1806, an exploring party led by Lieutenant Gabriel Moraga passed through this area. The diary of Father Pedro Muñoz noted an Indian village, "Tautamne," in a mountainous area. Tuolumne, according to Bancroft, is taken from the Indian word *talmalamne*, meaning "a group of stone huts or caves." Kroeber thinks this interpretation is unlikely, since California Indians did not build stone houses, but "the word *tawalimni*, which perhaps was really *Tawalamni* or *Tawalumni*, would easily give rise, in either English or Spanish, to Tuolumne," and that it was the name of a tribe of Indians, "possibly Miwok, but more probably Yokuts," living in the vicinity of the lower Tuolumne and Stanislaus Rivers as far up as Knight's Ferry. The river, meadows, canyon, and county now bear the name.

PREHISTORIC LANDMARKS

Table Mountain, frequently mentioned by Bret Harte in his stories, is a conspicuous feature of the Tuolumne County landscape. A particularly fine view of its long, level top is obtained while crossing Rawhide Flat on the road from Tuttletown to Jamestown. The topography in the Miocene period consisted of an andesite lava flow that filled the hollows. Table Mountain is a part of this huge mass of lava, a quarter of a mile wide on the average and forty miles long, that filled one of the ancient stream beds. Ages of erosion have cut away the banks that hemmed in the river, leaving the hard andesite mountain standing out in bold relief. Deep beneath this once-molten mass have been found bones of extinct animals, traces of early flora, and implements of stone. Waterworn pebbles, gravel, and smoothly polished gold nuggets have been taken from the ancient river channel by miners, who tunneled great distances into the heart of the mountain until it was honeycombed with subterranean passageways. It is said that even today, Table Mountain holds millions of dollars of gold within it.

Southeast of Dardanelle, a resort on SR 108, is the largest and oldest known specimen of the western juniper, called the Bennett Juniper for Clarence Bennett, who discovered it in 1932. Perhaps a thousand years old, it is over forty feet in circumference and about eighty-five feet tall. The venerable tree is reached by a seven-mile trail from Dardanelle or a twelve-mile dirt road via Niagara Creek and Eagle Meadow.

There are two groups of *Sequoia gigantea* in Tuolumne County, the South Grove of the Calaveras Big Trees and the Tuolumne Grove. The South Grove, seven miles southeast of the North Grove of the Calaveras Big Trees in Calaveras County (both of which are in the Calaveras Big Trees State Park) is reached only by trail. It is a magnificent stand of 974 giant trees, all over twelve feet in diameter. Among them is the Louis Agassiz, one of the largest of all the Big Trees. The Tuolumne Grove, inside the western boundary of Yosemite National Park about one mile north of SR 120, contains only a small number of trees.

In Pate Valley, a wooded flat in the Grand Canyon of the Tuolumne River below Muir Gorge, there are a number of Indian pictographs, the first of them discovered by Harnden and McKibbie while exploring the river in 1907. Colored with red ochre, they are painted on the face of a high cliff on Piute Creek a little way from its junction with the Tuolumne River. Near the middle of the precipice there is a small cave, partly natural and partly hollowed out by human hands, in which other pictographs may be seen.

SONORA PASS

In the early nineteenth century, the Sierra Nevada stood as an almost insurmountable barrier between the western American plains and the Pacific slope. The jagged crest on the eastern edge of Tuolumne County, which is also the eastern boundary line of parts of both Stanislaus National Forest and Yosemite National Park, was one of the most impassable stretches in the entire range. The great difficulty was neither in the ascent of the eastern side, nor in passing the summit, but rather in the western descent, which, though spoken of figuratively as a slope, is in reality a series of granite domes, lakes, and canyons with almost perpendicular walls.

Sonora Pass, in the northeastern corner of Tuolumne County near its conjunction with Alpine and Mono Counties, rises to an elevation of 9,624 feet. Wagons hauling supplies to the mines east of the Sierra began using this pass in 1864. It was also the route of the early passenger stage on its weekly trip from Sonora to Bodie. The Sonora-Mono Highway, SR 108, follows the old road approximately as it winds through scenic Stanislaus Forest, over the crest, and on down to Bridgeport, 110 miles from Sonora. Portions of the former roadbed can be seen clearly from the highway at several points. Historical signs have been placed near the summit and along the route to call attention to points of interest. Fourteen miles northeast of Sonora a monument has been placed commemorating the Sonora–Mono Road (SRL 422).

In 1841 the Bartleson-Bidwell party, the first overland group of American settlers to enter California by crossing the Sierra Nevada, used a pass located ten miles south of the present Sonora Pass. By the time the party had begun the western descent, the last ox had been consumed and the travelers had begun to eat crow and bobcat. In the attempt to add to their provisions, young John Bidwell left the party to hunt, planning to cut across country and rejoin them later. When night overtook him he found himself in a grove of large trees. In the darkness he had particular difficulty in getting around a fallen tree, the butt of which seemed to extend some twenty or more feet into the air. In later years he visited the North Grove of the Calaveras Big Trees and found what he believed was the same spot. However, since the route of the party followed the south side of the North Fork of the Stanislaus River, rather than the north side, it is likely that Bidwell discovered the South Grove rather than the North Grove.

The emigrant trails to the west of Sonora Pass were not easy to follow, and various parties became entangled in the vast labyrinth of canyons, mountains, and rivers through which it was necessary to travel. In the early 1850s a party of gold-seekers was caught in a heavy snowstorm on the eastern slope of the mountains. As a result, they were forced to abandon their wagons, but they finally succeeded in crossing the pass and finding a comparatively sheltered spot on the western side. From this place a few members of the party proceeded as far as the Jarboe ranch, about where the town of Tuolumne now is, and from there assistance was sent back to the men in camp. It is from this episode that Relief Valley got its name.

Among the first wagon trains to cross Sonora Pass were the Duckwall party and the Washington Trahern party, named after a Cherokee who led the group. The former, consisting of J. W. Duckwall, his wife, six children, and three other men, found themselves marooned on one of the granite domes southwest of Sonora Pass, but managed to extricate themselves by hitching one pair of oxen to the front of a wagon and three pair to the rear and letting the vehicles down the precipitous granite wall. The Duckwalls arrived at Upper Relief Valley on September 27, 1853. The Washington Trahern party, which had lost most of their wagons in crossing the summit, reached the valley a day later. No road has ever been built over this stretch of the old emigrant trail, and the country has remained primitive and isolated.

From Strawberry and Pinecrest to Burst Rock (also known as Birth Rock because in the natural chamber formed by the great boulder a baby girl was born to an emigrant mother) a trail follows the old emigrant road marked by trees on which, it is said, blazes made by the pioneers are still visible.

VIRGINIA PASS AND CONNESS PASS

Long before the Americans came, the passes of the High Sierra were used by Indians to reach the deer and acorns that abounded on the western side and the pine nuts on the eastern slopes or to get the choice larvae that are found at Mono Lake at certain seasons.

Two of the lesser-known passes that cross the eastern border of Tuolumne County and are reached only by trail are the Virginia and the Conness, both of which lead from Yosemite National Park into the Hoover Wilderness on the western side of Mono National Forest. The Hoover Wilderness, named in 1928 for President-elect Herbert Hoover, contains thirty square miles at the headwaters of Green and Lee Vining Creeks, and within it are Tioga, Conness, Excelsior, and Dunderberg Peaks, as well as several glacial lakes. Two of these lakes, lying close together not far from the summit, are the Hoover Lakes, so named in honor of Theodore J. Hoover, mining engineer (and brother of the president), who explored and mapped this region in the summers of 1904 and 1905 while in charge of the Standard Consolidated Mines at Bodie. Conness Peak was named in 1863 for John Conness, later United States senator, in appreciation for his efforts in promoting the bill that organized the California Geological Survey. Dominating the landscape, it lifts its majestic summit 12,565 feet above sea level.

TIOGA PASS

Of the several Sierra passes on the eastern border of Tuolumne County, the Tioga Pass is one of the most used at the present time. Over this pass the Tioga Road crosses the summit at an elevation of 9,941 feet. The pass is dominated on the southeast by Mount Dana, 13,050 feet elevation, named in 1863 by the Whitney Survey in honor of James Dwight Dana, professor of geology at Yale University from 1850 to 1894.

Mining carried on in the Tioga district by the Great Sierra Consolidated Silver Mining Company, incorporated in 1881, necessitated a road from Sonora to the summit. The Tioga Road, or the "Great Sierra Wagon Road," which was completed in 1883 at a cost of $61,000, was built in part over the Mono Trail, but from the point where the latter turned south toward Mono Pass, the Tioga Road was continued eastward to Tioga Pass. When the mines in this rugged eastern part of Yosemite National Park were closed in July 1884, the road also was abandoned. A few of the buildings at the mines can still be found in a fair state of preservation.

The Tioga Road was donated to the United States Department of the Interior in 1915 and is one of the most scenic in California. Passing south of the Hetch Hetchy Valley through Yosemite National Park via Lake Tenaya and Tuolumne Meadows, it crosses the park from east to west. At the first ranger station west of the pass is a plaque placed in 1924 honoring Stephen T. Mather, then director of the National Park Service.

THE GRAND CANYON OF THE TUOLUMNE

One of the most spectacular scenic canyons in the United States is the Grand Canyon of the Tuolumne, lying wholly within Tuolumne County, fifteen miles due north of Yosemite Valley. Within a distance of twenty miles the Tuolumne River descends this majestic gorge from the level of Tuolumne Meadows to Hetch Hetchy Valley, a drop of almost 5,000 feet, the greater part of which occurs within the two miles immediately west of the California Falls. John Muir described the marvelous beauty of the canyon's superb, cascading river:

> It is the cascades of sloping falls of the main river that are the crowning glory of the Canyon. . . . For miles the river is one wild, exulting, onrushing mass of snowy purple bloom, spreading over glacial waves of granite without any definite channel, gliding in magnificent silver plumes, dashing and foaming through huge bowlder-dams, leaping high in the air in wheel-like whirls . . . doubling, glinting, singing in exuberance of mountain energy.

Tuolumne Meadows, one of the most beautiful of the numerous alpine meadows found in the Sierra, lies at the junction of the Dana and Lyell Forks of the Tuolumne River about fifteen miles northeast of Yosemite Valley. It is surrounded on all sides by the highest peaks of the Sierra Nevada, and many trails wind up from it into the very heart of the range. Conness, Dana, Mammoth, and Lyell Peaks lie to the north and east. On Mount Lyell there is a small glacier, one of the southernmost in California, which is believed to be a remnant of larger and older glaciers that, among other things, carved Yosemite Valley. Cathedral Range, with its unique and picturesque Cathedral Peak, protects the southern boundary of the meadow. Out of the floor of the valley itself rises Lembert Dome, while at the lower end, at the entrance to the Tuolumne Grand Canyon, towers beautiful Fairview Dome. The Tuolumne Meadows Visitors Center, where the highway crosses Unicorn Creek in the middle of the meadows, is a striking building from 1934 originally used as the mess hall for the local Civilian Conservation Corps. It is built in the distinctive style found in many public buildings throughout the Sierra: cemented boulders forming a foundation and lower walls, and upright peeled logs framing a front porch or veranda.

Hetch Hetchy (originally written Hatchatchie), a deep valley at the lower end of Tuolumne Canyon, was discovered by Joseph Screech in 1850 while hunting game. The valley was then occupied by Indians. John Muir is the authority for the statement that the name is a Miwok word for a certain grass with edible seed that grew in the vicinity. The valley was visited in 1863 by Professor J. D. Whitney and in 1871 by John Muir, who called it the "Tuolumne Yosemite." Muir explored the valley later, in 1875, with Galen Clark. Over the protests of Muir and other conservationists, the city of San Francisco, in the early 1900s, asked the federal government for the right to dam the Tuolumne, flood the Hetch Hetchy Valley, and provide San Francisco with its water system. In 1913 President Woodrow Wilson and Secretary of the Interior Franklin Lane (a Canadian-born Californian) reversed previous federal denials of the request and allowed the Hetch Hetchy project to proceed. The O'Shaughnessy Dam, named for San Francisco's city engineer, was completed and the reservoir filled in 1923. The height of the dam was increased in 1938. The dam, giving a view onto the Hetch Hetchy Reservoir, is reached by road from SR 120 just west of the Big Oak Flat entrance station to Yosemite National Park. In 1988, Secretary of the Interior Donald Hodel caused a furor when he proposed that the dam be taken down and the valley drained and restored. Protests from the city of San Francisco so far seem to have defeated this scheme.

RIVER CAMPS

Activity on the bars of the Tuolumne and Stanislaus Rivers began early in 1849. Hawkins' Bar, below Jacksonville, was the site of the first river diggings on the Tuolumne. Its population increased from fifteen in April 1849 to 700 by the following September. Extensive plans for damming and diverting the river were made but had to be abandoned because of an unexpected rise in the flow of the water. By 1852 Hawkins' Bar was practically deserted.

The history of Swett's Bar, where mining was begun in November 1849, is typical. A company of men cut a race to divert the stream, but here, too, the sudden rise of water caused the project to be abandoned temporarily. In August 1850 the work was resumed, and after fifty-nine days of hard labor the dam was completed— only to be washed away that very evening. The process was repeated a third time, with the same result. The season being then too far advanced to resume the project, the work was laid aside for the year. In August 1851 the camp, although reduced to twenty-seven men, completed a dam in a few weeks, and for some time thereafter an ounce of gold per man was taken out each day.

During 1850 the river camps along the Tuolumne were among the largest in the county, thousands of miners being engaged in attempts to divert the river in order to mine its bed. Few of the camps, however, enjoyed any great prosperity, and all of them, Hawkins', Swett's, Stevens', Payne's, Hart's, Morgan's, Roger's, Signorita, York, and Texas Bars, have completely disappeared. Not a vestige of former days remains to show where the cabins of the miners once stood. Not even the bars themselves remain as they were, for the river has changed its course several times since the 1850s.

Along that part of the old channel now covered by Lake Don Pedro lay the bars of Don Pedro, Indian, and Red Mountain. From one claim at Don Pedro's Bar, gold valued at $100,000 was taken out before 1889, the cost of operation being only $5,000. In the presidential election of 1860 (in which Lincoln carried California), as many as 1,500 votes were cast at Don Pedro's Bar. Indian Bar, the scene of active mining in the 1850s, continued to exist until the building of the first Don Pedro Dam, in 1923.

Moccasin, once a thriving camp at the mouth of Moccasin Creek, is now the site of the Moccasin Creek Power House, a unit in the Hetch Hetchy water system.

WOODS' CROSSING

The first discovery of gold in Tuolumne County was made in August 1848 at Woods' Crossing on Woods'

St. James Episcopal Church, Sonora

Creek by a party of men led by James Woods. Charles Bassett, J. H. Rider, and James Savage were members of the party. The richness of the gold field proved remarkable, and for a time gold in the amount of two or three hundred dollars a day per man was taken out with pick and knife alone. It is said that more gold was taken from this creek than from any other stream of its size in California. Almost as famous were two branches, Sullivan's Creek and Curtis Creek.

At Woods' Crossing, on SR 49 one mile southwest of Jamestown, a small monument of gold-bearing quartz has been placed by the Tuolumne County Chamber of Commerce commemorating the finding of gold there. The spot at which the discovery was made is located 500 feet southeast of this marker where the old road crosses Woods' Creek.

SONORA

Very soon after the discovery of gold at Woods' Crossing, settlements were made at Jamestown and at Sonora, farther up Woods' Creek. Located in a famous gold region, Sonora is one of the most picturesque and beautiful of all the old mining towns in the Mother Lode. It is also a modern county seat and commercial center, a blend of different periods. Along Washington Street, some of the heavy iron shutters of earlier days

have been replaced by plate-glass windows, which display relics of the mining era and recently found gold nuggets as well as current merchandise.

Sonorian Camp, as it was first known, was located by a party of Mexicans who pushed up Woods' Creek beyond Woods' Crossing and were the sole occupants of this region for several months. In the spring of 1849 the first American settlers arrived, including R. S. Ham, who apparently assumed the office of alcalde, and George Washington Keeler. Others soon followed. In July 1849 some 1,500 immigrants, mostly from Mexico and Chile, poured into the camps of Tuolumne County, and by autumn there were 5,000 people in Sonora. The narrow streets were thronged and almost impassable on Sundays. A tax on foreigners, which incited a bloodless war in June 1850, brought an exodus that cut the population almost in half.

In spite of the frequent fires from which Sonora has suffered, some buildings of the Gold Rush days still remain in and about the town. At 286 South Washington Street is the Gunn house, the oldest residence in Sonora. Dr. Lewis C. Gunn, who had arrived in Jamestown in 1849, built the house and in 1851 brought his wife and family of young children from the East to live there. At that time the house, a two-story adobe, had a balcony across the entire front of the second story. The parlor at the left was used as a printing office. Here the first issue of the *Sonora Herald* came out on July 4, 1850. Across the hall was the county recorder's office, Dr. Gunn having been elected recorder in 1850. After the Gunn family moved to San Francisco in 1861, the house was converted into a hospital, and in 1899 was remodeled as a private residence. Only the middle part of the present structure comprises the original Gunn adobe. The house is now a motel and is a fine example of a building in keeping with its historic theme.

St. James Episcopal Church (SRL 139), built in 1859, is one of the most attractive small churches in California, and one of the oldest Episcopal churches in the state. It is easily seen at the north end of Washington Street, commanding a view over the business district. To the west, the Street-Morgan mansion stands across the way from the church; this outstanding Victorian home, built in 1896, has been converted to offices and is beautifully preserved. St. Patrick's Catholic Church (1862) is another beautiful old building still serving the community. The Tuolumne County courthouse, built in 1898 and set back from Washington Street by a small park, is an impressive structure suggesting the vitality that resurged in the town in the year that the railroad arrived. It was erected on the site of the first courthouse, a wood-frame building from 1854.

The Tuolumne County Museum and Historical Center at 158 West Bradford Street is housed in the old jail, which operated from 1857 to 1961; it has many interesting exhibits related to gold mining. The Tuolumne County Historical Society, which operates the museum, has printed guides for walking tours of the downtown area. The City Hotel (1852) was originally an adobe structure and has been extensively remodeled, now wearing an appearance of the 1890s. Other noteworthy public buildings are the Odd Fellows Hall at Washington and Dodge Streets and the Wells Fargo building at Washington and Linoberg Streets. The Opera Hall (1885) near the Gunn house on South Washington Street has been refurbished and is used for public performances. Old residences still standing (all of which are privately owned and not open to the public) are the Burden, Burgson, Rosasco, Cady, and Sugg homes, the latter two on the National Register of Historic Places.

On a hill at the east side of town beyond the silvery dome of the 1909 Sonora Grammar School at 251 South Barretta Street is the Masonic cemetery, on Golden Street off Cemetery Lane, in which the graves of early residents are shadowed by oak and cypress trees. A monument of gold-bearing quartz was placed here by Tuolumne Lodge No. 8, Fraternal and Ancient Order of Masons, of Sonora, the Sonora Welfare Club, and the Tuolumne County Chamber of Commerce in honor of Jacob Richard Stoker, 1820–96. The inscription reads in part: "His heart was finer metal than any gold his shovel ever brought to light." Dick Stoker was a Mexican War veteran who came to California in 1849. He was closely associated with Mark Twain and the Gillis Brothers on Jackass Hill in the 1860s, and was a member of Tuolumne Lodge No. 8. With a reputation for being just and fair, Dick settled many miners' disputes and served his community faithfully.

The Big Bonanza Mine in the heart of Sonora is the greatest pocket mine ever discovered. (A pocket mine is one that yields a large and usually compact amount of pay dirt in a very small area.) It is located on Piety Hill less than one hundred yards north of the St. James Episcopal Church and within a short distance of four other churches. It was first worked in 1851 by Chileans, who took out a large amount of surface gold. In the 1870s it was purchased by three partners, who worked it for years and then one day broke into a body of al-

Railtown 1897 State Historic Park, Jamestown

most solid gold. The next day they shipped gold valued at $160,000 to the San Francisco Mint. Within a week $500,000 was taken out and another half-million was mined before the property was again sold. There is a marker to this amazing mine nearby, at the corner of Snell and School Streets.

Among other mines in this vicinity were the San Giuseppe, located about a quarter of a mile northwest of the center of Sonora, and the Golden Gate, renowned for the pureness of its gold. It has been estimated that within a radius of two miles of Sonora, $41 million of gold has been mined.

JAMESTOWN AND ITS NEIGHBORS

Jamestown (SRL 431), also called Jimtown, lies in the shadow of Table Mountain about four miles southwest of Sonora on SR 108. Colonel George F. James, a lawyer from San Francisco, located at this point on Woods' Creek in 1848. James had a falling out with his neighbors, and after his departure the inhabitants changed the name of the settlement to American Camp. The first name, however, had more appeal to the miners and was revived. In the years 1890–1915, $30 million in gold was taken from the Jamestown area alone—evidence that the gold rush was not confined to 1849 and the 1850s.

The coming of the railroad in 1897 made Jamestown an important transportation center, although there was not much railroad activity beyond here. The Sierra Railroad Company continues to operate a fifty-seven-mile track between Oakdale in Stanislaus County and Standard, east of Sonora, which carries freight. The Railtown 1897 State Historic Park on Fifth Avenue in Jamestown displays some of the equipment this route has used, some housed in a six-stall roundhouse where four steam locomotives are kept. Managed and operated by the California State Railroad Museum in Sacramento, this operation in Jamestown is seasonal; in the summer months, the trains carry passengers for trips along part of the line on weekends.

On Main Street in Jamestown today's visitor sees old brick stores and hotels, many with attractive balconies. The building formerly occupied by the St. James Masonic Lodge has been partly remodeled and the original stone has been covered with stucco, but the thickness of the walls is evident at the entrance. It is located on the west side of Main, two doors north of the picturesque Emporium. The Methodist Episcopal church on Seco Street was built in 1852 and is still in use.

At Montezuma (SRL 122), three miles south of Jamestown on SR 49, mining operations were begun in the summer and fall of 1852. Deep and extensive mines in this neighborhood produced exceptionally pure gold. The old Fox Building at Montezuma has been rebuilt and is now a private dwelling. Remains of a cemetery are near the corral. Campo Seco (or Dry Diggins), Curtisville, Green Springs, Hardtack, Sullivan's Creek, and Yorktown were other long-gone camps in the vicinity of Jamestown.

At Quartz Mountain, south of Jamestown and east of SR 49, is the famous App Mine, which produced $6.5 million in gold until 1909. The mine was closed down a few years later, and in 1927 the town of Quartz was destroyed by fire. John App and others became interested in property on this mountain as early as 1856, when they located the quartz claim on the west side. App married Leanna Donner, one of the six Donner girls orphaned by the famous Donner Pass tragedy of 1847. Mrs. App, who reached the age of ninety-five, lived for seventy-eight years in Tuolumne County.

South of Quartz is Stent, formerly known as Poverty Hill, where an old cemetery remains. Even less can be seen at nearby Algerine.

Climbing Table Mountain west of Jamestown one comes to Rawhide, or Rawhide Flat, the location of the Rawhide Quartz Mine, which had a production record of over $6 million in gold until 1909. At one time this mine, owned by Captain William Nevills, was considered one of the greatest gold mines in the world. There has been much pocket mining in the vicinity of Rawhide.

Jeffersonville, a thriving town in the 1850s and a stage stop between Rawhide and Tuttletown, was the scene of extensive tunnel mining under Table Moun-

Miners' Ditch, Columbia

tain. Only a small graveyard at the top of a hill marks the site of the town. West of Jeffersonville is the site of French Flat, now overgrown with chaparral. The Humbug Mine, on the east slope of the mountain a little way from the road leading from Jamestown to Rawhide, was the richest of all the tunnel mines, with a total yield of more than $4 million; nuggets the size of hens' eggs were found there.

COLUMBIA

Columbia (SRL 123) was a city of several thousand people, one of the largest mining camps in California. From an area of 640 acres on the outskirts of the town, more gold was recovered from gravel than in any equal area in the Western Hemisphere. Most of the topsoil here, which averages from twenty to sixty feet in depth, was removed by hand cart, leaving an expanse of rocks, fantastic and unreal in appearance.

The rush for gold in California had few parallels. On March 27, 1850, Dr. Thaddeus Hildreth, his brother George, and some other miners made camp for the night under an oak tree in the vicinity of what is now Columbia. Rain during the night obliged the men to remain the next morning in order to dry their blankets, and while there, John Walker found "color" in a nearby gulch. The party remained and located at this promising point, which is where the bridge at the foot of Main Street crosses Columbia Gulch.

For a time the place was called Hildreth's Diggings, but was soon renamed Columbia. Almost from the first the camp was troubled by a lack of water. The winter of 1850–51 provided little rain to remedy the situation. In June 1851 the Tuolumne County Water Company was organized at Columbia. Its attempt to build a ditch to Five Mile Creek was at first frustrated, however, by the fact that there was insufficient waterpower to operate its sawmill. Heavy steam equipment had to be hauled to it, and by late November the mill was in operation. The ditch was completed by the following spring. In the meantime merchants were coming in to supply the needs of the 200 men working on the ditch. About the first of September 1851 a citizens committee was appointed to lay out the streets and lots, and subsequently the town was platted on its present site. It was incorporated in May 1854, only to be almost destroyed by fire two months later. The reconstructed buildings were substantial and more nearly fireproof. In the summer of that year another ditch company, the Columbia and Stanislaus Water Company, was formed, but eventually it was absorbed by the older company. Ultimately, after years of supplying the county with water for mining and irrigation, the Tuolumne County Water Company and its successors were absorbed by the Pacific Gas and Electric Company, which continues to furnish electricity for the entire county.

Families had begun to settle in Columbia as early as the fall of 1851, and soon gardens were planted and ranches begun in the vicinity. Two terribly destructive fires, in 1854 and 1857, were convincing reasons for rebuilding most of the public structures in brick or stone and embellishing them with iron shutters and doors. From January 1858 to January 1860 Columbia was illuminated by gas made from pitch, the lamps being set on cedar posts. Churches and public buildings were illuminated free. The gasworks were on the east side of Gold Street, midway between Washington and State Streets, about opposite the end of Fulton Street. After two years this unsatisfactory system was discontinued. The town was often spoken of as "Columbia, the Gem of the Southern Mines," because of the great extent of its rich placer deposits. With the decline of mining, its population shrank to a few hundred, but it never became a ghost town. The post office has operated continuously since November 16, 1852, although the old building was recently closed and the office now operates from a new facility to the west of the town.

As the centennial of the Gold Rush approached, the Mother Lode country began to attract the attention of

Wells Fargo Building, Columbia

historians, and Columbia was adjudged the best preserved of the old camps and the most worthy of restoration as a memorial to the pioneers and a piece of "living history" for the enjoyment and education of future generations. The old town was purchased by the state in 1945 and became Columbia State Historic Park. It has since been registered as a National Historic Landmark.

Columbia is a contemporary California town, but on a site that is deliberately maintained to present the outward appearance, as far as possible, of a town of the late 1850s. Among the oldest buildings in town are the adjacent Franklin & Wolf and Brainard buildings, which have a common wall. The Stage Drivers' Retreat and the Pioneer Saloon (Alberding's) are just two of the numerous establishments where locals gathered to slake their thirst and pass the time. The City Hotel, from 1856, is a successful establishment operated by Columbia College and is both a restaurant-and-hotel and a school for hotel management trainees. The view of Columbia from its second-floor balcony is a photographers' favorite. The Fallon Hotel and Theater have been restored and are likewise open for business; Owen Fallon built the oldest part of it in the fall of 1859. Nearby stands a replica of Eagle Cottage, the original of which was a boardinghouse in the middle 1850s. A stone monument on the west side of Broadway opposite the restored Masonic Hall bears a bronze tablet recounting major events in Columbia's history.

Todd & Company's Express maintained an office at Columbia at least as early as 1852, the year in which

William Daegener took charge, at a location unknown to historians. By September 1853 Todd had sold out to Wells Fargo & Co., and within the next few months the office was moved to the American Hotel. This was at the site of the present brick Wells Fargo Building, which Daegener built in 1858. Now thoroughly renovated and restored, it is another favorite subject for photographers. Wells Fargo operated there until 1914.

The little engine house contains one of the oldest pieces of fire-extinguishing apparatus in the state, the hand-pumper "Papeete," polished and painted to look as it did when it arrived in Columbia in December 1859. (It is said that the engine was constructed for use in Papeete, Tahiti, but the Columbia committee visiting San Francisco to purchase a municipal wagon prevailed upon the builder to sell it to Columbia instead.) The adjoining two-story building contained the office where four short-lived newspapers were printed.

The brick Columbia school on the hill was opened for its first term by John Graham on March 18, 1861, using furnishings from the old school. By September new desks and seats were all in place. Restoration of the schoolhouse was effected through the efforts of the California Teachers Association. On a hill beyond the school is the cemetery of Columbia Lodge No. 28, F. & A. M., which has been restored by the Grand Lodge, which also rebuilt the Masonic Hall in the town itself.

St. Ann's Church, a favorite subject for photographers and painters, crowns Kennebec Hill, overlooking the world's richest placer grounds, with the ghostlike rocks of the diggings encroaching to the very edge of the little cemetery. The church was built in 1856 with funds contributed by the miners. The walls of this historic church were made of brick fired in a kiln that was located on the Sonora-Springfield Road, while the timbers used in its construction were obtained from Saw Mill Flat about three miles southeast of Columbia. The belfry was added in 1857. The interior decorations and altar paintings are the work of pioneer hotelkeeper James Fallon, son of Owen Fallon. After having stood for half a century, the walls of the church were considered unsafe, and its doors were closed. With the support of the Knights of Columbus and the Native Sons of the Golden West, the structure was repaired and re-dedicated in 1906. Another restoration was made in the late 1980s.

Between Columbia and Vallecito was Parrott's Ferry (SRL 438) on the Stanislaus River. Thomas H. Parrott established it in 1860, and it operated until 1903, when the first bridge was built. An incised boulder at Parrott's Ferry Outlook reads:

> Inspiration Point: The Inspiration to revive the Ancient and Honorable Order of E Clampus Vitus, a benevolent society prominent in gold rush days, occurred fifty years ago to Carl I. Wheat as he travelled from Columbia down to Parrott's Ferry on the Stanislaus River. ECV Redivivus, now a fraternal historical society dedicated to preserving Western history and lore, has thirty-five active chapters throughout California and Nevada. Plaque dedicated May 26, 1980 [Memorial Day]. Co-sponsored by Matuca Chapter 1848, Quivira Chapter, Yerba Buena Capitulus Redivivus, New Helvetia Chapter, Paltrix Chapter, Lord Sholto Douglas Chapter. Credo Quia Absurdum.

GOLD SPRINGS

In the sands of a large spring, which is still visible about a mile and one-half northwest of Columbia, a Mr. Hatch and others discovered gold in April 1850. This spring and another were the source of a stream that was used for mining operations employing some three hundred miners. A camp boasting a two-story brick building, at least three food stores, several boardinghouses, a soda works, and a number of mechanics' shops and hardware stores, with an area population of 500, had grown up at the springs by 1856. It is said that its citizens were quiet, orderly, and enterprising. Several gardens and small ranches in the immediate vicinity supplied fresh fruits and vegetables to the miners at Columbia and Yankee Hill to the southeast, and to Red Dog, Dow's Flat, Heavy Tree Hill, Wayne's Bar, Simpson's Bar, Italian Bar, and Texas Bar to the north.

OTHER OLD SETTLEMENTS

Saw Mill Flat (SRL 424), so named because of the two sawmills established there to supply mining timbers in the early 1850s, was situated on a fork of Woods' Creek, three miles southwest of Columbia and one and one-half miles south of Yankee Hill. At first it was a great gathering place for Mexicans and Peruvians, and it is said that Joaquín Murieta, at that time a monte dealer, operated in the town, where injustices done to him by some Americans set him on his career of banditry and revenge.

Shaw's Flat (SRL 395), on the eastern edge of Table Mountain, was named by Mandeville Shaw, who planted an orchard there in 1849. Homes planted with fruit and ornamental trees give the place an attractive appearance today. The old miners' bell is displayed at the school. Immense fortunes were taken out of tunnels dug under Table Mountain, some beginning from Caldwell's Gardens, now vanished.

Brown's Flat, located on Woods' Creek one mile north of Sonora, had its beginning in 1851. Extensive hill and surface diggings independent of the creekbed were worked in the vicinity. Among these mines were the Ford, the O'Hara, the Page, and the Sugarman, the last-named producing crystallized gold of great beauty.

Squabbletown, a small camp farther north on Woods' Creek, has practically disappeared. Only a few old cabins show where the settlement once stood.

TUTTLETOWN

Tuttletown (SRL 124), about six miles west of Sonora on SR 49, was named for Judge A. A. H. Tuttle, who built a log cabin there in 1848. The earliest dwellings consisted of tents and *ramadas* or brush houses. It was a stopping place for packers carrying miners' supplies over the old Slumgullion Road from Angels Camp to Sonora, and by 1850 it was a flourishing camp. It has declined to a small hamlet.

JACKASS HILL

Jackass Hill, just west of Tuttletown, achieved notoriety in 1851 and 1852. The diggings were rich in coarse gold and excitement was intense. Hundreds rushed to the scene, and many a lucky miner made a "pile" in a few hours. Some claims of 100 square feet yielded as much as $10,000, and one quartz pocket produced from $100 to $300 a day for three years. Numerous small pocket mines made rich yields of ore.

The hill received its name from the braying of the jackasses in the pack trains that paused overnight on their way to and from the mines. As many as two hundred of the animals are said to have been picketed on the hill at one time.

Mark Twain spent five months on Jackass Hill in 1864–65 as the guest of William R. Gillis. A replica of the cabin (SRL 138) stands on the hilltop about one mile from Tuttletown. It is built around the old fireplace, which survived the destruction of the original cabin by fire in 1906. It is surrounded by modern homes and is set apart by a fence. A tablet telling the story of Jackass Hill was placed near the cabin in 1929 by the Tuolumne County Chamber of Commerce.

SPRINGFIELD

Springfield (SRL 432), a camp southwest of Columbia near the head of Mormon Creek, received its name from the fine springs there, which afforded sufficient water for the placer-mining operations of several hundred men who worked the rich gold claims in the vicinity. The miners often uncovered Indian mortars and pestles, showing that Indians had camped at the springs. The town, with its stores, shops, and hotels, was laid out around a plaza. The erection of a Methodist church before a gambling house was built makes Springfield unique in the annals of mining towns. It was noted for the quiet orderliness and sobriety of its citizens, many of whom worked in the mines under Table Mountain nearby. The site of the town is indicated by an abandoned brick schoolhouse, which formerly served as a church, and was an arsenal in the Civil War.

CHINESE CAMP

Ten miles southwest of Sonora is Chinese Camp (SRL 423), which in 1856 had a population of 1,000 and boasted a church; a bank; an express office; several stores and hotels; and two fraternal orders, the Masonic Lodge and the Sons of Temperance. Mining there consisted principally of surface diggings on the hilltop and in the valley. Water was brought to the mines in the vicinity from Woods' Creek by means of a flume and ditch.

A story explaining the origin of this old place name is that the town was founded by a ship's captain who deserted his vessel (the brig *Eagle*) in San Francisco Bay and brought his entire Chinese crew there to mine. A less dramatic version is that English prospectors employed Chinese miners there. A third story says that after gold became exhausted over the hill at Campo Salvado, the miners working there next joined the Chinese on the other side and named the new location after them. Around five thousand Chinese workers gave their name to the place, yet another story goes. There appears to be no Chinese population in the town today. The visitor can still see a few old stone and brick buildings with heavy iron doors typical of the early gold days. The Wells Fargo Building (SRL 140) has entirely vanished, although its iron doors are in the Wells Fargo Museum in San Francisco. On a hill at the edge of Chinese Camp is picturesque little St. Francis Xavier Catholic Church, built in 1854, restored in 1949, and further restored in

1976. The old one-room Chinese Camp School is at the same location.

Chinese Camp was the rallying place of the second big tong war in California. Two Mile Bar on the Stanislaus River was the scene of the incident that led to this war. Twelve members of the Sam-Yap Tong were working near six members of the Yan-Wo Tong when a huge stone rolled from one property to the other. Words and blows ensued. Calls went out for assistance. American blacksmiths in neighboring camps were engaged to make crude weapons—pikes, daggers, and tridents—and a few firearms were supplied from San Francisco. On September 26, 1856, 900 members of the Yan-Wo Tong went forth from Chinese Camp to meet 1,200 members of the opposing tong near Crimea Gorge. The battle took place amid the beating of gongs and the reverberations of random shots from inexperienced marksmen. The casualties were four killed and four wounded. American law officers finally arrested 250 of the combatants. The State Historical Museum at Sutter's Fort, Sacramento, has specimens of these locally manufactured weapons.

JACKSONVILLE

Jacksonville (SRL 419) on the Tuolumne River was established by Colonel Alden Jackson in June 1849 and by the summer of 1851 it ranked second only to Sonora. In the early 1850s Jacksonville was the scene of extensive river operations, including the building of great dams and wing dams at high cost in labor and materials. A modern dam finished off the town and its old orchards, which now lie at the bottom of Lake Don Pedro.

PRIEST'S HOTEL AND BIG OAK FLAT

Priest's Hotel (named after its original owner) was on the main road to Yosemite Valley in the 1860s. A wagon road over this route was not completed to the floor of the valley until 1874. The steep and winding road up Old Priest's Grade (now bypassed by SR 120) is one of the most picturesque in the Sierra, and one of the most challenging for the driver. The original Priest's Hotel and its successor have long disappeared from the site, simply known as Priest today. From a hill at about the middle of the settlement a panorama touching seven counties may be observed on a clear day.

About a mile from the hotel stood a famous landmark during mining days, the valley oak (*Quercus lobata*) from which Big Oak Flat (SRL 406) derived its name. This huge tree, eleven feet in diameter, was eventually killed by miners digging around its roots for gold.

James Savage, with a retinue of Indian laborers in 1850, was the first man to mine Big Oak Flat, originally called Savage Diggings. In the vicinity, the Lumsden, Big Oak Flat, Longfellow, Cosmopolite, and Mississippi Mines were notable producers. A large stone building, the Odd Fellows Hall, still stands at Big Oak Flat, as does the Wells Fargo Building, which is now on the National Register of Historic Places.

FIRST AND SECOND GARROTE

Groveland (SRL 446), formerly known as Garrote or First Garrote, on SR 120, the Big Oak Flat Road, is still a thriving community. Its original name refers to the hanging of a thief by early miners. On its main street stands the old Tannehill store, and at the opposite end of the block is the Masonic Hall, an old two-story adobe. About two miles above Groveland, near the edge of the Stanislaus National Forest, is Second Garrotte (SRL 460), a small mountain town. When the stage line opened on the Yosemite road in 1876, it is said that operators of the line wished to provide something of interest for travelers at the otherwise featureless stage stop; they selected a large oak and named it Hangman's Tree. Across the road from the marker and enclosed by a fence is a two-story frame house, formerly the home of Chaffee and Chamberlain, said to have been the originals of Bret Harte's stories. Mines in the vicinity of Second Garrote were the Kanaka, the Big Betsy, and the Mexican.

TUOLUMNE

Tuolumne, just west of the border of the Stanislaus National Forest, was a lumber center and terminus of the Sierra Railway. It is less than a mile from the old mining camp of Carter's, first known as Summersville (SRL 407), named in honor of Mrs. Elizabeth Summers, wife of an early settler. This area was home to the Miwok people, and just north of the town is the Tuolumne Rancheria, with about 150 inhabitants.

The Buchanan Mine ten miles east of Tuolumne has yielded more than $2 million over the years.

THE EAST BELT MINES

Mining activity in the East Belt began early in the 1850s. The Soulsby Quartz Mine at Soulsbyville was discovered by Benjamin Soulsby in 1856. It seems to have been worked exclusively by Cornish miners. By 1909 it had produced $7 million. Other mines in the vicinity were the Black Oak, the Live Oak, the Golden Treasure, and the Platt and Gilson. Soulsbyville (SRL 420) has always been a place of well-kept homes, pretty gardens, and law-abiding people, so the chroniclers say.

Over the lava ridge just east of Soulsbyville was Cherokee (SRL 445), near neighbor to Arastraville. The Confidence Mine at Confidence, thirteen miles northeast of Sonora on SR 108, was discovered in 1853 and was one of several good producers in this vicinity. This group of claims included the Independence, the Little Jessie, the Mary Ellen, and the Plowboy. The Excelsior Mine at Sugar Pine produced $420,000 worth of gold before the quartz vein was lost; many attempts to relocate the vein have failed.

Ventura County

Ventura County was organized in 1873 from Santa Barbara County. The city of Ventura has always been the county seat. Ventura is a shortened form of San Buenaventura, the name of the mission. The city is still officially known as San Buenaventura, although the post office has been designated Ventura since 1889.

CABRILLO'S ARRIVAL

Once there were many Chumash villages along the shore of what is now Ventura County. When Juan Rodríguez Cabrillo sailed up the coast in 1542, he came ashore on October 10 at a place where there was a large village called Shislolop. Impressed by the large, finely built boats of the Chumash people, Cabrillo called the place El Pueblo de las Canoas ("the town of the canoes"). The boats carried from fifteen to twenty persons, were built of boards hewn by hand, and were caulked with asphalt from the neighboring hills. Their boats, homes, implements, and utensils, as well as their mode of life, exhibited a skill in workmanship and a high level of culture that placed a distinguishing mark upon the Chumash people of Ventura and Santa Barbara Counties and of the Channel Islands.

The village at which Cabrillo landed may have been the one located at the foot of what is now Figueroa Street in Ventura. In the 1870s a kitchen midden was still visible very near the sea, about where Promenade Park is today. There is, however, some difference of opinion among historians as to the location of Pueblo de las Canoas, Mugu Lagoon southeast of Oxnard being noted as another possible site. Cabrillo remained at the village until October 13, when he sailed "six or seven leagues, passing along the shores of two large islands," anchoring off Rincon Point, then continuing in a northerly direction up the coast.

Relics of Chumash culture have been found throughout the region; some are preserved in the Ventura County Museum of History and Art located at 100 East Main Street in Ventura. Water baskets lined with native asphalt, skillfully wrought bowls and mortars, and finely shaped arrowheads are among the many interesting artifacts on display.

THE TRAIL OF PORTOLÁ

Leaving the campsite near Castaic in Los Angeles County on August 10, 1769, Captain Gaspar de Portolá and his men continued down the rich valley that was later called the Santa Clara, after a village that Father Juan Crespí had named, halting for the night on the banks of an arroyo in the vicinity of Rancho Camulos very near the county line. On the three succeeding days the tents were pitched near Indian villages in the neighborhood of Fillmore, Santa Paula, and Saticoy, where the friendly inhabitants gave the strangers gifts of seeds, acorns, and baskets of pine nuts in exchange for beads. Portolá's visit has been commemorated by markers at Warring Park in Piru (SRL 624) and the eastern edge of Santa Paula (SRL 727). On August 14 the party stopped near the site of Mission San Buenaventura, where a large ranchería was located. Father Crespí, who named the village La Asunción de Nuestra Señora, expressed the hope "that such a fine site, where nothing is lacking, will become a good mission." The next night found the travelers at a coastal village where the father wrote that the Indians "kept us awake playing all night on some doleful pipes or whistles." The name bestowed upon this place by the soldiers has persisted in Pitas ("whistles") Point, the location of Faria County Park. On August 16, Rincon Point was rounded and camp was made at a fishing village on Rincon Creek.

When Portolá's men again crossed the county on their way back from Monterey in 1770, their route was the shorter one followed by the present US 101 via Conejo Grade and Calabasas into Los Angeles.

ANZA'S TRAIL

Juan Bautista de Anza, on April 10, 1774, on his overland journey from Sonora to San Francisco, camped near Triunfo (a former post office at the junction of El Camino Real and the road to Lake Sherwood) in Russell Valley west of Calabasas. "Passing among many docile heathens," the party continued their march the next day, halting for the night near San Buenaventura on the river of the same name. Returning from the north a little later, Anza camped on April 29 east of Camarillo at the foot of Conejo Grade, this being his only stop in Ventura County on that trip. In 1776 Anza passed this way again as leader of the first overland emigrant trains to California. Retracing his former route, he made only one halt in Ventura County, near El Rio, on February 23.

MISSION SAN BUENAVENTURA

In the midst of these populous villages with their friendly people, halfway between San Diego in the south and Monterey on the north, Father Junipero Serra at length planted the ninth of the missions and named it San Buenaventura. Saint Bonaventure (Buenaventura, "good fortune") was healed by Saint Francis, and was a Franciscan theologian of the thirteenth century. This was the last mission to be founded by Serra, who died two years later. From the beginning of his work in California the padre presidente had contemplated the founding of a mission in the fruitful valley of San Buenaventura. But it was thirteen years after the founding of the first mission that Mission San Buenaventura was established, on March 31, 1782. In the vicinity of the Chumash village of Mitz-Khan-a-Khan, Father Serra put up the crude *enramada* for the celebration of the first Mass.

It was the custom, when a mission was dedicated, to put up a cross, not only as an emblem of faith but also as a sign to guide travelers to the mission. Along the coast a site was usually chosen that was visible both by land and by sea. At Ventura, the place selected was a lofty hill, La Loma de la Cruz ("the hill of the cross"), which rises immediately behind the mission church in the present city of Ventura.

For nearly fifty years Serra's cross (SRL 113) stood upon the hilltop above the mission. At last, however, rain and wind so weakened it that it fell. The old central timber was replaced by a new one, but the original scroll and crosspiece were retained. Thus it stood for another half-century until it was again blown down in 1875. After that, the hill was without a cross for thirty-eight years. The scroll of the original cross, however, was saved and is now preserved in the Ventura County Museum of History and Art. In 1913 a new cross was raised on the original hilltop site, now located within Grant Park.

Very soon after the first *enramada* was made, the first mission church was built. According to Captain George Vancouver, this was destroyed by fire. Church records indicate that if such was the case, the disaster occurred between December 9, 1791, and June 21, 1792. The site of this first church may have been at what is now the corner of Palm and Thompson Streets. There in 1792 a small chapel dedicated to San Miguel Arcángel was built to be used as the mission church while the principal church was being built at its present location at 211 East Main Street. This chapel was in use when the 1812 earthquake severely damaged the building, and in 1816 it was pulled down. Another chapel built nearby suffered from flood damage and its last ruins were removed in the 1870s.

Another chapel, dedicated to Santa Gertrudis, was built for the Chumash community at the entrance to Casitas Pass, about seven miles north of the mission. This chapel was used intermittently for many years until about 1868. Many Chumash of the area settled around the Chapel of Santa Gertrudis, and the great numbers of their little willow-thatched houses gave the name Casitas ("little houses") to the entire region. The site of the chapel now lies under the Ojai Freeway, by the turnoff to Foster Park.

The present mission church was begun early in 1793 but not completed for some years. Even before the dedication of the present mission structure on September 10, 1809, the mission garden had become famous. In the autumn of 1793, Vancouver, on his second visit to California, wrote in his journal about the gardens of San Buenaventura, describing them as "far exceeding anything" he had seen elsewhere in California. At a later date, Richard Henry Dana declared them to be "the finest in the whole country."

The old walled garden, now entirely vanished, was bounded approximately by Main Street on the north, Ventura Avenue on the west, Meta Street on the south, and Colombo Street on the east. The beautiful Ventura County Museum of History and Art (1977) at 100 East Main Street now occupies the northeast portion of the old mission garden.

The present mission structure on the north side of East Main Street (SRL 310) was at one time the center of what was considered to be one of the richest of all the missions, being especially noted for its horticulture. After the secularization of the missions, it suffered with the rest. It was roofless for many years after the earthquake of 1857 and, while in this condition, was abandoned. In 1868, the Chapel of Santa Gertrudis was being used in its stead.

In 1957 the interior of the church was restored, as nearly as possible, to its original condition, undoing the work of a regrettable earlier "restoration" that had obliterated much of its charm. Ceiling and flooring were torn out in 1957 to reveal the original beams and floor tiles. The crude but beautiful Chumash frescoes, which had been covered up by ornate scrollwork, unfortunately could not be saved, but a small section of them, which had escaped modernization, may be seen in the Father Serra Chapel. Many relics are on display in the mission museum, including part of the old wooden pupit, carved and painted by the Chumash, which had been torn out of the church in the earlier restoration, and the original confessionals, also showing their handiwork. Old records in Father Serra's handwriting and a pair of unusual wooden bells, probably used during the last three days of Holy Week and the only ones extant in the California mission chain, are also to be seen there.

A fascinating display at 113 East Main Street immediately to the west of the mission is the Mission Plaza Archaeological Interpretive Facility, opened in 1980. Several years before, a team of archaeologists sifted through 3,500 years of historical remains to piece together the life story of one city block. The adjacent Albinger Archaeological Museum has displays from the Oak Grove people of prehistoric times through the later settlers of Ventura, the Chumash, Spaniards, Mexicans, Americans, and Chinese. Outside, the excavated remains of four old mission buildings can be seen superimposed on the foundation of one of the first church structures, as well as middens and wells. Up Valdez Alley on the hill behind the facility are the remains of the excellent system of pipes and aqueducts built by the padres and their laborers to bring water from the Ventura River and San Antonio Creek to the fountains and fields of the mission. At the end of the system they built a settling tank and receiving reservoir (SRL 114), called "Cabeza del Caballo" from the horse's head that once adorned its waterspout. The area is now known as Eastman Park.

The great water ditch or stone aqueduct, which was also a part of the padres' seven-mile-long water system, was demolished by the floods and landslides of 1866–67. The massive ruins may still be seen near the mouth of the Cañada Larga, one-fourth of a mile east of the Ojai road on Cañada Larga Road.

THE CITY OF VENTURA

Standing on a slight elevation at the foot of La Loma de la Cruz, the mission church dominated the town that grew out from it westward to the Ventura River. Two irregular bridle paths formed the streets of the little settlement and along these the adobe homes were built, sometimes flat-roofed and covered with *brea*, sometimes tiled, and occasionally shingled. Only the Ortega adobe remains today.

Ortega Adobe, Ventura

Seventy years before the Ortega house was built on the east bank of the river, an adobe house had been erected on the Rancho Sespe near the site of Fillmore, twenty-eight miles east of Ventura. The unknown builders of this homestead were killed in an Indian conflict, leaving the house deserted and forgotten until 1857, when it was remembered by Miguel Emigdio Ortega, who wanted its sturdy timbers for his new home. The house was dismantled and the coveted timbers were hauled back to Ventura, where they were incorporated into the new house. In 1897, E. C. Ortega, son of the original builders, had occasion to repair the house. The center beam, brought from the Sespe house forty years before, was found to be in perfect condition and so solid that a 20-penny spike could not penetrate it more than a quarter of an inch.

In the flood of 1861–62, the swollen waters of the river swept away half of the Ortega adobe and a portion of the orchard of pear, peach, and fig trees. The remaining portion of the house is still in good condition and has been added to slightly at the eastern front end. It is owned by the city of Ventura and is open to the public at 215 West Main Street.

The first courthouse in Ventura was built on Santa Clara Street on what is now the site of the Ventura Unified School District Office. This courthouse proved inadequate to house the many county offices, and another site was chosen, at 501 Poli Street. Here in 1913 a larger courthouse, Roman Doric in style with a white marble façade, opened (SRL 847). A wooden statue of Father Serra, carved in 1936 by John Palo-Kangas, stood for many years in the plaza in front of the building. When sun, wind, and rain caused it to disintegrate, it was removed and replaced by a replica. Many years later, when new county offices were needed, an agreement was made whereby the City of San Buenaventura would take over this building and make it the City Hall, and the county offices would move to a new location to the east, just off SR 126. The San Buenaventura City Hall began its present life in 1973.

The Ventura Pier was built in 1872, before the railroad came, when the only practical way to move produce and freight was by sea. Then called the Ventura Wharf, it extends into the ocean from Harbor Boulevard, east of the end of California Street. Heavy seas have caused damage over the years—in 1914, a freighter was actually pushed through the pier by a gale—and today it is used for fishing and strolling.

Ventura has some notable structures from over a century ago. The Ewing Home at 605 Poli Street is now a law office. It was built in 1894 by Felix Ewing, the only judge in Ventura County at that time. The Sheridan House at 1029 Poli is a Craftsman bungalow house, a style very popular in southern California between 1895 and 1915. Selwyn Shaw, perhaps the best-known builder between 1885 and 1915, put up seven houses on the "Shaw" block between Ann and Hemlock on Poli and Buena Vista Streets, for his sons, his neighbors, and himself. The Pierpont Inn, at 550 Sanjon Road near Pierpont Bay, is the oldest hotel in the city, built in 1910.

Montalvo, now a part of the city of Ventura, was a rail stop on the Southern Pacific line when it came into Ventura County in 1887. This is one of two places in the state (the other being Villa Montalvo in Santa Clara County) named for Garcí Ordóñez de Montalvo. He wrote a sequel to the popular romance *Amadis de Gaula*, and gave it the name of *Las Sergas de Esplandián*, published in Seville in 1510. This "Exploits of Esplandián" includes an account of a fabulous island named California, whose Queen Calafia ruled a troop of Amazons. By the eighteenth century, the name California was being used to describe the territory on the Pacific Coast west and north of New Spain.

In the beginning all the lands around San Buenaventura belonged to the mission. After secularization of the missions, grants were made, and the people to whom the land was given began establishing homes and building their adobe *casas* throughout the county. These tracts were very large, those over four thousand acres being considered to be among the smaller units. Consequently, the country homes scattered over the entire area were few, and only a handful remain.

On what was formerly the Lower Ojai Rancho stands the López adobe, called the "Barracks" because it once defended the lower Ojai Valley against the threat of marauding Indians. Extensively renovated "but preserving a flavor of earlier days," it is beautifully situated on the

Olivas Adobe, Ventura

McCaleb Ranch just to the left of the highway about two and one-half miles northwest of Ojai.

RANCHO SAN MIGUEL AND THE OLIVAS ADOBE

Perhaps the best preserved of the historic adobes around Ventura is the Olivas adobe (SRL 115), which stands near the Santa Clara River about a mile east of Ventura Harbor on Olivas Park Drive. Don Raimundo Olivas, the original owner, was born in Los Angeles in 1801 and came to Santa Barbara as a soldier twenty years later. In 1841 he and another retired soldier, Felipe Lorenzana, received the grant of 4,693 acres that constituted Rancho San Miguel; Lorenzana sold his half to Dixie Thompson at a later date. This is roughly where the eastern part of the city of Ventura lies today.

The Olivas adobe is a long two-story building with balcony and veranda overlooking a walled garden below, and fields, park, and marshlands beyond. The Olivas family, with its twenty-one children, was famous for its fine entertainment and generous hospitality. Many stories are locally told of the place, such as the time that Olivas was surprised and robbed by bandits. The property remained in the Olivas family until 1899. In 1927 it was purchased by Major Max Fleischmann for use as a duck-hunting club. After his death the Fleischmann Foundation in 1963 donated the adobe and the surrounding land to the city for a museum and golf course. The adobe is open to the public.

RANCHO SANTA ANA

About nine miles north of Ventura, on Old Creek Road just east of SR 33, stands the Santa Ana Rancho adobe house of Don José de Arnaz. Don José was mayordomo of San Buenaventura at the time of John C. Frémont's arrival at the mission in 1846. Frémont, on his way south to the reconquest of Los Angeles, wished to gain possession of Mission San Buenaventura for the United States. He arrested Arnaz and tried to get information from him, but the Californian claimed that he was unable to give this information and was released. Until the publication in 1928 of the memoirs of Don José Arnaz, the site of General Frémont's camp while at Ventura was unknown or forgotten. Arnaz wrote that Frémont "established his camp on the west side of the mission orchard." This places the site of the camp south of Main Street near Garden Street. Arnaz's town house was on what is now West Main Street, midway between South Ventura Avenue and the river. In the late 1850s he moved to his Santa Ana Rancho, and his home in town became the American Hotel.

RANCHO CAMULOS

About thirty miles east of Ventura, on SR 126 near the Los Angeles county line, is one of the most famous adobes in California. Located on Rancho Camulos, it was the home of the Del Valle family until 1927, and is still privately owned. The land continues to be a working citrus ranch. Rancho Camulos ("juniper" in Ventureño Chumash) was originally a part of Rancho San Francisco, granted to Antonio del Valle in 1833 and 1839. The two properties became separate entities in 1869. The adobe was begun in 1853 and reached what is essentially its present plan in 1880. Travelers often stopped at Rancho Camulos, where the hospitality of the Del Valles was famous.

In 1882, Helen Hunt Jackson paid a brief visit to the adobe; when she wrote the first part of *Ramona* it was with this house in mind as the setting for the novel. The fame of the adobe became widespread when the book, published in 1884, became a best-seller. A monument (SRL 553) stands on the highway in front of the rancho complex. Rancho San Francisco is commemorated by a marker (SRL 556) just across the Los Angeles county line one-quarter mile south of the junction of SR 126 and I-5, south of Valencia.

The Northridge earthquake of 1994 was very destructive to the adobe and other buildings at Rancho Camulos, and as of 2000 their ruins, closed to the public, await a future restoration.

Piru, the closest town to Camulos, was founded by David Cook in 1887, during southern California's "triple boom" in health resorts, railroads, and real estate. Cook's beautiful mansion at 829 North Park Avenue burned in 1981 but was well restored. It continues to be a private residence. Cook, the son of a Methodist minister, also founded the Piru Methodist Church in 1887. The present church building at Center and Church Streets dates from 1890. It contains an organ that was shipped around the Horn in the 1860s to San Francisco, survived the disaster of 1906 there, and finally, with some refurbishment, was installed in this church in 1935. It may be the oldest operating organ in California.

RANCHO SIMI

SR 118 parallels SR 126 as a highway from Ventura to Los Angeles County. For much of its length it passes through the Simi Valley, location of the old Spanish Rancho Simi, the first grant made in Ventura County. The huge ranch, whose 113,009 acres made it one of California's largest, includes the valley and surrounding hills and a bit of Los Angeles County. The original grant was made in 1795 to Santiago Pico, who came to California in 1776 as a volunteer soldier with his wife and children. He died in 1815; his sons Patricio, Miguel, and Francisco Javier were regranted the rancho in 1821, under Mexican law. Around 1831, José de la Guerra of Santa Barbara, who also acquired part of adjoining El Conejo Rancho, acquired this property from the last of the Picos. The name "Simi" comes from the Chumash *Shimiji* or *Shimiyi*—"place" or "village."

Rancho Simi (SRL 979) is commemorated by a marker at Robert P. Strathearn Historical Park at 137 Strathearn Place in Simi Valley. Two rooms from an old adobe built here by the Picos around 1810 were later incorporated into the Strathearn family home and remain on the site. In 1889 the California Mutual Benefit Colony of Chicago advertised "Simiopolis" in Chicago and Cincinnati and sent out by rail twelve prefabricated "colony" houses for buyers. One of these stands today in the park. The first Simi Library, opened in 1930, is also located in the park and houses exhibits about local pioneer families and life.

The most recent addition to Simi Valley history is the Ronald Reagan Presidential Library at 40 Presidential Drive in Simi Valley. Dedicated in 1991, this houses materials from the two terms of this Illinois-born Californian. A full-size replica of the Oval Office in the White House is one feature, as is a great chunk of the Berlin Wall, which fell in 1989, several months after Reagan left the presidency to live in retirement in Los Angeles County.

THE OJAI VALLEY

Rancho Ojai ("moon" in Chumash) was a grant made to Fernando Tico in 1837. The land was broken up after the American conquest and became famous for its cattle and citrus crops. An early developer named the principal town "Nordhoff" in 1874, after Charles Nordhoff, whose travel writings about California stimulated much interest and immigration after the railroad made such things possible. During World War I, the name was changed to that of the valley.

Ojai is one of the most charming towns in California. With an agreeably mild climate, it is a resort, a cultural center, and a thriving agricultural community. Edmund Drummond Libbey, of the Toledo glass company, had discovered the place as a winter vacation spot, and beginning in 1915 made several additions to the area. He envisioned a planned community in the Mission Revival style of architecture. The Arcade, built on East Ojai Avenue in 1917, is a row of shops and restaurants, now owned by the city. The Ojai Post Office Tower and Portico (also 1917) on the opposite side of the avenue is a local landmark. Since 1950, the annual Ojai Music Festival has been held in the Libbey Park Bowl. The park on East Ojai Avenue was given to the town in 1916. The Ojai Valley Museum and Historical Society is housed in the former fire station at 109 South Montgomery Street.

SANTA PAULA

Where Sycamore Road joins SR 126, four miles east of Santa Paula, there stands a giant sycamore that was fully mature when John C. Frémont passed that way with his men on their march south to Los Angeles in 1846 (SRL 756). A long-standing landmark, it has seen service as a meeting place, an outdoor chapel, a post office, and, in October 1873, a polling place.

The city of Santa Paula was once part of Rancho Santa Paula y Saticoy, granted in 1834 and in 1840 to Manuel Jimeno Cesarin. American settlement began around 1870, when the town site was laid out, the water of Santa Paula Creek was diverted and used for irrigation, and E. B. Higgins put up a water-powered gristmill in what is now Mill Park on Ojai Road. In 1874, Nathan W. Blanchard supervised the first commercial plantings of citrus in Ventura County. By 1893, the Limoneira Company of Santa Paula began, which ultimately became the world's largest lemon ranch. The company helped make the California Fruit Growers'

Association successful and their brand name "Sunkist" a famous one. Lemons and other crops such as avocados continue to be important in the economic life of Ventura County.

From the 1880s to the 1930s, Santa Paula was also the center of some major oil fields. The Santa Paula Oil Museum at 1003 East Main Street, formerly the California Oil Museum, is housed in the building where the Union Oil Company of California was created in 1890, on the second floor of what was then the Santa Paula Hardware Company. This museum has a scope much larger than its name suggests, but the history of petroleum is paramount, and extremely interesting.

FILLMORE

Fillmore was named for J. A. Fillmore, who was superintendent of the Pacific Division of the Southern Pacific Railroad in 1887, when the tracks down the Santa Clara River valley arrived at this location, originally a freight stop. The town is on part of Rancho Sespe, a property with a troubled history; much of it is still farmland. The Fillmore Historical Museum is now located on a historic park at 350 Main Street in the center of the community. The four original buildings now moved to this location are the Southern Pacific Railroad depot from 1887, the 1892 Bardsdale Post Office, a 1905 Craftsman single-family house, and a Rancho Sespe employee two-story bunkhouse from 1919.

OTHER HISTORIC SPOTS IN VENTURA COUNTY

The town of Camarillo, usually associated with the nearby State Hospital and St. John's Seminary (location of the Edward E. Doheny Memorial Library), was named for Juan Camarillo, who purchased Rancho Calleguas from the heirs of the grantee, José Pedro Ruíz. The Camarillo family's home at 3771 Mission Oak Boulevard, built in 1892, remains as the family's private residence.

About eight miles east of Camarillo, at 51 South Ventu Road in Newbury Park, is the reconstructed Stagecoach Inn (SRL 659). The original white-frame two-story inn was built in 1876 by James Hammell as a stage stop under the name of the Grand Union Hotel. Moved to its present location in 1966 when the Ventura Freeway widened US 101, it burned down in 1970, but was completely rebuilt and reopened in 1976. It is the museum of the Conejo Valley Historical Society.

Fillmore City Hall, Fillmore

Nearby Moorpark was probably named for the Moorpark apricot, which flourished in this area around 1900. Most of this part of Ventura County has had the rapid changes of increased population dramatically thrust upon it. In 1955, Moorpark replaced its last hand-cranked telephone with a dial model. Four years later, it became the first town in the United States to receive all its electricity from a nuclear power plant!

Thomas A. Bard drilled the first oil well in Ventura County in 1865, later became the president of the Union Oil Company, and was a United States senator for the term 1899–1905. The little settlement of Bardsdale, just across the Santa Clara River from Fillmore, commemorates his name. Bard was also associated with the development of the Simi Valley and with Port Hueneme. According to W. W. Robinson, the port was once "the biggest California shipping point south of San Francisco," and, during World War II, it was the harbor through which was shipped "the major portion of all the supplies for our Armed Forces in the Pacific." Port Hueneme is the location of the Naval Construction Battalion Center, "Home of the Seabees"; the Seabee Museum, open to the public, commemorates this historic unit. The Port Hueneme Museum and Historical Society, in the former Bank of Hueneme Building at 220 North Market Street in Port Hueneme, has special displays on the pioneers of the region.

The nearby city of Oxnard now exceeds Ventura in population. It owes its early success to the incredible richness of its soil; lima beans and sugar beets were among the crops that flourished in abundance in the vicinity. The Oxnard Historical Society Museum at 424 South C Street is housed in the basement of the 1906 Carnegie Library.

Northern Ventura County is a ruggedly beautiful area included in Los Padres National Forest and with very few roads. The Sespe Condor Sanctuary north of Fillmore and Piru is dedicated to the preservation of the California condor, an endangered species.

Ventura County also includes two of the Channel Islands, Anacapa and San Nicolas. The lighthouse on Anacapa Island, built in 1932, was one of the last to be constructed in the United States. The Channel Islands National Park headquarters is in Ventura, and the visitors' center is at 1901 Spinnaker Drive in the Ventura Harbor area.

Yolo County

Yolo County was one of the original twenty-seven counties. Yolo, or Yodoy, was the name of a place inhabited by a group of Patwin Indians, and is said to mean "a place abounding in rushes." Fremont was the first county seat, from 1850 to 1851, when the honor was bestowed upon Washington, now West Sacramento. In 1857 the county seat was moved to Cacheville, now Yolo. Washington again became the county seat, in 1861. Another move was made in 1862, to Woodland, which since then has been the county seat.

THE TRAIL OF THE FUR HUNTER

In the marshlands west of the Sacramento River lived the Patwin or Southern Wintun people. To the south lay fertile, unbroken plains where game abounded. These plains were bounded on the north and south by Cache and Putah Creeks, while on the east flowed the great river, and on the west lay a range of hills. The area supported a fairly large indigenous population; some 147 archaeological sites have been recorded in Yolo County. The diseases brought by the white settlers devastated the native people, and there are no Patwin living today.

For hundreds of years, Patwin hunters roamed this region undisturbed. In 1808, Gabriel Moraga led a Spanish expedition that sailed up the Sacramento to what is now Sutter County, noting Indian villages along the river. A second upriver expedition was led in 1817 by Luís Argüello accompanied by Fathers Narciso Durán and Ramon Abella to look for mission sites in the Central Valley. They landed on the west bank of the river near the present town of Clarksburg and put up a cross on an oak tree there. In 1821, the last official Spanish expedition into the Central Valley was the first to pass overland through what is now Yolo County. Led by Luís Argüello, the party crossed what are now Solano and Yolo Counties before reaching the Sacramento River at a point in Colusa County in the vicinity of Grimes. Father Blas Ordaz, chaplain and chronicler of the expedition, noted the existence of an Indian ranchería by Putah Creek, near present-day Winters, and estimated its population at 400 souls.

Some time before 1830, Hudson's Bay Company trappers arrived and found this a rich field. They cached their furs along the river and smaller streams, one of which became known as Cache Creek. One of their camps, known to early settlers as French Camp, was situated in a grove of oaks on the north bank of Cache Creek one mile east of the present town of Yolo, formerly Cacheville.

In the spring and summer of 1830 another band of hunters, led by Ewing Young, trapped along the San Joaquin and Sacramento Rivers and remained for a time on Cache Creek. Two years later, on his way to Oregon, Young again passed through Yolo County territory, camping on Cache and Putah Creeks before proceeding to the coast and northward to Oregon by way of Putah Canyon.

Joseph Gale, who had come to California with Ewing Young in 1831, had a cattle rendezvous on Cache Creek in 1843. The need for more livestock in the Willamette Valley in Oregon was the incentive for a daring project begun by Gale in 1841. Undaunted by the difficulties of getting the cattle to Oregon, he set to work to construct an oceangoing vessel that he proposed to take to California and there exchange for livestock. With the help of Charles Wilkes, the Hudson's Bay Company equipped the vessel, and Gale, after passing a seaman's examination, was given a seaman's license. The schooner, *Star of Oregon*, was launched in May 1841, and toward the end of August 1842 Gale and his crew started down the Columbia River toward California. At San Francisco, José Y. Limantour, a Frenchman, purchased the ship in exchange for 350 cows.

Needing more men for the vast stock-driving venture over the mountains as well as for the Oregon settlement project, Gale waited until the spring of 1843 before starting north. Circulars had been sent out describing the advantages of the Willamette Valley for settlement, and by the middle of May, forty-two men, among them Jacob P. Leese, had gathered at Cache Creek. The Stars and Stripes floated for several weeks that spring from a tall cottonwood tree trimmed into the form of a flagstaff. The expedition finally started northward on May 14, driving 1,250 head of cattle, 600 horses and mules, and 3,000 sheep, most of which were safely guided over the northern mountain barrier after a journey of seventy-five days.

MEXICAN LAND GRANTS

Within what is now Yolo County, nine grants of land for permanent settlement were made by Mexican authorities between 1842 and the American conquest in 1846. Only five of these titles, however, were later confirmed by the United States government.

The first, Rancho Río de los Putos, was situated on both banks of Putah Creek in the vicinity of Winters. ("Los Putos" and "Putah" seem to be Spanish approximations of the name of a Patwin village.) The grant of four leagues was made to William Wolfskill, an American living in Los Angeles; it was occupied in July 1842 by his brother John, who began the plantings that would make him the father of the horticultural industry in northern California. While his initial plantings of vines and trees were on both sides of the creek, his permanent residence was on the south bank, in what became Solano County.

William Gordon, a native of Ohio who brought his family to California with the Workman-Rowland party in 1841, settled on Rancho Quesesosi in July 1842. This pioneering venture was located on a grant of two square leagues bisected by Cache Creek west of what is now Woodland. (The boundaries can be followed on County Roads 94B, 19, and 87 and SR 16.) "Uncle Billy" Gordon had been a trapper and hunter in New Mexico, "rough, honest, and hospitable." His place on Cache Creek became a "general rendezvous for settlers and hunters" from 1843 to 1846. James Clyman, in his diary for July 12, 1845, noted that at the time of his visit Gordon was the only permanent settler on Cache Creek. On this rancho the first wheat in Yolo County was grown. In a primitive building one mile from Gordon's home, the county's first school was started in 1847 with an enrollment of eight pupils. Gordon sold land and water rights to James Moore, who began construction in 1856 of the first irrigation dam and ditch system to utilize the natural water supply of Cache Creek, which flows out of Clear Lake in the mountains of Lake County.

Rancho Quesesosi, more commonly known as Gordon's Ranch, was sold in 1866, when William Gordon moved to Cobb Valley in Lake County, where he lived until his death in 1876. All that remains today is a family cemetery situated north of Cache Creek, near the former homesite on County Road 19 and marked with a plaque in 1948 by the Native Daughters of the Golden West.

The third grant made in Yolo County territory was given to Thomas M. Hardy, a Canadian, in 1843, and consisted of 26,637 acres along Cache Creek east of Gordon's Ranch, reaching as far as the Sacramento River. It was called Rancho Río Jesús María, an early name given to the upper Sacramento River. Hardy built a tule shack on the west bank of the Sacramento near the mouth of the Feather River, but he spent very little time there, having enlisted in military service under the Mexican government.

After Hardy's death by drowning in Suisun Bay in 1848 or 1849, his property was sold by the public administrator. Among those who purchased portions of the original rancho was James H. Harbin, who had come to this part of California in 1847. On Harbin's land the town of Fremont was laid out. In 1857 Harbin moved to Lake County, where he settled at the springs that bear his name.

Rancho Cañada de Capay was located on Cache Creek and was granted to Francisco Berryessa and his brothers, Santiago and Demisio, in 1846. (Kroeber says that Capay is from the Indian *capi*, meaning "stream.") Including more than 40,000 acres, this was the largest land grant wholly within the boundaries of Yolo County. This property was later taken over by incoming Americans, one of whom was George Dickson Stephens. In 1850 Stephens camped on Cache Creek on what he supposed was government land, but he afterward learned that it was part of the Berryessa grant. With his brother John he acquired the property in 1852 and erected an adobe building. This house, around which a larger frame structure was built as the needs of the family grew, is the only adobe standing within Yolo County today. This building is well preserved and is still occupied by Stephens's descendants. It stands half a mile south of SR 16 midway between Madison and Esparto; the wooden balcony and veranda overhang the adobe walls.

Almost simultaneously with the building of Moore's canal on Gordon's Ranch, another dam and ditch were begun by David Quincy Adams in 1857. The Adams Canal, which was completed in 1870, was laid out by Adams on Rancho Cañada de Capay, 4,693 acres of which he had purchased with money made in the mines of the Mother Lode during the years from 1849 to 1852. Adams built his canal for the purpose of irrigating 150 acres of alfalfa and forty acres of gardens cared for by Chinese. This alfalfa, probably the first to be grown in California, was raised from seed obtained by Adams from Chile, and nearly all of the alfalfa grown in northern California today is known as Chilean alfalfa. The Adams Dam, which was located on Cache Creek about two miles west and a little north of Capay, no longer exists, but a newer Capay Dam diverts water southward to the Winters Canal.

WASHINGTON (BRODERICK) AND WEST SACRAMENTO

In 1845 Rancho Nueva Flandria, the fifth Mexican grant in Yolo County, consisting of three square leagues of land bordering the west bank of the Sacramento River, was granted to John Schwartz, also called Jan Lows de Swart, an eccentric Flemish immigrant who had come to California with the Bidwell-Bartleson party in 1841.

In the spring of 1846 Schwartz sold 600 acres of his rancho to James McDowell, who had come overland with his wife and children in 1845. McDowell built a log house on the northwest corner of his ranch opposite the site of the present city of Sacramento, where he took his family to live. He died in 1849, and in 1850 his widow had a town site laid out on the land. This was the beginning of the little town of Washington, later known as Broderick.

When the town of Fremont began to decline in 1851, Washington became the center of commerce as well as of judicial and political activity in Yolo County. From 1851 to 1857 it was the county seat, and again from 1861 to 1862.

Washington was the site of the first Pacific Coast salmon cannery, established in the spring of 1864 on the west side of the Sacramento River opposite the foot of Sacramento's K Street. William and George Hume and Andrew Hapgood, fishermen from Maine, began with crude equipment in a converted cabin and scow, performing every operation by hand. During the first year, at least half the cans burst at the seams in cooking, but the partners managed to produce 2,000 cases of a dozen cans each, selling them at five dollars a case. As the business became more successful, other salmon canneries sprang up. By 1882, the peak year, there were twenty canneries along the Sacramento River and San Francisco Bay producing 200,000 cases of salmon a year. Decline set in when the number of salmon entering the Sacramento River was sharply reduced, a consequence of the silting of the river by hydraulic mining in the Sierra. In recognition of the fact that the multimillion-dollar salmon canning industry of the Pacific Coast is a direct outgrowth of this pioneering effort, the Department of the Interior has registered the site of Hapgood, Hume, and Company, just up the river from Tower Bridge, as a National Historic Landmark.

For several years most of the traffic from the northern and western sections of Yolo County passed through Washington. So great was its early promise that the citizens for a time had hopes of its becoming a great city. Later, with the transfer of growth and activity from Washington to Sacramento across the river, and with the coming of the railroad, which decreased its importance as a center of navigation, Washington's boom days ended. In 1987, Broderick, as Washington had come to be known, joined with the communities of Bryte, Southport, and West Sacramento to form the city of West Sacramento.

The eastern part of Yolo County is crisscrossed by a maze of roads, highways, railroad tracks, and bridges. The first bridge across the Sacramento River was a wooden wagon bridge constructed in 1857 between Washington and Sacramento's I Street. When the transcontinental railroad was completed in 1869, the bridge was rebuilt to accommodate railroad tracks. Today, the I Street Bridge is on the National Register of Historic Places, as is the Tower Bridge, a distinctive twin-towered motor vehicle bridge several blocks downstream, which leads directly to the state capitol.

Downriver from the two bridges is the Port of Sacramento, which was opened to ocean-going traffic in 1963. The port is the terminus of a 42.8-mile ship channel, thirty feet deep, that was constructed between West Sacramento and Collinsville in Solano County. No longer in operation, what was California's only inland navigation lock was on the barge canal here. Travelers on I-80 cross the Yolo Bypass on the three-mile-long Yolo Causeway. The bypass is an elaborate system to control flooding of 101,000 acres of the Sacramento Valley. The system, which was begun in 1911, extends from Shasta Dam to Rio Vista and includes 980 miles of levees, 438 miles of flood-control channels and canals, thirty-one bridges, six weirs, and seven bypasses. The Yolo Causeway is now a six-lane divided elevated highway, widened and reinforced in 1985–86. When it was constructed in 1916, it was the first all-year, all-weather road across what was then a vast wilderness of tules.

FREMONT

The town of Fremont was established in March 1849 on the west shore of the Sacramento River directly opposite the mouth of the Feather River. Jonas Spect, a native of Pennsylvania who had come overland to Oregon in 1847 and from there to San Francisco on the *Henry* early in 1848, put up a temporary store of tules, willow poles, and canvas; the site was within the boundaries of the Harbin Ranch. With the help of Indians, Spect established a ferry across the Sacramento River. A sandbar blocked the entrance to the Feather River at this point, making Fremont the head of navigation for travelers to Marysville and the northern mines.

With miners, teamsters, and packers constantly passing through on their way to the mining regions, Fremont grew by leaps and bounds, and at the height of its prosperity claimed a population of 3,000. But its promise was short-lived. In the winter of 1849 heavy storms washed away the town and the sandbar; the Feather River became navigable as far as Marysville, and commerce on both rivers passed Fremont by.

The loyal citizens of Fremont did not give up their town at once. They rebuilt their homes and businesses, and by means of effective lobbying succeeded in making it the first county seat in 1850. In July 1851, however, a popular vote took the seat of government to Washington, and Fremont gradually disappeared. Some of its buildings were moved to Knights Landing, some to Marysville, and others to newly established ranches in the vicinity. Soon empty lots were all that remained of the little river town. Today the site is privately owned farmland.

CACHEVILLE (YOLO)

In September 1849 Thomas Cochran camped on the north bank of Cache Creek about ten miles west of Fremont, on the site of the present town of Yolo, and put up a hotel for the accommodation of travelers along the west side of the Sacramento River. The place grew and became known as Cochran's Crossing. In 1853 James A. Hutton arrived and built a large, commodious house that he opened to the public. The hospitality of Hutton and his family became so well known that the name of the place was changed to Hutton's Ranch, or Travelers' Home. The old Hutton house is still standing at 325 Main Street. In 1857 the place became the county seat of Yolo County and was renamed Cacheville. The post office had been established under the name of Yolo in 1853.

Located in a rich farming region, Cacheville grew rapidly for a few years. In 1857 the *Yolo Democrat* newspaper (forerunner of the still-existing *Woodland Daily Democrat*) was established, and by 1860 the town's population of 1,995 made it the largest in the county. That same year the county seat was moved back to Washington and the town stopped growing. It exists today as a small commercial and social center of the surrounding farming area. The Methodist church, built in 1867, is still standing.

KNIGHTS LANDING

William Knight, a native of Baltimore, Maryland, who was said to have been educated as a physician, came to California with the Workman-Rowland party in 1841.

Snowball Mansion, Knights Landing

Yolo County Court House, Woodland

In 1843, he settled at a natural landing place on the Sacramento River later known as Knights Landing. In 1846 he received a grant to this land, but the title was never confirmed.

Knight's first home on the river ranch was made of tules and willow poles fastened with rawhide and plastered with mud. It was built in 1843 on the ancient Yodoy Indian mound. Since this site was at the junction of the lower Sycamore Slough with the Sacramento River, it proved suitable for a ferry, which was established by Knight soon after his arrival, and the place became an important landing and shipping point on the Sacramento. Knight later moved to Stanislaus County, where he founded Knight's Ferry; when he died there on November 9, 1849, his lack of business foresight resulted in his estate being lost to his intended heirs.

An attempt to start a town at Knights was made in 1849 under the name of Baltimore, but it never materialized because of disagreements over the sale of lots. In 1853, however, Charles F. Reed laid out another town site and the place was officially named Knights Landing. The same year, J. R. Snowball, Knight's son-in-law, and J. J. Perkins opened a general store on the Indian mound. Snowball was later elected judge and became a prosperous businessman and landowner. In 1877 he built an imposing two-story house, a prominent local landmark that still stands near the river.

Knights Landing, which is located about twelve miles northeast of Woodland, retained the early river-town atmosphere in the older portion of the settlement so perfectly that in the 1920s it was chosen by film directors as the locale for the making of Mississippi River scenes in *Showboat* and *Steamboat Round the Bend*. Most of the picturesque buildings along Front Street were de-

stroyed in a fire that swept the town in 1938; since then, the town has turned away from the river, although it is still a center for fishing and boating activities.

WOODLAND

The fine groves of oak trees just south of Cache Creek, where the city of Woodland now stands, were centrally located in the midst of an extensive and fertile region, which later became one of the principal agricultural belts of the county. "Uncle Johnny" Morris, a Kentuckian, was the first settler in what is now Woodland. He arrived with his family in November 1849 from Missouri and lived for two years in a log cabin on the south side of Cache Creek. During this time he planted two acres of the Mission variety of grapes, the first in the county. In 1851 he settled at what is now the corner of First and Clover Streets. He was joined two years later by Henry Wyckoff, who set up the first store in what he called "Yolo City." By 1857 Frank S. Freeman had purchased 160 acres and laid out a town that he envisioned as a trading center for one of the richest grain-growing counties in the nation. The following year he opened the town's first post office, which his wife, Gertrude, named Woodland.

Freeman donated a city block to the county when Woodland was chosen as county seat in 1862, and an imposing courthouse was erected there the following year; this was replaced by the present Neoclassical Revival structure in 1917. On the northwest corner of First and Main Streets is the brick commercial building Freeman built in the 1860s; across the street is the old Capitol Hotel building from 1868. The Woodland Opera House (SRL 851) at Second Street and Dead Cat Alley, first opened in 1896, is enjoying a revival as a performing theater.

Among the many fine old houses on College and First Streets built in the last quarter of the nineteenth century, the Gable House (SRL 864) at 659 First Street is an excellent example of what is often called Italianate architecture; it is on the National Register of Historic Places. The small wooden Gothic Revival church on First Street, from 1874, is one of the oldest public buildings in the county; originally a Congregational house of worship, it is today the Seventh Day Adventist Spanish Church.

CLARKSBURG

Clarksburg lies on the west bank of the Sacramento River in an area first settled by an adventurous German named Frederick Babel in 1849. Other farmers moved into the area, where the fertile soil produced rich crops. Floods, however, were an annual threat, and not until the second decade of the twentieth century were high levees and canals created that transformed this land into what was called "The Eden of California." The present town dates from the 1920s. On the River Road north of Clarksburg one can see some of the two-story houses built by Portuguese settlers before 1900; typically, the family living quarters were placed on the second floor in anticipation of floods. Near the Freeport Bridge, St. Joseph's Catholic Church, built in 1923 to replace a structure from 1886, is still an important element in the life of the Portuguese community.

DAVIS

Where the little town of Davisville grew up in the late 1860s and where the University of California at Davis draws thousands of students annually, Jerome C. Davis settled in the early 1850s. By 1864 his ranch totaled approximately 13,000 acres, more than 8,000 of which were fenced; he raised cattle, horses, and sheep, had extensive wheat fields, and raised profitable crops of peaches and grapes.

William Dresbach leased the Davis home in 1867 and made it into a hotel, which he called the Yolo House. As a settlement began to grow up, Dresbach named it Davisville. With the advent of the railroad the place became a thriving grain-shipping point. In 1868, however, when a branch of the California Pacific Railroad was extended north to Marysville, Davisville began to decline as a trade center, a decline hastened when

the Vaca Valley Railroad was constructed to Madison in 1875.

The rich farming lands that surrounded Davisville continued to be developed, however, and in 1905 the University Farm was established by an act of the state Legislature. The first buildings appeared there in 1907, the same year that the name of the Davisville post office was shortened to the present Davis. The first courses for adult farmers were given in the autumn of 1908, and the following January the farm school for young men and boys was opened. In 1922 it was officially organized as a branch of the College of Agriculture at the University of California at Berkeley. Even at this early date, a gradual shift had begun in the educational mission of the school. More and more courses not directly related to agriculture were offered, and finally, in 1951, these were combined into the College of Letters and Science. In 1959 Davis was authorized as a general campus of the University of California, and a graduate division was established in 1961.

WINTERS

The city of Winters is located on a tract of Rancho Río de los Putos, just above the old Wolfskill Ford, where a town was laid out by developers of the Vaca Valley Railroad in 1875. This independent line, initially built from Vaca Station, now Elmira, to Vacaville in 1869, was extended to the north bank of Putah Creek, with plans for connecting lines to Berryessa Valley and the north coastal lumber district through Cache Creek Canyon. A forty-acre town site was named for the former landowner, Theodore Winters, a well-known breeder of horses who had purchased a large tract of the Wolfskills' rancho in 1865.

Three brick business houses constructed in 1875–76 still stand in a one-block historic district. The Bank of Winters, organized locally in 1885 to finance the rapidly growing fruit industry, built a large facility in 1904, which still stands on the corner of Main Street and Railroad Avenue.

Seven miles west of Winters on SR 128 is scenic Putah Canyon, where the Putah Creek Canyon Turnpike, an early toll road to Berryessa Valley, was operated by the Adam See family from 1858 to 1875, when a county road was opened. Stone quarries in the upper canyon furnished grinding stones for some of the first gristmills in northern California as early as 1846. Later, stone for many public and private buildings was extracted from the Bertholet Quarry. Devil's Gate, a jagged rock outcropping at the head of Putah Canyon where Yolo, Napa, and Solano Counties meet, became the site of Monticello Dam, a federal reclamation project completed in 1957. The 304-foot-high concrete arched dam impounds the waters of Putah Creek, creating Lake Berryessa.

Yuba County

Yuba County was one of the original twenty-seven counties established in 1850. Nevada and Sierra Counties were later created from its territory. Marysville has been the only county seat.

There are two explanations for the name Yuba. According to one, the Gabriel Moraga expedition of 1808, while naming the rivers flowing from the Sierra into the great central valley, gave one the name of Río de las Uvas ("the grapes") for the wild grapes on its banks; "Yuba" is therefore a corruption of "Uvas." A second account says that Yuba was the ancestral village of a Maidu tribe, located where the Feather River was joined by a great river flowing from the mountains, and that this name was used for both the river and the county.

YUBA TRAILS

Before the arrival of explorers in the territory of what is now Yuba County, its trails were known only to the Maidu people. John C. Frémont, in his *Memoirs*, describes their villages as he saw them in 1846:

> We traveled across the valley plain, and in about sixteen miles reached Feather River, at twenty miles from its junction with the Sacramento, near the mouth of the Yuba, so called from a village of Indians who live on it. The Indians aided us across the river with canoes and small rafts. Extending across the bank in front of the village was a range of wicker cribs, about twelve feet high, partly filled with what is there the Indians' staff of life, acorns. A collection of huts, shaped like beehives, with naked Indians sunning themselves on the tops, and these acorn cribs, are the prominent objects in an Indian village.

Hudson's Bay Company trappers occasionally crossed the region during the years 1830–41. In the 1840s a branch of the old California Emigrant Trail crossed the high Sierra through Donner Pass and followed down the mountains to Johnson's Ranch, an outpost of civilization at that time, located on the Bear River about four miles east of where Wheatland now stands.

MARYSVILLE

A large portion of what is now Yuba County became a part of the princely domain of John A. Sutter after 1841, but, since the lands included on his map covered a much larger area than the Mexican laws allowed, he resorted to the practice of subletting parts of his estate to other settlers. Some of these farms were in what are now Sutter and Placer Counties, while others lay within the present boundaries of Yuba County.

The land on which the town of Marysville was later

founded was located on a part of Sutter's Ranch that was leased in the fall of 1842 to Theodore Cordua, a German, for a period of nineteen years. Cordua made it a stock ranch and in 1842–43 built an adobe dwelling, with a trading room and outbuildings, at what is now the foot of D Street in Marysville.

Cordua, described as "a fat, jolly, whist-loving man, popular with everybody," called his settlement "New Mecklenburg," from his birthplace, but his neighbors called it Cordua's Ranch. It stood on the California-Oregon Trail through the Sacramento Valley, and by 1846 travel over this route from Oregon had become so extensive that Cordua's adobe became an important way station and trading post for emigrants, hunters, and, later, miners. The adobe with its thick walls was destroyed by fire in 1851. In 1844, Cordua obtained a grant from the Mexican government of seven leagues of land north of the Yuba River in what is now Yuba County, but not included in his grant from Sutter.

Charles Covillaud, a Frenchman and a former employee of Cordua, purchased a half-share in the ranch at New Mecklenburg in 1848. The other half was sold in January 1849 to two brothers-in-law of Covillaud's wife; they were Michael C. Nye, who married Mrs. Harriet Murphy Pike, a survivor of the Donner party tragedy, and William Foster, also a member of the Donner party and husband of Sarah Murphy. Nye and Foster sold out to Covillaud in September 1849, and in October Covillaud in turn sold all but one-fourth to José Manuel Ramírez, John Sampson, and Theodore Sicard. Discovery of gold at Coloma in 1848 had brought a period of great development to the region, and a town was laid out in January 1850. Covillaud's wife, Mary Murphy Covillaud, another survivor of the Donner party, received the honor of having the new town named for her, Marysville.

Marysville became the actual head of navigation on the Feather River and a center of trade for the northern mines. Its location gave it a decided superiority over all other candidates for such a position on the river, above and below. The distance to the mines, north and east, was not great, and cargoes from the riverboats could be transported readily by pack-mule trains to the outlying gold fields. These proved to be rich producers, and as a result Marysville experienced a phenomenal growth.

Freight and passenger boats landed at a point adjoining the plaza, on Front Street between D and E Streets. Today the river, held in leash by stone-lined levees, actually flows above the city streets. In the early days the plaza looked down upon the stream and its rich bottomlands, which were originally covered with

Bok Kai Temple, Marysville

groves of cottonwood, willow, and sycamore, but which soon became dotted with the homes and orchards and vineyards of the early settlers. Hydraulic mining, however, changed the face of the entire countryside, burying homes and settlements beneath acres of debris, raising the bed of the river seventy feet or more, and necessitating the construction of miles of levees. Most of the buildings from mining days are now buried under suburban homes.

The Bok Kai Temple (SRL 889), one of the oldest Chinese temples in the state and the only one in the nation dedicated to the Chinese water god Bok Eye, was constructed in 1880 from a former bathhouse, replacing an earlier and smaller temple in the town. The roof of this sturdy brick shrine is now about on a level with the levee, which keeps the river from washing the whole structure down to the sea. It is still used by worshipers.

Among Marysville's many interesting old houses is the José M. Ramírez residence at 220 Fifth Street between B and C Streets. Of elaborate construction, with a marble basement and Gothic windows, it is known locally as "The Castle." It later became the home of W. T. Ellis, the father of the Marysville levee system, for whom Ellis Lake in downtown Marysville is named.

The brick house at 630 D Street is now the Two Rivers Maritime Museum. The house is said to have been built by Stephen J. Field, who had a remarkable career. Field, a young Connecticut lawyer who came to Marysville in 1849, worked with Sutter and several other prominent men in laying out the town of Marysville and in organizing the county as a political entity. He purchased 200 lots within the prospective city and named the first streets after his associates, Covillaud, Ramírez, Sampson, and Sicard. Later he became the first alcalde of the town, a state legislator, and, in 1857, chief justice of the California Supreme Court. President Abraham Lincoln appointed him to the United States Supreme

Court in 1863, where he served until 1897, making his the second longest tenure on that bench.

The old Aaron home at 704 D Street was willed to the city of Marysville and opened as the Mary Aaron Memorial Museum in 1960. The two-story building, built by architect and inventor Warren P. Miller in 1856, contains materials and displays on the history of Marysville from 1860 to 1890.

Marysville is one of the cities of California where modern priorities and interests have prevailed over the past, and most of the old buildings in the downtown area have been pulled down since 1960. One that has survived is St. Joseph's Catholic Church, built in 1855 at Seventh and C Streets, a handsome neo-Gothic structure. Father Florian Schwenninger, a Tyrolean-born Benedictine monk who did much work in the gold camps of the 1850s and early 1860s, particularly at Sawyer's Bar in Siskiyou County, spent his last years, 1866–68, at St. Joseph's. He is buried in the Marysville Cemetery as is Mary Murphy Covillaud.

Nearby Beale Air Force Base was established as Camp Beale in 1942. It was named for Edward Fitzgerald Beale, prominent in the history of Kern County, where he developed Rancho El Tejón; he was also the federal superintendent of Indian Affairs for the state of California.

GOLD BARS ON THE YUBA RIVER

The first prospectors in the Sierra worked along the rivers and especially on the sandbars, which were rich in gold. Like other gold-bearing streams, the Yuba River above Marysville was dotted thickly with river-bar settlements, with a camp every one or two miles. By some accounts, Jonas Spect was the first to find gold in the county, on June 2, 1848, at a place later known as Rose's Bar. Almost simultaneously Michael Nye and William Foster found pay gravel on Dry Creek near its junction with the Yuba.

In the fall of 1848 John Rose and William J. Reynolds opened a store at Rose's Bar, where they supplied the miners with goods from Sacramento as well as fresh beef and farm products from their ranch south of Marysville. In the spring of 1849 Rose's Bar was so overcrowded with miners that at a meeting called for the purpose it was decided to limit claims to 100 square feet per man. By 1850, 2,000 men were at work on this bar alone.

The floods of 1850 drove the miners away from the sandbars to higher ground, where more gold was un-covered. Gatesville, or Sucker Flat (virtually an extension of Rose's Bar away from the river), grew up at this time and had developed into a town of some importance by the time the bars along the river became depleted of their gold. Squaw Creek, another rich locality, enjoyed its brief heyday in common with such neighboring camps as Cordua, Sawmill, Lander's, and Kennebec bars. Opposite Lander's Bar near the mouth of Deer Creek was Malay Camp, worked by miners from the Malay Peninsula of Southeast Asia.

The richest of all the Yuba River bars was Parks' Bar, located two or three miles west of Rose's Bar. To this location came David Parks with his wife and children in September 1848. Since a man with a family was very unusual in the earliest camps, the place was named in his honor. Parks' Bar, which had become a populous camp by 1849, reached the height of its prosperity in 1852, when it rivaled Marysville for a time. When gold along the river became worked out, in 1855, decline set in, and Parks', as well as its neighbors, Barton's and Union Bars, was soon depopulated. Near Parks' Bar was Sicard's Bar, where Theodore Sicard was the first to find gold. The name Sicard Flat was given to the town that grew up about a mile back from the river.

The first mining camp of importance above Marysville was Swiss Bar, opposite Sand Flat, nine miles up the river. Little mining was done there before 1850, and the place was never the equal of Long Bar, a little farther up the river. Long Bar, in addition to being the longest bar on the Yuba, also boasted the longest period of success. It was occupied as early as October 1848, and the first organized body of miners to come to California from the outside stopped there in November. By 1851 there was a ferry in operation between Long Bar and Kennebec Bar across the river. Above Long Bar was Chimney Hill, and at the mouth of Dry Creek was Owsley's Bar, named for a Dr. Owsley, who mined there in the early days. After 1857 hydraulic mining slowly destroyed the old river bars and their camps along the Yuba. They became buried towns, lying at least seventy feet beneath the debris washed down from the titanic diggings in the Sierra.

Gold still lies in the bed of the Yuba River, and in later years extensive dredging took out vast amounts from the old tailings. In 1905 the Yuba Consolidated Goldfields began operations nine miles east of Marysville, with a capital of $12.5 million. The towns of Marigold and Hammonton, the later named after Wendell P. Hammon, moving spirit of the company, grew up, direct descendants of the mining camps of the 1850s.

During the depression of the 1930s the field was taken over by men, otherwise unemployed, who were learning to wield pan and rocker in approved pioneer style. On Parks' Bar alone, from fifty to one hundred people were mining by these primitive methods in the summer of 1932. Today, small portable dredges are often seen in operation along the Yuba and other streams coming from the Sierra highlands, and nearly every year reports are made of the finding of a choice nugget or other discovery.

"SPECULATIVE CITIES"

Population increased so rapidly in the fall of 1849 and in 1850 that land speculators saw possibilities of accumulating wealth by laying out cities on paper. Alonzo Delano said in 1854 of these early real estate booms: "There seemed to be a speculative mania spreading over the land, and scores of new towns were heard of which were never known, only the puffs of newspapers, the stakes which marked the size of lots, and the nicely drawn plot of the surveyor." Delano spoke from experience, for he took part in some of the speculation, buying lots in Marysville and losing half of his earnings in the operation. In an effort to recoup his losses he and a friend laid out a town on the Feather River twenty miles north of Marysville, but they were unable to attract population to their town.

Marysville, as it turned out, survived and became a thriving city. Linda, on the south bank of the Yuba River above Marysville, had a short boom, and a store there remained in business about two years. The arrival of the little stern-wheel steamer *Linda* at the site was the occasion for the establishment of the town in 1850, but its hope to become the head of navigation and to rival Marysville was never realized. The site is now buried more than thirty feet beneath the tailings washed down from the hydraulic mines in the hills, and the only reminder of this would-be city is the modern Marysville suburb called Linda.

Early in 1851, the *Linda* was converted to a dredge, probably the first in the history of California mining. *Linda* made it up the river as far as Owsley's Bar, and came to an unprofitable end.

SMARTSVILLE

The first building at Smartsville (SRL 321) was a hotel built in the spring of 1856 by a Mr. Smart. The Catholic church, which had first been organized at Rose's Bar by

Abandoned Church of the Immaculate Conception, Smartville

Father Peter Magagnotto, C.P., had its building erected here in 1861. The building burned in 1870, but another took its place next year. This Church of the Immaculate Conception is today abandoned and falling apart, but it still is a prominent feature in this tiny community. A historical oddity is that the post office designation has always been Smartville. Remains of the rich mines developed at Smartsville in the late 1850s, as well as scars of the hydraulic operations of the 1860s and 1870s, may still be seen in the surrounding hills. By 1878 the Excelsior Company at Smartsville had washed eight million cubic yards of detritus into the Yuba River, while ten times that amount remained in the company's claims when hydraulic activities ceased in 1884.

To the east of Smartsville is a great gash in the hillside, the site of the once-populous mining camp of Sucker Flat.

THE EMPIRE RANCH STATION

In the early 1850s, the heyday of stagecoaches before the advent of railroads, the California Stage Company carried passengers from one end of the state to the other. One of the many stations used by this company was maintained on the Empire Ranch near Smarts-

YUBA COUNTY

575

ville, where meals were served and horses changed. The old Empire Ranch Station stood there for over a century, one of the last remaining California Stage Company stops. Now only a pile of debris marks the site on the road to Beale Air Force Base just south of Smartsville and a stone's throw from SR 20. The barn, built in 1852 with rough hand-hewn timbers held together by wooden pegs, still stands across the road from the site of the station. Halfway up the hill, hidden among the oaks on the right side of the road, is a neglected graveyard. Beyond this graveyard on the opposite side is a cemetery that has seen more recent use.

In 1849 a Mr. Berry and his wife built a log cabin on the site of the later Empire Ranch Station, and by 1851 this location had become the rallying point for miners for miles around. Thomas Mooney and Michael Riley bought the place that year and established a trading post and hotel there. Sunday was a gala day at the Empire Ranch, when hundreds of miners gathered in a convivial mood.

TIMBUCTOO

Timbuctoo (SRL 320) is half a mile west of Smartsville, on Timbuctoo Road just north of the junction with SR 20. The first mining in this region was done as early as 1850 in the ravines nearby, one of which was named Timbuctoo after an African man who was one of the first miners in the locality. The town was started in 1855. In the years when hydraulic mining flourished, it was the largest town in the eastern part of Yuba County, with a population of 1,200 at the height of its prosperity.

The town bears a forlorn and neglected look today. The old Wells Fargo Express Building (also known as the Stewart Brothers Store), built in 1855, was restored in 1928 by the Native Sons of the Golden West. It has since collapsed, and the pile of bricks, which is all that is left, is fenced to prevent injuries. There are a few homes remaining. Looking about the site today, it is difficult to imagine it as it was in the days when it had a church, a theater, and the usual cluster of saloons, stores, and hotels.

BROWN'S VALLEY

On the old road to Downieville, thirteen miles northeast of Marysville and one mile north of SR 20, is Brown's Valley. An early settler named Brown, who came to this spot in 1850, discovered gold near a huge boulder adjoining the temporary camp he had set up.

After taking out over $12,000 in quartz, Brown "was satisfied to retire." Not long after his discovery four Frenchmen developed the famous Jefferson Mine in the vicinity; other rich discoveries followed rapidly, among them the Flag, the Donnebroge, the Pennsylvania, and the Sweet Vengeance mines. One of the first stamp mills to be erected in California was put up at the Sweet Vengeance Mine by a French company, which purchased the mine from Spaniards who had been milling the ore by means of an arrastra on Little Dry Creek.

Ruins of some of the old mills still rise above the shafts of once-prosperous mines, and within the town a store recalls the past. The present hamlet once possessed five hotels, twenty-four saloons, and numerous stores.

Along the old Marysville–Downieville road are the sites of many taverns and stage stations. Although all of them have vanished, a few survive in place names; for example, the Peoria Cemetery and Peoria Road are named after the long-gone Peoria House, about fifteen miles northeast of Marysville.

THE OREGON HOUSE

Where the branch turnpike to La Porte turned north from the Downieville Trail, twenty-four miles northeast of Marysville, the Oregon House was built in 1852. It became one of the most popular of the several hostelries along that trail, and many a traveler in search of gold found rest and entertainment awaiting him within its hospitable doors. The original Oregon House was destroyed by fire many years ago, but the name is preserved in a country post office, where County Road E-20 and Frenchtown Road meet.

INDIANA RANCH AND GREENVILLE

The Downieville Trail and, later, the first wagon road from the Oregon House to Camptonville went by way of Foster's Bar, passing through Indiana Ranch and the town of Greenville. Beyond the Oregon House several stopping places broke the loneliness of the old trail, among them the California House and the Keystone House, the latter a large hotel with a racetrack attached. Indiana Ranch was at one time a thriving town. It was first settled in 1851 by Peter Labadie, John Tolles, and the Page brothers from Indiana; the former two kept the first hotels in the place. After 1860 mining declined in the vicinity, and, although rich pockets have been found from time to time, none of them has proved lasting.

Greenville, now a tiny settlement on Oregon Hill

Road northwest of New Bullard's Bar Dam, was originally known as Oregon Hill. Gold was first found there in 1850, but the place did not become prosperous until a ditch was constructed to bring water to the diggings. The company responsible for building this ditch had nine members, and in order to let everyone know that it was no "one-horse" project that they were putting in, they named it the Nine-Horse Ditch.

BROWNSVILLE AND NORTHEASTERN YUBA COUNTY

Brownsville, located on what was known in early days as the Central Turnpike to La Porte, was named after I. E. Brown, who erected a sawmill in the vicinity in 1851. For a decade or more a number of sawmills and lumbering camps, as well as mining camps, existed in the surrounding country. Among these were the Sharon Valley Mills, two miles northeast, completed in 1853 by L. T. Crane; the Challenge Mills, a mile farther to the northeast, built in 1856; and the short-lived Washington and Page Mills, located on Dry Creek, south of Challenge.

Brownsville was a "temperance town" and in 1878 became something of an educational center with the establishment there of the Knoxdale Institute by Martin Knox and his wife, with Professor E. K. Hill acting as principal. Knox, in partnership with P. E. Weeks, had purchased Brown's mill in 1852 and conducted the business until 1857; they also ran a hotel there.

North and northeast from Challenge Mills to La Porte a number of stage stations were passed, all important stopping places on the way to the gold mines of northwestern Sierra County and Plumas County. Challenge is a small town served for nearly a century by its general store. Woodville, now Woodleaf, just south of the present Butte county line, was formerly known as Barker's Ranch, first settled in 1850 by Charles Barker. James Wood bought the place in 1858 and built a beautiful two-story brick hotel, the Woodville House, now a church youth camp.

Leaving Woodleaf behind, the traveler passes through a corner of Butte County at Clipper Mills and again enters Yuba County at Strawberry Valley, known to the Indians as "Pomingo." Once in the midst of a large mining area, the Strawberry Valley district included the rich diggings on Deadwood Creek, Kentucky Gulch, Rich Gulch, and Whiskey Gulch. The town of Strawberry Valley became a lively center of trade for the surrounding mines, and in the late 1850s its main street was lined with stores, dwellings, and saloons, the leading hostelry

Sacred Heart Catholic Church, Dobbins

being the Columbus Hotel, still standing with its old well. The buildings on one side of the street were originally in Butte County, while those on the opposite side were located in Yuba County, but in 1860 the Legislature moved the county line a short distance north. All that is left of the town today is in Yuba County.

DOBBINS

Located in the lovely foothill valley of Dobbins' Creek, Dobbins' Ranch was first settled in 1849 by William M. and Mark D. Dobbins. By 1850 it had become the terminus for the stage-carried express business of Langton's Pioneer Express. From that point the contents had to be transported over the mountains to Downieville on muleback. Turnpikes ultimately took the place of the narrow pack trails, and in 1860 Atchison and Rice, with others, constructed a road to Downieville by way of Dobbins' Ranch, Bullard's Bar, and Camptonville, a course followed today by Yuba County Road E-20. The pioneer store that still stands in the town of Dobbins was opened in 1867 by Dan Gattens and William Slingsby, who formed a partnership, maintaining a pack train on the Downieville Trail continuously for a number of years, and furnishing the surrounding country with supplies. Near the store in the middle of Dobbins is the Sacred Heart Catholic Church, built in 1897, beautifully refurbished for its centennial, and one of the most attractive restorations to be seen in the gold country.

Below Dobbins is the Colgate Power House, built by the founder of the Pacific Gas & Electric Company. In September 1899, it provided electricity over the longest transmission line in the world to Sacramento. In 1901 another record was broken with a 162-mile line from the powerhouse to Oakland.

The early miners of northeastern Yuba County had a wild and rugged country to contend with. Carl I. Wheat, in a note to the DeLong journals, describes this region as follows:

> The map of Northeastern Yuba County gives no hint of the wildly broken nature of the terrain. The general contour of the ridges suggests an old plateau, slightly tilted to the west, greatly cut away by erosion during recent geologic times. The Yuba River and its many branches have cut deeply into this old plateau, its gorges being from five hundred to over a thousand feet in depth. Oregon Creek canyon just south of Camptonville falls away on a grand scale. The "bars" were located along the rivers, with mountains towering up on both sides. The other towns and "diggins" were generally located on or near the tops of the highest ridges, where the miners discovered the rich, gold-bearing gravels left by the rivers of earlier geologic ages. To one familiar with this broken terrain, DeLong's active journeyings, to and fro, on foot and on muleback, take on a new significance. It is a heavily wooded country, and to become lost was, and is, very easy, if one were to leave the beaten paths. . . . The very names of many of the populous mining camps of these wild ridges have been lost, and in other localities only a lone cabin or an ancient apple tree remains to recall the teeming life of the early "fifties," for the pines have grown up even over the burying places of the dead, and Nature has hastened to take back her own.

The New Bullard's Bar Reservoir now covers most of the old mining sites in the area. Impounded by New Bullard's Bar Dam, 966,000 acre-feet of water are stored to operate generators in the powerhouse at the base of the structure. Bullard's Bar was named for a Dr. Bullard who had been shipwrecked off the California coast on his way from Brooklyn, New York, to the Sandwich Islands. He made his way here and turned to mining. Foster's Bar, the other historically important town of the region, was named for William M. Foster, a survivor of the Donner party tragedy, who established a store along the river in 1849. Both these places are now under the waters of the reservoir.

CAMPTONVILLE

Camptonville's present buildings date from after the Gold Rush, the town having been completely destroyed by fire several times. SR 49 passes it a quarter of a mile

Pelton Water Wheel Monument, Camptonville

to the west. In a fenced enclosure at the entrance to the town from the highway is a monument placed in 1929 by the Masons, with a plaque testifying that, "On this spot in 1878 Lester Allen Pelton invented the Pelton Water Wheel." This device greatly improved the efficiency of the revolving machine, and ultimately was used in other industrial activities. A miniature wheel surmounts the monument. Also within the enclosure is a memorial stone to Robert Campton (1820-84), a blacksmith for whom the town was named. William Bull Meek, "stage driver—Wells Fargo agent—mule skinner—teamster—merchant," is memorialized with a plaque placed by the E Clampus Vitus chapter that bears his name. A small building marked "Town Jail" completes this remarkable collection.

A hotel was built on the site of Camptonville as early as 1850, when it was on the main road from Marysville and Nevada City to Downieville, and pack-mule trains stopped there daily on their way to the higher mountains. The toll road via Foster's Bar was completed to Camptonville in 1854, and the California Stage Company began running stages that far in the following year. The first great boom, however, came to the town in 1852, when gold was discovered on Gold Ridge to the east. Among the new arrivals at that time was Campton. By 1866 Camptonville numbered 1,500 inhabitants and was the center for hydraulic operations that produced $500,000 annually. A plank road one mile long formed the main street of the town. This was lined by more than thirty stores, numerous hotels and boarding-houses, as well as the ubiquitous saloons. Most of this ground was soon washed out by the activities of giant hydraulic monitors. The place today is a charming village of perhaps six hundred residents.

Rich strikes other than that of Gold Ridge soon caused a number of settlements to spring up throughout the region. Two miles north of Camptonville a group of men from Galena, Illinois, found gold in 1852, and the camp that grew up there was known as Galena Hill, a sizable place by 1856, and abandoned soon thereafter. The site is on Weeds Point Road west of SR 49.

Young's Hill, three miles northwest, also had its beginnings in 1852 when William Young and his brother settled there. The camp is mentioned frequently in the diary of the writer Charles DeLong, who lived there for some time. By 1856 it was a thriving center of trade, with hotels, stores, saloons, blacksmith shops, and even a theater flanking its main street. Ramm's Ranch to the southwest was located early by John Ramm, who saw the value of the perpetual spring that existed on the spot, which he used to advantage later in growing grapes. Early settlers had found an Indian rancheria in the region.

JOHNSON'S RANCH (WHEATLAND)

Pablo Gutiérrez, an employee of John A. Sutter, received a grant of five leagues of land on the north side of Bear River in 1844. Here he built an adobe house at a point later called Johnson's Crossing, about three miles east of today's town of Wheatland.

Gutiérrez was killed late in 1844, and his grant and cattle were sold at auction by Captain Sutter, magistrate of the region. The land was purchased for $150 by William Johnson and Sebastian Kayser, Johnson taking the eastern half and Kayser the western half. Just below the crossing they built an adobe house.

This place came to be known as Johnson's Ranch (SRL 493), about four miles east of Wheatland. It was the first settlement reached by the argonauts who crossed the Sierra over that branch of the California Trail that went through Donner Pass and down the ridge north of Bear River into Yuba County. Here many footsore emigrants rested and obtained supplies.

Among them were seven members of the Donner party who succeeded in getting over the mountains in the winter of 1846–47, finally reaching Johnson's Ranch, where they sought aid for those snowbound at Donner Lake. Johnson was the first husband of Mary Murphy of the Donner party, who later married Charles Covillaud.

CAMP FAR WEST

Camp Far West was established upriver from Johnson's Ranch by the federal government in 1849 for the protection of American settlers in the Yuba region. Two companies of American soldiers were stationed there under the command of Captain Hannibal Day. The post was abandoned in 1852, and the site since then has been obliterated by dredges. The Camp Far West cemetery, about four miles east of Wheatland, has been marked by the Native Sons of the Golden West.

THE WHEATLAND RIOT

East of Wheatland was the Durst Ranch, scene of one of California's most famous riots. The ranch had first been planted with hops in 1874; by 1913 it was a major producer. Ralph Durst was the state's largest employer of migratory labor, and, in response to advertisements, as many as 2,800 men, women, and children showed up on August 1, 1913. They found that there were fewer jobs than people, pay was very low, and the company store gouged the workers for food and supplies. As was not unusual in California's labor camps at that time, sanitation and housing were woefully insufficient. There were, for example, only eight or nine crude toilets for these thousands of people.

On August 2, a protest meeting was called by the Industrial Workers of the World (IWW), and a strike was organized. This led to a confrontation between Durst and the IWW leader, Richard "Blackie" Ford; on August 3, the sheriff and his deputies were called out. A deputy fired a warning shot into the air, starting a full-scale riot by the outraged hop pickers that ended in the deaths of the sheriff, the district attorney, and two workers; about a dozen more people were injured. Ford and another IWW leader, Herman Suhr, were arrested, convicted of murder, and sentenced to life imprisonment.

The shock of this episode reverberated beyond Yuba County. Governor Hiram Johnson sent in the National Guard to keep order and created a Commission on Immigration and Housing to investigate the condition of migratory farm laborers. Although some legislative action resulted from the commission's report, written by Carleton Parker, it did virtually nothing to improve the condition of migratory workers in California, whose lives remained dismal and who continued to be exploited for decades. The influence of the IWW, which had already been labeled a radical organization, was all but wiped out in the Sacramento Valley.

Later in 1913, "General" Charles T. Kelley led unemployed migratory farm workers and unskilled workers in a march on Sacramento to demand legislative aid. Twenty years before, Kelley had led a California detachment (which included Jack London) in Coxey's Army's march on Washington, D.C. Like Coxey's Army, Kelley's Army was broken up by police officers on reaching its destination. The condition of itinerant agricultural workers continues to be an issue in California.

As in previous editions of *Historic Spots in California*, this bibliography lists references by county. There are, however, many writings in California history with a scope wider than that of a single county. To minimize repetition, this edition begins the bibliography with a series of listings by area—California in General, Coastal California, the Gold Country, the San Francisco Bay Area, and Southern California—followed by the counties in alphabetical order.

CALIFORNIA IN GENERAL

Akers, Charlene. *Open to the Public: A Guide to the Museums of Northern California.* Berkeley: Heyday Books and California Historical Society, 1994.

Atlas of California. Culver City: Pacific Book Center, 1994.

Bancroft, Hubert Howe. *California.* Vols. 18–24 of *The History of the Pacific States of North America.* San Francisco: The History Company, 1884–80. [Most of the California material was written by Henry L. Oak.]

Barth, Gunther. *Bitter Strength: A History of the Chinese in the United States, 1850–1870.* Cambridge: Harvard University Press, 1964.

Batman, Richard. *James Pattie's West: The Dream and the Reality.* Norman: University of Oklahoma Press, 1986.

Beasley, Delilah L. *The Negro Trail Blazers of California.* 1919. Reprint, San Francisco: R & E Associates, 1968.

Beck, Warren A., and Ynez D. Haase. *Historical Atlas of California.* Norman: University of Oklahoma Press, 1975.

Beilharz, Edwin. *Felipe de Nava, First Governor of California.* San Francisco: California Historical Society, 1972.

Biggs, Donald C. *Conquer and Colonize: Stevenson's Regiment in California.* San Rafael: Presidio Press, 1977.

Bolton, Herbert Eugene. *Anza's California Expeditions.* 5 vols. Berkeley: University of California Press, 1930.

———, ed. *Historical Memoirs of New California, by Fray Francisco Palou, O.F.M.* 5 vols. Berkeley: University of California Press, 1926.

Boutelle, Sara Holmes. *Julia Morgan, Architect.* New York: Abbeville Press, 1988.

Boyd, William Harlan. *Stagecoach Heyday in the San Joaquin Valley, 1853–1876.* Bakersfield: Kern County Historical Society, 1983.

Brooks, George R., ed. *The Southwest Expedition of Jedediah S. Smith: His Personal Account of the Journey to California, 1826–1827.* Glendale: Arthur C. Clark Co., 1977.

California Historical Landmarks. Sacramento: State of California, The Resources Agency, California State Parks, 1996.

Chartkoff, Joseph, and Kerry Kona Chartkoff. *The Archaeology of California.* Stanford: Stanford University Press, 1984.

Clark, George T. *Leland Stanford, War Governor of California, Railroad Builder, and Founder of Stanford University.* Stanford: Stanford University Press, 1931.

Cook, Sherburne F. *Colonial Expeditions to the Interior of California's Central Valley, 1800–1820.* Berkeley: University of California Press, 1960.

———. *The Conflict Between the California Indians and White Civilization.* Berkeley: University of California Press, 1943.

———. *Expeditions to the Interior of California's Central Valley, 1820–1840.* Berkeley: University of California Press, 1962.

———. *The Population of the California Indians, 1769–1970.* Berkeley: University of California Press, 1976.

de Roos, Robert. *The Thirsty Land: The Story of the Central Valley Project.* Stanford: Stanford University Press, 1948.

Eargle, Dolan H., Jr. *The Earth Is Our Mother: A Guide to the Indians of California, Their Locales, and Historic Sites.* San Francisco: Trees Company Press, 1986.

Farquhar, Francis P., ed. *Up and Down California in 1860–1864: The Journal of William H. Brewer.* 1930. Reprint, Berkeley and Los Angeles: University of California Press, 1966.

Fickeworth, Alvin A. *California Railroads, an Encyclopedia (1851–1992).* San Marino: Golden West Books, 1992.

Fowler, Harlan D. *Camels to California, a Chapter in Western Transportation.* Stanford: Stanford University Press, 1950.

Fox, Stephen. *John Muir and His Legacy: The American Conservationist Movement.* Boston: Little, Brown, 1981.

Frémont, John C. *The Expeditions of John Charles Frémont.*

581

Vol. 1, *Travels from 1838 to 1844*, edited by Donald Jackson and Mary Lee Spence. Vol. 2, *The Bear Flag Revolt and the Court-Martial*, edited by Mary Lee Spence and Donald Jackson. Vol. 3, *Travels from 1848 to 1854*, edited by Mary Lee Spence. Urbana: University of Illinois Press, 1970, 1973, 1984.

———. *Memoirs of My Life, Including in the Narrative Five Journeys of Western Exploration.* Chicago: Belford, Clarke & Co., 1887.

Garr, Daniel. "Power and Priorities: Church-State Boundary Disputes in Spanish California." *California History* 57 (1979): 364–75.

Geiger, Maynard J. *Franciscan Missionaries in Hispanic California, 1769–1848: A Biographical Dictionary.* San Marino: Huntington Library, 1969.

———. *The Life and Times of Fray Junipero Serra.* 2 vols. Washington, D.C., 1959.

Gelber, Steven M. "Working to Prosperity: California's New Deal Murals." *California History* 58 (1979): 98–127.

Goode, Kenneth. *California's Black Pioneers.* Santa Barbara: McNally & Loftin, 1973.

Gudde, Erwin G. *California Place Names: The Origin and Etymology of Current Geographical Names.* Fourth edition, revised and enlarged by William Bright. Berkeley: University of California Press, 1998.

Guest, Francis F. *Fermín Francisco de Lasuén, 1736–1803, a Biography.* Washington, D.C., 1973.

———. "Junipero Serra and His Approach to the Indians." *Southern California Quarterly* 67 (1985): 223–61.

———. "Municipal Government in Spanish California." *California Historical Society Quarterly* 46 (1967): 307–36.

Gutiérrez, Roman, and Richard J. Orsi, eds. *Contested Eden: California Before the Gold Rush.* Berkeley: University of California Press, 1998.

Haas, Lisbeth. *Conquests and Historical Identities in California, 1769–1936.* Berkeley: University of California Press, 1995.

Hague, Harlan. "'Here Is the Road': Indian as Guide." *The Californians* (Mar.–Apr. 1985), pp. 28–33.

Hart, James D. *A Companion to California.* 2d ed. Berkeley: University of California Press, 1987.

Hastings, Lansford Warren. *The Emigrants' Guide to California.* Facsimile of the 1845 edition with introduction and notes by Charles H. Corey. Princeton: Princeton University Press, 1932.

Heizer, Robert F. *Languages, Territories, and Names of California Indian Tribes.* Berkeley: University of California Press, 1966.

———, ed. *California.* Vol. 8 of *Handbook of North American Indians.* Washington, D.C.: Smithsonian Institution, 1978.

———, ed. *The Destruction of the California Indians, 1847–1865.* Salt Lake City and Santa Barbara: Peregrine Smith, 1974.

Heizer, Robert F., and Albert B. Elsasser. *The Natural World of the California Indians.* Berkeley: University of California Press, 1980.

Helfrich, Devere, Helen Helfrich, and Thomas Hunt. *Emigrant Trails West: A Guide to Trail Markers Placed by Trails West, Inc., Along the California, Applegate, Lassen, and Nobles' Emigrant Trails in Idaho, Nevada, and California.* Reno, Nev.: Trails West, Inc., 1984.

Herr, Pamela. *Jessie Benton Frémont: American Woman of the 19th Century.* New York: Franklin Watts, 1987.

Hine, Robert V. *California's Utopian Colonies.* 1953. Reprint, Berkeley: University of California Press, 1983.

Hittell, Theodore. *History of California.* 4 vols. San Francisco, 1885–97.

Hornbeck, David. "Land Tenure and Rancho Expansion in Alta California, 1784–1846." *Journal of Historical Geography* 4 (Oct. 1978).

Hornbeck, David, and Phillip Kane. *California Patterns: A Geographical and Historical Atlas.* Palo Alto: Mayfield Publishing, 1983.

Hundley, Norris, Jr. *The Great Thirst: Californians and Water, 1770s–1990s.* Berkeley: University of California Press, 1992.

Hutchinson, W. H. "Southern Pacific: Myth and Reality." *California Historical Society Quarterly* 48 (1969): 325–34.

Jackson, W. Turrentine, and Alan M. Peterson. *The Sacramento–San Joaquin Delta: The Evolution and Implementation of Water Policy, an Historical Perspective.* Davis: California Water Resources Center, University of California at Davis, 1977.

Jaeger, Edmund C. *The California Deserts.* Stanford: Stanford University Press, 1965.

Jelenik, Lawrence J. *Harvest Empire: A History of California Agriculture.* San Francisco: Boyd & Fraser, 1979.

Kelley, Robert. *Battling the Inland Sea: Floods, Public Policy, and the Sacramento Valley.* Berkeley: University of California Press, 1989.

Kroeber, A. L. "California Place Names of Indian Origin." *University of California Publications in American Archaeology and Ethnology* 12, no. 2 (1916–17).

Kroeber, Theodora. *Ishi in Two Worlds.* Berkeley: University of California Press, 1961.

Lapp, Rudolph. *Afro-Americans in California.* Rev. ed. San Francisco: Boyd & Fraser, 1987.

Liebman, Ellen. *California Farmland: A History of Large Agricultural Landholdings.* Totowa, N.J.: Rowman & Allenheld, 1983.

McGloin, John B. *California's First Archbishop: The Life of Joseph Sadoc Alemany, O.P., 1814–1888.* New York: Herder & Herder, 1966.

McGowan, Joseph A. *History of the Sacramento Valley.* 3 vols. New York: Lewis Historical Publishing Co., 1961.

MacMullen, Jerry. *Paddle-Wheel Days in California.* Stanford: Stanford University Press, 1944.

McWilliams, Carey. *California: The Great Exception.* New York: A. A. Wyn, 1950.

———. *Factories in the Field: The Story of Migratory Farm Labor in California.* 1939. Reprint, Santa Barbara and Salt Lake City: Peregrine Publishers, 1971.

Miller, Robert Ryal. *Juan Alvarado, Governor of California, 1836–1842.* Norman: University of Oklahoma Press, 1998.

Moratto, M. J. *California Archaeology.* New York: Academic Press, 1984.

Nadeau, Remi. *Ghost Towns and Mining Camps of California.* Los Angeles: Ward Ritchie Press, 1965.

Nevins, Allen. *Frémont, Pathmarker of the West.* New York: Longmans, Green, 1955.

Nunis, Doyce B. *The Hudson's Bay Company's First Fur Brigade to the Sacramento Valley: Alexander McLeod's 1829 Hunt.* Fair Oaks: Sacramento Book Collector's Club, 1968.

Osio, Antonio Maria. *The History of Alta California: A Memoir of Mexican California.* Translated and edited by Rose Marie Beebe and Robert M. Senkewicz. Madison: University of Wisconsin Press, 1996.

Powers, Stephen. *Tribes of California.* Berkeley: University of California Press, 1977.

Rawls, James J. *Indians of California: The Changing Image.* Norman: University of Oklahoma Press, 1984.

Rawls, James J., and Walton Bean. *California: an Interpretive History.* 7th ed. New York: McGraw-Hill, 1997.

Rice, Richard B., William A. Bullough, and Richard J. Orsi. *The Elusive Eden: A New History of California.* 2nd ed. New York: McGraw-Hill, 1996.

Robinson, W. W. *Land in California.* 1948. Reprint, Berkeley: University of California Press, 1980.

Rolle, Andrew W. *California, a History.* 6th ed. Arlington Heights, Ill.: Harlan Davidson, 1998.

Royce, Josiah. *California.* 1886. Reprint, New York: Alfred A. Knopf, 1948.

Salley, H. E. *History of California Post Offices, 1849–1976.* La Mesa: Postal History Associates, 1977.

Sanchez, Nellie Van de Grift. *Spanish and Indian Place Names of California.* San Francisco: A. M. Robertson, 1922.

Schoeneberger, William A., with Paul Sonnenburg. *California Wings: A History of Aviation in the Golden State.* Woodland Hills: Windsor Publishing Co., 1984.

Starr, Kevin A. *Americans and the California Dream, 1850–1915.* New York: Oxford University Press, 1973.

———. *The Dream Endures: California Enters the 1940s.* New York: Oxford University Press, 1997.

———. *Endangered Dreams: The Great Depression in California.* New York: Oxford University Press, 1996.

———. *Inventing the Dream: California Through the Progressive Era.* New York: Oxford University Press, 1985.

Sullivan, Maurice S. *The Travels of Jedediah Strong Smith.* Santa Ana: Fine Arts Press, 1934.

Thompson, John, and Edward A. Dutra. *The Tule Breakers: The Story of the California Dredge.* Stockton: Stockton Corral of Westerners International, 1983.

Uzes, Francois D. *Chaining the Land: A History of Surveying in California.* Sacramento: Landmark Enterprises, 1977.

Weber, David J. *The Mexican Frontier, 1821–1846: The American Southwest Under Mexico.* Albuquerque: University of New Mexico Press, 1982.

———. *The Spanish Frontier in North America.* New Haven: Yale University Press, 1992.

Weber, Francis J. *Documents of California's Catholic History.* Los Angeles: Dawson's Book Shop, 1965.

Weitze, Karen. *California's Mission Revival.* Los Angeles: Hennessey & Ingalls, 1984.

Wood, Raymund F. "Anglo Influence on Spanish Place Names in California." *Southern California Quarterly* 58 (1981): 392–413.

Ziebarth, Marilyn. "California's First Environmental Battle." *California History* 63 (1984): 274–79.

COASTAL CALIFORNIA

Bolton, Herbert Eugene. *Fray Juan Crespí, Missionary Explorer on the Pacific Coast, 1769–1774.* Berkeley: University of California Press, 1927.

———, ed. *Font's Complete Diary, a Chronicle of the Founding of San Francisco.* Berkeley: University of California Press, 1933.

Brandes, Ray, trans. and ed. *The Costanso Narrative of the Portolá Expedition.* Newhall: Hogarth Press, 1970.

Brown, Joseph E. *Monarchs of the Mist: The Story of Redwood National Park and the Coast Redwoods.* Point Reyes: Coastal Parks Association, 1982.

Burgess, Sherwood D. "Lumbering in Hispanic California." *California Historical Society Quarterly* 41 (1962): 237–48.

California Coastal Access Guide. Berkeley and Los Angeles: University of California Press, 1983.

Costo, Rupert, and Jeanette Henry Costo, eds. *The Missions of California: A Legacy of Genocide.* San Francisco: The Indian Historian Press, 1987.

Coughlin, Magdalen. "Boston Smugglers on the Coast, 1797–1821: an Insight into the American Acquisition of California." *California Historical Society Quarterly* 46 (1967): 99–120.

Dana, Richard Henry, Jr. *Two Years Before the Mast.* 1840. Reprint, ed. by Thomas Philbrick and with appendix, "Twenty-Four Years Later." New York: Penguin Books, 1985.

Doran, Adelaide LeMert. *Pieces of Eight: Channel Islands, a Bibliographical Guide and Source Book.* Glendale: Arthur H. Clark Co., 1981.

Ehlers, Chad, and Jim Gibbs. *Sentinels of Solitude: West Coast Lighthouses.* Portland, Ore.: Graphic Arts Center Publishing Co., 1981.

Engelhardt, Zephyrin. *The Missions and Missionaries of California*. Santa Barbara: Santa Barbara Mission, 1930.

Hutchinson, W. H. *California Heritage: A History of Northern California Lumbering*. Rev. ed. Santa Cruz: Forest Historical Society, 1974.

Jacobs, Julius L. "California's Pioneer Wine Families." *California Historical Quarterly* 54 (1975): 139–75.

Kelsey, Harry. *Juan Rodríguez Cabrillo*. San Marino: Huntington Library, 1986.

———. "Mapping the California Coast: The Voyages of Discovery, 1533–1543." *Arizona and the West* 26 (1984): 307–24.

Martin, Wallace. *Sail and Steam on the North California Coast, 1850–1900*. San Francisco: National Maritime Museum Association, 1983.

Mathes, W. Michael. *Vizcaíno and Spanish Expansion in the Pacific Ocean, 1580–1630*. San Francisco: National Maritime Museum Association, 1983.

Nickerson, Roy. *Robert Louis Stevenson in California: A Remarkable Courtship*. San Francisco: Chronicle Books, 1982.

Schrepfer, Susan R. *The Fight to Save the Redwoods: A History of Environmental Reform, 1917–1978*. Madison: University of Wisconsin Press, 1983.

Shanks, Ralph C., and Janetta Thompson Shanks. *Lighthouses and Lifeboats on the Redwood Coast*. San Anselmo: Costanso Books, 1983.

Smith, Wallace E. "The Reverend Stephen Bowers, 'Curiosity Hunter' of the Santa Barbara Channel Islands." *California History* 62 (1983): 26–37.

Stanger, Frank M., and Alan K. Brown. *Who Discovered the Golden Gate: The Explorers' Own Accounts*. San Mateo: San Mateo County History Association, 1969.

Taylor, Bayard. *Eldorado, Or Adventures in the Path of Empire; Comprising a Voyage to California, Via Panama; Life in San Francisco and Monterey*. 1850, 1864. Reprint, Lincoln: University of Nebraska Press, 1988.

Treutlein, Theodore E. "Fages as Explorer." *California Historical Quarterly* 51 (1972): 338–56.

———. "The Portolá Expedition of 1769–1770." *California Historical Society Quarterly* 47 (1969): 291–334.

———. *San Francisco Bay: Discovery and Exploration*. San Francisco: California Historical Society, 1968.

Underhill, Reuben L. *From Cowhides to Golden Fleece— A Narrative of California, 1832–1858—Based upon Unpublished Correspondence of Thomas Oliver Larkin, Trader, Developer, Promoter, and Only American Consul*. Stanford: Stanford University Press, 1939.

Wagner, Henry R. *Spanish Voyages to the Northwest Coast of America in the Sixteenth Century*. San Francisco: California Historical Society, 1929.

Weber, Francis J. "California's Caminito Real." *California Historical Quarterly* 54 (1975): 63–76.

Wheeler, Eugene, and Robert Kallman. *Shipwrecks, Smugglers, and Maritime Mysteries of the Santa Barbara Channel*. Santa Barbara: McNally & Loftin, 1985.

THE GOLD COUNTRY

Ambrose, Stephen E. *Nothing Like It in the World: The Men Who Built the Transcontinental Railroad, 1863–1869*. New York: Simon & Schuster, 2000.

Burnett, Peter H. *Recollections and Opinions of an Old Pioneer*. New York: D. Appleton & Co., 1880.

Clark, William B., ed. *Gold Districts of California*. San Francisco: California Division of Mines and Geology, 1970.

Denalo, A. *Life on the Plains Among the Diggings*. Buffalo, N.Y.: Miller, Orton, & Mulligan, 1854.

Farquhar, Francis P. *History of the Sierra Nevada*. Berkeley and Los Angeles: University of California Press, 1965.

Gay, Theresa. *James W. Marshall, the Discoverer of California Gold*. Georgetown, Calif.: Talisman Press, 1966.

Geologic Guidebook Along Highway 49: Sierra Gold Belt, the Mother Lode Country. San Francisco: State Division of Mines, 1948.

Giffen, Helen S., ed. *The Diaries of Peter Decker: Overland to California in 1849 and Life in the Mines, 1850–1851*. Georgetown, Calif.: Talisman Press, 1966.

Glasscock, C. B. *A Golden Highway: Scenes of History's Greatest Gold Rush Yesterday and Today*. Indianapolis: Bobbs-Merrill, 1934.

Greenland, Powell. *Hydraulic Mining in California: A Tarnished Legacy*. Spokane: Arthur H. Clark Co., 2001.

Gudde, Erwin G. *Bigler's Chronicle of the West: The Conquest of California, Discovery of Gold, and Mormon Settlement as Reflected in William Henry Bigler's Diaries*. Berkeley: University of California Press, 1962.

Holliday, J. S. *Rush for Riches: Gold Fever and the Making of California*. Oakland Museum of California and the University of California Press, 1999.

———. *The World Rushed In: The California Gold Rush Experience*. New York: Simon & Schuster, 1981.

Howard, Thomas Frederick. *Sierra Crossing: First Roads to California*. Berkeley: University of California Press, 1998.

Jackson, Joseph Henry. *Anybody's Gold: The Story of California's Mining Towns*. 1941. Reprint, San Francisco: Chronicle Books, 1982.

Jackson, W. Turrentine. "Wells Fargo Staging over the Sierra." *California Historical Society Quarterly* 49 (1970): 99–134.

Littlefield, Douglas R. "Water Rights During the California Gold Rush: Conflicts over Economic Points of View." *Western Historical Quarterly* 14 (1983): 415–34.

Masri, Allen. *The Golden Hills of California*. Vol. 1 (with Peter Abenheim), *A Descriptive Guide to the Mother Lode Counties of the Southern Mines*. Vol. 2, *A Descriptive*

Guide to the Mother Lode Counties of the Northern Mines. Santa Cruz: Western Tanager Press, 1979, 1983.

Rawls, James J., and Richard Orsi, eds. *A Golden State: Mining and Economic Development in Gold Rush California.* Berkeley: University of California Press, 1999.

Reading, Pierson Barton. "Journal of Pierson Barton Reading." *Quarterly of the Society of California Pioneers* 7, no. 3 (1930).

Sargent, Shirley, ed. *Seeking the Elephant, 1849: James M. Hutching's Journal.* Glendale: Arthur H. Clark Co., 1980.

Todd, Arthur Cecil. *The Cornish Miner in America: The Contribution to the Mining Industry by Emigrant Cornish Miners, the Men Called Cousin Jacks.* Glendale: Arthur H. Clark Co., 1967.

Wagner, Jack R. *Gold Mines of California: An Illustrated History of the Most Productive Mines with Descriptions of the Interesting People Who Owned and Operated Them.* Berkeley: Howell-North Books, 1970.

Weston, Otheto. *Mother Lode Album.* Stanford: Stanford University Press, 1948.

SAN FRANCISCO BAY AREA

Bean, Lowell John, comp. & ed. *The Ohlone Past and Present: Native Americans of the San Francisco Bay Region.* Menlo Park: Ballena Press, 1994.

Bowman, J. N. "Adobe Houses in the San Francisco Bay Region," in *Geologic Guidebook of the San Francisco Bay Counties.* San Francisco: Department of Natural Resources, Division of Mines, 1951.

Estudillo, Jesus M. *Sketches of California in the 1860s: The Journals of Jesus Maria Estudillo*, edited and annotated by Margaret Schlichtmann and Marie Wilson. Fredericksburg, Tex.: Awani Press, 1988.

Gifford, E. W. "Composition of California Shellmounds." *University of California Publications in American Archaeology and Ethnology* 12 (1916): 1–29.

Houston, Alan Fraser. "Cadwalader Ringgold, U.S. Navy, Gold Rush Surveyor of San Francisco Bay and Waters to Sacramento, 1849–1850." *California History* 79 (2001): 208–21.

Kemble, John Haskell. *San Francisco Bay: A Pictorial Maritime History.* 1957. Reprint, New York: Bonanza Books, 1979.

Kennard, Charles. *San Francisco Bay Area Landmarks: Recollections of Four Centuries.* Palo Alto: Tioga Publishing Co., 1987.

Kinnaird, Lawrence. *History of the Greater San Francisco Bay Region.* 3 vols. New York and West Palm Beach: Lewis Historical Publishing Co., 1966.

Milliken, Randall. *A Time of Little Choice: The Disintegration of Tribal Culture in the San Francisco Bay Area, 1769–1810.* Menlo Park: Ballena Press, 1995.

Nelson, Nils Christian. "Shellmounds of the San Francisco Bay Region." *University of California Publications in American Archaeology and Ethnology,* 8, no. 4 (1909).

Schwendinger, Robert J. *International Port of Call: An Illustrated Maritime History of the Golden Gate.* Woodland Hills: Windsor Publications, 1984.

Scott, Mel. *The San Francisco Bay Area: A Metropolis in Perspective.* 2nd ed. Berkeley: University of California Press, 1985.

Wilson, Mark A. *East Bay Heritage: A Potpourri of Living History.* San Francisco: California Living Books, 1979.

Wollenberg, Charles. *Golden Gate Metropolis: Perspectives on a Bay Area History.* Berkeley: University of California Press, 1985.

SOUTHERN CALIFORNIA

Bean, Lowell John. *Mukat's People, the Cahuilla Indians of Southern California.* Berkeley: University of California Press, 1972.

Bolton, Herbert Eugene. *Spanish Exploration in the Southwest.* Vol. 17 of *Original Narratives of American History.* New York: Scribner, 1916.

Hague, Harland H. "The Search for a Southern Overland Route to California." *California Historical Quarterly* 55 (1976): 150–61.

Hine, Leland D. *Baptists in Southern California.* Valley Forge, Pa.: Judson Press, 1966.

Johnson, Hank. *The Railroad That Lighted Southern California.* Long Beach: Anglo Books, 1965.

Lothrop, Gloria Ricci. *A Guide to Historical Outings in Southern California.* Los Angeles: Historical Society of Southern California and Associated Historical Societies of Los Angeles County, 1991.

Lyman, Edward L. "Outmaneuvering the Octopus: Atchison, Topeka, and Santa Fe." *California History* 67 (1988): 94–107, 145–46.

McWilliams, Carey. *Southern California Country: An Island on the Land.* New York: Duell, Sloan, and Pearce, 1946.

Moses, Vincent. "'Oranges for Health—California for Wealth': The Billion-Dollar Navel and the California Dream." *The Californians,* July-Aug. 1985, pp. 27–37.

Nunis, Doyce B., Jr., and Abraham Hoffman, eds. *A Southern California Historical Anthology.* Los Angeles: Historical Society of Southern California, 1975.

Orsi, Richard. "*The Octopus* Reconsidered: The Southern Pacific and Agricultural Modernization in California, 1865–1915." *California Historical Quarterly* 54 (1975): 197–220.

Pitt, Leonard. *The Decline of the Californios: A Social History of Spanish-Speaking Californians, 1846–1890.* 1966. Reprint, Berkeley: University of California Press, 1998.

Sherer, Lorraine M. *Bitterness Road: The Mojave, 1604 to 1860.* Menlo Park: Ballena Press, 1994.

Starr, Kevin. *Material Dreams: Southern California Through the 1920s.* New York: Oxford University Press, 1990.

Stowe, Noel J., ed. "Pioneering Land Development in the Californias: An Interview with David Otto Brant." *California Historical Society Quarterly* 47 (1968): 15–40, 141–56, 237–50.

Thompson, Gerald. *Edward F. Beale and the American West.* Albuquerque: University of New Mexico Press, 1983.

ALAMEDA COUNTY

Abeloe, William N. *St. Leander's, 1864–1964.* San Leandro: St. Leander's Church, 1964.

Bagwell, Beth. *Oakland, Story of a City.* Novato: Presidio Press, 1982.

Berkeley Gazette. Special Centennial Edition. Oct. 26, 1977.

Bernhardi, Robert. *The Buildings of Berkeley.* Oakland: Holmes Book Company, 1973.

———. *The Buildings of Oakland.* Oakland: Forest Hill Press, 1979.

Bowman, J. N. "The Peraltas and Their Houses." *California Historical Society Quarterly* 30 (1951): 217–31. Reprint, Oakland: Alameda County Historical Society, 2001.

Burgess, Sherwood D. "Oakland's Water War." *California History* 64 (1985): 34–41.

Davis, William Heath. *Seventy-Five Years in California.* 1889. Reprint, edited by Harold A. Small, San Francisco: John Howell Books, 1967.

Kennedy, Keith E. *George Washington Patterson and the Founding of Ardenwood.* Cupertino: California History Center and Foundation, 1995.

McArdle, Phil, ed. *Exactly Opposite the Golden Gate: Essays on Berkeley's History.* Berkeley: Berkeley Historical Society, 1983.

McCarthy, Francis F. *The History of Mission San Jose, California, 1797–1835.* 1958. Reprint, San Jose: Commission for the Restoration of the Mission San Jose, 1977.

Martin, Imelda. *Alameda: A Geographical History.* Alameda: Friends of the Alameda Free Library, 1977.

Mosier, Page, and Dan Mosier. *Alameda County Place-Names.* Fremont: Mines Road Books, 1986.

Newton, Janet. *Las Positas: The Story of Robert and Josefa Livermore.* Livermore: Ralph and Janet Newton, 1969.

———. *Stories of the Vineyards and Wineries of the Livermore Valley.* 2nd ed. Livermore: Janet Newton, 1987.

Noble, John Wesley. *Its Name was M.U.D.* Oakland: East Bay Municipal Utility District, 1970.

Pattiani, Evelyn Craig. *Queen of the Hills: The Story of Piedmont, a California City.* 1954. Reprint, Oakland: DiMaggio Publications, 1982.

Pettit, George A. *Berkeley: The Town and Gown of It.* Berkeley: Howell-North Books, 1973.

———. *History of Berkeley.* Oakland: Alameda County Historical Society, 1976.

Sandoval, John. *History of Washington Township.* Fremont: Washington Township Historical Society, 1986.

Schenck, William E. "The Emeryville Shellmound." *University of California Publications in American Archaeology and Ethnology* 23, no. 3 (1926).

Schwartz, Richard. *Berkeley 1900.* Berkeley: RSB Books, 2000.

Studer, Jack J. "The First Map of Oakland, California: An Historical Speculation as Solution to an Enigma." *California Historical Society Quarterly* 48 (1969): 59–72.

———. "Julius Kellersberger, a Swiss as Surveyor and City Planner in California, 1851–1857." *California Historical Society Quarterly* 47 (1968): 3–14.

Thompson & West. *Official Historical Atlas of Alameda County.* 1878. Reprint, Fresno: Valley Publishers, 1976.

Verbarg, Leonard. *Celebrities at Your Doorstep.* Oakland: Alameda County Historical Society, 1972.

Weber, David. *Oakland: Hub of the West.* Tulsa, Okla.: Continental Heritage Press, 1981.

Weber, Francis J., comp. and ed. *The Patriarchal Mission: A Documentary History of San Jose.* Los Angeles: Libra Press, 1986.

Willard, Ruth Hendricks. *Alameda County: California Crossroads.* Northridge: Windsor Publications, 1988.

ALPINE COUNTY

Alpine Heritage. Alpine County Centennial Book Committee, 1964.

Gianella, Vincent P. "Where Frémont Crossed the Sierra Nevada in 1844." *Sierra Club Bulletin* 44, no. 7 (Oct. 1959).

Quille, Dan de [William Wright]. "Snow-Shoe Thompson." *Overland Monthly* 8, no. 46 (Oct. 1886): 419–35.

Sprout, Jerry, and Janine Sprout. *Alpine Trailblazer.* 2nd ed. Markleeville: Diamond Valley Co., 1999.

White, Chester Lee. "Surmounting the Sierras, the Campaign for a Wagon Road." *California Historical Society Quarterly* 7 (1928): 3–19.

AMADOR COUNTY

Andrews, John R. *Ghost Towns of Amador.* Rev. ed. Fresno: Book Publishers, 1979.

Cenotto, Larry. *Logan's Alley: Amador County Yesterdays in Picture and Prose.* Vol. 3. Jackson: Cenotto Publications, 1999.

Garbarini, Evelyn. *The Kennedy Wheels.* Jackson: Amador Press-News, 1975.

Glover, Choice M. *History of Amador County, California.* Sutter Creek: C. M. Glover, 1987.

Mason, J. D. *History of Amador County, California.* Oakland: Thompson & West, 1881.

Noble, John Wesley. *Its Name was M.U.D.* Oakland: East Bay Municipal Utility District, 1970.

Zorbas, Elaine. *Fiddletown: From Gold Rush to Rediscovery.* Altadena: Mythos Press, 1997.

BUTTE COUNTY

Bidwell, Annie E. K. *Rancho Chico Indians*, 1891–1913. Dorothy J. Hill, ed. 1980. Reprint, Chico: Bidwell Mansion Cooperating Association, 1987.

Bidwell, John. *Echoes of the Past.* 1889. Reprint: California Department of Parks and Recreation, 1987.

Bleyhl, Norris A. *Three Military Posts in Northeastern California, 1849–1863.* Chico: Association for Northern California Records and Research, 1984.

Book, Susan W. *The Chinese in Butte County, California, 1860–1920.* San Francisco: R & E Research Associates, 1976.

Butte Remembers. Chico: Butte County Branch, National League of American Pen Women, 1973.

Dunn, Forest, comp. *Butte County Place Names: A Geographical and Historical Dictionary.* Chico: Association for Northern California Records and Research, 1977.

Joslyn, Evelyn. *Memoirs of the Lott-Sank Family.* Oroville, 1973.

Mansfield, George C. *History of Butte County, California, with Biographical Sketches.* Los Angeles: Historic Record Co., 1918.

Talbitzer, Bill. *Butte County: An Illustrated History.* Northridge: Windsor Publications, 1987.

———. *The Days of Old, the Days of Gold.* Oroville: Las Plumas Publications, 1973.

———. *Lost Beneath the Feather.* Oroville, 1963.

Wells's and Chambers's History of Butte County, California, 1882, and Biographical Sketches of Its Prominent Men and Pioneers. Reprint, Berkeley: Howell-North Books, 1973.

CALAVERAS COUNTY

An Album of Pioneer Schools of Calaveras County. San Andreas: Calaveras County Historical Society, 1986.

Castro, Kenneth M., and Doris Castro. *Murphys, California: Short History and Guide.* Murphys: Kenneth M. Castro, 1972.

Elliott, W. W. *Calaveras County Illustrated and Described.* 1885. Reprint, Fresno: Valley Publishers, 1976.

Fry, Walter, and John R. White. *Big Trees.* Stanford: Stanford University Press, 1930.

Merriam, John C. "The True Story of the Calaveras Skull." *Sunset* 24, No. 2 (1910): 153–58.

Noble, John Wesley. *Its Name Was M.U.D.* Oakland: East Bay Municipal Utility District, 1970.

Stewart, George R., Jr. *Bret Harte, Argonaut and Exile.* Boston: Houghton Mifflin, 1931.

Zumwalt, Eve Starcevich. *The Romance of Mokelumne Hill.* Fresno: Pioneer Publishing Co., 1991.

COLUSA COUNTY

Benet, George. *A Place in Colusa.* San Pedro: Singlejack Books, 1977.

Carter, Jane Foster. *If the Walls Could Talk.* Colusa: History Preservation Committee, 1988.

Green, Will S. *Colusa County, California.* 1880. Reprint, Willows: Elizabeth Eubank, 1950.

McCornish, Charles Davis, and Rebecca T. Lambert. *History of Colusa and Glenn Counties, California.* Los Angeles: Historic Record Co., 1918.

Young, Helen D. *Arbuckle and College City.* Fresno: Pioneer Publishing Co., 1978.

CONTRA COSTA COUNTY

Andrews, Edna May, et al. *History of Concord, Its Progress and Promise.* Concord: Concord Historical Society, 1986.

Bogue, Lucille. "O'Neill at Tao House: California's Best-Kept Secret." *The Californians*, July–Aug. 1986, pp. 34–39.

Bohakel, Charles A. *Historic Tales of East Contra Costa County.* Antioch: Charles Bohakel, 1984.

———. *The Indians of Contra Costa County.* Amarillo, Tex.: P & H Publishers, 1977.

———. *Mount Diablo, The "Devil" Mountain of California.* Rev. ed. Antioch: Charles Bohakel, 1975.

———. "Tragic Tales of the Mount Diablo Coalfields." *The Californians*, July–Aug. 1984, pp. 39–41.

Cole, Susan D. *Richmond: Windows to the Past.* Richmond: Wildcat Canyon Books, 1980.

Conley, Frances. *First Settlers: The Castros of Rancho San Pablo.* San Pablo: San Pablo Historical and Museum Society, 1980.

Contra Costa Sun. "How It All Began." Issues of July 15–17, 1977, July 5–7, 1978, and July 28, 1982.

Emanuels, George. *California's Contra Costa County.* Fresno: Panorama West Books, 1986.

———. *Walnut Creek, Arroyo de las Nueces.* Walnut Creek: Diablo Books, 1984.

Fink, Leonora Galindo. "The San Ramon Valley." *Contra Costa Chronicles* 1, no. 3 (1966): 17–27.

Hurwitz, Karen E. *The History of John Marsh and Rancho de los Meganos.* Martinez: Contra Costa Development Association, 1973.

Illustrations of Contra Costa County, California, with Historical Sketches by Smith and Elliott. 1879. Reprint, Fresno: Valley Publishers, 1979.

Kimball, Sandy. *Moraga's Pride: Rancho Laguna de los Palos Colorados.* Moraga: Moraga Historical Society, 1987.

Loud, Llewellyn L. "The Stage Mounds at Richmond,

California." *University of California Publications in American Archaelogy and Ethnology* 17, no. 6 (1924).

Lyman, George D. *John Marsh, Pioneer.* New York: Scribner & Sons, 1930.

Mollenkopf, Jacquelyn. "The Byron Rail Disaster." *California History* 61 (1983): 292–301.

Moore, Shirley Anne Wilson. *To Place Our Deeds: The African-American Community of Richmond, California, 1910–1963.* Berkeley: University of California Press, 1999.

Munro-Fraser, J. P. *History of Contra Costa County, California.* 1882. Reprint, Oakland: Brooks-Sterling Co., 1974.

Murdock, Dick. *Port Costa, 1879–1941: A Saga of Sails, Sacks, and Rails.* Port Costa: Murdock-Endom Publishers, 1977.

Nelson, N. C. "The Ellis Landing Shellmound." *University of California Publications in American Archaeology and Ethnology* 7, no. 6 (1910).

Noble, John Wesley. *Its Name was M.U.D.* Oakland: East Bay Municipal Utility District, 1970.

Rego, Nilda. *Days Gone By in Contra Costa County.* 2 vols. Pleasant Hill: Contra Costa Historical Society, 1997 and 1998.

Russi, Alice McNeil. "Elam Brown." *Contra Costa Chronicles* 1, no. 3 (1966), 4–16.

Sorrick, Muir. *The History of Orinda, Gateway to Contra Costa County.* 1970. Reprint, Orinda: Friends of the Orinda Library, 1987.

Whitfield, Vallie Jo. *History of Pleasant Hill, California.* Pleasant Hill: Whitfield Books, 1988.

Winkley, John. *Dr. John Marsh, Wilderness Scout.* Nashville, Tenn.: Parthenon Press, 1962.

DEL NORTE COUNTY

Bledsoe, A. J. *Indian Wars of the Northwest.* San Francisco, 1885.

Carranco, Lynwood. "Two Tragic Shipwrecks of the 1860s." *The Californians,* May–June 1987, pp. 9–21.

McBeth, Frances Turner. *Lower Klamath Country.* Berkeley: Anchor Press, 1950.

———. *Pioneers of Elk Valley.* Angwin: Pacific Union College Press, 1960.

Smith, Esther Ruth. *History of Del Norte County.* Oakland: Holmes Book Co., 1953.

EL DORADO COUNTY

Bradley, Glen D. *The Story of the Pony Express.* Chicago: A.C. McClurg & Co., 1913.

Davis, Leonard M. *Georgetown, Pride of the Mountains.* Roseville: Georgetown Divide Rotary Club, 1976.

Dillon, Richard. *Fool's Gold: The Decline and Fall of Captain John Sutter of California.* 1967. Reprint, Santa Cruz: Western Tanager Press, 1981.

Greuner, Lorene, comp. *Lake Valley's Past.* South Lake Tahoe: Lake Tahoe Historical Society, 1976.

Historic Places of Interest, Myths & Legends: Coloma, Lotus, Gold Hill. Placerville: Heritage Association of El Dorado County, 1995.

Paul, Rodman W. *The California Gold Discovery: Sources, Documents, Accounts and Memoirs Relating to the Discovery of Gold at Sutter's Mill.* Georgetown: Talisman Press, 1966.

Sanborn, Margaret. *The American, River of El Dorado.* New York: Holt, Rinehart, and Winston, 1974.

Yohalem, Betty, ed. *I Remember: Stories and Pictures of El Dorado County Pioneer Families.* Placerville: El Dorado County Chamber of Commerce, 1977.

Zauner, Phyllis. *Lake Tahoe.* Tahoe Paradise: Zanel Publications, 1982.

FRESNO COUNTY

Clough, Charles W., et al. *Fresno County in the Twentieth Century.* Fresno: Panorama West Books, 1986.

Clough, Charles W., and William B. Secrest Jr. *Fresno County: The Pioneer Years from the Beginnings to 1900.* Fresno: Panorama West Books, 1984.

Donelan, John. "Coalinga, 4:42 P.M." *California History* 64 (1986): 42–47.

Eaton, Edwin M. *Vintage Fresno: Pictorial Recollections of a Western Town.* Fresno: Huntington Press, 1965.

Fresno Bee. "Fresno Centennial Issue." Sept. 22, 1985.

Fresno Past and Present, 1885–1985. Fresno: Fresno City and County Historical Society, 1985.

Genini, Ronald. "Industrial Workers of the World and Their Fresno Free Speech Fight, 1910–1911." *California Historical Quarterly* 53 (1974): 100–114.

Imperial Fresno. Fresno, California. 1897. Reprint, Fresno: Fresno City and County Historical Society, 1979.

Johnston, Hank. *They Felled the Redwoods.* Glendale: Interurban Press, 1983.

M. Theo Kearney's Fresno County, California, and the Fruit Vale Estate. 1903. Reprint, Fresno: Fresno City and County Historical Society, 1980.

McFarland, J. Randall. *Centennial Selma: Biography of a California Community's First 100 Years.* Selma: Selma Enterprise, 1980.

McGee, Lizzie. *Mills of the Sequoias.* Visalia: Tulare County Historical Society, 1952.

Mathes, Pauline Peterson. *Kingsburg, California: Bit of Sweden in the Desert.* Fresno: Pioneer Publishing Co., 1991.

Rehert, Catherine Morison. *The Valley's Legends and Legacies.* 2 vols. Fresno: Word Dancer Press, 1996 and 1997.

Secrest, William B. [Sr.] "The Horrifying History of a Highwayman's Head." *The Californians,* Nov.–Dec. 1986, pp. 28–34.

———. *Joaquin, Bloody Bandit of the Mother Lode.* Fresno: Saga-West Publishing Co., 1967.

Teilman, I., and W. H. Shafer. *The Historical Story of Irrigation in Fresno and Kings Counties in Central California.* Fresno: Williams and Son, 1943.

Tweed, William C. *Sequoia–Kings Canyon: The Story Behind the Scenery.* Las Vegas: KC Publications, 1980.

Winchell, Lilbourne Alsip. *History of Fresno County and the San Joaquin Valley, Narrative and Bibliographical.* Fresno: Arthur H. Cawston, 1933.

GLENN COUNTY

McCornish, Charles Davis, and Rebecca T. Lambert. *History of Colusa and Glenn Counties, California.* Los Angeles: Historic Record Co., 1918.

Russell, Gene H. *Orland's Colorful Past.* Orland: Orland Community Scholarship Association, 1977.

HUMBOLDT COUNTY

Adams, Kramer A. *Covered Bridges of the West.* Berkeley: Howell-North Books, 1963.

Anderson, Mary. *Backwoods Chronicle: A History of Southern Humboldt [County], 1849–1920.* Redway: Southern Humboldt Press, 1985.

Beal, Laurence. *The Carson Mansion: America's First Victorian Home and the Man Who Built It.* Eureka: Times Publishing, 1973.

Bledsoe, A. J. *Indian Wars of the Northwest.* San Francisco, 1855.

Carranco, Lynwood. "Maritime Fiasco on the Northern California Coast." *California History* 60 (1981): 210–27.

———. "Two Tragic Shipwrecks of the 1860s." *The Californians,* May–June 1987, pp. 9–21.

Coy, Owen C. *The Humboldt Bay Region, 1850–1875: A Study in the Americanization of California.* Los Angeles: California State Historical Association, 1929.

Hoopes, Chad L. "Redick McKee and the Humboldt Bay Region, 1851–1852." *California Historical Quarterly* 49 (1970): 195–220.

Nelson, Byron, Jr. *Our Home Forever: A Hupa Tribal History.* Hupa: Hupa Tribe, 1978.

Sachs, Benjamin. *Carson Mansion and Ingomar Theater.* Fresno: Valley Publishers, 1979.

Woolfolk, John. "Pacific Lumber Shuts Historic Mill." *Contra Costa Times* (Dec. 9, 2001): 3–4.

Zahl, Paul A. "Finding the Mt. Everest of All Living Things." *National Geographic* 126 (July 1964): 10–51.

IMPERIAL COUNTY

Dowd, M. L. *Historic Salton Sea.* El Centro: Imperial Irrigation District, 1960.

Farr, F. C. *History of Imperial County.* Berkeley: Elms and Franks, 1918.

Farris, William H. *The 1847 Crossing of Imperial County, California, and Baja California, Mexico, by the U.S. Mormon Battalion.* El Centro: Imperial Valley College Museum Society, 1977.

Geisinger, Iva L. *Goldrock: Facts & Folktales.* Monterey: d'Angelo Publishing Co., 1973.

Gillett, Paul, and Peter Gillett. *Imperial Valley's Lost Gold.* Yuma, Ariz.: Southwest Printers, 1974.

Hanna, Phil Townsend. "The Wells of Santa Rosa of the Flat Rocks." *Touring Topics* 20 (Jan. 1928): 18–20, 31.

Harris, Elizabeth. *Townsite of Silsbee and Indian Well.* Holtville: Imperial Valley Pioneer Society, 1979.

James, George Wharton. *Wonders of the Colorado Desert.* Boston: Little, Brown, 1906.

Love, Frank. *Mining Camps and Ghost Towns Along the Lower Colorado in Arizona and California.* Los Angeles: Westernlore Press, 1974.

Porretta, Phil. "Locating the Site of Mission Bicuñer." *Biblio-Cal Notes* of the Southern California Local History Council (Fall 1977), pp. 24–39.

INYO COUNTY

Austin, Mary. *The Land of Little Rain.* 1903. Reprint, New York: Penguin, 1988.

Chalfant, W. A. *Death Valley.* Stanford: Stanford University Press, 1966.

Cronkhite, Daniel. *Death Valley's Victims: A Descriptive Chronology, 1849–1980.* 3d ed. Morongo Valley: Sagebrush Press, 1981.

DeDecker, Mary. *Mines of the Eastern Sierra.* Glendale: La Siesta Press, 1966.

Kahrl, William. "The Politics of California Water: Owens Valley and the Los Angeles Aqueduct, 1900–1927." *California Historical Quarterly* 55 (1976): 2–25, 98–120.

———. *Water and Power: The Conflict Over Los Angeles' Water Supply in the Owens Valley.* Berkeley: University of California Press, 1982.

Lingenfelter, Richard E. *Death Valley and the Amargosa: A Land of Illusion.* Berkeley: University of California Press, 1986.

McAdams, Cliff. *Death Valley, Past and Present: Guide and Reference Book.* Boulder, Colo.: Pruett Publishing Co., 1981.

Nadeau, Remi. *The Water Seekers.* New York: Doubleday, 1950.

Paher, Stanley. *Death Valley Ghost Towns.* Las Vegas: Nevada Publications, 1973.

Richards, Frederick L. "The Commander's House." *Westways,* Feb. 1965, pp. 16–17.

Rose, Dan. "The Legend of Winneduma." *Touring Topics* 19 (Aug. 1927): 35, 39.

Walton, John. "Picnic at Alabama Gates: The Owens Valley Rebellion, 1904–1927." *California History* 65 (1986): 192–207.

———. *Western Times and Water Wars: State, Culture, and Rebellion in California*. Berkeley: University of California Press, 1992.

Williams, George, III. *The Guide to Bodie and Eastern Sierra Historic Sites*. Riverside: Tree by the River Publishers, 1981.

KERN COUNTY

Bailey, Richard C. *Explorations in Kern*. Bakersfield: Kern County Historical Society, 1962.

———. *Heart of the Golden Empire: An Illustrated History of Bakersfield*. Woodland Hills: Windsor Publications, 1984.

———. *Heritage of Kern*. Bakersfield: Kern County Historical Society, 1957.

Bolton, Herbert Eugene. "In the South San Joaquin Ahead of Garcés." *California Historical Society Quarterly* 10 (1931): 211–19.

Boyd, William Harland. *A California Middle Border: The Kern River Country, 1772–1880*. Richardson, Tex.: Havilah Press, 1972.

———. *Kern County Wayfarers, 1844–1881*. Bakersfield: Kern County Historical Society, 1977.

———. *Land of Havilah*. Bakersfield: Kern County Historical Society, 1952.

Burmeister, Eugene. *The Golden Empire: Kern County, California*. Beverly Hills: Autograph Press, 1977.

Crowe, Earle. *Men of El Tejon*. Los Angeles: Ward Ritchie Press, 1957.

Darling, Curtis. *Kern County Place Names*. Bakersfield: Kern County Historical Society, 1988.

Gifford, E. W., and W. Egbert Schenck. "Archaeology of the Southern San Joaquin Valley, California." *University of California Publications in American Archaeology and Ethnology* 23, no. 1 (1925): 1–122.

Inside Historic Kern. Bakersfield: Kern County Historical Society, 1982.

Kreiser, Ralph F., and Thomas Hunt. *Kern County Panorama*. Bakersfield: Kern County Historical Society, 1961.

Ludeke, John. "The No-Fence Law of 1874: Victory for San Joaquin Valley Farmers." *California History* 59 (1980): 98–115.

Peirson, Emma. *Kern's Desert*. Bakersfield: Kern County Historical Society, 1956.

Robinson, W. W. *The Story of Kern County*. Bakersfield: Title Insurance & Trust Co., 1961.

Saunders, Charles Francis. *The Southern Sierras of California*. Boston: Houghton Mifflin, 1923.

Street, Richard Steven. "A Kern County Diary: The Forgotten Photographs of Carleton E. Watkins, 1881–1888." *California History* 61 (1983): 242–63.

Where the Railroad Ended: Delano Centennial Yearbook. Delano: Delano Historical Society, 1974.

KINGS COUNTY

Bolton, Herbert Eugene. "In the South San Joaquin Ahead of Garcés." *California Historical Society Quarterly* 10 (1931): 211–19.

Brown, James L. *Mussel Slough Tragedy*. 2nd ed. Hanford: Oldtown Towns, 1980.

———. *The Story of Kings County, California*. Berkeley: Lederer, Street, and Zeus, 1941.

Brown, Robert R. *History of Kings County*. Hanford: A. H. Cawston, 1940.

Buckner, Leona Kreyenhagen. *The Lemoore Story*. Lemoore: Lemoore Chamber of Commerce, 1962.

Mitchell, Annie. *Sites to See*. Fresno: Panorama West Books, 1983.

Preston, William L. *Vanishing Landscape: Land and Life in the Tulare Lake Basin*. Berkeley: University of California Press, 1980.

Teilman, I., and W. H. Shafer. *The Historical Story of Irrigation in Fresno and Kings Counties in Central California*. Fresno: Williams and Son, 1943.

LAKE COUNTY

Anderson, Winslow. *Mineral Springs and Health Resorts of California*. San Francisco: Bancroft Co., 1892.

Benson, William Ralganal. "Narrative of the Stone and Kelsey Massacre." *California Historical Society Quarterly* 11 (1932): 266–73.

Carpenter, Aurelius, and Percy H. Millberry. *History of Mendocino and Lake Counties*. Los Angeles: Historic Record Co., 1914.

Case, Suzanne D. *Join Me in Paradise: The History of Guenoc Valley*. Middletown: Guenoc Winery, 1982.

Harris, Harvey. *California's Medical Story*. San Francisco: J. W. Stacey, 1932.

History of Napa and Lake Counties, California. San Francisco: Slocum, Bowen & Co., 1882.

Lewis, Ruth, et al. *Stories and Legends of Lake County*. 1949 rev. ed; orig. pub. 1935. Reprint, Kelseyville: Lake County Historical Society, 1983.

Mauldin, Henry K. *Your Lakes, Valleys and Mountains: History of Lake County*. San Francisco: East Wind Printers, 1960.

LASSEN COUNTY

Dozier, Dave F. *Main Street, Susanville 1910*. Susanville: Lassen County Historical Society, 1979.

Fairfield, Asa Merrill. *Fairfield's History of Lassen County, California*. San Francisco: H. S. Crocker, 1916.

Fariss & Smith. *History of Plumas, Lassen, and Sierra Counties, California*. 1882. Reprint, Berkeley: Howell-North Books, 1971.

Purdy, Tim I. *Sagebrush Reflections: The History of Amedee and Honey Lake*. Stamford, Conn.: Distribution Publications, 1983.

Strong, Douglas H. *"These Happy Grounds," a History of the Lassen Region*. Red Bluff: Walker Lithograph, 1982.

Swartzlow, Ruby Johnson. *Lassen, His Life and Legacy*. 1964. Reprint, Mineral: Loomis Museum Association, 1972.

LOS ANGELES COUNTY

Acuna, Rodolfo. *A Community Under Siege: A History of Chicanos East of the Los Angeles River*. Los Angeles: Chicano Studies Research Center, University of California at Los Angeles, 1984.

Basten, Fred E. *Santa Monica Bay, Paradise By the Sea: A Pictorial History of Santa Monica, Venice, Marina del Rey, Pacific Palisades, Topanga, and Malibu*. 1975. Reprint, Crawfordsville, Ind.: General Publishing Group, 1997.

Belderain, Francisca Lopez. "First to Find Gold in California." *Touring Topics* 22 (Nov. 1930): 32–34.

Bottles, Scott L. *Los Angeles and the Automobile: The Making of the Modern City*. Berkeley: University of California Press, 1987.

Carpenter, Virginia L. *The Ranchos of Don Pacifico Ontiveros*. Fullerton: Friis-Pioneer Press, 1982.

Caughey, John, and LaRee Caughey, eds. *Los Angeles: Biography of a City*. Berkeley: University of California Press, 1976.

Dakin, Susanna B. *A Scotch Paisano in Old Los Angeles: Hugo Reid's Life in California, 1832–1852*. 1939. Reprint, Berkeley: University of California Press, 1978.

Davis, Mike. *City of Quartz: Excavating the Future in Los Angeles*. New York: Vintage, 1992.

"A Double Look at Utopia: Llano del Rio." 1. Aldous Huxley, "Ozymandias, the Utopia That Failed." 2. Paul Kagan, "Portrait of a California Utopia." *California Historical Society Quarterly* 51 (1972): 117–54.

Driver, Les. "Carrillo's Flying Artillery: The Battle of San Pedro." *California Historical Society Quarterly* 48 (1969): 335–49.

Fink, Augusta. *Time and the Terraced Land* [Rancho Los Palos Verdes]. Berkeley: Howell-North Books, 1966.

Fogelson, Robert M. *The Fragmented Metropolis: Los Angeles, 1850–1930*. Cambridge: Harvard University Press, 1967.

Gebhard, David, and Robert Winter. *Architecture in Los Angeles: A Complete Guide*. Layton, Utah: Gibbs M. Smith, 1984.

Goodwin, H. Marshall, Jr. "The Arroyo Seco: From Dry Gulch to Freeway." *Southern California Quarterly* 47 (1965): 90–94.

Grenier, Judson A., et al., eds. *A Guide to Historic Places in Los Angeles County*. Dubuque, Iowa: Kendall-Hunt Publishing Co., 1978.

Grenier, Judson A., with Robert C. Gillingham. *California Legacy: The James Alexander Watson–Maria Dolores Dominguez de Watson Family, 1820–1980*. Carson, Calif.: Watson Land Co., 1982.

Hager, Anna Marie. "A Salute to the Port of Los Angeles, from Mud Flats to Modern Day Miracle." *California Historical Society Quarterly* 49 (1970): 329–36.

Harrington, Marie. *Mission San Fernando: A Guide*. Mission Hills: San Fernando Valley Historical Society, 1971.

Johnson, Faye. "William S. Hart, Cowboy's Cowboy." *The Californians*, May–June 1986, pp. 39–43.

Kelsey, Harry. "A New Look at the Founding of Old Los Angeles." *California Historical Society Quarterly* 55 (1976): 326–39.

King, William E. *Mission San Gabriel: Two Hundred Years, 1771–1971*. San Gabriel: The Claretian Fathers, 1971.

Leadabrand, Russ. *A Guidebook to the San Gabriel Mountains of California*. Los Angeles: Ward Ritchie Press, 1963.

"Los Angeles, 1781–1981; A Special Bicentennial Issue." *California History* 60, no. 1 (1981).

McDowell, Don. *The Beat of the Drum: The History, Events and People of Drum Barracks, Wilmington, California*. Wilmington: Drum Barracks Civil War Museum, 1993.

Marquez, Ernest. *Port Los Angeles: A Phenomenon of the Railroad Era*. San Marino: Golden West Books, 1976.

Matson, Charles A. *Building a World Gateway*. Los Angeles: Pacific Era Publishers, 1945.

Meyer, Larry J., and Patricia L. Kalayjian. *Long Beach, Fortune's Harbor*. Long Beach: Historical Society of Long Beach, 1983.

Outland, Charles F. *Man-Made Disaster: The Story of St. Francis Dam*. Glendale: Arthur H. Clark Co., 1977.

Owen, J. Thomas. "The Church by the Plaza, a History of the Pueblo Church of Los Angeles." *Historical Society of Southern California Quarterly* 42 (1960): 5–28, 186–204.

Perry, Edward Casewell. *Burbank: An Illustrated History*. Northridge: Windsor Publications, 1981.

Pflueger, Donald H. *Covina: Sunflowers, Citrus, Subdivisions*. Covina: Donald H. Pflueger, 1964.

———. *Glendora: The Annals of a Southern California Community*. Claremont: Saunders Press, 1951.

Pomona Centennial History. Pomona: Centennial-Bicentennial Committee, 1976.

Queenan, Charles F. *Long Beach and Los Angeles, a Tale of Two Ports*. Northridge: Windsor Publications, 1986.

Quinn, Charles Russell. *History of Downey*. Downey: Elena Quinn, 1973.

Rand, Christopher. *Los Angeles, the Ultimate City.* New York: Oxford University Press, 1967.

Rios-Bustamente, Antonio, and Pedro Castillo. *An Illustrated History of Mexican Los Angeles, 1781–1985.* Los Angeles: University of California Press, 1986.

Rogers, Warren S. *Mesa to Metropolis: the Crenshaw Area, Los Angeles.* Los Angeles: Lorrin L. Morrison, 1959.

Rolle, Andrew. *Los Angeles: From Pueblo to City of the Future.* 2nd ed. Sacramento: MTL, 1995.

Rowland, Leonore. *The Romance of La Puente Rancho.* Covina: Neilson Press, 1958.

San Pedro, a Pictorial History. San Pedro: San Pedro Bay Historical Society, 1983.

Scheid, Ann. *Pasadena: Crown of the Valley.* Northridge: Windsor Publications, 1986.

Schiesl, Martin J. "City Planning and the Federal Government in World War II: The Los Angeles Experiment." *California History* 59 (1980): 126–43.

Tanner, John Douglas, Jr. "Campaign for Los Angeles— December 29, 1846, to January 10, 1847." *California Historical Society Quarterly* 48 (1969): 219–42.

U.S. Works Progress Administration, Writer's Program. *Los Angeles: A Guide to the City and Its Environs.* 1939. Rev. ed., New York: Hastings House, 1951.

Waddingham, Gladys. *The History of Inglewood.* Inglewood: Historical Society of Centinela Valley, 1994.

Weber, Francis J., comp. and ed. *The Mission in the Valley: San Fernando Rey de España.* Los Angeles, 1975.

———, comp. and ed. *The Pride of the Missions: A Documentary History of San Gabriel Mission.* Los Angeles: 1979.

Wright, Judy. *Claremont, a Pictorial History.* Claremont: Claremont Historic Resources Center, 1980.

MADERA COUNTY

Clough, Charles W. *Madera.* Fresno: Valley Publishers, 1968.

Crampton, C. Gregory, ed. *The Mariposa Indian War, 1850–51: Diaries of Robert Eccleston.* Salt Lake City: University of Utah Press, 1975.

Farquhar, Francis P. *Place Names of the High Sierra.* San Francisco: Sierra Club, 1926.

Foster, Doris, and Clyde Foster. "One Hundred Years of History—Foster's Hogue Ranch." *The Madera Historical Society Quarterly* 1 (1961): 1–7.

From Whence We Came. Madera: Friends of the Madera County Library, 1998.

Fry, Walter, and John R. White. *Big Trees.* Stanford: Stanford University Press, 1930.

LeConte, J. N. "The Devil's Postpile." *Sierra Club Bulletin* 8 (Jan. 1912): 170–73.

Matthis, Francois E. "Devil's Postpile and Its Strange Setting." *Sierra Club Bulletin* 15 (Feb. 1930): 1–8.

MARIN COUNTY

Andrews, Kenneth R. *Drake's Voyages.* New York: Scribners, 1967.

Armentrout-Ma, L. Eve. "Chinese in California's Fishing Industry, 1850–1914." *California History* 60 (1981): 142–57.

Bancroft Library Publications. *The Plate of Brass Reexamined* (1977). *Supplementary Report* (1979). Berkeley: Bancroft Library, University of California at Berkeley.

Carlson, Pamela McGuire, and E. Breck Parkman. "An Exceptional Adaptation: Camillo Ynitia." *California History* 65 (1986): 238–47.

Colley, Charles C. "The Missionization of the Coast Miwok Indians of California." *California Historical Society Quarterly* 49 (1970): 143–62.

Dwyer, John T. *One Hundred Years an Orphan: St. Vincent's Home for Boys at San Rafael, 1855–1955.* Fresno: Academy Library Guild, 1955.

Evans, Elliott A. P., and David W. Heron. "Isla de los Angeles: Unique State Park in San Francisco Bay." *California History* 66 (1987): 24–39.

Fairley, Lincoln. "Literary Associations with Mount Tamalpais." *California History* 61 (1982): 82–99.

"The Francis Drake Controversy: His California Anchorage, June 17–July 23, 1579." Marilyn Ziebarth, ed. *California Historical Society Quarterly* 53, no. 2 (1974).

Futcher, Jane, and Robert Conover. *Marin: The Place, the People.* New York: Holt, Rinehart, and Winston, 1981.

Glimpses of Belvedere and Tiburon: the Early Decades. Belvedere-Tiburon: The Landmarks Society, 1964.

Hanna, Warren L. *Lost Harbor: The Controversy Over Drake's California Anchorage.* Berkeley: University of California Press, 1979.

Heizer, Robert F. *Elizabethan California.* Ramona, Calif.: Ballena Press, 1974.

Kelsey, Harry. *Sir Francis Drake: The Queen's Pirate.* New Haven: Yale University Press, 1998.

Killion, Tom. *Fortress Marin.* San Rafael: Presidio Press, 1979.

McKenna, Clare V., Jr. "The Origins of San Quentin, 1851–1880." *California History* 66 (1987): 49–54.

Martin, N. B. "'Portus Novae Albionis': Site of Drake's California Sojourn." *Pacific Historical Review* 48 (1979): 319–31.

Mason, Jack. *Point Reyes: The Solemn Land.* Inverness: North Shore Books, 1970.

Mason, Jack, and Helen Van Cleave Park. *Early Marin.* Rev. ed. Inverness: North Shore Books, 1976.

Morison, Samuel Eliot. *The European Discovery of America.* Vol. 2, *The Southern Voyages, 1492–1626.* New York: Oxford University Press, 1974.

Pictorial History of Tiburon, a California Railroad Town. Belvedere-Tiburon, 1984.

Teather, Louise. *Discovering Marin: Historical Tour by Cities and Towns.* Fairfax: The Tamal Land Press, 1974.

Thrower, Norman J. W., ed. *Sir Francis Drake and the Famous Voyage, 1577–1580: Essays Commemorating the Quadricentennial of Drake's Circumnavigation of the Earth.* Berkeley: University of California Press, 1984.

Treganza, Adan E. "Old Lime Kilns Near Olema." *Geological Guidebook of the San Francisco Bay Counties.* San Francisco: State of California, Division of Mines, 1951, pp. 65–72.

MARIPOSA COUNTY

Burchfield, Chris. "Demolishing Two Mariposa Legends." *The Californians,* Nov.–Dec. 1986, pp. 42–43.

Clark, Galen. *The Yosemite Valley.* Yosemite Valley, 1911.

Crampton, C. Gregory, ed. *The Mariposa Indian War, 1850–51: Diaries of Robert Eccleston.* Salt Lake City: University of Utah Press, 1975.

"The Early Days in Yosemite," reprinted from the *Mariposa Democrat* of August 5, 1856, with introduction by Ansel F. Hall. *California Historical Society Quarterly* 4 (1925): 2–58.

Mendershausen, Ralph. *Treasures of the South Fork: A History and Guide for the South Fork of the Merced River in Mariposa County.* Mariposa: Ralph R. Mendershausen, 1983.

Muir, John. *The Yosemite.* New York: Century Company, 1912.

Phillips, Catherine Coffin. *Coulterville Chronicle: The Annals of a Mother Lode Mining Town.* 1942. Reprint, Fresno: Valley Publishers, 1978.

Sargent, Shirley. *Mariposa County Guidebook.* Yosemite: Flying Spur Press, 1984.

———. *Yosemite's Historic Wawona.* Yosemite: Flying Spur Press, 1984.

Trexler, Keith A. *The Tioga Road, a History: 1883–1961.* Rev. ed. Yosemite: Yosemite Natural History Association, 1975.

Wood, Raymund F. *California's Agua Fria.* Fresno: Academy Library Guild, 1954.

MENDOCINO COUNTY

Boynton, Searles R. *The Painter Lady: Grace Carpenter Hudson.* Eureka: Interface Corporation, 1978.

Carpenter, Aurelius O. *A History of Mendocino County.* 1914. Reprint, Mendocino: Pacific Rim Research, 1977.

Holmes, Alice, and Wilbur Lawson, eds. *Mills of Mendocino County.* Ukiah: Mendocino County Historical Society, 1996.

Kortum, Karl, and Roger Olmsted. "A Dangerous-Looking Place—Sailing Days on the Redwood Coast." *California Historical Society Quarterly* 50 (1971): 43–58.

Landsman, David, ed. *Mendocino County Historic Annals.* 2 vols. Mendocino: Pacific Rim Research, 1977.

MacDonald, Irene. *Littleriver's Yesterdays.* Fort Bragg: Mendocino Graphics, 1999.

Stebbins, Beth. *The Noyo: Being an Account of the History at the Mouth of the Noyo River, on the Mendocino County Coast of California, from 1852 into 1920 and a Little Beyond.* Mendocino: Bear and Stebbins, 1986.

MERCED COUNTY

Cabezut-Ortin, Delores J. *Merced County: The Golden Harvest.* Northridge: Windsor Publications, 1987.

DePertuis, Jeff. *Homes of Old Merced.* Merced: Merced Historical Society, 1987.

Outcalt, John. *History of Merced County.* Los Angeles: Historic Record Co., 1925.

Pimentel, Wayne. *Dogtown and Ditches: Life on the Westside.* Los Banos: Loose Change Publications, 1987.

Shumate, Albert. *Francisco Pacheco of Pacheco Pass.* Stockton: University of the Pacific, 1977.

Treadwell, Edward F. *The Cattle King.* New York: Macmillan, 1931.

Veronico, Nicholas. *Castle Air Museum.* Castro Valley: Pacific Aero Press, 1985.

MODOC COUNTY

Dillon, Richard. *Burnt-Out Fires: California's Modoc Indian War.* Englewood Cliffs, N.J.: Prentice-Hall, 1973.

French, R. A., comp., and Gertrude P. French, ed. *A Historical, Biographical, and Pictorial Magazine Devoted to Modoc County.* Alturas, 1912.

Sagebrush Corner—Opening of California's Northeast. New York: Garland Publishing, 1973.

Thompson, Erwin N. *Modoc War: Its Military History and Topography.* Sacramento: Argus Books, 1971.

MONO COUNTY

Bean, Betty. *Horsehoe Canyon: A Brief History of the June Lake Loop.* Bishop: Chalfant Press, 1977.

Briggs, Carl. "Goodbye, God: We're Going to Bodie." *The Californians,* July-Aug. 1986, pp. 30–32.

Cain, Ella M. *The Story of Bodie.* San Francisco: Fearon Publishers, 1956.

———. *The Story of Early Mono County.* San Francisco: Fearon Publishers, 1961.

Calhoun, Margaret. *Pioneers of Mono Basin.* Lee Vining: Artemisia Press, 1975.

Chalfant, W. A. *Gold, Guns, and Ghost Towns.* 1947. Reprint, Bishop: Chalfant Press, 1975.

DeDecker, Mary. *Mines of the Eastern Sierra.* Glendale: La Siesta Press, 1966.

Hart, John. *Storm Over Mono: The Mono Lake Battle and the California Water Future.* Berkeley: University of California Press, 1996.

Hoffman, Abraham. *Vision or Villainy: Origins of the Owens Valley–Los Angeles Water Controversy.* College Station, Tex.: Texas A & M Press, 1981.

Reed, Adele. *Old Mammoth.* Genny Smith, ed. Palo Alto: Genny Smith Books, 1982.

Russell, Carl P. "Early Mining Excitements East of Yosemite." *Sierra Club Bulletin* 13 (Feb. 1928): 40–53.

Von Blon, John L. "Rock Writings of the Owens Valley." *Touring Topics* 21 (May 1929): 14–17, 51.

Williams, George, III. *The Guide to Bodie and Eastern Sierra Historic Sites.* Riverside: Tree by the River Publishers, 1981.

———. *The Murderers of Convict Lake.* Riverside: Tree by the River Publishers, 1984.

MONTEREY COUNTY

Clark, Donald Thomas. *Monterey County Place Names: A Geographical Dictionary.* Carmel Valley: Kestrel Press, 1991.

Colton, Walter. *Three Years in California.* New York: A. S. Barnes & Co., 1850.

Dakin, Susanna B. *The Lives of William Hartnell.* Stanford: Stanford University Press, 1949.

Davenport, William. *The Monterey Peninsula.* Menlo Park: Lane Books, 1964.

Fink, Augusta. *Monterey: The Presence of the Past.* San Francisco: Chronicle Books, 1972.

———. *Monterey County: The Dramatic Story of Its Past.* Fresno: Valley Publishers, 1978.

Fisher, Anne B. *The Salinas: Upside-Down River.* New York: Rinehart, 1945.

Guinn, James Miller. *History and Biographical Record of Monterey and San Benito Counties.* Los Angeles: Historic Record Co., 1910.

Horne, Kibbey M. *A History of the Presidio of Monterey, 1770 to 1970.* Monterey: Defense Language Institute, 1970.

Howard, Donald M. *Prehistoric Sites Handbook: Monterey and San Luis Obispo Counties.* Carmel: Monterey County Archaeological Society, 1979.

King City, California: The First Hundred Years. King City: San Antonio Valley Historical Association, 1986.

Kirker, Harold. "The Larkin House Revisited." *California History* 65 (1986): 26–33.

Lewis, Betty. *Monterey Bay Yesterday.* Fresno: Valley Publishers, 1977.

O'Donnell, Mayo Hayes. *Monterey's Adobe Heritage.* Monterey: Monterey Savings and Loan, 1965.

Orth, Michael. "The Founding of Carmel." *California Historical Society Quarterly* 48 (1969): 195–210.

Perry, Frank. *Lighthouse Point: Reflections on Monterey Bay History.* Soquel: GBH Publishing, 1982.

Planer, Edward T. "The Short but Valuable Life of the M & SV RR," *Monterey Peninsula-Herald,* Oct. 19, 1975, pp. 4–11.

Root, Wendy. "Pacific Grove, California's Last Dry Town." *California Historian,* Summer 1996, pp. 17–21.

Smith, Frances Rand. *The Mission of San Antonio de Padua.* Stanford: Stanford University Press, 1932.

Smith, Gene A. "The War That Wasn't: Thomas ap Catesby Jones's Seizure of Monterey." *California History* 66 (1987): 104–14.

Spencer-Hancock, Diane, and William E. Pritchard. "El Castillo de Monterey, Frontline of Defense." *California History* 63 (1984): 230–41.

Stevenson, Robert Louis. *From Scotland to Silverado.* Edited by James D. Hart. Cambridge: Belknap Press of Harvard University, 1966.

Van Nostrand, Jeanne. *Monterey: Adobe Capital of California, 1770–1847.* San Francisco: California Historical Society, 1969.

Weber, Francis J., comp. and ed. *California's Sorrowful Mission: A Documentary History of Nuestra Señora de la Soledad.* Los Angeles: Archdiocese of Los Angeles Archives, 1986.

NAPA COUNTY

Archuleta, Kay. *The Brannan Story.* St. Helena: Illuminations Press, 1982.

Camp, Charles L., ed. *George C. Yount and His Chronicles of the West, Comprising Extracts from his "Memoirs."* Denver: Old West Publishing Co., 1966.

Dutton, Joan Perry. *They Left Their Mark: Famous Passages Through the Wine Country.* St. Helena: Illuminations Press, 1983.

Gregory, Tom. *History of Solano and Napa Counties, California.* Los Angeles: Historic Record Co., 1912.

History of Napa and Lake Counties, California. San Francisco: Slocum, Brown & Co., 1882.

Lapsley, James T. *Bottled Poetry: Napa Winemaking from Prohibition to the Modern Era.* Berkeley: University of California Press, 1996.

Stevenson, Robert Louis. *From Scotland to Silverado.* Edited by James D. Hart. Cambridge: Belknap Press of Harvard University, 1966.

Verardo, Denzil, and Jennie Verardo. *Napa Valley: From Golden Fields to Purple Harvest.* Northridge: Windsor Publications, 1986.

Weber, Lin. *Old Napa Valley: The History to 1900.* St. Helena: Wine Ventures Publishing, 1999.

NEVADA COUNTY

Best, Gerald M. *Nevada County Narrow Gauge.* Berkeley: Howell-North Books, 1965.

Browne, Juanita Kennedy. *Nuggets of Nevada County History*. Nevada City: Nevada County Historical Society, 1983.

California Mining Journal [featuring Nevada and Sierra county mines]. Vol. 1, no. 1 (Aug. 1931).

Comstock, David A. *Gold Diggers and Camp Followers: The Nevada County Chronicles, 1845–1851*. Grass Valley: Comstock-Bonanza Press, 1979.

Houghton, Mrs. Eliza Cook (Donner). *The Expedition of the Donner Party and Its Tragic Fate*. Chicago: A. G. McClurg & Co., 1911.

King, Joseph A. *Winter of Entrapment: A New Look at the Donner Party*. Toronto: P. D. Meany, 1992.

Lardner, W. B., and M. J. Brock. *History of Placer and Nevada Counties, California*. Los Angeles: Historic Record Co., 1924.

McGlashan, C. F. *History of the Donner Party, a Tragedy of the Sierra*. 1881. Reprint, Stanford: Stanford University Press, 1940, 1977.

Mann, Ralph. *After the Gold Rush: Society in Grass Valley and Nevada City, California, 1849–1870*. Stanford: Stanford University Press, 1982.

Meschery, Joanne. *Truckee, an Illustrated History of the Town and Its Surroundings*. Truckee: Rocking Stone Press, 1978.

Rourke, Constance. *Troopers of the Gold Coast, or the Rise of Lotta Crabtree*. New York: Harcourt, Brace, 1928.

Slyter, Robert I., and Grace I. Slyter. *Historical Notes of the Early Washington, Nevada County, California, Mining District*. Washington, Calif.: Robert I. Slyter, 1972.

Smith, Paul B. "Highway Planning in California's Mother Lode: The Changing Townscape of Auburn and Nevada City." *California History* 59 (1980): 204–21.

Stewart, George. *Ordeal by Hunger*. 1936. Reprint, New York: Washington Square Press, 1960.

Wells, Harry L. *History of Nevada County, California*. Oakland: Thompson & West, 1880. Reprint, Berkeley: Howell-North Books, 1970.

Wyckoff, Robert M. *The Compleat Pedestrian's Partially Illustrated Guide to Greater Nevada City*. 2nd ed. Nevada City: Nevada City Publishing Co., 1979.

———. *Walking Tours and Twice-Told Tales of Grass Valley*. Nevada City: Nevada City Publishing Co., 1979.

———, ed. *Never Come, Never Go! The Story of Nevada County's Narrow-Gauge Railroad*. Nevada City: Nevada City Publishing Co., 1986.

ORANGE COUNTY

Cleland, Robert G. *The Irvine Ranch*. 1952. Revised, with an epilogue by Robert V. Hine. San Marino: Huntington Library, 1984.

Dickson, Lucile E. "The Founding and Early History of Anaheim, California." *Annual Publications, History Society of Southern California* 2, part I (1918).

Friis, Leo J. *Campo Aleman: The First Ten Years of Anaheim*. Santa Ana: Friis-Pioneer Press, 1983.

———. *Historic Buildings of Pioneer Anaheim*. Santa Ana: Friis-Pioneer Press, 1983.

———. *Orange County Through Four Centuries*. Santa Ana: Friis-Pioneer Press, 1982.

Gibson, Wayne Dell. *Tomas Yorba's Santa Ana Viejo, 1769–1847*. Santa Ana: Santa Ana College Foundation Press, 1970.

Hallan-Gibson, Pamela. *The Golden Promise: An Illustrated History of Orange County*. Northridge: Windsor Publications, 1986.

Lee, Ellen K. *Newport Bay: A Pioneer History*. Newport Beach: Newport Beach Historical Society, 1973.

Marsh, Diann. *Anaheim's Architectural Treasury*. Anaheim: Anaheim Historical Society, 1973.

Meadows, Don. *Historic Place Names in Orange County*. Balboa Island: Paisano Press, 1966.

Miller, Edrick J. *The S.A.A.A.B. [Santa Ana Army Air Base] Story*. Costa Mesa: Edrick J. Miller, 1981.

Olin, Spencer, Jr. "Bible Communism and the Origins of Orange County." *California History* 58 (1979): 220–33.

O'Neill, Ynez Viola. "Father Serra Plans the Founding of Mission San Juan Capistrano." *California Historical Society Quarterly* 56 (1977): 46–51.

Osterman, Joseph D. "Venture, Gain, Loss and Change in Old El Toro's Orange County." *The Californians*, July–Aug. 1983, pp. 6–12.

Roley, Margaret, et al. *100 Years of Laguna Beach, 1876–1976*. Laguna Beach: Laguna Beach Historical Society, 1974.

Schultz, Elizabeth, ed. *Visiting Orange County's Past*. Santa Ana: Orange County Historical Commission, 1984.

Sleeper, Jim. *Santa Ana Mountains*. Trabuco Canyon: California Classics, 1976.

Smith, Gail Vinje, and William A. Allen. *The Picture History of Balboa Island, 1906–1981: A Celebration of the Diamond Jubilee*. Newport Beach: Gailliard Press, 1981

Weber, Francis J., ed. *The Jewel of the Missions: A Documentary History of San Juan Capistrano*. San Juan Capistrano: San Juan Capistrano Mission, 1976.

PLACER COUNTY

Davis, Leonard M. *Profiles Out of the Past: A Biographical History of Roseville*. Roseville: Roseville Community Projects, 1982.

Gilberg, M. E. *Auburn: A California Mining Camp Comes of Age*. Newcastle: Gilmer Press, 1986.

History of Placer County, California, with Illustrations and Biographical Sketches of Its Prominent Men and Pioneers. 1882. Reprint, Auburn: Placer County Historical Society, 1986.

Lardner, W. B., and M. J. Brock. *History of Placer and

Nevada Counties, California. Los Angeles: Historic Record Co., 1924.

Robie, Wendell. *Auburn: A Century of Memories.* Auburn: Placer County Historical Society, 1988.

Smith, Paul B. "Highway Planning in California's Mother Lode: The Changing Townscape of Auburn and Nevada City." *California History* 59 (1980): 204–21.

Zauner, Phyllis. *Lake Tahoe.* Tahoe Paradise: Zanel Publications, 1982.

PLUMAS COUNTY

Beckwourth, James P. *The Life and Adventures of James P. Beckwourth.* Edited by T. D. Bonner, 1856. Reprint, New York: Knopf, 1931.

Clappe, Louise Amelie Knapp Smith ("Dame Shirley"). *The Shirley Letters, Being Letters Written in 1851–1852 from the California Mines.* 1854. Reprint, Salt Lake City: Peregrine Smith, 1983.

Dunn, Mary E. Phelps. *A Review of the History of Plumas County and Explanation of Many Place Names.* 1960. Reprint, Quincy: Plumas County Historical Society, 1982.

Fariss & Smith. *History of Plumas, Lassen, and Sierra Counties, California.* 1882. Reprint, Berkeley: Howell-North Books, 1971.

Hall, Jacqueline, and JoEllen Hall. *Italian-Swiss Settlement in Plumas County, 1860–1920.* Chico: Association for Northern California Records and Research, 1973.

Little, Jane Braxton. *Plumas Sketches.* Canyondam: Wolf Creek Press, 1983.

Paul, Rodman W. "In Search of Dame Shirley." *Pacific Historical Review* 33 (1964): 127-46.

RIVERSIDE COUNTY

Ainsworth, Katherine. *The McCallum Saga: The Story of the Founding of Palm Springs.* Palm Springs: Palm Springs Desert Museum, 1973.

Beattie, George William. "Development of Travel Between Southern Arizona and Los Angeles, as Related to the San Bernardino Valley." *Annual Publications, Historical Society of Southern California* 13 (1925): 228-57.

Brumgardt, John R., and Larry L. Bowles. *People of the Magic Waters: The Cahuilla Indians of Palm Springs.* Palm Springs: ETC Publications, 1981.

DeStanley, Mildred. *The Salton Sea, Yesterday and Today.* Los Angeles: Triumph Press, 1966.

Eldridge, Fred, and Stanley Reynolds. *Our History: Corona, California Commentaries.* Corona: Heritage Committee, Corona Public Library, 1986.

Gunther, Jane Davies. *Riverside County, California, Place Names: Their Origins and Their Stories.* Riverside: J. D. Gunther, 1984.

Jackson, Helen Hunt. *Ramona.* 1884. Annotated, with introduction, by Antoinette May. San Carlos: Wide World Publishing/Tetra, 1989.

James, George Wharton. *Through Ramona's Country.* 1909. Reprint, Boston: Little, Brown, 1970.

Kennedy, Don H. "Ramona's People." *The Californians,* Sept.–Oct. 1986, pp. 46–49.

Klotz, Esther, and Joan H. Hall. *Adobes, Bungalows, and Mansions of Riverside, California.* Riverside: Riverside Museum Press, 1985.

Lopez, Barry. "California Desert, a Worldly Wilderness." *National Geographic* 171 (Jan. 1987): 42–78.

Moses, Vincent. "Machines in the Garden: A Citrus Monopoly in Riverside, 1900–1936." *California History* 61 (1982): 26–35.

Patterson, Tom. *Landmarks of Riverside.* Riverside: Press-Enterprise Co., 1964.

Robinson, John W., and Bruce D. Risher. *The San Jacintos: The Mountain Country from Banning to Borrego Valley.* Arcadia: Big Santa Anita Historical Society, 1993.

San Jacinto Valley, Past and Present. Hemet: Hemet–San Jacinto Genealogical Society, 1998.

Stonehouse, Merlin. *John Wesley North and the Reform Frontier.* Minneapolis: University of Minnesota Press, 1965.

Vickery, Joyce Carter. *Defending Eden: New Mexican Pioneers in Southern California, 1830–1890.* Riverside: Riverside Museum Press, 1977.

SACRAMENTO COUNTY

Blenkie, Joe. *Folsom-Auburn and the Mother Lode: Gold, Blood, Water.* Sacramento: Western Wonder Publications, 1976.

Bradley, Glen D. *The Story of the Pony Express.* Chicago: A. G. McClurg & Co., 1913.

Briens, Marvin. "Sacramento Defies the Rivers, 1850–1878." *California History* 58 (1979): 2-19.

Burns, John. *Sacramento: The Golden Heart of California.* Encinitas: Heritage Media Corp., 1999.

Chu, George. "Chinatowns in the Delta: The Chinese in the Sacramento–San Joaquin Delta, 1870-1960." *California Historical Society Quarterly* 49 (1970): 21–38.

Dillon, Richard. *Fool's Gold: The Decline and Fall of Captain John Sutter of California.* New York: Coward-McCann, 1967.

Eifler, Mark A. "Taming the Wilderness Within: Order and Opportunity in Gold Rush Sacramento, 1849–1850." *California History* 79 (2001): 192–207.

Gillenkirk, Jeff, and James Motlow. "This Was Our Place: Memories of Locke." *California History* 66 (1987): 170-87.

Graham, Kathleen Mary, et al., eds. *Historic Houses of the Sacramento River Delta.* Walnut Grove: Sacramento Delta Historical Society, 1984.

Hall, Carroll D., Hero Eugene Rensch, Jack R. Ryson, and Norman L. Wilson. *Old Sacramento: A Report on Its Significance to the City, State, and Nation, with Recommendations for the Preservation and Use of Its Principal Historic Structures and Sites.* 3 vols. Sacramento: State Division of Beaches and Parks, 1958, 1960.

Hume, Charles V. "First of the Gold Rush Theatres." *California Historical Society Quarterly* 46 (1967): 337–44.

Hussey, John A., ed. *Early Sacramento: Glimpses of John Augustus Sutter, the Hock Farm and Neighboring Indian Tribes, from the Journals of Prince Paul, H. R. H. Duke Paul Wilhelm of Wurttemburg.* Translated by Louis C. Butscher. Sacramento: Sacramento Book Collectors Club, 1973.

Lokke, Janet. "'Like a Bright Tree of Life': Farmland Settlement of the Sacramento River Delta." *California History* 59 (1980): 222–39.

McGowan, Joseph A., and Terry R. Willis. *Sacramento, Heart of the Golden State.* Woodland Hills: Windsor Publications, 1983.

Mellon, Steve. *Sacramento Then and Now.* Gibson, Pa.: Scripps Howard Publications, 1994.

Neasham, V. Audrey. *Old Sacramento, a Reference Point in Time.* Sacramento Historic Landmarks Commission, in cooperation with the Redevelopment Agency of the City of Sacramento, 1965.

Neasham, V. Audrey, and James E. Hensley. *The City of the Plain: Sacramento in the Nineteenth Century.* Sacramento: Sacramento Pioneer Foundation, 1969.

Owens, Kenneth, ed. *John Sutter and a Wider West.* Lincoln: University of Nebraska Press, 1994.

Severson, Thor. *Sacramento: An Illustrated History, 1839–1874.* San Francisco: California Historical Society, 1973.

Smith, Jesse M., ed. *Sketches of Old Sacramento.* Sacramento: Sacramento County Historical Society, 1976.

Thompson, John. "From Waterways to Roadways in the Sacramento Delta." *California History* 59 (1980): 144–59.

Wheat, Carl I. "A Sketch of the Life of Theodore D. Judah." *California Historical Society Quarterly* 4 (1925): 219–71.

Zauner, Phyllis. *Sacramento: A Mini-History.* Tahoe Paradise: Zanel Publications, 1979.

SAN BENITO COUNTY

Clough, Charles W. *San Juan Bautista: The Town, the Mission, and the Park.* Ed. by Bobbye Sisk Temple. Fresno: Word Dancer Press, 1996.

Flint, Dorothy. *Escarpment on the San Andreas: The Probing of a California Heritage.* Hollister: Marjorie Flint, 1978.

Hoyle, M. F. *Crimes and Career of Tiburcio Vasquez, the Bandit of San Benito County and Notorious Early California Outlaw.* Hollister: Evening Free Lance, 1927.

Iacopi, Robert. *Earthquake Country.* Menlo Park: Lane Books, 1964.

Jordan, David Starr. *The Days of a Man.* 2 vols. Yonkers, N.Y.: World Book Co., 1922.

Milliken, Ralph LeRoy. *San Juan Bautista, California, the City of History.* Los Banos: Los Banos Enterprise, 1961.

SAN BERNARDINO COUNTY

Beattie, George W. "Development of Travel Between Southern Arizona and Los Angeles, as Related to the San Bernardino Valley." *Annual Publications, Historical Society of Southern California* 13 (1925): 228–57.

———. "San Bernardino Valley in the Spanish Period." *Annual Publications, Historical Society of Southern California* 12, part III (1923): 10–28.

Beattie, George W., and Helen P. Beattie. *Heritage of the Valley.* Oakland: Biobooks, 1951.

Bishop, M. Guy. "The San Bernardino Mormon Colony: 'To Establish a Standard of Righteousness.'" *The Californians,* Sept.–Oct. 1987, pp. 12–17.

Black, Esther Boulton. *Rancho Cucamonga and Dona Merced.* Redlands: San Bernardino County Museum Association, 1975.

———. *Stories of Old Upland.* Upland: Chaffey Communities Cultural Center, 1979.

Casebier, Dennis. *Fort Pah-Ute, California.* Norco: Tales of the Mojave Road Publishing Co., 1974.

———. *The Mojave Road.* Norco: Tales of the Mojave Road Publishing Co., 1975.

Conley, Bernice Bedford. *Dreamers and Dwellers: Ontario and Neighbors.* Ontario: Stump Printing Services, 1982.

Davis, Mike. *City of Quartz* [Fontana chapter]. New York: Vintage, 1992.

Historical Landmarks of San Bernardino County. Redlands: San Bernardino County Museum, 1980.

Houston, Flora Belle. "When the Mormons Settled San Bernardino." *Touring Topics* 22 (Apr. 1930): 32–34, 52.

Keeling, Patricia J., ed. *Once Upon a Desert: A Bicentennial Project.* Barstow: Mojave River Valley Museum Association, 1976.

Kroeber, A. L., and C. B. Kroeber. *A Mojave War Reminiscence, 1854–1880.* Berkeley: University of California Press, 1973.

Lawrence, Eleanor. "Mexican Trade Between Santa Fe and Los Angeles, 1830–1848." *California Historical Society Quarterly* 10 (1931): 27–39.

Leadabrand, Russ. *A Guidebook to the Mojave Desert of California.* Los Angeles: Ward Ritchie Press, 1966.

———. *A Guidebook to the San Bernardino Mountains of California.* Los Angeles: Ritchie & Simon, 1973.

Lyman, Leo E. *San Bernardino: The Rise and Fall of a California Community.* Salt Lake City: Signature Books, 1995.

Moore, William G. *Redlands Yesterdays: A Photo Album, 1870–1920.* Redlands: Moore Historical Foundation, 1983.

Peirson, Emma. *The Mojave River and Its Valley.* Glendale: Arthur H. Clark Co., 1970.

Robinson, John W. *Mines of the San Bernardinos.* Glendale: La Siesta Press, 1977.

Robinson, W. W. *The Story of San Bernardino County.* San Bernardino: Title Insurance & Trust Co., 1962.

Schuiling, Walter C. *San Bernardino County: Land of Contrasts.* Woodland Hills: Windsor Publications, 1984.

———, ed. *Pleistocene Man at Calico.* Redlands: San Bernardino County Museum Association, 1979.

Swisher, John M. *Bits 'N Pieces of the Mojave Desert's Weathered Past.* Apple Valley: Phoenix Printing and Promotion, 1995.

———. *Mojave Rendezvous: True Old Desert Tales.* Apple Valley: Phoenix Printing and Promotion, 1997.

SAN DIEGO COUNTY

Berger, Dan, Peter Jensen, and Margaret C. Berg. *San Diego: Where Tomorrow Begins.* Northridge: Windsor Publications, 1987.

Booth, Larry, Roger Olmsted, and Richard F. Pourade. "Portrait of a Boom Town: San Diego in the 1880s." *California Historical Quarterly* 50 (1971): 363–94.

Brackett, R. W. *The History of San Diego County Ranchos.* San Diego: Union Title Insurance Co., 1960.

Brown, Joseph E. *Cabrillo National Monument.* San Diego: Cabrillo Historical Association, 1981.

Engstrand, Iris H. W. *San Diego: California's Cornerstone.* Tulsa, Okla.: Continental Heritage Press, 1980.

———. "Serra and the Founding of San Diego." *The Californians,* Sept.–Oct. 1984, pp. 24–26.

Hill, J. J. *History of Warner's Ranch and Its Environs.* Los Angeles, 1927.

Holland, F. Ross. *The Old Point Loma Lighthouse, San Diego.* San Diego: Cabrillo Historical Association, 1978.

Joyce, Barry Alan. *A Harbor Worth Defending: A Military History of Point Loma, San Diego.* San Diego: Cabrillo Historical Association, 1996.

Kuhn, Gerald C., and Francis P. Shephard. *Sea Cliffs, Beaches, and Coastal Valleys of San Diego County.* Berkeley: University of California Press, 1984.

Lemenager, Charles R. *Off the Main Road, San Vicente and Barona: A History of the Rancho Cañada de San Vicente y Mesa del Padre Barona.* Ramona: Eagle Peak Publishing Co., 1983.

Lindsay, Diana. *Our Historic Desert: The Story of the Anza-Borrego Desert.* San Diego: Copley Books, 1973.

McKeever, Michael. *A Short History of San Diego.* San Francisco: Lexikos, 1985.

MacMullen, Jerry. *They Came by Sea: A Pictorial History of San Diego Bay.* San Diego: Ward Ritchie Press, 1969.

MacPhail, Elizabeth C. *The Story of New San Diego and of Its Founder Alonzo E. Horton.* San Diego: San Diego Historical Society, 1979.

Mills, James. *Historical Landmarks of San Diego County.* San Diego: San Diego Historical Society, 1960.

O'Neal, Lulu R. *The History of Ramona, California, and Environs.* Ramona: Ballena Press, 1976.

Ryan, Frances B., and Lewis C. Ryan. *Escondido As It Was, 1900–1950.* Escondido: Frances B. and Lewis C. Ryan, 1980.

Stein, Lou. *San Diego County Place Names.* San Diego: Tofus Press, 1975.

Weber, Francis J., ed. *King of the Missions, a Documentary History of San Luis Rey de Francia.* Los Angeles, 1980.

———, ed. *The Pronto Mission, a Documentary History of San Diego de Alcalá.* Los Angeles, 1980.

SAN FRANCISCO COUNTY

Brant, Michelle. *Timeless Walks in San Francisco: A Historical Walking Guide.* San Francisco: Lompa-Brant, 1996.

Brechin, Gary. *Imperial San Francisco: Urban Power, Earthly Ruin.* Berkeley: University of California Press, 1999.

Browning, Peter, ed. *San Francisco/Yerba Buena From the Beginning to the Gold Rush, 1769–1849.* Lafayette, Calif.: Golden West Books, 1998.

Bullen, Isabel. "A Glimpse into the *Niantic's* Hold." *California History* 58 (1980): 326–33.

The California Star: Yerba Buena and San Francisco— Volume I, 1847–48; a Reproduction in Facsimile. Introduction by Fred Blackburn Rogers. Berkeley: Howell-North Books, 1965.

Cather, Helen V. *The History of San Francisco's Chinatown.* San Francisco: R & E Research Associates, 1974.

Chen, Yong. *Chinese San Francisco, 1850–1943: A Trans-Pacific Community.* Stanford: Stanford University Press, 2000.

Delgado, James. "A Dream of Seven Decades: San Francisco's Aquatic Park." *California History* 64 (1985): 272–82.

———. "'No Longer a Buoyant Ship'—Unearthing the Gold Rush Steamship *Niantic.*" *California History* 58 (1980): 316–25.

DeLuca, Richard. "'We Hold the Rock': The Indian Attempt to Reclaim Alcatraz Island." *California History* 62 (1983): 2–23.

Dicker, Laverne M. "The San Francisco Earthquake and Fire: Photographs and Manuscripts from the California Historical Society Library." *California History* 59 (1980): 34–65.

Doss, Margot Patterson. "Taking a Hike through History." *San Francisco Chronicle,* March 5, 1989.

Doughty, Robin W. "The Farallones and the Boston Men." *California Historical Quarterly* 53 (1974): 309–16.

Geiger, Maynard. "New Data on the Buildings of Mission San Francisco." *California Historical Society Quarterly* 46 (1967): 195–205.

Hittell, John W. *History of the City of San Francisco and Incidentally of the State of California*. 1878. Reprint, Berkeley: Berkeley Hills Books, 1999.

Jewett, Masha Zakheim. *Coit Tower, San Francisco*. San Francisco: Volcano Press, 1986.

Kurzman, Dan. *Disaster: The Great San Francisco Earthquake and Fire of 1906*. New York: William Morrow, 2001.

Langellier, John Phillip, and Daniel B. Rosen. *El Presidio de San Francisco: A History Under Spain and Mexico, 1776–1846*. Spokane: Arthur H. Clark Co., 1996.

Lewis, Oscar. *San Francisco: Mission to Metropolis*. 2nd ed. San Diego: Howell-North Books, 1980.

Lockwood, Charles. "Rincon Hill Was San Francisco's Most Genteel Neighborhood." *California History* 58 (1979): 48–61.

Loewenstein, Louis K. *Streets of San Francisco: The Origins of San Francisco's Street and Place Names*. San Francisco: Lexikos, 1984.

McGloin, John B. *San Francisco: The Story of a City*. San Rafael: Presidio Press, 1979.

Miller, Robert Ryal. *Captain Richardson: Mariner, Ranchero, and Founder of San Francisco*. Berkeley: La Loma Press, 1995.

Mullen, Kevin J. "San Francisco: City on the Wrong Side of the Bay." *The Californians*, Mar.–Apr. 1984, pp. 34–42.

Page, Charles Hall, et al. *Splendid Survivors: San Francisco's Architectural Heritage*. San Francisco: California Living Books, 1979.

Parker, Elizabeth L., and James Abajian. *A Walking Tour of the Black Presence in San Francisco During the Nineteenth Century*. San Francisco: San Francisco African-American Historical and Cultural Society, 1974.

Richards, Rand. *Historic San Francisco: A Concise History and Guide*. San Francisco: Heritage House Publishers, 1991.

Watkins, T. H., and R. R. Olmsted. *Mirror of the Dream: An Illustrated History of San Francisco*. San Francisco: Scrimshaw Press, 1976.

Weber, Francis J., comp. and ed. *Mission Dolores: A Documentary History of San Francisco Mission*. Los Angeles: Archdiocese of Los Angeles Archives, 1979.

SAN JOAQUIN COUNTY

Audubon, John W. *Audubon's Western Journal, 1849–1850*. Cleveland, Ohio: Arthur H. Clark, 1906.

Brotherton, I. N. ("Jack"). *The Annals of Stanislaus: River Towns and Ferries*. Santa Cruz: Western Tanager Press, 1982.

Curtis, Mrs. Dwight. *Old Cemeteries of San Joaquin County*. 2 vols. Stockton: San Joaquin Genealogical Society, 1960.

Davis, Olive. *Stockton: Sunrise Port on the San Joaquin*. Sun Valley, Calif.: American Historical Press, 1998.

Hardeman, Nicholas P. *Harbor of the Heartlands: A History of the Inland Seaport of Stockton, California, from the Gold Rush to 1985*. Stockton: Holt-Atherton Center for Western Studies, 1986.

Hillman, Raymond, and Leonard Covello. *Cities and Towns of San Joaquin County Since 1847*. Fresno: Panorama West Books, 1985.

Hittell, Theodore H. *The Adventures of James Capen Adams, Mountaineer Grizzly Bear Hunter of California*. 1906. Rev. ed. New York: Scribner, 1911.

Mazet, Horace S. "The Man Who Loved Grizzlies." *The Californians*, Sept.–Oct. 1985, pp. 27–35.

Minnick, Sylvia Sun. *Samfow: The San Joaquin Chinese Legacy*. Lodi: San Joaquin County Historical Society, 1988.

Schenck, W. Egbert. "Historic Aboriginal Groups of the California Delta Region." *University of California Publications in American Archaeology and Ethnology* 25, no. 4 (1929): 289–413.

Spencer, Horace A. *A Guide to Historical Locations in San Joaquin County*. 3d ed. Stockton: San Joaquin County Superintendent of Schools Office, 1978.

Tinkham, George H. *Index to History of San Joaquin County, California, 1923*. Compiled by Naomi McCallum Carey & Mary Diehl Thomason. Lodi: C-T Publications, 1991.

Wood, R. Coke, and Leonard Covello. *Stockton Memories*. Stockton: Valley Publishers, 1977.

SAN LUIS OBISPO COUNTY

Angel, Myron. *History of San Luis Obispo County*. 1883. Reprint, San Miguel: Friends of the Adobes, 1983.

Darling, Velva G. "Cave Landing, a San Luis Obispo County Scenic Spot." *Touring Topics* 18, Mar. 1926.

Howard, Donald M. *Prehistoric Sites Handbook: Monterey and San Luis Obispo Counties*. Carmel: Monterey County Archaeological Society, 1979.

Kocher, Paul H. *Mission San Luis Obispo de Tolosa, 1772–1972, a Historical Sketch*. San Luis Obispo: Blake Printing and Publishing, 1972.

Nasaw, David. *The Chief: The Life of William Randolph Hearst*. Boston: Houghton Mifflin, 2000.

Robinson, W. W. *The Story of San Luis Obispo County*. Los Angeles: Title Insurance & Trust Co., 1957.

Romney, Joseph B. *A Research Guide to the History of San Luis Obispo County, California*. Rexburg, Idaho: Milhollow Publications, 1985.

Swanberg, W. A. *Citizen Hearst*. New York: Scribner, 1961.

Weber, Francis J., comp. and ed. *Mission in the Valley of the Bears: A Documentary History of San Luis Obispo de Tolosa*. Los Angeles: Archdiocese of Los Angeles Archives, 1985.

Winslow, Carleton M., and Nickola L. Frye. *The Enchanted Hill: The Story of Hearst Castle at San Simeon.* Los Angeles: Rosebud Books, 1980.

SAN MATEO COUNTY

Atherton, F. D. *The California Diaries of Faxon Dean Atherton, 1836–9.* Edited by Doyce R. Nunis Jr. Special Publication 29. San Francisco: California Historical Society, 1964.

Atherton, Gertrude. *Adventures of a Novelist.* New York: Liveright, 1932.

Blum, Joseph A. "South San Francisco—the Making of an Industrial City." *California History* 63 (1984): 114–34.

Brown, Alan K. "Rivera at San Francisco, a Journal of Exploration, 1774." *California Historical Society Quarterly* 41 (1962): 325–41.

———. *Saw Pits in the Spanish Redwoods.* San Mateo: San Mateo County Historical Association, 1966.

Carter, Charles Franklin. "Duhaut-Cilly's Account of California in the Years 1827–28." *California Historical Society Quarterly* 8 (1929): 131–66, 306–36.

Chandler, Samuel C. *Gateway to the Peninsula: A History of the City of Daly City.* Daly City: Daly City Public Library, 1973.

Coastside Cultural Resources of San Mateo County, California. Redwood City: San Mateo County Department of Environmental Management, 1982.

Hynding, Alan. *From Frontier to Suburb: The Story of the San Mateo Peninsula.* Palo Alto: Star Publishing Co., 1983.

The Illustrated History of San Mateo County. 1878. Reduced facsimile, Woodside: Gilbert Richards, 1974.

Kauffman, Linda. *South San Francisco: A History.* South San Francisco, 1976.

Richards, Gilbert. *Crossroads: People and Events of the Redwoods of San Mateo County.* Woodside: Gilbert Richards, 1973.

Shumate, Albert. "Correspondence Concerning 'Murder, by God!'" *The Californians,* May–June 1986, pp. 6, 7, 51.

Stanger, Frank M. "'The Hospice' or 'Mission San Mateo.'" *California Historical Society Quarterly* 23 (1944): 247–58.

———. *Sawmills in the Redwoods: Logging on the San Francisco Peninsula.* San Mateo: San Mateo County Historical Association, 1967.

———. *South from San Francisco: San Mateo County, California, Its History and Heritage.* San Mateo: San Mateo County Historical Association, 1963.

Wyatt, Roscoe D. *Historic Names and Places in San Mateo County.* Redwood City: San Mateo County Title Insurance Co., 1947.

SANTA BARBARA COUNTY

Bookspan, Rochelle, ed. *Santa Barbara by the Sea.* Santa Barbara: McNally & Loftin, 1983.

Caldwell, Joyce Craven. *Carpinteria As It Was.* Carpinteria: Papillon Press, 1979.

Cullimore, Charles. *Santa Barbara Adobes.* Santa Barbara: Santa Barbara Book Publishing Co., 1948.

Geiger, Maynard. *Mission Santa Barbara, 1782–1965.* Santa Barbara: Franciscan Fathers of California, 1965.

Hageman, Fred C., and Russell C. Ewing. *An Archaeological and Restoration Study of Mission La Purísima Concepción.* Edited by Richard Whitehead. Santa Barbara: Santa Barbara Trust for Historic Preservation, 1980.

Harrington, John P. "Exploration of the Burton Mound at Santa Barbara, California." *Forty-Fourth Annual Report of the Bureau of American Ethnology.* Washington, D.C.: U.S. Government Printing Office, 1928, pp. 30–168.

Hawley, Walter A. *The Early Days of Santa Barbara, California: From the First Discoveries by Europeans to December 1846.* 1920. 3d ed., enlarged, edited by John C. Woodward. Santa Barbara: Santa Barbara Heritage, 1987.

Hudson, Travis. *Guide to Painted Cave.* Santa Barbara: McNally & Loftin, 1982.

Olmstead, Cresencia, and Dale Olmstead. *Mission Santa Ines: The Hidden Gem.* Solvang: Old Mission Santa Ines, 1995.

Rife, Joanne. *Where the Light Turns Gold: The Story of the Santa Ynez Valley.* Fresno: Valley Publishers, 1977.

Rogers, David Banks. *Prehistoric Man of the Santa Barbara Coast.* Santa Barbara: Santa Barbara Museum of Natural History, 1929.

Sandos, James A. "'Levantamiento!' The 1824 Chumash Uprising Reconsidered." *Southern California Quarterly* 57 (1985): 109–33.

Tompkins, Walker. *Old Spanish Santa Barbara.* Santa Barbara: McNally & Loftin, 1984.

———. *Santa Barbara History Makers.* Santa Barbara: McNally & Loftin, 1983.

———. *Stagecoach Days in Santa Barbara County.* Santa Barbara: McNally & Loftin, 1984.

———. *The Yankee Barbareños: The Americanization of Santa Barbara County, California, 1796–1925.* Ventura: Movini Press, 1999.

Weber, Francis J., comp. and ed. *Our Lady's Mission: A Documentary History of La Purísima Concepción.* Los Angeles: Libra Press, 1986.

———, ed. *Queen of the Missions: a Documentary History of Santa Barbara.* Hong Kong: Libra Press, 1979.

Whitehead, Richard S. *Citadel on the Channel: The Santa Barbara Royal Presidio, 1769–1798.* Spokane: Arthur H. Clark Co. and Santa Barbara Trust for Historic Preservation, 1995.

SANTA CLARA COUNTY

Allen, Peter C. *Stanford, from the Foothills to the Bay.* Stanford: Stanford Historical Society, 1980.

Arbuckle, Clyde, and Ralph Rambo. *Santa Clara County Ranchos.* San Jose: Rosicrucian Press, 1973.

Bowman, J. N. "The Peraltas and Their Homes." *California Historical Society Quarterly* 30 (1951): 217–31. Reprint, Oakland: Alameda County Historical Society, 2001.

Butler, Phyllis F. "New Almaden's Casa Grande." *California Historical Quarterly* 54 (1975): 315–22.

———. *The Valley of Santa Clara: Historic Buildings, 1792–1920.* Novato: Presidio Press, 1981.

Cupertino Chronicle. Cupertino: California History Center, De Anza College, 1975.

Curtis, James R. "New Chicago of the Far West: Land Speculation in Alviso, California, 1890–1891." *California History* 61 (1982): 36–45.

Douglas, Jack. *Historical Footnotes of Santa Clara County.* San Jose: San Jose Historical Museum, 1993.

Fox, Theron, ed. *After Harper's Ferry: John Brown's Widow— Her Family and the Saratoga Years.* Saratoga: Saratoga Historical Foundation, 1964.

Jacobson, Yvonne. *Passing Farms, Enduring Values: California's Santa Clara Valley.* Los Altos: Kaufmann, 1984.

Khorsand, Seonaid, and Alice Marshall. *Lingering Legacy: A Historical Tour Guide in and Around the Santa Clara Valley.* Cupertino: California History Center, De Anza College, 1973.

McKay, Leonard. *Luis Maria Peralta and His Adobe.* San Jose: Smith-McKay Printing Co., 1976.

McKevitt, Gerald. *The University of Santa Clara: A History, 1851–1977.* Stanford: Stanford University Press, 1979.

Palo Alto Times-Tribune. "Stanford Centennial Issue." Nov. 10, 1985.

Payne, Stephen M. *Santa Clara County: Harvest of Change.* Northridge: Windsor Publications, 1987.

Peck, Willys I. *Saratoga Stereopticon.* Cupertino: California History Center and Foundation, 1997.

Santa Clara County Heritage Resource Inventory. San Jose: Santa Clara County Historical Heritage Commission, 1979.

Spearman, Arthur Dunning. *The Five Franciscan Churches of Mission Santa Clara, 1777–1825.* Palo Alto: National Press, 1963.

Sullivan, Charles L. *Like Modern Edens: Winegrowing in Santa Clara Valley and Santa Cruz Mountains, 1798–1981.* Cupertino: California History Center, De Anza College, 1982.

Thompson & West. *Historical Atlas of Santa Clara County.* 1876. Reprint, San Jose: Smith & McKay Publishing Co., 1973.

Watson, Jeannette. *Campbell, the Orchard City.* Campbell Historical Museum Association, 1990.

Weber, Francis J. *The Laurelwood Mission: A Documentary History of Santa Clara de Asis.* Los Angeles: Dawson's Book Shop, n.d.

Weymouth, Alice Jenkins. *The Palo Alto Tree.* Stanford: Stanford University Press, 1930.

SANTA CRUZ COUNTY

Adams, Kramer A. *Covered Bridges of the West.* Berkeley: Howell-North Books, 1963.

Clark, Donald Thomas. *Santa Cruz County Place Names.* Santa Cruz: Santa Cruz County Historical Society, 1986.

Gant, Michael S., ed. *Santa Cruz, the Early Years: The Collected Historical Writings of Leon Rowland.* Santa Cruz: Paper Vision Press, 1980.

Greenberg, Leonard, et al. *Santa Cruz County, California, with Historical Sketch of the County.* Santa Cruz: Museum of Art and History at the McPherson Center, 1997.

Koch, Margaret. *Santa Cruz County, Parade of the Past.* Fresno: Valley Publishers, 1979.

———. *The Walk Around Santa Cruz Book.* Fresno: Valley Publishers, 1980.

Lewis, Betty. *Watsonville: Memories That Linger.* Fresno: Valley Publishers, 1977.

MacMullen, Jerry. "World War II's Strangest Naval Battle." *Westways* 48, no. 6 (June 1955): 10–11.

Sullivan, Charles L. *Like Modern Edens: Winegrowing in Santa Clara Valley and Santa Cruz Mountains, 1798–1981.* Cupertino: California History Center, De Anza College, 1982.

Weber, Francis J., ed. *Holy Cross Mission: A Documentary History of Santa Cruz.* Hong Kong: Libra Press, 1984.

Young, John V. *Ghost Towns of the Santa Cruz Mountains.* Santa Cruz: Paper Vision Press, 1979.

SHASTA COUNTY

Bleyhl, Norris A. *Three Military Posts in Northern California, 1849–1863.* Chico: Association for Northern California Records and Research, 1984.

Frisbie, Mabel Moores, and Jean Moores Beauchamp. *Shasta: The Queen City.* San Francisco: California Historical Society, 1973.

Giffen, Helen. *Man of Destiny: Pierson Barton Reading, Pioneer of Shasta County, California.* Redding: Shasta Historical Society, 1985.

Johnson, Paul C., and Mabel Moores Frisbie. "Shasta Revisited." *California Historical Quarterly* 51 (1972): 331–37.

Jones, William A. "Prosperity v. Pollution: The Shasta Copper Mining Controversy." *The Californians,* Mar.–Apr. 1985, pp. 34–37.

Lawson, John D. *Redding and Shasta County: Gateway to the Cascades.* Northridge: Windsor Publications, 1986.

Miller, Joaquin [Cincinnatus Heine Miller]. "The Battle of Castle Crags." *Leslie's Monthly,* Mar. 1893.

———. *Life Amongst the Modocs.* London: Richard Bentley & Son, 1875. Reprint, Berkeley: Heyday Books, 1996.

Neasham, Ernest R. *Fall River Valley . . . From the Earliest Times Until 1890*. Sacramento: Citadel Press, 1985.

Reminiscence of the Fort Crook Historical Society. Fall River Mills: Fort Crook Historical Society, 1965. Subsequently reprinted.

Strong, Douglas H. *"These Happy Grounds": A History of the Lassen Region*. Red Bluff: Walker Lithography, 1982.

SIERRA COUNTY

California Mining Journal [featuring Nevada and Sierra County mines]. Vol. 1, no. 1 (Aug. 1931).

Downie, Major William. *Hunting for Gold*. San Francisco: California Publishing Company, 1893.

Fariss & Smith. *History of Plumas, Lassen and Sierra Counties, California*. 1882. Reprint, Berkeley: Howell-North Books, 1971.

Sinnott, James J. *Alleghany and Forest City*. Downieville: James J. Sinnott, 1974.

———. *"Over North" in Sierra County*. Fresno: Mid-Cal Publishers, 1977.

———. *Sierra City and Goodyears Bar*. Downieville: James J. Sinnott, 1974.

SISKIYOU SOUNTY

Camp, Charles L., ed. *James Clyman: American Frontiersman*. San Francisco: California Historical Society, 1928.

Davies, Gilbert W., and Florence M. Frank, eds. *Fort Jones, 1852–1858*. Hat Creek: History Ink Books, 1994.

Dillon, Richard. *Burnt-Out Fires: California's Modoc Indian War*. Englewood Cliffs, N.J.: Prentice-Hall, 1973.

Hall, Ansel F. "Mount Shasta." *Sierra Club Bulletin* 12 (1926): 252–67.

Jones, David Rhys. "Pre-Pioneer Pathfinders, California-Oregon Trail, 1826–1846." *Motor Land* 29 (1931).

Jones, William A. "Yreka's Chinese and the Great Flood of '90." *The Californians*, Sept.–Oct. 1986, pp. 31–35.

Miller, Joaquin [Cincinnatus Heine Miller]. *Life Amongst the Modocs*. London: Richard Bentley & Son, 1875. Reprint, Berkeley: Heyday Books, 1996.

Palmberg, Walter H. *Copper Paladin: A Modoc Tragedy. A Story of the Two Principal Players of the Modoc Indian War of 1872–73*. Bryn Mawr, Pa.: Dorrance & Co., 1982.

Palmquist, Peter E. "Silver Plates Among the Goldfields: The Photographers of Siskiyou County 1850–1906." *California History* 65 (1986): 114–25.

Riddle, Jeff C. *The Indian History of the Modoc War*. 1914. Reprint, Eugene, Ore.: Urion Press, 1974.

Thompson, Erwin N. *Modoc War: Its Military History and Topography*. Sacramento: Argus Books, 1971.

Wells, Harry L. *History of Siskiyou County, California*. Oakland: Stewart & Co., 1881.

SOLANO COUNTY

Dillon, Richard. *Great Expectations: The Story of Benicia, California*. Benicia: Benicia Heritage Books, 1981.

Emparan, Madie Brown. *The Vallejos of California*. San Francisco: Gleeson Library Associates, 1968.

Gregory, Tom. *History of Solano and Napa Counties, California*. Los Angeles: Historic Record Co., 1912.

Lemmon, Sue, and E. D. Wichels. *From Sidewheelers to Nuclear Power: A Pictorial Essay Covering 123 Years at the Mare Island Naval Shipyard*. Vallejo: Mare Island Historical Record, 1984.

Limbaugh, Ronald H., and Walter A. Payne. *Vacaville: The Heritage of a California Community*. Vacaville: Vacaville City Council, 1978.

"Yee Ah Chong Remembers Vacaville's Chinatown." *California History* 63 (1984): 247–51.

Young, Wood. *Vaca-Peña Los Putos Rancho and the Peña Adobe*. Vallejo: Wheeler Printing & Publishing, 1965.

SONOMA COUNTY

Alexander, James B. *Sonoma Valley Legacy: Histories and Sites of 70 Historic Adobes in and around Sonoma Valley*. Sonoma: Sonoma Valley Historical Society, 1986.

Clar, C. Raymond. *Out of the River Mist: History of the Russian River Area and the Lumber Town of Guerneville*. Sacramento: Argus Books, 1973.

Claybourn, Hannah, et al. *Historic Homes of Healdsburg*. Healdsburg: Healdsburg Historical Society, n.d.

Donohoe, Joan Marie. "Agostin Haraszthy: A Study in Creativity." *California Historical Society Quarterly* 48 (1969), 153–64.

Emparan, Madie Brown. *The Vallejos of California*. San Francisco: Gleeson Library Associates, 1968.

Florence, Jack W., Sr. *Legacy of a Village: The Italian Swiss Colony Winery and People of Asti, California*. Phoenix: Raymond Court Press, 2000.

Heig, Adair. *History of Petaluma, a California River Town*. Petaluma and San Francisco: Scottwall Associates, 1982.

Lynch, Robert M. *The Sonoma Valley Story*. Sonoma: Sonoma Index-Tribune, 1997.

Munroe-Fraser, J. P. *History of Sonoma County*. 1880. Reprint, Petaluma: C. B. Verona, 1973.

Parmelee, Robert D. *Pioneer Sonoma*. Sonoma: Sonoma Index-Tribune, 1972.

Smilie, Robert S. *The Sonoma Mission*. Fresno: Valley Publishers, 1974.

Spencer-Hancock, Diane, and William E. Pritchard. "The Chapel at Fort Ross: Its History and Reconstruction." *California History* 61 (1982): 2–17.

Tuomey, Honoria, and Luisa Vallejo Emparan. "Historic Mount St. Helena." *California Historical Society Quarterly* 3 (1924): 171–77.

Weber, Francis J., comp. and ed. *Last of the Missions: A Documentary History of San Francisco de Solano.* Los Angeles: Archdiocese of Los Angeles Archives, 1986.

STANISLAUS COUNTY

Bare, Colleen S. *The McHenry Mansion: Modesto's Heritage.* Modesto: McHenry Museum Press, 1999.

Beard, Franklin. *The Way We Were Fifty Years Ago: East of Modesto to Empire and Beyond.* Modesto: McHenry Museum, 1985.

Branch, L. C. *History of Stanislaus County.* 1881. Reprint, Stanislaus County Historical Society, 1974.

Brotherton, I. N. ("Jack"). *The Annals of Stanislaus: River Towns and Ferries.* Santa Cruz: Western Tanager Press, 1982.

Criswell, John F. *Knight's Ferry's Century-Old Structures.* Knight's Ferry: John F. Criswell, 1981.

———. *Knight's Ferry's Golden Past.* Knight's Ferry: John F. Criswell, 1982.

Elias, Solomon P. *Stories of Stanislaus.* 1924. Reprint, Modesto: McHenry Museum Guild, 1979.

Gray, Thomas B. *Quest for Deep Gold: The Story of La Grange, California.* Modesto: Southern Mines Press, 1973.

Gray, Thorne B. *The Stanislaus Indian Wars: The Last of the California Northern Yokuts.* Modesto: McHenry Museum Press, 1993.

Lucas, Mildred D. *From Amber Grain to Fruited Plain: A History of Ceres and Its Surroundings.* Ceres: Ceres Unified School District, 1976.

Maino, Jeanette Gould. *One Hundred Years.* Modesto: Belt Printing & Lithography Co., 1970.

Orsi, Richard J. "Estanislao's Rebellion, 1829." In R. B. Rice, W. A. Bullogh, and R. J. Orsi, *The Elusive Eden: A New History of California.* New York: McGraw-Hill, 1996.

Patterson Irrigator. Diamond Jubilee of Patterson, 1909–1984. May 31, 1984 issue.

Tinkham, George H. *History of Stanislaus County, with Biographical Sketches.* 1921. Reprint, Modesto: McHenry Museum Guild, 1979.

SUTTER COUNTY

Bayless, Dorothy Martin. *Index to Thompson and West's 1879 History of Sutter County, California.* Sacramento: Dorothy M. Bayless, n.d.

Delay, Peter J. *History of Yuba and Sutter Counties, California.* Los Angeles: Historic Record Co., 1924.

Hendrix, Louise Butts. *Sutter Buttes, Land of the Histun Yani.* Yuba City: Louise B. Hendrix, 1980.

Hussey, John A., ed. *Early Sacramento: Glimpses of John Augustus Sutter, the Hock Farm and Neighboring Tribes, from the Journal of Prince Paul, H. R. H. Duke Paul Wilhelm of Wurttemburg.* Translated by Louis C.

Butscher. Sacramento: Sacramento Book Collectors Club, 1973.

Sullivan, Janet R., and Mary-Jane Zall. *The Survivors: Existing Homes and Buildings of Yuba and Sutter Counties' Past.* Marysville, 1974.

Thompson & West. *History of Sutter County.* 1879. Reprint, Berkeley: Howell-North Books, 1974.

TEHAMA COUNTY

Bruff, J. Goldsborough. *Gold Rush: The Journals, Drawings and Other Papers of J. Goldsborough Bruff, April 2, 1849–July 20, 1851.* Edited by Georgia Willis Read and Ruth Gaines. New York: Columbia University Press, 1944.

Grimes, Mary Lee. *The First Fifty Years: A Pictorial Essay of Tehama County, 1856–1906.* Red Bluff: Tehama County Heritage, 1984.

Hisken, Clara Hough. *Tehama: Little City of the Big Trees.* New York: Exposition Press, 1948.

Hislop, Donald L. *The Nomee Lackee Indian Reservation, 1854–1870.* Chico: Association for Northern California Records and Research, 1978.

Hitchcock, Ruth Hughes. *Leaves of the Past, 1828–1880: A Pioneer Register, Including an Overview of the History and Events of Early Tehama County.* Chico: Association for Northern California Records and Research, 1982.

Lewis, E. J. *Tehama County, California, with Historical Reminiscences.* San Francisco: Elliott & Moore, 1880.

Sherman, Edwin A. *Fifty Years of Masonry in California.* 2 vols. San Francisco: George Spaulding & Co., 1898.

Tehama County Memories. Red Bluff: Tehama County Genealogical and Historical Society, 1992.

Zelinsky, Edward Galland, and Nancy Olmsted. "Upriver Boats—When Red Bluff Was the Head of Navigation." *California History* 64 (1985): 86–117.

TRINITY COUNTY

Bell, Horace. *Tales of the Trinity, 1879–80.* Reprint, edited by Dewey and Nola Mosier. Weaverville: Trinity County Historical Society, 1983.

Cox, Isaac. *The Annals of Trinity County.* San Francisco: Commercial Book and Job Steam Printing Establishment, 1858.

Dale, Harrison Clifford. *The Ashley-Smith Explorations and the Discovery of a Central Route to the Pacific, 1822–1829, with Original Journals.* Cleveland, Ohio: Arthur H. Clark Co., 1918.

McDonald, Douglas, and Gina McDonald. *The History of Weaverville Joss House and the Chinese of Trinity County, California.* Medford, Ore.: McDonald Publishing, 1988.

Miller, William P. "Trinity County." Report by State Mineralogist. Sacramento: State Office, 1890.

Mosier, Dewey, and Nola Mosier. "The Giants and the Mountain—Mining Machines Make a Highway." *California History* 61 (1982): 188–95.

Trinity County Historic Sites. Weaverville: Trinity County Historical Society, 1981.

TULARE COUNTY

Bunch, Lonnie G., III. "Allensworth: The Life, Death, and Rebirth of an All-Black Community." *The Californians,* Nov.–Dec. 1987, pp. 26–33.

Fry, Walter, and John R. White. *Big Trees.* Stanford: Stanford University Press, 1930.

Gifford, E. W., and W. Egbert Schenck. "Archaeology of the Southern San Joaquin Valley, California." *University of California Publications in American Archaeology and Ethnology* 13, no. 1 (1926): 1–122.

McCraw, Donald J. "The Tree That Crossed a Continent." *California History* 61 (1982): 120–39.

McCubbin, J. C. *Papers on the History of the San Joaquin Valley, California.* Collected and edited by Raymund F. Wood. Fresno: California State University at Fresno Library, 1960.

McGee, Lizzie. *Mills of the Sequoias.* Visalia: Tulare County Historical Society, 1952.

Mitchell, Annie. *Jim Savage and the Tulareno Indians.* Los Angeles: Westernlore Press, 1957.

———. *A Modern History of Tulare County.* Visalia: Limited Editions of Visalia, 1974.

———. *Sites to See: Historic Landmarks in Tulare County.* Fresno: Panorama West Books, 1983.

———. *The Way It Was: The Colorful History of Tulare County.* Fresno: Valley Publishers, 1976.

O'Connell, Jay. *Co-operative Dreams: A History of the Kaweah Colony.* Van Nuys: Raven River Press, 1997.

Porterville Recorder. "The Porterville Museum, 20th Anniversary Issue." Nov. 9, 1985.

Robinson, W. W. *The Story of Tulare County and Visalia.* Los Angeles: Title Insurance & Trust Co., 1955.

Small, Kathleen. *History of Tulare County.* Chicago: S. J. Clarke Publishing Co., 1926.

Stewart, George W. *Big Trees of the Giant Forest.* San Francisco: A. M. Robertson, 1930.

Tweed, William C. *Sequoia–Kings Canyon: The Story Behind the Scenery.* Las Vegas: KC Publications, 1980.

TUOLUMNE COUNTY

Holmes, Roberta Evelyn. *The Southern Mines of California: Early Development of the Sonora Mining Region.* San Francisco: Grabhorn Press, 1931.

Lang, H. O. *A History of Tuolumne County, California.* 1882. Reprint, Columbia: Tuolumne County Historical Society, 1973.

Mark Twain's Sojourn in Tuolumne County, California: Genesis of a Literary Giant. Sonora: Tuolumne County Historical Society, 1988.

O'Neill, Elizabeth Stone. *Meadow in the Sky: A History of Yosemite's Tuolumne Meadows Region.* Fresno: Panorama West Books, 1983.

Paden, Irene D., and Margaret B. Schlichtmann. *The Big Oak Flat Road.* San Francisco: Lawton Kennedy, 1955.

Robertson, David. *East of Eden: A History of Art and Literature of Yosemite.* Yosemite: Yosemite Natural History Association, 1984.

Stewart, George R. *Bret Harte, Argonaut and Exile.* Boston: Houghton Mifflin, 1931.

Trexler, Keith A. *The Tioga Road: A History, 1883–1961.* 1961. Rev. ed. Yosemite Natural Historical Association, 1975.

VENTURA COUNTY

Bandurraga, Peter L., David W. Hill, and G. Belden Holland. *Ventura County's Yesterdays Today: Looking Back at Ventura County.* Ventura: Anacapa Publishing, 1980.

Belknap, Michael R. "The Era of the Lemon: A History of Santa Paula, California." *California Historical Society Quarterly* 48 (1968): 113–40.

Bicentennial San Buenaventura, 1782–1982. Ventura: San Buenaventura Mission, 1982.

Del Castillo, Richard Griswold. "The Del Valle Family and the Fantasy Heritage." *California History* 59 (1980): 2–15.

Engelhardt, Zephyrin. *San Buenaventura, the Mission by the Sea.* Santa Barbara: Mission Santa Barbara, 1930.

Fry, Patricia. *The Ojai Valley: An Illustrated History.* Ojai: P. L. Fry, n.d.

Havens, Patricia. *Simi Valley: A Journey Through Time.* Simi Valley: Simi Valley Historical Society and Museum, 1997.

Outland, Charles F. *Man-Made Disaster: The Story of St. Francis Dam.* Glendale: Arthur H. Clark Co., 1977.

Ricard, Herbert F. *Place Names of Ventura County.* Ventura: Ventura County Historical Society, 1972.

Robinson, W. W. *The Story of Ventura County.* Los Angeles: Title Insurance & Trust Co., 1956.

Smith, Wallace E. *This Land Was Ours: The Del Valles and Camulos.* Ventura: Ventura County Historical Society, 1977.

Triem, Judith. *Ventura County: Land of Good Fortune.* Northridge: Windsor Publications, 1985.

Weber, Francis J. *A History of San Buenaventura Mission.* Los Angeles: Roman Catholic Archdiocese of Los Angeles, 1977.

YOLO COUNTY

Clyman, James. "James Clyman, His Diaries and Reminiscences." Edited by Charles L. Camp. *California Historical Society Quarterly* 5 (1926): 109–28.

Gregory, Tom. *History of Yolo County, California, with Biographical Sketches.* Los Angeles: Historic Record Co., 1913.

Hill, Joseph J. "Ewing Young in the Fur Trade of the Far Southwest, 1822–1834." *Oregon Historical Society Quarterly* 24 (1923): 1–23.

History of Yolo County, California, Its Resources and Its People. Edited by William O. Russell. Woodland: Nelle S. Coil, 1940.

Larkey, Joann, ed. *Davisville '68: The History and Heritage of the City of Davis, Yolo County, California.* Davis: Davis Historical Landmarks Commission, 1969.

Larkey, Joann, and Shipley Walters. *Yolo County: Land of Changing Patterns.* Woodland: Yolo County Historical Society, 1987.

McDermott, Douglas, and Robert K. Sarlos. "The Woodland 'Hershey' Opera House: The End of an Era in California Theatre." *California Historical Society Quarterly* 48 (1969): 291–308.

Walking Tours of Historic Woodland. Woodland: City of Woodland, 1976.

Walters, Shipley, with Tom Anderson. *Knights Landing: The River, the Land, and the People.* Woodland: Yolo County Historical Society, 1992.

Walters, Shipley. *Woodland, City of Trees.* Woodland: Yolo County Historical Society, 1995.

Winters' Architectural Heritage. Winters: Winters Historic Landmarks Advisory Committee, 1985.

YUBA COUNTY

Bal, Peggy. *Pebbles in the Stream: A History of Beale Air Force Base and Neighboring Areas.* Chico: Easter Publishing Co., 1979.

Bleyhl, Norris A. *Three Military Posts in Northeastern California, 1849–1863.* Chico: Association for Northern California Records and Research, 1984.

Delay, Peter J. *History of Yuba and Sutter Counties.* Los Angeles: Historic Record Co., 1924.

The History of Yuba County. Marysville: Yuba County Historical Commission, 1976.

Smith, Louise A. *Reclamation: A History of the Linda-Olivehurst Area of California, 1850–1975.* Marysville: Louis A. Smith, 1975.

Sullivan, Janet R., and Mary-Jane Zall. *The Survivors: Existing Homes and Buildings of Yuba and Sutter Counties' Past.* Marysville, 1974.

Wells, Henry L., and William H. Chamberlain. *History of Yuba County, California.* Oakland: Thompson & West, 1879.

Wheat, Carl I. "'California's Bantam Cock'—The Journals of Charles E. DeLong, 1854–1863." Edited with an introduction by Carl I. Wheat. *California Historical Society Quarterly* 8, 9, 10 (1929–31): *passim.*

Bold page numbers indicate main entries; italic numbers indicate illustrations.

608

INDEX

INDEX

INDEX

634

Moutry, Riley, 442
Movie Road, 122
movies, *see* motion picture industry
Mowers-Goheen Museum, 492
Mowry's Landing, 3, 13
Mt., *see* entries at Mount
Mud Slough, 215
Mud Slough Wildlife Area, 215
Mud Springs (El Dorado Co.), 78, 83
Mud Springs (Los Angeles Co.), 323. *See also* Ciénega
Mugártegui, Fr. Pablo, 264
Mugu Lagoon, 559
Muir, John, xvi, 61, 62, 196, 479–81, **547**, 550–51
Muir Gorge, 549
Muir Grove, 546
Muir Woods National Monument, 196
Mule Creek State Prison, 36
Mule Hill, 344, 346
Muletown, 36, 470
Mulholland, William, 176
Mullett, A. B., 361
Municipal Art Gallery, 172
Municipal Pier, Hermosa Beach, 172
Muñoz, Fr. Pedro, 209–10, 548
Munras, Estévan, 230, 239, 382
Munro-Fraser, J. P., 58
Murderer's Bar, 76–77, 80, 99
Murderer's Gulch, 30
Murdock Ranch, 97
Murguía, José Antonio, 423
Murieta, Joaquín, 45, 89, 92, 203, 462, 556
Murieta Rocks, **92**
Muroc Air Force Base, 137
Muroc Army Air Field, 137
Muroc Dry lake, 137
Murphy, Daniel, 46
Murphy, Diana, 436
Murphy, Harriet, 573
Murphy, Helen, 371
Murphy, John, 46
Murphy, John W., 436
Murphy, Martin, 371, 435–36
Murphy, Martin, Jr., 306, 388, 430, 435
Murphy, Martin J. C., 436
Murphy, Mary, 573–74, 579
Murphy, Matilda Josephine (Mrs. Robert Burnett), 169
Murphy, Mr., 476
Murphy, Patrick, 388
Murphy, Sarah, 573
Murphy, Timoteo, 185–86, 190
Murphy cabin, 252
Murphy estate, 387–88
Murphy family, 26, **46–47**, 48
Murphy Historic Park, 430
Murphy's Bridge, 139
Murphy's Camp, 46
Murphy's Diggings, 46
Murphy's Hotel, 46, *47*
Murphy's Peak (Twenty-One Mile Peak), 436
Murphy-Townsend-Stevens party, 133, 375
Murray, James, 406

Murray, John, 406
Murray, John Jarvis, 406
Murray, Margaret, 406
Murray, Michael, 11
Murray, Welwood, 291
Murray Township, 11
Murry Park, 543
museums: African-American Museum and Library, Oakland, 22; Agua Mansa chapel, 329; Air Force Museum, Travis Air Force Base, 501; Air Force Test Flight Museum, 137; Alameda Historical Museum, 23; Albinger Archaeological Museum, 561; Allen Knight Maritime Museum, 233; Alta Schmidt House Museum, Orland, *100*; Amador Co., 32, *33*, 34–35; Amador-Livermore Valley Historical museum, 15; American Heritage, Museum of, 445; Angels Camp Museum, 44; Avila adobe museum, 154; Bangor Church museum, 42; Bank of Canton Pacific Heritage Museum, 361; Banning Residence Museum, 158; Battery Point Lighthouse Museum, 72, *73*; Benicia Historical Museum and Cultural Foundation, 495; Big Valley Historical Museum of Lassen County, 148; Blackhawk Museum, 59; Blume House Museum, 57; Borax Museum, 119; Boulder Creek, 462; Butte Co., 38, 40–42; Butte Valley Museum, 488; Cable Car Barn and Museum, 356; Calaveras Co., 44, 46–47, *48*; California Railway Museum, 502–3; California State Indian Museum, **304**; California State Railroad Museum, 312; Camel Barn Museum, 495; Campbell Historical Museum, 439; Carpinteria Valley, 409; Cherokee Museum, 41; Chico Museum, 38; Chinese Historical Society of America, Museum of, 366; City Museum, Redding, 470; Clarke Memorial Museum, 105; Clayton Museum, 67; Cloverdale, 514; Colusa Co., 50; Contra Costa Co., 54, 57, 59, 65, 67, 69; Corning Museum, 532; Crocker Art Gallery, *301*, 314; Cupertino Historical Museum, 443; Dai Loy Gambling Hall, 315; Del Norte Co., 72, 74; DeSaisset Museum, 423; Desert Museum, 135; Drum Barracks Civil War Museum, 158; Dublin Historic Preservation Association, 12; Dunsmuir Museum,

483; Eastern California Museum, 121, 123; El Cajón, 345; El Dorado Co., 75–76, 81–82, 88, 91; El Presidio de Santa Barbara State Historic Park, 411; Elverhoy Museum, 418; Eschscholtzia Parlor #122, Native Daughters of the Golden West Museum, 486; Ferndale Museum, 106; Fillmore Historical Museum, 565; Folsom Railroad Museum, 305; Forbes Mill Regional History Museum, 440; Fort Crook Historical Society, 472; Fort Guijarros Museum Foundation, 339; Fort Jones Museum, 486; Fort Point National Historic Site, 351; Fortuna Depot Museum, 106, *107*; Fountain-Tollman City Museum, 81; Fresno Co., 93, 95; Gatekeeper's Museum, 272; Gene Autry Western Heritage Museum, 169; George C. Page Museum of La Brea Discoveries, 162; Gilroy Historical Museum, 446; Glenn Co., *100*; Golden State Museum, 309; Guest House Museum (Fort Bragg), *207*; Haggin Museum and Art Gallery, 372; Harris-Lass Historic Museum, 439; Hayward Area Historical Society Museum, 16; Healdsburg Museum, 513; Hearst Memorial Mining Museum, 23; Heritage Junction Museum, 488; Heritage of the Americas Museum, 345; Hiller Aviation Museum, 404; Historical Society of Germans from Russia Museum, 93; Hoopa Tribal Museum, 103; Horace A. Sexton Memorial Museum, 416; *Hornet*, USS, *8*, 23–24; House of Pacific Relations, 341; Humboldt Co., 103–7; Imperial Co., 115; Indian Valley Museum (Taylorsville), *288*; Inyo Co., 119–21, 123; ItaloAmericano, 368; J. Paul Getty Museum, 172; Jack London State Historic Park, 515; Jackson Museum, Weaverville, 537; Judah L. Magnes Memorial Museum, 23; Junipero Serra Museum, 336; Kelley House Museum, *205*; Kelly-Griggs House Museum, Red Bluff, *530*, 532; Kern Co., 131, 134–37; Kings Co., 140; La Jolla Museum of Contemporary Art, 341; Lake Co., 145–46; Lake Tahoe Historical Society Museum, 88; Lassen Co., 148–49; Laws Railroad Museum, 120, 123; Leland Stanford Junior

Museum, 444; Lincoln Highway, 13; Little Landers Museum, 176; Lompoc Museum, 413; Lompoc Valley Historical Museum, 413; Loomis Museum, 464; Los Altos History House Museum, 432; Los Angeles Co., 154–55, 157–62, 164–66, 169, 171–73, 175–77; Los Gatos Museum Association, 440; Lower Lake Historical Schoolhouse Museum, 145; Luther Burbank House and Garden, 510; Madera Co., 180, *181*; Man, Museum of, 341; Marin Co., 182, 185–87, 189, 193; Marion Steinbeck Museum, 272; Mariposa Co., 199–200; Mark Abbot Memorial Lighthouse, 451; Markleeville, 28; Mary Aaron Memorial Museum, 574; McHenry Museum, Modesto, 521; Mendocino Co., 204–6, 208; Merced Co., 213; Mexican Museum, 368; Michael H. de Young Memorial Museum, 366; Mission Plaza Archaeological Interpretive Facility, 561; Mission San Juan Bautista, 316; Modoc Co., 220; Moffett Field Historical Museum, 430; Mojave River Museum, 332; Monterey Co., 228–32, **233**, 236, 239; Monteverde Store Museum, *33*; Mousley Museum of Natural History, 328; Mowers-Goheen Museum, 492; Napa Co., 243–44, 248, 251; Natural History Museum, 106; Needles Regional Museum, 331; Nevada Co., 252, 256, 259, 262; New Almaden Museum, 436; Norton Simon Museum, 164; Oakland Museum, 22; Ojai Valley Museum and Historical Society, 564; Old Cabin at Butte Valley Museum, Dorris, *489*; Old-Timers Museum, 46; Orange Co., 266, 268–69; Oregon City School Museum, *41*; Oxnard Historical Society Museum, 565; Pacific Lumber Company Museum, 106; Pardee Home Museum, 21; Patterson City Museum, 522; Petaluma Museum, 513; Phillips House Museum, 106; Pioneer Village Museum (Fresno Co.), 95; Pioneer Village Museum (Kern Co.), **134**; Pioneers' Museum (Imperial Co.), 115; Placer Co., 272, 275, 277–79; Plumas Co., 286–88; Port Hueneme Museum and Historical Society, 565; Porterville His-

INDEX

INDEX